ENGLISH DICTIONARY

Abbreviations used in the Dictionary

adj	adjective	*infin*	infinitive	*pt*	past tense
adv	adverb	*interj*	interjection	*r*	reflexive
aux	auxiliary	*n*	noun	*s*	singular
cap	capital	*neg*	negative	*sl*	slang
conj	conjunction	*pl*	plural	*tab*	taboo
def art	definite article	*poss*	possessive	*Tdmk*	trademark
esp	especially	*pp*	past participle	*US*	United States
f	feminine	*prep*	preposition	*v*	verb
indef art	indefinite article	*pres*	present tense	*vi*	verb intransitive
inf	informal	*pron*	pronoun	*vt*	verb transitive

Key to symbols used in pronunciation

Vowels

i	meet	u	put	ai	fly
ı	bit	u:	shoot	au	how
e	get	ʌ	cut	ɔı	boy
æ	hat	ə	ago	ıə	here
ɑ:	heart	ə:	sir	ɛə	air
ɔ	hot	ei	late	uə	poor
ɔ:	ought	ou	go		

Consonants

θ	thin	ʃ	ship	
ð	then	ʒ	measure	
ŋ	sing	tʃ	chin	
j	yes	dʒ	gin	

' indicates that the following syllable is stressed as in ago (ə'gou).
, placed under an *n* or *l* indicates that the *n* or *l* is pronounced as a syllable as in button ('bʌtn) and flannel ('flænl)

Irregular verbs

Infinitive	Past Tense	Past Participle	Infinitive	Past Tense	Past Participle
abide	abode *or* abided	abode *or* abided	**beware**[2]		
arise	arose	arisen	**bid**	bid	bidden *or* bid
awake	awoke *or* awaked	awoke *or* awaked	**bind**	bound	bound
			bite	bit	bitten *or* bit
be	was	been	**bleed**	bled	bled
bear[1]	bore	borne *or* born	**blow**	blew	blown
beat	beat	beaten	**break**	broke	broken
become	became	become	**breed**	bred	bred
begin	began	begun	**bring**	brought	brought
bend	bent	bent	**build**	built	built
bet	bet	bet	**burn**	burnt *or* burned	burnt *or* burned

THE COMPLETE HANDY REFERENCE

DICTIONARY
&
THESAURUS

CHANCELLOR
PRESS

Material in this book has previously appeared in
The Complete Handy Reference Dictionary Thesaurus Guide to English Usage (Chancellor Press, Octopus Publishing Group 1992)

This 2002 edition first published by Chancellor Press, an imprint of Bounty Books, a division of Octopus Publishing Group, 2–4 Heron Quays, London E14 4JP Reprinted 2003

Copyright © Octopus Publishing Group 2002

ISBN 0 7537 0643 1

A catalogue record for this book is available from the British Library

Printed in England by Mackays of Chatham

Infinitive	Past Tense	Past Participle	Infinitive	Past Tense	Past Participle
burst	burst	burst	have	had	had
buy	bought	bought	hear	heard	heard
can	could		hide	hid	hidden or hid
cast	cast	cast	hit	hit	hit
catch	caught	caught	hold	held	held
choose	chose	chosen	hurt	hurt	hurt
cling	clung	clung	keep	kept	kept
come	came	come	kneel	knelt	knelt
cost	cost	cost	knit	knitted or knit	knitted or knit
creep	crept	crept	know	knew	known
crow	crowed or crew	crowed	lay	laid	laid
cut	cut	cut	lead	led	led
deal	dealt	dealt	lean	leant or leaned	leant or leaned
dig	dug or digged	dug or digged	leap	leapt or leaped	leapt or leaped
do	did	done	learn	learnt or learned	learnt or learned
draw	drew	drawn	leave	left	left
dream	dreamed or dreamt	dreamed or dreamt	lend	lent	lent
			let	let	let
drink	drank	drunk	lie	lay	lain
drive	drove	driven	light	lit or lighted	lit or lighted
dwell	dwelt	dwelt	lose	lost	lost
eat	ate	eaten	make	made	made
fall	fell	fallen	may	might	
feed	fed	fed	mean	meant	meant
feel	felt	felt	meet	met	met
fight	fought	fought	mow	mowed	mown
find	found	found	must		
flee	fled	fled	ought		
fling	flung	flung	panic	panicked	panicked
fly	flew	flown	pay	paid	paid
forbid	forbade or forbad	forbidden or forbid	picnic	picnicked	picnicked
			put	put	put
forget	forgot	forgotten or forgot	quit	quitted or quit	quitted or quit
			read	read	read
forgive	forgave	forgiven	rid	rid or ridded	rid or ridded
forsake	forsook	forsaken	ride	rode	ridden
freeze	froze	frozen	ring	rang	rung
get	got	got	rise	rose	risen
give	gave	given	run	ran	run
go	went	gone	saw	sawed	sawn or sawed
grind	ground	ground	say	said	said
grow	grew	grown	see	saw	seen
hang[3]	hung or hanged	hung or hanged	seek	sought	sought
			sell	sold	sold

Irregular verbs

Infinitive	Past Tense	Past Participle	Infinitive	Past Tense	Past Participle
send	sent	sent	string	strung	strung
set	set	set	strive	strove	striven
sew	sewed	sewn or sewed	swear	swore	sworn
shake	shook	shaken	sweep	swept	swept
shall	should		swell	swelled	swollen or swelled
shear	sheared	sheared or shorn	swim	swam	swum
shed	shed	shed	swing	swung	swung
shine	shone	shone	take	took	taken
shoe	shod	shod	teach	taught	taught
shoot	shot	shot	tear	tore	torn
show	showed	shown	tell	told	told
shrink	shrank or shrunk	shrunk or shrunken	think	thought	thought
			throw	threw	thrown
shut	shut	shut	thrust	thrust	thrust
sing	sang	sung	traffic	trafficked	trafficked
sink	sank	sunk	tread	trod	trodden or trod
sit	sat	sat			
sleep	slept	slept	wake	woke	woken
slide	slid	slid	wear	wore	worn
sling	slung	slung	weave	wove	woven or wove
slink	slunk	slunk	weep	wept	wept
slit	slit	slit	will	would	
smell	smelt or smelled	smelt or smelled	win	won	won
			wind	wound	wound
sow	sowed	sown or sowed	wring	wrung	wrung
speak	spoke	spoken	write	wrote	written
speed	sped or speeded	sped or speeded			
spell	spelt or spelled	spelt or spelled			
spend	spent	spent			
spill	spilt or spilled	spilt or spilled			
spin	spun	spun			
spit	spat or spit	spat or spit			
split	split	split			
spread	spread	spread			
spring	sprang	sprung			
stand	stood	stood			
steal	stole	stolen			
stick	stuck	stuck			
sting	stung	stung			
stink	stank or stunk	stunk			
stride	strode	stridden			
strike	struck	struck			

[1] when *bear* means *give birth to* the past participle is always *born*

[2] used only in the infinitive or as an imperative

[3] the preferred form of the past tense and past participle when referring to death by hanging is *hanged*

A

a, an *indef art* one; each; every; any; some

aback *adv* **taken aback** taken by surprise; disconcerted; flabbergasted

abandon *vt* 1 leave behind with no intention of returning; desert; forsake 2 give up; fail to complete **abandon oneself (to)** yield; submit, or give in (to)

abashed *adj* ashamed; embarrassed

abate *vi* lessen; die down *vt* reduce; subdue; suppress **abatement** *n*

abattoir (ˈæbətwɑ:) *n* slaughterhouse

abbess *n* female head of nuns in an abbey or nunnery

abbey *n* 1 community of monks or nuns 2 buildings occupied by such a community 3 church attached to such a community

abbot *n* male head of monks in an abbey or monastery

abbreviate *vt* shorten (a word or phrase) **abbreviation** *n*

abdicate *vi,vt* renounce or relinquish (the throne, one's powers, etc) **abdication** *n*

abdomen *n* lower part of the body between the diaphragm and pelvis; belly **abdominal** *adj*

abduct *vt* take (a person) away unlawfully; kidnap **abduction** *n* **abductor** *n*

aberration *n* deviation from the usual, right, or natural course, condition, etc **aberrant** *adj*

abet *vt* (-tt-) assist or encourage in crime or wrongdoing

abeyance *n* **in abeyance** in a state of inactivity; suspended

abhor *vt* (-rr-) have an intense horror of; loathe; detest **abhorrence** *n* **abhorrent** *adj*

abide *vt* (abode *or* abided) tolerate; bear *vi* 1 stay; remain 2 reside; dwell **abide by** keep to; remain close or faithful to

ability *n* 1 power; capacity; means 2 competence; skill

abject *adj* 1 downcast; humiliated 2 despicable; shocking 3 humble **abjectly** *adv*

ablaze *adj* 1 on fire; in flames; burning fiercely 2 displaying strong passion or ardour

able *adj* 1 having the power, capacity opportunity, or means (to) 2 competent; skilled

ably *adv* **able-bodied** *adj* physically fit; strong

abnormal *adj* irregular; unnatural; deviant **abnormality** *n* **abnormally** *adv*

aboard *adv,prep* on or in(to) a ship, aircraft, etc

abode[1] *n* place of residence; dwelling; home

abode[2] *v a pt* and *pp* of **abide.**

abolish *vt* do away with; put an end to; ban **abolition** *n*

abominable *adj* loathsome; detestable; dreadful **abominably** *adv*

Aborigine (æbəˈridʒini) *n also* **Aboriginal** person belonging to a race of original native inhabitants, esp of Australia **Aboriginal** *adj*

abort *vt* 1 terminate (a pregnancy); perform an abortion on 2 cancel or destroy (a project, mission, etc) before completion *vi* 1 miscarry 2 fail to function successfully; terminate before completion **abortive** *adj* **abortion** *n* 1 operation carried out to remove a foetus from the womb 2 miscarriage 3 disastrous failure

abound *vi* exist or have in great quantity; be plentiful

about *prep* 1 of; concerning; relating to; connected with 2 near or close to; around **about to** ready or preparing to; on the point of ~about 1 approximately 2 nearby; close at hand 3 around; here and there; to and fro

above *adv* higher up; overhead *prep* 1 over; higher than 2 more or greater than 3 in authority over; superior to 4 beyond (suspicion, reproach, etc) *adj also* **above-mentioned** mentioned or written above or before **above all** more than anything **aboveboard** *adv* openly; without deception *adj* open; straightforward; honest; legal

abrasion *n* 1 wearing down by rubbing 2 graze on the skin **abrasive** *adj* 1 producing abrasion 2 harsh; grating *n* something used for wearing down or smoothing a surface

abreast *adv* side by side; level with **keep abreast of** keep up or up-to-date with

abridge *vt* cut (a novel, play, etc); condense **abridgement** *n*

abroad *adv* 1 in or to a foreign country 2 in circulation; at large

abrupt *adj* 1 unexpected and sudden 2 curt; short; brusque **abruptly** *adv* **abruptness** *n*

abscess n pus-filled sore

abscond vi leave without permission; run away, esp after committing a crime **absconder** n

absent adj ('æbsənt) 1 away; not in attendance 2 lacking; missing; not present v absent **oneself** (əb'sent) stay away **absence** n **absentee** n person, such as an employee or landlord, who is absent **absenteeism** n **absent-minded** adj forgetful or vague, esp when preoccupied **absent-mindedly** adv **absent-mindedness** n

absolute adj total; utter; complete **absolutely** adv

absolve vt release from blame, sin, obligation, etc ; pardon; exonerate **absolution** n

absorb vt 1 take in or soak up 2 assimilate 3 engross; engage fully **absorbent** adj **absorbing** adj **absorption** n

abstain vi 1 refrain from registering one's vote 2 refrain from indulging in certain pleasures, such as drinking alcohol **abstention** n withholding of one's vote **abstinence** n state or period of self-denial

abstract adj ('æbstrækt) having no material existence; not concrete, conceptual n ('æbstrækt) brief account, summary; résumé vt (əb'strækt) take away; remove **abstraction** n **abstract art** n art depicting ideas or objects through form, colour, and line rather than natural or actual representation

absurd adj ridiculous; silly; ludicrous **absurdity** n **absurdly** adv

abundant adj plentiful **abundance** n **abundantly** adv

abuse vt (ə'bju:z) 1 use or treat badly or unfairly; misuse 2 insult; be rude to n (ə'bju:s) 1 ill-treatment; misuse; violation 2 insulting behaviour or language **abusive** adj

abyss (ə'bis) n deep bottomless pit or gulf **abysmal** (ə'bizməl) adj 1 bottomless; deep 2 dreadful; shocking **abysmally** adv

academy n 1 school or college offering specialized training 2 association of distinguished scholars **academic** adj 1 relating to a university, college, etc 2 theoretical or intellectual rather than practical or technical n university teacher or researcher **academically** adv

accelerate vt,vi make or become faster; speed up **acceleration** n **accelerator** n control pedal in a motor vehicle that is used for regulating speed; throttle

accent n ('æksent) 1 type of pronunciation associated with a particular region, social class, etc 2 stress placed on a syllable or word 3 written or printed symbol occurring in some languages to indicate stress, vowel quality, etc 4 emphasis vt (ək'sent) stress; mark with an accent **accentuate** vt emphasize; draw attention to **accentuation** n

accept vt 1 take something that is offered; receive 2 agree (to); admit 3 tolerate; put up with **acceptable** adj **acceptance** n

access n 1 way in or to; approach 2 opportunity, means, or permission to enter, reach, use, etc **accessible** adj reachable; approachable

accessory n 1 one of an additional set of items 2 person who assists in or conceals knowledge of a crime

accident n unforeseen event or occurrence, often having unpleasant consequences **by accident** by chance, unexpectedly **accidental** adj **accidentally** adv

acclaim vt show approval by cheering; applaud; hail; praise n also **acclamation** enthusiastic approval; applause; praise

acclimatize vt,vi make or become conditioned or used (to) **acclimatization** n

accommodate vt 1 provide room or space for; house; shelter 2 adjust (to); reconcile **accommodation** n

accompany vt go with; escort; join in or take part in with **accompaniment** n 1 something that belongs or occurs with something else 2 music that is played to support a solo performance

accomplice n partner in crime or wrongdoing

accomplish vt achieve; attain; complete successfully **accomplished** adj talented; skilful; proficient, esp in social graces; refined **accomplishment** n 1 successful completion; achievement 2 skill; refinement; proficiency

accord vt,vi agree; correspond; match up (to) n harmony; agreement **of one's own accord** on one's own initiative; voluntarily **accordance** n **in accordance with** in agreement with; conforming to **according** adv **according to** 1 as laid down or stipulated by 2 as stated or shown by; on the evidence of 3 in relation to; dependent on **accordingly** adv 1 therefore; so 2 as the situation demands

accordion *n* portable box-shaped musical instrument with bellows and keys

accost *vt* 1 approach (someone) in order to converse, question, etc 2 solicit

account *n* 1 report of an event etc 2 explanation 3 banking service or a credit service at a store, etc 4 sum of money deposited at a bank 5 statement of money transactions 6 importance; esteem **on account** on credit **on account of** because of **on any/no account** for no reason whatever **take into account** or **take account of** allow for *vi* **account for** 1 give reasons for; explain 2 make a reckoning of; count 3 capture; kill **accountable** *adj* responsible (for) **accountant** *n* professional person who investigates the business and financial transactions of an individual or organization **accountancy** *n*

accumulate *vt,vi* amass or collect over a period of time; pile up **accumulation** *n* **accumulative** *adj*

accurate *adj* precise; correct; exactly right **accuracy** *n* **accurately** *adv*

accuse *vt* charge (a person) with a crime, mistake, fault, etc ; blame **accusation** *n*

accustom *vt* familiarize; acquaint; acclimatize

ace *n* 1 playing card having a single pip 2 pilot who has destroyed a large number of enemy aircraft 3 champion *adj sl* first-rate; excellent

ache *vi* 1 feel a steady dull pain 2 yearn; long (for) *n* steady dull pain

achieve *vt* accomplish; attain; gain **achievement** *n*

acid *n* sour-tasting chemical compound that turns litmus red and dissolves in water to produce hydrogen ions *adj* 1 sharp; sour-tasting 2 sarcastic; caustic **acidic** *adj* **acidity** *n*

acknowledge *vt* 1 recognize that something is true or right; admit 2 respond to **acknowledgment** or **acknowledgement** *n*

acne ('ækni) *n* skin disorder affecting mainly the face and upper part of the body, which become covered with pimples and blackheads

acorn *n* nut that is the fruit of the oak

acoustic *adj* relating to sound or the sense of hearing **acoustics** *n* 1 *s* branch of physics concerned with the study of sound-waves 2 *pl* properties of a concert hall, room, etc , that affect the way sounds are heard

acquaint *vt* inform; familiarize; introduce

acquaintance *n* 1 someone one knows, but not as a close or intimate friend 2 personal knowledge **acquaintanceship** *n*

acquiesce *vi* agree tacitly; assent; comply **acquiescence** *n* **acquiescent** *adj*

acquire *vt* obtain, esp gradually or with some effort; take possession of; get **acquisition** *n* **acquisitive** *adj* eager to possess

acquit *vt* (-tt-) pronounce not guilty; discharge **acquit oneself** perform; behave; conduct oneself

acre *n* unit of land area equal to approx 4000 sq m (4840 sq yds) **acreage** *n* total number of acres in any given area

acrobat *n* performer on a trapeze tightrope, etc , gymnast **acrobatic** *adj* **acrobatics** *n s* or *pl* gymnastic feats or exercises

across *prep,adv* 1 from one side to another 2 over on the other side (of) **come across** meet or discover unexpectedly

acrylic *adj* relating to a type of synthetic fibre

act *vi* 1 operate; function; behave; perform; do (something) 2 perform in a play 3 pretend; feign *vt* take the role of; play *n* 1 single deed; action 2 law passed by Parliament 3 major division of a play, opera, etc , consisting of a number of scenes 4 performer(s) in a show, circus, etc , or the performance itself

action *n* 1 process of doing something; act; deed 2 gesture; movement 3 mechanism; movement of mechanical parts 4 lawsuit

activate *vt* make active; stir; agitate; cause to react

active *adj* 1 in operation; functioning 2 taking a positive part 3 lively; busy **actively** *adv* **activist** *n* person working for a particular political cause

activity *n* 1 movement; motion 2 something that keeps one occupied or busy

actor *n* performer in the theatre, on television, or in films **actress** *f n*

actual *adj* having real existence; not imaginary **actually** *adv* really; as a matter of fact; in fact

actuary *n* expert adviser on insurance, pensions, etc **actuarial** *adj*

acupuncture *n* Eastern method of medical treatment using sharp needles to puncture certain areas of the skin

acute *adj* 1 having a keen sense of hearing, smell, etc 2 perceptive; quick-witted; shrewd 3 severe; critical 4 *med* reaching crisis point; not chronic **acute accent** *n* symbol placed over certain vowels in some languages, as in café **acute angle** n angle of less than 90° **acutely** adv **acuteness** n

adamant adj insistent; firm **adamantly** adv

Adam's apple n popular name for the thyroid cartilage of the larynx

adapt vt modify to suit a different purpose or situation vi adjust to a new environment or set of conditions **adaptable** adj **adaptation** n **adaptor** n

add vt,vi 1 put together; join; give as something extra 2 calculate the sum (of); total 3 state further; go on to say **add to** supplement; increase **addition** n **additional** adj extra **additive** adj,n

adder n viper

addict n ('ædikt) 1 person who has become physically dependent on something, esp a drug 2 enthusiast; fanatic **be(come) addicted to** (ə'diktid) be(come) totally dependent on **addiction** n **addictive** adj

address n 1 postal location of a house, office, etc 2 speech given before an audience vt 1 write the address on 2 speak directly to **addressee** n

adenoids pl n mass of enlarged tissue in the pharynx

adept adj skilful; adroit; deft **adeptly** adv **adeptness** n

adequate adj 1 sufficient; just enough; acceptable; satisfactory 2 able to cope; capable **adequacy** n **adequately** adv

adhere vi stick; hold vt stick; glue; gum **adhere to** keep to; uphold; observe strictly; abide by **adherent** adj **adhesion** n **adhesive** n substance such as glue, gum, or paste, used for sticking things together adj relating to such a substance

ad hoc adj used for a specified purpose

adjacent adj adjoining; situated beside; next to

adjective n part of speech qualifying a noun **adjectival** adj

adjoin vt be situated next to; border on **adjoining** adj

adjourn vt,vi discontinue or suspend (a meeting, court session, etc) with the intention of resuming at a later time **adjournment** n

adjudicate vi,vt judge; settle; select (a winner) **adjudication** n **adjudicator** n

adjust vt make a minor alteration to; modify; change vi change to fit in with new requirements; adapt **adjustable** adj **adjustment** n

ad-lib vi (-bb-) compose (a speech, lines in a play, etc) without previous preparation; improvise

administer vt 1 also **administrate** govern; control as an official 2 dispense; hand out; issue **administrative** adj **administrator** n **administration** n 1 management; control; process of governing 2 body of managers, governors, etc

admiral n highest ranking naval officer **admiralty** n state department responsible for naval affairs

admire vt have a high regard for; respect; look up to; approve of **admirable** adj **admiration** n **admirer** n

admit vt (-tt-) 1 grant entry to 2 confess; accept blame for 3 accept as true; agree to **admissible** adj acceptable; allowable **admission** n 1 permission or opportunity to enter 2 fee charged for entrance 3 confession 4 acknowledgment; acceptance **admittance** n right of entry; access

ado n fuss, confused excitement; commotion

adolescence n period between puberty and adulthood **adolescent** n adj

adopt vt 1 take (another person's child) into one's own family as a legal guardian 2 take up (someone else's suggestion, plan, etc) 3 give formal approval to; choose **adoption** n

adore vt love ardently; worship; have great affection for **adorable** adj **adoration** n

adorn vt decorate, embellish; enhance **adornment** n

adrenaline n hormone secreted in the body or produced synthetically that is used to accelerate heart action, raise blood sugar levels, etc

adrift adj 1 cut loose from a mooring; unattached; drifting 2 off the point; not concise

adroit adj skilfully quick; resourceful; adept **adroitly** adv **adroitness** n

adulation n 1 unqualified or uncritical praise 2 flattery 3 unquestioning devotion

adult n 1 person who is grown up or mature 2 fully grown animal or plant adj 1 mature; of age; fully grown 2 intended for adults **adulthood** n

adultery n extra-marital sexual intercourse

advance vi 1 move forwards or upwards; proceed 2 show improvement; progress vt 1 take further; move ahead 2 pay out (money) before it is due *n* 1 movement forwards 2 progress 3 amount paid before payment is due *adj* issued in advance **advancement** *n* **in advance** beforehand; ahead

advantage *n* favourable position, circumstances, etc ; privilege; benefit **advantageous** *adj*

adventure *n* an exciting journey or experience, usually involving risks or hazards **adventurous** *adj* daring; bold; willing to take risks **adventurously** *adv*

adverb *n* part of speech qualifying a verb **adverbial** *adj*

adverse *adj* hostile; in opposition; antagonistic **adversity** *n* distressing circumstances; misfortune

advertise *vt,vi* give public information (of goods for sale, vacancies, etc); announce **advertiser** *n* **advertisement** *n* public announcement in the press, on televison, etc ; note of goods for sale, etc

advice *n* opinion or recommendation given in order to help someone make a decision

advise *vt,vi* give advice (to), recommend **adviser** *n* **advisable** *adj* wise; worth recommending

advocate *vt* ('ædvəkeit) recommend; urge *n* ('ædvəkət) 1 supporter; believer 2 (in Scotland) barrister

aerial *n* system of conducting rods for receiving or transmitting radio or television signals; antenna *adj* of, in, or from the air **aerially** *adv*

aerodynamics *n* study of the behaviour of aircraft, missiles, etc , in relation to airflow **aerodynamic** *adj* **aerodynamically** *adv*

aeronautics *n* study of flight **aeronautic** or **aeronautical** *adj*

aeroplane *n* aircraft propelled by jet engines or propellers and kept aloft by aerodynamic forces

aerosol *n* container dispensing a fine spray of pressurized liquid, gas etc

aesthetic (i:s'θetik) *adj* 1 pleasing to one's sense of beauty 2 relating to aesthetics **aesthetics** *n* branch of philosophy concerned with the concept and study of beauty, esp in art

afar *adv* far away; from or at a distance

affair *n* 1 matter; concern; business 2 sexual relationship, esp an extra-marital one; liaison *pl n* personal, business, or political matters

affect¹ *vt* 1 influence; alter; cause to change 2 move; arouse emotionally

affect² *vt* feign; simulate; pretend **affectation** *n* falseness of manner or style; insincerity

affection *n* fondness; love; strong liking **affectionate** *adj* **affectionately** *adv*

affiliate *vt,vi* join or unite (with) as a member; associate **affiliation** *n*

affinity *n* 1 relationship, esp by marriage 2 close connection; resemblance 3 empathetic attraction; strong liking

affirm *vt,vi* testify as to truth or validity; substantiate; assent **affirmation** *n* **affirmative** *adj* positive; assertive *n* the answer 'yes'

affix *vt* (ə'fiks) fasten; attach *n* ('æfiks) prefix or suffix

afflict *vt* cause distress, pain, or suffering; torment **affliction** *n* 1 torment; grief 2 disease; sickness; disability

affluent *adj* wealthy; prosperous; rich **affluence** *n*

afford *vt* 1 have money, time, etc , to spare (for) 2 be able to risk 3 offer; provide; allow

affront *vt* insult or offend esp publicly *n* public insult; display of disrespect

afield *adv* far away; a long way off

afloat *adj,adv* 1 floating 2 solvent

afoot *adj,adv* under way; in the offing

aforesaid *adj* also **aforementioned** previously referred to

afraid *adj* 1 frightened; apprehensive; fearful 2 sorry; regretful

afresh *adv* from the beginning; again; anew

aft *adv* towards or at the stern

after *prep* 1 following; later than 2 in pursuit of 3 in spite of; in view of 4 concerning 5 in imitation of **after all** when everything is considered ~*adv* 1 behind 2 subsequently **take after** resemble ~*conj* subsequent to the time that **after-care** *n* help, treatment, supervision, etc , given to a person discharged from hospital or prison **after-effect** *n* delayed effect, esp of a drug **afterlife** *n* life after death **aftermath** *n* 1 period of devastation following a war, disaster, etc 2 disastrous consequence **afternoon** *n* period between midday and evening **afterthought** *n* thought or idea that occurs later or incidentally **afterwards** *adv* at a later time; subsequently

again *adv* 1 once more; any more 2 additionally; further; besides **again and again** repeatedly; many times

against prep **1** in contact with; next to; close to; up as far as **2** in opposition to; competing with **3** not in favour of **4** contrasting with **5** in order to prevent

age n **1** period of time during which a person or thing has existed **2** era; epoch; period **3** also pl inf a long time vi,vt grow or cause to grow or look old(er) **aged** adj **1** ('eidʒid) very old **2** (eidʒd) of the age of

agenda n list of items to be discussed or dealt with; programme

agent n **1** person representing or working on behalf of a client **2** something that produces a change or effect **agency** n **1** company providing services or goods and operating on behalf of a client **2** influence; mediating power

aggravate vt **1** make worse; exacerbate **2** irritate; annoy **aggravation** n

aggression n feeling or display of hostility, anger, etc **aggressive** adj **aggressively** adv **aggressor** n

aggrieved adj suffering from injustice; feeling unfairly treated

aghast adj horrified; dumbfounded; shocked

agile adj quick; alert; nimble **agility** n

agitate vt **1** shake or stir violently **2** worry; make anxious; trouble vi also **agitate for** publicly campaign and fight for **agitator** n

aglow adj glowing; shining; alight

agnostic n person who believes that an immaterial being such as God cannot be the subject of real knowledge **agnosticism** n

ago adv in the past

agog adj eager and excited

agony n intense and prolonged pain or suffering; torment; anguish **agonize** vi,vt suffer or cause agony or extreme distress

agrarian adj relating to agricultural land or landed property

agree vi **1** consent **2** correspond; match; tally **3** think or feel the same (as) **4** make a joint decision **5** suit; go well with vt **1** settle; arrange terms of **2** acknowledge; concede; consent to **agreeable** adj **1** willing to consent **2** pleasant **agreement** n **1** consent; permission **2** deal or contract between parties **3** accordance; harmony

agriculture n practice or study of farming **agricultural** adj **agriculturalist** n

ahead adv further on; in front; in advance **go ahead** continue; proceed; advance

aid vt,vi help; assist; facilitate n help; assistance; support **in aid of** for; in order to help

ailment n particular illness or disease

aim vt,vi **1** point or direct (a gun, etc) towards a target **2** direct (one's efforts, remarks, etc) towards a particular object **aim at** or **for 1** try to achieve; strive for **2** mean or intend for ~n **1** act of aiming **2** goal; target; purpose **aimless** adj having no particular goal or purpose **aimlessly** adv **aimlessness** n

air n **1** mixture of gases, consisting chiefly of nitrogen (78 per cent) and oxygen (21 per cent), that is essential for respiration **2** layer of air surrounding the earth; atmosphere **3** light breeze **4** impression or aura **5** bearing; manner **6** tune; melody **by air** transported by aircraft **clear the air** remove tension or discord **in the air** not yet settled **into thin air** without a trace; completely **on/off the air** being/not being broadcast **walk** or **tread on air** feel elated **airs** pl n affectations ~vt **1** expose to fresh air; ventilate **2** declare openly; make public vt,vi dry in warm air **airborne** adj in or supported or carried by air **airtight** adj preventing the passage of air into or out of; impermeable **airy** adj **1** open to the fresh air; well ventilated **2** carefree; unconcerned **3** light as air; graceful **4** insubstantial; speculative **airily** adv **airiness** n

air-conditioning n system for controlling flow and humidity of air within a building

aircraft n machine, such as an aeroplane, helicopter, or glider, that is capable of flight through the air

aircraft carrier n warship with special decks for operational aircraft

airfield n extensive level area for take-off and landing of aircraft

airforce n branch of a nation's armed services concerned with military aircraft

airgun n gun discharged by compressed air

air hostess n stewardess on an aircraft

airlift n transportation by air of people, food, etc, esp in an emergency when surface routes are cut vt transport using an airlift

airline n organization offering transportation by scheduled flights for people and cargo **airliner** n

airmail n **1** letters and parcels conveyed by

aircraft **2** system for sending such mail *vt* send (mail) by air

airport *n* system of buildings, runways, hangars, etc, providing facilities for aircraft, passengers, and cargo

air-raid *n* military attack by enemy aircraft

airship *n* self-propelled aircraft kept aloft by buoyancy

aisle *n* **1** gangway or open passageway separating blocks of seats in a theatre, church, etc **2** area on either side of a church, usually separated from the nave by a series of pillars and arches

ajar *adj,adv* partially open

alabaster *n* form of gypsum that is white and opaque or translucent, used for statues, ornaments, etc

alarm *n* **1** warning signal, such as a bell or shout **2** sudden fear or anxiety; panic; fright *vt* **1** frighten; shock; horrify **2** alert to possible danger

alas *interj* expression of regret, sadness, etc

albatross *n* large sea-bird with webbed feet

albeit *conj* even though; although

albino *n* person or animal with unnatural colouring in skin and eyes

album *n* **1** book used for the display of photographs, stamps, etc **2** long-playing record

alcohol *n* **1** intoxicating substance produced by fermenting sugar in a liquid **2** any drink containing such a substance **alcoholic** *adj* containing aicohol *n* person addicted to alcohol **alcoholism** *n* addiction to alcohol

alcove *n* recess or niche

alderman *n* senior councillor of a city or borough

ale *n* type of light-coloured beer

alert *adj* watchful; quick to respond **alertness** *n*

algebra *n* branch of mathematics in which numbers, quantities, and variables are represented by symbols whose manipulation is governed by generalized rules and relationships **algebraic** *adj*

alias *adv* also known as *n* assumed name; pseudonym

alibi *n* claim that someone accused of a crime was elsewhere at the time that it was committed

alien *adj* **1** foreign; strange **2** not part of; contrary *n* foreigner **alienate** *vt* estrange;

cast out; cause to become indifferent or detached, esp from society **alienation** *n*

alight[1] *adj* **1** on fire; lit up **2** bright; shining

alight[2] *vi* (alighted *or* alit) **1** dismount; get down (from) **2** settle or perch (on) **alight on** find unexpectedly; seize; light on

align *vt,vi* **1** bring into line (with); line up; straighten **2** form an alliance (with); cooperate **alignment** *n*

alike *adj* similar; appearing the same; resembling *adv* similarly; in the same way

alimentary canal (æli'mentəri) *n* system of organs in the body, including the stomach and intestines, through which food passes

alimony *n* allowance paid to one marriage partner by the other following a legal separation

alive *adj* **1** living; existing **2** active; vigorous

alkali ('ælkəlai) *n* chemical base that is soluble in water **alkaline** *adj*

all *adj* **1** every one of; the whole of **2** complete; total *adv* entirely; completely; totally **all but** very nearly; almost **all in all** taking everything into consideration **in all** altogether; in total

allay *vt* alleviate; assuage; appease; relieve

allege (ə'ledʒ) *vt* claim as true; assert; avow **allegation** (æli'geiʃən) *n*

allegiance (ə'li:dʒəns) *n* loyalty, esp to a sovereign; fidelity

allegory ('æligəri) *n* story, painting, etc in which moral values and other qualities are personified **allegorical** (æli'gɔrik|) *adj*

alleluia *interj,n* hallelujah

allergy ('ælədʒi) *n* physical reaction of the body caused by extreme sensitivity to certain substances **allergic** (ə'lə:dʒik) *adj*

alleviate *vt* relieve (pain or suffering); allay **alleviation** *n*

alley *n* **1** *also* **alleyway** narrow passageway or street **2** lane used in skittles, ten-pin bowling, etc

alliance *n* **1** treaty of mutual friendship and help between nations **2** relationship so formed **3** nations so involved **4** close relationship; union **allied** *adj* **1** joined by alliance; united **2** related; connected

alligator *n* large reptile, chiefly of the southern US, related to the crocodile but having a shorter broader snout

alliteration *n* repetition of the initial sound, usually a consonant, in a group of words

7

allocate vt assign; distribute; share out **allocation** n

allot vt (-tt-) allocate **allotment** n 1 plot of rented land for cultivation 2 assignment

allow vt 1 permit; let 2 set aside 3 grant; permit to have; concede **allow for** make provision for **allowable** adj permissible **allowance** n 1 regular amount of money paid to a dependant 2 sum of money allocated for certain tasks, responsibilities, etc 3 concession; toleration **make allowances for** 1 excuse 2 take into account

alloy n metallic material consisting of a mixture of metals, as in bronze and brass, or of metals and nonmetals, as in steel

allude v **allude to** refer indirectly to

allure vt entice; attract; fascinate n attraction; fascination **allurement** n

ally n ('ælai) 1 member of an alliance 2 sympathetic person; supporter vt,vi (ə'lai) unite; join (with)

almanac ('ɔːlmənæk) n book containing a calendar, with astronomical and astrological information, etc , for the year

almighty adj 1 omnipotent; supremely or divinely powerful 2 sl tremendous; great **the Almighty** n God

almond n 1 tree related to the plum and peach 2 smooth oval nut in a hard shell produced by this tree adj of an oval shape like an almond

almost adv nearly; close to; not quite

alms (ɑːmz) pl n money or gifts donated as charity to the poor **almshouse** n building founded to provide accommodation and food for the poor and aged

aloft adj,adv high up; overhead

alone adj,adv by oneself; by itself; apart; isolated; separate; unaccompanied

along prep 1 from one end to the other 2 on any part of the length of adv 1 onwards; forwards 2 together (with); accompanying **all along** all the time **alongside** adv,prep along the side of; beside; parallel to

aloof adj distant; haughty or reserved; uninvolved adv at a distance; with reserve

aloud adv using a normal speaking voice; not silently; out loud

alphabet n system of letters or other symbols used for writing in a particular language **alphabetical** adj following the order of the letters of the alphabet **alphabetically** adv

alpine adj relating to mountains or a mountainous region

already adv by now, by then; previously

Alsatian n breed of dog resembling a wolf in appearance and often used by the police or as a guard dog

also adv in addition; as well; too; besides

altar n 1 table in a Christian church at which the Eucharist is celebrated 2 table or platform used for offerings or sacrifices to a deity

alter vt,vi change; give or take on a new form or appearance; modify **alteration** n

alternate adj ('ɔːltɪ:nət) every other or second one; first one then the other vi,vt ('ɔːltəneit) switch repeatedly from one to the other; take or arrange in turn **alternately** adv **alternation** n **alternative** n the second of two possibilities or choices adj offering a choice between two things

although conj though; even though; in spite of the fact that

altitude n height of an aircraft, mountain, etc , esp that above sea level

alto n 1 male singing voice or musical instrument with a range between tenor and treble 2 contralto

altogether adv 1 completely; totally; absolutely; all; utterly; entirely 2 on the whole 3 added together; in total

aluminium n silvery metallic element extracted mainly from bauxite and widely used in lightweight alloys

always adv all the time; without exception; regularly

am v 1st person singular form of **be** in the present tense

amalgamate vi,vt join together; merge; unite; combine **amalgamation** n

amass vt,vi bring or come together; accumulate; collect

amateur n person who is an unpaid participator in an activity such as sport or the arts adj 1 not professional 2 also **amateurish** lacking in skill or polish; of a rather low standard

amaze vt fill with surprise or wonder; astonish; astound **amazement** n **amazingly** adv

ambassador n minister or diplomat sent abroad by the Government as an official representative

amber n yellowish-brown fossil resin often used for jewellery adj 1 of a yellowish-brown or dull orange colour 2 made of amber

ambidextrous adj able to use either hand with equal skill **ambidexterity** n

ambiguous adj having more than one possible meaning; open to interpretation **ambiguity** n **ambiguously** adv

ambition n 1 desire or will to achieve fame, power, position, etc 2 desired object or goal; aim **ambitious** adj **ambitiously** adv

ambivalent (æm'bivələnt) adj having conflicting or uncertain feelings; undecided **ambivalence** n **ambivalently** adv

amble vi 1 walk at an easy and leisurely pace; stroll; saunter 2 (of a horse) move slowly lifting both legs on the same side of the body together n leisurely pace

ambulance n vehicle designed and equipped to convey sick or injured people to hospital

ambush n 1 act of lying in wait in order to make a surprise attack 2 such an attack, the concealed place from which such an attack is launched, or the attackers themselves vt attack (an enemy) by ambush

amen interj word meaning 'so be it' spoken or sung at the end of a prayer, hymn, etc

amenable adj 1 willing; agreeable; responsive 2 legally responsible; answerable 3 capable of being tested or judged

amend vt rectify; correct; modify **make amends** make up (for); compensate **amendment** n

amenity n often pl useful service or facility intended to make life easier or more comfortable

amethyst n precious stone of crystallized quartz that is usually purple or mauve

amiable adj pleasant; likeable; friendly **amiability** n **amiably** adv

amicable adj friendly; not hostile **amicably** adv

amid or **amidst** prep among or amongst; in the midst of

amiss adj faulty; defective; wrong adv wrongly; incorrectly **take amiss** feel wronged or hurt (by), often unjustifiably

ammonia n colourless pungent gas, containing nitrogen and hydrogen, used in the manufacture of fertilizers and of other chemicals

ammunition n 1 bullets, missiles, etc, that can be fired from a gun or other offensive weapon 2 information or points of argument used against someone in debate, criticism, etc

amnesty n general pardon given esp to political prisoners

amoeba n microscopic single-celled animal having a constantly changing shape

among or **amongst** prep 1 in the middle of; surrounded by; in company with; together with 2 between; shared by

amoral (ei'mɔrəl) adj outside the sphere of morality **amorality** n

amorous adj concerned with or displaying love; affectionate **amorously** adv **amorousness** n

amorphous adj having no distinct form, shape, or structure

amount n 1 quantity; extent; whole 2 sum; total v **amount to** 1 add up to; come to 2 be equal or equivalent to; have the same function as

ampere n unit used to measure electric current

amphetamine n drug that stimulates the central nervous system, used for the relief of nasal congestion, hay fever, etc

amphibian n 1 cold-blooded animal, such as the frog or newt, that usually lives on land as an adult but breeds in water 2 vehicle able to function both on land and water **amphibious** adj

amphitheatre n large arena enclosed by rising tiers of seats

ample adj 1 plenty; more than enough; sufficient 2 of generous proportions; large **amply** adv

amplify vt increase the intensity of (an electrical signal) vt,vi explain in greater detail; expand (on) **amplification** n **amplifier** n electrical device, used in radios, televisions, etc, for reproducing a signal at increased intensity

amputate vt,vi sever (a limb or part of a limb) usually by surgery **amputation** n

amuse vt 1 entertain, esp by speaking or acting in a humorous way 2 keep pleasantly busy or occupied **amusement** n

an indef art used before an initial vowel sound and sometimes h See **a**.

anachronism n 1 representation of an object, event, etc, in too early a historical period; chronological error 2 something no longer useful or suitable in the present age **anachronistic** adj

anaemia n deficiency of red blood cells causing pale appearance of the skin, fatigue, etc **anaemic** adj

anaesthetic (ænis'θetik) n substance administered before an operation to produce loss of sensation or unconsciousness **anaesthetist** n (ə'ni:sθətist) person trained to administer anaesthetics **anaesthetize** vt (ə'ni:sθətaiz) administer anaesthetics

anagram n word or phrase whose letters can be transposed to form a new word or phrase

anal ('einəl) adj relating to the anus

analogy (ə'nælədʒi) n comparison that serves to draw attention to a similarity between things **analogous** (ə'næləgəs) adj

analyse ('ænəlaiz) vt break down (a substance, situation, etc) into constituent parts or stages for examination **analysis** n, pl **analyses** (ə'næləsi:z) **analytic** (ænə'litik) or **analytical** adj **analyst** ('ænəlist) n 1 person who analyses 2 psychoanalyst

anarchy ('ænəki) n 1 form of society in which established forms of government and law are not recognized 2 disorder; lawlessness **anarchist** n supporter of anarchy

anatomy (ə'nætəmi) n study or science of the physical structure of animals and plants **anatomical** (ænə'tɔmikəl) adj **anatomist** (ə'nætəmist) n

ancestor ('ænsestə) n person from whom one is descended; forefather **ancestral** (æn'sestrəl) adj **ancestry** ('ænsəstri) n

anchor n 1 heavy steel or iron object used for holding fast a vessel in the water 2 something that offers security and stability vt,vi hold fast with the anchor **anchorage** n 1 place where a vessel may be anchored or the fee charged 2 stability, firm or sound basis

anchovy ('æntʃəvi) n small fish of the herring family with a strong salty flavour

ancient adj 1 relating to a very early or remote historical period 2 very old

ancillary adj auxiliary; secondary; subsidiary

and conj 1 as well as; in addition to 2 then; after 3 also; too

anecdote ('ænikdout) n short witty account or story

anemone (ə'neməni) n 1 woodland plant producing white, red, or deep blue flowers 2 sea anemone

anew adv afresh; again

angel n 1 spiritual being in the Christian religion who is one of God's attendants and messengers, usually depicted as having human form with wings 2 sweet kind-hearted person **angelic** (æn'dʒelik) adj

anger n feeling of intense annoyance or irritation; rage vt make angry; enrage; infuriate

angle[1] n 1 difference in direction between two intersecting lines or planes, measured in degrees 2 shape formed by such lines or planes 3 projecting corner 4 point of view; aspect vt 1 move or place at an angle; bend into an angle 2 direct at a particular audience; bias

angle[2] vi 1 fish with a rod, line, and bait 2 also **angle for** seek (compliments, favours, etc), esp by devious means **angler** n

Anglican adj relating to the Church of England n member of the Church of England **Anglicanism** n

angry adj 1 extremely cross or annoyed; enraged 2 sore and inflamed **angrily** adv

anguish n intense anxiety and distress; agony; torment

angular adj 1 having sharp corners or many angles 2 bony; gaunt

animal n living organism capable of spontaneous movement; creature adj 1 relating to an animal or animals 2 physical as opposed to spiritual; carnal

animate adj ('ænimət) living; capable of spontaneous movement vt ('ænimeit) give life or movement to; make active **animation** n

aniseed n seed yielding an aromatic oil with a strong liquorice flavour, used in medicines, drinks, etc

ankle n joint that connects the foot and the leg

annex vt (ə'neks) 1 take possession of by conquest 2 join; attach; incorporate n ('æneks) also **annexe** additional building usually set apart from the main block of a hotel, hospital, etc

annihilate vt wipe out completely; destroy; obliterate **annihilation** n

anniversary n 1 date of a significant event which occurred in some previous year 2 celebration of this

announce vt declare; proclaim; make known **announcement** n **announcer** n person who introduces programmes, reads news bulletins, etc , on radio or television

annoy vt,vi irritate; bother; vex **annoyance** n

annual adj 1 occurring once a year 2 valid for one year 3 lasting for one growing season n

1 plant that lasts for one growing season only **2** book or periodical published in a new edition each year **annually** adv

annuity (ə'nju:iti) n sum of money paid out in instalments at regular intervals

annul (ə'nʌl) vt (-ll-) declare (a law, marriage contract, etc) invalid or no longer binding; revoke

anoint vt rub or smear with oil, esp ritually as an act of consecration **anointment** n

anomaly (ə'nɒməli) n something that is out of place or deviates from the common rule **anomalous** adj.

anonymous (ə'nɒnəməs) adj **1** sometimes shortened to **anon** having no acknowledged author **2** faceless; unknown **anonymity** (ænə'nimiti) n

anorak n waterproof jacket with a hood

another adj **1** additional; further **2** different; separate pron **1** one more **2** a different or new one **3** a comparable or similar one

answer n **1** reply or response (to a question) **2** solution (to a problem) vt, vi reply or respond (to); acknowledge vt ~solve **answer for** accept responsibility or blame for **answer to** match or correspond to (a description) **answerable** adj responsible; liable; accountable

ant n small insect that typically lives in a complex highly organized colony

antagonize vt provoke; incite; arouse hostility by attacking **antagonism** n **antagonist** n **antagonistic** adj

antelope n deer-like animal with hollow horns such as the gazelle or springbok

antenatal adj relating to the period of pregnancy; before birth

antenna (æn'tenə) **1** pl **antennae** (æn'teni:) one of a pair of sensitive organs on the head of an insect, crustacean, etc; feeler **2** pl **antennas** radio aerial

anthem n patriotic song; hymn of praise

anthology n collection of poems, stories, articles, etc

anthropology n study of mankind and man's social and cultural relationships **anthropological** adj **anthropologist** n

anti-aircraft adj designed for defence against enemy aircraft

antibiotic (æntibai'ɒtik) n chemical substance, such as penicillin, used to destroy certain bacteria adj relating to an antibiotic

antibody n protein in the blood that counteracts harmful bacteria

anticipate vt **1** realize or recognize beforehand; predict; foresee **2** expect; look forward to; await **anticipation** n

anticlimax n drop in mood from excitement to flatness, seriousness to absurdity, etc

anticlockwise adj, adv moving in a direction opposite to that followed by the hands of a clock

antics pl n playful jokes, tricks, or gestures

anticyclone n area of high atmospheric pressure producing calm settled weather

antidote ('æntidout) n substance or agent used to counteract harmful effects; remedy

antifreeze n substance that lowers the freezing point of a liquid, used esp in car radiators

antique n valuable piece of furniture, work of art, etc, belonging to an earlier period adj **1** old and valuable **2** antiquated **antiquated** adj obsolete; out-of-date; old-fashioned **antiquity** (æn'tikwiti) n **1** quality of being very old **2** period before the Middle Ages; distant past

anti-Semitic (æntisə'mitik) adj discriminating against Jews **anti-Semite** (ænti'semait) n **anti-Semitism** (ænti'semitizəm) n

antiseptic adj relating to the destruction of undesirable microorganisms; preventing decay n an antiseptic substance

antisocial adj **1** contrary to the norms of society **2** unsociable; shunning the company of others

antithesis (æn'tiθisis) n, pl **antitheses** (æn'tiθisi:z) direct contrast; opposite **antithetical** (ænti'θetikəl) adj

antler n branched bony outgrowth on the head of a male deer or similar animal

anus n opening at the lower end of the rectum

anvil n iron or steel block on which metal is hammered and shaped

anxious adj **1** nervous; worried; uneasy; apprehensive; tense **2** keen; eager **anxiety** n **anxiously** adv

any adj **1** some; several **2** whichever; no matter which **3** one of many; every **at any rate/in any case** anyway; moreover; besides; anyhow; however ~pron **1** anybody; anything **2** some adv at all; to an extent **anybody** pron, n a person; no matter who; anyone **anyhow** adv **1** besides; anyway **2** haphazardly; with no particular care or organization; not systematically **anyone** pron,n anybody **anything** pron,n a thing; no matter what or which; something ~adv at all; remotely **anyway** adv 1 in any case; well; besides; anyhow; after all 2 carelessly; anyhow **anywhere** adv 1 to or at any place 2 at all; anything

apart adv 1 separately; independently 2 into parts or pieces 3 at a distance; away **apart from** after considering; aside from; other than

apartheid (ə'pɑːtaid) n system of racial segregation, esp in South Africa

apartment n 1 chiefly US flat, usually in a block. 2 suite of rooms

apathy n lack of sympathy, feeling, interest, etc; listlessness; complete indifference **apathetic** adj

ape n short-tailed or tailless primate, such as the chimpanzee or gorilla

aperture n 1 opening or slit 2 diaphragm in a lens system that limits the diameter of a light beam entering a camera, etc 3 diameter of such a diaphragm

apex ('eipeks) n, pl apexes or apices ('æpisiːz) highest point; vertex; tip; pinnacle

aphid ('eifid) n small insect that feeds on plant juices

apiece adv each; for each one

apology n 1 statement expressing regret for an offence, error, failure, etc 2 poor substitute **apologetic** adj sorry; making an apology **apologetically** adv **apologize** vi make an apology or excuse

apostle (ə'pɒsəl) n one of Christ's twelve disciples

apostrophe (ə'pɒstrəfi) n written or printed symbol ( ) used to show omission of a letter or letters or to denote the possessive case

appal vt (-ll-) fill with abhorrence; shock; horrify; disgust

apparatus n equipment, machinery, tools, etc, required for a particular purpose

apparent adj 1 seeming; ostensible 2 evident; clear; obvious **apparently** adv

appeal vi 1 apply to a higher authority for the reversal of a decision 2 plead; beseech; call (for) 3 appear attractive (to); please n 1 application to a higher authority 2 plea; request; entreaty 3 attractiveness; ability to arouse interest **appealing** adj attractive; arousing interest, sympathy, pity etc

appear vi 1 come into view; become visible 2 arrive 3 seem; give the impression (of) 4

become clear or obvious; emerge 5 give a public performance 6 become available 7 present oneself in court, before a tribunal, etc **appearance** n 1 coming into view 2 arrival 3 outward manifestation; impression; aspect; look 4 public performance 5 attendance in court **keep up appearances** maintain an outward show of respectability, affluence, etc

appease vt 1 pacify; soothe 2 assuage; ease; allay; relieve **appeasement** n

appendix n, pl **appendixes** or **appendices** (ə'pendisiːz) 1 small blind functionless tube attached to the lower abdomen 2 section containing supplementary information at the end of a book **appendicitis** n inflammation of the appendix

appetite n 1 desire to satisfy bodily needs, esp for food 2 craving; capacity **appetizing** adj able to stimulate the appetite; tasty

applaud vi,vt 1 show appreciation (of) by clapping 2 commend; praise **applause** n

apple n edible round fruit with a red, green, or yellow skin

apply vt 1 use in a practical or appropriate way; employ; put into practice 2 cover with; put on 3 concentrate; give attention to vi 1 make a formal request (for a job, money etc) 2 be appropriate; have a bearing (on) **appliance** n piece of equipment; tool; machine; instrument **applicable** adj relevant; appropriate; able to be applied **applicant** n person applying for a job, place, etc ; candidate **application** n 1 formal request; claim 2 putting into practice (of relevant knowledge, skills etc) 3 act of applying (paint, ointment, etc) 4 close attention; concentration

appoint vt 1 select for a job, position, etc 2 assign, allocate 3 arrange for a particular time; fix **appointment** n 1 fixed meeting; engagement 2 selection or nomination for a job position, etc 3 job or position for which a person is selected

apportion vt share out; allot; distribute **apportionment** n

appraise vt estimate the quality or value of; assess **appraisal** n

appreciate vt 1 be grateful for; recognize the worth of 2 realize; understand; be aware of vi increase in value **appreciation** n **appreciable** adj considerable; large; enough to be assessed

apprehend vt **1** arrest and take into custody **2** be anxious about; fear; dread vt,vi comprehend; grasp **apprehension** n **1** anxiety; fear; caution; dread **2** understanding; conception **3** arrest **apprehensive** adj worried; anxious; cautious; uneasy; doubtful

apprentice n person under contract to an employer whilst learning a trade vt engage or place as an apprentice

approach vt,vi draw close or closer (to); near; advance vt **1** make contact with in order to obtain advice, a favour, etc **2** begin to tackle; start working on; deal with **3** approximate; come close to being n **1** act of drawing near; advance **2** initial contact; overture **3** method of working, acting, thinking, etc **4** approximation **5** way in or to; access **approachable** adj **1** accessible; able to be contacted **2** friendly; easy to get on with

appropriate adj (ə'proupriət) suitable for a particular purpose or set of circumstances; relevant; apt vt (ə'prouprieit) **1** take possession of; take for one's own use **2** set aside; allocate **appropriately** adv **appropriation** n

approve vt give consent for; sanction **approve of** have a favourable opinion of; believe to be good or right **approval** n **1** consent; permission **2** favourable opinion **on approval** on free trial before deciding whether or not to buy

approximate adj (ə'prɒksimət) roughly calculated; estimated; about right vt,vi (ə'prɒksimeit) come close to what is required or expected; be roughly right **approximately** adv

apricot n small fleshy fruit that is similar to the peach, with a soft reddish-orange skin

April n fourth month of the year

apron n **1** loose covering worn over the front of the body to protect one's clothes and tied round the waist **2** part of a stage that projects in front of the curtain

apse n semicircular domed recess situated at the east end of a church

apt adj **1** fitting; appropriate; to the point **2** likely; inclined; liable **3** quick to learn; clever **aptly** adv **aptitude** n talent, skill, or ability; flair

aquarium n, pl **aquariums** or **aquaria** (ə'kwɛəriə) tank or pool for fish and aquatic plants

Aquarius (ə'kwɛəriəs) n eleventh sign of the zodiac represented by the water carrier

aquatic adj relating to or living in water

aqueduct n channel constructed to direct a flow of water, esp one built as a bridge

arable adj (of land) able to be ploughed in order to produce crops

arbitrary adj **1** not fixed by law; discretionary **2** impulsive; capricious **arbitrarily** adv

arbitrate vt,vi settle (a dispute); mediate (between) **arbiter** or **arbitrator** n **arbitration** n

arc n **1** curved segment of a circle **2** something shaped like an arc, such as a rainbow **3** luminous electrical discharge between two electrodes vi form an arc

arcade n **1** series of arches and columns **2** covered passageway or gallery, esp one lined with shops

arch[1] n **1** curved structure built to bear a load over an opening **2** also **archway** opening, passageway, gateway, etc, with an arch **3** curve; bow **4** part of the sole of the foot between the ball and heel vt,vi **1** span with an arch; curve over **2** produce or form into a curve or bow

arch[2] adj **1** chief; principal **2** mischievous; cunning

archaeology (ɑːki'ɒlədʒi) n scientific study of ancient remains and artefacts **archaeological** (ɑːkiə'lɒdʒikəl) adj **archaeologist** (ɑːki-'ɒlədʒist) n

archaic (ɑː'keiik) adj no longer in current use; out-of-date; old; belonging to the past

archbishop n bishop having jurisdiction over an ecclesiastical province

archduke n prince of the imperial dynasty of Austria **archduchess** n **1** wife or widow of an archduke **2** princess of the imperial dynasty of Austria **archduchy** (ɑːtʃ'dʌtʃi) n territory ruled by an archduke or archduchess

archery n art of shooting with a bow and arrows **archer** n

archetype ('ɑːkitaip) n **1** prototype **2** ideal or completely typical example or model; standard type **archetypal** or **archetypical** (ɑːki'tipikəl) adj

archipelago (ɑːki'peləgou) n chain or scattered group of islands

architecture n **1** art of designing buildings and other constructions **2** style of building or design **3** buildings taken collectively

architect n 1 person trained in architecture 2 planner; organizer; mastermind

archives ('ɑːkaɪvz) pl n 1 collection of historical records and documents 2 place where such a collection is kept **archivist** ('ɑːkɪvɪst) n person in charge of archives

arctic adj 1 relating to regions surrounding the earth's North Pole 2 extremely cold

ardent adj fervent; zealous; vigorously enthusiastic; earnest; passionate **ardently** adv **ardour** n

arduous adj hard and laborious; extremely difficult; exhausting; requiring great effort **arduously** adv

are v plural form of **be** in the present tense

area n 1 extent of a specific surface, piece of ground, geometric figure, etc 2 open space; region; locality 3 section or part 4 range or scope of something

arena n 1 central area for performers in an amphitheatre, stadium, etc 2 scene of activity

argue vi quarrel; attack verbally vi,vt debate; have a heated discussion (about); present (a case) for or against; reason **argument** n **argumentative** adj quarrelsome; inclined to argue

arid adj 1 extremely dry and infertile; parched 2 dull; not stimulating **aridity** n

Aries ('eəriːz) n first sign of the zodiac represented by the ram

arise vi (arose; arisen) 1 rise; get up; stand up 2 come about; occur; happen; start

aristocracy n 1 class of privileged people of the highest rank; nobility 2 government by such a class **aristocrat** n **aristocratic** adj

arithmetic n (ə'rɪθmətɪk) 1 manipulation of numbers by addition, subtraction, multiplication, and division 2 mathematical calculations adj (ærɪθ'metɪk) also **arithmetical** relating to arithmetic

arm[1] n 1 upper limb extending from the shoulder to the wrist 2 sleeve 3 support for the arm on a chair or seat 4 anything resembling an arm in appearance or function **armchair** n easy chair with supports for the arms **armhole** n opening in a garment for the arm to pass through **armpit** n hollow under the arm where it joins the shoulder

arm[2] vt,vi 1 equip (with weapons and ammunition) 2 prepare (for a confrontation discussion, etc) **arms** pl n weapons; firearms

armament n 1 equipment for fighting; weaponry 2 armed force 3 preparation for a war or battle

armour n 1 protective covering of metal formerly worn in battle 2 hard protective shell or covering of certain animals **armour-plated** adj also **armoured** fitted with a protective covering of steel against bullets, shells, torpedoes, etc

army n 1 organized military force 2 horde; large organized group

aroma n distinctive smell given off by food, wine, perfume, etc **aromatic** adj

arose v pt of **arise.**

around prep 1 round the outside of; surrounding; enclosing 2 from place to place within; about; at various points on 3 round rather than straight across 4 at approximately; about adv 1 on all sides; in a circle 2 somewhere near; in the vicinity; about 3 round; with a circular movement **get around** travel widely; circulate

arouse vt stimulate; provoke interest, anger, etc ; in; awake vt,vi rouse; wake **arousal** n

arrange vt 1 put into some kind of order or pattern; form 2 fix; make plans for 3 come to agreement about; settle on 4 adapt (music) for a different instrument **arrangement** n **arranger** n

array n 1 arranged selection or display; assortment 2 dress; clothing vt 1 dress lavishly; adorn 2 arrange in order; set out

arrears pl n outstanding payments; accumulated debts **in arrears** behind in one's payments

arrest vt 1 seize and detain by lawful authority; apprehend 2 hinder; check; stop n 1 act of arresting or state of being arrested 2 hindrance; check; stoppage **under arrest** held in detention **arresting** adj attracting attention

arrive vi 1 reach a destination 2 happen; occur 3 inf achieve success **arrive at** reach **arrival** n

arrogant adj proud; haughty; conceited **arrogance** n **arrogantly** adv

arrow n 1 slender pointed missile shot from a bow 2 symbol used to indicate direction, etc

arsenic n poisonous brittle grey metallic element

arson n crime of maliciously setting fire to property

art n 1 process of creative activity, esp painting

and drawing **2** works resulting from such a process **3** creative or practical skill **arts** *n pl or s* university course(s) such as modern languages, literature, history, and philosophy

artefact *n also* **artifact** man-made object

artery *n* **1** thick-walled tubular vessel that conveys oxygenated blood from the heart **2** major road, railway, or other channel of communication **arterial** *adj*

artful *adj* cunning; crafty; ingenious **artfully** *adv*

arthritis *n* painful inflammation of a joint or joints **arthritic** *adj*

artichoke *n* **1** *also* **globe artichoke** thistle-like plant with large edible fleshy flower heads **2** *also* **Jerusalem artichoke** sunflower with an edible tuber

article *n* **1** small object; item **2** newspaper or magazine report **3** clause or section in a document **4** the words *a* or *an* (*indefinite articles*) or *the* (*definite article*) preceding a noun or noun phrase **articled** *adj* bound by written contract; apprenticed

articulate *v* (aː'tikjuleit) *vt,vi* speak clearly *vt* express precisely or coherently *adj* (aː'tikjulit) **1** fluent; coherent **2** able to speak **articulated** *adj* having two or more jointed or pivoted sections **articulation** *n*

artifact *n* artefact

artificial *adj* **1** man-made; synthetic **2** feigned; not spontaneous **artificial respiration** *n* method for restoring natural breathing **artificially** *adv*

artillery *n* **1** large-calibre guns; cannon **2** troops or military units trained in their use

artist *n* **1** creative person, esp a painter or sculptor **2** skilful practitioner of a craft, etc **3** professional performer **artistic** *adj* **1** creative; skilled **2** beautiful; aesthetically pleasing **3** relating to art **artistically** *adv*

as *conj* **1** when; just at the time that **2** in the manner that; like **3** that which; what; whatever **4** because; since *prep,conj* to the extent (that); of the same amount (that) *prep* in the role or capacity of

asbestos *n* any of several incombustible fibrous minerals used for thermal insulation and in flameproof and building materials

ascend *vt,vi* climb; mount; rise **ascent** or **ascension** *n* **the Ascension** ascent of Christ into heaven

ascertain *vt* determine by inquiry; discover; find out

ascribe *vt* attribute (a work of art, blame, etc); assign

ash[1] *n* widespread deciduous tree with compound leaves, winged seeds, and a durable wood used as timber

ash[2] *n* **1** grey powdery residue of something that has been burnt **2** fine material thrown from an erupting volcano **ashes 1** human remains after cremation **2** ruins **ashen** *adj* pallid **ashtray** *n* receptacle for cigarette ends, ash, etc

ashamed *adj* **1** full of shame (for); remorseful **2** reluctant or refusing (to)

ashore *adv,adj* towards or on land

aside *adv* **1** on or to one side **2** into a secluded place **3** out of one s thoughts, consideration, etc **4** in reserve **aside from** apart from ~*n* confidential or seemingly confidential statement

ask *vt,vi* **1** put a question to (concerning) **2** make a request for *vt* **1** enquire about **2** invite **ask after** request news of **ask for trouble/it** behave provocatively

askew *adv* at an angle, awry *adj* crooked

asleep *adj* sleeping **fall asleep** pass into a state of sleep

asparagus *n* young edible shoots of a plant of the lily family

aspect *n* **1** direction towards which something faces; outlook **2** appearance **3** point of view; angle

asphalt *n* dark naturally occurring material used in road surfacing and roofing materials *vt* cover with asphalt

aspire *vi* have ambitious plans desires etc; yearn for **aspiration** *n*

aspirin *n* mild pain-relieving drug, usually taken in tablet form

ass *n* **1** donkey **2** fool; stupid person

assail *vt* attack; assault **assailant** *n,adj*

assassinate *vt* murder (a public figure), esp for political reasons **assassin** *n* murderer; hired killer **assassination** *n*

assault *n* **1** violent or sudden attack **2** *law* threat of attack *vt* **1** make an assault on **2** rape

assemble *vt,vi* **1** come or bring together; collect **2** fit together, construct **assembly** *n*

assent *n* **1** agreement, acceptance **2** consent *vi* agree to; accept

assert vt 1 declare as true 2 insist upon; maintain **assert oneself** act authoritatively or boldly **assertion** n **assertive** adj

assess vt 1 determine the value or amount of; evaluate 2 judge the worth or importance of **assessment** n

asset n possession, quality etc , that is useful or of value **assets** pl n capital; property

assign vt 1 allot; give to; set apart for; fix 2 nominate; select for; appoint to **assignation** n arrangement to meet secretly or illicitly; tryst **assignment** n

assimilate vt vi 1 absorb or become absorbed; incorporate 2 adjust or become adjusted vt digest (food) **assimilation** n

assist vt vi help; give support (to); work in a subordinate capacity (for) **assistance** n **assistant** n

associate v (ə'sousiet) **associate with** vt link or connect (with) vi keep company (with) n (ə'sousit, -eit) 1 partner; colleague 2 acquaintance; companion adj (ə'sousiit) 1 having equal or nearly equal status with others 2 having only partial rights **association** n 1 connection 2 organized group; society

assorted adj 1 of various kinds; miscellaneous 2 classified; sorted **ill-assorted** badly matched **assortment** n

assuage vt make less severe; ease; lessen

assume vt 1 take for granted; accept; suppose 2 undertake; take on 3 adopt; feign; affect **assumed** adj 1 false; fictitious 2 taken for granted **assumption** n

assure vt 1 make certain; ensure 2 inform confidently; promise; guarantee **assurance** n 1 promise; guarantee 2 certainty 3 self-confidence 4 life or endowment insurance **assuredly** adv definitely

asterisk n symbol (*) used in print to indicate an omission, cross reference, etc vt mark with an asterisk

asthma ('æsmə) n disorder, often allergic, causing difficulty in breathing, wheezing etc **asthmatic** adj n

astonish vt fill with surprise or wonder; amaze; astound **astonishment** n

astound vt surprise greatly; astonish

astray adv,adj away from what is right or expected

astride adv adj prep with a leg on each side (of)

astrology n prediction of human characteristics, activities, etc , based on the motion and relative positions of celestial bodies **astrological** adj **astrologer** n

astronaut n person trained and adapted to space travel **astronautical** adj **astronautics** n

astronomy n study of the universe and the celestial bodies contained in it **astronomer** n **astronomical** or **astronomic** adj 1 relating to astronomy or the celestial bodies 2 huge; immense

astute adj cunning; sly; clever; perceptive; quick **astutely** adv **astuteness** n

asunder adv,adj apart; in(to) pieces

asylum n 1 temporary refuge; place of shelter; sanctuary 2 mental hospital

at prep 1 in; close to; next to 2 towards; in the direction of 3 towards or around a specified time 4 in a state of; engaged in 5 during 6 in exchange for; for the price of 7 about; concerning

ate v pt of **eat.**

atheism n disbelief in the existence of God **atheist** n

athlete n person skilled in running hurdling, shot putting, or other track and field sports **athletics** n track and field sports **athletic** adj

atlas n book containing maps

atmosphere n 1 gaseous layer surrounding the earth or other celestial body 2 air in an enclosed space 3 gaseous medium 4 prevailing mood; feeling 5 unit of pressure **atmospheric** adj

atom n 1 minute entity of which chemical elements are composed, consisting of a central nucleus around which electrons orbit 2 very small amount **atom bomb** also **atomic bomb** bomb in which energy is derived from nuclear fission **atomic** adj **atomic energy** n energy derived from nuclear fission or fusion **atomize** vt reduce (a liquid, such as perfume) to a fine spray by forcing it through a nozzle **atomizer** n

atone vi make amends (for a sin error etc); expiate **atonement** n

atrocious adj 1 extremely cruel; wicked; appalling; horrifying 2 inf of very poor quality **atrociously** adv **atrocity** n cruel and appalling act or behaviour

attach vt,vi join; connect; fasten vi 1 attribute;

ascribe **2** adhere; be inherent in **attached to 1** fond of; devoted to **2** assigned or brought in as a specialist **attachment** n

attaché n member of staff of an embassy or legation **attaché case** n small rectangular case for carrying documents, etc

attack vt **1** make a physical or verbal assault on; assail; set upon **2** seize upon; take up with vigour **3** act or play offensively **4** affect adversely n **1** physical or verbal assault **2** offensive action **3** bout of illness

attain vt,vi succeed in reaching; achieve; obtain; get **attainable** adj **attainment** n

attempt vt try (to do or accomplish something); endeavour n **1** effort, often unsuccessful **2** attack

attend vt,vi be present (at); go regularly (to) vi pay attention (to); listen (to) **attend to 1** deal with; handle; manage **2** look after; tend; minister **attendance** n **1** act of attending; presence **2** number of persons present **attendant** n person employed to assist, guide, look after, etc adj associated or accompanying **attention** n **1** concentrated thought **2** observation; notice **call** or **bring attention to** point out **pay attention to 1** take notice of; attend **2** take care of **stand to attention.** adopt a formal alert stance, esp on military occasions **attentive** adj **1** listening carefully; observant **2** thoughtful; polite

attic n room just below the roof; garret

attitude n **1** opinion; judgement; policy; disposition **2** position of the body; pose **strike an attitude** assume a theatrical pose

attorney n **1** person with legal authority to act for another **2** US lawyer

attract vt **1** excite pleasure, anticipation etc, in; fascinate **2** cause to approach; draw towards **attraction** n **attractive** adj **1** pleasing to look at; alluring; appealing **2** interesting; pleasing

attribute vt (əˈtribjuːt) **attribute to** consider as produced by, resulting from, or belonging to; ascribe to n (ˈætribjuːt) property; quality; feature **attribution** n

atypical (eiˈtipikəl) adj not typical; unrepresentative

aubergine n tropical plant with a deep purple egg-shaped fruit, eaten as a vegetable

auburn n,adj reddish-brown

auction n public sale in which items are sold to

the highest bidder vt sell by auction **auctioneer** n person conducting an auction

audacious adj **1** fearlessly bold **2** impudent; forward

audible adj able to be heard **audibly** adv

audience 1 group of spectators, listeners, etc **2** formal hearing or interview granted by someone in authority

audiovisual adj involving both hearing and sight

audit n professional examination of business accounts vt,vi examine by or perform audit(s) **auditor** n

audition n trial in which an actor, singer, musician, etc, demonstrates his ability or his aptitude for a role vt,vi give a trial hearing (to)

auditorium n, pl **auditoriums** or **auditoria** part of a theatre, hall, etc, where the audience is seated

augment vt,vi increase; enlarge; extend **augmentation** n

August n eighth month of the year

aunt n **1** sister of one's mother or father **2** wife of one's uncle

au pair n foreign girl who undertakes housework, etc, in return for board and lodging adv as an au pair

aura n **1** distinctive air or quality of a person or thing; charisma **2** apparent emanation surrounding an object, etc

aural adj relating to hearing

austere adj severe; strict; harsh; not luxurious **austerely** adv **austerity** n

authentic adj genuine; real; not faked; from a reliable source **authentically** adv **authenticity** n

author n **1** writer of a book, script, article, etc **2** originator; creator **authorship** n

authoritative adj possessing, exercising, or claiming authority **authoritatively** adv **authorize** vt empower; sanction; give permission for **authorization** n

authority n **1** power or right to command and enforce obedience **2** official body or group having such power **3** position commanding such power **4** delegated power **5** acknowledged expert or trustworthy written work **6** power or influence **authoritarian** adj favouring the enforcement of obedience; opposed to individual freedom; nondemocratic n an authoritarian person

autistic adj living in a fantasy world; abnormally introspective **autism** n

autobiography n person's biography written by that person; personal biography **autobiographical** adj

autograph n handwritten signature vt write an autograph in; sign

automatic adj 1 operated or regulated by mechanical means; self-acting 2 performed or produced without conscious thought or effort 3 inevitable n self-loading weapon firing continuously on depression of the trigger **automatically** adv **automation** n automatic operation of industrial processes or equipment

autonomous adj self-governing; self-sufficient; independent **autonomously** adv **autonomy** n

autumn n season between summer and winter

auxiliary adj additional; supporting; extra; ancillary n helper; assistant **auxiliary verb** verb used to express tense, mood, etc , of another verb

avail n **to** or **with no avail** in vain; without success v **avail oneself of** make use of; help oneself to

available adj obtainable; ready for use; accessible **availability** n

avalanche n 1 heavy fall of snow and ice down a mountainside 2 large pile or heap that has accumulated suddenly and rapidly

avenge vt,vi seek vengeance (for); punish in retaliation

avenue n 1 wide road or drive, esp one lined with trees 2 means of achieving; way; opening

average n 1 sum of a set of numbers or quantities divided by their total number; mean value 2 representative or typical amount, value etc **on average** typically; usually ~adj 1 typical, representative, usual 2 constituting or worked out as an average vt 1 perform or receive an amount calculated as an average 2 calculate an average vi amount to an average

averse adj disinclined, unwilling, against **aversion** n strong dislike; repulsion

aviary n enclosure or large cage for birds

aviation n art or science of flying aircraft **aviator** n airman; pilot

avid adj eager; enthusiastically dedicated or keen **avidity** n **avidly** adv

avocado (ævɔ'kɑːdəʊ) n also **avocado pear**

fleshy pear-shaped tropical fruit with a dark green or purple skin .

avoid vt keep away from or out of; evade; refrain from **avoidable** adj **avoidance** n

avow vt declare; claim; admit openly **avowal** n

await vt 1 wait for; expect 2 be ready or in store for

awake v (awoke or awaked; awaked) vt vi wake; wake up; rouse vt arouse, stir; stimulate

awaken vt,vi awake

award vt give as a prize; grant n prize; grant

aware adj conscious (of); having knowledge; well-informed **awareness** n

away adv 1 to or at a place further off 2 apart; at a distance; separately 3 out of one's possession 4 without hesitation; immediately 5 until there is nothing left **do away with** 1 abolish; get rid of 2 murder; kill **get away with** do without being noticed or caught ~adj absent; not at home

awe n feeling of absolute wonder, fear, reverence, etc vt fill with awe; dumbfound **awe-inspiring** adj overwhelming; magnificent; tremendous **awesome** adj capable of producing awe **awe-struck** adj also **awe-stricken** filled with awe

awful adj terrible; dreadful; very bad **awfully** adv inf very; extremely

awhile adv briefly; for a while

awkward adj 1 clumsy ungainly 2 difficult to deal with; tricky; inconvenient **awkwardly** adv **awkwardness** n

awl n small tool used for boring holes in leather wood, etc

awning n sheet of canvas attached to a frame to provide cover and protection from the weather

awoke v pt of **awake.**

awry (ə'raɪ) adj 1 crooked, askew 2 wrong, amiss

axe n chopping tool with a long handle and a broad blade **have an axe to grind** act from selfish motives or a vested interest ~vt 1 chop or fell with an axe 2 cut back or reduce drastically

axis n, pl **axes** ('æksiːz) 1 line about which something rotates or is symmetrical 2 reference line on a graph by which a point is located 3 main central stem of a plant

axle n rod or shaft that allows an attached wheel to revolve

azalea n flowering shrub related to the rhododendron

B

babble vi,vt **1** speak incoherently and continuously: chatter **2** burble; murmur n **1** fast incoherent speech **2** burbling sound; murmur

babe n baby

baboon n large monkey

baby n **1** newborn child; infant **2** newborn animal vt treat as a baby; lavish care on **babyish** adj **baby-sit** vi (-tt-) look after a baby for a short time while the parents are out **baby-sitter** n

bachelor n **1** unmarried man **2** person who holds a first degree from a university or college

bacillus n any of various rod-shaped bacteria

back n **1** that part of the body extending from the base of the neck to the buttocks **2** corresponding part of an animal **3** spine; backbone **4** side or part that is opposite the front; reverse **5** place furthest away from the front; rear **6** part of a garment that covers the back **7** defence player in football, hockey, etc **behind one's back** without one's knowledge; deceitfully **get/put one's back up** antagonize; provoke; anger ~vt **1** bet on to win **2** support; sponsor **3** provide a musical accompaniment for vt,vi move backwards; reverse **back down** withdraw a claim, challenge, etc ; admit fault **back onto** have the back or rear bordering on **back out** withdraw one's support **back up** support; encourage; confirm ~adv **1** backwards; towards the rear **2** in or into the past **3** to a previous or earlier place, state, condition, owner, etc **4** in reply; in return **back to front** with the back and front reversed **go back on** break (a promise) **take back** revoke; cancel ~adj **1** situated behind **2** from the past; overdue; not current

backbencher n British member of Parliament without a ministerial position

backbone n **1** spine **2** stamina; courage; spirit

backdate vt make effective from an earlier date

backfire vi **1** produce an explosion of fuel mixture in an internal-combustion engine **2** have unintended and unfortunate consequences

backgammon n board game for two players, each using fifteen pieces, which are moved according to the throws of two dice

background n **1** place, setting, scene etc , at the back or in the distance **2** person's class, education, experience, etc **3** context through which historical, political, or social events may be understood

backhand n stroke in tennis made with the back of the hand facing the direction of the shot **backhanded** adj **1** relating to a backhand **2** with underlying sarcasm

backing n **1** sponsorship; support **2** musical accompaniment

backlash n **1** recoil occurring when machinery parts are badly worn or faulty **2** hostile reaction; repercussions

backlog n accumulated work, arrears, etc , requiring attention

backside n inf buttocks; bottom

backstage adv **1** behind the stage, esp in the wings, dressing-rooms, etc **2** at the back of the stage adj taking place behind or at the back of the stage

backstroke n type of stroke made when swimming on one's back

backward adj **1** slow to learn or progress; underdeveloped **2** directed towards the back or rear **3** towards or fixed in the past **4** bashful; shy adv backwards **backwardness** n

backwards adv **1** towards the back or rear **2** in reverse **3** into the past **4** back to a poorer state or condition **know backwards** know thoroughly

backwater n **1** stretch of water cut off from the main stream **2** isolated place unaffected by changes occurring elsewhere

bacon n cured meat from the back or sides of a pig

bacteria pl n group of microscopic vegetable organisms causing putrefaction, fermentation, disease, etc **bacterial** adj

bad[1] adj **1** not good; below standard; poorer than average **2** disobedient; naughty **3** harmful; injurious **4** sinful; wicked **5** sick; unwell **6** not fresh; rotten **7** distressing; upsetting **8** unpleasant; distasteful **badly** adv **1** unsatisfactorily; poorly **2** very much; urgently; seriously **bad-tempered** adj cross; irritable

bad[2] *v a pt of* **bid.**

bade (beid bæd) *v a pt of* **bid.**

badge *n* 1 emblem worn or displayed to indicate rank, membership, etc 2 distinguishing mark or characteristic

badger *n* nocturnal burrowing animal with a black and white striped head *vt* pester

badminton *n* game similar to tennis played with lightweight rackets and a shuttlecock

baffle *vt* perplex, bewilder; stump; mystify

bag *n* 1 container of leather, paper, etc , used for carrying things in 2 loose or sagging fold of skin *v* (-gg-) *vt* 1 put into a bag 2 *inf* claim; seize first *vi* hang loosely; sag; bulge **baggage** *n* luggage **baggy** *adj* hanging loosely; not tight **bagginess** *n* **bagpipes** *pl n* musical instrument consisting of a set of reed pipes and a wind-bag **bagpiper** *n*

bail[1] *n* 1 sum of money that is pledged to secure the release of a person from custody on condition that he appears in court on a specified date 2 procedure allowing such a sum of money to be pledged *vt* **bail out** rescue (a person, company, etc) esp by giving financial assistance

bail[2] *n* small wooden bar placed across the stumps of a wicket

bail[3] *vt vi also* **bail out** remove (water) from the bottom of a boat with a bucket or can

bailiff *n* 1 official employed by a sheriff to serve writs collect fines, summon juries, etc 2 landowner s agent

bait *n* 1 things such as worms , maggots, etc , used by an angler to lure and catch fish 2 food or other enticement used to lure animals into a trap 3 enticement, temptation *vt* 1 prepare (a line or trap) with bait 2 lure; entice 3 taunt; persecute

bake *vi vt* cook (bread, cakes etc) in an oven **baker** *n* person who bakes or sells bread, cakes, etc **bakery** *n* 1 room where bread cakes, etc , are baked 2 baker s shop

balance *n* 1 apparatus for weighing consisting of two pans suspended from either end of a horizontal bar which has a central pivot 2 equilibrium 3 emotional or mental stability rationality 4 compatibility; equality of distribution; harmony 5 equality between credit and debit totals 6 remainder; amount left over **in the balance** not yet decided ~*vt* 1 weigh on a balance 2 keep or put in a state of balance 3 calculate the totals of *vi* have

equal totals *vt vi* place in or achieve equilibrium **balance sheet** *n* statement of accounts showing a company s financial position for a given period

balcony *n* 1 enclosed platform built on to the outside of a wall of a building usually with access from within 2 gallery of seats above the circle in a theatre

bald *adj* 1 having no hair, esp on the head 2 threadbare; badly worn 3 bare; having no vegetation 4 plainly expressed; blunt **baldly** *adv* **baldness** *n*

bale[1] *n* large bundle or package *vt* pack into a bale

bale[2] *vi* **bale out** make an emergency parachute jump

ball[1] *n* 1 spherical object used in games such as football, golf, or tennis 2 any spherical object 3 rounded fleshy part of the thumb, sole of the foot, etc **balls** *pl n sl* testicles **on the ball** aware; quick to react

ball[2] *n* grand social event with music and dancing, refreshments etc **have a ball** enjoy oneself enormously **ballroom** *n* hall or large room used for dancing

ballad *n* narrative poem that is usually set to music

ballast *n* 1 any heavy material used to stabilize a ship, balloon etc 2 mixture of gravel and sand used in building

ballerina *n* female ballet dancer

ballet *n* 1 theatrical dance form requiring a conventional and highly developed technique 2 performance in which a story is told through dance and mime 3 music written for such a performance 4 company of dancers

ballistics *n* study of the motion of projectiles **ballistic** *adj* relating to projectiles or ballistics

balloon *n* 1 inflatable coloured rubber bag used as a toy or for decoration 2 large impermeable bag filled with gas lighter than air that enables it to rise in the air, often having a basket for passengers, scientific instruments, etc *vi* fly in a balloon *vt, vi* inflate or swell

ballot *n* 1 system of voting using tickets, cards slips etc 2 tickets or cards used in voting 3 number of votes cast *vt vi* vote or put to the vote by ballot

bamboo *n* tropical treelike grass with hard hollow stems, which are often used for making furniture

ban *vt* (-nn-) prohibit, declare to be illegal

forbid n order or rule prohibiting certain goods, behaviour, etc

banal (bə'na:l) adj commonplace; trite; mundane

banana n tropical fruit that is long or crescent shaped with a thick yellow skin

band[1] n 1 small group of people 2 group of musicians, esp one playing woodwind, brass, and percussion instruments for dancing or marching v **band together** form into a united group

band[2] n 1 flat strip of cloth, rubber, metal, etc, used as a fastening or for decoration 2 coloured stripe 3 waveband

bandage n strip of cloth used to keep a dressing in place over a wound, support a sprain, etc vt cover with a bandage

bandit n outlawed robber

bandy adj bow-legged vt 1 exchange (words, blows etc) 2 throw or pass to and fro

bang n 1 loud noise as of an explosion; report 2 knocking noise 3 slam 4 sharp hit or blow vt, vi 1 make a loud explosive sound 2 knock loudly; rap 3 slam 4 hit, strike **banger** sl 1 sausage 2 old car 3 firework that explodes with a bang

bangle n ornamental band worn as a bracelet

banish vt 1 exile; expel 2 dispel **banishment** n

banister n support rail on a staircase

banjo n long-necked instrument of the guitar family with a circular body

bank[1] n 1 slope; embankment 2 large mound or pile vt also **bank up** form into a mound; heap up

bank[2] n 1 institution dealing in deposits and withdrawals of money loans, exchange of currencies, etc 2 building occupied by such an institution 3 place reserved for the safekeeping of some valuable commodity vt deposit in a bank vi have an account with a bank **bank on** rely on **bankbook** n book containing a record of a person's financial transactions with a bank **banker** n professional expert in banking; financier **banking** n business of running a bank or similar institution **bank holiday** n public holiday on which banks are traditionally closed **banknote** n paper note issued by a bank as money **Bank Rate** n rate of interest charged by the Bank of England to the banking system

bankrupt adj insolvent n person who is declared bankrupt by a court **bankruptcy** n

banner n 1 flag or ensign, esp one carried in a procession 2 something that represents a principle, particular cause, etc

banquet n lavish entertainment and feast given for a large number of guests

baptize vt, vi initiate into the Christian faith with the rite of immersing in or sprinkling with water **baptism** n **Baptist** n member of a Christian denomination believing in baptism as an expression of personal faith adj relating to such a denomination

bar n 1 straight piece of wood, metal, etc, used as part of an enclosure, lever, etc 2 stripe; band 3 slab of chocolate, soap, etc 4 barrier; obstruction 5 counter from which drinks or refreshments are served 6 room in a hotel or public house where alcoholic drinks are served 7 also **barline** vertical stroke on a stave in a musical score 8 notes or music occurring between such strokes **the Bar** professional body of barristers **barmaid** n woman employed to serve drinks in a hotel or public house **barman** n

barbarian n savage or uncivilized person adj uncivilized; not cultured **barbaric** adj also **barbarous** cruel; savage; brutal; inhuman **barbarism** n also **barbarity** cruelty; brutality; uncivilized behaviour

barbecue ('ba:bikju:) n 1 grid or grill used on an open fire for cooking meat, vegetables, etc 2 party held in the open air at which barbecued food is served vt cook on a barbecue

barber n person who cuts men s hair, trims beards, etc

barbiturate n drug used as a sedative

bare adj 1 unclothed; naked 2 uncovered; unadorned 3 plain; undecorated 4 having no vegetation 5 mere; hardly sufficient vt uncover, make bare **bareness** n **barefoot** adj, adv having no covering on the foot **barely** adv 1 hardly; only just; scarcely 2 austerely; not elaborately

bargain n 1 agreement between parties; deal 2 something bought cheaply; good buy **into the bargain** moreover; besides ～vi barter; haggle; make a deal **bargain for** be prepared for expect

barge n large flat-bottomed boat used esp for carrying cargo on canals vi 1 bump (into), collide; push rudely 2 interrupt; enter noisily

baritone n male singing voice or musical instrument with a range between bass and tenor

bark[1] n 1 loud cry of a dog or wolf 2 gruff angry voice vi,vt 1 (of a dog or wolf) utter a loud harsh cry 2 speak in a gruff voice

bark[2] n outer covering of the trunk and branches of a tree vt scrape the skin or outer layer of

barley n cereal plant with spiked ears used for food and to make malt for brewing and distilling **barley-sugar** n boiled sweet made from sugar

barn n farm building used for storing hay, housing livestock, etc

barnacle n crustacean that attaches itself to rocks, the timber of boats, etc

barometer n 1 instrument for measuring atmospheric pressure 2 anything that indicates or warns of change

baron n 1 nobleman of the lowest rank 2 inf magnate **baronial** adj **baroness** n 1 wife or widow of a baron 2 woman of a rank that is equivalent to that of a baron **baronet** n man of a rank between that of a baron and a knight **baronetcy** n

barracks n pl or s building used for the accommodation of soldiers

barrel n 1 cylindrical wooden or metal container 2 tube of a gun through which the bullet or shell is discharged vt put into a barrel

barren adj 1 infertile; sterile 2 unproductive; bare 3 dull; uninteresting **barrenness** n

barricade n obstruction hastily set up as a barrier against an advancing enemy vt block with a barricade

barrier n 1 gate fence, etc intended to prevent access 2 something that screens or protects 3 hindrance; impediment

barrister n lawyer having the right to practise in a court of law

barrow[1] n cart pushed by hand; wheelbarrow

barrow[2] n burial mound

barter vi vt trade by exchanging goods or commodities vi haggle n exchange of goods by bartering

base[1] n 1 bottom, support on which something is constructed or rests 2 foundation, basis 3 main ingredient or element 4 starting point 5 headquarters 6 establishment set up by the armed forces 7 marked position on a baseball pitch 8 sour-tasting chemical substance that

turns litmus blue vt 1 take as a foundation or starting point 2 locate; situate **baseball** n game for two sides of nine players each, on a diamond-shaped pitch using a hard ball and wooden bat **basement** n room or set of rooms built below ground level

base[2] adj 1 mean; despicable 2 inferior; worthless **baseness** n

bash inf vt hit hard; slog n rough blow **have a bash** try; attempt

bashful adj shy; embarrassed **bashfully** adv **bashfulness** n

basic adj 1 fundamental; main 2 elementary; primary 3 relating to a chemical base **basics** pl n fundamental or underlying principles **basically** adv

basin n 1 bowl used for mixing foods, holding liquids, etc 2 sink; washbasin 3 area of land drained by a river

basis n, pl **bases** ('beisiːz) 1 underlying principle; foundation 2 main part

bask vi 1 expose oneself to the warmth of the sun, a fire, etc 2 display enjoyment of publicity, glory, etc

basket n 1 receptacle made of cane, straw, etc 2 metal hoop with a net attached used as the goal in basketball **basketball** n game for two sides of five or six players each, using a large ball which must be shot through a metal hoop fixed to a board in order to score **basketry** n art of making baskets

bass[1] (beis) n 1 lowest range of male singing voice 2 musical instrument having the lowest range of its type 3 double bass

bass[2] (bæs) n, pl **bass** sea fish with a spiny dorsal fin; perch

bassoon n woodwind instrument that is lower in tone than an oboe and having a mouthpiece fitted with a double reed **bassoonist** n

bastard n 1 illegitimate child 2 inf unpleasant or cruel person

bat[1] n wooden implement used for hitting a ball in various games **off one's own bat** unassisted and on one's own initiative ~vi,vt (-tt-) strike or play with a bat **batsman** n, pl -**men** person who bats in cricket

bat[2] n small nocturnal mammal that is able to fly

batch n 1 quantity of loaves, cakes, etc, baked at the same time 2 set; group

bath n 1 large tub that is filled with water and used for washing the whole body 2 act of sitting or lying in a bath in order to wash oneself **3** water in a bath **baths** *pl n* building housing public baths, swimming pool, etc ~*vi,vt* wash in a bath **bathroom** *n* room containing a bath and often a toilet and washbasin

bathe *vi* **1** swim **2** have a bath *vt* **1** wash in order to cleanse or soothe **2** cover with light, colour, etc **bathing costume** *n* garment worn when bathing, swimming, etc

baton *n* **1** small stick used to conduct an orchestra **2** stick carried by the runner in a relay race **3** staff of office

battalion *n* military unit of three or four companies

batter[1] *vt,vi* beat severely and repeatedly; pound

batter[2] *n* mixture of flour, eggs, and milk used in cooking

battery *n* **1** electrical device used as the source of current in radios, torches, vehicles, etc **2** collection of cages for intensive rearing of chickens, turkeys, etc **3** unlawful attack on a person **4** prepared position for artillery, the artillery itself, or a military unit operating it **5** array; number

battle *n* **1** fighting between organized forces or armies **2** hard struggle; fight *vi* **1** fight in a battle **2** struggle; strive **battlefield** *n* site of a battle **battleship** *n* large armoured warship

battlement *n* parapet with indentations, used for defence

bauxite *n* claylike substance that is the chief ore of aluminium

bawl *vt,vi* shout or cry loudly; howl; bellow *n* howl

bay[1] *n* coastal inlet

bay[2] *n* **1** window area projecting beyond the face of a building **2** recess, alcove **3** area set aside for parking or loading and unloading a vehicle **4** storage area in an aircraft

bay[3] *n* type of laurel tree whose aromatic leaves are used as a seasoning

bay[4] *n* bark or deep cry of a hound **at bay 1** facing and warding off a pursuer **2** in check; at a distance ~*vt,vi* bark; howl

bay[5] *n* horse with a reddish-brown body and black mane and tail *adj,n* reddish-brown

bayonet *n* short blade attached to the muzzle of a rifle *vt* stab with a bayonet

be *vi* (*pres t s* am*, are, is; pl are pt s* was, were,

was; *pl* were *pp* been) **1** exist **2** occur; take place **3** equal; have the character of **4** remain; stay **5** continue to do or act *v aux* (used to form the passive)

beach *n* expanse of sand, pebbles, etc , on the seashore **beachcomber** *n* person who makes a living by collecting things washed ashore by the sea

bead *n* **1** small ball strung together with others to make a necklace, rosary, etc **2** small drop; globule *vt* decorate with beads

beak *n* horny jaw of a bird; bill

beaker *n* **1** glass for drinking from; tumbler **2** small glass cylinder used in chemical experiments

beam *n* **1** thick piece of timber or steel used to support a floor or roof; joist; girder **2** shaft of light; ray **3** radio or radar signal **4** radiant smile *vt,vi* **1** send out (a ray of light, radio signal, etc) **2** smile radiantly

bean *n* **1** type of plant producing pods containing seeds **2** pod or seeds of such a plant often eaten as a vegetable **full of beans** cheerful and energetic; ebullient

bear[1] *v* (bore; borne) *vt* **1** take the weight of; support **2** hold; carry **3** accept responsibility for **4** *pp* **born** give birth to **5** yield (fruit); produce **6** tolerate; endure **7** display; wear **8** possess; have **9** conduct (oneself) *vi* follow or move in the direction of **bring to bear** exert influence; effect **bear on 1** push or press against **2** be relevant to; relate to **bear out** confirm; furnish proof of **bear up** cope cheerfully; manage **bearer** *n*

bear[2] *n* **1** large carnivorous mammal with black, brown, or white shaggy fur **2** person who sells stocks and buys them back after the price has dropped

beard *n* **1** hair growth on the chin and sides of the face **2** tuft or growth resembling a beard

bearing *n* **1** person's carriage, posture, deportment, etc **2** relevance; significance **3** angle measured from north or some other fixed direction **4** machine part that supports or guides another moving part **bearings** *pl n* **1** position or direction determined by reference to fixed points **2** awareness of one's situation; orientation

beast *n* **1** animal, esp when distinguished from man **2** brutal person **beastly** *inf adj* disgusting, nasty **beastliness** *n*

beat *v* (beat; beaten) *vt* **1** strike hard; hit **2**

thrash; flog **3** hammer; bang **4** whisk; stir vigorously **5** flap; move up and down **6** defeat in a contest **7** do better than; surpass **8** overcome vi **1** throb; pulsate **2** pound; bang **3** produce a rhythmical sound **4** move up and down **beat up** assault and injure severely ~n **1** throb; pulsation **2** blow; bang; stroke **3** rhythmical sound **4** basic unit by which the duration of musical notes is measured **5** stressed syllable or note in poetry or music **6** type of popular music with a strongly marked rhythm and beat

beauty n **1** quality or qualities appealing to the senses or intellect and conforming to a certain standard of excellence, attractiveness, etc **2** exceptionally lovely woman **3** exceptionally good example of something **beautiful** adj **beautifully** adv

beaver n **1** aquatic rodent with webbed feet and a strong broad tail **2** fur of the beaver vi work hard and enthusiastically

because conj for the reason that; since **because of** on account of; due to

beckon vi,vt summon with a gesture of the hand or head n summoning gesture

become v (became; become) vi **1** grow, change, or develop into; start to be **2** happen (to); befall vt suit; make attractive **becoming** fetching; attractive

bed n **1** piece of furniture designed for sleeping on **2** small plot of ground for growing flowers or vegetables **3** bottom of the sea, a river, etc **4** layer of rock vt (-dd-) **1** plant in a bed **2** sl have sexual intercourse with **bed down** find a place to sleep **bedclothes** pl n covers used on a bed **bedding** n mattress, covers, pillows, etc , used on a bed **bedridden** adj confined to bed, esp through illness **bedroom** n room used for sleeping in **bed-sitter** n also **bed-sit** one-roomed accommodation, usually with cooking and washing facilities **bedspread** n top cover for a bed

bedraggled adj spattered with mud or dirt

bee n insect that produces wax and converts nectar into honey **have a bee in one's bonnet** be obsessed or fanatical **beehive** n box-like or domed construction for keeping bees in

beech n deciduous tree with a smooth bark and shiny oval leaves

beef n **1** meat from a cow, bull, etc **2** cow, bull, etc , used for its meat **beefy** adj **1** containing or having the flavour of beef **2** muscular and strong

been v pp of **be**.

beer n alcoholic drink made from malt and flavoured with hops

beet n **1** also **beetroot** plant with a round red root, which is eaten as a vegetable **2** also **sugar beet** plant with a whitish root, which is used as a source of sugar

beetle n insect with wings, which are modified to form a hard protective shell

befall vi,vt (befell; befallen) happen (to); occur, esp by chance

befit vt,vi (-tt-) be right or suitable (for)

before adv on a previous occasion; earlier prep **1** previous to **2** in front of **3** in the presence of conj **1** until or up to the time that **2** rather than; sooner than **beforehand** adj,adv early; in advance

befriend vt take care of as a friend

beg vt,vi (-gg-) **1** ask for (money, food, etc) **2** beseech; implore; plead (with) **beggar** n

begin vt,vi (-nn-) (began; begun) start; commence; bring into being **beginner** n person at an early stage of learning; novice **beginning** n start; starting place; early stage; outset **beginnings** pl n **1** origin; early background **2** early indication of potential or development

begonia n plant with showy red, green, or greyish leaves and red, yellow, or white flowers

begrudge vt resent; wish to deny; grudge

beguile vt,vi charm; bewitch; hoodwink

behalf n **on behalf of** in the name of; representing

behave vi **1** act; react; function **2** conduct (oneself) **behaviour** n

behead vt execute by severing the head; decapitate

behind adv,adj **1** following; after **2** in a place that is further back **3** behindhand prep **1** at the back of; beyond **2** not so advanced as **3** remaining; left over n inf buttocks **behindhand** adj,adv in arrears; late

behold vt,vi (beheld) see; look (at) interj look!

beige adj,n light greyish-brown; fawn

being n **1** living creature **2** existence; living state

belated adj arriving or happening too late **belatedly** adv

belch vi,vt **1** expel wind noisily from the stomach

through the mouth 2 send out in large quantities gush n 1 act of belching 2 blast burst

belfry n tower in which bells are hung

belie vt 1 give the wrong impression of 2 show to be false

believe vt, vi 1 consider to be true or right accept 2 think, assume vi subscribe to a particular faith **believe in** have faith in trust; be convinced of the existence of **believable** adj **believer** n **belief** n 1 something believed; opinion 2 creed, faith 3 trust; acceptance

belittle vt undervalue disparage

bell n 1 hollow metal instrument that produces a ringing sound when struck 2 electrical device that produces a ringing or buzzing sound **ring a bell** seem vaguely familiar

belligerent adj warlike, aggressive **belligerence** n **belligerently** adv

bellow vi vt roar loudly bawl n deep-throated roar or shout

bellows n pl or s device that expands and contracts to produce a strong draught of air

belly n 1 abdomen 2 stomach 3 part of something that bulges

belong v **belong to** 1 be owned by 2 be a member of 3 be part of a set with go with fit vi have an allotted place **belongings** pl n personal possessions

below adv at a place lower down, underneath prep lower or further down than under

belt n 1 strip of leather cloth etc worn round the waist 2 band, strip 3 region or zone with specific characteristics 4 slap blow sharp hit **below the belt** unfairly against the rules ~vt 1 fasten with a belt 2 sl strike, beat 3 also **belt out** sing play or shout loudly vi race travel fast **belt up** sl stop talking

bemoan vt vi moan (about) lament deplore

bemused adj 1 lost in thought 2 dazed, confused

bench n 1 long wooden or stone seat 2 work table, counter 3 seat occupied by a judge or magistrate

bend v (bent) vt 1 make into a bow or curved shape 2 turn or curve in a particular direction 3 subdue, coerce vi 1 curve 2 stoop bow n curve **round the bend** mad, crazy

beneath adv underneath below prep 1 con-

cealed under lower than 2 in an inferior or subordinate position than 3 unacceptable to

benefactor n person who donates a large sum of money, patron

benefit n 1 advantage, privilege, good 2 welfare or insurance payment vt vi do good to or be good for **beneficial** adj advantageous; helpful **beneficiary** n recipient of a legacy, annuity etc

benevolent adj 1 kindly, good-natured 2 charitable generous **benevolence** n **benevolently** adv

benign (bi'nain) adj 1 gentle, friendly 2 not malignant

bent v pt and pp of **bend**. adj 1 crooked; curved 2 sl dishonest corrupt **bent on** determined to ~n inclination; penchant

benzene n colourless sweet-smelling liquid containing carbon and hydrogen and used as a solvent

bequeath vt leave (money property, etc) esp by will **bequest** n something bequeathed

bereaved adj deprived (of) by death **bereavement** n

bereft adj deprived; completely lacking (in)

beret ('berei) n flat circular cap of wool felt etc

berry n soft stoneless fruit of various trees or bushes

berserk (bə'zə:k) adj in a frenzy wild and violent

berth n 1 sleeping place in a ship train caravan etc 2 mooring place vi vt moor; dock

beseech vt implore, entreat

beset vt (besetting beset) 1 trouble, plague 2 attack, assail

beside prep at the side of, adjacent to; by **beside oneself** overcome out of control **besides** adv 1 moreover furthermore, anyway 2 additionally as well prep in addition to, apart from

besiege vt 1 surround and attack (a city fortress etc) 2 assail with demands, requests etc

best adj 1 of the highest quality 2 most suitable or desirable adv in the best way n the highest possible standard; utmost **best man** n man who looks after a bridegroom **bestseller** n book or other product that sells exceptionally well

bestial adj 1 brutal; coarse and savage; carnal 2 relating to a beast

bestow vt give; confer; endow **bestowal** n

bet n 1 pledge between parties to pay a sum of money to the one who successfully predicts the outcome of a future event 2 sum of money pledged 3 predicted outcome 4 course of action vt vi (-tt-; bet) 1 place a bet (on); gamble 2 inf predict **betting shop** n premises of a bookmaker

betray vt 1 disclose information about or expose to an enemy 2 be unfaithful or disloyal to 3 show signs of; reveal inadvertently **betrayal** n

better adj 1 of a higher quality; superior 2 more suitable or desirable 3 no longer sick; recovering **better off** richer; having a greater advantage adv more; to a greater extent **had better** ought to; should ~n 1 the more excellent or desirable 2 superior; person of higher worth **get the better of** outwit; defeat ~vt improve upon **betterment** n improvement

between prep 1 in a space or interval separating two places, moments in time, etc 2 shared by 3 through joint effort or contribution adv in or towards the middle

beverage n any drink except water

beware vt vi be wary (of); take heed (of)

bewilder vt puzzle; confuse; perplex **bewilderment** n

bewitch vt charm as if by a spell; enchant

beyond prep 1 farther away than; on the far side of 2 outside the control or limits of adv farther away

biannual adj occurring twice a year **biannually** adv

bias n 1 prejudice; distorted outlook 2 tendency; inclination 3 diagonal line or cut **biased** adj partial; prejudiced

bib n 1 piece of cloth worn under the chin by a baby whilst eating 2 part of an apron, pinafore, etc. that covers the front of the body above the waist

Bible n collection of sacred writings of the Christian Church **biblical** adj

bibliography n list of works relating to a particular subject, author, etc **bibliographical** adj **bibliographer** n

biceps pl n muscles of the upper arm

bicker vi squabble; quarrel, esp over trivial matters

bicycle also **cycle** or **bike** n vehicle with two wheels propelled by pedalling vi ride a bicycle

bid v (-dd-; bad bade, or bid; bidden or bid) vt,vi 1 offer to buy for a certain sum, esp at an auction 2 ask; command vt express in greeting **bidder** n

bidet ('bi:dei) n small bath used for washing the genital area

biennial adj occurring once every two years or lasting for two years n plant with a two-year life cycle **biennially** adv

big adj 1 large; great; not small 2 important; substantial 3 generous adv with authority; in a big way

bigamy n crime of marrying another partner when a former marriage is still valid **bigamist** n **bigamous** adj

bigot n offensively intolerant or prejudiced person **bigoted** adj **bigotry** n

bike n,vi short for **bicycle.**

bikini n woman's two-piece bathing costume

bile n fluid secreted by the liver **bilious** adj suffering from excessive secretion of bile in the liver

bilingual adj able to speak two languages

bill[1] n 1 statement of money owed; invoice 2 law or act of Parliament in draft form 3 poster or notice 4 programme of events 5 US banknote vt 1 present an account to; invoice 2 put on a programme; schedule

bill[2] n bird's beak

billiards n game played with a long cue and a number of balls on a table usually fitted with pockets

billion n 1 (in Britain) one million million 2 (esp in the US) one thousand million

billow n 1 large sea-wave 2 surging mass vi, vt swell up; surge

bin n storage container

binary adj 1 composed of two parts 2 relating to the number two

bind v (bound) vt,vi 1 tie or entwine; wrap round tightly 2 cohere; stick vt 1 restrict; place under an obligation or contract 2 confine; trap; constrain 3 fasten together (pages) inside a cover 4 sew the edge of to prevent fraying, decoration, etc n inf restricting circumstance; constraint **binder** n folder with clasps for holding together loose sheets of paper **binding** n 1 cover of a book 2 edging material or tape adj restricting;

obligatory **bindweed** n plant that twines round a support or the stems of other plants

bingo n gambling game in which players match up numbers on a chart with those picked out at random

binoculars pl n optical instrument consisting of a pair of small telescopes joined together

biochemistry n study of the chemical compounds occurring in plants and animals **biochemical** adj **biochemist** n

biography n account of a person's life written by someone else **biographical** adj **biographer** n

biology n study of living organisms **biological** adj **biologically** adv **biologist** n

birch n tree with a slender grey or white trunk 2 bundle of birch twigs used as a whip vt flog; thrash

bird n warm-blooded feathered egg-laying vertebrate with forelimbs modified as wings

birth n 1 act of being born or producing offspring 2 origin; beginning 3 descent; lineage **birth certificate** n official document issued when a child's birth is registered **birth control** n method or practice of contraception **birthday** n anniversary of a person's birth **birthmark** n blemish on the skin formed before birth **birth rate** n ratio of live births in relation to a given population

biscuit n crisp flat cake made from baked dough

bisect vt 1 divide into two equal parts 2 split; cut across **bisection** n

bisexual adj able to respond sexually to a person of either sex n person who is bisexual

bishop n 1 high-ranking clergyman with authority over a diocese 2 chess piece able to move diagonally across squares of the same colour

bison n N American animal of the ox family with a shaggy coat and humped back; buffalo

bistro ('bi:strou) small restaurant or bar

bit[1] n 1 small piece or amount 2 short while a **bit** a little; somewhat; rather **bit by bit** gradually **do one's bit** do one's duty; contribute **every bit as** equally as **not a bit** not at all

bit[2] n 1 mouthpiece attached to a bridle for controlling a horse 2 metal drill used with a brace

bitch n 1 female dog 2 sl malicious woman vi

speak maliciously grumble **bitchy** adj **bitchiness** n

bite vt, vi (bit; bitten) 1 press, cut or sink into with the teeth 2 have a tendency to attack with the teeth, fangs, etc 3 sting; smart 4 corrode; eat into 5 take bait 6 grip; hold fast n 1 act of biting 2 piece bitten off; morsel 3 mark or swelling caused by biting 4 something to eat; snack 5 strong grip **biting** adj 1 harsh keen 2 sarcastic; hurtful

bitter adj 1 having a harsh taste 2 resentful; rancorous; deeply hostile 3 distressing; hard to bear 4 extremely cold; icy n type of beer with a strong flavour of hops **bitterly** adv **bitterness** n

bivalve n mollusc having two shells hinged together

bizarre adj weird; odd; strange

black adj 1 of the colour of coal, jet, etc 2 extremely dark, unlit 3 extremely dirty 4 grim; bleak 5 enraged; angry 6 dark-skinned **black market** n system of illicit trading **black pudding** sausage made from pork fat and blood ~n 1 dark colour having no hue 2 darkness 3 cap Negro; dark-skinned person **black and blue** heavily bruised ~vt 1 blacken 2 inf boycott; ban **black out** 1 obliterate 2 extinguish; plunge into darkness 3 pass out; lose consciousness **blackout** n 1 power failure 2 extinguishing of lights in cities etc , in order to prevent identification by enemy aircraft 3 temporary loss of consciousness or memory **blackness** n **blacken** vt, vi make or become black; darken vt defame

blackberry n edible purplish-black fruit of the bramble

blackbird n songbird in which the male has black plumage with a yellow beak and the female is brown

blackboard n large board that can be written on with chalk

blackcurrant n small round edible black berry that grows on a cultivated bush

blackguard ('blæga:d) n scoundrel; rogue

blackhead n spot with a black surface that clogs a pore on the skin

blackleg n person who acts against the interests of a trade union, esp by refusing to strike vi (-gg-) act as a blackleg

blackmail n crime of demanding payment in exchange for not disclosing discreditable infor-

mation vt threaten by means of blackmail
blackmailer n

blacksmith n craftsman who works with iron

bladder n sac in the body that functions as a receptacle for urine

blade n 1 sharp-edged or cutting part of a knife, sword, etc 2 long flat leaf of grass 3 shoulder blade 4 flat broad end of a propeller, oar, etc

blame n responsibility for a crime, error, fault, etc vt vi attribute blame (to); find fault (with) **blameless** adj innocent, faultless

blanch vt 1 make lighter in colour, bleach 2 plunge (vegetables, meat, etc) into boiling water vi become pale with fear, nausea, etc

blancmange (blə'mɒndʒ) n dessert made from milk, cornflour and flavouring

bland adj 1 not highly flavoured or seasoned 2 mild, temperate 3 unemotional, without passion **blandly** adv **blandness** n

blank adj 1 not written on or filled in 2 bare, undecorated 3 uncomprehending, expressionless 4 uninspired **blank verse** unrhymed verse ~ n 1 empty space 2 mental confusion 3 written or printed dash 4 gun cartridge having powder but no bullet **draw a blank** fail to obtain the required information during an investigation v **blank out** blot out; obliterate

blanket n 1 woollen bed cover 2 thick layer, cover vt cover up

blare vt vi 1 shout or sound loudly, proclaim 2 shine harshly n 1 loud noise; blast 2 blinding light; glare; blaze

blasé ('blɑːzeɪ) adj no longer capable of being shocked, excited, etc ; cool and sophisticated

blaspheme vi curse; swear; utter profanities vt act irreverently towards **blasphemous** adj **blasphemy** n

blast n 1 explosion 2 loud explosive noise, blare 3 strong sudden rush of air, flames, water, etc interj sl exclamation of anger, frustration etc vt vi 1 blow up; destroy by explosion 2 produce a sudden loud noise 3 force an opening (in); breach **blastoff** n launching of a rocket

blatant adj flagrant; conspicuous; undisguised **blatancy** n **blatantly** adv

blaze n 1 roaring fire; bright flame 2 bright light; glare 3 passionate display; outburst vi 1 burn vigorously, flare 2 glare; shine harshly

blazer n jacket, esp one worn as part of a school or club uniform

bleach vt vi whiten through heat or the action of chemicals n substance used for bleaching clothes, the hair, etc

bleak adj 1 desolate and exposed 2 grim; dismal, unfavourable **bleakly** adv **bleakness** n

bleat vt vi 1 (of a sheep or goat) utter a high-pitched cry 2 moan plaintively; whine; complain n cry of a sheep or goat

bleed v (bled) vi 1 lose blood 2 suffer extreme anguish vt 1 drain blood from 2 draw off (liquid, gas, etc) **bleeding** adj utter adv sl extremely; very

bleep n noise produced by an electronic device vi make a short high-pitched sound

blemish n 1 discoloured mark on the skin 2 stain or flaw vt spoil; mar; tarnish

blend vt vi 1 mix (different varieties of tea, tobacco etc) 2 combine (colours) 3 merge; form a mixture vi harmonize; mix well n blended mixture **blender** n machine for blending vegetables, liquids, etc

bless vt 1 make holy, consecrate 2 call for God's aid or protection for **blessed with** (blest) endowed or favoured with; granted **blessed** ('blesid) adj holy; sacred **blessing** n 1 statement or ceremony invoking God's aid or protection 2 divine gift; sanction 3 good fortune

blew v pt of **blow** .

blight n 1 plant disease caused by fungi, insects etc 2 something that mars or impedes growth vt 1 cause blight in 2 spoil; destroy

blind adj 1 deprived of the power of sight 2 unable or unwilling to understand or tolerate 3 made reckless by passion 4 concealed; unseen 5 closed at one end adv also **blindly** 1 without being able to see 2 without proper information or preparation vt 1 make blind 2 dazzle 3 deprive of reason or judgment n 1 length of material on a roller used as a shade for a window **blindness** n **blindfold** n strip of cloth placed over the eyes and tied at the back of the head vt place a blindfold over (the eyes)

blink vt vi 1 rapidly open and shut (the eyes) 2 flash on and off n 1 rapid opening and shutting of the eyes 2 flash; twinkle **blinkers** pl n 1 direction indicators on a motor vehicle 2 part of a horse's bridle that prevents sideways vision

bliss n state of ecstatic happiness **blissful** adj **blissfully** adv

blister n 1 small swelling or bubble on the skin produced by friction, burning, etc 2 bubble of paint vt, vi produce blisters

blithe adj 1 carefree; light-hearted 2 thoughtless; casual **blithely** adv **blitheness** n

blitz n heavy attack, such as an air-raid vt make an intensive attack on

blizzard n violent snowstorm

bloat vt, vi swell; inflate

blob n 1 drop of liquid, dirt, etc 2 blurred shape or form vt (-bb-) splash or mark with blobs

bloc n united group of countries, political parties, etc

block n 1 solid piece of stone, wood, etc ; slab; brick; chunk 2 building comprising a number of offices, flats, etc 3 group of things fastened together or arranged in rows 4 obstruction; obstacle; blockage 5 psychological or mental barrier vt also **block up** 1 obstruct; cause a blockage in; stop up 2 veto; impede; prevent **blockade** n obstruction, esp of a port or harbour by military forces vt obstruct with a blockade **blockage** n something that blocks, obstructs, or impedes

bloke n inf man

blond adj fair-haired n man with fair hair **blonde** f n **blondness** n

blood n 1 red fluid circulating through the veins and arteries of the body 2 lineage; descent **in cold blood** ruthlessly; in a calculated way **bloodcurdling** adj terrifying; ghastly **blood pressure** n pressure of the blood against the inner walls of the arteries **bloodshed** n violent killing; slaughter **bloodstream** n flow of blood through the body **bloodthirsty** adj sadistic delighting in violence **bloodthirstiness** n **bloody** adj covered or stained with blood; gory adj, adv sl damned; extremely vt stain with blood **bloodiness** n **bloody-minded** adj obstinate; pig-headed; perverse **bloody-mindedness** n

bloom n 1 flower(s); blossom 2 healthy glow 3 shiny surface of various fruits vi 1 flower; blossom 2 flourish; develop vigorously

blossom n flower(s), esp of a fruit tree vi 1 flower; produce blossom 2 begin to grow or develop

blot n 1 ink stain 2 eyesore 3 damage to one s character or reputation vt (-tt-) 1 stain; mark 2 use an absorbent material to soak up **blot**

out obscure completely; obliterate **blot one's copybook** spoil one's reputation or record; blunder **blotting paper** n absorbent paper used esp to soak up excess ink

blotch n stain; discolouration; patch vt, vi produce stains or patches **blotchy** adj

blouse n woman s garment that is similar to a shirt

blow[1] v (blew; blown) vt, vi 1 send out (air) through the mouth or nose; exhale 2 move through or by air or wind 3 produce the sound of a whistle, trumpet, the wind, etc 4 fuse; burn out **blow out** extinguish or be extinguished **blow over** subside; pass **blow up** 1 explode or cause an explosion 2 lose one's temper 3 inflate 4 enlarge (a photograph) ~n 1 expulsion of air; puff 2 act of blowing or sound produced by a whistle, trumpet, etc **blowy** adj windy; blustery

blow[2] n 1 heavy stroke or hit with the hand or a weapon 2 sudden shock or disappointment; setback **come to blows** start to fight

blubber n thick layer of subcutaneous fat of a whale, seal, etc vt, vi sob; cry noisily

blue n colour in the spectrum that is the colour of a clear sky **out of the blue** suddenly; without warning; from nowhere **the blues** 1 state of depression; dejectedness 2 type of music created by Black Americans ~adj 1 of the colour blue 2 depressed; unhappy 3 inf obscene **bluebell** n woodland plant with blue bell-shaped flowers **blue-blooded** adj of royal or aristocratic descent **blueprint** n 1 photocopy of plans or drawings 2 original model; prototype

bluff vt, vi feign confidence in order to deceive about one s true motives, resources, etc n act of deception **call someone's bluff** act in a way that forces someone to reveal his true motives, resources, etc ; challenge

blunder n stupid, tactless, or clumsy mistake vi 1 make a stupid or tactless mistake 2 move clumsily; stumble

blunt adj 1 not sharp; unable to cut well 2 outspoken; forthright; direct vt, vi make or become blunt(er) vt make less sensitive, dull **bluntly** adv **bluntness** n

blur vt, vi (-rr-) 1 make or become hazy, indistinct, or vague 2 smear; smudge n 1 something that is indistinct in outline or vague 2 smudge

blurt vt,vi also **blurt out** reveal (a secret), esp when confused or under pressure

blush vi become red in the face with embarrassment, shame, etc; flush n 1 reddening of the cheeks 2 hint of redness on a flower, fruit, etc

bluster vt,vi speak or act in a forceful and often boastful manner; swagger vi blow strongly; be windy **blustery** adj

boar n 1 wild pig 2 uncastrated male domestic pig

board n 1 plank of wood 2 shaped piece of wood or other material designed for a specific purpose, such as an ironing board or chess board 3 cardboard 4 notice board or blackboard 5 body of directors, governors, or other officials; committee 6 meals provided for residents in a hotel, hostel, etc **go by the board** be ignored or rejected **on board** on a ship, aircraft; etc; aboard ~vt,vi go on to a ship, aircraft etc; embark vt also **board up** enclose or cover with boards of wood vt provide lodgings for vi live in lodgings

boarder n 1 child at boarding school 2 lodger **boarding house** n small private establishment offering cheap accommodation **boarding school** n school with living accommodation for pupils **board room** n committee room where a board meets

boast vi exaggerate or speak proudly of one's own achievements or qualities; brag vt be the proud possessor of n exaggerated or proud statement **boastful** adj **boastfully** adv **boastfulness** n

boat n small vessel for travelling on water **in the same boat** in the same situation or predicament **miss the boat** miss an opportunity ~vi travel in a boat esp for pleasure

bob vt,vi (-bb-) 1 move up and down esp in a liquid 2 nod or jerk (the head) 3 bow or curtsy n 1 jerky movement 2 bow or curtsy

bodice n top part of a woman's dress

body n 1 the whole physical structure of a human being or other vertebrate 2 torso; trunk 3 corpse 4 main or central part 5 mass; expanse 6 corporate group of people 7 object or solid 8 consistency or fullness, esp of wine **bodily** adj physical; corporeal adv by lifting or using the body **bodyguard** n person giving physical protection to another **bodywork** n covering for the shell or framework of a vehicle

bog n 1 area of waterlogged land, usually of peat 2 sl lavatory **bogged down** unable to make progress, hindered **boggy** adj

bogus adj fake; sham

boil[1] vt,vi 1 produce gas or vapour from a liquid by the action of heat 2 cook by heating in liquid vi seethe; become agitated **boil down** reduce in quantity by boiling **boil down to** amount to; result in **boil over** overflow or spill whilst boiling n **on the boil** 1 approaching boiling point 2 in operation; functioning well **boiler** n vessel producing steam to drive an engine **boiling point** n 1 temperature at which a liquid boils 2 moment at which one loses one's temper or a situation becomes explosive

boil[2] n inflamed pus-filled sore on the skin

boisterous adj unruly; noisy and unrestrained **boisterously** adv **boisterousness** n

bold adj 1 courageous; unafraid; daring 2 clear; distinct **boldly** adv **boldness** n

bolster n long pillow or cushion vt also **bolster up** reinforce; encourage; boost

bolt n 1 metal bar used to fasten a door, window, etc 2 screw or pin used with a nut 3 clap of thunder or flash of lightning **make a bolt for it** run away quickly ~vt 1 secure or fasten with a bolt 2 eat hurriedly; gulp down vi 1 jump up suddenly 2 run off unexpectedly adv **bolt upright** with one's back straight and rigid

bomb n explosive device **go like a bomb** 1 travel at high speed 2 be highly successful ~vt,vi attack with bombs **bombard** vt 1 attack repeatedly with bombs, missiles, etc 2 direct series of questions, complaints etc at **bombardment** n **bombardier** (bɔmbə'diə) n noncommissioned officer below a sergeant in the Royal Artillery **bomber** n 1 aircraft designed to carry bombs 2 person who attacks with bombs **bombshell** n unexpected event causing great shock or distress

bond n 1 something that binds, such as a rope or chain 2 close intimate relationship; tie 3 obligation; duty 4 company or government certificate issued as a guarantee of repayment of money lent **bonded warehouse** warehouse storing imported goods until duty is paid **bondage** n slavery

bone n hard tissue that makes up the skeleton of the body **have a bone to pick** have something to criticize or quarrel about **make**

no bones about have no hesitation or doubt about ~*vt* remove the bones from (meat) **bonemeal** *n* animal food or fertilizer made from crushed bones **bony** *adj* 1 having many bones 2 having prominent bones 3 resembling a bone

bonfire *n* fire lit out of doors

bonnet *n* 1 hat kept in place with ribbons tied under the chin 2 hinged section at the front of a vehicle that covers the engine or luggage compartment

bonus *n* additional payment, dividend, etc

booby trap *n* 1 concealed or disguised explosive device intended to blow up when touched 2 object or trap used by a practical joker to surprise or scare an unsuspecting victim **booby-trap** *vt* (-pp-) set up a booby trap in or for

book *n* 1 set of printed pages bound together; volume 2 written work, such as a novel or textbook 3 pack of stamps tickets, etc **by the book** strictly according to the rules ~*vt,vi* reserve (a seat ticket etc) in advance *vt* record (a person's name) prior to prosecution on a minor charge **bookkeeping** *n* accounting system or practice of keeping records of business transactions **bookkeeper** *n* **booklet** *n* small book, brochure **bookmaker** *n* person running a business to accept bets esp in horseracing

boom *vi* 1 produce a deep resonant sound 2 thrive prosper *n* 1 deep resonant sound 2 period or state of prosperity

boomerang *n* curved piece of wood used as a missile and designed to follow a course back to the user when thrown

boor *n* uncouth coarse person **boorish** *adj*

boost *n* 1 push or shove upwards 2 increase; rise 3 encouragement, help *vt* 1 lift up with a push 2 increase, expand 3 improve; promote **booster** *n*

boot *n* 1 type of footwear usually covering the leg up to the knee 2 stout shoe worn for walking, climbing, playing football etc 3 luggage compartment in a vehicle usually situated at the rear 4 *inf* kick **the boot** *sl* dismissal, sack ~*vt* 1 kick 2 *also* **boot out** expel or dismiss unceremoniously

booth *n* 1 enclosed cubicle 2 covered stall at a market or fair

booze *inf n* alcoholic drink *vi* drink heavily

border *n* 1 stretch of land constituting a frontier or boundary 2 edge; margin 3 flower bed along the edge of a lawn, path, etc *vt vi* function as a border or boundary (to) **border on** 1 lie adjacent to 2 verge on come close to **borderline** *n* 1 boundary line 2 intermediate area or category *adj* marginal; in between

bore[1] *vt,vi* 1 drill (a hole) in 2 dig or make (a tunnel, shaft, etc) esp in order to extract oil, minerals, etc *n* 1 tunnel or shaft 2 hollow part of a gun barrel 3 calibre of a gun

bore[2] *vt* exhaust or frustrate by being dull, repetitious, etc *n* tedious or dreary person, task, etc **boredom** *n*

bore[3] *v pt of* **bear**[1].

born *v pt of* **bear**[1] (def 4) when used in the passive *adj* possessing a specified innate quality

borne *v pp of* **bear**[1].

borough *n* 1 town or district represented in Parliament 2 area having its own local council

borrow *vt,vi* 1 take or accept on loan 2 incorporate into one's own language; adopt **borrower** *n*

borstal *n* establishment for young offenders

bosom *n* 1 breast or chest, esp of a woman; bust 2 centre of love or comfort

boss *inf n* employer manager or foreman *vt vi* control or manage, esp domineeringly **bossy** *adj* overbearing; inclined to dominate **bossiness** *n*

botany *n* science or study of plants **botanical** *adj* **botanist** *n*

botch *vt,vi* bungle, make a bad job of *n* mess; clumsy repair

both *pron adj* each of two taken together *conj* **both...and...** firstly and secondly

bother *vt* disturb; worry; annoy; trouble *vi* concern oneself; take trouble or care *n* 1 fuss; commotion 2 trouble; anxiety *interj* exclamation of mild impatience or annoyance **bothersome** *adj*

bottle *n* long glass or plastic vessel with a narrow neck for holding liquids *vt vi* pour into a bottle **bottle up** repress or hide (emotions) **bottleneck** *n* something that restricts the flow of traffic goods on a production line, etc

bottom *n* 1 lowest part; base; foot 2 seabed riverbed etc 3 worst or most inferior position 4 *inf* buttocks **at bottom** fundamentally basically **get to the bottom of** investigate the truth or cause of ~adj lowest **bottomless** adj 1 extremely deep 2 seemingly endless or inexhaustible **bottommost** adj 1 very lowest 2 most basic

bough n branch of a tree

bought v pt and pp of **buy.**

boulder n large stone or rock

bounce vi vt 1 rebound or cause to spring back after striking or being thrown 2 jump or throw up and down; jerk vi (of a cheque) be returned by a bank as unacceptable n 1 rebound; springing back 2 jump; jerk 3 exuberance; ebullience **bouncing** adj very healthy or robust **bouncy** adj exuberant; high-spirited **bounciness** n

bound[1] v pt and pp of **bind.** adj **bound to** certain to; sure to **bound up with** or **in** closely involved with

bound[2] vi leap; spring n jump; bounce; leap

bound[3] vt restrict; limit n boundary; limit **boundless** adj inexhaustible; limitless

bound[4] adj heading towards; destined for

boundary n something that marks the edge or limit of an area of land

bouquet n 1 (bou'kei bu:-) bunch of flowers, esp one elaborately arranged or displayed 2 (bu:'kei) aroma of a wine

bourgeois ('buəʒwɑ) adj of the middle class esp when regarded as conservative and materialistic n member of the middle class **bourgeoisie** (buəʒwa:'zi:) n middle class

bout n 1 boxing contest; fight 2 short period; spell

boutique n small shop esp one selling clothes

bow[1] (bau) vt vi bend (the body or head) forwards as an act of respect submission etc vi yield; submit; comply **bow down** 1 yield 2 submit ~n bending of the body or lowering of the head

bow[2] (bou) n 1 weapon from which arrows are shot consisting of a supple piece of wood pulled into a curved shape by a taut string 2 rod strung with horsehair used for playing a violin, cello etc 3 decorative knot having two loops and two loose ends 4 curve, arc vi vt 1 draw a bow across (a violin, cello, etc.) 2 curve; bend **bow-legged** (bou'legid -'legd) adj having the legs curving outwards; bandy

bow[3] (bau) n front or forward end of a ship or boat

bowels pl n 1 intestines 2 deepest or innermost part

bowl[1] n shallow basin or dish **bowler** n also **bowler hat** hat with a hard rounded crown and narrow brim

bowl[2] n heavy ball used in bowls, tenpin bowling etc vt vi 1 roll (a ball) or travel smoothly along the ground 2 deliver (a ball) to the batsman in cricket **bowl along** travel fast and comfortably **bowl over** 1 knock to the ground 2 overwhelm, astound **bowler** n person who bowls in cricket **bowling** n tenpin bowling or skittles **bowls** n game played with weighted balls on a level grass pitch

box[1] n 1 flat-bottomed container sometimes with a lid 2 compartment for a small number of spectators, situated at the side of an auditorium 3 cubicle; booth 4 horsebox 5 witness box 6 section of printed matter enclosed within a border **the box** sl television ~vt pack into a box **box in** 1 enclose, board up 2 corner or jam so as to prevent movement **Boxing day** n first weekday after Christmas day **box office** n booking office in a theatre cinema, etc

box[2] vi vt 1 fight in a boxing match (against) 2 punch hit with the fist 1 blow of the fist; punch cuff **boxer** n 1 person who fights in a boxing match 2 breed of smooth-haired dog, similar to a bulldog **boxing** n sport in which two opponents fight with the fists using padded gloves

boy n male child **boyhood** n **boyish** adj **boyfriend** n male friend, esp one with whom one has a romantic relationship

boycott vt refuse to deal with (another nation group etc.) or buy (goods) n practice or instance of boycotting

bra n also **brassiere** woman's undergarment worn to support the bosom

brace n 1 tool into which a drill or bit is fitted for boring holes 2 beam or girder used for strengthening or supporting a wall 3 metal band fixed to the teeth to correct their alignment 4 pair, esp of game birds **braces** pl n pair of straps worn over the shoulders and fastened to the waistband of a pair of trousers ~vt strengthen or support with a brace; vt vi invigorate, freshen **brace oneself** prepare oneself for impending pain, shock etc

break

bracelet n ornamental chain or band worn round the wrist

bracken n type of large fern

bracket n 1 right-angled support for a shelf 2 one of a pair of written or printed symbols used to enclose additional information, etc 3 classified group of people, esp an income group vt 1 fix with a bracket 2 enclose within brackets 3 place in the same category

brag vi (-gg-) boast n card game similar to poker **braggart** n boastful person

braid n 1 plait 2 band of material made from plaited or twisted threads vt plait; interweave (strands)

Braille n system of writing using embossed dots enabling the blind to read by touch

brain n 1 mass of nerve fibre situated inside the skull, forming the main part of the central nervous system 2 also **brains** intelligence vt inf kill by striking violently on the head **brainwash** vt indoctrinate or condition totally **brainwave** n 1 voltage and current waves produced by the brain 2 brilliant idea or inspiration **brainy** adj inf intelligent

braise vt vi cook in a small amount of liquid in an airtight container

brake n device on a vehicle that stops or slows down the motion of the wheels vi,vt stop or slow down by applying the brake

bramble n bush with thorny stems esp a blackberry bush

branch n 1 limb of a tree or shrub that grows from the trunk or main stem; bough 2 sub-division; offshoot 3 local shop bank etc that is part of a larger organization vi 1 produce branches 2 also **branch off** sub-divide, diverge, fork **branch out** extend one's interests

brand n 1 class of product, esp one marketed under a trademark 2 type, variety, sort 3 identifying mark on cattle, sheep, etc 4 also **branding iron** iron rod that is heated and used for marking animals for identification 5 stigma vt 1 mark with a brand 2 denounce as; label 3 impress permanently on the mind; scar **brand-new** adj absolutely new and unused

brandish vt hold or wave (a weapon) threateningly or defiantly n triumphant wave; flourish

brandy n spirit distilled from the fermented juice of grapes

brash adj 1 coarse; loud 2 reckless impetuous **brashly** adv **brashness** n

brass n 1 yellowish-gold alloy of copper and zinc 2 family of musical instruments that includes the trumpet and trombone 3 engraved memorial tablet made of brass **get down to brass tacks** start to consider or discuss the most important aspects of an issue or situation **brassy** adj 1 of or like brass 2 vulgar and showy; shameless

brassiere n bra

brave adj courageous; not cowardly; bold vt face or tackle courageously; defy n warrior of an American Indian tribe **bravely** adv **bravery** n

brawl n noisy uncontrolled fight vi fight or quarrel noisily

brawn n 1 well-developed muscles 2 muscular strength 3 dish made of chopped meat from the head of a pig or calf and compressed into a mould

bray n 1 harsh cry of a donkey 2 shout or harsh laugh vi,vt 1 (of a donkey) utter a harsh cry 2 shout or laugh harshly

brazen adj 1 shamelessly defiant; bold 2 made of or like brass; brassy v **brazen out** face or carry out boldly or defiantly

brazil n also **brazil nut** nut with an edible kernel and hard rough shell that grows in a cluster inside a large capsule

breach n 1 infringement or violation of the terms of a contract or agreement 2 split between factions or parties 3 gap, hole; crack vt 1 infringe, violate 2 break open; make a hole in

bread n 1 food made from flour, milk yeast, etc, baked in the form of loaves or rolls 2 sl money **breadwinner** n person responsible for earning money to support a family

breadth n 1 measurement or extent from one side to another; width; broadness 2 extent 3 open-mindedness; tolerance

break v (broke, broken) vt,vi 1 shatter or separate into pieces; fragment; smash; burst 2 damage or cease to function 3 pause; adjourn; stop for a while vt 1 fail to keep (a promise, agreement, etc) 2 bankrupt; ruin financially 3 destroy, crush 4 fracture (a bone) 5 reveal or disclose (news, a secret, etc) 6 succeed in giving up (a habit) 7 surpass or improve on (a previous record, achievement, etc) 8 reduce the impact of vi

33

1 become known, be made public **2** change; come to an end **3** be overcome or overwhelmed with grief strain etc **4** (esp of the male voice at puberty) undergo a change *n* **1** fracture; split; crack **2** pause; recess; interval **3** disconnection, discontinuation **4** change of routine or habit **5** sudden escape **6** *inf* opportunity; stroke of luck **break away 1** escape **2** form or join a new group **breakaway** *n* **1** escape **2** split **break down 1** stop functioning because of mechanical failure **2** fail **3** collapse with emotion **4** analyse **breakdown** *n* **1** failure **2** mental collapse nervous breakdown **3** analysis; detailed account **break even** cover one's expenses with neither profit nor loss **break in(to) 1** force entry esp in order to steal **2** interrupt **3** tame and train (a horse) **break-in** *n* forced entry **break off 1** detach a piece (from) **2** discontinue (a relationship) **3** stop abruptly, esp when speaking **break out 1** escape (from prison) **2** begin suddenly or violently **3** develop (a rash pimples etc) **break through 1** penetrate **2** achieve after a long struggle **breakthrough** *n* important discovery or achievement **break up 1** disintegrate **2** split up; separate, part **break-up** *n* **1** disintegration **2** split separation **breakable** *adj* **breakage** *n* **1** act of breaking **2** the thing broken or its value

breakfast *n* first meal of the day *vi* eat breakfast

breast *n* **1** front part of the body from the neck to the abdomen, chest **2** mammary gland **3** centre of affection patriotic feelings etc **make a clean breast of** confess **breaststroke** *n* stroke in swimming performed face downwards with the arms and legs making circular movements

breath *n* **1** inhalation and exhalation of air **2** air inhaled or exhaled **3** slight gust of air or wind **4** hint; suggestion; vague rumour **out of breath** unable to breathe properly **take one's breath away** dumbfound; astound **under one's breath** in a low voice or whisper **breathless** *adj* out of breath **breathy** *adj* **breathtaking** *adj* amazing; thrilling

breathe *vt vi* **1** inhale and exhale (air) **2** whisper, murmur; blow gently **breather** *n inf* pause for rest **breathing space** *n* sufficient room to move or function

breed *vt,vi* (bred) **1** bear and produce (offspring) **2** propagate; reproduce **3** generate; give rise to *n* **1** group within a species having common characteristics **2** type; variety; brand **breeder** *n* **breeding** *n* **1** reproduction propagation **2** socially acceptable upbringing or background

breeze *n* light wind *vi inf* move about in a carefree manner **breezy** *adj*

brethren *n pl* of **brother**, esp in a religious context

brevity *n* briefness, conciseness

brew *vt,vi* **1** make (beer) by fermentation **2** make (tea coffee, etc) by infusion *vt* concoct *vi* **1** undergo fermentation or infusion **2** be in the process of formation *n* **1** brand of beer **2** concoction **brewery** *n* establishment where beer is brewed

bribe *n* payment offered in order to influence a person to act in one's favour esp illegally *vt,vi* persuade with a bribe **bribery** *n*

brick *n* **1** block of stone or baked clay used in building **2** small block of wood used as a toy **3** slab *vt also* **brick up** seal or enclose with bricks **bricklayer** *n* person skilled in building with bricks **bricklaying** *n* **brickwork** *n* construction with bricks

bride *n* woman preparing for marriage or recently married **bridegroom** *n* husband of a bride **bridesmaid** *n* female attendant who looks after the bride

bridge[1] *n* **1** construction spanning a river valley etc **2** top part of the nose **3** platform from which a ship is piloted or navigated **4** small block supporting the strings of a violin guitar etc **5** something that serves to connect *vt* **1** place a bridge over; span **2** form a connection between

bridge[2] *n* card game developed from whist

bridle *n* part of a harness including the headpiece bit and reins for controlling a horse *vt* **1** fit or control with a bridle **2** curb, check *vi* express contempt anger etc by drawing in the chin or jerking the head **bridlepath** *n* narrow track that is suitable for horses

brief *adj* **1** lasting a short time **2** concise **3** curt; abrupt *n* **1** document in which a solicitor sets out details of his client's case for a barrister **2** set of instructions **briefs** *pl n* short underpants or knickers ~*vt* prepare or instruct with a brief **briefly** *adv* **briefness** *n* **briefcase** *n* bag or case used to hold papers documents etc **briefing** *n* meeting

at which information and instructions are given esp for a military operation

brigade n 1 military unit forming part of a division 2 group of people trained to perform a special task **brigadier** (briga'dia) n army officer holding a rank below that of major general and above a colonel and usually in command of a brigade

bright adj 1 giving off a strong light 2 of a strong colour; vivid 3 shiny; gleaming 4 cheerful 5 inf clever; intelligent adv also **brightly** in a bright manner **brightness** n **brighten** vt vi make or become bright(er)

brilliant adj 1 shining brightly; glittering 2 extremely clever or talented 3 displaying great imagination 4 outstanding **brilliance** n **brilliantly** adv

brim n 1 rim of a cup, dish, etc 2 edge of a hat projecting from the crown vt vi (-mm-) fill or be full so as to overflow

bring vt (brought) 1 carry or convey (to or towards) 2 accompany 3 produce; yield 4 cause 5 force or persuade **bring about** cause to happen **bring back** reintroduce; restore **bring down** 1 force down 2 reduce 3 humiliate or depress **bring forward** 1 produce; present 2 fix for an earlier time **bring in** 1 introduce; initiate 2 yield; earn 3 include **bring off** achieve by striving or by taking risks **bring on** 1 cause to start; induce 2 help to develop; encourage **bring out** 1 cause to show or appear 2 publish **bring round** 1 make conscious again esp after fainting 2 persuade; convert; convince **bring up** 1 rear; educate from an early age 2 vomit 3 introduce or mention

brink n 1 edge of a high or steep place, body of water etc 2 threshold; verge

brisk adj 1 quick; lively 2 invigorating; fresh **briskly** adv **briskness** n

bristle n 1 short tough hair of an animal such as the pig 2 hair, wire fibre etc, of a brush 3 hair of a man's beard; stubble vi 1 (of fur hair, etc) stand on end; be stiff or rigid 2 display signs of annoyance, indignation, etc **bristle with** be crowded or overrun with **bristly** adj

brittle adj 1 easily broken, shattered, or cracked 2 irritable; short-tempered **brittleness** n

broach vt 1 introduce or suggest tentatively 2 pierce or open in order to draw off liquid; tap

broad adj 1 wide; not narrow 2 extensive 3 from one side to another; across; in width 4 general; not specific 5 direct; not subtle 6 crude; coarse; vulgar 7 displaying features of dialect or non-standard speech 8 tolerant **in broad daylight** openly, without attempting to conceal **broad bean** n bean having large flat seeds, which are eaten as a vegetable **broaden** vt,vi make or become broad(er), widen **broad-minded** adj having tolerant or liberal views; not bigoted **broad-mindedness** n

broadcast v (-cast or -casted) vt,vi transmit via radio or television vi appear on a radio or television programme vt 1 publicize 2 sow (seed) by hand n radio or television transmission or programme **broadcaster** n **broadcasting** n

brocade n heavy fabric woven with embossed designs

broccoli n type of cabbage having edible green or purple flower heads

brochure n pamphlet or booklet containing information, advertisements etc

broke v pt of **break**. adj penniless; bankrupt

broken v pp of **break**. **broken-hearted** adj overwhelmed with grief sorrow disappointment, etc

broker n agent for insurance, shares, securities loans, etc

bronchi ('brɔŋkaɪ) pl n s **bronchus** ('brɔŋkəs) also **bronchial tubes** two main branches of the windpipe **bronchial** adj **bronchitis** n inflammation of the bronchi

bronze n 1 reddish-gold alloy of copper and tin sometimes with zinc and lead added 2 statue or ornament of bronze adj 1 reddish-gold 2 also **bronzed** suntanned vt,vi make or become suntanned

brooch n ornamental pin or clasp fastened to the front of the clothing

brood n 1 group of young birds hatched at the same time 2 inf children in a family; offspring vt,vi 1 sit on and hatch (eggs) 2 think or worry (about) for a long time **broody** adj

brook n small stream

broom n 1 implement for sweeping with a head of bristles or fibres and a long handle 2 evergreen shrub with bright yellow flowers, that is able to grow on poor soil

brother n 1 son of the same parents as another 2 fellow member, comrade 3 unordained or lay male member of a religious order **brotherhood** n 1 relationship as a brother 2 fraternity; fellowship 3 religious community of men **brother-in-law** n pl **brothers-in-law** 1 husband of one's sister 2 brother of one's wife or husband 3 husband of the sister of one's wife or husband **brotherly** adj affectionate or loyal as a brother

brought v pt and pp of **bring**.

brow n 1 eyebrow 2 forehead 3 crest of a hill **browbeat** vt (-beat; -beaten) intimidate; oppress; bully

brown n the colour of earth; very dark orange or yellow adj 1 of the colour brown 2 suntanned vt, vi make or become brown **browned off** adj disillusioned; bored; fed up **brownish** adj

browse vi 1 look through or examine a book, items for sale, etc, unhurriedly or casually 2 feed on vegetation; graze

bruise n rupture of the blood vessels causing discoloration of the skin vt, vi 1 produce a bruise 2 offend; hurt the feelings (of)

brunette n woman or girl with dark hair adj dark; brown

brunt n full impact of force, shock, etc

brush n 1 implement with a head of bristles or fibres and a handle 2 stroke made with a brush 3 light touch 4 short unpleasant meeting or contact 5 fox's tail vt 1 wipe, clean, apply etc, with a brush 2 touch lightly **brush aside** dismiss as irrelevant; disregard **brush up** 1 revise; refresh the memory 2 make neat and tidy

brusque adj curt; brisk; abrupt **brusquely** adv **brusqueness** n

Brussels sprout n type of cabbage having small edible heads of tightly overlapping leaves growing on one stem

brute n 1 animal esp when contrasted with man; beast 2 cruel, tyrannical, or ignorant person adj **brute force/strength** sheer physical force/strength; brawn **brutal** adj cruel; savage; barbaric **brutality** n **brutally** adv

bubble n 1 globule of air or gas contained within a film of liquid 2 gurgling sound vt, vi form bubbles; effervesce vi gurgle

buck n a male of animals such as the rabbit, hare or deer vi rear in an attempt to unseat a rider vt unseat; throw off **buck up** 1 hurry 2 cheer up

bucket n container with a circular bottom and a handle **kick the bucket** die

buckle n 1 clasp with a prong used for securing a belt or strap 2 distorted curve; bulge; twist vt vi 1 fasten with a buckle 2 force or be forced out of shape through stress, heat etc; warp

bud n undeveloped flower or leaf shoot **nip in the bud** prevent the development of ~vi (-dd-) produce buds **budding** adj beginning to show talent; promising

Buddhism ('budizəm) n Eastern religion founded by Buddha, that teaches self-awareness through the denial of passion or desire **Buddhist** n adj

budge vt, vi move; shift

budget n 1 estimate of expected income and expenditure 2 money allocated for a project vt, vi 1 allow for or include in a budget 2 spend according to a budget; economize (on)

buffalo n 1 African animal of the ox family having curved horns 2 bison

buffer n 1 shock absorber fitted to a train or placed at the end of a railway track 2 person or thing that serves to reduce the threat of attack or lessen the impact of a collision

buffet[1] ('bʌfei) n 1 counter or table from which refreshments are served 2 refreshments set out for guests to help themselves

buffet[2] ('bʌfit) vt 1 blow or toss about; batter 2 fight or push through

bug n 1 type of insect that feeds on plant juices or the blood of animals 2 inf infection caused by certain microorganisms 3 concealed device, such as a microphone, used to obtain secret information 4 sl obsession; craze vt (-gg-) 1 annoy; bother; nag 2 conceal a microphone in

bugle n brass instrument similar to the trumpet but without valves vi play a bugle

build vt vi (built) 1 construct using materials such as brick stone or wood 2 commission or finance a construction vt 1 establish and develop (a business, etc) 2 create or design for a particular purpose **build up** 1 work on in order to strengthen, increase, or enhance 2 accumulate **build-up** n 1 gradual increase 2 promotion of a commodity **builder** n **building** n 1 construction having walls and a roof 2 business or process of constructing houses, shops, etc **building society** n company advancing loans for mortgages using funds deposited by investors **built-in** adj constructed as an integral part

bulb n 1 rounded organ of a plant, such as the tulip or onion, that grows underground 2 plant growing from such an organ 3 light bulb **bulbous** adj

bulge n swelling; protuberance vi swell; stick out

bulk n 1 large quantity or volume 2 greater part 3 cargo, esp before packaging 4 human body, esp when large or fat **bulky** adj large and cumbersome **bulkiness** n

bull n 1 adult male member of the ox family 2 male of animals such as the elephant or seal 3 person who buys stocks and sells them after the price has risen 4 sl also **bullshit** nonsense; exaggerated statement **bulldog** n breed of short-haired dog with a sturdy body, muscular legs, and a large head **bulldoze** vt 1 demolish or clear with a bulldozer 2 barge through; shove **bulldozer** n heavy tractor used for clearing rubble, earth, etc **bullfight** n public entertainment common in Spain, Portugal, and S America in which a matador fights a bull **bullfighter** n **bullring** n arena used for a bullfight

bullet n projectile discharged from a gun **bullet-proof** adj able to protect from bullets

bulletin n public notice or announcement giving official news or information

bullion n gold or silver, esp before it has been minted

bully vt,vi threaten or act violently towards someone weaker; intimidate n person who bullies

bum n sl buttocks

bump vt,vi 1 collide (with); bang (into); knock 2 injure or hurt by banging vi also **bump along** jolt; travel jerkily **bump into** meet unexpectedly **bump off** sl murder ~n 1 collision; jolt; knock 2 swelling; lump 3 small mound; bulge **bumpy** adj **bumper** n protective bar fitted to either end of a vehicle

bun n 1 small sweet baked roll 2 hair coiled into a knot at the back of the head

bunch n 1 number of things growing or arranged in a cluster 2 group of people; set vt,vi also **bunch up** gather together; cluster; huddle

bundle n pile of things loosely wrapped or tied together vt 1 also **bundle up** make into a bundle 2 push hurriedly out of sight

bung n stopper for a bottle, barrel, etc vt 1 also **bung up** stop up or seal with a bung; block 2 sl throw; chuck

bungalow n single-storeyed house

bungle vt,vi spoil by acting clumsily or incompetently; botch

bunk n 1 narrow bed, esp on a ship 2 also **bunk bed** one of a pair of beds fitted one above the other in a single framework

bunker n 1 storage container for coal, oil, etc 2 sand-filled hollow functioning as a hazard on a golf course 3 fortified underground shelter

buoy n anchored float used as a navigation guide or for mooring a vessel v **buoy up** 1 keep afloat 2 sustain optimism or cheerfulness in **buoyant** adj 1 able to float 2 optimistic; light-hearted **buoyancy** n **buoyantly** adv

burble vt,vi gurgle, babble n gurgling sound

burden n 1 heavy load 2 responsibility, suffering, etc , that is hard to cope with vt 1 overload; weigh down with 2 oppress, cause to suffer **burdensome** adj

bureau ('bjʊərəu) n pl **bureaux** ('bjʊərəu) or **bureaus** 1 agency or government department dealing in employment, tourist information, etc 2 writing desk fitted with drawers, pigeonholes, etc

bureaucracy (bjʊəˈrɒkrəsɪ) n 1 system of government or administration by paid officials rather than elected representatives 2 officials working within such a system 3 excessive use of official administrative procedures; red tape **bureaucrat** n **bureaucratic** adj

burglary n crime of breaking into a building at night with intent to commit certain offences **burglar** n **burgle** vt,vi commit burglary (in or on)

burial n burying, esp of a body at a funeral

burn v (burnt or burned) vt,vi damage or become damaged by fire, heat or acid vi 1 be combustible or inflammable 2 produce heat or light; blaze; glow 3 feel painfully hot or sore, smart 4 be consumed with desire, anger, jealousy, etc vt 1 use in order to produce heat or light 2 make (a hole, mark, etc) by fire, heat, or acid; scorch **burn out** 1 wear out by heat or friction 2 use up one s energy. become exhausted ~n 1 injury caused by fire, heat, or acid 2 mark or hole caused by burning **burning** adj 1 urgent; vital 2 intense; passionate

burrow n underground hole or tunnel dug by an animal for shelter vt,vi tunnel or dig deeply (into) vi delve; search

burst vt,vi (burst) break or split open, esp under pressure; explode **burst in(to) 1** enter noisily **2** interrupt rudely **burst into song/tears, etc.** start to sing, cry, etc ; loudly and suddenly ~n **1** split; rupture **2** sudden loud noise; explosion **3** spurt of activity, energy, etc ; surge

bury vt **1** place (a corpse) in a grave or tomb; inter **2** place underground **3** conceal by covering **4** embed; stick into **5** engross **6** repress; forget

bus n, pl **buses** or **busses** large motor vehicle scheduled to carry passengers along a fixed route vi,vt (-ss-) travel or carry by bus

bush n **1** large plant with woody stems; shrub **2** thick mass **the bush** area of rough uncultivated land, esp in Australia or S Africa; scrubland **beat about the bush** act evasively; prevaricate **bushy** adj **1** thick and shaggy **2** covered with bushes

bushel n unit of capacity equal to 2219 cubic inches **hide one's light under a bushel** be modest about one s abilities or skills

business n **1** commerce; trade **2** occupation; profession **3** commercial company; trading organization; firm **4** affair; matter; concern **business-like** adj conforming to certain standards of business procedure; efficient **businessman** n, pl **-men** man engaged in commerce or trade, esp as an executive **businesswoman** f n

bust[1] n **1** bosom or breast **2** sculpture depicting a person s head and shoulders

bust[2] vt,vi (busted or bust) **1** break; smash **2** ruin; make or become bankrupt **3** sl raid or search, esp in order to arrest **bust up 1** disrupt **2** split or part after a quarrel **bust-up** n **1** brawl **2** separation after a quarrel

bustle vt,vi hurry; be or make busy n busy activity; commotion

busy adj **1** fully occupied; active; engaged **2** crowded; bustling v **busy oneself** take up time with; occupy oneself **busily** adv **busybody** n person who gossips or meddles

but conj **1** however; yet; nevertheless **2** except; apart from; other than prep with the exception of **but for** without; were it not for ~adv merely; just **all but** almost; nearly

butane n flammable hydrocarbon gas used as a fuel

butcher n **1** person who prepares and sells meat **2** savage murderer vt **1** slaughter and prepare (meat) **2** murder, esp with a knife axe, etc ; slaughter; slay **butchery** n

butler n male servant, usually having special responsibility for wines

butt[1] n **1** blunt thick end of a rifle, tool, etc **2** cigarette end; stub

butt[2] n **1** person who bears the brunt of ridicule scorn, etc **2** mound situated behind the target on a shooting range **3** target

butt[3] vt,vi push hard with the head or horns ram **butt in** interrupt; interfere ~n violent push with the head or horns

butter n yellowish-white solid fat produced by churning cream vt spread with butter **butter up** flatter **buttercup** n wild flower with bright yellow petals **butterscotch** n brittle toffee made with butter and sugar

butterfly n **1** insect with large wings, which are often brightly coloured or patterned **2** person who is unable to settle or sustain interest in anything for very long

buttocks pl n fleshy lower part of the body on which a person sits; bottom

button n **1** small disc sewn on to a garment and able to pass through a buttonhole or loop as a fastening, or used for decoration **2** small knob that is pushed to operate a machine doorbell etc **3** anything small and round that resembles a button vt also **button up** fasten with a button **buttonhole** n **1** hole edged with stitching, through which a button is passed **2** flower or spray worn in a buttonhole vt **1** stitch round a buttonhole **2** corner in order to engage in conversation

buttress n **1** structure of stone or brick built to support a wall **2** source of strength or support vt **1** strengthen with a buttress **2** give moral support to

buxom adj having a full bosom; plump

buy vt,vi (bought) obtain in exchange for money; purchase **buy up** buy all that is available of a particular commodity ~n thing bought; purchase **buyer** n person who buys esp one purchasing merchandise for resale

buzz n **1** low continuous noise; hum **2** inf telephone call; ring **3** sl pleasant sensation caused by certain drugs, alcohol, etc vt vi **1** produce a low vibrating hum **2** signal or call using a buzzer **3** *inf* phone; ring *vi* **1** move hurriedly from place to place **2** produce an atmosphere of excitement **buzz off** go away; leave **buzzer** *n* electrical device producing a harsh continuous signal

by *prep* **1** through the agency, means, or authorship of **2** via; past **3** beside; close to; near **4** no later than **5** to a greater or lesser extent than **6** multiplied with **7** with a second dimension of **8** during; in the course of **by and by** eventually; after a while **by-election** *n* election held when a particular seat becomes vacant, as after the resignation or death of a Member of Parliament **bylaw** *n* law made by a local authority and operational only within its own area **bypass** *n* road constructed to direct the flow of traffic away from a town centre *vt* **1** go round in order to avoid **2** ignore (regulations, procedures, etc) in order to proceed without delay

C

cab *n* **1** driver s compartment of a lorry, bus, etc **2** taxi

cabaret (´kæbərei) *n* entertainment provided by a nightclub, restaurant etc

cabbage *n* vegetable with a short stalk and a head of green or purplish tightly packed leaves

cabin *n* **1** small functional house hut, or shelter **2** living quarters on a ship; berth **3** section of an aircraft for passengers or crew **cabin cruiser** *n* motor boat with cabin accommodation

cabinet *n* **1** piece of furniture for storing crockery, glassware medicine, etc; cupboard **2** filing cabinet **3** outer case of a radio or television set **the Cabinet** body of Government ministers responsible for policy-making

cable *n* **1** strong rope of twisted wire, hemp, etc **2** set of insulated wires used for conducting electricity **3** overseas telegram **4** *also* **cable stitch** knitting stitch producing a twisted pattern *vt,vi* send an overseas telegram (to)

cache (kæʃ) *n* hidden supply or store, esp of weapons

cackle *vi* **1** squawk like a hen **2** laugh or shriek raucously *n* **1** squawk **2** raucous laugh or shriek

cactus *n pl* **cacti** (´kæktai) *or* **cactuses** plant adapted to grow in desert regions with tough spiny stems and bright showy flowers

cadence *n* **1** sequence of chords marking the end of a musical phrase or section **2** modulation of the voice; intonation

cadet *n* young trainee, esp in the armed forces or police force

cadge *vt,vi* acquire or ask for without intending to pay; beg **cadger** *n* person who cadges

café *n* small restaurant serving snacks

cafeteria *n* self-service restaurant or canteen

caffeine *n* mild stimulant found in some plants, esp coffee

cage *n* **1** enclosure or box with bars used for confining animals or birds **2** lift in a mine shaft *vt* put or keep in a cage

cajole *vt,vi* wheedle; coax; persuade by flattery

cake *n* **1** sweet food made from flour, sugar, eggs, etc, and baked **2** flattish compact mass, as of soap **a piece of cake** *inf* something easily achieved or obtained ~*vt* cover with a hard dry mass

calamity *n* disaster; misfortune **calamitous** *adj*

calcium *n* silvery metallic element found in limestone, marble, and other rocks and in bones and teeth

calculate *vt,vi* work out mathematically *vt* **1** estimate; believe; suppose **2** design; plan; intend **calculating** *adj* ruthless; scheming **calculation** *n* **calculator** *n* electronic device used for mathematical calculation

calendar *n* **1** system for determining the length of a year, order of months, etc **2** chart showing the divisions of a year **3** list or diary of events and engagements

calf[1] *n, pl* **calves 1** young of cattle **2** young seal, whale, elephant, etc

calf[2] *n* fleshy part of the back of the lower leg

calibre *n* **1** diameter of a gun bore, bullet, etc **2** worth; merit

call *vt,vi* **1** shout out in order to summon, attract attention, etc **2** telephone; ring *vi also* **call on** visit *vt* **1** name; christen **2** describe as; label **3** convene (a meeting) **call for 1** fetch; collect **2** require; demand **call in 1** drop by on a visit **2** request the services of (a doctor, specialist, etc) **call off 1** cancel or postpone **2** order to stop attacking **call on 1** appeal to; request **call out 1** summon **2** bring out on strike **call to mind** recall **call**

up 1 conscript **2** reach by telephone ~n **1** characteristic cry of a bird or animal **2** shout **3** visit **4** telephone conversation **5** duty; obligation **6** demand; need **on call** available for duty **caller** n **callbox** n public telephone box **calling** n vocation **call-up** n conscription

callous adj cruelly indifferent to suffering **callously** adv **callousness** n

calm adj **1** not excited or anxious; serene; untroubled **2** peaceful **3** still; hardly moving n also **calmness** stillness; tranquillity; peace vt,vi also **calm down** make or become calm(er); quieten; soothe **calmly** adv

calorie n unit of heat energy, used esp for measuring the energy value of foods

came v pt of **come.**

camel n long-legged largely domesticated mammal with one or two humps on its back, commonly found in desert areas of N Africa

camera n **1** optical device for producing a photographic image **2** also **television camera** device for converting optical images into electrical signals **in camera** in private; not open

camouflage n **1** use of certain materials as a disguise to prevent a person, military equipment, etc , from being seen by an enemy **2** colour or markings of an animal that make it less conspicuous in a certain environment vt make less noticeable by use of camouflage

camp[1] n **1** site having tents, huts, etc , for use as temporary accommodation **2** military base housing soldiers temporarily; encampment **3** group of people with common political views vi also **camp out** live in a tent or other temporary living accommodation **camper** n **camping** n

camp[2] adj of a style that exaggerates or parodies what is thought to be appropriate homosexual behaviour n exaggerated or effeminate style of behaviour

campaign n **1** series of planned military operations **2** technical activities designed to promote a political cause or candidate, commercial product, etc vi mount a campaign; fight **campaigner** n

campus n area and buildings occupied by a university or college

can[1] v aux (pt could) **1** be able or willing to; know how to **2** have permission or opportunity to

can[2] n metal container or tin **carry the can** accept responsibility or blame ~vt (-nn-) put or store in a can

canal n **1** man-made waterway or channel for navigation, irrigation, etc **2** passage or duct in the body

canary n small yellow songbird of the finch family

cancel vt (-ll-) **1** prevent (a planned event) from taking place; call off **2** stop; discontinue **3** make invalid by crossing through or stamping with a special mark **cancel out** offset; compensate (for) **cancellation** n

cancer n malignant growth or tumour in the body **Cancer** fourth sign of the zodiac represented by the crab

candid adj honest; frank; open; fair **candidly** adv **candour** n

candidate n **1** person nominated or applying for a particular office, job, or position **2** person sitting an examination

candle n cylinder of wax with a central wick, which burns slowly when lit **burn the candle at both ends** exhaust oneself by living strenuously

cane n **1** pliant hollow stem of the bamboo or various palms, often used for making furniture **2** sugar cane **3** thorny stem of a raspberry or blackberry bush **4** thin rod used as a walking stick or as an implement for inflicting punishment vt,vi punish by beating with a cane

canine adj **1** of the dog family **2** like a dog

canister n cylindrical metal storage container; can

cannabis n **1** hemp plant **2** marijuana

cannibal n **1** person who eats human flesh **2** animal that feeds on its own kind **cannibalism** n **cannibalize** vt take parts from (motor vehicles, etc) to repair others

cannon n, pl **cannons** or **cannon** heavy mounted gun that discharges large shells v **cannon into** collide with; barge into

cannot v aux **1** be unable or unwilling to **2** be forbidden or have no opportunity to

canoe n small narrow portable boat propelled with a paddle vi travel or transport by canoe

canon n **1** ecclesiastical law **2** list of Christian saints **3** priest attached to a cathedral or various religious orders **4** moral principle; standard; criterion **5** musical form in which the same melody is introduced at overlapping intervals by two or more voices **canonical** adj **canonize** vt recognize officially as a saint

canopy n ornamental awning suspended above a throne, bed, etc

canteen n 1 restaurant for the use of employees of a company, children at school, etc 2 box of cutlery 3 flask carried by soldiers, campers, etc

canter n gait of a horse between a trot and a gallop vi,vt move or take at a canter

canvas n 1 hard-wearing waterproof material of flax or hemp 2 piece of such material used for painting on in oils

canvass vi,vt seek support or opinions from (potential voters, customers etc) **canvasser** n

canyon n deep narrow valley or gorge; ravine

cap n 1 flat closely fitting hat, sometimes with a peak 2 small lid or cover 3 natural or artificial covering of a tooth 4 also **dutch cap** diaphragm used as a contraceptive device vt (-pp-) 1 cover the top or surface of 2 outdo; top **to cap it all** in addition; on top; as a finishing touch

capable adj 1 having the potential or capacity for 2 able; competent **capability** n **capably** adv

capacity n 1 power to contain a quantity 2 amount that a container can hold; volume 3 maximum number that can be accommodated 4 ability to perform or behave in a particular way 5 power or function of an office or rank

cape¹ n short cloak

cape² n headland

capital n 1 city that is the seat of government of a country 2 wealth or assets, esp when used for investment or profit 3 also **capital letter** large or upper case form of a written or printed letter of the alphabet adj 1 inf excellent; first-class 2 carrying the penalty of death **capitalism** n economic system whereby private owners control the means of production and distribution **capitalist** adj,n **capitalize** vt 1 use, provide, or convert into capital 2 write or print in capital letters **capitalize on** exploit; take advantage of

caprice (kə'pri:s) n whim **capricious** (kə-'priʃəs) adj subject to or indicative of whim; changeable

Capricorn n tenth sign of the zodiac, represented by the goat

capsicum n tropical plant bearing edible fruit (peppers)

capsize vi,vt overturn; upset

capsule n 1 soluble shell enclosing a dose of oral medicine 2 pressurized compartment of a space vehicle 3 closed structure containing seeds, spores, or fruits **capsular** adj

captain n 1 person in charge of a vessel or aircraft 2 naval officer ranking above a commander and below a rear admiral 3 army officer ranking above a lieutenant and below a major 4 leader of a sports team vt act as captain of **captaincy** n

caption n 1 brief description accompanying an illustration 2 heading or title; headline, subtitle vt provide with a caption

capture vt 1 take prisoner 2 gain control or possession of n act of capturing **captivate** vt fascinate; charm; enchant **captivation** n **captive** n prisoner adj 1 imprisoned 2 restrained; confined **captivity** n

car n 1 small wheeled vehicle for personal transport 2 vehicle containing passengers, such as a railway carriage

carafe (kə'ræf, 'kæræf) n decorative bottle used for serving wine or water at the table

caramel n 1 burnt sugar used for flavouring and colouring 2 chewy kind of toffee

carat n 1 measure of the purity of gold in an alloy 2 measure of weight of precious stones, esp diamonds

caravan n 1 covered vehicle equipped for living in and capable of being drawn by a car, horse, etc 2 company of travellers in desert regions vi (-nn-) travel by caravan

caraway n Eurasian plant whose aromatic fruits (caraway seeds) are used in cooking

carbohydrate n organic compound, such as starch or sugar, containing carbon, hydrogen, and oxygen

carbon n 1 widely distributed nonmetallic element occurring as diamond, graphite, or charcoal and forming many organic and inorganic compounds 2 also **carbon paper** n paper coated on one side with a dark pigment, used to duplicate writing or typing **carbon dioxide** n colourless incombustible gas present in the atmosphere, formed during respiration and the combustion of organic compounds

carburettor n part of a petrol engine where the fuel is mixed with air

carcass n dead body, esp of an animal sold for food

card n 1 piece of stiff paper used for filing, as proof of identity or membership, advertising, etc 2 similar piece of paper, often illustrated, used for sending greetings, congratulations, etc 3 any of a set of cardboard pieces, marked with symbols, used for playing games or telling fortunes **a card up one's sleeve** thing or action kept in reserve to be used to gain an advantage **on the cards** probable; likely **put one's cards on the table** or **show one's cards** reveal one's intentions, plans, etc **cardboard** n thin stiff board made of paper pulp

cardigan n close-fitting woollen jacket

cardinal n senior dignitary of the Roman Catholic Church, ranking next below the Pope adj of prime importance; fundamental **cardinal number** n number denoting quantity rather than order **cardinal point** n one of the points of the compass, N, S, E, or W

care n 1 solicitous attention 2 caution 3 supervision; charge; responsibility 4 anxiety; trouble, worry **care of** at the address of ~vi feel interest or concern **care for 1** feel affection for 2 look after; tend 3 wish for; want **carefree** adj free from worry, anxiety, and responsibility **careful** adj 1 cautious; wary 2 meticulous; painstaking **carefully** adv **careless** adj 1 lacking sufficient thought or attention; negligent 2 unconcerned; indifferent **carelessly** adv **carelessness** n **caretaker** n person employed to look after and maintain a school, office, etc

career n 1 pursuit of a profession or occupation 2 course; progression vi move rapidly, esp in an uncontrolled way; hurtle

caress n light gentle stroke of affection vt stroke gently and affectionately, fondle

cargo n goods carried in a ship or aircraft; freight; load

caricature n satirical representation of a person that grossly exaggerates particular characteristics vt represent as a caricature

carnal adj sensual; not spiritual; of the flesh **carnal knowledge** n sexual intercourse **carnally** adv

carnation n cultivated flower having fragrant pink, white or red blooms

carnival n public celebration, festivities, and revelry, esp just before Lent

carnivorous adj meat-eating **carnivore** n meat-eating animal, esp a mammal

carol n joyous song, esp to celebrate Christmas vi (-ll-) sing joyfully

carpenter n person skilled in using wood in building, making furniture, etc vi,vt work as a carpenter **carpentry** n

carpet n 1 thick textile floor covering 2 thick layer or covering vt cover with or as if with a carpet

carriage n 1 horse-drawn four-wheeled vehicle 2 section of a train, often comprising several compartments 3 movable gun-support 4 part of a typewriter holding and moving paper. 5 deportment; bearing **carriageway** n road, or part of a road, used by vehicles

carrot n plant whose long orange root is eaten as a vegetable **carroty** adj orange

carry vt,vi take (something) from one place to another; transport; transmit; convey vt 1 hold; bear; keep 2 contain; include 3 sustain; keep in operation 4 influence **carry oneself** conduct oneself; behave **carry on** continue; persevere **carrier** n 1 person or thing that carries 2 also **carrier-bag** large paper or polythene bag with handles 3 person or animal carrying disease

cart n strong two-wheeled open vehicle used by farmers, tradesmen, etc vt,vi 1 transport in a cart 2 inf carry with difficulty

cartilage n strong flexible tissue often developing into bone; gristle **cartilaginous** adj

carton n small light container, esp of cardboard

cartoon n 1 simple humorous or satirical drawing 2 animated film 3 sketch made in preparation for a painting, tapestry, etc **cartoonist** n

cartridge n 1 small cylindrical case containing explosives, a bullet, or shot 2 large type of cassette for a tape recorder 3 film cassette 4 device fitted to the pickup arm on a gramophone that contains the stylus 5 removable container filled with ink for a fountain pen **cartridge paper** n strong white paper for drawing

carve vi,vt 1 shape with a knife, chisel, etc 2 cut (meat) into pieces or slices **carve up 1** inf injure by an attack with a knife 2 sl endanger by aggressive driving **carver** n **carving** n 1 act of carving 2 artefact carved from wood, stone, etc

cascade n 1 waterfall 2 something that falls in folds or drapes vi fall like a cascade

case[1] n box, container, or protective outer covering

case[2] 1 instance; circumstance; example 2 instance of a medical condition 3 legal suit, or grounds for suit 4 patient or client dealt with by a doctor, social worker, lawyer, etc 5 grammatical relationship of a noun, pronoun, or adjective to other parts of a sentence sometimes shown by inflectional endings **in case** in the event that **in any case** whatever happens

cash n money, esp in the form of notes and coins vt convert into cash **cash in on** inf profit from; exploit

cashier[1] n person employed to receive and pay out cash in a bank, shop, etc

cashier[2] vt discharge dishonourably from the army

cashmere n very fine soft woven hair of the Kashmir goat

casino n building equipped for gambling

casket n small box or case, esp for jewels

casserole n 1 heavy pan or dish for long slow cooking 2 meal cooked in a casserole vt cook in a casserole

cassette n sealed container holding spools of film, magnetic tape, etc , for use in a camera, tape-recorder, etc

cassock n long black tunic worn by various members of the clergy

cast vt (cast) 1 throw; hurl; fling 2 discard; shed; drop 3 project; direct 4 make (a vote) 5 allocate (parts) for a play 6 make (shape of metal, glass, etc) by pouring into a mould **cast off** discard; throw away; reject **castoff** n discarded thing or person **cast on/off** form the first/last row of stitches of a piece of knitting ~n 1 all the actors in a play 2 throw, as of dice 3 mould 4 casing for a broken bone 5 slight squint

castanets pl n pair of hollow shells of hard wood or ivory held in the hand and clicked together to accompany music and dancing

caste n 1 one of four hereditary social divisions in Hindu society 2 social class

castle n 1 large fortified building functioning as a fortress or stronghold 2 (in chess) rook **castellated** adj having battlements, turrets etc , as a castle

castrate vt remove the testicles of **castration** n

casual adj 1 accidental, not planned; chance 2 informal 3 not regular; temporary **casually** adv

casualty n victim of a serious accident battle etc

cat n 1 small domestic animal, kept esp as a pet 2 feline mammal, such as the lion, tiger, or leopard **cat's eye** n glass stud set into the road surface to mark traffic lanes as a guide to motorists at night

catalogue n comprehensive orderly list of books in a library, goods for sale, etc vt list or insert in a catalogue

catapult n 1 device for hurling small rocks and stones 2 equipment for launching aircraft from ships, etc vt throw or hurl as from a catapult

cataract n 1 powerful waterfall 2 heavy rainstorm or flood 3 eye disorder in which the lens becomes opaque

catarrh n inflammation of a mucous membrane in the nose or throat, as during a cold

catastrophe n major disaster; calamity **catastrophic** adj **catastrophically** adv

catch v (caught) vt 1 grasp (something that has been thrown or is falling) 2 capture; seize 3 discover by surprise; detect 4 board or take (a train, bus, etc) 5 hear or grasp the meaning of 6 contract (an infection or disease) 7 strike: hit 8 portray accurately or convincingly 9 make contact with; find 10 deceive; swindle vi,vt 1 ignite or become ignited by 2 become tangled (with) or hooked up (on) **catch on** 1 learn or grasp 2 become fashionable **catch up** 1 reach or get level with after following 2 make up (arrears, a backlog, etc) ~n 1 act of catching 2 something caught 3 device for fastening 4 inf difficulty; snag 5 inf highly eligible person 6 ball game **catchy** adj inf (esp of a tune) easy to remember or imitate

catechism n religious instruction, esp in a dialogue form

category n class; group; division **categorical** adj absolutely; definite; explicit **categorically** adv **categorize** vt place in a category; classify

cater vi provide food, entertainment, etc **cater for** supply whatever is necessary **caterer** n

caterpillar n 1 larva of a moth, butterfly etc 2

continuous band of steel plates fitted instead of wheels to a vehicle such as a tractor or tank

cathedral n principal church in a diocese

catholic adj widespread, liberal; of general interest **Catholic** adj, n Roman Catholic **Catholicism** n

catkin n cluster of small flowers of the willow, hazel, etc resembling a cat's tail

cattle pl n cows, bulls, etc, collectively

catty adj inf spiteful

caught v pt and pp of **catch.**

cauliflower n variety of cabbage cultivated for its large edible white flower head

cause n 1 something that produces an effect 2 motive; grounds; reason 3 general aim or set of ideals for which a person or group campaigns vt be the cause of; bring about; make happen **causal** adj **causation** or **causality** n

causeway n raised road or path over treacherous ground, water, etc

caustic adj 1 burning or corrosive 2 cutting, sarcastic **caustic soda** n sodium hydroxide

caution n 1 prudence; care; watchfulness 2 warning vt warn; advise caution **cautionary** adj advising caution; intended as a warning **cautious** adj careful; prudent; wary **cautiously** adv

cavalry n unit of troops, originally mounted on horseback but now equipped with armoured cars, tanks, etc

cave hollow area in a rock or under a cliff vt hollow out **cave in** collapse; give way; subside **cavern** n large underground cave **cavernous** adj

caviar n salted roe of the sturgeon, eaten as a delicacy

cavity n 1 hollow space 2 hollow part of a tooth caused by decay

cayenne n hot red pepper produced from capsicum seeds

cease vt,vi stop; end, discontinue; finish n **without cease** endlessly, continuously **ceasefire** n truce, esp a temporary one **ceaseless** adj incessant; endless

cedar n large coniferous evergreen tree with hard sweet-smelling wood

cede vt,vi concede or yield territory, rights, etc

ceiling n 1 upper surface of a room 2 upper limit of prices, wages, etc

celebrate vt 1 mark or honour with festivity and rejoicing 2 officiate at. a religious or public ceremony vi rejoice, make merry **celebrated** adj famous **celebrity** n 1 well-known or famous person 2 fame; renown; notoriety

celery n vegetable grown for its long greenish-white edible stalks

celestial adj heavenly; of the sky

celibate adj unmarried 2 abstaining from sexual intercourse n person who is celibate, esp one who has taken religious vows **celibacy** n

cell n 1 independent unit of an organism 2 small room occupied by a monk, prisoner etc 3 device producing or storing electric current by chemical action 4 small group working within a larger political or religious movement **cellular** adj

cellar n 1 underground room, used esp for storage 2 store of wine

cello n musical instrument of the violin family, held between the knees when played **cellist** n

Cellophane n Tdmk thin transparent packaging material

Celluloid n Tdmk inflammable material made from cellulose nitrate and camphor, used esp as a coating for film

cellulose n carbohydrate forming walls of plant cells

cement n 1 substance made from limestone and clay mixed with water that hardens to form concrete 2 substance used to fill cavities of the teeth vt 1 join or spread with cement 2 unite; bind together; strengthen

cemetery n burial ground, esp one not attached to a church

censor n person authorized to examine and ban material in films, books letters, etc considered to be harmful dangerous, or immoral vt act as a censor of **censorship** n **censorious** adj critical, harsh

censure n disapproval; blame, harsh criticism vt reprimand; criticize, blame

census n official population count

cent n 1 US coin equivalent to one hundredth of a dollar 2 coin of various other countries **per cent** by the hundred; in a hundred **hundred per cent** complete; absolute; total

centenary n hundredth anniversary adj relating to a period of a hundred years

centigrade adj relating to a temperature scale

on which the freezing point of water is 0° and its boiling point 100°

centime n 1 French coin equivalent to one hundredth of a franc 2 coin of various other countries

centimetre n one hundredth of a metre

centipede n small crawling animal having a body made up of several segments, each segment bearing a pair of legs

central adj 1 of the centre 2 principal; most important **central heating** n system of heating a building with radiators air vents, etc, connected to a central source **centralize** vt 1 bring to a central point 2 unite (several duties, powers, etc) under one central authority vi come to a central point **centralization** n

centre n 1 middle point of a circle, line, sphere. etc 2 main point or focus of interest, attention, administration, importance, etc vt,vi be concentrated (on); have a centre at or in **centre-forward** n player in football, hockey, etc, positioned at the centre of the front line **centre-half** n, pl **-halves** player in football, hockey, etc, positioned at the centre of the defence line

century n 1 one hundred years 2 one of the periods of a hundred years numbered before and since the birth of Christ 3 score of a hundred runs in cricket

ceramics n art of making pottery from clay, porcelain, etc **ceramic** adj,n

cereal n 1 crop yielding edible grain 2 breakfast dish made from cereals

ceremony n 1 formal or public act, religious rite, etc 2 formal politeness **stand (up)on ceremony** insist on exaggerated politeness or formality **ceremonial** adj ritual; formal; pertaining to ceremony n prescribed form of ceremonies; ritual **ceremonially** adv **ceremonious** adj elaborately correct, dignified, or precise **ceremoniously** adv

certain adj 1 sure; convinced; positive 2 definite; inevitable 3 indicating someone or something specific but unnamed **certainly** adv **certainty** n

certificate n written declaration of a fact, such as success in an examination, ownership of shares, public status, etc **certify** vt 1 declare; authorize; guarantee; endorse 2 declare officially to be insane

cervix n, pl **cervixes** or **cervices** (´sɜːvɪsiːz) 1 lower part of the uterus 2 neck **cervical** adj

chafe vt,vi rub until sore or roughened n soreness

chaffinch n small European songbird of the finch family

chain n 1 flexible line of connected metal links 2 range of mountains 3 series of connected events vt fasten or restrict with or as with a chain **chain reaction** 1 chemical or nuclear process in which the product of each step initiates the next step 2 series of rapid interconnected events **chain-smoke** vi smoke continuously, esp by lighting one cigarette from the stub of the last **chain-smoker** n **chain-store** n one of a number of shops owned and managed by the same organization

chair n 1 movable seat usually with four legs and a back, for one person 2 seat of dignity or authority 3 chairmanship 4 professorship vt preside over, act as chairman of **chairman** n, pl **-men** 1 principal director of a company 2 person presiding over a meeting, committee, etc **chairmanship** n

chalet n 1 wooden Swiss house with a steep overhanging roof 2 house or bungalow built in this style esp for holidays

chalk n 1 soft white rock consisting of calcium carbonate 2 piece of chalk or similar material used for writing or drawing vt,vi write or treat with chalk

challenge vt 1 invite to a duel or other contest 2 defy; dispute; call for an answer to n 1 summons to a contest 2 questioning of right; calling to account

chamber n 1 room esp a bedroom 2 meeting hall 3 enclosed cavity **chambers** pl barrister s or judge s conference rooms **chambermaid** n hotel maid in charge of bedrooms **chamber music** n music written for a small ensemble of solo instruments

chamberlain n 1 officer managing a royal household 2 high-ranking Court official

chameleon (kəˈmiːliən) n type of lizard capable of changing its skin colour to match its surroundings

champagne n type of sparkling French wine

champion n 1 winner; victor; person excelling all others 2 upholder of a cause adj excellent vt defend; stand up for **championship** n 1 competition or series of contests to find a champion **2** status or conduct of a champion

chance n **1** unexpected or inexplicable event **2** risk **3** possibility; opportunity **by chance** accidentally; fortuitously ~adj fortuitous; accidental vi,vt **1** happen (to) **2** risk; dare

chancel n eastern part of a church near the altar, reserved for the clergy and choir

chancellor n **1** chief minister or other high official **2** titular head of a university **Chancellor of the Exchequer** n principal government finance minister

chandelier n decorative branched fitting that hangs from a ceiling and supports a number of lights

change n **1** substitution of one thing for another; alteration; variance **2** money returned as balance for payment; coins of small value vt **1** alter; substitute; make different **2** give coins of smaller denomination in exchange for a larger coin or note vi become different vt,vi **1** put on (different clothes) **2** board (another train, bus etc) **changeable** adj

channel n **1** navigable part of a harbour, river bed, etc **2** comparatively narrow stretch of sea **3** radio or television waveband **4** tube; passage; groove **5** means of communication, commerce, etc vt (-ll-) **1** provide, use, or supply through a channel **2** direct; find an outlet for

chant n song, esp intoned sacred music vt,vi **1** sing esp in monotone **2** recite

chaos n disorder; confusion **chaotic** adj

chap¹ vt vi (-pp-) (of skin) roughen and crack through excessive cold, etc

chap² n inf man, fellow

chapel n **1** small subordinate church often attached to a college, institution etc **2** small part of a larger church containing a separate altar **3** association of printers or journalists

chaplain n clergyman attached to a particular household, institution, unit of soldiers, etc

chapter n **1** one of the principal divisions of a book **2** governing body of a cathedral

char¹ vt,vi (-rr-) scorch; singe; blacken; burn

char² n also **charwoman** or **charlady** inf person employed to do housework vi (-rr-) do rough housework

character n **1** sum of particular qualities distinguishing an individual **2** personality created by a writer **3** distinguishing feature,

mark, handwriting etc **4** eccentric or amusing person **characteristic** adj distinctive; typical n distinctive quality or trait **characteristically** adv **characterize** vt **1** distinguish (by); typify **2** portray; describe **characterization** n

charcoal n carbon made from burnt wood, coal, etc

charge n **1** price; liability to pay **2** accusation **3** responsibility; duty **4** quantity, esp of explosive with which anything is loaded **5** property of matter responsible for electrical phenomena and having two forms, positive and negative, which cause mutual attraction **6** sudden attacking rush **in charge of** with responsibility for ~vt,vi **1** demand as a price **2** rush aggressively towards vt **1** accuse **2** burden **3** load; fill up **4** supply (with electricity) **charge-hand** n workman or assistant in charge of others; foreman

chariot n two-wheeled horse-drawn vehicle formerly used for races and battle **charioteer** n

charisma n spiritual quality inspiring great devotion and trust **charismatic** adj

charity n **1** quality of love, kindness, or generosity; compassion **2** institution or organization founded for the benefit of others **charitable** adj **1** kind; lenient; generous **2** of a recognized charity

charm n **1** ability to fascinate and delight by personal qualities **2** magic spell, act trinket, etc , thought to bring good fortune vt vi **1** attract; delight; enthrall **2** enchant by magic **charming** adj delightful

chart n graph, plan, or map vt record progress by means of a chart

charter n document granting a right establishing a university, etc vt **1** establish by charter **2** let or hire, esp a ship or aircraft **chartered** adj regulated according to established rules

chase vt hunt; pursue; run after; drive away n pursuit; hunt

chasm n ('kæzəm) n deep gulf or inlet; abyss

chassis ('ʃæsi) n, pl **chassis** basic frame esp of a motor car, on which other parts are mounted

chaste adj pure or virtuous, esp sexually **chastity** n

chastise vt punish esp by beating **chastisement** n

chat vi (-tt-) talk in a friendly informal way n

easy informal conversation **chatty** adj inf talkative

chatter vi 1 talk rapidly and thoughtlessly 2 (of monkeys, birds, etc.) make an excited rapid rattling noise n 1 idle talk; gossip 2 rattling noise **chatterbox** n inf talkative person

chauffeur ('∫oufə) n person employed to drive another s car; driver vt act as chauffeur for

chauvinism ('∫ouvinizəm) n excessive aggressive patriotism **male chauvinism** belief of men in their superiority over women **chauvinist** n, adj

cheap adj 1 inexpensive; low in price 2 inferior; vulgar; shoddy **cheaply** adv **cheapness** n **cheapen** vt, vi decrease in price or quality

cheat vt defraud; swindle; trick vi attempt to succeed by dishonest means n person who cheats; fraud

check vt 1 restrain; hinder; halt 2 verify; test the truth of; inspect n 1 obstruction; hindrance 2 supervision; careful watch; verification 3 move in chess threatening the opponent's King 4 pattern of squares 5 US bill; account; cheque **checkmate** n stage in chess where a threat to the King cannot be countered vt defeat at checkmate **checkpoint** n place where traffic is halted and inspected by police, etc **check-up** n careful detailed examination, esp for medical purposes

cheek n 1 side of the face below the eye 2 inf impudence; rudeness; impertinence vt inf speak impertinently to **cheeky** adj inf impudent; saucy **cheekily** adv **cheekiness** n **cheekbone** n bone of the face just below the eye

cheer n 1 shout of approval or joy 2 entertainment; comfort 3 disposition; attitude vt comfort; encourage vi, vt shout with joy or approval **cheer up** become more cheerful **cheerful** adj happy; jovial; lively **cheerfully** adv **cheerfulness** n

cheese n protein-rich food of many varieties made from the curd of milk

cheetah n swift-running member of the cat family, resembling a leopard

chef n master cook

chemical adj pertaining to chemistry n substance made by or used in chemical processes **chemist** n 1 one qualified to sell drugs and medicine 2 researcher or student of chemistry **chemistry** n science concerned with the properties and interactions of elements and compounds

cheque n signed order, written generally on a printed form, to a bank to pay out money from a customer's account

chequer n pattern of squares **chequered** adj 1 variegated; diversified in colour 2 marked by fluctuations in fortune, nature, etc

cherish vt protect; preserve; hold dear; nurture

cherry n small red or yellow stone fruit

cherub n one of the orders of angels, generally depicted as a plump winged child

chess n game of skill for two players using thirty-two pieces (chessmen) on a board with sixty-four black and white squares

chest n 1 upper front part of the body 2 large strong box **chest of drawers** n piece of furniture fitted with a set of drawers, used esp for storing clothes or linen

chestnut n 1 deciduous tree (sweet-chestnut, bearing edible nut, or horse-chestnut, bearing inedible nut) 2 fruit of these trees 3 dark reddish-brown horse n, adj dark reddish-brown

chew vt, vi grind between the teeth **chew over** wonder; ruminate ~n act of chewing **chewing gum** n sweetened flavoured preparation of resin or gum for chewing

chick n 1 young bird, esp a chicken 2 sl girl

chicken n 1 fowl reared for its eggs and meat 2 inf young person adj sl cowardly **chickenpox** n mild infectious disease usually contracted by children, characterized by a blistery rash

chicory n plant whose leaves are used in salads and whose root is ground to flavour coffee

chief adj main; major; most important; principal n 1 leader; superior head of a department, organization, etc 2 also **chieftain** leader of a tribe or clan **chiefly** adv mainly; principally

chilblain n painful itchy red swelling on the hands and feet caused by extreme cold, bad circulation, etc

child n 1 young person; infant; boy or girl 2 son or daughter **childbirth** n act of giving birth to a child **childhood** n state or period of being a child **childish** adj immature; foolish; naive **childishly** adv **childlike** adj trusting or innocent like a child

chill n 1 coldness 2 slight cold preceding fever 3 discouraging influence vt, vi make or become cold or cool **chilly** adj 1 slightly cold; cool 2 unfriendly

chilli n pod of a capsicum, often dried and ground into the hot pungent spice, Cayenne pepper

chime n melodious sound as of bells, esp when ringing in sequence vt,vi 1 ring musically 2 agree; concur

chimney n construction allowing smoke to escape from a fireplace, furnace, etc

chimpanzee n small African ape

chin n part of the face below the mouth

china n crockery, esp made of fine porcelain

chink [1] n crevice, narrow opening; slit

chink [2] n sharp clinking sound, as of coins or glasses struck together vi clink; jingle

chip n 1 small fragment or splinter of glass, wood, etc 2 small oblong piece of deep-fried potato 3 small crack or missing piece in china, glass, etc 4 counter or token used in gambling games **have a chip on one's shoulder** bear a grudge ~vt (-pp-) 1 crack or break a small piece from 2 cut (potatoes) into oblongs 3 carve with a small tool **chip in** contribute

chiropody n treatment of minor foot disorders **chiropodist** n

chirp vi make the short shrill cry of a bird n chirping sound **chirpy** adj inf lively and cheerful

chisel n steel cutting tool with wedge-shaped edge used in carpentry, masonry, etc vi,vt (-ll-) cut or shape with a chisel

chivalry n 1 courtesy or protectiveness, esp as shown by men to women 2 code of behaviour of medieval knights **chivalrous** adj

chive n small plant of the onion family whose leaves are used as a seasoning in cooking

chlorine n greenish-yellow poisonous corrosive gaseous element used as a disinfectant and bleach

chlorophyll n green colouring matter present in plants, necessary for photosynthesis

chocolate n preparation of cocoa mixed with sugar, milk, etc, eaten as a sweet, used for flavouring, etc adj,n dark brown

choice n 1 act of choosing 2 variety or things to choose from 3 thing chosen adj of excellent quality; selected

choir n 1 body of singers performing in public, esp in a church 2 part of a church or cathedral reserved for singers above the nave

and below the altar **chorister** n member of a church choir

choke vt 1 throttle or obstruct the breathing of; suffocate 2 block; obstruct vi 1 become choked 2 become speechless through emotion n 1 action or sound of choking 2 valve controlling air supply, as in a carburettor

cholera n highly infectious, often fatal disease characterized by feverish vomiting and diarrhoea

choose vt select or take something in preference to something else vi decide; determine

chop [1] vt (-pp-) 1 cut with sharp blows 2 cut into small pieces n 1 act of chopping 2 slice of pork or lamb containing part of a rib **chopper** n axe or hatchet

chop [2] vi (-pp-) make a sudden change of direction or attitude **chop and change** change or alter repeatedly

chopstick n one of a pair of small sticks used, esp in the Far East, as an implement for eating

choral adj written for or sung by a choir or chorus

chord n 1 simultaneous sounding of several notes in music 2 string of a musical instrument 3 straight line linking two points on a curve

chore n routine or repetitive task, esp housework

choreography n art of dance composition and notation **choreographer** n

chorus n 1 group of performers speaking, singing, or dancing together, esp as separate from the action of a drama 2 combined speech or song, esp the refrain of a ballad etc vt,vi speak or sing as a group

chose v pt of **choose.**

chosen v pp of **choose.**

Christ n title given to Jesus acknowledging him to be the Saviour foretold in the Old Testament

christen vt give a name to, esp at a Christian baptismal service **christening** n ceremony of baptizing and naming a child in a church

Christian n one professing to follow the teaching of Christ adj 1 believing in Christ 2 charitable; forgiving; unselfish 3 of or pertaining to Christ **Christian name** n personal name, esp as given at a christening **Christianity** n Christian faith, teaching, spirit, or way of life

Christmas n celebration of the birth of Christ **Christmas Day** December 25th

chromatic adj 1 concerned with or having colours 2 relating to a musical scale consisting of semitones

chrome n chromium

chromium n silvery-white metallic element used for highly polished coatings on other metals

chromosome n small rod-like body found in living cells, responsible for the transmission of genetic information

chronic adj 1 (esp of a disease) of a long-standing or constantly recurring nature 2 inf dreadful; tedious; objectionable **chronically** adv

chronological adj in order of time; according to time of occurrence **chronologically** adv **chronology** n

chrysalis n pupa or insect larva, esp enclosed in a sheath during its resting stage

chrysanthemum n autumn-flowering garden plant with large blooms

chubby adj plump and round-faced **chubbiness** n

chuck vt,vi inf 1 throw; toss 2 give up **chuck out** 1 throw away or out 2 eject forcibly

chuckle n quiet burbling laugh vi laugh quietly

chunk n thick piece or portion **chunky** adj thick and bulky

church n 1 whole body of Christians or of one of the Christian denominations 2 building used for Christian or other religious services 3 the clergy **churchyard** n burial ground surrounding a church

churn n 1 vessel used for converting milk or cream into butter 2 large cylindrical container used for transporting milk vt,vi rotate or agitate vigorously, as in a churn **churn out** produce rapidly and in great quantity

chute n 1 sloping track or passage down which water, rubbish, laundry, etc, may be shot 2 narrow waterfall

chutney n sweet spicy relish made from pickled fruit and vegetables

cider n drink made from pressed fermented apples

cigar n roll of tobacco leaves for smoking

cigarette n shredded tobacco leaves rolled in thin paper for smoking

cinder n piece of burnt or charred wood, coal, etc

cinecamera n camera used for taking motion pictures

cinema n 1 the film industry 2 building in which films are shown

cinnamon n sweet pungent spice made from the bark of a type of laurel found largely in S and SE Asia

circle n 1 plane figure bounded by an unbroken line, which is at every point the same distance from the centre 2 ring 3 group of people with a common interest 4 gallery in a theatre vt,vi move round in a circle

circuit n 1 circular path, distance or way round 2 journey taken regularly through a specific area, esp by a judge or barrister in performance of professional duties 3 path of an electric current **circuitous** adj roundabout; long-winded; devious

circular adj 1 relating to a circle 2 round **circulate** vi,vt move or pass around **circulation** n 1 act of moving or passing around 2 movement of blood through veins and arteries 3 distribution or sale of newspapers, magazines, etc

circumcise vt cut off the foreskin **circumcision** n

circumference n outer rim of a circle

circumscribe vt 1 restrict or contain within certain limits 2 draw a line around

circumstance n incident; fact; detail **circumstances** n pl 1 facts attendant on or relating to others; condition; state 2 financial position **circumstantial** adj 1 of or derived from circumstances 2 fully detailed

circus n 1 group of travelling entertainers, clowns, acrobats, performing animals, etc 2 arena or amphitheatre 3 place where several roads converge

cistern n water tank, esp supplying water to a lavatory

cite vt 1 quote as an example or authority 2 summon to appear in court **citation** n 1 quotation 2 summons 3 mention, esp for bravery, in military dispatches

citizen n 1 resident of a city 2 member of a state **citizenship** n

citrus n genus of fruit trees including orange, lemon, and lime

city n large or important town, esp containing a cathedral **the City** financial centre of London

civic adj of a city or local community **civics** pl

n science of government, esp local government

civil *adj* 1 courteous; polite 2 of a citizen or the community 3 not military 4 (of legal proceedings, etc) not criminal; disputed between ordinary citizens **civil engineering** *n* branch of engineering concerned with designing and building roads, bridges, etc **civil engineer** *n* **civil service** *n* body of officials employed by the state in an administrative capacity **civil servant** *n* **civil war** *n* war between citizens of the same state

civilian *n* one not in the employ of the armed forces

civilization *n* 1 moral, social, intellectual, and artistic standards of a specific society 2 advanced nonbarbaric condition or society **civilize** *vt* bring out of a primitive condition; refine

clad *adj* clothed; dressed

claim *vt* 1 demand as a right 2 ask or call for *vt,vi* assert; maintain *n* 1 demand or request by right 2 that which is claimed or asserted 3 right or title **claimant** *n* person who makes a claim, esp in law

clam *n* edible bivalve shellfish *v* **clam up** refuse to speak

clamber *vi* climb, esp with effort or difficulty *n* awkward climb

clammy *adj* damp and sticky

clamour *n* raucous outcry; uproar *vi* demand vociferously **clamorous** *adj* **clamorously** *adv*

clamp *n* device used in carpentry, metalwork, surgery, etc , to hold things firmly in place *vt* fasten or hold with a clamp **clamp down on** *inf* suppress

clan *n* large family or tribal group, esp in Scotland **clansman** *n*

clandestine *adj* concealed; secret

clang *n* resounding metallic sound, as of a large bell *vt,vi* make or cause a clang **clanger** *n* *inf* blunder

clank *n* loud metallic sound, as of a heavy chain *vt,vi* make or cause a clank

clap *n* 1 sudden noise as of the palms of the hands brought sharply together 2 sound of thunder *vt,vi* (-pp-) 1 applaud with the hands 2 place (down) suddenly 3 throw (into prison, etc) **clapper** *n* tongue suspended inside a bell **like the clappers** very energetically or quickly

claret *n* red wine from Bordeaux

clarify *vt,vi* make or become clear **clarification** *n*

clarinet *n* musical wind instrument with a single reed **clarinetist** *n*

clarity *n* clearness

clash *n* 1 loud banging noise, as of colliding metal objects 2 opposition; dispute; conflict *vt* bang noisily together *vi* 1 strike against 2 come into opposition; conflict 3 (of colours) be displeasing or disharmonious when placed together

clasp *n* 1 hinged or interlocking fastening 2 embrace; grasp of the hand *vt* 1 fasten with a clasp 2 embrace; grasp with the hand

class *n* 1 kind; sort; category 2 social group defined according to occupation, position, wealth, birth, social status, etc 3 group of students or pupils undergoing the same course of instruction 4 division denoting standard of comfort in an aeroplane, train, etc *vt* form into or place in a class

classic *adj* widely recognized as standard, typical, or of great merit *n* work of art, esp literature, noted for its lasting excellence **classical** *adj* 1 of ancient Greece or Rome, esp in formalized literary or architectural style 2 (of music) belonging to great serious European tradition, esp if composed before 1800 **classics** *pl n* language, literature, and philosophy of ancient Greece and Rome **classicist** *n* student of classics

classify *vt* arrange in classes or categories; place in a class **classification** *n*

clatter *n* loud repetitive rattling noise *vt,vi* make or cause a clatter

clause *n* 1 part of a sentence with a subject, predicate, and finite verb 2 subsection in a legal contract, will, agreement, etc

claustrophobia *n* morbid dread of enclosed or confined places **claustrophobic** *adj*

claw *n* hard hooked nail of an animal or bird *vt* seize or tear with claws or nails

clay *n* heavy sticky fine-grained soil material, plastic when moist, and used in pottery, brick-making, etc

clean *adj* free from dirt, marks, impurity, guilt, disease, etc *adv* completely *vt* make clean **clean out** clean thoroughly; empty **clean up** 1 tidy 2 suppress crime, vice, etc 3 gain a large profit, advantage, etc **cleanliness** *n*

cleanse vt clean (something) thoroughly; make pure **cleanser** n

clear adj 1 unclouded; bright; transparent 2 obvious; distinct; straightforward 3 net; after deductions 4 without obstruction adv completely vt 1 clarify 2 empty 3 acquit; declare innocent 4 pass without touching 5 verify; justify 6 receive (net) vi become clear **clear off** or **out** leave hurriedly **clear up** 1 solve 2 tidy 3 become fine or sunny **clearance** n 1 act of clearing 2 space between moving and stationary objects 3 certificate permitting passage through Customs, esp of a ship **clear-headed** adj lucid; intelligent; sensible **clearing** n 1 act of making or becoming clear 2 area free from trees, esp in a forest

clef n musical symbol denoting pitch of the notes written on the stave

clench vt 1 grasp; grip; press (teeth, the fist, etc) firmly together 2 secure tightly; rivet

clergy n priests and ordained ministers of a Christian church **clergyman** n, pl **-men** priest, esp in the Church of England

clerical adj 1 of a clerk 2 of a clergyman; religious

clerk n 1 employee dealing with records, correspondence, etc, in an office 2 person holding a particular administrative position in local government, the law, etc

clever adj 1 intelligent; bright 2 ingenious; cunning **cleverly** adv **cleverness** n

cliché n hackneyed expression or phrase

click n short sharp sound, as of a latch closing vi,vt make a click

client n customer; person employing another for business or professional purposes **clientele** (kli:ɔn'tel) n clients

cliff n steep high rock, esp facing the sea

climate n 1 general weather conditions of a region 2 prevailing public attitude, economic situation, etc

climax n 1 ultimate culmination of a series of events 2 moment of supreme elation, terror, etc 3 orgasm **climactic** adj

climb vi,vt 1 ascend or go up using hands and feet; scale 2 rise; mount n 1 distance or route to be climbed 2 act of climbing **climb down** admit to having been wrong; withdraw

cling vi (clung) 1 adhere or stick to closely 2 refuse to abandon a belief, idea, etc

clinic n 1 hospital department or health centre for the diagnosis and treatment of specific disorders 2 private nursing home **clinical** adj 1 relating to a clinic 2 of, used, or carried out in a hospital 3 concerned with treatment of disease in the patient 4 not biased or emotionally involved

clink n 1 short ringing sound as of metal, glass, etc, struck together 2 sl prison vt,vi make a clink

clip [1] n 1 device for holding paper, etc, together 2 hairgrip vt (-pp-) fasten with a clip

clip [2] vt (-pp-) 1 trim; cut closely; shorten 2 smack; hit sharply n 1 act of clipping 2 piece clipped off 3 sharp blow 4 short extract from a film

clitoris n female sexual organ similar to a rudimentary penis **clitoral** adj

cloak n long loose sleeveless garment fastening at the neck vt disguise; mask **cloakroom** n room in a public building, etc, where coats are left

clock n instrument for telling or measuring time vt 1 time (a runner) 2 sl hit; strike **clock in** or **on/out** or **off** record the time of starting/finishing work **clockwise** adv in the same direction as the hands of a clock **clockwork** n mechanism of a clock or one working like that of a clock **like clockwork** with perfect regularity and precision

clog n heavy shoe with a sole and sometimes upper of wood vi (-gg-) (of drains, pipes, etc) become obstructed or blocked vt block; obstruct

cloister n 1 covered arcade surrounding a monastery quadrangle 2 monastery, abbey, or nunnery **cloistered** adj shut away; secluded

close adj (klous) 1 nearby; near 2 mean; stingy 3 stuffy; sultry 4 confined; restricted 5 thorough 6 intimate n (klous for 1,2; klouz for 3) 1 alley; dead-end street or road; enclosure 2 cathedral precinct 3 end adv (klous) tightly; leaving no space **close-up** n ('klousʌp) film-shot or photograph giving a detailed view ~v (klouz) vt 1 shut 2 pull together; unite 3 finish; end; complete vi come to an end; terminate **close in** surround and move in on **close down** terminate; cease functioning **close up** shut completely **closed-shop** n factory employing only union members **closure** n

closet n 1 small private room 2 cupboard 3 lavatory **closeted** adj shut away; kept secret

clot n 1 small solidified mass of blood, mud, etc 2 sl fool vt,vi (-tt-) form into clots; congeal; coagulate

cloth n 1 small piece of fabric used for polishing, mopping, covering, etc 2 woven fabric from which clothing, curtains, etc , are cut and sewn

clothe vt 1 provide with clothes; dress 2 cover; disguise **clothing** n clothes; garments in general **clothes** pl n 1 garments; materials fashioned to be worn on the person; dress 2 bed-coverings **in plain clothes** (of a policeman, etc) not wearing uniform

cloud n 1 visible mass of small droplets of water floating in the sky, from which rain or snow falls 2 mass of dust, smoke, etc , resembling a cloud 3 anything depressing or threatening vt,vi 1 fill or cover with clouds 2 make or become murky or opaque 3 fill or cover with gloom, doubt, etc **cloudy** adj 1 covered or scattered with clouds 2 opaque; not clear

clove[1] n dried flower-bud of an aromatic tropical tree, used as a spice

clove[2] n small bulb, esp of garlic, that forms part of a larger one

clover n small flowering plant with three-lobed leaves, often grown as cattle fodder

clown n comic fool, esp in a circus vi play the fool

club n 1 association of people with a common interest in a social, cultural, or sporting activity, etc 2 the building, etc , used by such a group 3 thick heavy stick 4 stick used in golf **clubs** pl n one of the four suits in cards ~vt (-bb-) beat with a club **club together** unite for a common end; contribute to a collection

cluck n sound made by a hen vi make such a sound

clue n 1 hint or suggestion leading to the solution of a mystery 2 information; idea **clueless** adj inf stupid

clump n 1 cluster of trees, bushes, etc 2 heavy tread vi 1 tread heavily 2 group together

clumsy adj 1 inclined to stumble, drop things, etc ; awkward 2 tactless; gauche **clumsily** adv **clumsiness** n

cluster n closely packed group, as of flowers, diamonds, stars, etc vi grow or be gathered together

clutch vt grasp or seize tightly n 1 grasp; grip 2 mechanical coupling device allowing gradual engagement of gears, etc 3 number of eggs laid at one time

clutter n confused jumble vt crowd with a confused or untidy mass

coach n 1 bus, esp one used for long trips 2 large horse-drawn carriage 3 railway carriage 4 tutor training people for exams, athletic events, etc vt prepare for examination, contest, etc ; train

coagulate vi solidify; clot; congeal **coagulation** n

coal n solid black mineral consisting of carbonized vegetation and mined for use as fuel **coalmine** n workings from which coal is obtained; pit

coalition n short-term alliance, esp between political parties

coarse adj 1 rough in texture; not fine 2 vulgar; base; impolite **coarsely** adv **coarseness** n

coast n land bordering the sea vi sail or drift along **coastal** adj **coastguard** n person employed to watch the coast and sea for ships in danger, smuggling, etc **coastline** n line of the shore, as seen from the sea or air or as shown on a map

coat n 1 outer garment with sleeves 2 hair, fur, etc , covering an animal; pelt 3 layer of paint, etc , on a surface vt cover with a layer

coax vt persuade, esp by soothing or flattery; cajole

cobble n rounded stone used for paving, road-making, etc vi,vt mend or repair clumsily or shoddily

cobbler n one who makes or mends shoes and boots

cobra n poisonous hooded snake found in Asia and Africa

cobweb n spider s web

cock n 1 male bird, esp of domestic fowl 2 water-tap 3 hammer of a gun 4 inf chap; fellow 5 sl penis vt 1 tilt; turn to one side; set at a jaunty angle 2 pull back the hammer of (a gun) **cocky** adj cheeky; self-assured; impudent **cockiness** n

cockle n edible bivalve mollusc with a heart-shaped shell

Cockney n 1 Londoner, esp one born within the sound of Bow Bells 2 dialect of a Cockney

cockpit n pilot's compartment in an aircraft

cockroach n brown or black insect with long antennae

cocktail n 1 drink made from a mixture of spirits and flavourings 2 dish made from mixed fruit or prawns, etc

cocoa n powder from the ground seeds of the cacao tree, used to make chocolate or to flavour drinks

coconut n large fruit of a tropical palm-tree, with edible flesh, juice resembling milk, and a hard hairy husk

cocoon n protective silky coating spun by various insect larvae before becoming pupae

cod n, pl **cod** large edible sea fish

coddle vt 1 boil lightly 2 pamper; indulge; be protective towards

code n 1 system of symbols for secret or esoteric communication 2 system of regulations, laws, social customs, or moral principles vt put into a code

codeine n pain-killing drug obtained from opium

coeducation n education of children of both sexes at the same school

coerce (kou'ə:s) vt persuade forcefully; compel **coercion** n **coercive** adj

coexist vi exist at the same time, esp in harmony **coexistence** n

coffee n drink made from the roasted ground seeds (beans) of the coffee tree adj,n light brown

coffin n wooden box in which a corpse is placed for burial

cog n one of the teeth on the rim of a wheel **cogwheel** n wheel fitted with cogs, used in engineering, etc, for transmitting movement; gearwheel

cognac n French brandy

cohabit vi live together as man and wife **cohabitation** n

cohere vi stick together; remain consistent **coherence** n **cohesion** n **coherent** adj clear; comprehensible; articulate; consistent

coil vt,vi wind in rings; twist n 1 piece of rope, string, etc, coiled into rings 2 coil of wire in an electrical circuit

coin n stamped metal disc used as official currency vt 1 form or stamp coins in a mint 2 invent (an expression or phrase) **coinage** n

coincide vi 1 occur at the same time or place 2 agree; concur **coincidence** n 1 act or state of coinciding 2 striking accidental concurrence of events

colander n large strainer for draining vegetables

cold adj 1 not hot; chilly; low in temperature 2 unfriendly; indifferent; unemotional n 1 lack of heat 2 acute nasal inflammation **coldly** adv **coldness** n **cold-blooded** adj 1 having a blood temperature varying with that of the surrounding water or air 2 unemotional; callous; ruthless **cold-bloodedly** adv **cold-bloodedness** n **cold war** n period or state of political and military hostility between nations, involving no armed conflict

collaborate vi 1 co-operate; work together 2 co-operate with an enemy **collaboration** n **collaborator** n

collapse vi 1 break or fall down; fail totally; give up 2 fold away n 1 breakdown; physical or mental exhaustion 2 falling down of a structure **collapsible** adj

collar n 1 part of a garment encircling the neck 2 leather strap worn round the neck by a dog, horse, etc vt inf seize; tackle **collarbone** n prominent frontal bone linking the ribs to the shoulder blades

colleague n associate, esp someone following the same profession as oneself

collect vt 1 gather together; seek out and acquire 2 solicit (money) for a cause 3 fetch; pick up **collection** n 1 group of objects collected together 2 act of collecting, esp for a charity, church, etc **collective** adj taken as a whole **collectively** adv

college n 1 place of higher or specialized education 2 autonomous group of people **collegiate** adj

collide vi 1 strike violently, crash into 2 come into conflict **collision** n

colloquial adj of informal everyday speech **colloquialism** n informal phrase; slang, idiom

colon n punctuation mark (:) used to indicate a definite pause or division in a sentence

colonel n military officer of a rank between lieutenant-colonel and brigadier

colony n group of settlers from another country **colonize** vt take over as a colony **colonial** adj from or of a colony n inhabitant of a colony

colossal adj extremely large; enormous; gigantic, huge

colour n 1 sense impression produced by light of different wavelengths, or the property of objects or light producing this 2 pigment; hue 3 skin pigmentation 4 quality of vividness or distinction 5 false quality **colours** pl *n* **1** military flag or standard **2** award for membership of a team **off colour** unwell ~*vt* **1** impart colour to **2** give a false or biased impression of *vi* take on a colour **coloration** *n* **colour-bar** *n* discrimination against people of coloured or dark-skinned races **colour-blind** *adj* unable to distinguish or identify specific colours **colour-blindness** *n* **coloured** *adj* **1** having a colour **2** (of a person) of a non-White race **3** deceptive; biased **colourful** *adj* **1** full of colour **2** picturesque; vivid

colt *n* young male horse

column *n* **1** tall pillar, esp one supporting a building **2** row or line of people, figures, etc **3** newspaper or magazine article or report **columnist** *n* journalist providing regular articles for a newspaper or magazine

coma *n* condition of very deep unconsciousness **comatose** *adj* **1** drowsy **2** in a coma

comb *n* **1** small toothed instrument for separating and tidying hair, wool, etc **2** group of wax cells made by bees **3** crest of certain birds, esp cocks *vt* **1** untangle and tidy hair, wool, etc **2** search thoroughly

combat *vt, vi* fight against; oppose *n* fight; struggle; battle **combatant** *n* **combative** *adj*

combine *vt, vi* (kəm'bain) join together; unite; amalgamate *n* ('kɔmbain) association of several similar companies, institutions, etc **combine harvester** *n* mechanical corn harvester **combination** *n* mixture; amalgamation

combustion *n* process of burning **combustible** *adj* capable of burning; flammable

come *vi* (came; come) **1** arrive; be delivered; reach **2** happen; occur **3** originate; be caused by **4** be available; be supplied **come across** discover or meet by chance **come back** return **come off** **1** become separated or broken **2** be successfully completed **come out** **1** emerge **2** be issued **3** erupt **come round** **1** recover consciousness **2** be persuaded **come to** **1** recover consciousness **2** amount to **come up** arise; appear **come up with** suggest; think of; produce **comeback** *n* **1** return or success after an absence or failure **2** retort **comedown** *n* **1** anticlimax **2** reduction in status, quality, etc

comedian *n* entertainer who performs comic songs or plays; tells jokes, etc

comedy *n* humorous, amusing, or light-hearted play

comet *n* heavenly body having a luminous head and a long tail, which always points away from the sun

comfort *n* **1** encouragement; relief **2** ease; peacefulness; lack of anxiety or pain *vt* relieve; console; cheer **comfortable** *adj* **1** providing or enjoying comfort **2** fairly affluent **comfortably** *adv*

comic *adj* **1** funny; amusing **2** relating to comedy *n* **1** comic person; comedian **2** children's paper consisting mainly of strip cartoons **comical** *adj* ridiculous; absurd; laughable **comically** *adv*

comma *n* punctuation mark (,) used to indicate a slight pause, to separate clauses, etc

command *vt* order; control; have authority or influence over; dominate *n* order; rule; authority; control **in command** in charge **commander** *n* **1** someone who commands; leader **2** naval officer ranking below a captain

commandeer *vt* take over or seize arbitrarily or by force, esp for military purposes

commandment *n* order; command **Ten Commandments** *pl n* laws given by God to Moses according to the Old Testament

commando *n, pl* **commandos** or **commandoes** soldier specially trained to carry out dangerous raids

commemorate *vt* celebrate the memory of; provide a memorial for **commemoration** *n*

commence *vt, vi* begin; start **commencement** *n*

commend *vt* **1** praise; recommend **2** entrust **commendable** *adj* **commendation** *n*

comment *n* brief, critical, or explanatory remark expressing an opinion, reaction, etc *vi* make a comment **commentary** *n* **1** series of comments, esp analysing a book **2** description of and comments on a sporting event, state occasion, etc., esp when broadcast **commentator** *n* one who provides a commentary, esp on radio or television

commerce *n* business; trade **commercial** *adj* relating to commerce or business **commercial traveller** *n* representative employed by a firm as a salesman

commission *n* **1** document conferring authority, position, agency, etc **2** body of people holding an enquiry and producing a report **3**

piece of work, esp a work of art, specifically ordered **4** percentage payment taken by an agent, salesman, etc *vt* **1** give authority to **2** put an order for **commissioner** *n* one holding or appointed by a commission

commit *vt* (-tt-) **1** entrust; charge with **2** perform; do; perpetrate (a crime, etc) **3** promise; pledge **4** send to prison or for further trial **commit oneself** take on an obligation or duty **commitment** *n*

committee *n* small group instructed by a larger organization to deal with specific matters

commodity *n* particular type of goods, produce, or merchandise

common *adj* **1** shared by or belonging to all or to many **2** usual; frequent **3** general; widespread **4** relating to the public **5** habitual **6** ordinary; familiar; well-known **7** coarse; vulgar; low *n* piece of land belonging to the community and available for public use **in common** in joint use; of mutual interest; shared **commonly** *adv* **commonness** *n* **common law** unwritten law based on custom or tradition **common sense** *n* practical sense; good judgment; normal mental capacity **commonplace** *adj* ordinary; not remarkable *n* trite remark; cliché **commonwealth** *n* **1** people of a state or nation, esp when viewed as a political entity **2** federation of self-governing units or former colonies

commotion *n* disturbance; public disorder; uproar

communal *adj* relating to or belonging to a commune or community; public; common

commune[1] *vi* (kə'mju:n) converse or act intimately or spiritually *n* ('kɔmju:n) intimate conversation; communion

commune[2] ('kɔmju:n) *n* **1** smallest administrative division of some countries, such as France or Belgium **2** group or small community organized to promote mutual interests and goals

communicate *vt* **1** give or transmit; impart **2** make known *vi* **1** exchange thoughts or information in a way that may be easily understood **2** be connected, as by a passage *vt,vi* administer or receive the Eucharist **communicant** *n,adj* **communication** *n*

communion *n* **1** participation; act of sharing **2** fellowship **3** intimate exchange of thoughts and feelings **Communion** *also* **Holy Communion** the Eucharist or its celebration

communism *n* belief or social system based on the doctrine that all goods, property, and means of production belong to the community or state **communist** *adj,n*

community *n* **1** group of people living in the same area or sharing a common culture **2** joint possession or ownership

commute *vi* travel regularly, usually over relatively long distances, from home to work *vt* reduce (a prison sentence, penalty, etc) *vt,vi* transform; substitute **commuter** *n*

compact[1] *adj* (kəm'pækt) **1** packed neatly and closely together **2** concentrated; dense **3** terse, pithy *vt* (kəm'pækt) pack closely together; condense; compress *n* ('kɔmpækt) small hinged container, usually with a mirror, for holding face powder **compactly** *adv* **compactness** *n*

compact[2] ('kɔmpækt) *n* agreement or contract between parties

companion *n* **1** mate; comrade **2** person who accompanies another or shares the same experience **3** something that matches another **companionable** *adj* **companionship** *n* fellowship; friendship

company *n* **1** gathering of persons, as for social purposes; group **2** guest or guests **3** association for business **4** officers and crew of a ship **5** infantry unit of two or more platoons **6** troupe of actors, dancers, or singers **part company** end association or friendship (with)

compare *vt* notice or identify similarities; liken *vi* be in relation to **comparable** *adj* capable or worthy of being compared **comparably** *adv* **comparative** *adj* **1** relating to or involving comparison **2** not absolute or positive; relative **comparatively** *adv* **comparison** *n*

compartment *n* **1** part or parts into which an enclosed space is partitioned or divided off; section; division **2** section of a railway carriage

compass *n* **1** instrument for determining bearings, usually by means of a magnetized needle that always points north **2** limit or scope **compasses** *pl n* small instrument with two hinged arms, used for drawing circles arcs, etc *vt* encircle; surround

compassion *n* deeply felt pity or sympathy **compassionate** *adj*

compatible *adj* **1** able to live or exist well or

harmoniously together **2** consistent; not contradictory **compatibility** n **compatibly** adv

compel vt (-ll-) **1** force or bring about by force **2** subdue, overpower

compensate vt,vi pay money (to) in acknowledgement of loss, damage, or injury, recompense vt offset vi modify or exaggerate one s behaviour to make up for a fault or shortcoming **compensation** n

compete vi strive against others **competitor** n **competition** n **1** competing, rivalry, opposition **2** contest to show worth or ability, often with a prize for the winner **competitive** adj **competitively** adv

competent adj **1** skilful, able; properly qualified **2** sufficient; adequate **competence** or **competency** n **competently** adv

compile vt assemble; make or put together (a book its parts, etc) from various materials or sources **compilation** n **compiler** n

complacent adj self-satisfied **complacency** n **complacently** adv

complain vi express unhappiness or lack of satisfaction; grumble, moan **complaint** n **1** statement of a grievance wrong, etc **2** illness

complement n **1** something that serves to complete or make whole or perfect **2** full allowance, quantity etc **complementary** adj

complete adj **1** whole finished, full; perfect **2** utter; absolute vt finish, make whole perfect, or full **completely** adv **completion** n

complex adj involved: intricate; complicated **2** having many facets or parts n **1** whole composed of many parts, often different or distinct **2** set of mental attitudes, often subconscious, that affect personality **complexity** n

complexion n **1** texture colour and quality of the skin, esp of the face **2** aspect; appearance

complicate vt make difficult intricate, or involved **complication** n

compliment n ('kɔmplimənt) remark expressing praise, admiration, respect, etc vt ('kɔmpliment) pay a compliment to; congratulate; praise **complimentary** adj **1** expressing a compliment; flattering **2** free of charge

comply vi do as one is asked; consent; conform **compliance** n **compliant** adj

component n essential or constituent part of something

compose vt **1** create or write (a literary or musical work) **2** constitute; make up **3** make of various parts or elements; fashion **4** set type in lines vi write music **compose oneself** calm or settle oneself **composer** n writer of music **composite** adj made up of different parts **composition** n **1** putting together of parts or elements to form a whole **2** parts that form the whole; make-up **3** piece of music **4** artistic creation **5** short essay esp one written at school **composure** n calmness of mind, serenity

compost n decomposed matter, manure etc , used as fertilizer

compound[1] adj ('kɔmpaund) composed of separate parts or substances vt **1** (kəm-'paund) assemble into a whole; combine **2** complicate, increase n ('kɔmpaund) **1** something formed by putting together separate substances, ingredients, or components **2** chemical substance composed of atoms of two or more elements held together by chemical bonds

compound[2] ('kɔmpaund) n enclosure containing houses or other buildings

comprehend vt,vi **1** understand; grasp **2** include **comprehensible** adj **comprehension** n **comprehensive** adj **1** inclusive covering everything; broad **2** able to understand fully n also **comprehensive school** state secondary school taking in pupils from a given area irrespective of ability

compress vt (kəm'pres) **1** force or squeeze together **2** make smaller in bulk size, etc n ('kɔmpres) pad or cloth for applying pressure moisture, etc , to a bodily part **compression** n

comprise vt contain; include; consist of

compromise n **1** settlement of a dispute or disagreement by giving up part of a claim **2** something between two extremes, courses of action, etc **3** exposure to jeopardy, suspicion loss of reputation, etc vi settle a dispute through a compromise vt expose to jeopardy, etc

compulsion n **1** impulse or urge that cannot be resisted **2** act of compelling **compulsive** adj acting on a sudden urge or impulse **compulsively** adv **compulsiveness** n **compulsory** adj **1** obligatory; required **2** compelling; employing compulsion **compulsorily** adv

computer n electronic apparatus that performs

calculations, processes data, etc., usually equipped with a memory and able to print out required information

comrade n 1 close associate or companion; mate 2 fellow member of a communist group or party **comradeship** n

concave adj curved inwards; being hollow and curved n concave surface or part

conceal vt 1 hide 2 keep secret **concealment** n

concede vt admit having lost vt,vi 1 acknowledge to be true 2 yield

conceit n excessive estimation of one s achievements, abilities, or worth; vanity **conceited** adj

conceive vt,vi 1 become pregnant with (a child) 2 form (an idea); imagine **conceivable** adj

concentrate vt,vi 1 direct (one's attention or energies) towards a particular objective 2 make or become less diluted; condense 3 place or be confined in a dense mass n concentrated solution **concentration** n **concentration camp** n (esp during World War II) place, such as a guarded compound, for the detention of political prisoners, racial minorities, etc

concentric adj having a common centre

concept n abstract notion; idea; thought **conceptual** adj **conception** n 1 fertilization; start of pregnancy 2 idea; concept 3 plan; design

concern vt be of interest to; relate to; affect; worry n 1 care; regard; anxiety; interest 2 affair; matter 3 business; firm; company **concerning** prep about; regarding; relating to

concert n ('kɔnsət) 1 public musical entertainment 2 agreement; union; harmony vt (kən-'sɔːt) plan together; arrange by agreement **concerted** adj

concertina n musical instrument with bellows and button-like keys

concerto (kən'tʃɛətou) n musical piece for solo instrument and orchestra

concession n 1 act of conceding or yielding 2 that which is conceded or yielded 3 franchise or privilege; grant **concessionary** adj

concise adj brief; terse; succinct **concisely** adv

conclude vt,vi bring or come to an end; finish vt 1 settle; arrange or agree finally 2 say or

declare in ending or finishing **conclusion** n **conclusive** adj

concoct vt 1 prepare with various ingredients; make a mixture of 2 make up; devise; invent **concoction** n

concrete adj 1 real; not abstract 2 relating to a specific object or case n building material formed from sand, cement, water, etc., that hardens as it dries vt cover over with concrete

concur vi (-rr-) 1 agree; have the same opinion 2 occur together; coincide **concurrent** adj

concussion n injury to the brain, caused by a blow, fall, etc., often causing loss of consciousness **concuss** vt cause concussion in

condemn vt 1 blame; find guilty 2 pronounce judicial sentence against 3 judge to be unfit for service or use **condemnation** n

condense vt 1 concentrate; make more solid compact, or dense 2 abridge; put into a few or fewer words 3 change (a gas or vapour) to a liquid, esp by cooling vi become liquid or solid **condensation** n anything condensed from a vapour, esp fine droplets of water on a window, etc., condensed from the atmosphere

condescend vi 1 lower oneself to the level of one's inferiors 2 be gracious or patronizing **condescension** n

condition n 1 state or mode of existence 2 state of health 3 stipulation; restriction **conditions** pl n 1 circumstances 2 terms of an agreement, contract, etc ~vt 1 accustom (someone) to 2 affect; change **conditional** adj tentative; not absolute; dependent on certain conditions **conditionally** adv

condolence n expression of sympathetic grief

condone vt overlook; forgive; pardon

conduct v (kən'dʌkt) vt,vi 1 transmit (heat electricity, etc) 2 control (an orchestra) during a performance or rehearsal vt 1 guide; lead 2 direct; manage; control n ('kɔndʌkt) 1 behaviour 2 execution or handling of business **conduction** n transfer of heat or electricity through a medium **conductor** n 1 director of an orchestra, choir, etc 2 leader; guide 3 person who collects fares from passengers on public transport vehicles 4 that which conducts electricity, heat, etc

cone n 1 solid figure with a circular base and tapering to a point 2 fruit of certain trees, such as the pine or fir **3** anything shaped like or resembling a cone

confectioner n person who makes or sells sweets, cakes, etc **confectionery** n **1** sweets chocolate etc **2** confectioner's trade or business

confederate adj (kən'fedərit) united; allied n (kən'fedərit) ally; accomplice vt, vi (kən-'fedəreit) unite in an alliance, conspiracy etc **confederation** or **confederacy** n

confer v (-rr-) vt grant as a favour, gift, honour, etc vi talk with; compare opinions

conference n meeting for discussion

confess vt, vi **1** admit or acknowledge (a crime, sin, etc) **2** concede; agree **confession** n **confessor** n priest who gives absolution to those who confess their sins

confetti n small bits of coloured paper for throwing at weddings, etc

confide vi also **confide in** divulge information (to); disclose in secret **confidence** n **1** feeling of trust, assurance, etc; firm belief **2** self-assurance **confident** adj **confidently** adv **confidential** adj secret; private **confidentially** adv

confine vt (kən'fain) **1** imprison; shut in **2** keep in bed or in the house **3** limit; keep within limits **confines** ('konfainz) pl n limits; restrictions **confinement** n

confirm vt **1** verify; substantiate; make valid **2** give a firm undertaking of **3** administer confirmation to **confirmation** n **1** verification **2** rite by which baptized persons are admitted into full membership of the Church

confiscate vt seize by authority; appropriate **confiscation** n

conflict n ('konflikt) **1** struggle; trial of strength **2** opposition or clash of interests, ideas, etc vi (kən'flikt) be inconsistent or at odds with; clash

conform vi also **conform to** comply (with); agree to certain standards, rules, etc; fit in (with) **conformist** n, adj **conformity** n

confound vt **1** baffle; perplex **2** mix up; confuse **confounded** adj **1** astonished; utterly confused **2** dreadful; irritating

confront vt **1** face; present **2** bring face to face with **confrontation** n

confuse vt **1** throw into disorder **2** mix mentally; obscure **3** bewilder; muddle **confusion** n

congeal vt vi **1** solidify by freezing or cooling **2** coagulate; stiffen **congealment** n

congenial adj **1** pleasing; agreeable **2** similar in disposition; compatible **congenially** adv

congenital adj existing at birth

congested adj **1** crowded; overcrowded; blocked **2** (of an organ or part) excessively suffused with blood **congestion** n

congratulate vt acknowledge the good fortunes or achievements of; praise; compliment **congratulation** n

congregate vi assemble; flock together; gather **congregation** n **1** act of congregating **2** assembly of people, esp those who gather in a church to worship

congress n **1** assembly; conference **2** legislative body **congressional** adj

conical adj also **conic** relating to or having the shape of a cone

conifer n tree, such as the pine or fir having evergreen needle-shaped leaves and bearing cones **coniferous** adj

conjugal adj marital; relating to husband and wife

conjugate vt ('kondʒugeit) inflect (a verb) in its various forms adj ('kondʒugit) joined together in pairs; coupled **conjugation** n

conjunction n **1** union; association **2** simultaneous occurrences; combination of events **3** part of speech joining words, phrases etc **conjunctive** adj

conjure vt also **conjure up 1** call or produce as if by magic **2** imagine; evoke; recall vi practice or perform tricks of illusion or magic **conjurer** n

connect vt, vi link; join; fasten together vt associate in the mind **connection** n **1** link, joining together **2** association; relationship **3** public transport, esp a train, timed to meet another train for the transfer of passengers **connections** pl n influential business or social contacts

connoisseur n person who is an expert esp in matters of taste and art

connotation n suggestion or implication of a word in addition to its chief meaning **connotative** adj

conquer vt, vi **1** overcome (an enemy) by force; defeat **2** surmount vt gain possession of by force; take over **conqueror** n **conquest** n

conscience n **1** mental sense of right and wrong **2** feeling of guilt **conscientious** adj **1**

paying attention to conscience; scrupulous **2** painstaking; hard-working **conscientiously** adv

conscious adj **1** aware of one s surroundings; awake **2** sensitive to or recognizing some truth, fact, etc **3** performed or registered with full awareness **4** intended; deliberate **consciously** adv **consciousness** n

conscript vt (kən'skrɪpt) enrol compulsorily into service esp in the armed forces; call up n ('kɒnskrɪpt) person who has been conscripted **conscription** n

consecrate vt **1** make sacred or holy; sanctify **2** devote; dedicate **consecration** n

consecutive adj in unbroken or logical order or succession **consecutively** adv

consent vi agree (to); give assent n **1** permission **2** agreement

consequence n **1** effect or result; conclusion **2** significance; importance **in consequence** as a result **consequent** adj

conservative adj **1** opposed to change, as in social or political conditions; traditional **2** moderate n person who is conventional or opposed to change **Conservative Party** n British political party which generally favours private enterprise **conservatively** adv

conservatory n glassed-in room for growing blooming or exotic plants, esp one attached to an outside wall of a house

conserve vt preserve; keep from decay, change etc n jam made with whole fruit **conservation** n preservation, esp of the natural environment

consider vt, vi **1** think about; reflect on; contemplate; examine **2** suppose; think to be; believe **3** look upon with respect, sympathy, etc **considerable** adj **1** somewhat large in amount, extent, or degree **2** important; great **considerably** adv **considerate** adj thoughtful; kind **consideration** n **1** thought; contemplation; reflection **2** payment; financial reward **3** thoughtfulness for others **4** importance **take into consideration** take into account; bear in mind **considering** prep in view of

consign vt **1** hand over formally; commit (to) **2** give over to another's custody; entrust **consignment** n

consist vi be composed or made up (of) **consistency** n **1** degree of solidity, density, or firmness **2** agreement; correspondence;

accordance; regularity **consistent** adj harmonious; not contradictory; regular **consistently** adv

console vt, vi comfort in distress or grief; cheer **consolation** n

consolidate vt, vi **1** make or become firm or solid; strengthen **2** combine; unite **consolidation** n

consonant n **1** speech sound made by constriction or stoppage of the breath stream **2** letter or symbol representing this, such as p t, or s

conspicuous adj easily seen; noticeable, standing out **conspicuously** adv

conspire vt, vi plot (an evil or criminal act) in secret vi act together; contribute in combination **conspiracy** n **conspirator** or **conspirer** n

constable n police officer of the lowest rank **constabulary** n local police force

constant adj **1** always present, happening, or continuing **2** unchanging; permanent n quantity or value that does not vary **constancy** n **constantly** adv

constellation n star group, esp one with a given name

consternation n dismay; anxiety

constipation n difficulty or infrequency in evacuating the bowels

constituency n body of electors or area served by a member of Parliament

constituent adj **1** serving to make up a whole; component **2** having power to elect n **1** component or essential part **2** elector; voter

constitute vt **1** set up; establish **2** be an element of; make up **3** appoint; make into **constitution** n **1** manner in which something is made up **2** state of physical or mental health **3** character; temperament; disposition **4** principles or laws by which a state is governed **constitutional** adj

constrain vt **1** compel **2** confine; restrain; restrict **constraint** n

constrict vt make narrower or tighter; compress **constriction** n

construct vt (kən'strʌkt) **1** put together; build; make **2** devise; formulate; fabricate n ('kɒnstrʌkt) something constructed; formulation **construction** n **constructive** adj useful; helpful

consul n official state representative, residing and performing administrative duties in a foreign city **consular** adj **consulate** n 1 premises occupied by a consul 2 period of office of a consul

consult vt seek advice or information from; refer to **consultant** n 1 person qualified to give expert professional advice 2 medical or surgical specialist **consultation** n

consume vt 1 use up 2 eat or drink up 3 destroy as by burning or decomposition 4 spend (time, money, etc), esp foolishly or wastefully 5 engross; absorb **consumer** n person who buys or uses a commodity or service **consumption** n

contact n 1 touching or being in touch 2 connection; association 3 person exposed to a contagious disease 4 person who may be useful to one socially or for business purposes vt,vi get in touch, be in contact, or communicate (with) **contact lenses** pl n optical lenses that fit directly on to the surface of the eye to correct visual defects

contagious adj 1 (of an infectious disease) transmitted directly or indirectly from one person to another 2 (of an infected person) able to spread disease to others 3 tending to spread or influence; catching **contagion** n

contain vt 1 hold; enclose 2 comprise; include; have room for **contain oneself** control or restrain oneself **container** n something able to hold a product, substance, etc ; receptacle

contaminate vt 1 make impure by mixture or contact; pollute 2 corrupt; spoil 3 make dangerous or worthless by being exposed to radioactivity **contamination** n

contemplate vt 1 gaze upon, esp thoughtfully 2 meditate on 3 intend; plan vi consider carefully; meditate **contemplation** n

contemporary adj 1 of roughly the same date or age 2 of the present; reflecting current styles, fashions, etc ; modern n person of the same age or time as another **contemporaneous** adj

contempt n 1 scorn 2 disrespect 3 lack of regard for authority, esp for the rules of a court or legal body **contemptible** adj **contemptuous** adj

contend vi struggle; fight for; compete vt assert; claim; maintain **contention** n

content[1] ('kɔntent) n 1 capacity 2 proportion of a substance contained; subject matter **contents** pl n 1 items placed in a container 2 list of chapters or divisions in a book

content[2] (kən'tent) adj 1 satisfied; happy 2 willing; resigned vt make content; please n also **contentment** happiness; satisfaction

contest n ('kɔntest) 1 competition; match 2 conflict; struggle vt (kən'test) fight for; dispute; struggle against **contestant** n person who takes part in a contest; competitor

context n 1 text or section preceding or following a particular passage, word, etc 2 facts or circumstances relating to an event, situation, etc ; background **contextual** adj

continent n major land mass of the earth **continental** adj **Continental** adj relating to the mainland of Europe or to Europeans n inhabitant of the mainland of Europe **continental quilt** n duvet

contingency n chance occurrence; unforeseen event or circumstance; possibility; eventuality **contingent** adj dependent upon an uncertain event or condition; possible n representative group in a body of people

continue vt,vi 1 go on; carry on; proceed (with) 2 remain existing; persist 3 resume; take up again **continual** adj occurring at regular intervals; constant; persistent **continually** adv **continuation** n 1 extended or connected part or section 2 prolonged action 3 resumption; renewal **continuity** n 1 continuous flow; logical sequence 2 complete film scenario, script, etc **continuous** adj without interruption; unbroken **continuously** adv

contour n outline or shape of a body or figure vt form the outline or shape of **contour line** n line on a map that passes through all points that have equal elevation

contraband n 1 illegal importing or exporting 2 smuggled goods

contraception n prevention of conception; birth control **contraceptive** adj serving to prevent conception n agent or device that prevents conception

contract n ('kɔntrækt) agreement, esp legally binding, between two or more persons, groups, etc v (kən'trækt) vt,vi 1 make or become smaller or more compressed 2 ('kɔntrækt) enter into or settle by agreement 3 draw or be drawn together vt 1 shorten by omitting parts, elements, etc 2 acquire (a disease, liability, etc) **contraction** n

contradict vt 1 state the opposite of (a statement, etc) 2 deny; refute vt,vi be inconsistent (with) **contradiction** n **contradictory** adj

contralto n female alto voice

contraption n strange or cumbersome invention, machine, etc

contrary adj 1 opposite 2 opposed in direction, tendency, or nature 3 perverse n exact opposite adv in opposition

contrast vt,vi show or display dissimilarity n ('kɔntra:st) striking difference or distinction

contravene vt 1 infringe; conflict with; violate 2 contradict; dispute **contravention** n

contribute vt,vi 1 pay with others to a common fund 2 supply or give as one's share in a discussion, task, etc **contribution** n **contributor** n **contributory** adj

contrive vt 1 devise; design 2 succeed in bringing about; manage vi,vt plot; conspire **contrivance** n **contrived** adj unnatural; not spontaneous

control vt (-ll-) 1 command; dominate 2 check; curb; restrain 3 verify or test by a standard comparison n 1 domination; command 2 restraint; check 3 standard of comparison **controls** pl n devices for regulating or guiding a machine, as an aircraft, car, etc

controversy n debate; dispute; argument **controversial** adj

convalesce vi recover from illness **convalescence** n period of recovery **convalescent** adj,n

convenience n 1 suitability; usefulness 2 personal comfort; ease 3 public lavatory **convenient** adj 1 well adapted to one's purpose; suitable 2 helpful; useful; handy **conveniently** adv

convent n 1 religious community, esp of nuns 2 buildings occupied by such a community

convention n 1 large assembly, conference, or formal meeting 2 traditionally observed custom or rule; norm **conventional** adj conforming to accepted standards

converge vi tend to meet or move towards the same point; approach **convergence** n **convergent** adj

converse (kən'va:s) vi talk or hold a conversation (with) **conversation** n talk; exchange of thoughts, opinions, etc

converse[2] ('kɔnva:s) adj opposite; reverse n statement with the terms of another, interchanged; opposite **conversely** adv

convert vt (kən'va:t) 1 modify or change into something different; adapt 2 change in outlook, religion, opinion, etc n ('kɔnva:t) person who has been converted, esp to a particular religion **conversion** n **convertible** adj capable of being converted n car with a folding or removable roof

convex adj curved outwards; bulging

convey vt 1 carry; transport 2 communicate **conveyance** n 1 transfer of property from one person to another 2 transportation **conveyor belt** n endless flexible belt used to convey goods, esp in a factory

convict vt (kən'vikt) prove or declare guilty n ('kɔnvikt) imprisoned criminal

conviction n 1 firm belief; certainty 2 verdict of guilt

convince vt satisfy by argument or evidence; persuade

convoy n 1 escort of naval vessels, armed forces, etc, provided for protection 2 group of vehicles moving together

cook vt,vi 1 prepare (food) by roasting, boiling, etc 2 subject or be subjected to heat; burn n person who prepares food, esp professionally **cooker** n oven; stove **cookery** n art or practice of cooking

cool adj 1 somewhat cold 2 unexcited; calm 3 lacking interest or friendliness vt,vi make or become cool(er) n cool part, place, time, etc **cool one's heels** be kept waiting **coolly** adv **coolness** n

coop n pen or cage for poultry vt also **coop up** confine in a small space

cooperate vi work together; act jointly **cooperation** n **cooperative** adj helpful; willing to cooperate n joint enterprise based on collective principles

coordinate vt (kou'ɔ:dineit) bring into order as parts of a whole; combine harmoniously adj (kou'ɔ:dinit) combined; harmonious n (kou-'ɔ:dinit) combination

cope vi deal with; manage satisfactorily

copper[1] n 1 soft reddish lustrous metal, used in electrical wiring, plumbing, etc 2 coin made or formerly made of copper adj,n red or reddish-gold

copper[2] n sl policeman

copulate vi have sexual intercourse **copulation** n

copy n 1 reproduction or imitation; duplicate 2 single specimen of a book 3 matter for

printing vt, vi **1** make a copy (of); duplicate **2** imitate **copyright** n exclusive legal right to produce or dispose of copies of a literary or artistic work over a given period of time vt secure a copyright on

coral n **1** hard red or white substance secreted by sea polyps, often forming reefs or islands **2** polyps producing this **3** ornament, etc fashioned from coral

cord n **1** thin rope or thick string **2** ribbed fabric, such as corduroy vt furnish or fasten with cord

cordial adj sincere; warm; hearty n concentrated fruit juice **cordially** adv

cordon n **1** ornamental cord or badge **2** line of police, troops, etc , guarding an area

corduroy n thick cotton fabric with a corded or ribbed surface

core n **1** central or innermost part of anything **2** middle part of an apple or other fleshy fruit, containing the seeds vt remove the core of

cork n **1** porous outer bark of a certain tree (cork oak), used for making bottle stoppers, floats, etc **2** piece of cork used as a bottle stopper vt stop up with a cork **corkscrew** n device for extracting corks from bottles, usually consisting of a sharp pointed metal spiral

corn[1] n **1** edible grain, esp the small hard seeds of cereal plants **2** US maize **cornflakes** n breakfast cereal made from flakes of roasted maize **cornflour** n finely ground flour from maize, used mainly to thicken gravies, sauces, etc **cornflower** n blue flower commonly found growing in cornfields

corn[2] n horny growth on the toe or foot, caused by friction of shoes

corner n **1** angle or area formed when two sides, surfaces, or lines meet **2** nook; secluded place vt **1** force or drive into a difficult position **2** establish a monopoly

cornet n **1** brass musical instrument with three valves, similar to but smaller and more mellow than a trumpet **2** cone-shaped wafer for ice cream

coronation n ceremony of crowning a monarch

coroner n public official in charge of an inquest in cases of suspicious death

coronet n small crown

corporal[1] adj relating to the body; physical

corporal[2] n noncommissioned officer below a sergeant in the army or airforce

corporation n **1** body of persons usually in business legally authorized to function as an individual **2** municipal authority or council **corporate** adj

corporeal adj physical; material; not spiritual

corps (kɔː) n **1** military unit comprising several divisions **2** group of dancers, actors etc **3** body of officials esp diplomats

corpse n dead human body

corpuscle ('kɔːpʌsəl) n small free-floating cell present in the blood

correct vt **1** set right **2** point out faults or errors **3** neutralize; counteract adj **1** factual; true; accurate **2** proper; conforming to a custom or standard **correction** n **correctly** adv

correlate vt, vi have or bring into mutual relation n either of two related things that imply each other **correlation** n

correspond vi **1** conform; match **2** be similar or equivalent **3** communicate by exchanging letters **correspondence** n **1** agreement; conformity **2** communication by letters **correspondent** n **1** person who communicates by letters **2** person employed by a newspaper, etc , to cover a special area or to report from a foreign country adj similar

corridor n long passageway connecting rooms, railway compartments, etc

corrode vt eat away; eat into the surface of **corrosion** n **corrosive** adj, n

corrupt adj **1** dishonest; open to bribery **2** depraved; evil **3** rotten; putrid; tainted vt **1** cause to be dishonest **2** pervert; debase **3** taint **corruptible** adj **corruption** n

corset n close-fitting stiffened undergarment that supports and shapes the stomach worn esp by women

cosmetic n preparation to beautify the complexion or the hair adj relating to cosmetics

cosmic adj relating to or forming part of the universe

cosmonaut n Soviet astronaut

cosmopolitan adj **1** relating to all parts of the world; worldwide **2** widely travelled; urbane n person who is widely travelled or sophisticated

cosmos n **1** universe **2** harmonious system; order

cost n **1** price of something **2** loss; sacrifice; penalty **3** expenditure of time, labour, money, etc **at all costs** or **at any cost** regardless of the cost ~vt (cost) **1**, have as the price **2** result in a loss, sacrifice or penalty **3** determine or estimate the cost of **costly** adj

costume n style of dress, esp one indicating a particular period, nationality, etc

cosy adj snug; comfortable n padded cover for keeping a teapot, boiled egg, etc warm **cosily** adv

cot n **1** child s bed with high sides **2** portable bed or hammock

cottage n small house, esp in the country

cotton n **1** plant producing white downy fibres that cover its seeds **2** thread or cloth produced from these fibres v **cotton on** realize; grasp **cotton-wool** n raw bleached cotton, esp as used for surgical dressings

couch n upholstered furniture that seats two or more persons vt express in a particular style

cough vi expel air from the lungs with effort and noise **cough up** sl produce; hand over ~n act or sound of coughing

could v pt of **can.**

council n administrative or legislative body, esp one elected to govern a town or district **councillor** n

counsel n **1** advice; guidance **2** barrister **3** consultation; debate vt (-ll-) give advice to recommend **counsellor** n adviser

count[1] vt vi **1** enumerate; add; reckon up; calculate **2** list or name numerals in sequence vt take into account; consider vi be of importance; matter **count on** rely or depend on **count out** exclude ~n **1** reckoning; calculation **2** total number **countdown** n period immediately before firing a missile, launching a spacecraft, etc , timed by counting backwards to zero **countless** adj innumerable

count[2] n nobleman of certain European countries corresponding to a British earl

counter[1] n **1** table or other surface on which money is counted, business transacted, etc **2** long narrow table at which food is served **3** small disc used as a token **under the counter 1** conducted in a secret or dishonest manner **2** reserved for special persons, favoured clients, etc

counter[2] adv in the opposite or reverse direction adj n opposite vt,vi oppose; contradict

counterattack n military attack launched just after an enemy attack vt vi make such an attack (on)

counterfeit adj not genuine; fake; forged vt imitate with intent to deceive; forge n something counterfeited

counterfoil n stub of a cheque, receipt, etc , kept as a record

counterpart n person or thing having an identical or equivalent function

countess n **1** wife or widow of a count or earl **2** woman of a rank equivalent to a coun or earl

country n **1** nation; territory; state **2** population of a nation **3** land of birth or residence **4** rural area as opposed to a town

county n major administrative, political, or judicial division of certain countries or states

coup (ku:) n successful and often unexpected attack, stroke, etc

couple n **1** pair **2** two people in a relationship **a couple of** a small number of; a few ~vt **1** link or fasten together **2** associate mentally vi **1** associate in pairs **2** unite sexually; copulate

coupon n detachable slip or ticket used when ordering goods, claiming discount, etc

courage n capacity to deal with danger; bravery; boldness **courageous** adj **courageously** adv

courgette n small vegetable marrow

courier n **1** special or express messenger **2** person employed to take care of tourists and their travel arrangements

course n **1** movement in space or time **2** direction of movement; route **3** type of action or conduct **4** duration **5** area or stretch of land over which a race is run, golf is played, etc **6** series of lessons, sessions, etc **7** any of the sequential parts of a meal **in the course of** during **of course** certainly, in fact ~vi move or flow quickly

court n **1** also **courtyard** space enclosed by buildings **2** area marked off or enclosed for playing games, such as tennis or squash **3** household or establishment of a sovereign **4** body with judicial powers; tribunal **5** building or room in which a trial or tribunal is held **6** attention; homage vt vi **1** seek the affection of (a member of the opposite sex) **2** seek the approval or support of **court card** n playing card that is a king, queen, or jack; face card **court-martial** n pl **courts-martial** court of officers for trying naval, airforce, or army offences **courtship** n courting of a woman

courtesy n polite behaviour or disposition **courteous** adj

cousin n son or daughter of one's uncle or aunt

cove n 1 small inlet; sheltered bay 2 nook or recess

covenant n 1 agreement; bargain 2 sealed contract or one of its clauses vt,vi agree to or enter into a covenant

cover vt 1 place or spread over 2 overlie 3 shield or conceal 4 include 5 protect by insurance 6 report (an event) for a newspaper, etc n 1 anything that covers 2 funds to meet possible liability or loss **coverage** n extent, amount, or risk covered

cow n 1 female of the ox family, esp one kept by farmers for milk 2 female of certain other animals, such as the elephant, whale, and seal **cowboy** n herdsman in charge of cattle on the western plains of North America, esp one on horseback

coward n person given to fear **cowardice** n **cowardly** adj **cower** vi crouch in fear or shame; tremble

coy adj shy; modest; slow to respond esp deliberately **coyly** adv **coyness** n

crab n 1 ten-legged shellfish 2 flesh of the crab, used as food 3 ill-tempered person 4 species of small apple vi (-bb-) criticize, find fault

crack vi,vt 1 break into pieces; form fissures 2 make or cause to make a sharp sound 3 change suddenly in tone; become hoarse vt 1 strike sharply 2 inf open; break into 3 inf find the solution to 4 tell (a joke) vi also **crack up** have a physical or mental breakdown n 1 sharp explosive noise 2 split or fissure **cracker** 1 thin crisp biscuit 2 exploding firework 3 paper and cardboard Christmas toy that emits a bang when pulled apart **crackle** n 1 sound of rapid repeated cracking 2 network of fine cracks vi emit a sharp cracking sound

cradle n 1 infant's bed 2 supporting frame 3 origin or home vt hold in or as if in a cradle

craft n 1 skilled trade 2 manual skill 3 cunning 4 boat; vessel **craftsman** n **craftsmanship** n **crafty** adj cunning; artful **craftily** adv

crag n rugged projecting rock or rock mass

cram v (-mm-) vt fill or pack tightly vt,vi 1 study

intensively, as just before an examination 2 eat greedily

cramp[1] n sudden painful involuntary contraction of a muscle

cramp[2] n clamp for holding things together vt 1 hold with a cramp 2 hem in; keep within too narrow limits; hinder **cramp someone's style**, hinder someone from doing his best, etc

crane n 1 large wading bird with long legs, neck, and bill 2 machine for moving heavy objects vi stretch the neck (for a better view)

crash n 1 violent noisy impact, fall, etc 2 burst of mixed loud sound, such as thunder 3 sudden downfall or collapse vi,vt 1 make or cause to make a crash 2 fall or strike with a crash 3 involve or be involved in a collision

crate n large packing case vt pack in a crate

crater n 1 bowl-shaped cavity or depression, such as one made by a meteorite on the earth or moon or by an exploding bomb 2 mouth of a volcano **cratered** adj

crave vt,vi have a strong desire (for) ; yearn (for) **craving** n

crawl vi 1 move along on the ground etc , on the stomach or on the hands and knees 2 move or progress very slowly 3 creep or go stealthily or abjectly 4 behave abjectly n 1 act of crawling 2 also **front crawl** fast swimming stroke

crayfish n freshwater shellfish resembling a lobster

crayon n stick of coloured chalk or wax used for drawing

craze n 1 mania; tremendous liking 2 temporary fashion vt 1 impair mentally; drive insane 2 make small cracks in vi become insane **crazy** adj 1 insane; mad 2 eccentric; peculiar 3 unsound; shaky 4 inf wildly enthusiastic or excited (about) **crazily** adv **craziness** n

creak vi make a sharp squeaking or grating sound n such a sound **creaky** adj

cream n 1 fatty part of milk 2 dish or delicacy resembling or made of cream 3 creamlike substance esp a cosmetic 4 best part of anything n adj yellowish-white vt 1 beat (a mixture, etc) until light and smooth 2 remove the cream from 3 apply a cream to **creamy** adj

crease n 1 line made by folding 2 wrinkle vt,vi make or develop creases

create vt 1 bring into being 2 give rise to 3 make; produce **creation** n 1 act of creating or state of being created **2** something created, esp an original design, work of art, etc **3** universe and all living creatures **creative** adj having the ability to create; original; inventive **creativity** n

creature n **1** living being, esp an animal **2** contemptible or pitiful person

crèche n **1** nursery for infants **2** model of the Nativity scene

credible adj believable; worthy of belief

credit n **1** system of doing business without immediate receipt or payment of cash **2** power to purchase items, services, etc , by deferred payment **3** money at one's disposal in a bank, etc **4** belief; trust **5** source of honour, reputation, etc **6** good name; reputation **7** influence; respect; commendation **8** acknowledgement of authorship, direction, performance, etc vt **1** believe; trust; have faith in **2** attribute; acknowledge **3** give credit for **credit card** n card that identifies and authorizes the holder to obtain goods or services on deferred payment **creditor** n person, etc , to whom money is owed

creep vi (crept) **1** move like a snake; crawl **2** move stealthily, quietly, or very slowly **3** feel a shrinking shivering sensation due to fear, repugnance, etc n **1** creeping movement **2** sl servile or unpleasant person **creeps** pl n feeling of fear, repugnance, etc **creeper** n plant, such as ivy, that trails over ground, etc , by means of roots, tendrils, etc , along its stem

cremate vt dispose of (a corpse) by burning **cremation** n **crematorium** n place where corpses are cremated

crept v pt or pp of creep

crescent n **1** waxing or waning moon **2** narrow curved and pointed figure or symbol **3** curved row of houses

cress n plant of the mustard family, whose leaves are used in salads or as a garnish

crest n **1** comb or tuft on an animal's head **2** plume on top of a helmet **3** top of a wave, mountain ridge, etc **4** reach or lie on the top of vi form or rise into a crest **crestfallen** adj dejected

crevice n fissure, narrow split or crack

crew n persons that man a boat, ship, aircraft, etc

crib n **1** child s cot **2** barred rack for fodder vt,vi (-bb-) inf copy unfairly; plagiarize

cricket[1] n chirping leaping insect

cricket[2] n **1** team game played on a grass pitch with bats, ball, and wickets **2** inf fair play

cried v pt or pp of **cry.**

crime n **1** serious violation of the law **2** wicked act; sin; grave offence **3** inf senseless or foolish act **4** unlawful acts in general **criminal** n person guilty or convicted of crime adj **1** relating to or involving crime or its punishment; guilty of crime **2** wicked; senseless

crimson n,adj deep rich red

cringe vi cower; crouch; shrink back n act of cringing

crinkle vt,vi,n **1** wrinkle; twist **2** rustle

cripple n lame or disabled person vt **1** disable; maim; make a cripple of **2** damage, esp financially **crippling** adj damaging

crisis n, pl **crises** (ˈkraisiːz) **1** time of acute danger, stress, suspense, etc **2** turning point; decisive moment

crisp adj **1** brittle; dry; crackling **2** brisk **3** clear-cut; sharp; lively **4** fresh n fine slice of fried potato **crisply** adv **crispness** n

criterion n, pl **criteria** (kraiˈtiəriə) standard of judgement or comparison; test

critic n **1** person who passes judgment or criticizes **2** expert in assessing the merits of works of art, literature, drama, etc **critical** adj **1** given to judging, fault-finding, etc **2** of great importance; decisive **3** involving suspense or risk **4** relating to critics or criticism **critically** adv **criticism** n **1** severe judgment; disapproval **2** assessment; review; analysis; evaluation **criticize** vt,vi **1** judge severely; censure **2** examine critically; evaluate

croak n deep hoarse cry or sound vi,vt utter or speak with a croak **croakily** adv **croaky** adj

crochet n type of knitting done with a single hooked needle vt,vi do such work

crockery n china or earthenware vessels

crocodile n **1** large predatory amphibious reptile of the tropics, with armour-like skin, long tapering snout, and massive jaws **2** long line of schoolchildren

crocus n small bulbous plant with yellow, purple, or white flowers

crook n **1** criminal; swindler **2** hooked staff **3** sharp turn or bend vt bend; curve; make a crook in **crooked** adj **1** bent; curved **2** set at an angle; askew **3** inf dishonest

crop n 1 cultivated produce 2 harvest of this 3 group of things occurring together 4 pouch in a bird s gullet 5 stock of a whip 6 hunting or riding whip 7 closely cut head of hair vt (-pp-) 1 clip; cut short; cut off 2 raise or harvest produce **crop up** inf occur, arise etc , unexpectedly

croquet n lawn game played with wooden balls and mallets and wire hoops

cross n 1 upright stake with a transverse bar 2 model, mark, or figure of a cross esp as a Christian emblem or symbol of Christianity 3 sign of the Cross made with the hand 4 intermixture of breeds, qualities, etc 5 misfortune; trouble **the Cross** 1 cross on which Jesus died 2 model or picture of this ~vt 1 place so as to intersect 2 make the sign of the Cross on or over 3 pass across 4 meet and pass 5 mark with lines across 6 oppose; thwart 7 modify a breed of animals or plants by intermixture vi 1 intersect 2 pass over adj 1 out of temper 2 transverse 3 intersecting 4 contrary; adverse **cross-examine** vt examine a witness already examined by the other side **cross examination** n **cross-eyed** adj having a squint **cross-fire** n 1 sharp verbal exchange 2 crossing of two or more lines of fire **crossing** n 1 act of crossing 2 intersection of roads, rails, etc 3 special place for crossing easily, safely, etc **cross-question** vt cross-examine **cross-reference** n reference from one word, part etc in a book to another vt vi also **cross-refer** make a cross-reference **crossword** n puzzle in which words are written horizontally and vertically in numbered spaces according to numbered clues

crotchet n musical note or symbol equal to quarter of a semibreve **crotchety** adj inf cross, quick-tempered

crouch vi 1 huddle down close to the ground floor etc 2 cringe; fawn n crouching position

crow[1] n large black bird with glossy feathers

crow[2] vi 1 inf boast 2 utter a shrill cry

crowd vi flock together vi 1 cram or pack 2 fill with people n large number; throng **crowded** adj

crown n 1 monarch s headdress 2 wreath for the head 3 royal power 4 former coin 5 top, as of the head 6 completion; perfection vt 1 put a crown on 2 make a king or queen 3

honour; reward; invest with dignity, etc 4 bring to completion or perfection **crown prince** n male next in line to the throne

crucial adj decisive; critical

crucifix n cross esp one with a figure of Jesus crucified on it **crucifixion** n crucifying, esp of Jesus **crucify** vt 1 put to death by nailing or tying to a cross 2 treat severely; torment

crude adj 1 in the natural or raw state 2 unfinished; rough 3 without grace; unpolished 4 blunt; vulgar **crudely** adv **crudeness** or **crudity** n **crude oil** n petroleum before it is made into petrol or other products

cruel adj 1 delighting in the pain or suffering of others; heartless 2 enjoying the infliction of pain on others 3 distressing; painful **cruelty** n

cruise vi 1 sail about, esp for pleasure 2 fly drive, etc , at moderate speed n act of cruising **cruiser** n armed high-speed naval ship of light or medium displacement

crumb n small particle; fragment esp of bread vt break into or cover with crumbs

crumble vt,vi 1 break into small fragments 2 decay; fall to pieces n baked fruit pudding with a crumbled cake-like topping

crumple vt,vi,n crease, wrinkle

crunch vt,vi crush, grind or chew noisily n 1 act or sound of crunching 2 sl critical moment

crusade n also **Crusade** medieval Christian war to recover the Holy Land from the Turks 2 campaign in favour of a cause vi participate in a crusade

crush vt 1 compress so as to break bruise, or crumple 2 break into small pieces 3 defeat utterly n 1 act of crushing 2 crowded mass esp of people

crust n 1 hard outer surface of bread 2 any hard or firm outer part deposit or casing 3 surface of the earth vt,vi cover with or form a crust **crusty** adj 1 having or like a crust 2 ill-tempered **crustily** adv

crustacean n hard-shelled animal with antennae, usually living in water such as a crab or lobster

crutch n 1 support for a lame person that fits under the armpit 2 something needed for moral or physical support

crux n 1 real issue 2 hard problem

cry vi 1 weep; shed tears 2 cry out; shout 3

(esp of animals) utter a characteristic sound *vt* utter or implore loudly **cry for** beg for **cry off** break a promise; withdraw from an agreement ~*n* 1 loud utterance 2 call of an animal or bird 3 fit of weeping **a far cry** 1 long way 2 very different

crypt *n* underground chamber or vault, esp one beneath a church, used for burials, etc **cryptic** *adj* secret; hidden; mysterious

crystal *n* 1 transparent piece of mineral 2 form of certain substances having a definite internal structure and external surfaces that intersect at characteristic angles 3 very clear glass 4 cut-glass vessels 5 something made of or resembling crystal **crystalline** *adj* **crystallize** *vt,vi* 1 form into crystals 2 become or cause to be definite or certain

cub *n* 1 young of certain animals, such as lions or bears 2 inexperienced person

cube *n* 1 regular solid figure bounded by six equal squares 2 cube-shaped or nearly cube-shaped block 3 product obtained by multiplying a number by itself twice **cubic** *adj* 1 having the shape of a cube 2 relating to volume or volume measure 3 having three dimensions

cubicle *n* small room or walled-off space, as for sleeping, dressing, studying, etc

cuckoo *n* widely distributed bird named from the sound of its call

cucumber *n* long fleshy green edible fruit commonly used in salads

cuddle *vt* hug; fondle *vi* lie close *n* hug; affectionate embrace

cue[1] *n* 1 words or actions used as a guide or signal 2 hint

cue[2] *n* long tapered rod with a soft tip used to strike the ball in billiards, etc

cuff[1] *n* end of a sleeve; wrist-band **off the cuff** without preparation; improvised

cuff[2] *vt* hit with the open hand *n* such a blow

culinary *adj* relating to or used in cooking or the kitchen

culprit *n* guilty person; offender

cult *n* 1 system of religious worship 2 devotion to or pursuit of some object

cultivate *vt* 1 raise (crops) on land; grow 2 develop; improve; refine **cultivation** *n*

culture *n* 1 intellectual, behavioural, and artistic ideas, beliefs, etc of a particular group, time, or place 2 particular form or stage of civilization 3 development and training of the

mind 4 refinement of taste, manners, etc 5 cultivation **cultural** *adj* **cultured** *adj* 1 refined 2 grown in an artificial medium

cumbersome *adj* 1 troublesome; vexatious 2 clumsy; unwieldy

cunning *n* 1 dexterity; skill 2 skill in deceit or evasion *adj* having such qualities or characteristics **cunningly** *adv*

cup *n* 1 drinking vessel, esp one with a handle 2 any cup-shaped formation, depression, cavity, etc 3 prize in the shape of a cup 4 fruit-flavoured wine, cider, etc **one's cup of tea** what especially or particularly suits one; what one likes ~*vt* (-pp-) form (one's hand) into a hollow shape

cupboard *n* closed cabinet, usually with shelves

curate *n* assistant to a parish priest or vicar

curator *n* person in charge of a museum, a specific collection etc

curb *n* 1 check or means of restraint; control 2 framework or border that encloses *vt* restrain; control; check

curd *n* substance obtained by coagulating milk, used as food or in cheese-making **curdle** *vt vi* form into curd

cure *vt* 1 heal; remedy 2 preserve (fish, skins, etc) *n* 1 remedy 2 course of medical treatment 3 restoration to health

curfew *n* 1 restriction on movement after nightfall or a signal indicating that this is to be enforced 2 time at which such a signal is given

curiosity *n* 1 eagerness to know; inquisitiveness 2 strange, rare, or odd object

curious *adj* 1 eager to know; inquisitive 2 prying; tending to meddle 3 exciting interest 4 odd; eccentric **curiously** *adv*

curl *vt,vi* bend into a curved shape or spiral *n* 1 spiral lock of hair 2 spiral or curved form, state, or motion **curly** *adj* **curling** *n* game played on ice with large rounded stones

currant *n* small seedless raisin

currency *n* 1 time during which anything is current 2 state of being in use 3 money

current *adj* 1 in general use or circulation 2 going on; not yet superseded *n* 1 moving body of water or air 2 flow of something, such as a river 3 movement of electric charge through a conductor or the rate of its flow

curry *n* 1 oriental dish flavoured with hot spices

2 spicy seasoning *vt* add curry to (food) while cooking

curse *n* 1 obscene or profane utterance 2 utterance designed to destroy or harm someone 3 affliction; bane; scourge *vi* swear *vt* 1 abuse by uttering curses at 2 call on supernatural powers to bring harm to (someone)

curt *adj* 1 short 2 rudely brief **curtly** *adv* **curtness** *n*

curtail *vt* cut short; end **curtailment** *n*

curtain *n* 1 cloth, etc , hung as a screen in front of a window or door 2 screen between the audience and a stage 3 end to an act or scene *vt* provide or cover with a curtain

curtsy *n* formal woman s bow made as a sign of respect, greeting, etc *vi* make such a bow

curve *n* 1 line with no straight parts 2 bend in a road, etc 3 curved form or object *vt, vi* bend in a curve **curvature** *n*

cushion *n* 1 bag or pad filled with soft stuffing or air, used to sit on lean against, etc 2 something that absorbs shocks, jolts, etc *vt* provide or protect with a cushion

custard *n* cooked dessert of flavoured eggs and milk

custody *n* 1 safe-keeping; guardianship 2 imprisonment **custodian** *n* person having custody of someone or something

custom *n* 1 established or habitual practice, usage, etc 2 business patronage 3 customers of a shop, business, etc **customs** *pl n* 1 duties levied on certain imports 2 area in an airport, etc , where such duties are collected **customary** *adj* usual **customer** *n* 1 buyer; patron 2 *inf* fellow, chap

cut *vt* (-tt-; cut) 1 sever; penetrate 2 divide; separate 3 detach, trim, or shape by cutting 4 abridge; shorten 5 ignore (someone) 6 strike (with a whip, sword etc) **cut down** 1 reduce 2 fell (trees) 3 *inf* kill **cut it fine** leave very small margin of time etc **cut off** 1 discontinue supply of (gas, etc) 2 interrupt 3 separate; isolate **cut out** 1 cut (pieces, etc) from something 2 remove 3 suit or equip for 4 cease to operate **cut up** 1 chop into small pieces 2 *inf* upset; distress ~*n* 1 act or result of cutting 2 incision 3 engraving 4 piece cut off 5 division **a cut above** superior to *adj* **cut and dried** settled **cut-price** *adj* below the normally charged price **cutting** *n* 1 act of cutting or thing cut

off or out 2 newspaper clipping 3 piece cut from a plant for replanting

cute *adj* 1 quaint; sweet 2 clever; sharp **cutely** *adv* **cuteness** *n*

cuticle *n* skin at the edges of the nails

cutlery *n* 1 knives and other cutting implements 2 eating implements

cutlet *n* small piece of meat, esp for frying or grilling

cycle *n* 1 recurrent or complete series or period 2 development following a course of stages 3 series of poems, etc 4 short for **bicycle**. *vi* 1 move in cycles 2 ride a bicycle **cyclic** or **cyclical** *adj* **cyclist** *n* person who rides a bicycle

cyclone *n* system of winds moving round a centre of low pressure

cygnet *n* young swan

cylinder *n* 1 tube-shaped figure, usually with a circular base 2 piston chamber of an engine **cylindrical** *adj*

cymbal *n* saucer-shaped piece of brass used as a musical instrument of percussion

cynic *n* sceptical or distrusting person **cynical** *adj* **cynicism** *n*

cypress *n* coniferous tree having dark foliage and durable wood

cyst *n* abnormal sac containing bodily secretions

czar *n* tsar

D

dab *vt vi* (-bb-) touch gently; apply with a light touch *n* 1 gentle blow 2 small lump of soft substance

dabble *vt, vi* move about in water or other liquid *vi* engage in some activity in a superficial manner **dabbler** *n*

dad *n inf* father

daffodil *n* variety of yellow narcissus

daft *adj* silly; feeble-minded

dagger *n* short stabbing weapon with a double-edged blade

daily *adj* performed, occurring, etc every day *adv* every day *n* 1 daily newspaper 2 non-resident domestic help

dainty *adj* 1 pretty; elegant 2 fastidious; delicate **daintily** *adv* **daintiness** *n*

dairy *n* place for keeping, processing, or supplying milk and milk products **dairy farm** n farm producing milk and milk products

daisy n small white-petalled flower with a yellow centre

dam[1] n barrier to hold back water vt (-mm-) obstruct or hold back with a dam

dam[2] n female parent, esp of an animal

damage vt,vi injure; harm; impair; spoil n harm; injury **damages** pl n financial compensation awarded by law for loss or harm

dame n lady, esp a mistress of a household or school **Dame** title of a female member of an order of knighthood

damn vt 1 curse; doom; condemn to hell 2 censure interj expression of anger or annoyance **damnable** adj 1 deserving condemnation 2 wretched **damnation** n state of being damned

damp adj moist; slightly wet n moisture vt also **dampen** 1 moisten 2 depress; discourage

damson n small purple fruit of the plum family

dance n 1 sequence of rhythmical steps usually performed to music 2 social gathering for dancing vt,vi 1 perform (a dance) 2 move quickly energetically or gracefully **dance attendance (on)** attend constantly **dancer** n

dandelion n plant with bright yellow flowers and leaves with jagged edges

dandruff n flakes of scurf formed on the scalp

danger n exposure to risk of harm; peril; risk **dangerous** adj **dangerously** adv

dangle vt vi swing loosely, hang freely

dare vt vi be brave enough (to do something) vt challenge; defy n challenge to do something **daring** adj bold adventurous n boldness, audacity

dark adj 1 without light 2 deeply tinted brown or almost black 3 mysterious secret evil n 1 absence of light; night 2 ignorance; secrecy **darkness** n **darken** vt vi make or become dark(er)

darling n person greatly loved; favourite adj greatly loved or desired

darn vt vi mend (a hole in fabric) by stitching over n repair so made

dart n 1 small pointed missile such as a short arrow 2 swift sudden movement 3 short seam or tuck in a garment vi vt move swiftly and suddenly, shoot out **darts** n game in which darts are thrown at a circular board (dartboard)

dash vi rush hastily vt 1 hurl; thrust; knock violently 2 discourage; ruin n 1 sudden rush 2 small quantity, esp as a flavouring in food or drink 3 punctuation mark (-) used to indicate a pause change of subject, etc 4 energy; vigour **dashing** adj 1 showy; stylish 2 impetuous; spirited **dashboard** n instrument panel of a motor vehicle

data n s or pl facts, figures, statistics, etc, used as a basis for discussion or calculation

date[1] n 1 day on which an event occurs or a statement of this in days, months, and years 2 inf appointment; rendezvous 3 person with whom one has an appointment vt 1 determine the date of 2 inf make an appointment esp with a member of the opposite sex **date from** originate from a certain date

date[2] n sweet oblong single-stoned fruit of the date palm

daughter n 1 female offspring esp in relation to her parents 2 any female descendant **daughter-in-law** n pl **daughters-in-law** son s wife

dawdle vi move slowly, loiter; fall or lag behind **dawdler** n

dawn n 1 period during which the sun rises; daybreak 2 beginning vi 1 begin to grow light 2 begin to appear or develop **dawn upon** become evident to

day n 1 period between sunrise and sunset 2 period of 24 hours beginning at midnight **daybreak** n dawn **daydream** n pleasant sequence of thoughts or musing while awake vi have daydreams **daylight** n light from the sun

daze vt stupefy bewilder stun n state of being dazed or stunned drowsiness

dazzle vt 1 blind temporarily with brilliant light 2 confuse or surprise with brilliance beauty etc

dead adj 1 without life having died 2 dull; numb; resembling death 3 extinct; no longer active **deaden** vt make insensible, numb dull the vitality of **deadline** n time by which some task must be completed **deadlock** n complete standstill in which further progress is impossible **deadly** adj 1 fatal poisonous 2 like death

deaf adj 1 lacking or deficient in the sense of hearing 2 unwilling to listen **deafen** vt 1 make deaf 2 make impervious to sound **deafness** n

deal v (dealt) vt vi distribute esp playing cards to the players vt inflict: deliver vi do business: trade **deal with** manage settle ~n 1 business transaction 2 distribution of playing cards 3 inf amount **dealer** n

dean n 1 head clergyman of a cathedral 2 college or university official

dear adj 1 much loved: precious 2 expensive costly n someone much loved adv at high cost **dearly** adv **dearness** n

death n 1 end of life state of being dead 2 dying 3 cause of death **deathly** adj resembling death, lifeless, pale

debase vt undervalue, lower in value: degrade

debate n 1 formal public discussion 2 argument, controversy vt vi discuss argue (about) **debatable** adj open to discussion, questionable

debit n 1 record in an account of money owed 2 debt; something owed vt record as money owing; charge

debris n wreckage, fragments

debt n 1 something owed 2 obligation **in debt** 1 owing money 2 having an obligation **debtor** n person who is in debt to another

decade n period of ten years

decadent adj 1 declining or deteriorating esp morally 2 corrupted **decadence** n

decant vt pour liquid gently from one vessel to another **decanter** n glass vessel for serving wine

decapitate vt sever or chop off the head of **decapitation** n

decay vi 1 decompose rot 2 deteriorate decline n 1 decomposition 2 deterioration, decline

decease n death vi die

deceive vt vi mislead deliberately delude, cheat **deceit** n **deceitful** adj **deceitfully** adv

December n twelfth month of the year

decent adj 1 respectable proper, modest 2 inf fairly good, adequate **decency** n **decently** adv

deceptive adj tending to deceive or give a false impression **deception** n

decibel n unit for measuring intensities of sounds

decide vt give judgment on, settle vi make up one's mind, conclude **decided** adj 1 certain, definite 2 resolute **decidedly** adv

deciduous adj 1 (of leaves teeth etc) shed

periodically 2 (of trees) shedding leaves annually

decimal adj based on the number ten numbered or proceeding by tens n also **decimal fraction** fraction having a denominator that is a power of ten written with a dot in front of the numerator

decipher vt 1 decode 2 make out the meaning of

decision n 1 judgment settlement, conclusion 2 firmness determination **decisive** adj 1 conclusive, deciding 2 resolute firm **decisively** adv

deck n 1 horizontal platform forming the floor of a ship bus etc 2 pack of cards vt adorn decorate **deckchair** n portable folding chair with a canvas back

declare vt vi 1 announce formally proclaim assert 2 state that one has an income, goods etc on which duty or tax must be paid 3 close an innings in cricket before all the wickets have fallen **declaration** n

declension n 1 change in form of a noun pronoun or adjective depending on its case 2 decline, deterioration

decline vt vi 1 slope downwards 2 deteriorate decay 3 refuse n gradual deterioration loss of strength vigour etc

decode vt interpret from a code; decipher

decompose vt vi putrefy rot, decay **decomposition** n

decorate vt 1 embellish adorn 2 restore with new paint wallpaper etc 3 invest with a medal badge etc **decoration** n **decorative** adj **decorator** n

decoy n something used to attract others into a trap, lure

decrease vt vi diminish make or grow less reduce n process of or amount of lessening reduction

decree n official decision, judgment or law vt vi command; judge order

decrepit adj worn out old and useless

dedicate vt 1 devote solemnly or wholly 2 set apart for a special purpose 3 inscribe or address as a compliment **dedication** n

deduce vt draw as a conclusion from given facts, infer **deduct** vt take away subtract **deduction** n 1 act of deducting 2 amount deducted 3 logical reasoning from given facts 4 the conclusion reached

deed n 1 something done action exploit 2

legal document stating terms of a contract, rights etc

deep adj 1 extending far down, in, or across 2 at or of a specified distance down or in 3 profound; intense; serious 4 absorbed; engrossed 5 low-pitched 6 dark-coloured adv also **deeply** so as to be deep n deep place, esp in the sea **deepness** n **deepen** vt,vi make or become deep(er) **deep-freeze** n refrigerator to keep food fresh for long periods **deeply** adv strongly; profoundly; extremely **deep-seated** adj firmly established; not superficial

deer n, pl **deer** ruminant the male of which has deciduous antlers

deface vt spoil the appearance or surface of; disfigure **defacement** n

defame vt injure the good name or reputation of, as by libel, slander, etc **defamation** n **defamatory** adj

default n 1 absence; want 2 failure to act or appear vi fail to act or appear as required **defaulter** n

defeat vt conquer; vanquish; overcome; beat n act of being beaten or conquered

defect n ('di:fekt) failing; blemish; imperfection; fault; flaw vi (di'fekt) desert one s country, duty, etc; switch allegiance **defection** n **defector** n **defective** adj imperfect; faulty; deficient

defend vt,vi 1 protect against attack 2 justify, as in answer to a legal charge **defence** n **defences** pl n 1 fortifications 2 self-protective attitudes **defensive** adj protective; resisting attack **defensively** adv

defer[1] vt,vi (-rr-) postpone; put off

defer[2] vi (-rr-) make concessions; submit (to) **deference** n respectful submission to another s will **deferential** adj

defiant adj stubbornly or aggressively hostile; insolent **defiance** n **defiantly** adv

deficient adj incomplete; defective; lacking **deficiency** n

deficit n lack or shortage esp of money

define vt 1 mark out; show the limits of 2 describe exactly; give the meaning of

definite adj 1 certain; fixed; exact 2 clear distinct **definite article** n the word the **definitely** adv

definition n 1 act of defining 2 brief description or explanation esp of a word or phrase 3 quality of distinctness or clarity

deflate vt,vi 1 release air from or lose air 2 reduce economic inflation 3 lessen the dignity or conceit of **deflation** n **deflationary** adj

deflect vt,vi turn or move at an angle **deflection** n

deform vt spoil the shape of; make ugly; disfigure **deformation** n **deformity** n

defraud vt cheat; swindle; deprive by fraud

defrost vt remove ice from

deft adj skilful; nimble **deftly** adv **deftness** n

defunct adj obsolete, no longer used

defy vt 1 challenge, resist stubbornly 2 disobey

degenerate vi (di'dʒenəreit) decline in standard or qualities; deteriorate adj (di'dʒenərət) degraded; depraved n (di'dʒenərət) degenerate person **degeneration** or **degeneracy** n

degrade vt,vi 1 reduce in grade or rank 2 lower in character; debase; humiliate **degradation** n

degree n 1 grade; stage; relative position; extent 2 academic rank awarded for proficiency or as an honour 3 unit of measurement in temperature scales 4 unit of angular measure; 1/360th part of a complete turn

dehydrate vt remove water from **dehydration** n

deity n god or goddess

dejected adj depressed; despondent; sad; miserable

delay vt cause to be late; postpone vi be late; linger n act of delaying; fact or period of being delayed; postponement

delegate vt ('deligeit) 1 send or elect as a representative 2 entrust to as a deputy n ('deligət) representative, deputy, agent **delegation** n 1 number of delegates in a group 2 act of delegating

delete vt strike out; erase; remove **deletion** n

deliberate vi (di'libəreit) reflect, consider carefully adj (di'libərət) 1 intentional; purposeful 2 slow in deciding; cautious **deliberately** adv **deliberation** n

delicate adj 1 finely made or prepared; pleasing 2 sensitive; easily hurt or damaged 3 refined; fastidious **delicacy** n 1 sensitivity; tact 2 refinement; gracefulness 3 attractive and tasty food **delicately** adv

delicatessen n shop specializing in foreign food, cooked meats delicacies, etc pl n the foods sold

delicious adj 1 pleasing, esp to the senses of taste or smell 2 delightful

delight vt give great pleasure to **delight in** take pleasure in ~n intense pleasure or joy or a cause of this **delightful** adj **delightfully** adv

delinquency n neglect of duty; wrongdoing; petty crime **delinquent** n,adj

deliver vt 1 set free; liberate 2 hand over or distribute (mail, goods etc) 3 give forth; discharge 4 pronounce; utter 5 assist at the birth of **deliverance** n liberation; rescue **delivery** n 1 delivering of mail goods a speech, etc 2 childbirth

delta n fan-shaped area of land at the mouth of a river

delude vt deceive; mislead **delusion** n **delusive** adj

deluge n violent flood vt rush upon or at, as a flood inundate

delve vt,vi 1 dig 2 also **delve into** research deeply (into)

demand vt 1 ask for; claim; request urgently 2 require; need n pressing request or requirement

democracy n 1 government by the people, esp by majority vote; equality of rights 2 state or community so governed **democrat** n **democratic** adj

demolish vt destroy; pull down **demolition** n

demon n 1 devil; evil spirit 2 cruel or wicked person **demonic** adj

demonstrate vt show by reasoning or practical example; prove, explain vi manifest opposition or sympathy in public; make a protest **demonstrable** adj **demonstration** n **demonstrator** n

demoralize vt 1 lower the morale of; cause to lose courage 2 harm morally; corrupt

demure adj modest; reserved; sedate **demurely** adv

den n 1 wild animal s retreat or resting place 2 hiding-place of thieves 3 private room for work

denial n 1 contradiction 2 refutation; rejection 3 refusal of a request

denim n strong cotton fabric

denomination n 1 name or designation 2 class of units in money, weights, etc 3 name of a group of people, esp a religious sect

denominator n lower number in a fraction; divisor **common denominator** n something

possessed in common by all members of a group

denote vt 1 mark out; distinguish 2 stand for; indicate **denotation** n

denounce vt 1 condemn strongly or publicly 2 inform against 3 repudiate

dense adj 1 thick; closely packed 2 opaque 3 inf stupid **density** n 1 thickness 2 mass per unit volume

dent n small hollow left by a blow or by pressure vt,vi make a dent in or become marked by a dent

dental adj of or relating to the teeth **dentist** n person who treats decayed teeth fits false teeth, etc **dentistry** n **denture** n set of false teeth

deny vt 1 declare to be untrue; contradict 2 reject; repudiate 3 refuse **deny oneself** abstain from

deodorant n substance that counteracts offensive smells

depart vi 1 go away, leave 2 die **departure** n

department n 1 subdivision, branch; separate section of an organization 2 field of activity special concern

depend v **depend (up)on** 1 be conditional or contingent on 2 rely on; trust **dependable** adj reliable **dependant** n person relying upon another for maintenance or support **dependent** adj **dependence** n

depict vt represent in words or pictures; portray, describe **depiction** n

deplete vt exhaust, empty, reduce **depletion** n

deplore vt 1 regret deeply; lament 2 disapprove of **deplorable** adj

deport vt expel from a country; banish **deportation** n

deportment n manner of standing walking etc ; bearing

depose vt remove from office, esp from a high position vi bear witness, testify **deposition** n

deposit vt 1 set down 2 put aside for safekeeping or as a pledge of faith n 1 money entrusted to a bank etc , or as part-payment of a transaction 2 layer of ore or sediment in the earth **depository** n place for safekeeping esp a store for goods

depot n 1 store or military headquarters 2 central garage for buses

deprave vt corrupt morally; pervert **depravity** n

deprecate vt express disapproval of

depreciate vt, vi 1 lower or fall in price or value 2 disparage **depreciation** n

depress vt 1 press down; lower 2 lessen the activity of 3 make humble or gloomy **depression** n 1 lowered surface; hollow 2 low spirits; dejection 3 state or period of reduced economic activity; slump 4 region of low barometric pressure in the atmosphere

deprive vt prevent from possessing or using; take away from **deprivation** n

depth n 1 distance downwards; deepness 2 intensity or extent, as of emotion 3 profundity of thought or explanation 4 lowness of pitch 5 most extreme or intense point **out of one's depth** unable to understand or cope with a subject, situation etc **the depths** pl n 1 deepest part 2 condition of low spirits or dejection

deputize vi vt act or appoint as an agent or representative **deputation** n body of persons sent to represent others **deputy** n assistant; representative, delegate

derail vt cause (a train) to leave the rails **derailment** n

derelict adj abandoned, in a poor condition; dilapidated n something abandoned **dereliction** n neglect esp of duty

deride vt mock at, scorn **derision** n **derisive** adj

derive vt obtain or receive from vi originate (from); be descended (from) **derivation** n **derivative** n adj

derogatory adj insulting, not complimentary; damaging

descend vt vi move, come, or bring down vi 1 move or slope downwards 2 originate (from) **descendant** n person descended from another, offspring **descent** n 1 descending; going down 2 downward slope or path 3 ancestry; transmission by inheritance

describe vt 1 give a detailed account of, esp in words 2 trace or mark out **description** n **descriptive** adj

desert[1] ('dezət) n waterless and uninhabited region adj barren; lonely

desert[2] (di'zə:t) vt abandon; leave vi leave service esp the army without permission **deserter** n **desertion** n

desert[3] (di'zə:t) n something deserved, as a reward or punishment

deserve vt be entitled to by conduct or qualities; merit vi be worthy

design vt 1 plan; make sketches for 2 intend n 1 plan; scheme; project 2 art of making designs or patterns **designer** n

designate vt ('dezigneit) 1 indicate; point out; name 2 appoint to office adj ('dezignət) appointed to but not yet holding office **designation** n

desire vt 1 wish for greatly; yearn for; want 2 request n 1 longing craving; urge; appetite 2 request 3 thing or person desired **desirable** adj

desist vi refrain; cease; stop

desk n table with a flat or sloping writing surface

desolate adj ('desələt) 1 abandoned; lonely 2 dreary; gloomy vt ('desəleit) 1 lay waste; destroy 2 make unhappy **desolation** n

despair n loss of hope; hopelessness; despondency vi lose hope

desperate adj 1 very serious or dangerous; beyond hope 2 reckless; violent; careless of risk **desperation** n

despise vt feel contempt for; scorn **despicable** adj

despite prep in spite of

despondent adj dejected, lacking hope or courage **despondency** n

despot n tyrant; cruel ruler or master **despotic** adj

dessert n fruit, confectionery, etc, served as the final course of a meal **dessertspoon** n spoon of a size between a tablespoon and a teaspoon

destine vt 1 determine the future of; doom 2 set apart for a special purpose; intend **destination** n place towards which a person travels or a thing is sent; end of a journey **destiny** n 1 fate; supernatural or divine power 2 that which is destined to happen

destitute adj in extreme poverty; penniless **destitution** n

destroy vt demolish, annihilate; ruin **destruction** n **destructive** adj

detach vt separate; disconnect **detached** adj 1 disconnected 2 aloof; impartial **detachment** n

detail n small part of a whole; item; fact; piece of information **in detail** thoroughly; fully

— vt **1** give particulars of **2** appoint for special duty

detain vt **1** keep waiting, prevent from leaving; delay **2** keep possession of withhold **3** hold in custody **detainee** n **detention** n

detect vt **1** notice, see **2** find out discover **detection** n **detective** n person esp a policeman who investigates crimes

deter vt (-rr-) discourage or dissuade from action, esp by fear of consequences **deterrent** n adj

detergent n cleansing substance adj cleansing

deteriorate vt, vi make or become worse, degenerate **deterioration** n

determine vt **1** be the cause of or deciding factor in **2** set limits to fix vi resolve decide **determination** n

detest vt dislike intensely loathe, hate **detestable** adj

detonate vt, vi explode **detonation** n **detonator** n detonating device

detour n diversion deviation from a usual route

detract vt disparage **detract from** diminish spoil

devalue vt reduce the value of **devaluation** n

devastate vt destroy wholly demolish **devastation** n

develop vi evolve, grow open out vt **1** bring to a more advanced stage **2** bring forth reveal **3** treat (photographic film) to make the image visible **development** n

deviate vi diverge, turn away from what is normal or expected **deviant** adj n

device n **1** mechanical contrivance apparatus appliance or machine **2** plot scheme

devil n **1** demon wicked fiend **2** sl lively or energetic person rascal **the Devil** personification of evil, Satan **devilish** adj

devious adj **1** roundabout, winding erratic **2** deceitful

devise vt **1** invent contrive **2** bequeath

devoid adj **devoid of** empty (of) lacking in

devolve vt to delegate or transfer (power, responsibility, etc) vi to be transferred **devolution** n the act of devolving, esp the transfer of government from a central to a regional organisation

devote vt give up wholly esp to some cause or person, dedicate **devotion** n **1** great loyalty dedication **2** religious worship **devotee** n

devour vt **1** eat greedily consume **2** absorb mentally with great eagerness

devout adj **1** pious **2** earnest solemn

dew n droplets of moisture deposited on ground surfaces at night

dexterous adj skilful deft clever **dexterity** n

diabetes (daiə'tis) n disease of the pancreas characterized by allergy to sugar and abnormal discharge of urine **diabetic** adj n

diagonal adj joining two opposite corners slanting oblique n diagonal line **diagonally** adv

diagram n sketch drawing or plan used esp to illustrate or demonstrate something **diagrammatic** adj

dial n **1** graduated face or disc on a watch compass or other instrument **2** numbered disc on a telephone vt (-ll-) call using a telephone dial

dialect n regional variation of a language

dialogue n **1** conversation **2** passage of written work in conversational form

diameter n **1** straight line across a circle passing through the centre **2** length of this line thickness

diamond n **1** very hard precious stone of pure carbon **2** equilateral parallelogram **3** playing card of the suit marked with a red diamond-shaped pip or the symbol itself

diaphragm n **1** muscular membrane between the chest and the abdomen **2** thin vibrating disc in certain instruments **3** contraceptive device inserted over the mouth of the cervix to act as a barrier to sperm

diarrhoea (daiə'riə) n abnormal looseness of the bowels

diary n daily record of events or book in which such a record is kept

dice n pl or s small cube with faces marked with between one and six spots used in games of chance vt cut into small cubes **dice with** gamble with deal with recklessly

dictate vt (dik'teit) **1** say or read for another to write down **2** prescribe command n ('dikteit) authoritative command **dictation** n act of dictating for another to write down or the matter so dictated **dictator** n absolute ruler **dictatorial** adj of or resembling a dictator autocratic **dictatorship** n **1** office of or government by a dictator **2** country so ruled

dictionary n **1** book containing an alphabetical list of words and their meanings pronunciation etc **2** reference book relating to a particular subject, with items listed in alphabetical order

did v pt of **do.**

die vi (dying) cease to live; perish **die down** gradually diminish or become less forceful

diesel n internal-combustion engine fuelled by oil or a vehicle driven by this

diet n 1 regulated allowance of food, esp one prescribed for slimming or medical reasons 2 the food a person normally eats vi to eat a special diet

differ vi be unlike; disagree **difference** n degree of differing or point in which things differ; disagreement **different** adj **differently** adv **differentiate** vi 1 constitute a difference between 2 become unlike; diverge vt distinguish between **differentiation** n

difficult adj not easy; hard to do or understand **difficulty** n

dig v (-gg-; dug) vt,vi cut into or remove earth, esp with a spade; excavate vt poke or prod n 1 prod 2 sarcastic remark 3 archaeological excavation

digest vt (di'dʒest) 1 dissolve (food) in the stomach for bodily absorption 2 classify or summarize to aid mental assimilation 3 reflect on; absorb n ('daidʒest) 1 summary 2 publication containing condensed versions of other articles, books, etc **digestion** n natural assimilation of food into the bodily system

digit n 1 any number from nought to nine 2 finger or toe

dignified adj stately; exalted, noble

dignity n 1 stateliness, gravity; distinction of mind or character 2 high office or title

digress vi stray from the main point or theme of a story, argument, etc **digression** n

dike n, vt dyke

dilapidated adj decayed; neglected; in ruins **dilapidation** n

dilemma n situation in which alternative choices are equally unattractive; difficult predicament

diligent adj industrious; conscientious **diligence** n

dilute vt reduce the strength of by adding water, water down **dilution** n

dim adj 1 not bright; indistinct; obscure 2 also **dim-witted** inf stupid, not intelligent vt,vi (-mm-) make or become dim(mer)

dimension n measurement of length, breadth, height, etc ; extent; size

diminish vt,vi make or become smaller or less;

lessen; reduce **diminutive** adj extremely small

dimple n small hollow, esp in the surface of the skin on the face

din n loud continuous noise vt (-nn-) 1 subject to din 2 repeat (facts, opinions, etc) insistently

dine vi eat dinner vt entertain at dinner

dinghy n small open boat

dingy adj 1 shabby; dirty 2 badly lit; gloomy **dinginess** n

dinner n 1 chief meal of the day 2 formal banquet

dinosaur n large extinct reptile

diocese ('daiəsis) n district under a bishop's jurisdiction **diocesan** (dai'ɔsizən) adj

dip vt (-pp-) 1 submerge briefly in liquid; immerse 2 lower vi 1 sink briefly under the surface of a liquid 2 slope downwards n 1 act of dipping 2 downward slope 3 bathe

diphthong n union of two vowel sounds in one syllable

diploma n document conferring some privilege, title, or qualification

diplomacy n 1 management of international relations 2 tact or skill in dealing with others **diplomat** n person engaged in international diplomacy **diplomatic** adj

direct vt 1 give orders; manage; control 2 give directions to; point; indicate a route to adj straight; straightforward; immediate **direct object** n word in a sentence receiving the direct action of the main verb **direction** n 1 instruction; command 2 course to which anything moves, faces, etc **director** n 1 person who directs, esp the production of a film or play 2 member of a board controlling a company or organization **directory** n book listing names with addresses, telephone numbers, etc

dirt n 1 any unclean substance; filth: 2 soil; earth **dirty** adj

disable vt incapacitate; cripple **disability** n **disabled** adj

disadvantage n unfavourable circumstance or situation; handicap

disagree vi 1 differ in opinion; dissent 2 be incompatible **disagreeable** adj **disagreement** n

disappear vi vanish; go out of sight **disappearance** n

disappoint vt fail to fulfil the desires or expectations of; frustrate **disappointment** n

disapprove vt, vi fail to approve; have an unfavourable opinion (of) **disapproval** n

disarm vt 1 deprive of weapons; make defenceless 2 win over; conciliate vi lay down weapons; reduce national military forces **disarmament** n

disaster n extreme misfortune; calamity **disastrous** adj

disc n 1 thin flat circular plate 2 inf gramophone record **disc jockey** n person who plays recorded music on the radio, at parties, etc

discard vt, vi throw out; cast off; reject

discern vt see clearly; detect; distinguish **discerning** adj having good taste; discriminating **discernment** n

discharge vt (dis'tʃɑːdʒ) 1 release; send forth 2 dismiss 3 unload n ('distʃɑːdʒ) 1 matter discharged 2 state of being discharged; release

disciple n follower; loyal pupil

discipline n 1 obedience and orderliness; self-control 2 training or system of rules that produces such conduct vt 1 subject to strict rules of conduct; train 2 punish

disclose vt reveal; make known **disclosure** n

disconcert vt upset; take aback; dismay

disconnect vt break connection between; separate

disconsolate adj unhappy; lacking hope or comfort

discontinue vt, vi cease to continue; leave off

discord n lack of harmony; disagreement; strife

discotheque n public place for dancing to recorded pop music

discount n ('diskaunt) reduction in the price of anything vt (dis'kaunt) 1 reduce the value or price of 2 leave out of consideration; ignore

discourage vt 1 lessen the courage or confidence of; dishearten 2 oppose by expressing disapproval; deter **discouragement** n

discover vt 1 find out; learn about 2 uncover; reveal **discoverer** n **discovery** n

discreet adj careful; prudent; tactful

discrepancy n difference; inconsistency; variance

discrete adj separate; distinct

discretion n 1 prudence; tact 2 freedom to act or choose as one likes

discriminate vt, vi 1 make or see distinctions; distinguish 2 treat persons, groups, etc as different from others **discrimination** n

discus n heavy disc thrown in athletic contests

discuss vt argue or write about in detail; debate **discussion** n

disease n illness; condition of impaired health

disembark vt, vi set or go ashore from a ship; land

disfigure vt spoil the appearance of; deform **disfigurement** n

disgrace n shame; dishonour vt bring shame or discredit on; humiliate

disgruntled adj discontented; sulky

disguise vt conceal the true nature or appearance of; misrepresent n clothing, make-up, etc , worn to give a false appearance

disgust n extreme dislike; loathing; repugnance vt cause disgust in; offend greatly

dish n 1 shallow vessel or basin for food 2 particular variety or preparation of food

dishearten vt discourage; make despondent

dishevelled adj untidy; scruffy; bedraggled

dishonest adj not honest; insincere; deceitful **dishonesty** n

dishonour n 1 state of shame or disgrace 2 cause of this vt 1 bring shame or discredit on; disgrace 2 treat with disrespect 3 fail to pay (a debt, etc) **dishonourable** adj

disillusion vt cause to lose illusions; disenchant **disillusionment** n

disinfect vt free from infection; remove infectious germs from; sterilize **disinfection** n **disinfectant** n substance that prevents or removes infection

disinherit vt deprive of inheritance **disinheritance** n

disintegrate vt, vi break into fragments; crumble **disintegration** n

disinterested adj impartial; objective; free from selfish or private motives

disjointed adj 1 disconnected 2 incoherent

dislike vt feel aversion to; disapprove of n aversion; disapproval

dislocate vt put out of joint; displace **dislocation** n

disloyal adj not loyal; unfaithful **disloyalty** n

dismal adj gloomy; depressing; dreary **dismally** adv

dismantle vt take apart, esp carefully or piece by piece

dismay vt fill with alarm or fear n apprehension; anxiety

dismiss vt 1 send away; discharge from a job 2 give only brief consideration to **dismissal** n

disobey vt refuse or fail to obey **disobedience** n **disobedient** adj

disorder n 1 lack of order or organization; confusion 2 breach of the peace; riot 3 illness; ailment **disordered** adj upset, disturbed; badly arranged **disorderly** adj unruly; badly organized

disown vt refuse to acknowledge; repudiate

disparage vt speak scornfully of; belittle **disparagement** n

dispassionate adj without emotion or prejudice; objective

dispatch vt 1 send off 2 finish off n 1 sending off 2 speed; promptness 3 official message or report

dispel vt (-ll-) clear away; make disappear; scatter

dispense vt 1 deal out; administer 2 make up (medicines) **dispense with** do without; get rid of **dispensary** n place where medicines are made up

disperse vt vi scatter; spread widely **dispersal** n

displace vt 1 move out of place 2 remove from office 3 take the place of **displacement** n

display vt exhibit; show; expose to view n 1 exhibition 2 ostentatious show

dispose vt 1 arrange; set in order 2 make willing or inclined **dispose of** get rid of; deal with **disposal** n **disposition** n 1 arrangement 2 inclination; tendency 3 temperament

dispossess vt deprive of rights possessions, etc

disprove vt prove false; refute

dispute v (di'spju:t) vi,vt argue debate, or disagree vt 1 doubt or question the truth of 2 compete to win (something) n ('dispju:t) argument; quarrel

disqualify vt 1 make ineligible or unsuitable 2 ban from competing in sports, etc , for a breach of the rules 3 deprive of legal or other rights etc **disqualification** n

disregard vt 1 take no notice of; ignore 2 treat with no respect n lack of respect

disrepute n ill repute **disreputable** 1 discreditable 2 shabby

disrespect n have or show no respect for n lack of respect or courtesy **disrespectful** adj

disrupt vt 1 cause chaos or disorder 2 interrupt the continuity of **disruption** n **disruptive** adj

dissect vt 1 cut up and examine (an animal or plant) 2 analyse in detail **dissection** n

dissent vi 1 disagree 2 express views opposing established or orthodox doctrines, esp of a church **dissension** n **dissenter** n

dissimilar adj not similar; different **dissimilarity** n

dissolve vi vt 1 disperse or cause to disperse into a solution 2 dismiss (a company, organization, etc) vi vanish **dissolution** n

dissuade vt discourage from an intention by persuasion

distance n length of a space between two points **keep (someone) at a distance** refuse to allow someone to become friendly **keep one's distance** behave in a reserved or formal way **distant** adj 1 far away 2 remote 3 reserved

distaste n dislike **distasteful** adj unpleasant, objectionable

distil v (-ll-) vt 1 boil (a liquid) and condense the vapour 2 purify by this process 3 obtain the essential part of something vi undergo distillation **distillation** n **distillate** n product of distillation **distillery** n place where alcoholic spirits are produced

distinct adj 1 easily understood; clear 2 noticeable **distinct from** different, not the same as **distinction** n 1 act of distinguishing things as different or distinct 2 mark of difference 3 mark of superiority or excellence **distinctive** adj of distinguishing characteristic

distinguish vt 1 be able to see a difference; discriminate 2 characterize 3 recognize, perceive **distinguish oneself** do something with distinction

distort vt 1 twist, deform 2 give an untrue impression of **distortion** n

distract vt 1 divert the attention of 2 confuse; disturb 3 entertain or amuse **distraction** n **distractive** adj

distraught adj 1 agitated or bewildered 2 frantic

distress vt cause acute mental or physical discomfort n 1 state of acute anxiety or anguish 2 state of danger extreme discomfort, etc

distribute vt 1 give out in shares; allot 2 spread; scatter 3 divide into groups or categories **distribution** n

district n geographical, political, or administrative region

distrust vt have no trust in; suspect n lack of trust

disturb vt 1 interrupt; disrupt 2 cause disorder; disarrange 3 cause worry or anxiety **disturbance** n 1 act of disturbing or being disturbed 2 disturbing of the public peace

ditch n narrow trench dug for drainage purposes vi repair or dig ditches vt inf throw away; abandon

ditto n the same as above; used in accounts, lists, etc , to save repetition

divan n 1 low backless cushioned couch set against a wall 2 also **divan bed** type of bed with an enclosed base and no visible frame

dive vi 1 jump into water headfirst or in a controlled fashion 2 throw oneself forward headlong 3 (of a submarine) submerge vi,vt 1 move in a steep downward path through the air n 1 act of diving 2 inf shabby disreputable café, pub, etc **diver** n

diverge vi 1 turn off and go in different directions; move apart 2 differ **divergence** n

diverse adj varied; different **diversify** vt,vi make or become diverse **diversification** n

divert vt,vi turn (a person or thing) from a previously intended course vt distract **diversion** n 1 act of diverting 2 temporary detour caused by repairs, etc , on a road 2 distraction; amusement

divide vt,vi 1 separate or split into two or more parts 2 distribute 3 find out how many times a number is contained in another vt cause a disagreement (between)

dividend n 1 money paid to shareholders as interest, profit, etc 2 number to be divided by another

divine adj 1 relating to God, a god, or theology 2 sacred; religious; heavenly vt,vi guess or discover intuitively **divinely** adv **divinity** n 1 state or quality of being divine 2 god; deity 3 theology

divisible adj able to be divided

division n 1 act of dividing 2 part of a unit or whole 3 administrative or legislative body 4 military unit larger than a regiment

divorce n 1 legal termination of a marriage 2 total or radical separation vt,vi obtain a divorce (from) vt separate **divorcé(e)** n man (woman) who is divorced

divulge vt reveal; disclose; let out (a secret, etc)

dizzy adj 1 experiencing a sensation of confusion, being unsteady, or whirling; giddy 2 causing such a sensation **dizzily** adv **dizziness** n

do v (does; did; done) vt 1 perform; act 2 deal with; complete 3 serve; provide 4 fix; arrange 5 have as a job or occupation 6 inf swindle; defraud vi 1 suffice; be accepted 2 manage; cope 3 make progress v aux used in certain interrogative, negative, or emphatic statements **do in** sl kill; murder **do up** 1 tie; fasten 2 make smart **make do (with)** manage with what is available ~n inf function; social event

docile adj willing to be trained; tame; gentle; obedient

dock[1] n area or wharf for mooring, loading, repairing ships, etc vt,vi bring or come in to dock; moor **docker** n person employed to load and unload cargo **dockyard** n enclosure with docks for repairing, equipping, or building ships

dock[2] n 1 solid part of an animal's tail 2 stump remaining after clipping a tail vt 1 cut (an animal's tail) 2 deduct from

dock[3] n section in a lawcourt where the accused is seated

doctor n 1 person qualified to practise medicine 2 person holding the highest diploma or degree of a university vt 1 treat medically 2 falsify; adulterate

doctrine n 1 teaching of a school, church, political group, etc 2 dogma; belief

document n ('dɔkjumənt) printed or written evidence or information ('dɔkjument) furnish with evidence, references, etc **documentation** n **documentary** adj relating to a document n detailed factual film

dodge vi,vt move quickly, so as to avoid; evade n clever plan or move

does v 3rd person singular of **do** in the present tense

dog n domesticated or wild four-footed animal of various breeds vt (-gg-) pursue steadily; tail; hound **dog-collar** n inf clergyman's collar **dogged** ('dɔgid) adj persistent; stubborn; tenacious

dogma n system of beliefs, such as those of a church; doctrine **dogmatic** adj 1 relating to

dogma 2 asserting beliefs or opinions with persistent arrogance **dogmatically** adv

dole n money or food given charitably or for maintenance **on the dole** receiving unemployment benefit v **dole out** give or share out; distribute

doll n 1 child's toy in the image of a person 2 sl attractive girl or young woman v **doll up** dress up in fine clothes

dollar n unit of currency of the US and various other countries, comprising 100 cents

dolphin n sea mammal resembling but larger than a porpoise

domain n 1 territory ruled over as by a sovereign 2 field of interest influence etc; province

dome n large high rounded roof

domestic adj 1 relating to the home or household matters 2 not foreign 3 (of animals) tame **domestic science** n study or art of cooking needlework household management etc **domesticate** vt tame; train for domestic purposes **domesticity** n home life, matters concerning the home or a household

dominate vt vi 1 rule; control; govern 2 be the most important or conspicuous feature (of) **domination** n **dominant** adj 1 prevailing having power authority, or priority 2 prominent most important **dominance** n **domineer** vi behave in an overbearing or arrogant manner **dominion** n 1 sovereignty governing authority rule 2 land controlled by a government; domain 3 name formerly given to the self-governing countries of the Commonwealth of Nations

domino n, pl **dominoes** small rectangular brick marked with various combinations of spots for use in various games

donate vt give **donation** n gift esp for charity v **do**. **donor** n person making a donation

done v pp of **do**.

donkey n 1 long-eared member of the horse family, used esp as a beast of burden ass 2 sl fool

doodle vi,vt draw or scribble casually esp while attending to some other matter n scribbled drawing or shape **doodler** n

doom n 1 fate; destiny 2 unfavourable judicial sentence; condemnation vt 1 sentence; condemn 2 destine to an unhappy end or fate

door n 1 hinged or sliding structure fitted across

a passage or entrance 2 also **doorway** entrance to a building room, etc

dope n 1 kind of varnish used for waterproofing 2 drug, esp a narcotic 3 sl information 4 sl stupid person, dunce vt,vi drug or take drugs **dopey** adj also **dopy** 1 drugged; drowsy 2 stupid

dormant adj inactive

dormitory n large room containing a number of beds

dormouse n pl **dormice** hibernating rodent similar to but smaller than a squirrel

dorsal adj relating to or on the back

dose n 1 amount of a medicine, etc to be given or taken at one time 2 bout; spell vt give medicine or doses (to) **dosage** n 1 giving of medicine in doses 2 amount of medicine to be given

dot n small point or spot speck vt (-tt) 1 mark with dots spot 2 place a dot over a letter after a musical note etc

dote vi be silly or mentally weak **dote on** be excessively fond of **dotage** n silliness or childishness in old age; feeble-mindedness

double adj 1 two of a kind together of two kinds 2 twice as much 3 having two functions uses etc 4 suitable for two 5 having extra weight thickness width etc 6 ambiguous adv 1 twice 2 in pairs n 1 something or someone exactly like another 2 quantity that is twice that of another 3 sharp backward turn or bend 4 evasion, trick shift vt vi 1 make or become twice as great 2 multiply by two 3 fold in half 4 turn sharply **double up** be contorted with pain laughter etc **double bass** n largest instrument of the violin family **double-cross** vt betray n betrayal **double-dutch** n inf nonsense, gibberish **doubly** adv to twice the extent

doubt vt 1 hesitate to accept, fail to believe immediately 2 suspect n uncertainty lack of conviction or belief **no doubt** probably presumably **doubtful** adj **doubtless** adv adj

dough n flour or meal mixed with water and kneaded before baking **doughnut** n small round cake made of dough and sugar and fried in deep fat

douse vt vi also **dowse** plunge into water immerse, drench vt extinguish (a light)

dove n bird belonging to the pigeon family

dowdy adj drab, shabby

down[1] adv 1 from a higher to a lower place or

position **2** to or at the bottom; towards or on the ground **3** below the horizon **4** from an earlier to a later time **5** into a worse physical or mental condition *prep* **1** towards at, in, or near a lower place, rank, condition, etc **2** in the same direction as; with *adj* dejected; miserable; depressed

down² *n* **1** fine soft feathers of young ducks or other birds **2** fine hair

downcast *adj* **1** looking or directed downwards **2** dejected

downfall *n* **1** ruin; destruction **2** cause of overthrow or destruction **3** falling, as of rain or snow

downhearted *adj* dejected in spirits; depressed

downhill *adv* down a hill; downwards *adj* descending; sloping

downpour *n* heavy fall of rain

downright *adj* in plain terms; straightforward *adv* absolutely; thoroughly

downstairs *adv* **1** down the stairs **2** towards or on a lower floor *adj* relating to or situated on a lower floor *n* lower floor

downstream *adv* down or in the direction of flow of a stream *adj* farther down or moving with the current

downtrodden *adj* trodden or trampled down; oppressed

downward *adj* moving or extending from a higher to a lower place **downwards** *adv* from a higher place to a lower; in a descending course

dowry *n* money, goods, or property that a woman brings to her husband at marriage

dowse *vt,vi* douse

doze *vi* sleep lightly or for a short time *n* light or brief sleep

dozen *n* group of twelve **dozens** *pl n* many

drab *adj* **1** of a dull colour **2** monotonous; not exciting

draft *n* **1** first or rough copy; outline, sketch, etc **2** detachment of soldiers **3** conscription **4** written order for money *vt* **1** prepare a first or rough copy of **2** send or select (a detachment of soldiers) **3** conscript; recruit

drag *v* (-gg-) *vt,vi* **1** pull draw or be drawn along **2** trail **3** search or sweep with a net hook, etc *vi* move slowly; lag **drag out** prolong, esp unnecessarily ~*n* **1** device used for dragging **2** something that slows movement or progress **3** *sl* something or someone that is tedious or a waste of time **4**

inf puff or inhaling of a cigarette **in drag** (of a man) wearing women s clothing

dragon *n* **1** fire-breathing monster usually depicted as a winged reptile **2** *inf* fierce or fiery person, esp a woman; tyrant **dragonfly** *n* long-bodied insect with large delicate wings

drain *vt* **1** draw off (liquid) so as to empty or leave dry **2** exhaust; consume utterly; empty *vi* **1** flow out or away **2** become dry or empty *n* **1** pipe, channel or ditch for drawing off water, sewage, etc **2** steady depletion or expenditure **drainage** *n* **1** act or process of draining **2** system of pipes or channels for draining **3** substance drained **draining board** *n* sloping surface beside a sink on which wet dishes, etc , are placed to dry **drainpipe** *n* pipe channelling water, sewage, etc

drake *n* male bird of the duck family

dram *n* **1** unit of weight, equal to one sixteenth of an ounce **2** small amount of alcoholic drink; tot

drama *n* **1** story performed by actors; play **2** plays collectively **3** compelling event or series of events **dramatic** *adj* **1** relating to or resembling drama **2** vivid; forceful **dramatically** *adv* **dramatics** *pl n* acting by an amateur company **dramatist** *n* person who writes drama; playwright **dramatize** *vt* **1** act out or put into the form of a drama **2** express vividly or forcefully or in an exaggerated manner

drank *v pt of* drink.

drape *vt* cover, esp with cloth or fabric *vt,vi* hang in folds (about) *n* arrangement of folds **draper** *n* person who deals in cloth, linen, etc **drapery** *n* **1** cloth or other fabrics **2** business of a draper

draught *n* **1** current of air esp in an enclosed space **2** act of pulling or that which is pulled **3** quantity drunk in one go **4** drawing of beer wine etc , from a barrel or cask **5** dose of medicine **draughts** *n* game played with round flat pieces on a board marked off in squares **draughtsman** *n pl* **-men** **1** person skilled in mechanical drawing **2** *also* **draught** piece used in draughts

draw *v* (drew; drawn) *vt,vi* **1** pull; haul; drag **2** bring or come nearer; approach **3** portray in lines; sketch *vt* **1** pull out; extract; withdraw; take **2** inhale **3** infer; deduce **4** describe **5** obtain by lot **6** attract *vi* **1** finish a game with an equal score for both sides, tie **2** permit the circulation of air **draw on 1** use as a resource **2** approach **draw up** draft (a will contract, etc) ~*n* **1** attraction **2** raffle, lottery **3** game ending in a tie **drawback** *n* disadvantage **drawbridge** *n* bridge that can be raised

drawer *n* sliding compartment in a desk, chest etc **drawers** *pl n inf* underpants or knickers

drawing *n* **1** art or practice of portraying in lines; sketching **2** image or sketch so done **drawing pin** *n* short pin with a flat head, fixed by pushing with the thumb **drawing room** *n* room for the reception or entertaining of guests; living room

drawl *vt,vi* speak slowly, esp with elongated vowel sounds *n* such speech

dread *vt* anticipate with great fear or apprehension *n* great apprehension or fear; terror **dreadful** *adj* **1** causing dread **2** *inf* unpleasant bad **dreadfully** *adv inf* terribly, awfully; very

dream *n* **1** sequence of thoughts or images during sleep **2** something hoped for **3** vision *vi,vt* (dreamt or dreamed) have dreams (of)

dreary *adj* gloomy, not exciting, dull **dreariness** *n*

dredge *n* device for bringing up mud and other material from the bottom of a river, etc *vt* bring up, clean, etc , with a dredge

dregs *pl n* sediment

drench *vt* wet completely, soak

dress *vt,vi* put clothes on or arrange for show decorate, adorn **1** prepare (meat fish, etc) by trimming, gutting etc **4** treat (a wound, etc) by applying a dressing *n* **1** clothing **2** female outer garment consisting of a bodice and skirt **3** formal evening wear **dress circle** *n* first gallery above the floor in a theatre or cinema **dressmaker** *n* person skilled in making dresses **dress rehearsal** *n* final rehearsal of a stage production, in which the actors appear in full costume

dresser[1] *n* kitchen sideboard.

dresser[2] *n* person assisting an actor with costume changes

dressing *n* **1** sauce applied to various foods **2** stuffing **3** something applied to a wound to aid healing **dressing-gown** *n* loosely fitting robe or gown usually worn over night attire **dressing-room** *n* special room esp in a theatre where one dresses **dressing-table** *n*

small table usually with a mirror for cosmetics etc

drew *v pt of* **draw.**

dribble *vi vt* **1** flow or allow to flow in small drops, trickle **2** propel (a ball) with a series of small kicks *n* drop trickle

drier *n* appliance for drying clothes, hair etc

drift *n* **1** snow sand etc piled up by the wind **2** general meaning. **3** deviation from a plan course, etc **4** general movement progress etc *vi* **1** be carried as by air or water currents **2** move without purpose or direction **driftwood** *n* wood carried ashore by water

drill[1] *n* **1** tool or device for boring holes **2** routine exercises or training *vt vi* **1** bore (a hole) in **2** exercise esp by repetition

drill[2] *n* **1** small trench for seed **2** machine or device for sowing seed in drills

drink *v* (drank, drunk) *vt, vi* swallow (liquid) *vt* **1** absorb take in **2** consume (alcoholic drinks) *n* **1** amount of liquid suitable for consumption, beverage **2** alcohol

drip *vi, vt* (-pp-) fall or let fall in drops *n* process of dripping or that which falls by dripping **drip-dry** *adj* (of clothing, etc) drying without creases if hung up when wet **dripping** *n* fat that drips from a roasting joint

drive *vt,vi* (drove, driven) **1** move by force power etc **2** urge onward, compel **3** control or steer (an animal vehicle etc) **4** transport or be transported in a vehicle **5** move or fix by striking hitting etc *n* **1** act of driving **2** trip in a vehicle **3** road esp a private one leading to a house **4** energy. force. motivation **driver** *n*

drivel *vi* (-ll-) **1** let secretions flow from the mouth or nose dribble **2** talk or act foolishly *n* nonsense silly talk

drizzle *vi* rain lightly *n* fine rain

droll *adj* witty satirical, wry

dromedary *n* camel with one hump

drone *n* **1** male bee **2** idle person **3** deep buzz or hum **4** monotonous voice tone etc *vi* **1** buzz or hum continuously **2** speak in a low monotonous voice

drool *vi* **1** gloat. gush **2** drivel dribble

droop *vi vt* bend or hang down limply sag *vi* become disheartened languish *n* drooping state or condition

drop *n* **1** small spherical amount of liquid globule **2** very small amount of anything **3** steep descent fall **4** distance through which something falls 5 round sweet v (-pp-) vt,vi 1 fall or permit to fall 2 lower; decrease; sink vt 1 cease to consider or discuss 2 mention casually 3 allow (passengers, goods, etc) to disembark or be unloaded 4 omit; cease to make use of **drop in** make a casual visit **drop off** 1 fall asleep 2 decline; decrease **drop out** cease to compete complete one s education, etc **dropout** n person who rejects society s norms fails to complete an educational course, etc

drought n prolonged period during which no rain falls

drove [1] v pt of **drive.**

drove [2] n herd or flock, esp when on the move

drown vt,vi kill or die by suffocating in water vt 1 overpower; extinguish; destroy 2 cover completely; flood 3 shut out (sound); muffle

drowse vi,vt be or make sleepy n condition of being sleepy or half asleep **drowsy** adj 1 sleepy or sluggish 2 inducing sleep; soporific **drowsily** adv **drowsiness** n

drudge vi work hard; slave n person doing menial work **drudgery** n hard menial work; toil

drug n substance, esp a narcotic vt (-gg-) 1 mix a drug or drugs with (food, drink, etc) 2 administer a drug (to)

drum n 1 percussion instrument having skin, etc , stretched tightly over a hollow chamber 2 large cylindrical container for oil, water etc vt vi (-mm-) 1 beat or play (a drum) 2 beat, tap, or strike continuously vt instil by insistent repetition **drummer** n

drunk adj 1 also **drunken** intoxicated; inebriated 2 emotionally overcome n also **drunkard** person who is drunk esp habitually

dry adj 1 not wet or moist 2 having little or no rainfall and 3 thirsty or causing thirst 4 not yielding milk water etc 5 not stimulating; dull 6 caustically clever or witty 7 not permitting the legal sale or consumption of alcohol vt vi make or become dry(er) **dry-clean** vt clean with chemical solvents rather than water

dual adj 1 relating to two or a pair 2 having two parts, double **dual carriageway** n major road with opposite lanes separated by a barrier area of grass etc **duality** n **dually** adv

dubious adj causing doubt suspicious questionable

ducal adj relating to a duke or duchy

duchess n 1 wife or widow of a duke 2 woman holding a rank equivalent to that of a duke **duchy** n territory ruled by a duke or duchess

duck [1] n wild or tame edible bird with webbed feet **duckling** n young duck

duck [2] vi 1 bend down or lower suddenly; bob 2 plunge temporarily under water 3 avoid; dodge

duct n channel or tube for conveying liquid, secretions, etc **ductile** adj 1 (of gold, copper, etc) capable of being drawn out into wire or hammered very thin 2 flexible; pliant

due adj 1 payable at once 2 fitting; usual; proper; adequate 3 expected to arrive or be ready **due to** attributed or ascribed to ~n fair share **dues** pl n fee; charges

duel n 1 fight with pistols, swords, etc , between two persons 2 contest between two parties vi (-ll-) fight a duel

duet n composition for two musicians or performers

dug v pt and pp of **dig.**

duke n 1 nobleman ranking next below a prince 2 ruler of a small state (duchy)

dulcimer n percussion instrument having a set of strings, which are struck with hammers

dull adj 1 lacking intelligence; stupid 2 having no feelings; insensible 3 not clear or sharp 4 tedious 5 moving slowly; sluggish 6 overcast 7 blunt vt vi make or become dull **dullness** n **dully** adv

duly adv as expected properly; in a fitting manner

dumb adj 1 incapable of uttering speech sounds 2 temporarily unable to speak 3 silent 4 sl stupid **dumbfound** vt amaze into silence astound **dumbly** adv **dumbness** n

dummy n 1 model of a human being used esp for displaying clothes 2 imitation; copy 3 inf inactive or silent person 4 rubber teat sucked by a baby

dump vt 1 throw down in a pile or heap 2 unload dispose of n 1 place where rubbish is dumped; tip 2 inf messy dirty, or ugly place room etc **down in the dumps** depressed, dejected miserable **dumpling** n ball of dough cooked in a stew, etc **dumpy** adj short and fat plump

dunce n person who is slow to learn or mentally dull

dune n ridge or hill of sand

dung n excrement; manure

dungeon n underground cell or prison, esp in a castle

duplicate adj ('dju:plikət) 1 resembling or exactly like another 2 occurring in pairs, double n ('dju:plikət) exact copy vt ('dju:-plikeit) reproduce exactly; copy **duplication** n **duplicator** n machine for producing stencilled copies

durable adj resisting decay or wear; lasting **durability** n

duration n period of time that something lasts

during prep 1 throughout the period, existence, or activity of 2 in the course of

dusk n period of the evening before darkness falls; twilight **dusky** adj 1 dark-skinned 2 dim; shadowy

dust n dry fine particles of earth, mineral deposits, etc vt, vi wipe the dust (from) vt sprinkle; powder **dusty** adj **dustbin** n container for refuse, ashes, etc **duster** n cloth used to wipe dust from furniture, etc **dustman** n, pl **-men** person employed to remove refuse, empty dustbins, etc

duty n 1 obligation, esp of a moral or legal nature 2 allocated work or task 3 tax on imported or exported goods; tariff **on/off duty** at work/not at work, esp as a nurse, doctor, soldier, etc **duty-free** adj requiring no duty to be paid **dutiful** adj respectful; obedient **dutifully** adv

duvet ('du:vei) n quilt for a bed, padded with feathers, down, etc; continental quilt

dwarf n, pl **dwarfs** or **dwarves** 1 person of exceptionally small stature or size 2 plant or animal of a smaller type than average 3 supernatural being in the form of a small ugly man vt 1 restrict the growth of 2 cause to appear relatively small, insignificant, etc, by comparison

dwell vi (dwelt or dwelled) reside as a permanent occupant; live (in) **dwell (up)on** emphasize; concentrate on **dwelling** n place where someone lives; abode; house

dwindle vi grow gradually less in size, number, etc; decrease

dye n substance used for colouring fabric, the hair, etc v (dyeing, dyed) vt colour (fabric, hair, etc) with a dye vi become coloured with a dye

dying v pres p of **die**. **dying to/for** having a strong desire to/for

dyke n also **dike** 1 embankment for holding back sea or river water 2 ditch; trench vt hold back or drain with a dyke

dynamic adj 1 relating to force or energy; not static 2 forceful; ambitious **dynamically** adv **dynamics** n branch of science concerned with forces and their effects on motion

dynamite n high explosive of nitroglycerine and other substances

dynamo device that converts mechanical energy into electrical energy

dynasty n 1 unbroken line of hereditary rulers of the same family 2 period of their rule

dysentery n disease of the intestines

dyslexia n condition leading to impaired reading ability **dyslexic** adj, n

E

each adj, pron, adv every separate one considered individually

eager adj 1 strongly desirous 2 keen; willing **eagerly** adv **eagerness** n

eagle n large bird of prey having very keen eyesight

ear[1] n 1 one of two organs of hearing, situated on either side of the head 2 sense of hearing or appreciation of sound, esp music 3 attention **be all ears** be listening attentively **eardrum** n membrane in the inner part of the ear that vibrates when struck by sound waves **earmark** vt designate for a special purpose **earphone** n small loudspeaker placed in or over the ear for listening to a radio or telephone communication **earring** n jewellery worn on or hanging from the ear lobe

ear[2] n spike of a cereal plant containing the seed

earl n British nobleman ranking next above a viscount

early adj, adv 1 before the expected or appointed time 2 at or near the beginning of a period or season **earliness** n

earn vt, vi gain (money, etc) by working vt deserve **earnings** pl n wages or salary

earnest adj 1 sincere; serious 2 zealous; determined **earnestly** adv

earth n 1 third planet from the sun, lying between Venus and Mars and orbited by the moon, on which life has developed; world 2 surface of this planet 3 soil; ground 4 home of a fox, etc **5** connection of an electrical apparatus to the ground, assumed to be at zero voltage **down-to-earth** sensible; realistic **earthenware** n domestic pottery of coarse baked clay **earthly** adj **1** of the earth or world **2** likely; conceivable **earthquake** n violent natural movement of the earth's crust; tremor **earthworm** n worm that lives in and eats soil **earthy** adj coarse; basic; crude

earwig n small insect having pincers on the tail

ease n **1** freedom from work, pain, or exertion; comfort; relaxation **2** lack of difficulty (in doing something) vt,vi make or become less painful, difficult, etc

easel n frame for supporting a blackboard or artist's canvas

east n **1** one of the four cardinal points of the compass situated to the front of a person facing the sunrise **2** part of a country, area, etc , lying towards the east adj also **eastern** of, in, or facing the east adv,adj **easterly** **1** towards the east **2** (of winds) from the east **easterner** n **eastward** adj facing or moving towards the east **eastwards** adv in the direction of the east

Easter n annual Christian festival in the spring, celebrating Christ's resurrection

easy adj **1** requiring little effort; not difficult **2** relaxed; comfortable **3** tolerant; casual **easily** adv **easiness** n **easygoing** adj tolerant; relaxed

eat v (ate; eaten) vt,vi consume (food) through the mouth; have (a meal) vt **1** corrode; wear away **2** use up in great quantities

eavesdrop vi (-pp-) listen secretly to a private conversation **eavesdropper** n

ebb n **1** tidal falling back of the sea away from land **2** decline; decay vi **1** flow back from the land **2** decline; diminish; wane

ebony n hard almost black wood, obtained from a tropical or subtropical tree

ebullient adj fervent; enthusiastic; full of life **ebullience** n

eccentric adj **1** not having the same centre; having a noncentral axis **2** unconventional; odd n eccentric person **eccentricity** n

ecclesiastic adj also **ecclesiastical** of or relating to the Church or clergymen n clergyman

echo n, pl echoes **1** sound like or repeating a first sound, caused by reflection of sound waves by a solid object **2** anything that repeats or mimics vt,vi reverberate; repeat; imitate

éclair n cake made of light pastry and filled with cream

eclipse n phenomenon in which light from one heavenly body is blocked by another, esp a **solar eclipse**, where the moon moves between the earth and the sun vt **1** cause an eclipse of **2** throw into obscurity; surpass

ecology n **1** relationship between natural things and their surroundings, and the effect of technology on this **2** study of this **ecological** adj **ecologist** n

economic adj **1** of or relating to economics **2** worth doing; profitable **3** economical **economical** adj **1** frugal; thrifty **2** not wasteful; giving value for money **economically** adv **economics** n study of the causes of and relationships between production, exchange, distribution, and consumption **economize** vt,vi reduce expenditure or consumption to save money **economy** n **1** arrangement or condition of trade, production, and commerce of an area **2** thrift; frugality

ecstasy n **1** intense joy; bliss **2** state of extreme religious fervour **ecstatic** adj

edge n **1** outer side or margin **2** cutting side of a blade **3** keenness; sharpness **4** slight advantage **on edge** tense ~vt **1** sharpen **2** be or provide the border of vi vt move gradually; inch **edgy** adj tense

edible adj that may be eaten; not poisonous; not disgusting to the palate

edit vt **1** prepare (a manuscript) for publication **2** prepare the final form of (a film)

edition n set of books, newspapers, etc , printed at the same time **editor** n **1** person who edits **2** person who directs content and coverage of a newspaper, etc **editorial** adj of or relating to the task of an editor n newspaper article containing the opinions of its editor

educate vt **1** give teaching to; instruct **2** bring up; raise **3** refine; improve **education** n **1** process of gaining knowledge; training; schooling **2** state of being educated **3** upbringing **educational** adj

eel n snakelike fish

eerie adj frighteningly strange; weird; ghostly **eerily** adv **eeriness** n

effect n **1** change produced by an action; result **2** impression on the mind, eyes, etc **in effect**

actually; virtually **take effect** start; become operative ~vt bring about; cause **effective** adj 1 producing a result, esp a considerable one 2 causing a pleasant or striking effect or impression 3 taking effect **effectively** adv

effeminate adj (of a man) like a woman; not masculine or virile

effervesce vi (of a liquid) give off bubbles of gas; fizz **effervescent** adj 1 bubbling; fizzy 2 merry, lively **effervescence** n

efficient adj producing the desired effect without waste; competent; effective **efficiency** n **efficiently** adv

effigy n model or solid representation of a person

effort n 1 exertion of energy 2 attempt; try **effortless** adj needing or using little effort; easy **effortlessly** adv

egg [1] n 1 oval object consisting of the embryo of birds, reptiles, etc within a protective shell 2 egg of certain birds, esp hens, eaten as food

egg [2] v **egg on** encourage or incite; urge; persuade

ego n 1 the self; part of the mind that is conscious of itself 2 self-centredness; conceit **egocentric** adj self-centred; conceited **egoism** n characteristic of thinking only of oneself; self-centredness **egoist** n **egoistic** adj **egotism** n characteristic of talking only or too much about oneself; arrogance; conceit **egotist** n **egotistic** or **egotistical** adj

eiderdown n 1 fine down from the eider duck 2 bed cover or quilt filled with down feathers etc

eight n 1 number equal to one plus seven 2 group of eight things or people 3 also **eight o'clock** eight hours after noon or midnight adj amounting to eight **eighth** adj 1 coming between seventh and ninth in sequence n 1 eighth person, object etc 2 one of eight equal parts, one divided by eight adv after the seventh

eighteen n 1 number that is eight more than ten 2 eighteen things or people adj amounting to eighteen **eighteenth** adj,adv n

eighty n 1 number equal to eight times ten 2 eighty things or people adj amounting to eighty **eightieth** adj,adv,n

either adj,pron one or each of two conj used to introduce a choice between alternatives adv (after negatives) as well; furthermore; anyway

ejaculate vt,vi 1 say (something) suddenly; exclaim 2 discharge; eject **ejaculation** n

eject vt throw out; expel; send forth; discharge **ejection** n

eke v **eke out** cause to last; supplement; draw out

elaborate adj (i'læbərət) complicated; intricate; detailed vt,vi (i'læbəreit) make more detailed; give further explanation of **elaborately** adv **elaboration** n

elapse vi (of time) pass; go by

elastic adj easily stretched; flexible; able to return to its original shape after being distorted etc n material made elastic by interwoven strips of rubber, used in clothes **elasticity** n

elated adj very happy and excited; overjoyed; high-spirited **elatedly** adv **elation** n

elbow n 1 joint between the forearm and upper arm 2 part of a coat etc, covering this **elbow grease** n inf hard work ~vt push (one's way) through towards, etc

elder [1] adj older of two, esp two brothers or sisters; senior n 1 older person 2 official in some churches **elderly** adj old, aged

elder [2] n bush or small tree with whitish flowers and purple or black berries

eldest adj oldest of three or more people

elect vt appoint or choose by voting vi choose; decide **elector** n **election** n process of choosing and voting for candidates for office esp for Parliament

electric adj 1 also **electrical** of, relating to or worked by electricity 2 charged with emotion; tense **electrically** adv

electrician n person whose job is to install or mend electrical equipment

electricity n 1 phenomenon caused by motion of electrons or by excess of electric charge 2 electric current; electric charge

electrify vt 1 supply with or adapt to work by electric power 2 startle, shock, thrill **electrification** n

electrocute vt kill by passing an electric charge through the body **electrocution** n

electrode n metal plate or wire by which an electric current enters or leaves a device

electron n elementary particle with negative electric charge that moves round the nucleus of an atom

electronic adj relating to or operated by the conduction of electrons through a vacuum gas or semiconductor **electronics** n 1 s study and technology of electronic equipment 2 pl circuits in electronic equipment

elegant adj tasteful refined graceful **elegance** n **elegantly** adv

element n 1 constituent part 2 chemical substance that cannot be broken down into simpler substances by chemical reactions 3 small amount suggestion **elements** pl n 1 weather rain, wind etc 2 basic ideas **elemental** adj

elementary adj 1 easy, simple basic 2 relating to the earliest stages of teaching or development

elephant n largest land mammal found in India and Africa having a trunk and two tusks of ivory **elephantine** adj enormous

elevate vt 1 make higher in physical position, raise lift up 2 promote in rank 3 make more refined or cultured **elevation** n 1 act of elevating or state of being elevated 2 altitude, height **elevator** n US lift (def 2)

eleven n 1 number that is one greater than ten 2 eleven things or people adj amounting to eleven **eleventh** adj adv n

elf n pl **elves** small magical being in human form fairy **elfin** adj

eligible adj having the necessary qualities or qualifications to be chosen suitable

eliminate vt get rid of remove **elimination** n

elite n select group of people

ellipse n geometric figure having an oval shape **elliptical** adj also **elliptic** oval-shaped

elm n tall deciduous tree

elope vi run away with one s lover to get married secretly **elopement** n

eloquent adj speaking persuasively or expressively **eloquence** n **eloquently** adv

else adv 1 other different 2 more **or else** otherwise if not **elsewhere** adv to in or at another place

elucidate vi explain the meaning or clarify **elucidation** n

elude vt 1 escape from avoid capture 2 escape (a person s mind or memory) **elusive** adj 1 hard to find catch or see 2 evasive

emaciated adj very thin esp through starvation or illness **emaciation** n

emanate vi come from originate from **emanation** n

emancipate vt free from slavery or legal or social restraint esp by giving the right to vote **emancipation** n

embalm vt preserve (a corpse) by removing internal organs and applying chemicals etc

embankment n artificial mound or ridge piled up to carry a railway etc or hold back water as along a river

embargo n pl **embargoes** order prohibiting ships from entering or leaving port veto prohibition (esp on trade)

embark vi vt go or put on board a ship aircraft etc **embark on** begin start **embarkation** n

embarrass vt 1 cause awkwardness or shyness in disconcert 2 hinder hamper **embarrassment** n

embassy n 1 ambassador s official residence 2 staff of an ambassador 3 mission or message of an ambassador

embellish vt 1 make more beautiful decorate adorn 2 add greater detail or description to **embellishment** n

ember n piece of wood or coal in a dying fire glowing cinder

embezzle vt misuse or misappropriate (money in one s care) defraud **embezzlement** n **embezzler** n

embitter vt cause to feel bitterness or rancour

emblem n sign or symbol representing an idea principle etc **emblematic** adj

embody vt 1 represent in physical form 2 include comprise **embodiment** n person or thing representing a quality etc personification

emboss vt impress (a raised design lettering etc) on (a surface)

embrace n clasp hug vt vi hug as to show affection or welcome vt 1 take up (a religion etc) adopt 2 include cover

embroider vt vi sew (a pattern) on to (fabric) using coloured silks and fancy stitches vt add untrue details to **embroidery** n

embryo n 1 unborn young of animals during early stages of development 2 early stage of development **embryonic** adj

emerald n bright green precious stone n adj bright green

emerge vi 1 come into view as from concealment appear 2 become revealed or known **emergence** n **emergent** adj beginning to develop

emergency n unforeseen and dangerous situation requiring immediate action crisis

emigrate vi leave a country to live permanently in another **emigrant** n,adj **emigration** n

eminent adj 1 famous and respected; distinguished; high; exalted 2 outstanding or obvious **eminence** or **eminency** n **eminently** adv

emit vt (-tt-) give forth; make (sounds, etc) **emission** n

emotion n feeling, esp strong feeling; anger, hate, love, etc **emotional** adj given to strong or changeable emotion **emotionally** adv **emotive** adj arousing emotion; provocative

empathy n ability to imagine and share the feelings of another person

emperor n ruler of an empire

emphasis n 1 calling of special attention to an important fact etc ; stress 2 accent on a particular or important word phrase in music etc **emphasize** vt represent as important; give emphasis to; lay stress on; **emphatic** adj 1 stressed; accented 2 sure; decided **emphatically** adv

empire n group of territories or countries ruled by one person or government

empirical adj based on experience or experiment; not theoretical **empirically** adv

employ vt 1 hire (a person) to work for money, provide work for 2 make use of 3 occupy, use **employment** n **employee** n person hired to work for money **employer** n person firm, etc , employing people

empower vt invest with the power (to); authorize

empress n 1 female ruler of an empire 2 wife or widow of an emperor

empty adj 1 containing nothing unoccupied 2 lacking significance or feeling meaningless, dull 3 lacking force or substantiation vt vi discharge, vacate leave empty, evacuate **emptiness** n **empty-handed** adj 1 carrying nothing 2 having won or gained nothing **empty-headed** adj not thinking deeply about important matters, silly

emu n large flightless Australian bird

emulate vt imitate (a person or thing admired or envied); try to equal **emulation** n

emulsion n 1 mixture in which one liquid is suspended in the form of tiny droplets in another 2 household paint consisting of an emulsion of oil paint in water 3 light-sensitive coating on photographic film or plates **emulsify** vt vi make into or become an emulsion

enable vt make able (to); make possible for (a person) to do something

enact vt 1 make into a law or statute 2 represent on or as if on a stage, perform **enactment** n

enamel n 1 opaque glossy substance applied by fusion to metal for protection or decoration 2 glossy paint 3 protective outer layer of the teeth vt (-ll-) coat or decorate with enamel

enchant vt 1 cast a magic spell on, charm 2 be delightful or fascinating to; bewitch **enchantment** n

encircle vt 1 make a circle round; surround 2 pass round (the waist etc)

enclose vt 1 place within a surround, wall etc shut in 2 put in an envelope for posting esp as an additional item **enclosure** n 1 act of enclosing or something enclosed 2 fencing off of land esp common land 3 area of a sports ground, etc reserved for spectators officials or others

encore interj call from an audience to a performer to repeat a piece of music etc or perform an additional item n song or item so performed

encounter vt 1 meet unexpectedly come across 2 be faced or confronted with n meeting or confrontation

encourage vt cause to feel more hopeful or confident **encouragement** n

encroach vi overstep the proper limits intrude on (another s property area of responsibility etc)

encumber vt 1 weigh down; be a burden to 2 hamper; impede **encumbrance** n

encyclopedia n reference book or books giving information on a wide range of topics or on one particular subject **encyclopedic** adj

end n 1 final or last part; furthest point 2 conclusion or completion 3 aim, object 4 death **at a loose end** having nothing to do **in the end** finally, at last ~ vi vt come or bring to an end; finish, conclude **endless** adj without end; never ceasing **endlessly** adv

endanger vt bring into danger put at risk

endeavour vt vi try hard (to do something); attempt n act of trying, attempt

endemic adj always present in a particular country or area

endorse vt 1 sign the back of (a cheque etc) 2 enter a motoring offence in (a driving licence) 3 support, uphold **endorsement** n

endow vt 1 give money or property to (a college, etc) 2 bestow (beauty, kindness, etc) upon; bless with **endowment** n

endure vi last; continue in existence vt tolerate; bear **endurance** n **endurable** adj bearable **enduring** adj longlasting

enemy n 1 person hostile to or hated by one; foe; opponent; antagonist 2 nation with which one is at war

energy n 1 capacity to do work 2 physical strength; vitality; force **energetic** adj **energetically** adv

enfold vt fold in; hold tightly; embrace

enforce vt 1 force (a law) to be carried out or obeyed 2 force; compel **enforcement** n

engage vt 1 hire; employ 2 promise; pledge esp to marry someone 3 occupy 4 begin fighting against; attack vt,vi (of gears, etc) lock in position; mesh **engagement** n 1 state of being engaged; act of engaging 2 appointment to meet; date 3 military encounter; battle

engine n 1 machine able to convert energy into mechanical work 2 railway locomotive 3 any mechanical apparatus or device **engineer** n 1 person skilled in a branch of engineering 2 someone in charge of engines, esp on a ship 3 planner or organizer vt 1 plan, supervise, or construct as an engineer 2 plan or arrange skilfully; contrive **engineering** n 1 practical application of scientific knowledge in the design, construction or management of machinery, roads bridges, buildings etc 2 planning or contrivance

engrave vt 1 cut (letters, designs etc) into a hard surface 2 print from an engraved and inked surface 3 make a deep impression on **engraver** n **engraving** n 1 print made from an engraved surface 2 engraved surface 3 art of engraving

engross vt occupy the attention of; absorb

engulf vt swallow up **engulfment** n

enhance vt raise in importance or prominence; heighten; intensify **enhancement** n

enigma n 1 puzzle; riddle 2 baffling or perplexing person situation etc **enigmatic** or **enigmatical** adj **enigmatically** adv

enjoy vt 1 take pleasure in 2 have the use or benefit of; possess **enjoy oneself** feel pleasure amusement, satisfaction etc **enjoyable** adj **enjoyment** n

enlarge vt vi make or become larger, increase in

size scope, extent, etc **enlarge on** or **upon** treat more fully **enlargement** n

enlighten vt impart knowledge or information to, esp to free from ignorance, superstition, etc **enlightenment** n

enlist vt,vi 1 enrol in some branch of the armed forces 2 secure or join in support of a person, cause, etc **enlistment** n

enmity n hatred between enemies; hostility; animosity

enormous adj very great; huge; gigantic **enormity** n **enormously** adv

enough adj adequate for the purpose; sufficient n adequate amount; sufficiency adv 1 sufficiently; adequately; tolerably 2 fully

enquire vt vi 1 ask questions or seek information (about) 2 inquire **enquiry** n 1 act of enquiring 2 question 3 inquiry

enrage vt fill with rage; anger

enrich vt 1 make wealthy or wealthier 2 make more splendid in appearance; adorn 3 increase the value or quality of

enrol v (-ll-) vt place (a name) or write the name of (a person) on a list register, etc vt,vi make or become a member enlist **enrolment** n

ensemble (aːnˈsɑ mbəl) n 1 collection of parts 2 group of performers 3 outfit; set of matching clothes and accessories

ensign n 1 flag of a nation, regiment, etc 2 badge or emblem of office

enslave vt make a slave of **enslavement** n

ensue vi come about or follow esp as a consequence

ensure vt 1 make sure or certain 2 make safe; secure

entail vi have as a consequence; inevitably involve **entailment** n

entangle vt 1 catch or snare in a mesh, net, etc 2 make tangled 3 involve in difficulties complications, etc **entanglement** n

enter vt,vi 1 come or go in(to) 2 penetrate, pierce 3 be or cause to be admitted (to) vt 1 put into; insert 2 become a member of 3 write down in a record, list, etc 4 begin upon **enter into** take part in; become a party to **enter upon** 1 begin; set out on 2 come into enjoyment or possession of

enterprise n 1 undertaking or project, esp an important one 2 boldness daring, or adventurousness; initiative 3 commercial undertaking; business

entertain vt,vi 1 divert, amuse, or interest 2

give hospitality (to); receive (guests) vt consider; cherish **entertainment** n

enthral vt (-ll-) captivate; enchant **enthralment** n

enthusiasm n intense interest, admiration, approval, etc.; zeal; fervour **enthusiast** n **enthusiastic** adj **enthusiastically** adv **enthuse** vi display enthusiasm

entice vt lure or attract by exciting hope of reward gratification etc.; tempt **enticement** n **enticingly** adv

entire adj 1 whole; complete; undivided; unbroken; intact **entirely** adv **entirety** n

entitle vt 1 give a particular title or name to 2 give a right, claim or legal title to **entitlement** n

entity n 1 something that has real existence; thing; object 2 being; existence

entrails pl n 1 internal organs of an animal, esp the intestines 2 internal parts of anything

entrance[1] ('entrans) n 1 act of entering 2 place of entry such as a doorway passage etc 3 admission 4 act or instance of an actor coming on stage

entrance[2] (en'trɑːns) vt delight; charm captivate; enthral

entreat vt vi beseech; implore; beg **entreaty** n

entrench vt 1 fortify or defend by digging trenches 2 establish firmly and securely **entrenchment** n

entrepreneur (ɑ ntrəprə'nɜː) n someone who sets up and organizes business enterprises

entrust vt give into the care of; trust with; invest or charge with a duty etc

entry n 1 act or instance of entering 2 place for entering, esp a passageway or hall entrance 3 access or admission 4 entering of an item in a record ledger, etc or the item entered 5 contestant in a race competition etc

entwine vt vi twist or tangle together; interweave (with)

enumerate vt 1 mention or specify one by one as in a list; itemize 2 count **enumeration** n

enunciate vt vi say or pronounce (a word or words) vt state declare or proclaim, esp clearly and carefully **enunciation** n

envelop (en'veləp) vt 1 wrap or cover up 2 surround, enclose or engulf 3 obscure; conceal **envelopment** n

envelope ('envələup) n 1 covering or container for a letter 2 any enclosing structure, etc

environment n all the external influences surroundings, conditions etc.; immediately affecting a person or other organism **environmental** adj

envisage vt contemplate as actual or real; visualize

envoy n 1 diplomatic representative ranking just below an ambassador 2 any messenger or agent

envy n 1 feeling of discontent caused by the possessions, status etc., of someone else 2 desire to have or enjoy an advantage possession, etc., of another 3 object of such feelings vt view with envy **enviable** adj **envious** adj **enviously** n

enzyme n any of numerous organic substances that are produced in living cells and act as catalysts for biochemical changes

epaulet n also **epaulette** decorative shoulder piece, esp as worn on military uniforms

ephemeral adj lasting only for a short time; transitory; fleeting

epic n 1 long narrative poem in formalized style relating the exploits of a hero or heroes 2 film novel, etc resembling this in style or content

epidemic adj spreading rapidly among people in a certain area n widespread occurrence of a disease etc

epilepsy n disorder of the nervous system characterized by convulsions and usually, loss of consciousness **epileptic** adj n

epilogue n 1 speech made to an audience at the end of a play by one of the actors 2 concluding part of a novel television or radio broadcast etc

episcopal adj 1 of or relating to a bishop 2 governed by bishops

episode n 1 incident or occurrence in the course of a series of events 2 digression in a narrative piece of music etc 3 instalment of a book play, etc serialized on television or radio **episodic** adj

epitaph n 1 inscription on a tomb or other monument 2 anything serving as a memorial

epitome (ɪ'pɪtəmɪ) n 1 summary, abstract 2 representative or typical characteristic **epitomize** vt 1 summarize; abstract 2 typify

epoch n 1 period of time esp one considered as distinctive; era 2 beginning of an important era in the history of anything

equable adj 1 uniform or steady in effect,

operation, motion, etc ; unvarying **2** tranquil;
even; serene

equal adj **1** as great as another in extent, size.
degree, etc ; equivalent **2** having the same
rank, value, quality, etc . as another **3** evenly
proportioned **4** uniform; equable **5** adequate
in quantity, powers, ability, etc **6** smooth;
even; level *n* someone or something equal to
another *vt* (-ll-) be equal to or the same
as **equality** *n* **equalize** *vt* make equal *vi*
reach a score equal to an opponent's

equate *vt* **1** treat or regard as equal or
equivalent **2** put in the form of an equation
equation *n* **1** mathematical expression of the
equality of two quantities **2** representation in
symbols of a chemical reaction

equator *n* circle round the earth dividing the
Northern hemisphere from the Southern
hemisphere **equatorial** adj

equestrian adj **1** of or relating to horses,
horsemen, or the skill of riding **2** on horseback *n* rider on horseback, esp an entertainer
or competitor

equilateral adj having all sides equal

equilibrium *n* **1** state of poise or balance
prevailing when equal and opposing forces,
influences, etc . counter each other in effect **2**
mental composure or stability

equinox *n* either of the two dates in the year, at
the beginning of spring and autumn, when
day and night are of equal length

equip *vt* (-pp-) provide with necessary equipment, skills, etc **equipment** *n* **1** equipping or
being equipped **2** collection of tools,
implements, resources etc necessary for a
task or undertaking

equity *n* **1** fairness; impartiality **2** system of law
co-existing with and supplementing Common
Law **3** total ordinary shares of a limited
company **equitable** adj

equivalent adj **1** equal in value, significance
force, etc **2** corresponding in meaning.
function, etc *n* something equivalent
equivalence *n*

equivocal adj **1** uncertain; ambivalent **2**
ambiguous; debatable

era *n* **1** period of time with its own distinctive
flavour trends characteristics etc ; age:
epoch **2** system of dating from a particular
event, etc in the past

eradicate *vt* wipe out; destroy; obliterate
eradication *n*

erase *vt* **1** rub or scratch out (something
written) **2** remove all trace of; wipe out
eraser *n*

erect adj **1** upright; vertical **2** raised or directed
upwards **3** stiff or firm *vt* **1** build, construct
or elevate **2** set up; establish **erection** *n*

ermine *n* **1** stoat with a brown summer coat and
white winter fur **2** white fur of the animal
used to trim judges' robes, etc **3** rank or
functions of a judge

erode *vt* wear or eat away by gradual action
erosion *n*

erotic adj of, relating to, or exciting sexual
desire **eroticism** *n*

err *vi* **1** be mistaken; make an error **2** deviate
from a moral code; sin

errand *n* short task entrusted to someone, esp a
short journey to deliver or fetch something

erratic adj **1** irregular; random **2** irresponsible
unpredictable

error *n* **1** something incorrect; mistake **2** sin

erudite adj learned; having great knowledge or
wisdom **erudition** *n*

erupt *vi* **1** (of a volcano) emit lava, etc **2** burst
out; emit suddenly **eruption** *n*

escalate *vt,vi* increase by stages or in intensity
escalator *n* moving staircase consisting of
steps in an endless belt

escape *vt,vi* **1** free oneself from; get away
(from) **2** avoid (harm, punishment, etc) *vi*
become free; leak out *vt* be forgotten by;
elude *n* **1** act of escaping or means by which
this occurs **2** sport, pastime or other release
from pressure or reality **escapism** *n*
avoidance of unpleasant reality by fantasy
etc **escapist** adj,n

escort *n* ('eskɔ:t) **1** person or group acting as
guard or protection for others on a journey **2**
man accompanying a woman to a social
function *vt* (e'skɔ:t) accompany as an escort

esoteric adj **1** restricted to a specialized group
2 difficult to understand; obscure in meaning

especial adj **1** outstanding; notable; special **2**
particular **especially** adv

espionage *n* spying; obtaining secret infor
mation

esplanade *n* wide level road or walk, esp one
constructed along the shore

essay *n* **1** ('esei) short prose composition **2**
(e'sei) attempt; try; test *vt vi* (e'sei) attempt
try; test

essence *n* **1** characteristic fundamental feature

or nature of something **2** oil or other constituent of a plant, extracted as a perfume, flavouring, etc **essential** adj **1** highly important; indispensable; necessary **2** constituting the essence; fundamental **3** absolute; perfect n something that is essential

establish vt **1** make secure or permanent **2** found; bring about **3** set up in a position, business, etc **4** cause to be accepted **establishment** n **1** act or an instance of establishing something **2** permanent large business or government organization **3** institution **4** small business premises, club, hotel, etc **5** large private household **the Establishment** n group of people and institutions thought of as holding the power in a country

estate n **1** country property with extensive land **2** new building development, for housing or light industry **3** person s collective assets and liabilities **4** position in society; social standing **estate agent** n person whose business is the management, lease, and sale of houses and land **estate car** n car with a long body and rear doors, designed to carry goods as well as passengers

esteem vt **1** think highly of; respect **2** consider; regard n judgment or opinion, esp a favourable one

estimable adj **1** deserving respect; worthy **2** able to be estimated; calculable

estimate vt ('estimeit) **1** calculate roughly; gauge n ('estimət) **1** approximation **2** judgment **estimation** n **1** act or result of estimating **2** regard; esteem

estuary n tidal mouth of a river

etch vt **1** produce (a design, picture, etc) on a metal plate by cutting into a wax coating and removing exposed metal with acid **2** eat away by chemical action **etching** n etched plate or a print made from this

eternity n **1** endless time **2** time after death **eternal** adj **1** lasting for ever; timeless; without end **2** continual; incessant **eternally** adv

ether ('i:θə) n **1** volatile highly flammable liquid formerly used as an anaesthetic **2** hypothetical weightless substance once thought to permeate all space **ethereal** (i'θiəriəl) adj **1** light and airy **2** spiritual; heavenly

ethics n **1** s branch of philosophy concerned with moral conduct, right and wrong, etc **2** pl

moral principles; rules or standards of conduct **ethical** adj **ethically** adv

ethnic adj **1** relating to a group of people of a particular culture, religion, language, etc **2** relating to the racial classification of man

etiquette n customs and rules determining good behaviour; manners

etymology n study of the derivation of words and changes in their meaning and form **etymological** adj **etymologist** n

eucalyptus n tree native to Australasia yielding an aromatic oil, which is used medicinally

Eucharist n **1** Christian sacrament of communion, commemorating the Last Supper **2** consecrated bread or wine offered at communion

eunuch n male who has been castrated

euphemism n **1** socially acceptable word or phrase used in place of one considered offensive or impolite **2** practice of using euphemisms **euphemistic** adj

euphoria n feeling of bliss or elation **euphoric** adj

euthanasia n act of killing a person, esp one experiencing intense pain or suffering; mercy killing

evacuate vi,vt leave or remove from (an unsafe place) vt empty; discharge; vacate **evacuation** n

evade vt avoid; escape; elude

evaluate vt **1** determine the quantity or worth of **2** judge critically; appraise **evaluation** n

evangelist n preacher, esp one not attached to a particular church **Evangelist** any one of the four writers of the Gospels **evangelical** adj **1** relating to the Gospels **2** relating to certain Protestant groups that stress the importance of personal religious experiences and missionary work

evaporate vt,vi **1** change from a solid or liquid state to a vapour **2** lose or cause to lose some liquid, leaving a concentrated residue **3** disappear; vanish **evaporation** n

eve n **1** evening or day before a holiday, festival, etc **2** period immediately preceding an event

even adj **1** level; flat; plane **2** uniform; regular **3** calm; placid **4** equally balanced; fair **5** (of numbers) divisible by two **6** exact adv **1** still; yet **2** used to emphasize comparative forms **3** used when the content of a phrase or sentence is unexpected **4** used to modify a statement or add precision to it vt,vi make or become even;

balance **evenly** adv **even-tempered** adj calm; not easily upset or angered

evening n 1 latter part of the day or early night 2 concluding or final period

event n 1 anything that takes place; occurrence 2 outcome; result 3 sports contest

eventual adj final; ultimate; last **eventually** adv

ever adv 1 at any time 2 by any possibility 3 always **evergreen** adj (of trees, shrubs, etc) having foliage that remains green throughout the year n evergreen tree or shrub **everlasting** adj 1 endless; unending 2 perpetual; of long duration **evermore** adv always; forever; constantly

every adj 1 each 2 all possible **every other** every second or alternate **everybody** pron each person; everyone **everyday** adj 1 daily 2 commonplace; ordinary 3 suitable for normal days; not special **everyone** pron each person; everybody **everything** pron 1 each thing, aspect, factor, etc 2 a great deal; something very important **everywhere** adv towards or in all places, parts, etc

evict vt eject or expel (a person) from a house, building, etc **eviction** n

evidence n proof; ground for belief **evident** adj apparent; obvious; plain **evidently** adv

evil adj 1 wicked; sinful 2 harmful; malicious 3 offensive; vile n wickedness; sin; depravity

evoke vt 1 summon; call forth 2 excite; provoke **evocation** n

evolution n 1 natural process of very gradual continuous change in all plants and animals 2 development; unfolding **evolutionary** adj

evolve vt,vi develop; unroll vi undergo evolution

ewe n female sheep

exacerbate vt 1 aggravate; heighten 2 exasperate; irritate; provoke **exacerbation** n

exact adj 1 completely correct 2 precise 3 very same; particular 4 rigorous; strict vt 1 extort 2 demand; require authoritatively **exactly** adv

exaggerate vt,vi represent (something) as being greater or more than it really is vt make more noticeable **exaggeration** n

exalt vt 1 raise, elevate 2 praise **exaltation** n

examine vt 1 inspect; observe 2 investigate; study 3 test (a person's skill, knowledge, etc) **examiner** n **examination** n 1 act of being examined 2 questions or tasks intended to test skill or knowledge 3 medical inspection of the body

example n 1 specimen; sample 2 someone or something worthy of emulation 3 precedent

exasperate vt irritate; provoke; incense **exasperation** n

excavate vt,vi 1 dig out 2 hollow out 3 expose (buried objects) by digging **excavation** n **excavator** n machine for digging and moving soil, gravel, etc

exceed vt,vi be greater than (another) vt overstep the limit of **exceedingly** adv very; greatly

excel v (-ll-) vt,vi surpass; be superior to vi do extremely well (in)

excellency n term of address used for ambassadors, governors, high-ranking government officials, etc

excellent adj of the best quality; thoroughly good and praiseworthy **excellence** n

except prep with the exception of; save vt exclude; omit **exception** n 1 act of being excepted 2 instance to be excepted; unusual situation, person, thing, etc **exceptional** adj 1 relating to an exception; irregular 2 having higher than average intelligence, skill, talent, etc **exceptionally** adv

excerpt n selected passage from a book; extract

excess n (ek'ses) 1 surplus 2 amount, degree, etc , by which something is exceeded by another adj ('ekses) over and above what is normal, necessary, or required **excessive** adj **excessively** adv

exchange vt 1 barter; trade for something 2 interchange; trade (information) 3 replace; substitute n 1 act of exchanging 2 anything that substitutes for or replaces something offered 3 argument 4 central office or station 5 place where brokers, dealers, etc , buy and sell securities and certain commodities

exchequer n 1 department of the treasury dealing with accounting 2 treasury or government department of a country, state, etc , controlling financial matters

excise n ('eksaiz) 1 tax levied on certain commodities or for certain licences 2 branch of the civil service responsible for collecting such taxes vt (ek'saiz) impose excise on; tax; levy

excite vt 1 arouse; awaken; provoke 2 stir up;

instigate **3** disturb; agitate **excitable** adj
excitement n

exclaim vt cry out; shout **exclamation** n **1** act
of exclaiming; outcry **2** interjection; emphatic
word, phrase, or sentence **exclamation
mark** n punctuation mark (!) used after an
exclamation

exclude vt **1** keep out; bar **2** deny inclusion or
consideration of **exclusion** n **exclusive** adj
1 barring or excluding everything else **2** sole;
not shared; individual **3** fashionable; select
exclusively adv

excommunicate vt bar (someone) from church
membership or receiving certain sacraments
excommunication n

excrete vt (of an animal) discharge (waste,
such as urine, sweat, etc) from the body
excrement n waste matter, esp solid,
discharged from the body **excreta** pl n waste
matter discharged from the body

excruciating adj agonizing; tortuous; intensely
painful

excursion n **1** short journey, pleasure trip, or
outing **2** group or party taking an excursion

excuse vt (ik'skju:z) **1** pardon; forgive **2** justify
or make allowances for **3** exempt or release
(from) n (ik'skju:s) **1** justification; reason **2**
explanation offered to explain bad behaviour,
rudeness, etc **3** pretext; pretence **excusable**
adj

execute vt **1** kill, esp following a legal decision;
put to death **2** perform; achieve; carry out **3**
administer; enforce **execution** n **executive**
adj relating to administration, the execution of
a duty, etc n person or group running or
administrating a company, project, etc
executor (ig'zekjutə) n person who carries out
a duty, esp someone responsible for dealing
with the provisions of a will

exempt vt release or excuse from a duty,
obligation, etc adj released from a duty,
obligation, etc **exemption** n

exercise n **1** physical exertion, esp for the
purpose of training or to maintain health **2**
task undertaken to improve one's skill or
competence **3** operation or use of one's
power, right, etc vt, vi give exercise to or take
exercise vt **1** use; employ **2** put into action;
carry out **3** exert; wield

exert vt use the power of (strength, influence,
etc); exercise **exert oneself** make an effort;
strive **exertion** n

exhale vi, vt breathe out; force (air) out of the
lungs **exhalation** n

exhaust vt **1** drain; empty; consume completely
2 use, discuss, etc , to the full n **1** gases that
are expelled from an engine as waste **2**
expulsion of such gases **exhaustion** n **exhaustive** adj **exhaustively** adv

exhibit vt **1** present for viewing or inspection **2**
indicate; disclose; demonstrate n something
presented for public viewing **exhibitor**
n **exhibition** n **1** act of exhibiting **2** public
show or display **exhibitionism** n practice of
or tendency towards showing off or drawing
undue attention to oneself in public
exhibitionist adj, n

exhilarate vt enliven, animate; stimulate
exhilaration n

exhume vt dig up (a corpse) after burial

exile n **1** banishment; ostracism **2** banished
person; outcast vt banish; expel (from a
country)

exist vi **1** be; have reality **2** endure; continue **3**
be present in a particular place or situation
existence n life; state of being **existent** adj

exit n **1** way out **2** departure; withdrawal vi go
out or away; depart

exonerate vt **1** absolve; acquit **2** release;
exempt **exoneration** n

exorbitant adj excessive; extravagant; enormous **exorbitantly** adv

exorcize vt deliver from evil spirits, demons,
etc **exorcism** n **exorcist** n

exotic adj unusual; foreign; not native

expand vt, vi **1** make or become greater in size,
range, scope, etc **2** swell; fill out; extend **3**
develop (a theme, story, etc) **expansion**
n **expansive** adj **expanse** n continuous
surface that extends or spreads; stretch

expatriate vt (eks'peitrieit) **1** banish; exile **2**
move (oneself) away from one's own country
adj (eks'peitriit) **expatriated** n (eks'peitriit)
expatriated person **expatriation** n

expect vt **1** consider as probable **2** await; look
forward to **3** rely on; require; want vt, vi be
pregnant (with) vi suppose; anticipate
expectant adj **expectation** n **1** act of
expecting **2** goal; aim; hope **3** something
expected or anticipated

expedient adj **1** proper; suitable **2** advantageous; profitable **expediency** n

expedition n **1** organized journey for exploration, hunting, etc **2** group or party on such a journey

expel vt (-ll-) eject; drive out; ban

expend vt use up; spend; consume **expenditure** n money spent; outgoings

expense n **1** cost; charge; outlay **2** something costing a great deal **expensive** adj costly; high-priced; dear

experience n **1** direct personal observation, knowledge practice, etc **2** specific situation that one has undergone **3** process of gaining knowledge, esp when not through study **4** acquired knowledge vt **1** undergo; encounter **2** feel; be moved by **experienced** adj fully trained or qualified; expert

experiment n **1** trial test or examination to discover something by observation **2** original or new attempt vi perform an experiment **experimental** adj **experimentation** n **experimenter** n

expert n person having great knowledge experience skill, etc in a particular subject adj **1** relating to an expert **2** knowledgeable; specialist; skilled **expertise** n specialist skill or knowledge

expiate vt atone for; redeem **expiation** n

expire vi **1** end; terminate; conclude **2** exhale **3** die **expiry** n termination lapsing; end

explain vt vi **1** make clear or understandable **2** interpret; expound **3** account for; justify **explanation** n **explanatory** adj **explicable** adj

expletive n exclamation; swearword or curse

explicit adj **1** clear precise; definite **2** open; unreserved **explicitly** adv

explode vt vi **1** burst, blow up **2** destroy or be destroyed by bursting vi suddenly or violently display anger, rage etc **explosion** n **1** act of exploding **2** any rapid or very large increase as in population **explosive** adj **1** characterized by or capable of explosion **2** potentially violent turbulent or dangerous n substance or device capable of exploding **explosively** adv

exploit n ('eksplɔit) heroic act deed or feat vt (ik'splɔit) **1** take unjust advantage of **2** utilize fully **exploitation** n **exploitative** adj

explore vt investigate thoroughly and methodically vt,vi go to or into (distant lands, areas, etc) to investigate **exploration** n **explorer** n

exponent n person or thing that functions as an example, representation, or symbol

export vt,vi **1** sell or send (goods) out of a country for foreign sale n ('ekspɔːt) commodity sold or sent to a foreign country **exporter** n

expose vt **1** uncover; disclose, lay open **2** subject; make liable **3** make familiar with **4** subject (camera films, etc) to light **exposure** n **1** act of exposing **2** direction in which the main wall of a house or building faces **3** frame of photographic film that has been exposed to light

expound vt explain in detail

express vt **1** utter; verbalize; speak **2** represent or symbolize as in a painting piece of music, etc adj **1** clear; plain; definite **2** special, particular n train, bus etc stopping only at major stations **expression** n **1** verbal communication **2** manifestation, representation **3** saying; phrase; term **4** look on the face that expresses a particular emotion **expressionless** adj **expressive** adj conveying emotion **expressly** adv particularly; especially; explicitly

exquisite adj delicate, refined; excellent, rare **exquisitely** adv

extend vt,vi **1** stretch;' reach out; spread **2** prolong or last (for) vt **1** offer; give **2** expand, broaden **extension** n **1** act of extending **2** additional room(s) built on to a house etc **3** additional telephone apparatus connected to a central switchboard or having the same number as another **4** delay or additional period **extensive** adj **1** wide large **2** comprehensive; far-reaching **extensively** adv **extent** n degree to which something extends range; scope

exterior n outside; outward appearance adj outer, outside external

exterminate vt annihilate, destroy or kill **extermination** n

external adj **1** situated at or coming from the outside; outer **2** foreign; alien **3** (of medicines etc) not to be taken internally **externally** adv

extinct adj **1** (of plants, animals, etc) no longer existing **2** obsolete; out-of-date **3** (of volcanoes) inactive; incapable of further eruption **extinction** n

extinguish vt **1** put out or suppress (fire, lights, etc) **2** destroy completely **extinguisher** n

extort vt obtain by force or threats **extortion** n

extra adj additional; supplementary n 1 something additional 2 special edition of a newspaper 3 actor taking part in crowd scenes, etc

extract vt (ik'strækt) 1 draw or pull out; remove 2 derive or develop (an idea, theory, etc) 3 select (from a written work) n ('ekstrækt) 1 quotation; excerpt 2 essence; vital principle or substance **extraction** n

extramural adj related to but not under direct control of an academic institution

extraneous (ik'streiniəs) adj not strictly necessary or central; external; extra

extraordinary adj remarkable; unusual; amazing **extraordinarily** adv

extravagant adj 1 wasteful 2 free or generous 3 excessive; inordinate; exorbitant 3 ornate; fussy **extravagance** n **extravagantly** adv

extreme adj 1 greatest; highest; most intense 2 immoderate; unreasonable 3 drastic; radical 4 most distant or remote; utmost n 1 highest or greatest degree 2 upper or lower limit of a scale, range, etc **extremely** adv **extremity** n 1 utmost or farthest point or degree 2 end part of a limb; hand or finger or foot or toe

extricate vt disengage; clear; set free (from) **extrication** n

extrovert n gregarious outgoing person adj also **extroverted** gregarious; outgoing; not shy

exuberant adj 1 joyful; vigorous; lively 2 lavish; prolific; abundant **exuberance** n **exuberantly** adv

exude vt,vi emit, ooze; gush

eye n 1 organ of sight 2 also **eyesight** sight; vision 3 gaze; look; glance 4 ability to inspect, judge, or observe 5 aperture in a camera, etc through which light can pass 6 small hole in a needle, etc 7 calm centre of a hurricane, tornado etc 8 bud on a potato, etc vt inspect carefully; scrutinize **eyeball** n round ball-shaped part of the eye **eyebrow** n 1 fringe of hair growing on the ridge above the eye 2 ridge above the eye; brow **eye-catching** adj stunning; attracting attention **eyelash** n short hair growing out of the edge of the eyelid **eyelid** n fold of skin that can be closed over the eyeball **eye-opener** n revelation; startling occurrence **eye shadow** n cosmetic applied to colour the eyelids and

draw attention to the eyes **eyesore** n extremely ugly or offending building, object, etc **eyestrain** n fatigue and tiredness of the eye **eye-witness** n someone who has been present at and has observed a particular event

F

fable n 1 tale with a moral, whose characters are often animals 2 fictional story or account

fabric n 1 woven or knitted cloth 2 structure or basis, as of society, personality, etc **fabricate** vt 1 manufacture or construct, esp by putting together components 2 invent; give a false account of **fabrication** n

fabulous adj 1 wonderful; marvellous 2 almost impossible; unbelievable 3 mythical **fabulously** adv

facade (fa'sa:d) n 1 front of a building, esp when considered for its artistic merit 2 image that a person presents, esp when misleading

face n 1 front part of the head, including the mouth, nose, eyes, etc 2 particular expression of the face 3 outward attitude or pose, as of self-confidence 4 any outward appearance 5 most prominent or front part, as of a cliff, building, etc 6 dial of a clock or watch 7 flat surface of something, such as a coin, crystal, etc **save/lose face** maintain/lose one s dignity or prestige ~vt,vi position or be positioned to point in a particular direction vt 1 come into contact with; meet 2 confront; challenge 3 apply to or cover (a surface) **face up to** accept and deal with realistically **faceless** adj anonymous **facelift** n 1 surgical operation to tighten the skin on the face and improve the appearance 2 any improvement in appearance, as by decoration; renovation **facepack** n cream or paste applied to the face to improve the skin **face value** n 1 stated monetary value 2 apparent value or meaning of something **facial** adj relating to the face n cosmetic treatment for the face

facet n 1 flat surface of a polished gem 2 aspect of a situation, subject, or personality

facetious (fa'si:ʃəs) adj meant or attempting to be amusing, sometimes inappropriately **facetiously** adv

facile adj 1 easy; simple 2 glib; superficial; too easy

facility n 1 ease or skill 2 equipment or means

enabling execution of an action **facilitate** vt make easier or simpler

facsimile (fæk'simili) n exact copy; reproduction

fact n something that actually happened, existed, or exists; provable statement **in fact** or **as a matter of fact** really; truly **factual** adj true or truthful; actual

faction n dissenting group within a larger group

factor n 1 something that contributes towards a result 2 number that can be divided into another number evenly

factory n building equipped with manufacturing machinery

faculty n 1 ability or power, as the senses, etc 2 department of a university or its staff

fade vt, vi make or become pale, less clear, etc **fade out** disappear gradually

fag n 1 difficult chore 2 sl cigarette vt, vi (-gg-) also **fag out** make or become tired through arduous work; exhaust

Fahrenheit adj relating to a temperature scale on which the freezing point of water is 32° and its boiling point 212°

fail vi, vt have no success (at) vi 1 become inoperative; break down 2 be inadequate or insufficient 3 omit; forget vt 1 judge to have failed 2 disappoint; let down n instance of failing **without fail** certainly; definitely **failing** n inadequacy; fault **failure** n person or thing that fails

faint adj 1 lacking in clarity, contrast, etc 2 without conviction; weak; feeble 3 feeling as though one is going to lose consciousness 4 cowardly; timid vi lose consciousness for a short time n short period of loss of consciousness **faint-hearted** adj cowardly; timid

fair¹ adj 1 impartial; just; without bias 2 conforming to regulations 3 (of a person) having light colouring 4 beautiful or unblemished 5 acceptable; good 6 sunny; cloudless **fair and square** legitimate; correct **fairness** n fairly adv 1 moderately; rather 2 justly; deservedly **fair-minded** adj just; impartial

fair² n 1 event, usually out of doors, with various entertainments and sideshows 2 cattle market 3 gathering of people dealing in similar products for trade purposes **fairground** n place where a fair is held

fairy n imaginary being having small human

form and supernatural or magical powers **fairytale** n a story containing imaginary or supernatural characters, usually intended for children

faith n 1 belief; trust 2 any religion **faithful** adj 1 loyal; true 2 remaining close to the original **faithfully** adv **faith-healing** n healing by means of supernatural or religious powers

fake vt, vi forge; pretend n counterfeit; forgery adj not real; counterfeit

falcon n bird of prey, which is sometimes trained for sport

fall vi (fell; fallen) 1 descend quickly; drop 2 collapse from an upright position 3 decrease; decline 4 diminish in tone 5 extend towards a lower level; hang down 6 be defeated or overthrown; submit 7 pass into sleep or a similar condition 8 occur at a specified time 9 be transferred 10 be classified into **fall back on** have recourse to for support **fall for** inf 1 be deceived by 2 develop a deep affection for **fall in with** 1 become acquainted with 2 agree to **fall on one's feet** emerge successfully from a precarious situation **fall out** quarrel; disagree ~n 1 act or instance of falling or dropping 2 lowering; decline 3 distance over or through which something falls 4 capture or decline of a city, civilization, etc **falls** pl n waterfall; cataract **fallout** n descent of particles of radioactive substances, which contaminate the air after a nuclear explosion

fallacy n incorrect opinion or belief; deceptive notion **fallacious** adj

fallible adj 1 liable to make mistakes or be deceived 2 likely to contain errors

fallow adj (of land) left uncultivated for one or more seasons

false adj 1 untrue; incorrect 2 unfaithful; given to deceit 3 synthetic; not genuine; artificial **falsehood** n lie or fallacy **false pretences** pl n forgeries and misrepresentations for illegally obtaining money, property, etc **falsify** vt 1 make false or incorrect, esp to mislead 2 prove incorrect; disprove

falsetto n male voice pitched within a range that is higher than normal adj, adv using such a voice

falter vi hesitate; waver; stumble vt say with hesitation; stammer

fame n state of being well known; reputation **famed** adj acknowledged; recognized

familiar adj 1 well-known or easily recognizable 2 often used or frequented; customary **familiar with** well acquainted with **familiarize** vt make knowledgeable about a subject, place, etc

family n 1 group consisting of parents and their children 2 group of related people 3 any interrelated group of things

famine n widespread shortage of food, esp because of drought or crop failure

famished adj extremely hungry; starved

famous adj 1 well-known; celebrated 2 inf fantastic; splendid

fan[1] n 1 device for causing a flow of air for cooling, such as a folding wedge-shaped device held in the hand 2 anything shaped like a fan vt,vi (-nn-) 1 cool by means of a fan 2 also **fan out** spread or move in the shape of a fan; separate

fan[2] n enthusiastic admirer of a pop star, actor, etc

fanatic n 1 person with extreme and irrational dedication to a cause 2 inf person dedicated to a particular pastime **fanatical** adj

fancy adj 1 elaborate, decorated, or ornamental 2 high in quality 3 coming from the imagination n 1 whim; pleasure 2 poetic imagery vt 1 imagine; picture in the mind 2 like; be attracted to **fancy dress** n costume worn for a masquerade **fanciful** adj 1 not factual; imaginary 2 produced creatively or imaginatively

fanfare n short musical piece played on trumpets

fang n long pointed tooth, as of a snake or dog

fantasy n 1 unrestrained imagination 2 something imagined, esp when bizarre 3 imagined sequence that fulfils some unsatisfied need; daydream 4 hallucination 5 notion that is not based on fact **fantastic** adj 1 strange or eccentric in design, appearance, etc 2 exaggerated or incredible 3 inf very large or great 4 inf fabulous; splendid

far adv 1 at, to, or from a long way or great distance 2 at or to a distant time 3 very much **as far as** to the point that **by far** by a great deal **far and near** or **far and wide** everywhere; over a great distance or area **far gone** 1 in an advanced condition 2 mad; crazy 3 inf drunk **far out** sl strange; unconventional **in so far as** to the extent that ~adj 1 long way away 2 extending or protruding a great distance 3 remote; isolated **far-away** adj 1 distant; removed 2 preoccupied; daydreaming **far-fetched** adj improbable; exaggerated **far-off** adj distant; remote **far-reaching** adj having extensive effects or importance

farce n 1 form of drama in which characters, plot, etc, are presented as highly comical or ridiculous 2 absurdly silly event or situation **farcical** adj

fare n 1 amount of money paid for a journey, etc 2 menu; type of food

farewell interj,n goodbye

farinaceous adj made of or containing flour or grain

farm n tract of land, with buildings, used for the rearing of livestock or cultivation of crops vi,vt rear livestock or cultivate (land) for a living **farm out** distribute **farmer** n **farmyard** n enclosed area adjacent to farm buildings

farther adv 1 to or at a distant place or time; further 2 in addition (to) **farthest** adv to or at the most distant place or time; furthest adj most remote in place or time

fascinate vt make curious or interested; captivate **fascination** n

fascism n ideology or government that is authoritarian and undemocratic **fascist** adj,n

fashion n 1 style of dress, makeup, etc 2 custom; behaviour 3 kind; type vt make or form **fashionable** adj relating to a current trend, style, or fashion

fast[1] adj 1 moving or able to move rapidly; quick 2 lasting only a short period 3 (of a timepiece) indicating a more advanced time than is accurate 4 promiscuous 5 retaining colour; not prone to fading adv 1 quickly; rapidly; swiftly 2 securely; tightly 3 soundly

fast[2] vi abstain from food, esp for religious reasons or as a protest n also **fasting** abstinence from food

fasten vt,vi attach; secure; tie

fastidious adj difficult to please; fussy

fat n 1 greasy semi-solid chemical substance 2 animal tissue containing such substances adj 1 overweight; obese 2 containing fat 3 thick 4 rewarding or promising **fatten** vt,vi make or become fat(ter) **fatty** adj

fatal adj 1 leading to death 2 disastrous, tragic **fatality** n 1 accident that has resulted in death 2 person so killed 3 condition causing death

fate n 1 force or power that determines events 2 fortune; destiny **fated** adj determined by fate **fateful** adj awful; dreadful

father n 1 male parent 2 person who has founded a field of study, movement, etc vt be the father (of) **father-in-law** n, pl **fathers-in-law** father of one's husband or wife

fatherland n person's native country or that of his ancestors

fathom n unit used to measure depth of water, equal to 6 feet vt 1 measure the depth of (water) 2 probe into (a problem, situation etc) and discover its meaning

fatigue n 1 tiredness; weariness 2 strain, esp in fibres, metals etc vt make tired or weak

fatuous adj silly; foolish

fault n 1 flaw; defect 2 mistake 3 misdemeanour; wrong 4 accountability for a mistake or error **at fault** to blame **find fault** criticize; find a mistake in **to a fault** excessively ~vt find a mistake in **faulty** adj

fauna n, pl **faunas** or **faunae** ('fɔːniː) all animal life of a particular time or region

favour n 1 kind gesture of good will 2 good will 3 partiality 4 token or gift **in favour of** 1 commending 2 to the advantage of vt 1 prefer 2 advocate or endorse **favourable** adj advantageous; encouraging **favourably** adv **favourite** adj given preference to over others; best liked n someone or something regarded preferentially

fawn[1] n young deer adj,n greyish or yellowish brown

fawn[2] vi seek attention or favour servilely

fear n 1 feeling of alarm or terror 2 something causing this 3 reverence 4 anxiety, apprehension **for fear of** so as to avoid ~vt,vi feel fear (of) **fearless** adj **fearful** adj 1 afraid 2 inf very great

feasible adj 1 able to be done 2 suitable or likely **feasibility** n

feast n 1 lavish meal; banquet 2 periodic religious celebration 3 something lavishly pleasing vi 1 eat at a feast 2 take extreme pleasure in vt 1 provide with a feast 2 please; delight

feat n deed or action esp when noteworthy

feather n one of the external structures that form a bird's outer covering vt cover or fill with feathers **feathery** adj

featherweight n 1 boxer of a weight under 126 lbs 2 something extremely lightweight or of little consequence

feature n 1 part of the face such as mouth, eyes, etc 2 characteristic or quality 3 full-length cinema film 4 particular article in a periodical vt 1 distinctive characteristic of vt offer as or make a feature; give main importance to

February n second month of the year

feckless adj weak; ineffectual

federal adj 1 relating to a league of nations or states 2 relating to a system of government in which states retain a degree of autonomy under a central government **federally** adv **federate** vi vt join in a federation or league **federation** n

fee n amount of money due for a service; right of entrance, etc

feeble adj 1 weak or exhausted, either physically or mentally 2 deficient in strength or force **feeble-minded** adj lacking in intelligence

feed v (fed) vt 1 offer food or other essential materials to 2 offer as food vi eat n 1 food esp as for infants, livestock, etc 2 amount of food or material allowed **fed up** disgruntled with a particular situation

feel v (felt) vt 1 sense or examine by touching 2 experience (an emotional or physical sensation) 3 have an emotional or physical reaction to vi produce a sensation as specified **feel for** sympathize with **feel like** want **feel up to** be well enough to ~n 1 instance of feeling 2 nature of something as perceived by touch or by intuition **feeler** n organ in some animals especially adapted for touch **feeling** 1 ability to experience a sensation or a sensation itself 2 mood; attitude; emotion 3 impression; premonition adj 1 sensitive; sympathetic 2 showing emotion

feet n pl of **foot.**

feign vt pretend; invent; imitate

feint n deceptive movement, action etc vi make such a movement

feline adj 1 of the cat family 2 like a cat n animal in the cat family

fell[1] v pt of **fall.**

fell[2] vt bring down or cause to fall

fellow n 1 man; boy 2 companion; colleague 3

member of the same class, kind, etc **4** member of a learned society **fellowship** n **1** sharing of interests, activities, etc **2** group sharing such things; brotherhood **3** position of being a fellow, esp in a learned society, university, etc **4** religious communion

felon n criminal **felony** n

felt[1] v pt and pp of **feel.**

felt[2] n fabric whose fibres have not been woven but joined together by pressure

female n person or animal of the sex that conceives and gives birth adj designating a female **feminine** adj **1** considered suitable to or representative of women or girls **2** of a grammatical gender normally denoting females **feminism** n **1** ideology or movement that advocates the equality of women **feminist** n,adj

fence n **1** structure enclosing an area or forming a barrier **2** inf distributor of illegally obtained goods **on the fence** indecisive; neutral ~vt build a fence around or on vi **1** participate in the sport of fencing **2** evade questions or arguments **fencing** n sport or activity of fighting with swords

fend v **fend off** ward off (something) **fend for** provide for; support

ferment vt,vi (fə'ment) undergo or cause fermentation n ('fɔːment) **1** agent, such as yeast, that causes fermentation **2** tumult; commotion **fermentation** n chemical reaction in which sugar is changed into alcohol by action of microorganisms

fern n plant with green feathery leaves that forms spores

ferocious adj fierce; savage

ferret n weasel-like animal used for hunting rabbits and rats vt **1** drive out from cover **2** also **ferret out** find; search out; seek

ferry n boat or service used for transportation across a body of water vt,vi transport or travel over water

fertile adj **1** able to produce young **2** capable of sustaining vegetation **fertility** n **fertilize** vt **1** cause the union of (a female reproductive cell) with sperm or a male reproductive cell **2** make fertile **fertilizer** n substance added to soil to increase crop yield

fervour n ardour, zeal; passion **fervent** adj

fester vi **1** form pus **2** become gradually resentful, bitter, etc

festival n **1** celebration or feast **2** series of

cultural performances **festivity** n **1** gaiety, merry-making **2** feast or celebration

festoon n **1** decorative chain of flowers, foliage etc ; garland **2** something that resembles a festoon vt,vi decorate with or form festoons

fetch vt **1** go and get; bring **2** cost or sell for **fetching** adj becoming or charming

fete (feit) n **1** festival or celebration, esp in aid of charity **2** holiday vt **1** entertain **2** celebrate with a fete

fetid adj smelling stale or rotten

fetish n **1** object believed to have magic powers in certain cultures **2** object or activity to which one is blindly devoted

fetlock n part of a horse s leg above the hoof

fetter n chain fastened to the ankle; shackle vt restrain with fetters; shackle

feud n long bitter hostility between two families, factions, etc vi participate in a feud

feudal adj of a social system based on land ownership and on ties between lords and vassals **feudalism** n

fever n **1** abnormally high body temperature **2** disease characterized by fever **3** extreme excitement **feverish** adj

few adj not many; small number of n small number **quite a few** large number

fiancé n engaged man **fiancée** f n

fiasco n disaster; absolute failure

fib inf n harmless lie vi (-bb-) tell fibs **fibber** n

fibre n **1** yarn or cloth or the filaments from which they are made **2** thread; filament **3** structure or substance **4** character; nature **fibreglass** n **1** fabric made from pressed or woven glass fibres **2** material made by binding glass fibres with synthetic resin

fickle adj not faithful; changeable

fiction n **1** literary works not based on fact **2** falsehood; lie **3** act of lying **fictional** adj **fictitious** adj not genuine; false

fiddle n **1** inf violin **2** inf illegal or fraudulent dealing or arrangement vi **1** play on a fiddle **2** fidget or tamper with vt do something deceptively or illegally

fidelity n **1** faithfulness or devotion to duty, a cause person etc ; loyalty **2** truthfulness **3** faithfulness of reproduction in sound recording

fidget vi **1** be restless or uneasy **2** play with or handle something in a restless manner **fidgety** adj

field n **1** open plot of land, esp one for pasture

or crops **2** tract of land on which sports are played; pitch **3** battleground **4** area rich in minerals, etc **5** area of knowledge, study, etc **6** area away from normal working quarters where new data or material can be collected **7** the side that is not batting in a game of cricket *vt* stop or recover (the ball) in cricket **fieldwork** *n* work done away from normal working quarters for purposes of research, investigation, etc

fiend *n* **1** evil spirit **2** wicked or cruel person **3** *inf* fanatic; addict **fiendish** *adj* cruel; wicked

fierce *adj* savage; wild; ferocious

fiery *adj* **1** of or like fire **2** emotional; passionate **3** causing a feeling of burning

fifteen *n* **1** number that is five more than ten **2** fifteen things or people *adj* amounting to fifteen **fifteenth** *adj,adv,n*

fifth *adj* coming between fourth and sixth in a sequence *n* **1** one of five equal parts; one divided by five **2** fifth person, object, etc *adv* after the fourth

fifty *n* **1** number equal to five times ten **2** fifty things or people *adj* amounting to fifty **fiftieth** *adj adv,n*

fig *n* plant bearing sweet fleshy fruit, which is sometimes dried

fight *n* **1** battle; combat **2** quarrel; conflict **3** boxing contest *vt,vi* (fought) **1** struggle against (a person) in physical combat **2** contend with (a person, situation, etc) **3** support or campaign (for) **4** box **fighter** *n*

figment *n* invention; fiction

figurative *adj* not literal; metaphorical

figure *n* **1** symbol for a number **2** amount; number **3** shape; form **4** person **5** pattern; design *vt,vi* **1** calculate **2** mark with a pattern, diagram, etc *vi* be important; feature **figure out** *inf* solve; think out **figurehead** *n* person who is an apparent leader, but with no real power

filament *n* **1** thin wire inside a light bulb **2** single strand of fibre

file[1] *n* **1** holder for the orderly storage of documents **2** correspondence or information on a particular subject, person, etc **3** row or line **on file** in a file; recorded ~*vt* **1** keep or put in a file **2** institute (a legal suit) *vi* proceed in a row **filing cabinet** *n* cabinet designed for orderly storage of documents

file[2] *n* **1** hand tool with a blade that has small cutting teeth **2** nailfile

filial *adj* of or suitable to a son or daughter

fill *vt* **1** make full to capacity **2** extend; permeate **3** insert material into (an opening) **4** fulfil (a requirement) **5** cover, as with writing, etc **6** do or perform the duties of (a job) **7** hire or elect for **fill in 1** supply information on a form **2** be a substitute for **3** insert **4** fill up (a hole, gap, etc) **fill out** become or make fuller *n* **one's fill** enough; one's limit

fillet *n* piece of boneless meat or boned fish *vt* remove the bones from (meat or fish)

filly *n* female horse or pony of under four years

film *n* **1** cellulose that has been specially treated for making photographs, negatives, etc **2** sequence of pictures projected onto a screen in a cinema or transmitted on television, etc **3** thin layer or coating *vt* take moving pictures with a cinecamera *vt,vi* cover or be covered with a film

filter *n* **1** substance or device through which fluid is passed to remove particles, impurities, etc **2** device which allows only certain signals, kinds of light, etc , to pass through *vt,vi* pass through a filter *vi* become known or occur slowly

filth *n* **1** dirt, squalor, or pollution **2** obscenity **filthy** *adj*

fin *n* wing-like organ of a fish, used for locomotion

final *adj* **1** last; ultimate **2** decisive; conclusive **finally** *adv* **finalize** *vt* conclude or arrange

finance (fi'næns, 'fainæns) *n* study or system of public revenue and expenditure *vt* provide funds for **finances** *pl n* monetary affairs, resources, etc **financial** *adj* **financially** *adv* **financier** *n* person engaged in finance, esp on a large scale

finch *n* small bird that feeds mainly on seeds

find *vt* (found) **1** discover or come upon **2** become aware of **3** regard or consider as being **4** determine; arrive at (a conclusion) **5** provide *n* lucky discovery, bargain, etc

fine[1] *adj* **1** superior in quality, skill, or ability **2** pleasurable **3** minute, powdered, or thin **4** (of weather) clear and dry **5** in good health or condition **6** subtle or acute **7** refined; well-mannered *adv* *inf* very well; in good health **finely** *adv* **fine arts** *pl n* painting, sculpture, architecture, etc

fine[2] *n* amount of money paid as a penalty for a crime offence, etc *vt* impose a fine on

finery *n* showy or elaborate dress, jewellery, etc

finesse (fi'nes) n delicate or subtle skill

finger n any of the five appendages attached to the hand vt handle; touch with the fingers **fingermark** n smudge made by a finger **fingerprint** n impression of the pattern on the underside of the end joint of a finger

finish vt,vi end; complete; conclude; terminate vt 1 use up; consume 2 perfect 3 put a finish on n 1 final stage, completion; conclusion; end 2 surface or texture of a material or a preparation used to produce this 3 refinement; elegance

finite adj bounded or limited

fiord n also **fjord** narrow inlet of the sea between high cliffs

fir n coniferous tree with needle-like leaves

fire n 1 state of burning or combustion 2 mass of burning material 3 any device for heating a room 4 something that resembles a fire 5 discharge of a firearm 6 passion or enthusiasm 7 liveliness or brilliance vt,vi (of a firearm or explosive) discharge or be discharged vt 1 inf terminate (someone's) employment 2 expose to heat, as clay in a kiln 3 provide the fuel for **firearm** n weapon from which a bullet, etc , is propelled by means of an explosion **fire brigade** n group of persons trained in fire-fighting **fire drill** n practice of emergency measures to be taken in case of fire **fire engine** n motor vehicle equipped with fire-fighting apparatus **fire-escape** n staircase or other means of escape in the event of a fire **fireman** n, pl -men man specially trained in fire-fighting **fireplace** n recess in a wall for a fire **fire station** n building where fire engines are housed and where firemen are stationed **firework** n device made from combustible material that is lit for entertainment **firing squad** n group of men who carry out a death sentence by shooting

firm[1] adj 1 hard; solid 2 stationary; secured 3 settled; established 4 steadfast resolute **firmly** adv **firmness** n

firm[2] n business concern; company

first adj coming before all others adv 1 before any other 2 for the first time n 1 beginning 2 highest honours degree **first aid** n emergency medical aid administered before professional help is available **first-class** adj best or most expensive; belonging to the highest grade adv by first-class means **first-hand** adj,adv from the original source **first person** n form of a pronoun or verb when the speaker is the subject **first-rate** adj of the best kind or class

fiscal adj relating to state finances

fish n, pl **fish** or **fishes** 1 any of a large group of aquatic animals, usually having gills and fins 2 flesh of this animal used for food vi 1 catch or attempt to catch fish 2 also **fish out** obtain from an inaccessible place 3 angle, draw out, as by hinting or questioning vt fish in (a particular body of water) **fisherman** n, pl -men man who catches fish for a living **fishmonger** n person who sells fish

fission n 1 breaking into parts or bits 2 also **nuclear fission** splitting of the nucleus of atoms, used in atom bombs and as a source of energy

fist n closed or clenched hand

fit[1] vt,vi (-tt-) 1 make or be suitable or well adapted for 2 be proper or correct for 3 adjust to make (something) appropriate 4 qualify or make competent 5 alter (clothing) for a particular person adj 1 suitable or well adapted 2 competent 3 healthy; well 4 worthy 5 ready or inclined to n 1 way in which something fits 2 something that fits 3 process of fitting **fitting** adj appropriate; suitable

fit[2] n 1 attack; seizure; convulsion 2 period or spell of emotion, activity, etc **fitful** adj coming on in or characterized by sudden irregular spells

five n 1 number equal to one plus four 2 group of five persons, things, etc 3 also **five o'clock** five hours after noon or midnight adj amounting to five

fix vt,vi fasten; secure; attach vt 1 settle; determine 2 assign; allot 3 repair; mend; correct n 1 inf predicament; dilemma 2 sl injection of a narcotic **fixation** n compulsive preoccupation with or concentration on (a particular object, idea, etc) **fixture** n 1 household appliance that is firmly or permanently attached 2 person regarded as being permanently installed in a particular place, position, etc 3 scheduled football match, sports meeting, etc

fizz vi bubble; effervesce n 1 hiss 2 effervescence 3 drink containing soda water or sparkling wine

fizzle vi 1 hiss; make bubbling sounds 2 inf also **fizzle out** die out after an energetic start

fjord n fiord

flabbergasted adj amazed; astonished

flabby adj 1 without firmness; soft 2 having limp flesh 3 lacking vitality; listless **flabbiness** n

flag¹ n piece of cloth decorated with an emblem or symbol vt (-gg-) 1 decorate with flags 2 signal with flags

flag² vi (-gg-) become limp or weak; tire

flagon n vessel for holding liquids

flagrant adj blatant; glaring

flair n 1 ability or aptitude 2 style; elegance

flake n thin layer or piece vt,vi 1 peel off in flakes or chips 2 cover with flakes **flaky** adj

flamboyant adj showy; ostentatious; extravagant **flamboyance** n

flame n 1 blaze or fire 2 ardour; passion vt,vi burn vi flash; be inflamed

flamingo n, pl **flamingos** or **flamingoes** large wading bird with bright pinkish red plumage and long legs

flammable adj capable of burning; inflammable

flan n open tart, either savoury or sweet

flank n 1 part of the body of man or animals between the ribs and hip 2 cut of beef from this area 3 either side of a body of armed troops, ships, etc vt,vi 1 place or be next to 2 go round the flank of (an enemy)

flannel n 1 light fabric with a short nap 2 piece of cloth used for washing the body 3 inf evasive speech, explanation, etc vt (-ll-) clean or polish with a flannel

flap v (-pp-) vt,vi swing or flutter vi panic; become agitated or upset n 1 action or sound made by flapping 2 flat sheet attached at one end, used to cover an opening, etc 3 inf state of panic or distress

flare vt,vi 1 burn with an unsteady or sudden flame 2 spread outwards in a wedge shape vi develop quickly; break out **flare up** suffer a sudden outburst of anger, violence, etc ~n 1 sudden burst of flame, sometimes used as a signal 2 spreading or tapering section 3 sudden burst of emotion, etc

flash n 1 flame; flare 2 outburst 3 instant; moment 4 display adj also **flashy** 1 ostentatious or gaudy 2 counterfeit; false vi 1 move quickly; race 2 occur suddenly 3 send out a sudden intermittent bright light vt 1

send a signal or message by means of a **flash** 2 inf display ostentatiously **flashback** n abrupt change of scene to one earlier in time in a play, film, etc **flashbulb** n bulb producing a bright flash used to take photographs **flashlight** n 1 source of intermittent or flashing light 2 electric torch

flask n bottle or similar container for liquids

flat¹ adj 1 horizontal; level; even or smooth 2 low; prostrate 3 collapsed or deflated 4 unqualified; outright 5 dull; lifeless 6 insipid; stale 7 pointless 8 having a pitch below the true pitch; half a semitone below a specified note adv 1 horizontally 2 absolutely; definitely n 1 flat surface, piece of land, etc 2 deflated tyre 3 flat musical note **flatfish** n, pl **-fish** fish that swims horizontally and has both eyes on the uppermost side of the body, such as plaice, sole, etc **flat-footed** adj having feet with flattened arches **flatten** vt,vi make or become flat

flat² n room or set of rooms in a building, used as a self-contained dwelling

flatter vt,vi 1 praise insincerely or immoderately 2 show to advantage 3 please by paying compliments or attention to **flattery** n

flaunt vt,vi 1 show off 2 wave or flutter

flautist n person who plays the flute

flavour n 1 taste 2 seasoning or extract 3 essence; characteristic quality 4 smell; aroma vt give a flavour to **flavouring** n seasoning

flaw n defect; imperfection; blemish **flawless** adj

flax n plant producing fibres used in the manufacture of linen, paper, etc

flea n small blood-sucking insect, a parasite on mammals and birds, noted for its ability to leap

fleck n speck; spot

flee vt,vi (fled) run away (from)

fleece n 1 woollen coat of a sheep, etc 2 something resembling this vt 1 shear (a sheep) 2 swindle

fleet¹ n 1 large number of warships functioning as a unit 2 nation's navy 3 group of aeroplanes, motor vehicles, ships, etc , operated by the same company

fleet² adj moving quickly; fast **fleeting** adj passing quickly; transitory

flesh n 1 soft body tissue of animals or man 2 skin; body surface 3 thick pulpy part of a fruit or vegetable 4 man's physical nature, as opposed to his spiritual side **5** one s family **fleshy** adj

flew v pt of **fly**¹.

flex vt,vi bend n insulated cable for connecting an appliance with a source of electricity **flexible** adj **1** pliable; supple **2** adaptable or yielding **flexibility** n

flick n sudden light stroke vt strike, move, or remove with a sudden jerky movement **the flicks** pl n inf cinema

flicker vi,n **1** flash; glimmer **2** flutter; flap

flight¹ n **1** act, ability, or manner of flying **2** route taken by an airborne animal or object **3** trip or journey or or on an aircraft or spacecraft **4** soaring mental digression **5** fin fitted to a dart, arrow, etc , to stabilize its flight **6** set of steps or stairs **flighty** adj irresponsible; frivolous or erratic

flight² n act of fleeing, as from danger

flimsy adj **1** weak or insubstantial **2** (of paper, fabrics, etc) thin

flinch vi **1** withdraw suddenly, as if from pain or shock; wince **2** avoid; shirk

fling v (flung) vt **1** toss or hurl, throw forcefully **2** cast aside; abandon vi move quickly and violently n **1** instance of flinging **2** period of unrestrained or irresponsible behaviour **3** any of several lively Scottish dances

flint n **1** hard dark grey stone **2** small piece of this stone used for striking fires

flip v (-pp-) vt toss lightly or carelessly vt,vi move with a jerky motion; flick n **1** tap, flick **2** alcoholic drink containing egg **flipper** n **1** broad flat limb of certain aquatic animals, used for swimming **2** paddle-like device worn on the feet for use in swimming

flippant adj impertinent or impudent **flippancy** n

flirt vi **1** behave as if one is amorously attracted to another person **2** trifle or toy (with an idea, situation, etc) **flirtation** n **flirtatious** adj

flit vi (-tt-) **1** dart; skim along, flutter **2** pass or pass away quickly n rapid movement; flutter

float vt vi **1** suspend or be suspended on the surface of a liquid **2** move lightly through the air or through a liquid **3** come or bring to mind vaguely vt **1** circulate (a rumour idea, etc) **2** offer (stocks, bonds, etc) for sale on the market n **1** something that floats **2** small floating object attached to a fishing line **3** light electrically powered vehicle, as for delivering milk, etc

flock¹ n **1** group of sheep, goats, birds, etc , that keep or are kept together **2** crowd of people vi **1** gather or cluster together **2** go or attend in large numbers

flock² n **1** tuft of wool, cotton, etc **2** wool remnants used for mattress stuffing, etc

flog vt (-gg-) **1** beat or whip **2** sl sell

flood n **1** overflowing of water on usually dry ground **2** great outpouring or gush **3** rising tide vt,vi **1** cover or be covered in quantities of water **2** overflow or cause to overflow **3** overwhelm or be overwhelmed with a great quantity of something **4** cover or fill completely; saturate vi flow copiously; gush **floodlight** n artificial light that illuminates an area evenly vt illuminate with or as if with a floodlight

floor n **1** lowest horizontal surface of a room, compartment, etc **2** storey **3** bottom of a river, ocean, cave, etc **4** area used for a particular purpose vt,vi cover with or make a floor vt **1** knock over or down **2** defeat or confound **floorboard** n board in a wooden floor

flop v (-pp-) vi,vt **1** fall or drop quickly or clumsily **2** flap; flutter clumsily vi inf fail n failure

flora n, pl **floras** or **florae** ('flɔːriː) **1** plant life of a particular area or time period **2** catalogue of such plant life **floral** adj of flowers **florist** n person who sells flowers or plants

flounce¹ vi move or go with angry or jerky movements n instance of flouncing

flounce² n ruffle used to ornament a garment, etc

flounder¹ vi stumble or plod; move or act with difficulty

flounder² n common marine flatfish

flour n powdered wheat or other grain, used in baking and cooking vt **1** make into flour or a fine powder **2** sprinkle or cover with flour

flourish vi **1** thrive; prosper **2** wave in the air n **1** ostentation; show **2** embellishment **3** showy musical passage

flout vt,vi mock; show contempt (for)

flow vi **1** (of liquids) move in a stream; circulate **2** move or proceed as if in a stream **3** hang loosely **4** abound n **1** act or rate of flowing **2** current; stream **3** continuity **4** amount that flows **5** outpouring; flood; overflowing

flower n 1 blossom or a plant that bears a blossom 2 finest period, part, example, etc 3 ornament or embellishment vi 1 bear flowers; blossom 2 mature; develop fully vt cover or adorn with flowers **flowery** adj 1 covered with flowers 2 ornate; highly embellished

flown v pp of **fly**¹.

fluctuate vi waver; change; vary **fluctuation** n

flue n pipe or passage conducting hot gases, air, etc , from a fireplace or boiler

fluent adj 1 speaking or writing a foreign language well 2 spoken or written well and with ease 3 flowing, smooth, or graceful **fluency** n **fluently** adv

fluff n light downy particles or material vt,vi make or become fluffy or like fluff **fluffy** adj

fluid n 1 liquid substance 2 (in physics) liquid or a gas adj 1 capable of flowing 2 changing; not stable

flung v pt and pp of **fling**.

fluorescent adj giving off light by the influence of radiation, electrons etc ; luminous **fluorescence** n

fluoride n 1 chemical compound of fluorine 2 sodium fluoride added to the water supply to reduce tooth decay

fluorine n yellow poisonous corrosive gaseous element

flush¹ vt,vi 1 blush or make blush; glow 2 flow or cause to flow with water, etc vt excite; exhilarate n 1 blush, rosy colour; ruddiness 2 emotion; exhilaration 3 hot feeling; fever

flush² adj,adv level; even adj 1 inf affluent 2 inf plentiful; easily obtainable 3 vigorous 4 full; almost overflowing

fluster vt vi make or become nervous or confused n state of nervousness or confusion

flute n 1 musical wind instrument made of wood or metal 2 narrow rounded channel or groove as in pillars, etc vt cut flutes in

flutter vt,vi 1 wave or flap 2 make or be nervous; fluster vi 1 fall or move with irregular motion 2 move uneasily or aimlessly n 1 flap; wave 2 state of nervousness 3 excitement; sensation 4 distortion of higher frequencies in record-players radios, etc 5 inf gamble, wager

flux n 1 flow 2 continuous change

fly¹ v (flew; flown) vi 1 move through the air; take wing; soar 2 move quickly or rapidly 3 vanish; disappear vt vi 1 travel in or operate (an aircraft) 2 float; glide; flutter 3 transport or be transported by aircraft n strip of fabric concealing the zip on trousers **flyover** n road intersection having a bridge that passes over another road

fly² n any of certain two-winged insects, such as the housefly

foal n horse, ass, etc , less than one year old vt,vi (of horses, etc) give birth (to)

foam n 1 mass of tiny bubbles, as soap suds 2 sweat of a horse 3 frothy saliva 4 lightweight porous substance made from rubber, plastic, etc ,vt produce foam; froth; lather

focus n, pl **focuses** or **foci** ('fousai) 1 point to which light converges or from which it appears to diverge by the action of a lens or curved mirror 2 central point, as of attraction or interest vt,vi 1 bring or come to a focus 2 concentrate (on) **focal** adj

fodder n feed for livestock

foe n enemy; opponent

foetus n young of an animal or person while still developing in the womb

fog n 1 cloudlike mass of water vapour near the ground 2 bewilderment; confusion vt,vi (-gg-) 1 surround or be surrounded with fog 2 blur; confuse, obscure **foggy** adj **foghorn** n loud horn used to signal warning to ships, etc in foggy weather

foible n slight weakness or fault; failing

foil¹ vt frustrate; thwart

foil² n thin flexible metal sheet

foil³ n light flexible sword used in fencing

foist vt impose or force (unwanted or inferior goods, etc)

fold¹ vt vi bend or double (paper etc) over itself vt 1 position (the arms) with one round the other 2 wrap up 3 wind, bend; enclose vi inf fail; flop n 1 section or mark made by folding 2 act of folding

fold² n enclosure for livestock, esp sheep

foliage n leaves of a plant

folk n 1 people in general 2 family, relatives **folkdance** n traditional dance having common or popular origins **folklore** n traditional legends, proverbs, etc , of a people **folksong** n 1 song whose words and music have been passed down through the common people 2 composition imitating such a song **folktale** n traditional legend or tale

follicle n small cavity or gland, such as that from which a hair grows

follow *vt, vi* 1 go or come after 2 result from; ensue 3 comprehend or understand 4 watch closely; monitor *vt* 1 accompany 2 keep to (a path, road, etc); trace 3 comply with; observe; conform to 4 be interested in **follower** *n*

folly *n* 1 foolishness 2 elaborate nonfunctional building erected to satisfy a whim, fancy, etc

fond *adj* 1 affectionate; loving 2 doting; indulgent **be fond of** have a liking for; be pleased by **fondness** *n*

fondant *n* creamy sugary paste, used for sweets, icing, etc

fondle *vt* touch or handle tenderly or with affection

font *n* receptacle for baptismal water in a church

food *n* 1 substance, esp when solid, eaten for nourishment 2 something that provides nourishment or stimulation

fool *n* 1 senseless, silly, or stupid person 2 jester, buffoon *vt* deceive; trick; take in *vi* act like a fool; joke or tease **fool (around) with** behave stupidly or irresponsibly with **foolish** *adj* 1 silly; senseless 2 unwise; thoughtless **foolishly** *adv*

foot *n; pl* **feet** 1 part of the end of the leg below the ankle 2 similar part in animals 3 unit of length equal to 12 inches (30 48 centimetres) 4 anything resembling a foot in form or purpose 5 bottom or base 6 way of walking **on foot** walking or running **football** *n* any of various team games in which a ball is kicked towards a goal **footballer** *n* **footbridge** *n* bridge for pedestrians **foothold** *n* 1 place capable of providing support for a foot 2 secure situation or position **footing** *n* 1 foothold 2 foundation or base 3 status or level **footlights** *pl n* row of lights along the front of the stage floor in a theatre **footnote** *n* note printed on the bottom of a page giving additional information to the main text **footprint** *n* mark made by a foot **footwear** *n* articles worn on the feet, as shoes boots etc

for *prep* 1 with the intention of 2 intended to belong to 3 towards 4 over or across 5 in support of 6 to obtain 7 suited to 8 over a particular period or length of time 9 instead of 10 because of 11 with regard to a norm 12 as 13 at a particular time 14 to join in 15 in spite of *conj* because

forage *n* 1 fodder 2 search for food *vt, vi* search for food etc

forbear *vt, vi* (-bore; -borne) abstain or refrain (from)

forbid *vt* (-dd-; -bad *or* -bade; -bidden) 1 prohibit 2 hinder

force *n* 1 strength; intensity; energy 2 power or might 3 power to affect; influence 4 organized military group 5 group of people organized for a particular purpose 6 violence; coercion 7 effectiveness; potency 8 influence producing motion or strain in an object or material *vt* 1 compel or oblige 2 obtain through effort or by overpowering 3 propel or drive 4 break down or open; overpower 5 impose; urge upon 6 strain; labour **forceful** *adj* **forcefully** *adv* **forcible** *adj* having or done through force **forcibly** *adv*

forceps *pl n* surgical pincers

ford *n* area of a river, etc, shallow enough to be crossed on foot, horseback, etc *vt* cross (a river etc) in this manner

fore *adj* at or towards the front *n* front section or area *adv* at or towards the bow of a ship or boat

forearm[1] ('fɔːrɑːm) *n* part of the arm between the elbow and wrist

forearm[2] (fɔːrˈɑːm) *vt* arm beforehand

forebear *n* ancestor

forecast *vt, vi* predict; foretell *vt* herald; anticipate *n* prediction; estimate

forecourt *n* court in front of a building petrol station, etc

forefather *n* ancestor; forebear

forefinger *n* finger next to the thumb; index finger

forefront *n* most outstanding or advanced position

foreground *n* nearest part of a scene or view

forehand *adj* 1 made or relating to the right side of a right-handed person or the left side of a left-handed person 2 foremost; most important *n* forehand stroke in tennis squash, etc

forehead *n* part of the face between the hairline and eyebrows

foreign *adj* 1 in, from dealing with or relating to another country people or culture 2 not familiar; alien 3 not coming from or belonging to the place where found 4 not pertinent or applicable; inappropriate **foreigner** *n*

foreleg n one of the front legs of a four-legged animal

forelock n lock of hair growing above the forehead

foreman n pl **-men** person who supervises workers

foremost adj adv first in order prominence, etc

forensic adj relating to courts of law

forerunner n 1 predecessor; forebear 2 herald

foresee vt (-saw; -seen) see or realize beforehand; anticipate

foresight n 1 prudence forethought or precaution 2 forecast

forest n 1 large tree-covered tract of land 2 anything resembling this in appearance density etc

forestall vt 1 thwart or foil beforehand 2 anticipate; consider in advance

foretaste n vt sample or taste in advance

foretell vt (-told) predict prophesy

forethought n foresight anticipation

forfeit n 1 fine or penalty 2 something lost in order to pay a fine or penalty vt surrender or lose (something) as a forfeit **forfeiture** n

forge[1] n 1 place or furnace where metal is heated and worked 2 device for hammering heated metal into shape vt 1 hammer (heated metal) into a form 2 make or produce 3 invent or make up (a story etc) 4 duplicate or copy (a signature money etc) **forgery** n act or result of illegally duplicating (a signature money etc)

forge[2] vi move ahead or make progress esp slowly and with difficulty

forget v (-got -gotten) vt vi fail to remember or recall vt 1 neglect or ignore 2 leave behind unintentionally **forget oneself** 1 behave improperly 2 forget one's position or station

forgive vt vi (-gave -given) 1 pardon; excuse acquit 2 cease to blame or harbour ill will (for) **forgiveness** n

forgo vt (-went, -gone) do without; deny oneself

fork n 1 pronged instrument for holding and lifting esp one used at table or in gardening 2 branching or dividing of a road river etc 3 tuning fork vi vt divide as or with a fork

forlorn adj 1 abandoned deserted, forsaken 2 desolate miserable

form n 1 shape, structure 2 variety, type 3 nature 4 printed document with blank spaces to be filled in 5 long backless bench 6 class

in a school 7 conventional social behaviour 8 formula; conventional procedure 9 fitness or level of performance as in a sport vt vi 1 make into or assume a particular shape arrangement or condition 2 develop 3 constitute; make up **formation** n

formal adj 1 relating or adhering to set conventions rituals behaviour, etc 2 precise or symmetrical in form **formally** adv **formality** n 1 something done solely for the sake of custom or appearance 2 state of being formal 3 rigorous observation of ceremony protocol etc

formation n 1 forming 2 arrangement as of a group of soldiers aircraft etc

formative adj 1 relating to growth or development 2 giving form

former adj previous n first of two things mentioned **formerly** adv

formidable adj 1 fearful; threatening, menacing 2 difficult to resolve conquer etc 3 awe-inspiring

formula n, pl **formulas** or **formulae** ('fɔːmjuliː) 1 standard procedure or method for doing or expressing something 2 mathematical relationship expressed esp in the form of an equation 3 representation of the chemical structure of something **formulaic** adj **formulate** vt express in exact form or formula **formulation** n

forsake vt (-sook, -saken) 1 leave, desert, abandon 2 renounce; forgo

fort n also **fortress** fortified building or enclosure **hold the fort** maintain or control during the absence of those usually in charge

forte (fɔːt 'fɔːteɪ) n person's strong point or particular ability

forth adv 1 forwards, onwards 2 out or away from **forthcoming** adj 1 happening soon imminent 2 willing to talk, open; forward

fortify vt strengthen or enrich **fortification** n

fortnight n two weeks fourteen days **fortnightly** adv every two weeks

fortress n fort

fortune n 1 amount of great wealth; bounty 2 fate, destiny 3 good luck **fortunate** adj lucky; happy, favourable **fortunately** adv **fortune-teller** n person who predicts future events

forty n 1 number equal to four times ten 2 forty things or people adj amounting to forty **fortieth** adj,adv n

forum n. pl **forums** or **fora** ('fɔːrə) 1 meeting
for discussion 2 court or tribunal

forward adv 1 onward; ahead; in advance 2
out or forth adj 1 well-advanced; ahead 2
ready; prompt; eager 3 bold; impertinent 4
radical; progressive 5 early; premature n an
attacking player in certain team games vt
send (a letter) on to a new address **forwards**
adv 1 towards the front; ahead 2 into the
future

forwent v pt of **forgo.**

fossil n 1 remains or impression of a plant or
animal of an earlier geological age 2 inf
old-fashioned person or thing **fossilize** vt, vi
make into or become a fossil

foster vt 1 promote; encourage; further 2 bring
up; rear; nourish 3 cherish; care for **foster-
parent** n person who takes care of another's
child

fought v pt and pp of **fight.**

foul adj 1 offensive; disgusting; repulsive 2
filthy; squalid; polluted 3 stormy; tempestuous 4 wicked; shameful; infamous 5
obscene; smutty; profane 6 unfair; dishonourable; underhanded n breaking of the rules (of
a sport, game, etc) vt 1 soil; defile; stain 2
commit a foul on vt vi entangle or clog adv
unfairly **foul play** n unfair or underhanded
goings-on or behaviour

found[1] v pt and pp of **find.**

found[2] vt set up; establish; organize vt vi base
(on) **founder** n **foundation** n 1 base or
basis, 2 supporting base of a building structure, etc 3 organization or institution supported by an endowment 4 cosmetic used to
cover the skin

founder vt vi sink; fill with water vi 1 break
down or collapse 2 stumble or fail

foundry n place where metal is cast

fountain n 1 jet or gush of water 2 decorative
structure producing jets of water **fountain
pen** n pen with a built-in ink reservoir or
cartridge

four n 1 number equal to one plus three 2
group of four persons, things, etc 3 also **four
o'clock** four hours after noon or midnight adj
amounting to four **fourth** adj coming
between third and fifth in sequence adv after
the third **four-poster** n bed having a post at
each corner and sometimes a canopy **foursome** n group of four

fourteen n 1 number that is four more than ten

2 fourteen people or things adj amounting to
fourteen **fourteenth** adj, adv, n

fowl n 1 hen or cock; chicken 2 any bird that is
hunted as game or used or bred for food 3
flesh of these birds

fox n 1 undomesticated doglike mammal having
pointed ears and muzzle and a bushy tail 2
fur of this animal 3 sly or crafty person vt inf
trick or perplex **foxhound** n hound trained
and kept for foxhunting **foxhunting** n sport
in which people on horseback pursue a fox
that is being chased by a pack of hounds

foxglove n wild flower having trumpet-like
purple or white flowers

foyer ('fɔiei) n lobby or entrance hall

fraction n 1 small part of something 2 quantity
that is not a whole number, often expressed as
one number divided by another **fractional**
adj being a part, esp a small part

fracture n act of breaking or something broken,
esp a bone vt, vi break

fragile adj easily broken, marred, or damaged;
frail **fragility** n

fragment n ('frægmənt) 1 broken-off part; chip
2 incomplete portion or part vt, vi (fræg'ment)
break into fragments or bits **fragmentation**
n

fragrant adj perfumed; sweet-smelling; aromatic **fragrance** n

frail adj 1 weak; delicate; feeble 2 fragile;
breakable; brittle **frailty** n

frame n 1 supporting structure of anything 2
form; basis 3 surrounding structure such as a
border around a picture or mirror 4 small
glass structure for growing plants 5 single
picture in a film or television transmission vt 1
surround with a frame 2 support with a
frame 3 form the basic outlines of (a plan
theory etc) 4 sl incriminate (someone) by
falsifying evidence **framework** n 1 basis or
outline 2 structure that supports or sustains

franc n monetary unit of France Belgium,
Switzerland and several other countries

franchise n 1 rights of citizenship esp the right
to vote 2 privilege granted by the government 3 permission to market a product in a
specified area

frank adj 1 straightforward; honest candid 2
blunt unrestrained; outright 3 undisguised,
avowed vt mark (mail) so as to authorize for
free delivery

frankfurter n thin smoked sausage made of

beef or pork that is served hot, usually in a roll

frantic adj agitated; frenzied; raving **frantically** adv

fraternal adj 1 of or relating to a brother 2 brotherly; showing affection or support **fraternally** adv **fraternity** n 1 group of people with common interests or goals 2 brotherhood; brotherly consideration and affection **fraternize** vi associate or be friendly (with) **fraternization** n

fraud n 1 deceit; trickery; deception 2 something false or forged; counterfeit 3 person who practises fraud. **fraudulent** adj

fraught adj abounding in; full of

fray¹ n noisy argument or brawl

fray² vt, vi 1 unravel or wear away 2 strain; vex, annoy 3 rub or rub against

freak n 1 deformed person, animal, or plant 2 abnormal or odd thing, event, etc 3 sl person deeply interested in something

freckle n small brownish spot on the skin vt, vi cover or be covered with freckles

free adj 1 at liberty; independent 2 not restricted or regulated 3 clear; immune, or exempt 4 easy; firm or unimpeded 5 loose, unattached 6 available; unoccupied 7 costing nothing; without charge 8 frank or open 9 liberal; generous vt (freed) 1 liberate; set free; release 2 exempt 3 rid; clear adv 1 also **freely** in a free manner 2 without cost **freedom** n 1 state or quality of being free; liberty 2 immunity or privilege 3 ease. facility 4 frankness 5 familiarity; lack of formality **freehand** adj done by hand without the use of other aids **freehold** n absolute ownership of land, property, etc **freeholder** n **freelance** n also **freelancer** self-employed writer, artist etc adj relating to a freelance adv in the manner of a freelance **free will** n doctrine that people have free choice and that their actions are not predetermined

freeze v (froze; frozen) vt, vi 1 change into a solid by a drop in temperature 2 cover, be or become covered or blocked with ice 3 attach (to) 4 be or cause to be motionless through terror, fear, surprise etc 5 be or make very cold vt 1 preserve (food) by subjecting to extreme cold 2 stabilize and prevent increases in (prices, incomes, etc) n fixing of levels of prices, incomes etc **freezer** n refrigerator in which food can be deep-frozen; deep freeze

freezing point n temperature at which a liquid freezes

freight n 1 cargo; shipment; load 2 transportation of goods

French bean n thin green seed pod used as a vegetable

French dressing n salad dressing made from oil and vinegar and usually seasoned

French horn n coiled brass instrument with a mellow tone

French window n door made of glass and wood that opens outwards

frenzy n wild excitement or enthusiasm; rage vt make very excited; enrage **frenzied** adj

frequent adj ('fri:kwənt) 1 occurring often and at short intervals 2 habitual; usual vt (fri'kwent) visit regularly or repeatedly **frequently** adv **frequency** n 1 state of being frequent 2 rate of occurrence 3 rate of repetition of a periodic process per unit time

fresco n, pl **frescoes** or **frescos** technique or example of wall-painting in which pigments are applied to the plaster before it has dried

fresh adj 1 new; recent 2 additional; more 3 (of food) not preserved in any way 4 (of water) not salt adv in a fresh manner **freshly** adv **freshness** n **freshen** vt, vi make or become fresh **freshwater** adj relating or indigenous to fresh water

fret¹ vt, vi (-tt-) 1 worry; irritate; vex 2 wear away, erode 1 annoyance; irritation; vexation 2 erosion; eating away **fretful** adj

fret² n ornamental geometric pattern vt (-tt-) adorn with such a pattern **fretsaw** n fine narrow saw with a curved frame used for cutting designs **fretwork** n interlacing geometric designs cut in thin wood

friar n male member of a religious order supported by alms

friction n 1 resistance met when two surfaces are rubbed together 2 discord; conflict

Friday n sixth day of the week

fridge n inf refrigerator

friend n 1 companion, intimate 2 acquaintance; colleague 3 ally **friendly** adj 1 relating or fitting to a friend 2 amicable or helpful **friendliness** n **friendship** n 1 being friends or a friend 2 goodwill; benevolence

frieze n ornamental band or border on a column, wall, etc

fright n scare; alarm, dismay **look a fright** look terrible or grotesque **frighten** vt 1 scare terrify 2 cause to worry or feel apprehensive about something **frightful** *adj* dreadful; terrible **frightfully** *adv* 1 dreadfully; terribly 2 *inf* very

frigid *adj* cold in manner, feeling, temperature, etc **frigidity** *n*

frill *n* 1 decorative ruffle 2 trimming; ornamentation *vt* decorate with frills

fringe *n* 1 border or edging having hanging thread, tassels, flaps etc 2 section of hair cut short to hang over the forehead 3 outer region; margin *vt* provide with a fringe *adj* additional; supplementary

frisk *vi,vt* move about playfully *vt* *inf* search or rob (a person) by examination of clothing **frisky** *adj*

fritter[1] *vt* waste (money, time, etc)

fritter[2] *n* type of pancake dipped in batter and deep-fried

frivolity *n* gaiety; revelry; merriment **frivolous** *adj* 1 unimportant; trifling; petty 2 idle; silly; foolish

frizz *vt,vi* make or become tightly curled or kinky **frizzy** *adj*

frizzle[1] *vt,vi* frizz *n* tight wiry curl

frizzle[2] *vi* emit a hiss or sizzling noise *vt* cook (meat, etc) until crisp and dry

fro *adv* from or back **to and fro** back and forth

frock *n* 1 dress 2 monk s cloak *vt* install (a cleric) in office

frog *n* smooth-skinned web-footed amphibian **have a frog in one's throat** speak hoarsely **frogman** *n, pl* **-men** underwater diver

frolic *n* gaiety or merry occasion *vi* (-ck-) act in a lively playful manner **frolicsome** *adj*

from *prep* 1 indicating the original place or circumstance 2 starting at 3 indicating a distance between (two places) 3 indicating removal or restraint

front *n* 1 forward position or side that is usually closest to a viewer or user 2 beginning or opening part or section 3 leading position 4 separating area between two different masses of air 5 *inf* cover; outward appearance 6 alliance coalition *vt vi* face (on) **frontal** *adj* **frontally** *adv*

frontier *n* 1 unexplored or unsettled area 2 boundary

frost *n* 1 (formation of) ice particles that are white in appearance 2 below-freezing temperature 3 *inf* coldness of attitude, manner, etc *vt,vi* coat or be coated with frost or

something similar **frostbite** *n* injury to the body caused by exposure to extreme cold **frostbitten** *adj* **frosty** *adj*

froth *n,vi,vt* foam

frown *vi,n* scowl **frown on** disapprove of

froze *v pt* of **freeze. frozen** *v pp* of **freeze.**

frugal *adj* economical; thrifty **frugality** *n* **frugally** *adv*

fruit *n* 1 produce of a plant, usually eaten raw or cooked as a sweet 2 result; product *vi* bear fruit **fruit machine** *n* gambling machine with pictures of fruits as variables **fruitful** *adj* prolific; fertile; productive **fruitfully** *adv* **fruitfulness** *n* **fruitless** *adj* 1 yielding nothing; useless 2 barren; sterile **fruitlessly** *adv* **fruition** (fru:'iʃən) *n* 1 fulfilment or maturity 2 bearing of fruit

frustrate *vt* baffle; disconcert; foil **frustration** *n*

fry *vt,vi* cook in oil or fat

fuchsia ('fju:ʃə) *n* ornamental plant or shrub yielding hanging red, purple, or white flowers

fudge *n* thick sweet made of butter, sugar, cream, and flavouring

fuel *n* substance that can be used to supply energy *vt,vi* (-ll-) provide with or receive fuel

fugitive *n* person who flees or hides

fulcrum *n, pl* **fulcrums** or **fulcra** ('fulkrə) 1 pivot 2 support; prop

fulfil *vt* (-ll-) 1 carry out; complete 2 perform; do; obey 3 satisfy; gratify 4 complete; terminate **fulfilment** *n*

full *adj* 1 filled to capacity 2 having eaten as much as one can 3 entire; complete 4 enjoying all rights and privileges 5 ample or plump **full of** preoccupied with ~*adv* also **fully** entirely; exactly *n* **in full** in entirety **to the full** to capacity **full-length** *adj* 1 relating to the complete length; unabridged 2 (of dresses and skirts) reaching the floor **full stop** *n* punctuation mark ( ) used to mark the end of a sentence **full-time** *adj adv* relating to or lasting normal working hours

fumble *vi* 1 handle something clumsily 2 grope; find one s way clumsily *vi vt* utter (something) in an awkward manner **fumbler** *n*

fume *vi* storm; rage *vt,vi* smoke; give off (smoke) *n* smoke, vapour

fun *n* enjoyment; pleasure; amusement **make fun of** ridicule; tease **funfair** *n* fair; amusement park

function *n* 1 purpose; special or natural activity

2 formal gathering 3 variable factor *vi* perform (as) **functional** *adj* 1 relating to a function 2 useful rather than decorative or ornamental **functionally** *adv*

fund *n* store or reserve esp of money resources, etc *vt* supply with a fund or funds

fundamental *adj* 1 basic; underlying; principal 2 original; first *n* principle; rule **fundamentally** *adv*

funeral *n* burial ceremony

fungus *n, pl* **fungi** (ˈfʌndʒaɪ) plant lacking chlorophyll, such as a mould, mushroom etc

funnel *n* 1 hollow tapering apparatus for transferring a substance to a more narrow-necked container 2 something shaped like a funnel *vt,vi* 1 pour through a funnel 2 direct or channel 3 fix attention or focus (on)

funny *adj* amusing; comical; humorous **funnily** *adv*

fur *n* 1 dense coat of an animal 2 *inf* sediment caused by hard water *v* (-rr-) *vt* decorate with fur *vi,vt inf* cover or be covered with sediment

furious *adj* raging; angry; violent **furiously** *adv*

furnace *n* apparatus equipped to produce steam, etc , by burning fuel

furnish *vt* 1 provide furniture, carpets, etc , for 2 equip or supply (with)

furniture *n* movable items such as tables, chairs, or beds, found in a house, office, etc

furrow *n* 1 trench 2 groove or line, esp in the forehead *vt,vi* make or become wrinkled or lined

further *adv* 1 *also* **furthermore** moreover 2 to a greater degree or distance *adj* more *vt* assist; help along **furthest** *adv* to the most extreme degree or place *adj* most

furtive *adj* secret; sly **furtively** *adv*

fury *n* 1 passion; anger; frenzy 2 violence; turbulence

fuse[1] *vi,vt* 1 melt 2 combine; blend *n* safety device in plugs, electric wiring, etc **fusion** *n* act of fusing; coming together

fuse[2] *n* combustible wire or device leading to and capable of setting off an explosive *vt* provide with a fuse

fuselage *n* body of an aeroplane

fuss *n* activity; ado; bustle *vi* worry; be unduly preoccupied with **fussy** *adj* 1 fussing; worrying 2 preoccupied with petty details 3 particular

futile *adj* 1 ineffective; useless; unsuccessful 2 trivial; frivolous **futility** *n*

future *n* 1 time that is yet to come 2 prospects *adj* yet to come

fuzz *n* 1 fluffy or curly hairy mass 2 blur *vt,vi* make or become like fuzz **fuzzy** *adj*

G

gabble *vi,vt* speak rapidly and inarticulately *n* rapid inarticulate speech

gable *n* triangular part of a wall immediately below that part of a pitched roof that juts out

gadget *n* ingenious, novel or useful tool device, or appliance **gadgetry** *n* gadgets collectively

gag[1] *n* something placed in or over the mouth in order to silence or control *vt* (-gg-) place a gag on

gag[2] *n inf* comedian s joke

gaiety *n* jollity; light-heartedness; merriment

gaily *adv* in a gay manner; light-heartedly

gain *vt* 1 obtain; acquire, win; earn 2 reach, attain *vi* 1 increase; gather speed 2 profit *n* 1 advantage; win; profit 2 increase; advancement **gainful** *adj* profitable

gait *n* manner of walking

gala *n* special performance or display; festival

galaxy *n* 1 large grouping of stars, such as the Milky Way 2 impressive group of famous people **galactic** *adj*

gale *n* strong wind

gallant *adj* (ˈgælənt) 1 dashing and brave; courageous 2 (ˈgælənt, gəˈlænt) chivalrous *n* (ˈgælənt) 1 brave knight or nobleman 2 attentive suitor **gallantly** *adv* **gallantry** *n*

galleon *n* large sailing ship originally used by Spain

gallery *n* 1 building or room(s) exhibiting works of art 2 block of seats above the circle in a theatre 3 upper floor or section opening out on to the interior of a hall, church, etc

galley *n* 1 ship s kitchen 2 warship propelled by oars 3 long tray for holding metal type

gallon *n* measure of liquid equal to approx 4 5 litres (8 pints)

gallop *n* 1 the fastest gait of a horse or similar animal 2 rapid movement or course *vi,vt* ride at a gallop *vi* race; move rapidly

gallows *s n* wooden structure used for execution by hanging

galore adv in abundance

galvanism n process of producing electricity by chemical action **galvanize** vt 1 coat with a metal by galvanism 2 stimulate into action **galvanic** adj

gamble vi vt 1 place a bet (on); stake 2 risk, hazard, speculate vi play at games of chance, esp in order to win money n risk, something of uncertain outcome; chance **gambler** n

game n 1 something played for amusement or sport 2 match; contest 3 certain wild animals that are hunted for sport or food vi take part in games of chance such as roulette adj willing; plucky **gamekeeper** n person employed to take care of animals, fish, etc, on an estate, to prevent poaching, etc

gammon n lower end of a side of bacon

gander n male goose

gang n 1 group of people esp one engaged in unlawful activity 2 band of workers v **gang up (on)** band together in order to attack **gangster** n armed criminal usually operating in a gang

gangrene n death and putrefaction of part of a living organism caused by lack of blood supply

gangway n 1 aisle or passageway separating blocks of seats 2 movable bridge placed between a ship and the quay

gaol n vt jail **gaoler** n

gap n 1 opening, hole or space between two things 2 interval, pause

gape vi 1 stare in a stupid way with astonishment etc 2 be wide open n 1 open mouthed stare 2 split, hole, breach

garage n 1 small building or shelter for a vehicle esp a car 2 commercial premises selling petrol, repairing motor vehicles etc service station

garble vt give a muddled or misleading account of

garden n 1 plot of land adjoining a house where flowers, vegetables etc are cultivated 2 small park vi engage on work in a garden **gardener** n **gardening** n

gargle vi rinse out the mouth and throat with liquid which is kept moving by the action of air drawn up from the lungs n mouthwash, rinse

gargoyle n carved stone face usually of a grotesque form and often functioning as a waterspout

garish (ˈgɛərɪʃ) adj gaudy, vulgar in taste, colour etc

garland n flowers, leaves etc woven into a ring and worn for decoration round the neck or on the head vt decorate with a garland

garlic n plant with a pungent bulbous root which is used as a seasoning

garment n item of clothing

garnish vt add extra decoration, seasoning etc to (food) n trimmings or seasoning used to decorate or enhance the flavour of food

garrison n military establishment where troops are stationed vt station (troops etc) in a garrison

garter n elasticated band worn round the leg to hold up a stocking or sock

gas n 1 substance such as nitrogen, oxygen or carbon dioxide that has no fixed volume or shape 2 fuel in the form of gas vt (-ss-) poison or asphyxiate with gas **gaseous** (ˈgæsɪəs, ˈgeɪʃəs) adj

gash n deep cut, wound or tear vt cut deeply, slash

gasket n asbestos sheet used as a seal in an engine cylinder

gasp vi 1 struggle to breathe, pant 2 catch one's breath in surprise, shock etc 3 inf crave, long (for) n 1 sudden sharp intake of air 2 strangled cry of surprise, etc

gastric adj relating to the stomach

gastronomic adj relating to the art of good eating **gastronomy** n

gate n wooden or metal structure forming a barrier across an opening in a fence, wall, etc **gatecrash** vt vi force one's way into (a party, meeting etc) as an uninvited guest **gatecrasher** n

gâteau n pl **gâteaus** or **gâteaux** (ˈgætou) rich cake decorated with cream, fruit, nuts etc

gather vi vt 1 collect together in a crowd or group; assemble; congregate 2 increase in speed, intensity etc 3 draw thread through material to form pleats or folds vt 1 amass, accumulate, collect 2 pick or pluck (flowers, berries etc) 3 assume, understand, believe **gathering** n assembly of people, congregation

gauche (gouʃ) adj awkward, clumsy; ill at ease **gaucheness** n

gaudy adj brightly coloured, showy, garish **gaudiness** n

gauge (geidʒ) n 1 instrument for measuring

speed, temperature, pressure, etc **2** standard or criterion **3** thickness of metal **4** width of a railway track *vt* **1** measure or estimate the measurement of **2** assess; judge

gaunt *adj* thin and bony; haggard; angular

gauze *n* thin loosely woven fabric used for surgical dressings, curtains, etc

gave *v pt* of **give.**

gay *adj* **1** cheerful; bright; light-hearted; merry **2** vivid; of a bright colour *adj,n sl* homosexual

gaze *vi* stare fixedly or for a considerable time *n* fixed or long look or stare

gazelle *n* small antelope of Africa and Asia

gear *n* **1** mechanism consisting of a set of toothed wheels, such as that on a motor vehicle used for transmitting motion from the engine to the road wheels **2** the engaging of a particular gear **3** *inf* equipment or apparatus required for a particular activity *vt* set up or arrange one thing to fit in with another

geese *n pl* of **goose.**

gelatine *n also* **gelatin** yellowish protein obtained by boiling animal bones and skin, used in the manufacture of glue, jellies, etc **gelatinous** *adj*

gelignite *n* type of dynamite

gem *n also* **gemstone** jewel created from a polished stone

Gemini *n* third sign of the zodiac, represented by the Twins

gender *n* **1** category, such as masculine, feminine, or neuter, into which nouns may be placed in some languages **2** sexual identity

gene *n* part of a chromosome carrying hereditary information

genealogy *n* **1** descent through a line of ancestors; lineage **2** family tree **genealogical** *adj*

general *adj* **1** not specific or particular; broad **2** common; widespread; usual **3** vague; indefinite *n* military officer of a rank below that of field marshal **general election** *n* nationwide election held to elect parliamentary representatives **generalize** *vi,vt* come to a general conclusion from particular statements or facts **generalization** *n* **generally** *adv* **1** usually **2** widely, commonly **general practitioner** *n* doctor dealing with a wide range of cases rather than specializing in any particular area of medicine

generate *vt* **1** create **2** produce (electricity) **generation** *n* **1** production; creation **2**

whole range of people within the same general age group **3** particular genealogical stage **4** span of about 30 years **generator** *n* machine producing electrical energy

generic *adj* **1** relating to a genus **2** representing a whole group or class

generous *adj* **1** unselfish; not mean; kind **2** tolerant; liberal **3** ample; lavish **generosity** *n* **generously** *adv*

genetic *adj* relating to genes or genetics **genetics** *n* study of heredity

genial *adj* amiable; friendly; warm **geniality** *n*

genitals *pl n* male or female sexual organs **genital** *adj*

genius *n* **1** person of exceptionally high intelligence or talent **2** remarkable talent or ability

genteel *adj* displaying extremely refined manners or taste

gentile *n* non-Jewish person, esp a Christian *adj* non-Jewish

gentle *adj* **1** not rough or violent **2** mild **3** docile; tame **4** gradual **gentleness** *n* **gently** *adv* **gentleman** *n, pl* **-men 1** man who is cultured and well-mannered **2** aristocrat or nobleman

genuine *adj* **1** real; authentic; not false or artificial **2** sincere **genuinely** *adv*

genus ('dʒenəs, 'dʒiːnəs) *n, pl* **genera** ('dʒenərə) biological subdivision containing one or more species

geography *n* **1** study of the features of the earth's surface **2** physical features of a region **geographer** *n* **geographical** *adj*

geology *n* study of the composition and evolution of the earth **geological** *adj* **geologist** *n*

geometry *n* branch of mathematics concerned with the properties of figures in space **geometric** *or* **geometrical** *adj*

geranium *n* garden or house plant having pink, scarlet, or white flowers and roundish leaves

germ *n* any microbe that causes disease

German measles *n* contagious disease characterized by a rash and swelling of the glands

germinate *vi,vt* **1** develop through warmth and moisture from a seed into a plant **2** create; spring up **germination** *n*

gesticulate *vi* make wild or broad gestures **gesticulation** *n*

gesture *n* **1** movement of the arms or head **2**

act of friendship, sympathy, etc *vi,vt* express by means of gestures

get *v* (-tt-; got) *vt* **1** obtain; acquire; gain possession of **2** fetch **3** cause to happen or be done **4** *inf* grasp; understand **5** make; force; persuade *vi* **1** become; grow **2** start **3** go; proceed **get about** *or* **around 1** be active **2** move about; circulate **get across** communicate so as to be understood **get ahead** progress; continue **get along 1** manage; cope **2** succeed **get at 1** reach **2** intend; imply **get away** escape **get away with** remain undetected or unpunished **get by** just about manage to cope adequately **get down 1** descend **2** depress; make unhappy **get down to** begin to concentrate on **get off 1** dismount or disembark **2** be permitted to leave **3** escape punishment **get on 1** board (a bus, train, etc) **2** mount (a horse, etc) **3** make successful progress **4** have a friendly relationship (with) **get over** recover from; come to terms with **get round 1** cajole; persuade; bribe **2** solve or resolve (a difficulty, problem, etc) by using a different technique or approach **get round to** find time to **get through (to) 1** contact by telephone **2** make (someone) understand or listen **get up 1** stand up **2** get out of bed **3** organize; arrange **get up to** engage in, esp when not being watched or controlled **getaway** *n* escape

geyser *n* **1** natural hot spring **2** gas-fuelled water heater

ghastly *adj* dreadful; shocking; gruesome; horrific

gherkin *n* small cucumber used for pickling

ghetto *n*, *pl* **ghettos** *or* **ghettoes 1** poor district or quarter in a city; slum area **2** (formerly) poor Jewish quarter in a city

ghost *n* supernatural being believed to be a dead person's soul, which returns to haunt the living; spirit *vt,vi* write (a book) for another person who is then acknowledged as the author

giant *n* **1** abnormally tall person **2** prominent or powerful person **3** one of a race of huge mythological people with superhuman powers *adj* huge; enormous

gibberish *n* nonsense; gabbling speech

gibbon *n* small long-armed ape

giddy *adj* **1** dizzy **2** frivolous **giddiness** *n*

gift *n* **1** present; donation **2** talent **gifted** *adj* talented

gigantic *adj* very large; huge

giggle *vi* laugh in a silly or uncontrolled manner *n* silly laugh; chuckle

gild *vt* (gilded *or* gilt) coat with gold, gold paint, etc

gill[1] (gil) *n* respiratory organ of aquatic animals

gill[2] (ʒil) *n* liquid measure equal to one quarter of a pint

gimmick *n* device or method used to gain publicity, promote sales, etc

gin *n* alcoholic drink made by distilling barley or rye and flavoured with juniper berries

ginger *n* plant whose pungent root is used as a flavouring for drinks, confectionery, etc *n,adj* reddish-orange; auburn *v* **ginger up** *inf* enliven; give energy to

gingerly *adv* cautiously; warily; uncertainly

gingham *n* cotton fabric patterned with coloured checks or stripes

Gipsy *n* Gypsy

giraffe *n* African mammal with a mottled hide and very long neck

girder *n* iron or steel beam; joist

girdle *n* **1** cord or thin belt worn round the waist **2** light corset **3** band or circle *vt* **1** fasten with a girdle **2** encircle

girl *n* **1** female child; young woman **girlish** *adj* **girlhood** *n* **Girl Guide** *n* female member of an organization with aims similar to those of the Scouts

giro *n* banking system whereby transfers between accounts may be made by special cheques

girth *n* **1** leather strap secured under a horse's belly to hold a saddle in position **2** measurement of circumference *vt* secure with a girth

give *v* (gave; given) *vt* **1** present as a gift; donate **2** place into the hands of; offer; hand **3** provide; supply **4** be the cause of **5** transmit or transfer **6** yield; produce **7** *also* **give out** emit or radiate **8** grant; award; confer **9** pay; offer to buy for **10** set aside; allow; spare **11** act as the host for (a party, meal, etc) **12** administer (drugs, a punishment, etc) **13** communicate; make known; tell **14** inflict; cause to suffer **15** utter *vi* **1** donate **2** be flexible or elastic **3** *also* **give way** collapse or break under strain or pressure **give away 1** dispose of; offer for no payment **2** reveal; disclose **give in** submit;

surrender **give up** abandon; cease to do, study, care for, etc ~*n* elasticity; flexibility

glacier *n* mass of ice extending over a large area **glacial** *adj*

glad *adj* happy, pleased **gladly** *adv* **gladness** *n* **gladden** *vt, vi* make or become glad; cheer

gladiolus *n pl* **gladioli** (glædiˈɒulai) or **gladioluses** plant with long narrow leaves and one stem bearing a brightly coloured flower

glamour *n* attraction or attractiveness; allure; glittering charm **glamorous** *adj* **glamorize** *vt* make attractive or glamorous; exaggerate the charms of; idealize

glance *vi* 1 take a brief look 2 flash; shine **glance off** bounce off sharply ~*n* 1 brief look; glimpse 2 quick movement of the eyes 3 flash; spark

gland *n* one of various organs in the body that secrete different substances **glandular** *adj*

glare *vi* 1 shine fiercely or dazzlingly 2 stare angrily; glower; scowl *n* 1 harsh blinding light; dazzle 2 angry look

glass *n* 1 hard brittle transparent material used in windows vessels etc 2 drinking vessel made of glass 3 mirror 4 telescope *vt* glaze **glasses** *pl n* 1 spectacles 2 binoculars **glasshouse** *n* greenhouse or conservatory **glassy** *adj* of or like glass

glaze *vt, vi* 1 fit with glass 2 apply or have a thin glassy coating *n* shiny coating, esp on ceramics

gleam *n* beam of light; glow *vi* shine; beam; glow

glean *vt, vi* 1 gather (remnants of corn) after reaping 2 collect painstakingly

glee *n* mirth; cheerfulness; joy **gleeful** *adj* **gleefully** *adv*

glen *n* (in Scotland) narrow valley

glib *adj* smooth but insincere in manner **glibly** *adv* **glibness** *n*

glide *vi, vt* move smoothly and noiselessly *n* smooth flowing movement **glider** *n* aircraft without an engine that moves according to air currents

glimmer *vi* shine dimly or faintly *n* 1 faint light 2 slight hint or suggestion of hope, intelligence etc

glimpse *n* fleeting look; glance; brief view *vt* see very briefly; get a partial view of

glint *n* flash; sparkle; gleam *vi* sparkle; glitter

glisten *vi* sparkle; shine brightly

glitter *vi* shine brilliantly; flash; twinkle *n* sparkle; twinkle

gloat *vi* take malicious pleasure in one's own greed, another's misfortune, etc

globe *n* 1 the earth 2 model of the earth 3 spherical object; ball **global** *adj* **globule** *n* small drop, particle, or bubble

gloom *n* 1 dim light; semi-darkness, shadow 2 pessimism, cynicism; despondency; depression **gloomy** *adj* **gloomily** *adv*

glory *n* 1 state of being highly honoured, revered, etc.; exaltation 2 magnificence, splendour 3 fame; renown **glorify** *vt* exalt, treat with great reverence; worship or admire **glorification** *n* **glorious** *adj* 1 overwhelmingly beautiful; magnificent 2 stunning 3 highly distinguished; great **gloriously** *adv*

gloss *n* 1 bright or reflective surface or appearance; sheen; lustre 2 *also* **gloss paint** type of paint giving a smooth shiny finish *vt* polish; shine **gloss over** try to hide, cover up mistakes, etc **glossy** *adj* shiny

glossary *n* explanatory list of specialist or technical terms or words

glove *n* covering for the hand with individual sections for each finger and the thumb *vt* cover with a glove

glow *vi* 1 burn with a steady light; shine warmly or brightly 2 radiate excitement pride enthusiasm, etc *n* steady bright light; blaze **glow-worm** *n* small beetle, the female of which possesses organs that give off a luminous greenish light

glower (ˈglauə) *vi* scowl, frown, stare angrily *n* angry stare; scowl

glucose *n* type of sugar obtained from grapes and other fruits

glue *n* substance used as an adhesive made from gelatine, resin, etc *vt* 1 stick with glue 2 attach firmly

glum *adj* disconsolate unhappy, gloomy, sullen **glumly** *adv* **glumness** *n*

glut *n* surfeit; excess *vt* (-tt-) supply with an excess amount; provide with too much *vi* gorge, overeat **glutton** *n* 1 excessively greedy person, one who habitually overeats 2 fanatic **gluttony** *n*

gnarled *adj* twisted and knotty, misshapen, lumpy

gnash *vt* grind or clench (the teeth); grate *n* grinding action or sound

gnat *n* small mosquito

gnaw *vt,vi* **1** bite continuously (on); chew **2** corrode; wear away **3** torment persistently *n* act of gnawing

gnome *n* mythological being living underground and having a dwarflike appearance

go *v* (went; gone) *vi* **1** move; proceed **2** function; work; operate **3** depart; leave **4** make a trip or take a walk with a particular purpose **5** vanish; disappear **6** extend as far as; reach **7** become **8** be put; belong **9** be ordered; have as a sequence **10** be used for **11** fail; break down; collapse **12** attend; be a member of **13** be decided (by) **14** be able to fit **15** be applicable or relevant **16** be awarded **17** be allowed to escape *vt* **1** take or follow (a route, path, etc) **2** travel (a specified distance) **go against** defy; infringe **go down 1** descend **2** be reduced **3** deflate **4** be received or appreciated by an audience **go for 1** aim at **2** attack suddenly **go in for** take up as a hobby, career, etc **go off 1** explode **2** cease to be interested in **3** happen **4** (of food) turn bad **go on 1** proceed; continue **2** criticize or nag incessantly **3** appear (on stage, TV, etc) **4** take place; occur **go out 1** be extinguished **2** cease to be fashionable **3** attend a social function **go over 1** repeat; re-examine **2** cross **3** be communicated **go slow** work slowly to enforce one's demands for more pay, etc **go through 1** suffer; have to bear; experience **2** make a search of **3** inspect **go under** succumb; sink **∼n 1** turn **2** *inf* energy; drive **go-between** *n* person acting as a messenger between parties; intermediary

goad *n* **1** sharp pointed stick used for driving cattle **2** provocation; stimulus *vt* **1** drive or prod with a goad **2** urge; incite; provoke

goal *n* **1** area between two posts through which a ball must pass in games such as football or hockey in order to score **2** winning post on a race track **3** point scored by getting a ball through the goal **4** aim; object; target **goalkeeper** *n* player who guards the goal area

goat *n* brownish-grey mammal often domesticated for its milk or wool **get one's goat** irritate; annoy

gobble[1] *vt,vi* eat quickly or greedily; gulp; bolt

gobble[2] *vi* (of a turkey cock) make a harsh gurgling sound *n* harsh gurgling sound

goblet *n* drinking vessel with a long stem

goblin *n* mythological being that is malevolent or mischievous; demon

god *n* **1** supernatural being having power over mankind who is worshipped and revered; deity **2** any object of worship or idolatry **God** *n* spiritual being who is the creator and ruler of mankind *interj* exclamation of disgust, horror, surprise, etc **the gods** highest gallery in a theatre **godchild** *n, pl* **-children** child for whom a godparent acts **goddaughter** *n* female godchild **godfather** *n* male godparent **godfearing** *adj* intensely religious; pious **godless** *adj* **1** having no religious beliefs **2** wicked; evil **godmother** *n* female godparent **godparent** *n* person who acts as a sponsor for a child at baptism **godsend** *n* timely and fortunate event or gift **godson** *n* male godchild

goddess *n* **1** female god **2** extremely beautiful woman

goggle *vi* **1** stare stupidly; gape **2** roll the eyes **goggles** *pl n* protective covering worn over the eyes

going *n* **1** departure; leaving **2** manner of travelling *adj* thriving **going** being to intending to

gold *n* **1** valuable yellow metal used for coins, jewellery, etc **2** coins of this metal **3** wealth; money; riches *adj,n* bright yellowish-orange **golden** *adj* **1** made of gold **2** of the colour of gold **3** valuable; precious **golden syrup** *n* kind of treacle of a pale golden colour **goldfinch** *n* European finch with gold and black plumage **goldfish** *n* reddish-gold freshwater fish **goldmine** *n* **1** place where gold ore is mined **2** source of great wealth **goldsmith** *n* craftsman who works with gold

golf *n* sport played on a grass course with the aim of driving a small ball into a succession of holes with a long club **golfer** *n*

gondola *n* long narrow open boat traditionally used on the canals in Venice **gondolier** *n* person who makes a living by transporting passengers in a gondola

gone *v pp* of **go**.

gong *n* percussion instrument consisting of a large metal disc, which is struck with a hammer

gonorrhoea (gonəˈriə) *n* type of venereal disease

good *adj* **1** of a high quality; not bad **2** obedient; not naughty **3** pleasing; attractive **4** virtuous **5** efficient; suitable **6** kind;

benevolent **7** beneficial **8** correct; accurate **9** able; competent **10** fitting; apt **11** considerable **12** safe; not harmful **13** full; complete *n* **1** use; point **2** benefit; advantage **3** virtue **for good** for ever; definitely and finally **Good Friday** *n* Friday before Easter when Christ's Crucifixion is commemorated **good-humoured** *adj* affable; in a good mood **good-looking** *adj* handsome; attractive **good-natured** *adj* kind; genial; easygoing **goods** *pl n* **1** merchandise; products **2** items; articles **3** possessions; property **good will** *n* **1** generosity; kindness **2** assets, such as clientele, reputation, etc , taken into consideration when a business is bought or sold

goose *n*, *pl* **geese 1** web-footed bird that is similar to but larger than a duck **2** foolish or timid person

gooseberry *n* small edible green berry that grows on a bush with thorny stems

gore[1] *n* blood that flows from a wound

gore[2] *vt* stab and wound by ramming with horns or tusks

gorge *n* **1** steep-sided river valley; ravine **2** lavish feast *vi*, *vt* stuff (oneself) with food; overeat; glut

gorgeous *adj* very beautiful; magnificent; wonderful

gorilla *n* large African ape

gorse *n* prickly evergreen shrub with bright yellow flowers

gory *adj* **1** covered with blood **2** bloodthirsty; involving bloodshed **3** horrifying

gosh *interj* exclamation of surprise

gosling *n* young goose

gospel *n* something taken as the truth; doctrine **Gospel** *n* one of the first four books of the New Testament, namely Matthew, Mark, Luke, and John

gossip *vi* talk, esp in a way that spreads scandal, rumours, etc *n* **1** act of gossiping **2** casual or malicious talk; news; scandal **3** person who gossips

got *v pt* and *pp* of **get. have got** possess; hold; own **have got to** must

gouge *vt* **1** carve a deep hole in with a sharp instrument **2** tear or scoop out

goulash *n* stew seasoned with paprika that is a traditional Hungarian dish

gourd *n* large fruit of various plants, having a tough outer skin and a large number of seeds

gourmand *n* glutton

gourmet *n* connoisseur of good food and wine

govern *vt*, *vi* **1** rule; reign (over); control **2** participate in a government *vt* **1** check; restrain **2** determine; influence completely

governess *n* woman employed as a tutor in a private household **government** *n* **1** control; rule **2** body of representatives who govern a country, state, etc **governor** *n* **1** ruler, esp of a colony, province, etc **2** person in charge of a prison **3** chief controller of a state in the US **4** *inf* boss **governorship** *n*

gown *n* **1** woman's dress, esp for evening wear **2** loose light garment, often signifying academic or official status; robe

grab *vt*, *vi* (-bb-) **1** take hold of hastily, clumsily or greedily; seize; snatch **2** take possession of by force; confiscate *n* **1** act of grabbing **2** mechanical device for gripping large objects

grace *n* **1** elegance, beauty, or charm of movement, style, etc **2** good will; magnanimity; mercy **3** short prayer of thanks offered before or after a meal *vt* serve to add elegance or beauty to; adorn **graceful** *adj* **gracefully** *adv* **gracious** *adj* **1** elegant; dignified **2** benevolent; courteous; kind *interj* *also* **good gracious!** expression of surprise or alarm

grade *n* **1** position on a scale or in a category **2** mark or score awarded in an examination test, etc *vt* **1** place in a category according to size, quality, etc **2** award a mark or score to **gradation** *n* **1** step or stage within a system or on a scale **2** gradual progression or transition

gradient *n* slope of a road, railway, etc measured by the increase in height per distance travelled

gradual *adj* **1** slowly changing **2** not steep **gradually** *adv*

graduate *vi* ('grædju:eit) **1** receive a degree or diploma from a university, college, etc **2** change gradually; move along a scale **3** progress *n* ('grædju:it) person holding a degree, diploma, etc **graduation** *n*

graffiti *pl n* scribbled messages or drawings on walls, public buildings, etc

graft *n* **1** small plant shoot that is united with another plant in order to produce a new plant **2** transplanted bone or skin tissue *vt*, *vi* **1** propagate by means of a graft **2** transplant or be transplanted

grain *n* **1** fruit or seed of a cereal plant **2** cereal crops **3** small particle or granule of sand, sugar, etc **4** pattern, texture, or arrangement of layers of a piece of timber, rock, etc **5** minute quantity or proportion

gram n also **gramme** metric unit of weight equivalent to approx 0 035 ozs

grammar n **1** system of rules governing the correct use of a language **2** branch of linguistics concerned mainly with syntax and word formation **grammar school** n (in Britain) state secondary school that selects pupils at the age of eleven by means of examination **grammatical** adj relating or conforming to the rules of grammar **grammatically** adv

gramophone n machine for playing records, having a turntable, amplifier, and pick-up arm fitted with a stylus; record player

granary n storage place for grain

grand adj **1** impressively large; magnificent; tremendous **2** haughty; elegant **3** marvellous; great **4** admirable; worthy **5** final and complete n also **grand piano** large piano whose strings are arranged horizontally rather than vertically **grandeur** n **grandly** adv **grandchild** n grandson or granddaughter **granddaughter** n daughter of one s son or daughter **grandfather** n father of one s father or mother **grandmother** n mother of one's father or mother **grandparent** n grandfather or grandmother **grandson** n son of one's son or daughter **grandstand** n covered block of seats for spectators at a race meeting, football match, etc

granite n hard greyish-white crystalline rock

granny n inf grandmother

grant vt **1** give as a favour **2** admit; concede **3** give (a sum of money) n sum of money given for research, education, etc

granule n small grain **granular** adj

grape n small sweet green or purple fruit that is eaten raw, dried, or pressed to make wine **grapevine** n **1** vine producing grapes **2** informal or underground information network

grapefruit n large round citrus fruit with a yellow peel

graph n chart or diagram for depicting the relationship between variables, particular sets, quantities etc **graphic** adj **1** clearly or imaginatively expressed **2** relating to writing or drawing **3** in graph form

graphite n soft black carbon used in pencils, electrodes, etc

grapple vi struggle physically; wrestle; tussle **grapple with** attempt to deal with (a problem, difficult situation, etc) ~n **1** iron hook **2** grip in wrestling; hold

grasp vt,vi **1** take hold (of) firmly in the hands; grip; clasp vt understand; comprehend n **1** firm grip **2** knowledge; understanding **3** power to dominate

grass n **1** plant with green spiky blades **2** lawn, field, or pasture of such plants **3** sl marijuana vt,vi sow with grass vi sl act as an informer, esp to the police **grassy** adj **grasshopper** n greenish-brown insect renowned for its characteristic chirping sound produced by friction of the hind legs against the wings **grass roots** pl n **1** section of the population regarded as representing true political or public opinions at a local level **2** underlying or essential principles

grate [1] vt cut or shred (cheese, vegetables, etc) by rubbing against a rough surface vt,vi **1** produce a harsh squeak by scraping **2** annoy; jar n harsh squeak

grate [2] n iron structure or rack placed in a fireplace to hold fuel and allowing air to circulate underneath

grateful adj thankful; appreciative of kindness a gift, opportunity, etc **gratefully** adv

gratify vt **1** seek or obtain satisfaction of (one s desires); indulge **2** please; make happy **gratification** n

grating n cover or guard made of a network of metal bars; grille

gratitude n feeling or expression of appreciation; thankfulness

gratuity n gift of money, tip **gratuitous** adj **1** free of charge **2** not asked for or solicited; unjustified

grave [1] n trench or hole dug in the ground for a coffin **have one foot in the grave** be feeble or near to death

grave [2] adj **1** serious, solemn **2** dangerous bad **gravely** adv

gravel n coarse mixture of fragments of rock

gravity n **1** force of attraction between objects with mass, exerted by the earth moon etc to pull objects towards their centre **2** seriousness; solemn importance **gravitate** vi **1** be drawn by the force of gravity **2** be attracted to a certain place **gravitation** n

gravy n stock or juice produced by cooking meat, often thickened for a sauce

graze[1] vi,vt feed or allow to feed on grass or other vegetation in a pasture

graze[2] vt,vi touch lightly; scrape vt produce a scratch or cut on the skin by scraping n abrasion; scratch

grease n 1 melted animal fat 2 lubricant; oil vt 1 cover or smear with grease 2 lubricate **greasy** adj **greasepaint** n waxy substance used by actors as make-up for the stage

great adj 1 large; big; huge; vast; tremendous 2 excellent 3 famous 4 important; significant 5 impressive; grand **greatly** adv **greatness** n

greed n 1 desire to overeat; gluttony 2 desire to take more than one's fair share of wealth, power, etc **greedy** adj **greedily** adv

green n 1 colour of grass; spectral colour 2 grass pitch or field · adj 1 of the colour green 2 inexperienced; naive 3 jealous; envious 4 unripe **greenery** n green vegetation; foliage **greenfly** n green aphid **greengage** n fruit of the plum family with a yellowish-green skin **greengrocer** n person who sells fruit and vegetables **greengrocery** n **greenhouse** n shed with walls and roof mainly of glass, used for housing and cultivating plants **greens** pl n leaves of green vegetables, such as cabbage or spinach

greet vt 1 welcome 2 send good wishes to 3 be present at the arrival of; meet **greeting** n statement or act of welcome, good wishes, etc

gregarious adj enjoying other people's company; sociable

grenade n small explosive shell thrown by hand or fired from a gun

grey n colour between black and white, having no hue adj 1 of a grey colour 2 having grey hair 3 dull; gloomy **greyish** adj **greyhound** n breed of smooth-haired dog with a slender body and pointed muzzle, often used for racing

grid n 1 network of squares printed or placed over a map or drawing 2 network of electricity cables water pipes etc

grief n sorrow; distress; remorse **grief-stricken** adj suffering intense grief; heart-broken **grievance** n complaint; feeling of being hurt or offended **grieve** vi vt feel or cause great sorrow or distress

grill n rack or section of an oven on or under which food is cooked vt,vi cook on or under a grill vt inf interrogate; cross-question

grille n framework of metal bars forming an ornamental screen or grating

grim adj 1 bleak; unpleasant; formidable 2 stern; unbending; severe **grimly** adv

grimace n facial expression of disgust, hatred etc vi screw up the face in a grimace

grime n 1 soot 2 dirt **grimy** adj

grin n broad happy smile vi,vt (-nn-) smile with the lips widely parted

grind vt,vi (ground) 1 crush or pound into powder or small particles 2 sharpen (a blade) or smooth by friction 3 oppress; enslave 4 grate or gnash (the teeth) n hard toil repetitious routine **grinder** n appliance for grinding coffee beans, etc

grip n 1 firm hold of a body; grasp 2 strength of the fingers 3 handle of a racquet or bat 4 understanding; comprehension 5 holdall; bag **get** or **come to grips with** learn to control; master; tackle ~vt,vi (-pp-) 1 hold firmly; clasp 2 mesmerize; enthrall

gripe vi moan; nag; complain vi,vt feel or cause sudden pain

gristle n cartilage, esp when present in meat

grit n 1 small pieces of gravel, sand, etc 2 inf courage; stamina v **grit one's teeth** (-tt-) 1 clench the teeth 2 bear suffering bravely and without complaint

groan n 1 low cry of pain, distress, disappointment, etc 2 harsh noise made by the wind 3 complaint; grumble vi vt 1 utter or sound like a groan 2 complain; moan

grocer n shopkeeper selling food, household articles, etc **grocery** n trade or business of a grocer **groceries** pl n items purchased from a grocer

groin n part of the body where the legs join the abdomen

groom n 1 person employed to look after horses 2 bridegroom vt 1 rub down (a horse) 2 keep (hair, clothes, etc) clean and neat 3 train or instruct for a particular role

groove n 1 narrow channel cut into the surface of something; rut; furrow 2 monotonous routine vt cut a groove (into)

grope vi 1 search by touch; handle uncertainly; fumble 2 seek (a solution) with difficulty n fumbling touch

gross adj 1 offensively fat 2 vulgar; crude 3 excessive; extreme 4 before deductions n 1 *pl* **gross** quantity of 144 (12 dozen) **2** majority; bulk *vt* earn before deductions **grossly** *adv*

grotesque *adj* extremely ugly; bizarre·

grotto *n* small cave; cavern

ground[1] *n* **1** surface of the earth; land; soil **2** enclosure or pitch **3** area of knowledge; field **down to the ground** perfectly; entirely ~*vt* **1** prevent the take-off of (an aircraft) **2** give basic but thorough instructions to **grounds** *pl n* **1** justification; valid reasons **2** land attached to a large house, castle, etc **3** coffee dregs **groundsheet** *n* waterproof sheet used when camping in a tent **groundsman** *n*, *pl* **-men** caretaker or gardener employed on an estate, park, sports ground, etc **groundwork** *n* basic preparation for a job or project

ground[2] *v pt* and *pp* of **grind.**

group *n* number of people or things placed or classed together; set *vt*, *vi* form into a group or set; assemble

grouse[1] *n* game bird with reddish-brown or black plumage

grouse[2] *vi* grumble; nag; complain *n* complaint; grievance

grove *n* area of trees; plantation

grovel *vi* (-ll-) **1** humiliate oneself; behave in a servile manner **2** crawl in an undignified manner

grow *v* (grew; grown) *vi* **1** become larger taller etc ; mature **2** increase in size or number **3** develop; arise; become *vt* produce; bring forth; yield **grow up** become adult **grown-up** *n* adult person *adj* mature; adult **growth** *n* **1** process of growing **2** amount by which something grows **3** increase; development **4** cancer or tumour

growl *vt*, *vi* **1** (esp of an animal such as a dog) utter a low warning or hostile sound **2** say in a low angry voice *vi* rumble; grumble *n* low hostile sound

grub *n* **1** larva of certain insects, esp a beetle **2** *sl* food *vt*, *vi* (-bb-) dig or root (in)

grubby *adj* dirty; grimy soiled **grubbiness** *n*

grudge *n* grievance feeling of resentment *vt* resent; feel grieved about; begrudge **grudgingly** *adv*

gruelling *adj* extremely strenuous, exhausting; taxing; rigorous

gruesome *adj* ghastly; horrible; spine-chilling

gruff *adj* rough in manner or voice; rough **gruffly** *adv*

grumble *vt*, *vi* express dissatisfaction; groan; complain *vi* rumble *n* **1** expression of discontent; groan **2** rumble

grumpy *adj* inclined to grumble; cross; bad-tempered **grumpiness** *n*

grunt *vi*, *vt* **1** (esp of a pig) snort **2** say in a low incoherent manner *n* **1** snort **2** low incoherent noise

guarantee *n* **1** statement that goods supplied conform to a certain standard or that they will be repaired or replaced **2** formal undertaking to honour another s debts **3** assurance that something is right or will happen *vt* give a guarantee of; assure; undertake **guarantor** *n* person giving a guarantee

guard *vt*, *vi* **1** keep watch (over) in order to defend, protect, or prevent entry or escape **2** shield; protect *vt* restrain; control **guard against** take precautions to avoid ~*n* **1** person who guards, esp a warder **2** military or police escort **3** sentry; keeper **4** person officially in charge of a train **5** safety device fitted to a machine, fire, etc **6** safeguard; precaution **on/off one's guard** alert or watchful/unwary **guarded** *adj* cautious **guardian** *n* **1** person having custody of another, esp a minor **2** defender; protector; keeper

guerrilla *n* also **guerilla** member of a group of fighters waging war against regular military forces, using tactics of ambush, sabotage, etc

guess *vt* *vi* **1** attempt to judge or find an answer or solution (to) without having sufficient information; estimate **2** give the right answer (to); discover correctly *n* attempt at solving; estimate **guesswork** *n* **1** process of guessing **2** conclusion reached by guessing

guest *n* **1** person invited as a visitor **2** person whom one entertains or treats to a meal **3** person staying at a hotel **guesthouse** *n* small private hotel or boarding house

guide *vt* **1** lead; show the way to; conduct **2** influence; direct **3** steer; control the movement of *n* **1** person who guides, esp one who conducts tourists or sightseers round places of interest **2** also **guidebook** book giving information on places of interest **3** book containing practical information on a subject; manual **4** also **guideline** suggested principle or standard **5** Girl Guide **guidance** *n*

guild n 1 society of craftsmen or merchants of the Middle Ages 2 association; society

guile n cunning; slyness; deceit **guileless** adj

guillotine n 1 execution device used to behead people 2 machine fitted with a sharp blade for cutting and trimming paper, metal, etc vt use a guillotine on

guilt n 1 fact of having committed a criminal or other offence 2 deep feeling of shame or remorse at having been responsible for a crime, error, omission, etc **guiltless** adj **guilty** adj **guiltily** adv

guinea n former. British gold coin worth 21 shillings (£1 05)

guinea pig n 1 small tailless rodent often kept as a pet or used for experiments 2 person used as the subject of experiment

guitar n long-necked musical instrument, usually with six strings which are plucked **guitarist** n

gulf n 1 large bay or inlet of the sea 2 chasm or abyss 3 great discrepancy; irreconcilable difference vt engulf

gull n a seabird with white or grey plumage and webbed feet

gullet n 1 oesophagus 2 throat

gullible adj easily cheated or taken in **gullibility** n

gulp vt,vi 1 swallow (food) quickly and noisily; bolt 2 inhale noisily; choke. gasp n act of gulping

gum¹ n 1 sticky substance produced by various plants and used as an adhesive 2 chewing gum v (-mm-) vt stick with gum vt,vi also **gum up** smear or become smeared with gum; clog

gum² n pink fleshy tissue in which the teeth are rooted

gun n any type of weapon capable of discharging bullets or shells from a barrel **jump the gun** begin too soon or without adequate preparation **stick to one's guns** keep to one's opinions or principles; persevere ~vt (-nn-) also **gun down** shoot at with a gun **gun for** pursue with determination **gunman** n, pl **-men** person who uses a gun to commit a crime **gunpowder** n explosive mixture of sulphur, charcoal and saltpetre **gunrunning** n smuggling of firearms **gunrunner** n

gurgle vi 1 (esp of flowing water) make a bubbling or rushing sound 2 produce a throaty chuckle; bubble n gurgling sound

guru n Hindu or Sikh religious teacher

gush vt,vi 1 pour out with great force; flow; stream 2 utter with exaggerated enthusiasm or sentiment n sudden stream or flow

gust n blast of wind, smoke, etc

gut n 1 alimentary canal or any part of it 2 strong type of thread made from an animal's intestines vt (-tt-) 1 remove the entrails of (fish) 2 reduce to a shell; destroy **guts** pl n 1 intestines or bowels 2 courage; tenacity; determination 3 essential part; core

gutter n drainage channel at the side of a road or attached to the eaves of a roof

guy¹ n 1 inf man 2 effigy of Guy Fawkes that is burnt on Nov 5th

guy² n rope or chain used to keep a tent, mast, etc , in position

guzzle vt,vi eat or drink greedily or noisily

gymkhana (dʒim'kɑ:nə) n horseriding event in which competitors are judged for their skill or speed in various contests

gymnasium n, pl **gymnasiums** or **gymnasia** (dʒim'neiziə) building or hall equipped with gymnastic apparatus and also used for various indoor sports **gymnastics** n method of physical training that includes exercises in balance, vaulting, etc **gymnast** n **gymnastic** adj

gynaecology n branch of medicine concerned with diseases peculiar to women **gynaecological** adj **gynaecologist** n

gypsum n white mineral consisting of calcium sulphate, used to make plaster of Paris

Gypsy n also **Gipsy** member of a nomadic race living in many parts of Europe and N America

gyrate (dʒai'reit) vi rotate **gyration** n

H

haberdasher n shop or shopkeeper selling pins, thread, lace, etc **haberdashery** n

habit n 1 custom; usual practice or way of behaving 2 type of garment worn by monks nuns, etc **habit-forming** adj causing addiction **habitual** adj 1 usual; customary 2 having a specified habit or addiction **habitually** adv

habitable adj fit to be lived in

hack¹ vi,vt cut chop or strike roughly or clumsily vi inf cough dryly and spasmodically n rough cut or blow **hacksaw** n saw for cutting metal, consisting of a narrow blade in a U-shaped frame

hack [2] n 1 horse that can be hired 2 old overworked horse 3 writer or journalist who produces poor work fast and for little money **hackneyed** adj unoriginal; said too often; trite

had v pt and pp of **have**.

haddock n, pl **haddock** common N Atlantic food fish, related to the cod

haemorrhage n profuse bleeding vi to bleed profusely

hag n ugly old woman; witch

haggard adj looking ill, tired, or pale; gaunt

haggis n Scottish dish of sheep s offal and oatmeal boiled in a sheep s stomach

haggle vi dispute noisily (over) a price, etc wrangle

hail [1] n 1 also **hailstones** pellets of frozen rain 2 shower of hail 3 profusion or shower of insults, abuse, or bullets vi fall as hail

hail [2] vt 1 greet or salute 2 call out to; attract the attention of **hail from** be a native of n shout; greeting

hair n 1 threadlike growth on or from the skin of mammals 2 mass of hairs, esp that on the human head **hair's breadth** very short distance or margin **keep your hair on!** keep calm! **let one's hair down** act informally and without reserve **not turn a hair** show no fear or surprise **split hairs** make petty unimportant distinctions **hairy** adj **hairdo** n arrangement of a woman s hair, esp by a hairdresser **hairdresser** n 1 person who cuts and arranges hair 2 shop employing such persons **hairdressing** n **hairgrip** n also **hairpin** clip for securing women's hair **hairpiece** n false hair worn to hide baldness, etc **hair-raising** adj frightening; terrifying

half n, pl **halves** 1 amount obtained by dividing a whole into two equal or nearly equal parts 2 either of the parts 3 half a pint, esp of beer **better half** one's wife or husband **go halves** share equally ~adv 1 to the extent of a half 2 partially; nearly adj amounting to a half in number pron amount of half in number **half-and-half** adj neither one thing nor the other **half-back** n player or position in rugby, soccer, etc, behind the forwards **half-baked** adj foolish; not properly thought out **half-breed** n 1 person having parents of different races; half-caste 2 domestic animal having parents of different breeds adj relating to a half-breed **half-brother** n brother related through only one parent **half-caste** n,adj half-breed **half-hearted** adj not enthusiastic **half-heartedly** adv **half-sister** n sister related through only one parent **half-term** n point or holiday in the middle of a scholastic term **half-time** n point or interval in the middle of a football match, etc **halfway** adv,adj equally far from two points **halfwit** n 1 idiot; cretin 2 stupid or foolish person **halfwitted** adj

halibut n, pl **halibut** large N Atlantic flat fish, important as a food fish

hall n 1 large room for dining, lectures, etc 2 public building for dances, meetings, etc 3 also **hallway** passage or room leading from an entrance to other rooms 4 large country house 5 students residence, hostel, or college

hallelujah interj,n, also **alleluia** cry of praise to God

hallmark n 1 stamp of an official body on a silver or gold article, indicating its purity 2 typical characteristic proving authenticity; distinguishing feature

hallowed adj 1 holy; consecrated 2 revered; respected

Hallowe'en n Oct 31st, eve of All Saints Day, when witches are supposed to ride at night and graves give up their dead

hallucination n 1 alleged but imaginary perception of an object, sound, etc, because of illness or through taking certain drugs 2 act of such perception **hallucinate** vi experience hallucinations

halo n 1 circle of light around the head of Christ, an angel saint, etc, as shown in paintings 2 circle of light around the sun or moon, caused by refraction by ice particles

halt vi,vt stop n 1 act of stopping; stop 2 place, as on a train or bus route, at which it stops briefly

halter n 1 rope by which horses, etc, can be led or tethered 2 also **halterneck** neckline of a woman s dress that leaves the back bare

halve vt 1 divide in half; share equally 2 cut by half

ham n 1 salted, sometimes smoked meat from the thigh of a pig 2 back of the thigh; thigh and buttocks 3 actor who overacts 4 amateur radio operator **ham-fisted** adj clumsy

hamburger n fried cake of seasoned minced beef often served in a bread roll

hammer n 1 tool with a head fitted at right angles to a handle for driving in nails, beating metal, etc 2 any device for striking, knocking, etc 3 heavy metal sphere with a flexible wire handle, thrown by athletes **go at it hammer and tongs** argue or fight fiercely ~vt, vi strike or pound with a hammer vt 1 strike violently 2 defeat conclusively 3 criticize severely **hammer away at** work hard to do or produce **hammer in(to)** teach by repetition **hammer out** settle or work out after much discussion or dispute

hammock n bed of canvas, rope, etc : suspended between two supports

hamper¹ vt prevent from moving or working easily; hinder; impede

hamper² n basket or case in which food and other things can be packed

hamster n tailless ratlike animal with pouched cheeks, kept as a pet

hand n 1 part of the arm below the wrist 2 help, assistance, role 3 manual worker, labourer 4 indicator esp on a clock 5 single game at cards or the cards so dealt 6 position or direction **change hands** pass to another owner **a free hand** complete freedom **from hand to mouth** precariously in poverty **hand and foot** completely **hand in glove** in close cooperation **in good hands** well cared for **in/out of hand** under/beyond control **on/at/to hand** near; close by **on the other hand** in contrast **take in hand** discipline; control **wash one's hands of** disclaim responsibility **win hands down** win easily ~vt 1 pass to; give 2 also **hand on, hand down** pass on, transmit **handbag** n small bag for carrying personal items, etc **handbook** n book of useful hints or information manual; guide **handbrake** n manual brake on cars, etc **handful** n 1 small amount or number 2 person that is difficult to control **handmade** adj made by a person rather than a machine **hand-pick** vt select very carefully **handstand** n vertical upside-down position maintained by balancing on one's hands **handwriting** n 1 writing done by hand, 2 individual's style of handwriting **handwritten** adj

handicap n 1 something that hinders, disadvantage; defect; drawback 2 mental or physical defect or disability 3 disadvantage given to certain sports competitors to equalize everybody's chances vt (-pp-) be a disadvantage to **handicapped** adj

handicraft n skilled manual work, often artistic, such as pottery

handiwork n 1 skilled or artistic manual work 2 result of someone's actions or plans

handkerchief n piece of absorbent material on which to blow or wipe one's nose

handle n part of a tool, machine, case, etc by which to hold, carry, or control it **fly off the handle** lose one's temper ~vt 1 hold or feel with one's hands 2 control or use (a machine, etc) 3 deal with; cope with; manage **handlebars** pl n metal crosspiece by which a bicycle, etc is steered

handsome adj 1 good-looking 2 generous or ample **handsomely** adv

handy adj 1 useful; easy or convenient to use 2 capable of doing manual jobs well 3 easily accessible **handyman** n, pl -**men** person adept at odd jobs

hang vi vt (hung or hung) 2 hanged or hung) 1 suspend or be suspended from above 2 execute or be executed by strangling with a noose vt 1 suspend by a hook, attach, fix or stick in position 2 keep (meat esp game) suspended until ready for eating **hang around** or **about** linger, wait without purpose **hang back** hesitate **hang on** vt wait, persevere; cling to **hang out** 1 live, frequent 2 display, hang outside **hang up** replace (telephone receiver) n **get the hang of** understand or begin to be able to do **hanger** n coathanger **hangover** n after-effects of excessive drinking, esp a headache

hanker vi desire persistently; yearn (for) **hankering** n lingering desire or wish

haphazard adj happening or arranged without planning, by chance, or at random adv also **haphazardly** by chance; at random

happen vi occur take place, esp by chance **happen to (one)** befall; affect **happen to** chance to (be, do, know, etc) **happening** n occurrence; event, esp a social one characterized by spontaneity

happy adj 1 feeling, indicating, or causing contentment, pleasure or joy 2 fortunate 3 willing (to) 4 suitable; apt 5 mildly drunk **happily** adv **happiness** n

harass vt annoy, pester or pursue (someone)

continually **harassed** adj nervous; irritated; bothered **harassment** n

harbour n 1 sheltered coastal area providing safe anchorage for ships, etc 2 place for shelter or safety vt 1 give refuge to (a hunted criminal, etc); shelter 2 cherish or maintain secretly vi take shelter (in)

hard adj 1 not easily cut, dented, etc; rigid 2 difficult to do or understand 3 violent or strenuous; arduous 4 unfair; harsh or strict; severe; distressing 5 unfeeling or insensitive 6 (of water) impairing the lathering of soap **hard and fast** strict; rigid **hard cash** paper money and coins rather than cheques, etc **hard to come by** difficult to obtain **hard drugs** addictive drugs **hard of hearing** deaf or slightly deaf **hard up** having little money ~adv 1 with force; violently 2 with effort or vigour 3 closely; with careful scrutiny **hard at it** working strenuously **hard put to** finding difficulty in **harden** vt,vi 1 make or become hard(er) 2 make or become insensitive or accustomed to pain or suffering

hardback n book with stiff cardboard covers

hardboard n sheeting formed from compressed sawdust and woodchips, used as a building material, etc

hard-boiled adj 1 (of eggs) boiled until the whole inside is solid 2 cynical; callous

hard-headed adj practical or shrewd, esp in business **hard-headedness** n

hard-hearted adj not feeling or showing sympathy for the sufferings of others; cruel **hard-heartedly** adv **hard-heartedness** n

hardly adv scarcely; not quite; barely

hardship n lack of material comforts; deprivation; suffering

hardware n 1 household utensils, tools, etc; ironmongery 2 computer equipment

hardy adj 1 able to tolerate difficult physical conditions; tough; robust 2 (of plants) able to survive outdoors all year round

hare n animal resembling a rabbit but having longer legs and ears vi rush (about, after, etc), esp in a confused manner **harebrained** adj stupid; rash; foolish

hark vi listen (to) **hark back** revert (to a previous question or topic)

harm n damage or injury vt cause damage or injury to **harmful** adj

harmonic adj relating to or characterized by harmony n component of a musical note whose frequency is a multiple of the note's pitch **harmonically** adv with or in harmony **harmonics** n study of musical sounds

harmonica n small musical instrument played by blowing into a small case in which metal reeds are set; mouth-organ

harmony n 1 pleasant relationship of musical sounds 2 friendly agreement in personal relationships 3 pleasant arrangement, as of colours **harmonious** adj **harmoniously** adv **harmonize** vt vi come or bring into harmony; reconcile vi sing or play in harmony (with) **harmonization** n

harness n 1 complete set of straps and other parts fitted to a working horse 2 fitment for a baby, etc, used for controlling, guiding, etc vt 1 put a harness on (a horse) 2 gain control over (a form of energy etc)

harp n triangular musical instrument played by plucking or drawing the fingers over strings v **harp on** talk repeatedly about

harpoon n spear with a line attached that is fired or thrown when hunting whales, etc vt,vi catch (whales, etc) using a harpoon

harpsichord n pianolike musical instrument

harsh adj 1 not soft; coarse; rough 2 severe; cruel; unkind 3 jarring on the senses; strident; too bright or loud **harshly** adv **harshness** n

harvest n 1 act of cutting and gathering ripe crops 2 the crop itself 3 result; product vt, vi 1 gather in ripe crops 2 get the benefit from

has v 3rd person singular of **have** in the present tense

hashish n also **hash** intoxicating drug prepared from dried leaves, flower tops, etc, of Indian hemp

hasten vi,vt hurry or cause to hurry; rush **haste** n 1 speed; hurry; urgency 2 rashness **hastily** adv **hasty** adj

hat n shaped covering for the head **keep (something) under one's hat** keep secret **old hat** old-fashioned; no longer novel

hatch[1] vi,vt to emerge or cause to emerge from an egg vt also **hatch up** think up (a plot, surprise, or idea)

hatch[2] n 1 small door covering an opening in a wall, esp between two rooms 2 cover for an opening on the deck of a boat or ship providing access below decks

hatchet n small axe **bury the hatchet** make peace after a quarrel

hate vt, vi dislike fiercely; abhor n 1 *also* **hatred** feeling of strong dislike or abhorrence 2 person or thing so disliked **hateful** adj loathsome

haughty adj proud and arrogant; condescending; supercilious **haughtily** adv **haughtiness** n

haul vt vi pull or drag along with great effort; transport n 1 something hauled 2 act of hauling or the effort involved 3 distance hauled or travelled 4 result or amount obtained from an enterprise

haunch n part of the body from the hip to the thigh

haunt vt vi visit as or be visited by a ghost vt 1 go to habitually; frequent 2 be continually in the thoughts of; obsess 3 pester 4 pervade n place one frequents

have v (3rd person s present has pp and pt had) vt 1 be characterized by 2 own possess 3 hold, keep 4 experience or undergo 5 bear (children or young) 6 eat or drink (something) 7 take or receive 8 must; be forced (to) 9 cause to happen or be done 10 tolerate; put up with allow 11 cheat or deceive v aux (used to form the perfect and pluperfect tenses) **have had it** be near death no longer usable tolerable etc **have on 1** wear 2 fool; hoax

haven n 1 place of shelter; refuge 2 harbour

haversack n canvas bag carried on the back or over the shoulder while hiking, etc

havoc n disorder or confusion

hawk n type of small long-tailed bird of prey

hawthorn n thorny tree or bush with white pink or red flowers

hay n dried grass used as fodder **hayfever** n allergic reaction to inhaled pollen or dust causing sneezing runny eyes etc **haystack** n pile of hay in a field **haywire** adj **go haywire** go badly wrong, become disorganized

hazard n 1 danger; peril; risk 2 something causing danger or risk; obstacle vt 1 risk; gamble 2 venture (an opinion etc) **hazardous** adj

haze n 1 light mist that impairs visibility 2 vague or confused state of mind **hazy** adj 1 slightly misty 2 dimly or imperfectly remembered or remembering **hazily** adv **haziness** n

hazel n small tree producing edible nuts adj, n light to medium brown

he pron male person or animal

head n 1 part of the body above the neck 2 intelligence; mental power 3 chief person; commander; ruler 4 highest or foremost point or part; top 5 pl **head** person or animal considered as a unit in a group 6 short for **headmaster** or **headmistress** **bite someone's head off** rebuke sharply **come to a head** reach a critical point **give someone his head** allow greater freedom **go to one's head** make proud, rash etc **head over heels (in love)** madly in love **keep/lose one's head** keep calm/become flustered **not make head nor tail of** completely fail to understand **off one's head** crazy **over someone's head** to someone of greater authority ~vt vi be form or put at the head of vt hit (a football) with one's head **head for** be directed towards (a place trouble etc) **heady** adj intoxicating, affecting the mind or senses

headache n 1 pain in the head 2 troublesome person or thing

headgear n any covering for the head

heading n title at the beginning of an article chapter of a book etc

headland n area of land jutting out to sea; cape

headlight n *also* **headlamp** powerful light on the front of a car etc

headline n words in large or heavy type at the top of a newspaper article

headlong adv *also* **headfirst** 1 with the head foremost 2 rashly; impetuously

headmaster n chief male teacher in a school **headmistress** f n

headphones pl n pair of receivers fitted over the ears for communications purposes

headquarters pl n chief office of a military force or other organization

headstrong adj 1 obstinate wilful 2 rash impetuous

headway n 1 movement forward by a vessel 2 progress as in a struggle or problem

heal vt cure, restore to health vi (of a wound) close up

health n 1 person s general bodily condition 2 condition of being well freedom from illness 3 general condition of a business, country, etc **healthy** adj 1 in good health 2 conducive to good health **3** promising or encouraging **healthily** adv

heap n **1** jumbled mass; pile; mound **2** also **heaps** great deal **3** something no longer useful vt place (things) in a heap

hear (heard) vt, vi **1** perceive (sound) with the ears **2** become informed (about news) vt listen to **hear from** receive news, etc, from **hear of 1** obtain news or information about **2** allow the possibility of **hear out** allow (a person) to finish what he is saying **hear, hear!** exclamation of agreement, approval, etc **hearing** n **1** sense by which one hears; ability to hear **2** range in which a person may be heard **3** chance or opportunity to be heard

hearse n car or carriage for carrying a corpse for burial or cremation

heart n **1** muscular internal organ that pumps blood round the body **2** symbolic seat of love sympathy, or courage; these feelings themselves **3** soul; inner thoughts **4** centre; core **5** heart-shaped symbol **6** playing card marked with one or more red hearts **hearts** pl or s n suit of cards each marked thus **after someone's own heart** exactly of the type someone likes or approves of **break someone's heart** upset or disappoint someone, esp in love **by heart** from memory **heart of hearts** inmost feelings **heart to heart** (discussion that is) intimate **set one's heart on** want very much **take to heart** be greatly influenced by **wear one's heart on one's sleeve** make one's feelings, esp of love, very obvious **with all one's heart 1** with deep love **2** willingly

heart attack n sudden very painful, often fatal, malfunction of the heart

heartbeat n single pulsation of the heart

heartbroken adj very unhappy disappointed etc

hearth n **1** place where a domestic fire is lit **2** the whole fireplace **3** the home

heartless adj cruel; unfeeling; unsympathetic **heartlessly** adv

hearty adj **1** jovial, cheerful **2** cordial; sincere **3** in good health; vigorous n fellow, comrade **heartily** adv

heat n **1** form of energy resulting from the motion of atoms and molecules in an object etc **2** degree of hotness, esp when great **3** hot weather **4** strong or deep feeling, anger; enthusiasm **5** pressure intensity **6** period of sexual excitement in female animals **7** preliminary race or contest vt, vi make or become hot vi become agitated or nervous **heated** adj **heater** n domestic appliance for heating rooms, water, etc **heatwave** n period of very hot weather

heath n **1** area of open uncultivated ground **2** heather

heathen adj **1** not believing in the same god or religion as oneself; pagan **2** uncivilized; barbaric n person who is heathen

heather n also **heath** small evergreen plant having small purplish or white bell-shaped flowers **heathery** adj

heave vt, vi pull or drag (something heavy); haul vt **1** throw with great effort **2** give out (a sigh, etc) vi **1** move up and down rhythmically **2** retch n act of heaving

heaven n **1** abode of God, the angels, and the good after death **2** great happiness; intense pleasure **3** place or state that induces this **4** also **heavens** sky **move heaven and earth** do everything possible to effect **heavenly** adj

heavy adj **1** of great or considerable weight **2** difficult to move or lift because of weight **3** serious; weighty; considerable **4** difficult to bear, fulfil, digest, read, etc **5** violent; of great force n **1** role of a villain in a play or film **2** actor playing this **heavily** adv **heaviness** n **heavyweight** n boxer who weighs 175 pounds or more

Hebrew n **1** language of the ancient Jews and modern Israel **2** Jew; Israelite

heckle vt, vi try to disconcert a public speaker by continual taunts **heckler** n

hectic adj **1** very busy or active **2** hurried and confused; agitated **hectically** adv

hedge n **1** closely planted row of bushes and small trees forming a fence etc **2** barrier vt **1** provide or surround with a hedge **2** give an answer that does not reveal one's true thoughts **hedge one's bets** make a safe bet, investment, etc to protect oneself **hedgehog** n small animal with long prickles on its back

heed vt vi take careful notice of n **1** attention notice **2** caution; care **take heed!** be careful!

heel[1] n **1** back part of a the foot **2** part of a sock stocking etc that covers the heel **3** part of a shoe or boot beneath the heel **4** despicable man **Achilles' heel** person s only weak point **down at heel** shabbily dressed **cool one's heels** be kept waiting **take to one's heels** run away **to heel** under control ~vt repair the heel of (a shoe)

heel[2] vi also **heel over** 1 tilt to one side; list 2 fall to the ground

hefty adj 1 strong and muscular 2 forceful

height n 1 distance from bottom to top 2 altitude 3 most successful point; culmination 4 most extreme or exaggerated form **heights** high place or point **heighten** vt,vi 1 make or become higher 2 accentuate; be increased

heir n 1 male person who inherits the wealth, rank, etc, of another when the latter dies 2 successor, as to a tradition **heiress** f n **heirloom** n object passed down to succeeding generations in a family

held v pt and pp of **hold**.

helicopter n aircraft powered by large overhead horizontally rotating blades

helium n light inert rare gaseous element

hell n 1 abode of Satan; place of eternal damnation for the wicked after death 2 extreme suffering; torture; difficulty 3 place or situation causing this **a hell of a** very much of a **for the hell of it** for fun **give someone hell** 1 cause much trouble to 2 scold severely **like hell** 1 very much, fast, etc 2 certainly not

hello interj exclamation of greeting, surprise, etc

helm n 1 steering device on a boat; tiller or steering-wheel 2 position of control or authority **helmsman** n

helmet n 1 soldier's protective metal headgear worn during battle 2 protective headgear worn by miners, firemen motorcyclists, etc

help vt,vi 1 give assistance (to), aid 2 cause improvement in vt 1 be of use in (doing) 2 avoid (doing); prevent oneself from 3 serve with food or drink **it can't be helped** it cannot be avoided or rectified **help oneself** (to) 1 take without permission payment etc 2 serve oneself **help out** give assistance to esp in time of need ~n 1 assistance aid, cooperation 2 domestic servant **helper** n **helpful** adj **helpfully** adv **helpless** adj 1 weak; dependent 2 powerless

hem n edge of a piece of cloth or clothing turned over and sewn vt (-mm-) sew a hem on **hem in** surround; encircle

hemisphere n 1 half a sphere 2 half of the earth **hemispherical** adj

hemp n 1 tough-fibred Asian plant from which the drug cannabis is obtained 2 cannabis 3 rope or coarse cloth made from the fibres

hen n 1 female bird, esp a chicken 2 old woman **hen party** n gathering for women only

hence adv 1 and so; therefore; for this reason 2 from this time forward 3 from this place

henna n reddish dye for hair, etc, obtained from an Asiatic shrub

her adj belonging to a female person pron that particular woman or girl **herself** r pron 1 her own self 2 her normal self

herald n 1 official who makes public or ceremonial announcements 2 person or thing that indicates the approach of something vt usher in; proclaim

heraldry n practice and rules governing official coats of arms, etc **heraldic** adv

herb n plant, such as parsley, that can be used as a flavouring in cooking, as a medicine, etc **herbal** adj **herbaceous** adj relating to plants with fleshy stems that die down after flowering **herbivore** n animal feeding on plants **herbivorous** adj

herd n 1 large group of wild or domestic animals that live and feed together 2 mass of people, rabble vt vi 1 gather or be gathered into a herd 2 drive or be driven (forward or back) **herdsman** n man who tends a herd

here adv 1 in or to this place 2 at this point in time or space **here and there** 1 in or to several places 2 scattered around **be neither here nor there** be irrelevant or unimportant ~n this place

heredity n 1 biological process by which characteristics etc are transmitted from parents to children in the genes 2 characteristics so transmitted **hereditary** adj

heresy n belief or doctrine, esp religious that is contrary to established order **heretic** n person originating or believing a heresy **heretical** adj **heretically** adv

heritage n 1 culture or tradition passed on to successive generations 2 something inherited at birth esp property or family characteristics

hermit n 1 person living completely alone to pray or undergo mystic experiences 2 person who lives a solitary life, recluse **hermitage** n dwelling of a hermit

hero n, pl **heroes** 1 man admired for his courage, nobleness, or fortitude 2 central male character in a book, play, or film 3 person who suffers much without complaint **heroic** adj **heroically** adv **heroine** f n **heroism** n

heroin n addictive narcotic drug obtained from morphine

heron n long-legged wading bird

herring n, pl **herring** or **herrings** marine food fish **red herring** misleading fact or argument

hers pron belonging to her **herself** r pron her own self; her normal self

hesitate vi pause through doubt; waver; falter; be unwilling (to) **hesitancy** n **hesitant** adj **hesitation** n

heterosexual n person sexually attracted to members of the opposite sex **heterosexuality** n

hexagon n six-sided geometric figure **hexagonal** adj

hibernate vi (of animals) spend the winter in a sleeplike state **hibernation** n

hiccup n also **hiccough** one of a series of sudden involuntary coughlike noises vi (-pp-) also **hiccough** experience such a spasm; make such a noise

hide 1 vt (hid; hidden) 1 keep from sight; conceal 2 keep secret vi conceal oneself n place where someone is concealed, esp for observing birds

hide 2 n skin of some large animals, usually hairless, esp when tanned **tan someone's hide** beat or flog someone

hideous adj 1 extremely ugly 2 morally repulsive 3 of an extreme nature **hideously** adv

hiding 1 n act or place of concealment

hiding 2 n 1 beating or thrashing 2 conclusive defeat in a contest

hierarchy n strictly graded structure, as of society or some other system **hierarchical** adj

high adj 1 having or being at a considerable or specified height 2 being at a peak; considerable; relatively great in value or amount 3 important, exalted 4 main; chief 5 noble; lofty; admirable 6 slightly intoxicated by liquor or drugs **high and dry** stranded; abandoned **high and low** in every place possible **high time** the correct or appropriate time ~adv 1 at or to a high point or place 2 for considerable gambling stakes n 1 high point;

peak 2 high place **highly** adv greatly; considerably

highbrow adj relating to very intellectual tastes in music, literature, art, etc n person having such tastes

high-fidelity adj reproducing sounds electronically without distortion

high jump n athletic event in which competitors leap over a high, continuously elevated bar **be for the high jump** be in trouble **high-jumper** n

highland n also **highlands** hilly or mountainous region, esp in Scotland

highlight n 1 small concentration of light on something shiny 2 best or most impressive or enjoyable part vt 1 put highlights in 2 put emphasis on; accentuate

highness n 1 condition of being high 2 honorary address to a royal person

highway n public road, esp a main road

hijack vt 1 board and capture (an aeroplane, etc) and threaten to destroy it or kill its passengers unless one's demands are met 2 steal (a lorry, etc) with its load n instance of hijacking **hijacker** n

hike n long walk or walking holiday in the country; ramble vi go for a hike **hiker** n

hilarious adj very funny; causing much amusement **hilariously** adv **hilarity** n

hill n 1 elevated area of ground; small mountain 2 slope, as in a road **hilly** adj

him pron that particular man or boy **himself** r pron 1 his own self 2 his normal self

hind adj in or at the back or rear; posterior **hindsight** n ability to guess or act correctly when looking back on an event

hinder vt cause obstruction or delay to; impede **hindrance** n 1 obstruction; delay 2 person or thing causing this

hinge n 1 joint by which a door, lid, etc, is attached to a frame, container, etc, so that it can open and close 2 central fact or argument on which all else depends vi **hinge on** depend on

hint n suggestion; piece of helpful advice vt,vi make suggestions (about)

hip n side of the body from the upper thigh to the waist

hippopotamus n, pl **hippopotamuses** or **hippopotami** (hɪpəˈpɒtəmaɪ) very large thick-skinned African mammal living in and around rivers.

hire vt obtain the temporary use or services of, for payment n 1 act of hiring 2 charge of hiring

his pron belonging to him

hiss vi 1 produce a whistling sound like a prolonged s vt,vi display scorn or disapproval (for) by making such a noise n such a noise

history n 1 development and past events of a country, etc 2 study concerned with this 3 book, play, or other chronological account about past events **make history** do something important or influential **historian** n scholar or student of history **historic** adj 1 important or memorable in history 2 also **historical** relating to history

hit vt,vi (-tt-; hit) 1 give a blow to; knock; strike 2 reach (a target, etc) vt 1 come upon by chance; find 2 wound; injure **hit it off with** get on well (with somebody) **hit on** or **upon** guess or find (an answer, etc) by chance **hit out (at** or **against)** speak angrily or critically (about) ~n 1 blow or knock 2 act of reaching a target 3 great success

hitch vt pull up roughly vt,vi 1 fasten or become fastened (on to); become entangled or caught 2 procure (a lift) from a driver n 1 abrupt pull 2 unexpected difficulty or obstacle causing a delay 3 type of knot **hitched** adj married **hitch-hike** vi 1 procure free travel in a motor vehicle 2 travel around by such means **hitch-hiker** n

hive n 1 structure in which bees are kept 2 bees kept in a hive 3 very busy or industrious place vt gather (bees) into a hive

hoard n 1 accumulated store, often hidden or secret 2 hidden or buried treasure 3 also **hoards** great quantity (of) vt,vi amass (a hoard) **hoarder** n

hoarding n 1 temporary wooden fence on which advertising posters are often stuck 2 structure intended for posters, etc

hoarse adj 1 coarse and husky; raucous 2 having a harsh voice, esp from shouting or due to a cold **hoarsely** adv

hoax n mischievous deception; practical joke vt,vi play a hoax on

hobble vi walk lamely or clumsily; limp vt tie together two legs of a horse, etc , to prevent it from straying n clumsy or lame walk

hobby n favourite leisure occupation; pastime

hockey n 1 team game in which a ball is hit

128

with curved wooden sticks into opposing goals 2 ice hockey

hoe n long-handled horticultural tool with transversely set blade, used to weed, break up ground, etc vt,vi weed, break up, etc , with a hoe

hoist vt raise or lift, esp using a mechanical device n 1 act of hoisting 2 device for doing this

hold[1] (held) vt 1 grasp, grip, or support 2 reserve or keep; maintain; control 3 have; occupy; use 4 contain 5 cause to take place; conduct 6 think that; consider vi 1 withstand 2 remain in a certain attitude or condition; remain valid 3 maintain beliefs, etc 4 refrain; forbear **hold back** restrain; hesitate **hold down** keep a job, esp when difficult **hold forth** talk at length or pompously **hold good** remain valid **hold off** 1 keep or stay at a distance 2 stay aloof **hold on** 1 cling to 2 wait **hold one's own** maintain one's position, as in an argument **hold one's tongue** say nothing **hold out** 1 resist successfully; remain firm 2 last; be sufficient **hold up** 1 cause delay in 2 rob threatening with a gun **holdup** n 1 delay 2 armed robbery **hold water** remain true or logical under analysis **hold with** agree with out of principle ~n 1 act or method of holding 2 something to grasp 3 control or influence **get hold of** 1 grasp 2 get in contact with **holdall** n large bag or case

hold[2] n cargo storage area below the deck of a vessel

hole n 1 empty or hollow space in something; cavity; gap; opening; rupture or tear 2 animal's burrow 3 squalid or dingy room or house 4 dull place 5 predicament; difficulty **make a hole in** use up a large part **pick holes in** find faults with ~vt,vi produce a hole in

holiday n 1 time or period of rest from work, esp when spent away from home 2 day of rest or recreation, esp a public one 3 day for celebrating a religious event; festival vi spend a holiday

hollow adj 1 having an empty interior or a cavity inside 2 having a depression in it; sunken 3 insincere; flattering 4 without substance; unreal 5 dull or muffled 6 hungry n 1 hollow part of something 2 sunken place; depression; cavity 3 shallow valley vt also

hollow out scoop out a hollow in *adv* in a hollow way **beat hollow** defeat completely **hollowness** *n*

holly *n* evergreen tree or shrub having shiny prickly leaves and red berries

hollyhock *n* tall garden plant having large showy open flowers

holster *n* leather case for a pistol

holy *adj* **1** of God or a religion; sacred **2** worshipped as sacred; sanctified **3** saintly; pious **holiness** *n* condition of being holy **Holiness** title or term of address of the Pope

homage *n* **1** loyalty; allegiance; reverence **2** act of respect or reverence rendered to someone

home *n* **1** place where a person lives; family residence **2** place where something originated or is situated **3** native country or town **4** institution for the old or infirm **at home** feeling comfortable **at home with** familiar with ~*adv* **1** at or towards home **2** to a required point, target, etc **come/bring home to** realize/cause to realize fully **homely** *adj* plain; simple; unpretentious **homeliness** *n* **homesick** *adj* feeling great longing or nostalgia for one's home or native country **homework** *n* pupil's work that is to be done outside school hours

homosexual *n* person sexually attracted to members of his or her own sex *adj* relating to such people **homosexuality** *n*

honest *adj* **1** not lying, deceiving, or cheating **2** not given to stealing or other criminal activities **3** sincere; open; frank **4** trustworthy or conscientious **honestly** *adv* **honesty** *n*

honey *n* **1** sweet liquid made from nectar by bees **2** something sweet soothing, flattering, etc **honeycomb** *n* **1** waxy structure of hexagonal cells in which bees store their honey and eggs **2** intricate system of passages and tunnels **honeymoon** *n* holiday of a newly married couple *vi* spend one's honeymoon (in) **honeysuckle** *n* sweet-smelling climbing shrub

honorary *adj* **1** given or conferred as an honour **2** acting or done without pay

honour *n* **1** good reputation; public esteem; integrity; respect **2** person or thing bringing honour **3** mark of respect, etc **4** act of courtesy **5** title or address, esp of a judge **do the honours** act as host ~*vt* **1** treat with honour; show respect or courtesy for **2** confer an honour on **3** keep a promise or bargain **4**

accept as valid **honourable** *adj* **honourably** *adv*

hood *n* **1** loose covering for the head and neck **2** collapsible or removable cover for a car or pram **3** hood-shaped structure **hooded** *adj* (of the eyes) half closed

hoof *n* horny part of the foot of horses, cows, etc

hook *n* **1** small implement curved or bent at one end, by which something is hung, pulled. fastened, etc **2** something shaped like a hook **3** swerving blow or stroke **off the hook** out of trouble or difficulty ~*vt* **1** connect, hang, fasten, catch, etc with a hook **2** put in the shape of a hook; crook **hooked on** addicted to

hooligan *n* wild, violent, or destructive person, vandal **hooliganism** *n*

hoop *n* circular band or ring, used as a binding, toy, etc *vt* bind with a hoop

hoot *vi* **1** make or give out a hollow noise like the cry of an owl **2** laugh noisily **3** express derision with a hoot *n* **1** such a noise **2** cause of great amusement **hooter** *n* **1** mechanical device giving out a hoot as a time signal **2** *inf* nose

hop[1] *vi* (-pp-) **1** jump on one leg **2** move by hopping or jumping **hop it!** go away! ~*n* **1** act of hopping **2** short distance or journey **3** small dance **on the hop** unprepared

hop[2] *n* climbing plant whose flowers are used in flavouring beer

hope *n* **1** desire, expectation **2** person or thing expected to bring desired success, etc *vt,vi* wish (for); expect or trust (that) **hopeful** *adj* **hopefully** *adv*

horde *n* large number or group; throng, gang *vi* gather together in a horde

horizon *n* **1** line where the sea or land appears to meet the sky **2** limit of a person's hopes, intellect, or ambition **horizontal** *adj* parallel to the horizon; lying flat; level **horizontally** *adv*

hormone *n* biochemical substance produced in certain glands and secreted into the blood to trigger or stimulate certain processes **hormonal** *adj*

horn *n* **1** hard pointed growth projecting from the head of certain animals **2** drinking vessel made from a hollowed horn **3** curved projection **4** metal musical wind instrument **5** siren or hooter on a car, etc **draw in one's**

horns reduce one's expenditure ~*vt* injure with a horn

hornet *n* large wasp

horoscope *n* astrological prediction

horrible *adj* 1 causing horror or great fear 2 horrid **horribly** *adv*

horrid *adj* 1 unpleasant; nasty; cruel 2 shocking; repulsive **horridly** *adv*

horrify *vt* cause to feel horror; shock **horrific** *adj*

horror *n* 1 great fear; disgust 2 thing causing such feeling 3 ugly thing 4 annoying or disagreeable person **horror-struck** *adj* overwhelmed with horror

hors d'oeuvres *n* (ɔ:'də v) course before the main course of a meal, esp a light savoury or appetizing fruit dish

horse *n* 1 large hoofed domestic animal that may be ridden or used as a draught animal 2 wooden frame for drying or airing clothes 3 large wooden box over which gymnasts vault **dark horse** person with hidden or unknown merit **flog a dead horse** work at or revive a lost or hopeless cause *vi* **horse about** act noisily or foolishly **horsy** *adj* 1 relating to a horse 2 interested in horses and riding **horsebox** *n* large trailer or van for transporting horses **horse chestnut** *n* large tree with clusters of white or red flowers and shiny brown nuts enclosed in a prickly case **horsepower** *n* unit of power, as of a car engine **horseradish** *n* plant whose pungent root is made into a thick sauce

horticulture *n* growing of flowers, fruit, and vegetables; gardening **horticultural** *adj* **horticulturist** *n*

hose *n* long narrow flexible pipe for transporting liquids, directing water, etc *vt* direct water at

hospitable *adj* offering a friendly welcome to guests; sociable **hospitably** *adv* **hospitality** *n*

hospital *n* institution where the sick or injured are cared for or treated by doctors, nurses, etc

host[1] *n* 1 person who receives and entertains guests 2 person who runs an inn, hotel, etc 3 animal or plant on which parasites live

host[2] *n* also **hosts** large number of people, such as an army

hostage *n* person seized and kept under threat until his captors' demands are fulfilled

hostel *n* residential house or hall for students, hikers, or workers

hostess *n* 1 female host 2 female attendant on an aeroplane, etc

hostile *adj* showing enmity or opposition; aggressive; unfriendly **hostility** *n*

hot *adj* 1 having a high temperature; very warm 2 highly spiced; pungent 3 violent; passionate 4 recently occurring, discovered, etc; following closely **hot air** meaningless or boastful talk **hot stuff** person or thing exciting or excellent **hot water** trouble ~*adv* in a hot manner; hotly **blow hot and cold** repeatedly enthuse then hesitate *vt,vi* (-tt-) **hot up** make or become more exciting, powerful, etc **hotly** *adv* with ardour or deep feeling **hot-blooded** *adj* passionate **hot dog** *n* hot sausage in a bread roll or sandwich **hothouse** *n* artificially heated greenhouse **hot-tempered** *adj* losing one's temper easily

hotel *n* building offering accommodation and service to travellers, etc

hound *n* 1 dog that hunts by following the scent of its quarry 2 despised person *vt* pursue or persecute ruthlessly

hour *n* 1 unit or period of time; sixty minutes 2 correct or appointed time 3 destined time, as of a person's death **hours** *pl n* 1 normal time of operation, as of a shop 2 long time **the eleventh hour** the last possible moment **hourly** *adj* 1 occurring or done every hour 2 measured by the hour

house *n* (haus) 1 building designed for living in; residence; home 2 building used for a special purpose 3 household 4 important or noble family 5 part of a school 6 business firm 7 legislative assembly 8 theatre audience **bring the house down** cause great merriment or applause **get on like a house on fire** get on very well **on the house** free **safe as houses** very safe ~*vt* (hauz) 1 contain; enclose 2 put in a house; provide shelter for

housebound *adj* unable to leave the house

household *n* those living together in a house **household word** or **name** very well-known name, as of a product

housekeeper *n* 1 woman hired to cook and look after someone else's house 2 woman servant in charge of other servants in a large household **housekeeping** *n* 1 domestic management 2 money allowed or required for this

houseman n, pl **-men** junior resident doctor in a hospital

House of Commons n lower house of the British legislative assembly consisting of representatives elected by the people; parliament

House of Lords n upper house of the British legislative assembly consisting of non-elected hereditary peers and life peers and acting also as the supreme court of judicial appeal

housewife n, pl **-wives** married woman who stays at home to run the house instead of working

housing n 1 houses collectively 2 provision of houses by the government, etc

hover vi 1 remain suspended in air, almost motionless 2 remain close, as to help or protect **hovercraft** n passenger craft that moves above a water or land surface on a cushion of air

how adv 1 in what way or manner; by what method or means 2 in what condition 3 to what extent or degree 4 why; for what reason 5 to what a great degree or amount **however** conj nevertheless; in spite of this adv in any way; by whatever means

howl vi 1 make a prolonged mournful cry 2 cry loudly 3 laugh uncontrollably n 1 loud or mournful cry 2 loud laugh **howler** n ridiculous or amusing mistake

hub n 1 centre of a wheel from which the spokes radiate 2 central point, as of activity

huddle vi,vt crowd or be crowded together, as for warmth or protection n confused heap **in/into a huddle** in/into a private discussion

hue n 1 attribute of colour that enables different colours, red, yellow, blue, etc, to be distinguished 2 colour; shade **hue and cry** public outcry

huff n angry, offended, or sulky fit of temper **huffish** or **huffy** adj

hug v (-gg-) vt,vi clasp affectionately; cuddle vt keep close to n affectionate clasp; cuddle

huge adj extremely large; vast; immense **hugely** adv very much

hulk n 1 old, useless, abandoned, or partially dismantled ship 2 large clumsy person **hulking** adj large and clumsy

hull n basic frame of a ship, without masts, etc

hum v (-mm-) vi 1 make a continuous musical sound like singing but with the mouth shut 2 make a prolonged low buzzing noise 3 be alive with activity, rumour, etc vt sing (a tune, etc) by humming n 1 sound like a prolonged 'm 2 low buzz or drone 3 sound of great activity

human adj 1 relating to man or mankind 2 having or appealing to human kindness, weakness, etc n also **human being** person; man or woman **humane** adj sympathetic; merciful; kind; compassionate **humanely** adv **humanity** n 1 mankind 2 compassion for others

humble adj 1 not proud or conceited; modest 2 unimportant or lowly; subjected; submissive vt 1 cause to feel humble; shame 2 make humble or lowly **eat humble pie** apologize in a humble way **humbly** adv

humdrum adj commonplace; dull; monotonous

humid adj damp; moist **humidity** n

humiliate vt cause to feel humble, foolish or ashamed **humiliation** n

humility n condition of being humble; meekness; modesty

humour n 1 ability to see or appreciate what is funny 2 humorous or amusing quality 3 temper; mood vt indulge someone's whims or ideas **humorous** adj causing laughter; funny; amusing; droll; witty **humorously** adv

hump n 1 natural lump on the backs of camels 2 rounded deformity on the back of humans 3 any curved protuberance, such as a small hill vt lift clumsily vt,vi arch

hunch n suspicion; intuitive guess vt 1 draw (one's shoulders) up, as when sitting 2 thrust out or arch (one's back) **hunchback** n 1 lumplike deformity on the back 2 person with such a deformity

hundred n 1 number equal to ten times ten 2 hundred things or people **hundreds** very many adj consisting of or amounting to a hundred or about a hundred **hundredth** adj,adv,n **hundredweight** n measure of weight equal to 112 pounds; one twentieth of a ton

hung v pt and pp of **hang**.

hunger n 1 sensation that one needs or desires to eat 2 lack of food; famine 3 deep desire or need; craving vi 1 feel hungry 2 lack food **hunger for** or **after** desire or crave **hunger-strike** n refusal to eat, as when in prison, as a protest **hungry** adj

hunt vt,vi 1 chase or pursue wild animals to kill them for food or sport 2 search (for); seek vt chase or pursue a criminal, etc **hunt down**

capture after pursuing ruthlessly ~n 1 practice or instance of hunting animals 2 group of people and working animals so involved 3 search; pursuit **hunter** n

hurdle n 1 light frame used as a temporary fence 2 framelike barrier over which an athlete (**hurdler**), show jumper, etc , must **leap** 3 problem to be overcome; obstacle vi,vt jump over (hurdles) in a race

hurl vt 1 throw with great effort or force 2 shout; yell

hurrah interj,n also **hurray** exclamation of pleasure or applause

hurricane n 1 very strong wind 2 violent storm; tropical cyclone

hurry vi,vt 1 move or cause to move more quickly or with haste 2 do quickly n 1 haste; bustle 2 need for haste; urgency

hurt vt,vi (hurt) 1 cause physical pain or injury (to) 2 offend; distress 3 affect adversely; damage n 1 pain; injury; wound 2 harm; damage adj 1 injured 2 offended

hurtle vi rush violently; move very fast

husband n man to whom a woman is married

hush vt,vi 1 make or become quiet or silent 2 make or become soothed **hush up** keep secret; suppress ~n quiet; silence interj be quiet!

husk n dry outer covering of some seeds vt remove the husk from

husky adj hoarse or whispery **huskily** adv

hustle vt,vi hurry along or be hurried along roughly vi act quickly and efficiently n rush of activity; bustle; jostling

hut n small wooden building, esp a temporary or ramshackle one

hutch n small wooden cage for pet rabbits, etc

hyacinth n plant that grows from a bulb and produces a spike of white, pink, or blue fragrant flowers in spring

hybrid n 1 plant or animal that is a cross between two different species or varieties 2 blend of two dissimilar things

hydraulic adj 1 worked by the flow or pressure of fluids, esp water 2 relating to fluids and their use in engineering **hydraulics** n study of fluid flow

hydrocarbon n organic compound containing only carbon and hydrogen

hydro-electric adj relating to the generation of electricity by the force of falling water **hydro-electricity** n

hydrogen n inflammable gas that is the lightest element and occurs in water and most organic compounds

hyena n doglike carnivorous animal

hygiene n 1 cleanliness; healthy practices 2 science of preserving health **hygienic** adj

hymn n religious song; song of praise to God

hyphen n mark (-) in writing or printing used to compound two words or syllables or when a word is split at the end of a line **hyphenate** vt insert a hyphen in **hyphenation** n

hypnosis n 1 induced relaxed state of semiconsciousness during which a person will obey suggestions or commands made to him 2 hypnotism **hypnotic** adj 1 having the power to hold the attention; fascinating 2 of or like hypnosis; lulling or trancelike **hypnotism** n induction of hypnosis **hypnotist** n **hypnotize** vt 1 induce hypnosis in 2 fascinate; dominate the will or mind of

hypochondria n obsessive concern with one's own health **hypochondriac** adj,n

hypocrisy n 1 feigning of beliefs or feelings one does not have; insincerity 2 false virtue **hypocrite** n **hypocritical** adj **hypocritically** adv

hypodermic n 1 syringe or needle used to administer injections below the skin 2 such an injection adj relating to the tissue area below the skin

hypothesis n 1 idea or suggestion put forward for discussion or verification; proposition **hypothetic** or **hypothetical** adj not based on facts **hypothetically** adv

hysterectomy n surgical removal of the womb or part of the womb or uterus

hysteria n 1 neurotic uncontrollable outbursts of panic or other emotions 2 any uncontrollable emotion **hysterical** adj 1 relating to hysteria 2 extremely funny **hysterically** adv

I

I pron used as the subject to refer to oneself

ice n 1 water frozen until solid 2 ice-cream vt 1 produce ice in; freeze 2 put icing on (a cake) 3 chill (a drink) with ice **iceberg** n large floating mass of ice in the sea **ice-cream** n dessert made of flavoured frozen cream, custard, etc **ice lolly** n confectionery consisting of flavoured ice on a short stick **ice**

hockey n team game similar to hockey, played on ice **ice rink** n an area of ice for skating, esp one kept frozen artificially **ice-skate** vi skate on ice n 1 shoe fitted with a narrow metal runner for skating on ice 2 such a runner

icicle n thin tapering piece of hanging ice

icing n mixture of fine sugar (icing sugar) and water, egg whites, etc , spread over cakes as a decoration

icon n sacred image of Christ, saints, angels, etc

icy adj 1 so cold as to cause ice 2 relating to ice 3 (of roads) slippery 4 unfriendly; aloof; distant **icily** adv **iciness** n

idea n 1 mental concept; anything thought of in the mind 2 opinion; belief 3 plan or suggestion 4 impression of what something is like

ideal adj 1 of the best that could be imagined; perfect 2 conforming to a notion of excellence or purity n 1 standard of excellence or complete perfection 2 principle or aim that is pure or noble 3 concept of perfection in a person, object, etc **ideally** adv **idealistic** adj 1 having or cherishing ideals or high-minded principles 2 relating to such principles **idealist** n,adj **idealism** n **idealize** vt 1 consider that (a person or thing) conforms to an ideal or standard of excellence 2 present or write about (a person or thing) as if ideal **idealization** n

identical adj exactly the same **identically** adv **identify** vt recognize or prove the identity of **identify with** associate oneself or give support to (a group, person, etc) **identity** n 1 fact of being who one is or what something is 2 exact sameness

ideology n body of related ideas or doctrines of a religious, political, or economic system **ideological** adj **ideologically** adv

idiom n 1 phrase or expression meaning something other or more than its literal meaning 2 language restricted to a particular type of speaker, period, group, etc **idiomatic** adj **idiomatically** adv

idiosyncrasy n individual and unusual tendency or characteristic **idiosyncratic** adj

idiot n 1 foolish or stupid person 2 mentally subnormal person **idiotic** adj foolish; silly **idiotically** adv

idle adj 1 not doing anything; inactive 2 (of a machine) not in use 3 lazy 4 vain or ineffectual; useless 5 frivolous vi,vt waste (time) doing nothing vi (of an engine) turn over gently while not providing drive **idleness** n **idly** adv

idol n 1 image, esp a sculpture, of a god or something that is worshipped as a god 2 a god of another religion from one's own 3 very popular or admired person or thing, esp a pop star or film star **idolatry** n 1 worship of idols 2 excessive admiration **idolater** n **idolatrous** adj **idolize** vt treat or worship as an idol

idyllic adj charmingly simple, peaceful, or poetic **idyllically** adv

if conj 1 in case that; supposing that 2 whether 3 even though; allowing that

igloo n Eskimo's dome-shaped hut made of blocks of hard snow

ignite vt,vi 1 set or be set on fire; kindle 2 cause or reach a temperature at which combustion takes place 3 arouse the passion of or be so aroused **ignition** n 1 act or fact of igniting 2 starting system in an internal-combustion engine

ignorant adj 1 lacking knowledge 2 lacking education or upbringing **ignorance** n

ignore vt 1 fail to notice or take into account; disregard 2 refuse to acknowledge or greet

ill adj 1 in bad health; sick 2 bad; wicked 3 hostile; malicious 4 rude 5 unfavourable; indicating misfortune **ill at ease** embarrassed; uneasy ~adv badly n misfortune; harm **ill-bred** adj lacking good manners or refinement, badly brought up **illness** n 1 state of being ill; sickness; ill health 2 specific complaint or disease **ill-treat** vt treat cruelly or carelessly; abuse **ill-treatment** n **ill will** n feeling of dislike, jealousy, or hatred; malice

illegal adj not in accordance with the law; unlawful **illegally** adv

illegible adj not able to be read; badly written; partially obliterated

illegitimate adj 1 born of parents who are not married to each other 2 contrary to the law; unlawful **illegitimacy** n

illicit adj not permitted or authorized; unlawful **illicitly** adv

illiterate adj 1 unable to read or write 2 ignorant, uneducated, or uncultured **illiteracy** n

illogical adj 1 contrary to logic; irrational 2 not thinking logically **illogically** adv

illuminate vt 1 light up; provide light for 2 clarify 3 decorate with bright gay lights or floodlighting 4 decorate (a manuscript) by adding painted ornamentation **illumination** n

illusion n 1 something that is falsely or mistakenly thought to exist or be so 2 deception; delusion; hallucination 3 conjuring trick **illusionist** n conjurer **illusory** adj based on illusion; not real; deceptive

illustrate vt 1 provide pictures for (a book, talk, etc) 2 provide examples for; clarify **illustration** n

illustrious adj eminent

image n 1 representation or likeness of a person or thing 2 exact likeness 3 view of an object as seen in a mirror, lens, etc 4 mental concept; idea 5 figure of speech, esp a metaphor or simile in poetry, etc 6 way the personality or character of a person, company, etc, is presented to others, esp the general public 7 symbol; emblem **imagery** n 1 metaphorical language 2 repetition or use of certain symbols, as in a cultural tradition

imagine vt, vi 1 form a mental image or idea (of) 2 suppose; believe **imaginary** adj created by the imagination; not real **imagination** n 1 power or ability to create mental concepts or images 2 act of imagining 3 baseless or fanciful belief or idea **imaginative** adj 1 having considerable powers of creative imagination 2 relating to or characterized by imagination **imaginatively** adv

imbecile n idiot

imitate vt 1 copy the behaviour, appearance, etc, of; take as a model 2 impersonate or mimic 3 be or look like **imitation** n 1 act of imitating 2 impersonation or copy adj made of a synthetic material

immaculate adj 1 completely free from dirtiness or untidiness 2 free from sin; pure **immaculately** adv

immature adj 1 not yet fully grown or developed 2 lacking adult judgment or stability **immaturity** n

immediate adj 1 without delay; instant 2 very close or near 3 without another intervening; next **immediacy** n **immediately** adv

immense adj 1 very large; vast; huge 2 very great in number, quantity, etc **immensely** adv 1 to an immense degree 2 very greatly; very much **immensity** n

immerse vt 1 put into water or other liquid; plunge or steep 2 absorb or engross 3 involve (someone) in an affair; entangle 4 baptize (a person) by plunging him in a river, special bath, etc **immersion** n

immigrate vi come to a country other than one's own in order to take up permanent residence **immigration** n **immigrant** n person who immigrates

imminent adj likely to happen very soon **imminence** n **imminently** adv

immobile adj 1 not moving; still or fixed 2 not capable of moving or being moved **immobility** n **immobilize** vt make incapable of moving **immobilization** n

immoral adj not in accordance with morals; against moral laws **immorality** n

immortal adj 1 never dying or ceasing 2 never forgotten **immortality** n

immovable adj unable to be moved or altered; rigid **immovably** adv

immune adj 1 protected from a disease, etc, esp because of previous exposure or inoculation 2 not affected or moved emotionally (by) 3 free or safe (from) **immunity** n **immunize** vt render immune to a disease **immunization** n **immunology** n science dealing with immunity to disease

imp n 1 mischievous small fairy; sprite; goblin 2 naughty, impudent, or mischievous child **impish** adj

impact n ('impækt) 1 act of one object colliding with another 2 force with which an object collides with something 3 effect or impression vt (im'pækt) press forcefully into something or together

impair vt reduce the effectiveness, value, or strength of **impairment** n

impart vt give (information, news, enthusiasm etc) to

impartial adj not favouring either side; fair; disinterested; not biased **impartiality** n **impartially** adv

impatient adj 1 not willing to wait or delay 2 irritated; vexed 3 intolerant (of) **impatience** n **impatiently** adv

impeach vt 1 charge with (a crime, esp of treason) 2 cast doubt on; call in question 3 accuse or try to discredit **impeachment** n

impeccable adj without fault; perfect **impeccably** adv

impediment n 1 something that prevents something happening or working properly; obstacle 2 speech defect, such as a stammer or lisp

imperative adj 1 urgent or necessary; essential 2 commanding; authoritative 3 designating that form of a verb used in commands n 1 command 2 form of a verb used in commands

imperfect adj not perfect; defective, faulty, or incomplete **imperfection** n defect or flaw

imperial adj 1 relating to an emperor or empire 2 commanding in manner; majestic **imperialism** n form of government in which one state establishes and extends its rule over foreign lands and people **imperialist** n,adj

impermeable adj impervious

impersonal adj 1 not personal; formal; unfriendly 2 (of verbs) limited in use to the third person singular form with it as the subject 3 (of pronouns) not specifying; indefinite **impersonally** adv

impersonate vt pretend to be (another person) **impersonation** n

impertinent adj rude; cheeky; impudent **impertinence** n **impertinently** adv

impervious adj 1 no; absorbing liquid; watertight 2 not affected by criticism, etc ; insensitive

impetuous adj done or acting without due consideration; rash **impetuosity** n **impetuously** adv

impetus n 1 driving force or momentum 2 incentive

impinge vi come into contact or collision (with) **impinge (up)on** 1 have an effect or bearing on 2 encroach or infringe on **impingement** n

implement ('impləmənt) n tool; instrument vt ('impləment) put (a law, etc) into force **implementation** n

implicit adj 1 implied though not expressly stated 2 unquestioning; unqualified; absolute **implicitly** adv

implore vt beg or plead

imply vt 1 state or show in an indirect way 2 insinuate; suggest; hint at 3 indicate as a logical consequence **implication** n

import vt (im'pɔ:t) 1 bring (goods) into a country from another for resale, etc 2 mean;

signify n ('impɔ:t) 1 imported commodity 2 act or practice of importing 3 importance 4 meaning; consequence **importer** n

important adj 1 of significance or consequence; notable 2 wielding power or influence 3 pompous; self-satisfied **importance** n **importantly** adv

impose vt 1 force to comply with 2 force to pay (a tax) 3 take advantage of 4 foist (one's company) on **imposition** n **imposing** adj of grand or impressive appearance or nature

impossible adj 1 not possible; unable to be done 2 difficult to deal with; annoying **impossibility** n **impossibly** adv

impostor n person who pretends to be someone else in order to cheat or defraud

impotent adj 1 not able to act; powerless or helpless 2 (of men) not able to have an erection of the penis **impotence** or **impotency** n **impotently** adv

impound vt 1 take legal possession of; confiscate 2 confine; enclose

impress vt 1 have a great effect or influence on the mind or feelings of 2 cause to remember 3 press a mark into; stamp **impressive** adj producing a great or lasting effect; remarkable **impressively** adv

impression n 1 effect on the mind or feelings 2 idea or memory, esp when vague or general 3 mark or stamp left when something is pressed on something 4 imitation or impersonation 5 printing of a book, esp a subsequent one with no amendments **impressionable** adj easily impressed **impressionism** n late 19th-century movement in the arts, using effects of light, sound, form, etc , to give a general impression of the subject

imprint vt (im'print) 1 stamp or print on to 2 make a lasting impression on n ('imprint) 1 mark or print on something 2 publisher's or printer s mark, as on the title page of a book

improbable adj unlikely; not very probable **improbability** n

impromptu adj,adv made or done without preparation, rehearsal, or consideration n short piece of music

improper adj 1 not proper; not conforming to rules of etiquette, morality, etc 2 unsuitable; inappropriate **improperly** adv

improve vi,vt become or make better or more valuable **improvement** n

improvise vt,vi 1 make or do (something)

without preparation or proper materials **2** play (music) without rehearsal or with the addition of one's own embellishments **improvisation** n

impudent adj rude; cheeky; insolent; impertinent **impudence** n **impudently** adv

impulse n **1** sudden desire for something, whim **2** thing that drives or forces something to happen **3** electrical signal in certain machines **impulsive** adj done or acting on impulse **impulsively** adv

impure adj **1** not pure; mixed with other substances **2** not chaste; indecent **impurely** adv **impurity** n

in prep **1** on the inside of; within **2** at or to (a place) **3** during **4** according to **5** involved with **6** through the medium of; using **7** made of **8** wearing adv **1** inside; on the interior **2** at home **3** so as to have power **4** so as to be fashionable **5** accepted as a friend **in for** going to receive or experience **in on** knowing about n **ins and outs** complicated details

inability n lack of ability, power, or means

inaccurate adj not accurate; wrong; incorrect **inaccuracy** n **inaccurately** adv

inadequate adj **1** not adequate; insufficient **2** not able to cope or deal with a task, etc **inadequacy** n **inadequately** adv

inadvertent adj **1** done, said, etc., by accident **2** not paying attention; careless, heedless **inadvertently** adv

inane adj **1** having no sense; silly **2** having no content; empty; void **inanely** adv **inaneness** or **inanity** n

inarticulate adj **1** not able to voice one's thoughts or feelings fluently **2** not clearly said or expressed **inarticulately** adv

inasmuch adv **inasmuch as** since, because

inaugurate vt **1** declare open or in use with ceremony **2** install in office ceremonially **inaugural** adj **inauguration** n

incapable adj **1** not able (to) **2** not capable; lacking the necessary powers **incapacity** n **incapacitate** vt render incapable or unfit; disable

incendiary adj **1** relating to fires, esp intentional fires **2** stirring up strong feelings, esp of revolt against authority n **1** person who illegally sets fire to buildings, etc **2** person who stirs up revolt, violence, etc **3** type of bomb causing fires

incense[1] n ('insens) substance that gives off sweet or aromatic smells when burnt

incense[2] vt (in'sens) enrage

incessant adj never-ending; constant; ceaseless **incessantly** adv

incest n illicit sexual intercourse between closely related members of the same family **incestuous** adj

inch n unit of length equal to one twelfth of a foot or 2 54 centimetres vi move forward very slowly

incident n event or occurrence **incidence** n degree or scope of occurrence of something **incidental** adj **1** happening at the same time as or as a natural part of **2** not specially planned; chance; casual **3** less important or significant **incidentally** adv **1** in an incidental manner **2** by the way

incisor n tooth adapted for cutting

incite vt stir up in; inflame; urge on **incitement** n

incline v (in'klain) vt,vi **1** slope or slant **2** tend or cause to tend towards vt **1** bend or bow (the head, etc) **2** influence (someone) towards; dispose n ('inklain, in'klain) slope, gradient **inclination** n

include vt **1** contain as a part or member; comprise **2** regard as a part of a category, class, etc **inclusion** n **inclusive** adj

incognito adj,adv in disguise; under an assumed identity

incoherent adj not easy to understand because of being rambling, inconsistent or illogical **incoherently** adv

income n money gained, esp regularly, from work done investments etc

incompatible adj **1** not able to agree or remain on friendly terms together **2** not capable of or suitable for existing, working, etc (with or together) **incompatibility** n

incompetent adj **1** lacking the necessary skill or knowledge **2** not capable or able; inefficient n person who is incapable or inefficient **incompetence** or **incompetency** n **incompetently** adv

incongruous adj out of place; irrelevant; not suitable **incongruously** adv

inconsistent adj **1** not consistent **2** changing one's opinions often **3** not agreeing or compatible **inconsistency** n **inconsistently** adv

inconvenient adj not convenient; causing

trouble or difficulty **inconvenience** n **inconveniently** adv

incorporate vt,vi unite, blend, or mix into another body or thing **incorporation** n

increase vt,vi (in'kri:s) make or become more, larger, or greater; multiply; enlarge n ('inkri:s) **1** act or fact of increasing **2** amount increased by **increasingly** adv more and more

incredible adj **1** not able to be believed; unlikely or amazing **2** very surprising; extraordinary **incredibly** adv

incubate vt (of birds, reptiles, etc) sit on eggs to hatch them vi **1** (of eggs) hatch **2** undergo incubation **incubation** n **1** hatching of eggs **2** stage of a disease between infection and the appearance of symptoms **incubator** n **1** heated apparatus in which delicate or premature new-born babies are protected **2** similar device for hatching eggs, growing bacteria, etc

incur vt (-rr-) bring upon oneself; become liable or responsible for

indecent adj **1** shameful; immodest **2** improper or unseemly **indecency** n **indecently** adv

indeed adv **1** certainly **2** in fact interj really!

indefinite adj **1** not clearly or exactly stated, limited or defined **2** not precise or fixed; vague; unsure **3** (of pronouns) impersonal **indefinite article** n a' or an' **indefinitely** adv **1** in an indefinite manner **2** for an unknown, esp a long, period of time

indent vt **1** put or cut notches or regular recesses in **2** set lines (such as the first line of a paragraph) in printed or written matter further from the margin than the rest **indentation** n **1** act of indenting **2** notched part as formed **3** series of such notches or recesses

independent adj **1** not under the control or authority of someone or something else; free; self-governing **2** not relying or dependent on other people or things; self-sufficient **3** without any connection (with) or reference (to) **independence** n **independently** adv

index n, pl **index** or **indices** ('indisi:z) **1** alphabetical list of names, subjects, etc , at the end of a book, indicating where or on what page they are mentioned **2** pointer on a dial, etc **3** indication; sign vt provide an index for (a book) **index finger** n finger next to the thumb

indicate vt **1** show, as by sign or gesture; point

out **2** imply; mean **indication** n **indicative** adj suggestive (of); meaning or implying (that) adj,n (of or designating) grammatical mood of verbs expressing simple statements, not wishes, etc **indicator** n **1** person or thing that indicates, esp a directional signal on a car **2** chemical substance that changes colour when certain reactions take place

indifferent adj **1** not caring (about); not interested (in) **2** mediocre **indifference** n **indifferently** adv

indigenous adj originally belonging (to); native

indigestion n **1** inability to digest food or difficulty in digesting **2** pain in the stomach caused by this **indigestible** adj not easy to digest

indignant adj righteously angry, as at something one considers justifies anger **indignantly** adv **indignation** n

indirect adj not direct, straightforward, or explicit **indirectly** adv

individual adj of, for, or characteristic of one particular person or thing n **1** single person, as distinguished from a group **2** any person **individuality** n **individually** adv

indoctrinate vt teach (someone) rigidly so that he does not question or think for himself **indoctrination** n

indolent adj lazy; idle **indolence** n **indolently** adv

indoor adj done or suitable for inside a house or other building **indoors** adv in, into, or inside a house or other building

induce vt **1** have the effect of; cause; produce **2** persuade or influence **inducement** n

indulge vi,vt yield to or satisfy (a desire, whim, etc) vt pamper; spoil **indulgence** n **indulgent** adj

industry n **1** system of manufacturing goods using mechanization **2** particular branch of this; trade **3** hard work or diligent application **industrial** adj relating to industry **industrially** adv **industrialism** n **industrialist** n **industrialize** vt bring industry, factories, etc , to **industrialization** n

inebriate vt intoxicate

inept adj **1** not suitable or appropriate **2** stupid; slow, as to learn **ineptly** adv **ineptness** n **ineptitude** n **1** ineptness **2** inept remark, etc

inequality n state or instance of a person or

thing being unequal, esp in having fewer rights or advantages

inert adj 1 not showing movement, activity, or change; sluggish 2 not chemically active **inertly** adv **inertia** n lack of activity or movement

inevitable adj unavoidable; certain to happen **inevitability** n **inevitably** adv

inextricable adj unable to be separated, parted, or solved **inextricably** adv

infallible adj 1 never failing; always successful, correct, or effective 2 certain; inevitable **infallibility** n **infallibly** adv

infamous ('infamas) adj 1 notorious; disreputable 2 shocking; scandalous **infamy** n

infant n 1 small child 2 person under eighteen and therefore not legally independent or responsible; minor **infancy** n 1 period of being an infant 2 early stages of development **infantile** adj childishly immature

infantry n foot soldiers

infatuated adj wildly or foolishly in love or obsessed, esp temporarily **infatuation** n

infect vt 1 transmit a disease or germs to 2 communicate a feeling to 3 pollute; contaminate **infectious** adj **infection** n 1 act of infecting or state of being infected 2 disease or organism causing disease

infer vt (-rr-) deduce; conclude **inference** n

inferior adj lower in position, rank, value, or quality n person lower in rank or authority; subordinate **inferiority** n

infernal adj 1 of, like, or found in hell or the underworld 2 wicked; diabolical 3 annoying; confounded **infernally** adv

infest vt (of vermin, pests, etc) swarm over or into; overrun **infestation** n

infidelity n 1 unfaithful or disloyal act or behaviour 2 adultery

infiltrate vt enter (a country, political group, etc) gradually and stealthily as to subvert it **infiltration** n **infiltrator** n

infinite adj without end or limit; boundless or countless **infinity** n **infinitely** adv 1 without limit or end 2 extremely; very

infinitive n grammatical form of verbs, usually preceded by to, and not indicating tense, person, or subject

infirm adj 1 in poor health; ill or weak 2 not resolute; uncertain **infirmity** n

inflame vt 1 cause a part of the body, etc , to become red and swollen, as when hit or infected 2 anger or excite 3 make more intense or worse **inflammable** adj 1 likely to ignite; easy to burn 2 excitable **inflammation** n 1 act of inflaming or state of being inflamed 2 swelling or redness

inflate vt,vi 1 fill with gas; blow or swell up 2 raise (prices) or increase in price **inflation** n persistent fall in the value of money leading to continuously rising prices **inflationary** adj

inflection n 1 modulation of tone and stress in speech 2 alteration in the form of a word to denote a grammatical change, as in the tense, number, case, etc

inflict vt make (a person) suffer, undergo, or endure (something unpleasant); impose **infliction** n

influence vt have an impression on; affect; persuade, often indirectly n 1 power to influence others 2 person or thing that influences **influential** adj

influenza n also inf flu contagious viral disease characterized by fever, breathing difficulties, and muscular aches and pains

influx n sudden abundant flow or large increase

inform vt 1 tell; instruct; impart knowledge (to) 2 give character to; inspire **inform on** reveal a person's activities, esp secret or discreditable ones, to a higher authority **informer** n person who informs on others **information** n knowledge acquired from another source; news; relevant facts **informative** adj

informal adj casual; easy-going; not formal **informality** n **informally** adv

infringe vi go beyond the limits or boundaries of vt break or disobey (a law or rule) **infringement** n

infuriate vt annoy or irritate intensely

infuse vt impart; inspire vt,vi soak or steep in a liquid, esp to extract flavour **infusion** n

ingenious adj inventive; cleverly contrived; resourceful; cunning **ingenuity** n

ingenuous adj innocent or naive; not sophisticated

ingredient n constituent; something that forms part of a mixture

inhabit vt live or reside in **inhabitable** adj **inhabitant** n person living in a place; occupier

inhale vt,vi draw into the lungs; breathe in

inherent adj existing as an essential part (of) **inherently** adv

inherit vt,vi have as a legacy; become heir (to)

vt possess (a family trait); derive from one s family **inheritance** *n*

inhibit *vt* prevent; restrain; hold back **inhibition** *n*

inhuman *adj* cruel; barbarous; unfeeling **inhumanity** *n*

initial *adj* existing at the beginning or outset; early, first *n* first letter of a name *vt* (-ll-) sign one's initials on

initiate *vt* (i'nifieit) 1 begin; originate 2 introduce; admit *n* (i'nifiit) initiated person **initiation** *n*

initiative *n* 1 capacity to be enterprising and efficient 2 first step; introductory move

inject *vt* 1 drive (liquid) into living tissue using a syringe 2 introduce vigorously **injection** *n*

injure *vt* hurt; harm; damage **injury** *n* 1 damage 2 wound 3 something causing damage or offence

injustice *n* 1 lack of fairness; practice of being biased or unjust 2 wrong, unjust act

ink *n* coloured liquid used in writing, printing, etc

inkling *n* hint; vague idea; notion

inland *adj* 1 situated in the interior of a country or region; away from the coast 2 operating inside a country, domestic *adv* towards an inland area *n* interior of a country or region **Inland Revenue** *n* 1 money obtained by taxes and duties levied within a country and on residents living abroad 2 government body that collects and administers this money

inmate *n* 1 person confined to an institution 2 occupant

inn *n* public house esp one that serves meals and offers lodgings

innate *adj* inherent in one's nature **innately** *adv*

inner *adj* 1 situated or occurring further in inside, or within 2 not superficial; hidden

innings *n pl* or *s* turn of a batsman or team of batsmen in cricket

innocent *adj* 1 ignorant of evil; uncorrupted; naive, unsophisticated 2 not guilty 3 not harmful *n* innocent person **innocence** *n* **innocently** *adv*

innocuous *adj* totally harmless

innovation *n* a newly introduced device, procedure method or change **innovate** *vt,vi* make an innovation

innuendo *n. pl* **innuendoes** malicious or obscene implication or reference

innumerable *adj* too many to be calculated; countless

inoculate *vt,vi* introduce a vaccine into the body to immunize against a specific disease **inoculation** *n*

input *n* amount, material, or data put into or supplied to a machine, factory, project, etc

inquest *n* 1 judicial inquiry, esp one into an unnatural death 2 any official investigation

inquire *vi* investigate; request information *vt,vi* enquire **inquiry** *n* 1 investigation; official examination of the facts 2 enquiry

inquisition *n* lengthy, thorough, and painful investigation or interrogation **The Inquisition** tribunal set up by the Roman Catholic Church to abolish heresy **inquisitor** *n*

inquisitive *adj* 1 fond of inquiring into other people s affairs; curious 2 eager to learn **inquisitively** *adv* **inquisitiveness** *n*

insane *adj* 1 mentally ill or out of control; mad; crazy 2 dangerously foolish **insanely** *adv* **insanity** *n*

insatiable *adj* unable to be satisfied; voracious; greedy

inscribe *vt* write engrave, or mark (names words, etc) **inscription** *n*

insect *n* 1 invertebrate animal or class of animals with six legs, a segmented body, and wings, such as beetles, butterflies, flies, and ants 2 *inf* any similar animal such as a spider **insecticide** *n* substance used to kill insects

insecure *adj* 1 not balanced; wobbly; unsafe 2 lacking confidence or stability **insecurely** *adv* **insecurity** *n*

inseminate *vt* implant semen into (a female) **insemination** *n*

insensible *adj* 1 insensitive, indifferent 2 unconscious; unable to experience sensations

insensitive *adj* 1 thick-skinned, not sensitive 2 heartless; cruel; ruthless

insert *vt* put or place in, among, or between introduce into **insertion** *n*

inside *n* 1 inner area, surface, or side; interior 2 *inf* stomach *adj* relating to the inside *adv* 1 on or in the inside; indoors 2 *inf* in prison *prep also* **inside of** within; on the inside of

insidious *adj* 1 secretly spreading; tending to corrupt or destroy 2 intended to trap; treacherous **insidiously** *adv* **insidiousness** *n*

insight *n* 1 perception; discernment; sympathetic understanding **2** sudden revealing glimpse

insinuate vt **1** imply or hint (something unpleasant) **2** introduce covertly or gradually **insinuation** n

insist vt,vi **1** declare or assert emphatically or repeatedly **2** demand strongly, persist in urging **insistence** n **insistent** adj persistent; demanding attention

insolent adj insulting; impertinent; rude **insolence** n **insolently** adv

insoluble adj **1** not soluble **2** unable to be solved

insolvent adj unable to meet debts; bankrupt n insolvent person **insolvency** n

insomnia n inability to get to sleep **insomniac** n person suffering from insomnia

inspect vt examine; scrutinize; look into; investigate **inspection** n **inspector** n **1** person, esp an official, who inspects **2** police officer inferior in rank to a superintendent and superior to a sergeant

inspire vt **1** stimulate; fill with creative or intellectual urges or impulses **2** arouse; excite **3** communicate or produce by superhuman influence **inspiration** n **1** artistic genius or impulse **2** sudden bright idea

instability n lack of stability, esp in mood or character

install vt **1** fix (apparatus) in position ready for use **2** place in office **3** settle; set (oneself) down **installation** n

instalment n one portion of something that appears, is sent, or paid in parts at regular intervals or over a period of time

instance n example; illustration of a general statement or truth **for instance** for example **in the first instance** to begin with; firstly

instant adj **1** occurring immediately or at once; immediate; urgent **2** requiring little or no preparation n **1** precise moment **2** brief time **instantaneous** adj occurring or done immediately or with little delay **instantaneously** adv **instantly** adv immediately; at once

instead adv as an alternative **instead of** in place of; rather than

instep n **1** top part of the foot between the toes and ankle **2** part of a shoe, etc that covers the instep

instigate vt stir up; urge; incite; bring about **instigation** n **instigator** n

instil vt (-ll-) gradually introduce (ideas, values, etc) into the mind **instillation** n

instinct n **1** innate impulse or feeling **2** mode of behaviour that is innate and not learned or acquired through experience **instinctive** adj **instinctively** adv

institute vt establish; start up n society or establishment, esp for promoting the arts or sciences or for education **institution** n **1** act of instituting **2** established law, procedure, custom, or practice **3** establishment set up for educational, medical, social, or corrective purposes **institutional** adj

instruct vt teach; direct; order **instruction** n **1** act of instructing **2** information **instructions** pl n directions as to use, etc ; orders **instructive** adj informative

instrument n **1** implement; tool; mechanical device **2** object played to produce music **3** person exploited by another as a means to an end **instrumental** adj **instrumentalist** n person who plays a musical instrument **instrumentation** n arrangement of music for instruments; orchestration

insubordinate adj disobedient; rebelling against authority n insubordinate person **insubordination** n

insular adj **1** inward-looking, narrow-minded; remote; aloof **2** relating to an island **insularity** n

insulate vt **1** protect against heat or sound loss or the passage of electric current by means of nonconducting material **2** isolate or separate by means of a barrier **insulation** n

insulin n hormone secreted by the pancreas to control blood sugar levels

insult vt (in'sʌlt) speak or act in order to hurt a person s pride or dignity; abuse n ('insʌlt) insulting remark or action

insure vt **1** safeguard against loss damage illness, etc , by paying insurance **2** ensure **insurance** n **1** act, system, or business of insuring **2** state of being insured **3** money paid to provide financial compensation in the event of illness, injury, loss of or damage to property, etc **4** financial protection so obtained

intact adj **1** whole; complete **2** unharmed; untouched

intake n amount or number taken in, admitted or consumed

integer ('intidʒə) n whole number

integral adj 1 being an essential part (of) 2 complete; entire

integrate vt combine or mix parts to make a whole; coordinate; unify **integration** n

integrity n 1 uprightness; honesty; soundness of character 2 unity; wholeness

intellect n 1 ability to absorb knowledge and think rationally; intelligence 2 person of great intelligence; brilliant mind **intellectual** adj 1 relating to the intellect 2 having or revealing great powers of mind n person of high intellect and cultural tastes, esp one interested in ideas

intelligence n 1 ability to learn, to reason, and to use the mental faculties 2 information, esp secret information about an enemy **intelligent** adj possessing or showing intelligence; clever **intelligently** adv **intelligible** adj comprehensible; capable of being easily understood

intend vt have as a purpose, mean

intense adj 1 extreme 2 strenuous; strong 3 violent, deeply felt; passionate 4 unable to relax, tense **intensely** adv **intensify** vt vi make or become stronger, greater, brighter or more extreme **intensification** n **intensity** n 1 quality or state of being intense 2 strength; power, concentration **intensive** adj 1 thorough and organized; exhaustive, concentrated 2 requiring and using large amounts of labour or capital **intensively** adv

intent adj 1 determined; resolved having in mind 2 concentrating (on) n purpose, motive **to all intents and purposes** as good as more or less; pretty well **intention** n aim; purpose; plan of action; design, motive **intentional** adj meant, on purpose **intentionally** adv

inter (in´tə) vt (-rr-) bury

interact vi have an effect upon other things influence **interaction** n

intercept vt stop or seize during transit; interrupt the progress of **interception** n

interchange vt vi 1 exchange; switch 2 substitute; alternate n 1 exchange alternation 2 motorway junction of interconnecting roads and bridges **interchangeable** adj

intercourse n 1 dealings; interchange of ideas benefits, etc 2 also **sexual intercourse** copulation

interest n 1 curiosity; concern involvement 2 cause of such a feeling 3 pursuit; pastime;

hobby 4 personal advantage 5 right, share, or claim, as in a business 6 charge or payment for a financial loan vt arouse the curiosity of; take an interest in **interested** adj 1 having or showing interest 2 personally involved

interfere vi meddle; concern oneself with others affairs **interfere with** have a bad effect on; impede; hinder; molest **interference** n 1 act of interfering 2 interruption of broadcast signals by atmospheric conditions, etc

interim n time between; time that has elapsed; meantime adj temporary

interior n 1 inside esp of a house or room 2 inland regions of a country adj of, on or in the interior

interjection n exclamation; sudden interrupting remark **interject** vt interpose, interrupt with

interlock vi, vt lock together join firmly or inextricably

interlude n 1 intermission; interval 2 intervening period or episode of contrasting activity

intermediary n go-between; mediator adj 1 acting as an intermediary 2 intermediate

intermediate adj coming or existing between; in between

intermission n 1 short interval; pause between the parts of a performance, film show etc 2 respite; rest

intermittent adj occurring at intervals; sporadic; periodic **intermittently** adv

intern vt confine to a particular area, camp or prison esp during wartime **internee** n

internal adj 1 concerning the interior workings or inside of something 2 domestic; within a country 3 essential, intrinsic **internally** adv

international adj of between or shared by a number of countries n 1 member of a national team 2 international match or contest

interpose vt vi 1 put in or between; interrupt (with) 2 intervene; mediate

interpret vt vi 1 translate 2 reveal the meaning or significance of 3 take to mean understand **interpretation** n **interpreter** n person who makes an immediate verbal translation of speech

interrogate vt ask (a prisoner or suspect) a series of questions; cross-examine, cross-question **interrogation** n **interrogator** n **interrogative** adj 1 questioning; in the form of a query **2** describing a word, such as *who* or *which*, used in or forming a question *n* interrogative word

interrupt *vt,vi* **1** stop the flow, passage or progress (of) **2** break in (on); disturb *vt* obstruct **interruption** *n*

intersect *vt,vi* divide by crossing; cut across; cross **intersection** *n* **1** act of intersecting **2** place or point where two things cross

interval *n* **1** period of time between two events, acts, or parts; intermission **2** intervening space

intervene *vi* **1** occur or come between **2** interfere or step in in order to prevent, hinder, or protest **intervention** *n*

interview *n* **1** formal meeting or discussion **2** conversation between a journalist and a newsworthy person **3** article resulting from this *vt* have an interview with **interviewer** *n*

intestines *pl n* portion of the digestive tract between the stomach and anus **intestinal** *adj*

intimate¹ ('intimit) *adj* **1** close, dear; being a good friend **2** deep; profound, private **3** sexual; having sexual relations *n* close friend **intimacy** *n*

intimate² ('intimeit) *vt* hint; imply

intimidate *vt* **1** frighten; make nervous or timid; bully **2** discourage by threats **intimidation** *n*

into *prep* **1** in; to the inside of **2** to; from one point or condition to another

intolerable *adj* **1** unbearable; unendurable **2** extremely annoying **intolerably** *adv*

intolerant *adj* not tolerant; narrow-minded; bigoted **intolerance** *n*

intonation *n* **1** variation of pitch in the speaking voice **2** correct pitching of musical notes

intoxicate *vt* **1** make drunk; inebriate **2** excite; inflame; exhilarate **intoxication** *n*

intransitive *adj* describing a verb that does not take or need a direct object

intricate *adj* complex; complicated; difficult to work out or solve **intricacy** *n* **intricately** *adv*

intrigue *n* ('intri:g) **1** plot; conspiracy; secret plan **2** illicit love affair *v* (in'tri:g) *vt* fascinate; stimulate the curiosity or wonder of *vi* plot; conspire

intrinsic *adj* real; fundamental; essential **intrinsically** *adv*

introduce *vt* **1** bring in; put forward **2** bring

into use; first establish **3** present and identify (a stranger) to another or others; make acquainted **4** insert **introduction** *n* **1** act of introducing **2** something introduced **3** preface; foreword; opening **4** preliminary guide; basic handbook **introductory** *adj*

introspective *adj* mentally inward-looking; aware of and critical of one's mental processes

introvert *n* withdrawn or introspective person

intrude *vt,vi* force (one's presence, etc.) uninvited **intruder** *n* **intrusion** *n* **intrusive** *adj*

intuition *n* **1** ability to perceive and understand things instinctively **2** knowledge acquired through this ability; hunch **intuitive** *adj* using or revealing powers of intuition rather than logic or rationality **intuitively** *adv*

inundate *vt* flood; overwhelm; swamp **inundation** *n*

invade *vt,vi* attack or forcibly enter (another's country or territory) *vt* violate; intrude or encroach on **invader** *n* **invasion** *n*

invalid¹ ('invali:d) *n* sick, disabled, or permanently bedridden person *vt also* **invalid out** send home or ↓ure (military personnel) because of ill health or injury

invalid² (in'vælid) *adj* not valid; not legally justifiable or effective **invalidate** *vt* render invalid **invalidation** *n*

invaluable *adj* of great worth or usefulness; priceless

invariable *adj* constant; unvarying; not changing; usual **invariably** *adv* always; constantly

invent *vt* **1** think up (something untrue or imaginary) **2** design or devise (something new or original) **inventor** *n* **invention** *n* **1** act of inventing **2** thing invented **3** ability to invent; ingenuity **inventive** *adj* good at thinking up or creating new ideas or things; ingenious

invert *vt* turn upside down; put back to front; reverse **inverse** *adj* inverted; back to front; contrary **inversion** *n*

invertebrate *adj* having no backbone *n* invertebrate animal

invest *vt,vi* put in (money, capital, time, effort, etc.) in order to make a profit *vt* **1** endow; provide **2** confer a rank or office upon with ceremony **investor** *n* **investiture** *n* ceremonial conferring of office **investment** n 1 act of investing 2 thing invested

investigate vt make enquiries about; look into; examine; inquire into **investigation** n **investigator** n

invincible adj unconquerable

invisible adj 1 incapable of being seen 2 hard to see; not conspicuous **invisibility** n

invite vt 1 request (a person) to be present or take part 2 ask for (comments, questions, etc) 3 court; provoke **invitation** n 1 act of inviting 2 spoken or written request for a person's presence

invoice n bill listing goods sold or services rendered with prices charged vt present with or make an invoice of

invoke vt summon the powers of; appeal or call for **invocation** n

involve vt 1 include 2 embroil; entangle 3 engross 4 entail; mean **involvement** n

inward adj 1 inner 2 existing in the mind or emotions; situated within **inwardly** adv inside; deep down **inwards** adv towards the inside or middle

iodine n chemical element found in seawater and seaweed and used in photography and the manufacture of antiseptics and dyes

ion n positively or negatively charged atom or group of atoms **ionize** vt,vi convert into ions

iridescent adj shimmering with rainbow colours **iridescence** n

iris n 1 circular coloured area around the pupil of the eye 2 garden plant with narrow leaves and purple or yellow flowers

iron n 1 malleable magnetic metallic element that is easily corroded and widely used in alloyed form, esp steel 2 heated appliance for removing creases from clothes, etc 3 iron or steel tool, usually heated 4 great hardness, strength, or resolution 5 golf club with a metal head vt,vi remove creases from (clothes, etc) with a hot iron **iron out** settle; put right **Iron Curtain** n the ideological, cultural, and social barrier that exists between the Soviet dominated countries of Eastern Europe and most of Western Europe **ironmonger** n person selling hardware, tools, etc **ironmongery** n 1 hardware, tools, etc 2 shop or business of an ironmonger

irony n 1 subtle use of words to imply a meaning opposite to the literal one 2 incongruous usually unfortunate situation or

sequence of events **ironic** or **ironical** adj **ironically** adv

irrational adj not rational or consistent; illogical **irrationality** n **irrationally** adv

irreconcilable adj not capable of being reconciled or made compatible **irreconcilably** adv

irregular adj 1 not occurring regularly 2 not symmetrical; uneven; not uniform 3 contravening customs, rules, or laws 4 not following the usual grammatical pattern **irregularity** n **irregularly** adv

irrelevant adj not relevant or applicable **irrelevance** n

irresistible adj 1 impossible to resist 2 extremely delightful or charming; fascinating **irresistibly** adv

irrespective adv **irrespective of** not taking into consideration; regardless of

irresponsible adj not behaving in a responsible manner; unreliable **irresponsibly** adv

irrevocable (i'revəkəbl) adj unable to be reversed; unalterable **irrevocably** adv

irrigate vt keep (land) constantly supplied with water using ditches, pipes, etc **irrigation** n

irritate vt 1 annoy; exasperate 2 sore; itch; chafe **irritation** n **irritable** adj easily annoyed

is v 3rd person singular form of **be** in the present tense

Islam n 1 Muslim faith based on a belief in one God, Allah, and on the teachings of his prophet, Mohammed, set down in the Koran 2 Muslim culture; Muslim world **Islamic** adj

island n 1 area of land surrounded by water 2 anything resembling an island in being isolated from its surroundings **islander** n **isle** n small island

isolate vt 1 set apart or keep separate 2 put in quarantine **isolation** n

issue vi 1 emerge; come, go, or pour out 2 result; be derived vt 1 give out; offer; distribute 2 publish n 1 something issued at one time, such as stamps or copies of a magazine or journal 2 outflow; discharge 3 disputed point; question; topic 4 result 5 offspring **at issue** in dispute; under discussion **take issue** disagree; dispute

it pron 1 that or this thing, animal, group, etc , when not specified or identified precisely or when previously mentioned 2 used as the subject with impersonal verbs such as 'rain', 'snow', etc **3** used as the subject or object when referring to a following clause or phrase

italic *adj* in or denoting a style of type with letters sloping to the right *n also* **italics** italic type, sometimes used to isolate or emphasize a word or phrase

itch *n* **1** irritating sensation of the skin causing a desire to scratch **2** constant craving; restless desire *vi* have or feel an itch **itchy** *adj*

item *n* **1** one unit or object from a list or collection **2** piece of news or information **itemize** *vt* list

itinerary *n* **1** detailed plan of a journey; route **2** account of a journey **itinerant** *adj* travelling from place to place *n* itinerant worker

its *adj* belonging to it **itself** *r pron* of its own self

ivory *n* hard smooth cream-coloured highly prized material forming the tusks of the elephant, walrus, etc

ivy *n* trailing evergreen plant with shiny leaves

J

jab *vt,vi* (-bb-) poke, thrust, stab *n* **1** sharp thrust or poke **2** *inf* injection

jack *n* **1** tool used for raising heavy objects esp a vehicle **2** lowest court card in a pack; knave *vt,vi also* **jack up** raise by using a jack **jackpot** *n* accumulated sum of money given as a prize

jackal *n* wild animal of the dog family

jackdaw *n* large black bird of the crow family

jacket *n* **1** short coat **2** *also* **dust jacket** detachable paper cover of a book **3** skin of a baked potato

jade *n* semiprecious hard stone of a green or whitish colour, valued as a gemstone

jaded *adj* worn out or stale; weary

jagged ('dʒægɪd) *adj* having rough sharp points or edges

jaguar *n* wild animal of the cat family resembling the leopard

jail *or* **gaol** *n* prison *vt* imprison **jailer** *n*

jam¹ *v* (-mm-) *vt* **1** crush or squeeze into a confined space; cram; clog **2** *also* **jam on** apply (brakes) suddenly and forcefully *vt,vi* stick or become stuck; wedge *n* congestion or blockage, esp of a number of vehicles on the road

jam² *n* preserve made by boiling fruit and sugar together

jangle *vi,vt* produce a harsh or discordant metallic ringing sound *n* harsh metallic ringing sound

janitor *n* caretaker; porter; warden

January *n* first month of the year

jar¹ *n* glass or earthenware vessel used for preserves, pickles, etc

jar² *vi,vt* (-rr-) **1** vibrate with an unpleasant grating sound **2** grate (on the nerves) *n* jolt; grating vibration

jargon *n* **1** idiomatic or specialized language developed by a particular group, trade, or profession **2** any talk or writing difficult to understand

jasmine *n* shrub of the olive family having sweet-scented yellow, red, or white flowers

jaundice *n* disease caused by excessive bile pigment in the blood characterized by a yellowing of the skin **jaundiced** *adj* affected or distorted by prejudice, jealousy, etc

jaunt *n* **1** short trip or excursion **2** spree; carefree adventure

jaunty *adj* sprightly; brisk; lively **jauntily** *adv*

javelin *n* long slender spear thrown as a field event in athletics

jaw *n* bony structure forming the bottom of the face or head in which the teeth are set **jaws** *pl n* gripping part of a machine, tool, etc ~*vi inf* gossip, chatter **jawbone** *n* either of the two bones of the jaw

jazz *n* popular music of Negro origin, often improvised and making use of syncopation

jealous *adj* experiencing strong feelings of resentment or envy, esp towards a rival in love **jealously** *adv* **jealousy** *n*

jeans *pl n* trousers of a strong cotton or denim material

jeep *n* open-sided motor truck used esp by military personnel

jeer *vi* shout insults; scorn; scoff; mock *n* mocking remark or shout; taunt

jelly *n* **1** type of confectionery made from gelatin, sugar and fruit flavouring **2** gelatinous substance produced when meat is boiled **jellyfish** *n* small marine creature with tentacles and a soft gelatinous body

jeopardize *vt* place at risk; endanger **jeopardy** *n*

jerk *vt* pull or push sharply; tug *vi* move quickly

and suddenly; jolt **n 1** sharp tug **2** spasm **jerky** adj **jerkily** adv **jerkiness** n

jersey n **1** woollen jumper **2** type of knitted fabric **Jersey** breed of dairy cattle

jest n witty or amusing joke or trick vi joke light-heartedly **jester** n **1** clown or fool formerly employed at the court of a king or nobleman **2** joker in a pack of cards

Jesuit ('dʒezjuɪt) n member of a religious order (Society of Jesus) founded by Ignatius Loyola

Jesus n also **Jesus Christ** founder of Christianity

jet[1] n **1** fast stream of water, gas etc , forced by pressure through a nozzle **2** aircraft propelled by a jet of gas

jet[2] n type of hard black coal used for jewellery **jet black** adj,n deep glossy black

jetty n small pier

Jew n person belonging to or following the religion of the race which is descended from the ancient Israelites **Jewish** adj

jewel n precious stone worn or used for adornment; gem **jewellery** n items such as necklaces, rings or brooches; jewels **jeweller** n

jig[1] n **1** lively folk-dance **2** music for such a dance usually in triple time vi vt (-gg-) **1** dance or play (a jig) **2** bounce or jog up and down

jig[2] n cutting tool or a guide for such a tool **jigsaw** n also **jigsaw puzzle** puzzle consisting of a number of specially shaped pieces of cardboard or wood, which interlock to make up a complete picture

jiggle vt,vi jerk or shake up and down; rattle

jilt vt forsake (a lover, intended husband or wife, etc)

jingle vt,vi produce a light ringing sound; tinkle n **1** light metallic sound **2** catchy tune or song

job n **1** employment; occupation; work **2** specific task; assignment **a good job** a fortunate thing or occurrence

jockey n professional rider of racehorses vt,vi also **jockey for** jostle; manoeuvre

jocular adj given to joking; jolly **jocularity** n

jodhpurs ('dʒɔdpəz) pl n type of close-fitting trousers worn when riding a horse

jog v (-gg-) vi **1** knock or push lightly; nudge; jerk **2** move slowly but steadily, trot or plod vt stimulate (the memory) n nudge; light blow

joggle vt vi jolt; jerk; jiggle, shake, jog n slight shake or jolt

join vt vi **1** bring or come together; fasten; connect **2** become a member (of) **3** also **join up** enlist (in) vt also **join in** accompany; take part in with n seam **joinery** n craft of making wooden doors window frames etc **joiner** n

joint n **1** connection of two parts or components **2** junction at which two bones connect **3** large piece of meat including a bone **4** inf marijuana cigarette **5** inf bar or club **6** inf place adj shared; combined vt cut up (meat) into joints **jointly** adv

joist n steel or timber beam or girder

joke n something done or said to cause amusement or laughter; jest vi speak or act amusingly or wittily **joker** n **1** person who jokes **2** one of two extra cards in a pack with a picture of a clown or jester

jolly adj cheerful; funny; jovial adv very **jollity** n

jolt vt,vi shake or bump sharply; lurch; jerk n **1** sudden sharp jerk **2** shock

jostle vi,vt push or move so as to gain more room or a better position n rough push

journal n **1** periodical; newspaper or magazine **2** diary or logbook recording daily events **journalism** n art or practice of writing for the press **journalist** n

journey n process of travelling or distance travelled; trip; voyage; excursion vi travel; take a trip

jovial adj hearty; jolly; good-humoured

joy n delight; pleasure; gladness **joyful** or **joyous** adj **joyfully** adv

jubilant adj joyful; rejoicing; triumphant **jubilance** or **jubilation** n

jubilee n celebration of a particularly significant anniversary

Judaism n Jewish religion or tradition

judge n **1** person presiding over a trial in a court of law **2** person who chooses the winner(s) of a competition; adjudicator **3** critic assessor vt,vi act as a judge (for) **judgment** or **judgement** n **judicial** adj relating to a judge court of law, or justice **judiciary** adj relating to judgment n **1** method or administration of justice **2** judges collectively **judicious** adj wise, well-judged, sensible **judiciously** adv

judo n Japanese sport embracing certain principles of self-defence by unarmed combat

jug *n* vessel with a handle and spout or lip, used for holding or serving liquids

juggernaut *n* large articulated lorry

juggle *vi,vt* **1** perform tricks (with) by tossing and catching (various objects) **2** manipulate or rearrange, esp in order to deceive **juggler** *n*

juice *n* liquid from fruit, vegetables, etc **juicy** *adj* **1** containing plenty of juice **2** suggesting scandal **juiciness** *n*

jukebox *n* coin-operated record-player found mainly on commercial premises

July *n* seventh month of the year

jumble *vt,vi* mix up; place or be out of sequence *n* muddled heap or mixture **jumble sale** *n* sale of second-hand articles which have been donated, esp in aid of charity

jump *vi* **1** leap into the air, spring **2** move involuntarily, esp in reaction to a noise, shock, etc **3** jerk **4** increase, rise, or switch suddenly *vt* leap over or across; clear **jump at** take advantage of or seize (an opportunity) eagerly ~*n* **1** leap; spring **2** obstacle to be cleared by jumping **3** spasm; jerk **4** sudden increase, rise, or switch **jumpy** *adj* nervous; tense

jumper *n* garment fitting the upper part of the body, often made of wool; sweater

junction *n* **1** joining place or point of intersection **2** place where railway lines converge or intersect **3** point of contact between different electrical circuits

juncture *n* **1** critical point in time **2** junction; connection

June *n* sixth month of the year

jungle *n* **1** area of land in tropical regions, having thick dense vegetation and undergrowth **2** situation or environment characterized by ruthless competition, lack of law and order, etc

junior *adj* of a lower rank or status, not senior *n* person who is younger or of a lower rank or status; subordinate **junior school** *n* school for children after primary but before secondary levels

juniper *n* conifer producing pungent purple cones, which are used in medicines, distilling, etc

junk[1] *n* discarded articles regarded as worthless; rubbish; trash **junkie** *n* also **junky** *sl* drug addict

junk[2] *n* flat-bottomed square-sailed ship of Chinese origin

junta *n* **1** self-appointed group that seizes political power **2** administrative council in some parts of Latin America

Jupiter *n* largest of the planets, orbiting between Mars and Saturn

jurisdiction *n* legal power, authority or administration

jury *n* **1** body of persons required to hear evidence and deliver a verdict at a trial **2** panel of judges **juror** *n* member of a jury

just *adj* **1** fair in the administration of justice; impartial; unbiased **2** deserved, proper *adv* **1** a moment earlier; recently **2** exactly; precisely **3** barely; hardly **4** at the same time (as) **5** merely; only **justly** *adv*

justice *n* moral or legal correctness, fairness, lawfulness **do justice to** treat according to merit

justify *vt* give sufficient or valid reasons for; uphold; defend **justifiable** *adj* **justification** *n*

jut *vi* (-tt-) also **jut out** stick out; extend beyond a particular point; protrude

jute *n* strong natural fibre used for ropes or sacking

juvenile *adj* **1** immature; young; childish **2** intended for young people *n* young person, child or adolescent **juvenile delinquency** *n* criminal behaviour by young offenders **juvenile delinquent** *n*

juxtapose *vt* place immediately next to **juxtaposition** *n*

K

kaftan *n* also **caftan** traditional loose full-length tunic of the Near East

Kaiser *n* (formerly) German emperor

kaleidoscope (kəˈlaɪdəskoup) *n* sealed tube containing at one end pieces of coloured glass whose reflections produce patterns when the tube is turned or shaken

kangaroo *n* Australian marsupial with powerful hind limbs and a broad tail

karate (kəˈrɑːtɪ) *n* Oriental system of self-defence by unarmed combat employing smashes, chops, or kicks with the hands, elbows, head, or feet

kebab *n* Middle Eastern dish of small cubes of

meat and vegetables cooked on a skewer over a charcoal grill

keel n timber or plate running along the length of the bottom of a ship's hull **on an even keel** maintaining a steady course; stable v **keel over** capsize; overturn

keen adj 1 enthusiastically willing or interested 2 anxious; eager 3 perceptive; observant; shrewd 4 having a sharp cutting edge 5 bitingly cold 6 intense; strong **keen on** very interested in **keenly** adv **keenness** n

keep v (kept) vt 1 hold in one's possession; retain 2 detain 3 maintain in a particular state or condition 4 own and look after or care for 5 abide by; observe; comply with 6 store; have in stock 7 restrain; deter; prevent 8 provide for; earn money for 9 make a record in vi 1 remain; stay 2 carry on; continue to 3 stay fresh **keep on** 1 continue to employ 2 nag; persist 3 proceed **keep to** proceed as planned; stick or adhere to **keep up (with)** maintain the same rate of progress (as) ~n 1 cost of maintaining 2 fortified central tower of a castle **keeper** n 1 person in charge of animals in a zoo 2 museum or gallery attendant 3 warder; jailer **keeping** n **in keeping with** in accordance with; conforming or appropriate to **keepsake** n memento, token gift or souvenir

keg n small barrel

kennel n 1 small shed for housing a dog 2 also **kennels** establishment breeding and caring for dogs

kerb n edge of a pavement

kernel n edible central part of a nut or fruit stone

kestrel n small falcon

kettle n metal vessel with a lid, spout, and handle, used for boiling water **kettledrum** n large percussion instrument having a hollow body with a skin stretched tightly over the top

key n 1 metal instrument cut and shaped to fit a particular lock 2 lever on a typewriter 3 lever on a piano and certain woodwind instruments 4 set of notes in a musical scale 5 crucial piece of information, component, etc 6 guide to coded information or symbols used adj most important or vital **keyed up** tense with anticipation **keyboard** n set of levers or keys on a piano, typewriter, etc

khaki ('ka:ki) adj,n yellowish-brown, often used as the colour for military uniforms

kibbutz (ki'buts) n, pl **kibbutzim** (kibut'si:m) collective farm in Israel

kick vt,vi strike or aim (at) with the foot vi raise or shake the feet or legs **kick up** create (a fuss, trouble, etc) ~n 1 blow or jerky movement of the foot 2 inf thrill **kick-off** n start of play in football

kid[1] n 1 young goat 2 inf child; young person 3 soft goatskin

kid[2] vt,vi (-dd-) inf deceive by teasing; hoax

kidnap vt (-pp-) seize and carry off (a person), esp in order to obtain ransom **kidnapper** n

kidney n one of a pair of bodily organs that filters the blood and removes waste products which are discharged to the bladder as urine **kidney bean** n reddish-brown kidney-shaped bean

kill vt,vi 1 cause the death (of) 2 destroy completely 3 inf cause pain, suffering, etc, to; exhaust **kill time** find something to do whilst waiting ~n act of killing, esp a hunted animal or prey **killer** n

kiln n large oven used for baking clay, bricks, etc

kilogram n also **kilogramme** or **kilo** one thousand grams (approx 2 2 lbs)

kilometre ('kilomi:tə, ki'lomitə) n one thousand metres (approx 0 6 miles)

kilowatt n one thousand watts

kilt n pleated tartan skirt, traditionally worn by Highland Scotsmen

kimono n full-length wide-sleeved dress with a wide sash, traditionally worn by Japanese women

kin n also **kindred** one s relatives

kind[1] adj 1 also **kind-hearted** friendly; generous, helpful, considerate 2 mild; not harmful **kindness** n **kindly** adj sympathetic; warm-hearted adv 1 in a kind manner, sympathetically 2 please

kind[2] n sort; type; class

kindergarten n nursery group or school for children under primary school age

kindle vt 1 set light to 2 arouse or excite (interest, passion, etc) vi catch fire

kindred adj 1 of one s kin 2 compatible, in sympathy n kin

kinetic adj relating to motion

king n 1 male monarch or sovereign 2 most influential or prominent person or thing 3 highest court card ranking above a queen and often below an ace 4 key chess piece, able to

move one square at a time in any direction
kingdom n 1 nation ruled by a king or queen;
realm 2 one of three major divisions into
which animals, plants, or minerals may be
classified **kingfisher** n fish-eating river bird
having bright blue and orange plumage
king-size adj also **king-sized** of a larger than
average size

kink n 1 twist, loop, or curl in a piece of rope,
string, hair, etc 2 inf perversion vi,vt form
into kinks; bend; curl **kinky** adj sl sexually
deviant; perverted

kiosk n 1 public telephone booth 2 small
open-fronted shop selling newspapers,
cigarettes, etc

kipper n herring or similar fish that has been
salted and smoked

kiss vt,vi caress or touch with lips as a token of
love, affection, reverence, etc n act of kissing

kit n 1 items of clothing and equipment issued to
a member of the armed forces 2 equipment or
tools used by a workman sportsman, etc 3
collection of parts sold for assembly by the
purchaser vt (-tt-) also **kit out** supply or issue
with a kit

kitchen n room equipped for cooking **kitchen
garden** n garden where vegetables, herbs,
etc , are grown

kite n 1 light framework of wood, paper, etc ,
that can be flown in the air at the end of a
long string 2 type of hawk

kitten n young cat

kitty n pooled sum of money; fund

kiwi n large bird native to New Zealand that is
unable to fly

kleptomania n compulsion to steal **kleptomaniac** n,adj

knack n skilful or intuitive ability; aptitude; flair

knave n 1 jack in a pack of cards 2 rogue;
scoundrel

knead vt shape and mould (dough, clay etc)
with the hands

knee n joint connecting the upper and lower
leg **kneecap** n flat bone at the front of the
knee **kneedeep/kneehigh** adj so deep/high
as to reach the knees

kneel vi (knelt or kneeled) rest or bend with the
knees on the ground

knickers pl n woman s undergarment covering
the lower half of the body

knife n, pl **knives** cutting implement consisting
of a sharpened blade set into a handle vt stab

or wound with a knife **on a knife-edge** in a
state of extreme tension or anxious anticipation

knight n 1 medieval nobleman of high military
rank 2 person honoured by the sovereign with
a non-hereditary rank below that of the
nobility 3 chess piece usually in the shape of
a horse s head **knighthood** n rank of a
knight

knit vi,vt (-tt-; knitted or knit) 1 make (a
garment, fabric, etc) by winding and looping
wool or yarn round two or more long needles
in a particular way 2 join together; mesh;
interlock **knitwear** n knitted garments

knob n 1 rounded handle on a door, drawer
etc 2 round switch on a radio, TV set, etc 3
lump; swelling **knobbly** adj also **knobby**
lumpy; bumpy; having knobs

knock n 1 blow; bang; tap 2 tapping noise
vt,vi 1 tap; bang; hit; strike 2 produce a
tapping sound; rattle 3 inf criticize; find fault
(with) **knock about or around** 1 travel
around 2 be in a group (with) 3 beat,
batter **knock down** 1 hit and push over 2
sell in an auction 3 reduce in price **knock
off** sl 1 finish work 2 pilfer, steal 3 complete
hurriedly 4 deduct **knock out** 1 cause to
lose consciousness 2 exhaust; tire **knockout**
n 1 blow that renders (someone) unconscious
2 contest in which competitors are eliminated
by heats 3 person of stunningly attractive
appearance 4 overwhelming experience
knock up 1 assemble quickly 2 rouse;
waken **knocker** n hinged metal bar attached
to a door and used for knocking

knot n 1 tight loop tied in a piece of rope,
string, ribbon, etc 2 small bunch of people 3
irregular lump in a piece of wood 4 unit used
to measure the speed of a ship or aircraft
equal to one nautical mile per hour vt vi (-tt-)
form into a knot; tangle; tie

know v (knew; known) vt,vi 1 be aware or
certain of (a fact) 2 understand; have
experience (of) vt 1 be acquainted or familiar
with 2 have a grasp of or skill in 3 be able to
distinguish **know how to** have the skill (to): have the
skill (to) **knowhow** n inf skill; ability
knowing adj 1 shrewd; aware 2 intentional;
deliberate **knowingly** adv **knowledge** n 1
information or facts 2 experience; awareness,
consciousness 3 familiarity; understanding 4

learning; wisdom **knowledgeable** adj well-informed **knowledgeably** adv

knuckle n joint of the finger v **knuckle down** get on with a task **knuckle under** submit to authority or pressure

kosher adj conforming to the requirements for the preparation of food under Jewish law

kung fu n Chinese system of self-defence combining the principles of both karate and judo

L

label n 1 slip of paper, card, etc, affixed to luggage, a parcel etc, for identification, tag 2 name or description vt (-ll-) 1 affix a label to 2 describe as, name

laboratory n room or building equipped for scientific experiments, manufacture of drugs, etc

laborious adj 1 requiring great effort or hard work 2 painstaking; hardworking **laboriously** adv

labour n 1 work; toil, task 2 period of childbirth 3 body of people available for employment; workers vi 1 work hard; toil 2 move with difficulty, struggle vt go into excessive detail about **labourer** n unskilled manual worker **Labour Party** n British political party representing the interests of the working class and trade unions

labrador n breed of dog with a golden or black coat

laburnum n small tree bearing clusters of drooping yellow flowers

labyrinth n 1 complex network of paths tunnels caves etc 2 complicated system situation etc

lace n 1 delicate fabric woven from cotton silk etc 2 cord for fastening a shoe or boot vt 1 also **lace up** tie (footwear) with a lace 2 add a dash of alcohol to **lacy** adj

lack n deficiency absence shortage vt vi be without or short (of)

lacquer n 1 resinous substance for varnishing wood 2 hairspray vt, vi coat or spray with lacquer

lad n inf boy or young man

ladder n 1 framework for climbing consisting of two uprights fitted with horizontal bars or rungs 2 flaw in knitting where vertical threads

have unravelled 3 means of moving within a social structure vt produce a ladder in (stockings, tights, etc)

laden adj 1 loaded; weighed down 2 overburdened

ladle n spoon with a long handle and deep bowl for serving soups stews, etc vt also **ladle out** serve by using a ladle

lady n woman, esp one who is wealthy or noted for her good manners **Lady** title rank, or form of address of certain female members of the nobility **ladylike** adj refined and well-mannered as befits a lady **Your/Her Ladyship** n form of address used to/of certain women with the rank of Lady

ladybird n small beetle having a red back with black spots

lag[1] vi (-gg-) fall behind n interval, lapse

lag[2] vt (-gg-) protect (pipes, etc) with insulating material

lager n type of beer stored in a cool place and served chilled

laid v pt and pp of **lay** .

lain v pp of **lie** .

laity n persons who are not members of the clergy, laymen

lake n inland expanse of water

lamb n young sheep or its meat

lame adj 1 unable to walk properly, crippled or limping 2 feeble, unconvincing vt make lame, cripple **lame duck** n liability, worthless cause etc

lament (lə'ment) vi, vt express great sorrow or grief (for); mourn n song or poem expressing grief or mourning **lamentable** ('læməntəbəl) adj deplorable

lamp n device producing light by electricity, oil etc usually having a shade for protection

lance n 1 long spear 2 also **lancet** sharp surgical knife vt pierce with a lance **lance corporal** n noncommissioned officer of the lowest rank in the British Army

land n 1 solid mass forming the earth s surface 2 country nation 3 soil, ground 4 domain sphere vi 1 arrive on the shore or ground after a journey by ship or aircraft, disembark 2 come to the ground after falling or jumping vt 1 bring (a ship) to shore or (an aircraft) to the ground 2 catch (a fish) 3 obtain (a job contract etc) vt vi place or be in a difficult situation **landing** n 1 flat area at the top of a flight of stairs 2 act of bringing a ship or aircraft to land **landlady** n 1 woman who rents out rooms to tenants or guests 2 female owner or manager of a public house **landlord** n 1 person who owns and rents out property, land, rooms, etc 2 male owner or manager of a public house **landmark** n 1 prominent feature of the landscape 2 significant historical event or achievement **landscape** n 1 scenery of an area 2 painting, drawing, etc, depicting this vt vi design and lay out (a park, garden, etc)

lane n 1 narrow road, esp in the country 2 marked division of a motorway, racing track, etc 3 prescribed route for shipping or aircraft

language n 1 structured system of speech sounds used by a community 2 written form of such a system 3 any system of communication 4 style of expression of speech or writing

languid adj lacking energy; weakened; listless; inert **languish** vi become languid; lose strength through neglect, deprivation, etc **languor** n

lanky adj tall and thin

lantern n lamp with a light enclosed in a glass case

lap[1] n 1 part formed by the area from the waist to the thighs when a person is sitting down 2 comfortable or safe place

lap[2] vt, vi (-pp-) 1 drink by licking up with the tongue 2 wash gently against with a soft slapping sound **lap up** take in (information) greedily ~n gentle slapping movement or sound

lap[3] n one circuit of a racing track vt (-pp-) 1 wrap round; overlap; envelop 2 overtake so as to be one or more laps ahead

lapel n front part of a garment that folds back to join the collar

lapse n 1 error; deviation; aberration; fault 2 decline to a lower standard 3 interval or passing of time vi 1 decline; fall into disuse 2 cease to subscribe to or be a member of a club, organization, religion, etc 3 elapse; pass slowly vt cancel the subscription of

larceny n theft

larch n type of deciduous conifer

lard n pig fat melted down for use in cooking vt 1 smear with lard 2 embellish (a speech, story, etc)

larder n room used for storing food; pantry

large adj 1 of considerable size, weight, extent,
150

etc; great; big **at large** 1 free; unchecked 2 on the whole; generally **largely** adv mostly; to a great extent

lark[1] n small songbird; skylark

lark[2] n piece of fun or mischief; prank; spree v **lark about** act mischievously

larva n, pl **larvae** (ˈlɑːvi) immature form of an insect such as the butterfly or an animal such as the frog **larval** adj

larynx n organ containing the vocal cords situated at the base of the tongue **laryngitis** n inflammation of the larynx resulting in temporary loss of voice

lascivious (ləˈsɪvɪəs) adj lewd; lustful; lecherous

laser n electronic device for producing a narrow parallel very intense beam of light of a single wavelength

lash[1] n 1 whip, esp the flexible part or thong 2 stroke of a whip 3 cutting remark 4 beating or impact of waves, rain, etc 5 eyelash vt 1 whip; thrash 2 scold; criticize sharply 3 strike forcefully and repeatedly 4 move like a whip **lash out** 1 attack wildly 2 spend extravagantly

lash[2] vt bind with ropes

lass n inf girl or young woman

lasso n, pl **lassoes** or **lassos** long rope with a noose for catching horses, etc vt catch with a lasso

last[1] adj 1 coming at the end; final 2 most recent; latest 3 one remaining 4 ultimate; most conclusive adv 1 at the end; after the rest 2 most recently n person or thing at the end **at last** finally; eventually **lastly** adv as a conclusion

last[2] vi 1 exist or continue for a specified time 2 endure; remain useful or in good condition; keep **lasting** adj permanent; continuing

latch n bar or lever for securing a door or gate vt fasten with a latch **latch on (to)** inf 1 attach oneself to 2 grasp; come to understand

late adj 1 not punctual 2 happening or continuing after the normal or expected time 3 occurring towards the end of a period, stage, etc 4 former; recent 5 deceased adv 1 after the expected time 2 at an advanced stage **lately** adv also **of late** recently

latent adj present but not yet developed or apparent; potential **latency** n

lateral adj directed to or coming from the side

lathe n machine for holding and shaping or cutting wood, metal, etc

lather n 1 foam produced by soap or detergent; suds 2 frothy sweat, esp of a horse vi,vt produce lather; foam; froth

latitude n angular distance north or south of the equator

latrine n lavatory, esp a temporary one for use at a camp site, barracks, etc

latter adj 1 relating to the second of two things 2 occurring in the second half **latterly** adv lately

lattice n network of strips of wood, metal, etc, arranged to form a pattern of squares, diamonds, etc

laudable adj praiseworthy; commendable

laugh vi,vt utter a sound of amusement, scorn, etc **laugh at** make fun of; mock n 1 single sound uttered in amusement, scorn, etc 2 inf something that is fun to do or watch **laughable** adj ridiculous **laughter** n act or sound of laughing

launch[1] vt 1 send (a ship) into the water for the first time 2 send (a rocket) into space 3 propel; hurl 4 start off on a new course or enterprise **launch into** start without hesitation or introduction

launch[2] n small open motorboat

launder vt,vi wash and press or iron (clothes, sheets, etc) **Launderette** n Tdmk public laundry equipped with coin-operated machines **laundry** n 1 place where clothes, sheets, etc, are laundered 2 items to be laundered

laurel n evergreen tree with smooth broad aromatic leaves; bay **laurels** pl n honours; credit for achievement **rest on one's laurels** cease to strive after having attained victory or success

lava n molten rock from an erupting volcano

lavatory n water-closet or the room where it is situated; toilet

lavender n bush bearing fragrant mauve flowers n,adj mauve

lavish adj done on a generous scale; abundant; lush vt bestow; spend generously **lavishly** adv

law n 1 binding regulation laid down by a government, council, or sovereign 2 scientific rule or principle 3 code of behaviour **the law** 1 legal profession 2 body of legal regulations 3 inf police **lay down the law** behave domineeringly, dogmatically, or tyrannically **law-abiding** adj obedient according to the law **lawful** adj permitted by law; legal; legitimate **lawsuit** n instance of bringing a case before a court of law; action **lawyer** n practising member of the legal profession

lawn n area of grass laid out in a garden or park **lawn-mower** n machine for cutting grass

lax adj 1 not strict 2 loose; slack 3 having open or loose bowels **laxative** n medicine taken to relieve constipation

lay[1] v (laid) vt 1 place gently on the ground or a surface; rest; deposit 2 set (a table) for a meal 3 fit (a carpet) 4 place a bet on; stake 5 tab copulate with vt,vi produce (eggs) **lay down** surrender; sacrifice; relinquish **lay off** 1 dismiss (workers) temporarily 2 sl stop; desist **lay on** provide; organize **lay out** 1 spread out, arrange for display 2 prepare (a body) for burial 3 spend **lay up** incapacitate **layabout** n lazy person **layby** n parking space at the side of a road **layout** n arrangement of material for a book, newspaper, etc

lay[2] v pt of **lie**.

lay[3] adj relating to people, duties, etc, concerned with the laity **layman** n, pl **-men** 1 person who is not a member of the clergy 2 person who has an amateur rather than a professional knowledge of something

layer n 1 coating spread over a surface 2 stratum; band 3 strip placed over or resting on another 4 shoot of a plant pegged underground so that it will produce its own roots vi,vt form or place in layers vt propagate by means of a layer

lazy adj not inclined to work; idle; inactive **lazily** adv **laziness** n **laze** vi,vt be lazy; spend (time) idly

lead[1] (led) n 1 tough malleable bluish-grey metal, used for pipes, as a roofing material, etc 2 graphite used for pencils **leaden** adj 1 made of lead 2 heavy or sluggish

lead[2] (li:d) v (led) vi,vt 1 show the way (to); guide; conduct 2 act as the leader or head (of); control 3 be in or take first place; be ahead (of) vi 1 be a means of reaching 2 follow a particular direction vt live; follow (a particular way of life) **lead astray** persuade to do wrong; corrupt **lead on** entice; provoke **lead up to** move towards; prepare for; approach ~n 1 clue; hint; guideline 2 position in front or ahead of others 3 main role in a play, film, etc 4 flex, cord, or cable for an electrical appliance 5 leash **leader** n 1 person in charge; head of a political party, movement etc 2 person in a winning position 3 principal violinist in an orchestra 4 editorial in a newspaper **leadership** n **leading** adj main, principal; chief

leaf n, pl **leaves** 1 flat photosynthetic organ of a plant 2 page of a book **turn over a new leaf** make a fresh start by reforming one's behaviour ~vi produce leaves **leaf through** glance through (a book papers etc) by turning the pages quickly **leaflet** n 1 advertisement or notice printed on a single sheet of paper 2 small undeveloped leaf

league n 1 political alliance; coalition 2 association of sports teams **in league (with)** conspiring (with); allied (to) ~vt vi bring or come together in a league

leak n 1 crack or hole through which liquid gas etc, escapes 2 disclosure of confidential information vi vt 1 escape or allow to escape through a leak 2 divulge, disclose **leaky** adj **leakage** n process of leaking or the amount leaked

lean¹ vt,vi (leaned or leant) place or be in a sloping position; tilt, incline **lean on** 1 rest against; use for support 2 rely or depend on 3 sl threaten, intimidate **lean towards** favour; have a bias towards **leaning** n tendency, bias; inclination

lean² adj 1 (of meat) having very little fat 2 thin; skinny 3 not productive, barren; of a poor quality or standard **leanness** n

leap vi,vt (leapt or leaped) 1 jump or spring high into the air, bound 2 increase sharply n 1 high or sudden jump 2 abrupt change of position **leap at** take advantage of eagerly **leapfrog** n game in which one person bends over for another to leap or vault over him vi (-gg-) 1 play leapfrog 2 move erratically **leap year** n year having one day (i e Feb 29th) more than the usual 365

learn vi,vt (learned or learnt) 1 acquire knowledge (of) or skill by studying or being taught 2 experience 3 obtain information (of); hear (about) **learned** ('lə:nid) adj scholarly, wise, having great learning **learning** n academic knowledge or study; scholarship

lease n contract drawn up between a landlord

and tenant vt grant or take possession of by lease **leasehold** adj held by lease n tenure by lease **leaseholder** n

leash n strap for attaching to a dog's collar as a means of control, lead vt attach a leash to

least adj smallest in amount or importance n smallest amount **at least** 1 as a minimum 2 even if nothing else **not in the least** not at all; not in the slightest; not to any extent ~adv of the lowest amount

leather n strong material made from the cured hide of certain animals **leathery** adj of or resembling leather

leave¹ v (left) vt,vi 1 go away or depart (from) 2 cease to attend 3 cease to be a member (of) or participant (in) vt 1 forget to take; lose 2 deposit; place 3 result in 4 cause a visible sign (of) 5 bequeath 6 cause to remain 7 fail to complete; postpone 8 keep open free or vacant 9 abandon; forsake **leave out** omit fail to consider

leave² n 1 permission 2 time off from duty or work **take one's leave (of)** depart (from), say goodbye (to)

leaves n pl of **leaf.**

lecherous adj lewd, lascivious lustful **lecher** n **lechery** n

lectern n stand for the Bible in a church

lecture n 1 formal talk given to instruct an audience, esp as part of a university course 2 rebuke, reproof, scolding reprimand vt vi deliver a lecture (to) **lecturer** n **lectureship** n

ledge n narrow horizontal shelf projecting from a wall window cliff, etc

ledger n book in which credits and debits of an account are recorded

leech n 1 blood-sucking wormlike animal living usually in water 2 person who lives off another's efforts

leek n vegetable related to the onion having a long edible greenish-white bulb

leer vi stare lustfully mockingly or slyly n lascivious, mocking, or sly look **leery** adj

left¹ v pt and pp of **leave** .

left² adj of or on the side of a person or thing that is turned towards the west when facing north adv towards the left side n direction location, or part that is on the left side **the Left** party or political group following radical or socialist policies **left-hand** adj on the side towards the left **left-handed** adj using the left hand for writing, etc **left wing** n the Left adj **left-wing** relating to the left wing

leg n 1 limb used for walking, standing, running etc 2 upright support of a chair, table, etc 3 part of a garment covering the leg 4 particular stage of a journey race, or competition **not have a leg to stand on** be unable to defend oneself; have no justifiable case **on its/one's last legs** about to disintegrate or collapse; worn out **pull someone's leg** hoax; tease; deceive jokingly v **leg it** (-gg-) walk, go on foot

legacy n gift of property left by will; bequest

legal adj 1 relating to law 2 authorized or required by law; legitimate, lawful **legality** n **legally** adv **legalize** vt make legal; sanction by law **legalization** n

legend n traditional story popularly believed to concern actual people or events **legendary** adj known from legend; renowned

legible adj written so as to be clear to read, easily deciphered

legion n 1 military unit of Ancient Rome comprising several thousand soldiers 2 vast number; multitude

legislate vi vt formulate officially and pass laws (about) **legislation** n **legislative** adj **legislator** n **legislature** n body of statesmen who pass laws; parliament

legitimate adj 1 permitted by law; legal 2 conforming to rules; allowable; permissible 3 logical, justifiable 4 born of parents who are legally married **legitimacy** n **legitimately** adv

leisure n period outside working hours free time **at leisure** when free, at a convenient time **leisurely** adj without haste; unhurried adv at an easy or unhurried rate or pace

lemon n sharp-tasting citrus fruit with a bright yellow skin n adj bright light yellow

lend vt (lent) 1 give with the expectation of repayment or return, loan 2 add to the quality or character of; impart **lend a hand** help, cooperate; assist **lender** n

length n 1 measurement of something from one end to another 2 time taken from beginning to end; duration 3 piece of cloth rope wire etc **at arm's length** at a distance; apart **at length** 1 in great detail for a long time 2 eventually **lengthen** vt vi make or become longer **lengthways** adj adv also **lengthwise**

measured from one end to another **lengthy** adj long and detailed

lenient adj not strict; inclined not to punish severely **leniency** n **leniently** adv

lens n piece of transparent material with curved surfaces for converging or diverging a beam of light

Lent n period of forty days before Easter, traditionally observed by Christians as a time for fasting and penitence

lentil n plant producing brownish-orange seeds, which are eaten as a vegetable, used to thicken soups, etc

Leo n fifth sign of the zodiac, represented by the Lion

leopard n large animal of the cat family having a yellowish coat with black markings

leprosy n infectious disease characterized by skin inflammation and disfigurement **leper** n person suffering from leprosy

lesbian n woman who has a sexual relationship with someone of her own sex; female homosexual **lesbianism** n

less adj,adv not as much; to a smaller extent; not as often prep minus pron a smaller amount **lessen** vt,vi make or become less; reduce; decrease **lesser** adj smaller; less important

lesson n 1 period of time spent learning or teaching 2 something that is learned or taught 3 short reading from the Bible given during a service

lest conj in case; for fear that; so as to avoid

let vt (-tt-; let) 1 allow; permit 2 rent or hire (accommodation etc) **let alone** 1 leave alone 2 not to mention; apart from **let down** 1 lower; take down 2 deflate 3 disappoint; fail to keep a promise **let (someone)** inform; tell **let off** 1 excuse; pardon, refrain from punishing 2 cause to explode 3 release allow to escape **let on** divulge; tell reveal **let out** 1 allow to leave 2 divulge; leak 3 alter (a garment) so as to be larger 4 utter; emit **let up** cease become less persistent **let-down** n disappointment; anticlimax

lethal adj likely to cause death; highly dangerous

lethargy ('leθədʒɪ) n extreme lack of energy or vitality; inertia. sleepiness; idleness sluggishness **lethargic** (lɪ'θɑːdʒɪk) adj

letter n 1 written message or account that is

sent to someone **2** written or printed alphabetical symbol or character **letter of the law** the law when interpreted literally **lettering** n art or practice of inscribing letters

lettuce n vegetable with broad green leaves used in salads

leukaemia n disease in which an excessive number of white corpuscles in the blood is produced

level adj **1** having an even surface or plane; horizontal **2** not tilted or sloping **3** equal; even **4** also **level-headed** calm and sensible; not inclined to panic n **1** measured height or altitude **2** flat even surface or area **3** standard or status; grade **4** instrument or device for measuring or checking that something is horizontal or level **5** layer; stratum **on the level** inf honest straightforward ~vt (-ll-) **1** make level or horizontal; line up **2** equalize; bring to the same standard or status; even up **3** raze; demolish **4** take aim with; point **5** direct (a remark, gaze, etc) **levelly** adv **levelness** n **level crossing** n intersection of a road and railway track

lever n **1** bar or rod used to move a heavy object, set machinery in motion, etc **2** means of persuasion or coercion vt,vi use a lever (on); prise **leverage** n **1** force or action of a lever **2** means of exerting power or influence

levy n tax; duty; toll vt,vi impose a levy (on)

lewd adj **1** lecherous; lustful **2** vulgar; crude; obscene; indecent

liable adj **1** obliged by law; subject (to) **2** likely; apt; inclined **liability** n **1** legal obligation **2** likelihood; probability **3** tendency; inclination **4** responsibility; burden, disadvantage; drawback

liaison n **1** close working relationship; association; cooperation **2** illicit sexual relationship **liaise** vi work together; cooperate

liar n person who tells lies

libel n **1** written defamatory statement **2** crime of publishing such a statement vt (-ll-) publish libel about **libellous** adj

liberal adj **1** tolerant, esp on political or religious matters **2** progressive; enlightened **3** generous; free **Liberal** n member or supporter of the Liberal Party **Liberal Party** n British political party advocating individual freedom and occupying a position to the right

of the Labour Party but to the left of the Conservative Party

liberate vt set free; release; emancipate **liberation** n

liberty n freedom from restraint, restriction, or control **take liberties (with)** take unfair advantage (of)

Libra n seventh sign of the zodiac, represented by the Scales

library n **1** room or building housing a collection of books **2** collection of films, documents, etc **librarian** n person working in a library **librarianship** n

libretto n text of an opera, operetta, etc

lice n pl of **louse**.

licence n **1** official document or certificate of authorization **2** permission granted by an authority **3** misuse of freedom; lack of self-control **4** allowable deviation from a particular convention esp in art or literature **license** vt grant or authorize a licence (for) **licensee** n person holding a licence, esp to sell alcoholic drinks

lichen ('laikən, 'litʃən) n moss-like plant that grows on tree-trunks, rocks, etc

lick vt,vi **1** touch or stroke with the tongue **2** inf beat or defeat soundly **3** inf thrash; flog **lick into shape** improve or groom by special training or instruction ~n **1** stroke of the tongue **2** inf pace; rate; speed

lid n **1** cover for a container **2** eyelid

lie[1] n untrue statement, esp one deliberately intended to deceive vi (lying) tell a lie or lies

lie[2] vi (lying; lay; lain) **1** be stretched out or placed in a horizontal position; rest **2** be situated **3** be buried **4** be the responsibility (of) **lie in** remain in bed for longer than usual **lie low** remain in hiding

lieu (luː) n **in lieu of** instead of, in place of

lieutenant (lef'tenənt) n **1** military officer of a rank below that of captain **2** naval officer of a rank below that of lieutenant commander **lieutenant colonel** n military officer of a rank below that of colonel **lieutenant commander** n naval officer of a rank below that of commander

life n, pl **lives 1** condition of existing or being alive; being **2** also **lifetime** period of existence; length of time lived **3** all living things **4** biographical account **5** liveliness; vivacity; vitality **6** way of living; mode of existence **7** maximum prison sentence that can be awarded **come to life 1** recover consciousness; be revived **2** become lively or animated **lifeboat** n boat used for searching for those in distress at sea or one carried by a ship in case of emergency **lifeguard** n person who patrols the shore, attends a swimming pool, etc for the safety of swimmers **lifelike** adj resembling something real **lifeless** adj **1** dead **2** motionless; seemingly dead **3** dull; uninspired **lifeline** n **1** rope used in life-saving **2** something that ensures survival **lifelong** adj lasting throughout one's life; permanent **life-saving** n practice or method of rescuing someone in distress, esp at sea adj able to save life

lift vt **1** take or carry upwards; pull up; haul; raise **2** turn or direct upwards **3** put into a happy or cheerful mood; gladden **4** exalt; elevate **5** revoke or cancel (a ban, restriction, etc) **6** inf steal; shoplift **7** inf copy or borrow (an idea, piece of text etc) **8** dig up (plants) vi **1** move upwards; rise **2** (of fog, mist, etc) clear; disperse n **1** act of lifting or raising **2** boxlike compartment driven hydraulically, mechanically or by electricity that moves vertically between floors of a building **3** free ride in someone else's vehicle **4** something that gives one energy or makes one cheerful or happy **lift-off** n launching of a rocket; blast-off

light [1] n **1** brightness emitted by the sun, a lamp etc **2** daylight **3** source of illumination **4** match etc that produces a flame **5** aspect; context; view **6** enlightenment; knowledge **7** small window pane **bring/come to light** make/become known or apparent **in the light of** taking into account; with the knowledge of **set light to** ignite or kindle **shed** or **throw light on** clarify; explain ~adj **1** not dark; illuminated **2** of a pale or pastel shade or colour **3** fair-haired vt vi (lit or lighted) **1** set light to, ignite **2** provide with light or illumination **light up 1** illuminate; make bright **2** apply a match to **3** cause to sparkle or shine; brighten **light bulb** n glass bulb containing a metal filament, which lights up when an electrical current is passed through it **lighten** vt,vi brighten, make or become light(er) **lighter** n device producing a flame for lighting cigarettes, etc **lighthouse** n tower situated on or near the coast that sends

out a powerful light as a guide or warning to shipping

light [2] adj **1** not heavy; weighing little **2** not forceful; gentle; not hard **3** of a small amount; slight **4** not overpowering; subtle **5** buoyant **6** also **light-headed** giddy; faint; dizzy **7** also **light-hearted** cheerful; not serious; happy **8** not severe or strict; lenient **9** airy; spongy; porous **10** not classical or highbrow **11** nimble; graceful or quick **12** not arduous; simple or easy **make light of** treat as unimportant; make no fuss about ~adv without being weighed down; comfortably vi (lighted or lit) settle or perch; alight **light (up)on** come across by chance; discover **lightly** adv **lightness** n **lighten** vt,vi **1** make or become less heavy **2** make or become more cheerful, optimistic, etc ; lift **lightweight** adj **1** light in weight **2** not intellectually demanding; superficial n boxer whose weight is between 126 lbs and 135 lbs

lightning n electricity discharged in the atmosphere producing a flash of light and usually accompanied by thunder **like lightning** with tremendous speed

like [1] prep **1** very similar to; in the manner of; the same as **2** for example; such as **3** as though; as if **feel like 1** desire; want; be tempted or inclined to **2** have the sensation of; resemble; feel similar to **like-minded** adj having the same or similar views or opinions **liken** vt compare; draw an analogy or find a resemblance (between) **likeness** n **1** resemblance; similarity **2** representation in a painting, photograph, etc **likewise** adv **1** similarly; in the same way **2** moreover, furthermore; also

like [2] vt be fond of; find pleasing, attractive, agreeable, etc vi,vt wish; prefer; choose

likely adj probable; to be expected; liable adv probably; possibly **likelihood** n

lilac n hardy shrub having fragrant purple, mauve or white flowers

lilt n **1** rhythmic or melodious quality in speech or music **2** tune or song with such a quality vi,vt sing, speak, or sound with a lilt

lily n bulb producing large white, purple, yellow, or orange flowers **lily-of-the-valley** n small plant having fragrant white bell-shaped flowers and broad leaves

limb n **1** part of the body attached to the trunk,

such as an arm or leg **2** branch; bough (**out**) **on a limb** isolated and vulnerable

limbo n **1** supposed state of those who have died without being baptized **2** state of being unwanted, cast aside, or without a proper place

lime¹ n **1** also **quicklime** calcium oxide; white substance made from limestone **2** also **slaked lime** calcium hydroxide; white substance produced by adding water to quicklime vt treat with lime **limelight** n **in the limelight** attracting a great deal of public notice or acclaim **limestone** n whitish rock composed of calcium carbonate

lime² n green-skinned citrus fruit similar to a lemon

limerick n humorous five-lined poem

limit n **1** extent to which something is possible or permissible **2** most acceptable amount; minimum or maximum **3** boundary vt place a restriction on **limitation** n restriction; limiting circumstance

limp¹ vi walk in an abnormal way because of injury or disablement; be lame n act of limping

limp² adj **1** sagging; not rigid; floppy **2** feeble; weak

limpet n marine mollusc having a conical shell that clings to rocks, etc

line¹ n **1** mark drawn in pencil, paint, etc, across a surface **2** groove; crease; furrow **3** row; column **4** outline; edge **5** boundary; limit **6** cable, rope, cord, or string used for a particular purpose **7** means of transport; route **8** railway track **9** policy; method or system **10** direction taken by a missile **11** field of research; area of interest **12** single horizontal row of written or printed words vt **1** draw lines on **2** produce grooves or furrows in **3** form a row along; border **line up 1** set in a straight or orderly row or line **2** provide; organize

line² vt provide with an inside covering or layer of material

lineage n line of descent from a common ancestor

linear ('liniə) adj **1** relating to a line **2** made up of lines **3** of one dimension only

linen n **1** strong fabric of woven flax **2** sheets, tablecloths, etc, made esp of linen

liner n ship designed to carry a large number of passengers

linger vi **1** be reluctant to hurry away; stay behind; loiter **2** remain or persist, esp as a memory

lingerie ('lɑːnʒərɪ) n women's underwear and nightwear

linguist n **1** person who is able to speak one or more foreign languages skilfully **2** student of linguistics **linguistic** adj relating to language, linguistics, or speech **linguistics** n study of the structure or history of language

lining n material used to line a coat, curtain, etc

link n **1** single loop forming part of a chain **2** connecting part or piece in a mechanism **3** connection or relationship between people, different places, times, etc vt, vi form a link (**between**); connect; relate

linoleum n also **lino** material having a canvas backing coated with linseed oil, cork, etc, used as a floor covering

linseed n seed of flax from which oil is extracted

lion n **1** large mammal of the cat family, the male of which has a shaggy mane **2** powerful or strong person **lioness** f n

lip n **1** one of two fleshy parts surrounding the opening of the mouth **2** that part of the rim of a jug, etc, that channels liquid being poured out **3** sl impudent remark **lip-read** vi vt (-read) interpret (speech) by following a person's lip movements **lipstick** n cosmetic used to add colour to the lips

liqueur n sweet alcoholic drink generally taken after a meal

liquid n substance that can flow but cannot easily be compressed adj **1** relating to a liquid; capable of flowing **2** harmonious; flowing **3** (of assets) readily convertible into cash **liquidate** vt **1** settle (debts) **2** dissolve (a company) by realizing assets in order to pay off creditors, shareholders, etc **3** dispose of (an enemy, spy etc) by violent means **liquidize** vt, vi also **liquefy** make or become liquid

liquor n any alcoholic drink esp a spirit

liquorice n black substance extracted from the root of a shrub for use in medicines, confectionery, etc

lira ('lɪərə) n, pl **lire** ('lɪərɪ) or **liras** standard monetary unit of Italy

lisp n manner of pronunciation in which s and z sound like th (θ and ð) vt, vi pronounce or speak with a lisp

list[1] n record or statement placing a number of items one after the other vt place on a list; make a list of

list[2] vi (of a ship) lean to one side n leaning to one side

listen vi 1 pay attention or concentrate in order to hear 2 take notice; heed **listener** n

listless adj not energetic; lethargic; weary

lit v a pt and pp of **light**[1] and **light**[2].

literal adj 1 not metaphorical 2 interpreted or translated word for word **literally** adv

literary adj concerning literature, authorship, or scholarship

literate adj able to read and write **literacy** n

literature n body of written material, such as novels, poetry, or drama

lithe adj supple; moving easily or gracefully

litmus n type of vegetable dye that turns red in acids and blue in alkalis

litre n unit of volume equal to one thousand cubic centimetres

litter n 1 rubbish or refuse that is dropped or left lying about, esp in a public place 2 set of offspring produced by a sow, bitch, etc , at one birth vt 1 cover or make untidy with litter 2 scatter or be scattered untidily on

little adj 1 small; tiny; not big or tall 2 not important; trivial 3 brief; not lasting long pron not much adv not often; hardly at all **a little** pron a small number or quantity adv to a small extent **little by little** gradually

live[1] (liv) vi 1 exist; be alive; have life 2 have one's home (in); reside; stay 3 continue, flourish 4 make a living vt 1 spend (one's life) 2 have as a fundamental part of one s life **live up to** match (required standards or expectations)

live[2] (laiv) adj 1 alive; not dead; living 2 stimulating; interesting 3 (of a shell, cartridge etc) not yet exploded 4 broadcast directly without being previously recorded 5 carrying electric current **livestock** n s or pl animals kept or reared on a farm, such as cattle, pigs, or poultry

livelihood n means of earning a living

lively adj 1 active; having energy; vigorous 2 busy; fully occupied 3 alert; quick 4 bright; cheerful **liveliness** n

liver n reddish-brown organ situated below the diaphragm in the body that secretes bile, neutralizes toxic substances, etc

livid adj 1 extremely angry; furious 2 discoloured, as when bruised

living adj still alive; not yet dead or extinct n 1 livelihood 2 way of life **living room** n room in a house used for recreation, receiving guests, etc

lizard n reptile having four limbs, a long tail, and a scaly body

llama n mammal related to but smaller than a camel, valued for its fleece

load n 1 something carried or transported 2 cargo 3 burden; weight of responsibility, etc 4 inf large amount; lot; heap vt, vi 1 place a load on or in (a lorry, ship, etc) 2 burden 3 put ammunition in (a gun)

loaf[1] n, pl **loaves** baked bread in a particular shape

loaf[2] vi pass time idly; lounge; loiter

loan n something lent, such as a sum of money or a book from a library **on loan** borrowed ~vt, vi lend

loathe vt hate; detest; abhor **loathsome** adj detestable; abhorrent

lob vt, vi (-bb-) hit or bowl (a ball) so as to form a high arc n ball hit or bowled in such a way

lobby n 1 entrance hall, waiting room, or corridor 2 group seeking to persuade officials, members of parliament, etc , to support or oppose a particular policy or piece of legislation vt, vi seek to influence as a lobby

lobe n 1 lower fleshy part of the ear 2 subdivision of certain organs such as the lung or brain

lobster n large edible crustacean with long claws or pincers

local adj 1 belonging to or concerning a particular district or locality 2 affecting a particular part of the body n 1 person belonging to the locality 2 inf public house nearest to one s home or place of work **locality** n neighbourhood; vicinity; district **localize** vt 1 limit to a particular part of the body 2 make local

locate vt 1 look for and find the position of 2 situate; place; position **location** n 1 place; site; position 2 act of locating or finding 3 place other than a studio where a film is shot

loch n (in Scotland) lake or narrow sea inlet

lock[1] n 1 device for securely fastening a door, drawer, box, etc , operated usually by means of a key 2 section of a canal or river enclosed within a barrier or gate, which can be opened or shut to control the water level 3 wrestling hold in which a limb or the head is unable to move *vt,vi* **1** fasten or become secure with a lock **2** jam; fix so as to be unable to move **3** interlock

lock² *n* length or curl of hair from or on the head

locker *n* cupboard provided esp in a public building, used for storing personal property, clothes, etc

locket *n* small case containing a portrait, memento, etc , attached to a chain and worn as a necklace

locomotion *n* power of motion **locomotive** *n* engine driven by steam, electricity, or diesel power, used to draw a train along a railway track

locust *n* insect of the grasshopper family that travels in swarms stripping vegetation over a wide area

lodge *vt,vi* **1** provide or be provided with accommodation, esp in a private household **2** embed or become embedded (in); wedge *vt* **1** make (a formal complaint) **2** deposit for safekeeping *n* **1** small house located near or at the gate of a park, estate, etc **2** cabin or house used by hunters, skiers, etc **lodger** *n* person lodging in a private household **lodgings** *pl n* accommodation, such as rented rooms in a private household

loft *n* **1** room or space immediately below the roof of a house **2** upper floor of a barn, stable, etc , where hay is stored **3** building constructed as a shelter for racing pigeons **lofty** *adj* **1** high and imposing **2** idealistic; noble **3** haughty; arrogant

log *n* **1** section of a felled branch or tree trunk **2** regular or daily record kept during a voyage, flight, etc *vt* (-gg-) **1** fell or saw (logs) **2** record as a log **logbook** *n* book in which records or logs are kept

logarithm *n* power to which a base number, usually 10, is raised to give a specified number, tabulated as an aid to calculation **logarithmic** *adj*

logic *n* **1** branch of philosophy concerned with determining the validity of particular statements according to certain principles of reasoning **2** consistency of method or practice; validity of reasoning **logical** *adj* **logically** *adv*

loins *pl n* lower part of the back and sides of the body

loiter *vi* lurk; linger; move about aimlessly **loiterer** *n*

loll *vi* laze; lounge *vt,vi* droop; sag; hang loosely

lollipop *n* **1** boiled sweet on a small stick **2** ice lolly

lonely *adj* **1** without friends; isolated; alone **2** remote; desolate **loneliness** *n* **lone** *adj* solitary; single

long¹ *adj* **1** of considerable extent from one end to another; not short **2** lasting for a considerable time. **3** of a particular length or duration **4** having a large number of entries parts, etc **in the long run** over a long period *adv* for a particular time **as long as** on condition that; provided that **before long** after a short time; soon **for long** for a long time **no/any longer** no/any more **long-sighted** *adj* **1** able to see clearly at a distance **2** having imagination or foresight **long-standing** *adj* having been in effect over a long period **longwinded** *adj* using an excessive number of words; tediously long

long² *v* **long for** crave; yearn for; desire **longing** *n*

longevity *n* relatively long life span or state of living to a great age

longitude *n* angular distance east or west of a standard meridian (through Greenwich)

loo *n inf* lavatory or toilet

look *vi* **1** *also* **look at** direct the eyes (towards) in order to see **2** *also* **look at** begin to examine; attend (to) **3** seem; appear; be likely to be **4** face; overlook **5** *also* **look for** search (for); seek **6** *also* **look through** read; glance at; scan *vt* **1** direct one's gaze at; stare or glance at **2** have the appearance of being correspond to **look after** take care of; tend be in charge of **look down on** regard as inferior or worthy of contempt **look forward (to)** anticipate with pleasure **look out** be cautious; heed **look up** begin to improve **look up to** admire; respect ∼*n* **1** act of looking **2** appearance; impression **lookout** *n* **1** person placed on guard, to watch out for danger, etc **2** *inf* matter for personal concern. affair **looks** *pl n* physical appearance

loom¹ *n* machine for weaving by hand or mechanically

loom² *vi* **1** approach or appear menacingly **2** give an impression of greatness; dominate

loop *n* shape of a circle, oval, spiral, etc

formed by string, wire, etc ; coil *vt,vi* form a loop

loophole *n* flaw or ambiguity in a law, contract, etc , that enables one to evade obligations, penalties, etc

loose *adj* **1** not tight; slack **2** not fastened or fitted securely **3** not put in a bundle or tied together **4** free; not confined **5** not compact **6** approximate; rough **7** promiscuous **8** not careful; sloppy **9** not controlled **at a loose end** having nothing in particular to do; not occupied ~*adv also* **loosely** in a loose man ner *vt* **1** liberate; set free; allow to escape **2** loosen; slacken **loosen** *vt,vi* make or become loose(r); slacken; unfasten

loot *n* money, property, etc , stolen or seized, esp during a battle or riot *vt,vi* steal; plunder **looter** *n*

lop *vt* (-pp-) chop or sever (branches, a limb etc) swiftly and in one movement

lopsided *adj* tilted to one side, uneven or crooked; not symmetrical

lord *n* nobleman **Lord 1** title, rank or form of address of certain male members of the nobility **2** title of certain high officials in the Church or of the law **the Lord 1** God **2** Jesus Christ **the Lords** House of Lords **v lord (it) over** be master of; dominate **lordship** *n* rank of a lord **Your/His Lordship** form of address used to/of certain men with the rank of Lord and also bishops and judges of the high court

lorry *n* motor vehicle for carrying heavy loads transporting goods, etc ; truck

lose *v* (lost) *vt* **1** drop or leave (something) and be unable to find it again **2** decrease in power, speed etc **3** be deprived of as through death, accident etc **4** be unable to maintain (a particular state belief, etc) **5** fail to take advantage of or use *vt vi* **1** fail to win, suffer defeat (in) **2** (of a watch clock etc) be slow (by) **loser** *n* **loss** *n* act of losing or that which is lost **at a loss** helpless; incapable

lot *pron* **a lot** a large number or quantity much or many; a great deal *n* **1** group, collection, bunch **2** assigned task **3** article or set of items in an auction **draw lots** select at random by using tickets slips etc *adv* **a lot 1** to a great extent **2** often; regularly

lotion *n* liquid preparation used as a skin cleanser, antiseptic, etc

lottery *n* **1** system of raising money by selling

tickets, one or more of which are drawn at random to entitle the holder to a prize **2** situation governed by luck or chance

lotus *n* **1** mythical fruit that induces laziness or forgetfulness **2** variety of tropical water lily

loud *adj* **1** of a relatively high volume of sound; not quiet **2** of a vulgar style; garish *adv also* **loudly** in a loud manner **out loud** aloud **loudness** *n* **loud-mouthed** *adj* rude; abusive brash **loudspeaker** *n* device for converting electrical signals into sound that can be heard over a wide area

lounge *n* **1** sitting room **2** room or area at an airport hotel etc where one may sit or wait **3** *also* **lounge bar** saloon bar *vi* laze, move or sit idly

louse *n, pl* **lice** wingless bloodsucking insect that is a parasite of mammals **lousy** *adj* **1** infested with lice **2** *inf* very bad; awful

lout *n* uncouth person

love *n* **1** feeling of deep passion desire affection or fondness **2** score of nil in tennis, squash etc **make love (to)** have sexual intercourse (with) ~*vt vi* feel love (for) **lover** *n* **lovesick** *adj* pining, suffering through love

lovely *adj* **1** giving pleasure, nice, highly enjoyable **2** beautiful, attractive **loveliness** *n*

low¹ *adj* **1** not tall or high, relatively close to the ground **2** close to the bottom of a particular scale grade etc poor **3** inferior below average **4** mean, despicable **5** depressed or ill **6** almost empty, having only a small amount left **7** deep and quiet *adv* towards or into a low position state or condition **lie low** remain hidden esp to avoid capture **lowness** *n* **lowbrow** *adj* relating to a style or taste esp in the arts that is not very sophisticated or intellectual not highbrow **lower** *vt vi* **1** decrease reduce **2** move downwards **lower case** *n* printed letters of the alphabet that are not capitals **lowland** *n* region or area that is relatively flat **lowlander** *n*

low² *vt vi n* (of cattle) moo

loyal *adj* faithful maintaining allegiance, patriotic **loyally** *adv* **loyalty** *n*

lozenge *n* **1** small tablet eaten as a sweet for medicinal purposes **2** diamond-shaped equilateral figure

LSD *n* **lysergic acid diethylamide**; synthetic hallucinatory drug

lubricate vt apply oil or grease to **lubrication** n **lubricant** n lubricating substance; oil adj serving to lubricate

lucid adj 1 expressed in a way that is easily understood; clear 2 shining; bright **lucidity** n

luck n 1 state of affairs, event etc , apparently occurring at random; chance; fortune 2 good fortune **lucky** adj having or bringing good luck; fortunate **luckily** adv fortunately

lucrative adj profitable

ludicrous adj absurd; ridiculous

lug vt (-gg-) pull or carry with effort; drag

luggage n suitcases bags etc carried on a journey; baggage

lukewarm adj 1 tepid; moderately warm 2 not enthusiastic

lull vt soothe; make calm or drowsy n brief respite or period of tranquillity **lullaby** n soothing song intended to lull a child to sleep

lumbago n backache

lumber[1] n 1 (esp in North America) timber or logs 2 large unwanted furniture or other household articles vt 1 store or fill with household lumber 2 inf burden with an unpleasant duty boring person etc **lumberjack** n (esp in North America) person who fells trees and cuts timber

lumber[2] vi move clumsily and heavily

luminous adj reflecting light

lump n 1 solid mass usually irregular in shape 2 swelling; bump vt also **lump together** place in or consider to be one group or mass **lumpy** adj having many lumps; bumpy

lunar adj relating to the moon

lunatic n insane person **lunacy** n madness insanity

lunch n also **luncheon** midday meal vi eat lunch

lung n one of a pair of respiratory organs situated in the thorax that oxygenates the blood

lunge n 1 thrust of a sword in fencing 2 sudden forward movement vi make or move with a lunge

lupin n plant with a tall stem bearing bright flowers of various colours

lurch[1] vi stagger; sway jerk or jog violently n sudden violent jerk or stagger

lurch[2] n **leave in the lurch** abandon at a critical time; forsake

lure vt entice in order to trap; tempt

lurid adj 1 sensational; shocking; scandalous 2 having strange bright colours

lurk vi loiter; lie in wait; remain hidden

luscious adj 1 gorgeous; delightful 2 having a rich flavour; succulent

lush adj 1 characterized by rich dense growth; luxuriant; abundant 2 luxurious

lust n 1 strong sexual desire 2 craving; passion; greed **lustful** adj consumed with lust **lusty** adj robust, hearty; vigorous

lustre n brightness or gloss of a surface; sheen, shine, radiance **lustrous** adj

lute n pear-shaped stringed instrument of the 14th–17th centuries, related to the guitar **lutenist** n

luxury n 1 condition of having all that one needs to gratify one s desires 2 item not regarded as a necessity **luxuriant** adj abundant, lush **luxurious** adj providing luxury **luxuriously** adv

lynch vt (of a mob) hunt down and kill without legal trial

lynx n long-eared wild cat inhabiting forest regions in parts of Europe North America and Africa

lyre n stringed instrument of ancient Greece resembling a small harp

lyric adj relating to a style of poetry expressing personal feelings, originally recited to a lyre accompaniment **lyrical** adj 1 expressive of the emotions of love sorrow, etc 2 enthusiastically eloquent **lyrics** pl n words of a song

M

mac n short for **mackintosh.**

macabre (mə'ka brə) adj suggesting or associated with death frightening

macaroni n type of pasta shaped into thin tubes

mace[1] n 1 hammer-like medieval weapon with a spiked metal head 2 ceremonial staff that is a symbol of office

mace[2] n spice produced from nutmeg

machine n 1 apparatus that performs useful work using applied forces 2 mechanism such as a car or aeroplane 3 highly organized controlling body vt vi use a machine to shape cut or work on something **machine gun** n automatically loaded and repeatedly firing gun **machine-gun** vt (-nn-) shoot at with a machine gun **machinery** n 1 machines or machine parts 2 system or way of organization **machinist** n person who makes or works on machines

mackerel n pl **mackerel** or **mackerels** marine food fish with a silvery belly and green stripes on its back

mackintosh n light coat worn esp as protection from rain, raincoat

mad adj 1 mentally disturbed, insane 2 eccentric crazy 3 inf extremely pleased angry enthusiastic noisy etc **drive** or **make someone mad** annoy **go mad** become very excited angry pleased etc **madly** adv **madness** n **madden** vt vi anger excite irritate

madam n polite form of address to a woman

made v pt and pp of **make**.

Madonna n Virgin Mary esp when painted or a statue

madrigal n 1 love poem or song 2 part song performed usually by six or seven voices without musical accompaniment

magazine n 1 paper-covered periodical containing contributions from various writers and usually illustrated 2 place where arms explosives etc are stored 3 replaceable metal containers for cartridges inserted into some automatic guns or rifles

maggot n larva of a housefly etc often breeding in decaying matter

magic n 1 art of producing certain effects with the help of supernatural forces witchcraft 2 art of producing seemingly inexplicable results by means of tricks 3 mysterious power or agency adj 1 relating to magic 2 also **magical** as if by magic miraculous enchanting **magician** n person who is skilled in tricks or in spells

magistrate n person who officiates in a lower court of law justice of the peace **magisterial** adj 1 relating to a magistrate 2 dictatorial authoritative

magnanimous adj generous noble not petty **magnanimity** n **magnanimously** adv

magnate n wealthy highly influential person esp in industry

magnet n piece of iron or steel that can attract iron or steel objects and point north when suspended **magnetic** adj 1 relating to a magnet or magnetism 2 attractive alluring **magnetism** n 1 science or attractive properties

of magnets 2 charm; attractiveness **magnetize** vt 1 make magnetic 2 attract

magnificent adj remarkable; splendid **magnificence** n **magnificently** adv

magnify vt 1 make apparently larger esp by means of a lens or microscope 2 exaggerate **magnification** n

magnitude n 1 size extent 2 importance significance

magnolia n shrub or tree with large usually sweet-smelling creamy-pink flowers

magpie n bird with a long tail black-and-white plumage and a chattering call

mahogany n tropical American tree the hard reddish-brown wood of which is used for furniture

maid n 1 girl 2 female servant **old maid** old unmarried woman spinster **maiden** n young single woman **maiden aunt** n unmarried aunt **maiden name** n family name before a woman marries **maiden speech** n first speech

mail n 1 letters parcels etc sent or received by post 2 postal service **mailing list** n list of names and addresses of persons to whom specific information is regularly sent **mail order** n order and delivery of goods by post

maim vt disable cripple

main adj chief principal most important n also **mains** principal pipe or cable for gas water or electricity supply **mainly** adv **mainland** n land mass such as a country or continent excluding its islands **mainspring** n 1 chief spring of a clockwork mechanism 2 driving force chief motivation **mainstream** n leading trend

maintain vt 1 keep going keep in fair condition support 2 assert **maintenance** n 1 act or way of keeping or supporting a person or thing 2 financial support as after a divorce

maize n tall annual grass grown for its yellow grain used as food and fodder and for its oil

majesty n grandness splendour stateliness **Majesty** term of address for a queen or king or the spouse or widow of a sovereign **majestic** adj stately dignified

major adj 1 of greater importance extent size etc 2 of or relating to a musical scale in which the third and fourth and the seventh and eighth notes are a semitone apart n military officer ranking below a lieutenant colonel and above a captain **major general** n military officer ranking above a brigadier

majority n 1 greater number, part, etc ; more than half 2 number by which a winning vote in an election, etc , exceeds the runner-up 3 state or time of reaching full legal age

make v (made) vt 1 create; produce; construct; form; prepare; establish 2 cause to be, become, or seem 3 cause; force 4 amount to; constitute 5 earn; acquire 6 develop into 7 do; perform 8 appoint vt, vi cause to become or become (happy, sad, merry, etc) n brand; style; way things are made **on the make** inf seeking an easy profit or conquest **make do (with)** be content with; improvise with **make for** go towards **make good** 1 repair 2 be successful in **make it** achieve or reach a goal **make off (with)** go or run off (with) **make out** 1 understand 2 see; discern 3 write out or fill in (a cheque, etc) 4 attempt to establish; represent as **make up** 1 complete; form 2 invent; compose; fabricate 3 reconcile or become reconciled 4 apply cosmetics to the face, esp for theatrical effect **make-up** n 1 cosmetics 2 person's constitution or personality **make up for** compensate or atone for **make up one's mind** decide; resolve

make-believe n pretence; fantasy

makeshift adj provisional; acting as a substitute n makeshift object, method, etc

maladjusted adj not adjusted or adapted properly to personal environment **maladjustment** n

malaria n infectious tropical disease transferred by mosquitoes and characterized by chills and high fever

male adj 1 of or related to the sex that produces young by fertilizing the female masculine 2 composed of or for men or boys n male person or animal

malevolent adj harmful, evil, spiteful malicious **malevolence** n **malevolently** adv

malfunction vi fail to function properly n failure to function properly

malice n intention to inflict harm on another, spite **malicious** adj **maliciously** adv

malignant adj 1 inclined to cause suffering showing ill will 2 (of disease) likely to cause death if not treated successfully **malign** vt insult slander adj evil **malignancy** n

malleable adj (esp of metal) easily shaped or treated

mallet n hammer-shaped tool, usually with a wooden head

malnutrition n defective or inadequate nutrition

malt n grain, often barley, soaked then dried for use in brewing beers or distilling spirits

maltreat vt treat in an abusive or cruel manner **maltreatment** n

mammal n any of the class of warm-blooded animals whose offspring are fed by mother's milk **mammalian** adj

mammoth n huge extinct elephant adj huge; immense

man n, pl **men** 1 human male adult 2 individual; person 3 mankind 4 husband or lover 5 workman; male employee 6 piece in draughts, chess, etc **man in the street** n person considered as representative of an average member of society **to a man** 1 unanimously 2 completely; utterly ~vt (-nn-) supply with people for a specific purpose **manly** adj denoting conduct and qualities expected of a man **manliness** n

manage vt, vi control; be in charge (of); handle vt succeed in; be successful in vi cope **manageable** adj **management** n 1 managing techniques 2 body of persons in charge of a business 3 administration **manager** n person managing or controlling a business, etc **manageress** f n **managerial** adj

mandarin n 1 high-ranking official in imperial China 2 high-ranking or pompous official 3 small orange-like fruit **Mandarin** n official Chinese dialect

mandate n 1 authorization; official command 2 sanction or support given to a government by the electorate **mandatary** ('mændətərı) n person, body, or state holding a mandate **mandatory** ('mændətərı) adj 1 having the nature or command of a mandate 2 compulsory

mandolin n musical instrument of the lute family with eight strings tuned and plucked in pairs

mane n long growth of hair on the back of the neck of a horse, lion etc

mange n contagious skin disease of domestic animals esp dogs **mangy** adj 1 having mange 2 scruffy

mangle[1] vt **1** disfigure as by severe cuts, etc; mutilate **2** spoil by errors

mangle[2] n machine with two rollers used for removing water from and smoothing clothes, etc vt put through a mangle

mango n, pl **mangos** or **mangoes** pear-shaped tropical fruit with sweet yellowish flesh, borne on an evergreen tree

manhandle vt **1** treat roughly; use physical violence on **2** use physical rather than mechanical force

manhole n hole, covered by a lid, that serves as an access to a sewer, pipe, etc

mania n **1** excessive excitement **2** obsession or excessive liking for something **3** condition characterized by abnormal excitement and often manifestations of violence **maniac** n **1** person showing excessive enthusiasm for something; fanatic **2** mad person; lunatic **manic** adj relating to mania

manicure n care or treatment of hands and fingernails vt treat (fingernails) by cutting, varnishing, etc

manifest adj quite apparent and obvious; visible vt reveal clearly **manifest itself** show itself; appear **manifestation** n **manifestly** adv

manifesto n written declaration by a sovereign or body of people proclaiming certain principles or rights

manifold adj of many parts, aspects, or uses; varied **manifoldly** adv

manipulate vt **1** operate skilfully; use; handle **2** exercise shrewd control over; influence cleverly **3** exercise treatment on **manipulation** n **manipulator** n

mankind n human race

man-made adj artificially produced

manner n **1** way something happens or is done **2** style **3** particular way a person behaves towards others **4** kind; sort **manners** pl n social conduct **mannerism** n gesture, speech habit, etc, particular to an individual

manoeuvre (məˈnuːvə) n planned, calculated, or strategic movement, as in a war; clever plan vt,vi **1** make or perform manoeuvres **2** move or cause to move into a desired direction or position

manor n **1** feudal territorial unit occupied and worked by serfs paying rent in crops and service to their lord **2** also **manor house**

residence of the lord with its grounds **3** mansion on an estate

manpower n number of people needed or supplied for something

mansion n large stately residence; manor house

manslaughter n unlawful but unintentional killing of a person

mantelpiece n structure above and around a fireplace, often incorporating a shelf

mantle n **1** loose sleeveless cloak **2** something covering or concealing **3** net-like luminous cover over a gas lamp vt cover with or in a mantle

manual adj of the hands; done or operated by hand; not mechanical n book containing fundamentals of a subject; textbook; handbook **manually** adv

manufacture n **1** commercial production or processing of goods, usually on a large scale **2** manufactured product vt,vi make (goods); produce; process vt fabricate; concoct **manufacturer** n

manure n animal excrement used for fertilizing soil vt apply manure to (soil)

manuscript n author's original piece of writing or document before its printing

many adj much more than few; numerous n,pron large number of people or things

map n two-dimensional representation of a geographical area vt (-pp-) produce a map of

maple n deciduous tree or shrub with hard close-grained wood, used for furniture, etc

mar vt (-rr-) spoil; ruin

marathon n **1** long-distance race run over a distance of 42 km **2** any long and trying task or contest

marble n **1** hard, usually veined, limestone rock, used in a polished form, esp in architecture **2** small glass ball **marbles** n game played with such balls

march vi **1** walk with regular steps in an orderly military fashion **2** proceed steadily vt force to go or march n **1** act or instance of marching **2** distance or route marched **3** piece of music composed for marching

March n third month of the year

marchioness n (maːˈʃənes) wife or widow of a marquess

mare n female horse

margarine n food product, similar to butter, usually made from vegetable fats

margin n **1** border **2** empty space on the sides

of a text **3** vertical line bordering this **4** limit of something **5** tolerable excess **marginal** *adj* **1** relating to a margin **2** close to a limit **3** insignificant **marginally** *adv*

marguerite *n* garden plant resembling a large daisy

marigold *n* plant having orange or yellow flowers

marijuana (mæri'waːnə) *n* dried hemp leaves or flowers smoked for euphoric effect

marinade *n* **1** seasoned mixture of vinegar or wine with oil in which meat, vegetables, etc, are steeped before cooking **2** food thus steeped **marinate** *vt, vi also* **marinade** soak (meat, fish, etc) in marinade

marine *adj* **1** of or relating to the sea and sea life **2** of navigation and shipping or the navy *n* **1** soldier trained to serve both on land and the sea **2** sea vessels collectively

marital *adj* relating to marriage

maritime *adj* **1** relating to the sea, shipping, or navigation **2** of a place or area by the sea

marjoram *n* plant with sweet-scented leaves, which are used in cooking

mark[1] *n* **1** visible trace on a surface, such as a stain, dot, scratch, etc **2** sign or symbol indicating or distinguishing something **3** figure or letter evaluating a piece of work, examination, etc **4** distinguishing quality **5** target *vt* **1** put a mark on **2** distinguish, characterize, indicate, or show, as by a mark **3** select; designate *vt vi* **1** stain; scratch **2** evaluate and correct (an examination paper, essay, etc) **marked** *adj* **1** noticeable; evident **2** watched with suspicion singled out **markedly** *adv* **marksman** *n, pl* **-men** a person who shoots a gun skilfully and accurately

mark[2] *n* German monetary unit

market *n* **1** place usually with outdoor stands, where food, clothes, etc, are sold **2** area of trade in certain goods **3** demand for goods *vt, vi* offer for sale **market garden** *n* establishment where fruit and vegetables are grown for sale **market research** *n* research into consumers needs and preferences

marmalade *n* jelly-like preserve usually made from oranges

maroon[1] *n, adj* brownish-red

maroon[2] *vt* abandon or isolate on an island etc, without resources

marquee *n* large tent used for exhibitions, etc

marquess *n also* **marquis** ('maːkwis) nobleman ranking below a duke and above an earl or count **marquise** (maːˈkiːz) *n* wife of a marquess

marriage *n* **1** relationship or legal bond between a man and woman, making them husband and wife **2** harmonious union of two things

marrow *n* **1** soft nutritious tissue inside bones that is vital for production of certain blood cells **2** *also* **vegetable marrow** plant with a long, rounded, and usually green striped fruit eaten as a cooked vegetable **marrowbone** *n* bone containing marrow used in cooking, esp for making stock

marry *vi* become husband and wife *vt* **1** make (a person) one's spouse; join or take in marriage **2** unite

Mars *n* fourth planet from the sun, lying between earth and Jupiter **Martian** *adj*

Marseillaise (maːsəˈleiz) *n* French national anthem

marsh *n* low, poorly drained, and usually very wet ground **marshy** *adj*

marshal *n* **1** highest military rank in certain countries **2** official in charge of ceremonies parades, etc *vt* (-ll-) **1** arrange in proper order **2** assemble **3** conduct

marshmallow *n* sweet with a soft spongy texture

marsupial *n* any of the group of mammals including the kangaroo, whose young are carried in and complete their development in a pouch

martial *adj* relating to war

martin *n* kind of swallow

martini *n* drink made of gin and vermouth

martyr *n* person who endures suffering out of religious or some other conviction *vt* kill torture, or persecute as a martyr **martyrdom** *n*

marvel *n* something wonderful *vi vt* (-ll-) feel wonder or surprise (at) **marvellous** *adj* wonderful; excellent **marvellously** *adv*

Marxism *n* political theory describing the historical change of capitalism into a classless society as the outcome of the struggle of the working classes against their exploitation **Marxist** *n, adj*

marzipan *n* sweet paste of ground almonds and sugar, moulded into small fruits or used in cakes, etc

mascara *n* cosmetic for painting eyelashes

mascot n object believed to bring luck

masculine adj 1 relating to or characteristic of a man 2 of a grammatical gender normally denoting males **masculinity** n

mash n 1 mixture of warm water and crushed grain, etc, used as fodder, in brewing, etc 2 mashed potatoes vt crush into a soft pasty mass

mask n 1 facial covering, worn, esp as a disguise 2 pretence; disguise vt 1 put a mask on 2 disguise; hide

masochism n condition in which a person suffers voluntarily in order to experience pleasure, esp sexual **masochist** n **masochistic** adj

mason n person who works with building stone **masonry** n profession or work of a mason

masquerade n 1 ball, etc, where people wear masks, costumes, and other disguises 2 pretence; false show vi wear a disguise

mass[1] n 1 bulk of matter that is not particularly shaped 2 large number or quantity of something 3 measure of the amount of matter in a body vt,vi form or gather into a large crowd **mass media** pl n newspapers, television, radio, etc, informing and influencing the public **mass-produce** vt manufacture on a very large scale **mass production** n

mass[2] n 1 also **Mass** celebration of the Eucharist, esp in the Roman Catholic Church 2 music composed for this occasion

massacre n ruthless killing, esp of innocent people; slaughter vt kill indiscriminately

massage n treatment of muscles in order to relax them by rubbing and kneading vt give a massage to **masseur** n person who practises massage **masseuse** f n

massive adj 1 large and solid 2 considerable

mast n 1 vertical pole for supporting a vessel's sails and rigging 2 any high upright pole

mastectomy n surgical removal of a breast

master n 1 person who controls others 2 expert in a special field 3 employer of servants 4 male teacher 5 form or mould for making duplicates; original vt 1 become highly skilled in 2 gain control over; overcome **masterful** adj 1 highly capable; skilful 2 showing authority; dominant **mastermind** n person who creates or plans a major project or activity vt plan with great skill **masterpiece** n great work of art; example of excellence or skill

masturbate vi,vt excite oneself or another to orgasm by manipulation or rubbing of the genitals **masturbation** n

mat[1] n 1 piece of fabric, used to cover floors, stand or sit on, wipe shoes on, etc 2 piece of material placed under vases, plates, etc 3 tangled mass vi (-tt-) become tangled

mat[2] adj matt

matador n man who kills the bull in bullfights

match[1] n slender strip of wood with a coated head that bursts into flame when rubbed

match[2] n 1 person or thing that resembles or corresponds to another 2 contest; team game 3 marriage or person eligible for marriage vt 1 equal or be equal to 2 be the match of 3 make to fit or correspond; adapt vi correspond in shape, size, colour, etc harmonize **matchless** adj incomparable; having no equal

mate n 1 one of a couple or pair, esp a pair of breeding animals 2 husband or wife 3 friend; one's equal; fellow worker 4 officer of a merchant ship ranking below a captain vt,vi 1 join or pair 2 (of animals) unite in order to produce young

material n 1 stuff or substance of which anything is made 2 raw data; facts 3 cloth; fabric **materials** pl n elements or tools required to make or perform something ~adj 1 composed of matter; not spiritual; relating to physical well-being or wealth 2 essential; important **materialist** n person who values possessions and physical well-being more than ideas or spiritual beliefs **materialism** n **materialistic** adj **materialize** vi,vt appear or cause to appear out of nothing vi assume solid, material, or bodily form; become fact

maternal adj 1 relating to a mother or mothers; motherly 2 related through a mother **maternalistic** adj

maternity n state of being a mother adj relating to mothers or the period of their pregnancy

mathematics n science concerned with the logical study of space, numbers relationships, etc, using various forms of analysis and special symbols **mathematical** adj **mathematician** n

matinée n afternoon or first evening performance at a theatre, cinema, etc

matrimony n state of being married **matrimonial** adj

matrix n, pl **matrices** ('meitrisi:z) 1 mould for

casting or shaping objects **2** anything that encloses or gives form to something

matron n **1** married woman, esp one of at least middle age **2** woman in charge of nurses or domestic arrangements in a school, hospital, or other institution **matronly** adj of or like a matron; dignified

matt adj also **matte, mat** dull; without lustre; not shiny

matter n **1** stuff or substance of which the physical universe is composed **2** any physical or bodily substance **3** topic or issue; thing; concern **4** difficulty or trouble **5** content of a book, etc vi be of significance or importance

mattress n flat case filled with soft or firm supporting material, used as a bed or placed on a bed frame

mature adj **1** fully developed; ripe **2** complete in growth; grown-up **3** characteristic of an adult; mentally developed; sensible **4** perfected; complete vi,vt become or make mature **maturity** n

maudlin adj over-sentimental; tearfully drunk

maul vt treat roughly; attack savagely; injure badly

mausoleum n **1** stately building used as a tomb or housing tombs **2** large depressing building

mauve n,adj pale bluish purple

maxim n condensed general truth or principle of conduct

maximum adj greatest; highest n pl **maximums** or **maxima** (ˈmæksɪmə) greatest or highest amount, extent, degree etc **maximize** vt **1** increase to a maximum **2** make the most of

may v aux (pt might) **1** be able or permitted to **2** be likely or probable that **maybe** adv perhaps, possibly

May n fifth month of the year **May Day** n first day of May, celebrated with various festivities parades, etc **maypole** n decorated pole around which persons dance on May Day

mayonnaise n thick dressing for salads etc consisting usually of egg yolk oil and vinegar

mayor n official head of a town corporation **mayoress** f n

maze n **1** intricate network of interconnecting paths passages, etc **2** confused state

me pron form of I when used as the object

meadow n grassland, often used for grazing or growing hay

meagre adj lacking quality or quantity; insufficient; scanty; thin

meal[1] n **1** food, esp when eaten at regular times during the day **2** occasion or time of eating

meal[2] n coarsely ground grain, used esp as fodder

mean[1] vt,vi (meant) **1** signify; intend; intend to express; denote **2** be resolved to; be serious about

mean[2] adj **1** stingy; petty; not generous **2** low in quality, character, rank, or performance **3** not important; having little consequence **4** offensive, nasty **meanly** adv **meanness** n

mean[3] adj **1** halfway between two extremes, values, numbers, etc; intermediate **2** average n anything intermediate or between two extremes values, etc; average

meander (miˈændə) vi wander; move about aimlessly; follow a winding course n winding course of a river or stream

meaning n **1** significance; import **2** sense of a word, phrase, etc; definition **meaningful** adj **meaningless** adj

means pl n **1** method for achieving a purpose or function **2** financial or material resources **by all means** certainly; without fail or hesitation **by no means** most definitely not; on no account, not at all

meantime n intervening time adv also **meanwhile** during or in an intervening time; at the same time

measles n **1** infectious viral disease producing a red rash, common in childhood **2** German measles

measure n **1** size, quantity, extent etc of something determined by comparing it with a standard **2** unit of size quantity etc **3** criterion **4** vessel or instrument for determining size quantity etc **5** certain amount extent or degree **6** regular beat or movement in music poetry, etc, rhythm **for good measure** as something extra; as an addition **take measures** do things to achieve some goal or purpose ~vt determine the size or quantity of, judge, estimate vi have a specified measure **made to measure** (of clothes) fitted to the individual **measure up** live up to expectations; be adequate for **measurement** n

meat n **1** flesh of animals used as food often excepting fish and poultry **2** edible part of anything **3** main principle of something; essence

mechanical adj **1** relating to machinery **2** operated or produced by machines; automatic **3** not requiring thought; spontaneous **mechanic** n person skilled in repairing, building, or using machinery **mechanics 1** s n study of the action of forces on physical bodies and the motions they produce **2** pl n technical aspects or workings of something

mechanism n **1** machine or its structure or parts **2** means by which a machine works **3** way in which anything works or operates

mechanize vt **1** make mechanical **2** substitute mechanical power as a source of production or energy **3** operate by machines or machinery **mechanization** n

medal n flat piece of metal, usually round, with a design or inscription to commemorate an event or given as an award **medallion** n **1** large medal **2** circular decorative design or panel

meddle vi **1** also **meddle in** concern oneself with things that are not one's business **2** also **meddle with** interfere; tamper

media pl n newspapers, radio, and television; collective means of communication

medial adj also **median** relating to or situated in the middle **median** n middle point, part, value, etc ; dividing line or plane

mediate vt **1** settle; reconcile **2** serve as the medium for communicating, conveying, etc vt,vi intervene to bring about a reconciliation or compromise **mediation** n

medicine n **1** practice and profession of preserving or restoring health **2** drugs or other agents used to treat bodily diseases or disorders **medicinal** adj **medical** adj **1** relating to medicine **2** relating to treatment that does not require surgery n physical examination by a doctor **medication** n **1** use of medicine or medical agents **2** drug or other medical agent

medieval adj **1** relating to the Middle Ages **2** inf primitive; crude

mediocre adj between good and bad; of only average quality or excellence; ordinary **mediocrity** n

meditate vi engage in deep mental reflection; contemplate vt think about doing; plan **meditation** n **meditative** adj

medium n **1** means; agency **2** middle degree or

quality; mean **3** substance through or in which something is transmitted, conveyed, or effected **4** material used by an artist **5** environment **6** person claiming to be able to communicate with spirits **7** pl **media** means of mass communication, such as the press, radio, or television adj average; intermediate

meek adj humble; submissive; lacking in spirit; mild **meekly** adv

meet v (met) vt **1** encounter; come across **2** be present at the arrival point of **3** satisfy; handle; cope with vi come together; come into contact; join vt,vi **1** be introduced (to) **2** gather for a meeting, etc (with) **3** fight; confront n assembly of people and animals prior to a hunt **meeting** n **1** coming together; encounter **2** gathering; assembly of persons, esp for a common cause **3** joining of things

megaphone n instrument shaped like a funnel, used to amplify the voice or direct sound

melancholy n depression; sadness; tendency to be morose adj depressing; sad; gloomy **melancholic** adj

mellow adj **1** not harsh; rich and full **2** genial; warm **3** rendered receptive and friendly, as through advancing years, alcoholic drink, etc vt,vi make or become mellow

melodrama n **1** play or drama displaying violent or exaggerated emotions **2** over-emotional language or behaviour **melodramatic** adj

melody n **1** agreeable or pleasing music or tune **2** recognizable sequence of musical notes **melodic** adj relating to melody **melodious** adj pleasing to listen to; tuneful

melon n plant of the gourd family, the edible fruit of which has a hard rind and juicy flesh

melt vi,vt **1** liquefy by heat; thaw; pass or convert from solid to liquid **2** soften; dissolve **3** disappear; disperse **4** blend; merge n act of melting or state of being melted **melting point** n temperature at which a solid becomes liquefied

member n **1** person who belongs to a group, society, or organization **2** distinct part of a whole **3** limb or other bodily organ **membership** n **1** state of being part of a group or society **2** total number of persons who are part of a group, etc

membrane n thin pliable sheet of tissue that lines, connects, or covers an organ or part

memento n, pl **mementoes** or **mementos** reminder; souvenir; keepsake

memoir n record of facts or events written from experience or gathered through research **memoirs** pl n biography or autobiography; published reminiscences

memorable adj easily or worthy to be remembered

memorandum n, pl **memorandums** or **memoranda** (memə'rændə); also **memo 1** note to aid the memory **2** short informal communication to colleagues, business firms, clients, etc

memorial n object or custom in memory of a person, event, etc; monument adj preserving the memory of a person or event; commemorative

memory n **1** faculty of recalling to mind or recollecting **2** something remembered **3** capacity to remember **4** commemoration **5** part of a computer where information is stored **memorize** vt commit to memory

men n pl of **man.**

menace n something that threatens or constitutes a threat vt threaten; intimidate

menagerie n exhibition of caged animals

mend vt **1** repair; make whole; put right **2** make better; improve; correct vi improve in health n improvement; repair **on the mend** recovering; improving in health

menial adj lowly; servile n servile person; domestic servant

menopause n time of life during which women cease to menstruate, usually between the ages of 45 and 50

menstrual adj relating to the monthly discharge from the womb of blood and cellular material in women **menstruate** vi produce menstrual discharge **menstruation** n

mental adj **1** relating to the mind or intellect; done or existing in the mind **2** sl insane; mad; crazy **mental hospital** n institution for treating persons with disorders of the mind **mentality** n mental or intellectual capacity; mind

menthol n substance obtained from peppermint oil, used esp as a flavouring

mention vt speak of; refer to n remark about or reference to a person or thing

menu n **1** list of dishes available to be served, with their prices **2** dishes served

mercantile adj **1** relating to merchants or commerce; commercial **2** engaged in commerce or trade

mercenary adj working simply for reward or gain n professional soldier serving a foreign country

merchandise n **1** goods or commodities bought and sold in commerce or trade **2** stock of a store vt, vi buy and sell; promote the sale (of)

merchant n wholesale trader, esp with foreign countries **merchant bank** n bank chiefly involved in foreign commerce **merchant navy** n **1** ships of a nation engaged in commerce **2** officers and crews of merchant ships

mercury n heavy silvery toxic metallic element, normally liquid, used in thermometers, barometers, etc **Mercury** nearest planet to the sun **mercurial** adj lively; changeable

mercy n **1** compassion; kindness; pity **2** forgiveness of an injustice, transgression, or injury by someone with the power to inflict punishment **3** act of compassion, kindness, etc **at the mercy of** completely in the power of; defenceless **merciful** adj compassionate **mercifully** adv **merciless** without mercy; cruel **mercilessly** adv

mere adj nothing more than; only **merely** adv

merge vt, vi **1** blend; mingle **2** combine; unite **merger** n commercial combination of two or more companies

meridian n **1** position of the sun at noon **2** highest point or period of development of something **3** imaginary circle encompassing the earth and passing through both poles adj **1** relating to a meridian **2** relating to or at noon

meringue (mə'ræŋ) n **1** mixture of sugar and beaten egg whites, slightly browned, used as an icing, etc **2** small cream-filled cake of meringue

merit n **1** worth; excellence **2** commendable quality vt be worthy of **meritorious** adj

mermaid n mythical sea creature with the head arms, and torso of a woman and the tail of a fish

merry adj **1** joyous; cheerful; festive; happy; gay **2** slightly drunk **merry-go-round** n fairground amusement consisting of a rotating platform fitted with models of animals, cars, etc, on which one may ride; roundabout **merrily** adv **merriment** or **merriness** n

mesh n net; network vt catch in a mesh vi **1**

(of gearwheels) engage **2** merge; blend; harmonize

mesmerize vt **1** hypnotize **2** fascinate greatly

mess n **1** untidy state or condition **2** state of confusion or disorder **3** difficult or embarrassing situation **4** place where military personnel, etc , take their meals **5** meals taken by military personnel, etc **6** inf person who is untidy sloppy, or dirty vt also **mess up** make dirty or untidy **mess around** or **about** busy oneself in an ineffective or aimless manner

message n **1** spoken or written communication **2** moral conveyed in a literary or artistic work **messenger** n person who conveys a message, does errands, etc

metabolism n sum of the chemical changes in an animal or plant that result in growth, production and use of energy, etc **metabolic** adj

metal n **1** chemical element, such as iron, tin, or silver, that is usually lustrous, easily worked, and often a good conductor of heat and electricity **2** alloy **metallic** adj **metallurgy** n study and technology of metals **metallurgical** adj **metallurgist** n

metamorphosis n **1** complete change in form **2** marked change in character, etc **3** relatively rapid transformation of certain larvae into adult form, as tadpole to frog **metamorphic** adj

metaphor n figure of speech in which a word is applied to something for which it does not literally stand **metaphorical** adj

meteor n small body from space that burns up in the earth s atmosphere producing a bright streak **meteoric** adj **1** relating to meteors **2** rapid; transient **meteorite** n larger body able to reach earth

meteorology n study of the earth s atmosphere, climate, and weather **meteorological** adj **meteorologist** n

meter n measuring or recording instrument or device vt measure with a meter

methane n inflammable gas occurring in natural gas and used as a fuel and in chemical manufacture

method n **1** way of doing something **2** systematic or orderly procedure **methodical** adj systematic; orderly

Methodist n adherent of the Christian beliefs and tenets (Methodism) of a Protestant nonconformist denomination founded by John Wesley adj relating to Methodists or Methodism

meticulous adj extremely careful about small details

metre n **1** unit of length equal to 1 09 yards **2** rhythmic arrangement of syllables in verse **metric** adj **metric system** n system of scientific units based on the metre, the kilogram or gram and the second **metrication** n conversion to the metric system

metropolitan adj **1** relating to or characteristic of the capital or any large city **2** relating to the characteristics or attitudes of a city dweller; sophisticated **metropolis** n chief or major city; capital

miaow n sound a cat makes vi make such a sound

mice n pl of **mouse.**

microbe n microorganism esp one causing disease; germ

microorganism n microscopic animal or plant, such as a bacterium or virus

microphone n instrument for converting sound waves into electrical currents or voltages that can then be amplified

microscope n instrument for magnifying very small objects, usually consisting of at least two lenses mounted in a tube **microscopic** adj visible only under a microscope; tiny

midday n noon

middle adj **1** equidistant from two extremes; intermediate; mean **2** central n **1** something intermediate or equidistant from two extremes **2** central area of the body; waist **middle-aged** adj relating to the age between youth and old age; aged about 40 to 65 **Middle Ages** n historical period now usually regarded as being from about the fifth to the late fifteenth century **middle class** n generally well-educated class of people in commerce the professions, etc , who often hold conformist views **middle-class** adj relating to the middle class

midget n **1** very small person **2** anything unusually small of its kind

midnight n middle of the night; 12 o clock at night

midst n middle; central part, stage, or point **in the midst of** surrounded by; among

midwife n, pl **-wives** woman who assists others in childbirth **midwifery** n

might[1] v pt of **may**. v aux used to express likelihood or possibility

might[2] n strength; power **mighty** adj

migraine n severe headache

migrate vi 1 leave one country, region, etc., to settle or work in another 2 (of certain birds, animals, etc.) move seasonally from one region to another **migrant** n **migration** n **migratory** adj

mike n sl microphone

mild adj 1 moderate; gentle; not harsh or drastic 2 not having a sharp taste **mildly** adv

mildew n destructive fungus or fungal disease that attacks plants or objects exposed to damp

mile n 1 unit of length equal to 1760 yards or 1 61 kilometres 2 also **miles** great distance **mileage** n 1 total number of miles travelled 2 distance in miles between two points 3 travel expenses based on a given sum per mile **mileometer** n device for measuring and recording the number of miles travelled **milestone** n 1 roadside stone showing number of miles to the next large city or town 2 important event or turning point in history, a person's life, etc

militant adj 1 aggressive; forceful 2 engaged in warfare n aggressive person **militancy** n

military adj relating to the armed forces, soldiers, or warfare n soldiers collectively; armed forces

milk n 1 whitish liquid produced in the mammary glands of female mammals, used to feed their young 2 cow's or goat's milk, used as food 3 whitish juice of various plants or fruits **cry over spilt milk** regret or complain about something that cannot be undone or remedied ~vt 1 extract milk from the udder of 2 draw off from **milkman** n, pl -**men** person who sells or delivers milk **Milky Way** n faint band of light in the night sky that consists of millions of stars and is part of our galaxy

mill n 1 machinery for grinding grain into flour 2 machinery for manufacturing paper, textiles, steel, etc 3 building containing such machinery 4 small machine for grinding pepper corns, coffee beans, etc vt grind, work, or shape in or as if in a mill **millstone** n 1 either of two large round slabs of stone

between which grain, etc., is ground 2 heavy emotional burden

millennium n, pl **millenniums** or **millennia** (mi'lenia) thousand years

millet n cereal grass cultivated for its small seeds or grain

milligram n one thousandth of a gram

millimetre n one thousandth of a metre

million n 1 number or numeral, 1 000 000, equal to 1000 multiplied by 1000 2 also **millions** extremely large number or amount 3 million units of money, etc adj amounting to a million **millionth** adj,n **millionaire** n 1 person worth a million pounds, dollars, etc 2 very rich person

mime n 1 art or practice of wordless acting 2 person who performs wordless acting vt,vi act or express in mime

mimic n person or animal that imitates or copies others vt (-ck-) imitate in action, speech, etc; copy; caricature **mimicry** n

minaret n slender tower of a mosque, from which the faithful are called to prayer

mince vt 1 cut or chop into small pieces 2 utter with affected carefulness vi speak or act in an affected way n minced meat

mind n 1 thinking faculties or consciousness 2 intellect 3 memory 4 person of great intelligence 5 sanity; reason 6 way of thinking; opinion; temper 7 attention **bear in mind** continue to remember **be of one mind** be in total agreement with **be of two minds** be undecided **make up one's mind** decide **out of one's mind** mad; highly agitated; confused **take (someone's) mind off** help (someone) stop worrying about something distract ~vt,vi 1 object (to); be upset or concerned (about) 2 pay attention (to) 3 be careful (about) vt attend to; look after **mind out** be careful; watch

mine[1] pron that belonging to me

mine[2] n 1 deep hole or shaft in the ground for extracting coal, metals, etc 2 associated buildings, etc 3 underground or surface deposit of minerals 4 rich source of something 5 explosive device, detonated on impact vt,vi 1 dig or extract (minerals) from a mine 2 make a mine in or under

mineral n 1 inorganic substance that occurs in the earth and has a definite chemical composition 2 nonliving matter **mineralogy** n study of minerals **mineral water** n 1 water containing dissolved minerals or gases **2** fizzy nonalcoholic drink

minestrone (mini'strouni) n Italian soup containing vegetables, etc

mingle vt,vi **1** blend; mix; combine **2** mix in company

miniature n **1** very small painting, esp a portrait **2** model, copy, etc, greatly reduced in size adj small-scale; reduced; tiny

minim n musical note half the length of a semibreve

minimum n least possible or lowest quantity, number, degree, etc **minimal** adj **minimize** vt **1** reduce to or estimate at a minimum **2** belittle; underestimate

mining n act, process, or industry of extracting minerals, coal, etc, from mines

minister n **1** person authorized to conduct religious services; clergyman **2** person in charge of a government department **3** diplomatic representative vi give aid or service (to) **ministerial** adj

ministry n **1** functions or profession of a clergyman or clergymen **2** profession or department of a government minister **3** building in which government offices are located **4** act of giving service

mink n **1** animal of the weasel family with highly valued brownish fur **2** garment made of mink fur

minor adj **1** lesser in size, extent, significance, etc **2** of or relating to a musical scale in which the second and third and the fifth and sixth notes are a semitone apart n **1** person under full legal age **2** person or thing of inferior importance, rank, etc **minority** n **1** smaller number, part, etc; less than half **2** group whose race, religion, etc, is different from most others in the same country or community **3** state or period of being under full legal age

minstrel n medieval musician or singer

mint[1] n **1** aromatic herb **2** sweet with a peppermint or similar flavouring

mint[2] n **1** place where money is officially minted **2** large amount, esp of money vt,vi make (coins and paper money) under government authority **mint condition** perfect condition

minuet n **1** slow stately dance in triple time **2** music in the rhythm of this dance

minus prep **1** less by the deduction of;

decreased by **2** without; lacking adj **1** indicating deduction or subtraction **2** negative **3** lacking n also **minus sign** symbol denoting subtraction

minute[1] ('minit) n **1** one sixtieth of an hour; 60 seconds **2** short time **3** one sixtieth of a degree of angular measure **4** memorandum **up to the minute** current; very latest; modern **minutes** pl n summary of a meeting

minute[2] (mai'nju:t) adj **1** very small **2** insignificant; trivial **3** precise; detailed **minutely** adv

miracle n **1** supernatural event **2** something wonderful; marvel **miraculous** adj

mirage n **1** optical illusion caused by intense heat, etc **2** something unreal or illusory

mirror n **1** polished surface that reflects images of objects, esp glass backed with metal **2** any reflecting surface, as of water **3** something that gives a true representation or portrayal vt reflect or represent faithfully

mirth n merriment; festive or joyous gaiety

misbehave vi behave badly **misbehaviour** n

miscarriage n **1** expulsion of a foetus from the womb before it is capable of living independently **2** failure to carry out or attain a desired result **miscarry** vi **1** undergo a miscarriage **2** fail; go wrong

miscellaneous adj **1** varied; mixed; assorted **2** having various qualities or aspects; many-sided **miscellany** n miscellaneous collection

mischance n bad luck; misfortune; unlucky accident

mischief n **1** teasing or annoying conduct **2** source of annoyance or harm **mischievous** adj **mischievously** adv

misconceive vt,vi misunderstand; interpret incorrectly **misconception** n

misconduct n improper conduct

misdeed n evil or criminal deed

miser n person who hoards money **miserly** adj

miserable adj **1** extremely unhappy or uncomfortable **2** causing misery **3** characterized by wretched poverty and neglect **4** pitiable **miserably** adv **misery** n condition or cause of great suffering or distress

misfire vi **1** fail to fire correctly or on time **2** fail to be successful or have a desired effect n failure to fire

misfit n **1** person who does not fit in socially

with others **2** something that does not fit properly

misfortune n bad luck; calamity

misgiving n feeling of fear, doubt or mistrust

misguided adj mistaken; misled

mishap n unlucky or unfortunate accident

mislay vt (-laid) put something in a place later forgotten

mislead vt (-led) lead astray; deceive, esp by giving incorrect or inadequate information or advice

misplace vt **1** lose; put in the wrong place **2** place or bestow unwisely or improperly

misprint n mistake in printing

miss[1] vt **1** fail to hit, find, reach, notice, catch, etc **2** also **miss out** omit; pass over **3** notice or regret the absence of **4** fail **5** escape; avoid vi **1** (of an engine) fail to fire **2** fail to hit or attain something **miss the boat** fail to take advantage of an opportunity ~n failure

miss[2] n girl; young woman **Miss** form of address for an unmarried young woman or girl

missile n object or weapon that can be thrown or fired, esp a rocket-propelled weapon

mission n **1** group of persons sent to a foreign country as envoys or missionaries **2** official business or task of an envoy or missionary **3** aim or calling in life **4** military operation against an enemy **5** any duty esp one that has been assigned **missionary** n person sent to convert natives or primitive peoples to his religion, educate them, etc

mist n **1** water vapour in fine drops; thin fog **2** something that blurs or dims vt, vi be, become, or make dim or blurred **misty** adj

mistake n error in thought or action vt (-took, -taken) **1** form a wrong opinion about; misunderstand **2** take (a person or thing) for another; confuse

Mister n form of address for an adult male; normally written Mr

mistletoe n evergreen plant with white berries that grows as a partial parasite on other trees

mistress n **1** woman teacher **2** woman who employs others **3** woman with whom a man has a continuing sexual relationship outside marriage

mistrust n lack of trust vt regard with lack of trust; distrust

misunderstand vt vi (misunderstood) fail to understand correctly or properly **misunder-**

standing n **1** failure to understand **2** slight quarrel

misuse n (mis'ju:s) wrong or improper use vt (mis'ju:z) **1** use wrongly **2** treat badly

mitre n **1** bishop's tall pointed hat **2** corner joint formed by two pieces of wood, etc , that meet at equal angles vt join so as to make a mitre joint

mitten n glove with one compartment for the four fingers and a separate one for the thumb

mix vt, vi combine; blend vi associate with others freely or easily vt form by blending **mix up 1** confuse **2** blend **mixture** n **1** product of mixing **2** combination of two or more ingredients, elements, types, qualities, etc **mix-up** n confusion; muddle

moan n low sound, usually indicating pain or suffering vi, vt **1** utter or say with a moan **2** grumble; complain

moat n deep wide ditch, originally filled with water, round a castle or town

mob n disorderly crowd of people vt (-bb-) crowd round; attack in a crowd

mobile adj **1** capable of movement **2** easily moved **3** expressive n ornament consisting of a delicate hanging construction of balanced parts, which move with the air current **mobility** n **mobilize** vt **1** prepare (armed forces) for active service **2** organize for a task **3** put into motion or use vi be ready or assembled for battle

mock vt, vi make fun of by imitating; scoff or jeer (at) **mockery** n **1** ridicule **2** derisive action or imitation

mode n manner; style; method; fashion

model n **1** representation of an object made to scale **2** pattern to be followed; design; style **3** person or object worthy of imitation **4** person who poses for an artist, etc **5** person who wears and displays clothing for potential customers v (-ll-) vt, vi **1** make a model (of) **2** form or work (clay, etc) **3** wear and display (clothing) for potential customers vi pose for an artist, etc

moderate adj ('mɒdərit) **1** not going to extremes **2** of medium quantity, quality, or extent; not excessive n ('mɒdərit) person of moderate views vt, vi ('mɒdəreit) make or become less violent or excessive **moderately** adv

modern adj relating to or characteristic of

present and recent time **modernize** vt make modern; bring up to date **modernization** n

modest adj 1 unassuming; shy; not vain. 2 free from pretension; not showy 3 moderate **modestly** adv **modesty** n

modify vt 1 make small changes in 2 tone down 3 qualify 4 make less severe **modification** n

modulate vt 1 vary the tone, pitch, or volume of 2 regulate; adjust; soften vi change from one musical key to another **modulation** n

module n 1 separable compartment of a space vehicle 2 standard or unit of measurement 3 removable framework or assembly

mohair n yarn or fabric made from the soft silky hair of the Angora goat or made to resemble it

moist adj damp; slightly wet **moistly** adv **moisten** vt, vi make or become moist **moisture** n 1 water or other liquid diffused as a vapour or condensed on a surface 2 dampness **moisturize** vt give or restore moisture to

mole[1] n small dark birthmark on the skin

mole[2] n small nocturnal burrowing animal with a smooth silky pelt

molecule n simplest unit of a chemical compound, consisting of two or more atoms **molecular** adj

molest vt 1 disturb or annoy by interfering with 2 interfere with improperly, esp sexually

mollusc n soft-bodied invertebrate, such as the snail, oyster, or octopus, usually with a hard shell

molten adj liquefied by intense heat

moment n 1 very short space of time 2 appropriate time **at the moment** now **in a moment** 1 soon; shortly 2 quickly; instantly **momentary** adj lasting a moment **momentarily** adv **momentous** adj important

momentum n 1 mass multiplied by velocity of a moving body 2 impetus; driving strength

monarch n sovereign head of a country; king or queen **monarchic** or **monarchical** adj **monarchy** n 1 form of government in which authority is vested, constitutionally or traditionally, in the monarch 2 country of a monarch

monastery n house occupied by a community of monks **monastic** adj relating to monks or their way of life

Monday n second day of the week

money n 1 official medium of exchange of a country, consisting of coins and paper currency of various denominations 2 amount or sum of money; income 3 funds; assets **monetary** adj relating to money

mongrel n dog of mixed breeds

monitor n 1 pupil appointed to special duties in a school 2 person who warns or advises 3 control or checking device on a machine or system 4 person who officially listens to and records foreign broadcasts vt listen to in order to record or check

monk n member of a male community, having taken final religious vows

monkey n 1 long-tailed primate usually living in forests 2 mischievous child vi also **monkey around** or **about** play or fool (with)

monochrome n something of one colour or in black and white

monogamy n custom or state of being married to only one person at a time **monogamous** adj

monologue n 1 prolonged talk by a single speaker 2 dramatic work or part to be performed by one speaker

monopoly n exclusive control or possession of a trade, privilege, etc **monopolize** vt obtain or exercise sole control or possession of

monosyllable n word of one syllable **monosyllabic** adj

monotone n sound, note, or voice of an unvaried pitch **monotonous** adj lacking variation; dull; tedious **monotonously** adv **monotony** n

monsoon n 1 seasonal wind of S Asia and the Indian Ocean, blowing from the southwest in summer 2 rainy season that accompanies the wind from this direction

monster n 1 legendary animal of a combination of forms 2 grossly deformed animal or plant 3 evil person 4 something huge **monstrous** adj 1 very great; huge 2 ugly; hideous 3 outrageous; revolting

month n any of the 12 periods into which a year is divided **monthly** adj 1 occurring, done, etc, once a month 2 lasting a month adv once a month

monument n 1 something, esp a statue, that commemorates 2 statue, structure, etc, of historical importance 3 written record **monumental** adj 1 colossal; massive; stupendous 2 relating to or serving as a monument

moo n sound a cow makes vi make a sound like a cow

mood[1] n 1 state of mind and feelings 2 depressed or sulky state of mind **moody** adj changeable in mood

mood[2] n form of a verb that indicates a particular function, such as the imperative, subjunctive, conditional, etc

moon n 1 cratered and mountainous body that revolves around the earth in about 27 3 days, changing in apparent shape 2 apparent shape of the moon; phase vi also **moon around** or **about** go about idly, dreamily, listlessly, etc **moonlight** n light from the sun reflected from the moon to the earth

moor[1] n also **moorland** tract of open waste land, often hilly and covered with heather **moorhen** n black red-billed water bird living on river etc

moor[2] vt,vi secure or fasten (a ship, etc) with cables or ropes or be secured so **mooring** n place for securing a vessel **moorings** pl n ropes, etc , used in securing a vessel

mop n sponge or bundle of yarn, cloth, etc , fastened to the end of a handle for cleaning floors, etc vt (-pp-) also **mop up** clean or wipe with a mop

mope vi be depressed **mope about** or **around** act aimlessly **mopes** pl n dejected state

moped n motorized bicycle

moral adj 1 relating to or concerned with right and wrong conduct; ethical 2 of good conduct; virtuous; honest n practical lesson, esp one taught by a fable or other story **morally** adv **morale** (ma'ra:l) n discipline and spirit of a group of persons **morality** n 1 virtuous conduct 2 moral principles **moralize** vi interpret or explain in a moral sense; derive a moral from vi make moral reflections; talk about morality **morals** pl n personal conduct, or principles

morbid adj 1 gloomy; unpleasant 2 unhealthy **morbidly** adv

more adj 1 greater in quantity, number, or degree 2 additional; extra n additional quantity, number, or degree adv to a greater extent; in addition **more or less** approximately, roughly **moreover** adv besides; further

morgue n room or building where dead bodies are taken to await identification before burial

morning n early part of the day, usually up to noon or lunchtime

moron n 1 mentally deficient person 2 foolish person **moronic** adj

morose adj sullen; gloomy; unsociable

morphine n drug to relieve severe pain

Morse Code n signalling system in which numbers and letters are represented by combinations of dots and dashes

mortal adj subject to or causing death n human being **mortality** n 1 condition of being subject to death 2 large loss of life 3 frequency of death; death rate

mortar n 1 mixture of lime, sand, and water for holding bricks and stones together 2 vessel in which substances are pounded or ground 3 short cannon for throwing shells at high angles vt fix or plaster with mortar

mortgage n conveyance of property pledged as security for a debt until the loan is repaid vt pledge (property) by mortgage

mortify vt 1 humiliate 2 subdue by self-denial **mortification** n

mortuary n place where dead bodies are temporarily kept before burial

mosaic n picture or pattern made of small pieces of coloured stone, glass, etc

Moslem n, adj Muslim

mosque n Muslim place of worship

mosquito n, pl **mosquitoes** or **mosquitos** blood-sucking insect that can transmit a disease such as malaria

moss n small plant that grows in dense clumps on moist surfaces **mossy** adj

most adj greatest in size, number, or degree; nearly all n greatest amount or degree **at (the) most** not over; at maximum **make the most of** use to the greatest advantage ~adv in the greatest degree **mostly** adv mainly; almost entirely; usually

motel n roadside hotel, often consisting of private cabins with parking space in front

moth n usually nocturnal insect similar to the butterfly **motheaten** adj decrepit; damaged; filled with holes

mother n 1 female parent 2 head of a religious community of women vt care for or protect as a mother **motherhood** n state or qualities of being a mother **mother-in-law** n, pl **mothers-in-law** mother of one's husband or wife **mother superior** n head of a religious community of women

motion n 1 movement 2 manner or power of movement 3 formal proposal at a meeting **in motion** in operation, functioning ~*vi* make a gesture, as with the hand *vt* direct or guide by a gesture **motionless** *adj* not moving; still

motive n 1 reason; cause; intention; incentive 2 chief idea in a work of art *adj* causing motion or action **motivate** *vt* provide with a motive **motivation** n

motor n 1 engine 2 machine that transforms electrical into mechanical energy to produce motion *vi* travel by car **motorboat** boat powered by a motor **motor car** n car **motorcycle** n also **motorbike** two-wheeled road vehicle, heavier and more powerful than a moped **motorist** n person who drives a (motor) car **motorway** n main road with separate carriageways of several lanes and limited access

motto n, pl **mottoes** or **mottos** 1 saying adopted as a rule of conduct 2 short phrase or sentence inscribed on a coat of arms, etc

mould[1] n 1 hollow form or container in which molten metal, plastic, etc , is cast or shaped 2 anything cast or shaped in a mould 3 character; type *vt* form; shape; model

mould[2] n fungal growth caused by dampness, mildew **mouldy** *adj*

moult *vi,vt* shed (feathers, skin, fur, etc) n act or process of moulting

mound n 1 pile, as of earth or stones; heap 2 small hill *vt* form into a mound

mount[1] *vt,vi* 1 go up; ascend; climb 2 get up on (a horse, platform, etc) *vt* 1 set at a height or elevation 2 provide with or place on a horse 3 fix in a setting, backing, or support *vi* rise; increase n 1 act of . mounting 2 something mounted 3 setting, backing, or support on which something is mounted

mount[2] n mountain, hill

mountain n 1 natural and usually very high and steep elevation of the earth s surface 2 large pile or heap **mountainous** *adj* **mountaineer** n person who climbs mountains *vi* climb mountains

mourn *vi* feel sorrow *vt* grieve for

mouse n, pl **mice** small long-tailed rodent **mousy** *adj* 1 like or suggestive of a mouse 2 (of hair) fair but not blond(e)

mousse n dish made with whipped cream, beaten eggs, etc

moustache n hair growing on the upper lip

mouth n (mauθ) 1 cavity between the lips and the throat, containing the teeth, tongue, etc , in which food is chewed and speech sounds are formed 2 opening into anything hollow 3 entrance to something 4 part of a river where its waters empty into a sea, lake, etc *v* (mauð) *vt* form (words) with the lips without speaking *vi* declaim **mouthpiece** n 1 end of something intended to be put between or near the lips 2 person who speaks for others **mouth-watering** *adj* appetizing

move *vt,vi* 1 change the place or position (of) 2 stir *vt* 1 propose 2 affect with emotion *vi* 1 change one's place of residence 2 make progress; advance n act of moving; movement **get a move on** *inf* hurry up **movable** *adj* capable of being moved; not fixed **movement** n 1 process or act of moving 2 moving parts of a mechanism, as of a watch 3 main division of a musical work, esp of a symphony 4 group engaged in or activities directed towards some goal or end 5 trend

mow *vt,vi* (mowed; mown or mowed) cut or cut down (grass, grain, etc) **mower** n

Mr abbreviation for **Mister.**

Mrs abbreviation for **mistress**; used as a form of address for a married woman

much *adj* in great quantity or degree n 1 large amount 2 notable or important matter or thing *adv* in or to a great degree **as much** exactly that **make much of** 1 make sense of 2 give importance to **not much of** not really **not think much of** have a poo opinion of

muck n 1 manure 2 filth; dirt *vt* make dirty **muck about** *sl* mess or fool about **muck in** *sl* join in to achieve something **muck out** *sl* clean out; remove muck from **muck up** *sl* ruin, spoil **mucky** *adj*

mud n wet soft earth **mudguard** n guard over a wheel to protect against mud **mudslinging** n reckless accusations or abuse **muddy** *adj* 1 covered with or abounding in mud 2 mudlike in colour or texture 3 vague; obscure; not clear *vt,vi* make or become muddy

muddle *vt* 1 confuse; bewilder 2 mismanage; mix up in a confused way **muddle through** succeed in spite of inadequate planning, etc ~*n* muddled state or condition; mess

muffle *vt* 1 wrap or cover up with something

warm 2 wrap up to deaden sound 3 deaden (sound) 4 conceal *n* something that muffles

mug *n* 1 large drinking cup with a handle 2 *sl* face or mouth 3 fool; gullible person *vt,vi* (-gg-) *sl* attack and rob **mug up** obtain (information) or study during a short intensive period **mugger** *n sl* person who assaults and robs someone

mulberry *n* tree that bears dark red edible berries

mule[1] *n* sterile offspring of a mare and a donkey **mulish** *adj* stubborn

mule[2] *n* slipper with an exposed heel

multiple *adj* have many parts, elements, etc *n* quantity that contains another quantity an exact number of times

multiply *vt,vi* 1 find the mathematical product of two or more numbers or quantities 2 increase or cause to increase in number or amount **multiplication** *n*

multitude *n* 1 great number of persons; crowd; throng 2 the common people

mum *n inf* mother

mumble *vt,vi* speak or utter indistinctly *n* indistinct talk or sound

mummy[1] *n* dead body preserved by embalming or other techniques **mummify** *vt* preserve as a mummy

mummy[2] *n inf* mother

mumps *n* contagious viral disease, esp of children, marked by a swelling of the glands in the neck

munch *vt,vi* chew vigorously and often noisily

mundane *adj* ordinary; everyday; common

municipal *adj* relating to the local government of a city or town **municipality** *n* city or town with local self-government

mural *n* painting executed on a wall

murder *n* 1 unlawful and deliberate killing of a human being 2 *inf* difficult or unpleasant task *vt* 1 kill 2 *inf* ruin; destroy *vi* commit murder **murderer** *n* **murderess** *f n*

murmur *n* 1 low and continuous sound 2 grumble; complaint *vt* utter in a low voice *vi* 1 make a murmur 2 complain

muscle *n* 1 specialized body tissue that produces movement by contracting 2 strength; brawn **muscular** *adj*

muse *vi* ponder, meditate; be lost in thought

museum *n* building housing objects or illustrations of art, science, history, etc , for observation and study

mushroom *n* fungus esp an edible variety, having a cap on the end of a stem *vi* 1 increase, grow, or expand rapidly 2 gather mushrooms

music *n* 1 organization of vocal or instrumental sounds into a pleasing or stirring rhythm or harmony 2 sequence of pleasing sounds 3 art of producing music 4 record of notes for reproducing music **musical** *adj* 1 relating to music 2 liking or skilled in music *n* light stage or film entertainment with songs and dancing **musician** *n* composer or performer of music

Muslim *n also* **Moslem** adherent of Islam *adj also* **Moslem** relating to the religion or culture of Islam

muslin *n* fine cotton fabric

mussel *n* mollusc with a dark elongated hinged shell

must *v aux* be obliged to; be certain to; be resolved to *n* something imperative

mustard *n* strong-flavoured yellowish or brownish paste or powder prepared from the seeds of the mustard plant, used as a condiment and seasoning

mute *adj* 1 silent; soundless 2 dumb; not capable of speech *n* person unable to speak *vt* deaden the sound of; soften

mutilate *vt* injure, disfigure or make imperfect as by damaging parts, removing a limb, etc **mutilation** *n*

mutiny *n* revolt or rebellion against authority, esp by soldiers or sailors *vi* engage in mutiny **mutinous** *adj*

mutter *vt,vi* utter indistinctly or in a low tone; mumble *n* muttered sound; complaint

mutton *n* flesh of mature sheep, used as food

mutual *adj* done, felt, possessed, etc by each of two with respect to the other; common to both or all **mutually** *adv*

muzzle *n* 1 open end of the barrel of a firearm 2 projecting nose and mouth of an animal 3 device placed over the mouth of an animal to prevent it from biting *vt* 1 put a muzzle on 2 prevent from speaking

my *pron* belonging to or associated with me **myself** *pron* reflexive or emphatic form of **me** or **I**.

myrrh (mɔ:) *n* aromatic gum exuded from certain shrubs, used as perfume, incense, etc

mystery *n* secret, puzzling, or obscure thing **mysterious** *adj* **mysteriously** *adv*

mystic n person who claims spiritual knowledge or insight, as by following mysticism **mystical** adj also **mystic** 1 of hidden, spiritual, or occult nature or significance 2 mysterious 3 relating to mysticism **mysticism** n belief in direct communion with God and awareness of divine truth by means of contemplation and love alone

mystify vt 1 bewilder; confuse; perplex 2 make obscure or mysterious **mystification** n`

mystique n atmosphere of mystery associated with or investing certain activities, doctrines, arts, etc

myth n 1 ancient story or legend, usually with supernatural characters or events 2 imaginary or fictitious event, person, or thing **mythical** adj **mythology** n 1 collection of myths 2 study of myths **mythological** adj

N

nag vt,vi (-gg-) annoy, pester, or be troubled with constant complaints, reminders, worries, or pain

nail n 1 narrow flat-headed piece of metal hammered in as a means of joining or for use as a peg 2 hard horny covering on the tip of a finger or toe **as hard as nails** cold; ruthless; tough **hit the nail on the head** describe exactly; pinpoint (a problem, situation, etc) ~vt 1 join or fasten with a nail 2 inf get hold of (a person); catch **nail down** make (a person) declare his aims or opinions **nailfile** n small metal file for shaping fingernails

naive adj 1 unsophisticated; ingenuous 2 credulous; gullible **naively** adv **naiveté** or **naivety** n

naked adj without clothes or protection; bare **nakedly** adv **nakedness** n

name n 1 word or words by which a person or thing is known or identified 2 reputation 3 inf celebrity vt 1 give a name to; identify 2 declare (a price, terms, etc) **namely** adv that is to say **namesake** n person or thing having the same name as another

nanny n 1 woman employed to look after children, esp in a private household 2 inf grandmother

nap[1] n short period of sleep esp during the day vi (-pp-) sleep for a short period

nap[2] n surface fibres on cloth

napalm n jellied mixture of petrol and acids used in bombs, etc

nape n back of the neck

napkin n square of cloth or paper used for protecting clothes and wiping the mouth and fingers during meals

nappy n square of cloth or disposable pad worn by a baby to absorb excreta

narcissus n, pl **narcissi** (nɑːˈsisai) bulb producing yellow or white flowers

narcotic n addictive drug, such as morphine, that induces sleep and dulls the senses adj inducing sleep or insensibility

narrate vt relate or tell (a story) **narration** n **narrator** n **narrative** n story; account adj consisting of or relating to a narrative

narrow adj 1 measuring little across 2 strict; accurate 3 bigoted; not liberal 4 limited; restricted vt,vi make or become narrow or narrower **narrowly** adv **narrowness** n **narrow-minded** adj having rigid and narrow views

nasal adj 1 relating to the nose 2 (of sounds) formed by breathing through the nose

nasturtium n garden plant having orange, yellow, or red flowers and roundish leaves

nasty adj 1 unpleasant 2 spiteful 3 offensive; disgusting **nastily** adv **nastiness** n

nation n 1 country; land 2 large group of people having a common cultural background, history, and language **nationwide** adj,adv throughout the country

national adj 1 relating to a country as a whole 2 typical of a particular country 3 controlled by the government **nationally** adv **national anthem** n country's official song **national insurance** n state scheme to provide financial aid during unemployment, sickness, widowhood, etc **national service** n compulsory military training **nationalism** n patriotism; belief in national unity **nationalist** n,adj **nationality** n citizenship of a particular country **nationalize** vt transfer (an industry or property) to public ownership and control **nationalization** n

native adj 1 relating to the place of birth or origin 2 innate 3 indigenous 4 relating to the indigenous population n 1 person born or living in or animal found in a certain country or area 2 person belonging to a race of original inhabitants of a country **nativity** n 1

177

birth 2 *also* **nativity play** play or artistic representation of the birth of Christ

natural *adj* 1 produced by, present in, or relating to the physical world; not artificial 2 innate 3 normal, to be expected; automatic 4 unaffected 5 not domesticated or civilized *n* 1 *inf* person naturally equipped for a particular skill or job 2 musical note or key that is neither sharp nor flat **naturally** *adv* **natural gas** *n* gas formed like oil in natural deposits and burned for cooking, heating, etc **natural history** *n* study of animals and plants **natural science** *n* science, such as chemistry or zoology, that is concerned with laws and processes of the external physical world **naturalize** *vt,vi* 1 confer or adopt citizenship of a country 2 introduce or adapt to another country or area **naturalization** *n*

nature *n* 1 external physical world and its laws plants and animals 2 character or temperament; characteristics 3 kind or sort

naughty *adj* 1 mischievous 2 indecent; suggestive **naughtily** *adv* **naughtiness** *n*

nausea *n* 1 feeling of sickness; desire to vomit 2 absolute disgust **nauseous** *adj* **nauseate** *vt* 1 induce a feeling of sickness 2 disgust; repel

nautical *adj* relating to ships, seamen or navigation

naval *adj* relating to the equipment personnel or activities of a navy

nave *n* central seating area of a church up to the chancel

navel *n* small pit in the abdomen left by the severed umbilical cord

navigate *vt vi* direct or plan the course or route of (a ship, car etc) *vt* 1 follow the course of (a river) 2 sail across **navigator** *n* **navigable** *adj* 1 (of water) deep enough to admit ships 2 able to be navigated **navigation** *n* 1 theory and practice of navigating 2 shipping

navy *n* 1 fleet of warships with sea aircraft 2 personnel of the fleet **navy blue** *n,adj* dark blue

near *prep* at or within a short time or distance *adj* 1 close in position or time 2 intimate; dear 3 only just avoided; narrow *adv* close (to) **nearness** *n* **nearby** *adj* close by, not far away **nearly** *adv* almost **nearside** *n* the side of a car, traffic lane etc ; nearest to the kerb **near-sighted** *adj* short-sighted

neat *adj* 1 tidy carefully arranged 2 skilful;

deft 3 well-planned; clever 4 precise 5 undiluted **neatly** *adv* **neatness** *n* **neaten** *vt* make neat; tidy up

necessary *adj* 1 essential; needed 2 logical **necessarily** *adv* **necessity** *n* 1 essential requirement 2 pressing need 3 logical consequence

neck *n* 1 part of the body connecting the head and shoulders 2 *also* **neckline** part of a garment round the neck and shoulders 3 long narrowed portion of land, slender part of a bottle, etc **neck and neck** abreast in a race or contest **stick one's neck out** act defiantly and risk censure ~*vi inf* kiss and cuddle lengthily (with) **necklace** *n* neck ornament

nectar *n* 1 sweet liquid that bees obtain from certain flowers for making honey 2 very sweet, soothing drink

née (nei) *adj* having a maiden name of; born

need *vt* require; lack *vi* be obliged to; be necessary to *v aux* **need I, you, he?, etc.** must I, you, he?, etc **I, you, he, etc., need not** I, you, he, etc do/does not have to ~*n* 1 circumstances in which something is needed 2 misfortune, poverty 3 requirement **needy** *adj* poor

needle *n* 1 sharp pointed sliver of steel with a hole at one end to take thread for sewing 2 plastic or metal rod for knitting 3 gramophone stylus 4 indicator arrow on a compass dial, etc 5 pointed part of a hypodermic syringe 6 sharply pointed leaf of a conifer **needlework** *n* hand-sewing

negate *vt* 1 deny 2 cancel out; make void **negation** *n*

negative *adj* 1 indicating *no* not affirmative 2 not productive or positive 3 indicating opposition or disapproval 4 denoting numbers less than zero 5 with light and dark areas reversed 6 designating the electrical charge carried by an electron *n* 1 word(s) indicating a denial or refusal 2 negative number 3 negative photographic plate

neglect *vt* 1 fail to care for 2 omit; overlook *n* act or result of neglecting **negligent** *adj* careless; not paying proper attention **negligence** *n* **negligently** *adv* **negligible** *adj* so minor as to be not worth considering **negligibly** *adv*

négligé ('negliʒei) *n* woman's dressing gown usually of a light or flimsy material

negotiate *vi* reach an agreement through discussion *vt* **1** settle through discussion **2** successfully come through or deal with (an obstacle) **3** obtain cash settlement for **negotiation** *n* **negotiator** *n*

Negro *n, pl* **Negroes** black-skinned person of African descent

neigh *vi* (of a horse) produce a braying sound *n* cry of a horse; bray

neighbour *n* **1** person living nextdoor or nearby **2** thing situated near or adjacent to another *v* **neighbour on** border on; adjoin **neighbourhood** *n* (people living in) the vicinity; surrounding area

neither *adj,pron* not either (one) *conj* nor yet

neon *n* gaseous element used in strip lighting and advertising display

nephew *n* son of one's brother or sister, or of one's husband's or wife's brother or sister

nepotism *n* favouritism shown to relatives in unfairly procuring positions or promotion for them **nepotist** *n*

Neptune *n* outer giant planet lying beyond Uranus

nerve *n* **1** bundle of fibres that connects the central nervous system with all parts of the body transmitting sensory and motor impulses **2** courage; confidence **3** *sl* impudence; cheek **nerves** *pl n* anxiety; hysteria; irritability **get on one's nerves** irritate **nervy** *adj* anxious; tense **nerve-racking** *adj* causing emotional strain; worrying

nervous *adj* **1** tense; excitable **2** timid; anxious **3** vigorous, spirited **4** relating to the nerves **nervous breakdown** *n* severe mental and emotional collapse **nervous system** *n* body mechanism coordinating internal functions and external impulses

nest *n* **1** shelter made of twigs, grass, etc, where birds, reptiles, mice, etc, lay eggs or give birth **2** protective or comfortable place in which young animals are reared *vi* **1** make a nest **2** look for nests **nest egg** *n* savings

nestle *vi* cuddle, settle comfortably

net[1] *n* **1** *also* **netting** open mesh of knotted string, wire, etc, used for catching fish, birds, etc, or to protect against birds, insects, etc **2** mesh barrier dividing playing areas in tennis and other games or to enclose a goal area *vt,vi* (-tt-) **1** catch or cover with nets **2** snare **3** construct a net **netball** *n* sport in which goals are scored by throwing a ball into a net **network** *n* **1** complex connected pattern

or system of wires, roads, etc **2** series of linked radio or television stations

net[2] *adj* remaining after deductions *vt* (-tt-) earn as net profit or income

nettle *n* plant with toothed leaves and stinging hairs *vt* irritate

neurosis *n* nervous disorder involving irrational anxiety, obsessions, or other abnormal behaviour **neurotic** *adj* **1** relating to a neurosis or to the nerves **2** prone to anxiety or hysteria *n* neurotic person

neuter *adj* **1** of neither masculine nor feminine gender **2** sexually underdeveloped **3** deprived of sexual organs *n* neuter word, animal, plant, etc *vt* make neuter

neutral *adj* **1** impartial; not taking sides **2** belonging to neither side **3** having no definite characteristics **4** neuter **5** neither alkali nor acid **6** neither positive nor negative **7** (of gears) not engaged *n* **1** person, country, etc, who favours no side or who does not take part in an argument, war, etc **2** (of gears) state of being not engaged **neutrality** *n* **neutralize** *vt* **1** make neutral **2** render powerless; deaden

neutron *n* minute uncharged particle occurring in the nuclei of all atoms except hydrogen

never *adv* **1** at no time **2** not at all **never mind!** don't worry! **well I never!** how surprising!

nevertheless *adv* even so; in spite of that

new *adj* **1** of recent origin or existence; not old; freshly produced **2** recently acquired or discovered **3** modern; novel; different **4** another **new at** or **to** unaccustomed to; unfamiliar with ~*adv also* **newly** freshly; recently **newcomer** *n* recently arrived person; beginner **New Year** *n* **1** coming year **2** first or first few days of January

news *s n* **1** current information about recent events **2** broadcast information about local, national, and international events **newsagent** *n* shopkeeper who sells newspapers, journals, etc **newspaper** *n* daily or weekly publication containing news, features, specialist information, and advertisements **newsreel** *n* filmed report of current events

newt *n* small lizard-like amphibian

next *adj* **1** following; subsequent **2** adjacent; neighbouring **3** closest *adv* after this or that

nib *n* pointed writing end of a pen

nibble n 1 small bite 2 morsel vt,vi take a nibble (at); eat in nibbles

nice adj 1 pleasant; attractive 2 good; virtuous 3 refined 4 precise; subtle; delicate **nicely** adv

niche n 1 alcove or recess, often used for shrines or statues 2 suitable or comfortable place or position

nick n tiny notch **the nick** sl jail **in the nick of time** just in time ~vt 1 make a nick in 2 sl steal; pinch

nickel n 1 hard silvery metal used for plating and coin-making 2 US five-cent coin

nickname n name by which a person is known affectionately or mockingly vt give a nickname to

nicotine n narcotic found in tobacco

niece n daughter of one's brother or sister, or of one's husband's or wife's brother or sister

nigger n abusive Negro

night n period of time between evening and morning; darkness **nightclub** n place of entertainment open at night providing food and drink **nightdress** n also **nightgown** woman's sleeping garment **nightly** adv 1 during the night 2 every night **nightmare** n 1 terrifying dream 2 frightening experience, trauma **night-time** n period of darkness between sunset and sunrise **night watchman** n person employed to guard premises at night

nightingale n red-brown European songbird noted for its nocturnal trilling song

nil n nothing

nimble adj agile; deft; quick **nimbly** adv

nine n 1 number equal to one plus eight 2 group of nine persons, things, etc 3 also **nine o'clock** nine hours after noon or midnight adj amounting to nine **nine days wonder** something that causes short-lived excitement or admiration **ninth** adj coming between eighth and tenth in sequence n 1 ninth person, object, etc 2 one of nine equal portions; one divided by nine adv after the eighth

nineteen n 1 number that is nine more than ten 2 nineteen things or people **talk nineteen to the dozen** talk fast and unceasingly ~adj amounting to nineteen **nineteenth** n,adj,adv

ninety n 1 number equal to nine times ten 2 ninety things or people adj amounting to ninety **ninetieth** adj,adv,n

nip vt,vi (-pp-) 1 catch, pinch, or bite sharply 2 check the growth (of) vi inf go quickly; pop n 1 small bite or pinch 2 touch of frost **nippy** adj cold; sharp; frosty

nipple n 1 suckling teat of a breast or bottle 2 device similar in shape or function to a nipple

nit n 1 egg of a head louse or other parasite 2 sl fool

nitrogen n colourless gas forming 78 per cent of the air and used esp in the manufacture of fertilizers

nitroglycerine n unstable chemical used in dynamite and other explosives

no adv 1 not any; not one 2 not in any way; not at all 3 not 4 expressing denial, refusal, etc n statement of denial, refusal, etc ; negative

noble adj 1 courageous; worthy; high-minded 2 aristocratic 3 stately; splendid n also **nobleman** member of the nobility; aristocrat; peer **nobility** n 1 hereditary class of the highest status; aristocracy 2 moral courage, worthiness, or endurance

nobody pron 1 no-one 2 person of no importance or of low birth

nocturnal adj of, occurring in, or active during the night **nocturnally** adv

nod vt,vi (-dd-) bend (the head) forward to indicate (agreement or approval) vi doze n nodding motion

noise n sound **noisy** adj loud **noisily** adv **noisiness** n

nomad n 1 member of a tribe constantly on the move in search of new pasture 2 habitual wanderer; roamer **nomadic** adj

nominal adj 1 not actual; existing in name only 2 very small; token **nominally** adv

nominate vt 1 propose as a candidate 2 appoint **nomination** n **nominee** n person who is nominated

non- prefix indicating negation, absence, etc

nonchalant adj coolly casual; offhand **nonchalance** n **nonchalantly** adv

nondescript adj having no distinguishing characteristics; dull

none pron 1 not any (of them or it) 2 no part or section 3 no such person adv not at all; in no way

nonentity n 1 insignificant person or thing 2 non-existent thing

nonsense n 1 meaningless or foolish words or ideas 2 trifle **nonsensical** adj

noodle n thin strip of pasta

nook n secret or sheltered corner or hiding place

noon n midday; 12 o clock in the daytime

no-one pron no person at all; nobody

noose n loop of rope with a slipknot to tighten it, used esp for execution by hanging

nor conj also not; not either

norm n 1 usual or recognized standard or pattern 2 expected or potential output

normal adj 1 usual; ordinary; average 2 not physically or mentally handicapped **normality** n **normally** adv

north n 1 one of the four cardinal points of the compass situated to the left of a person facing the sunrise 2 part of a country, area, etc , lying towards the north adj also **northern** of, in, or facing the north adv,adj also **northerly** 1 towards the north 2 (of winds) from the north **northerner** n **northeast** n point situated midway between the north and east adj also **northeastern** of, in, or facing the northeast adv,adj also **northeasterly** 1 towards the northeast 2 (of winds) from the northeast **northward** adj facing or moving towards the north **northwards** adv in the direction of the north **northwest** n point situated midway between north and west adj also **northwestern** of, in, or facing the northwest adv,adj also **northwesterly** 1 towards the northwest 2 (of winds) from the northwest

nose n 1 central projection in the face used for breathing and smelling 2 ability to smell out or discover **be led by the nose** follow blindly **keep one's nose to the grindstone** work persistently **pay through the nose** pay too much **poke one's nose into** interfere in **turn one's nose up (at)** reject contemptuously **under one's (very) nose** in one's presence, in full view ~vt,vi smell or sniff (at)

nostalgia n 1 sentimental longing for things past 2 homesickness **nostalgic** adj

nostril n one of the two openings of the nose

nosy adj unpleasantly inquisitive **nosiness** n

not adv expressing negation, denial, refusal, etc

notable adj important; remarkable; conspicuous n important person **notably** adv

notation n 1 act or process of organizing a

scheme of signs that represent scientific, musical, or other concepts 2 such a scheme or method

notch n V-shaped cut in a piece of wood, etc vt cut a notch in, esp as a way of keeping count **notch up** score

note n 1 short written record, summary, or comment 2 short letter 3 piece of paper money 4 written promise to pay 5 (symbol indicating) a musical sound of a certain pitch 6 distinction; fame; importance 7 notice; attention 8 certain quality vt 1 make a note of 2 take note of; observe **noteworthy** adj 1 deserving attention; worth noting 2 remarkable

nothing n 1 not anything; no thing 2 no part 3 something of no importance or value 4 something requiring no effort 5 zero; nought **for nothing** 1 free of charge 2 with no purpose **think nothing of** do without hesitation ~adv not in any way

notice vt,vi 1 observe; take note of 2 comment on, esp favourably n 1 attention; observation 2 piece of displayed written information 3 public announcement 4 warning 5 official announcement or notification of the termination of employment 6 critical review **at short notice** with little warning or preparation time **noticeable** adj

notify vt let (a person) know; inform officially **notification** n

notion n impression; view; idea; concept **notional** adj 1 expressing a concept; not based on fact 2 nominal

notorious adj infamous; having a bad reputation **notoriety** n **notoriously** adv

notwithstanding adv nevertheless prep conj in spite of

nougat n chewy white sweet containing nuts

nought n zero; nothing **noughts and crosses** n game played on a criss-cross grid in which the object is to get three noughts or crosses in a row

noun n word used to denote a thing, person, concept, act, etc

nourish vt 1 give food to 2 encourage or harbour (feeling) **nourishment** n food

novel[1] adj new and different **novelty** n 1 quality of being novel 2 cheap often gaudy small article for sale

novel[2] n sustained work of prose fiction longer than a short story **novelist** n

November n eleventh month of the year

novice n 1 beginner; learner 2 nun or monk who has not yet taken final vows

now adv 1 at present 2 immediately; this minute 3 recently 4 presently 5 at this point; currently 6 consequently **now and then** every so often; occasionally ~conj also **now that** since; as a consequence of **nowadays** adv these days; in modern times

nowhere adv not in any place; not anywhere **get nowhere** be unsuccessful; fail to achieve something

noxious adj poisonous

nozzle n tube or spout through which liquid or gas is let out

nuance n subtle variation in meaning, shade, etc

nuclear adj 1 of, forming, or relating to the nucleus or central core 2 relating to the structure or splitting of atoms **nuclear fission/fusion** n splitting of a heavy atom/fusion of light atoms attended by enormous release of energy **nuclear physics** n science relating to the behaviour of atoms **nuclear reactor** n device for generating power from nuclear fission **nuclear weapon** n bomb or missile using energy from nuclear fission or fusion

nucleus n, pl **nuclei** ('nju:kliai) or **nucleuses** 1 central or most active part of a movement, organization, etc 2 positively charged central mass of an atom consisting of protons and neutrons

nude adj naked n naked figure, esp one depicted in a painting, sculpture, etc **in the nude** naked **nudity** n

nudge n deliberate slight push with the elbow; prod vt give a nudge (to)

nugget n 1 small hard irregularly shaped lump, esp of gold 2 small valuable piece

nuisance n thing or person causing annoyance, trouble, or offence

null adj 1 without value or feeling 2 having no legal force **null and void** legally invalid **nullity** n **nullify** vt make null **nullification** n

numb adj without feeling, sensation, or emotion vt make numb or insensitive **numbness** n

number n 1 mathematical concept of quantity, each unit of which has a unique value, enabling them to be used in counting 2 numeral 3 sum; quantity; aggregate 4 one of a series; issue 5 short musical piece 6 exclusive article **a number of** several **number one** oneself **without** or **beyond number** too many to be counted ~vt 1 assign a number to 2 add up to 3 enumerate; list **numberless** adj countless; innumerable

numeral n symbol or group of symbols, such as 6 or VI, denoting a number

numerate adj ('nju:mərət) able to understand and use mathematical concepts vt ('nju:məreit) number; count **numeracy** n

numerical adj relating to or consisting of numbers **numerically** adv

numerous adj great in number; abundant

nun n woman who has taken final vows in a religious order **nunnery** n community of nuns; convent

nurse n 1 person trained and employed to care for the sick under the direction of doctors 2 woman employed to look after very small children vt,vi 1 act as a nurse (to) 2 suckle vt cherish; foster; nurture; encourage **nursing home** n small privately run hospital for convalescent, aged, or chronically ill patients

nursery n 1 playroom 2 place for growing or stocking plants **nursery rhyme** n traditional children's song or verse **nursery school** n school for children under five; kindergarten

nurture vt foster; rear; feed n upbringing, education

nut n 1 hard shelled fruit with a single sometimes edible kernel 2 small regularly shaped metal block with a central threaded hole used for securing bolts 3 sl fanatic; enthusiast 4 sl insane or peculiar person **nuts** sl adj crazy **nutcracker** n also **nutcrackers** device having pincers for cracking nutshells **nutmeg** n seed of an East Indian tree, ground as a spice **nutshell** n woody covering of a nut kernel **in a nutshell** precisely; concisely expressed

nutrient n nourishing substance taken in, esp by a plant

nutrition n 1 digestion and assimilation of food 2 feeding; nourishment **nutritious** adj nourishing; health-giving

nuzzle vt,vi rub or push (against) with the nose

nylon n synthetic plastic fibre or material made from it **nylons** pl n woman's stockings

nymph n 1 minor Greek or Roman goddess inhabiting and guarding trees, rivers, etc 2 beautiful young girl

O

oak n deciduous acorn-bearing tree with hard wood and jagged leaves

oar n wooden pole with one end flattened into a blade, used to propel a boat through water **put one's oar in** interfere **oarsman** n pl **-men** one who rows with an oar

oasis n, pl **oases** (ou'eisi:z) fertile area in a desert

oath n 1 solemn binding declaration of the truth of one's statement 2 casual use of a solemn word or name in anger or irritation; swearword **on** or **under oath** sworn to tell the truth

oats pl n grains of a hardy cereal plant, widely used as human and animal food **sow one's wild oats** indulge in pleasures, esp irresponsible sexual relationships, while young **oatmeal** n coarse flour made from oats used for porridge, biscuits, etc

obese adj extremely fat; gross **obesity** n

obey vt,vi do what is commanded by a person, law, instinct, etc **obedient** adj ready and willing to obey; dutiful **obedience** n **obediently** adv

obituary n notice of death, esp in a newspaper, often including a short biography

object n (ˈɔbdʒekt) 1 thing discernible by the senses 2 aim, goal, or intention vt,vi (əbˈdʒekt) oppose, disapprove, or protest against **objection** n 1 act of or reason for objecting 2 feeling or statement of dislike or disapproval **objective** adj 1 separate; detached 2 impartial; viewed fairly and dispassionately n point or situation to be aimed at; goal **objectively** adv **objectivity** n

oblige vt 1 allow no choice; insist or force 2 do a favour for 3 make indebted to **obligation** n duty enforceable by law, morality, a contract, promise, etc **obligatory** (əˈbligətəri) adj necessary and binding

oblique 1 slanting away from the horizontal or vertical 2 indirect; devious; not straightforward **obliquely** adv

obliterate vt leave no trace of; destroy; blot out **obliteration** n

oblivion n state of forgetfulness or lack of awareness **oblivious** adj 1 absent-minded;

unaware 2 unaffected by; impervious to **obliviously** adv

oblong n figure, esp a rectangle, longer than it is broad adj shaped like an oblong

obnoxious adj 1 repulsive; causing disgust 2 extremely rude or insulting

oboe n woodwind instrument having a mouthpiece fitted with a double reed **oboist** n

obscene adj offending against decency or morality; vulgar; lewd **obscenely** adv **obscenity** n

obscure adj 1 vague; enigmatic; not easily understood 2 dim; gloomy; indistinct 3 not famous or well-known **obscurely** adv **obscurity** n

observe vt,vi 1 see, notice, or watch 2 keep to the rules of a custom, law, religion, etc 3 remark or comment **observer** n **observance** n adherence to the rules of law, religion, custom, etc **observant** adj attentive; taking notice **observation** n 1 careful watching; recognizing and noting 2 comment or remark **observatory** n building used for astronomical observation

obsess vt be an obsession of; preoccupy **obsessive** adj **obsession** n fixed idea or addiction that fascinates and preoccupies the mind to an exaggerated or dangerous extent

obsolete adj out-of-date; antiquated; disused **obsolescent** adj becoming obsolete **obsolescence** n

obstacle n any snag or obstruction hindering progress or action

obstinate adj stubborn; hard to persuade; unyielding **obstinacy** n **obstinately** adv

obstruct vt,vi 1 block off; prevent access or progress 2 impede or delay any action **obstruction** n

obtain vt,vi gain possession (of); get; secure or acquire **obtainable** adj

obtrusive adj interfering; impertinent **obtrusion** n

obtuse adj dull; blunt; not sharp or acute **obtuse angle** n angle greater than 90° but less than 180°

obvious adj evident; clear; apparent **obviously** adv

occasion n 1 particular time of an event, ceremony, etc 2 suitable opportunity or chance 3 reason; need **rise to the occasion** display the necessary or suitable qualities ~vt give rise to; bring about or cause **occasional** adj infrequent; sporadic **occasionally** adv

Occident n the West, esp W. Europe and America **Occidental** adj,n

occult adj supernatural; magical; mysterious **the occult** n supernatural or magical knowledge or experience

occupy vt 1 take or hold possession of (a country, building etc.) 2 employ **occupant** n one who possesses or lives in a particular place **occupancy** n **occupation** n 1 employment, pastime; job 2 state or act of occupying or being occupied

occur vi (-rr-) 1 happen; take place 2 exist; be found at 3 come into the mind **occurrence** n

ocean n one of the five vast areas of sea surrounding the continents of the globe **oceanic** adj

octagon n geometric figure, design, building, etc., having eight sides **octagonal** adj

octane n inflammable hydrocarbon present in petrol **high-octane** adj denoting a superior grade of petrol

octave n 1 range of eight notes in a musical scale 2 set of eight

October n tenth month of the year

octopus n, pl **octopuses** or **octopi** ('ɔktəpai) eight-armed mollusc

odd adj 1 strange; bizarre; peculiar 2 uneven; irregular 3 (of a number) not divisible by two **odd man out** one remaining when others have formed a pair, class, group etc **oddly** adv **oddity** n 1 strangeness; peculiarity 2 remarkable or unlikely event, person, object, etc **oddment** n scrap; remnant; leftover **odds** pl n 1 chances; possibilities 2 ratio between two stakes in a wager **at odds** in disagreement **odds and ends** small miscellaneous scraps

ode n poem addressed to a particular person or object

odious adj hateful; loathsome **odium** n

odour n smell; fragrance

oesophagus (iːˈsɔfəgəs) n, pl **oesophagi** (iːˈsɔfəgai) tube running from the pharynx to the stomach; gullet

oestrogen n female sex hormone

oestrus n period of sexual receptiveness in most female mammals

of prep 1 belonging to 2 originating from 3 created or produced by 4 from the period relating to 5 made with 6 containing; holding 7 towards or away from a specified place 8 that is the same as 9 for 10 separated from

off prep 1 so as to be away or distant from 2 not present at or attending to 3 removed or deducted from 4 no longer interested in 5 by the means of adv 1 distant; away 2 so as to be removed or rid of 3 so as to stop or disengage adj 1 cancelled or postponed 2 not attached 3 not working or turned on **on the off chance** with the possibility or hope

offal n edible internal organs or parts of an animal

offend vt cause displeasure or pain to vi sin; do wrong **offence** n 1 crime or infringement of the law 2 any cause of anger, grievance, or pain **to take/give offence** to be/cause hurt **offensive** adj aggressive; repellent obnoxious n attack

offer vt give; present or hold out for acceptance vi volunteer; be available or on hand n 1 act of offering 2 something offered

offhand adj 1 impromptu; unprepared 2 casual, impolite

office n 1 position of authority esp public or governmental 2 place of business 3 government department 4 rite or religious service **officer** 1 person holding a responsible position in a government, club, organization etc 2 holder of a commission in the armed forces 3 policeman **official** n one who holds an office adj 1 authorized or vouched for 2 relating to an office **officially** adv **officious** adj bossy; interfering

offing n **in the offing** in view; near; likely to happen

off-licence n shop licensed to sell alcoholic drink for consumption off the premises

off-peak adj,adv at a less popular or less busy time

off-putting adj discouraging; repelling

offset vt (-tt-, -set) compensate for; balance out

offshore adj,adv from or far from the shore or land

offside adj in a part of a football field, etc between the ball and the opponents goal, where it is not allowable to kick the ball n the right-hand side of a vehicle, horse, etc

offspring 1 child or children 2 any issue or result

offstage *adj,adv* not visible to the audience in a theatre

often *adv* frequently; repeatedly

ogre *n* 1 monstrous man-eating giant of fairy tales and folklore 2 cruel person; tyrant

oil *n* viscous liquid obtained from many mineral and vegetable sources, lighter than and insoluble in water **burn the midnight oil** work or study until late at night ~*vt* apply oil to **oily** *adj* **oil painting** *n* 1 picture painted in oil-based paints (oils) 2 art or practice of painting such pictures **oilskin** *n* cloth or clothing treated with oil to make it waterproof

ointment *n* soothing or medicated cream applied to the skin

old *adj* 1 aged; having existed for many years 2 out-of-date; obsolete; belonging to an earlier age; stale **old age** *n* last years of life **old-fashioned** *adj* out-of-date; obsolete; quaint **old hand** *n* experienced person

olive *n* small oily Mediterranean fruit eaten either unripe (green olive) or ripe (black olive) *n,adj also* **olive green** brownish green

omelette *n* eggs beaten together, fried, and flavoured with herbs, vegetables, cheese, etc

omen *n* sign supposedly prophesying a future event

ominous *adj* threatening; suggesting future trouble

omit *vt* (-tt-) leave out; fail to do **omission** *n*

omnibus *n* bus *adj* containing several assorted ingredients, items, etc

omnipotent *adj* all-powerful **omnipotence** *n*

on *prep* 1 placed or being in contact with the top or surface of 2 supported by or attached to 3 during a particular day 4 close to or by the side of; along 5 being broadcast by or performed at 6 at the time or occasion of 7 with the support of 8 concerning; about 9 by means of *adv* 1 so as to work or function 2 so as to be covered with 3 ahead **on and off** sporadically **on and on** repeatedly; continuously ~*adj* 1 taking place; planned 2 attached 3 working; functioning; performing

once *adv* 1 on a single occasion 2 in the past **at once** 1 immediately 2 simultaneously **once and for all** finally

one *adj* 1 single; individual 2 only 3 being a united entity *n* 1 the smallest whole number represented by the symbol 1 or I 2 a particular or specified single person, thing, example, etc 3 *also* **one o'clock** the first hour after noon or

midnight *pron* 1 a person; any person; each person 2 *formal* I or me **one another** each other; one to or with the other **oneself** *r pron* 1 a or any person's own self 2 yourself **be/feel oneself** be/feel normal, natural, etc **one-sided** *adj* unfairly biased **one-way** *adj* 1 allowing traffic in one direction only 2 not reciprocal

onion *n* vegetable whose rounded pungent bulb is used in cooking

onlooker *n* spectator; observer

only *adj* being a single one or one of few; sole *adv* 1 exclusively; solely 2 merely; just *conj* but; however

onset *n* beginning; start; attack

onslaught *n* violent assault

onus *n* responsibility; duty; burden

onward *adj* moving forwards **onwards** *adv* forwards; towards the front

onyx (´ɔniks) *n* quartz having bands or layers of different colours

ooze *vi,vt* seep; leak; flow gradually

opal *n* quartz-like mineral characterized by iridescent colours, often used as a gemstone

opaque *adj* obscure; transmitting no light **opacity** *n*

open *adj* 1 not closed or sealed 2 allowing access 3 ready or available for business or trade 4 free from obstruction 5 vacant; unoccupied; free 6 not yet settled or decided 7 candid; honest; not prejudiced 8 vulnerable; liable *vt,vi* 1 make or become open 2 undo; unfold 3 start; give an introduction (to) *vt* 1 disclose; reveal 2 declare officially to be open to the public *n also* **the open air** outdoors; outside **in the open** so as to be known or made public **openly** *adv* **openness** *n* **open-ended** *adj* limitless **opener** *n* gadget for opening tins, bottles, etc **open-handed** *adj* generous **open-hearted** *adj* frank, sincere **opening** *n* 1 gap; space 2 start; beginning 3 opportunity; chance **open-minded** *adj* not biased or prejudiced; liberal **open-mouthed** *adj* astonished; aghast **open-plan** *adj* having few or no internal walls to separate rooms

opera *n* musical drama, largely or wholly sung **operatic** *adj*

operate *vi,vt* 1 work or function 2 perform surgery (on) **operative** *adj* **operator** *n* **operation** *n* 1 working; action; function; effect 2 instance of surgery **operational** *adj*

operetta n short, light, or comic opera

ophthalmology n branch of medicine dealing with eye disorders **ophthalmologist** n

opinion n judgment; view; belief **opinionated** adj dogmatic; stubborn **opinion poll** n organized questioning to determine public opinion on a particular issue

opium n narcotic sedative, or stimulant drug prepared from juice of certain poppies. **opiate** n drug containing opium adj made from opium; inducing sleep

opponent n antagonist; one who opposes adj opposing; adverse

opportunity n favourable chance or occasion **opportune** adj lucky; well-timed

oppose vt set against; resist; obstruct or contest **opposite** adj 1 facing; in front of 2 opposed or contrary (to) n opposite person or thing; antithesis adv,prep in an opposite position, direction, etc **opposite number** n person holding a similar or equivalent position in another country, company, etc **opposition** n 1 resistance; hostility 2 state or position of being opposite 3 most distant positioning of two stars or planets **the Opposition** major political party not in office

oppress vt 1 weigh down or overwhelm 2 persecute severely **oppression** n **oppressive** adj 1 harsh; cruel 2 (of weather) sultry

opt vt choose; settle for; decide between **option** n 1 choice; alternative 2 right, freedom, or opportunity to purchase **optional** adj not obligatory

optical adj relating to the eyes; visual **optician** n person who makes or sells glasses, lenses, etc

optimism n feeling or belief that the best will happen; hopefulness **optimist** n **optimistic** adj

opulent adj rich; lavish; sumptuous **opulence** n

or conj 1 with the alternative of 2 and also; as well as

oral adj 1 spoken 2 relating to the mouth

orange n round juicy citrus fruit with reddish-yellow peel n,adj reddish-yellow **orangeade** n orange-flavoured fizzy drink

oration n eloquent public speech or address **orator** n **oratory** n

orbit n 1 path followed around a planet or star by a satellite 2 sphere of influence 3 eye socket **orbital** adj

orchard n enclosed area of fruit trees

orchestra n 1 company of instrumental musicians 2 also **orchestra pit** semicircle between the stage and seats in a theatre **orchestra stalls** pl n front seats in a theatre **orchestral** adj **orchestrate** vt arrange (music) for an orchestra **orchestration** n

orchid n one of a family of perennial plants with complicated specialized, often exotic, flowers

ordain vt 1 decree; order 2 appoint as a priest or minister **ordination** n

ordeal n severe trial of stamina or endurance

order n 1 arrangement; sequence 2 command; rule 3 tidiness 4 class or group 5 religious body **in order** 1 in a proper state or condition 2 correct or appropriate **in order to** so as to; with the intention or purpose of ~vt 1 command; instruct 2 arrange; organize 3 send for **orderly** adj methodical; tidy; well-controlled n 1 soldier serving an officer 2 attendant in a hospital

ordinal number n number, such as first, second, etc , that denotes order, quantity, or rank in a group

ordinary adj usual; common; familiar; plain n **out of the ordinary** unusual; exceptional **ordinarily** adv

ore n mineral from which metal may be obtained

organ n 1 differentiated part of an animal or plant performing a particular function 2 large musical wind instrument with a keyboard and pipes, often used in churches 3 means or method of communication **organist** n

organic adj 1 relating to or derived from plants or animals 2 inherent; structural 3 (of food) grown without application of any non-organic fertilizer, pesticide, etc 4 relating to chemical compounds of carbon **organically** adv

organism n any animal, plant, bacterium, or virus

organize vt arrange, group, classify, or prepare vi form a political group, union, etc **organization** n 1 organized group, system, company, etc 2 act of organizing

orgasm n culmination of a sexual act characterized by ejaculation in the male and vaginal contractions in the female

orgy n drunken riotous revelry **orgiastic** adj

Orient n the East or the countries of Asia **Oriental** adj,n

orientate vt find the bearings of in relation to surroundings, conditions, etc **orientation** n

origin n source; beginning; starting point **original** adj 1 existing since the beginning 2 new; not copied; novel; creative n the source from which copies, translations, etc , are made **originate** vt, vi start or initiate; have as a source **origination** n

Orlon n Tdmk lightweight synthetic fibre used for clothing, etc

ornament n ('ɔ:nəmənt) 1 decoration; adornment 2 item or article used for show vt ('ɔ:nəment) embellish; decorate **ornamentation** n **ornamental** adj decorative

ornate adj elaborately or flamboyantly decorative

ornithology n study of birds **ornithologist** n

orphan n child whose parents have died adj bereaved of parents vt leave bereaved of parents **orphanage** n institution for bringing up orphans

orthodox adj having sound, correct, or established views, esp in religion **orthodoxy** n

orthopaedic adj intended to cure deformity

oscillate vi 1 move from side to side as a pendulum 2 waver; fluctuate **oscillation** n

ostensible adj apparent; seeming **ostensibly** adv

ostentatious adj showy; flamboyant; vulgar **ostentation** n

osteopath n one who manipulates the bones and muscles in order to cure diseases **osteopathy** n

ostracize vt isolate, shun, or bar from society **ostracism** n

ostrich n large fast-running long-necked bird that is native to Africa

other adj alternative; remaining; different; additional **on the other hand** alternatively **the other day** recently ~pron second or additional person or thing adv **other than** 1 in addition to; apart from 2 in a different way from **others** pl pron remaining, different, or additional ones **otherwise** conj or else adv in a different way; in other respects adj different

otter n fish-catching aquatic mammal having a smooth coat and webbed feet

ought v aux 1 have an obligation or duty 2 need; will be wise or advised 3 will be likely or liable 4 will be pleased

ounce n unit of weight equal to one sixteenth of a pound (approx 28 grams)

our adj belonging to us **ours** pron something or someone belonging to us **ourselves** r pron 1 our own selves 2 our normal selves

oust vt eject or dispossess; usurp or replace

out adv 1 away; towards the outside 2 not present 3 no longer in power 4 on strike 5 not accurate 6 available to the public 7 not alight or switched on 8 no longer in fashion 9 so as to eliminate or omit 10 so as to project or protrude 11 so as to appear 12 acting with the intention of 13 into a state of unconsciousness prep away through **out-of-date** adj old-fashioned; obsolete

outboard motor n engine that can be attached to the exterior of a small boat

outbreak n eruption, epidemic, or sudden appearance

outburst n sudden or violent expression of feelings

outcast n one rejected by society; exile

outcome n result; consequence

outcry n eruption of public protest

outdo vt (-does; -did; -done) excel or surpass

outdoor adj used or existing outdoors **outdoors** adv in the open air; outside any building

outer adj external; further out **outermost** adj furthest out or away **outer space** n vast untravelled area beyond the known planets

outfit n 1 complete equipment, such as a suit of clothes, for a specific purpose 2 inf gang; group of people **outfitter** n shop or dealer selling men's clothes

outgoing adj 1 resigning; retiring; departing 2 extrovert; gregarious n expenditure

outgrow vt (-grew; -grown) 1 grow larger or taller than 2 grow too large for **outgrowth** n something growing from a main stem, part, etc

outhouse n shed; small building separate from larger one

outing n excursion; pleasure trip

outlandish adj extraordinary; eccentric; bizarre

outlaw n fugitive from justice; bandit vt ban; prohibit

outlay n expenditure vt (-laid) spend; expend

outlet n 1 means of escape, expression, etc 2 market or shop handling a particular commodity

outline n 1 rough sketch or draft 2 silhouette

vt **1** produce an outline of **2** give a preliminary account of

outlive *vt* live longer than; survive

outlook *n* **1** mental attitude; point of view **2** prospect; forecast

outlying *adj* remote; on the outside; far away

outnumber *vt* surpass in number; be more than

outpatient *n* non-resident patient who visits hospital for treatment

outpost *n* position or station far away from headquarters

output *n* quantity or amount produced by a factory, industry, person, etc

outrage *n* **1** atrocity; intolerable act **2** indignation or anger over such an act *vt* shock; scandalize **outrageous** *adj* **1** monstrous; appalling; horrifying **2** absurdly ridiculous **outrageously** *adv*

outright *adj* **1** direct; thorough **2** blatant; total *adv* at once; completely

outshine *vt* (-shone) be more successful than; surpass; overshadow

outside *n* outer surface or side *adj* exterior; on the outside *adv* out of doors; not inside *prep* beyond **outsider** *n* **1** one not belonging to a particular group, society, party, etc **2** competitor in a race, etc, considered to have very little chance of winning

outsize *adj* larger than average

outskirts *pl n* outer surrounding area or district; suburbs

outspoken *adj* exceedingly frank and candid; forthright

outstanding *adj* **1** prominent; conspicuous; exceptional **2** not yet paid

outstrip *vt* (-pp-) **1** do better than; surpass **2** run faster than

outward *adj* **1** towards the outside **2** superficial; apparent; external *adj,adv* away from home **outwardly** *adv* ostensibly; apparently; on the surface **outwards** *adv* out; away from the centre

outweigh *vt* be more important, valuable, or heavy than

outwit *vt* (-tt-) defeat by superior cunning or ingenuity

oval *adj* egg-shaped *n* something that is oval

ovary *n* **1** one of the two female reproductive organs producing eggs **2** part of a flower containing ovules

ovation *n* enthusiastic applause

oven *n* compartment enclosed by metal, brick, etc, and heated for baking, roasting, etc; kiln; furnace

over *prep* **1** above; higher than **2** on the top or surface of; so as to cover **3** across; on the other side of **4** during **5** in excess of; more than **6** throughout **7** about; concerning **8** recovered from; finished with **9** better than **10** superior in rank to **11** by means of **12** whilst occupied with *adv* **1** across **2** throughout; during **3** from start to finish **4** so as to fall or bend **5** so as to remain **6** so as to be finished **over and over (again)** repeatedly *~n* series of six balls bowled in cricket

overall *adj,adv* including or considering everything *n* light coat or apron worn to protect clothes from dirt **overalls** *pl n* hard-wearing trousers with a high front and straps over the shoulders

overbearing *adj* domineering, bossy

overboard *adv* over the side of a boat or ship **go overboard** enthuse

overcast *adj* cloudy; gloomy

overcharge *vt,vi* charge too much money

overcoat *n* heavy coat

overcome *vt* (-came, -come) **1** conquer; vanquish; get the better of **2** overwhelm; affect totally

overdo *vt* (-does; -did; -done) **1** do something to excess; exaggerate **2** cook for too long

overdose *n* too large a dose

overdraw *vt,vi* (-drew; -drawn) draw from a bank more money than exists to one's credit **overdraft** *n* amount by which debit exceeds credit in a bank account

overdue *adj* late, past the time when due

overeat *vi* (-ate; -eate n) eat excessively; gorge

overestimate *vt* value too highly

overfill *vt* flood, fill too full

overflow *vt* (-flowed; -flown) flow over the edge of; reach beyond the limits of; be excessively full of *n* **1** flood or profusion **2** outlet for excess water

overgrown *adj* covered with vegetation, weeds etc

overhang *vt,vi* (-hung) jut over *n* jutting ledge

overhaul *vt* **1** check thoroughly for faults **2** repair; renovate; restore *n* check-up service

overhead *adv,adj* above the head, in the sky **overheads** *pl n* regular unavoidable expenses of administration

overhear vt (-heard) eavesdrop; hear words intended for others by accident or design

overjoyed adj ecstatic; thrilled; delighted

overland adj,adv mainly or entirely by land

overlap vt,vi (-pp-) 1 extend partly beyond the edge of 2 coincide partly n overlapping part or area

overlay vt (-laid) 1 cover the surface of 2 cover; disguise with n something laid over as a cover, decoration, etc

overleaf adv on the other side of the page

overload vt load, fill, or weigh down excessively

overlook vt 1 view from a higher place 2 disregard or take no notice of; choose to ignore

overnight adv,adj 1 during the night 2 all night 3 lasting for one night

overpower vt 1 conquer by superior strength, weight, etc 2 subdue; overwhelm; overcome

overrate vt overestimate

overreach vt 1 reach or extend too far for comfort 2 outwit

overrule vt rule against or annul by virtue of greater authority

overrun vt (-nn-, -ran; -run) 1 swarm over and take possession of; infest 2 extend beyond

overseas adv,adj abroad; across the sea

overshadow vt 1 cast a shadow over 2 outshine

overshoot vt (-shot) shoot or go over or beyond

oversight n 1 omission; mistake; failure to take into account 2 supervision

oversleep vi (-slept) sleep longer than intended

overspill n surplus esp of the population of a town

overstep vt (-pp-) exceed; go beyond (a limit, constraint, etc)

overt adj openly done; public; not concealed **overtly** adv

overtake vt (-took; -taken) 1 catch up with and pass 2 come up on suddenly

overthrow vt (-threw; -thrown) 1 defeat utterly 2 overturn; demolish n defeat; ruin

overtime n time worked beyond usual working hours or payment for this

overtone n implication; suggestion

overture n 1 instrumental prelude to an opera, ballet, etc 2 opening negotiations or approach

overturn vt upset, overthrow, or abolish

overweight adj heavier than permissible or normal n excess weight

overwhelm vt 1 conquer by superior might 2 overpower emotionally **overwhelmingly** adv

overwork vt,vi work or cause to work too hard n excess work

overwrought adj over-excited: in a state of nervous agitation

ovulate vi produce and discharge an egg from an ovary **ovulation** n

ovule n part of a plant that contains the egg cell, which develops into a seed after fertilization

owe vt be indebted for; be under an obligation **owing to** because of

owl n nocturnal bird of prey with a large head and eyes, small hooked beak, and a hooting cry

own adj relating to oneself, itself, etc **get one's own back** take revenge **hold one's own** succeed in keeping one's position; acquit oneself well **on one's own** by oneself; independently ~vt possess; have **own up** confess **owner** n **ownership** n

ox n pl oxen castrated male of domestic cattle **oxtail** n tail of an ox used esp in soups and stews

oxygen n colourless tasteless gaseous element present in air, water, and most minerals **oxygenate** vt,vi also **oxygenize** fill with oxygen

oyster n edible marine bivalve mollusc

P

pace n 1 single step or its approximate length 2 speed, esp of walking or running **put through one's paces** test (someone) for speed, talent, etc ~vi walk with a regular step vt measure out (distance) by pacing

pacifism n opposition to or nonparticipation in warfare or violence **pacifist** n,adj **pacify** vt calm; soothe; placate; appease

pack n 1 bundle; load; heap 2 container; small package, as of cigarettes 3 set of playing cards 4 group of wolves, hounds, etc 5 gang of people 6 forwards in a Rugby team **pack of lies** false story ~vt,vi arrange (clothes, etc) in a case etc vt 1 form into a bundle, roll up; put away 2 crowd into; press together; cram **3** make compact **pack off** send away **send packing** send away abruptly; dismiss **packhorse** n horse used to carry supplies, goods, etc

package n **1** parcel; object or objects in a container, wrapping, etc **2** group of separate items, services, ideas, etc . offered for sale or acceptance as a single unit vt make a package of or for; wrap **packaging** n materials or containers and wrappings used to package goods

packet n **1** small package **2** sl large sum of money

pact n agreement; treaty; contract

pad[1] n **1** piece of material used to fill out, cushion, or protect **2** fleshy cushion on the underside of an animal's paw or foot **3** covering or guard to protect part of the body **4** sheets of writing paper fastened together **5** sl flat or residence, esp a small one vt (-dd-) **1** stuff, fill, or protect with soft cushion-like material **2** expand or extend with irrelevant or unnecessary information **padding** n

pad[2] vt,vi (-dd-) traverse on foot; trudge n soft dull sound

paddle[1] n **1** short oar flattened at one or both ends used without rowlocks in small boats, canoes, etc **2** structure or implement shaped like a paddle **3** spell of paddling vt,vi move on water using a paddle

paddle[2] vi dabble one's feet or hands in shallow water n act or instance of paddling

paddock n **1** small field used for grazing horses **2** enclosure where racehorses assemble before a race

paddyfield n also **paddy** field used for growing rice

padlock n detachable lock having a hinged loop released by a key vt secure with a padlock

paediatrics n branch of medicine dealing with children and childhood diseases **paediatric** adj **paediatrician** n

pagan adj heathen; relating to a religion other than Christianity, Judaism, or Islam n pagan person

page[1] n one side of a leaf of a book, newspaper, etc.

page[2] n **1** attendant in a hotel, etc **2** junior servant of a king or nobleman **3** boy attendant at a wedding vt summon by calling out a name over a public address system

pageant n lavish public spectacle, procession, or play, esp of historical significance **pageantry** n

pagoda n Oriental temple with a tower of concave sloping roofs

paid v pt and pp of **pay.**

pain n **1** physical or mental distress or discomfort **2** sl also **pain in the neck** irritating or annoying person or thing vt hurt; cause to feel physical or mental distress **painful** adj **painfully** adv

painstaking adj careful; meticulous **painstakingly** adv

paint n colouring or covering matter on or for a surface vt **1** apply paint or liquid to **2** represent or depict in words vt,vi portray or design using paint **painter** n **painting** n **1** picture; artist's representation in paint **2** art or procedure of applying paint to a canvas

pair n **1** two matched objects designed to be used or worn together **2** two persons, animals, things, etc , normally found together **3** single object consisting of two similar interdependent parts vt,vi arrange in twos; make a pair

pal n inf friend; mate; chum v (-ll-) **pal up** inf become friends

palace n present or former residence of a royal family, bishop, or archbishop **palatial** adj

palate n **1** roof of the mouth **2** sensitive or refined sense of taste, esp for wine **palatable** adj **1** agreeable to the taste **2** acceptable to the mind

pale adj **1** light in shade; lacking in colour **2** faint; dim vi lose importance or significance (before) **paleness** n

palette n **1** flat board used by artists for mixing colours **2** range of colours used by a particular artist or school of painters

pallid adj pale; sickly looking **pallor** n

palm[1] n cushioned underside of the hand between the fingers and wrist v **palm off** (on) pass to or impose by trickery; get rid of

palm[2] n tropical and subtropical tree with a straight branchless trunk and a crest of large fan-shaped leaves at the top **Palm Sunday** n Church festival on the Sunday before Easter commemorating Christ's triumphal entry into Jerusalem

palmistry n practice or skill of foretelling the future by inspecting lines on the palm of the hand **palmist** n

pamper vt spoil; over-indulge

pamphlet n leaflet or short publication containing information of current interest

pan n **1** metal or earthenware vessel in which food is cooked or served **2** container resembling such a vessel vt vi (-nn-) wash (sand gravel, etc) in a pan to separate out any gold, silver, etc **pancake** n thin round cake of batter that is fried on both sides

pancreas n gland situated near the stomach that secretes insulin

panda n large black and white bearlike mammal that is native to China

pander v **pander to** minister to or gratify vices weakness, etc

pane n sheet of glass cut to fit a window or door

panel n **1** section of a wall, door, etc , when framed, raised, or sunk **2** vertical strip of material in a dress skirt, etc **3** small group of persons meeting for a specific purpose vt (-ll-) cover with or provide panels for

pang n sharp stabbing pain

panic n fear or terror, often resulting in rash ill-considered behaviour vi,vt (-ck-) feel or cause to feel panic **panic-stricken** adj

panorama n uninterrupted view of a landscape spread over a wide area **panoramic** adj

pansy n **1** garden plant with white yellow, purple, or red flowers **2** sl homosexual

pant vi vt gasp for breath vi long or yearn (for) n gasping noise

panther n leopard, esp a black leopard

pantomime n traditional English Christmas entertainment for children

pantry n room adjoining a kitchen with shelves for storing provisions etc

pants pl n undergarment covering area of the body from the waist to the thighs

papal adj relating to the Pope or his official function

paper n **1** material produced by processing wood, rags, etc , used for books packaging etc **2** examination; essay report **3** newspaper vt cover with paper or wallpaper **paperback** n book in a cheap edition with a paper cover **paperclip** n piece of twisted wire used to fasten single sheets of paper together **paperwork** n routine clerical work

papier-mâché n pulped paper used in making models, masks etc

papist n abusive follower of the Pope and the Roman Catholic faith

paprika n powdered sweet red pepper

par n **1** equality; equal or even footing; average or usual value or level **2** (in golf) standard score **at par** (of shares, etc) at face value **on a par with** equal or equivalent to

parable n story designed to illustrate a moral or philosophical point; allegory

parachute n device that assumes an umbrella shape to slow down the descent of a person jumping from an aircraft. etc vi,vt descend or land by parachute

parade n **1** procession, march **2** show; ostentatious display **3** promenade vi walk or march (through) in or as in a procession vt flaunt; exhibit openly

paradise n heaven; state of bliss

paradox n **1** statement that appears selfcontradictory or absurd **2** person or thing having self-contradictory qualities **paradoxical** adj **paradoxically** adv

paraffin n light oil distilled from petroleum, used for domestic heating and as aircraft fuel

paragraph n subdivision of the printed page containing several sense-connected sentences and indicated by indentation of the first word

parallel adj **1** remaining equidistant to infinity **2** similar, analogous n **1** comparable situation **2** circle marking a degree of latitude vt (-ll-) compare with; correspond to

paralyse vt **1** immobilize or cripple through damage to or destruction of a nerve function **2** transfix; make immobile **paralysis** n, pl **paralyses** (pə'ræliːsiːz) pathological condition of crippling due to loss of muscle control **paralytic** adj,n

paramount adj chief; supreme, most important

paranoia n mental disorder characterized by delusions of grandeur persecution etc **paranoid** adj,n

parapet n low protective wall built along the edge of a balcony bridge etc

paraphernalia n **1** equipment, assorted personal possessions **2** complicated procedure; rigmarole

paraphrase vt express the sense of a passage by using other words n passage thus reworded

parasite n **1** animal or plant depending on another for sustenance **2** person who lives off others **parasitic** adj

paratrooper n member of an army unit trained in parachute jumping

parcel n wrapped object, esp. in paper vt (-ll-) 1 make a parcel of 2 divide (up); apportion

parch vt vi dry up vt make thirsty

parchment n 1 skin of a sheep or goat processed for use as paper 2 old document

pardon vt 1 forgive; excuse 2 waive legal consequences of an offence for (a prisoner) n 1 forgiveness 2 waiver of a penalty

pare vt peel; skin; trim **pare down** make smaller or more compact

parent n 1 mother or father 2 animal or plant that has produced one of its kind **parental** adj **parenthood** n state of being a parent

parenthesis n pl **parentheses** (pə'renθısi:z) either of a pair of characters used to separate or enclose matter in a written or printed text

parish n ecclesiastical subdivision of a county with its own church and clergyman

park n large enclosed area of land laid out for ornamental or recreational purposes vt vi position or leave (a car etc) in a place temporarily vt inf put or leave

parliament n democratic assembly of elected representatives constitutionally empowered to govern by legislation following free discussion **parliamentary** adj

parlour n sitting room or lounge

parochial adj 1 relating to a parish 2 provincial; limited; narrow

parody n 1 imitation of a work or of an author or musician's style with comic or satirical intent 2 poor imitation; travesty vt imitate; mock

parole n 1 early or temporary release from prison on condition of good behaviour 2 period of such release vt grant parole to

parrot n brightly coloured tropical bird capable of imitating human speech

parsley n mildly aromatic herb with curly green leaves

parsnip n white tapering root vegetable

parson n clergyman; minister **parsonage** n residence of a clergyman

part n 1 portion; piece; segment; component 2 role; responsibility; duty 3 actor's role 4 melodic line in choral or orchestral music 5 also **parts** region; area **take part in** become involved in; join in ~vt, vi 1 divide; separate; come, break, or take apart 2 leave or stop seeing one another; keep apart **part with** give up; relinquish ~adv partially; in part **partly** adv **parting** n 1 leave-taking; separa-

tion 2 division; splitting up 3 line between two sections of hair that have been combed in opposite directions **part-time** adj, adv for or during less than normal working time

partake vi (-took; -taken) 1 participate 2 have or receive a share or portion

partial adj 1 incomplete; relating to a part 2 biased; unfair 3 having a liking for; fond of **partially** adv

participate vi take part (in); share (in) **participant** n **participation** n

participle n adjective derived from various verb forms e.g. laughing, loving, given or written

particle n 1 tiniest visible portion; speck 2 microscopic body of matter

particular adj 1 relating to a single person, object, etc 2 extraordinary; notable 3 careful; fastidious; exact **particulars** pl n details; features **particularly** adv

partisan n 1 supporter of a party, cause, etc 2 guerrilla fighter in enemy-occupied territory

partition n 1 division; separation into parts 2 structure erected to separate rooms, areas, etc vt divide into parts; separate

partner n 1 associate; colleague; member of a partnership 2 one of a pair in dancing, cards, etc vt join with someone, esp in a game or dance **partnership** n legal relationship between two or more persons operating a joint business venture

partridge n small European game bird

party n 1 group united by a common belief or purpose, esp political 2 social gathering 3 person or persons involved in a legal action

pass vt, vi 1 go by or through; move ahead or on; proceed 2 move or cause to move 3 exchange or be exchanged 4 undergo (an exam, trial etc) with favourable results 5 elapse or allow to elapse vt 1 hand over; transfer; throw 2 surpass; exceed 3 pronounce; utter 4 adopt; approve (legislation, etc) vi happen; occur; come to an end **pass out** faint ~n 1 favourable examination result without honours 2 ticket; authorization, etc to enter or leave at will; without charge, etc 3 critical position 4 narrow passage between mountains 5 amorous advance **passable** adj 1 able to be crossed; passed, etc 2 mediocre; fairly good **password** n prearranged word used as a code for entry, etc

passage n 1 corridor; channel; route 2 state of transit; voyage; journey 3 section of a book, etc **passenger** n 1 person travelling in but not controlling a motor vehicle boat, etc 2 sl person in a team etc who does not do his share of the work

passion n 1 intense or ardent emotion 2 strong liking or enthusiasm 3 object of such liking **passionate** adj **passionately** adv

passive adj 1 inactive, inert; not participating 2 submissive yielding 3 denoting a sentence or construction in which the logical subject of a verb is the recipient of the action **passively** adv

Passover n Jewish festival commemorating the deliverance of the Hebrews from Egypt

passport n official document issued by a country that identifies the bearer permits his travel abroad and requests safe passage while there

past adj 1 relating to an earlier time, gone by, just over finished 2 previous, former 3 relating to a verb tense used to express an action or condition occurring in the past n 1 period prior to the present past time 2 person s past life career activities etc prep beyond adv by ago **past participle** n verb form functioning as an adjective or used with an auxiliary verb to denote past or completed action, e g *grown, written,* or *spoken*

pasta n food such as spaghetti macaroni etc made from a flour and water dough and boiled

paste n 1 pliable malleable or sticky mess 2 preparation of meat fish etc mashed to a spreadable consistency 3 glue adhesive vt stick fix or cover with paste

pastel n 1 crayon made from colour pigments and gum 2 drawing made with these crayons adj pale light

pasteurize vt partially sterilize (milk beer etc) by heating in order to kill bacteria limit fermentation etc **pasteurization** n

pastime n recreation amusement hobby

pastoral adj 1 of the country rural 2 (of land) used for grazing 3 peaceful idyllic 4 relating to a clergyman or his duties

pastry n 1 flour paste used for pies tarts etc 2 baked foods

pasture n 1 grass etc suitable for grazing cattle 2 meadow field vt put to pasture

pasty[1] ('peisti) adj 1 relating to paste 2 (of a person s appearance) pale unhealthy white skinned

pasty[2] ('pæsti) n small pie filled with meat vegetables, etc

pat[1] vt (-tt-) 1 tap; touch lightly 2 stroke softly; caress 3 flatten by beating gently n light blow; slap; tap

pat[2] adj 1 apt; perfect 2 presumptuous; glib adv 1 exactly; perfectly 2 aptly

patch n 1 piece of material used to repair something 2 irregular or small area piece, plot of land etc 3 protective covering for an eye etc vt repair, mend **patchwork** n 1 patches of material stitched together to form a pattern 2 something made of different parts, pieces etc

pâté n paste or spread made from liver meat fish etc

patent ('pætnt) n 1 government permit granting sole rights for an invention process etc for a set period of time 2 something under such a permit adj ('peitnt) obvious, evident **patent leather** n leather treated to produce a hard lacquered appearance ~vt obtain a patent for

paternal adj 1 fatherly characteristic of a father 2 pertaining to a father or a father s side of a family **paternally** adv **paternity** n 1 fatherhood 2 descent from a father

path n 1 also **pathway** track worn by pedestrians animals etc 2 walk in a park garden etc 3 means procedure course of action

pathetic adj 1 pitiful evoking sadness 2 inf poor of low quality **pathetically** adv

pathology n study of diseases **pathological** adj **pathologist** n

patience n ability to persevere or endure without complaint

patient n person under the care of a doctor dentist etc adj marked by or exhibiting patience **patiently** adv

patio n paved area adjoining a house

patriarch n 1 male head of a family tribe etc 2 elder senior member of a community 3 any of several Old Testament personages regarded as a father of the human race 4 bishop of the Eastern Orthodox Church **patriarchal** adj

patriot n person who loves his country intensely **patriotic** adj **patriotism** n

patrol n 1 regular inspection of an area or building to ensure security orderliness etc 2 person or persons carrying out this inspection

3 military detachment with the duty of reconnaissance *vt,vi* (-ll-) take part in a patrol (of)

patron *n* **1** regular customer of a shop, etc **2** one who offers financial support to a cultural or educational enterprise **patronage** *n* **1** support given by a patron **2** trade given a business by its customers **3** power to bestow political favours, make appointments, etc **patronize** *vt* **1** visit regularly; support **2** behave condescendingly (towards someone) **3** be a benefactor of; sponsor

patter[1] *n* **1** glib inconsequential speech **2** rapidly delivered lines of a salesman, comedian, etc **3** *inf* jargon, expressions used by a clique *vi,vt* talk glibly, rapidly, etc

patter[2] *vi* **1** make a sound like tapping **2** walk with a patter *n* light tapping sound

pattern *n* **1** design; arrangement **2** example; model; plan **3** usual way of doing something *vt* model after a pattern; imitate

pause *n* temporary stop or break *vi* **1** stop temporarily **2** hesitate; linger

pave *vt* **1** cover (a road, etc) with a hard surface **2** prepare; facilitate **pavement** *n* paved path for pedestrians alongside a road

pavilion *n* **1** building on a sportsground housing changing rooms, etc **2** large tent erected temporarily at fairs, weddings, etc **3** summerhouse, light ornamental building or structure

paw *n* foot of certain mammals esp cats and dogs *vi,vt* touch or strike with a paw or leg *vt inf* caress clumsily; grope

pawn[1] *vt* leave (an article) as security in exchange for a loan until repayment is made **pawnbroker** *n* person who lends money on security of personal possessions

pawn[2] *n* **1** chessman of least value whose second and subsequent moves are limited to one square in a forward direction **2** manipulated person

pay *v* (paid) *vt,vi* give (money, etc) to for, or in return for; recompense **2** discharge (a debt, etc) **3** *also* **pay off** be profitable or worthwhile; benefit *vt* **1** bestow; give **2** make (a visit, etc) **pay back** repay (a loan, etc) **2** retaliate against **pay for** suffer or be punished because of **pay off** pay wages of and discharge **2** pay in total ~ *n* **1** money paid for work; salary; wages **2** paid employment **payment** *n* **1** act of paying **2** sum of money paid **3** due reward **payoff** *n* **1** *inf* outcome;

climax of events **2** full payment **payroll** *n* **1** list of employees to be paid and their salaries or wages **2** total of or amount equal to a company's salary or wage expenditure

pea *n* annual climbing plant whose round green seeds are eaten as a vegetable

peace *n* **1** state of amity; absence of war **2** tranquillity; period of rest or quiet **peaceful** *adj* **peacefully** *adv*

peach *n* tree yielding a round juicy yellowish fruit with down-covered skin *n,adj* bright pinkish-yellow

peacock *n* brightly coloured male of a large pheasant with a crested head and a tail which can fan out to display bright blue and green markings **peahen** *f n*

peak *n* **1** any pointed edge or projection **2** top of a mountain; summit **3** projecting brim of a cap **4** sharp increase or the highest point or value reached *vi* reach the highest point or value **peaked** *adj*

peal *n* loud resounding sound, such as bells ringing laughter or thunder *vt,vi* sound with a peal; ring out

peanut *n* edible seed rich in food value and yielding oil

pear *n* tree yielding a sweet juicy fruit whose shape is rounded and tapers towards the stalk

pearl *n* **1** smooth lustrous creamy precious gem formed on the inside of a clam or oyster shell or synthesized **2** highly valued person or thing **pearly** *adj*

peasant *n* **1** agricultural labourer; countryman; rustic **2** *inf* uncultured and unsophisticated person **peasantry** *n*

peat *n* solid partially carbonized and decomposed vegetable matter used as a garden fertilizer and a fuel **peaty** *adj*

pebble *n* small rounded stone *vt vi* pave or cover with pebbles **pebbly** *adj*

peck *vt* **1** strike with the beak or something sharp **2** *inf* kiss quickly on the cheek *n* **1** quick strike or blow **2** *inf* quick kiss on the cheek

peckish *adj inf* hungry

peculiar *adj* strange, odd; unusual **peculiar to** special or specific to **peculiarity** *n* **peculiarly** *adv*

pedal *n* foot lever of a machine, bicycle, piano, etc *vt,vi* (-ll-) **1** operate by using pedals **2** ride a bicycle

peddle *vt,vi* sell from door to door; hawk **pedlar** *n*

pedestal *n* 1 plinth or base supporting an upright object 2 position of superiority or eminence

pedestrian *n* person who goes about on foot *adj* plodding; dull; unimaginative

pedigree *n* 1 record of an animal's ancestors, kept esp for animals of good breeding 2 animal of pedigree stock 3 ancestral line **pedigreed** *adj*

peel *n* rind; outer layer of fruit, vegetables, etc *vt,vi* strip or whittle (off) an outer skin or surface

peep *vi* 1 look quickly or furtively 2 appear briefly or partially *n* quick look or glance

peer[1] *n* 1 member of the nobility 2 person equal in rank or social standing **peerage** *n* 1 nobility as a group 2 position, rank, or title of a peer

peer[2] *vi* 1 look closely or intently (at) 2 appear partially; peep

peevish *adj* irritable; bad-tempered **peevishly** *adv* **peevishness** *n*

peg *n* 1 small piece of wood or metal used for hanging or fastening things 2 pin or stake pushed into the ground, a scoreboard, or other surface 3 pin on a guitar, violin, etc , used for tuning the strings 4 hinged or grooved pin for hanging clothes on a line **take down a peg** teach a lesson; humble **off the peg** (of clothes) ready-made ~*vt* (-gg-) 1 pierce with or insert a peg 2 secure with a peg

pejorative *adj* deprecatory; uncomplimentary

pelican *n* water bird with white plumage and a large beak with a pouch used for catching fish

pellet *n* 1 small ball of something solid 2 piece of shot

pelmet *n* wood or fabric used to conceal a curtain rail

pelt[1] *n* skin or hide of a fur-bearing animal

pelt[2] *vt* assail with a shower of missiles, blows, abuse, etc *n* blow; knock; stroke

pelvis *n* cavity or structure found in the lower part of the trunk in most vertebrates **pelvic** *adj*

pen[1] *n* instrument with a pointed nib used for writing with ink **penfriend** *n* person, often living in a different country with whom one corresponds **penknife** *n* small folding knife usually carried in the pocket

pen[2] *n* small enclosure for farm animals *vt* (-nn-) enclose in a pen; confine

penal *adj* relating to punishment, esp for breaking a law **penal code** *n* body of criminal law **penalize** *vt* 1 punish; subject to penalty 2 handicap; disadvantage 3 award a point or points to an opposing team **penalization** *n* **penalty** *n* 1 punishment; price exacted as a punishment 2 loss; suffering 3 free kick at goal afforded to one football team because of a breach of rules by the other **penance** *n* 1 self-imposed punishment 2 regret; sorrow

pence *n pl of* **penny** (def 3)

penchant ('pɑːnʃɑːn) *n* liking; strong inclination

pencil *n* writing instrument consisting of a thin rod of graphite encased in wood *vt* (-ll-) write or draw with a pencil

pendant *n* 1 hanging ornament, esp on a necklace 2 hanging lamp or chandelier

pending *adj* about to be decided, confirmed, completed, etc *prep* while waiting for

pendulum *n* suspended weight that swings back and forth under the influence of gravity

penetrate *vt,vi* 1 pass into or through 2 enter or permeate *vt* 1 see through 2 unravel; understand *vi* be understood **penetrable** *adj* **penetration** *n*

penguin *n* large flightless black and white aquatic bird of Antarctica

penicillin *n* antibiotic drug produced from a mould and capable of preventing the growth of certain bacteria

peninsula *n* strip of land jutting into the sea **peninsular** *adj*

penis *n* male organ of copulation

penitent *adj* repentant, remorseful *n* penitent person **penitence** *n* **penitently** *adv*

penniless *adj* having no money; very poor; destitute

penny *n* 1 *also* **new penny** bronze coin worth one-hundredth of a pound sterling 2 former bronze coin worth one-twelfth of a shilling 3 *pl* **pence** unit of currency of such a value **not worth a penny** worthless **spend a penny** *inf* urinate

pension *n* periodical payment by state or employer to the retired, disabled, widowed, etc *vt* grant a pension to **pensioner** *n* person receiving a pension

pensive adj engaged in serious or sad thought **pensively** adv

pentagon n five-sided figure **pentagonal** adj

penthouse n subsidiary structure attached to the main part of a building, often a small house or flat on the roof

penury n poverty; destitution

people pl n 1 human beings in general 2 racial group 3 one's family vt populate; fill as with people

pepper n 1 pungent condiment made from the dried berries of a pepper plant 2 red or green slightly pungent fruit of other types of pepper plant vt flavour with pepper **peppercorn** n dried berry of the pepper plant **peppermill** n instrument for grinding peppercorns **peppermint** n 1 aromatic and pungent herb of the mint family 2 lozenge flavoured with oil from this mint

per prep 1 for each 2 by means of

perambulator n formal pram

perceive vt 1 see; discern 2 be or become aware of 3 understand **perceivable** adj

per cent adv in each hundred

percentage n 1 number forming a proportion in each hundred 2 interest paid per hundred

perception n 1 process or power of becoming aware of something 2 insight; discernment **perceptible** adj noticeable; discernible **perceptive** adj 1 able or quick to notice 2 intelligent **perceptively** adv

perch[1] n, pl **perch** edible spiny-finned freshwater fish

perch[2] n 1 pole, bar, or branch for birds to roost or sit on 2 secure seat in a high position vi, vt sit or place on a perch

percolate vi, vi filter or trickle (through) vi gradually become known **percolator** n apparatus for percolating water through coffee grounds

percussion n 1 impact; collision 2 production of noise by striking or tapping 3 musical instruments, such as the drum, that are struck to produce a note

perennial adj 1 continuing through the year or from year to year 2 (of plants) living more than two years 3 perpetual **perennially** adv

perfect adj ('pɜ:fikt) faultless; complete; functioning correctly; exact vt (pə'fekt) make perfect or complete; finish **perfection** n **perfectly** adv

perforate vt vi make a hole or holes through,

often in a line for easy separation **perforation** n

perform vt, vi 1 do; carry out; complete 2 act **performer** n **performance** n 1 act of performing; carrying out of something 2 piece of work; exhibition or entertainment 3 manner or achievement in working

perfume n 1 sweet-smelling substance applied to the body 2 pleasant odour; fragrance vt impart fragrance to

perhaps adv maybe; possibly

peril n danger; risk **perilous** adj **perilously** adv

perimeter n circumference; boundary; length of outline of a plane figure

period n 1 stretch of time; phase; era 2 interval between recurrent phases 3 full stop 4 inf menstruation **periodic** adj **periodical** adj periodic; issued or occurring at roughly regular intervals n magazine published at stated intervals of more than one day **periodically** adv

peripheral adj 1 of or on the circumference, boundary, or outskirts 2 of less than central importance **periphery** n

periscope n tube with mirrors for viewing objects above eye level

perish vt destroy; ruin; cause to decay vi 1 die; decay; be ruined or destroyed 2 distress with hunger and cold **perishable** adj

perjure vt **perjure oneself** lie deliberately under oath **perjurer** n **perjury** n

perk v **perk up** 1 look up jauntily 2 make (oneself) smarter 3 recover spirits or energy n inf legitimate extra gain attached to a job, not included in wages

permanent adj lasting or intended to last indefinitely n also inf **perm** artificially induced and long-lasting waving of the hair **permanently** adv

permeate vt, vi spread through, pervade, or be pervaded **permeation** n

permission n act of permitting; allowing; consent **permissible** adj **permissive** adj granting permission or liberty; lenient; tolerant **permissively** adv **permissiveness** n

permit vt, vi (pə'mit) (-tt-) grant leave; allow; concede; make possible n ('pɜ:mit) written permission; warrant; licence

permutation n 1 changing of the order of a set of objects 2 each arrangement of these objects

peroxide n 1 oxide containing more oxygen than normal oxide 2 inf hydrogen peroxide, an antiseptic and bleach

perpendicular adj upright; vertical; at right angles (to) n vertical position; perpendicular line **perpendicularly** adv

perpetual adj 1 never ceasing; not temporary 2 continuously blooming through the growing season 3 applicable or valid for ever or for an indefinite time **perpetually** adv **perpetuate** vt 1 make perpetual 2 prolong indefinitely 3 preserve from extinction or oblivion **perpetuity** n quality or condition of lasting indefinitely

perplex vt confuse; present difficulties or intricacies to bewilder; tease with suspense or doubt **perplexity** n

persecute vt 1 harass; treat cruelly; persistently attack **persecution** n

persevere vi continue in spite of obstacles; keep on striving **perseverance** n

persist vi 1 continue firmly or obstinately, esp against opposition 2 continue to exist; remain **persistence** n **persistent** adj **persistently** adv

person n 1 human being 2 body of a person **in person** physically present or active **personal** adj 1 one's own; individual; of private concern 2 relating to bodily appearance 3 offensive to an individual; insulting **personally** adv **personality** n 1 state of having an identity 2 celebrity 3 total intellectual, emotional, or physical qualities of an individual, esp as presented to others **personify** vt 1 regard as a person 2 embody; symbolize in human form **personification** n

personnel n persons engaged together in some work; work force

perspective n 1 method of portraying relative size and distance of objects on a plane surface 2 relative importance and true relationship of facts, ideas, etc

perspex n tough transparent unsplinterable plastic material

perspire vi,vt exude moisture through skin pores; sweat **perspiration** n

persuade vt induce by argument; cause to believe; convince **persuasion** n **persuasive** adj **persuasively** adv

pert adj 1 forward; saucy; cheeky 2 open; brisk; flourishing **pertly** adv

pertain vi 1 belong as part of; be connected

with 2 have reference or relevance to 3 be suitable for or appropriate to **pertinent** adj **pertinently** adv

perturb vt disturb greatly; cause alarm or anxiety to **perturbation** n

pervade vt penetrate; diffuse through the whole of; permeate **pervasion** n **pervasive** adj

perverse adj obstinately turning aside from right or truth; unreasonably contradictory **perversely** adv **perversion** n **pervert** vt,vi (pə'və:t) turn from proper use or sense; corrupt or be corrupted n ('pə:və:t) one who is thought to deviate in sexual desires or practice **perversion** n

peseta n monetary unit of Spain

peso n monetary unit of Argentina, Mexico, the Philippines, and various other countries

pessimism n tendency to look on the worst side of things; despondency **pessimist** n **pessimistic** adj

pest n 1 troublesome or destructive person, etc 2 insect, fungus, etc , destructive of cultivated plants **pesticide** n chemical for destroying pests

pester vt cause slight but repeated annoyance to

pet[1] n 1 tame animal kept as a companion, etc 2 favourite; dearly loved and pampered person, esp a child; darling v (-tt-) vt treat as a pet; pamper; fondle vi indulge in amorous caressing

pet[2] n childish fit of aggrieved sulkiness; huff vi (-tt-) be peevish; sulk

petal n leaflike part, sometimes brightly coloured, of a flower

peter v **peter out** gradually diminish to nothing; fade away

petition n 1 humble or solemn entreaty 2 formal request to an authority often signed by a number of persons vt,vi make or receive a humble or formal request

petrify vt,vi 1 turn into or become like stone, fossilize 2 fix in amazement or horror

petrol n inflammable liquid from refined petroleum, used esp as fuel in motor-vehicle engines

petroleum n dark thick oily mixture of hydrocarbons, other organic compounds, etc , found in rock deposits

petticoat n woman s underskirt

petty adj 1 unimportant; trivial; insignificant 2 contemptible, spiteful, or mean over small matters **petty cash** n cash fund in an office for small items of receipt or expenditure **petty officer** n noncommissioned naval officer **pettiness** n

petulant adj peevishly impatient, irritated, or capricious **petulance** n **petulantly** adv

pew n enclosed compartment or fixed bench with a back and sides, as in a church

pewter n 1 alloy of tin and lead and sometimes other metals 2 vessel, plate, or utensil made of pewter

pfennig n, pl **pfennigs** or **pfennige** ('pfeniɡə) West German copper coin equal to one hundredth of a mark

phallus n 1 male sexual organ; penis 2 representation of the penis **phallic** adj

phantom n 1 supernatural apparition; ghost; immaterial form 2 visual illusion

pharmacy n 1 art or practice of preparing and dispensing medicines 2 chemist's dispensary **pharmacist** n **pharmaceutical** adj relating to medical drugs

pharynx n cavity behind nose and mouth forming the upper part of the gullet and the opening into the larynx

phase n 1 transitory stage in a cycle 2 appearance of a moon or planet at a particular stage of its orbit 3 aspect or appearance of anything at any stage vt separate into stages of activity or development **phase out** bring to terminal stage; extinguish gradually; discontinue

pheasant n 1 long-tailed game bird, brightly coloured in the male 2 flesh of this bird as food

phenomenon n pl **phenomena** (fə'nominə) 1 anything perceived by the senses; observed event 2 anything striking or exceptional **phenomenal** adj of or like a phenomenon; extraordinary; exceptional; remarkable **phenomenally** adv

philanthropy n benevolence; active generosity in social action; love of mankind **philanthropic** adj **philanthropist** n

philately n study and collection of postage and revenue stamps **philatelist** n

philosophy n 1 study of the ultimate nature of existence 2 any specified system of thought in this 3 general mental and moral outlook on life; reasoning **philosopher** n **philosophical** adj 1 relating to philosophy or philoso-

phers 2 calmly reasonable; wise 3 stoical; bearing misfortune well

phlegm (flem) n 1 thick slimy fluid secreted in the throat and chest and discharged by coughing 2 apathy; sluggish indifference **phlegmatic** (fleg'mætik) adj 1 not easily excited or perturbed; placid 2 sluggish; apathetic; stolid **phlegmatically** adv

phobia n fear, often irrational; dread; dislike

phoenix n bird fabled to burn itself to death every 500 years and be reincarnated from its own ashes

phone n, vt, vi short for **telephone.**

phonetic adj relating to the sounds of spoken language **phonetically** adv **phonetics** n study of speech sounds

phoney adj counterfeit; unreal; insincere

phosphate n chemical salt containing phosphorus, used in fertilizers

phosphorescent adj emitting a faint light, similar to fluorescence, esp after bombardment by radiation **phosphorescence** n

phosphorus n nonmetallic chemical element having an unreactive red form and a toxic inflammable phosphorescent white form, used in matches

photo n short for **photograph.**

photocopy vt reproduce an exact copy of by a photographic process n copy produced in this way

photogenic adj suitable for and making a pleasing photograph

photograph n image of something produced by the action of light on chemically sensitized surfaces vt make a photographic image of **photographer** n **photography** n art or process of producing photographs **photographical** adj

phrase n 1 group of words forming a subdivision of a sentence 2 idiomatic expression vt choose fitting words to express **phrasebook** n collection of idioms and commonly used phrases of a language

physical adj 1 pertaining to the natural world of matter and energy or its study 2 relating to the body **physically** adv **physical education** n promotion of bodily fitness by exercising the body

physician n doctor; person legally qualified to treat disease by medicines but not surgery

physics n study of the properties of matter and energy **physicist** n

physiology n study of physical processes in living beings **physiological** adj **physiologist** n

physiotherapy n treatment of disease, weakness, or disability by exercise, massage, heat, etc **physiotherapist** n

physique n bodily appearance and constitution

pi n ratio of the circumference of a circle to its diameter, equal to about 3 142

piano n keyboard instrument with strings struck by hammers **pianist** n

piccolo n small high-pitched woodwind instrument of the flute family

pick[1] vt,vi 1 choose; select carefully 2 gather (fruit, etc) vt 1 poke at with the fingers 2 provoke 3 steal from (a pocket, etc) **pick and choose** select with excessive care **pick at** nibble at food, esp due to loss of appetite **pick on** select, esp to blame or be unpleasant to **pick out 1** select 2 recognize; distinguish; make obvious **pick up 1** lift or gather in the hands 2 improve 3 take on (passengers, etc) 4 learn gradually and casually 5 inf meet casually and get acquainted 6 inf arrest ~n 1 choice; selection 2 best choice **pickpocket** n one who steals from others' pockets **pick-up** n 1 device for converting vibrations, as of a record-player stylus, into electric current 2 recovery 3 act of picking up or one picked up

pick[2] n 1 also **pickaxe** tool having a long cross-bar with sharp or pointed ends, used for breaking up stone, etc 2 any sharp or pointed instrument for picking

picket n 1 striker or group of strikers outside their workplace to dissuade other workers from working 2 vigil in a public place by a person or group expressing political or social protest vt,vi surround with or act as a picket

pickle n 1 brine or vinegar solution in which food is preserved 2 vegetable so preserved 3 inf plight vt preserve in pickle **pickled** adj sl drunk

picnic vi (picnicking; picnicked) take a casual meal outdoors for pleasure n 1 meal so eaten 2 outing for such a purpose

pictorial adj 1 having or expressed by pictures 2 relating to painting or drawing 3 magazine comprising mainly pictures **pictorially** adv

picture n 1 two-dimensional arrangement of lines and colours intended to have aesthetic value 2 embodiment; representation; mental image 3 impressive sight 4 film shown at a cinema 5 vivid verbal description **in the picture** well-informed; in possession of the facts **the pictures** pl n cinema ~vt depict or represent in a picture the mind, or in words

picturesque adj suitable for a picture graphic; quaint

pidgin n trade language or jargon having elements from two or more languages

pie n dish of meat, fish, vegetables, or fruit baked with a pastry covering **easy as pie** very easy

piece n 1 part or item of a whole; bit; portion 2 example; specimen 3 musical, artistic, or literary composition 4 small object, as used in board games **go to pieces 1** lose one's self-control 2 disintegrate **piecemeal** adv bit by bit; in pieces **piecework** n work paid according to the amount done rather than the time taken v **piece together** assemble; fit together; mend

pier n 1 jetty; landing stage; breakwater 2 column supporting an arch or bridge 3 load-bearing brickwork between windows or doors

pierce vt 1 penetrate; make a hole in; enter or force a way into 2 be seen, heard, or felt through 3 afflict; touch or move deeply

piety n willing and devout observance of religious duties; devotion to God

pig n 1 domesticated mammal with thick bristly skin and a long snout, bred for its meat 2 coarse, dirty, or greedy person **pig in a poke** something bought without examination **pigheaded** adj stupidly stubborn; obstinate **pigheadedly** adv **pig-iron** n iron in rough bars as first extracted from its ore **piglet** n young pig **pigsty** n 1 pen in which pigs are kept 2 very untidy or dirty house or room **pigtail** n hair twisted into a bunch to form a plait or hang loose

pigeon n widely distributed bird of the dove family **pigeonhole** n 1 small compartment for storing or classifying papers 2 compartment of the mind 3 entrance to a dovecote or pigeon's nest vt 1 put in a pigeonhole 2 put aside; defer considering 3 classify methodically

piggyback n ride astride someone's back or shoulders adv on someone's back or shoulders

pigment n paint; any colouring matter; substance giving colour to living tissue **pigmentation** n coloration by pigments

pike n, pl **pike** large voracious freshwater fish with a pointed snout

pilchard n small food fish, similar to the herring

pile¹ n 1 heap of objects 2 inf large sum or amount of money, work, etc vt,vi also **pile up.** heap up; collect into a mound vi move quickly and haphazardly as in a group **pile-up** n inf accumulation of things, esp of cars as a result of a multiple crash, traffic jam, etc

pile² n post driven into the ground to support a structure **piledriver** n 1 machine for driving piles into the ground 2 (in games) powerful stroke; kick

pile³ n 1 fine soft hair; down 2 raised yarn on cloth such as velvet or towelling

pilfer vt,vi steal petty articles in small quantities

pilgrim n 1 person journeying to a shrine for religious reasons 2 wanderer **pilgrimage** n journey to a sacred or revered place **Pilgrim Fathers** pl n original settlers of New England

pill n oral medicine formed into or contained in a small ball, capsule, etc **bitter pill** something disagreeable that has to be accepted **the pill** contraceptive pill

pillar n 1 column supporting a structure or standing alone as a monument 2 person who is a prominent supporter **pillar-box** n short hollow red pillar in which letters are posted; letter box

pillion n seat for a second person on a horse or motorcycle behind the rider or driver adv on a pillion

pillow n soft cushion to support a sleeper's head; padded support vt rest one's head; serve as a pillow for **pillowcase** n washable cover for a pillow

pilot n 1 person qualified to conduct ships in harbours, channels, etc 2 person qualified to operate flying controls of an aircraft 3 person steering a ship vt steer; navigate; guide **pilot scheme** preliminary, experimental, or trial approach or procedure

pimento n red pepper used for stuffing olives, in salads, and as a vegetable

pimple n small swelling on the skin **pimply** adj

pin n 1 short stiff pointed piece of wire with a rounded or flat head 2 anything resembling a pin in form or function 3 brooch; badge vt (-nn-) 1 fasten, attach, or secure by a pin 2

hold or fix in position; immobilize **pin down** 1 force to keep a promise, agreement, etc 2 define exactly **pin on** attribute to; blame **pinpoint** n 1 point of a pin 2 anything very tiny or minute vt locate; define very exactly **pinstripes** n repeated narrow stripes in a material pattern, etc **pin-up** n 1 picture of a nude or seminude girl pinned up on wall 2 one whose picture is thus displayed

pinafore n apron **pinafore dress** n sleeveless dress worn over a jumper, etc

pincers pl n 1 gripping tool with jaws and handles on a pivot 2 pair of grasping clawlike parts, as in a crab **pincer movement** n attack by two converging forces

pinch vt,vi 1 squeeze sharply between finger and thumb or be squeezed between two hard objects 2 inconvenience or be inconvenienced by a lack (of something) vt 1 sl steal 2 sl arrest n 1 squeeze 2 emergency 3 small amount **at a pinch** if absolutely necessary

pine¹ n coniferous tree with evergreen needle-shaped leaves

pine² vi 1 become feeble from mental or physical suffering 2 languish with longing; yearn (for)

pineapple n tropical plant yielding a large edible fruit having yellow flesh and a tuft of leaves on top

Ping-Pong n Tdmk table-tennis

pinion n small wheel with teeth engaging with a larger wheel or rack, one imparting motion to the other

pink adj,n pale red; light rose n garden plant resembling the carnation

pinnacle n 1 small ornamental turret or spire 2 slender mountain peak 3 highest point or degree vt 1 set on a pinnacle 2 adorn with pinnacles

pint n 1 measure of liquid capacity equal to an eighth of a gallon (0 57 litre) 2 inf this amount of beer

pioneer n one of the first to attempt, explore, research, or colonize; one who takes the lead vt,vi be or act as a pioneer

pious adj devout; faithful in religious duties **piously** adv

pip¹ n small seed of fleshy fruits

pip² n shrill note repeated as a signal in broadcasting or telephoning

pip³ n spot on a playing card, domino, or die

pipe n 1 tube for conveying water, etc 2 vessel

for smoking loose tobacco **3** simple wind instrument **4** note of a bird; shrill voice **pipes** pl n bagpipes ~vt **1** convey by pipe **2** provide pipes or piping for **3** play on a pipe **pipe down** make less noise **pipe up** begin to speak unexpectedly **pipedream** n wishful daydream; futile hope or plan **pipeline** n **1** long line of pipes conveying water or oil **2** direct communication line **in the pipeline** on the way

piquant adj **1** pleasantly pungent; tasty **2** rousing keen interest **piquancy** n

pique n ill-feeling; resentment; anger vt **1** annoy; offend **2** arouse (interest, etc)

pirate n **1** one who attempts robbery or unlawful capture of ships at sea **2** privately owned radio transmitter or operator without a licence **3** one who infringes copyright or trading rights vt infringe copyright or trading laws **piracy** n

pirouette n act of spinning on tiptoe, esp in dancing vi spin thus

Pisces n twelfth sign of the zodiac, represented by the Fishes

pistol n small hand gun

piston n short cylinder moving to and fro in a cylindrical tube as part of an engine or pump

pit n **1** hole; sunken area; depression **2** mine shaft **3** sunken area for an orchestra in front of a stage **4** area near a race track in which cars are serviced or refuelled **pit of the stomach** hollow below the breastbone ~vt, vi (-tt-) make a hole in or become marked with hollows **pit against** set to fight against; match against **pitfall** n hidden danger or unexpected difficulty

pitch[1] vt, vi **1** throw; fling **2** set up (camp); erect (a tent) vt **1** set the slope or level of **2** give a particular slant or character to **3** sing or play (a note, etc) accurately vi toss up and down, as by waves n **1** slope; gradient **2** playing field **3** frequency of a musical note **4** inf persuasive sales talk **pitchfork** n long-handled two-pronged fork for pitching hay vt **1** lift and throw with a pitchfork **2** assign work or responsibility to hastily or roughly

pitch[2] n black viscous tarry liquid that sets hard on cooling and is used for roads, paths, etc vt apply pitch to

piteous adj arousing pity; pathetic

pith n **1** core of spongy tissue in plant stems, feathers, etc **2** white fibre inside the rind of

oranges, lemons etc **3** essence; concentrated meaning; importance **4** physical strength; mastery **pithy** adj

pittance n meagre allowance or portion

pituitary gland n small gland in the brain that controls or influences hormone action

pity n **1** compassion for suffering and the misfortunes of others; mercy **2** cause of disappointment or regret vt feel pity for **pitiful** adj **1** arousing pity; pathetic; miserable **2** contemptible **pitifully** adv **pitiless** adj merciless; cruel

pivot n **1** pin or fixed point on which something turns **2** person or thing on which all depends vt, vi mount or turn on a pivot vi depend on

pizza n Italian dish consisting of a breadlike base with a topping of tomato sauce, cheese, and garnishes

placard n public notice, written or printed display vt **1** publicize by a placard **2** fix a placard to

placate vt appease the hostility or resentment of

place n **1** geographical point; location; area **2** position; state; rank **3** space; room; seat **4** house; residence **5** duty; right **6** job; appointment **7** relative position in a race **go places** inf become successful **out of place** unsuitable; inappropriate **in place of** instead of **take place** occur; happen ~vt **1** put or set in a particular or suitable position or order **2** identify by some past link **3** make; put **4** appoint **place with** put under the care of

placenta n mass of tissue within the womb by which a connection is made between the foetus and the mother and which is discharged after birth **placental** adj

placid adj calm; unruffled **placidly** adv

plagiarize vt, vi steal from writings or ideas of another and use as one's own **plagiarism** n **plagiarist** n

plague n **1** deadly highly infectious epidemic disease **2** calamity; curse **3** troublesome or annoying person or thing vt be a persistent trouble to; pester

plaice n edible flatfish having a brown body marked with orange spots

plaid n cloth with a tartan or a chequered pattern

plain n **1** tract of level land; open country **2** simple knitting stitch adj **1** level; flat; even **2** clear; obvious **3** simple; not ornate, decorated, or embellished **4** neither beautiful nor ugly **5** outspoken; straightforward *adv also* **plainly** distinctly; bluntly; frankly **plain-clothes** *adj* (of police, etc) wearing ordinary clothes as opposed to a uniform **plain sailing** *n* smooth and unhindered progress

plaintive *adj* mournful; lamenting; complaining **plaintively** *adv*

plait *n* braid in which three or more strands or bunches of hair, etc are passed over one another in turn *vt* braid; intertwine

plan *n* **1** scheme; project; method **2** map of an area **3** diagram of a structure *vt,vi* (-nn-) **1** make a plan of or for; devise methods of doing **2** regulate by a central authority

plane¹ *n* **1** level or even surface **2** level of existence or standard of performance, etc **3** short for **aeroplane**. *adj* level; flat *vi* skim over a water surface

plane² *n* tool for levelling or smoothing surfaces, cutting grooves, etc *vt* **1** use a plane on **2** shave off by means of a plane

planet *n* nonluminous celestial body that orbits around a star, esp the nine bodies, including earth, that orbit around the sun **planetary** *adj*

plank *n* long broad length of cut timber *vt* cover or supply with planks

plankton *n* small animals and plants that inhabit the surface of a body of water and on which many larger animals feed

plant *n* **1** living organism that synthesizes its own food from inorganic substances and lacks sense organs and powers of locomotion **2** any herbaceous plant, as distinct from a tree or shrub **3** factory; manufacturing works **4** *inf* person or thing introduced into a group, place etc , to throw guilt on innocent people *vt* **1** put in the ground to grow **2** establish; fix **plantation** *n* large estate, esp in tropical countries where crops are grown **planter** *n* **1** owner or supervisor of a plantation **2** decorative holder for a house plant

plaque *n* **1** ornamental plate or disc intended to be mounted or hung for display **2** hard white deposit that forms around the teeth

plasma *n* clear yellowish fluid part of blood or lymph in which cells are suspended

plaster *n* **1** mixture of sand lime and water that is applied to walls and ceilings to make them smooth **2** self-adhesive bandage for minor wounds *vt* cover or coat with or as if

with plaster **plaster of Paris** *n* hard refined plaster suitable for use in sculptures, casts etc

plastic *n* widely used synthetic material that can be moulded into a desired shape when soft *adj* **1** made of plastic **2** pliable; elastic **3** easily influenced **plastic surgery** *n* surgery concerned with the repair sometimes cosmetic of external tissue

Plasticine *n Tdmk* soft modelling material

plate *n* **1** shallow dish or receptacle **2** thin coating of metal, esp gold or silver **3** item or items coated with gold or silver **4** illustration or print in a book **5** thin sheet, esp of glass *vt* coat with a thin layer of metal **platelayer** *n* person who lays and maintains railway tracks

plateau *n* **1** large level area of high land **2** long stable period during development

platform *n* **1** raised area, as for a speaker at a meeting **2** waiting area at a railway station, etc **3** statement of policy or plan of a political party, etc

platinum *n* pliable silvery precious metal that is very durable and much used, esp in jewellery

platonic *adj* without physical desires

platter *n* large dish or plate, used esp for serving food

plausible *adj* reasonable, likely, or believable **plausibility** *n* **plausibly** *adv*

play *vt,vi* **1** occupy or amuse oneself (in a game, sport, etc) **2** fill a particular role in a team game **3** act as; imitate **4** operate a musical instrument, radio, record player, etc , or be operated *vt* **1** compete with **2** act the part of **3** give a dramatic performance of *n* **1** drama, dramatic production **2** games, diversions, etc **3** manner or way of playing **4** fun; light-heartedness **5** liberty of action; scope **playable** *adj* **player** *n* **playboy** *n* man who devotes himself to the pursuit of irresponsible pleasures **playground** *n* outdoor area for children to play in **playgroup** *n* nursery group for very young children **playhouse** *n* **1** theatre for live drama **2** toy house for children **playing card** *n* one of a pack of fifty-two cards having a set value in one of the four suits into which the cards are divided **playing field** *n* field used for playing team games **playmate** *n* companion in play, esp for children **playschool** *n* playgroup **playwright** *n* writer of plays; dramatist

plea n 1 sincere claim or appeal 2 something pleaded on behalf of a defendant in a legal trial

plead vt, vi 1 appeal (to); beseech; implore 2 offer an argument (for) vt 1 give as an excuse or justification 2 declare oneself as being (guilty or not guilty) in a court of law

pleasant adj pleasing; agreeable; enjoyable **pleasantly** adv **please** vt, vi gratify or delight (someone) adv used in making polite requests, asking favours, etc **pleasure** n 1 delight; happiness; enjoyment 2 something giving these things

pleat n permanent fold or repeated crease in a fabric, esp in skirts or dresses vt make pleats in

plectrum n, pl **plectrums** or **plectra** ('plektrə) implement or pick for plucking a musical string

pledge n 1 solemn oath or promise 2 guarantee; security 3 token; symbol vt 1 promise solemnly 2 give as a pledge vt bind or secure by a pledge

plenty n 1 enough; adequate supply 2 abundance; profusion; large number adj enough; very many **plentiful** adj

pliable adj 1 flexible; easily bent 2 compliant; yielding; manageable

plight n dilemma; difficult situation

plimsoll n rubber-soled canvas shoe worn for sport

plod v (-dd-) vt, vi walk along in a slow dogged manner vi work slowly and steadily n act or sound of plodding

plonk n inf cheap wine

plop n sound made by dropping an object into water v (-pp-) vt, vi drop or make fall with a plop vi make a plop

plot[1] n 1 secret plan; outline; scheme 2 story of a play, novel, etc v (-tt-) vt, vi plan or conspire secretly vt chart (a course) or make a map of

plot[2] n small patch of ground

plough n device for turning over soil when planting crops vt, vi till or make a furrow with a plough

pluck vt 1 pick off (feathers, flowers, etc) from 2 draw sound from (the strings) of (a musical instrument) by pulling them 3 pull; tug n courage **plucky** adj brave; courageous

plug n 1 piece of material used to fill a hole or stop up a gap 2 device that connects an electrical appliance to an electricity supply 3 inf unscheduled advertisement for or mention of a product vt (-gg-) 1 attach to an electricity supply by means of a plug 2 stop up or fill 3 inf mention favourably or advertise

plum n small tree bearing purple or green fruit with an oval stone adj inf comfortable; pleasant

plumage n feathers on a bird

plumb n lump of heavy material, esp when attached to a length of string (**plumbline**) and used to ensure that a wall, etc, is vertical vt measure the depth of (the sea, etc) with or as if with a plumb

plumber n person who installs and repairs water pipes, baths, sinks, etc **plumbing** n 1 profession of a plumber 2 pipes and other appliances connected with the supply of water to a building

plume n feather, esp a long ornamental one

plump[1] adj fleshy; chubby; fat vt, vi make or become plump

plump[2] vi fall or drop heavily or noisily **plump for** choose; select

plunder vt, vi steal (from) by force; rob n 1 anything stolen or taken by force; loot 2 act of plundering

plunge vt, vi 1 thrust or be thrust, esp into a liquid 2 bring or be brought suddenly (into a certain condition) 3 rush madly in a certain direction 4 throw oneself enthusiastically (into) n 1 act of plunging 2 leap; mad dash

plural adj consisting of or relating to more than one n 1 linguistic number category in which plural nouns are placed 2 plural form of a noun

plus prep added to; with adv or more n also **plus sign** sign indicating addition

plush adj also **plushy** very comfortable and expensive; luxurious

Pluto n ninth and furthest known planet from the sun

ply[1] vt 1 travel regularly around (an area) selling (goods, etc) 2 supply continuously 3 work at; engage in

ply[2] n layer of material, esp wood, or a strand of yarn **plywood** n material consisting of layers or strips of wood glued together

pneumatic adj relating to or operated by air, esp compressed air

pneumonia n disease marked by inflammation of the lungs, usually caused by bacteria or a virus

poach¹ *vi,vt* **1** catch or take (game, fish, etc)
illegally **2** trespass; encroach **3** steal; pinch
poacher *n*

poach² *vt* cook in gently boiling liquid

pocket *n* **1** small pouch or bag, esp one sewn
into a garment **2** cavity; hollow **3** isolated
area of group of people **out of pocket**
having made a financial loss ~*vt* steal;
appropriate **pocket money** *n* small weekly
sum of money given by parents to a child

pod *n* fruit of the pea, bean, and related plants

poem *n* composition usually written in regular
rhythmic lines and often employing rhyme,
metaphor, etc , to stimulate the imagination
poetic *adj* **poet** *n* writer of poems **poetess**
n f **poetry** *n* **1** verse **2** art or work of a poet
3 poetic qualities

point *n* **1** sharp tapering end **2** any projection,
esp a tapering one, such as a piece of land
jutting out into the sea **3** mark or dot made
by something with a sharp point **4** punctuation
mark or accent used in writing, esp a full
stop **5** something that has a position but no
spatial extent **6** definite place on a scale;
specific moment **7** stage in a course of action,
procedure, etc , esp an important or decisive
stage **8** element or part of something, esp
the most essential part, as of a topic, joke, etc
9 reason; aim; meaning; significance **10** unit
of counting used in scoring games. mark **on
the point of** about to commit the act of
make a point of insist on as being important
point of view outlook; personal position or
attitude **stretch a point** be prepared to make
an exception to one's usual practice **to/off
the point** relevant/irrelevant **point-blank** at
a range so close that one cannot miss;
directly ~*vt,vi* direct or aim (one's finger,
etc) at *vt also* **point out 1** indicate the
position of **2** turn someone's attention to *vi*
indicate or face in the direction of **pointed**
adj **1** having a point **2** referring obviously to
someone or something, emphatic; incisive
pointer *n* **1** something used for pointing **2**
indicator on a dial **3** hint; suggestion **4** breed
of hunting dog **pointless** *adj* lacking
relevance, meaning, significance, etc

poise *n* **1** calmness of manner; composure **2**
balance; stability *vt,vi* **1** balance or be balanced **2** hold a position. esp in mid-air;
hover

poison *n* substance that causes illness or death

because of its chemical properties *vt* **1** kill or
injure by administering poison **2** put poison
into (food, water, etc) **poisonous** *adj*

poke *vt,vi* **1** probe; prod; pierce **2** push or
thrust *n* prod; push; thrust

poker¹ *n* metal rod used for stirring the embers
of a fire

poker² *n* gambling card game

pole¹ *n* long usually slender cylindrical rod used
for support, measurement, propulsion, etc
pole-vault *n* athletic event in which a competitor propels himself over a high bar by
means of a pole *vt,vi* perform the pole-vault
over a barrier

pole² *n* **1** either of the two extreme ends of the
axis of a planet or other globe **2** two ends of a
magnet, terminals of an electric battery, etc
Pole Star star almost directly over the earth's
North Pole **polar** *adj* **polarize** *vt,vi* form
into two or more distinct opposing groups

polemic *n* controversial dispute or argument or
an article, essay, etc , containing this *adj also*
polemical of or concerning a polemic

police *n* **1** authority in a country responsible for
keeping order, preventing crime, and enforc-
ing laws **2** members of this authority *vt*
control or keep law and order in **policeman**
n, pl **-men** police officer **police station** *n*
headquarters of a local branch of the police

policy¹ *n* **1** course or line of action, esp one
adapted by a government in running state
affairs **2** wise or sensible way of doing things

policy² *n* document stating the details of a
contract between an individual and an
insurance company

polio *n also* **poliomyelitis** acute infectious
disease, usually of children, that can paralyse
various muscle groups

polish *vt,vi* put a shine on something *vt*
improve (one's language, manners, etc) *n* **1**
substance applied to something to make it
smooth or shiny **2** shine or smoothness
resulting from polishing **3** act of polishing **4**
elegance or superior quality, as of a person's
behaviour

polite *adj* **1** demonstrating good manners and
good behaviour; courteous **2** refined and
elegant **politely** *adv* **politeness** *n*

politic *adj* **1** wise **2** clever; cunning

political *adj* **1** of or connected with politics or a
party in politics **2** of or relating to a state
government or its administration **politically**

adv **politician** *n* person concerned with politics, esp one who holds a public office in a government **politics** *n* **1** *s* science or profession concerned with government **2** *pl* political affairs, principles, or ideas

polka *n* **1** lively Bohemian dance **2** music composed for this dance *vi* dance a polka

poll *n* **1** mass vote, as at an election **2** number of votes cast **3** list of people drawn up for voting or taxation purposes **4** *also* **opinion poll** process in which a selection of people are interviewed as a means of assessing public opinion *vt* **1** receive votes in an election **2** interview to test public opinion

pollen *n* dustlike material produced by flowering plants that serves as a fertilizing agent **pollinate** *vt* transfer pollen to (a plant) for purposes of fertilization **pollination** *n*

pollute *vt* **1** make foul or poisonous; contaminate **2** corrupt the morals of **pollutant** *n* something that pollutes **pollution** *n*

polygamy *n* practice of marrying or the situation of being married to more than one woman at a time **polygamist** *n* **polygamous** *adj*

polygon *n* geometric figure having three or more sides

polymer *n* substance containing long chains of atoms joined together, as in cellulose, plastics, synthetic fibres, etc

polyp *n* **1** type of individual of such organisms as corals or sea anemones, having tentacles and a mouth **2** *also* **polyps** small pathological growth, as in the nose

polytechnic *n* type of college of higher education originally set up to teach scientific subjects but now also teaching social sciences

polythene *n* widely used type of plastic *adj* made of polythene

pomegranate *n* large round usually red fruit with a tough rind and inner parts divided into chambers containing edible seeds

pommel *n* **1** raised front end of a saddle **2** knob on the top of a sword

pomp *n* **1** stately splendour **2** ostentation or empty show; vain display **pompous** *adj* **1** overdignified; self-important **2** ostentatious or inflated **pompously** *adv*

pond *n* small lake; pool

ponder *vt, vi* reflect or think deeply; meditate

pony *n* small horse

poodle *n* breed of dog having thick curly hair

pool[1] *n* **1** small body of water; pond; puddle **2** any small amount of liquid **3** still deep part in a river

pool[2] *n* **1** group or association of mutually cooperative members **2** combination of things, esp a set of services or financial facilities shared by a number of people or groups **3** all the stakes in a game *vt, vi* combine to form a pool **the pools** *n* system of betting on the results of football matches

poor *adj* **1** having or characterized by little wealth or resources **2** deficient in something necessary or desirable; inferior; unsatisfactory; scanty *n* **the poor** poor people in general **poorly** *adv* badly *adj inf* ill

pop[1] *v* (-pp-) *vt, vi* **1** make or cause to make a short sharp sound **2** burst open or cause to burst open with a pop *vi* come or go quickly *n* **1** popping sound **2** nonalcoholic fizzy drink **pop off 1** depart **2** die suddenly **pop the question** propose marriage *~adv, interj* with or expressing a popping sound **popcorn** *n* type of maize that bursts and puffs up when roasted

pop[2] *n* type of music usually having a distinctive and persistent rhythmic beat and making extensive use of electronically aided instruments

Pope *n* head of the Roman Catholic Church

poplar *n* tall tree of the willow family having a spirelike appearance

poppy *n* plant bearing red, orange, or white flowers

popular *adj* **1** liked or enjoyed by a large number of people **2** of or connected with the people **3** normal among or suitable for the people **popularity** *n* **popularly** *adv* **populate** *vt* **1** live in; inhabit **2** introduce a population into; people **population** *n* people considered collectively, esp all the people living in a town, city, country, etc

porcelain *n* type of delicate pottery; china

porch *n* **1** exterior roofed entrance to a house **2** veranda

porcupine *n* animal of the rodent family whose body is covered with stiff sharp spines or quills

pore[1] *v* **pore over** think or ponder deeply about; study

pore[2] *n* tiny opening, esp in the skin or a leaf, to allow the passage of perspiration or other moisture

205

pork n flesh or meat obtained from pigs **porker** n pig being fattened for slaughter

pornography n literature or art dealing with obscene subjects and intended to arouse sexual desires **pornographic** adj

porous adj full of little holes like a sponge, which allow the passage of water or air

porpoise n aquatic mammal with a blunt snout, related to the whale

porridge n breakfast dish consisting of oatmeal, water, and often milk

port[1] n a place, city, etc, where ships may load or unload cargoes

port[2] n left side of a ship or aeroplane for someone facing towards the front

port[3] n sweet fortified usually dark red wine

portable adj able to be carried easily by hand n portable object

porter[1] n person employed to carry people's luggage, as at a railway station or hotel

porter[2] n dark bitter ale

portfolio n 1 large flat case for carrying documents, drawings, etc 2 collection of documents concerned with a government department 3 office of a government minister 4 list of securities held by a person, bank, etc

porthole n opening in a ship's side fitted with glass to let in air and light

portion n 1 piece; share 2 amount of food served to one person vt 1 give as a share 2 divide or share

portrait n 1 picture of a person, usually a painting 2 lively written description of a person **portraiture** n 1 art of producing portraits 2 portraits collectively

portray vt 1 play the part of (someone), as in a play 2 describe a person or his character **portrayal** n

pose n 1 way of standing or behaving deliberately adopted to give an effect 2 pretence vi 1 act (as something one is not) 2 stand or sit in a certain way to be photographed or painted vt ask (a question); present (a problem)

posh adj inf 1 smart; showing style 2 upper-class; snobbish

position n 1 place 2 situation or condition 3 opinion; attitude 4 way of standing, sitting, etc 5 job; employment; office; rank vt 1 put into place 2 find the place of **positional** adj

positive adj 1 definite 2 certain; sure 3 real, true, or actual 4 useful or helpful 5 hopeful;

optimistic 6 denoting numbers greater than zero 7 designating or having the electric charge of a proton 8 (of a photograph) corresponding in colour or tone to the scene photographed n positive photograph, electric terminal, etc **positively** adv

possess vt have or control; own **possessed** adj mad or frenzied, esp when under the control of an evil spirit **possession** n 1 something one owns 2 act of possessing or state of being possessed 3 condition of occupying property 4 overseas colony **possessive** adj 1 concerning possession 2 selfishly dominating or controlling a person 3 denoting the case or form of a word used to indicate possession n possessive case or a pronoun in it

possible adj 1 able to exist, occur, be done, etc 2 that may perhaps happen 3 potential n person or thing that is possible **possibly** adv **possibility** n something that is possible **possibilities** pl n likely prospects

post[1] n 1 stout wooden pole driven into the ground, esp to support a roof, gate, or door 2 place where a race starts or ends vt 1 put up (a notice) on a wall, etc 2 announce to the public by putting up a notice or sign

post[2] n 1 job or duty 2 place where a soldier carries out his duties 3 fort or military camp 4 remote settlement vt 1 assign a task or duty to 2 send to (a military camp) 3 appoint to (a certain job)

post[3] n 1 national system or organization for carrying letters, parcels, etc 2 letters and parcels handled for delivery; mail 3 act or time of collecting or delivering mail vt send through the post **keep posted** keep informed **postage** n money paid for the use of the post **postal** adj **postal order** n money order that can be bought or cashed only at a post office **postbox** n box in which letters are placed for collection **postcard** n card sometimes having a picture on one side, used to send short messages **postman** n pl **-men** official who delivers letters

poster n placard esp used as an advertising announcement

posterior adj placed or following behind something else n buttocks

posterity n future generations

postgraduate adj relating to studies carried out

by a student who has already gained his first degree *n* postgraduate student

posthumous *adj* 1 happening or produced after a person's death 2 published after an author's death **posthumously** *adv*

postmortem *n* 1 medical examination of a corpse to find out the cause of death 2 analysis of reasons for failure of a plan, etc, of something after it is over *adj,adv* after death

postpone *vt* delay; put off; defer **postponement** *n*

postscript *n* additional note added at the end of a letter or document, after the signature

postulate *n* ('pɔstjulit) 1 idea or principle temporarily adopted as the basis of an argument, etc; assumption 2 unproved or self-evident scientific statement *vt* ('pɔstjuleit) 1 claim; demand 2 adopt as a postulate

posture *n* 1 way of standing or walking 2 situation or condition *vi* act in an unnatural way to achieve an effect

posy *n* small bunch of flowers

pot[1] *n* 1 round vessel or container 2 vessel used for cooking food or from which tea or coffee is served 3 jar **go to pot** fall into a state of ruin **pot shot** easy shot with a gun, etc ~*v* (-tt-) *vt,vi* 1 place plants, etc, in a pot 2 put food in jars to preserve it *vt* strike (a billiard ball) into a pocket

pot[2] *n* marijuana

potassium *n* soft silvery-white metallic element whose compounds are much used in drugs and fertilizers

potato *n pl* **potatoes** tuber of certain plants used as a vegetable

potent *adj* 1 powerful; strong; influential 2 (of men) able to perform sexually **potency** *n*

potential *adj* 1 capable of existing, becoming effective, etc 2 not yet using one's power *n* capacity or ability not yet realized or used **potentiality** *n* **potentially** *adv*

pothole *n* 1 small pit in a road 2 deep hole in rock, often large enough to be explored **potholer** *n*

potion *n* drink of a medicinal, magical, or poisonous nature

potter[1] *n* person who makes pottery

potter[2] *vi* move or act aimlessly

pottery *n* 1 earthenware vessels 2 material from which such vessels are made 3 factory where pots are made

pouch *n* 1 small bag, esp one for carrying money food, tobacco, etc 2 baglike or pocket-like part of the body on certain animals, esp the one in which kangaroos, wallabies, etc, carry their young

poultice *n* soft moistened mass applied to the body for medicinal purposes *vt* place a poultice on

poultry *n* domesticated fowls **poulterer** *n* person who sells poultry and game

pounce *vi* leap suddenly (upon); swoop *n* sudden leap or swoop

pound[1] *vt,vi* beat with a succession of heavy blows *vt* reduce to dust; crush *vi* thump; throb *n* thump

pound[2] *n* 1 unit of weight, divided into sixteen ounces, equivalent to 0 45 kilograms 2 basic unit of British currency or the system of currency used in Great Britain (**pound sterling**) and several other countries

pound[3] *n* enclosure, esp one for sheltering, confining, or catching animals

pour *vt,vi* 1 flow or cause to flow out 2 emit or cause to emit continually and quickly 3 rain heavily

pout *vi* push out the lips as when angry, sullen, etc *vt* say in a sulky manner *n* 1 act or gesture of pouting 2 sulk

poverty *n* state or condition of being poor; lack of wealth **poverty-stricken** *adj* without means; destitute

powder *n* 1 solid substance in the form of tiny loose particles, usually produced by grinding or crushing 2 type of powder used as a cosmetic medicine, etc *vt,vi* make into or become a powder, crush or be crushed *vt* apply powder to **powdery** *adj*

power *n* 1 ability or means to do something 2 capacity of mind or body 3 strength, energy, or force 4 control; influence; authority 5 country or state having international influence 6 divine or supernatural being 7 rate at which work is done or energy is transferred *vt* 1 provide energy, force, etc, for 2 provide with an engine or motor **powerful** *adj* **powerfully** *adv* **powerless** *adj*

practicable *adj* able to be done or used

practical *adj* 1 concerned with practice or action 2 capable of or suitable for use 3 concerned with the ordinary activities in the world 4 inclined towards actual or useful work; not philosophical or interested in theory

5 aware of possibilities; experienced **practically** adv **1** almost; nearly **2** in a practical manner

practice n **1** custom; habit **2** exercises done to gain skill in something **3** action that corresponds to a theory **4** work or clients of a lawyer, doctor, etc **practise** vt,vi **1** do as a habit or do repeatedly to gain skill **2** train (at) **3** take an action that corresponds to a theory **4** work as a lawyer, doctor, etc **practitioner** n person who works at a profession, esp a doctor

pragmatic adj **1** making judgments based on causes and results **2** acting in a practical manner **pragmatically** adv

prairie n large usually fertile area of grassland without trees

praise vt **1** show approval or admiration for **2** give glory to (God, etc) n **1** admiration or approval **2** glory or homage expressed to God **praiseworthy** adj

pram n wheeled carriage for a baby

prance vi **1** jump or move by jumping from the hind legs, as a horse does **2** walk about pompously; swagger n jump; spring; swagger

prank n childish trick

prattle n meaningless chatter vi chatter meaninglessly

prawn n edible marine animal resembling but larger than a shrimp

pray vt,vi make an earnest request for, esp to God or a god; make a prayer **prayer** n **1** earnest request made to God or a god **2** special set of words used in praying **3** strong wish or desire

preach vt,vi **1** speak publicly on a religious theme or in support of a religion **2** give strong moral encouragement (to); advocate **3** give unwelcome moral advice (to) **preacher** n

precarious adj insecure; unsafe; uncertain **precariously** adv **precariousness** n

precaution n action taken to stop something unpleasant or dangerous from happening **precautionary** adj

precede vt **1** go in front of **2** be earlier than **3** be more important or of higher rank than **precedence** n **1** act of preceding **2** relative importance or rank **3** right resulting from rank birth, or important office **precedent** n earlier case or decision that is taken as

guidance in dealing with subsequent situations

precept n rule or guide for behaviour; maxim

precinct n enclosed area, esp the grounds of a cathedral, school, etc

precious adj **1** valuable; of great price **2** well loved **3** affected; excessively refined adv very **preciously** adv

precipice n high, vertical, and steep cliff

precipitate (pri'sipiteit) vt **1** cause to happen before required or expected; hasten **2** throw down; hurl **3** cause dissolved matter to separate from solution in solid form n (pri-'sipitit) solid precipitated matter **precipitation** n

précis n shortened form of a longer statement document, etc vt make a summary of

precise adj **1** accurate; exact **2** clear; definite **precisely** adv **precision** n

precocious adj advanced in development

preconceive vt form an opinion beforehand **preconception** n

predator n **1** animal that lives by hunting and killing other animals for food **2** plunderer; thief **predatory** adj

predecessor n person who precedes someone else in a particular office, job, or duty

predestine vt decide the fate of beforehand **predestination** n

predicament n awkward or dangerous situation

predicate n ('predikit) **1** part of a sentence that contains what is said about the subject **2** statement relating to something vt ('predikeit) declare as a characteristic **predication** n **predicative** adj

predict vt describe future events before they happen; foretell; prophesy **predictable** adj **prediction** n

predominate vi **1** be the most numerous **2** have the most power or strength **predominance** n **predominant** adj

pre-eminent adj better than anyone or anything else; excellent; very distinguished **pre-eminence** n **pre-eminently** adv

preen vt,vi **1** (of a bird) clean and straighten the feathers with the beak **2** prepare or dress oneself tidily **3** show self-satisfaction

prefabricate vt manufacture parts or sections of (a building, etc) ready for assembling and erection

preface n **1** written introduction in a book; foreword **2** similar introduction to a speech or play *vt* introduce with a preface **prefatory** *adj*

prefect *n* senior pupil with some authority over other pupils at a school

prefer *vt* (-rr-) 1 like better 2 give special attention to 3 present or make (a statement charge, etc) 4 promote **preferable** *adj* **preference** *n* 1 preferring or being preferred 2 something preferred 3 advantage or right granted to particular people, countries, etc **preferential** *adj*

prefix *n* affix added to the beginning of a word to alter or otherwise affect its meaning *vt* attach at the beginning of something

pregnant *adj* 1 (of a woman or female animal) being with child or young 2 full of; abounding in 3 very significant **pregnancy** *n*

prehistoric *adj* of or occurring in the period before history was written down

prejudice *n* 1 judgment or opinion reached prematurely or on insufficient evidence 2 unfavourable opinion or bias *vt* 1 cause to be prejudiced; bias 2 injure; harm **prejudicial** *adj*

preliminary *adj* occurring beforehand; introductory *n* first action or occurrence; introductory or preparatory step event, etc

prelude *n* 1 short piece of music esp introducing an opera, suite, or fugue 2 any introduction *vt* form a prelude or introduction to

premarital *adj* before marriage

premature *adj* before the right time; too early

premeditate *vt* think of or decide upon beforehand; plan **premeditation** *n*

premier *adj* of the highest importance; first; leading *n* prime minister

premiere *n* first showing or performance of a film, play, etc

premise *n* 1 *also* **premiss** assumption 2 introduction to a document, such as a lease **premises** *pl n* house or other building, including the grounds ~*vt* state as a premise

premium *n* 1 prize; bonus 2 additional payment to a standard rate, wage, etc 3 amount paid periodically to renew an insurance policy **at a premium** very valuable **premium bond** government bond that pays no interest but offers the chance of monthly cash prizes

preoccupied *adj* 1 concentrating on one thought above others; engrossed; absorbed **preoccupation** *n*

prepare *vt,vi* 1 make or become ready or suitable for something 2 make; manufacture; construct 3 equip **preparatory** *adj* **preparation** *n* 1 preparing or being prepared 2 something prepared, esp a medicine or cosmetic 3 *also inf* **prep** school work done by a pupil at home; homework

preposition *n* word placed before a noun or pronoun indicating relationship in time, space, etc **prepositional** *adj*

preposterous *adj* ridiculous; stupid; absurd **preposterously** *adv*

prerogative *n* privilege, right

Presbyterian *adj* relating to a Protestant Church governed by elders (presbyters), traditionally following the teachings of Calvin *n* member of such a Church

prescribe *vt,vi* 1 order or require (medicine, treatment, etc) 2 make certain rules about **prescription** *n* 1 written instructions issued by a doctor indicating required medicine, treatment, etc 2 act of prescribing

presence *n* 1 state or condition of being present 2 closeness; nearness 3 demeanour; bearing 4 dignity; importance **presence of mind** ability to act quickly and intelligently when faced by difficulty or danger

present[1] *n* ('prezant) *adj* 1 being here within sight or hearing 2 being at a particular place at a certain time 3 existing now, indicating this time now *n* 1 time being lived through now 2 tense in a language indicating this **presently** *adv* soon; before long **present participle** *n* verb form functioning as an adjective or used with an auxiliary verb to denote continuous action e g *changing living, or speaking*

present[2] *n* ('prezant) gift *vt* (pra'zent) 1 give esp formally; bestow 2 introduce, esp in a formal way 3 organize (a performance, etc) 4 show to the public 5 offer or put forward for consideration, etc 6 raise (a weapon) in salute **presentation** *n* **presentable** *adj* fit to be introduced, displayed, etc

preserve *vt* 1 keep safe or undamaged 2 save from decay, change, etc *n* 1 preserved food, such as jam 2 area of country protected or kept private, as for hunting 3 right; privilege **preservation** *n* **preservative** *n,adj*

president *n* 1 person having highest authority in a republic 2 someone presiding over an assembly, society, company, etc **presidency**

n **preside** *vi* 1 sit in authority over a meeting, debate, etc 2 exercise control or authority

press [1] *vt,vi* 1 apply weight, force, or pressure to, so as to squeeze, crush, flatten, etc 2 obtain liquid, juice, oil, etc , by pressure 3 hold close; grasp 4 attack hard, as in battle 5 insist on; compel; urge; entreat 6 oppress; harass 7 *iron* **press on** continue with an activity ~*n* 1 machine for printing 2 newspapers and magazines collectively 3 machine for exerting pressure, as in extracting liquids 4 large crowd of people **press stud** *n* fastener for clothes having two parts pressed together

press [2] *vt* force into service, esp military service **pressgang** *n* men formerly employed to force people into the army or navy ~*vt* force (someone) into doing something

pressure *n* 1 act of pressing 2 force exerted by pressing; force per unit area acting on a surface 3 compulsion; constraint 4 cause of distress; burden **pressure group** *n* group of people seeking to influence public opinion, government, etc **pressure cooker** *n* special pot in which food is cooked at a high temperature under pressure **pressurize** *vt* 1 maintain normal air pressure in (an aircraft cabin, etc) 2 urge or compel, esp to a course of action

prestige *n* 1 high reputation gained through success, rank, etc ; status 2 power to influence and impress **prestigious** *adj*

presume *vt,vi* 1 assume; suppose 2 dare or venture, esp with excessive boldness **presumption** *n* **presumable** *adj* **presumably** *adv*

pretend *vt,vi* 1 feign or affect (to do or be something) 2 lay claim to, esp dubiously 3 state or profess falsely 4 venture; attempt 5 fancy or imagine oneself as being **pretender** *n* 1 claimant to a throne, inheritance, etc 2 someone who pretends **pretence** *n*

pretentious *adj* 1 claiming or attempting things beyond one's ability 2 affecting dignity, importance, etc 3 ostentatious; showy **pretentiousness** *n* **pretentiously** *adv* **pretension** *n* 1 laying claim to something 2 dubious or unsupportable claim, esp made indirectly, to some merit, importance, etc 3 pretentiousness

pretext *n* pretended reason or motive that conceals the real one; excuse

pretty *adj* 1 attractive, charming, or appealing in a delicate way 2 neat; dainty 3 *inf* fine; good 4 *inf* considerable **a pretty penny** great deal of money ~*adv* fairly; quite **prettily** *adv* **prettiness** *n*

prevail *vi* 1 be or prove dominant, effective, superior, etc ; be victorious 2 be used or exist widely; predominate **prevail on** persuade

prevalent *adj* used or occurring widely; common **prevalence** *n*

prevaricate *vi* make misleading statements; answer evasively **prevarication** *n*

prevent *vt* make impossible; hinder; stop **prevention** *n* **preventive** *adj*

preview *n* advance showing of a play, film, exhibition, etc , before presentation to the public *vt* see in advance

previous *adj* 1 before something else in time or position; prior 2 *inf* too early; premature **previously** *adv*

prey *n* 1 animal hunted for food 2 habit of hunting for prey 3 victim, as of an enemy, illness, etc *v* **prey on** 1 hunt for food 2 make profits out of; exploit 3 have a destructive or depressing influence (on); weigh heavily (on)

price *n* 1 amount of money, goods, etc , for which something is bought or sold 2 cost at which something is acquired 3 value; worth *vt* 1 set a price on 2 estimate or find out the price of **priceless** *adj* 1 valuable beyond price; invaluable 2 *inf* very funny or absurd **pricey** *adj inf* expensive

prick *vt* pierce; puncture; make holes in with a sharp point *vi,vt* feel or cause to feel sharp mental or physical pain; sting **prick up one's ears** listen attentively ~*n* 1 pricking or being pricked 2 small injury or puncture caused by a sharp point 3 sharp painful sensation 4 *sl* penis **prickle** *n* 1 small sharp thorn or spine 2 tingling or prickling sensation *vt,vi* tingle **prickly** *adj*

pride *n* 1 self-respect based on a true sense of personal worth 2 arrogance about or exaggerated belief in one's own merits, achievements, etc 3 satisfaction 4 source of pride, esp something splendid 5 group of lions **take pride in** be proud about

priest *n* minister who officiates at religious

ceremonies and rituals **priestess** f n **priest-hood** n

prim adj excessively formal or proper in attitude or behaviour

primary adj 1 first or most important 2 simple; elementary; basic; fundamental **primarily** adv **primary colours** pl n three colours, for example red, green, and blue, that can be combined to give any other colour **primary school** n school for children below the age of eleven (or sometimes nine)

primate n 1 high-ranking clergyman, such as an archbishop 2 member of the order of mammals that includes man, apes, and monkeys

prime adj 1 first or most important; primary 2 excellent; very good 3 necessary; essential n period when something is at its best or strongest, usually the earliest period vt,vi 1 put explosive into 2 fill with food 3 supply with information **prime minister** n chief minister; leader of the government **prime number** n number, such as seven, able to be divided only by itself and one **primer** n 1 book for beginners 2 cap or tube containing explosive used to set off a charge 3 first coat of paint

primitive adj 1 at the beginning of development 2 barbarous; savage 3 not sophisticated; rough; simple n primitive person or thing

primrose n wild plant bearing pale yellow flowers n,adj pale yellow

prince n 1 son or close male relative of a king or queen 2 nobleman 3 ruler of a minor state **princely** adj **princess** n 1 daughter or close female relative of a king or queen 2 wife of a prince

principal adj 1 chief; main 2 of the highest rank n 1 person who plays a leading part in an activity 2 head of a university, college, or school 3 capital sum that is borrowed or lent at interest **principally** adv

principality n rule of a prince or the country or state over which he rules

principle n 1 basic rule, esp one that governs one's life 2 fundamental truth or doctrine 3 important element of something · 4 moral behaviour

print vt,vi 1 produce (letters, text, pictures, etc) by pressing inked types, plates, etc, directly onto paper 2 publish (a book, magazine, etc) in this way 3 write in separated letters or

block capitals 4 produce a picture from a negative 5 leave (a mark, etc) by or as if by pressing or stamping n 1 printed text 2 picture produced from an engraved or etched plate or a photographic negative 3 cloth with a pattern printed on it 4 mark made by or as if by pressure **out of print** (of a book, etc) sold out; not available **printable** adj fit to appear in print **printer** n

prior[1] n head of a monastery

prior[2] adj 1 coming before; earlier 2 of greater importance **prior to** before; previous to **priority** n 1 greater importance; superiority 2 state of being earlier 3 condition of being or right to be dealt with earlier

priory n religious house presided over by a prior, often attached to an abbey

prise vt lift or open by means of a lever, etc

prism n 1 solid figure usually having rectangular sides and triangular ends of equal size 2 triangular prism of transparent material, used esp for splitting light into its component colours **prismatic** adj

prison n 1 building used for the confinement of convicted criminals 2 any place of confinement **prisoner** n criminal or other captive kept in prison

private adj 1 not public or official; secret; confidential 2 connected with an individual; personal 3 out of the way; isolated n soldier of the lowest army or marine rank **privacy** n **privately** adv

privet n evergreen shrub commonly used for hedges

privilege n 1 right granted to a person or group 2 advantage connected with such a right vt grant a privilege to; give a special advantage to

prize[1] n 1 reward won in a competition 2 something valuable captured in war, etc

prize[2] vt hold in high estimation; place a high value on

probable adj likely to occur or be true **probability** n likelihood, esp when mathematically calculated **probably** adv

probation n 1 period during which a person is tested for his ability or suitability 2 system by which a convicted offender is set free on condition that he reports regularly to an official and behaves well **probationary** adj

probe vt,vi seek for information; investigate; examine n 1 investigation 2 surgical instrument used to probe wounds, etc **3** spacecraft capable of exploration

problem n **1** difficult issue or situation **2** matter deserving profound consideration **3** question requiring a solution by calculation **problematic** adj

procedure n **1** method of doing something; technique **2** established manner of behaviour in a given situation **3** rules governing the conduct of business, as in parliament **procedural** adj

proceed vi **1** go forward; advance **2** start or continue a course of action **proceed from** be the result of **proceed against** bring a legal action against **proceeds** pl n profit from a sale, etc

process n **1** series of connected actions; course of action **2** method by which legal action is conducted **3** method of making or manufacturing something **4** bone, organ, or part that sticks out or projects vt **1** preserve (food), as by drying, freezing, etc **2** use special methods to manufacture or do something

procession n **1** large number of people moving along in an ordered manner **2** long series of things or events

proclaim vt announce or make known officially or openly **proclamation** n

procreate vt, vi give birth to or produce (offspring) **procreation** n **procreator** n

procure vt **1** get; obtain **2** bring about; cause **procurement** n

prod vt (-dd-) **1** poke; nudge **2** urge, encourage; rouse; stir n **1** poke; nudge **2** reminder

prodigy n **1** wonder; marvel; miraculous event or thing **2** person, esp a child, having exceptional ability or talent **prodigious** adj **1** enormous **2** extraordinary; wonderful

produce v (prəˈdjuːs) vt, vi bring forth; bear; yield vt **1** cause, bring into existence **2** manufacture or make **3** organize or finance (a play, film, etc) **4** bring out; show n (ˈprɒd-juːs) anything that is produced brought forth, or made, esp fruit or crops **producer** n **production** n **product** n **1** something produced **2** result of multiplying two or more numbers **productive** adj able to produce, esp effectively or efficiently **productivity** n

profane adj **1** showing contempt or disrespect for sacred or holy things **2** vulgar or coarse, esp in language vt **1** defile or otherwise spoil (something holy, sacred, or pure) **2** treat with

callous disrespect **profanely** adv **profanity** n

profess vt **1** declare or claim in public **2** pretend; declare falsely

profession n **1** job or career for which special training and mental skills are required **2** body of people in a particular profession **3** public declaration or claim **professional** adj **1** connected with a profession or those who practise it **2** earning one's living by playing a sport n professional person

professor n **1** head of a teaching department in a university or similar institution **2** someone who professes a religious belief

proficient adj skilled; capable; expert; experienced **proficiency** n

profile n **1** view or drawing of a face seen from the side **2** outline or sectional drawing **3** journalistic character outline of someone; brief biography vt give, present, or draw an outline of

profit n **1** advantage, benefit **2** money left over after the necessary expenses of a transaction have been paid vt, vi **3** gain advantage (from) **2** be of advantage **3** obtain profits **profitable** adj

profound adj **1** extremely deep **2** felt deeply; strong; intense **3** requiring considerable concentration; obscure; difficult **profoundly** adv **profundity** n

profuse adj **1** unrestrained, lavish, generous **2** very plentiful; abundant to the point of excess **profusely** adv **profusion** n

programme n **1** list of items or events in a theatrical performance, concert, etc , or at a meeting **2** performance consisting of several items or parts **3** radio or television broadcast **program** n list of operations and data used in or prepared for a computer vt, vi (-mm-) prepare data for a computer **programmer** n

progress n (ˈprougres) **1** forward motion **2** advance; development; increase or growth vi (prəˈgres) **1** move forward; advance **2** improve; get better **progression** n **progressive** adj **1** characterized by progress **2** supporting political or social reforms; enlightened **3** increasing regularly, accumulative n person supporting social and political reform **progressively** adv

prohibit vt forbid or prevent, esp by law; stop; ban; restrict **prohibition** n **prohibitive** adj

project n (ˈprɒdʒekt) scheme being planned or

already being worked on *v* (prə'dʒekt) *vt vi* stick out, protrude, jut out *vt* **1** throw; thrust; drive forward **2** cast (the mind) forward to think about the distant future, plan ahead **3** shine light or an image on something as with a film projector **projection** *n* **projectile** *n* object propelled through the air, missile **projectionist** *n* person who works a projector at a cinema **projector** *n* machine for projecting films or picture slides on a screen

proletariat *n* social class that owns no property and earns its living by the sale of its labour, working class

proliferate *vt vi* bring or come forth in increasing abundance, produce or reproduce more and more **proliferation** *n* **prolific** *adj* **1** plentiful, abundant **2** producing much **3** having numerous offspring

prologue *n* **1** section of a book, play, poem etc that comes before the main part, introduction **2** any preliminary to something more important

prolong *vt* make longer in time or space

promenade *n* **1** place along which one may walk, esp near the sea **2** short walk, stroll *vi* walk along freely, stroll

prominent *adj* **1** famous, well-known **2** obvious, clear **3** projecting, sticking out **prominence** *n* **prominently** *adv*

promiscuous *adj* **1** indiscriminate, esp in sexual relations **2** confused, lacking order, casual **promiscuity** *n* **promiscuously** *adv*

promise *n* **1** declaration; vow **2** assurance given to do or not to do something **3** grounds or hope for future excellence, achievement, etc *vt, vi* make a promise (of)

promote *vt* **1** advance to a higher or more important rank, position, etc **2** encourage the development, progress, or growth of **3** work to make successful, acceptable or popular **promotion** *n*

prompt *adj* **1** quick to act, respond, or do **2** punctual **3** acted on or accomplished without delay *vt* **1** instigate; incite **2** inspire *vi vt* provide or help by providing cues or suggestions *n* act of prompting or something that prompts **promptly** *adv*

prone *adj* lying with the face or front of the body downwards, stretched out **prone to** liable, inclined, or disposed (to)

prong *n* pointed end, as of a fork; spike; narrow projection

pronoun *n* word such as *you, my, who,* or *someone,* used as a substitute for a noun

pronounce *vt, vi* make a speech sound, esp in a specific manner, utter, articulate *vt* state formally, declare officially *vi* voice an opinion (on) **pronounced** *adj* obvious, marked **pronouncement** *n* declaration **pronunciation** *n* act or manner of making speech sounds esp with regard to correctness

proof *n* **1** irrefutable evidence, reasoning or facts **2** anything that serves to establish validity or truth **3** trial, demonstration, test **4** alcoholic strength proved or maintained by certain standards *adj* of standard or proved strength or quality **proof against** unable to be penetrated, invulnerable **proofread** *vt vi* (-read) read and correct (trial printed matter)

prop[1] *n* **1** rigid support such as a beam or pole **2** person or thing giving support *vt* (-pp-) **1** also **prop up** prevent from caving in or falling, support **2** place or rest against something

prop[2] *n* object placed on stage or used by actors

propaganda *n* false, biased or self serving information usually designed to harm or discredit another person, group etc

propagate *vt* **1** cause to increase or multiply **2** reproduce or transmit in reproduction **3** spread *vi* **1** breed; multiply **2** move (through); be transmitted **propagation** *n*

propel *vt* (-ll-) cause to move forwards, drive **propeller** *n* powered device usually consisting of blades mounted on a revolving shaft, for propelling aircraft, ships, etc

proper *adj* **1** suitable; appropriate; right, apt **2** having good manners, correct **3** within the technical or strict meaning of a term etc **properly** *adv* **proper noun** *n* also **proper name** noun that refers to a specific person, place, or thing

property *n* **1** possession(s) **2** piece of land, estate **3** ownership **4** quality or characteristic associated with something

prophecy ('prɒfisi) *n* **1** prediction **2** divine revelation **3** prophetic declaration **prophesy** ('prɒfisai) *vt* **1** predict; proclaim; foretell **2** reveal by divine inspiration *vi* declare what is to come **prophet** *n* **1** person who speaks by divine inspiration **2** person who predicts future events etc **3** inspired leader etc **prophetic** *adj*

proportion *n* **1** relative size or magnitude; ratio

comparative relation **2** symmetry; harmony **3** part of a whole; share; portion **proportions** pl n size ~vt adjust or arrange proportions of **proportional** adj

propose vt **1** submit for consideration; suggest **2** recommend for membership, office, etc **3** intend; plan to do vi make a proposal of marriage **proposal** n **1** act of proposing **2** plan; scheme **3** offer of marriage

proposition n **1** suggested plan; scheme **2** statement; assertion **3** point or subject offered for discussion vt suggest a plan, scheme, etc, to

proprietor n person who owns a business

propriety n **1** suitability; correctness; aptness **2** good conduct

propulsion n **1** act of propelling or state of being propelled **2** impulse; force

prose n speech, writing, or printed matter, esp as distinguished from poetry

prosecute vt bring legal action against vi seek legal redress **prosecutor** n **prosecution** n **1** act of prosecuting or state of being prosecuted **2** lawyers acting for the Crown in a criminal lawsuit

prospect n **1** expectation; probability; future outlook **2** scenic view; outlook **prospects** pl n chances of success, good fortune, etc ~vt, vi search, esp for oil or valuable minerals; explore **prospective** adj anticipated; expected; likely

prospectus n statement or pamphlet giving details of a coming event or of school or academic courses or describing an organization, etc

prosperous adj **1** successful; flourishing **2** having plenty of money, well-off **3** favourable; promising **prosperity** n wealth; success **prosper** vi be successful, thrive

prostitute n woman who charges money for sexual intercourse vt **1** offer (oneself) for sexual intercourse for money **2** sell for immediate gain, put to a base or unworthy use **prostitution** n

prostrate adj ('prɔstreit) **1** lying with the face downwards **2** helpless; defenceless; exhausted vt (prɔ'streit) **1** throw (oneself) down in an act of submission, humility etc **2** force or throw to the ground **3** render helpless; overcome

protagonist n leading character, actor, participant, spokesman, etc

protect vt guard; defend; shield from harm, etc **protection** n **protective** adj

protégé n person under the protection or guidance of another

protein n type of complex organic compound, found esp in meat, eggs, and milk, essential for metabolism

protest n ('proutest) **1** serious or formal objection, disapproval, or dissent **2** act of objecting or declaring formally vt, vi (prou-'test) **1** object; complain **2** affirm seriously or solemnly

Protestant n member or adherent of any of various Christian Churches outside the Roman Catholic Church

protocol n etiquette, esp in formal or diplomatic situations

proton n stable positively charged particle that occurs in the nucleus of an atom

prototype n first model, design, or pattern; original

protrude vt, vi project or thrust out **protuberance** n

proud adj **1** feeling intensely pleased with an achievement, etc **2** showing or having self-esteem, often excessive **3** very creditable **proudly** adv **proudness** n

prove vt **1** demonstrate to be true or genuine **2** test; verify; demonstrate by using, etc **3** show to be as expected or specified vi turn out (to be)

proverb n short common saying, expressing a general truth **proverbial** adj

provide vt **1** equip; supply; furnish **2** yield vi supply money or means of support (for) **providing** conj also **provided** on condition (that)

province n **1** administrative division of a country **2** area of learning, interest or activity **provinces** pl n parts of a country distinct from the leading financial, cultural or government centres **provincial** adj **1** relating to a province; not national **2** lacking sophistication; rustic n unsophisticated person

provision n **1** supplying of something needed **2** arrangement in advance **3** stipulation **4** something provided **provisions** pl n food and other necessities **provisional** adj temporary, serving only a limited function, need etc

proviso n condition stipulation

provoke vt **1** make angry, irritate; enrage **2**

arouse; move to action **3** cause to happen; induce **provocation** n **provocative** adj

prow n front part of a ship or boat; bow

prowess n **1** bravery; courage **2** accomplishment, esp showing unusual ability

prowl vt,vi move about stealthily, esp in search of something n act of prowling

proximity n nearness; near neighbourhood

prude n person who is excessively prim or modest **prudish** adj

prudent adj **1** wisely cautious or careful **2** showing caution, good judgment, etc **prudence** n

prune¹ n dried plum, dark brown in colour

prune² vt **1** trim; cut off, esp from trees and shrubs **2** remove (excesses, etc)

pry vi look inquisitively; enquire closely or furtively; examine with intrusive curiosity

psalm n religious song or hymn

pseudonym n false name used by a writer, etc , to conceal his identity

psychedelic adj relating to or producing a joyful state of expanded consciousness

psychiatry n branch of medicine concerned with treating mental illness **psychiatric** adj **psychiatrist** n

psychic adj **1** relating to the mind or mental activities **2** relating to unusual mental powers, such as telepathy **3** involving a nonphysical force or influence

psychoanalysis n technique or system of bringing subconscious conflicts into awareness **psychoanalyst** n **psychoanalyse** vt treat by psychoanalysis

psychology n scientific study of mental attitudes and human or animal behaviour **psychologist** n **psychological** adj **1** relating to psychology **2** arising in the mind; irrational

psychopath n person suffering from severe mental and emotional instability **psychopathic** adj

psychosis n serious mental illness **psychotic** adj

psychosomatic adj relating to a physical disorder that is caused or aggravated by the emotional state

pub n inf also **public house** building licensed for the sale and consumption of alcoholic drinks **publican** n person responsible for running a pub

puberty n age at which a person becomes sexually mature

public adj **1** relating or belonging to the people of a community, country, etc **2** general; available to all; not private n **1** people in general **2** followers; admirers **public relations** n business or activity of promoting goodwill for an organization, individual, etc **public school** n private independent fee-paying school

publication n act or product of publishing

publicity n **1** state or condition of being generally known **2** business, activity, or methods of informing the public about a person, product, campaign, etc

publicize vt make public; bring to general notice

publish vt,vi produce and issue (books, etc) for sale vt make known to the public **publisher** n

pucker vt,vi gather into wrinkles or folds n uneven fold; wrinkle

pudding n **1** cooked dish of various ingredients, such as suet or sponge with fruit or meat **2** course following the main meal; sweet; dessert

puddle n small pool of water or other liquid

puff n **1** brief burst of air, smoke, vapour, etc ; gust of wind **2** draw at a cigarette, cigar, or pipe vi,vt **1** send out puffs of air, smoke, etc **2** also **puff up** or **out** swell; inflate **3** smoke vi breathe in short gasps, pant

pull vt,vi tug (at) forcefully; haul; jerk vt **1** move forward by means of or using force; draw **2** tear or rip (apart, out, etc) **3** remove from the natural or normal position by pulling **pull apart** criticize severely **pull faces** grimace **pull a fast one** trick; deceive **pull in 1** draw into a station, kerb etc , and stop **2** attract **pull off** succeed in accomplishing something **pull oneself together** regain self-control **pull one's weight** make a significant contribution towards a common task **pull out** withdraw; abandon; leave **pull someone's leg** tease **pull strings** use personal influence **pull through** recover **pull up 1** stop **2** draw level in a race ~n act or force of pulling **pullover** n sweater; jumper

pulley n wheel for raising weights by pulling downwards on a cord, etc , passing over its grooved rim

pulp n **1** mass of soft moist matter **2** moist

215

mixture of wood particles, rags, etc., from which paper is made *vt,vi* reduce or be reduced to pulp

pulpit *n* raised stand or platform from which a clergyman preaches

pulsate *vi* beat or throb, esp rhythmically; quiver; vibrate **pulsation** *n* **pulse** *n* 1 periodic throbbing of the arteries, caused by successive contraction and relaxation of the heart 2 transient change in voltage, current, etc

pulverize *vt,vi* grind or pound to a fine powder or be so reduced *vt* demolish

pump *n* machine for forcing liquids or gases to a different level, container, etc., for reducing fluid pressure, etc *vt,vi* raise, clear, inflate, etc., with a pump *vt* 1 move up and down repeatedly 2 elicit by repeated questioning 3 question for information

pumpkin *n* large orange-coloured edible gourd

pun *n* play on words, esp those with similar sounds *vi* (-nn-) make puns

punch[1] *n* 1 sharp forceful blow, esp with the fist 2 forcefulness; drive 3 tool for stamping, piercing, etc *vt* 1 hit sharply, esp with the fist 2 prod; poke 3 stamp, pierce, etc, with a punch

punch[2] *n* drink usually made in quantity by mixing wine or spirits with fruit, spices, etc

punctual *adj* on time; prompt **punctuality** *n*

punctuate *vt* 1 mark (sentences, etc) with full stops, commas, brackets, etc 2 give emphasis to; stress 3 interrupt at intervals *vi* use punctuation **punctuation** *n* 1 various marks inserted in sentences, etc, to clarify meaning 2 act of punctuating

puncture *n* 1 tiny hole made by pricking or piercing 2 loss of pressure in a tyre resulting from this *vt* 1 prick; pierce 2 deflate by a puncture

pungent *adj* 1 smelling or tasting sharp or acrid 2 caustic; biting **pungency** *n* **pungently** *adv*

punish *vt* 1 inflict a penalty on; make to suffer for some offence, fault, etc; discipline 2 hurt; injure **punishment** *n*

punt[1] *n* boat with a flat bottom, moved by aid of a pole *vt,vi* propel (a boat) by using a pole

punt[2] *vi,n* gamble; bet

pup *n* young dog, seal, or similar animal

pupa *n pl* **pupae** ('pjuːpiː) inactive stage of

development of an insect, between larva and adult forms **pupal** *adj*

pupil[1] *n* student; schoolchild

pupil[2] *n* variable aperture in the iris of the eye through which light enters

puppet *n* 1 figure with movable limbs controlled by strings or wires; marionette 2 person, group, etc, under the control of another

puppy *n* 1 young dog 2 conceited young man

purchase *vt* buy; obtain by payment *n* 1 something bought 2 act of buying 3 leverage 4 hold; grip **purchase tax** *n* tax levied on purchased goods, being added to the selling price

pure *adj* 1 not contaminated; free from mixture with anything else 2 simple; not complicated 3 innocent; chaste 4 mere **purely** *adv* entirely; solely **purity** *n*

purgatory *n* 1 place where souls of the dead go for punishment of earthly sins before entering heaven 2 state or condition of temporary pain, suffering, etc

purge *vt* 1 cleanse; remove by cleaning 2 rid of waste, unwanted elements, etc; clear; eliminate; remove *vi* become cleansed, purified, etc *n* 1 act of purging 2 something that purges 3 *also* **purgative** drug or agent aiding defecation

purify *vt,vi* make or become pure *vt* free from undesirable elements, etc **purification** *n*

Puritan *n* member of an extreme reform group of 16th- and 17th-century Protestants **puritan** *n* person who is excessively strict, esp in matters of religion or morals **puritanical** *adj*

purl *n* knitting stitch that is an inverted plain stitch *vt,vi* knit in purl

purple *n,adj* reddish-blue or bluish-red **purplish** *adj*

purpose *n* 1 end or aim towards which any view, action, etc, is directed; intention 2 reason **on purpose** intentionally

purr *n* low murmuring sound, as made by a contented cat *vi* utter such a sound

purse *n* small pouch or bag for holding coins, etc

pursue *vt* 1 trail; follow closely; chase 2 attend 3 seek to gain or accomplish 4 continue (with or on) **pursuit** *n* 1 act of pursuing 2 hobby; pastime

pus *n* yellowish-white matter discharged from an infected wound

push *vt,vi* 1 press (against) forcefully; impel by

pressure **2** urge; promote *vt* thrust (away, through, forward, etc) with or by force **pushed (for)** *inf* short of ~*n* **1** act of pushing **2** *inf* drive; self-assertion **3** *inf* special effort **4** *inf* dismissal **pushchair** *n* small chair on wheels for carrying infants

pussy *n inf* cat

put *vt* (-tt-; put) **1** place, deposit, lay, set, or cause to be in any position, situation, or place **2** render; transform **3** express; propose **put across** *or* **over** communicate **put (it) at** estimate (it) as **put away 1** store **2** save **3** imprison; lock up **put down 1** record; write **2** quell **3** kill (an animal) **put forward** suggest; propose **put off 1** delay; defer **2** discourage **3** switch off **put on 1** dress in **2** assume; adopt **3** wager, bet **4** switch on **put out 1** annoy; disturb **2** extinguish; switch off **put up 1** build **2** accommodate **3** provide; give **put up with** tolerate **stay put** remain; not move

putrid *adj* **1** rotten; decaying **2** having a foul smell **3** *inf* awful; of poor quality **putrefy** *vi,vt* rot; decompose **putrefaction** *n*

putt *vt,vi* hit a golfball so that it rolls towards the hole *n* putted stroke **putting** *n* game like golf involving putted strokes only

putty *n* pliable material that sets rigid, used for holding panes of glass in frames, etc *vt* repair fill, etc , with putty

puzzle *vt,vi* confuse or perplex or be confused or perplexed **puzzle over** strain to discover a solution; expend effort to find a meaning` ~*n* **1** something that poses a problem to be worked out **2** something that perplexes **3** jigsaw

PVC *n* polyvinyl chloride: man-made plastic material, either flexible or rigid, with a wide variety of uses

Pygmy *n* member of a central African hunting people of small stature **pygmy** very small person

pyjamas *pl n* loose trousers and jacket for sleeping in

pylon *n* tall structure, used esp to convey high-voltage electric cables over open country

pyramid *n* **1** solid figure consisting usually of a square base and triangular sloping faces that meet at the top **2** enormous pyramid-shaped stone monument, esp of ancient Egypt

Pyrex *n Tdmk* heat-resistant glass or glassware

python *n* large snake that kills its prey by squeezing

Q

quack [1] *n* harsh cry of a duck *vi* make such a sound

quack [2] *n* medical practitioner who is unqualified or unreliable

quadrangle *n* **1** quadrilateral **2** *also inf* **quad** quadrilateral courtyard esp within a school **quadrangular** *adj*

quadrant *n* quarter section of a circle

quadrilateral *n* figure with four sides and four angles *adj* having four sides and four angles

quadruped *n* animal with four legs *adj* having four legs

quadruple *vt,vi* increase fourfold *adj* **1** four times as much **2** having four members, parts, etc

quadruplet *n* **1** *also inf* **quad** one of four children born at the same time to the same mother **2** group having four members or parts

quail [1] *n* small game bird

quail [2] *vi* shrink with dread or fear; tremble

quaint *adj* pleasingly odd or old-fashioned **quaintly** *adv*

quake *vi* tremble or shake *n inf* short for **earthquake.**

Quaker *n* member of a pacifist Christian sect advocating simplicity of worship, dress, etc

qualify *vt,vi* make or become suitable, appropriate, or acceptable (for) *vi* reach a required standard or level *vt* **1** restrict or modify (a statement proposal, etc) **2** temper or moderate **qualification** *n*

quality *n* **1** distinguishing attribute or characteristic **2** degree of fineness or excellence **3** excellence **4** accomplishment **qualitative** *adj*

qualm *n* pang of conscience; misgiving

quandary *n* dilemma; perplexed turmoil

quantify *vt* assess or ascertain the amount of **quantification** *n*

quantity *n* **1** amount **2** large amount

quarantine *n* careful isolation imposed on people, animals, etc , to prevent the spread of an infectious disease *vt* put into quarantine; isolate

quarrel *n* **1** disagreement or dispute **2** cause for complaint *vi* (-ll-) argue or disagree; squabble; dispute

quarry[1] *n* shallow mine or pit from which stone, slate, etc . is excavated *vt* mine (stone, etc) from a quarry

quarry[2] *n* animal, person, or other object of pursuit; game; prey

quart *n* liquid or dry measure equal to two pints (approx 1 1 litres) and one quarter of a bushel respectively

quarter *n* 1 one of four equal parts or portions; one divided by four 2 *US* twenty-five cents or a coin having this value *vt* 1 cut or divide into quarters 2 place or provide someone, esp soldiers, with lodgings **quarterly** *adj,adv* **quarterdeck** *n* rear section of the upper deck of a ship, often reserved for officers **quartermaster** *n* 1 petty officer on a ship responsible for steering, signals, etc 2 officer, esp in the army, responsible for the provision of food, clothing, lodging, etc **quarters** *pl n* living accommodation

quartet *n* group of four persons or things, esp four singers or musicians

quartz *n* common colourless crystalline mineral

quash *vt* 1 subdue; suppress 2 annul or invalidate (a decision, law, etc)

quaver *n* musical note lasting one eighth the time of a semibreve *vi* quiver; quake; tremble

quay *n* man-made landing place to which ships may come to load or unload; wharf

queasy *adj* 1 feeling or causing nausea; sickly 2 ill at ease **queasily** *adv* **queasiness** *n*

queen *n* 1 female monarch or wife of a king 2 woman, thing, etc , regarded as very fine or outstanding 3 fertile female in a colony of wasps, bees, ants, etc 4 court card whose value is higher than the jack and lower than the king 5 most powerful chess piece able to move any distance in a straight or diagonal line 6 *sl* homosexual male **queenly** *adj*

queer *adj* 1 odd; peculiar; strange 2 *sl* homosexual *n sl* homosexual *vt sl* ruin or spoil **queerly** *adv*

quell *vt* suppress; subdue; calm

quench *vt* 1 satisfy (a thirst, etc) 2 extinguish or smother something such as a fire

query *n* 1 question 2 point of doubt 3 question mark *vt,vi* raise (a question); ask for (an answer or clarification)

quest *n* search or hunt, esp one carried on fervently *vi* engage in a quest; search

question *n* 1 request for information, a decision, clarification, etc 2 point of doubt; uncertainty 3 problem or matter for discussion; issue *vt,vi* ask questions (of) *vt* cast doubt upon; challenge **beyond question** indisputable **call into question** cast doubt upon **out of the question** impossible **question mark** *n* mark (?) used at the end of a sentence, phrase, or word to indicate a question **questionnaire** *n* written list of questions used to gather information, obtain opinions, etc

queue *n* line of people or things waiting their turn to do or obtain something *vi* form or wait in a queue

quibble *n* trivial or petty objection, criticism, evasion, etc *vi* argue about trivial points; evade by petty criticism or objection

quick *adj* fast or sudden; swift *adv* rapidly; swiftly *n* sensitive flesh at the edge of a fingernail or toenail **the quick and the dead** the living and the dead **cut to the quick** hurt or offend deeply **quicken** *vt,vi* 1 hasten; accelerate 2 stimulate; revive **quicksand** *n* soft wet sand into which objects are liable to sink **quicksilver** *n* mercury **like quicksilver** moving very swiftly **quickstep** *n* 1 quick marching step 2 fast ballroom-dancing step **quick-tempered** *adj* having a hasty or hot temper; easily angered **quick-witted** *adj* thinking swiftly; alert

quid *n, pl* **quid** *sl* pound (money)

quiet *adj* 1 free from harsh noise or disturbance 2 tranquil; calm 3 subdued; restrained *n* calmness; stillness; tranquillity **quietly** *adv* **quieten** *vt,vi* also **quiet** make or become quiet; subdue; ease

quill *n* 1 large feather from the wing or tail of a bird 2 such a feather made into a pen for writing 3 one of the spines of a hedgehog, porcupine, etc

quilt *n* bed covering made of two layers of material filled with some soft fabric and sewn together *vt,vi* make a quilt (of)

quinine *n* alkaline substance originally obtained from the bark of a tree and used medicinally, esp in treating malaria

quintet *n* group of five persons or things, esp five singers or musicians

quirk *n* 1 unusual or odd trait or characteristic 2 sudden twist or turn

quit *vt,vi* (-tt-; quitted *or* quit) 1 stop; cease 2

give up; relinquish; resign **3** discharge (a debt, etc) **4** depart (from); leave

quite adv **1** wholly or entirely **2** inf fairly; moderately **3** positively interj expression of agreement or concurrence

quiver[1] vi shake; tremble; quake n act of quivering; tremble

quiver[2] n case or sheath for holding arrows

quiz n series of questions, often taking the form of a competition between two or more people vt (-zz-) question closely

quizzical adj **1** comical or odd **2** questioning; perplexed **3** teasing **quizzically** adv

quoit n ring of rubber, metal, etc , used in a game by being thrown at an upright peg in an attempt to encircle it

quota n prescribed share or amount of something that is allotted to or expected from a person, group, etc ; allotment

quote vt **1** repeat (a passage, sentence, etc) from a written or spoken source **2** cite as an example **3** state the price or cost of vi use a quotation or quotations n quotation **quotation** n **1** also **quote** something quoted **2** act of quoting **quotation marks** pl n punctuation marks and ' or '' and ' used to enclose and indicate a quotation

R

rabbi n **1** Jewish priest **2** scholar and teacher of the Jewish law

rabbit n small burrowing animal of the hare family with long ears, a short tufty tail, and soft fur vi hunt rabbits

rabble n noisy crowd or throng; mob

rabid adj **1** fervent; wildly enthusiastic **2** raging; violent **3** relating to or having rabies

rabies n fatal viral disease that is transmitted by the bite of an infected animal, esp a dog

race[1] n **1** contest of speed between people or animals in running, swimming, driving, etc **2** any contest in which people compete to be the first to do or achieve something vi **1** take part in a race **2** hurry; go quickly vt **1** run a race or compete with **2** cause (a horse, car, etc) to take part in a race **racecourse** n track on which races, esp horseraces, are held **racehorse** n horse trained and used for racing

race[2] n **1** group of people connected by common ancestry or blood **2** subdivision of mankind to which people belong by virtue of their hereditary physical characteristics **3** any group of people, plants, or animals regarded as a distinct class **race relations** pl n relationships between people of different races, esp within a single society **racial** adj of or relating to race or races **racially** adv

rack n **1** framework, holder, or container; storage or display unit **2** former instrument of torture on which people were tied and stretched vt **1** torture on the rack **2** torment **3** arrange on or in a rack **rack one's brains** strive to remember or understand something

racket[1] n **1** noisy disturbance; uproar **2** sl any illegal or dishonest scheme, activity, business, etc

racket[2] n bat used in tennis, squash, etc , consisting of a rounded frame across which strings are stretched **rackets** n kind of tennis played in a walled court

radar n system for determining the presence and position of an object, such as a ship, by transmitting a beam of radio waves and measuring the direction and time taken for the echo to return from the object

radial adj **1** branching out from a central point; radiating **2** of or relating to a radius

radiant adj **1** glowing with heat or brightness; shining **2** glowing with happiness, joy, hope, etc **3** emitted in rays

radiate v ('reidieit) vt,vi **1** emit radiation vt transmit or give out a particular emotion or feeling vi spread or branch out from a central point adj ('reidiit) having rays or radiating from a centre **radiation** n **1** emission of energy in the form of light, heat, sound, electrons, etc **2** energy so emitted and propagated **3** radiate arrangement **radiator** n **1** heating device through which hot air, water, steam, etc , passes **2** device by which a car engine is kept cool

radical adj **1** basic; fundamental **2** essential; complete **3** favouring fundamental political, social, or other reforms **4** of or arising from a root n person favouring radical reforms

radio n **1** transmission of information by waves transmitted through the atmosphere **2** device for receiving radio broadcasts; wireless **3** broadcasts so received vt,vi transmit a message, etc , by radio

radioactivity n spontaneous disintegration of

unstable atomic nuclei with the emission of radiation **radioactive** adj undergoing or relating to radioactivity

radish n small crisp white or red root of a plant of the mustard family, usually eaten raw

radium n radioactive metallic element

radius n, pl **radii** ('reidiai) or **radiuses** 1 line from the centre of a circle or sphere to its perimeter or surface 2 length of such a line 3 any radiating or raylike part 4 circular area defined by the length of its radius 5 range or extent of experience, influence, activity, etc

raffia n fibre obtained from the leafstalks of a Madagascan palm, used for weaving baskets, matting, etc

raffle n scheme for raising money in which tickets give the purchaser the chance of winning a prize, the winning tickets being randomly selected vt offer as a prize in a raffle

raft n buoyant material, such as logs, fastened together into a platform to transport goods or people by water

rafter n sloping timber or beam on which a roof is supported

rag[1] n 1 scrap of cloth; torn, dirty, or worthless fragment 2 sl newspaper or magazine, esp one of poor quality **rags** pl n old or tattered clothing **ragged** adj 1 rough, tattered, or torn 2 uneven; jagged 3 irregular or imperfect

rag[2] vt (-gg-) 1 tease or play jokes on 2 scold n 1 joke or escapade 2 organized series of games, events, etc , by students to publicize the collection of money for charity

rage n 1 extreme anger; fury 2 violence or intensity of fire, wind, disease, etc 3 intensity of emotion, appetite, or enthusiasm 4 anything arousing widespread enthusiasm vi 1 display violent anger 2 move, continue, prevail, etc , with great intensity or violence

raid n surprise attack, esp one undertaken to capture goods, personnel, etc vt,vi make a surprise attack (on)

rail n 1 horizontal bar of wood or metal acting as a barrier, support, etc 2 fence 3 one of a pair of parallel metal bars laid as a track for trains, etc 4 railway transportation vt enclose with a rail; fence **railing** n fence or framework of rails **railway** n 1 permanent track of rails on which trains may transport passengers, goods,

etc 2 complete network of such tracks together with stations, land, etc

rain n 1 drops of water falling from clouds, condensed from atmospheric water vapour 2 an instance of this; shower 3 rapid heavy fall or occurrence of anything vt,vi fall or cause to fall as or like rain vt give (praise, gifts, etc) in large quantities **rain cats and dogs** rain very heavily **rainbow** n banded arc of spectral colours visible in the sky during or just after a shower of rain **rainfall** n 1 fall of rain; shower 2 amount of water falling as rain, snow, etc , in a given area within a given period of time

raise vt 1 elevate; lift up 2 build; erect 3 bring up for consideration 4 initiate or inspire; provoke 5 bring up (children, etc); rear 6 collect or gather 7 increase in degree, size, intensity, etc 8 evoke; suggest 9 promote in rank, dignity, etc 10 summon up 11 bring back to life 12 remove or lift (a ban, siege, etc)

raisin n sweet dried grape

rajah n king, prince, or chief, esp in India

rake n tool with a long handle and teeth or prongs at one end used for gathering leaves, etc vt 1 gather, collect, or smooth with a rake 2 gather in or collect up 3 search through carefully vi use a rake **rake up** bring up or reveal (something, esp from the past)

rally vt,vi 1 reassemble 2 bring or come together for some common purpose vi 1 gather to support or assist a person, cause, etc 2 regain strength or vigour; recover n 1 recovery 2 gathering of people supporting a cause, taking part in a sporting event, etc

ram n 1 male sheep 2 device used to batter, crush, or drive against something vt (-mm-) 1 strike or crash against with great force 2 force, cram, or press

ramble vi 1 wander about; stroll 2 grow in or follow a meandering course 3 talk or write aimlessly or incoherently n walk taken for pleasure **rambler** n

ramp n sloping surface joining two levels

rampage vi rush about wildly or destructively n wild, violent, or destructive behaviour **on the rampage** very angry; engaged in destructive behaviour

rampant adj 1 rife; unchecked 2 violent in opinion, action, etc

rampart n 1 mound of earth, usually surmounted by a parapet, fortifying a castle, fort, etc 2 any defence or protection

ramshackle adj loosely constructed or held together; shaky; derelict

ran v pt of **run**.

ranch n large farm, esp in America, for rearing cattle, horses, or sheep **rancher** n

rancid adj having an unpleasant stale smell or taste; rank

rancour n angry resentment; bitterness

random adj happening, done, etc, without aim or purpose; chance; haphazard n **at random** without choice, purpose, method, etc **randomly** adv

rang v pt of **ring**.

range n 1 limits within which variation is possible 2 extent or scope 3 possible distance of movement, flight, etc 4 place with targets for shooting practice 5 chain of mountains 6 row or line 7 class, set, or series 8 large cooking stove vt 1 arrange in order, esp in rows or lines 2 dispose or place in a particular group, class, etc 3 travel through or over; roam vi 1 vary within specified limits 2 extend or run, esp in a given direction 3 roam or wander (over) 4 occur within a certain area or time 5 have a particular range

rank[1] n 1 position or standing in a scale or graded body 2 row or line, esp of soldiers vt 1 arrange in a row or rank 2 assign to a certain position, station, class, etc vi hold a certain position **rank and file** n body of soldiers in an army or people in any other organization, as opposed to the officers or leaders **ranks** pl n soldiers as opposed to officers

rank[2] adj 1 growing vigorously or producing luxuriant vigorous growth 2 having a strong unpleasant smell or taste 3 utter; complete **rankly** adv **rankness** n

rankle vi annoy; hurt one's pride

ransack vt 1 search thoroughly or energetically 2 plunder

ransom n 1 redeeming of a kidnapped person, captured goods, etc, for a price 2 price paid or demanded vt release from captivity, detention, etc, by paying the price demanded

rant vi shout angrily; rage

rap vt,vi (-pp-) 1 knock, strike, or tap, esp quickly 2 also **rap out** say sharply n 1 quick

light blow; tap 2 sound of this 3 sl blame or punishment, esp a prison sentence

rape n 1 crime of having sexual intercourse with a woman without her consent 2 act of taking by force vt,vi commit rape (on) **rapist** n

rapid adj quick; fast; swift **rapids** pl n part of a river where the water flows very swiftly **rapidity** n **rapidly** adv

rapier n sword with a slender pointed blade used for thrusting

rapt adj 1 enthralled; enchanted 2 totally absorbed or engrossed

rapture n ecstatic delight; joy; pleasure **rapturous** adj

rare[1] 1 seldom occurring, found, experienced, etc 2 remarkable or unusual, esp in excellence 3 of low density **rarely** adv **rarity** n

rare[2] adj not completely cooked; underdone

rascal n 1 scoundrel; rogue 2 mischievous child or animal **rascally** adj,adv

rash[1] adj hasty in speech or action; reckless

rash[2] n skin eruption, as of spots

rasher n thin slice of bacon

rasp vt,vi grate; sound harsh n harsh grating sound

raspberry n shrub of the rose family producing small juicy red edible fruit

rat n 1 long-tailed rodent resembling but larger than the mouse 2 sl despicable person **smell a rat** be suspicious about ~v (-tt-) **rat on** sl desert or betray (friends, a cause, etc)

rate n 1 quantity, amount, degree, etc, relative to a unit of something else 2 price 3 speed of movement, action, etc 4 tax paid by householders, companies, etc, to cover the supply of local services and amenities vt 1 appraise the value or worth of 2 esteem; consider 3 deserve 4 determine (prices, etc) at a certain rate vi 1 be classed or ranked 2 have status, value, position, etc

rather adv 1 more readily; preferably 2 somewhat; quite 3 with more reason, justice, etc 4 more accurately or properly 5 on the contrary

ratio n fixed numerical relation between two similar magnitudes; proportion

ration n fixed allowance; share vt 1 apportion; share out 2 restrict to or provide with rations

rational adj 1 of, relating to, or based on reason 2 able to reason 3 reasonable; sensible **rationality** n **rationally** adv **ration-**

alize vt 1 make rational; justify unconscious behaviour 2 make (an industry, process, etc) more efficient; streamline vi think in a rational manner; reason

rattle vi,vt make or cause to make a series of short sharp sounds; vibrate noisily vi also **rattle on** chatter vt 1 say or do rapidly 2 sl confuse or disturb (someone) n 1 rapid succession of short sharp sounds 2 device producing a rattling sound, such as a baby's toy

raucous adj rough or harsh sounding **raucously** adv

ravage n 1 violent destructive action 2 devastation; damage vt damage or devastate vi cause great damage

rave vi,vt talk or utter wildly or incoherently vi also **rave about** talk or write very enthusiastically (about) n 1 act of raving 2 extravagant praise

raven n large bird of the crow family with shiny black plumage and a harsh cry adj,n shiny black

ravenous adj 1 extremely hungry 2 greedy for praise, recognition, etc **ravenously** adv

ravine steep valley; gorge; canyon

ravioli n small pieces of pasta enclosing chopped meat, etc , usually served in a tomato sauce

ravish vt 1 seize and carry away forcibly 2 rape 3 enrapture

raw adj 1 not cooked 2 in a natural state; unprocessed 3 inexperienced 4 painfully open or exposed, as a wound 5 crude; vulgar 6 harsh; unfair; unpleasant **rawness** n

ray n 1 narrow beam of light, etc 2 tiny amount of hope, comfort, etc ; spark 3 line or structure radiating from a centre vi,vt radiate

rayon n man-made textile or fibre made from cellulose

raze vt demolish or destroy (buildings, etc) completely

razor n instrument fitted with cutting edges, used esp for shaving hair

reach vt 1 get to; arrive at; attain; come to 2 establish contact with 3 amount to; total vt,vi extend as far as **reach for** stretch up or out for in order to grasp and bring closer ~ n 1 act of reaching 2 range; extent covered

react vi 1 reciprocate 2 respond to a stimulus 3 act in opposition or in reverse 4 interact **reaction** n 1 reciprocal action, movement, or

tendency 2 response to a stimulus 3 response to an event, idea, etc 4 tendency or movement in politics towards extreme conservatism 5 interaction between chemicals **reactionary** adj relating to reaction, esp in politics n reactionary person

read v (read) vt,vi 1 apprehend the meaning of (letters, words, etc) 2 also **read out** utter (printed or written matter) aloud 3 be occupied in reading 4 study (a subject) 5 learn of by reading vt 1 interpret 2 register; indicate 3 predict; foretell vi have a certain wording **read between the lines** deduce an implied meaning not openly stated ~ n act of reading **reader** n

readjust vt adjust again or afresh; rearrange; readapt

ready adj 1 fully prepared 2 willing 3 prompt; quick 4 inclined; apt 5 likely or liable (to) 6 immediately available **get ready** 1 prepare 2 dress oneself n **at the ready** in position **readily** adv willingly; without delay

real adj 1 true; genuine; authentic 2 actual; not imaginary or fictitious **really** adv 1 in fact; actually 2 truly; genuinely **reality** n **realism** n interest in or concern for the real or actual **realist** n **realistic** adj **realistically** adv

realize vt,vi comprehend; appreciate; be aware vt 1 bring to fruition 2 convert into cash vi be sold for; bring as proceeds; gain **realization** n

realm n 1 kingdom; domain 2 region or sphere in which something rules or predominates

reap vt,vi cut or harvest (grain) vt obtain as a result or recompense

rear[1] n 1 back part of anything 2 position behind or in the rear 3 buttocks adj of, at, or in the rear **rear admiral** n naval officer ranking immediately below a vice-admiral **rearguard** n military detachment that brings up and protects the rear, esp in retreat

rear[2] vt 1 care for and bring to maturity 2 lift; erect vi rise up on the hind legs **rear up** rise up in anger, resentment, etc

reason n 1 ground, cause, or motive 2 justification; explanation 3 mental ability of logical argument 4 good sense 5 sanity vi,vt 1 think or argue logically (about) 2 conclude or infer (that) 3 urge or persuade by reasoning **reasonable** adj 1 amenable to reason 2 based on reason; sensible or sound **3** able to reason **4** not excessive; moderate **reasonably** adv

reassure vt allay (fears, doubts, etc); restore confidence or tranquillity to **reassurance** n

rebate n return of part of an amount paid for goods, a service, etc

rebel n ('rebal) person who defies authority or control vi (ri'bel) (-ll-) resist; oppose **rebel against** show or feel strong aversion (for) **rebellion** n **rebellious** adj

rebound vt,vi (ri'baund) spring back or cause to spring back n ('ri:baund) act of rebounding; recoil

rebuff vt treat scornfully; turn away; snub n rejection; abrupt dismissal

rebuke vt,n reprimand

recalcitrant adj unwilling to submit; wayward; wilful; stubborn **recalcitrance** n

recall vt **1** remember **2** call back **3** revoke or withdraw n **1** act or instance of recalling **2** memory

recede vi **1** move back; retreat **2** become more distant **3** slope backwards **4** withdraw from a bargain, promise, etc **5** decline in value, etc

receipt n **1** written acknowledgement of payment or delivery **2** act of receiving; fact of being received vt mark (a bill) as paid vt,vi write or give a receipt for **receipts** pl n amount received

receive vt **1** take into one's possession; gain; get **2** encounter, experience, or undergo **3** bear; sustain **4** gain knowledge of; learn **5** welcome; admit vi **1** receive something **2** buy and sell stolen goods **receiver** n **1** someone or something that receives **2** device for converting electrical signals into their desired form

recent adj occurring, appearing, done, etc , just before the present time; fresh; not remote **recently** adv

receptacle n **1** container **2** portion of a plant stem bearing a flower or flower head

reception n **1** act of receiving or being received **2** manner of being received **3** formal social gathering **4** area in an office, hotel, etc , where visitors are received **5** quality attained in receiving radio signals, etc **receptionist** n person employed to receive visitors, answer the telephone, etc **receptive** adj able, quick, or willing to receive suggestions, requests, etc

recess (ri'ses, 'ri:ses) **1** part or area that is set back; alcove **2** also **recesses** secluded inner

place or area **3** US temporary break; holiday vt **1** place in a recess **2** make a recess in or of

recession n **1** withdrawal **2** receding part **3** decline or falling off in business activity

recipe n formula or method, esp for preparing a dish in cookery

recipient n person who receives

reciprocal adj **1** given, felt, etc , on both sides; mutual **2** given, done, etc , in return n reciprocal relationship; equivalent; counterpart **reciprocate** vt,vi **1** do, feel, etc , (something similar) in return **2** give and receive; interchange

recite vt,vi repeat aloud, as from memory vt read or narrate before an audience **recital** n **1** musical performance, poetry reading, etc **2** detailed account; statement; description

reckless adj careless of consequences; heedless; rash **recklessly** adv

reckon vt,vi add (up); calculate vt consider; regard as; think **reckon with 1** settle accounts with **2** take into consideration

reclaim vt **1** render useable for cultivation, habitation, etc **2** recover from waste products **3** bring back from error, sin, etc **reclamation** n

recline vi,vt lean back or cause to lean back **reclinable** adj

recluse n hermit

recognize vt **1** identify; know again **2** perceive; realize **3** acknowledge or accept the existence, truth, etc , of **4** show appreciation of by a reward, etc **recognition** n **recognizable** adj

recoil vi **1** draw or shrink back, as in fear, horror, etc **2** spring back when released, as a firearm **3** rebound or react upon n act or instance of recoiling

recollect vt,vi recall; remember **recollection** n

recommend vt **1** speak or write of favourably; commend **2** urge as advisable; advise **3** entrust to **4** make acceptable or likeable **recommendable** adj **recommendation** n

recompense vt **1** compensate, repay, or reward **2** compensate for (a loss, etc) n compensation; repayment; remuneration

reconcile vt **1** make no longer opposed or hostile **2** settle **3** make consistent or compatible **reconciliation** n

reconstruct vt **1** rebuild **2** recreate from surviving information **reconstruction** n

record v (ri'ko:d) vt **1** set down for future reference, esp in writing **2** produce in a lasting form, as on magnetic tape **3** register; indicate vi record music, etc n ('reko:d) **1** written account **2** something preserving evidence of the past **3** aggregate of past achievements, actions, etc ; career **4** attainment, occurrence, etc , that surpasses all others **5** flat disc with a spiral groove played on a gramophone to reproduce music, etc **6** list of a person's crimes **on record** stated or known publicly **recorder** n wind instrument similar to the flute

recount vt **1** relate or tell in detail **2** enumerate

recover vt **1** regain; retrieve; reclaim **2** secure compensation for; make up for vi **1** regain health, composure, balance, etc **2** get back to a former or normal position, state, etc **recovery** n

recreation n **1** refreshment and relaxation afforded by exercise, a pastime, etc **2** hobby, exercise, or other diversion providing this **recreational** adj

recriminate vi accuse one's accuser **recrimination** n

recruit n recently enlisted member, esp of the armed forces vt,vi enlist (new personnel, etc) **recruitment** n

rectangle n four-sided figure with four right angles **rectangular** adj

rectify vt set or put right; remedy; correct **rectification** n

rector n clergyman of a parish formerly returning tithes **rectory** n residence of a rector

rectum n lower end of the intestine

recuperate vi recover from illness or fatigue vt recover (financial losses) **recuperation** n

recur vi (-rr-) **1** occur again; be repeated **2** return to the mind, in conversation, etc **recurrence** n

red n **1** colour of the spectrum that is the colour of fresh blood, ripe tomatoes, etc **2** also **Red** someone who is radical in politics, esp a communist **in the red** in debt **see red** become very angry ~adj of the colour red **reddish** adj **redness** n **redcurrant** n shrub bearing small red edible berries **redden** vt,vi make or become red vi blush **red-handed** adj,adv in the act of performing a deed,

committing a crime, etc **red tape** n complicated official or administrative procedure

redeem vt **1** buy or get back; recover; pay off **2** convert (bonds, etc) into cash **3** fulfil (a pledge, etc) **4** make amends for **5** deliver from sin **redemption** n

redress vt set right; remedy; repair; adjust n compensation; reparation

reduce vt,vi make or become smaller or less; diminish; decrease vt **1** bring or force into a certain state, form, etc **2** lower; weaken; subdue **reduction** n

redundant adj **1** excessive; superfluous; unnecessary **2** deprived of a job through being superfluous, etc **redundancy** n

reed n **1** hollow straight stem of any of various tall grasses **2** vibrating piece of cane or metal in some wind instruments **3** wind instrument that sounds by means of a reed

reef n narrow ridge of sand, rocks, etc , at or just under the surface of water

reek vi smell strongly or unpleasantly; stink vt emit (smoke, etc) n strong unpleasant smell

reel[1] n cylinder, frame, or spool on which thread, wire, film, etc , may be wound vt wind on a reel **reel off** say, write, or produce easily and quickly

reel[2] vi sway; rock; stagger; whirl n act of reeling; stagger

refectory n large communal dining hall

refer v (-rr-) vt,vi direct attention, etc , (to) vt submit; assign **refer to 1** be concerned with; relate to **2** resort to for help, information, etc **3** mention or allude (to) **referee** n **1** person to whom something is referred for decision **2** umpire in certain games **3** person who supplies a written reference vi act as a referee **reference** n **1** act of referring **2** mention or allusion **3** direction of attention to a person or thing **4** written statement as to character, abilities, etc **5** relation; regard **referendum** n, pl **referendums** or **referenda** (refə'rendə) referring of legislative measures to the direct vote of the electorate for approval or rejection

refine vt,vi **1** make or become fine; purify; separate out **2** make or become more polished, elegant, etc **refined** adj **refinement** n **refinery** n establishment for refining oil, sugar, etc

reflation n government action taken to stimulate the economy **reflationary** adj

reflect vt,vi **1** cast or throw back light, heat, etc

2 produce an image (of) *vt* **1** mirror; express; reproduce **2** rebound; bring as a consequence *vi* *also* **reflect on 1** think about; contemplate **2** cast credit, dishonour, etc , on **reflection** *n* **reflector** *n* surface or device that reflects light, heat, sound, etc

reflex *n* involuntary reaction; automatic response **reflexive verb** *n* verb having an identical subject and direct object

reform *vt* improve by removing abuses, inequalities, etc ; change for the better *vi,vt* abandon or cause to abandon (evil habits, crime, etc) *n* act or instance of reforming; improvement **reformation** *n*

refract *vt,vi* appear to bend or be bent by the action of light or other waves **refraction** *n*

refrain[1] *vi* keep oneself from; forbear

refrain[2] *n* recurring phrase or verse

refresh *vt,vi* revive; restore; renew *vt* stimulate or revive (the memory) **refreshment** *n* food or drink **refreshments** *pl n* light meal

refrigerator *n* cabinet in which food, drink, etc , may be kept at a low temperature **refrigerate** *vt,vi* freeze, chill, or keep cool in a refrigerator **refrigeration** *n*

refuge *n* **1** shelter or protection from danger, trouble, etc **2** place or person affording this **refugee** *n* person who flees from warfare, persecution, etc , esp to a foreign country

refund *vt* (ri'fʌnd) pay back; reimburse *n* ('ri:fʌnd) repayment; sum repaid

refuse[1] (ri'fju:z) *vt* decline to do, accept, give, grant, etc *vi* withhold or decline acceptance, consent, compliance, etc

refuse[2] ('refju:s) *n* rubbish; waste

refute *vt* prove to be false or in error

regain *vt* **1** win or get back; recover **2** reach or attain again

regal *adj* **1** of, like, or befitting a king; royal **2** stately; dignified; elegant

regard *vt* **1** consider; look upon; take into account; heed **2** have or display respect for; esteem **3** relate to; concern *vt,vi* look steadily (at) *n* **1** attention; heed **2** respect; esteem **3** reference; connection **regards** *pl n* greetings

regardless *adj* heedless or careless (of) *adv* without regard for expense, difficulties, etc

regatta *n* event in which yachts and other boats are raced

regent *n* person ruling in a kingdom during the

minority, illness, incapacity, etc , of the sovereign **regency** *n,adj*

regime *n* **1** system or method of government **2** prevailing system or authority

regiment *n* ('redʒimənt) **1** military unit of ground forces commanded by a colonel **2** large quantity *vt* ('redʒiment) organize strictly, esp into disciplined groups **regimentation** *n*

region *n* **1** part; area; district **2** range; scope **3** sphere of activity **regional** *adj*

register *n* **1** official record or list of names, items, etc **2** book in which this is kept **3** range of a voice or an instrument *vt,vi* enter in a register **2** record **3** show by facial expression, reaction, etc **registration** *n* **registrar** *n* official keeper of a register or record

regress *vi* **1** move or go backwards **2** revert to a former, esp worse, state **regression** *n* **regressive** *adj*

regret *vt* (-tt-) **1** feel sorrow or remorse for **2** remember with sadness or remorse **3** mourn *n* **1** remorse **2** sorrow or grief, esp for a loss **regretful** *adj* **regrettable** *adj*

regular *adj* **1** usual; normal **2** conforming to a rule, principle, etc **3** symmetrical **4** recurring at fixed times or distances; unvarying; periodic **5** habitual *n* **1** soldier in a permanent army **2** habitual customer or visitor of a place **regularity** *n* **regularly** *adv*

regulate *vt* **1** control by rule, principle, etc **2** adjust to function accurately, conform to some standard, etc ; put in order **regulatory** *adj* **regulation** *n* **1** rule; law; requirement **2** control; adjustment

rehabilitate *vt* **1** restore to normal by treatment or training **2** restore to a former position or standing **rehabilitation** *n*

rehearse *vt,vi* practise in private before giving a public performance **rehearsal** *n*

reign *n* **1** period of rule, esp of a sovereign **2** dominance or rule *vi* **1** rule as a sovereign **2** prevail; predominate

reimburse *vt* repay or refund, esp for expense incurred, time lost, etc **reimbursement** *n*

rein *n* **1** long narrow strap fastened to a bit for controlling a horse **2** restraint; curb **give free rein to** allow complete freedom or licence ~*vt* **1** put a rein on **2** check; guide

reincarnation *n* **1** belief that the soul returns after death in a new bodily form **2** rebirth of the soul in a new body **3** new bodily form taken

reindeer n, pl **reindeer** large deer having branched antlers, found in arctic regions

reinforce vt strengthen; give support to; stress **reinforcement** n

reinstate vt restore to a former state or position

reject vt (ri'dʒekt) refuse to take, keep, accept, grant, etc n ('ri:dʒekt) something rejected as imperfect, useless, etc **rejection** n

rejoice vt, vi make or become joyful; gladden

rejuvenate vt, vi make or become young again; restore or be restored in vigour, freshness, etc **rejuvenation** n

relapse vi 1 fall or slip back to a former state or condition **2** become ill again after apparent recovery n act of relapsing

relate vt 1 tell of; recount **2** establish or perceive connection or relationship vi refer to; have relation to **relation** n 1 connection; association **2** kinship **3** relative **4** reference; respect **5** narration **relations** pl n connections, feelings, etc, between people, countries, etc **relationship** n connection; relation; mutual response

relative adj 1 considered or existing in relation to something else; comparative **2** related to; connected with **3** relevant **4** proportionate n someone connected to another by birth or marriage **relatively** adv **relative pronoun** n word, such as who or which, that introduces a subordinate clause and refers back to a previous word or words

relax vt, vi 1 make or become less rigid, tense, or firm **2** make or become less strict, severe, or intense **3** rest from or cease (work effort, worry, etc) **relaxation** n

relay n 1 fresh supply or group of horses, men, etc, relieving others **2** also **relay race** race between teams, each member covering part of the distance before being relieved by another **3** broadcast; transmission vt broadcast; transmit

release vt 1 free; let go; give up; surrender **2** permit to be issued, published, etc **3** discharge n 1 act of releasing; discharge **2** something released for public sale, exhibition, publication, etc

relent vi become less severe, firm, or harsh; soften; abate **relentless** adj ruthless

relevant adj to the point; pertinent **relevance** or **relevancy** n

reliable adj dependable; trustworthy **reliability** n **reliant** adj dependent; trusting **reliance** n

relic n 1 something associated with or surviving from the past **2** object treasured in remembrance **3** something associated with a saint, martyr, etc, revered as holy

relief n 1 easing or alleviation of pain, distress, etc **2** feeling resulting from this **3** anything that eases **4** aid; assistance **5** pleasing change **6** release from a post or duty **7** person taking over **8** raising of a siege **9** elevation of figures, forms, etc, from a flat surface or the appearance of this **10** distinct contrast **relieve** vt 1 ease; lessen; alleviate **2** help; aid **3** free from anxiety, etc **4** break the monotony of **5** bring into relief; provide contrast **6** release from duty; take over the duties of **7** deprive

religion n 1 belief in and worship of a god or gods **2** a particular system of belief and worship **3** associated ritual, conduct, doctrines, etc **4** anything revered or zealously pursued **religious** adj 1 relating to religion **2** pious **3** conscientious; scrupulous **religiously** adv

relinquish vt 1 give up; abandon **2** let go; release **3** surrender

relish vt take delight in; enjoy; look forward to n 1 enjoyment; keen anticipation **2** appetizing taste or flavour **3** sauce; spicy food

relive vt experience again through the imagination or memory

reluctant adj unwilling; marked by unwillingness **reluctance** n **reluctantly** adv

rely v **rely on** trust in; depend on; have confidence in

remain vi 1 stay behind in a place **2** be left over or behind **3** continue to be **remains** pl n 1 remnants; relics; surviving fragments **2** dead body; corpse **remainder** n 1 something remaining or left over **2** quantity remaining after subtraction or division

remand vt send (a prisoner or accused person) back to prison pending further inquiries or proceedings n act of remanding or state of being remanded **remand home** n home for juvenile offenders

remark n comment; observation vt, vi say; comment (about) vt notice; perceive **remarkable** adj worthy of notice; striking; unusual **remarkably** adv

remedy n 1 medicinal cure or treatment 2 cure or correction for a wrong, evil, etc 3 legal redress vt 1 cure or heal 2 put right; correct; redress **remedial** adj

remember vt retain in or recall to the memory vi hold in one's memory **remembrance** n memory; keepsake

remind vt cause to remember or think of again **reminder** n thing that reminds

reminiscence n thing remembered or act of evoking old memories **reminiscent** adj

remiss adj negligent; at fault

remission n 1 forgiveness; pardon 2 reduction of a prison sentence

remit v (-tt-) vt 1 send, esp money 2 pardon; refrain from inflicting (a sentence, etc) vt,vi slacken **remittance** n money sent; payment

remnant n fragment; remainder; relic

remorse n feeling of deep regret, guilt, etc **remorseful** adj **remorseless** adj 1 relentless 2 not penitent

remote adj 1 far away; removed; isolated 2 slight; unlikely **remotely** adv

remove vt 1 take away or off; withdraw 2 dismiss from a post or appointment **removal** n

remunerate vt grant as earnings, reward, etc ; pay or repay **remuneration** n **remunerative** adj

renaissance n revival esp of learning **the Renaissance** n period of radical artistic, scientific, and social development in Europe from the 14th to 16th centuries

renal adj relating to the kidney

render vt 1 give back; return 2 serve; present for approval, action, etc ; supply with 3 give a version or interpretation of; represent 4 melt down **rendition** n

rendezvous n meeting place or time of meeting vi meet by appointment

renew vt,vi make or become new again; revive vt 1 restore; replace; repair; renovate 2 grant for a further period 3 begin again **renewal** n

renounce vt 1 give up; abandon, esp formally 2 disown; break ties with **renunciation** n

renovate vt make fit or habitable again; restore **renovation** n

renown n fame; great distinction; notoriety

rent n regular payment for the use of land, a house, buildings, etc vt grant or use in exchange for rent; hire **rental** n amount charged or paid in rent

rep n short for (sales) **representative** or **repertory** (company)

repair vt 1 mend; restore; renew 2 make up for; make good; remedy n 1 mend 2 act or process of repairing **reparation** n compensation; amends; remedy

repartee n witty reply or retort

repatriate vt send (someone) back to his own country **repatriation** n

repay vt,vi (-paid) 1 pay back; refund 2 return (a kindness, compliment, etc)

repeal vt annul; revoke; cancel n annulment; cancellation

repeat vt say or do again; reproduce; echo n second performance; something repeated **repeatedly** adv

repel vt (-ll-) 1 drive or force back or away; resist 2 disgust **repellent** adj 1 revolting; disgusting 2 unpleasant n substance used to keep flies, pests, etc , away

repent vi,vt feel penitent (about); regret (one's sins) **repentance** n **repentant** adj

repercussion n 1 indirect or unintended consequence or result 2 recoil

repertoire n stock of plays, songs, etc , that a theatrical company, singer, etc , can offer

repertory n 1 theatrical company performing a selection of plays, operas, etc , over a relatively short period 2 repertoire; stock

repetition n 1 act of repeating or being repeated 2 something said or done again **repetitious** adj repeated in a boring manner **repetitive** adj 1 having a constant rhythm or beat 2 characterized by repetition

replace vt 1 put back 2 find or be a substitute for **replacement** n

replenish vt fill up or supply again

replica n copy or reproduction, esp of a work of art

reply vi,vt answer; respond n answer; response

report vt,vi 1 relate 2 make, give, or bring back an account (of) 3 take down or write for publication vt name as an offender; inform against vi present (oneself), register (with) n 1 rumour 2 account of something 3 bang; sharp noise **reporter** n person who reports, esp for a newspaper

repose vi,vt take rest or give rest to; recline; relax n 1 rest; sleep; relaxed state 2 tranquillity; composure

represent vt 1 depict; stand for; symbolize 2 act as a deputy or agent for 3 portray; describe **representation** n **representative** adj serving to represent; typical n 1 person or thing that represents or typifies 2 also **sales representative** person selling a company's products 3 agent; delegate

repress vt keep down or under **repressive** adj **repression** n 1 restraint 2 exclusion of thoughts and tendencies from consciousness

reprieve vt 1 suspend execution of 2 relieve temporarily from harm, punishment, etc n 1 respite from punishment 2 temporary relief

reprimand n sharp rebuke; severe scolding vt give a reprimand to

reprint vt print again; print a new copy of n reproduction or copy of something previously printed

reprisal n retaliation; vengeful action

reproach vt scold; rebuke n scolding; rebuke **reproachful** adj

reproduce vt 1 produce again 2 make a copy of; duplicate; imitate vt,vi produce (offspring) **reproduction** n **reproductive** adj

reptile n cold-blooded egg-laying vertebrate, such as a snake, lizard, or turtle **reptilian** adj

republic n form of state in which supreme power rests in the people and their elected representatives **republican** adj,n

repudiate vt 1 reject 2 disown; cast off **repudiation** n

repugnant adj distasteful; offensive **repugnance** n

repulsion n distaste; aversion **repulsive** adj

reputation n 1 what is generally thought about a person or thing 2 good repute **reputable** adj of good repute; respectable **repute** n reputation, esp a favourable one **reputed** adj considered; reckoned

request n act of asking for something or a thing asked for; demand vt ask for (something) or ask (someone) to do something, esp a favour

requiem n 1 mass for the dead 2 music composed for this

require vt 1 need 2 demand; order **requirement** n

rescue vt save or deliver from danger, etc n delivery or release from harm or danger

research n investigation, esp into a scientific field in order to discover facts vt,vi investigate **researcher** n

resemble vt look like or be similar to **resemblance** n

resent vt feel indignant at; dislike; be bitter about **resentful** adj **resentment** n

reserve vt 1 hold back; set apart; keep for future use 2 book (tickets, seats, etc) in advance n 1 something reserved 2 part of an army, etc , kept back for use in emergency 3 self-restraint; lack of familiarity **in reserve** kept back for future use **reservation** n 1 act of reserving; something reserved 2 advance booking 3 qualification; limitation **reserved** adj 1 set aside for future use; held back 2 booked in advance 3 quiet; self-restrained; reticent

reservoir n 1 place functioning as a store 2 place for holding a large quantity of water

reside vi dwell; have as one's home; live **reside in** live in; be present or inherent **residence** n state of residing or the place where a person resides **resident** adj residing n person staying in a place permanently or for a long time **residential** adj relating to housing, residences, etc ; not commercial

residue n what is left over; remainder **residual** adj

resign vt give up; surrender; relinquish vi give up an office, commission, employment, etc **resign oneself (to)** accept as unavoidable **resignation** n

resilient adj 1 elastic; rebounding 2 capable of recovering quickly from a shock, injury, etc **resilience** n

resin n 1 sticky substance manufactured or obtained from various plants or trees 2 synthetic substance used in making plastics, varnish, etc

resist vt,vi 1 withstand; oppose 2 overcome (a temptation) **resistance** n **resistant** adj

resit vt (-tt-, -sat) take (an examination) again after failing it

resolute adj firm; determined **resolutely** adv

resolution n 1 firmness; determination; resolve 2 act or state of resolving or being resolved 3 decision of a court 4 vote of an assembly, etc 5 explanation; solution

resolve vt 1 make clear 2 determine; decide 3 form by a vote or resolution 4 find a solution to (a problem, etc) 5 agree to (an action, course, etc) formally vt,vi separate into component parts; analyse n 1 something resolved 2 determination; strong intention

resonance n increase or prolonging of vibrations, as of sound **resonant** adj **resonate** vi,vt undergo or cause resonance

resort vi also **resort to** go for help to; turn to n holiday or recreation place

resound vi echo; ring; continue sounding

resource n skill in devising means **resources** pl n 1 means of supplying a want 2 supplies, etc , that can be drawn on **resourceful** adj

respect n 1 reference; relation 2 deference; esteem 3 point or aspect vt treat with esteem; admire **respectable** adj **respectability** n **respectful** adj **respective** adj relating to two or more persons or things regarded individually **respectively** adv individually in the order mentioned

respite ('respit) n 1 delay 2 period of rest or relief 3 suspension of execution; reprieve

respond vi 1 answer; reply 2 react **response** n

responsible adj 1 liable to answer for something 2 of good credit or position **responsibility** n

responsive adj 1 answering, making reply 2 acting in response

rest[1] n 1 quiet repose; sleep 2 refreshing break from activity 3 freedom or relief 4 calm; tranquillity 5 stopping or absence of motion 6 prop or support; something that steadies 7 pause in music, rhythm, etc vi,vt 1 take rest or give rest to 2 support or steady or be supported or steadied **restful** adj **restless** adj 1 unable to remain at rest 2 uneasy, unquiet 3 never still or motionless 4 without rest 5 characterized by constant activity

rest[2] n 1 remainder; that which is left 2 others, everyone else vi remain; continue to be

restaurant n place where meals are bought and eaten

restore vt 1 build up again; repair; renew 2 establish again 3 give back **restoration** n **restorative** adj,n

restrain vt check; hold back; repress **restraint** n

restrict vt,vi place limits (on); confine; restrain **restriction** n **restrictive** adj

result n 1 thing caused or produced; effect; outcome; consequence 2 solution; answer 3 final score vi be the result **result in** end in

resume (ri'zju:m) vt,vi start to take up again after an interval or pause vt occupy (a seat) again **resumption** n

résumé ('rezju:mei) n summary, esp of one's career or background

resurrect vt 1 bring to life again 2 use again; express new interest in **resurrection** n

retail n sale of goods in small quantities to the public, usually through a shop; not wholesale adv sold in such a way vt,vi sell or be sold by retail **retailer** n

retain vt 1 keep back; continue to hold 2 hold in the mind or memory 3 continue to employ; keep for future use **retention** n **retentive** adj

retaliate vi fight back; answer an attack **retaliation** n

retard vt hold back or slow down the development of; delay **retardation** n

retch vi attempt or begin to vomit

reticent adj reserved; modest; shy; not forthcoming **reticence** n

retina n, pl **retinas** or **retinae** ('retini:) membrane of the eyeball that is sensitive to light and transmits images to the brain

retire vi 1 leave one's employment at the end of one's working life 2 go to bed 3 leave or withdraw vt cease to employ after a certain age **retirement** n

retort[1] vi,vt reply rudely or abruptly; answer back n rude or angry reply

retort[2] n round glass vessel with a long neck attached at an angle, used esp in a laboratory for distilling or heating certain substances

retrace vt 1 follow (a route) again in exactly the same way 2 go over again; recount or recall

retract vt,vi 1 draw or pull inwards 2 withdraw (an earlier statement, promise, etc); go back on **retractable** or **retractible** adj **retraction** n

retreat vi 1 move back esp from an advancing army 2 seek shelter or refuge n 1 act of retreating 2 safe place; refuge; haven; sanctuary

retribution n punishment; revenge

retrieve vt 1 fetch, find again; recover; regain 2 rescue from difficulty or harm **retrieval** n

retrograde adj also **retrogressive** 1 moving or pointing backwards; reverse 2 tending to retrogress or decline into a worse condition **retrogress** vi 1 move backwards; recede 2 revert; decline; deteriorate **retrogression** n

retrospect n **in retrospect** looking back in time; with hindsight **retrospective** adj

return vi 1 come or go back to a former place

situation, etc **2** reappear **3** reply; answer back *vt* **1** give, send, or take back **2** respond to; react to; acknowledge **3** yield as a rate of interest **4** elect by voting *n* **1** act of coming or going back **2** yield on investment; revenue. **3** reappearance **4** form to be filled in for tax purposes **returnable** *adj*

reveal *vt* **1** display; show **2** divulge; disclose; betray **revelation** *n* dramatic or sudden disclosure of the truth, esp as revealed by God to mankind

revel *v* (-ll-) **revel in** derive enormous satisfaction or pleasure from; bask in **revels** *pl n also* **revelry** merrymaking; festivities

revenge *n* act of retaliation to offset a previous crime or wrong; vengeance *vt* avenge; retaliate for

revenue *n* income, esp from taxation or goods sold

reverberate *vi* vibrate noisily; resound; echo **reverberation** *n*

reverence *n* feeling or act of deep respect, esp towards something sacred **Reverence** title used when addressing a priest or high-ranking clergyman **reverent** *adj* **revere** *vt* treat with reverence; idolize or worship

reverse *vt* **1** change the direction or order of; turn back **2** revoke; alter (a former decision, attitude, etc) *vi* drive or move backwards *n* **1** opposite side of a coin, sheet of paper, etc **2** gear engaged on a vehicle for moving backwards **3** opposite of what has been stated *adj* opposite **reversal** *n* **1** turning round; reversing **2** revoking of a law, etc ; cancellation

revert *vt* return to a former state or condition **reversion** *n*

review *vt* **1** look back over; examine, check, or consider again **2** give a critical report of (a book, play, etc) *n* **1** critical report **2** general analysis or report; survey **reviewer** *n*

revise *vt* **1** alter (one's attitudes, opinions, etc) **2** rewrite *vi,vt* study in preparation for an examination **revision** *n*

revive *vt,vi* **1** bring or return to consciousness **2** introduce again; restore **revival** *n*

revoke *vt* cancel, esp a law or rule; repeal

revolt *vi* rebel; protest or act against authority *vt* disgust; repel *n* rebellion; uprising; mutiny **revolting** *adj* disgusting; repulsive

revolution *n* **1** large-scale rebellion resulting in the overthrowing of those in power and radical social and political change **2** dramatic change **3** movement around a point or axis; orbit or rotation **revolutionary** *n* person in favour of or working for political revolution *adj* **1** relating to political revolution **2** radical, changing dramatically **3** revolving or rotating **revolutionize** *vt* cause a radical change in; alter dramatically

revolve *vt,vi* move around a point or axis; orbit or rotate **revolve around** be centred on or totally engaged with **revolver** *n* small firearm capable of discharging several shots before reloading

revue *n* light entertainment with music, satirical or comic sketches, etc

revulsion *n* **1** repugnance; feeling of extreme distaste or hatred **2** violent withdrawal or recoil

reward *n* **1** something, such as a sum of money or prize, awarded in acknowledgment of a particular deed, act of service, etc **2** profit; gain; benefit *vt* repay; give a reward to **rewarding** *adj* satisfying

rhetoric *n* **1** art of public speaking; oratory **2** eloquence **rhetorical** *adj* **1** relating to rhetoric **2** concerned more with style or effect of language than with meaning or content **rhetorical question** *n* question to which no answer is required, used esp as a literary device for its dramatic effect

rheumatism *n* inflammation of the muscles, joints, etc **rheumatic** *adj*

rhinoceros *n* large mammal inhabiting tropical or subtropical regions, having one or two horns and a tough hide

rhododendron *n* evergreen shrub having showy red, pink, or white flowers

rhubarb *n* plant with large flat leaves and edible pink stalks

rhyme *n* **1** identical or similar form of sounds occurring esp at the end of two or more words, e g *try* and *buy* or *relieve* and *believe* **2** verse using rhymes *vi,vt* occur or make use of as a rhyme

rhythm *n* **1** alternation of strong and weak stress or beats in music, speech, etc **2** recurring pattern or form of movement, flow, etc **rhythmic** *or* **rhythmical** *adj*

rib *n* **1** one of the curved bones forming the wall of the chest **2** anything resembling such a bone **3** ridged stitch in knitting *vt* (-bb-) **1**

knit using alternate plain and purl stitches **2** *inf* tease; make fun of in a gentle way

ribbon *n* **1** strip of satin, cotton, etc., used for decoration, trimming, etc **2** long narrow strip of land, water, etc **3** narrow band impregnated with ink for use on a typewriter or similar machine

rice *n* type of grass whose grains are used as a staple food

rich *adj* **1** having a large amount of money; wealthy **2** having an abundant supply **3** sumptuous; luxurious **4** having a high proportion of cream or fat **5** having a full flavour or consistency **6** of a deep or vivid colour **richly** *adv* **richness** *n* **riches** *pl n* wealth; valuable possessions

rickety *adj* liable to collapse or break

rickshaw *n* two-wheeled passenger vehicle drawn by hand, traditionally used in parts of Asia

rid *vt* (-dd-; rid or ridded) free; clear away completely **get rid of** dispose of entirely; do away with; banish or abolish **good riddance (to)** *n* welcome relief (from)

riddle[1] *n* complicated puzzle or problem in the form of a verse or question employing puns, hidden meaning, etc

riddle[2] *vt* make a series of holes in

ride *v* (rode; ridden) *vi* **1** be carried on the back of a horse, donkey, etc **2** travel in a vehicle **3** *inf* continue without interference. *vt* **1** travel by sitting on an animal's back **2** drive or propel (a vehicle) *n* journey on horseback, in a vehicle, etc **take for a ride** swindle; defraud **rider** *n* **1** person who rides **2** additional remark, observation, etc

ridge *n* **1** long elevated stretch of land, range **2** furrow; raised or projecting section **3** area of high atmospheric pressure between two depressions

ridicule *n* mockery; scorn. *vt* treat as absurd; mock; deride **ridiculous** *adj* stupid, extremely silly; absurd; ludicrous **ridiculously** *adv*

rife *adj* prevalent; rampant; widely distributed

rifle[1] *n* firearm that is effective over a relatively long range, having spiral grooves cut inside a long barrel

rifle[2] *vt* ransack; loot; plunder

rift *n* **1** crack or opening caused by a geological fault **2** split or disagreement

rig *vt* (-gg-) **1** equip (a vessel) with sails, masts etc **2** fix (prices, an election, etc) by

fraudulent means **rig up** construct or set up, esp in a makeshift fashion ~*n* **1** arrangement of sails masts, etc **2** equipment or installation used in drilling for oil or gas

rigging *n* ropes, chains, etc., supporting sails or masts on a ship

right *adj* **1** correct; accurate **2** true; of an expected standard **3** suitable; appropriate **4** normal **5** on the side of the body opposite the heart **6** conservative or reactionary *adv* **1** accurately, correctly, properly **2** directly; all the way **3** completely; totally **4** towards the right side **5** immediately *n* **1** legal or moral entitlement; due **2** direction, location, or part that is on the right side **3** conservative or reactionary group *vt* correct; restore *vt,vi* make or become upright again **rightly** *adv* **rightful** *adj* proper; entitled; justified **right angle** *n* angle of 90° **right-hand** *adj* on the side towards the right **right-handed** *adj* using the right hand for writing, etc **right wing** *n* political group representing conservative attitudes *adj* **right-wing** relating to the right wing

righteous ('raitʃəs) *adj* virtuous, pious, upright **righteousness** *n*

rigid *adj* **1** straight and stiff; not flexible **2** strict; not allowing variation **rigidity** *n* **rigidly** *adv*

rigour *n* harshness, severity; hardship **rigorous** *adj* **rigorously** *adv*

rim *n* outer or top edge of a container, wheel, etc

rind *n* **1** tough outer skin of certain fruits; peel **2** hard layer or coating of a piece of bacon or cheese

ring[1] *n* **1** circle **2** band worn on the finger **3** circular course track route, etc **4** group of people in a circle **5** circular arena, esp for a circus performance **6** raised platform for a boxing match *vt,vi* **1** encircle, surround **2** fit rings on (birds etc) for identification **ringleader** *n* main organizer, esp of crime etc **ringlet** *n* long curl of hair **ringside** *n* seats nearest the ring at a boxing or wrestling match

ring[2] *v* (rang; rung) *vt,vi* **1** produce a clear metallic sound **2** sound (a bell) **3** *also* **ring up** telephone; call *vi* **1** resound **2** experience a vibrating hum in the ears **ring true/false** sound right/wrong ~*n* **1** sound produced by a bell, telephone, etc 2 echo 3 telephone call 4 quality; characteristic; hint

rink n building or arena used for ice-skating

rinse vt wash through in water, esp in order to remove soap n 1 application of clean water 2 temporary dye for the hair; tint

riot n 1 public disturbance causing a breakdown of law and order; uprising 2 showy display; blaze 3 inf hilarious occasion or person vi participate in a riot **rioter** n **riotous** adj uproarious; disorderly

rip vt, vi (-pp-) tear clumsily or violently n torn part; split **rip off** sl 1 cheat; overcharge 2 steal **rip-off** n sl 1 swindle 2 exploitation for profit

ripe adj 1 ready to be eaten or harvested 2 fully matured 3 having reached the appropriate stage of development **ripen** vi, vt become or make ripe

ripple n 1 slight movement of liquid; small wave 2 continuous gentle sound vi 1 form small waves; undulate 2 gently rise and fall

rise vi (rose; risen) 1 move upwards; ascend 2 stand up; arise 3 get out of bed 4 progress to a higher rank or status 5 become more cheerful, animated, etc 6 increase in price or value 7 rebel; revolt 8 be able to tackle or cope n 1 pay increase 2 upward movement or progression; ascent 3 slope; incline **give rise to** cause; produce

risk n possibility of harm, loss, etc ; gamble; chance vt take a chance on; gamble; hazard **risky** adj

rissole n ball of minced meat fried with a coating of egg and breadcrumbs

rite n formal ceremony having deep religious or cultural significance **ritual** adj relating to rites n 1 formalized procedure for performing certain rites or ceremonies 2 rigid routine

rival n person organization, etc , in competition with others vt (-ll-) 1 compete with 2 be equal to **rivalry** n

river n 1 body of fresh water flowing usually into the sea or a lake 2 flow; stream

rivet n short bolt or nail vt fasten with rivets **riveted** adj unable to move or avert one s gaze; fixed

road n 1 also **roadway** stretch of prepared land for vehicles 2 street 3 way

roam vi, vt wander freely (over); travel widely n leisurely walk; ramble **roamer** n

roar vi (esp of lions) utter a loud noise vi, vt 1 bellow; produce a loud angry or wild sound 2 burn fiercely vi 1 loud cry of a lion bull etc 2 angry or wild noise of a crowd the wind etc **roaring trade** brisk profitable trade

roast vt vi 1 cook in an oven 2 brown, scorch n joint of meat for roasting

rob vt (-bb-) 1 steal from 2 deprive of **robbery** n stealing by force or by threat of violence **robber** n

robe n long loose gown, often signifying office held vt, vi dress, esp officially

robin n small brown songbird the male of which has a red breast

robot n man-like machine capable of performing certain human tasks and functions

robust adj strong, healthy, vigorous **robustly** adv

rock[1] n 1 large solid mass of minerals 2 cliff; boulder, large stone 3 hard stick of sugar **on the rocks** 1 in serious financial trouble 2 served with ice cubes **rock-bottom** n lowest possible level **rockery** n also **rock garden** area in which small plants grow between specially placed rocks **rocky** adj having or strewn with rocks

rock[2] vt, vi sway, move gently from side to side shake **rocker** n curved wooden or metal support for a rocking-chair, cradle, etc **off one's rocker** mentally unbalanced **rocky** adj shaky; unsteady

rocket n cylindrical object propelled at speed into the sky to launch spaceships, direct bombs, or act as a warning or decorative firework vi move like a rocket

rod n 1 long straight stick of wood bar of metal etc 2 also **fishing rod** rod used to suspend a line over water

rode v pt of **ride.**

rodent n mammal such as a rat vole or squirrel, with four strong incisors for gnawing and no canine teeth

roe n 1 also **hard roe** 1 mass of eggs in a female fish 2 also **soft roe** sperm of a male fish

rogue n villain; rascal; scoundrel; criminal **roguery** n **roguish** adj

role n 1 actor s part 2 function, task

roll vt, vi 1 move along by rotating, turn over 2 move on wheels 3 billow, undulate 4 rotate; move up and down 5 sway or move from side to side 6 form into a ball or cylinder coil 7 produce a loud noise; roar vi pass; move onwards vt use a roller on **roll in** or **up**

arrive, turn up ~*n* **1** act of rolling **2** something rolled into a cylinder or ball **3** small round or oblong of baked dough **4** undulation **5** roar **6** rapid drumbeat **rollcall** *n* calling of names to check attendance **rolling pin** *n* cylindrical kitchen utensil for rolling pastry dough etc

roller *n* **1** cylindrical part of a machine for pressing, rolling, winding etc **2** small cylindrical hair-curler **3** long swelling wave **roller-skate** *n* skate with wheels *vi* move on roller-skates

Roman Catholic *n* member of that part of the Christian Church owing allegiance to the Pope *adj* relating to the Roman Catholic Church **Roman Catholicism** *n*

romance *n* **1** love affair, idealized love **2** inclination for adventure, excitement, etc **3** atmosphere of mystery, nostalgia, etc **4** love story, esp remote and idealized **5** heroic medieval legend, verse, etc **6** flight of imagination or fancy *vi* tell extravagant or untrue stories **romantic** *adj* **1** concerned with or given to romance **2** fantastic extravagant, imaginative *n* person with romantic views **romanticize** *vt vi* attach romantic qualities to an otherwise unromantic object story, etc

romp *vi* frolic and play together, esp boisterously **romp home** win easily ~*n* boisterous game **rompers** *pl n* one-piece garment for a young child

roof *n* **1** upper covering of a building, vehicle, etc **2** top limit, highest point **hit the roof** become furious **raise the roof 1** complain noisily **2** cause confusion ~*vt* cover with a roof

rook[1] **1** black raucous gregarious type of crow **2** *sl* swindler, cheat *vt sl* swindle, cheat, overcharge **rookery** *n* tree-top colony of rooks

rook[2] *n also* **castle** chess piece that can move forwards, backwards, or sideways over any number of empty squares

room *n* **1** unoccupied space **2** partitioned part of a building with a specific purpose **3** opportunity, scope **make room** clear a space, bring about an opportunity **roomy** *adj* spacious

roost *n* bird's perch or sleeping place **rule the roost** be in charge, dominate ~*vi* settle for sleep

root[1] *n* **1** part of a plant anchoring it to the

ground and through which it absorbs water and nutrients **2** essential element, basic part or cause, origin **3** one of a specified number of equal factors of a number or quantity *vi* **1** form roots, become established **2** have a basis or origin (in) **root out 1** dig out **2** remove, destroy

root[2] *v* **root about** *or* **around** search (for)

rope *n* thick twisted cord **give enough rope** allow enough freedom **know the ropes** be familiar with the method, rules etc ~*vt* catch or tie with rope **rope in** persuade to take part, enlist **rope off** partition or enclose with a rope **ropy** *adj sl* meagre, of poor quality

rosary *n* **1** series of Roman Catholic prayers, counted on a string of beads **2** beads so used

rose[1] *n* **1** prickly shrub or climbing plant having red, yellow, pink, or white flowers, often fragrant **2** rose-shaped ornament, window etc *n adj* deep pink **bed of roses** luxurious state **through rose-coloured spectacles** *or* **glasses** with unjustified optimism **rosette** *n* **1** cluster of ribbons in the shape of a rose, often worn or presented as a trophy **2** carving in the shape of a rose **rosy** *adj* **1** rose-coloured **2** promising, hopeful

rose[2] *v pt of* **rise.**

rot *vi,vt* (-tt-) decay or cause to decay, deteriorate putrefy *n* **1** decay, corruption **2** disease causing localized decay in plants, animals, timber, etc *n,interj inf* nonsense! rubbish!

rota *n* list of duties, names, etc which may be performed or used in rotation

rotate *vt,vi* **1** move or cause to move on an axis, spin **2** recur or cause to recur in regular succession **rotation** *n* **rotary** *adj* **1** turning like a wheel, moving round an axis **2** acting by rotation **rotor** *n* rotating part of a machine

rotten *adj* **1** unsound, decayed putrefied **2** corrupt, contemptible **3** *inf* unfortunate, annoying, badly done

rouge *n* pink cosmetic powder for the cheeks

rough *adj* **1** not smooth coarse, uneven **2** turbulent, violent **3** unkind, rude **4** harsh, grating **5** unfinished, casual **rough and ready** primitive but effective **rough and tumble** *or* **rough house** disorderly brawling behaviour **rough diamond** person who is worthy but lacking refinement **rough on 1** unfortunate for **2** severe towards ~*n* **1** rough

ground 2 preliminary sketch, stage, etc
v **rough it** live primitively **rough up 1** *sl*
attack; beat up 2 produce a preliminary
sketch, etc **roughen** *vt,vi* make or become
rough **roughly** *adv* 1 in a rough way 2
approximately **roughness** *n*

roulette *n* gambling game in which bets are laid
on which numbered socket a ball will find
when dropped onto a rotating wheel

round *adj* 1 circular; ring-shaped; spherical;
curved 2 complete; whole *n* 1 habitual
journey; single circuit, turn, session, etc 2
meeting; session 3 outburst; volley 4
distribution of drinks to members of a group 5
song in which voices sing in turn *adv,prep* 1
continuously 2 around; about; from place to
place 3 in a reverse or sideways direction 4
with a circular movement 5 so as to arrive 6
so as to be conscious again **round the bend**
crazy **get round** persuade; overcome *~vt,vi*
make or become round, curved, etc *vt* go or
move around **round off** bring to completion
round on attack *esp* verbally **round up**
gather or collect together **roundup** *n*
gathering, collection

roundabout *n* 1 merry-go-round at a fairground
2 road junction where traffic circulates in only
one direction *adj* indirect; circuitous

rouse *vt,vi* 1 waken from sleep; stir 2 incite to
fury, passion, etc ; provoke **rousing** *adj*
exciting; thrilling; vigorous

route *n* course or way to be followed to a
destination *vt* direct along or plan (a particular route)

routine *n* regular unvarying repeated course of
action

rove *vt,vi* stray; wander ramble

row¹ (rou) *n* line of several persons, objects
etc

row² (rou) *vt,vi* propel by oars *vt* carry or
transport in a boat propelled by oars *vi* take
part in races in such a boat *n* act or instance
of rowing

row³ (rau) *n* 1 noisy brawl; squabble 2 disturbance; noise; din *vi* quarrel noisily

rowdy *adj* noisily boisterous and exuberant
rowdiness *n*

royal *adj* 1 of or relating to a king or queen;
regal; majestic 2 splendid; lavish; magnificent **royally** *adv* **royalty** *n* 1 the rank of a
king or queen 2 member(s) of a reigning
family 3 share of profits made on the sale of

books, records, etc . paid to the author,
composer, etc

rub *vt,vi* (-bb-) 1 move a hand, cloth, etc .
briskly or forcefully over the surface (of);
polish; smooth 2 irritate; grate **rub (it) in**
emphasize **rub off on** affect through
association **rub out** obliterate; erase **rub up**
polish; improve **rub up the wrong way**
annoy *~n* act of rubbing; massage

rubber *n* 1 elastic material made from the milky
juice of certain tropical trees or synthesized 2
piece of rubber used to erase pencil marks,
etc

rubbish *n* 1 waste materials; litter 2 nonsense

rubble *n* loose fragments of stone, rock, etc
esp from demolished buildings

ruby *n* deep red precious stone *n,adj* deep red

rucksack *n* large bag carried on the back by
walkers, etc

rudder *n* vertical pivoted piece of wood, metal,
etc , at the stern of a boat or aircraft, used to
steer it

rude *adj* 1 impolite; impertinent 2 primitive;
unsophisticated 3 vulgar; coarse **rudely** *adv*
rudeness *n*

rudiments *pl n* 1 basic elements; first principles
of a subject 2 undeveloped form **rudimentary** *adj* undeveloped; primitive, elementary

rueful *adj* regretful; repentant **ruefully** *adv*

ruff *n* 1 starched lacy collar or frill 2 prominent
growth of feathers or hair around the neck of a
bird or animal

ruffian *n* rogue, villain; bully

ruffle *vt,vi* 1 disturb, wrinkle, rumple 2 annoy
or become annoyed 3 erect (feathers) in
anger or display *n* frill at the neck or wrist

rug *n* 1 small thick carpet 2 thick woollen
blanket

rugby *n also* **rugby football** *or* **rugger** form of
football in which players may use their hands
to carry the ball or to tackle opponents

rugged *adj* 1 uneven rough; craggy 2 strong,
unbending, harsh **ruggedly** *adv* **rugged-
ness** *n*

ruin *n* 1 collapse, devastation, total destruction
2 complete loss of social financial or moral
reputation *vt* bring to ruin; spoil; destroy
ruins *pl n* remains of a partly destroyed or
derelict building, etc **in ruins** destroyed;
decayed **ruinous** *adj*

rule *n* 1 regulation, law, maxim, code of discipline; procedure 2 period of control,

authority, etc **as a rule** generally **work to rule** decrease efficiency or output by observing rules precisely ~vt,vi 1 govern; dominate 2 decree (that); decide officially (that) vt draw a straight line **rule out** exclude **ruler** 1 person who rules 2 instrument for measuring, drawing straight lines, etc

rum n alcoholic drink distilled from sugar cane

rumble vi make a low rolling noise, as of distant thunder vt sl see through; guess correctly **rumble along** or **past** move or pass making a rumble ~n low rolling noise

ruminant n any of various cud-chewing, hoofed animals, such as the cow, sheep, or deer **ruminate** vi 1 chew the cud 2 meditate; ponder; consider carefully

rummage vt,vi ransack; search (through)

rumour n hearsay; gossip; unverified talk

rump n rear part of a person or animal; buttocks

rumple vt,vi crease; crumple; ruffle

run v (-nn-; ran; run) vi 1 proceed on foot at a fast pace 2 gallop or canter 3 make a quick journey 4 function; operate 5 be valid; endure or last 6 go; proceed 7 be inherited from 8 fall in a stream; flow 9 spread; become diffused vt 1 do whilst running 2 roll; push; drive 3 cover quickly 4 operate; manage; control 5 be affected by 6 cause to flow **run across** or **into** meet unexpectedly **run away** escape; abscond **run down 1** slow down 2 find or capture 3 criticize; speak badly of **run for** seek election for **run out** become exhausted; have no more **run to** be adequate for ~n 1 act or pace of running; race 2 continuous series 3 sort; type 4 unlimited freedom or access 5 strong demand 6 score of one in cricket **in the long run** eventually; after a long while **on the run** escaping from the police, etc

rung[1] n bar forming a spoke of a wheel, step of a ladder, crosspiece on a chair, etc

rung[2] v pp of **ring**.

runner n 1 person that runs; athlete 2 lateral shoot of a plant 3 narrow strip of wood, metal, or cloth on which something is supported or runs **runner bean** n climbing bean plant with scarlet flowers and long edible green pods **runner-up** n competitor finishing just after the winner

running adj 1 continuous; without interruption 2 taken at a run 3 moving easily; flowing n 1

condition of the ground on a race course 2 management; operation **in/out of the running** with a/no chance of winning

runny adj discharging liquid; streaming

runway n 1 long wide track used by aircraft for landing or taking off 2 ramp 3 channel; groove

rupture n act of bursting; state of being burst or broken; breach; split vt,vi break; burst

rural adj 1 of the countryside 2 rustic

rush[1] vi,vt hurry or cause to hurry; hasten; proceed recklessly vi come, flow, etc, quickly vt make a sudden attack on n sudden speedy advance **rush hour** n time of day when traffic is heaviest

rush[2] n plant growing in wet places, the stems of which can be used for chair seats, baskets, etc

rust n powdery brownish coating formed on iron and steel by the action of air and moisture vi,vt become or make rusty; corrode **rusty** adj 1 covered in rust; corroded 2 inefficient through disuse; spoilt by neglect **rustiness** n

rustic adj unsophisticated; rural; simple n 1 country dweller 2 unsophisticated person

rustle vi,vt make or cause to make a soft sound, as of dry leaves, silk, etc vt steal (cattle, etc) **rustle up** improvise; procure hastily ~n rustling sound

rut n 1 sunken furrow in a path or track; groove 2 dreary or boring way of life

ruthless adj without mercy or pity; cruel; heartless **ruthlessly** adv **ruthlessness** n

rye n cereal grain used as animal fodder and for making flour and whisky

S

Sabbath n day set aside for rest and worship, Saturday for Jews and Sunday for Christians

sabotage n deliberate destruction for political, military, or private ends vt destroy or disrupt by sabotage **saboteur** n

saccharin n intensely sweet powder used as a non-fattening sugar substitute adj cloyingly sweet

sachet n small sealed bag containing perfume, shampoo, etc

sack n 1 large coarse bag made of flax, hemp, etc, used for coal, flour, corn, etc 2 inf dismissal from employment *vt inf* dismiss from employment

sacrament *n* religious ceremony (Baptism, Matrimony, Holy Orders, etc) regarded as conferring an outward sign of inward divine grace **sacramental** *adj*

sacred *adj* holy; dedicated to God; inviolate **sacredly** *adv* **sacredness** *n*

sacrifice *vt* 1 give up (something) so that greater good or a different end may result 2 offer to or kill in honour of a deity *n* 1 offering of something to a god 2 giving or offering up (anything), esp with a worthy motive **sacrificial** *adj*

sacrilege *n* desecration of a sacred place, person, or thing **sacrilegious** *adj*

sad *adj* 1 sorrowful; dejected; downcast 2 unfortunate **sadly** *adv* **sadness** *n* **sadden** *vt,vi* make or grow sad

saddle *n* rider's seat fitted to a horse, bicycle, etc *vt* 1 put a saddle on 2 load or burden (with)

sadism *n* perversion in which pleasure, esp sexual pleasure, is derived from inflicting pain **sadist** *n* **sadistic** *adj*

safari *n* expedition, esp for hunting big game

safe *adj* 1 secure; free from danger 2 dependable; reliable **safe and sound** unharmed ~*n* strong box for keeping valuables secure against theft **safely** *adv* **safeguard** *n* proviso; precaution *vt* protect; guard **safekeeping** *n* custody

safety *n* security; freedom from danger or risk **safety belt** *n* strong strap to secure a passenger in the seat of an aircraft, car, etc **safety pin** *n* bent pin with the point protected by a guard **safety valve** *n* 1 machine valve that opens when pressure becomes too great for safety 2 harmless outlet for anger, passion, etc

sag *vi* (-gg-) 1 droop; bend; sink 2 give way under weight or pressure

saga *n* 1 heroic prose tale in old Norse literature 2 long chronicle, esp of generations of one family

sage[1] *n* very wise man *adj* of great wisdom, discretion, prudence, etc **sagacity** *n* **sagely** *adv*

sage[2] *n* grey-green aromatic herb widely used in cookery

Sagittarius *n* ninth sign of the zodiac, represented by the Archer

said *v pp* and *pt* of **say**

sail *n* 1 large sheet of canvas, etc , spread to catch the wind and propel a boat 2 arm of a windmill 3 trip in a sailing vessel *vt,vi* 1 move by sail power; travel by sea 2 glide or pass smoothly and easily **set sail** start on a voyage **sail close to the wind** narrowly avoid danger, ruin, etc **sailor** *n* member of ship's crew **good/bad sailor** one not/very liable to seasickness

saint *n* holy person canonized or famous for extreme virtue **saintly** *adj*

sake *n* purpose; benefit; behalf **for the sake of** for the advantage or purpose of; in order to help, protect, etc

salad *n* cold meal of vegetables seasoned and served raw **fruit salad** mixture of raw fruits **salad dressing** *n* mixture of oil, vinegar, seasoning, herbs, etc , used to flavour salad

salamander *n* lizard-like creature of the newt family

salary *n* fixed payment given periodically for non-manual work **salaried** *adj* earning a salary

sale *n* 1 exchange of goods for money 2 fast disposal of unwanted stock at reduced prices or by auction **saleable** *adj* easy to sell **salesman** *n*, *pl* **-men** person employed to sell **saleswoman** *f n* **salesmanship** *n* skill in persuading customers to buy

saline *adj* of or containing salt **salinity** *n*

saliva *n* spittle; colourless odourless juice secreted into the mouth, esp for moistening food **salivate** *vi* produce saliva, esp in excess **salivation** *n*

sallow *adj* 1 with skin of a pale yellow colour 2 unhealthy looking

salmon *n*, *pl* **salmon** or **salmons** large fish, popular as a food, that goes up rivers to spawn **salmon pink** *n,adj* orange-pink colour of salmon flesh

salon *n* 1 large elegant reception room 2 regular gathering of distinguished guests 3 exhibition of paintings 4 premises or shop where dressmakers, hairdressers, etc , receive clients

saloon *n* 1 large public room in a hotel, ship, train, etc 2 *also* **saloon bar** more comfortably furnished bar room in a public house 3 car with an enclosed body

salt *n* 1 white crystalline compound, sodium chloride, used as food seasoning, preservative, etc **2** any crystalline compound formed from an acid and base *vt* season or treat with salt **salt-cellar** *n* small container for holding salt **saltpetre** *n* nitrogen compound used in explosives, fertilizers, etc

salute *n* gesture of greeting, recognition, or respect *vt,vi* make a salute (to)

salvage *n* act of or reward for saving a ship, property, etc , from destruction or waste *vt* save from loss or destruction

salvation *n* act of saving from loss, destruction, or sin

salve *vt* anoint, heal, or soothe *n* ointment; balm; whatever soothes or heals

same *adj* **1** identical **2** indicating no change *adv* **the same** in an identical manner; with no change **all the same** even so; in spite of that; nevertheless ~*pron* that same or identical thing or person

sample *n* specimen; example; small quantity showing properties of something *vt* test or try a sample

sanatorium *n*, *pl* **sanatoria** (sænə'tɔːriə) *or* **sanatoriums** **1** hospital, esp for convalescent, tubercular, mentally unbalanced, or chronically ill patients **2** place where sickness is treated in a school, college, etc

sanctify *vt* make holy or sacred; revere

sanction *vt* allow; authorize; confirm *n* **1** penalty or reward intended to enforce a law **2** confirmation; authorization; permission

sanctity *n* holiness; sacredness

sanctuary *n* **1** recognized place or right of refuge **2** part of a church beyond the altar rails **3** protected reserve for birds, animals, etc

sand *n* mass of tiny fragments of crushed rocks covering deserts, seashores, etc *vt* rub with sandpaper **sandpaper** *n* heavy paper coated with sand or other abrasive and used for smoothing, polishing, etc **sandy** *adj* **1** covered with sand **2** of the colour of sand

sandal *n* open shoe secured by straps

sandwich *n* two slices of bread enclosing jam, meat, etc *vt* squeeze (one thing) between two others

sane *adj* of sound mind; sensible; rational **sanely** *adv* **sanity** *n*

sang *v* pt of **sing.**

sanitary *adj* concerning or conducive to health, esp in regard to cleanliness and hygiene **sanitary towel** *n* absorbent pad for use during menstruation **sanitation** *n* sanitary methods and equipment, esp concerning sewage disposal drainage, clean water, etc

sank *v* pt of **sink.**

sap *n* vital juice, esp of plants *vt* (-pp-) drain the sap or energy from **sapling** *n* young tree

sapphire *n* gemstone, usually brilliant blue, akin to the ruby *adj* brilliant blue

sarcasm *n* mocking sneering, or ironic language **sarcastic** *adj* **sarcastically** *adv*

sardine *n* young pilchard often packed tightly with others and tinned in oil

sari *n* Indian or Pakistani woman's garment worn over a blouse, consisting of a long bolt of cloth that is wrapped around the waist and over the shoulder

sash[1] *n* band of material worn around the waist or over the shoulder

sash[2] *n* sliding frame holding panes of glass in a window

sat *v* pt and pp of **sit.**

Satan *n* the Devil **satanic** *adj*

satchel *n* small bag with shoulder straps, esp for holding school books

satellite *n* **1** heavenly body or spacecraft revolving round a planet or star **2** disciple; hanger-on; underling

satin *n* glossy closely woven silk fabric *adj* of or like satin

satire *n* **1** use of irony, ridicule, or sarcasm to mock or denounce **2** literary work exhibiting this **satirical** *adj*

satisfy *vt,vi* fulfil the needs or wishes of *vt* be sufficient for; give enough to; appease **satisfaction** *n* **satisfactory** *adj*

saturate *vt* imbue or soak completely; cause to be thoroughly absorbed in **saturation** *n*

Saturday *n* seventh day of the week

Saturn *n* outer giant planet lying between Jupiter and Uranus and having a system of rings around its equator

sauce *n* **1** liquid poured over food to add piquancy or relish **2** *inf* cheeky impudence **saucy** *adj* **1** cheeky; impertinent; bold **2** smart; pert **saucily** *adv* **sauciness** *n*

saucepan *n* long-handled cooking pan

saucer *n* **1** shallow indented dish placed under a cup **2** anything of similar shape

sauna *n* also **sauna bath** **1** steam bath **2** room used for this

saunter *vi* wander idly; stroll; amble *n* gentle stroll; ramble

sausage n short tube, esp of animal gut, stuffed with minced seasoned meat

savage adj ferocious; violent; uncivilized n 1 primitive person 2 one with savage characteristics; brute vt attack and wound

save[1] vt rescue or protect from evil, danger, loss, damage, etc vt,vi 1 store up; set aside for future use 2 be economical or thrifty **savings** pl n sum of money set aside for future use

save[2] prep except; not including

saviour n one who saves another person, etc , from serious trouble; redeemer **Saviour** n Christ

savoury adj not sweet but with a pleasant appetizing taste n savoury course of a meal

saw[1] n tool with a long toothed metal blade used for cutting wood, etc vt,vi use a saw (on) **sawdust** n tiny fragments of wood produced by sawing and used in packaging, etc

saw[2] v pt of **see**.

saxophone n brass wind instrument with a single reed and about twenty keys **saxophonist** n

say vt,vi (said) 1 state, utter, or speak in words 2 declare; tell; repeat 3 assure; take as an example n 1 chance or turn to speak 2 authority **saying** n maxim; proverb; something commonly said

scab n 1 crust formed over a healing wound 2 sl blackleg

scaffold n 1 temporary raised platform, esp for supporting workmen 2 platform on which criminals are executed **scaffolding** n scaffold or system of scaffolds

scald vt 1 burn with hot liquid 2 clean or cook with boiling water 3 bring (milk, etc) almost to boiling point n burn caused by hot liquid

scale[1] n 1 graded table used as a scheme for classification or measurement 2 series of musical notes ascending at fixed intervals 3 range; compass; scope vt clamber up; climb **scale down** make smaller proportionately

scale[2] n 1 one of the small thin plates protecting fish, reptiles, etc 2 thin film or layer vt,vi peel off (scales) **scaly** adj dry; flaky; hard

scale[3] n 1 dish forming one side of a balance 2 also **scales** weighing machine

scalp n skin covering the head vt tear off scalp and hair from

scalpel n small surgical knife

scampi pl or s n large prawns

scan v (-nn-) vt 1 scrutinize carefully 2 glance briefly over 3 cast a beam over 4 classify (verse) by metre vi follow metrical pattern n act of scanning

scandal n 1 act or behaviour outraging public opinion 2 malicious gossip; slander **scandalize** vt shock by scandal **scandalous** adj **scandalously** adv

scant adj scarcely enough; not plentiful **scanty** adj meagre; inadequate

scapegoat n one forced to bear the blame for others' faults

scar n mark left by a wound vt (-rr-) mark with a scar

scarce adj in short supply; rare **make oneself scarce** inf go away **scarcely** adv 1 hardly; barely; only just 2 not quite **scarcity** n

scare vt startle; frighten away; alarm n sudden or unreasonable panic **scary** adj inf frightening **scarecrow** n device, often resembling a man, to frighten birds away from crops

scarf n, pl **scarves** piece of material worn over the head or around the neck

scarlet adj brilliant red

scathing adj scornful; showing contempt

scatter vt strew; sprinkle; throw loosely about vi disperse; separate **scatter-brained** adj easily distracted; unable to concentrate

scavenge vt,vi search through litter and rubbish and take (anything of value) **scavenger** n

scenario n outline of the plot of a film or play

scene n 1 setting for an action, play, film, etc 2 short division of an act in a play or film 3 description of an incident 4 noisy public outburst **behind the scenes** not for public view or knowledge **scenery** n 1 theatrical backdrops, properties, etc 2 natural features of landscape **scenic** adj 1 concerning natural scenery 2 dramatic; theatrical

scent n 1 individual smell, aroma, or fragrance 2 mixture of fragrant essences; perfume 3 sense of smell vt 1 perceive odour of 2 sense; suspect 3 impart scent to

sceptic n one unwilling to believe and inclined to question or doubt **sceptical** adj **scepticism** n

sceptre n staff carried as a symbol of regal or imperial power

schedule n 1 timetable; order of events 2

inventory or list *vt* make a schedule of; plan; arrange **on schedule** as arranged; on time

scheme *n* 1 planned systematic arrangement 2 cunning plot *vt,vi* plan; contrive; plot

schizophrenia *n* psychosis marked by delusions and inability to distinguish fantasy from reality and often leading to a double personality **schizophrenic** *adj,n*

scholar *n* 1 learned person 2 student or holder of a scholarship **scholarly** *adj* studious; learned; intellectually thorough **scholarship** *n* 1 grant awarded to a promising student 2 erudition; learning

school[1] *n* 1 place of education, esp for children 2 group of students of a particular branch of learning 3 followers or imitators of a particular theory, artist, etc *vt* 1 instruct 2 control **scholastic** *adj* of schools, learning, etc

school[2] *n* large body of fish, whales, etc

schooner *n* 1 swift two-masted sailing ship 2 large beer or sherry glass

science *n* knowledge or branch of knowledge obtained by experiment, observation, and critical testing **science fiction** *n* fiction based on imagined sensational changes or developments of environment, space travel, etc **scientific** *adj* 1 to do with science 2 systematic, careful, and exact **scientist** *n*

scissors *pl n* cutting tool with two pivoted blades

scoff[1] *vi* mock or jeer; show scorn and derision *n* expression of contempt

scoff[2] *vt sl* eat greedily ravenously, or quickly *n sl* food

scold *vt* find fault with; reprimand

scone *n* small round plain cake eaten with butter and jam

scoop *n* 1 small short-handled shovel 2 journalist s exclusive story *vt* hollow out or lift as with a scoop

scooter *n* 1 child's two-wheeled vehicle with handles and a platform, propelled by pushing against the ground with one foot 2 small low-powered motorcycle

scope *n* range; extent; field of action

scorch *vt,vi* 1 burn slightly, so as to discolour but not destroy 2 dry up with heat; parch

score *n* 1 tally or record of relative charges, achievements, or points gained 2 incised line 3 written musical composition 4 set of twenty *vt* 1 gain and record points 2 furrow

or mark with lines 3 orchestrate *vi inf* achieve a success **know the score** know the hard facts **scoreboard** *n* board on which a score is recorded

scorn *vt* 1 despise; hold in contempt 2 refuse contemptuously; disdain *n* derision; contempt; mockery **scornful** *adj* **scornfully** *adv*

Scorpio *n* eighth sign of the zodiac, represented by a scorpion

scorpion *n* member of the spider family with pincers and a joined head and thorax

scoundrel *n* rascal; villain; rogue

scour[1] *vt* clean or polish thoroughly by rubbing *n* act of scouring **scourer** *n*

scour[2] *vt* search thoroughly through

scout *n* one sent out or ahead to bring back information *vi* act as scout **Scout** *also* **Boy Scout** boy belonging to an organization founded to encourage high principles, self-reliance, etc

scowl *vi* frown angrily or sullenly *n* bad-tempered sullen frown

scramble *vi* make one s way fast and awkwardly, esp to race others to a goal *vt* 1 mix or muddle 2 alter the frequencies of (a radio message, etc) so as to render it unintelligible *n* 1 undignified rush 2 motorcycle race over rough ground **scrambled eggs** eggs beaten and cooked

scrap *n* 1 morsel; fragment 2 rubbish; leftovers 3 *inf* fight; quarrel *vt* (-pp-) discard; throw away **scrapbook** *n* blank book into which newspaper cuttings, photographs, etc, are pasted **scrap iron** *n* fragments of metal useful only for remelting

scrape *vt* smooth or damage by rubbing with a sharp edge **scrape through** succeed by a narrow margin **scrape up** *or* **together** gather with difficulty, diligence, or thrift ~*n* 1 scratch 2 *inf* awkward predicament

scratch *vt,vi* 1 mark or cut with something sharp or be susceptible to such marking 2 rub the nails over (the skin) to relieve itching *vt* cancel; erase *n* mark or sound made by scratching **from scratch** from the very beginning **up to scratch** *inf* acceptable; up to standard **scratchy** *adj* 1 marked with scratches 2 ragged; irregular 3 irritable

scrawl *vt,vi* scribble; write fast and unintelligibly *n* illegible writing

scream *vt,vi* shriek or cry out in a high loud

voice *n* **1** piercing cry **2** *inf* hilarious joke **screamingly** *adv* hilariously

screech *vi* cry out in a harsh shrill voice *n* sound made by screeching

screen *n* movable board or partition acting as a room divider, surface to project films, protection from heat or observation, etc *vt* **1** hide or shelter **2** display on a cinema or television screen **3** subject to tests to determine weakness, disease, qualities, etc **screenplay** *n* script for a film

screw *n* spiral grooved metal shaft used as a fastening device **have a screw loose** be mentally deficient **put the screws on** extort by blackmail ~*vt* fasten; tighten; compress with a screw **screw,vi tab** have sexual intercourse (with) **screw up 1** tighten firmly with a screw **2** twist; distort; crumple **3** summon up **screwdriver** *n* tool with metal wedge-shaped blade, which slots into the groove on the head of a screw to turn it **screwy** *adj sl* crazy

scribble *vt,vi* write carelessly, fast, or meaninglessly *n* careless or meaningless writing **scribbler** *n*

script *n* **1** text of a film, play, speech, etc **2** handwriting or print resembling It **scriptwriter** *n* one who writes scripts dialogues, television series, etc

scripture *n* the Bible **scriptural** *adj*

scroll *n* **1** roll of parchment or paper **2** ornamental design resembling a scroll

scrounge *vt,vi inf* cadge; sponge; wheedle or scrape together **scrounger** *n*

scrub[1] *vt,vi* (-bb-) clean by rubbing hard with a brush and water *n* act of scrubbing

scrub[2] *n* landscape of low stunted trees, bushes, and shrubs

scruffy *adj* untidy; unkempt; messy **scruffily** *adv* **scruffiness** *n*

scruple *n* moral doubt or hesitation *vi* hesitate because of scruple

scrupulous *adj* conscientious; attentive to details **scrupulously** *adv*

scrutinize *vt* examine closely, critically, or in great detail **scrutiny** *n*

scuffle *n* close confused struggle or fight *vi* fight in a disorderly manner

scullery *n* small room for rough kitchen work, dish washing, etc

sculpture *n* **1** art of making figures, statues, etc , by carving or moulding **2** work or works

made in this way **sculpt** *vt,vi* make a sculpture (of) **sculptor** *n*

scum *n* **1** foam on the surface of a liquid **2** worthless or disgusting residue

scurf *n* crust of small flakes of dead skin, esp on the scalp; dandruff

scythe *n* implement with a large curved blade for cutting grass *vt* cut with a scythe

sea *n* **1** continuous expanse of salt water that covers most of the earth's surface **2** large body of salt water partially bounded by land **3** large lake **4** condition, turbulence, waves, etc , of an ocean or sea **5** something suggestive of the sea in being vast or overwhelming **at sea 1** on the ocean **2** confused **go to sea** become a sailor **2** start an ocean voyage **put to sea** leave port

sea anemone *n* common marine animal whose arrangement of tentacles resembles a flower

seacoast strip of land bordering on an ocean or sea

seafront *n* area of a seaside resort directly facing the sea and having a promenade, hotels, etc

seagull *n* gull frequenting the sea or coast

seahorse *n* **1** marine fish that swims in an upright position and has a head shaped like that of a horse **2** walrus

sea-kale vegetable having broad green leaves

seal[1] *n* **1** impression on wax or metal serving as an authorization, guarantee, etc **2** anything used to close tightly to prevent leaking or opening *vt* mark, attest, or close firmly with a seal **set the seal on** formally conclude

seal[2] *n* carnivorous marine mammal with flippers, a short tail, and a long body covered in dense fur **sealskin** *n* close short furry hide of the seal, sometimes used for clothing

sea-level *n* level of the sea midway between high and low tide

sea-lion *n* large seal having visible external ears

seam *n* join formed by sewing together or attaching two pieces of material **seamy** *adj* squalid

seaman *n, pl* **-men** sailor, esp below the rank of officer **seamanship** *n* skill or techniques of ship management, operation, and navigation

seaplane *n* aeroplane equipped to land on or take off from the water

search *vt,vi* examine, probe, or investigate closely hoping to find something *n* investigation; exploration; enquiry **search me!** si I have no idea! **searchlight** n lamp emitting a strong beam of artificial light used to scan an area, the sky, etc

seashore n seacoast

seasick adj nauseated by the movement of a vessel at sea **seasickness** n

seaside n seacoast adj relating to or located at the seacoast

season n 1 one of the four climatic divisions of the year 2 appropriate time; short spell **in season** 1 (of game, fish foxes, etc) allowed to be legally hunted or caught 2 ripe; ready for use ~vt 1 flavour with salt, pepper, etc 2 accustom; mature **seasonable** adj appropriate to the moment or occasion; timely **seasonal** adj occurring at or changing with the season **seasoned** adj 1 experienced 2 flavoured; tempered **seasoning** n 1 food flavouring, such as salt, pepper, or herbs 2 processing of timber **season ticket** n ticket valid for repeated use over a set period

seat n 1 chair or part of a chair, place to sit 2 position in Parliament, a council, etc to which one is elected or appointed 3 basis, central location or site 4 manner of sitting (on a horse, etc) 5 buttocks, bottom vt place on a seat; accommodate in a chair or chairs **seat-belt** n safety belt

seaweed n plant or alga growing in the ocean

seaworthy adj (of a vessel) fit for sailing **seaworthiness** n

secluded adj hidden or shut off from observation or company **seclusion** n privacy solitude

second[1] adj 1 coming between the first and the third 2 another; additional; extra 3 alternate, alternative adv in second place n person or thing in second place vt support (another's proposal or nomination) **secondly** adv **second best** adj inferior to the best **second-class** adj of second or inferior class, quality, etc **second-hand** adj not new; having belonged to another **second nature** n habit or tendency that has become automatic or instinctive **second-rate** adj of inferior quality or value; shoddy

second[2] n 1 period of time equal to one sixtieth of a minute 2 moment; instant 3 unit by which time is measured

secondary adj subordinate; of less importance;

coming second **secondary school** n school teaching children over the age of eleven

secret adj concealed; hidden; private; not made known n whatever is made or kept secret **secrecy** n **secretly** adv **secret agent** n spy

secretary n 1 one employed to help with correspondence, keep records, etc 2 principal assistant to a minister, ambassador, etc **secretarial** adj

secrete vt (of a gland cell, etc) produce and release (substances such as saliva, etc) **secretion** n

secretive adj reticent; given to undue secrecy; uncommunicative

sect n group of people following a particular leader or holding specific views **sectarian** n, adj

section n division or portion; part vt cut or separate into parts

sector n 1 part of a circle bounded by two radii and an arc 2 area; part; scope of activity

secular adj temporal, lay, not spiritual or monastic n priest bound by no monastic rule

secure adj 1 safe, free from danger 2 reliable, certain 3 not movable vt 1 make safe certain or sure 2 obtain **securely** adv **security** n 1 safety, freedom from anxiety danger, or want 2 pledge, document, or certificate of ownership; bond or share 3 precautions against espionage, theft, etc

sedate adj 1 calm, placid, tranquil 2 staid dignified **sedately** adv **sedateness** n **sedation** n act of calming or state of calmness induced by sedatives **sedative** adj calming soporific n sedative drug

sediment n dregs or residue at the bottom of a liquid **sedimentary** adj

seduce vt 1 entice, lure, or tempt, esp into evil 2 persuade to have sexual intercourse **seducer** n **seduction** n **seductive** adj

see[1] v (saw; seen) vi 1 have the power of sight 2 find out, investigate 3 attend (to) vt 1 look at; perceive; be aware of; observe 2 experience 3 visit 4 realize; consider 5 discover 6 consult 7 make sure; check; take care vt, vi understand; comprehend **see through** 1 fail to be deceived by 2 finish, remain with until completion

see[2] n office or diocese of a bishop

seed n 1 tiny cell containing an embryonic plant 2 germ; first principle vt 1 sow 2 remove the seed from **run to seed** deteriorate; decay **seedling** n young plant grown from seed

seedy adj shabby

seek vt,vi (sought) look for; try to find; search (for)

seem vi appear to be; give the impression of being **seeming** adj apparent **seemingly** adv **seemly** adj appropriate; decent

seep vi ooze; percolate; leak through **seepage** n

seesaw n plank so balanced that children seated on either end can ride up or down alternately vi move or vacillate like a seesaw

seethe vi surge or be agitated (with extreme fury, excitement, etc)

segment n 1 part of a circle bounded by a chord and arc 2 section; portion vt,vi divide into segments **segmentary** adj **segmentation** n

segregate vt separate from others; isolate; group apart, esp racially **segregation** n

seize vt take possession of, esp suddenly or by force. **seize up** become jammed or stuck **seizure** n 1 act of seizing 2 sudden attack of illness; fit

seldom adv rarely; only occasionally

select vt choose; pick out for preference by choice; exclusive **selection** n 1 act or result of choice; discrimination 2 item or items selected 3 scope or range of selected items **selective** adj 1 able to select or discriminate 2 tending to select very carefully **selectively** adv

self n, pl **selves** 1 person or thing regarded as individual 2 personality or ego

self-assured adj confident; not shy **self-assurance** n

self-aware adj able to view oneself objectively **self-awareness** n

self-centred adj preoccupied with oneself; selfish **self-centredness** n

self-confident adj having confidence in oneself **self-confidence** n

self-conscious adj shy; embarrassed **self-consciously** adv **self-consciousness** n

self-contained adj 1 reserved; absorbed in oneself 2 (of accommodation) complete; not approached through another's property

self-discipline n control of one's own

behaviour, emotions, etc **self-disciplined** adj

self-employed adj working for oneself; freelance

self-expression n voicing or demonstrating one's own personality or beliefs

self-interest n desire for benefit or advantage to oneself

selfish adj motivated by self-interest; showing little regard for others. **selfishly** adv **selfishness** n

self-pity n pity for oneself; feeling of being sorry for oneself **self-pitying** adj

self-portrait n picture painted by an artist of himself

self-respect n pride; dignity; integrity

self-righteous adj excessively confident in one's own merits, judgment, etc; hypocritical **self-righteously** adv. **self-righteousness** n

self-sacrifice n subordination of one's own desires or rights to another's

selfsame adj (the) very same; exactly the same

self-satisfied adj smug; conceited

self-service adj (of a restaurant, shop, etc) where the customer serves himself

self-sufficient adj 1 needing nothing from outside oneself 2 economically independent **self-sufficiency** n

self-will n obstinacy **self-willed** adj

sell vt (sold) 1 exchange for money 2 betray for an ignoble motive 3 extol; praise the virtues of **sell off** sell cheaply to clear stock **sell out** 1 sell whole stock in trade 2 betray for profit **sell up** 1 sell a debtor's goods in settlement 2 sell a business

Sellotape n Tdmk transparent adhesive cellulose tape vt attach, stick down, etc, with adhesive tape

selves n pl of **self.**

semaphore n means of signalling by flags vt,vi signal using flags

semen n fluid and cells produced by the male reproductive organs

semibreve n musical note equal to two minims or four crotchets

semicircle n half a circle **semicircular** adj

semicolon n punctuation mark (;) showing a sentence division that is stronger than a comma but less marked than a colon

semiconductor n substance whose electrical conductivity increases with added impurities, used in transistors and other electronic components

semidetached *adj* (of a house) joined to another on one side

semifinal *n* last round of a tournament before the final **semifinalist** *n*

seminar *n* class of advanced students working on a specific subject

semiprecious *adj* (of stones) valuable, but not rare or valuable enough to be classed as precious

semiquaver *n* musical note half the length of a quaver

semitone *n* musical interval between a note and its sharp or flat

semolina *n* particles of fine hard wheat used for making milk puddings, pasta, etc

senate *n* also **Senate** 1 legislative or governing body of ancient Rome, modern British universities, etc 2 upper house of government of the US, Australia, Canada, etc **senator** *n*

send *vt* (sent) 1 cause (mail, goods, a message, etc) to be transmitted or taken 2 direct; convey 3 drive or force into a particular condition or state **send for** ask to come; demand the services of

senile *adj* weak or deteriorating through old age **senility** *n*

senior *adj* older, higher, or more experienced or advanced *n* one who is senior **seniority** *n*

sensation *n* 1 feeling; perception through the senses 2 public or melodramatic excitement **sensational** *adj* exciting; thrilling; startling **sensationally** *adv*

sense *n* 1 faculty of sight, hearing, smell, touch, or taste 2 sensation; feeling 3 awareness; perception 4 intelligence; common sense 5 meaning or definition, esp of a word or phrase **make sense** be logical, reasonable, or coherent ~*vt* 1 feel; be aware of 2 comprehend, esp intuitively **senseless** *adj* 1 meaningless; motiveless; foolish 2 unconscious

sensible *adj* 1 wise; reasonable; practical 2 aware 3 appreciable by the senses **sensibly** *adv* **sensibility** *n* delicacy or capacity of emotional, mental, or moral responses

sensitive *adj* 1 easily affected by another's emotions, actions, plight, etc 2 easily irritated by certain stimuli **sensitively** *adv* **sensitivity** *or* **sensitiveness** *n*

sensual *adj* 1 relating to the senses 2 seeking pleasure or gratification of the senses 3 voluptuous; licentious **sensuality** *n* **sensually** *adv*

sensuous *adj* relating or pleasing to the senses **sensuously** *adv* **sensuousness** *n*

sent *v pt* and *pp* of **send.**

sentence *n* 1 number of words forming a grammatical unit, usually containing a subject, predicate, and finite verb 2 punishment allotted to an offender in court *vt* pronounce judgment on (a person) in a court of law

sentiment *n* thought or opinion at least partly dictated by emotion **sentimental** *adj* 1 overemotional; mawkish 2 having romantic or tender feelings **sentimentality** *n*

sentry *n* soldier, etc, posted to stand guard

separate *v* ('sepəreit) *vt* set or keep apart; divide *vi* go, move, or live apart *adj* ('seprit) distinct; divided; individual **separable** *adj* **separately** *adv* **separation** *n*

September *n* ninth month of the year

septic *adj* putrefying because of the presence of bacteria

sequel *n* result; consequence; whatever succeeds, follows, or happens next

sequence *n* 1 order of succession; series 2 scene from a film **sequential** *adj* **sequentially** *adv*

sequin *n* tiny sparkling piece of foil used to decorate clothing

serenade *n* piece of music traditionally played at night by a lover under his lady's window *vt* entertain with a serenade

serene *adj* tranquil; calm; placid **serenely** *adv* **serenity** *n*

serf *n* medieval farm labourer or peasant bound to the land **serfdom** *n*

sergeant *n* 1 noncommissioned officer ranking above a corporal 2 police officer ranking between constable and inspector **sergeant-major** *n* highest grade of noncommissioned officer

serial *adj* forming a series; in instalments *n* story told in instalments **serialize** *vt* divide (a story, film, etc) into instalments or episodes

series *n, pl* **series** sequence; succession of things, episodes, etc, with similar characters, subjects, or purposes

serious *adj* solemn; grave; earnest; not comic or frivolous **seriously** *adv* **seriousness** *n*

sermon *n* speech, esp one delivered from a pulpit, with a strong scriptural or moral lesson

serpent n snake **serpentine** adj 1 relating to serpents 2 twisting; convoluted

servant n person employed to serve another

serve vt,vi 1 work for; wait upon 2 be of use to; help 3 act or offer as a host 4 deliver (the ball) in certain games 5 spend (a specified period of time, enlistment, etc) vt 1 obey or honour 2 deliver (a summons, etc) to **serve someone right** be an appropriate punishment ~n act or turn of delivering the ball in certain games

service n 1 work, position, or duty of a servant 2 religious rite or ceremony 3 supply, maintenance, or repair 4 set of dishes, etc 5 act of serving or turn to serve the ball in tennis, etc 6 supply or system of a public utility 7 branch of government or public employment 8 help; assistance (**the**) **services** pl n Army, Navy, and Air Force ~vt do maintenance work on **serviceable** adj useful; durable but not decorative **service station** n roadside garage providing petrol and repair services

serviette n table napkin

servile adj 1 of servants or slaves 2 menial; cringing **servility** n

session n period during which a court, Parliament, etc sits, universities function, or meetings or interviews take place

set v (-tt-; set) vt 1 place, position, put 2 cause or prompt 3 fix; regulate; mend 4 make firm or hard 5 put (hair) in rollers, etc , to produce waves or curls 6 bring into contact with fire; ignite; light 7 establish as a standard record, etc 8 require the completion of (an examination, task, etc) vi 1 become firm or hard; solidify 2 (of the sun) fall below the horizon 3 (of bones, etc) mend **set about** begin to deal with **set in** become established **set off** or **out** begin a journey; leave **set up** start (a business scheme, etc), establish; found ~adj 1 fixed; settled; determined; not alterable 2 ready; prepared n 1 group of people, class 2 number of things that match or are designed to be used together 3 scenery used for a play 4 studio or area used when making a film, TV broadcast, etc **setback** n relapse; check; halt **setting** n frame, background, scenery, environment, etc , in which anything is set

settee n long upholstered seat with a back and arms; couch; sofa

settle vt 1 place at rest or in comfort, peace, order, etc 2 decide finally 3 give money to; resolve (debts) vi 1 subside; come to rest; sink 2 take up residence 3 reach a decision **settle down** take up a settled normal established way of life **settle for** agree to accept **settle in** adapt to a new environment, circumstances, etc **settle up** balance accounts; pay **settlement** n 1 act or state of settling, paying, etc 2 group of social workers in an underprivileged community 3 newly established colony 4 sinking or subsidence

seven n 1 number equal to one plus six 2 group of seven persons, things, etc 3 also **seven o'clock** seven hours after noon or midnight adj amounting to seven **seventh** adj coming between sixth and eighth in sequence n 1 seventh person, object, etc 2 one of seven equal parts; one divided by seven

seventeen n 1 number that is seven more than ten 2 seventeen things or people adj amounting to seventeen **seventeenth** adj,adv,n

seventy n 1 number equal to seven times ten 2 seventy things or people adj amounting to seventy **seventieth** adj adv,n

sever vt,vi separate; cut; end **severance** n

several adj 1 more than one; a few 2 separate; distinct; various

severe adj 1 harsh; strict; violent 2 grave; serious 3 unadorned; plain, austere **severely** adv **severity** n

sew vt,vi (sewed; sewn or sewed) work on; fasten join, embroider, etc , with a needle and thread; stitch

sewage n used water supply containing domestic refuse and waste matter **sewer** n underground pipe or drain for carrying sewage **sewerage** n provision or system of sewers

sex n 1 characteristics distinguishing male from female 2 males or females 3 sexual desires instincts, or intercourse

sextet n 1 group of or work composed for six musicians 2 group of six

sexual adj relating to sex or sex organs **sexuality** n awareness of one's own sexual characteristics

sexy adj sexually attractive or stimulating **sexily** adv **sexiness** n

shabby adj 1 worn; dilapidated; ragged 2 despicable; dishonourable **shabbily** adv **shabbiness** n

shack n rough hut

shade n 1 comparative darkness caused by shelter from light or sun 2 screen against light 3 gradation of colour 4 small amount; tiny degree vt shield from light; darken **shady** adj 1 out of bright sunlight 2 inf dishonest; of dubious reputation

shadow n 1 dark outline of an object placed in front of light or sun 2 mere insubstantial copy 3 constant companion vt 1 shade from light 2 follow closely and secretly **shadowy** adj **shadow cabinet** n group of leading Opposition politicians determining policy should their party return to power

shaft n 1 long straight narrow rod, handle, beam of light, column, etc 2 vertical passage into a mine

shaggy adj unkempt; tangled **shaggily** adv

shake v (shook; shaken) vt agitate; move with small fast gestures vi tremble; be agitated **shake off** get rid of **shaky** adj unreliable; precarious; wobbling

shall v aux used to express future probability or intention

shallot n small onion similar to but milder than garlic

shallow adj 1 not deep 2 not profound; superficial **shallowness** n

shame n 1 feeling of humiliation caused by guilt, failure, disgrace, etc 2 sense of modesty, pride, or dignity 3 disappointing or unlucky event vt bring shame upon **put to shame** cause to feel inferior **shameful** adj **shamefully** adv **shamefaced** adj embarrassed; humiliated; ashamed

shampoo n preparation for washing hair, carpets, upholstery, etc vt rub clean with shampoo

shamrock n type of small three-leaved plant, used as the Irish emblem

shandy n drink made by mixing beer with lemonade or ginger beer

shanty[1] small roughly built cabin or shack

shanty[2] n rousing sailors' song

shape n 1 external appearance of an object or figure; outline; form 2 condition; situation; state **take shape** begin to develop or take on a definite form ~vt 1 make a particular shape of 2 develop; fit **shapeless** adj not having the proper or appropriate shape **shapely** adj well shaped

share n 1 part; portion or division given to or

contributed by an individual 2 fixed equal part of a company's capital vt divide into shares **share out** distribute; allot **shareholder** n one holding a share, esp in a company

shark n large long-bodied voracious and often dangerous marine fish

sharp adj 1 having a fine edge or point; cutting; piercing 2 acid; shrill, painful; intense 3 clear-cut 4 quick; lively 5 artful; dishonest 6 (in music) above true pitch; a semitone higher than the note adv 1 punctually 2 too high in pitch **look sharp** **sharp-sighted** adj 1 having excellent eyesight 2 shrewd; sharp-witted **sharpen** vt, vi become or make sharp

shatter vt, vi 1 smash or break into fragments 2 wreck; exhaust; destroy

shave vt, vi scrape off a superficial layer, esp of facial hair n act of shaving **close shave** narrow escape; near miss

shawl n folded square of material worn loosely around the shoulders or wrapped around a baby

she pron female person; the 3rd person singular as the subject

sheaf n, pl **sheaves** 1 large bundle of cereal crops tied together after reaping 2 bundle of papers

shear vt (sheared; shorn or sheared) clip or cut off hair or wool, esp from sheep **shears** pl n cutting implement resembling large scissors

sheath n tightly fitting case or covering for a blade, insects' wings, etc **sheathe** vt enclose in a sheath

shed[1] vt (-dd-; shed) cast off; let fall; pour out **shed light on** reveal; illuminate

shed[2] n small simple building; hut

sheen n glow; radiance; lustre

sheep n, pl **sheep** wild or domesticated ruminant mammal reared for meat and wool **black sheep** rogue **sheepish** adj embarrassed through being wrong, etc **sheepishly** adv **sheepdog** n dog trained to herd sheep **sheepskin** n skin of a sheep used for rugs, coats, etc

sheer[1] adj 1 perpendicular; very steep 2 unqualified; complete; utter adv 1 vertically 2 outright

sheer[2] vi swerve; deviate **sheer off** 1 move away 2 snap off with a clean break

sheet[1] 1 large thin rectangle of cotton, linen,

nylon, etc , for a bed **2** thin rectangular piece of paper, metal, etc

sheet[2] n rope attached to a sail of a boat

sheikh n head of an Arab family or tribe **sheikhdom** n area ruled by a sheikh

shelf n, pl **shelves** horizontal board set into a wall, bookcase, cupboard, etc **on the shelf** (usually of a woman) not married and unlikely to be so

shell n **1** hard outer case enclosing an egg, nut, shellfish, tortoise, etc **2** framework; outline **3** explosive device fired from heavy guns vt **1** remove shell from **2** bombard **shell out** inf pay **shellfish** n aquatic mollusc or crustacean with a shell

shelter n place or thing providing safety from weather, attack, danger, etc vt shield; protect vi take cover

shelve vt **1** provide with or put on a shelf **2** postpone indefinitely

shepherd n one who guards and herds sheep vt guide and herd like a shepherd **shepherdess** f n

sherbet n fizzy drink or powder for making it

sheriff n chief Crown officer of a county, responsible for keeping the peace, administering courts, etc

sherry n fortified wine, esp from Spain

shield n **1** broad piece of armour carried to protect the body **2** anything serving as shelter, protection, or defence vt protect; screen

shift vt, vi move; change position (of) vi manage; make do n **1** movement; change of position **2** period of work on a rota or relay system **3** undergarment

shilling n former British coin or unit of currency worth five new pence

shimmer vi glisten; gleam with faint diffuse light n faint light

shin n **1** front of the human leg below the knee **2** beef from the lower part of the leg vi climb up (a tree, rope, etc) quickly, using only the arms and legs

shine vi (shone) **1** give off or reflect light; beam; glow **2** excel; be conspicuous or animated vt (shined) polish (shoes, etc) n sheen; lustre **shiny** adj

ship n large floating sea-going vessel vt (-pp-) carry or send by ship **shipment** n **1** cargo; goods shipped together **2** shipping goods **shipping** n **1** business of transporting goods

by sea **2** number of ships, esp of a country or port **shipshape** adj well-ordered; clean; neat **shipwreck** n destruction or loss of a ship at sea vt, vi cause or suffer shipwreck; ruin **shipyard** n dock or yard where ships are built and repaired

shirk vt, vi evade (duties or obligations) **shirker** n

shirt n loose garment covering the top half of the body, esp with sleeves, collar, and cuffs **shirty** adj sl bad-tempered; irritable

shiver vi tremble or quiver with cold, excitement, or fear n tremble; shivering motion

shock[1] n **1** alarming startling experience **2** violent collision or impact **3** bodily condition of near or complete collapse because of rapid falling of blood pressure **4** also **electric shock** condition resulting from bodily contact with a strong electric current vt shake or alarm by violent impact, frightening experience, improper outrageous behaviour, etc **shock absorber** n device for diminishing vibration in vehicles

shock[2] n thick shaggy mass, esp of hair

shoddy adj of inferior quality; cheap and nasty n cloth made from scraps of other materials **shoddily** adv **shoddiness** n

shoe n **1** outer covering for the foot **2** anything resembling a shoe vt (shod) provide shoes for

shone v pt and pp of **shine**.

shook v pt and pp of **shake.**

shoot v (shot) vt, vi **1** fire (a gun) **2** propel (a bullet, arrow, etc) **3** send out suddenly; project **4** sprout; put out buds **5** photograph or film vt injure or kill with a gun vi hunt game for sport with a gun n **1** young branch or sprout **2** hunting or shooting party **3** inclined plank or trough down which water, rubbish, coal, etc , may be thrown; chute **good/bad shot** good/bad marksman

shop n **1** place where goods are sold **2** place where industrial work is carried out **on the shop floor** amongst the workers in a factory, workshop etc **talk shop** discuss one's own occupation or job ~vi (-pp-) visit shops to buy goods **shop around** compare values at different shops **shopkeeper** n owner or manager of a shop **shoplifter** n one who steals goods from a shop **shoplifting** n **shop steward** n trade union's elected departmental delegate

shore[1] *n* land bordering a river, lake, or sea

shore[2] *vt* support or prop up (a building, ship, etc) *n* prop

shorn *v pp* of **shear.**

short *adj* 1 of relatively little length; not long or tall 2 lasting for a little while; brief 3 brusque; abrupt; curt 4 not plentiful; sparse; inadequate; insufficient 5 abbreviated; cut *adv* abruptly *n* **in short** as a summary; briefly **shorts** *pl n* short trousers, worn esp when participating in certain sports **shortness** *n* **shortage** *n* lack; deficiency **shortbread** *n* crisp biscuit made from butter, flour, and sugar **shortcoming** *n* failure; deficiency **shorten** *vt, vi* decrease; reduce **shorthand** *n* system of symbols used for writing at speed **shorthanded** *adj* short of staff; undermanned **shortlived** *adj* transitory; brief **shortly** *adv* 1 soon; in a short time 2 briefly; abruptly **short-sighted** *adj* 1 unable to see clearly at a distance 2 without imagination or foresight **short-sightedly** *adv* **short-sightedness** *n* **short-tempered** *adj* liable to lose one's temper easily; irritable **short-term** *adj* immediate future

shot *n* 1 act of shooting or the missile shot 2 photograph 3 attempt; try 4 hypodermic injection **be/get shot of** be/get rid of **like a shot** with great speed **shot in the arm** encouragement **shot in the dark** mere guess ~*adj* of changing colour *v pt* and *pp* of **shoot. shotgun** *n* smooth bore gun firing small shot

should *v aux* 1 used to express obligation, duty, or likelihood 2 used to form the conditional tense 3 used in indirect speech

shoulder *n* 1 part of the body where the arm is attached 2 corresponding part in animals and birds 3 prominent part of a hillside, bottle, vase, etc 4 roadside verge **give the cold shoulder** to snub **rub shoulders with** mix with; get to know ~*vt* 1 push, lift, or jostle with the shoulder 2 accept (responsibility) **shoulder-blade** *n* broad flat bone of the upper back

shout *n* loud cry or call *vt, vi* utter (with) a shout

shove *vt, vi* push; thrust; jostle *n* hard push **shove off** 1 push a boat away from the shore 2 *sl* leave

shovel *n* broad often short-handled spade for lifting coal, earth, etc *vt* (-ll-) move with or as if with a shovel

show *v* (showed; shown) *vt* 1 display; allow to be seen 2 conduct; guide 3 reveal; indicate 4 demonstrate; instruct 5 prove; give evidence of *vi* 1 be able to be seen; be revealed or displayed 2 be evident; prove **show off** behave in a pretentious way ~*n* 1 exhibition or display 2 entertainment with dancers, singers, etc **show business** *n* profession of theatrical entertainers, variety artists, etc **showcase** *n* glass-fronted display cabinet **showdown** *n* open conflict or challenge **show-jumping** *n* horse-jumping displayed in competition **showmanship** *n* skill in displaying goods, theatrical productions, etc , to the best advantage **showroom** *n* room in which goods may be viewed

shower *n* 1 short fall of rain, bullets, blows, etc 2 large supply; abundant flow 3 bathroom fitting from which water is sprayed from above *vt* fall or pour out, as in a shower **showery** *adj* **showerproof** *adj* impervious to showers

shrank *v pt* of **shrink.**

shred *n* strip; fragment *vt* (-dd-; shredded or shred) cut or tear into shreds

shrew *n* 1 small mammal resembling a mouse and also having an elongated snout 2 bad-tempered woman

shrewd *adj* 1 discerning; astute; wise 2 cunning; sly **shrewdly** *adv* **shrewdness** *n*

shriek *n* high piercing cry or scream *vt, vi* utter (with a shriek)

shrill *adj* high-pitched, piercing, and insistent *vt, vi* utter in a shrill manner **shrillness** *n* **shrilly** *adv*

shrimp *n* 1 tiny edible crustacean smaller than and similar to a prawn 2 *inf* small person

shrine *n* 1 place hallowed by associations with a saint 2 casket containing holy relics

shrink *vi* (shrank, shrunk or shrunken) become smaller; contract, esp when wet **shrink (back) from** recoil or flinch from; shun

shrivel *vi* (-ll-) *also* **shrivel up** become shrunken, withered, and wrinkled

shroud *n* 1 sheet wrapped around a dead body 2 anything that veils or wraps round 3 set of ropes forming parts of a ship s rigging *vt* cloak or cover (in secrecy, antiquity, etc)

Shrove Tuesday *n* day of confession and subsequent merrymaking before Lent

shrub *n* low bush with no central trunk **shrubbery** *n* area or group of shrubs

shrug *vt,vi* (-gg-) raise the shoulders to express indifference, doubt, or dislike *n* act of shrugging **shrug off** shake off with indifference

shrunk *v* a *pp* of **shrink.**

shrunken *v* a *pp* of **shrink.**

shudder *n* shiver, esp with horror, fear, etc *vi* 1 tremble as with horror 2 vibrate

shuffle *vt,vi* 1 move slowly without lifting the feet from the ground 2 mix randomly, esp playing cards *n* act of shuffling

shun *vt* (-nn-) avoid; stay away from

shunt *vt,vi* 1 divert (a train) to another track 2 bypass; sidetrack *inf* move; go away *n* 1 act of shunting 2 electrical conductor diverting current

shut *v* (-tt-; shut) *vt* 1 move (a door, the eyes, mouth, etc) so as to be no longer open; close 2 fasten; secure; lock or bolt 3 cease to operate, trade, etc *vi* become closed **shut up** 1 become silent 2 lock up or in **shutter** *n* 1 wooden or metal window covering 2 device controlling light admitted to a camera lens

shuttlecock *n* small piece of cork, plastic, etc , stuck with feathers and struck by a racket in badminton, etc

shy *adj* bashful; timid; lacking self-confidence *vi* move (away from); recoil (from) **shyly** *adv* **shyness** *n*

sick *adj* 1 unwell; ill 2 inclined to vomit 3 gruesome; macabre **sick of** tired of; bored with **sicken** *vi,vt* become or make sick, weary, or disgusted **sickening** *adj* nauseating; annoying **sickly** *adj* 1 prone to ill-health; feeble 2 so sweet as to be nauseating **sickness** *n* 1 illness; disease 2 vomiting; nausea

side *n* 1 one of the surfaces of an object 2 that part of something other than the top and bottom or back and front 3 surface of a piece of paper, cloth, etc 4 left or right part of the body, face, etc 5 area to the left or right of the centre of something 6 one of the teams or groups in a match, competition, debate, etc 7 facet; aspect; part **side by side** together; in juxtaposition **take sides** favour one side more than the other in a dispute *v* **side with** take sides with one rather than the other **sideboard** *n* piece of dining-room furniture holding or displaying plates, cutlery, etc **sideboards** *pl n* side whiskers on the face

side effect *n* secondary unplanned and often undesirable effect of an action, drug, etc **sideline** *n* subsidiary or additional occupation **sideshow** *n* minor show or fairground entertainment **sidestep** *vt* (-pp-) neatly evade; avoid or step aside from **sidetrack** *vt* lead away from a subject; divert **sideways** *adv, adj* on or towards one side **siding** *n* short stretch of railway track used for shunting

sidle *vi* 1 move sideways; edge along 2 fawn; cringe

siege *n* attempt to conquer a fortified place by surrounding and preventing access to it

sieve *n* utensil with a perforated container for straining liquids, separating coarse from fine grains, or pulping solids *vt* put through a sieve; sift

sift *vt* 1 pass through or separate with a sieve 2 examine minutely

sigh *n* long deep breath expressing weariness, sadness, relief, etc *vt,vi* utter (with) a sigh

sight *n* 1 ability or power to see; vision 2 something seen or viewed 3 something that is messy, ugly, or untidy; mess 4 appearance 5 *inf* a lot; much more **at first sight** on the first occasion of seeing ~*vt* see; observe; spot **sightless** *adj* blind **sightread** *vt,vi* (-read) read, play, or sing music at first sight **sightseeing** *n* visiting tourist attractions, beauty spots, etc **sightseer** *n*

sign *n* 1 symbol 2 gesture; gesticulation 3 hint; implication; clue; trace 4 recognizable symptom 5 advertisement or notice *vt,vi* 1 write one's name or signature (on) 2 signal; communicate with signs **sign on** *or* **up** enrol; enlist

signal *n* visible or audible sign, esp prearranged or well-known *vt,vi* (-ll-) make signals (to)

signature *n* 1 signed name, esp for use as authentication 2 act of signing 3 mark showing key and time at the beginning of a musical score **signature tune** *n* tune used to announce and identify a particular performer or programme on stage, radio, television, etc

significant *adj* meaningful; noteworthy; important **significance** *n* **significantly** *adv* **signify** *vt* mean; indicate; be a sign of *vi* matter; be important

silence *n* absence of sound, speech, or communication *vt* make silent; suppress **silencer** *n* device rendering car exhaust, a gun, etc , more quiet **silent** *adj* without a sound; noiseless; quiet **silently** *adv*

silhouette *n* outline figure, esp in black on a white background *vt* show in silhouette

silk *n* fine soft fibre spun by silkworms and woven into fabric **silkworm** *n* caterpillar of the mulberry-eating moth, which spins silk **silky** *adj* soft, fine, and gleaming like silk **silkiness** *n*

sill *n* ledge or slab below a window or door

silly *adj* foolish; fatuous; imprudent; unwise **silliness** *n*

silo *n* granary

silt *n* sediment left by water in a river, harbour, etc *vt, vi* fill (up) with silt

silver *n* 1 white shining malleable valuable metallic element, widely used in coinage, jewellery, tableware, electrical contacts, alloys, etc 2 also **silverware** cutlery, dishes, etc , made from silver or an alloy of silver *adj* 1 made of silver 2 of the colour of silver **silver wedding** *n* twenty-fifth wedding anniversary **silvery** *adj* 1 looking like silver 2 having a clear soft sound

similar *adj* like, resembling; exactly the same **similarity** *n* **similarly** *adv*

simile *n* figure of speech in which two apparently unlike things are compared

simmer *vt, vi* 1 cook slowly at boiling point 2 have emotions (esp anger) barely in check **simmer down** calm down ~*n* state of simmering

simple *adj* 1 easy; plain; ordinary 2 not complex 3 mere **simple-minded** *adj* ingenuous; foolish **simple-mindedly** *adv* **simple-mindedness** *n* **simplicity** *n* condition of being simple **simplify** *vt* make less complicated; clarify **simplification** 3 absolutely

simulate *vt* feign or reproduce (a situation, condition, etc) **simulation** *n*

simultaneous *adj* occurring at the same time **simultaneously** *adv*

sin *n* moral or religious offence *vi* (-nn-) commit a sin **sinful** *adj*

since *adv* from that time until now; subsequently; ago *prep* after; from the time of *conj* 1 from the time that 2 because; seeing that

sincere *adj* honest; straightforward; genuine **sincerely** *adv* **sincerity** *n*

sinew *n* tendon joining a muscle to a bone **sinewy** *adj* wiry; muscular

sing *vi vt* (sang; sung) 1 utter (words or a tune) melodiously; produce musical notes 2 celebrate in poetry **singer** *n*

singe *vt, vi* scorch or burn (the surface, edge, or end of) *n* slight burn

single *adj* 1 individual; only one 2 separate; solitary 3 unmarried 4 unique *n* 1 short gramophone record played at 45 revolutions per minute 2 one-way train or bus ticket 3 single thing, event, etc **singles** *pl n* tennis match, etc , between two players *v* **single out** select from many for a specific purpose **singly** *adv* **single-handed** *adj* alone; unaided **single-minded** *adj* intent; with one driving force or set aim **single-mindedly** *adv* **single-mindedness** *n*

singular *adj* 1 indicating a single person, place, or thing 2 odd; extraordinary; unusual **singularity** *n* **singularly** *adv*

sinister *adj* malignant; suggestive of evil

sink *v* (sank; sunk) *vt, vi* 1 submerge 2 drop; lower 3 lower or become lower in cost, value, etc *vi* 1 pass (into) a state, condition, etc 2 become weaker, unwell, etc *vt* drive (a stake, post, etc) into the ground *n* fitted basin for washing, etc **sink or swim** fail or succeed

sinner *n* one who commits sin

sinus *n* bodily cavity or passage, esp communicating with the nose **sinusitis** *n* inflammation of the sinus

sip *vt, vi* (-pp-) drink in small mouthfuls *n* small mouthful of liquid

siphon *n* 1 bent pipe or tube for drawing off liquids 2 bottle for dispensing soda water, etc , by means of a siphon *vt, vi* draw (off) using a siphon

sir *n* title used in a formal letter or to address a knight, baronet, or a man superior in age, rank, dignity, etc

siren *n* apparatus producing a loud wailing noise or signal

sirloin *n* upper part of a loin of beef

sister *n* 1 daughter of the same parents as another 2 nun 3 nurse in charge of a hospital ward **sisterhood** *n* community of nuns or other women **sister-in-law** *n, pl* **sisters-in-law** brother's wife or husband's or wife's sister **sisterly** *adj*

sit *v* (-tt-; sat) *vi* 1 be in the position of having one's buttocks resting on the ground, a chair, etc 2 be placed; rest 3 be a member (of a committee, etc) *vt* 1 seat; place in a sitting

position **2** allocate a place at table to *vt,vi*
take (an examination) **sit-in** *n* mass
occupation of premises as a form of protest

site *n* place, setting, or ground on which a
building, town, etc stands *vt* locate

sitting *n* **1** session; business meeting **2** time
spent posing for a portrait, etc **sitting room**
n room used for sitting comfortably; living
room

situated *adj* **1** located; sited **2** placed with
respect to money, housing, or other con-
siderations **situation** *n* **1** position; condition
2 job

six *n* **1** number equal to one plus five **2** group of
six persons, things, etc **3** *also* **six o'clock** six
hours after noon or midnight **at sixes and
sevens** confused; in a muddle ~*adj* amounting to six **sixth** *adj* coming between fifth
and seventh in sequence *n* **1** sixth person,
object, etc **2** one of six equal parts; one
divided by six *adv* after the fifth

sixteen *n* **1** number that is six more than ten **2**
sixteen things or people *adj* amounting to
sixteen **sixteenth** *adj,adv,n*

sixty *n* **1** number equal to six times ten **2** sixty
things or people *adj* amounting to sixty
sixtieth *adj,adv,n*

size *n* **1** extent; dimensions; importance **2**
measurement categorizing individual proportions *vt* categorize by size **size up** judge
roughly; weigh up **sizable** *adj* of considerable size or importance

sizzle *vi* **1** hiss and splutter as during frying **2**
inf be very hot *n* sizzling noise

skate[1] *n* boot fitted with a blade or wheels
allowing the wearer to glide smoothly over ice
or other hard surfaces *vi* move on or as if on
skates **skate on thin ice** deal with or be in a
precarious situation **skater** *n*

skate[2] *n* large flatfish with an elongated snout

skeleton *n* **1** framework of bones within a
human or animal body **2** outline, sketch,
nucleus or framework of anything **skeleton
in the cupboard** secret domestic disgrace

sketch *n* **1** rough or unfinished drawing, draft
or outline **2** very short usually amusing play
vt vi draw or outline roughly **sketchy** *adj*
incomplete, rough, inadequate **sketchily**
adv

ski *n* **1** one of two long narrow pointed pieces of
wood, metal, etc , attached to boots allowing
wearer to slide quickly over snow **2** short for

water-ski. *vi* (skiing; skied *or* ski'd) travel on
skis **skier** *n* **ski-lift** *n* seats slung on a cable
transporting skiers up slopes

skid *n* **1** wooden or metal support on which a
ship, aeroplane, car, etc , may be rested,
moved, or slid **2** act of skidding *vi* (-dd-) (of
a vehicle, etc) slide sideways, esp out of
control **skid row** haunt or condition of
vagrants, drunkards, etc

skill *n* accomplishment; craft; expert knowledge
skilled *adj* **skilful** *adj* **skilfully** *adv*

skim *vt* (-mm-) **1** remove scum, cream, etc ,
from the surface of a liquid **2** pass over
lightly, scarcely touching **skim over** *or*
through read cursorily; glance at **skimmed
milk** milk without cream

skin *n* **1** tissue forming the outer covering of the
body **2** outer covering of a fruit **3** leather pelt
obtained from an animal **4** layer; thin coating
vt (-nn-) remove the skin of or from **skinny**
adj unpleasantly thin **skin-tight** *adj* extremely close-fitting

skip *vt,vi* (-pp-) **1** jump or hop lightly, esp from
one foot to the other or over a twirling rope **2**
omit; leave out *n* skipping movement

skipper *n* captain of a ship, aircraft, etc

skirmish *n* small unplanned fight or clash, as
between hostile armies, etc *vi* engage in a
skirmish

skirt *n* **1** woman's garment extending downwards from the waist or this part of a dress **2**
edge; extremity; border *vt* pass around or
along the edge of

skittle *n* bottle-shaped target used in ninepin or
tenpin bowling

skull *n* bony framework of the head enclosing
the brain

skunk *n* small carnivorous black North American
mammal with bushy tail, white-striped back,
and a gland that sprays a powerful offensive
scent

sky *n* upper atmosphere; heavens; apparent
canopy of air seen from the earth **sky-high**
adj,adv extremely high **skylark** *n* lark that
sings while hovering in the air *vi inf* indulge
in practical jokes, frolics, etc **skyscraper** *n*
very tall building of many storeys

slab *n* thick flat piece of stone, metal, cake,
chocolate, etc

slack *adj* **1** loose; not taut or stretched; limp **2**
lazy; remiss *n* slack part of a rope **slacks** *pl*
n trousers for casual or informal wear

slacken vi,vt 1 make or become slack(er) 2 relax; abate; delay

slam vt,vi (-mm-) shut or put down violently and noisily n noise of something slammed

slander n false, defamatory, or injurious report vt injure by spreading false malicious gossip **slanderer** n **slanderous** adj

slang n colloquial language not regarded as good, educated, or acceptable vt berate abusively **slanging match** bitter exchange of verbal insults

slant vt,vi 1 slope; turn obliquely 2 write or present (material) in a biased or prejudiced manner n 1 slope 2 angle of approach, attitude

slap n blow with hand or anything flat **slap in the face** insult; rebuff ~vt (-pp-) smack; strike with a slap **slapdash** adj careless; haphazard **slapstick** n rough boisterous comedy

slash vt,vi 1 cut with long violent random strokes 2 economize or reduce drastically n long cut or slit

slat n narrow strip of wood, metal, etc

slate n 1 dull grey fine-grained rock that can be split into smooth even pieces 2 thin piece of this used as a writing tablet, roofing tile, etc

slaughter n killing, esp of many people or animals at once; massacre vt 1 kill or slay ruthlessly, esp in large numbers 2 kill (an animal) for market **slaughterhouse** n place where animals are killed for market, abattoir

slave n 1 person legally owned by another 2 person forced to work against his will 3 person under the control or influence of someone or something vi work like a slave **slavery** n 1 state or condition of being a slave 2 extremely hard unrewarding work

sledge n vehicle on runners for transporting goods or people over snow; sleigh

sledgehammer n large heavy hammer

sleek adj 1 smooth and glossy 2 suave; elegant vt make smooth and glossy **sleekly** adv **sleekness** n

sleep n resting state during which the body is relaxed and consciousness is suspended vi (slept) take rest in sleep **sleep on it** postpone a decision overnight **sleepless** adj **sleepily** adv **sleepiness** n **sleepy** adj **sleeper** n 1 one who sleeps 2 horizontal beam supporting the rails of a railway track 3 sleeping car or compartment on a train

sleepwalk vi walk while asleep **sleepwalker** n

sleet n rain falling as half-melted hail or snow vi fall as sleet

sleeve n 1 part of a garment covering the arm 2 tube covering a rod, pipe, etc 3 cover for gramophone record **up one's sleeve** held secretly in reserve

sleigh n sledge, esp one pulled by horses

slender adj 1 slim; thin 2 meagre; insufficient

slice n 1 thin flat piece cut from something 2 utensil for lifting and serving fish, etc vt 1 cut into slices 2 cut a slice from 3 hit (a golfball, tennis ball, etc) so that it curves in flight

slick adj 1 sleek; smooth 2 deft; cunning **slickness** n

slide v (slid) vt,vi 1 move or glide smoothly over a surface 2 move or be moved unobtrusively vi 1 pass gradually 2 slip or fall **let slide** allow to take a natural course ~n 1 transparent photograph 2 smooth inclined surface for children, goods. etc , to slide down 3 clasp for the hair **slide-rule** n mechanical device used for calculating

slight adj 1 frail; slim; flimsy 2 insignificant; unimportant vt snub; hurtful act vt disregard; treat as if of no importance **slightly** adv a little; somewhat

slim adj 1 slender; thin 2 small; slight; meagre vi (-mm-) try to lose weight by means of diet, exercise, etc **slimmer** n **slimness** n

slime n thin oozing mud or anything resembling it **slimy** adj 1 resembling or covered with slime 2 vile; repulsive

sling n 1 piece of material for supporting an injured arm hand, etc 2 band or pocket attached to strings for throwing stones hoisting or supporting weighty objects, etc vt (slung) 1 throw casually 2 support with or hang from a sling

slink vi (slunk) move stealthily and quietly, sneak **slinky** adj 1 close-fitting 2 sinuous and graceful

slip[1] v (-pp-) vi 1 slide, glide 2 become unfastened or less secure 3 lose one's balance grip, etc 4 become less efficient careful etc 5 move quietly or without being noticed 6 forget; make a mistake vt 1 pull or push easily or hastily 2 drop; let fall **slip up** make a mistake ~n 1 sliding; act of slipping 2 mistake; small error 3 petticoat **slipway** n sloping area from which a vessel is launched

slip[2] *n* narrow strip of wood, paper, etc

slipper *n* loose comfortable indoor shoe

slippery *adj* 1 so smooth, greasy, etc , as to make slipping likely 2 elusive; unstable **slipperiness** *n*

slit *n* 1 long cut 2 narrow opening *vt* (-tt-) 1 make a long cut in 2 cut into long strips

slither *vi* slide unsteadily

slog *vi,vt* (-gg-) 1 hit violently 2 work hard and determinedly *n* 1 long spell of hard work 2 heavy blow

slogan *n* catchy word or phrase used in advertising, etc

slop *n* 1 liquid waste 2 semiliquid unappetizing food *vt,vi* (-pp-) spill carelessly and messily **sloppy** *adj* 1 messy; careless; untidy 2 muddy, slushy, or watery 3 sentimental; maudlin **sloppily** *adv* **sloppiness** *n*

slope *n* 1 inclined surface 2 deviation from the horizontal; slant *vi* have or take a sloping position or direction

sloshed *adj inf* drunk

slot *n* groove, channel, or slit into which a bolt, coin, etc , may fit or be inserted *vt* (-tt-) 1 make fit into 2 provide with or pass through a slot **slot together** fit neatly together

slovenly *adj* 1 careless; slipshod 2 lazy and dirty **slovenliness** *n*

slow *adj* 1 taking a long time 2 not quick; gradual 3 behind correct time 4 dull-witted or unresponsive *vt* delay; retard **slow down or up** lessen; slacken in speed **slowly** *adv* **slowness** *n*

slug small shell-less mollusc, destructive to garden plants

sluggish *adj* lazy; slow-moving **sluggishly** *adv* **sluggishness** *n*

sluice *n* sliding gate or valve controlling a flow of water in a channel, drain, etc *vt,vi* flush or wash down with running water

slum *n* squalid overcrowded housing

slump *n* 1 sudden fall or decline 2 economic depression *vi* 1 collapse in a heap 2 suddenly lose value

slung *v pt* and *pp* of **sling.**

slunk *v pt* and *pp* of **slink.**

slur *vt,vi* (-rr-) 1 sound (words) indistinctly 2 pass over lightly 3 disparage *n* 1 smudge; blur 2 indistinct noise 3 slight, insult, or blame

slush *n* 1 watery mud or snow 2 excessive sentimentality **slushy** *adj*

sly *adj* 1 cunning 2 devious; deceitful **slyly** *adv* **slyness** *n*

smack[1] *vt* strike sharply with the palm of the hand **smack the lips** make a smacking sound with the lips ~*n* act or sound of smacking *adv inf* immediately; directly

smack[2] *n* slight trace or flavour *vi* suggest; have the flavour (of)

small *adj* not large; of little size, strength, importance, quantity, etc **feel small** feel humiliated **small talk** polite trivial conversation ~*n* narrow part (of the back, etc) - **smallness** *n* **smallholding** *n* small farm or rented plot of agricultural land **small-minded** *adj* petty; narrow-minded **smallpox** *n* serious contagious disease causing eruptions and subsequent scars on the skin

smart *adj* 1 fashionable; elegant 2 clever, ingenious; witty *vi* feel sharp pain or resentment **smartly** *adv* **smartness** *n* **smarten** *vt* make cleaner, tidier, more fashionable, etc

smash *vt,vi* 1 shatter; break into fragments 2 hit or throw violently *n* 1 sound or act of smashing 2 violent collision, esp of motor vehicles **smashing** *adj inf* wonderful; excellent

smear *n* 1 dirty greasy mark 2 slur on one's reputation 3 specimen taken for pathological testing *vt* 1 spread or cover with something thick or greasy 2 discredit publicly 3 blur by smearing

smell *n* 1 odour; stink; fragrance 2 ability to distinguish smells 3 suggestion; hint *vt* detect or distinguish by the sense of smell *vi* give off a smell **smell out** discover by investigation **smell a rat** become suspicious **smelly** *adj* having a strong or unpleasant smell

smile *vi* turn up the corners of the lips to express pleasure, approval, amusement, etc *n* act of smiling; happy expression **smilingly** *adv*

smirk *vi* give an unpleasant, knowing, silly, or self-satisfied smile *n* act of smirking; smirking expression

smock *n* full long loose shirt

smog *n* combination of smoke and fog **smoggy** *adj*

smoke *n* 1 visible cloud of fine particles given off during burning 2 cigarette, cigar, etc *vi* give off smoke *vi vt* inhale fumes of burning tobacco in a cigarette, pipe, etc *vt* cure (meat, fish, etc) by treatment with smoke **smoker** *n* 1 person who smokes tobacco 2 train compartment where smoking is allowed **smoky** *adj*

smooth *adj* 1 having an even surface 2 level; even 3 unruffled; calm 4 easy; comfortable *vt,vi also* **smoothen** make or become smooth *vt* 1 soothe; comfort 2 facilitate; make easy or easier **smoothly** *adv* **smoothness** *n*

smother *vt* 1 suffocate; prevent access of air with a thick covering, heavy smoke, etc 2 suppress or conceal

smoulder *vi* 1 burn slowly without a flame 2 exist in a suppressed or undetected condition

smudge *n* smear; dirty mark *vt* mark or be marked with a smudge; smear

smug *adj* self-satisfied; complacent **smugly** *adv* **smugness** *n*

smuggle *vt,vi* import or export (goods) illegally *vt* bring or take in secretly or illegally **smuggler** *n*

smut *n* 1 particle of soot or dust 2 small dark mark 3 bawdiness; obscenity **smutty** *adj*

snack *n* light quick meal

snag *n* small problem, hitch, drawback, etc *vt* (-gg-) 1 hinder; prevent 2 catch or tear on a small sharp protuberance

snail *n* small slow-moving hard-shelled mollusc

snake *n* 1 long scaly legless reptile with a forked tongue and neither eyelids nor ears 2 treacherous deceitful person

snap *vt,vi* (-pp-) 1 bite suddenly 2 speak sharply or irritably 3 shut or break suddenly **snap up** seize hastily ~*n* 1 act or sound of snapping 2 simple card game 3 *inf* snapshot **snapshot** *n* informal photograph

snarl *vi* growl, speak, or show the teeth threateningly or angrily *n* act, sound, or expression of snarling

snatch *vt,vi* seize or grab suddenly, violently, or when an opportunity arises *n* 1 act of snatching 2 fragment or bit

sneak *vi* move or creep in a furtive cowardly or underhand way *vt* take secretly; steal *n* one who sneaks

sneer *n* cynical contemptuous expression or remark *v* **sneer at** scorn; mock

sneeze *vi* eject sudden convulsive involuntary breath through the nose **not to be sneezed at** not to be treated as insignificant ~*n* act or sound of sneezing

sniff *vi* inhale sharply and noisily through the nose *vt* smell **sniff at** show scorn ~*n* act or sound of sniffing

snip *vt,vi* (-pp-) clip or cut off with or as with scissors *n* 1 act of snipping 2 small piece snipped off

snipe *vi* shoot at an enemy or enemies from a concealed position *n* long-billed wading bird **sniper** *n*

snivel *vi* (-ll-) 1 have a runny nose 2 whine or whimper tearfully *n* act or sound of snivelling **sniveller** *n*

snob *n* one who admires and imitates those he considers his superior in class, wealth, or rank and who despises his inferiors **snobbish** *adj* **snobbery** *n*

snooker *n* game resembling billiards using fifteen red balls and six of other colours

snoop *vi* pry; investigate secretly **snooper** *n*

snooty *adj* supercilious; haughty; disdainful **snootily** *adv* **snootiness** *n*

snooze *n* short sleep; cat nap *vi* doze; take a snooze

snore *vi* breathe noisily while asleep *n* act or sound of snoring

snort *vi* exhale noisily and sharply through the nose, often in anger *n* act or sound of snorting

snout *n* 1 animal's projecting nose 2 part of machinery, etc, resembling a snout

snow *n* atmospheric vapour frozen and falling as flakes of white crystals *vi* shower or fall as snow. **snowed under** overwhelmed with work, problems, etc **snowed up** confined in a house, car, etc, by fallen snow **snowy** *adj*

snowdrop *n* tiny white-flowered bulbous plant of eerly spring

snub *vt* (-bb-) humiliate or slight pointedly or sarcastically *n* snubbing act or rebuff **snub-nosed** *adj* having a short turned-up nose

snuff[1] powder (esp tobacco) inhaled through the nose

snuff[2] *vt* extinguish (a candle)

snug *adj* cosy, comfortable, and warm **snugly** *adv*

snuggle *vt,vi* cuddle closely together or into blankets, etc, for warmth and comfort

so *adv* 1 to such an extent; very 2 in such a manner 3 consequently; then 4 also; as well **and so on** and continuing; et cetera ~*pron* 1 something similar 2 as anticipated *adj* correct; right; true **so-and-so** *n* 1 particular but unnamed person **2** awkward or difficult person; nuisance

soak vt,vi steep or be steeped in liquid vt drench; permeate **soak up** draw into itself; absorb ~n **1** act of soaking **2** heavy down-pour

soap n substance used for cleansing, forming a lather with water **soap opera** n serialized drama, esp broadcast on daytime television ~vt **1** rub with soap **2** inf flatter **soapy** adj

soar vi rise upwards; fly or glide at great height n act of soaring

sob v (-bb-) vi catch one s breath noisily in involuntary spasms as a result of emotion; weep; cry vt utter while sobbing n act of sobbing

sober adj **1** not drunk **2** temperate in the use of intoxicants **3** moderate; well-balanced **4** serious; sedate vt,vi make or become sober **soberly** adv **sobriety** or **soberness** n

sociable adj **1** friendly **2** fond of or conducive to social interaction **sociability** n **sociably** adv

social adj **1** of or concerning interaction or relations between persons **2** forming a society, group, or community **3** gregarious; convivial **4** pertaining to fashionable circles n gathering for companionship **socially** adv **social class** n members of a community sharing a similar position in economic and social structure **social security** n scheme(s) providing for the welfare of the public **social work** n social service to improve the welfare of the public **social worker** n

socialism n political and economic theory of society which tends towards centralized planning and ownership of the means of production, distribution, and exchange and operation of the free market **socialist** adj,n

society n **1** group sharing territory, language, customs, laws, and political and economic organization **2** fellowship; companionship **3** any group of people organized for a purpose **4** rich, aristocratic, and exclusive social group

sociology n study of human societies, their structure, organization, and customs **sociological** adj **sociologist** n

sock[1] n short stocking **pull one's socks up** make greater efforts

sock[2] vt,n sl punch; hit

socket n **1** device which receives an electric plug **2** natural or artificial indentation functioning as a receptacle

soda n term applied to compounds of sodium **soda-water** n aerated solution of sodium bicarbonate

sodium n soft silvery reactive metallic element

sofa n upholstered couch with a back and arms

soft adj **1** yielding; malleable; smooth **2** gentle **3** lenient **4** tender; sympathetic **5** (of sound) low in volume **6** (of colour) not very bright **7** inf feeble-minded; foolish **softly** adv **softness** n **soften** vt,vi make or become soft(er) **soft-hearted** adj easily moved to tenderness, pity, etc **soft-heartedly** adv **soft-heartedness** n **software** n written or printed data used in the operation of computers; program

soggy adj soaked; marshy, sodden **soggily** adv **sogginess** n

soil[1] n top layer of the earth, composed of organic and inorganic substances; ground

soil[2] vt,vi make or become dirty, stained, or polluted

solar adj **1** of or from the sun **2** measured by the movement of the earth relative to the sun **3** radiating like the sun's rays **solar system** n our sun with the planets, asteroids, comets, etc , that revolve round it **solar plexus** n network of nerves radiating from behind the stomach

sold v pt and pp of **sell.**

solder n alloy with a low melting temperature used for joining metals vt join, mend, or patch with solder

soldier n noncommissioned member of an armed force v **soldier on** keep fighting or struggling towards something **soldierly** adj

sole[1] n flat underside of a foot, shoe, etc vt put a sole on

sole[2] n edible flatfish

sole[3] adj only; single; solitary **solely** adv

solemn adj **1** grave; serious **2** marked by formal or religious ceremony; arousing awe and reverence **3** impressive; dignified; pompous **solemnity** n **solemnly** adv

solicit vt,vi **1** ask (for) persistently **2** make unlawful sexual offers or requests (to)

solicitor n lawyer who prepares deeds, manages cases, and who acts in lower courts only but prepares cases for barristers

solicitous adj considerate; concerned; eager; anxious **solicitude** n

solid adj 1 firm; compact 2 having three dimensions; not hollow 3 heavy; strongly built 4 reliable; steady 5 unanimous n solid substance; substance that is neither liquid nor gaseous **solidity** n **solidly** adv **solidarity** n unanimous whole-hearted coherence in action or attitude **solidify** vt vi make or become solid

solitary adj 1 existing, living or going without others 2 happening, done, or made alone 3 secluded 4 lonely; single; sole **solitary confinement** n isolation of a prisoner from all others **solitude** n absence of company; seclusion

solo n 1 musical composition for a single voice or instrument 2 card game in which players act individually and not in partnership 3 flight during which the pilot is unaccompanied adv alone; by oneself **soloist** n

solstice n time of year when the sun reaches its farthest points north and south of the equator, producing the shortest or longest day

soluble adj 1 capable of being dissolved in liquid 2 capable of being solved **solubility** n

solution n 1 method or process of solving a problem 2 explanation or answer 3 liquid containing a dissolved solid

solve vt find the correct solution to; settle; clear up; explain

solvent adj 1 able to pay debts 2 able to dissolve another substance n liquid capable of dissolving another substance **solvency** n ability to pay off debts

sombre adj dark; dismal; gloomy **sombrely** adv **sombreness** n

sombrero n wide-brimmed hat with a tall crown, traditionally worn in Spain and Latin America

some adj 1 certain (people or things) 2 a few; a number; an amount or quantity 3 particular proportion pron a number of people or things adv about; approximately **somebody** pron 1 particular but unnamed person 2 important or famous person **somehow** adv 1 in some way or other 2 for some reason **someone** pron somebody **something** pron particular but unnamed thing, action characteristic, etc **something like** approximately; about; almost adv to a certain extent **sometime** adv on some occasion; at some time **sometimes** adv occasionally; from time to time **somewhat**

adv to a certain extent; rather **somewhere** adv 1 in or to some particular but unspecified place 2 placed approximately

somersault n 1 leap or roll in which one turns heels over head 2 complete reversal of opinion or attitude vi make a somersault

son n 1 male offspring, esp in relation to his parents 2 any male descendant **son-in-law** n, pl **sons-in-law** daughter s husband

sonata n musical composition of three or four movements and featuring a solo instrument

song n 1 musical piece that is sung 2 songs in general 3 characteristic call of certain birds **song and dance** inf fuss

sonic adj 1 relating to sound 2 having a speed approximately equal to the speed of sound

sonnet n poem of fourteen lines with a set rhyming pattern

soon adv in a short time; without delay; quickly **as soon as** at the moment that

soot n black powdery substance given off by burning coal, wood, etc **sooty** adj

soothe vt calm; comfort; allay

sophisticated adj 1 refined or cultured in taste and manner; urbane 2 attractive to refined tastes 3 over-refined; unnatural 4 (of machines, etc) complex **sophistication** n

soprano n 1 highest range of an adult female voice 2 singer capable of this range of notes 3 part written for this voice

sordid adj 1 filthy; squalid 2 degrading; base 3 greedy or selfish **sordidly** adv **sordidness** n

sore adj 1 painful; tender; inflamed 2 grieved, vexed or bitter n injured or diseased spot; wound **soreness** n **sorely** adv severely; distressingly; greatly

sorrow n mental pain caused by loss or misfortune **sorrowful** adj **sorrowfully** adv

sorry adj 1 feeling pity, regret, sadness sympathy, etc 2 pitiful; miserable 3 poor; shabby interj expression of apology

sort n 1 class; kind; type 2 character; nature **sort of** inf in some way; rather **out of sorts** not in good health or spirits ~vt, vi 1 classify 2 group (with) **sort out** 1 separate out 2 solve (a problem); resolve (a situation) 3 inf punish; reprimand

soufflé n light fluffy dish made with eggs

sought v pt and pp of **seek.**

soul n 1 immortal spiritual part of man 2 innermost depth, being, or nature; core 3 nobler feelings and capacities of the human being; conscience 4 person 5 music derived from Black American gospel singing **soul-destroying** adj eroding identity; sapping effort or vigour; making inhuman **soulful** adj having, expressing, or affecting deep or lofty feelings **soulfully** adv **soulless** adj inhuman; mechanical; lacking emotion or identity

sound[1] n 1 noise perceptible to the ear 2 mere noise without meaning vt, vi 1 cause or emit a sound 2 signal by a sound vi seem; give an impression of being **soundless** adj **soundlessly** adv

sound[2] adj 1 in good condition; healthy; whole and complete 2 reasoned; prudent; reliable 3 (of sleep) deep; unbroken **soundly** adv **soundness** n

soup n liquid food made by boiling meat or vegetables in water **in the soup** sl in trouble or difficulties

sour adj 1 sharp or acid to the taste; not sweet 2 turned or rancid 3 embittered; morose **sour grapes** pretending to dislike what one cannot have **sourly** adv **sourness** n

source n 1 spring; origin; starting point or cause 2 document or work providing authority, validity, or inspiration

south n 1 one of the four cardinal points of the compass situated to the right of a person facing the sunrise 2 part of a country, area, etc , lying towards the south adj also **southern** of, in, or facing the south adv,adj also **southerly** 1 towards the south 2 (of winds) from the south **southerner** n **southeast** n point situated midway between the south and east adj also **southeastern** of, in, or facing the southeast adv,adj also **southeasterly** 1 towards the southeast 2 (of winds) from the southeast **southward** adj facing or moving towards the south **southwards** adv in the direction of the south **southwest** n point situated midway between south and west adj also **southwestern** of, in, or facing the southwest adv,adj also **southwesterly** 1 towards the southwest 2 (of winds) from the southwest

souvenir n memento or keepsake by which memory of some person, place, or event is cherished

sovereign n 1 monarch; supreme ruler 2 former English gold coin worth a pound adj 1 supreme; utmost 2 excellent **sovereignty** n

sow[1] (sou) v (sowed; sown or sowed) vt,vi scatter or put (seeds, plants, etc) in the ground vt disseminate; suggest **sower** n

sow[2] (sau) n adult female pig

soya bean n seed of an east Asian plant, rich in oil and protein

spa n resort having mineral water springs in its locality

space n 1 three-dimensional expanse 2 period of time or the distance between events, places, etc 3 blank or unused area 4 universe; area beyond the earth s atmosphere vt arrange at or divide into intervals **spacecraft** n vehicle launched into space for research purposes, exploration, etc **spacious** adj having ample room; extensive; wide **spaciously** adv

spade[1] n digging tool with a broad flat blade

spade[2] n playing card of the suit marked with a black heart-shaped pip and a stem or the symbol itself

spaghetti n pasta in the form of long thin cords

span n 1 extent of something stretched out; stretch of space or time 2 distance between two points, as between pillars, supports of arches, bridges, etc vt 1 extend; stretch across 2 measure with an extended hand

spaniel n breed of medium-sized dog with long drooping ears and a silky coat

spank vt strike with the open hand, a slipper, etc , esp on the buttocks; slap n blow or series of blows with the flat of the hand, etc ; smack

spanner n tool for manipulating nuts and bolts **spanner in the works** deliberate hindrance; sabotage

spare vt 1 be merciful to; refrain or release from punishment, suffering, etc 2 give away freely; be able to do without adj 1 left over; not used or needed; extra 2 freely available; kept in reserve 3 lean; thin 4 scanty; meagre n spare part **sparing** adj thrifty; economical

spark n 1 glowing particle thrown out by a burning substance 2 brief flash of light, as that accompanying an electric discharge 3 vitality; life vi emit sparks vt 1 produce (sparks) 2 kindle; excite

sparkle vi 1 glitter; twinkle; emit sparks or flashes 2 be gay, clever, or witty n 1 act of glittering; brilliance 2 gaiety; wit; lively intelligence **3** appearance of effervescence, as in champagne

sparrow n any of various small brown birds

sparse adj thinly distributed; scanty **sparsely** adv **sparseness** or **sparsity** n

spasm n **1** involuntary muscular contraction **2** strong but short-lived movement, action, or emotion **spasmodic** adj **1** intermittent; not continuous **2** relating to spasms **spasmodically** adv

spastic adj suffering from spasms and lack of muscular control due to damage to the brain n person who suffers so

spat v pt and pp of **spit.**

spatial adj of, in, or concerning space or the placement of objects in space **spatially** adv

spatula n broad blunt-bladed knife or flattened spoon

spawn n eggs of fish, frogs, molluscs, etc , laid in water vt,vi deposit (eggs)

speak v (spoke; spoken) vi **1** utter words; talk **2** give a speech, lecture, sermon, etc vt declare; pronounce **nothing to speak of** nothing worth mentioning **so to speak** as one might put it **speak for** speak on behalf of **speak for oneself** express personal views **speak up** speak so as to be sure to be heard **speak up for** speak in favour of; defend **speaker** n

spear n **1** long weapon consisting of a shaft with a sharp pointed head **2** anything so shaped vt,vi kill or pierce with a spear

spearmint n aromatic garden mint or the flavour of this

special adj **1** distinctive; peculiar; for a particular purpose **2** detailed; exceptional n special thing or person **specially** adv **specialist** n person having comprehensive knowledge of a subject, etc ; authority **speciality** n particular characteristic, product, etc , for which a person, shop, etc , is renowned **specialize** vi limit oneself to one particular area for intensive study **specialization** n

species n, pl **species** group of animals or plants of the same genus, capable of interbreeding

specific adj **1** of or particular to one definite kind or type **2** explicit; precise; exact **specifically** adv **specify** vt **1** make explicit; mention particularly **2** set down as a requisite **specification** n

specimen n individual, object, or portion regarded as typical or a sample for purposes of study or collection

speck n small spot; minute particle vt mark with specks

spectacle n **1** exhibition; show; pageant **2** unusual or ridiculous sight **spectacles** pl n glasses worn to correct vision, etc **spectacular** adj impressive; outstanding; amazing n flamboyant show **spectacularly** adv

spectator n person watching a show, contest, etc ; onlooker

spectrum n **1** range of colours in order of wavelength produced when sunlight is split into colours on passing through a prism **2** wide range; graduated series **spectral** adj

speculate vi **1** theorize; reflect; make conjectures **2** take risks, esp in buying and selling, in the hope of quick gain **speculation** n **speculative** adj **speculator** n

speech n **1** that which is spoken; language **2** act or faculty of speaking; manner of speaking **3** oration; talk addressed to an audience **speechless** adj **1** temporarily deprived of speech **2** unable to speak

speed n rate of movement; quickness; velocity v (sped or speeded) vi,vt move rapidly or quickly vi drive a vehicle at high speed or in excess of the speed limit vt **1** further; hasten **2** send forth with good wishes **speedy** adj. **speedily** adv

spell[1] v (spelt or spelled) vt,vi say or write in order the letters that constitute (a word) vt **1** (of letters) form; make up **2** amount to **spell out** explain in very simple and exact terms

spell[2] n **1** magical formula or incantation **2** enchantment; irresistible attraction **spellbound** adj under a spell or influence; fascinated

spell[3] n short period of time; bout

spend vt (spent) **1** give; pay out **2** expend; use; exhaust **3** pass (time) **spendthrift** n person who wastes money

sperm n **1** semen **2** male reproductive cell

sphere n **1** ball; globe **2** scope; range **3** field of activity or influence; world **spherical** adj

spice n **1** strong aromatic and pungent seasoning of vegetable origin **2** that which adds excitement or interest vt season with spice **spicy** adj **spicily** adv **spiciness** n

spider n eight-legged insect-like animal that spins webs to catch prey **spidery** adj **1** spider-like **2** having thin angular lines

spike n sharp pointed rod, esp of metal vt fix or pierce with a spike **spiky** adj

spill vt,vi (spilt or spilled) **1** allow (liquid) to fall, esp by accident **2** overflow or cause to overflow **spill the beans** reveal a secret ~n **1** fall from a vehicle, horse, etc **2** spilling

spin vt,vi (spun) **1** rotate rapidly **2** draw out and twist (wool, etc) into thread **3** (of spiders, etc) form webs or cocoons n **1** act or speed of rotating **2** inf pleasure drive in a vehicle, etc

spine n **1** backbone surrounding and protecting nerve tissue **2** long thin ridge **3** spiked extremity on a plant, fish, etc **4** bound edge of a book **spinal** adj **spiny** adj **spine-chilling** adj terrifying **spineless** adj **1** having no spine **2** weak; irresolute

spinster n unmarried woman

spiral n **1** curve that winds around and away from a fixed point or axis **2** upward or downward trend in prices, wages, etc adj resembling a spiral; twisting v (-ll-) vt,vi take or make into a spiral course or shape vi increase or decrease with ever-growing speed

spire n **1** tall slender tower tapering to a point **2** long slender flower or stalk; shoot

spirit n **1** moving force; inner life; soul **2** underlying meaning; true significance **3** vitality; courage **4** mood **5** any distilled alcoholic beverage **6** active essence of a drug, compound, etc **spirited** adj lively; animated **spirited away** adj mysteriously or secretly carried off

spiritual adj **1** of or like a spirit or soul **2** religious; sacred **3** ideal; unworldly; not materialistic n American Negro religious song originating in the time of slavery **spiritually** adv

spit[1] n saliva v (-tt-; spat or spit) vt,vi eject (something) from the mouth vi drizzle lightly and irregularly

spit[2] n spike for roasting meat

spite n malevolence; vindictiveness; desire to injure **in spite of** notwithstanding; in defiance of ~vt injure or grieve maliciously **spiteful** adj **spitefully** adv

splash vt,vi **1** scatter or cause (a liquid) to scatter; spatter **2** fall or cause to fall on in drops or waves n **1** act or sound of splashing **2** liquid splashed **3** mark so made **make a splash** cause a sensation

splendid adj **1** magnificent; brilliant **2** inf excellent; very good **splendidly** adv **splendour** n glory; brilliance; magnificence

splint n rigid piece of wood tied to a limb to keep a broken bone in place vt support with splints

splinter n sliver of wood, glass, metal, etc vt,vi break up into splinters **splinter group** n members who break away from a main group.

split vt,vi (-tt-; split) **1** break or divide into separate pieces, groups, etc **2** break off from a whole **3** tear; rend **4** separate because of disharmony, disagreement, etc **5** share or divide among persons **6** sl go away; leave n **1** act or process of splitting **2** result of splitting; division; gap

splutter vi **1** gasp and spit jerkily **2** speak incoherently as in rage **3** eject drops of liquid n act or noise of spluttering

spoil v (spoilt or spoiled) vt **1** damage, destroy, or impair the beauty, usefulness, or value of **2** cause (a child, etc) to become selfish by excessive indulgence vi deteriorate **spoils** pl n plunder; booty **spoil-sport** n person who spoils the enjoyment of others

spoke[1] v pt of **speak**.

spoke[2] n **1** bar radiating from the hub towards the rim of a wheel **2** rung of a ladder

spoken v pp of **speak**.

spokesman n, pl -men person authorized to speak on behalf of others

sponge n **1** pad of any porous elastic substance **2** marine animal with fibrous skeleton **3** act of applying or removing liquid with a sponge **4** light baked or steamed pudding vt,vi **1** apply a sponge to absorb; wipe off **2** inf live or obtain by presuming on the generosity of others **spongy** adj

sponsor vt **1** vouch for good character of; act as surety **2** act as godparent **3** finance; fund n person who sponsors **sponsorship** n

spontaneous adj **1** impulsive; uninhibited; unconstrained **2** produced of itself without external cause **spontaneity** n **spontaneously** adv

spool n small cylinder, bobbin, or reel for winding yarn, photographic film, etc, on

spoon n utensil consisting of a small bowl on a handle vt,vi transfer with or as if with a spoon

sporadic adj occasional; occurring irregularly **sporadically** adv

sport n **1** activity or game indulged in for pleasure **2** amusement; fun; joke **3** inf good-humoured person vt wear conspicuously

sporty adv **sportive** adj merry; playful
sports car n low-bodied usually two-seater car with high acceleration **sportsman** n 1 person fond of sport 2 one who bears defeat, inconvenience, etc; cheerfully **sportsmanship** n

spot n 1 small mark or patch 2 small area or quantity 3 skin blemish **in a spot** in difficulties **soft spot** liking; fondness ~vt (-tt-) 1 mark with spots 2 notice; observe; discover **spotless** adj 1 without blemish 2 very clean **spotlight** n strong beam of light focused on one spot **spotty** adj having spots, esp on the face

spouse n wife or husband of someone

spout n 1 narrow projecting tube through which contents of a vessel are poured 2 jet of liquid vt,vi pour out conspicuously

sprain vt twist or wrench muscles or ligaments (of a foot, hand, etc) without dislocation of a joint n 1 act of spraining muscles 2 swelling and pain caused by this

sprang v pt of **spring.**

sprawl vi 1 lie or sit with stretched-out limbs 2 be spread untidily over a wide area n 1 act or position of sprawling 2 untidy spread esp of buildings

spray[1] n 1 fine drops of liquid blown through the air 2 apparatus for doing this vt,vi squirt, disperse, or become spray

spray[2] small shoot or branch of a plant; sprig

spread vt,vi (spread) 1 extend or cause to extend or cover widely; stretch or be stretched 2 circulate n 1 extent 2 act or degree of spreading or the area covered 3 feast or substance for spreading on bread, etc

spree n lively outing; session of reckless activity or amusement

sprig n small shoot; twig

sprightly adj vivacious; brisk; lively **sprightliness** n

spring v (sprang; sprung) vi 1 leap; jump 2 bounce; rebound; recoil 3 move suddenly or violently 4 have as a cause; originate; start 5 produce shoots, leaves, etc ; sprout vt 1 leap over; jump 2 produce suddenly n 1 leap; jump; bounce 2 season following winter and preceding summer 3 coil of wire, metal, etc , that cushions impact, causes movement of parts in a mechanism, etc 4 natural flow of water forced by pressure from underground **spring-clean** n thorough house-cleaning associated with springtime vt clean in this way **springy** adj 1 elastic; resilient; well-sprung 2 able to leap or recoil

springbok n African antelope

sprinkle vt vi scatter in small drops n small quantity dispersed in drops; light shower

sprint vi race or run very fast for a short distance n short race at full speed

sprout vt develop (shoots or buds) vi begin to grow; send forth n 1 young bud or shoot 2 short for Brussels sprout

sprung v pp of **spring.**

spun v pt and pp of **spin.**

spur n 1 spiked or pointed device on the heel of a rider's boot for urging a horse on 2 incitement; stimulus 3 projecting small branch or hill range **on the spur of the moment** on impulse ~vt,vi (-rr-) goad; hasten

spurt vt,vi 1 make a sudden intense effort 2 send out a sudden jet or stream; spout n 1 brief spell of intense activity 2 sudden jet of liquid

spy n secret agent watching others and collecting information vi 1 watch 2 ascertain; detect

squabble vi dispute in a noisy way n petty quarrel; wrangle **squabbler** n

squad n 1 small group of soldiers 2 group or working party acting together

squadron n 1 group of military aircraft 2 group of warships forming part of a fleet

squalid adj sordid; dirty; uncared for **squalidly** adv **squalor** n state of being squalid; repulsive dirtiness

squander vt spend carelessly and wastefully.

square n 1 right-angled figure having four equal sides 2 total obtained by multiplying a number by itself 3 area of land courtyard, etc , usually bounded on four sides by buildings adj 1 of the shape of a square 2 broad and straight 3 relating to a measurement of area 4 equal or fair adv so as to be square vt 1 form into a square 2 multiply (a number) by itself 3 make equal or fair **square with** be equal or in agreement with; match up to **squarely** adv **squareness** n

squash vt,vi crush or become crushed into or as if into a pulp n 1 drink made from diluted fruit juice 2 ball game played with racquets 3 crushed mass or tight-packed crowd

squat vi (-tt-) 1 sit down with knees bent up and heels against buttocks; crouch 2 occupy a building or land without the consent of the legal owner *adj* short and thick **squatter** *n*

squawk *vi* utter a loud raucous cry *n* loud harsh cry

squeak *vi* emit shrill note or cry *n* shrill weak cry or grating noise **squeaky** *adj* **squeakiness** *n*

squeal *vi* utter a long shrill cry of pain, terror, or excitement *n* long shrill cry

squeamish *adj* easily distressed, shocked, or disgusted; too sensitive

squeeze *vt,vi* 1 subject or be subjected to pressure; press or be pressed out 2 pack tightly; cram 3 extort by threats *n* 1 act of squeezing; state of being tightly pressed or packed 2 government restrictions placed on commercial or financial activities

squid *n* edible marine mollusc having a slender body and triangular tail fins

squiggle *n,vi* twist; wriggle

squint *vi* 1 be unable to focus both eyes in the same direction 2 look obliquely; glance *n* 1 defect in the alignment of the eyes 2 sidelong or stealthy glance

squire *n* country landowner, esp of an old established family *vt* attend or escort (a lady)

squirm *vi* 1 twist and turn; wriggle 2 feel embarrassed or humiliated *n* wriggling movement

squirrel *n* 1 small nimble bushy-tailed rodent 2 *inf* person who hoards

squirt *vt,vi* eject or be ejected in a stream *n* jet; stream

stab *v* (-bb-) *vt* 1 wound or pierce with a pointed weapon 2 give a sharp throbbing pain *vt,vi* jab or strike (at) *n* act of stabbing; blow or wound

stable[1] *adj* 1 firmly established or steady; unchanging 2 not easily upset or overturned; constant **stably** *adv* **stability** *n* quality or state of being stable; steadiness **stabilize** *vt,vi* make or become stable or permanent **stabilizer** *n*

stable[2] *n* 1 building where horses, etc, are kept 2 group of horses, etc, kept by a particular owner or trainer *vt,vi* provide with or keep in a stable

stack *n* orderly pile or heap *vt* 1 place in a stack; heap 2 load; fill **stack the cards** dishonestly or unfairly arrange (something) against the interests of others

stadium *n, pl* **stadiums** *or* **stadia** ('steidiə) sports arena

staff *n, pl* **staffs** *or* (for 3–6) **staves** 1 people employed by a company, individual, authority, etc 2 officers appointed to assist a commanding officer 3 rod; stick 4 flag pole 5 something capable of sustaining or supporting 6 series of horizontal lines used in musical notation *vt* provide with a staff

stag *n* adult male deer **stag party** *n* social gathering of men only

stage *n* 1 elevated or allocated arena on which a performance takes place 2 theatrical profession 3 stopping place on a journey 4 level or period of development *vt* 1 put (a play, etc) on the stage before an audience 2 do for effect; contrive dramatically 3 arrange and carry out **stage manager** *n* person who organizes rehearsals, scenery, staging, etc, of a play

stagger *vi,vt* move or walk unsteadily; totter *vt* 1 startle; shock 2 arrange at intervals *n* unsteady movement; tottering gait **staggeringly** *adv*

stagnant *adj* 1 still; not flowing 2 foul; putrid from standing still 3 inert; languid **stagnantly** *adv* **stagnate** *vi* 1 cease to flow; putrefy 2 fail to develop; become sluggish **stagnation** *n*

stain *n* 1 discoloration; spot; blemish 2 dye or tint *vi,vt* soil or discolour *vt* 1 taint 2 colour or dye **stainless** *adj* **stained glass** *n* glass coloured by metallic pigments fused into its surface

stair *n* one in a series of steps **stairs** *pl n* series of steps from one level to another **staircase** *n* flight of stairs usually having a banister and containing structure

stake[1] *n* 1 pointed stick or post for fixing into the ground 2 post to which persons were tied and burnt to death *vi* 1 tie or join with or to a stake 2 mark a boundary with stakes *vt* 1 register (a claim) to a plot of land, rights, etc 2 support by tying to a stake

stake[2] *n* 1 money risked in gambling 2 amount that may be won **at stake** in danger of being lost; at risk, at stake ~*vt* bet; wager; risk

stale *adj* 1 (of food, etc) not fresh; altered by age 2 out of condition or practice **staleness** *n*

stalemate *n* 1 one type of draw in a game of

chess **2** deadlock *vt* cause to suffer a stalemate

stalk[1] *n* **1** stem of a plant **2** slender support; shaft

stalk[2] *vt,vi* **1** walk stealthily (after); go after (prey) **2** walk stiffly or haughtily

stall *n* **1** place for a single animal in a stable **2** bench, table, booth, or barrow for displaying goods for sale **3** theatre seat on the ground floor **4** church seat. esp for the choir **5** covering for a finger or toe *vt,vi* **1** stop (a car, motor, etc) or make stop because of incorrect adjustment or handling **2** put off; evade; delay

stallion *n* male horse. esp one kept for breeding

stamina *n* power of endurance; strength

stammer *n* speech defect in which particular sounds are uttered falteringly and sometimes repeated involuntarily *vi,vt* speak or say with a stammer; utter brokenly

stamp *vt,vi* crush or tread (on) heavily with the feet *vt* **1** make a mark, symbol, or design on **2** affix a postage stamp to **3** make a deep impression; scar **stamp out** suppress or abolish completely ∼*n* **1** heavy tread or pressure with the feet **2** *also* **postage stamp** small piece of paper printed with a design, for affixing to mail as proof of postage paid **3** seal, symbol, or mark **4** device for producing a particular symbol or mark **5** characteristic quality

stampede *n* **1** sudden rush of frightened animals **2** any impulsive action by a mass of people *vi,vt* flee or cause to flee in panic *vt* press a person into rash action

stand *v* (stood) *vi* **1** be erect with the feet supporting the weight of the body **2** move into such a position; rise; get up **3** be positioned or located **4** have a particular point of view **5** remain; stay; adhere (to) **6** be a candidate; be nominated *vt* **1** place; position; rest **2** take the strain of; bear **3** tolerate; put up with **4** treat; pay for **5** be subjected to (a trial) **stand by 1** be ready to act if needed **2** remain loyal to **stand down** give up a post, claim, etc **stand for** represent; tolerate **stand out** be conspicuous or prominent **stand up for** defend; protect; fight for ∼*n* **1** platform **2** article or piece of furniture for supporting something **3** stall at a market, exhibition, etc **4** position or point of view to

be defended **stand-by** *n* person or thing that may be relied upon in an emergency

standing *n* **1** rank; status; reputation **2** duration; length of experience, etc *adj* **1** erect **2** permanent or continuing **3** stagnant

standstill *n* complete cessation of movement or progress

standard *n* **1** guideline; example **2** principle; integrity **3** flag; banner; emblem **4** commodity on which a monetary system is based **5** fruit or rose tree having a straight stem and no lower branches *adj* serving as or conforming to a standard; average; accepted **standardize** *vt* cause to conform to a standard; remove variations from **standardization** *n*

stank *v pt of* **stink**.

stanza *n* group of lines of verse forming a division of a poem

staple[1] *n* bent length of wire for fastening *vt* fasten with a staple or staples **stapler** *n*

staple[2] *n* **1** basic essential food **2** grade of fibre in wool, flax, etc *adj* basic; indispensable; standard

star *n* **1** incandescent body in outer space seen in the night sky as a twinkling light **2** figure with five or six pointed rays **3** highly popular public entertainer **4** asterisk **5** planet influencing one's luck according to astrology; fate *vt* (-rr-) **1** mark or cover with stars **2** play the leading part or present as the leading performer **3** mark with an asterisk **starfish** *n* star-shaped invertebrate fish **starry** *adj*

starboard *n,adj* right-hand side of a vessel when one is facing forward

starch *n* **1** carbohydrate present in many plants and vegetables **2** this substance used as a stiffener after laundering fabrics *vt* stiffen with starch **starchy** *adj* **starchily** *adv* **starchiness** *n*

stare *vi* look with fixed eyes *n* act of staring

stark *adj* **1** bleak; harsh; grim **2** unelaborated; blunt *adv* completely **starkly** *adv* **starkness** *n*

starling *n* small gregarious bird with blackish feathers

start *vt* **1** begin; set up **2** set in motion *vi* jump involuntarily as because of fright *n* **1** beginning; a jerk; jump **starter** *n*

startle *vt* give a shock to; alarm; take aback *vi* feel slight shock or alarm; be taken aback **startlingly** *adv*

starve vi vt 1 die or make die from lack of food 2 suffer or make suffer from hunger vi be very hungry **starvation** n

state n 1 condition; situation; circumstances 2 form; structure 3 political community under a government 4 status; rank 5 splendour; dignified style 6 inf distressed or anxious condition vt declare; specify; utter **stately** adj imposing; magnificent; dignified **stateliness** n **statement** 1 act of stating 2 something stated 3 formal account 4 financial account in detail

statesman n wise revered politician **statesmanlike** adj **statesmanship** n skill and abilities involved in being a statesman

static adj 1 at rest unmoving 2 not causing movement 3 relating to interference in reception of radio signals n disturbance in radio or television reception caused by electrical disturbances

station n 1 fixed stopping place for a bus, train etc 2 position; status 3 office or headquarters of the police, etc vt assign a place or post to **station-master** n official in charge of a railway station

stationary adj fixed; still; permanently located

stationer n person who sells writing materials, etc **stationery** n writing materials, esp notepaper and envelopes

statistics pl n numerical data used to make analyses s n study of the analysis of numerical data **statistical** adj relating to numerical data **statistically** adv **statistician** n expert in statistics

statue n sculpture or representation of a person, group, or an animal

stature n 1 height of a person or animal standing upright 2 moral or intellectual greatness

status n 1 official or social position 2 prestige, high rank **status quo** the existing situation **status symbol** object desired or owned for prestige purposes

statute n 1 act, law, or decree made by Parliament or some other legislative body 2 rule laid down by an institution or authority **statutory** adj prescribed; authorized by statute

stave n 1 strip of wood, esp on the side of a barrel 2 series of five lines on which music is written **staves** pl of **staff** (defs 3–6)

stay[1] vi remain or be (for a time) vt check; delay **stay the course** be able to finish in spite of difficulties ~ n 1 period of time spent; visit 2 postponement

stay[2] n support; prop; rope or cable supporting a ship s mast, etc **stays** pl n corsets

steadfast adj 1 unwavering 2 resolute; loyal **steadfastly** adv **steadfastness** n

steady adj 1 firmly balanced or supported 2 regular; controlled; fixed 3 constant 4 reliable; sober vt,vi make or become steady **steadily** adv **steadiness** n

steak n thick slice of meat or fish

steal v (stole; stolen) vt 1 unlawfully take away (another person s property) 2 obtain secretly; snatch vi 1 thieve 2 move quietly and unobtrusively; creep **stealth** n furtive behaviour; secrecy; evasion **stealthy** adj **stealthily** adv

steam n 1 vapour produced by boiling water 2 mist left by water vapour **get up steam** become excited or emotional **let off steam** release pent-up emotion or energy harmlessly ~ vi 1 emit steam 2 move by steam power vt cook, iron, etc , using steam **steamy** adj

steel n 1 widely used strong hard alloy of iron and carbon 2 quality of toughness 3 steel weapon, esp a sword vt toughen; strengthen **steel oneself** prepare oneself (to do something difficult or unpleasant) **steely** adj 1 of or like steel 2 unwavering

steep[1] adj 1 rising or sloping sharply; precipitous 2 exorbitant; outrageous **steeply** adv **steepness** n **steepen** vi become steep(er)

steep[2] vt soak thoroughly; immerse

steeple n spire **steeplechase** n horse race in which ditches, fences, etc , must be jumped

steer vt guide; direct the course of (a vehicle etc) vi manoeuvre; guide **steer clear of** keep away from

stem[1] n 1 stalk of a plant 2 anything resembling a stalk, such as the shaft of a pipe or wine glass 3 unchanging part of a word to which inflexions are added v (-mm-) **stem from** arise out of

stem[2] (-mm-) vt stop the flow of; plug

stencil n sheet of card, paper, or metal in which patterns or lettering have been cut in order to transfer the design to a further sheet or sheets vt (-ll-) use or apply with a stencil

Sten gun n lightweight machine gun

step n 1 movement made by lifting the foot;

pace **2** manner of walking, dancing, etc **3** single section of a flight of stairs **4** single grade or stage on a scale **5** short distance **step by step** gradually **take steps (to)** begin to control; initiate action (on) ~vi (-pp-) move by steps; walk **step on it** trample on; walk on or rest the foot on **2** inf accelerate; go fast **step up** increase; intensify activity **step-ladder** n folding ladder with wide flat rungs

stepbrother n son of one's stepmother or stepfather by another marriage

stepdaughter n daughter of one's spouse by another marriage

stepfather n man married by one's mother after the death or divorce of one's father

stepmother n woman married by one's father after the death or divorce of one's mother

stepsister n daughter of one's stepmother or stepfather by another marriage

stepson n son of one's spouse by another marriage

stereo adj short for **stereophonic.** n apparatus for reproducing stereophonic sound **stereophonic** adj (of music, etc) recorded through separate microphones and relayed through separate loudspeakers to give an impression of natural distribution of sound

stereotype n **1** conventionalized idea, conception, or person that lacks variation or individuality **2** solid metal printing plate cast from a mould made from movable type

sterile adj **1** free from live bacteria **2** unable to produce offspring, seeds, or crops; barren; unproductive **sterility** n **sterilize** vt **1** destroy bacteria in **2** render incapable of producing offspring, seeds, or crops **sterilization** n

sterling adj **1** relating to British money **2** (of silver) conforming to a special standard **3** valuable; reliable; excellent n British money

stern[1] adj strict; severe; grim **sternly** adv **sternness** n

stern[2] n **1** back section of a ship or aircraft **2** rear; rump

stethoscope n medical instrument for listening to the sounds of the body

stew vt cook by long slow boiling or simmering n dish, usually of meat, cooked by stewing

steward n **1** person organizing the catering, seating, and sleeping arrangements, esp on a ship; passenger attendant **2** estate or household manager; organizer or helper at a public function, etc **stewardess** n female attendant on a ship or airliner

stick[1] v (stuck) vt **1** join or attach by using glue, paste, nails, pins, etc **2** pierce; prod; thrust **3** put or place carelessly or absent-mindedly vi **1** become fixed, attached, or jammed; wedge **2** remain close to **stick out 1** protrude; jut **2** be conspicuous **stick to** concentrate on for a length of time; adhere to **stick up for** defend or support (a person, one's rights, etc) **sticky** adj **1** tending to stick **2** covered with glue, paste, etc **3** inf awkward; tricky

stick[2] n **1** wooden rod; thin detached branch; staff or cane **2** rod used in certain sports **3** anything resembling a stick in shape

stiff adj **1** difficult to move, bend, or twist; rigid; not flexible **2** (of persons) not moving easily; formal; not at ease socially **3** strong **4** (of prices) high **stiff upper lip** stoicism ~n sl corpse **stiffly** adv **stiffness** n **stiffen** vt, vi make or become stiff **stiffening** n substance used to stiffen something

stifle vt **1** suffocate; choke **2** suppress; put down vi **1** die from suffocation; choke **2** have a suffocating impression

stigma n **1** mark or sign of disgrace; social blot **2** that part of a flower that receives pollen **stigmata** pl n marks of Christ's crucifixion **stigmatize** vt denounce; brand

stile n permanent set of steps or railings for climbing over a hedge, fence, etc

still[1] adv **1** even now; yet **2** even more conj in spite of that adj **1** quiet; hushed; calm; not agitated **2** not fizzy vt calm; subdue n single photograph taken from a film **stillborn** adj **1** born dead **2** (of ideas, etc) conceived but not put into practice **still life** n painting or photograph of inanimate things

still[2] n apparatus for distilling liquids by vaporizing and condensing

stilt n **1** one of a pair of poles with platforms for the feet for walking above the ground **2** supporting pole or pillar for a house, pier, etc **stilted** adj stiff; artificial; pompous

stimulate vt **1** persuade; encourage; arouse **2** inspire; excite mental activity in **3** increase **stimulation** n **stimulant** n **1** anything, esp a drink or drug, that produces extra mental or physical activity **2** stimulus; spur **stimulus** n, pl **stimuli** ('stimjulai) something that encourages, persuades, spurs on, or excites a response

sting vt,vi (stung) 1 hurt by piercing the skin and secreting poison 2 feel or cause to feel a piercing pain 3 hurt (a person's feelings) 4 sl extort money (from), esp by overcharging n 1 act of or pain from stinging 2 part of an insect, fish, or plant that causes a sting

stink vi (stank or stunk; stunk) 1 smell disgusting or offensive 2 inf (of a situation) be offensive or unpleasant n disgusting smell **stinker** n offensive person or thing

stint n fixed amount; quota (of work) vt give small amounts to reluctantly; be ungenerous towards

stipulate vt,vi insist (on) as a condition of agreement; require **stipulation** n

stir v (-rr-) vt 1 move or agitate (a mixture) with a spoon, etc 2 move (slightly) 3 rouse; incite vi move; become active n 1 stirring movement 2 disturbance; sensation

stirrup n hooped metal footrest hanging either side of a horse's saddle

stitch n 1 one unit in a row of sewing or knitting 2 particular kind of stitch 3 loop of thread used in surgery to close a wound, etc 4 inf piercing pain in one's side vt,vi sew using stitches

stoat n small fur-covered mammal similar to but larger than a weasel

stock n 1 store or supply of goods 2 persons, animals, etc, having a common ancestor 3 livestock 4 unspecified number of shares 5 liquid derived by cooking meat, bones, etc, in water 6 flower having purple or white scented flowers vt keep in supply; store **stockbreeding** n breeding and rearing of livestock **stockbroker** n person whc deals professionally in stocks and sheres **stock exchange** n place or association for the buying and selling of stocks and shares **stockpile** n store set aside for future use vt,vi build a stockpile (of) **stocktaking** n making of an inventory of goods or assets in a shop or business

stocking n tight-fitting nylon, woollen, or cotton covering for the leg and foot

stodge n inf heavy not easily digestible food **stodgy** adj thick and heavy; unpalatable; turgid

stoical adj bearing suffering without showing

pain or emotion; being resigned to one's lot **stoically** adv **stoicism** n

stoke vt,vi tend and pile fuel into (a fire or furnace)

stole[1] v pt of **steal.**

stole[2] n woven or knitted shawl, scarf, or fur collar worn round the shoulders

stolen v pp of **steal.**

stomach n 1 principal digestive organ lying between the gullet and the intestines 2 appetite vt 1 digest 2 bear; tolerate

stone n 1 hard compact rock material, used in building, etc 2 lump of rock 3 jewel 4 hard-shelled part of certain fruit 5 anything resembling a stone or made of stone 6 unit of weight equal to 14 pounds (6 3 kilograms) adj made of stone vt 1 throw stones at 2 remove stones from **stony** adj 1 made of, covered with, or like stone(s) 2 hostile; cold **stony broke** completely penniless

stood v pt and pp of **stand.**

stool n 1 backless seat for one person; footstool 2 solid excreta

stoop vt,vi bend (one's head and body) forward and down vi lower oneself morally; demean oneself n 1 act of stooping 2 habitually bent posture

stop v (-pp-) vt,vi cease; bring or come to an end; halt vt 1 discontinue; cut off; prevent 2 prevent the passage of air, liquid, etc, through; block; plug **stop off** call (at); visit ~n 1 halt; end; finish 2 place at which a bus, train, etc, stops to let passengers enter or leave 3 full stop **stopgap** n temporary measure or substitute in an emergency, etc **stoppage** n 1 act of stopping; state of being stopped 2 obstruction 3 cessation of work **stopper** n 1 person or thing that stops 2 plug for a bottle or vessel vt close with a stopper **stopwatch** n watch that can be stopped and restarted for timing races, etc

store n 1 stock set aside for future use; reserve supply; accumulation 2 shop with several departments 3 place where stock is kept **in store** 1 expected to happen 2 set aside **set store by** value greatly ~vt make a store of **store up** reserve for a future occasion; stock up **storage** n keeping of stocks of goods for future use

storey n floor or level of a building

stork n large long-legged long-billed wading bird

storm n 1 weather condition including a strong wind and often rain and thunder 2 sudden outburst of noise, feelings, etc **storm in a teacup** a lot of fuss over something unimportant **take by storm** 1 capture (a fortress) by a sudden massed attack 2 bowl over; captivate ~vt attack and capture suddenly vi rage **stormy** adj violent; tempestuous; relating to or portending a storm

story n 1 tale; short narrative 2 plot of a novel, etc 3 inf lie; fib

stout adj 1 fat; portly 2 strong; sturdy 3 brave n strong dark ale **stoutly** adv **stoutness** n

stove n device for cooking or heating, using gas, electricity, paraffin, etc

stow vt put away; store **stowaway** n person who hides on a ship or aircraft in order to avoid paying the fare

straddle vt, vi stand or sit with one leg on either side (of); stand or sit astride

straggle vi 1 sprawl; be scattered 2 fall behind the main group; continue in small irregular groups

straight adj 1 not crooked or curved 2 direct 3 rigid or erect 4 honest; correct adv 1 directly; in a straight line 2 honestly **straight away** immediately **straighten** vt, vi make or become straight **straighten out** 1 make straight 2 sort out or deal with (a problem) **straightforward** adj 1 uncomplicated; not difficult 2 honest; open

strain[1] vt, vi harm by stretching, exerting force, etc; stress vt 1 filter (a liquid) 2 make tense; demand excessive effort of n tension; stress; act or instance of straining; demand

strain[2] n 1 breed 2 hereditary trait or tendency

strand[1] n single thread from a wire, rope, etc

strand[2] vt, vi run aground; beach **stranded** adj abandoned; cut off; left helpless ~n beach; shore

strange adj 1 odd; peculiar 2 unfamiliar; unusual; extraordinary 3 foreign **strangely** adv **strangeness** n **stranger** n person foreign to or not familiar with a particular place area or society

strangle vt kill by throttling **strangler** n **stranglehold** n 1 choking grip 2 force that suppresses freedom of movement or growth

strap n thin strip esp of leather and with a buckle, for holding objects together vt (-pp-) 1 bind with a strap 2 beat with a strap

strategy n overall plan of attack or campaign,

esp military; set of tactics **strategic** adj relating to or important to an overall strategy

stratum n, pl **strata** ('stra:tə) or **stratums** 1 layer of rock 2 level of society

straw n 1 single dried stem of grain 2 such stems used as a material for baskets, mats, etc, for packing, or as bedding for cattle, etc 3 narrow tube of paper or plastic used for drinking **the last straw** a final blow that makes a situation no longer tolerable

strawberry n creeping plant bearing soft reddish edible fruit

stray vi wander; digress; err; go astray n homeless animal or child adj strayed; lost; scattered

streak n 1 narrow irregular stripe (of colour, etc) 2 flash (of lightning) 3 slight surprising tendency or trace vt mark with streaks vi 1 dash 2 inf run naked in public in order to amuse or shock **streaky** adj **streakiness** n

stream n 1 flow (of water, blood, etc); current 2 brook 3 educational division according to ability vi 1 flow in a steady stream; pour out 2 (of hair, a flag, etc) wave in the air vt divide (children) into educational groups according to ability **streamline** vt 1 design (cars, aircraft, etc) in a smooth narrow shape to give minimum air resistance 2 remove inefficient areas from an operation or process

street n road with houses along one or both sides **streets ahead** wholly superior **up one's street** in one's line or area of interest

strength n 1 quality of being strong; power; force 2 support; aid 3 effectiveness 4 potency; degree of concentration **on the strength of** based on; relying on **strengthen** vt, vi make or become strong(er)

strenuous adj vigorous; diligent; energetic **strenuously** adv **strenuousness** n

stress n 1 anxiety or distress caused by pressure or tension 2 importance; weight; emphasis 3 emphasis put on a word or syllable 4 deforming force applied to an object vt emphasize; put the stress on

stretch vt pull or push out; extend; pull taut vi 1 extend; be elastic 2 flex one's muscles n 1 act of stretching 2 expanse 3 continuous period of time 4 sl term of imprisonment **stretcher** n framework covered in canvas etc, and used for transporting the sick or injured

strict adj 1 accurate; precisely defined 2 stern;

severe; requiring complete obedience **strictly** adv **strictness** n

stride n long step **take in one's stride** cope with easily and without worrying ~vt,vi (strode; stridden) walk (over) in strides

strident adj harsh; grating

strike v (struck) vt 1 hit; touch violently; collide with; beat 2 light (a match) 3 occur to; remind; seem to 4 reach suddenly or unexpectedly vt,vi chime vi 1 attack 2 collide 3 take part in a strike **strike out** 1 delete; cross out 2 embark on a new venture **strike up** begin; set up, establish ~n 1 stoppage of work by employees in support of a claim; etc 2 discovery of oil, etc

string n 1 twine or cord used for tying, binding, etc 2 string-like object such as a tendon or fibre 3 taut cord of wire, catgut, etc, fitted to a musical instrument and producing a note when caused to vibrate 4 linked series; chain; line **strings** pl n stringed instruments of an orchestra **no strings attached** with no restricting factors or conditions **pull strings** use influence in order to better oneself ~vt (strung) fit strings to; thread **string along** keep happy with false promises **string out** 1 spread out over a long area 2 make (something) last a long time

stringent adj strict, harsh, rigorous **stringency** n **stringently** adv

strip[1] v (-pp-) vt 1 remove (the covering outer layer or clothes) from; lay bare 2 take (an engine, etc) apart vi remove one's clothes **striptease** n cabaret act in which the performer seductively removes clothing piece by piece

strip[2] n narrow band; long piece **strip cartoon** cartoon made up of a sequence of drawings

stripe n 1 band of contrasting colour or texture 2 band worn to show military rank **striped** adj marked with stripes

strive vi (strove, striven) try hard, endeavour; labour (to do something)

strode v pt of **stride**.

stroke[1] n 1 hit, blow 2 single controlled movement in sports such as tennis, golf, etc 3 style of swimming 4 individual mark made by a brush or pen 5 one of a series of movements 6 apoplexy, damage to the brain's blood supply causing paralysis 7 oarsman facing the cox 8 chime of a clock

stroke[2] vt caress with the hand; smooth n act of stroking

stroll vi walk for pleasure, saunter n leisurely walk

strong adj 1 physically powerful; forceful; difficult to break down, overcome, capture, or injure 2 sound; healthy; vigorous 3 positive, persuasive, drastic; effective; convincing 4 concentrated; intense adv **going strong** doing well; flourishing **strongly** adv **stronghold** n 1 fortress; garrison 2 area where something prevails or has gained control **strong-minded** having a powerful will, able to resist temptation

struck v pt and pp of **strike**.

structure n 1 way in which things are put together; internal organization, make-up 2 something constructed, esp a building vt give structure or form to; organize **structural** adj **structurally** adv

struggle vi 1 fight hand to hand, wrestle; grapple 2 labour; make great efforts endeavour n fight; strenuous effort

strum vt,vi (-mm-) play (a stringed instrument) idly; sound a few chords (on)

strung v pt and pp of **string**. adj **highly strung** very nervous or tense

strut[1] vi (-tt-) walk proudly to show off; swagger. n pompous gait

strut[2] n supporting bar of wood, iron, etc; slat, rung

stub n piece left after something has been used or worn down, esp a cigarette end or counterfoil of a ticket or cheque vt (-bb-) accidentally strike (one's foot or toe) against **stub out** crush and extinguish (a cigarette)

stubborn adj obstinate, difficult to persuade or influence; strong-willed **stubbornly** adv **stubbornness** n

stuck v pt and pp of **stick**.

stud[1] n 1 ornamental heavy-headed nail or peg, flat knob 2 button-like device for fastening collars or fronts to shirts 3 threaded pin or bolt vt (-dd-) 1 put studs into 2 dot or cover (with jewels stars etc)

stud[2] n 1 establishment for breeding pedigree animals esp horses 2 horse or group of horses kept for breeding

student n person who studies esp one following a course at a college or institute of further education

studio n 1 artist's or craftsman's workroom 2

place where broadcasts, recordings, or films are made **studio couch** sofa that doubles as a bed

studious adj 1 hard-working; fond of studying 2 deliberate

study vt 1 examine closely; peer at 2 give special attention to; learn about; devote oneself to (a particular subject) vi follow a course of instruction; devote oneself to learning from books n 1 act or process of studying; learning 2 book etc . produced by study 3 room intended for study, reading, etc **studied** adj deliberate; intentional; carefully considered; elaborately executed

stuff n any type of material or substance vt 1 cram full, overfill 2 fill with stuffing vi overeat **stuffing** n 1 material with which objects are stuffed 2 seasoned filling for meat, poultry, vegetables, etc

stuffy adj 1 close poorly-ventilated; oppressive 2 inf prim and proper; easily shocked **stuffily** adv **stuffiness** n

stumble vi trip and lose one s balance **stumble on** or **across** discover by chance; come across ~n act of stumbling **stumbling block** obstacle, something that causes hesitation or doubt

stump n 1 portion remaining after the main part of a limb or tree has been removed 2 one of the three posts of a cricket wicket vt inf puzzle, outwit vi walk slowly and heavily **stump up** inf produce or come up with (money)

stun vt (-nn-) 1 knock senseless, make unconscious 2 amaze or shock **stunning** adj inf extremely attractive

stung v pt and pp of **sting**.

stunk v pt and pp of **stink**.

stunt[1] vt impede the growth or development of

stunt[2] n dangerous sensational or acrobatic feat, anything done to attract attention or publicity **stunt man** n person employed to perform dangerous feats in films or for entertainment

stupid adj foolish, silly not clever, dim-witted **stupidity** n **stupidly** adv

sturdy adj strong, stout, solid **sturdily** adv **sturdiness** n

sturgeon n large edible fish whose roe is eaten as caviar

stutter n speech impediment causing hesitation

or constant repetition of a word or syllable; stammer vt,vi speak or say with a stutter

sty[1] n pen for pigs

sty[2] n small inflamed swelling on an eyelid

style n 1 characteristic manner or fashion, esp of practising a particular art, craft, or sport 2 fashion; mode 3 elegance, luxury, grandeur 4 form; kind; sort 5 title; mode of address vt fashion or shape (hair, clothes, etc) **stylist** n **stylistic** adj relating to artistic style **stylish** adj fashionable; smart

stylus n 1 sapphire or diamond point used as a gramophone needle 2 pointed writing or engraving instrument

subconscious n area of one s mind memory and personality of which one is not aware adj unconscious; stemming from the subconscious **subconsciously** adv

subcontract n (sʌbˈkɒntrækt) agreement assigning part of the work specified in a contract to another party vt,vi ('sʌbkɒntrækt) make a subcontract (regarding) **subcontractor** n person accepting a subcontract

subcutaneous adj situated or introduced beneath the skin

subdue vt suppress, put down, quieten

subject n ('sʌbdʒɪkt) 1 something dealt with; object of study, analysis discussion examination, etc ; topic 2 citizen under the authority of a state or ruler 3 grammatical term for word(s) about which something is predicated or for the noun or pronoun acting as the doer of the verb in a sentence 4 central musical theme of a composition **subject to** adj 1 liable or prone to 2 owing allegiance to 3 conditional; dependent adv conditionally ~vt (sʌbˈdʒɛkt) 1 force to experience or undergo 2 bring under the control (of) **subjection** n **subjective** adj 1 influenced by or arising from personal feelings rather than external evidence 2 (in grammar) of the subject **subjectively** adv

sublime adj 1 of great moral or spiritual worth, majestic; awe-inspiring, supreme 2 utter extreme n anything majestic or inspiring awe vt,vi change directly from a solid to a gas **sublimely** adv

submachine gun n lightweight automatic gun

submarine n vessel that can operate underwater adj relating to or intended for use below water level

submerge vt place under water, flood, cover

with liquid *vi* dip or go under water **submergence** *or* **submersion** *n*

submit *vt, vi* (-tt-) **1** surrender; yield **2** put forward for consideration; suggest **submit to** give in to; allow oneself to be under the control of **submission** *n* **1** act of submitting **2** suggestion **submissive** *adj* timid and yielding

subnormal *adj* mentally handicapped; below average intelligence

subordinate *adj* (sə'bɔːdinit) **1** junior; inferior in rank, position, or importance **2** (in grammar) subsidiary; dependent on a main clause *n* (sə'bɔːdinit) person in an inferior position or rank *vt* (sə'bɔːdineit) **1** reduce to a lower rank or position; assign to a lesser place **2** subdue **subordination** *n*

subscribe *vt, vi* pledge a regular sum of money (to) *vi* **subscribe to 1** agree to buy (a magazine, etc) regularly **2** approve of; agree with **subscriber** *n* **subscription** *n* **1** act of subscribing **2** amount subscribed **3** regular monetary contribution

subsequent *adj* later; following or coming afterwards **subsequently** *adv*

subservient *adj* **1** showing exaggerated feelings of humility; obsequious **2** serving an end; useful as a means **subservience** *n*

subside *vi* **1** sink in collapse **2** die down; decrease **subsidence** *n*

subsidiary *adj* supporting; supplementary; secondary *n* thing that is subsidiary, esp a company that is part of a group

subsidy *n* state grant for an industry, cultural organization, etc ; official financial assistance **subsidize** *vt* support with a subsidy; assist financially

substance *n* **1** stuff; matter; material **2** chief part; importance; essence; gist **3** worth; value; foundation **substantial** *adj* **1** ample; large; considerable **2** solid; well-established; wealthy **substantially** *adv* **substantiate** *vt* provide proof of (a claim, charge, etc); establish; show to be true

substitute *vt* put (one person or thing) in place of another *vi* serve as *n* person or thing substituted **substitution** *n*

subtitle *n* **1** title, often explanatory subsidiary to the main one **2** caption translating dialogue in a foreign film *vt* provide a subtitle for

subtle *adj* **1** delicate; slight; not gross; hard to

detect or perceive **2** ingenious; perceptive; complex **subtlety** *n* **subtly** *adv*

subtract *vt* take (an amount) away from; deduct **subtraction** *n*

suburb *n* residential area on the outskirts of a town or city **suburban** *adj* **1** conventional; narrow-minded **2** relating to a suburb

subway *n* **1** underground passage enabling pedestrians to cross a busy road **2** *US* underground railway

succeed *vi* achieve one s purpose; be able; manage *vt* come after; follow and take the place or position of

success *n* **1** achievement of one s purpose **2** achievement of fame and wealth **3** triumph; anything that succeeds **successful** *adj* **successfully** *adv*

succession *n* **1** series of things coming one after another **2** act or process of succeeding to a title or position **successive** *adj* happening one after another or in sequence **successively** *adv* **successor** *n* person taking over the position or rank of another

succulent *adj* **1** juicy **2** fleshy-leaved, as a cactus **succulence** *n* **succulently** *adv*

succumb *vi* **1** yield or give in, esp to powerful persuasion **2** die

such *adj* **1** of a particular kind **2** so much or so many *pron* **1** those who or that which **2** the same **as such 1** by or in itself **2** in that role or capacity **such as** for example; like ~*adv* this or that amount of person **suchlike** *pron* things of a similar sort *adj* similar; of that sort

suck *vt, vi* draw (liquid) into the mouth by action of the lips and tongue *vi* **1** draw milk (from a mother s breast, an udder etc) **2** absorb; draw up (liquid) **3** hold in the mouth and lick **4** make sucking actions *n* act of sucking **sucker** *n* **1** person that sucks **2** *sl* person easily deceived **3** device or organ usually disc-shaped that sticks to surfaces by suction **4** shoot growing from the root of a plant

suckle *vt, vi* give or suck milk from the breast

suction *n* **1** action or process of sucking **2** force causing a flow of liquid or gas or the adhesion of two surfaces

sudden *adj* unexpected; happening quickly or without warning *n* **all of a sudden** unexpectedly **suddenly** *adv* **suddenness** *n*

suds *pl n* froth on the surface of soapy water; lather

sue vt,vi take legal action (against) **sue for** beg; petition (for)

suede n soft leather with a velvety surface

suet n hard fat found round the kidneys of sheep and cattle

suffer vt,vi **1** endure; undergo mental or physical pain **2** bear; tolerate **suffer from** be ill, usually periodically, with **suffering** n mental or physical pain; anguish

sufficient adj enough; adequate for the purpose **sufficiency** n **sufficiently** adv

suffix n letter(s) or syllable(s) put at the end of a word to change its part of speech, meaning, or grammatical inflexion

suffocate vt kill by preventing or restricting breathing; smother vi suffer restriction of one s breathing; die through lack of air; stifle **suffocation** n

sugar n sweet crystalline white or brown carbohydrate obtained from plants such as sugar cane or sugar beet vt sweeten or coat with sugar **sugary** adj **sugar beet** n plant from the roots of which sugar is obtained **sugar cane** n tall tropical grass from the canes of which sugar is obtained

suggest vt vi **1** propose; submit for consideration **2** imply; intimate **3** evoke; bring to mind; make (a person) think of **suggestible** adj easily persuaded by suggestion **suggestion** n **1** proposal; act of suggesting **2** hint; trace **3** implication **4** production of an idea through association **suggestive** adj **1** provoking thoughts (of) **2** having sexual overtones or implications

suicide n **1** act of intentionally killing oneself **2** person who has committed suicide **3** action likely to ruin oneself or one s interests **suicidal** adj

suit vt **1** be convenient for; be acceptable to; satisfy **2** (of clothes, colours, etc) look attractive on or with **3** be or make appropriate **4** equip; adapt n **1** matching jacket and trousers or skirt **2** matching set or series, esp of playing cards **3** court case involving a claim **4** wooing **follow suit** copy; follow the example **suitable** adj appropriate; proper; fitting **suitably** adv **suitability** n **suitor** n **1** one who courts a woman **2** petitioner **suitcase** n portable case for luggage

suite n **1** set of rooms **2** set of furniture designed for one room **3** group of attendants; retinue **4** musical work of several connected movements, esp based on dance forms

sulk vi show offence or resentment by refusing to speak or cooperate n act of sulking **sulky** adj glumly withdrawn; sullen **sulkily** adv **sulkiness** n

sullen adj silently unfriendly or uncooperative; morose and resentful; gloomy **sullenly** adv **sullenness** n

sulphur n yellow nonmetallic element, used in making sulphuric acid **sulphurous** adj

sultan n Moslem ruler, esp the head of the Turkish empire

sultana n **1** sweet seedless raisin **2** wife, mother, or daughter of a sultan

sultry adj **1** hot and humid **2** sexually exciting; voluptuous

sum n **1** result obtained from addition; total or whole **2** amount of money **3** simple arithmetical problem vt (-mm-) find the sum of **sum up** make a summary; review; appraise; judge **summary** n review of the main points; précis adj hasty and unceremonious **summarily** adv **summarize** vt make a summary of

summer n season of the year between spring and autumn **summery** adj characteristic or suggestive of summer

summit n **1** highest point; peak **2** zenith; highest point, esp of a career **summit conference** n high level discussion(s) between governments

summon vt demand the presence of; call forth; call upon **summons** n order to appear, esp in court ~vt issue a summons to

sumptuous adj lavish; luxurious **sumptuously** adv

sun n star about which the earth rotates and from which it receives heat and light v (-nn-) **sun oneself** expose one s body to the sun's warmth **sunflower** n tall plant with large yellow flowers **sunglasses** pl n spectacles with tinted lenses for protection from the sun's rays **sunny** adj **1** exposed to the sun; full of or characterized by sunshine **2** cheerful **sunrise** n **1** daily appearance of the sun above the eastern horizon **2** time when this occurs **sunset** n **1** daily disappearance of the sun below the western horizon **2** time when this occurs **sunshine** n also **sunlight** light and warmth received from the sun

Sunday n first day of the week; day of Christian worship

sundry adj various; miscellaneous **sundries** pl n miscellaneous articles; extras

sung v pp of **sing**.

sunk v pt and pp of **sink**. **sunken** adj 1 situated below the surface; lying underwater; hollowed into the ground or floor 2 fallen in

super adj inf splendid; wonderful; first-rate

superannuation n retirement pension **superannuated** adj obsolete; out of date; antiquated

superb adj excellent; splendid **superbly** adv

superficial adj shallow; perfunctory; of or on the surface; not probing or thorough **superficiality** n **superficially** adv

superfluous (su'pə:fluəs) adj more than is wanted; unnecessary; left over **superfluity** n **superfluously** adv

superhuman adj greater or more intense than seems humanly possible

superimpose vt place (something) on top of something else

superintendent n 1 official in charge of an institution department, building, etc 2 highranking police officer **superintend** vt supervise; direct

superior adj 1 greater; higher; better 2 excellent; of high quality; high-ranking 3 disdainful; conceited; indifferent n person above one in rank or status **superiority** n

supermarket n large self-service food store

supernatural adj 1 existing outside or beyond the laws of nature; magical; ghostly 2 unnatural n **the supernatural** supernatural creatures and happenings

supersonic adj travelling faster than sound

superstition n irrational or uninformed belief or fear, esp in or of the supernatural or magic **superstitious** adj **superstitiously** adv

supervise vt,vi 1 direct (work and workers); control 2 act as a tutor (to) **supervision** n **supervisor** n

supper n light evening meal

supple adj easily bent or manipulated; physically agile; flexible **suppleness** n

supplement n ('sʌplimənt) 1 something added to complete or extend something else 2 additional section of a book, newspaper, etc vt ('sʌpliment) add to; make supplements to **supplementary** adj

supply vt 1 provide; keep provided with 2 fulfil;

satisfy n 1 stock; amount stored; something supplied 2 availability or production of goods, esp in relation to demand **supplies** pl n stored goods; provisions

support vt 1 hold up; bear the weight of 2 back; stand up for; favour the cause of; assist 3 maintain financially; provide for 4 tolerate n 1 act of supporting 2 person or thing that supports **supporting** adj secondary; not principal

suppose vt,vi imagine; be inclined to think, assume **supposition** n **supposed** adj presumed **supposed to** expected or obliged to **supposedly** adv said or thought to be

suppress vt 1 put down; crush 2 keep concealed; withhold; stifle **suppression** n **suppressive** adj

supreme adj most powerful; absolute; highest; greatest **supremely** adv **supremacy** n state of being supreme; dominance

surcharge n extra amount added to the main bill, total, or cost vt 1 impose a surcharge 2 overload

sure adj 1 convinced; having no doubt, confident 2 certain, inevitable 3 reliable; proven **make sure (of)** 1 satisfy oneself (about). check 2 make certain ~interj inf certainly! of course! **surely** adv 1 in a sure way 2 certainly; without doubt. **surety** n 1 pledge; guarantee; guarantor 2 certainty

surf n foam made by waves breaking along the shoreline; breakers vi engage in surfing **surfing** n sport of riding large waves while balancing on a board

surface n 1 topmost or outer covering, layer, or edge 2 outward appearance vt provide with a surface; improve the surface (of) vi rise to the surface; emerge

surfeit n excessive or superfluous amount, overabundance; excess, esp of food consumed

surge vi drive or press forward in a rush or flood n surging action; gush; swell; onrush

surgeon n 1 doctor who performs medical operations 2 military or police doctor **surgery** n 1 medical treatment involving operations 2 doctor s consulting-room; hours for visiting a doctor **surgical** adj used in or relating to surgery

surly adj bad-tempered and unhelpful; sullen

surmount vt overcome (an obstacle or problem);

climb over *vt,vi* be above; place on top of **surmountable** *adj*

surname *n* hereditary family name

surpass *vt* excel; outdo; exceed; transcend **surpassing** *adj* extraordinary

surplus *n* **1** excess amount **2** portion that remains after needs have been supplied expenses subtracted, etc *adj* extra, left over; no longer needed

surprise *vt* **1** astonish; amaze **2** take unawares *n* **1** something unexpected **2** amazement; astonishment **surprised** *adj* revealing or expressing surprise **surprising** *adj* causing surprise **surprisingly** *adv*

surrender *vt,vi* yield; give in; give up; abandon *n* act of surrendering

surreptitious *adj* done clandestinely; furtive; deliberately concealed **surreptitiously** *adv* **surreptitiousness** *n*

surround *vt* encircle; extend right round; crowd around **surrounding** *adj* situated around or nearby **surroundings** *pl n* environment; objects or area immediately surrounding one

survey *vt* (sə'vei) **1** scan; look over carefully **2** measure and record the area, elevations, and other geographical features of a piece of land **3** make a detailed inspection of the condition of a building, etc *n* ('sə:vei) **1** act or process of surveying **2** review; analysis **3** surveyor's report **surveying** *n* study or practice of surveying land **surveyor** *n* person employed to survey areas of land or buildings

survive *vt,vi* continue to exist (following); come through; outlive **survival** *n* **survivor** *n*

susceptible *adj* **1** prone (to); easily affected or influenced (by); easily stricken by emotion; sensitive **susceptibility** *n* **1** quality of being susceptible to **2** weakness (for)

suspect *vt,vi* (sə'spekt) **1** believe to be true without proof; have a feeling (about); suppose **2** be doubtful about **3** think (a person) guilty of *n* ('sʌspekt) person thought to have committed a crime etc *adj* ('sʌspekt) dubious; arousing suspicion

suspend *vt* **1** hang (one object from another); hang from above **2** postpone; defer; delay; keep unresolved **3** remove temporarily from office etc withdraw (someone's privileges) **suspension** *n* **1** act of suspending; condition of being suspended **2** postponement; temporary dismissal **3** mixture consisting of one substance dispersed in small particles in

another **suspension bridge** *n* bridge suspended from steel cables hung between two towers

suspense *n* feeling of tension; state of uncertainty

suspicion *n* **1** act of suspecting; doubt or mistrust **2** hint; trace; vague idea **suspicious** *adj* **1** dubious; likely to cause suspicion **2** mistrustful; doubtful; likely to suspect **suspiciously** *adv*

sustain *vt* **1** keep alive; maintain **2** support; hold up **3** endure; suffer; bear **4** give strength to **sustenance** *n* nourishment; food

swab *n* **1** piece of cotton wool, etc , used in medicine to absorb liquid, blood, etc , or to take specimens **2** mop; cloth used for washing floors, etc *vt* (-bb-) mop up; wash down

swagger *vi* strut about; show off; behave conceitedly *n* swaggering walk or manner

swallow[1] *vt,vi* **1** take into the stomach through the throat; gulp **2** *inf* believe or accept (something unlikely) **swallow up** consume; engulf —*n* act of swallowing

swallow[2] *n* small migratory bird with a forked tail

swam *v pt of* **swim.**

swamp *n* permanently waterlogged ground, often overgrown *vt* **1** drench with water; fill with water and sink **2** overwhelm; flood **swampy** *adj*

swan *n* large long-necked water-bird **swan-song** final appearance; last work or contribution

swank *vi* boast; show off *n* **1** person who swanks **2** act of swanking **swanky** *adj*

swap *vt,vi* (-pp-) *also* **swop** *inf* exchange (one thing for another) *n* **1** act of exchanging **2** thing exchanged

swarm *n* **1** dense mass of insects, esp bees **2** large crowd or throng *vi* **1** flock or surge; be crowded (with) **2** (of bees) leave the hive in a swarm with a new queen

swat *vt* (-tt-) strike or slap (an insect, etc) with the hand, a newspaper etc *n* sharp slap

sway *vt,vi* **1** swing, move or bend to and fro; lean to one side **2** persuade; influence *n* **1** act of swaying **2** rule; power **hold sway** rule (over) be in control; dominate

swear *vi* (swore, sworn) **1** use obscene or insulting language; utter curses or oaths **2** declare or promise solemnly; make a binding legal promise or oath **swear by** 1 take an oath on (a sacred object, etc.) 2 rely on absolutely **swearword** n socially unacceptable word; profane or obscene word

sweat n 1 moisture secreted from the pores of the skin; perspiration 2 inf hard work; trouble vi 1 exude sweat; perspire 2 inf work hard; labour

sweater n woollen garment covering chest, back and arms; jersey; jumper; pullover

swede n pale orange root vegetable related to the turnip

sweep vi vt (swept) 1 clean or clear with a broom brush etc 2 proceed or move rapidly (through) 3 extend; curve n 1 sweeping movement 2 person who cleans chimneys **sweeper** n

sweet adj 1 tasting sugary; not sour 2 kind likeable; charming; cute n 1 any type of small confection made principally from sugar 2 pudding; dessert **sweetly** adv **sweetness** n **sweeten** vt 1 make sweet(er) 2 make more acceptable **sweetheart** n person who loves and is loved in return; darling **sweet pea** n climbing garden plant with sweet-smelling flowers

swell vt, vi (swelled; swollen) expand; bulge out; increase in size, volume, etc n 1 act of swelling 2 waves; action of waves when not breaking 3 gradual increase in sound **swelling** n 1 act of swelling 2 something swollen, esp a bruised or infected area of the body **swollen-headed** adj conceited

swerve vi make a sudden or abrupt sideways turn n act of swerving

swift adj speedy; rapid; prompt n small widely distributed bird capable of fast sustained flight **swiftly** adv

swig inf vt, vi (-gg-) swallow; take gulps (from) n draught; gulp

swill vt, vi 1 drink large quantities (of) 2 wash or slop down n liquid food for animals, esp pigs

swim v (swam; swum) vi 1 move in or under water by movement of the body, limbs, tail, or fins, etc 2 float; drift; appear to swim 3 feel dizzy; swirl vt cross by swimming n act or period of swimming

swindle vt, vi obtain by fraud; cheat; exploit unfairly n instance of swindling **swindler** n

swine n, pl **swine** 1 pig 2 brutish or beastly person

swing vt vi (swung) 1 move; sway; rock back and forth 2 whirl about 3 veer; turn **swing round** turn suddenly in a sweeping movement ~n 1 swinging movement or action 2 seat suspended on ropes etc on which a person can swing himself

swipe n lunging blow vt vi 1 make a swipe (at) 2 inf seize, steal

swirl vi move round in a slow whirl; eddy or series of curves n 1 swirling action 2 eddy; whirl

swish n whistling sound as of a thin rod swung through the air; rustle; hiss vi, vt make a swishing sound (with)

switch vt, vi exchange; transfer; shift; make a change **switch on/off** turn on/off (an electric appliance, etc.) ~n 1 act of switching 2 device for turning an electrical appliance, etc on or off 3 thin flexible cane or whip **switchboard** n device fitted with many switches esp one used for relaying telephone calls

swivel vt, vi (-ll-) turn (round) on a pivot n device for joining two objects to allow one to move independently of the other

swollen v pp of **swell**.

swoop vt, vi plunge or sweep down (on), as of a bird of prey, esp to attack or carry off n act of swooping

swop vt, vi, n swap

sword n weapon with a long pointed blade set in a handle **swordfish** n edible marine fish with a long pointed jaw resembling a sword **swordsman** n person skilled in the use of a sword

swore v pt of **swear**.

sworn v pp of **swear**.

swot vt, vi (-tt-) inf study hard esp for an examination n person who swots

swum v pp of **swim**.

swung v pt and pp of **swing**.

sycamore n any of various kinds of deciduous tree having large indented leaves

syllable n word or part of a word uttered as a single unit of sound

syllabus n, pl **syllabuses** or **syllabi** ('sɪləbaɪ) outline of work to be studied; summary of a course

symbol n sign or object that represents something else, esp something abstract **symbolic** adj **symbolically** adv **symbolism** n the use of symbols to express abstract concepts, esp in the arts **symbolize** vt represent; stand for; act as a symbol of

symmetry n harmonious balance between parts; regularity or correspondence of a pattern within a whole **symmetrical** adj

sympathy n quality of feeling for people's suffering or understanding their attitude; compassion; understanding **sympathetic** adj 1 having sympathy 2 understanding; congenial **sympathetically** adv **sympathize** vi share a person's feelings, esp during suffering; have understanding; show sympathy **sympathizer** n one who approves of or sanctions a cause, political party, etc, without being a member or an active supporter

symphony n major orchestral composition in three or more movements

symptom n 1 physical or mental change indicative of or due to a malfunction 2 any sign indicative of a change, disorder, or condition **symptomatic** adj

synagogue n place of worship and instruction for members of the Jewish religion

synchronize vt, vi work, operate, or occur at the same time or in harmony **synchronization** n **synchronous** adj

syndicate n 1 association of people carrying out a business or joining in an enterprise 2 agency that sells articles, etc, to several newspapers for simultaneous publication vt publish through a syndicate

syndrome n combination of symptoms or signs indicating a certain condition or disorder

synopsis n, pl **synopses** (si'nɔpsi:z) brief summary, précis, or outline, esp of the plot of a novel, play, etc

synthesis n, pl **syntheses** ('sinθəsi:z) combination or fusing of parts into a whole; whole thus formed **synthetic** adj 1 artificial; false; man-made 2 produced by or relating to a synthesis **synthesize** vt

syphilis n serious contagious type of venereal disease **syphilitic** adj

syringe n device for sucking in liquid and/or forcing it out in a spray or jet, esp one used for injecting fluid into the body vt clean out or spray using a syringe

syrup n thick solution of sugar and water or juice; treacle **syrupy** adj

system n 1 group of coordinating parts forming a whole 2 carefully organized set of related

ideas or procedures **systematic** adj methodical; regular; following a system

T

tab n small flap or strip of cloth, paper, etc **keep tabs on** keep a check or watch on

tabby adj (of cats) brown or grey with dark stripes or blotches n tabby cat

table n 1 piece of furniture with a flat top and legs or supports, usually high enough to sit at 2 organized list, chart, index, etc **turn the tables on** place in an inferior or losing position ~vt put forward for future discussion **tablespoon** n large spoon used for serving food **table tennis** n game played with round bats and a small light ball on a table fitted with a low net

tablet n 1 pill 2 inscribed stone slab or plaque 3 cake (of soap)

taboo n also **tabu** act, object, or word that is forbidden in a particular society or religion adj forbidden

tack n 1 large-headed short nail for fastening things 2 direction taken by a sailing ship according to the angle of the wind 3 method of approach; course of action vt 1 fasten with tacks 2 sew together with loose temporary stitching; gather together loosely vi steer a course along a different tack

tackle n 1 gear or equipment, esp for fishing 2 set of ropes used in a pulley system 3 (in rugby football) act of seizing a player's legs so that he will give up the ball 4 attempt to get the ball from another player in football vt 1 attempt or attack (something difficult) 2 approach or deal with (a difficult or unwilling person, situation, etc) 3 perform a tackle on in football

tact n sensitivity to other people's feelings or to situations that require delicate and discreet handling **tactful** adj **tactfully** adv

tactic n manoeuvre, act directed towards a goal **tactics** pl n strategy, plan of action **tactical** adj **tactically** adv

tadpole n completely aquatic stage in a frog's or toad's life during which the legs develop and the tail and gills disappear

taffeta n strong stiff satin-like cloth

tag n small label or identity disc vt (-gg-) label;

identify **tag along** accompany; go along (with)

tail n 1 end part of an animal's body that is an elongation of the backbone 2 back or end part, section, or projection **turn tail** flee; run away ~vt, vi 1 follow and observe (a person's actions), esp without being noticed 2 take the tail from **tail off** gradually diminish or deteriorate **tails** s n side of a coin not bearing the sovereign's head

tailor n 1 person employed to make garments which require careful fitting, esp those for men 2 person selling men's clothes vt, vi 1 make and fit (suits, etc) 2 adapt; alter to suit individual needs

taint n trace of some defect, infection, corrupting influence etc vt infect; stain; poison; spoil

take vt (took, taken) 1 receive or accept (something offered) 2 bring into one's possession; help oneself to; remove 3 accompany to a particular destination 4 capture; seize 5 grasp; grip; hold 6 eat, drink or swallow (medicine, tablets, etc) 7 steal 8 select; use 9 transmit; transport; convey 10 keep a record of 11 last; be the time required for 12 require; be necessary for 13 have accommodation for 14 regard; consider 15 subtract; deduct 16 study **take in** deceive; swindle **take off** 1 remove 2 become airborne 3 impersonate; mimic **take on** accept as a duty or commitment **take out** 1 extract; delete 2 escort 3 acquire (a licence, insurance, etc) **take over** assume control **take to** find pleasure in; develop a liking or skill for **take up** pursue; adopt; become involved in **take-off** n 1 act of jumping or lifting off the ground 2 satirical imitation **take-over** n act of taking over and assuming control, esp of a business, government etc **takings** pl n money obtained in the course of business during a particular period

talcum powder n very fine scented body powder

tale n story; narrative; legend **tell tales** 1 report another's misdoings 2 tell lies

talent n ability; skill; special gift or aptitude

talk vi, vt 1 communicate by means of speech 2 discuss; express by speaking 3 chatter; gossip n 1 manner of speaking 2 speech or brief lecture 3 gossip **talkative** adj tending to talk a lot; chatty

tall adj large in height; not small **tall order** difficult commission **tall story** or **tale** n unlikely or exaggerated account or story

tally vi correspond, agree vt add up; reckon n 1 reckoning; score; bill 2 notched stick for recording numbers

talon n claw, esp of a bird of prey

tambourine n small shallow drum with metal discs which clink when shaken

tame adj 1 (of animals) not wild, not aggressive towards or frightened of humans 2 unexciting; unadventurous vt make tame

tamper vi interfere; meddle

tan n adj light brown n skin browned by the sun vt, vi (-nn-) 1 make or go brown 2 turn (hides) into leather

tang n sharp taste

tangent n straight line that touches but does not intersect a curve **go off at a tangent** digress, change the subject or line of thought **tangential** adj 1 relating to tangents 2 connected but irrelevant

tangerine n type of small sweet orange

tangible adj 1 able to be touched 2 visible; factual; real

tangle n muddle; confused web of knots; intricate mass vt, vi make into a tangle; muddle

tango n Latin-American ballroom dance

tank n 1 large container for keeping or storing liquids 2 large armour-plated military vehicle

tankard n large mug with a handle, used esp for beer

tanker n ship or lorry built for carrying liquids in bulk

tantalize vt tease by offering or presenting something desirable that cannot be attained

tantrum n hysterical fit of bad temper

tap[1] vt vi (-pp-) strike a quick gentle blow (on) n tapping action or sound **tap dancing** n style of dancing involving complicated heel and toe tapping steps

tap[2] n device with a screw and washer for controlling the flow of liquid from a pipe or container **on tap** constantly available ~vt (-pp-) 1 sap; drain off; extract 2 fit a bugging device to (a telephone etc) so as to intercept or overhear calls

tape n 1 strip of flexible resistant material for binding, mending etc 2 length of tape stretched across the finishing line of a race track or cut symbolically to open a fête, etc 3 strip of plastic magnetized recording tape vt 1 bind or stick together with tape **2** record on tape **tape-measure** n length of tape marked off with measurements; flexible rule **tape-recorder** n device for recording sound on magnetic tape

taper vt,vi make or become gradually thinner at one end; tail off n very thin candle

tapestry n heavy fabric having a picture or design woven by hand in coloured threads

tar n thick black sticky coal-based substance used in road building, wood preserving, etc ; vt,vi (-rr-) cover with tar

target n **1** object or person to be aimed at or attacked **2** goal or objective

tariff n **1** tax or list of taxes levied on imported goods **2** fixed schedule of charges or prices

tarnish vt,vi spoil the shine or lustre (of) n loss of shine or lustre

tart[1] adj **1** sharp to the taste; acid **2** sarcastic

tart[2] n **1** small pie or flan with a sweet filling **2** sl prostitute

tartan n woollen plaid fabric in different patterns and colours corresponding to those of various Highland Scottish clans

task n particular job or piece of work; chore **take to task** reprove; censure

tassel n ornamental knot with a bunch of loose threads

taste vt,vi **1** sense the flavour (of) with one's tongue **2** try; have a short experience of **3** have the flavour (of) n **1** flavour **2** sense by which one perceives flavour **3** ability to make aesthetic judgment; discernment **4** fineness or elegance of style, manners, etc **5** particular preference **6** small amount; trace; hint **tasteful** adj elegant; fitting **tasteless** adj **1** not strongly flavoured; insipid **2** not tasteful; tactless **tasty** adj good to eat

tattoo[1] vt permanently mark (the skin) by putting indelible stains into pricked designs n design made by tattooing

tattoo[2] n **1** military entertainment involving marching and music, usually at night **2** signal sounded on a drum or bugle recalling soldiers to their quarters for the night **3** continuous drumming

taught v pt and pp of **teach.**

taunt vt jeer at; provoke; tease n jeer; insulting remark

Taurus n second sign of the zodiac, represented by the Bull

taut adj tightly stretched; having no slack; tense **tautness** n

tavern n public house; inn

tax n **1** money demanded by law to be paid according to income, assets, goods purchased or imported, etc **2** difficult or onerous obligation, demand, etc ; burden vt **1** impose a tax on **2** put a burden on; strain **taxation** n system of imposing taxes or the amount of tax payable

taxi n car with a driver for public hire vi (of aircraft) move along the ground on landing or before take-off vt cause (an aircraft) to taxi

tea n **1** evergreen shrub grown in East Asia for its pungent leaves **2** drink made from infusing dried tea leaves in boiling water **3** meal between lunch and supper at which tea is drunk **tea-cloth** n also **tea-towel** cloth for drying dishes

teach vt,vi (taught) instruct; give lessons (in); show (a person) how to do something **teacher** n **teaching** n **1** ability to teach; knowledge or practice of teaching **2** set of doctrines

teak n large tree found in SE Asia with hard orange-brown wood, used for furniture, etc

team n **1** group of people working together, esp in order to compete against others **2** group of horses, dogs, etc ; pulling together v **team up with** join with in order to pool resources and work in harmony

tear[1] (tiə) n also **teardrop** drop of salty liquid that falls from the eye **tearful** adj **1** liable to cry **2** sad **tear-gas** n type of gas that makes the eyes water, used to disperse rioting crowds, etc

tear[2] (teə) v (tore; torn) vt,vi divide; split; rip vi hurry; rush **tear down** pull down; destroy **tear off 1** pull or pluck off, esp violently **2** inf do in a great hurry **tear up 1** divide into small pieces, strips, etc **2** pull up; destroy ~n torn hole; slit

tease vt,vi **1** torment by joking; mock; make fun of **2** draw out; comb out; disentangle n person given to teasing others

teat n **1** nipple **2** feeding nipple on a baby's bottle

technical adj **1** relating to a technique, method, or skill **2** relating to specialized industrial or mechanical skills and crafts or to technology **technically** adv

technician n person skilled in the technical

processes of a particular craft, science, or industry

technique n 1 method of performing some skill; system of practical procedures 2 practical skill

technology n 1 application of scientific ideas to industry or commerce 2 methods and equipment so used **technological** adj **technologist** n

tedious adj 1 boring; monotonous 2 tiresome **tediously** adv **tedium** n

tee n 1 small peg that supports a golf ball for the first stroke at each hole 2 elevated area from which this stroke is played v **tee off** 1 drive the ball from the tee 2 start

teenager n person aged between 13 and 19; adolescent

teeth n pl of **tooth**. **get one's teeth into** begin to cope with or tackle seriously **teethe** vi (esp of babies) produce teeth

teetotal adj refusing to drink or serve alcoholic drinks **teetotaller** n teetotal person

telegram n message transmitted by telegraph

telegraph n method of or apparatus for transmitting messages using radio signals or electric impulses sent along wires vt,vi send a telegram to **telegraphy** n

telepathy n human communication through scientifically inexplicable channels; mind-reading **telepathic** adj

telephone n system or apparatus for verbal communication over a distance, usually using electric impulses sent back and forth along a wire vt,vi call or talk to by telephone; phone **telephonist** n operator of a telephone switchboard

telescope n 1 optical instrument using lenses or mirrors to magnify distant objects 2 instrument, esp one using radio or light waves, to study astronomical bodies vt,vi make or become shorter, compressed, or crushed **telescopic** adj

television n 1 process of or apparatus for using high-frequency radio waves to transmit and receive visual images with accompanying sound 2 radio broadcasts received on a television **televise** vt,vi record or broadcast by means of television

telex n telegraph service or apparatus for transmitting printed messages

tell v (told) vt,vi inform; let know vt 1 relate; recount; express in words; describe 2 order;

instruct 3 disclose; reveal; confess vi reveal secrets; inform against someone **can tell** be able to discover, understand, distinguish, etc **tell off** scold **telltale** adj betraying; serving to reveal something hidden n person given to informing on others

temper n 1 state of mind; mood 2 angry fit; rage; tendency to become angry vt 1 modify; moderate; alleviate 2 strengthen (metal) by sudden changes of temperature

temperament n nature; disposition; person's style of thinking and behaviour **temperamental** adj 1 given to violent changes of mood; excitable 2 unreliable

temperate adj 1 mild in temperature 2 moderate; restrained; even-tempered

temperature n 1 measured or approximate degree of hotness of something 2 fever

tempestuous adj stormy; violent

temple[1] n 1 place of worship dedicated to a particular deity 2 sacred place

temple[2] n flat area on either side of the forehead

tempo n speed at which a conductor or performer chooses to play a piece of music

temporal adj existing in or limited by time; not spiritual; earthly **temporally** adv

temporary adj intended to be used for a short time; not permanent; passing **temp** n inf person not employed on a permanent basis **temporarily** adv

tempt vt persuade or induce (a person) to try or do something undesirable; attract; seduce; influence **temptation** n

ten n 1 number equal to one plus nine 2 group of ten persons, things, etc 3 also **ten o'clock** ten hours after noon or midnight adj amounting to ten

tenacious adj holding or sticking firmly; stubbornly persisting **tenaciously** adv **tenacity** n

tenant n person who occupies a house, flat, farm, etc, for payment of rent **tenancy** n state of being a tenant or the period during which this occurs

tend[1] vt look after; care for

tend[2] vi be inclined or likely (to); have the effect of **tendency** n

tender[1] adj 1 soft; delicate; not hardy 2 gentle; loving; compassionate 3 painful when touched; sensitive 4 easily chewed 5 youthfully innocent; vulnerable **tenderly** adv ten-

demess n **tender-hearted** adj easily moved to pity **tenderize** vt,vi make (food) soft and easy to chew

tender[2] vt vi offer for acceptance or settlement n offer of goods or services at a fixed rate

tendon n band or sheet of fibrous tissue by which muscle is attached to bone

tendril n threadlike shoot of a plant enabling it to cling to a support while climbing

tenement n 1 rented room or flat in a block, esp one in a poor quarter of a city 2 property held by a tenant

tennis n game for two or four players played by hitting a ball over a net with rackets

tenor n 1 general meaning, tone, direction 2 instrument or male voice with a range between that of baritone and alto

tense[1] adj 1 anxious; in suspense; overwrought 2 taut; strained; stretched vt make tense **tensely** adv **tenseness** n **tensile** adj able to be stretched **tension** n 1 stretching or state of being stretched or strained 2 excitement; suspense 3 anxiety or unease caused by suppressed emotion

tense[2] n form of a verb indicating the time of action

tent n canvas portable shelter for camping, etc

tentacle n slender flexible organ of various invertebrates, used for feeding, grasping, etc

tentative adj 1 hesitating; cautious 2 provisional

tenth adj coming between ninth and eleventh n 1 tenth person, object, etc 2 one of ten equal parts; one divided by ten adv after the ninth

tenuous adj 1 thin; slender; flimsy 2 subtle; weak

tenure n holding of land or office

tepid adj 1 slightly warm; lukewarm 2 unenthusiastic

term n 1 period of time for which something occurs or is in force, as a period of teaching in a college, school, etc 2 word used in specialized field 3 end of pregnancy **terms** pl n 1 conditions of an agreement, bargain, etc 2 relationships between people **come to terms** form an agreement; reconcile **in terms of** as expressed by ~vt define (something) as; call

terminology n set of terms specific to any particular field of study **terminological** adj

terminate vt,vi bring or come to an end **termination** n **terminal** adj of, at, or mark-

ing an end or limit; final n 1 end of a transport route 2 either end of an open electrical circuit **terminally** adv

terminus n, pl **termini** (ˈtɜːmɪnaɪ) or **terminuses** 1 boundary points; final point reached 2 end of a railway, airline, or bus route

terrace n 1 raised bank or walk in a garden 2 flat area cut into a slope, often for crop cultivation 3 balcony; flat rooftop 4 row of similar adjoined houses

terrestrial adj 1 of or on earth; earthly 2 living or growing on land rather than in the sea or air

terrible adj 1 causing terror; appalling; very bad 2 inf excessive, outstanding **terribly** adv

terrier n small dog of various breeds originally used in hunting out animals underground

terrific adj 1 frighteningly large; instilling terror 2 inf amazingly good, enjoyable **terrifically** adv

terrify vt cause terror in, frighten

territory n area regarded as owned by the state or a social group or individual or animal **territorial** adj **territorially** adv

terror n 1 extreme fear 2 anything causing fear or dread 3 inf nuisance; troublesome person **terrorist** n person employing organized violence and intimidation to obtain political objectives **terrorism** n **terrorize** vt manipulate by inspiring terror

terse adj concise, curt

Terylene n Tdmk type of synthetic fibre used as textile yarn

test n any critical trial or examination to determine the merit or nature of something vt conduct a test on; examine **test case** n legal case that establishes a precedent **test match** n international cricket match **test-tube** n glass tube used in conducting chemical experiments

testament n 1 one of the two major divisions of the Bible (the Old Testament and the New Testament) 2 act of testifying, as to religious faith 3 (in law) will

testicle n one of two glands in males producing sperm and male sex hormones

testify vi, vt bear witness; affirm; give evidence

testimony n evidence; proof; declaration **testimonial** n 1 written testimony of character

2 gift presented as a tribute or token of respect

tether n rope or chain by which an animal is secured **at the end of one's tether** at the end of one s patience or ability to withstand ~vt fasten with a tether; tie

text n **1** main section of written or printed words of a book as distinguished from illustrations, the index, etc **2** passage from the Bible **textual** adj **textbook** n book used as a standard source for a particular course of study

textile n woven fabric or cloth

texture n **1** surface, arrangement of strands, etc of a material, esp as perceived by the sense of touch **2** quality, esp of music

than conj **1** expressing the second stage of a comparison **2** expressing an alternative after rather, sooner, etc

thank vt **1** express gratitude to **2** blame **thankful** adj **thankless** adj **thanks** pl n interj expression of gratitude relief etc

that adj relating to the person or thing specified, esp one further away than or different from another pron **1** the particular person or thing so specified **2** who(m) or which adv so, to such an extent conj introducing a noun clause **that's that** there is no more to be said or done

thatch n arrangement of straw reeds etc used as a roof covering vt vi cover with a thatch

thaw vt, vi **1** melt after being frozen **2** make or become less hostile frigid etc n period or process during which snow or ice melts

the def art preceding a noun adv used for emphasis or to express a comparative amount or extent

theatre n **1** building in which plays operas etc are performed **2** lecture hall **3** also **operating theatre** room equipped for carrying out surgery **4** drama **5** business of working in or for a theatre **theatrical** adj

theft n crime of stealing another s property

their adj belonging to them **theirs** pron those things belonging to them

them pron those people or things **themselves** r pron **1** their own selves **2** their normal selves

theme n **1** main idea or concept with which a work of art discussion, etc is concerned; topic **2** recurring melody

then adv **1** at the particular time referred to **2** immediately afterwards; next **3** in that case adj functioning at that time n that time

theology n study of religion and the nature of God **theological** adj **theologian** n—

theorem n statement that is to be proved by logical reasoning

theory n **1** system or formula as an explanation of a particular phenomenon **2** body of abstract ideas or principles esp as distinguished from practice **theoretical** adj **theoretically** adv **theorize** vi speculate; formulate a theory

therapy n course of treatment designed to cure various disorders of the body or mind **therapeutic** adj **therapist** n

there adv **1** in to at, or towards that place **2** at that point pron used with forms of be can etc to introduce a sentence or clause n that position interj expression of consolation victory pride etc **thereabouts** adv also **thereabout** in that approximate place or position **thereafter** adv after that time, from then on **thereby** adv thus, by those means **therefore** adv so, consequently for that reason **thereupon** adv at which point, after which

thermal adj of or relating to heat n rising current of warm air

thermodynamics n study of the relationships between work heat and other forms of energy

thermometer n any instrument used to measure temperature

thermonuclear adj involving fusion of two atomic nuclei with consequent production of large amounts of heat **thermonuclear bomb** n hydrogen bomb

Thermos flask n also **Thermos** Tdmk container with double walls enclosing a vacuum to prevent heat transfer used for keeping food or drink hot or cold

thermostat n automatic device to maintain a room enclosure etc at a constant temperature **thermostatic** adj **thermostatically** adv

these adj form of **this** used with a plural noun

thesis n pl **theses** ('θiːsiːz) **1** original work submitted by a candidate for an academic degree **2** hypothesis proposition

they pron **1** two or more persons or things when used as the subject in a sentence or clause **2** people in general

thick adj 1 relatively deep wide or fat not thin 2 measured by width or diameter 3 densely layered, arranged, etc 4 not watery or runny 5 inf stupid 6 having a broad accent **a bit thick** unfair; unreasonable **through thick and thin** throughout both good and bad periods adv also **thickly** so as to be thick **thickness** n **thicken** vt vi make or become thick(er) **thick-skinned** adj 1 insensitive, esp to criticism 2 having a thick hide or outer layer

thief n, pl **thieves** person committing theft **thieve** vt, vi commit theft; steal

thigh n that part of the leg above the knee

thimble n small cap worn over the fingertip whilst sewing

thin adj 1 relatively narrow, not thick 2 slim, slender, not fat 3 not densely layered arranged, etc ; sparse 4 watery or runny 5 lacking depth of quality; not rich adv also **thinly** so as to be thin vt vi (-nn-) 1 make or become thin(ner) 2 dilute **thinness** n **thin-skinned** adj sensitive, esp to criticism

thing n 1 inanimate object; entity 2 course or action; act; deed 3 person or animal, esp when referred to with affection, sympathy etc **have a thing about** be preoccupied with **the thing** fashionable trend **things** pl n 1 possessions 2 points; matters, ideas 3 conditions or circumstances

think v (thought) vi use one s mind or power of reason vt vi 1 believe; consider 2 be aware (of); regard **think about** 1 reflect or ponder on 2 also **think of** have an opinion of **think of** 1 bring to mind; imagine or remember 2 plan; anticipate; consider —n inf concentrated effort to examine or analyse an idea, suggestion etc

third adj coming between second and fourth in sequence n 1 third person object etc 2 one of three equal parts one divided by three 3 gear above second on a motor vehicle adv 1 after the second 2 also **thirdly** as a third point **third party** n person only marginally involved in a case or affair **third person** n category of pronouns or verbs other than the person speaking or addressed **third rate** adj also **third-class** of a very poor standard; mediocre

thirst n 1 desire for water or other liquids 2 craving; yearning vi have a thirst (for) **thirsty** adj

thirteen n 1 number that is three more than ten 2 thirteen things or people adj amounting to thirteen **thirteenth** adj, adv, n

thirty n 1 number equal to three times ten 2 thirty things or people adj amounting to thirty **thirtieth** adj adv, n

this adj relating to the person or thing specified, esp one closer than or different from another pron the particular person or thing so specified adv to a specified extent

thistle n plant with a purple flower and prickly leaves

thong n thin strip of leather used in a whip, as a fastening, etc

thorax n, pl **thoraxes** or **thoraces** (ˈθɔːrəsiːz) 1 part of the body containing the heart lungs etc ; chest 2 part of an insect bearing the wings and legs

thorn n 1 sharp woody point occurring on a stem or leaf 2 bush esp the hawthorn, having thorns **thorny** adj 1 having thorns 2 difficult to solve

thorough adj 1 completed carefully and painstakingly, meticulous 2 utter, absolute **thoroughly** adv **thoroughness** n **thoroughbred** n animal of a pure breed; pedigree adj relating to such an animal **thoroughfare** n 1 road or street 2 access passage

those adj form of **that** used with a plural noun

though conj in spite of the fact that although **as though** as if —adv nevertheless; on the other hand

thought v pt of **think**, n 1 idea notion concept, etc produced by thinking 2 act or process of thinking 3 attention consideration 4 body of ideas relating to a particular period movement etc **thoughtful** adj 1 considerate 2 engaged in thought **thoughtfully** adv **thoughtfulness** n **thoughtless** adj tactless careless inconsiderate **thoughtlessly** adv **thoughtlessness** n

thousand n 1 number equal to ten times one hundred 2 thousand people or things **thousands** pl n huge number adj amounting to a thousand **thousandth** adj, adv, n

thrash vt 1 flog whip beat 2 defeat overwhelmingly vi make a violent movement with the arms or legs esp in water **thrash out** settle by debate or intense discussion —n beating; violent blow

thread n 1 strand of cotton, yarn, wool etc 2 spiral groove of a screw, bolt, etc 3 central

idea running through a story, argument, etc
vt **1** pass (a thread) through (a needle) **2** make (a way) through (obstacles, etc)

threadbare *adj* **1** worn; having no pile or nap **2** shabby; poor

threat *n* **1** statement or indication of future harm, injury, etc **2** person or thing likely to cause harm, injury, etc ; danger **threaten** *vt,vi* make threats (to); be a threat (to); menace

three *n* **1** number equal to one plus two **2** group of three persons, things, etc **3** *also* **three o'clock** three hours after noon or midnight *adj* amounting to three **three-dimensional** *adj also* **3-D** having three dimensions; solid or apparently solid **threesome** *n* group of three; trio

thresh *vt,vi* beat or shake (corn) so as to separate the grain from the husks **thresher** *n* person or machine that threshes

threshold *n* **1** slab or board placed at a doorway or entrance **2** starting point or verge **3** point at which a stimulus produces an observable effect

threw *v pt of* **throw.**

thrift *n* economic or careful use of resources **thrifty** *adj*

thrill *n* **1** tingle of excitement; flush of enthusiasm; intense emotion or sensation **2** event causing this *vt,vi* cause or experience a thrill **thriller** *n* book, film, etc , arousing strong excitement and suspense

thrive *vi* **1** grow healthily and well **2** prosper

throat *n* **1** front of the neck **2** passage connecting the mouth and stomach **3** narrow part, passage, or opening **cut one's throat** pursue a disastrous course **jump down someone's throat** attack verbally with sudden vehemence **ram down someone's throat** assert or force upon without allowing response **throaty** *adj* hoarse, as if with a sore throat

throb *vi* (-bb) beat strongly and rhythmically *n* strong pulsating beat

throne *n* **1** monarch s, pope s, or bishop s seat **2** sovereign power

throng *n* crowd; mass of people *vi vt* form or fill with a throng

throttle *n* valve that regulates an engine s fuel supply *vt* **1** choke; strangle **2** regulate or restrict (power supply)

through *prep* **1** along the length of; from one
end to the other of **2** in one side and out of the other side of **3** during; from the beginning to the end of **4** via **5** with the influence of; by the means or agency of **6** because of *adv* **1** from one side or end to another **2** from start to finish **3** throughout; completely **4** no longer functioning or successful **throughout** *prep* right through; during the whole of *adv* in every part

throw *v* (threw; thrown) *vt,vi* **1** send (a missile) through the air **2** toss; fling *vt* **1** baffle; perplex; confuse; take aback **2** place in a particular situation **throw away** discard as useless; reject; get rid of **throw out 1** eject; remove by force **2** expel; dismiss **throw up 1** vomit **2** produce unexpectedly **3** leave or reject (a job) ~*n* **1** act of throwing **2** toss, pitch

thrush *n* songbird with brown plumage and speckled underparts

thrust *vt,vi* **1** push with force **2** stab; pierce **3** force (a situation) upon (someone) *n* **1** violent lunge or push **2** force of the propulsion of an engine **3** *inf* ruthless drive to succeed

thud *n* dull heavy sound of impact *vi* (-dd-) make such a sound

thumb *n* **1** short thick digit of the human hand **2** corresponding digit in other mammals **rule of thumb** practical method based on experience **under the thumb of** (someone s) control ~*vt* **1** mark or touch with the thumb **2** use the thumb as a signal esp as a hitch-hiker

thump *n* **1** dull heavy blow **2** sound made by such a blow *vt,vi* strike; pound; beat

thunder *n* loud rumbling noise caused by movement of air after lightning *vi,vt* **1** make a sound like thunder; roar **2** speak loudly and angrily **thunderous** *adj* **thunderstorm** *n* thunder and lightning accompanied by heavy rain

Thursday *n* fifth day of the week

thus *adv* **1** in the meantime **2** to this extent or degree **3** therefore

thwart *vt* prevent; frustrate

thyme (taim) *n* fragrant herb with a minty odour

thyroid *n also* **thyroid gland** gland whose hormones regulate metabolism and growth

tiara *n* jewelled head ornament worn by women

tick[1] *n* **1** light tapping or clicking noise of a watch, clock, etc **2** mark or symbol used to indicate approval or acknowledgement of having been noted *vi* make a ticking sound *vt* mark with a tick **tick off** rebuke; scold **tick over** (of an engine) idle

tick[2] *n* any of a number of parasites of warm-blooded animals

ticket *n* **1** card or slip indicating right to entry, service, etc **2** price label **3** slip issued for any of certain motoring offences

tickle *vt* **1** touch lightly so as to cause laughter, pleasure, etc **2** amuse; please *vi* tingle; be the location of an itching sensation *n* itching sensation **ticklish** *adj* **1** susceptible or sensitive to tickling **2** precarious; difficult to handle

tide *n* **1** twice daily movement of the sea caused by the gravitational pull of the moon **2** turning point in time *v* **tide over** enable to cope until help or relief comes **tidal** *adj*

tidy *adj* neat; orderly *vt,vi* make tidy **tidily** *adv* **tidiness** *n*

tie *v* (tying) *vt* **1** fasten with a knot, bow, etc **2** bind or secure with string, rope, etc **3** restrict the freedom or mobility of *vi* **1** fasten **2** obtain an equal score or number of marks as someone else; draw *n* **1** fastening such as string or rope **2** obligation; restriction of freedom, etc; commitment **3** draw; equal score **4** shaped piece of material worn with a shirt, fastened in a large knot at the throat

tier *n* **1** row (of seats, etc) above and slightly behind another or others **2** level; layer

tiger *n* Asiatic feline mammal with a yellow and black striped coat

tight *adj* **1** taut; not loose **2** fitting snugly; constricting **3** compact **4** strict; hard **5** *inf also* **tight-fisted** stingy; mean; miserly **6** *inf* drunk **tightly** *adv* **tightness** *n* **tighten** *vt,vi* make or become tight(er) **tightrope** *n* taut rope or wire on which an acrobat performs **tights** *pl n* close fitting sheer garment covering the lower part of the body, legs, and feet

tile *n* thin flat slab used for covering roofs, floors, etc *vt* cover with tiles

till[1] *prep* until

till[2] *n* box or receptacle into which money is put behind the sales counter in a shop, etc

till[3] *vt* cultivate or work (land) **tillable** *adj*

tiller *n* lever attached to a rudder

tilt *vi,vt* incline; slant; lean *n* slope; inclination

timber *n* wood cut into planks for use in building *vt* provide with timber

time *n* **1** system that relates successive events, occurrences, or changes in terms of the past, present, or future **2** measurement by means of a clock **3** period; age **4** period for which something lasts; duration **5** tempo **6** instance; moment **7** experience of an event, emotion, etc **8** leisure; freedom from other tasks or duties **9** period allotted or taken to complete something **10** occasion **from time to time** occasionally **in time** not late or overdue **on time** at precisely the time fixed; punctual ~*vt* **1** keep a record of (the amount of time needed or taken) **2** fix the time of **time bomb** *n* bomb detonated by a timing device **timekeeper** *n* person or mechanism that records time **timely** *adj* happening at a fortunate or suitable time **times** *prep* multiplied by *pl n* period; era **timetable** *n* schedule of times of events, arrivals, departures, etc

timid *adj* easily frightened; shy **timidity** *n* **timidly** *adv*

timpani *pl n* kettledrums

tin *n* **1** soft silvery metal **2** container for food, etc, made of iron and plated with tin *vt* (-nn-) **1** cover with tin **2** preserve (food) in airtight containers

tinge *vt* colour faintly *n* **1** faint colour or tint **2** small trace; hint

tingle *vi* experience a prickling or mildly vibrating sensation *n* prickling feeling; mild vibration

tinker *n* itinerant craftsman who mends or sells pots and pans *vi* **1** work as a tinker **2** work in a haphazard fashion **3** meddle; interfere (with)

tinkle *n* light metallic bell-like sound *vi,vt* make or produce such a sound

tinsel *n* ornamental string of glittering metal threads used as a festive decoration

tint *n* **1** shade of a colour produced by mixture with white **2** dye; pigment *vt* give a tint to; colour; dye

tiny *adj* very small; minute

tip[1] *n* end; extremity, esp of anything tapering to a point **tiptoe** *vi* walk very quietly *n* **on tiptoe** standing or walking on the balls of the feet; straining to reach up

tip[2] *v* (-pp-) *vt,vi* lean or tilt to one side *vt* **1** pour out or dump by tipping the container **2**

touch or raise (one's hat) **tip over** topple; overturn ~**n** place where rubbish is dumped

tip³ *n* 1 extra payment in appreciation of services rendered 2 useful hint or advice *vt,vi* (-pp-) give a tip (to) **tip off** give a tip-off to **tip-off** *n* advance warning or confirmation of advantage to the recipient

tipsy *adj* inebriated; tight; slightly drunk

tired *adj* 1 weary; suffering from fatigue; sleepy 2 bored; fed up; no longer interested **tire** *vt,vi* make or become tired **tireless** *adj* unwearying **tiresome** *adj* wearying; trying; irritating

tissue *n* 1 finely woven thin paper 2 substance consisting of cells forming the structure of plants and animals

tithe *n* (formerly) tenth part of agricultural produce, levied as a tax

title *n* 1 name by which a person or thing may be distinguished 2 heading by which a novel, play, etc, is known 3 position or mode of address, esp of a member of the nobility 4 legal right to possess something

to *prep* 1 in the direction of 2 as far as 3 into the state of 4 giving the result of 5 near or in contact with 6 in comparison with 7 with the extent of 8 conforming with 9 for use with or on 10 in the opinion of 11 until 12 into the possession of 13 used before the infinitive form of a verb *adv* 1 fixed; closed 2 into consciousness **to and fro** alternately backwards and forwards **to-do** *n* fuss; bother; commotion

toad *n* 1 small tailless greenish-brown amphibian with a dry warty skin 2 unpleasant person **toadstool** *n* umbrella-shaped fungus living on dead organic matter

toast¹ *n* slice of bread browned by heat on each side *vt,vi* crisp; brown under heat

toast² *vt* drink to the health of (a person, etc) *n* drink in honour of a person, country, etc, or words proposing such a drink

tobacco *n* 1 tall annual plant with large broad leaves 2 cured leaves of this plant used in cigarettes, cigars, etc **tobacconist** *n* person or shop selling tobacco

toboggan *n* small sledge used on snow slopes for winter sport *vi* ride on a toboggan

today *n* this present day *adv* 1 now; on this very day 2 nowadays; at the present time

toddle *vi* walk with an unsteady uneven gait, as a child learning to walk **toddle along** *inf* go

at an easy unhurried pace **toddler** *n* child between the ages of one and three approximately, who is beginning to walk

toe *n* 1 digit of the foot 2 part of a shoe, stocking, etc, covering this *v* **toe the line** obey; do as one is told **toenail** *n* nail covering the toe

toffee *n* sweet made of boiled sugar **toffee-apple** *n* apple coated in toffee **toffee-nosed** *adj sl* snobbish; conceited

together *adv* 1 in close proximity 2 in the company of one or more other persons 3 simultaneously; at the same time

toil *vi* 1 work hard and long 2 proceed slowly and with difficulty *n* labour; hard work

toilet *n* 1 process of washing, combing one's hair, etc 2 lavatory; W C **toilet water** *n* dilute solution of perfume

token *n* 1 something used to represent or serve as a substitute 2 symbol; gesture 3 small gift; memento 4 metal or plastic voucher used in place of money *adj* 1 serving as a token 2 in name only; having little practical effect

told *v pp* and *pt* of **tell.**

tolerate *vt* allow; permit; endure **tolerable** *adj* bearable **tolerably** *adv* moderately; to a certain extent **tolerance** *n* 1 also **toleration** forbearance; fair-mindedness; freedom from bigotry 2 degree to which something can withstand specified conditions, etc

toll¹ *n* 1 payment exacted for use of a bridge, road, etc, in certain circumstances 2 price paid; number or amount sacrificed

toll² *vt,vi* ring or cause to ring with slow heavy strokes

tomato *n, pl* **tomatoes** juicy red fruit usually served as a vegetable with seasoning

tomb *n* place where the dead are buried or laid out in a hollow chamber

tomorrow *n* 1 the day after today 2 the future *adv* on the day after today

ton *n* measure of weight equivalent to 2240 pounds (approx 1016 kilograms)

tone *n* 1 quality of a musical note 2 pure musical note 3 manner of speaking, writing, etc, indicating attitude or emotion 4 general physical or moral condition 5 shade of colour; tint *v* **tone down** reduce; soften; calm **tonal** *adj* **tonality** *n* system of musical keys, esp in traditional Western music

tongs *pl n* instrument consisting of two hinged arms for grasping objects

tongue n 1 flexible organ in the mouth used in eating and in forming speech 2 language; method or tone of speaking 3 anything shaped like a tongue **tongue in cheek** insincerely or ironically **tongue-tied** adj 1 suffering from a speech defect 2 speechless; inarticulate **tongue-twister** n phrase or sentence that is difficult to pronounce because of unusual sound combinations

tonic n 1 medicine used to stimulate and invigorate 2 anything with this effect 3 key on which a musical work is primarily based

tonight n the night of the present day adv on this night or evening

tonsils pl n pair of oval-shaped organs situated on each side of the back of the throat **tonsillitis** n enlargement or inflammation of the tonsils due to infection

too adv 1 also; in addition; as well 2 to an excessive extent

took v pt of **take.**

tool n 1 instrument used in making or doing something; implement 2 person used to serve another's purpose 3 useful device; means vt, vi use a tool (on)

tooth n, pl **teeth** 1 hard projection in the jaws of humans and most vertebrates, used for biting, chewing, etc 2 any similar projection, as on a comb **toothbrush** n brush used for cleaning the teeth

top[1] n 1 highest point; peak 2 upper part 3 highest position 4 cap or cover of a bottle, jar, box, etc **blow one's top** lose one's temper ~adj best; highest vt (-pp-) 1 take the top off 2 cover or form the top of 3 surpass **top up** add extra liquid to so as to fill **top hat** n tall cylindrical hat worn by men on formal occasions **top-heavy** adj 1 disproportionately heavier or thicker above than below and thus unstable 2 with too much emphasis on certain parts **topmost** adj highest **topsoil** n uppermost and most fertile layer of the earth's crust

top[2] n small shaped object made to balance by spinning on a point, used esp as a toy

topic n subject; theme **topical** adj of current interest

topography n detailed geographical description or representation of the features of an area

topple vi, vt fall or cause to fall over; overturn vt overthrow; depose

topsy-turvy adj, adv 1 upside down 2 confused; muddled

torch n 1 burning material held on a stick 2 device carried by hand for giving light, usually operated by a battery

tore v pt of **tear** .

torment n ('tɔ:ment) severe mental or physical distress; anguish vt (tɔ:'ment) 1 torture; distress 2 pester; harass

torn v pp of **tear** .

tornado n, pl **tornadoes** or **tornados** violent storm of short duration with a characteristic rotating movement and funnel-shaped cloud

torpedo n, pl **torpedoes** self-propelled missile carried by a submarine for use against ships vt hit with or as if with a torpedo

torrent n 1 rapidly flowing stream of large quantities of water 2 any copious rapid flow, as of words, abuse, etc **torrential** adj

torso n trunk of the human body

tortoise n slow-moving reptile with a bony shell and scaly head and legs

tortuous adj 1 twisting; winding; snakelike 2 devious; unnecessarily complicated

torture n 1 severe pain inflicted as a punishment or method of persuasion 2 any extreme physical or mental distress vt 1 inflict torture on 2 cause extreme agony, pain, or distress in **torturous** adj

Tory n supporter of the Conservative party adj belonging or relating to this party

toss vt 1 throw into the air 2 move (the head, hair, etc) upwards with a jerk vt, vi 1 move about or up and down quickly and in an irregular manner; pitch; jerk 2 move restlessly, as in sleep 3 also **toss up** spin (a coin) in the air to decide something **toss off** finish quickly ~n act of tossing or being tossed

tot[1] n 1 small child 2 small measure of alcoholic liquor

tot[2] v **tot up** (-tt-) add up; count

total n 1 complete whole as compared with a part 2 final figure obtained by addition adj 1 complete; final 2 absolute; unrestrained vt, vi (-ll-) add up (to)

totalitarian adj (of a government) characterized by absolute authority, allowing no opposition **totalitarianism** n

totem n object, esp an animal regarded as having special significance for a clan, tribe etc **totem-pole** n carved post used as a totem by North American Indians

totter vi 1 walk unsteadily 2 be in a precarious state

touch vt,vi 1 bring or come into contact with 2 bring the hand into contact with; feel 3 also **touch (up)on** allude to; mention in passing vt 1 affect; influence 2 deal with; be associated with 3 sl borrow money from n 1 sense by which objects in contact with the body are felt 2 act of touching, esp a light brush or blow 3 small amount of something 4 knack; ability 5 sl act of borrowing money or the person borrowed from **in touch** 1 aware 2 having correspondence or contact (with) **touched** adj 1 emotionally moved 2 slightly mad **touching** adj producing pity or sympathy; moving **touchy** adj easily offended

tough adj 1 strong; hard-wearing 2 hardy; robust; capable of suffering hardship 3 (of food) difficult to chew 4 stubborn; uncompromising 5 difficult 6 vicious; rough n ruffian; lout **toughness** n **toughen** vt make tough(er); strengthen

toupee n small patch of false hair worn to cover a bald spot

tour n journey through several places, usually for sightseeing vt,vi make a tour (through) **tourism** n business catering for the needs of tourists **tourist** n person, esp a holiday-maker, visiting a city, foreign country, etc

tournament n 1 medieval contest between armed horsemen 2 organized competition involving several matches, as in tennis, chess, etc

tow vt pull along behind, as with a rope n act of towing

towards prep also **toward** 1 in the direction of 2 close to; in the vicinity of 3 as a contribution to

towel n cloth or paper for drying things **throw in the towel** surrender; concede ~vt,vi (-ll-) dry with a towel **towelling** n type of absorbent cloth used for towels

tower n tall cylindrical or square-shaped construction, forming part of a church, castle, etc **tower of strength** strong reliable person **in an ivory tower** insulated from reality ~vi rise up to great heights **tower above** or **over** 1 be much higher than 2 be greatly superior to

town n 1 group of houses, shops, etc, larger than a village and smaller than a city 2 inhabitants of a town **go to town** act in a wholehearted or unrestrained manner **town clerk** n official in charge of civic records **town hall** n public building used as the administrative centre of a town

toxic adj poisonous

toy n 1 plaything of a child 2 trifle; something treated lightly adj 1 relating to or like a toy 2 (esp of a dog) bred specially to be smaller in size than average v **toy with** 1 play or trifle with 2 consider; ponder about

trace vt 1 follow (a track, path, etc) 2 discover or find by careful searching 3 copy by overlaying a transparent sheet and marking the lines 4 draw; sketch n 1 trail; track 2 sign showing former presence of something 3 small amount; vestige

track n 1 mark or marks left by the passage of something; trail 2 path 3 path designed for guiding something, as in a railway 4 course on which races are held 5 series of metal plates fitted instead of wheels to vehicles such as tractors, tanks, etc vt,vi follow the track of **track down** find by searching **tracksuit** n loose-fitting garment fastened at the neck, wrists, and ankles, worn by athletes in training

tract[1] n 1 large area of water or land; expanse 2 bodily structure or system serving a specialized function 3 bundle of nerve fibres

tract[2] n treatise or pamphlet

tractor n vehicle with large wheels or tracks for use esp on farms

trade n 1 business; commerce 2 interchange of goods and money on an agreed basis 3 skilled manual craft vt,vi exchange for money or other goods; barter vi engage in a business **trade in** give in part exchange for something **trade on** exploit **trader** n **trademark** n 1 mark or name registered by a manufacturer for a product 2 characteristic trait **tradesman** n pl **-men** 1 person engaged in trade, esp a small shopkeeper 2 skilled worker **trade union** n association of people engaged in the same trade pledged to protect standards of wages, working conditions, etc

tradition n beliefs and practices passed down from earlier generations **traditional** adj **traditionally** adv

traffic n 1 motor vehicles using a road 2 movement of ships, aircraft, etc 3 trade, commerce vi (-ck-) trade (in), esp illicitly

tragedy n 1 prose or drama with an inevitable unhappy ending 2 sad event; great misfortune **tragic** adj 1 in the style of a tragedy 2 sad; moving; calamitous **tragically** adv

trail n track left behind by a person, animal, or thing vt 1 drag or pull behind 2 track; pursue 3 hang loosely vi 1 walk wearily with lagging steps 2 hang or grow downwards **trailer** n 1 vehicle attached to and pulled by another 2 series of short extracts used to advertise a film

train n 1 number of railway carriages or wagons coupled together and drawn by an engine 2 succession of things, persons, or events 3 part of a gown or robe trailing behind vt 1 impart skill or knowledge to 2 teach (an animal) to obey commands or perform tricks 3 encourage (plants) to grow as required 4 point (a gun, camera, etc) at vi 1 receive instruction 2 exercise regularly to increase fitness **trainee** n **trainer** n

traipse vi trudge; follow a long or circuitous route; wander about aimlessly; trek n long tiring walk or journey

traitor n person who betrays a trust, esp one who commits treason **traitorous** adj

tram n passenger car running on a metal track on a road **tramlines** pl n 1 tracks on which trams run 2 parallel lines on a tennis court marking the boundaries of the singles court

tramp vi walk with heavy tread vi vt walk (a certain distance) as for recreation n 1 itinerant vagrant living by casual work or begging 2 sound of someone tramping 3 walk, esp a long recreational walk

trample vt vi tread under foot; crush with the feet

trampoline n gymnasium apparatus consisting of a sheet attached to a framework by springs, used for jumping performing somersaults etc vi exercise on a trampoline

trance n dreamlike semi-conscious state produced by hypnotism drugs etc

tranquil adj calm; peaceful; unruffled **tranquillity** n **tranquillize** vt make tranquil; calm down **tranquillizer** n drug used to reduce anxiety

transact vt vi perform; carry out (something, esp a business deal) **transaction** n

transatlantic adj 1 across or beyond the Atlantic Ocean 2 relating to North America

transcend vt vi excel; surpass; exceed tran-scendent adj **transcendental** adj of or connected with the philosophy of seeking after truth by exploring the inner self **transcendentalism** n

transcribe vt copy out in writing **transcription** n

transfer vt, vi (træns'fɜː) (-rr-) 1 move from one place to another 2 change from one position, job, responsibility, etc, to another 3 make over (power, responsibility, etc) to another n ('trænsfɜː) 1 act of transferring 2 prepared design or picture on paper that can be transferred to another surface

transform vt, vi change in character, nature, shape, etc **transformation** n

transfusion n transfer of blood from one person to another or injection of other fluids to make up loss of blood **transfuse** vt give a transfusion of

transient adj transitory

transistor n small electronic component made of certain solid materials **transistorized** adj (of a piece of electronic equipment) using transistors rather than valves

transit n 1 act of crossing or being conveyed from one place to another 2 act of moving across **transition** n 1 change from one place or set of circumstances or conditions to another 2 process of continuous change or development **transitory** adj changing; of limited duration

transitive adj designating a verb that takes a direct object

translate vt, vi 1 express in another language 2 interpret, explain the meaning of **translation** n **translator** n

translucent adj allowing light to pass through but not allowing a clear image of an object to be seen

transmit vt (-tt-) 1 send across, pass on, communicate 2 act as a condition or medium for **transmission** n **transmitter** n device used to broadcast radio or television signals

transparent adj 1 transmitting rays of light clear 2 easily seen or detected **transparently** adv **transparency** n 1 quality of being transparent 2 transparent photographic print projected or viewed by transmitted light

transplant vt (træns'plɑːnt) 1 dig up and plant elsewhere 2 transfer (living tissue or an organ) from one person to another n ('trænsplɑ:nt) act of transplanting or something transplanted

transport n ('trænspɔ:t) 1 means of conveying a person or thing from one place to another 2 vehicle used for this purpose vt (træn'spɔ:t) 1 carry; move from one place to another 2 carry away, as with emotion

transpose vt 1 cause to exchange positions 2 rewrite (music) in a different key **transposition** n

trap n 1 device for catching an animal 2 trick to place someone in an unfavourable position 3 hazard; pitfall 4 device to prevent passage of gas, impurities, etc 5 light open horse-drawn carriage 6 stall from which greyhounds are released for a race 7 also **trap door** door in a floor or ceiling vt (-pp-) catch or remove by means of a trap **trapper** n person who traps animals for fur

trapeze n apparatus used by gymnasts or acrobats, consisting of two suspended ropes carrying a horizontal crossbar

trash n 1 rubbish, refuse 2 anything considered worthless or shoddy

trauma n violent emotional shock or experience **traumatic** adj

travel v (-ll-) vi 1 go on a journey, make a trip 2 go abroad frequently or regularly 3 move; proceed 4 move from place to place selling goods vt cover (a specified distance) **traveller** n 1 person who travels 2 person employed to travel in goods; travelling salesman **travels** pl n trips or journeys, esp abroad

traverse vt, vi cross from one side or corner to another n act of crossing over or through

trawl n large net pulled behind a boat to catch fish vi vt catch (fish) with a trawl **trawler** n fishing boat equipped with a trawl

tray n flat piece of wood, metal, etc, often with a raised edge, for carrying objects

treacherous adj 1 deceitful; betraying a trust 2 dangerous; hazardous **treachery** n

treacle n thick sticky syrup obtained by refining sugar

tread v (trod; trod or trodden) vi, vt put the foot down on (something) or apply pressure to (something) with the foot vi walk vt 1 walk on (a path, road, etc) 2 mark a floor with (mud, dirt, etc) carried on the feet **tread on** 1 oppress 2 crush; stamp out ∼n 1 act or manner of treading 2 part of a tyre that

makes contact with the ground, usually having a patterned surface to improve the grip 3 horizontal part of a step

treason n disloyalty to a sovereign or the state

treasure n object or collection of objects of value vt value or regard greatly; cherish **treasurer** n person in charge of funds of a society, group, etc **treasury** n storehouse for treasure **the Treasury** government department responsible for finance

treat vt 1 deal with; handle 2 prescribe medicine or medical care for 3 act towards or regard 4 buy something for 5 act upon; apply a process to n 1 entertainment or a gift paid for by someone else 2 something producing joy or pleasure **treatment** n 1 act or manner of treating a person or thing 2 course of medical care

treaty n formal agreement between nations

treble vt, vi multiply or be multiplied by three n soprano or a voice or instrument in this range adj threefold; multiplied by three

tree n perennial plant with a thick trunk of wood topped by branches and leaves

trek vi (-kk-) make a long slow journey, esp through difficult country n journey of this kind

trellis n framework of criss-crossed bars used as a plant support, decorative screen, etc

tremble vi 1 shake or quiver, as from cold, fear, etc 2 be afraid 3 vibrate n act or an instance of trembling

tremendous adj 1 overpowering; astonishing 2 inf great; considerable **tremendously** adv

tremor n trembling; shaking; quivering

trench n 1 narrow ditch dug in the ground 2 ditch with soil parapets, used by soldiers during battle vi, vt dig a trench (in)

trend n 1 movement or tendency in a particular direction 2 inf fashion **trendy** adj inf up-to-date; fashionable

trespass vi 1 intrude upon private property without permission 2 encroach upon n act of trespassing **trespasser** n

trestle n structure consisting of a beam with hinged legs, used to support a plank, table top etc

trial n 1 test; experiment 2 trying experience; hardship 3 formal inquiry in court

triangle n 1 plane figure bounded by three straight lines 2 steel musical instrument of this shape sounded by striking with a small rod **triangular** adj

tribe n 1 group of people, usually primitive, with a common ancestry, culture, etc 2 group of related animals or plants **tribal** adj

tribunal n 1 court of justice 2 board or group appointed to settle any matter in dispute

tributary n small river flowing into a larger one

tribute n 1 payment in money or kind made by one ruler or country to another as an act or submission 2 mark or expression of respect

trick n 1 action or device intended to deceive 2 skill; knack 3 prank; joke 4 cards played in one round vt,vi deceive; delude; cheat **trickery** n **tricky** adj 1 crafty; deceitful 2 difficult; complicated

tricycle n vehicle with three wheels propelled with pedals

trifle n 1 small object 2 matter of little value or importance 3 cold dessert sweet consisting of layers of cream, custard, fruit, and sponge v **trifle with** act insincerely towards

trigger n 1 device releasing the spring mechanism of a gun 2 any device that sets off or initiates something vt also **trigger off** set off; cause; initiate

trill n high-pitched vibrating sound vi,vt utter or sing with a trill

trim vt (-mm-) 1 make neat or tidy, as by clipping 2 cut away (superfluous material) from adj 1 neat; tidy 2 smart; in good condition n 1 correct condition; good order 2 act of trimming, esp the hair **trimmings** pl n additional decoration or garnish

trio n group of three, esp three singers or musicians

trip n 1 journey; excursion 2 stumble or fall 3 mistake; slip 4 sudden starting of a mechanism v (-pp-) vi,vt 1 stumble or cause to stumble 2 make or cause to make a mistake 3 release (a mechanism) or (of a mechanism) be released vi dance; skip

tripe n 1 white lining of the stomach of a ruminant, used for food 2 sl rubbish; worthless material

triple adj 1 three times as great, threefold 2 of three parts or kinds n anything that is a group of three vt,vi multiply or be multiplied by three **triplet** n 1 one of three children born at the same birth 2 any one of a group of three

tripod n stand with three legs, for supporting a camera, etc

trite adj commonplace; hackneyed

triumph n 1 victory 2 notable achievement; great success vi 1 gain a victory; win 2 achieve great success 3 rejoice in something; exult **triumphant** adj 1 victorious 2 exultant

trivial adj insignificant; of no account **triviality** n

trod v pt and a pp of **tread**. **trodden** v a pp of **tread.**

trolley n 1 small hand-drawn wheeled vehicle for carrying goods, dishes, etc 2 wheel on the end of a pole running on an overhead cable, used to draw electric current to drive a bus (trolleybus) or tram

trombone n long brass instrument, usually having a moving slide to control the notes **trombonist** n

troop n 1 body of soldiers 2 group of people or animals vi march or proceed in a group **troops** pl n soldiers

trophy n memento of a victory; prize; award

tropic n one of two lines of latitude, either 23°28' north (tropic of Cancer) or 23°28' south (tropic of Capricorn) of the equator **tropical** adj relating to the tropics **tropics** pl n region between these lines of latitude

trot n 1 pace between walking and running 2 pace of horses with diagonal pairs of legs moving together vi (-tt-) move with a trot **trot out** produce; introduce **trotter** n 1 horse bred for trotting 2 foot of a pig or certain other animals

trouble n 1 disturbance; uneasiness 2 affliction; distress 3 person or thing causing trouble or worry 4 care; pains; effort vt afflict; annoy; inconvenience vi take pains; bother; make an effort

trough (trɔf) n 1 long narrow vessel holding food or drink for animals 2 area of low barometric pressure

troupe n group of performers

trousers pl n garment designed to cover the legs and lower part of the body

trout n, pl **trout** or **trouts** brownish speckled edible fish of the salmon family

trowel n 1 flat-bladed tool with a pointed end, used to spread mortar 2 hand tool used by gardeners vt (-ll-) use a trowel on

truant n child absenting himself from school without permission **truancy** n

truce n temporary cessation of hostilities by mutual agreement

truck n strong vehicle for carrying heavy loads

trudge vi walk wearily n long or tiring walk

true adj 1 relating to truth; in accordance with facts; not false 2 legitimate; rightful 3 real; genuine 4 exact; precise; correct 5 faithful; reliable **truly** adv 1 sincerely; honestly; truthfully 2 really; absolutely

trump n card of a suit ranking above the others for the duration of a game or round vt,vi defeat by playing a trump

trumpet n long funnel-shaped brass wind instrument, usually having three valves vi make a loud noise similar to that of a trumpet **trumpeter** n

truncheon n short wooden club used esp by policemen

trundle vt,vi roll along or propel on or as if on wheels or castors

trunk n 1 large strong box with a hinged lid for storing or transporting goods 2 main stem of a tree 3 human body excluding the head and limbs; torso 4 main telephone line 5 long flexible snout of an elephant **trunk call** n long distance call on a main telephone line

trust n 1 belief in someone's honesty or something's reliability 2 responsibility 3 good faith 4 association of companies combining for trade **hold in trust** take legal charge for benefit of another ~vt,vi place or have trust (in) **trustee** n person holding property or money in trust for another **trustworthy** adj deserving of trust; reliable; dependable

truth n fact statement or concept that is known to be true or can be verified **truthful** adj given to speaking the truth **truthfully** adv

try vt,vi 1 attempt or make an effort to do (something) 2 test, as by experiment vt 1 irritate; strain 2 subject to a trial **try on** put (a garment) on to test the fit ~n 1 attempt; effort 2 score of four points in rugby made by grounding the ball behind the opponent's line

tsar n also **czar** Russian emperor

T-shirt n short-sleeved shirt without buttons or collar

tub n 1 small barrel 2 bath esp one filled by hand **tubby** adj shaped like a tub; chubby; rotund

tuba n large low-pitched brass instrument

tube n 1 long hollow cylinder 2 narrow flexible container for toothpaste, etc **the Tube** London's underground railway **tubular** adj

tuber n thick underground stem of certain plants on which buds are formed at or below ground level

tuberculosis n disease produced by bacteria attacking body tissues, esp the respiratory tract

tuck vt,vi 1 fold under 2 push or fit into a small space 3 draw (the legs or arms) in close to the body 4 make folds in (a material) **tuck in** eat heartily ~n 1 small fold sewn into a garment 2 position in which the knees are drawn up close to the chest

Tuesday n third day of the week

tuft n bunch of strands, hairs, etc

tug vt,vi (-gg-) pull sharply or with force n 1 act of tugging 2 small boat used to tow larger boats **tug-of-war** n, pl **tugs-of-war** sporting contest between two teams, each holding one end of a rope and trying to pull the other over a line between them

tuition n instruction; teaching

tulip n bulb producing a brightly coloured bell-shaped flower on a single upright stem

tumble vi,vt 1 fall or cause to fall; topple 2 move in an ungainly manner 3 roll or toss about 4 decrease or lose value sharply n fall **tumbler** n 1 acrobat who performs somersaults, etc 2 stemless drinking glass

tummy n inf stomach

tumour n local swelling from a benign or malignant growth

tumult ('tju:mʌlt) n noisy or violent disturbance as of a crowd; uproar **tumultuous** adj

tuna n also **tunny** large ocean fish of the mackerel family with pinkish edible flesh

tune n 1 sequence of musical notes forming a melody 2 piece of music song, etc **out of/in tune** having the incorrect/correct pitch **out of/in tune with** unsympathetic/sympathetic to ~vt 1 adjust (a musical instrument) so as to obtain the correct pitch 2 adjust (a radio, etc) so as to obtain the correct setting 3 adjust (a car engine) to improve performance **tune in** adjust a radio to receive a particular programme **tune up** (of an orchestra) check instruments to ensure that they are in tune before performing **tuneful** adj melodious **tunefully** adv **tuning fork** n device with two prongs, which produce a sound of a set pitch when vibrated

tunic n loose-fitting kneelength garment

tunnel n underground passage vi vt (-ll-) make a tunnel (through)

turban n 1 headdress consisting of a long scarf wound around a cap, traditionally worn by men in parts of N Africa, India, etc 2 woman's hat resembling this

turbine n engine in which a wheel is turned by the direct force of steam, water, etc

turbulent adj 1 restless; disturbed; tumultuous 2 (of liquids) not flowing smoothly; agitated **turbulence** n

tureen (tjuˈriːn) n large dish from which soup is served

turf n, pl **turves** or **turfs** 1 ground covered with short close-growing springy grass 2 single piece of grass and soil cut from the ground **the turf** horseracing ~vt cover with turf **turf accountant** n bookmaker; person who takes legal bets on horseraces

turkey n large domesticated bird used for food

turmoil n state of confusion or anarchy; turbulence

turn vt, vi 1 rotate; move around; spin 2 face or cause to face a different direction 3 go around (a corner) 4 move in a different direction 5 change (into a specified state or condition); transform vt 1 move (a page) over so as to display the other side 2 dig or plough (the soil) 3 shape on a lathe 4 reach (a specified age) vi 1 become sour, rancid, etc 2 change colour **turn away** send away; refuse **turn down** 1 refuse 2 reduce the volume or intensity of 3 fold down **turn in** 1 hand in; deliver 2 go to bed 3 finish; give up **turn off** 1 branch off; deviate 2 cause to stop operating 3 sl repel; disgust **turn on** 1 cause to operate 2 produce automatically 3 sl arouse; attract 4 attack without warning 5 sl initiate, esp into the use of drugs **turn out** 1 stop (a light, gas burner, etc) operating 2 produce; make 3 expel 4 become; develop into 5 assemble; gather 6 dress; array 7 clear out the contents of **turn over** 1 move so as to reverse top and bottom; shift position 2 start (an engine) 3 deliver; hand over 4 (of an engine) function correctly 5 handle (a specified amount of stock or money) in a business **turn tail** run away; flee **turn to** have recourse to; seek help from **turn up** 1 appear; attend 2 be found or discovered as if by chance 3 increase the volume or intensity

of 4 point upwards ~n 1 act or instance of turning 2 one of a number of successive periods during which different people have the right or responsibility of doing something 3 short spell of work etc 4 distinctive style 5 something done to affect someone 6 need; requirement 7 inf shock; surprise 8 short walk **at every turn** on all occasions; in all directions **to a turn** perfectly **turn-off** n road branching off from a main road **turn-out** n 1 group of people appearing at a gathering 2 output 3 style in which someone is dressed or something is equipped 4 act of clearing out the contents of something **turnover** n 1 small pastry containing fruit or jam 2 amount handled, produced, used, etc, during a specified period **turntable** n 1 revolving circular table of a record player 2 revolving platform for turning a locomotive **turnup** n 1 cloth folded up at the bottom of a trouser leg 2 chance occurrence

turnip n vegetable having a rounded purplish edible root

turpentine n also inf **turps** oily resin of several types of conifers, used in mixing paints

turquoise n opaque greenish-blue stone adj, n blue-green

turret n 1 small round or square tower attached to a larger building 2 revolving structure for a gun on a ship, tank, etc

turtle n large marine reptile similar to a tortoise

turves n a pl of **turf.**

tusk n long pointed tooth of an elephant, walrus, etc , protruding from the closed mouth

tussle vi, n struggle; scuffle; fight

tutor n 1 private teacher 2 university teacher in charge of the studies of individual students or small groups **tutorial** n teaching session run by a university tutor

twang n resonant sound of the type produced by plucking a string vi, vt produce a twang

tweed n rough woollen fabric made from interwoven colours, used esp for clothing

tweezers pl n small metal tongs, used to lift small objects or pull out splinters hairs, etc

twelve n 1 number equal to one plus eleven 2 group of twelve people, things, etc 3 also **twelve o'clock** noon or midnight adj amounting to twelve **twelfth** adj coming between eleventh and thirteenth in sequence adv after the eleventh n 1 twelfth person, thing, etc 2 one of twelve equal parts; one divided by twelve

twenty n 1 number equal to twice ten 2 twenty things or people adj amounting to twenty **twentieth** adj,adv,n

twice adv 1 two times 2 multiplied by two 3 on two occasions 4 doubly; two times as much or many

twiddle vt,vi twirl; turn to and fro; fidget (with)

twig n small shoot of a branch of a tree or bush vt (-gg-) inf catch the significance of

twilight n evening light as the sun is setting; dusk

twin n 1 one of two children born at one birth 2 one of any identical or closely related pair adj relating to a twin or pair vt (-nn-) bring together as a couple or pair; match exactly

twine n string made up of twisted strands vt,vi wind; coil; entwine

twinge n 1 sudden shooting pain 2 sudden pang as of conscience, regret, etc

twinkle vi 1 sparkle; glitter; flash intermittently 2 move lightly and rapidly n single flash; gleam

twirl vt,vi revolve or cause to revolve; turn in rapid circles n single rapid turn or flourish

twist vt,vi 1 alter in shape by a rotating or screwing motion; wrench; contort 2 wind or twine vt 1 alter or misinterpret the meaning of 2 inf deceive; cheat vi 1 rotate or turn sharply 2 writhe n 1 twisting movement; turn; rotation 2 anything twisted, as in a spiral 3 unexpected turn of events

twitch vt,vi 1 make spasmodic or convulsive muscle movements 2 pull; jerk; pluck n act of twitching; jerk

twitter vi,vt chirp; produce a continuous chattering sound vi tremble

two n 1 number equal to one plus one 2 group of two persons, things, etc 3 also **two o'clock** two hours after noon or midnight adj amounting to two **two-faced** adj hypocritical; deceitful **twosome** n 1 pair; couple, esp when exclusive of others 2 game with two players **two-way** adj 1 operating in two directions 2 reciprocal; of mutual benefit

tycoon n wealthy powerful businessman

type n 1 kind; sort 2 class; category 3 block of material carrying relief characters for printing 4 printed characters considered collectively vt,vi use a typewriter (for) vt assign to a type; classify **typecast** vt (-cast) cast (an actor) in

a part similar to parts he has played before

typewriter n machine for printing characters on paper, operated by pressing keys, which strike an ink-impregnated ribbon **typical** adj 1 characteristic; normal or average 2 showing the essential properties of a category **typically** adv **typify** vt represent; be typical of **typist** n person who uses a typewriter, esp a person employed to type

typhoid n also **typhoid fever** infectious intestinal disease caused by bacilli growing in contaminated food or water

typhoon n violent cyclonic storm occurring in the W Pacific Ocean

tyrant n harsh ruler or master; despot **tyranny** n **tyrannical** adj **tyrannize** vt treat tyrannically; terrorize

tyre n solid or air-filled rubber tube held round the circumference of a vehicle wheel

U

ubiquitous adj present everywhere **ubiquity** n

udder n external organ of cows, goats, etc, through which milk is secreted

ugly adj 1 unpleasant to look at; repulsive; offensive 2 threatening; angry **ugliness** n

ukulele n four-stringed instrument resembling but smaller than a guitar

ulcer n open sore on the skin or an internal membrane, which is slow to heal

ulterior adj 1 further away in time or space; distant 2 not disclosed; deep-seated

ultimate adj 1 last; final 2 most desirable or significant n 1 basis; final stage 2 best; greatest; most desirable **ultimately** adv eventually; in the end **ultimatum** n final proposal of terms whose rejection will cancel further negotiations; deadline

ultraviolet n invisible radiation having wavelengths between that of violet light and x-rays

umbrella n portable collapsible object used as protection against rain or sun

umpire n impartial person who enforces rules and settles disputes in cricket, tennis, etc vt,vi act as umpire (for)

umpteen adj inf large number of; countless

unaccompanied adj 1 alone 2 singing or playing without instrumental accompaniment

unanimous *adj* having the support and agreement of all concerned **unanimity** *n* **unanimously** *adv*

unarmed *adj* without weapons

unavoidable *adj* inevitable

unaware *adj* ignorant; not aware **unawares** *adv* by surprise; without warning or previous knowledge

unbalanced *adj* not sane; mentally disturbed

unbearable *adj* intolerable; beyond endurance **unbearably** *adv*

unbend *vt,vi* (-bent) 1 straighten 2 *inf* relax or become relaxed, friendly, etc **unbending** *adj* 1 stiff; rigid 2 stubborn; formal

unbutton *vt,vi* undo the buttons (of) 2 *inf* unbend

uncalled-for *adj* unwarranted; out of place; gratuitously rude

uncanny *adj* weird; strange; irrational

uncertain *adj* doubtful; undecided; variable; unpredictable **uncertainty** *n*

uncle *n* brother of one's father or mother; aunt's husband

uncomfortable *adj* 1 not comfortable 2 uneasy; awkward; embarrassing

unconscious *adj* 1 unaware; unintentional 2 having lost consciousness; insensible; in a faint, coma, etc *n* part of the mind concerned with instincts, impulses, repressed feelings, etc , not normally accessible to the conscious mind **unconsciously** *adv*

unconventional *adj* not conforming; bizarre; eccentric

uncouth *adj* ill-mannered; awkward; boorish

uncut *adj* 1 entire; not abridged 2 natural; unpolished and without facets

undecided *adj* uncertain; hesitant; in two minds

undeniable *adj* definite; obviously true **undeniably** *adv*

under *prep* 1 below the surface of; beneath; in a lower position than 2 covered or concealed by 3 lower in rank than; inferior to 4 less in price or value than 5 with the classification of 6 in; according to 7 influenced by; subject to *adv* 1 in or to a lower or inferior place or position 2 younger than 3 less than *adj* lower; low; inferior

underclothes *pl n* underwear

undercoat *n* coat of paint below the top or final coat *vt* apply an undercoat to

undercover *adj* secret; disguised

undercut (-tt-; -cut) *vt vi* sell at lower prices than competitors

underdeveloped *adj* 1 not fully developed; developing; of unrealized potential 2 primitive; backward

underdone *adj* lightly cooked; rare

underestimate *vt* (ʌndərˈestimeit) estimate at too low a value; underrate *n* (ʌndərˈestimət) estimate that is too low

underfoot *adv* 1 under the feet; on the ground 2 in a subservient position

undergo *vt* (-goes; -went; -gone) experience; submit oneself to; endure; suffer

undergraduate *n* student who has not yet taken a degree

underground *adj,adv* 1 below ground level 2 secret; hidden *n* 1 secret political resistance movement 2 underground railway

undergrowth *n* shrubs and plants growing under trees in a wood, etc

underhand *adj* sly; dishonest; furtive *adv* secretly; fraudulently

underline *vt* 1 draw a line under 2 stress; emphasize

undermine *vt* 1 tunnel beneath; wear away 2 destroy or weaken by subtle or insidious methods

underneath *adv,prep* below; beneath; lower than *n* lower part

underpants *pl n* man's undergarment covering the waist to the thighs

underpass *n* road or path crossing underneath another road, a railway, etc ; subway

underrate *vt* underestimate; rate too low

understand *v* (-stood) *vt,vi* know or grasp the meaning (of); comprehend; realize *vt* 1 infer; believe 2 sympathize with; tolerate **understanding** *n* 1 sympathy 2 comprehension; intelligence 3 agreement; pact *adj* sympathetic; wise

understatement *n* expression with less force or completeness than merited or expected **understate** *vt* express by understatement; minimize

understudy *n* actor or actress prepared to take another's part when necessary *vt* be ready to act as understudy to; learn a part as understudy

undertake *vt* (-took; -taken) commit oneself (to); attempt to; accept; promise **undertaker** *n* person who arranges funerals **undertaking** *n* 1 task; venture 2 promise

undertone n 1 low, suppressed, or hidden tone of voice or feeling 2 pale or subdued colour

undervalue vt place too low a value on

underwear n clothing worn under outer clothing, next to the skin; underclothes

underweight adj of less than average or required weight

underwent v pt of **undergo.**

underworld n 1 place of departed spirits 2 section of society controlled by criminals, gangsters, etc

underwrite vt (-wrote; written) accept liability; insure; guarantee **underwriter** n

undesirable adj not desirable; unpleasant; offensive

undo v (-does; -did; -done) vt,vi open; loosen; unfasten vt 1 cancel; reverse 2 ruin the reputation of

undoubted adj certain; sure **undoubtedly** adv

undress vt,vi remove the clothes (of) n state of being naked or partly clothed

undue adj excessive; unnecessary **unduly** adv

undulate vi move in a wavelike or rolling manner **undulation** n

unearth vt dig up, uncover; reveal; bring to light **unearthly** adj 1 ethereal; supernatural; uncanny 2 ridiculous; unreasonable

uneasy adj anxious; apprehensive; uncomfortable; awkward **uneasily** adv

unemployed adj 1 out of work 2 not in use n those without jobs **unemployment** n **unemployment benefit** n regular payments made to the unemployed; dole

unequal adj not equal, similar, or uniform; not evenly balanced **unequal to** lacking necessary strength, ability, etc , to **unequalled** adj supreme; without rivals **unequally** adv

uneven adj 1 not level or straight; rough 2 not uniform or well balanced; patchy 3 odd; not divisible by two **unevenly** adv

unfailing adj dependable; continuous; certain

unfair adj not fair; unjust; dishonest **unfairly** adv **unfairness** n

unfaithful adj 1 not faithful; disloyal 2 adulterous 3 inaccurate; unreliable

unfamiliar adj strange; not known or experienced **unfamiliar with** having little knowledge of

unfit adj 1 not fit; unhealthy 2 unsuitable; incapable; not worthy

unfold vt,vi 1 spread or open out 2 reveal or be revealed; relate; develop

unfortunate adj unlucky; unsuccessful; undesirable; regrettable **unfortunately** adv

ungainly adj awkward; gauche; clumsy

unhappy adj 1 not happy; sad; miserable 2 unfortunate; unlucky 3 tactless **unhappily** adv **unhappiness** n

unhealthy adj 1 not healthy; sick; diseased; abnormal 2 threatening physical, mental, or moral damage; harmful

unicorn n fabulous animal resembling a white horse with a single horn projecting from its forehead

uniform adj exactly similar in appearance, quality, degree, etc ; unvarying; regular n distinctive outfit worn by all members of a school, nursing staff, police force, etc **uniformity** n **uniformly** adv

unify vt,vi make or become one; unite **unification** n

unilateral adj one-sided; of, affecting, or carried out by one side only

uninterested adj not interested; bored **uninteresting** adj arousing no interest; dull

union n 1 act or condition of becoming united or joined together 2 association or confederation of people, companies, countries, etc , formed for the common good 3 trade union **Union Jack** n national flag of Great Britain, combining the crosses of the patron saints Andrew, Patrick, and George

unique adj 1 single; sole 2 unequalled; remarkable **uniquely** adv **uniqueness** n

unison n **in unison** 1 sounding or speaking the same notes or words simultaneously 2 in agreement

unit n 1 single item; undivided entity 2 standard amount such as the metre or second, by which a physical quantity, such as length or time, may be measured 3 small part of a larger scheme, organization, etc 4 apparatus; mechanical assembly; functional system

unite vt,vi 1 join together; combine; cooperate 2 unify; come or bring to agreement **unity** n 1 state of being united; amalgamation; continuity; harmonious agreement 2 the number one

universe n 1 whole system of matter, energy, and space, including the earth, planets, stars, and galaxies 2 field of human experience **universal** adj 1 relating to all mankind, to nature, or to every member of a specific group **2** widespread; general; applicable to most situations, conditions, etc

university *n* institution of higher education empowered to confer degrees and having research facilities

unkempt *adj* not cared for; neglected; untidy; messy

unkind *adj* not kind; inconsiderate; hurtful **unkindly** *adv* **unkindness** *n*

unknown *adj* not known, recognized, or identified *n* unknown thing, state, etc

unlawful *adj* against the law; illegal

unless *conj* except on condition or under the circumstances that

unlike *adj* not like; dissimilar; different *prep* not like; not typical of

unlikely *adj* not likely; improbable

unload *vi,vt* remove a load (from) *vt* sell in bulk

unlucky *adj* not successful; unfortunate; bringing misfortune or failure

unnatural *adj* **1** not natural; artificial; unusual; abnormal; forced **2** wicked; vile

unnecessary *adj* not necessary; superfluous

unofficial *adj* not official or confirmed; informal **unofficially** *adv*

unorthodox *adj* not orthodox; unconventional

unpack *vt,vi* remove (items) from a case, box, package, etc

unpleasant *adj* not pleasant; nasty; impolite; disagreeable **unpleasantly** *adv* **unpleasantness** *n*

unravel *v* (-ll-) *vt* **1** disentangle; undo a piece of knitting **2** sort out; straighten *vi* become unravelled

unreasonable *adj* not guided by reason; not justified; excessive; illogical

unrest *n* state of discontent; disturbance; anxiety

unruly *adj* difficult to control; not disciplined; wild; disorderly

unscrew *vt* **1** unfasten or loosen by turning a screw **2** loosen or detach by rotating *vi* become unscrewed

unsettle *vt* disturb; make uncertain or insecure; upset

unsightly *adj* unpleasant to look at; ugly

unsound *adj* not stable or reliable

unstable *adj* **1** not firm or reliable, esp mentally or emotionally **2** decomposing spontaneously;

radioactive **3** readily decomposing into other chemicals

unsteady *adj* not steady or firm; rocky; precarious **unsteadily** *adv*

untidy *adj* not tidy; disordered; slovenly *vt* make untidy; mess up **untidily** *adv* **untidiness** *n*

untie *vt* (-tying) unfasten; undo (a knot)

until *prep* during the time preceding; up to the time of *conj* up to the time or stage that **not...until** only when

untrue *adj* **1** not true; incorrect; false **2** unfaithful **3** diverging from a standard, rule, etc

untruth *n* lie; falsehood **untruthful** *adj* **1** given to lying **2** untrue

unusual *adj* not usual or common; strange; remarkable **unusually** *adv*

unwarranted *adj* uncalled for; unnecessary

unwell *adj* sick; ill

unwieldy *adj* difficult to handle or use; awkward; clumsy; cumbersome

unwind *vt,vi* (-wound) **1** unroll; uncoil; slacken; untangle **2** relax; calm down

unworldly *adj* **1** unearthly; spiritual **2** not sophisticated; not materialist

unworthy *adj* not worthy or deserving; lacking merit **unworthily** *adv*

unwrap *vt* (-pp-) remove the wrapping from

up *adv* **1** in or to a higher position; further away from the ground **2** in or to a higher status or rank **3** into a hotter condition **4** into a more intense emotional state **5** no longer in bed **6** so as to be equal to **be up to 1** be the responsibility of **2** be secretly engaged in **up against** involved in a struggle with; face to face with **up to date 1** modern; fashionable; current **2** complete up to the present time; not in arrears ~*prep* **1** to a higher position on **2** further along **3** to a place level with *adj* moving or directed towards the top or north *n* **ups and downs** fluctuations; alternate good and bad periods ~*v* (-pp-) *vi* rise; get or stand up *vt* make larger; increase or raise

upbringing *n* education and rearing of children

upheaval *n* great disturbance; commotion; eruption

uphill *adj* **1** going or sloping upwards **2** very difficult and exhausting *adv* upwards; towards higher ground

uphold *vt* (-held) maintain or defend against opposition; sustain

upholstery *n* **1** coverings, padding, springs,

etc , of chairs, sofas, etc **2** business, trade, or skill of upholstering **upholster** *vt,vi* provide or work with upholstery **upholsterer** *n*

upkeep *n* **1** maintenance; keeping in good condition **2** cost of maintenance

uplift *vt* **1** elevate; raise **2** raise spiritually, morally, etc ; exalt *n* **1** raising; elevation **2** improvement; encouragement; enlightenment **3** moment of joy

upon *prep* on; on top of

upper *adj* **1** higher in position, rank, status, etc **2** further upstream or inland **upper hand** position of control **~n** upper part of a shoe, boot, etc , above the sole **on one's uppers** reduced to desperate poverty **uppermost** *adj* highest in position, power, etc *adv* in the highest position, rank, etc

upright *adj* **1** vertical; erect **2** honest; worthy; righteous *adv* vertically *n* **1** vertical post, beam, etc **2** *also* **upright piano** piano with vertical strings

uproar *n* **1** loud clamorous noise **2** angry protest **uproarious** *adj* **1** hilarious **2** accompanied by uproar; tumultuous **uproariously** *adv*

uprising *n* revolt; rebellion

uproot *vt* **1** dig up by the roots **2** displace or remove from native surroundings **3** destroy

upset (-tt-; -set) *vt,vi* **1** overturn; knock or be knocked over; spill **2** distress; disturb; confuse **3** make or become ill *n* **1** act of upsetting **2** quarrel; disturbance *adj* **1** annoyed; unhappy; disturbed **2** overturned **3** ill; sick

upshot *n* consequence; outcome

upside down *adj* **1** turned over completely; inverted **2** confused; chaotic *adv* in an upside down position or fashion

upstairs *adv* up the stairs; to, in, or on a higher level *n* upper part or floor

upstream *adv,adj* against the current of a river; nearer or towards the source

upward *adj* facing or moving towards a higher place, level, etc **upwards** *adv* **1** to or towards a higher place, level, etc **2** onwards; further along a scale **upwards of** more than

uranium *n* radioactive metallic element, used in nuclear reactors

Uranus *n* outer giant planet lying between Saturn and Neptune

urban *adj* relating to a town or city

urbane *adj* sophisticated; suave; refined

urge *vt* **1** entreat; plead with; press; strongly advise **2** drive or force forward *n* impulse; strong tendency; yearning **urgent** *adj* pressing; demanding immediate action or attention **urgency** *n* **urgently** *adv*

urine *n* fluid containing waste products excreted by the kidneys that is stored in the bladder before being discharged from the body **urinate** *vi* discharge urine **urination** *n*

urn *n* **1** large metal container for heating and dispensing tea, etc **2** vase or vessel, esp for holding the ashes of a dead person

us *pron* form of **we** when used as the object

use *vt* (ju:z) **1** employ; put to some purpose **2** handle; treat **3** exploit **4** expend; consume *v aux* **used to** expressing past habits or regular occurrences **use up** finish; exhaust **used to** *adj* accustomed to; in the habit of **~n** (ju:s) **1** act of using; state of being used; usage **2** right of using **3** need; purpose; point of using **4** custom; familiar practice **usage** *n* manner of use; employment; treatment **useful** *adj* of use; convenient; serviceable; helpful **usefully** *adv* **usefulness** *n* **useless** *adj* of no use or help; incompetent; hopeless

usher *n* **1** person employed to show people to their seats **2** minor official at a law court, parliament, etc *vt* **1** act as usher to; escort; lead in or to **2** precede; herald **usherette** *n* female usher in a cinema, theatre, etc

usual *adj* habitual; customary; ordinary **usually** *adv*

usurp *vt* oust or take forcibly; seize without legal authority **usurper** *n*

utensil *n* tool or implement, esp used in cookery

uterus *n* womb; organ in female mammals where an embryo develops

utility *n* **1** usefulness **2** something useful or practical **3** *also* **public utility** public service, such as the railway or electricity supply **utilize** *vt* make practical or worthwhile use of

utmost *adj* *also* **uttermost** furthest; outermost; maximum; most extreme *n* greatest possible amount, degree, extent, etc ; best

utter[1] *vt,vi* give audible voice to; say or speak

utter[2] *adj* extreme; complete; total; absolute **utterly** *adv*

V

vacant *adj* 1 empty; unoccupied; not in use 2 blank; stupid **vacantly** *adv* **vacancy** *n* 1 position, job, etc, that is not yet filled 2 stupidity; blankness **vacate** *vt* make empty; leave **vacation** *n* holiday period for universities, law courts, etc

vaccinate *vt* produce immunity against a specific disease by inoculating with vaccine **vaccination** *n* **vaccine** *n* dead microorganisms used in vaccination to produce immunity by stimulating antibody production

vacillate *vi* 1 oscillate; fluctuate 2 waver; hesitate; prevaricate **vacillation** *n*

vacuum *n* 1 space devoid of air or containing air or other gas at very low pressure 2 feeling of emptiness **vacuum cleaner** *n* equipment for removing dust, etc, by suction **vacuum flask** *n* container in which the contents are kept at constant temperature by means of the insulating effect of the vacuum between its two walls

vagina (vəˈdʒaɪnə) *n* passage from an exterior orifice to the uterus in female mammals **vaginal** *adj*

vagrant *n* person with no fixed abode or job; tramp *adj* wandering; unsettled; erratic **vagrancy** *n*

vague *adj* lacking precision or clarity; uncertain; indefinite **vaguely** *adv* **vagueness** *n*

vain *adj* 1 conceited; excessively proud of one's appearance, possessions, etc 2 useless; futile; worthless; empty **in vain** to no purpose **vainly** *adv*

valiant *adj* brave; strong; heroic **valiantly** *adv*

valid *adj* based on truth, logically sound; having legal force **validity** *n* **validate** *vt* confirm; make valid **validation** *n*

valley *n* 1 trough between hills, often containing a river 2 land area drained by a river

value *n* 1 worth; market price; fair equivalent 2 quality that makes something estimable, desirable, or useful 3 degree of this quality *vt* 1 assess the value of; assign a value to 2 esteem; prize **valuable** *adj* 1 of great worth; costing much money 2 very useful; having admirable qualities, etc *n* article of high value

valve *n* 1 device or structure that seals opens or regulates fluid flow, usually in one direction 2 electronic device in which current flows in one direction only, used esp to amplify signals 3 device on some brass instruments by which the tube length and hence pitch may be varied

vampire *n* creature of folklore that rises by night from the grave to suck the blood of humans

van *n* 1 covered motor vehicle for transporting or delivering goods 2 railway wagon for luggage, goods, etc

vandal *n* person who deliberately destroys or spoils something of value **vandalism** *n* **vandalize** *vt* destroy by vandalism

vanilla *n* flavouring obtained from the bean of a tropical climbing orchid

vanish *vi* disappear; become invisible; cease to exist

vanity *n* 1 exaggerated opinion of oneself; conceit; excessive pride 2 worthlessness; futility

vapour *n* 1 moisture in the air, seen as mist, smoke, clouds, etc 2 substance in a gaseous state, esp when its temperature is below its boiling point **vaporize** *vt* *vi* turn into or become a vapour

variable *adj* liable to change; not constant; inconsistent; unreliable *n* something that can change value, etc

variant *adj* showing discrepancy or difference; varying *n also* **variance** different form of the same thing; variation; deviation

variation *n* 1 change; modification 2 departure from a standard type or norm

variety *n* 1 state or quality of having many forms or versions; diversity; versatility 2 different form or version of something 3 assorted collection 4 theatrical presentation of assorted turns

various *adj* several; of different kinds; displaying variety **variously** *adv*

varnish *n* 1 oil-based solution that dries to provide a hard glossy skin 2 glossy surface so produced 3 superficial attractiveness *vt* 1 coat with varnish 2 conceal under superficial gloss

vary *vt* make different; alter; diversify; modify *vi* become different or altered; disagree; deviate

vase *n* ornamental container, often used for holding flowers

vasectomy *n* sterilization of men by surgical cutting of the spermatic duct

vast *adj* boundless; immense; exceedingly great **vastly** *adv* **vastness** *n*

vat *n* large vessel or cask for holding or storing liquids

Vatican *n* **1** palace and principal residence and administrative centre of the Pope, in Rome **2** Papal authority

vault[1] *vi,vt* spring; leap over, esp with the aid of the hands or a pole *n* act of vaulting

vault[2] *n* **1** underground room, often a burial chamber **2** arched roof or ceiling **3** strongroom in which valuables may be safely stored **vaulted** *adj* arched ~*vt vi* cover with, construct, or curve like a vault

veal *n* calf's flesh, prepared as food

veer *vi,vt* change direction or course; swing round

vegetable *n* **1** plant having various parts that may be used for food **2** *inf* person entirely dependent on others due to loss of mental faculties, etc

vegetarian *n* person who eats no meat but only vegetable foods and sometimes fish, eggs, and dairy produce **vegetarianism** *n*

vegetation *n* plants in a mass; plant life **vegetate** *vi* lead a boring, empty, inactive life

vehement *adj* marked by strong feelings; forceful; passionate; emphatic **vehemence** *n* **vehemently** *adv*

vehicle *n* **1** means of transport or communication; conveyance **2** medium for conveying or expressing ideas, etc **vehicular** *adj*

veil *n* **1** covering for a woman's head or face **2** something flat that covers or conceals *vt* cover with a veil; conceal; disguise

vein *n* **1** vessel conducting oxygen-depleted blood to the heart **2** fluid-conducting vessel in plant leaves **3** fine tube in the framework of an insect's wing **4** streak in marble, wood, etc **5** trait in a person's character

velocity *n* speed; rate of change of position; rate of motion

velvet *n* **1** silk, cotton, or nylon fabric with soft thick pile on one surface **2** soft smooth surface or covering

vendetta *n* private feud; rivalry

veneer *n* **1** thin layer of wood, plastic, etc , bonded to a surface **2** superficial covering *vt* cover with veneer

venerate *vt* worship; have great respect or reverence for **veneration** *n*

venereal disease *n* disease transmitted by sexual intercourse

vengeance *n* infliction of injury in return for injury suffered; revenge **with a vengeance** thoroughly **vengeful** *adj* vindictive; desiring revenge

venison *n* deer's flesh prepared as food

venom *n* **1** poison, esp that of a snake **2** spite **venomous** *adj*

vent *n* narrow opening or outlet; ventilating duct **give vent to** allow free expression of ~*vt* give expression to

ventilate *vt* **1** allow free passage of air into, drive stale or foul air out **2** expose to public examination and discussion **ventilation** *n*

venture *n* hazardous or speculative course of action; attempt *vt* **1** risk **2** dare to put forward *vi also* **venture out** brave the dangers of something

Venus *n* conspicuous bright planet lying between Mercury and the earth

veranda *n also* **verandah** covered terrace along the outside of a house

verb *n* word expressing action, occurrence, or existence **verbal** *adj* **verbally** *adv* **verbatim** *adj* word for word **verbiage** *n* excess of words **verbose** *adj* using an excessive number of words **verbosity** *n*

verdict *n* conclusion of a jury, decision

verge *n* **1** limit; boundary; edge, margin **2** grass border *v* **verge on** approach; border on

verger *n* person acting as an official attendant and usher in a church

verify *vt* ascertain or confirm the truth of **verifiable** *adj* **verification** *n*

vermin *pl n* **1** animals, esp rodents, that are destructive or dangerous to man **2** obnoxious people; scum

vermouth *n* white wine flavoured with aromatic herbs

vernacular *n* **1** spoken language or dialect of a people **2** jargon or idiom

versatile *adj* capable of many activities or uses; adapting readily **versatility** *n*

verse *n* **1** subsection of a poem; stanza **2** metrical composition of a line of poetry **3** poetry as opposed to prose **4** unit into which chapters of the Bible are divided **versed** *adj* acquainted with; skilled in

version *n* one of a number of possible accounts, renderings, or interpretations

vertebrate n animal having a backbone adj having a backbone

vertex n, pl **vertexes** or **vertices** ('vɜːtɪsiːz) apex; topmost point; meeting point of two intersecting lines

vertical adj 1 upright; at right angles to the horizon 2 extending at right angles from a surface; directly above or overhead n vertical line or position **vertically** adv

verve n vigour; zest

very adv used to add emphasis to an adjective adj used with a noun to give emphasis to a quality inherent in the meaning of the noun

vessel n 1 container or receptacle, esp for a liquid 2 ship or boat, usually large 3 tube for conducting fluid in animals or plants

vest n undergarment covering the upper half of the body vt invest, confer on, or endow with (rights, property, etc) **vest in** place in the control of

vestige n faint trace or hint of proof, evidence, etc

vestment n ceremonial garment as worn by clergy

vestry n room in or attached to a church where vestments and church documents are kept

vet n short for **veterinary surgeon**. vt (-tt-) examine, check

veteran n 1 person with great or long experience in something 2 old and experienced soldier **veteran car** n old car constructed before 1905 or sometimes before 1919

veterinary surgeon n also **vet** person having specialized medical training in the treatment of sick or injured animals

veto vt forbid absolutely; withhold assent; reject n, pl **vetoes** 1 right to veto, esp the passing of a law 2 act of vetoing

vex vt distress; tease; annoy; agitate **vexation** n

via prep through; by way of

viable adj 1 capable of sustaining existence 2 capable of being effected, validated etc; feasible; workable **viability** n

viaduct n structure bridging a valley etc, bearing a road or railway

vibrate vt,vi 1 move rapidly to and fro, oscillate; quiver 2 resound; resonate **vibration** n

vicar n clergyman of a parish having the same spiritual status as a rector **vicarage** n residence of a vicar

vicarious adj deriving one's own pain pleasure,

etc from another's experiences **vicariously** adv

vice[1] n evil practice or trait; wickedness; immorality; bad habit

vice[2] n adjustable tool for gripping an object that is being worked on

vice-chancellor n active head of a university

vice-president n president's immediate deputy

vice versa adv conversely

vicinity n surrounding or adjacent area, neighbourhood; proximity

vicious adj wicked; cruel; violent; harsh; spiteful **viciously** adv **viciousness** n

victim n object of attack, person suffering from an accident or from ill treatment by others **victimize** vt make a victim of **victimization** n

victory n defeat of an enemy; success in a contest or struggle **victor** n person gaining victory; winner **victorious** adj

video-tape n magnetic tape on which television programmes, films, etc, may be recorded for subsequent transmission

view n 1 act of seeing or observing; examination; inspection 2 prospect of the surrounding countryside, etc 3 range or field of vision 4 mental attitude; opinion 5 survey 6 intention **in view of** considering ~vt,vi watch, esp a film or television; inspect; judge **viewer** n **view-finder** n device in a camera through which the area to be photographed can be established

vigil n act of or time spent keeping watch, esp at night **vigilance** n alertness; watchfulness **vigilant** adj

vigour n energy; power; strength; forcefulness; good health **vigorous** adj **vigorously** adv

vile adj 1 disgusting; despicable 2 abominable; shameful; sinful 3 unpleasant; objectionable

vilify vt speak ill of; abuse **vilification** n

villa n luxurious house esp one by the sea or in the country

village n 1 group of rural dwellings with a smaller population than that of a town 2 inhabitants of a village **villager** n

villain n 1 wicked person; scoundrel; evil-doer 2 character whose evil is central to the plot in a story, play, etc **villainous** adj

vindictive adj vengeful; spiteful **vindictively** adv

vine n woody climbing plant, esp one bearing grapes **vineyard** n plantation of grapevines

vinegar n sour-tasting acidic liquid used for pickling, as a seasoning, etc

vintage n 1 age as an indication of quality 2 time of origin 3 harvesting or harvest of grapes and the making of wine 4 wine obtained from grapes grown in a specified year, esp one of good quality adj 1 old and of good quality 2 dated **vintage car** n old car, esp one built between 1919 and 1930

vinyl adj containing an organic group of atoms that form the basis of many plastic and resins

viola n four-stringed instrument resembling but slightly larger than a violin

violate vt 1 do violence to; abuse; defile; treat disrespectfully 2 rape or assault 3 disregard or break (a rule, promise, etc) **violation** n

violence n 1 assault; use of excessive unrestrained force 2 great force; intensity; fervour **violent** adj 1 impetuously forceful; overwhelmingly vehement 2 using or needing great physical strength **violently** adv

violet n 1 small purple spring flower 2 spectral colour of a bluish-purple hue adj of a violet colour

violin n musical instrument having a hollow wooden waisted body and four strings, played with a bow **violinist** n

viper n small venomous snake; adder

virgin n person, esp a woman, who has never had sexual intercourse adj 1 also **virginal** pure; chaste 2 in the original condition; untouched; not yet used, cultivated, etc **virginity** n

Virgo n sixth sign of the zodiac, represented by the Virgin

virile adj sexually potent; displaying traditional masculine characteristics **virility** n

virtual adj existing in effect or essence, but not in fact **virtually** adv in effect; practically

virtue n 1 goodness; moral excellence 2 chastity; sexual purity **by virtue of** by reason of; on the grounds of **virtuous** adj

virus n microorganism causing various infectious diseases **viral** adj

visa n stamp or endorsement on a passport permitting the bearer to enter a particular country

viscount ('vaikaunt) n nobleman ranking between a baron and an earl in the British peerage **viscountess** n wife or widow of a viscount

viscous adj thick; sticky; slow to flow **viscosity** n

visible adj 1 capable of being seen 2 apparent; obvious **visibility** n 1 state of being visible 2 clearness of the atmosphere; range of vision

vision n 1 act or power of seeing; sight; range of sight 2 beautiful person or object 3 mystical experience or prophetic dream 4 imagination; foresight

visit vt, vi go or come to see for pleasure, business, etc; call (on) n act of visiting; call **visitor** n

visual adj of or by sight; capable of being seen; visible **visually** adv **visualize** vt form a clear mental image of

vital adj 1 necessary to or sustaining life; living 2 lively 3 very important; essential **vitality** n strength; vigour; energy **vitally** adv critically

vitamin n substance found in food and essential in small quantities to health

vivacious adj lively; sprightly; full of vitality **vivaciously** adv **vivacity** n

vivid adj 1 very bright; intense 2 graphic; distinct; clear 3 vigorous; lively **vividly** adv

vivisection n practice of performing surgical operations on living animals, esp for medical research

vixen n female fox

vocabulary n 1 total number of words used or understood by a person, group, etc, or contained in a language 2 listing of words or phrases given with meanings, translations, etc

vocal adj 1 relating to or produced by the voice 2 readily disposed to express opinions; outspoken **vocalist** n singer **vocal cords** pl n vibrating membranes in the larynx that are responsible for vocal production

vocation n 1 course of action or occupation to which a person feels called by God, duty, or conscience 2 profession or occupation, esp when viewed as a career **vocational** adj

vodka n traditional Russian alcoholic drink distilled from rye or potatoes

voice n 1 sound produced by the vocal cords 2 tone, quality, etc, of a voice; person's characteristic speech sounds 3 musical sound of a singing voice 4 faculty of speech or singing 5 expression of opinion vt express

void adj 1 empty; vacant 2 not binding; null; invalid vt make empty, invalid, or ineffective *n* **1** empty space **2** painful awareness of a lack of something or someone

volatile *adj* **1** changeable; lively but unstable **2** readily forming a vapour

volcano *n, pl* **volcanoes** *or* **volcanos** outlet in the earth's crust for erupting subterranean matter (lava, rocks, dust, and gases), which forms into a conical mountain **volcanic** *adj*

vole *n* small rodent resembling a rat

volition *n* power or exercise of the will

volley *n* **1** series of things discharged simultaneously or rapidly **2** return of a ball in cricket, tennis, etc , before it bounces *vt,vi* **1** return (a ball) before it bounces **2** discharge in a volley

volt *n* unit for measuring voltage **voltage** *n* force producing an electric current in a circuit

volume *n* **1** measure of the space occupied by or enclosed inside something; quantity; amount **2** intensity of sound **3** book; one of a series of books forming one work **voluminous** *adj* **1** sufficient to fill many volumes **2** ample; large

voluntary *adj* **1** done willingly or by one's own choice or desire; not compulsory **2** given or offered for no payment; supported by donations **voluntarily** *adv* **volunteer** *vi* **1** freely offer (oneself, one's help, etc) for something; enlist for service without compulsion *n* person who makes a voluntary offer or enlists voluntarily

voluptuous *adj* full of or suggesting sensual pleasure; alluring; provocative **voluptuously** *adv*

vomit *vi,vt* eject the contents of the stomach through the mouth *n* **1** matter ejected **2** act of vomiting

voodoo *n* religious cult, esp of Negroes in Haiti, involving belief in spirits, who possess the worshippers, and other rituals

vote *n* **1** indication of preference or opinion; formal decision **2** right to express such **3** act of voting *vt* **1** determine, decide on, or elect by a vote or general opinion **2** *inf* suggest *vi* express one's preference, etc , by a vote **voter** *n*

vouch *vi* *also* **vouch for** guarantee; confirm; bear witness to **voucher** *n* **1** written evidence supporting a claim **2** ticket acting as a substitute for cash

vow *n* solemn promise; pledge **take vows** enter and commit oneself to a religious order

~*vt,vi* make a vow (that); solemnly promise (to)

vowel *n* speech sound represented by the letters a, e, i, o, u, or a combination of these

voyage *n* journey of some distance, esp by water *vi* make a voyage

vulgar *adj* **1** lacking in taste; crude; coarse; unrefined **2** of the common people **vulgarity** *n*

vulnerable *adj* open to attack or injury; easily hurt **vulnerability** *n*

vulture *n* **1** large predatory bird, feeding mainly on dead flesh **2** person who preys on others

vulva *n, pl* **vulvae** ('vʌlviː) *or* **vulvas** external female genitals

W

wad *n* **1** mass of soft material **2** bundle; roll *vt,vi* (-dd-) pack, pad, or stuff with a wad **wadding** *n* material for padding, packing, etc

waddle *vi* take short steps, swaying from side to side *n* swaying walk

wade *vi* **1** step forward through water, mud, etc **2** progress with difficulty; labour *vt* cross by wading

wafer *n* **1** thin light crisp biscuit **2** thin disc of bread or biscuit used in the Eucharist

waft *vi,vt* convey or cause to move smoothly through the air, over water, etc *n* **1** whiff or scent carried through the air **2** rush of air

wag *vt,vi* (-gg-) move or cause to move from side to side or up and down *n* act of wagging

wage *n* rate of pay for a job, manual work, etc *vt* engage in; carry on **wager** *n,vt,vi* bet; stake **wages** *pl n* payment for a job; earnings

waggle *vt,vi,n* wag

wagon *n* four-wheeled vehicle, such as a cart or open lorry

wail *vi* lament; moan, express grief in long plaintive cries *n* cry of grief

waist *n* **1** narrowest part of the human body between the ribs and hips **2** *also* **waistband** part of a garment covering the waist **3** narrow middle part of an object, such as a violin **waistcoat** *n* sleeveless close-fitting garment covering the chest and back **waistline** *n* **1** junction of the skirt and bodice of a garment **2** level of or length around a waist

wait *vt,vi* defer action; remain in the same place

(until, for etc); delay or be delayed *vi* act as a waiter or waitress *n* act or period of waiting **lie in wait** prepare an ambush **waiter** *n* male person employed to serve meals and wait at table in restaurants, etc **waitress** f *n*

waive *vt* refrain from insisting on, claiming, or enforcing; defer

wake[1] *vi,vt* (woke; woken) *also* **wake up** disturb or be disturbed from sleep or inactivity; arouse; excite *n* vigil beside a corpse before the funeral **waken** *vt,vi* rouse or be roused; wake

wake[2] *n* 1 disturbed water waves produced by a moving boat, etc 2 disturbed track left by a hurricane, etc

walk *vi* 1 move, pass through, or travel to on foot at a moderate pace 2 stroll; ramble; hike *vt* 1 pass through, pace, or traverse on foot 2 cause to walk; accompany **walk out** *v* 1 go on strike 2 leave or abandon as a protest **walkout** *n* industrial strike **walk out on** *inf* abandon; desert **walk over** *v* 1 beat or win easily 2 *inf* take advantage of **walkover** *n* easy victory; unopposed win ~*n* 1 act or manner of walking 2 leisurely excursion 3 path; route

wall *n* 1 upright construction of brick, stone, etc , forming part of a room or building, marking a boundary, etc 2 containing surface or membrane 3 barrier *vt* surround, divide, fortify with, or confine within a wall **wallflower** *n* 1 cultivated plant with fragrant yellow, brown, or red flowers 2 *inf* spectator at an essentially participatory event **wallpaper** *n* paper, usually decorated, for pasting to a wall or ceiling *vt,vi* cover with wallpaper

wallet *n* folding case for bank notes, etc

wallop *inf* *vt,vi* beat soundly; thrash *n* heavy blow

wallow *vi* 1 indulge or delight (in) 2 roll about in mud, etc *n* act of wallowing

walnut *n* tree yielding highly esteemed hardwood for furniture, etc , and a nut with a wrinkled shell and edible kernel

walrus *n* amphibious mammal related to the seal, having two long tusks

waltz *n* 1 dance in three-four time performed in pairs 2 music for this dance or having this rhythm *vi* dance the waltz

wand *n* slender and supple stick used as symbol of power or authority

wander *vi* 1 roam without purpose or plan; stroll; meander 2 deviate from the line of argument 3 become delirious; talk incoherently *n* ramble **wanderer** *n* **wanderlust** *n* urge to travel

wane *vi* diminish in observed size, esp after a peak; decrease; decline *n* act of waning

wangle *inf* *vt,vi* manipulate to suit oneself; use craft or irregular means to achieve ends *n* act or instance of wangling

want *vt* feel a need for; long for *vt,vi* need; desire **want for** lack ~*n* 1 something wanted 2 lack; shortage **in want** destitute, requiring help

war *n* 1 armed conflict between nations, groups of people, etc 2 bitter conflict; hostility *vi* (-rr-) make war; fight **warfare** *n* act or process of waging war **warlike** *adj* 1 hostile; belligerent 2 military

warble *vi,vt* sing with trills *vi* produce a quavering note *n* sound of such singing

ward *n* 1 hospital room with beds for patients 2 area of a city, borough, etc , for administrative purposes 3 minor entrusted to the care of a guardian or a court of law **ward off** protect against **warden** *n* 1 guardian; guard; custodian 2 superintendent or head of certain colleges and schools **warder** *n* person in charge of prisoners in a gaol **wardress** f *n*

wardrobe *n* 1 cupboard in which clothes are kept 2 range and extent of clothing or costumes of an individual or theatrical group

warehouse *n* building used for storage of goods before their sale, distribution, etc **wares** *pl n* goods for sale

warm *adj* 1 having or maintaining a pleasant temperature; moderately hot 2 affectionate; kind 3 enthusiastic; passionate; lively 4 red, yellow, or orange coloured 5 near to discovery, guessing, etc *vt,vi* 1 *also* **warm up** raise or be raised to medium temperature 2 make or become livelier or happier **warm to** become enthusiastic about or friendly towards ~*n* process of warming **warm up** 1 make receptive to a performance on television, etc 2 exercise before a sporting contest 3 run until operating conditions are achieved *n* **warm-up** process of warming up **warmly** *adv* **warmth** *n* **warm-blooded** *adj* able to maintain a constant body temperature **warmhearted** *adj* generous; sympathetic; kindly

warn *vt,vi* 1 give an indication of approaching

danger, adverse results, etc ; threaten **2** advise against or in advance **warning** n indication of a likely course of events or state of affairs; caution

warp vt, vi **1** twist or cause to twist out of shape; distort **2** make or become full of misconceptions; pervert n **1** threads running along the length of woven material **2** distortion of wood, etc , caused by heat, damp, etc

warrant n **1** authorization, esp for police to make an arrest, search property, etc **2** guarantee vt authorize; guarantee vt, vi declare; affirm **warrant officer** n officer in the armed services holding a rank, authorized by warrant, between commissioned and non-commissioned officers

warren n **1** interconnecting underground tunnels inhabited by rabbits **2** overcrowded living quarters

warrior n man who is skilled in or experienced in warfare or fighting

wart n horny protuberance on the skin **warty** adj

wary adj cautious; careful of deception or danger **warily** adv **wariness** n

was v 1st and 3rd person form of **be** in the past tense

wash vt, vi make or become clean using water and usually soap vt **1** remove with soap and water **2** flow over **3** cover with a thin layer of paint etc vi inf bear examination **wash away** move or remove by the force of water ~n **1** act of washing **2** collection of articles for washing **3** flow or wake of water **4** medical lotion **washing** n clothes, etc , washed or to be washed **wash-out** n inf total failure

washer n flat ring under a bolt head or nut to distribute pressure or provide a seal

wasp n winged stinging insect, usually with black and yellow stripes on its body

waste vt use carelessly; squander **waste away** deteriorate in health; dwindle ~n **1** misuse; neglect act of wasting **2** something squandered, neglected, discarded, worthless, superfluous, etc **3** rubbish **wasteful** adj causing or tending to waste

watch vt, vi **1** look (at) or observe carefully or closely **2** wait attentively (for); keep a lookout (for) **3** guard vi keep guard or vigil n **1** small mechanism, worn esp on the wrist, registering the passage of time **2** act or

instance of watching; period of vigil **3** person or persons performing this duty **watchdog** n dog kept for guarding property **watchful** adj vigilant; awake

water n colourless liquid that consists of hydrogen and oxygen and forms ice below its freezing point and steam above its boiling point **2** impure water, as found in rivers, oceans, etc **3** large expanse of water **4** solution of something in water vt **1** supply or add water to; make wet **2** irrigate **3** dilute vi **1** (of the mouth) secrete saliva at the sight of food **2** (of the eyes) secrete tears

watercolour n **1** painting in water-soluble pigments **2** those pigments

watercress n freshwater plant with edible leaves

waterfall n precipitous descent of water in a river course

watering-can n vessel with a handle, spout, and nozzle for watering plants, etc

water lily n aquatic plant whose large leaves and showy flowers float on the surface of water

waterlogged adj saturated with water

watermelon n melon plant bearing large edible fruit with reddish watery flesh

waterproof adj not allowing water through n waterproof garment; raincoat vt make waterproof

water-ski vi travel over the surface of water on skis holding a rope pulled by a speedboat n ski used for this purpose **water-skier** n

watertight adj **1** impervious to water **2** irrefutable; allowing no points of dispute

waterworks n **1** establishment for supplying water to a community **2** sl shedding of tears **3** sl urinary system

watery adj **1** of, like, or containing water **2** weak; pale; insipid

watt n unit of electrical mechanical, and thermal power

wave n **1** undulation on the surface of a liquid, esp the sea **2** any undulation, as in the hair **3** oscillating disturbances by which radio energy, sound energy, light energy, etc , is carried through air or some other medium **4** surge of events, emotions, people, etc **5** to-and-fro movement of the hand expressing greeting, etc vt vi move or cause to move to and fro vi greet or signal by a wave vt **1** direct by a wave **2** set waves in (hair)

waveband n range of wavelengths used in radio transmission **wavelength** n distance between two successive peaks of an energy wave **wavy** adj undulating; full of waves; swaying to and fro

waver vi 1 be unsteady 2 oscillate; vary 3 hesitate; falter

wax¹ n solid or viscous insoluble natural substance that softens at low temperatures vt smear or rub with wax **waxy** adj

wax² vi become larger or apparently larger; increase

way n 1 route; direction; path 2 progress; distance; journey 3 manner; style; method; characteristic behaviour, etc 4 condition; state **by the way** incidentally **give way (to)** 1 yield 2 stop for **in a way** in certain respects **in the way** impeding progress **out of the way** 1 so as not to obstruct 2 unusual 3 not easily accessible **under way** in progress; in motion **wayside** n edge of a road or route

waylay vt 1 intercept so as to attack; ambush 2 detain in order to speak with

wayward adj wilful; capricious; selfish

we pron used as the subject to refer to oneself and another person or all other people including oneself

weak adj 1 not strong; frail 2 very diluted; insipid 3 below expected standard 4 lacking moral, mental, or political strength **weakly** adv **weakness** n **weaken** vt, vi make or become weaker; reduce or be diminished in stature, strength, or resolve **weak-kneed** adj lacking resolution or firmness; timid **weakling** n person or animal that gives way easily or lacks strength **weak-minded** adj 1 mentally deficient 2 lacking resolution; easily persuaded **weak-willed** adj easily deterred, dissuaded, or distracted

wealth n 1 aggregate of valuable property; affluence; riches 2 abundance **wealthy** adj

weapon n object, device, or other means used for attack or defence or to injure another

wear v (wore; worn) vt 1 be dressed in; have on 2 carry; bear; display; present vt, vi 1 produce or be produced by constant rubbing, long use, etc; impair or deteriorate 2 reduce or be reduced to a certain condition n 1 act of wearing 2 clothing 3 damage; wastage caused by use 4 lasting quality **wearable** adj

weary adj 1 tired; reduced in strength or patience 2 tedious; causing or caused by fatigue vt, vi make or become tired or impatient **wearily** adv **weariness** n

weasel n 1 small nimble carnivorous animal with a long slender brownish body 2 treacherous, furtive, or sharp-featured person

weather n local current atmospheric conditions of temperature, humidity, cloudiness, rainfall, wind, etc vt come safely through vt, vi expose or be exposed to the air or the weather

weave v (wove or weaved; woven or weaved) vt, vi 1 interlace by passing threads alternately below and above other threads 2 make fabric in this way 3 create or move by winding in and out vt 1 construct; fabricate 2 introduce; combine n texture or pattern of a woven fabric **weaver** n

web n 1 something woven 2 fine filmy net spun by a spider to trap its prey 3 membrane between the digits of a bat, duck, etc **webbed** adj

wedding n marriage ceremony

wedge n 1 piece of solid material tapering towards one end 2 anything of this shape vt 1 fix firmly by positioning a wedge 2 split; force apart vt, vi squeeze or be squeezed into a space

Wednesday n fourth day of the week

weed n 1 wild prolific plant, esp one growing where it is not wanted by man inf person of puny stature 3 sl tobacco; cigarette vt, vi remove weeds from (ground)

week n 1 period of seven days, usually from Sunday to Saturday 2 working days of the week **weekday** n any day of the week except Sunday and usually Saturday **weekend** n period from Friday night to Sunday night

weep v (wept) vi, vt 1 shed tears of sorrow, joy, etc; grieve (for) 2 exude moisture n act of grieving or crying

weft n threads running across the width of woven material

weigh vt 1 ascertain the weight of 2 compare against; counterbalance 3 have a weight of 4 estimate weight by holding or balancing in the hands 5 consider carefully 6 draw in an anchor vi 1 have weight; be heavy 2 be considered important or to have value **weigh down** press down; oppress **weigh out** measure by weight ~n process of weighing

weighbridge n machine for weighing vehicles and their loads

weight n 1 heaviness 2 standardized piece of metal used for weighing 3 force by which a mass is attracted by gravity to the earth 4 anything heavy or oppressive 5 power; impressiveness; significance vt load with a weight **weighty** adj **weight-lifting** n sport consisting of competitive attempts at lifting increasingly heavier weights

weird adj odd; uncanny; unreal **weirdly** adv

welcome n cordial greeting or reception adj agreeable; giving pleasure; gladly received; willingly permitted **make welcome** treat hospitably ~vt greet cordially; be glad of

weld vt join (metals, plastics, etc) by applying heat or pressure; unite vt,vi bring or be brought together n welded joint or union

welfare n 1 well-being; state or condition of life; freedom from want, sickness, or ignorance 2 work or plans to improve people's welfare

well [1] n 1 underground source of water; spring 2 deep sunken shaft through which oil, water, gas, etc, may be extracted vi pour forth; flow; gush

well [2] adv 1 satisfactorily; correctly; thoroughly 2 intimately 3 clearly; easily 4 with reason or consideration 5 fully; abundantly 6 generously; kindly; with care **as well** also; too; in addition adj 1 healthy 2 right; favourable; satisfactory interj expression of surprise, etc **well-being** n state of good health, happiness, etc; good **well-bred** adj of good stock; properly reared; having good manners, etc **well-built** adj of generous proportions and stature **well-known** adj celebrated; famous; notorious **well-off** adj rich; fortunate **well-spoken** adj 1 speaking with a sociably acceptable accent 2 spoken fittingly or appropriately **well-worn** adj 1 thoroughly used 2 trite; hackneyed

wellington n also **wellington boot** knee-length footwear, esp of rubber

went v pt of **go**.

wept v pt and pp of **weep**.

were v 1 2nd person singular and 1st, 2nd, and 3rd person plural form of **be** in the past tense 2 form of **be** in the subjunctive

west n 1 one of the four cardinal points of the compass situated to the rear of a person facing the sunrise 2 part of a country, area, etc, lying towards the west adj also **western** of,

in, or facing the west adv,adj also **westerly** 1 towards the west 2 (of winds) from the west **western** n story, film, etc, taking place in the American West during pioneering times **westerner** n **westward** adj facing or moving towards the west **westwards** adv in the direction of the west

wet adj 1 covered or saturated with liquid; not yet dry 2 rainy 3 inf sentimental; feeble; lacking spirit; naive vt (-tt-) make wet n rain; moisture; dampness **wetness** n

whack vt strike; hit n 1 sharp blow or the sound of this 2 inf share **whacked** adj inf exhausted **whacking** n beating adj inf very large

whale n very large marine mammal that breathes through a blowhole on its head vi hunt whales

wharf n, pl **wharves** or **wharfs** landing-stage for mooring, loading, and unloading boats vt,vi 1 berth 2 unload (cargo)

what adj,pron used as an interrogative to request further information adj that which interj exclamation of surprise, dismay, etc **whatever** pron 1 anything or all that 2 what adj,pron whichever; no matter which adj at all

wheat n cereal grass or its grain used for flour to make bread, etc

wheedle vt,vi persuade by devious means; cajole

wheel n 1 circular frame attached by radial supports to a central axis around which it rotates, used to aid movement, transportation, etc 2 thing of similar shape or function vt,vi 1 move on wheels; push along 2 change direction; pivot **wheelbarrow** n barrow supported on one wheel in front and two legs behind, which may be lifted by two handles **wheelchair** n chair on two wheels, used by invalids, etc

wheeze vi breathe with difficulty, making a rattling or hissing sound n 1 sound of difficult breathing 2 inf ruse; clever scheme; dodge

whelk n edible marine mollusc with a snail-like shell

when adv 1 at what time 2 in or during which period conj at the time that pron from or until what time **whenever** conj,adv at any or whatever time that adv when

where adv 1 in, at, or to what or which place or position 2 from which place conj to or in the place or situation that **whereabouts** adv in what place, near where n place where something or someone is located or hidden **whereas** conj but; though; while **whereby** adv by which means **whereupon** conj,adv at which point **wherever** conj,adv in or to any or whatever place that adv where

whether conj used to introduce an indirect question, esp implying an alternative or choice and sometimes substitutable by if

which adj,pron used as an interrogative to request further information esp so as to distinguish between things pron used to introduce a relative clause when referring to inanimate objects **whichever** adj pron 1 any one(s) that 2 no matter which

whiff n 1 puff, gust 2 slight smell vt vi 1 puff 2 smell

while conj also **whilst** as long as; during the time that; at the same time as; although n space of time v **while away** spend or pass idly

whim n caprice; fancy **whimsical** adj capricious; fanciful

whimper n feeble cry **whine** vi utter a whimper; plaintively moan or whine

whine n 1 wailing high-pitched cry or note 2 undignified complaint vi vt make or utter in a whine

whip v (-pp-) vt 1 beat with a lash to punish or cause (a horse etc) to move forward 2 whisk into froth vi move or act quickly **whip out** produce suddenly ~n 1 lash on a handle for whipping 2 stroke of a lash 3 person responsible for a political party's discipline 4 call on members to vote according to party policy 5 confection of whipped ingredients **whip-round** n informal collection of money for a present, etc

whippet n thin long-legged dog similar to a greyhound

whir vi (-rr-) move rapidly with a buzzing sound

whirl vi,vt 1 move or cause to move in a circle; spin very fast 2 move away quickly vi swing round quickly n 1 rapid circular movement; rush, agitation 2 state of bewilderment **whirlpool** n circular current of water **whirlwind** n moving spiral of air into which surrounding air can be drawn

whisk vt 1 move or remove swiftly and lightly; brush, swing, or toss briskly 2 beat lightly introducing air so as to make froth vi move or

pass quickly n 1 rapid sweeping motion 2 light stiff brush 3 instrument for beating eggs, etc

whisker n 1 firm sensitive hair at the side of an animal s mouth 2 hairs on a person s upper lip or side of the face

whisky n alcoholic drink, distilled esp from malted barley

whisper vi,vt 1 speak in very low tones mur mur 2 converse in secret vi spread rumours n 1 soft speech murmur; rustle 2 hint rumour

whist n card game played in pairs

whistle vi make a shrill sound by forcing breath through almost sealed lips or teeth or air through a crack etc vt use this method for rendering a tune n 1 sound of whistling 2 device making a similar sound

white n 1 colour of fresh snow, having no hue 2 something coloured or characteristically white adj 1 of the colour white or nearly white, pale, colourless 2 pure unblemished **White** n person with a pale skin colour esp a European adj having skin colour of Europeans **whiten** vt make white vi grow pale **whitewash** n substance for whitening walls, etc vt 1 cover with whitewash 2 inf gloss over; conceal (errors faults, etc)

whiting n marine food fish

Whitsun n 1 also **Whit Sunday** seventh Sunday after Easter when the Christian Church celebrates Pentecost, the inspiration of the disciples by the Holy Spirit 2 week following Whit Sunday

whiz vi,vt (-zz-) 1 move quickly, making a buzzing whirring sound 2 inf move or go rapidly n buzzing sound

who pron 1 what or which person 2 used to introduce a relative clause when referring to a person or people **whoever** pron 1 anyone at all that 2 no matter who 3 who

whole adj complete; total; undamaged healthy adv in a complete or unbroken piece n entire or undivided thing; total of all parts **wholehearted** adj sincerely and enthusiastically felt, done etc **wholeheartedly** adv **wholesale** n sale of goods in bulk rather than retail selling adj 1 relating to sales in bulk 2 large-scale; indiscriminate adv on a wholesale basis **wholesome** adj 1 containing good value 2 healthy in body mind morals etc 3 conducive to such **wholly** adv completely; altogether

whom pron form of **who** as the object

whooping cough n infectious disease characterized by bouts of coughing, respiratory difficulties, etc

whore (ho:) n female prostitute

whose pron belonging to whom; of whom or which

why adv,conj for what reason; from what cause

wick n stringlike cord that burns in a candle

wicked adj 1 sinful; evil; extremely bad 2 mischievous; roguish **wickedly** adv **wickedness** n

wickerwork n craft of making furniture, etc, from twisted twigs or branches, or the objects so made

wicket n 1 three pointed stumps with two bails resting on top, at which the bowler aims in a game of cricket 2 strip of turf between two wickets 3 batsman or batsman's turn 4 small gate or door **wicketkeeper** n

wide adj 1 broad; of considerable dimension from side to side 2 roomy; extensive; including much adv 1 to the full extent 2 widely **widely** adv over a large area or extent; considerably; spreading far from **widen** vt,vi make or grow wide(r) **widespread** adj found over a considerable area; distributed far

widow n woman whose husband has died and who has not remarried **widower** m n

width n 1 distance or measurement between sides 2 state of being wide

wield vt hold and use; possess; exercise

wife n, pl **wives** female partner in a marriage; married woman **wifely** adj

wig n hairpiece for the whole head made of artificial or real hair

wiggle vt vi move or cause to move to and fro jerkily n wiggling movement

wigwam n light conical dwelling used by North American Indians

wild adj 1 uncivilized; undomesticated or uncultivated 2 uncontrolled; boisterous; extremely excited or angry 3 untidy; dishevelled 4 lacking judgment; random; erratic; fantastic **wildly** adv **wildness** n **wildlife** n animals, birds, plants, etc, that are undomesticated and live in their natural habitat

wilderness n large desolate area uncultivated and uninhabited region

wilful adj headstrong; obstinately self-willed **wilfully** adv

will[1] v aux 1 used to form the future tense 2 used to emphasize an intention 3 used to express willingness or ability 4 used to express probability or likelihood

will[2] n 1 faculty by which decisions are made 2 conscious choice; intention; inclination; moral strength 3 intended distribution of one's property at death 4 legal document expressing this vt,vi 1 bequeath in a will 2 compel by using the will; desire **willpower** n strength of mind; firmness; control

willing adj without reluctance; in agreement; eager; cooperative **willingly** adv **willingness** n.

willow n tree with slender pliant branches and long slender leaves, often found near rivers **willowy** adj flexible; graceful; slender

wilt vt,vi droop, as through lack of moisture, energy, etc ; fade

win v (-nn-; won) vi reach a goal, esp before anyone else; come first vt secure or gain by effort or contest; obtain by gambling **win over** persuade ~n act of winning; victory; success **winner** n

wince vi draw back; flinch n involuntary movement resulting from pain, etc

winch n hauling or hoisting machine consisting of a drum on a rotating axle

wind[1] (wind) n 1 current of air usually moving with speed 2 gas produced in the alimentary canal 3 empty meaningless words 4 wind instruments in an orchestra 5 inf hint; suggestion **get/put the wind up** become frightened or alarmed/frighten or alarm **in the wind** about to happen ~vt cause to be short of breath **windbag** n 1 sl person who talks a lot but says little of interest 2 bag in bagpipes from which air can be squeezed to maintain a continuous sound **windfall** n 1 fruit blown off a tree 2 unexpected good fortune often a receipt of money **wind instrument** n musical instrument played by blowing or using an air current **windmill** n mill with rotating sails driven by wind power **windpipe** n passage between the mouth and lungs through which breath is inhaled or exhaled **windscreen** n protective plate of glass in front of a vehicle **windswept** adj exposed to or disordered by wind **windy** adj like, characterized by, or exposed to wind

wind[2] (waind) v (wound) vt **1** turn; twist; **2** also **wind up** tighten the spring of (a watch, etc) by turning something **3** make into a ball; coil vi change direction constantly; meander

windlass n machine with a revolving cylinder for hauling or hoisting vt hoist by means of a windlass

window n **1** opening in a wall, etc , to let in air and light **2** frame of a window or the glass in it **window-dressing** n **1** displaying of goods in a shop window **2** art of doing this **3** skill in emphasizing the best features of something **window-shop** vi (-pp-) scrutinize goods in shop windows without buying

wine n alcoholic drink made from fermented grape juice or sometimes from other fruits

wing n **1** limb or organ by which a bird, insect, etc , flies **2** similarly shaped structure on an aeroplane **3** any side structure, as of a building or stage **4** player on the extreme right or left of the forward line in football, etc **wing-commander** n airforce officer similar in rank to lieutenant colonel or naval commander **wingspan** n length from tip to tip of wings

wink vi, vt **1** rapidly shut and open (one or both eyes), often to convey complicity, etc n act or instance of winking

winkle n edible shellfish v **winkle out** extract with difficulty

winter n coldest season of the year adj of, like, happening, used, or sown in winter vi spend the winter (in) vt feed and shelter (animals) through winter **wintry** adj

wipe vt clean or dry by drawing a cloth over or rubbing lightly **wipe out** obliterate ~n act of wiping; clean, rub

wire n **1** flexible strand or rod of metal or a group of strands plaited or twisted together **2** insulated wire for carrying an electric current **3** inf telegram vt join, fasten, support, protect, equip, etc , with wire vi telegraph **wireless** n radio adj sinewy; tough

wise adj **1** having knowledge, perception, or judgment; clever **2** sensible, discreet **3** sl knowing the whole situation; warned about **wisdom** n **wisely** adv

wish vt **1** desire; long for **2** request; want vt, vi express or have a desire for n **1** desire **2** thing desired **wishful** adj desirous; hoping

wisp n **1** thin strand or streak of something **2** small bundle of straw, hay etc

wisteria n climbing plant with blue flowers hanging in clusters

wistful adj yearning, with little hope of satisfaction; thoughtful **wistfully** adv

wit n **1** ability to think quickly and pertinently and say clever amusing things **2** person with this ability **3** also **wits** intelligence; resourcefulness

witch n **1** woman believed to have supernatural powers through contact with evil spirits **2** ugly malevolent woman **witchcraft** n craft or practice of supernatural powers for evil purposes

with prep **1** in the company of **2** by means of; using **3** bearing; possessing **4** displaying; showing **5** in relation to **6** among; in the midst of **7** at the same time as

withdraw v (-drew; -drawn) vi draw back or away; retire vt take out; take back; retract; remove **withdrawal** n **withdrawn** adj unsociable; very reserved

wither vi, vt shrivel; dry (up); fade; decay **withering** adj crushingly sarcastic

withhold vt (-held) keep from; hold back; restrain; refuse to grant

within adv inside; internally; indoors prep **1** not out of or beyond **2** in; inside; to the inner part of

without adv outside prep **1** outside **2** not having; free from; in the absence of **3** beyond the limits of conj unless; but

withstand vt (-stood) maintain; endure; oppose successfully

witness n **1** person who is present and perceives a fact or event **2** person who gives evidence, esp in court **3** person who attests another's signature vt, vi give testimony; observe personally; act as witness **witness box** n place in a lawcourt where witnesses give evidence

witty adj capable of verbal wit; amusing **wittily** adv

wives n pl of **wife.**

wizard n **1** man having supernatural powers; magician **2** ingenious person; expert **wizardry** n

wobble vi **1** move unsteadily; rock; shake; tremble **2** be uncertain; vacillate n unsteady motion **wobbly** adj

woke v pt of **wake. woken** v pp of **wake.**

wolf n, pl **wolves 1** gregarious carnivorous predatory animal of the dog family **2** person who is greedy and cunning **cry wolf** raise a false alarm ~*vt also* **wolf down** eat rapidly and ravenously

woman *n, pl* **women** 1 adult female human being 2 women collectively **womanhood** *n* **womanly** *adj*

womb *n* uterus

won *v pt and pp of* **win.**

wonder *n* 1 emotion of delighted surprise and admiration 2 object or person that excites this **no wonder** not surprising(ly) **work wonders** achieve great results ~*vt,vi* 1 be curious or seek to find out (about) 2 doubt 3 marvel (at) **wonderful** *adj* 1 amazing 2 *inf* very good; marvellous **wonderfully** *adv*

wonky *adj sl* unsound; shaky; not right or well

wood *n* 1 collection of growing trees and other plants over an extensive area 2 hard fibrous material in the trunks and branches of trees, used as a building material, in furniture, etc **woody** *adj* **wooden** *adj* 1 made of wood 2 stiff; clumsy 3 showing no emotion 4 stupid; insensible **woodpecker** *n* bird with a chisel-like bill, which it uses for drilling the bark of trees for insects **woodwind** *n* section of an orchestra containing wind instruments with the exception of brass instruments **woodwork** *n* anything made of wood; carpentry **woodworm** *n* 1 larva of certain beetles laid in, boring through, and eating wood 2 resulting damage in wooden furniture, etc

wool *n* 1 hair-covering of sheep and other animals 2 yarn spun from this 3 garment, etc, made from the yarn **woollen** *adj* made from wool *n also* **woollens** woollen cloth or garments **woolly** *adj* 1 made of or like wool 2 lacking clearness or precision *n* jersey

word *n* 1 unit of spoken language or a written symbol of this, expressive of some object, idea, or relation 2 brief conversation; remark 3 news; message 4 decree; promise; recommendation **have words** argue **in a word** in short ~*vt* express in words; phrase **wordy** *adj* using too many words **word-perfect** *adj* memorized accurately

wore *v pt of* **wear.**

work *n* 1 effort exerted in purposeful activity; expenditure of energy 2 task; occupation for gain; employment 3 product of one's efforts; creation 4 place of employment or where activity takes place *vt* 1 bring into action;

effect 2 handle; shape *vi* 1 labour; expend energy; be occupied; be employed (at or in) 2 behave in a desired way when started; operate; function **worked up** *adj* angry; excited **work out** solve; develop **working class** *n* workers, usually implying those in manual work **workman** *n, pl* **-men** labourer; skilled manual worker **workmanlike** *adj* efficient; of a high standard **workmanship** *n* level of competence or skill in a product **workshop** *n* place where goods are made, manual work is carried on, etc

world *n* 1 universe; all that exists 2 earth and its inhabitants; part of the earth 3 mankind; public; society 4 present state of existence; public-life; sphere of interest or activity; environment 5 materialistic standards or system; secular life 6 large amount or quantity **worldly** *adj* 1 familiar with public life and the ways of society 2 adhering to materialistic standards; not idealistic or religious **worldliness** *n* **worldwide** *adj* extending over or applying to the whole planet

worm *n* 1 long slender usually limbless invertebrate animal, esp an earthworm 2 internal parasite *vt* wriggle; squirm; make (one's way) slowly or secretly; extract insidiously

worn *v pp of* **wear.** *adj* 1 well used; long used; exhausted 2 worried; haggard

worry *vi* be anxious; fret *vt* make anxious; disturb; pester; harass; be a trouble to *n* 1 act of worrying 2 cause of this

worse *adj* less good; poorer in health; more inferior or severe in condition or circumstances *adv* in a worse way; with more severity **worsen** *vt,vi* make or become worse

worship *v* (-pp-) *vt* 1 accord religious honour and supreme esteem to 2 adore; idolize *vi* attend religious worship *n* 1 act of worshipping; religious service 2 adoration; devotion

worst *adj* of the extreme degree of badness *adv* in the worst way *n* worst part, state, etc; least good part *vt* get an advantage over; defeat

worth *adj* 1 having a value of 2 deserving; justifying *n* intrinsic value; value in money; merit **worthwhile** *adj* warranting the time, effort, etc; sufficiently important **worthy** *adj*

of sufficient merit: deserving: commendable
worthily adv

would v aux form of **will** in the past tense.
conditional, or subjunctive

wound[1] vt,vi (wu nd) hurt; injure n injury

wound[2] v (waund) pt and pp of **wind** .

wove a pt of **weave**. **woven** a pp of **weave**.

wrangle vi argue; dispute doggedly n angry
dispute

wrap vt (-pp-) cover; fold round or together;
wind; envelop in vi 1 enfold 2 package n 1
covering, such as a shawl or rug 2 single turn
or fold

wreath n 1 arrangement, often circular, of
intertwined leaves and flowers, often in
memory of a deceased person; garland 2 wisp
or curl of smoke or vapour **wreathe** vt vi
twist; entwine; interweave

wreck vt ruin; damage or destroy, sabotage n 1
ship that has foundered or sunk 2 broken or
damaged remains after a disaster; destruction
3 person enfeebled mentally or physically
wreckage n 1 act of wrecking 2 remains of a
wrecked thing or person

wren n small brown songbird with short erect
tail

wrench vt pull sharply and with a twist; force
by violence; sprain; distort vi undergo violent
pulling, tugging, or twisting n 1 act of
wrenching; twist; sprain 2 difficult parting;
pain at parting 3 adjustable spanner

wrestle vi,vt struggle to overcome vi contend
in an organized fight by holding and throwing,
without punching n bout of wrestling;
struggle **wrestler** n **wrestling** n

wretch n 1 miserable unfortunate person 2
worthless despicable person **wretched** adj 1
miserable; dismal 2 of poor quality; contemptible

wriggle vi,vt squirm or make short twisting
movements **wriggle into/out of** inf insinuate oneself deviously into or extricate oneself
out of n act, motion, or shape of wriggling
movement

wring v (wrung) vt,vi twist and squeeze out
moisture (from) vt 1 twist 2 clasp in anguish
3 grip in a friendly manner 4 extract n act of
wringing

wrinkle n small ridge or furrow on a surface;
crease vt,vi crease

wrist n 1 joint between the hand and lower arm

2 part of a garment covering this **wristwatch**
n watch worn at the wrist

writ n legal or formal document summoning or
requiring a person to take some course of
action

write v (wrote, written) vt,vi 1 mark letters
words, numbers etc , usually on paper, to
communicate ideas thoughts etc 2 correspond (with) by letter 3 be an author (of)
vt state in a letter book etc **write down** or
out put in writing **write off** consider a loss
or failure **write-off** n complete loss or
failure; wreck **write up** describe or bring up
to date in writing **write-up** n written account
in a newspaper etc of a book, film, etc
review **writing** n 1 written work book etc 2
act of writing 3 style of handwriting

writhe vi 1 twist or roll about as if suffering
pain squirm 2 suffer mentally

wrong adj 1 not correct accurate or true.
mistaken 2 wicked; unjust 3 not suitable; not
wanted n injustice, wrong action **in the
wrong** mistaken adv also **wrongly** in a
wrong way **get wrong** 1 misunderstand 2
produce an incorrect answer —vt do injustice
or harm to, think ill of unjustifiably **wrongdoing** n improper illegal, or immoral action
wrongdoer n

wrought iron adj malleable pure iron, often
drawn out into decorative shapes

wry adj 1 twisted, contorted 2 ironical; dryly
humorous **wryly** adv

X

xenophobia n irrational fear or hatred of for
eigners or things foreign or strange

xerography n copying process in which images
are produced using electrically charged surfaces

Xerox n Tdmk process or machine employing
xerography

Xmas n Christmas

X-ray n 1 wave of radiation of considerable
energy that can penetrate matter used esp in
medical diagnosis and treatment 2 image,
esp of bone structure, produced on film
sensitive to X-rays vt,vi irradiate with X-rays

xylophone n musical instrument consisting of a
graduated series of wooden bars struck by
wooden hammers

Y

yacht n light sailing vessel for racing, cruising, etc vi sail in a yacht **yachtsman** n, pl **-men** person who keeps or sails a yacht

yank vt, vi pull sharply; jerk n sharp tug

yap n short sharp high-pitched bark; yelp vi (-pp-) 1 bark in yaps 2 inf chatter stupidly or at length

yard¹ n 1 unit of length, equivalent to 0 91 metres (three feet) 2 piece of material of this length **yardstick** n 1 graduated stick, one yard long, used for measuring 2 any standard used for comparison

yard² n enclosed area, usually adjoining a building and having a hard surface

yarn n 1 continuous thread made from twisted fibres of wool, cotton, synthetic materials, etc 2 story spun out to some length vi tell stories

yawn vi 1 breathe in through a wide open mouth, usually as a result of tiredness or boredom 2 be open wide n act of yawning

year n 1 also **calendar year** period of time of 365 days (or 366 in a leap year) from Jan 1 to Dec 31 2 period of twelve months 3 period of time (365 256 days) taken by the earth to complete one orbit of the sun **yearly** adj, adv

yearn vi 1 have a great longing; crave 2 feel pity or tenderness **yearning** n

yeast n fungus or a preparation of this fungus used in brewing and for raising bread

yell vi, vt scream; shout loudly n scream of anger, pain, or excitement; loud cry

yellow n spectral colour, as that of gold or a daffodil adj 1 of the colour yellow 2 inf cowardly

yelp n short sharp cry of pain, surprise, or excitement, esp by a dog vi utter a yelp

yes adv, interj expression of affirmation, consent, etc n affirmative reply

yesterday n day before today adv 1 on or during yesterday 2 not long ago

yet adv 1 up to that or this time 2 now; at this moment 3 still; even conj but; nevertheless; however

yew n coniferous tree with dark needle-shaped leaves and red cones

yield vt 1 produce; supply 2 give up under pressure; concede vi submit; give way under pressure; comply n amount yielded; product

yodel vi, vt (-ll-) alternate in singing between a normal and falsetto voice n song in this style **yodeller** n

yoga n philosophy and practice of type of oriental meditation **yogi** n person who practises yoga

yoghurt n also **yogurt, yoghourt** thickly clotted milk curdled by bacteria

yoke n 1 wooden neckpiece holding together two draught oxen 2 something resembling this 3 fitted part of a garment, esp for the chest and shoulders 4 oppressive force; slavery 5 bond of union vt put a yoke on; join together

yolk n yellow centre of an egg

yonder adv over there adj distant but in sight

you pron 1 used to refer to one or more persons addressed directly, excluding the speaker 2 people in general; one

young adj having lived a relatively short time; undeveloped; immature; not old pl n young people; offspring **youngster** n young person or animal

your adj belonging to you **yours** pron something or someone that belongs to or is associated with you **yourself** r pron, pl **-selves** 1 of your own self 2 your normal self

youth n 1 age between childhood and adulthood; early life 2 quality or condition of being young, inexperienced, etc 3 young man 4 young people collectively **youthful** adj fresh; vigorous; optimistic; buoyant

Z

zeal n enthusiasm, fervour; passionate ardour

zebra n black-and-white striped animal of the horse family, originating in Africa **zebra crossing** n black-and-white striped path used by pedestrians to cross a road

zero n nought; nothing; nil; figure 0; point separating positive and negative values or quantities, as on a temperature scale

zest n 1 gusto; keen interest; obvious enjoyment 2 anything that gives added zest

zigzag n 1 line that forms a series of sharp alternately right and left turns 2 something having this form vt, vi (-gg-) move or cause to move along such a line

zinc n hard bluish-white metal, used esp in alloys and in galvanizing iron

zip n **1** interlocking fastener for openings in clothes **2** whizzing sound **3** energy; vigour v (-pp-) vt also **zip up,** fasten with a zip vi **1** hurry or rush (through, etc) **2** move with a whizzing sound

zither n musical instrument consisting of numerous strings stretched over a wooden frame

zodiac n belt or zone of the heavens divided into twelve parts, each accorded a sign, in which the paths of the sun, moon, and planets appear to lie

zone n area; region; belt; characteristic or distinctive section, as of the earth vt divide into or mark with zones

zoo n enclosure where wild animals are kept for display to the public, for breeding, etc.

zoology n scientific study of animals and animal life **zoological** adj **zoologist** n

zoom vi,vt produce a loud buzzing noise vi move or rise rapidly

THESAURUS
OF ENGLISH WORDS

Introduction

A thesaurus is a book of words arranged according to ideas. You use it when you can think of an idea but cannot find the exact word to express it or when you have a word in mind that isn't close enough to the one you really want. This is where a thesaurus comes in: it gives words in lists according to the ideas they stand for.

This thesaurus covers the central part of the vocabulary of English – the 'core' of the language we all use most of the time – and groups this under 990 categories, each representing a different idea. It does not include highly technical words, but does reflect the fact that the English language used today is becoming more colloquial. By looking up a word in the index and referring to one of the categories in the book you will find a list of words with a similar meaning and you will then be able to choose the one you want.

The first thesaurus was written by Peter Mark Roget (1779–1869), and published in 1852. Its full original title was *The Thesaurus of English Words and Phrases Classified and Arranged so as to Facilitate the Expression of Ideas and Assist in Literary Composition.* It has since been published in many editions and the concept has been taken over and used for other languages. Many changes have been made in writing this thesaurus: categories have been re-ordered, many have been given more intelligible names, and there is a thorough coverage of new words that have entered the language. A large number of older words and phrases have been rejected as no longer used.

This thesaurus is written for those who use language – those who speak and write English and want to use a variety of words, for those who solve crosswords, and for those who just like browsing through its pages to pore over the richness of the language. After all, the word 'thesaurus' itself comes from the Greek word for 'treasure', and we hope that something of the deep resources of the language will be discovered in these pages.

M. H. Manser

How to use this thesaurus

Imagine that you have a word in mind, let us say, 'beautiful'. You have used this word already and don't want to use it again, or you want something more expressive. The first thing to do is to look up this word – 'beautiful' – in the index. The index is arranged in alphabetical order. Every entry in the index consists of a word or words, a part of speech, and a number or numbers. Parts of speech have been abbreviated as follows: *n.* = noun; *adj.* = adjective; *vb.* = verb; *adv.* = adverb; *prep.* = preposition. The numbers refer to categories. The entry for 'beautiful' looks like this:

beautiful adj. 844

If you turn to category **844** in the main part of the book and look under the appropriate part of speech – here *adj.* – you will find a list of alternative words that you can use: beautiful, attractive, good-looking, ... Some of the entries in the index have numbers printed in a darker, bold type. These show the main references for particular words.

The words listed have slightly different meanings from each other. If you are not familiar with a word it would therefore be advisable to look up the word in a good modern dictionary before using it. Otherwise you may risk using the word in the wrong context. Two further abbreviations are used. Informal or colloquial words are marked as (*inf.*) and slang words (*sl.*). At the end of many entries there are cross-references to other categories (e.g. see also **56, 112**). These can usefully be followed up to find further lists of related words. You should also consult the words given at the other parts of speech in an entry, as some words there may suggest others to you.

If you look at the adjacent categories, too, you will find further help or perhaps the possibility of using a word meaning something opposite, e.g., the categories **534 resolution, 535 perseverance, 536 irresolution.**

A list of the 990 categories is given after the index and you can check that the number of the category you are looking up is the one you want.

Plan of categories

Thesaurus

1 Abstract Relations

A Existence

1 existence

n. existence, being, essence, self-existence, reality, actuality, presence; subsistence, givenness, historicity, factuality; actualization, creating, becoming, potentiality, possibility; ontology, existentialism, metaphysics, realism.

fact, truth, *fait accompli*, real thing, entity, vital principle.

adj. existing, being, in being, in existence, afoot, given, uncreated; ontological, metaphysical; extant, living, current, present, standing, surviving; subsisting, subsistent, obtaining, prevailing, prevalent; real, actual, true, authentic, genuine, mere, objective; essential, substantial, substantive, self-existing, self-existent, intrinsic, factual.

vb. be, exist, have being, live, breathe, abide, remain, stay, prevail, be so, be the case; subsist, obtain; consist in, inhere in, reside in; stand, find itself, lie, be situated, be found; occur, take place, happen, continue, go on, endure, last.

adv. actually, really, in fact, in reality.

2 non-existence

n. non-existence, inexistence, non-being, nonentity, nothingness, nullity, nihility, neverness; vacuum, vacuity, emptiness, void, blank; extinction, destruction, abolition, obsolescence.

adj. non-existent, void, vacuous, blank; extinct, dead, obsolete, vanished; unreal, wrong, untrue, false, specious, imaginary, fictitious, hypothetical, groundless, unfounded.

vb. come to nothing, pass away, die, vanish, disappear, dematerialize, evaporate, dissolve; bring to nothing, nullify, destroy, abolish, kill.

3 material existence

n. materiality, substantiality, actuality, essentiality, reality, objectivity, substantivity, corporeity, corporality, concreteness, solidity, tangibility.

substance, thing, body, solid, stuff, matter, entity, flesh and blood (*inf.*).

adj. material, substantial, actual, solid, corporeal, objective, substantive, concrete, physical, real, natural; visible, tangible.

see also 327

4 non-material existence

n. immateriality, insubstantiality, inessentiality, intangibility.

shadow, token, dream, vision, apparition, spirit, illusion, optical illusion, mirage, breath, mist, vapour, wisp.

adj. immaterial, insubstantial, abstract, intangible, imponderable, airy, vaporous, ethereal, spiritual, ghostly, spectral, bodiless, disembodied, visionary, shadowy, vague.

see also 328

5 being according to internal form

n. intrinsicality, inherence, inwardness, internality, essentiality, immanence.

essence, substance, basis, being, soul, fundamental, principle, quality, quintessence, essential, heart, core, character, nature, constitution, structure, make-up, bearing, framework, frame; attribute, element, aspect, quality, feature, manner, temper, temperament, mood, humour, disposition, personality, particularity, idiosyncrasy, endowment, heredity, gene.

adj. intrinsic, essential, inherent, inward, central, fundamental, immanent, implicit, internal, original, integral, innate, distinctive, specific, characteristic, particular, peculiar, unique; native, genetic, hereditary, inborn, congenital, ancestral.

vb. inhere, be intrinsic; internalize.

see also 223, 224

6 being according to external form

n. extrinsicality, externality, objectivity, outwardness, transcendence, projection, extrapolation; accessory, external.

adj. extrinsic, external, objective, transcendent, exterior, outward, extraneous, foreign, independent, additional, outside.

vb. be extrinsic, transcend, surpass; make extrinsic, objectify, project, extend, extrapolate.

see also 222, 825

7 absolute state

n. state, standing, condition, station, status, case, position, stand, rank, class, degree, estate, style, fashion, mode, aspect, facet, posture, attitude.

8 circumstance

n. circumstance, circumstances, situation, environment, surroundings, setting, background, backdrop, *milieu,* context, how the land lies, ambience, atmosphere, climate; conditions, factors, details, items, features, particulars, requirements, necessities; cause, reason, motives, grounds.

adj. circumstantial, modal, surrounding, environmental, contextual, incidental, background, contingent; detailed, itemized, particular.

adv. under the circumstances, this being the case, incidentally, under these conditions, in the event of.

B Relation

9 relation

n. relation, relatedness, association, relationship, arrangement; connection, link, dependence, involvement, implication, bearing; relativity, correspondence, analogy, correlation; relevance, suitability, appositeness.

adj. relative, related, connected, involved, arranged, linked, bearing upon, concerning, belonging, appertaining; reciprocal, mutual; analogous, comparable; relevant, suitable, apposite, appropriate, proper, applicable, pertinent.

vb. be related to, concern, refer to, touch upon, bear upon, deal with, treat, have to do with, apply, hold true for, be a factor in; relate, associate, link, refer; correspond to, be analogous to; belong, pertain.

adv., prep. concerning, regarding, as regards, on, about, with reference to, with respect to, on the subject of, in the matter of, à propos, re, in re.

10 absence of relation

n. irrelation, dissociation, unrelatedness, non-involvement, independence, arbitrariness; disproportion, difference, misfit, irreconcilability, irrelevance, unsuitability, inconsequence.

adj. unrelated, independent, unconcerned, uninvolved, unconnected, inappropriate, incongruent; isolated, arbitrary, free, unallied, unilateral; irrelevant, unsuitable, inapplicable, inapposite, inconsequential.

vb. be unrelated to, have no relation with, not concern, have no bearing upon, have nothing to do with, not be one's business.

adv. by the way, incidentally.

11 kindred relations

n. consanguinity, blood relationship, blood, ties of blood, kinship, kindred, relations, relatives, kith and kin; ancestry, parentage, antecedents, forbears, patrimony, heritage, lineage; descent, descendants; affiliation; children, offspring, issue, progeny; sibling, brother, sister, twin, cousin, uncle, aunt, nephew, niece, parent, father, mother; kinsman, clansman, fellow, compatriot; family, matriarch, patriarch, fatherhood, paternity, motherhood, maternity, brotherhood, fraternity, sisterhood, sorority; in laws; household, one's folks (*inf.*), home, family circle; race, stock, generation, strain, breed, line, side, clan, tribe, stirps.

adj. related, akin, kindred, consanguineous; parental, maternal, paternal, brotherly, fraternal, sisterly, sororal, cousinly, avuncular; collateral, allied; ethnic, racial, minority, tribal.

vb. be related to, be akin, generate, adopt, affiliate.

12 correlation

n. correlation, relation, correspondence, mutuality, reciprocity, interchange, interrelation, interdependence, interaction, interplay, exchange, alternation, equivalence.

adj. correlative, reciprocal, reciprocating, mutual, relative, corresponding, equivalent, interchangeable.

vb. correlate, interrelate, interconnect, interplay, interact, reciprocate, correspond, alternate.

adv. correlatively, mutually, reciprocally, alternately.

13 identity

n. identity, identicalness, oneness, sameness, selfsameness, equality, unity, homogeneity, uniformity, invariability, interchangeability.

adj. same, identical, one, very, constant, invariable, unchangeable, unvarying, homogeneous; like, alike, indistinguishable; equivalent, duplicate, equal, twin.

vb. be identical, coincide, coalesce, equate; not distinguish, not know from Adam.

14 absolute difference

n. contrariety, inequality, inequity, contrariness, oppositeness, adverseness; incompatibility, irreconcilability; contradiction, inconsistency, polarity, antithesis.

adj. contrary, different, contrasting, inconsistent, contradictory, mutually exclusive, opposite, reverse, diametrical, adverse, opposing.

vb. be contrary, differ, contrast, contradict, oppose, go against the grain; clash.

adv. on the other hand, on the contrary, contrariwise, conversely, in the opposite way.

15 variance

n. variance, difference, variation, unlikeness, heterogeneity, diversity; disparity, deviation, divergence, deflection, discrepancy, disagreement; differentiation, discrimination.

variant, irregularity, special case.

adj. different, unlike, unidentical, dissimilar, variable, changeable, varying, variant; heterogeneous, diverse, indiscriminate; changed, modified; contrasting, incongruous, contrary, deviating, divergent, disparate, incompatible.

vb. differ, vary, change, modify; diverge, deviate; differentiate, discriminate, distinguish.

16 uniformity

n. uniformity, homogeneity, constancy, sameness, invariability, stability, regularity; symmetry, evenness, unity, congruity; conformity; monotony, routine, ritual, standardization, stereotype.

adj. uniform, homogeneous, same, consistent, invariable, steady, stable, regular, symmetrical, even, unchanging, unvarying; monotonous, routine, standardized, stereotyped.

vb. be uniform, accord, conform; make uniform, characterize, standardize, normalize, level, smooth.

17 non-uniformity

n. non-uniformity, heterogeneity, inconstancy, variability, diversity, instability, irregularity, asymmetry, unevenness, disunity, incongruity.

adj. non-uniform, heterogeneous, inconsistent, variable, diversified, motley, unsteady, irregular, asymmetrical, uneven, changing, varying, incongruous.

18 similarity

n. similarity, likeness, resemblance, affinity, analogy, similitude; disguise, camouflage; correlation, comparison,

equivalent, correspondence; counterpart.

adj. similar, like, alike, resembling, twin, analogous, à la, equivalent, typical, representative; lifelike, realistic, faithful, true, exact, simulating, imitative; camouflaged, disguised, mock.

vb. be similar, look like, seem, pass for, take after, approximate; liken, assimilate to, imitate; answer to the description of.

19 dissimilarity

n. dissimilarity, difference, unlikeness, dissimulation, diversity, disparity; variety, variation.

adj. dissimilar, different, unlike, disparate, incongruent; atypical; unrealistic, inexact.

vb. be unlike, differ from, bear no resemblance, have nothing in common with.

20 imitation

n. imitation, imitativeness, copying, representation, portrayal, mimicry, impersonation, caricature, parody; simulation, patterning; likeness, replica, reflection, portrait, echo, copy, reprint, facsimile, counterpart; translation, paraphrase, interpretation; cribbing, plagiarism; counterfeit, forgery, fake, sham.

imitator, simulator, ape, copycat (*inf.*), parrot, conformist, sheep, mimic, impersonator; translator, paraphraser, interpreter; plagiarist; forger, counterfeiter, faker.

adj. imitative, apish, parrot-like, counterfeit, pseudo-, sham, fake, mock, phoney (*sl.*); modelled on, based on.

vb. imitate, emulate, portray, depict, represent, simulate, do likewise, take after, follow suit, take a leaf out of someone's book; parrot, take off (*inf.*), send up (*inf.*), mimic, parody, caricature; repeat, mirror; pretend, disguise; copy, quote, reproduce, paraphrase, translate; crib, plagiarize; counterfeit, fake.

21 non-imitation

n. originality, creation, creativeness, inventiveness, ingenuity, independence, newness, novelty, individuality, authenticity, genuineness; real thing.

adj. unimitative, uncopied, underived, authentic, primary, genuine, creative, inventive, original, independent, first hand, incomparable, unique, rare, exceptional.

22 copy

n. copy, reprint, facsimile, reproduction, transcript, translation, paraphrase, interpretation, crib, forgery; semblance; study, representation, portrait, echo; parody, caricature, travesty; counterpart, duplicate, replica, reflection, likeness, impression, dummy, cast, tracing, model, transfer; analogue, correlate.

23 prototype

n. prototype, archetype, type, primitive form, original; precedent, first occurrence; principle, basis, standard, pattern, frame of reference, criterion; blueprint, design, plan, example, instance, illustration; dummy, mockup; model, poser, sitter, mannequin; die, stamp, mould, shell, negative, plate, mint.

vb. be an example, set an example; act as a mould; model for, sit, pose; typify, exemplify.

24 agreement

n. agreement, understanding, harmony, unity, integration, uniformity, unanimity, consensus, unison, accord, concord, correspondence, concurrence, consonance; coincidence, congruity; reconciliation, sympathy; treaty, contract.

adj. agreeing, like-minded, unanimous, agreed, corresponding, conforming, concurrent, coinciding, concerted, harmonious, unifying, consonant, concurring, united, collective, undisputed, in step, in concert, of one accord, with one voice, sympathetic, reconcilable, compatible, consistent.

vb. agree, concur, assent, accord, tally, harmonize, match, reconcile, coincide, correspond, fit in with, dovetail, square with, synchronize, adapt, adjust, go hand in hand with, say yes to, see eye to eye, get along with, get on with, click (*inf.*), hit it off (*inf.*); keep in with (*inf.*), keep on the right side of (*inf.*).

see also **643, 699**

25 disagreement

n. disagreement, discord, misunderstanding, division, tension, dissidence, argument, dispute, contention, quarrel, disunion, dissension, strife; discrepancy, dissonance, dissimilarity, disparity, incongruence.

adj. disagreeing, differing, disputing, contradictory, inconsistent, incongruous, out of character, disproportionate, at odds, at variance, at loggerheads, out of step; hostile, inimical, factious, dissenting, non-conformist.

vb. disagree, object, not accept, say no to, speak against, contradict, defy, reject; oppose, fight, quarrel, dispute, come into conflict with, come up against; not conform, be contrary to.

see also **642**

C Quantity

26 quantity

n. quantity, amount, number, sum, extent, scope, expanse, size, dimensions, measure; length, breadth, width, height, depth, volume, capacity, area; mass, bulk, weight; mouthful, handful, spoonful, dose, portion, lot, batch, deal, whole, heaps (*inf.*), masses (*inf.*), load (*inf.*), abundance, profusion, greatness, magnitude, largeness.

adj. quantitative, quantified, measured, some, any.

vb. quantify, measure.
see also 32

27 relative quantity

n. degree, level, grade, point, stage, measure, rate, proportion, ratio, scale, measure, standard, comparison, criterion; extent, scope, range, intensity, frequency, size, speed, shade, nuance, tint; gradation, graduation, calibration, measurement.

adj. graded, graduated, calibrated, measured, scaled, comparative, proportional, relative; gradual, tapering, shading off, fading.

vb. graduate, grade, measure, calibrate; compare, rank, classify; taper off, shade off, fade, narrow, reduce, lessen, thin out.

adv. gradually, in stages, little by little, step by step.

28 equality

n. equality, parity, uniformity, sameness, equivalence, equalization, equation, adjustment, equilibrium, balance, symmetry, steadiness, synonymity, six of one and half a dozen of the other (*inf.*), six and two threes (*inf.*).

equivalent, draw, tie, dead heat, stalemate, no decision; counterpart, opposite number, equal, complement, twin, double, peer; synonym.

adj. equal, equivalent, equilateral, regular, symmetrical, fifty-fifty, on equal terms, even, level, flush, parallel, reciprocal, uniform, comparable, commensurate, proportionate, coextensive, tantamount, synonymous.

vb. be equal, agree with, coincide, suffice, rank with, match, rival, meet, touch, live up to, measure up to, come up to, be the equivalent of, keep pace with, come to the same thing, go halves; tie, draw, balance.

equalize, make equal, adjust, square.

29 inequality

n. inequality, disparity, non-uniformity, unlikeness, disproportion, dissimilarity, deviation, divergence, dissemblance, inferiority, shortcoming, deficiency; unevenness, imbalance, lopsidedness, unsteadiness.

adj. unequal, disparate, non-uniform, uneven, odd, inferior, deficient, insufficient, inadequate; disproportionate, lopsided, top-heavy, crooked, overbalanced.

vb. be unequal, outclass, outstrip, have the advantage, fall short of, not come up to, not hold a candle to (*inf.*).

30 mean

n. average, mean, golden mean, medium, happy medium, median, balance, norm, par, middle term, middle point, midpoint, centre, halfway, middle, compromise.

adj. mean, average, median, middle, grey, intermediate, halfway, lukewarm, middling, fair to middling, medium; typical; mediocre, run of the mill.

vb. average out, take the average, split the difference, strike a balance, go halfway.

31 compensation

n. compensation, weighting, equalization, balance, counterbalance, ballast, allowance, amends, costs, damages, remuneration, reimbursement, indemnification, indemnity, reparation, restitution, recompense, repayment, refund, offset, satisfaction, atonement, requital.

adj. compensatory, indemnificatory, restitutory, balancing.

vb. compensate, make amends, balance, neutralize, equalize, counterbalance, counteract, overcompensate, pay costs, indemnify, remunerate, recompense, reimburse, redeem, refund, recoup, satisfy, make up for, make reparation, allow for, set off, offset, take back.

32 greatness

n. greatness, largeness, bigness, vastness, enormity, immenseness, magnitude, size, bulk; spaciousness; might, mightiness, power, strength, intensity; amplitude, fullness, plenitude.

great quantity, profusion, abundance, masses, lots, quantities, oodles (*inf.*), stacks (*inf.*); excess, redundance, superfluity, superabundance.

adj. big, large, great, considerable, numerous, massive, enormous, vast, colossal, huge, sizeable; tall, lofty, high, towering; strong, mighty, powerful, energetic; ample, plentiful, abundant, profuse, plenteous, copious; noble, sublime, high, stately, exalted; remarkable, notable, unspeakable; extensive, far-reaching, widespread, prevalent, sweeping, universal, worldwide; marvellous, exceptional, surpassing, wonderful, overwhelming, unbelievable, stupendous, astounding.

vb. be great, be big, be large; mount,

soar, tower, exceed, rise above, transcend.

adv. enormously, vastly, highly, on a big scale, in a big way; heavily, strongly, mightily, powerfully, actively; greatly, very, much, in a great measure, extremely, exceedingly, considerably; plenteously, plentifully, abundantly, immeasurably, unspeakably, ineffably, awfully (*inf.*), tremendously; excessively, inordinately, immoderately; unbelievably, exceptionally.

see also 75

33 smallness

n. smallness, littleness, tininess, diminutiveness, minuteness; shortness, slightness, slenderness; meagreness, scantiness, paucity, scarcity, fewness, sparseness, rareness.

small quantity, dash, trace, *soupçon*, shade, morsel, crumb, iota, jot, tittle; point, dot, spot, fleck, speck, grain, atom, particle, modicum, chip, flake, shred, bit, rag, fragment, trifle.

adj. small, little, diminutive, minimal, infinitesimal, imperceptible, tiny, minute, miniature; slim, slender, thin, slight, scanty, meagre, insufficient, few, sparse, rare, inconsiderable, minor, trifling; modest, poor, pitiful.

adv. slightly, little, to a small extent, faintly, on a small scale, in a small way; humbly, modestly; scarcely, hardly, barely, pitifully.

see also 76

34 superiority

n. superiority, supremacy, dominance, transcendence, excellence, perfection, nobility, sublimity, eminence, pre-eminence; advantage, privilege, prerogative, favour, upper hand, head start, start.

superior, better, elder, master, overlord, chief, boss, **management**, senior, top dog (*inf.*).

adj. superior, eminent, upper, higher, greater, major; better, preferred, surpassing, exceeding; supreme, pre-eminent, greatest; first, chief, principal, main, capital, leading, mainline, cardinal, paramount; best, excellent, superlative, first-class, matchless, unrivalled, unsurpassed, beyond compare.

vb. be superior, rise above, tower, transcend, exceed, excel, surpass, eclipse, top, cap, overshadow, outmatch, get the better of, lord it over; prevail, predominate; have the advantage, have the edge on (*inf.*).

adv. eminently, superlatively, prominently, above all, *par excellence*, principally, especially, particularly.

35 inferiority

n. inferiority, deficiency, imperfection, shortcoming; mediocrity, poorness; lowliness, subordination, subjection, back seat (*inf.*).

inferior, subordinate, servant, slave, junior, auxiliary, accessory, workers, poor relation, underdog (*inf.*).

adj. inferior, low, lower, junior, minor, lesser, subordinate, secondary, accessory, auxiliary, ancillary, unclassified; lowly, humble, menial, subject, obedient; deficient, mediocre, substandard, imperfect, worse, worst, common, below par, not a patch on (*inf.*).

vb. be inferior, fall short of, not come up to, not compare with, not come near, want, lack, not hold a candle to (*inf.*); take a back seat (*inf.*).

see also 571

36 increase

n. increase, rise, augmentation, growth, progression, development, spread, proliferation, build-up, prolon-

gation, extension, expansion, enlargement, escalation, magnification, heightening, swelling, incorporation, merger, cumulative effect, snowball (*inf.*).

adj. increasing, rising, growing, progressing, developing, proliferating, expanding, escalating, enlarging, intensifying, cumulative, crescent.

vb. increase, grow, rise, gain; thrive, flourish; multiply, enlarge, magnify, amplify, aggrandize; develop, escalate, boost, build, build up, expand, swell, add, compound, upsurge, strengthen, intensify, accumulate, accrue, snowball (*inf.*); prolong, lengthen, broaden, widen, thicken, deepen, heighten; enhance; exacerbate, aggravate.

37 decrease

n. decrease, decline, fall, drop, reduction, wane, restriction, restraint, curtailment, paring, pruning, squeeze; fade-out, regression, depression, depreciation, shortening.

adj. decreasing, falling, declining, reducing, dwindling, fading, on the wane.

vb. decrease, lessen, fall, drop, diminish, moderate, subside, decline, abate, recede, dwindle, wane, shrink, ebb, drain away, tail off; peter out, taper off; deteriorate; reduce, restrain, limit, check, curb, curtail, cut back, economize, consume, use up, shorten, trim, squeeze, compress, erode, dilute, quell.

38 numeration

n. numeration, numbering, enumeration, counting, count, census, figuring, reckoning, calculation, computation; mathematics, arithmetic, algebra, geometry, trigonometry, calculus, analysis; addition, subtraction, multiplication, division; statistics, figures, data, tables, measurements; abacus, ready reckoner, computer, electronic brain, microprocessor, calculator; addend, subtrahend, product, quotient.

adj. numerable, countable, calculable, computable, statistical, numbered, mathematical, arithmetical, algebraical, geometrical, analytical.

vb. number, count, tell, score, tally, cast, enumerate, poll; calculate, add, total, subtract, multiply, divide, compute, figure, work out, reckon, estimate; inventorize, list; classify; measure.

39 number

n. number, numeral, figure, digit, cipher, integer, whole number, prime number, symbol, character, sign, notation; function, variable, expression, formula; fraction, denominator, numerator, decimal, power, root.

adj. numerical, arithmetical, even, odd, prime, whole, positive, negative, rational, irrational, transcendental, exponential, integral, digital, decimal, binary; multiple, reciprocal, fractional.

40 addition

n. addition, summation, total; increase, enlargement, annexation, accession, accretion, accruing, supplement; prefixion, suffixion, affixation.

adj. additional, additive, adopted, extra, new, further, added, fresh, other, extraneous, accessory, auxiliary, supplementary.

vb. add, add up, sum, total; append, annex, attach, tack on, clap on (*inf.*), slap on (*inf.*), join, insert, contribute, supplement, increase, accumulate; accrue; affix, suffix, prefix, infix.

adv. in addition, moreover, furthermore, further, besides, as well, also, additionally, extra, and, too, over and above, in conjunction with.

41 thing added

n. adjunct, addition, attachment, fixture, extension, accretion, accession, accessory, appurtenance, increment, rise, interest, bonus, contribution, supplement; qualification, rider; annexe, wing; *addendum,* appendix, appendage, postscript, note; prefix, suffix, infix.

42 subtraction

n. subtraction, deduction, removal, withdrawal, curtailment, reduction, decrease, outback, deletion, discount; amputation; abbreviation.

vb. subtract, deduct, take away, detract from, remove, exclude, withdraw, withhold, cut back; unload, unpack; shorten, abbreviate, delete; sever, amputate.

adv., prep. minus, without, with the exception of, bar, excepting, save.

43 thing subtracted

n. deduction, decrement, cut, decrease, reduction, rebate, discount, allowance, credit, depreciation, remission, forfeit, write-off; loss, shortcoming, defect.

44 remainder

n. remainder, rest, remnant, vestige, remains, residue, relic, hangover; result; balance, surplus, excess, margin; left-overs, waste, garbage, rejects, salvage, debris, sediment, dregs, slag, scum, leavings, clippings, crumbs, pairings, trimmings, castoffs.

adj. remaining, left, left over, over, residual, surviving; outstanding, carried over; surplus, unused, spare, to spare, superfluous; outcast.

45 mixture

n. mixture, mingling, combination, fusion, infusion, amalgamation, merger, integration; adulteration, transfusion.

blend, compound, composite, composition, conglomeration, amalgam, alloy, tincture, admixture; medley, miscellany, patchwork, pastiche, jumble, tangle, pot-pourri, *mélange*, mishmash, gallimaufry; hybrid, mongrel.

adj. mixed, composite, fused, merged, combined, united, amalgamated, half-and-half; stirred, blended, heterogeneous, adulterated, hybrid, mongrel; miscellaneous, assorted, motley, varied, jumbled, hotch-potch.

vb. mix, mix up, join, fuse, alloy, merge, combine, unite, amalgamate, conjoin, mingle, intermingle, stir, transfuse, shake, scramble; adulterate, water down; jumble; be mixed, permeate, infect, infiltrate; interbreed, cross with.

46 freedom from mixture

n. simpleness, purity, homogeneity, simplicity, plainness, purification, sifting, elimination.

adj. simple, pure, clean, clear, plain, uniform, absolute, homogeneous, uncomplicated, unadulterated, unqualified; mere, only, sheer.

vb. simplify, purify, unmix, unscramble, disentangle, eliminate, sift, winnow.

47 junction

n. junction, joining, connection, union, reunion, contact, tying, fastening, coupling, merging, fusion, bonding, marriage, concatenation; assemblage, structure, tie-up.

adj. joined, connected, linked, coupled, allied, married, wed, attached, fixed, secure, tied, hooked, stuck, firm, fast, close, rooted; tight, inextricable, inseparable; united, together, whole.

vb. join, attach, fix, stick on, affix, bolt, nail, screw; connect, link, make contact, span, bridge; put together, merge, fuse, combine, marry, juxtapose, cement; secure, tie, hook, couple, fasten, bind, splice, yoke, harness, knit, string, tether, clamp, clinch, twist; assemble, confederate, band together; dovetail, fit, set; unite, become one, meet, converge; unify, associate, ally with.

48 separation

n. separation, disconnection, dissociation, disjoining, detachment, segregation, disunion, disengagement, removal, withdrawal, dislocation, dismemberment, severance, division, cut, parting, divorce; dissolution, integration, break-up, dissection, breakdown, analysis; rupture, fracture, cleavage; burst, puncture, blowout.

adj. disjoined, discontinuous, unattached, unconnected; separable, detachable, divisible; apart, distinct, discrete, detached, divorced, isolated, alone, broken, fractured, in pieces, interrupted, torn, rent, cut, split, dismembered.

vb. separate, part, disunite, detach, disengage, break away, set apart, keep apart, disconnect, partition, demarcate, hive off, divide, subdivide, dissociate, divorce, isolate; disintegrate, decompose; fracture, rupture, break, fragment; unravel, disentangle; uncouple, unhitch, dislocate, unbind, loose, free, set free, release; tear, undo, rend; cut, dissect, hew, fell, reap, dice, chop, snip, slit, split, burst, puncture, sever, saw, chip, dissect, behead, carve; distribute, disperse; diverge; decollate.

49 bond

n. bond, link, connection, channel, passage, bridge; line, cable, string, rope, cord, chain, thread, ribbon, band, bandage, ligature, strip, girdle, belt, harness, lace, braid, tie, plait; knot, fastening, zip, hook, hook and eye, nut, bolt, screw, clasp, coupling; joint, junction, nexus, node, weld, seam, splice, swivel, hinge; adhesive, fixative, glue, paste, cement, epoxy, sticky tape.

50 coherence

n. coherence, cohesion, cohesiveness, consistency, adhesiveness; continuity, attachment, solidarity, inseparability, indivisibility.

adj. cohesive, adhesive, sticky, clinging, tenacious; inseparable, indivisible, inextricable, close, compact, solid.

vb. cohere, hold, hold fast, hold together; congregate; fit tight; adhere, stick, cleave, cling, fasten, unite, glue, gum, paste, weld, solder; hug, embrace, grasp, clasp, grip, clinch.

see also 332

51 incoherence

n. incoherence, non-coherence, non-adhesion, separability, divisibility, looseness, laxity.

adj. non-adhesive, slippery, loose, disconnected, lax, runny, inconsistent.

vb. unstick, unglue, detach, disjoin, disunite, peel off; come unstuck, fall apart, shake.

52 combination

n. combination, coalescence, fusion, mixture, synthesis, amalgamation, merger, integration, union, incorporation, embodiment, association, affiliation.

adj. combined, linked, integrated, connected, synchronized, harmonious, unified.

vb. combine, join, link, integrate, fuse, put together, merge, consolidate,

unify, compound, group, incorporate, embody, coalesce, amalgamate; mix, blend, absorb; harmonize, synchronize; affiliate, cooperate, work together; kill two birds with one stone; make the best of both worlds, have one's cake and eat it.

see also 639

53 decomposition

n. decomposition, resolution, dissolution, analysis, breakdown, disintegration; decentralization; destruction; decay, putrefaction, corrosion, rottenness, putrescence, mould, rot, blight, mildew.

adj. decomposed, rotten, off, bad, rancid.

vb. decompose, resolve, break down, analyse, reduce, simplify, dissolve, dissect, atomize; decentralize, disband; disintegrate, break up; degenerate, waste away, decay, erode, corrode, rust, rot.

see also 588

54 whole

n. wholeness, completeness, entirety, totality, unity, comprehensivity, inclusiveness, panorama, catch-all; all, everyone, everybody, everything, total, whole, aggregate, sum, ensemble.

adj. whole, all, every, entire, full, complete, single, integral, total, universal, aggregate, gross, outright, inclusive, undivided, indivisible, inseparable, indissoluble; comprehensive, all-inclusive, all-embracing, sweeping, extensive, widespread, far-reaching, omnibus, wholesale, indiscriminate, blanket, catch-all, compendious, encyclopedic; intact, solid, perfect, safe, good, unbroken, undamaged, unblemished, unimpaired, flawless.

adv. wholly, entirely, completely,

altogether, a hundred per cent, all in all.

55 part

n. part, portion, share, cut, division, section, sector, segment, compartment, department, class, group, family, branch; genus, phylum; piece, fragment, bit, scrap; detail; splinter, sliver, chip, chunk, lump, wedge, slice; instalment, part payment, foretaste, down-payment, deposit; excerpt, extract; constituent, component, factor, element, member, ingredient, integral part; aspect, facet, feature.

adj. in parts, fragmentary, broken, in bits and pieces, defective; partial, incomplete, half-finished; constituent, integral, inherent, built-in, inclusive.

vb. part, divide, separate, allot, share.

adv. partly, piecemeal, in part, bit by bit.

see also 73, 717

56 completeness

n. completeness, wholeness, fullness, plenitude, saturation, one's fill, replenishment, refill; entirety, universality, comprehensivity, nothing lacking, nothing to add, integration; perfection, integrity, soundness; last touch, finish.

adj. complete, full, utter, entire, whole, plenary, all, gross, replete; comprehensive, exhaustive; absolute, extreme, thorough, thoroughgoing, radical, sweeping, wholesale, unqualified, unconditional; integral, perfect; abounding, profuse, brimful, saturated, swamped, drowned, sated, laden.

vb. be complete, come to maturity, culminate; overflow, bulge; make complete, consummate, add, perfect; conclude, fulfil; fill, replenish, top up, soak, overwhelm, saturate, swamp, drown; cloy, glut, gorge, sate, cram, pack, stuff.

adv. completely, wholly, entirely, fully, utterly, perfectly, altogether, quite, undividedly, exclusively, absolutely, out and out; hook, line, and sinker; with a vengeance, from beginning to end.

see also 659

57 incompleteness

n. incompleteness, defectiveness, deficiency, shortcoming, deficit, shortage, shortfall, omission, defect, want, need, lack, break, decrease.

adj. incomplete, defective, imperfect, deficient, short, lacking, not enough, sparing, depleted; superficial, unfinished, half-done, under construction, in preparation, in progress; imperfect, sketchy, meagre, skimpy, scrappy, rough.

vb. be incomplete, lack, want.

adv. incompletely, partially, imperfectly, inadequately.

see also 660

58 composition

n. composition, constitution, organization, make-up; nature, character, condition, quality, personality; design, pattern; compilation.

vb. constitute, compose, form, make up, comprise, consist, comprehend, include, incorporate, belong to, be a component of; arrange, mix, organize, systematize, construct, compile, assemble, devise, design, plan, write.

59 unity

n. unity, oneness, wholeness, homogeneity, unification, integration, uniqueness, singularity, individuality, singleness, isolation, solitude, indivisibility.

unit, item, bit, piece, one, point,

entity, whole, entirety; assembly, system.

adj. one, singular, individual, peculiar, specific, special; sole, single, only, unique, unprecedented, unequalled, *sui generis,* indivisible; lone, alone, lonely, lonesome, homeless, rootless, on one's own, single-handed, unaccompanied.

60 accompaniment

n. accompaniment, togetherness, concomitance, coexistence, society, association, partnership, cooperation, fellowship.

concomitant, accessory, adjunct, attachment, appendage, belongings, appurtenance, attendant, complement; satellite; *sine qua non;* coincidence; consequence.

adj. accompanying, concomitant, coexistent, attendant, accessory, connected, related, associated, belonging, attending, coincidental, incidental, ancillary; contemporary, concurrent, synchronous, simultaneous; symptomatic; united.

vb. accompany, be found with, exist with, happen with, coexist, belong, characterize, coincide, be connected with, go hand in hand, go together, be related, follow.

adv. together, hand in hand, collectively.

61 duality

n. duality, dualism, doubleness, double-sidedness; two, deuce, pair, couple, couplet, twosome, tandem.

adj. dual, duple, dualistic, binary, both, twin, paired, duplex, bilateral, bipartite, bipartisan, bi-.

vb. pair, couple, match, mate, dualize; combine.

62 duplication

n. duplication, doubling, reduplication, repetition, iteration, encore, copy.

adj. double, duplicate, twofold, twin, second.

vb. double, repeat, twin, duplicate, reduplicate, copy.

adv. twice, again, once more.

63 bisection

n. bisection, halving, forking, bifurcation; half, hemisphere, dichotomy; dividing line, equator.

adj. bisected, half, bifurcated, semi-, demi-, hemi-.

vb. bisect, halve, cut in two, divide, split, sunder, bifurcate; go halves; diverge, fork.

64 triality

n. triality, trinity; three, triad, threesome, trio, triplet, trilogy, triangle.

adj. three, tertiary, tripartite, trilateral, triangular, triplex, triform, tri-; triune.

65 triplication

n. triplication, triplicity, hat trick.

adj. treble, threefold, triplicate, third.

vb. treble, triple, triplicate.

66 trisection

n. trisection, tripartition, third, trichotomy.

vb. trisect, cut in three.

67 quaternity

n. quaternity; four, tetrad; square, quadrilateral, quadrangle; quartet, foursome, quadruplet, tetragon.

adj. four, quaternary, quaternal; quadratic, biquadratic, square, quadrilateral, quadri-, tetra-.

68 quadruplication

n. quadruplication, quadruplicity.

adj. fourfold, quadruplicate, fourth, quadruple.

vb. quadruple, quadruplicate.

69 quadrisection

n. quadrisection, quadripartition; fourth, quarter, quart.

vb. quadrisect, quarter, cut in four.

70 five and over

n. five, fiver, pentad, quintuplet, pentagon, quintet, quincunx, Pentateuch; six, half a dozen, hexad, sextuplet, hexagon, sextet; seven, heptad, septuplet, heptagon, septet; eight, octad, octagon, octet, octave; nine, ennead, nonagon, enneagon, nonet; ten, decade, decagon; double figures; eleven, endecagon; twelve, dozen, dodecagon; thirteen, baker's dozen; teens; twenty, score; hundred, century, centenary; three figures, treble figures; gross; thousand, grand, millenium; ten thousand, myriad; million; billion; trillion.

adj. five, quintuple; six, sextuple; seven, septuple; eight, octuple; ten, decimal; twelve, duodecimal; -fold.

71 multisection

n. multisection, quinquesection.

vb. multisect, quinquesect.

72 plurality

n. plurality, plural, number, multiplicity, variety, abundance, some; majority.

adj. plural, pluralistic, pluralistical, multiple, many, some, numerous; more.

73 fraction

n. fraction, fragment, part, section, portion, segment.

adj. fractional, partial, fragmentary, constituent, sectional.

see also 55, 717

74 zero

n. zero, nil, nought; nothingness, nullity, void; nothing, none, no one, nobody; no score, duck, love.

adj. zero, null, not one.

75 multitude

n. multitude, numerosity, multiplicity; great amount, quantity, lot; great number, hundreds, thousands, myriads, millions; crowd, mob, army, throng, flock, legion, host, posse; plenty, a great deal, abundance, profusion, bonanza (*inf.*); majority, main part, mass, bulk, main emphasis, weight.

adj. many, not a few, several, considerable, numerous, manifold, countless, legion; much, sufficient, enough, ample, galore (*inf.*); profuse, abundant, overflowing, prevalent, plentiful; crowded, populous, peopled; dense, teeming with, alive with, thick.

vb. be many, crowd with, throng with, flock, mass, swarm with, teem with, crawl with; overflow with; pack, stuff; outnumber.

76 fewness

n. fewness, paucity, scarcity, sparseness, thinness, rarity; a few, handful, smattering, sprinkling; remnant, minority, insufficiency, absence, lack.

adj. few, not many, sparse, scant, thin, inconsiderable, negligible, infrequent, few and far between.

vb. diminish, reduce, lessen; lack, need.

77 repetition

n. repetition, recurrence, repetitiveness, reappearance; reproduction, copy, duplication; renewal, resumption; reiteration, rehearsal, recapitulation.

repeat, encore, replay; reprint, reissue, rehash.

adj. repeated, reiterated, restated, reworded, retold; reproduced, remade, redone, copied; repetitious, repetitive, boring.

vb. repeat, reiterate, restate, reword, retell, iterate; recite, say after, echo; rehearse, go over, take it from the top (*inf.*); recapitulate; redo, remake, renew, rework, remodel; rehash, revive; reissue, republish, copy; reoccur, reappear.

adv. again, over again, anew; ditto, encore; repeatedly.

78 infinity

n. infinity, endlessness, limitlessness; eternity; infinitude, perpetuity.

adj. infinite, immense, vast, untold, boundless, endless, immeasurable, unexhaustible, interminable; countless, numberless, unnumbered; eternal, perpetual.

vb. go on and on, know no bounds.

adv. infinitely, *ad infinitum*, without end.

D Order

79 order

n. order, organization, arrangement, array, state of order; tidiness, orderliness, neatness; method, pattern, regularity, system; uniformity, routine, habit; discipline.

adj. orderly, organized, methodical, systematic, regular, harmonious; under control, businesslike; neat, tidy, shipshape, well-ordered.

vb. order, organize, harmonize; take shape, fall into place.

adv. in order, all right, all correct, O.K., orderly, systematically, methodically.

80 disorder

n. disorder, disarrangement, muddle, clutter, mess, disarray, disharmony, disorderliness, untidiness; chaos, crisis; confusion, disturbance, shambles, Bedlam, mix-up.

turmoil, tumult, turbulence, agitation, to-do, ferment, storm, upheaval, *mêlée*, *fracas*, uproar, hullabaloo, frenzy, row, riot; anarchy, unruliness.

adj. orderless, out of order, unorganized, disorganized, in disarray, out of order, untidy; unsystematic, unmethodical, irregular, non-uniform; incoherent, muddled, confused, mixed up (*inf.*), disconnected; chaotic; tumultuous, turbulent; anarchical, lawless.

adv. confusedly, anyhow, irregularly, in disorder, higgledy-piggledy, upside down.

81 arrangement

n. arrangement, ordering, reduction to order, composition, preparation, organization, reorganization, regulation, marshalling, disposal, distribution; plan, method, system.

adj. arranged, well-arranged, ordered, organized, well-organized, methodical, regular, systematic, well-regulated, classified, sorted; coordinated, connected, disposed; disciplined; disentangled, unravelled, straightened out.

vb. arrange, plan, prepare, compose, put in order, set in order, reduce to order, array, dispose; assign, set, establish, formulate, coordinate, line up, regulate, marshal, range; organize, systematize, standardize, formalize, coordinate, connect; collocate; classify, pattern; disentangle, unravel, untwist, uncoil, straighten out; put one's own house in order.

82 disarrangement

n. disarrangement, derangement, disorganization, dishevelment, discomposure; irregularity, tangle, entanglement.

adj. disarranged, discomposed, disorganized, disorderly.

vb. disturb, disorganize, disorder, jumble, shuffle, mix up, muddle, derange, upset, unsettle; agitate, disconcert, discompose; ruffle, dishevel; confuse, perturb, confound, trouble; disperse, scatter; destroy, disrupt, dislocate; disband; overturn, overthrow; stir up, put the cat among the pigeons (*inf.*).

83 list

n. list, enumeration, classification, record, register, catalogue, directory, file; statement, schedule, agenda, table; roll, roll-call; roster, rota; enrolment; inventory, stock list, checklist; programme, prospectus, syllabus, synopsis; index, table of contents, bibliography, thesaurus, dictionary, glossary, lexicon.

vb. list, enumerate, catalogue, itemize, classify; enter, register, book, inscribe, record, file, log; enrol, enlist, matriculate; schedule.

84 precedence

n. precedence, antecedence, priority, precedency, previousness; coming before, anteriority; pre-eminence, precedent, preference, superiority.

adj. preceding, precedent, antecedent, anterior; previous, earlier, former, foregoing, prior, aforementioned.

vb. come before, go before, go ahead, precede, have precedence, take pre-

cedence; lead, be in front, head, place before; herald, pioneer, forerun, blaze the trail (*inf.*), clear the way, show the way, set the fashion; preface, introduce, prelude, preamble, usher in.

adv. before, in advance, above.

85 sequence

n. sequence, going after, following, placement, succession; successiveness, consequence; order, series, progression, set, string, row, chain, train, flow, concatenation.

adj. following, succeeding, ensuing, resulting, subsequent, successive, consequent; next, later, posterior; sequential, consecutive, serial; connected.

vb. come after, go after, go behind; ensue, follow, result; place after, append; succeed, come next, supersede, displace, supplant, become heir to.

adv. after, afterwards, behind, subsequently.

86 precursor

n. precursor, predecessor; pioneer, herald, vanguard, scout, pathfinder, forerunner, harbinger; parent, ancestor, forbear.

precedent, antecedent; prelude, preliminary, introduction, prologue, foreword, preface, exordium, prolegomena, preamble; prefix; authoritative example; preparation.

adj. precursory, preliminary, prefatory, introductory; exploratory, preparatory.

87 sequel

n. sequel, consequence, effect, result, end, issue, outcome, upshot, aftermath; after-effect, by-product, spin-off; inference, deduction, conclusion; afterthought, second thoughts; follow-up; continuation, tail, tailpiece, supplé-

ment, postscript, epilogue, appendage;
suffix.

88 beginning

n. beginning, start, commencement,
outset, onset, outbreak; foundation,
establishment, origination, invention,
birth, origin, genesis, cause, source,
root, spring; infancy, primitiveness,
youth; starting-point, square one.

inauguration, initiation, début,
coming out, unveiling, *première*, opening, inception.

preliminaries, introduction, prelude,
foreword, preface; rudiments, first
principles, ABC, primer, basics.

adj. beginning, first, starting, initial,
maiden; introductory; precursory,
opening, inaugural; foundational, elementary, fundamental, basic, rudimentary; original, embryonic, primitive.

vb. begin, start, commence, go
ahead, make a beginning, make a start,
kick off (*inf.*); come into existence,
arise, break out, burst forth, rise, be
born, see the light of day; make one's
début, come out; undertake, do, set
about, tackle, enter upon, set in
motion, start up, get under way, start
the ball rolling, activate; take the first
step, break the ice; begin again, go
back to square one (*inf.*).

initiate, conceive, introduce, found,
establish, institute, inaugurate, open,
originate, invent.

adv. initially, in the first place, first,
ab initio, at the outset, to begin with,
for a kick-off (*inf.*).

see also 605

89 end

n. end, conclusion, close, termination, ending, finish, stop, cessation,
completion, closure, adjournment,
dissolution; expiration, death, decease,
demise; retirement; finale, swan song,

last word, death blow, curtains (*inf.*),
finis, end of the line (*inf.*).

extreme, extremity, terminus, terminal, furthest point, achievement;
consummation, perfection, culmination, climax, *dénouement;* goal, limit,
point, boundary, top, peak, summit,
head, bottom, base, tail; postscript,
epilogue, appendage.

adj. ending, final, last, ultimate,
terminal, concluding, consummate,
ended, settled, concluded; extreme.

vb. end, finish, stop, conclude,
terminate, cease, discontinue, desist,
refrain, come to an end; expire, breathe
one's last, die; run out, run its course,
come to a close, draw to a close, break
off; settle, determine, bring to an end,
put an end to, dispose of, suspend,
postpone, cancel, bring to a standstill,
arrest, quell; switch off, wind up; end
up.

adv. finally, lastly, at last, in
conclusion, ultimately.

see also 144

90 middle

n. middle, midpoint, centre, middle
distance, equidistance, halfway house;
pivot, heart, kernel, core; focus, focal
point; average, mean, median; midst,
thick of things.

adj. middle, centre, central, mid,
equidistant, halfway, medial, intermediate; focal; mean, average;
moderate, neutral, compromising.

adv. in the middle, midway, halfway,
in between.

91 continuity

n. continuity, continuousness, con-
secutiveness, progression, continuance,
one thing after another, constancy,
flow, succession, endlessness, perpetuation, perpetuity; routine, daily
round, monotony; sequence, queue,

crocodile, procession, march, cortège, column, train, suite, retinue, single file, tail, tailback.

adj. continuous, consecutive, running, serial, successive, progressive, constant, endless, perpetual, sustained, persisting, unbroken, uninterrupted; regular.

vb. continue, carry on, maintain, sustain, remain, succeed, follow in a line; file, march, parade, queue; endure.

adv. continuously, in succession, successively, in file, in train.

92 discontinuity

n. discontinuity, disconnectedness, disjunction; interruption, intervention, break, interval, intermission, pause, breather, rest, stop-over; gap, missing link.

adj. discontinuous, disconnected, unconnected, interrupted, broken; intermittent, irregular, infrequent, few and far between; spasmodic, jerky, uneven, desultory.

vb. discontinue, break, interrupt, pause, stop over; disconnect.

adv. at intervals, irregularly, in fits and starts, discontinuously.

see also 200

93 position in a series

n. term, serial position, order, rank, grade, station, position, situation, status, standing, footing, level, tier, rung, degree.

94 assemblage

n. assemblage, bringing together, juxtaposition, mobilization.

gathering, assembly, association, collection, company, society; circle, clique; meeting, reception, party; council, committee, conference, congress, commission, convention, congregation, convocation, symposium.

group, body, mass, crowd, throng, mob, crush, huddle, band, gang, troop, horde; team, cast, crew, squad; swarm, colony, herd, flock, pack, brood, shoal, school; set, cluster, bunch, lot, batch, bundle.

adj. gathered, assembled, met, convened; crowded, dense, swarming.

vb. gather, assemble, meet, come together, associate, congregate, converge, rendezvous; group, crowd, throng, rally, flock in, pour in; swarm, huddle, bunch; accumulate, pile up, amass; collect, bring together, call up, summon, convene, muster, round up.

95 dispersion

n. dispersion, dispersal, scattering, dissemination, broadcasting, dissipation, diffusion, divergence, decentralization.

adj. dispersed, scattered.

vb. disperse, scatter; disseminate, broadcast, sow, seed; sprinkle, strew, spread, dissipate; separate, divide; shed, distribute, propagate, dispense, dole out, dispel, diffuse, decentralize, disband; evaporate; sprawl, diverge.

96 focus

n. focus, focal point, centre; meeting place, forum, market, club, rendezvous; heart, hub, centre of interest, headquarters, nerve centre; Mecca, promised land.

vb. focus, converge, concentrate, centre, attract, draw attention.

see also 224

97 class

n. class, sort, kind, type, category, section, division, group, grouping, department, branch; mark, brand, make; strain, breed, line, family, genus, species, phylum, caste; hierarchy, rank.

classification, categorization, specification, taxonomy, systematization, list.

adj. classificatory, taxonomic.

vb. class, sort, classify, categorize, hierarchize, rank, grade, group, divide.

98 inclusion

n. inclusion, admission, reception, incorporation, embodiment, composition.

adj. inclusive, comprehensive, all-inclusive, all-embracing, overall, wholesale, sweeping.

vb. include, admit, incorporate, embody, comprehend, comprise, consist of, constitute, contain, involve, take in, entail, embrace, enclose, subsume.

99 exclusion

n. exclusion, exclusiveness; omission, rejection, ejection; prohibition, boycott, embargo, blockade; eviction, dismissal, suspension, expulsion, excommunication, ostracism, segregation, apartheid; bar, ban, closed shop, lock-out.

adj. exclusive, restrictive, segregated, prohibitive.

vb. exclude, omit, leave out, remove, eliminate, except, disregard; disqualify, reject, dismiss, suspend, deport, banish, expel, excommunicate, send to Coventry, ostracize; feel left out, feel out of things; restrict, forbid, prohibit, bar, segregate, ban, black, blacklist, boycott; prevent, preclude, obviate.

prep. except, excluding, apart from, save, bar.

100 extraneousness

n. extraneousness, foreignness; outsider, foreigner, alien, stranger,

immigrant, expatriot, migrant, emigrant, refugee; newcomer, guest, visitor; squatter, interloper, invader.

adj. extraneous, extrinsic, external, outward, outside; foreign, alien, strange, immigrant; exotic, imported, borrowed, adopted, introduced, naturalized; alienated, estranged.

101 generality

n. generality, universality; ubiquity; broadness; generalization, abstraction, observation, simplification, overview; average man, man in the street, everybody, every mother's son (*inf.*), all the world and his wife (*inf.*).

adj. general, overall, universal, global, catholic; worldwide, international, cosmopolitan; typical, representative, generic; broad, wide; comprehensive, widespread, ubiquitous, blanket, average.

vb. be general, prevail, predominate; generalize, expand, broaden; conclude, infer.

102 speciality

n. speciality, particularity, originality, individuality, peculiarity, distinctiveness, uniqueness, idiosyncrasy, characteristic.

particulars, specifications, details, minutiae.

adj. special, particular, peculiar, especial, distinct, unique, original, *sui generis*, individual, individualistic, characteristic, idiosyncratic; specific, precise.

vb. specify, define, particularize, itemize, designate, enumerate, go into detail; single out, isolate, put one's finger on (*inf.*).

103 rule

n. rule, regulation, law, direction,

instruction, ordinance, code, order, precept, norm, principle, maxim, proposition, formula, guide, criterion, model, standard, procedure, system, convention.

adj. regulated, normative, prescriptive; legislative; formulaic, conventional.

see also **626, 954**

104 diversity

n. diversity, variation, variousness, heterogeneity, multiformity, variability, difference; medley, mixture, variety, miscellany.

adj. diverse, diversified, various, manifold, heterogeneous, multifarious, motley, irregular; different, disparate, variable, changeable.

see also **45**

105 conformity

n. conformity, correspondence, congruity, consistency, coincidence, compatibility, agreement, affinity, resemblance, similarity, adjustment, acclimatization.

conformist, conventionalist, traditionalist, loyalist, conservative.

adj. conforming, agreeing, harmonious, corresponding, appropriate, applicable, consonant; similar, resembling, well-matched, conformable, adaptable, adjustable, compatible, consistent.

vb. conform, comply, agree, accord; accommodate, adapt, adjust, fit, suit, integrate, bend, square, accustom, acclimatize, harmonize, reconcile; follow, obey, observe, fall into line, toe the line, adhere to.

106 unconformity

n. unconformity, difference, contrast, dissimilarity, disagreement, inconsistency, incongruity, incompatibility; nonconformity, unorthodoxy, heresy, schism; eccentricity, peculiarity, unconventionality, abnormality, irregularity.

nonconformist, dissenter, rebel, angry young man, separatist, demonstrator, maverick; eccentric, crank; homosexual, queer (*sl.*), gay (*sl.*), lesbian.

adj. unconformable, different, dissimilar, inconsistent, incongruous, incompatible, inappropriate, inapplicable; nonconformist, unorthodox; heretical, dissident, unconventional, eccentric, peculiar, abnormal, irregular, unusual, unfamiliar.

E Time

107 time

n. time, duration, continuance, extent, life, span, season, date.

adj. temporal; dated.

vb. elapse, pass; continue, last; spend time, employ, fill, occupy oneself, use, what do with oneself, while away, idle, fritter, squander; happen, occur, transpire.

adv., prep. during, when, while, whilst, in the course of, throughout, in the process of; meanwhile, in the meantime, in the interim.

see also **109**

108 absence of time

n. timelessness, neverness, nothingness, eternity.

adv. never, at no time, never again, nevermore.

109 period

n. period, era, epoch, time, season, interval, phase, age, generation; term, span, spell, stint, stretch; cycle; second, minute, hour, day, week, fortnight, month, year, leap year, decade, decennium, jubilee, centenary, millenium, aeon.

adj. periodic, seasonal, recurring, recurrent, cyclic, regular.

110 course of time

n. course of time, lapse of time.

vb. elapse, pass, lapse; flow, proceed, run, fly.

see also 109

111 contingent duration

adv., prep. as long as, provisionally, for the present, for the time being.

112 long duration

n. lifetime, ages, eternity, month of Sundays (*inf.*), prolongation, permanence; endurance.

adj. long-term, long-standing, long-lasting, abiding, lasting, durable, permanent; enduring, steadfast, unyielding, persistent, surviving.

vb. last, endure, continue, stay, persist, remain, abide, never end, prevail, persevere; survive, outlive, outlast, outstay, live on, linger.

113 short duration

n. transience, ephemerality, evanescence, impermanence; brief period, flash in the pan (*inf.*), nine days' wonder (*inf.*).

adj. transient, transitory, brief, temporary, quick, short, short-term, momentary, short-lived; fading, passing, fleeting, cursory, ephemeral, evanescent, impermanent, perishable, before one can say Jack Robinson (*inf.*).

vb. be transient, pass, pass away, fly, fleet, flit, fade, vanish, disappear.

114 endless duration

n. perpetuity, endlessness, eternity, infinity, everlastingness, timelessness, immortality, constancy, endurance.

adj. perpetual, eternal, endless, interminable, continual, unceasing, incessant, unremitting, infinite ever-lasting, enduring, around-the-clock, timeless, ageless, immortal, incorruptible, imperishable; perennial.

vb. perpetuate, immortalize, eternalize, preserve, keep alive; never end, go on forever.

adv. always, forever, on and on, perpetually.

115 point of time

n. instantaneousness, suddenness, abruptness; instant, second, moment, flash, jiffy (*inf.*), twinkling, point of time.

adj. instantaneous, immediate, spontaneous, sudden, abrupt, prompt, punctual.

adv. instantaneously, instantly, immediately, at once, directly, forthwith, without delay, promptly, suddenly, abruptly, at the drop of a hat, on the spur of the moment.

116 chronometry

n. chronometry, horology, chronology, timing, timekeeping, dendrochronology; date, day, time; local time, summer time, daylight saving.

timepiece, timekeeper, chronometer, clock, alarm clock, digital clock, watch, wristwatch, digital watch, stopwatch, hour-glass, sun-dial, egg-timer; time-signal, pips, siren, hooter; calendar, schedule, timetable, diary, journal, register, almanac, chronicle, annals, log, memoirs.

adj. chronological, horological, temporal, horometrical, chronometrical.

vb. time, date; put the clocks back, put the clocks forward, set the alarm, wind up, keep time, gain, lose; clock in, clock out.

117 anachronism

n. anachronism, wrong date, misdating, mistiming, parachronism, prochronism.

adj. anachronistic, misdated, undated; early, beforehand; late, overdue.

vb. misdate, antedate, predate, postdate.

118 priority

n. priority, antecedence, anteriority, previousness; pre-existence, preoccurrence; precedent, antecedent, foretaste, preview.

adj. prior, earlier, before, preceding, previous, anterior, past, antecedent, ahead of; pre-existing; one-time, ex-, retired, former; foregoing, abovementioned, above, aforesaid.

vb. go before, come before, precede, forerun, antecede, herald.

see also **84, 124**

119 posteriority

n. posteriority, succession, subsequence; sequel, follower, successor.

adj. following, subsequent, later, after, coming after, next, posterior; designate, elect, to-be; consequential, resulting.

vb. come after, go after, succeed, ensue, follow, result.

see also **85, 123**

120 present time

n. contemporaneity; present time, present moment, present, the time being, this day and age, modern times, today.

adj. present, contemporary, modern, current, present-day, latest, newest, actual, contemporaneous, existent.

adv. now, at present, at the moment, today, nowadays, right now, at this moment in time.

121 different time

n. different time, not now, other time.

adv. not now, yesterday, earlier, tomorrow, later, sometime, sooner or later, at one time or other, at a different time.

122 synchronism

n. synchronism, simultaneousness, coexistence, concurrence, coincidence, contemporaneity; same age; contemporary, own generation, peers, fellows, year, class, set.

adj. synchronous, contemporary, concurrent, coincident, coexistent, simultaneous, contemporaneous; accompanying.

vb. synchronize, coexist, exist together, coincide; accompany.

adv. at the same time, simultaneously, concurrently, in phrase, in step.

123 future

n. futurity, future, tomorrow, time to come; prospect, fate; the shape of things to come; afterlife, world to come, next world, hereafter.

adj. future, later, coming, to come, approaching, unfolding, at hand; prospective, designate; imminent, impending; likely, expected, inevitable.

vb. lie in the future, be near, draw near, approach; impend, threaten.

adv. tomorrow, in the future, in the course of time, hereafter.

124 past

n. past, history, antiquity, prehistory, archaism; retrospection, memory; olden times, yesterday good old days (*inf.*).

adj. past, historical, ancient, prehis

toric, primitive, proto-; gone, bygone, lost, forgotten, no more; former, late, old, once, one-time, ex-, retired, sometime, erstwhile.

vb. be past, have run its course, have had its day (*inf.*), be a thing of the past.

adv. yesterday, formerly, in the past, ago, of old.

125 newness

n. newness, modernity, renovation, modernization, novelty, innovation.

fad, craze, passing fancy, vogue, fashion, the latest thing (*inf.*), all the rage (*inf.*), the last word (*inf.*), the in-thing (*inf.*); innovator, pioneer, leader, futurist, trendsetter, pacesetter, *avant-garde*, upstart, fledgling.

adj. modern, new, novel, current, topical, recent, original; contemporary, present-day, up-to-the-minute, up-to-date, brand-new, just out, hot off the press (*inf.*); newfangled (*inf.*); untraditional, in fashion, in vogue, stylish, chic, smart, modish, trendy (*inf.*), in (*inf.*), *à la mode, avant-garde;* advanced, forward-looking, progressive, ultra-modern, streamlined, futuristic, space-age; convenient, automatic, electronic; fresh, virgin, budding, inexperienced.

vb. modernize, bring up to date, adapt, renew, reissue, republish, refurbish, renovate, streamline, update; innovate.

adv. recently, newly, lately, afresh, anew, of late.

126 oldness

n. oldness, antiquity; obsolescence, extinction, decay, deterioration, decline; maturity, ripeness; tradition, footsteps; old age, senility, infirmity.

adj. old, archaic, prehistoric, antique, ancient, primitive, primeval,

aboriginal, extinct; time-worn, time-honoured, venerable, forgotten, antediluvian, distant, former, unrecorded, of earliest time; old-fashioned, antiquated, obsolete, obsolescent, outmoded, discarded, disused, unstylish, *passé*, out of date, old hat (*inf.*), out of fashion, behind the times, anachronistic, dated, outdated; traditional, handed down, established, customary, Victorian; dilapidated, secondhand, used, decrepit, decayed, faded; patched, mended, in holes, rusty, motheaten.

see also 30

127 morning; spring; summer

n. morning, morn, a.m., sunrise, dawn, daybreak, break of day, cockcrow, the small hours, forenoon, matin, matins, aurora; noon, midday, meridian; spring, springtime, springtide, flowering, budding; summer, summertime, summertide, midsummer, Indian summer, St. Luke's summer, St. Martin's summer.

adj. morning; spring, springlike, vernal; summer, summery, aestival.

128 evening; autumn; winter

n. p.m., afternoon, evening, eventide, eve, evensong, vesper, vespers; sunset, sundown, twilight, dusk, dimness, half-light, gloaming, curfew, night, nightfall, nighttime; midnight, witching time of night, dead of night; autumn, fall, harvest; winter, wintertime, wintertide, midwinter.

adj. afternoon, vespertine, evening; crepuscular; night, nocturnal; autumn, autumnal; wintry, winter, brumous.

129 youth

n. youth, youthfulness, young blood, juniority, juvenility; infancy, tender age, childhood, adolescence, puberty, pubescence, boyhood, girlhood, school-going age, teens, boyishness, girlishness, next generation; freshness, salad days, awkward age, growing pains, younger generation, immaturity, inexperience, callowness, greenness, prime, spring, springtime; minority, wardship, nonage, pupilage.

adj. young, youthful, boyish, girlish, childlike, teenage, adolescent, pubescent, in one's teens; formative, budding, flowering, unwrinkled, ageless, tender, developing; childish, unripe, green, callow, awkward, raw, unfledged, immature, inexperienced, puerile, juvenile; minor, under-age, infant, younger, minor, junior, youngest.

see also 131

130 age

n. age, oldness, old age, senility, second childhood, senescence, seniority, dotage, infirmity; middle age, middle years, older generation; responsibility, experience, wisdom, maturity, caution.

adj. old, aged, elderly, advanced in years, senile, senescent, matured, seasoned, grey, balding, wrinkled, toothless; superannuated; inactive, infirm, debilitated, feeble, enfeebled, doddery, decrepit, moribund, dying, with one foot in the grave; experienced, qualified, expert, respected, venerable; major, senior, older, elder, oldest, eldest, first-born.

vb. age, grow old, decline, progress, advance in years, have seen better days, show one's age; superannuate; mellow, develop, mature.

see also 132

131 infant

n. baby, babe, infant, suckling, mite, toddler, tot, bairn; child, youngster,

kid, brat (*sl.*); young person, juvenile, pupil, schoolchild, minor, teenager, adolescent, student; boy, schoolboy, lad, junior, master; young man, youth, stripling, fellow; girl, schoolgirl, young lady, lass, miss.

adj. baby, newborn, childlike; infantile, babyish, childish, puerile, juvenile; boyish, girlish; adolescent, youthful, teenage, pubescent; immature, naive, innocent, spontaneous.

132 veteran

n. old person, elder, senior, retired person, old age pensioner, senior citizen, dependant; veteran, patriarch, old hand (*inf.*), old timer (*inf.*), grand old man, elder statesman; old woman, matriarch.

133 adulthood

n. adulthood, years of discretion, manhood, womanhood, maturity, age of majority, majority.

adult, grown-up, man, woman.

adj. adult, grown-up, manly, womanly, mature, responsible; marriageable.

vb. come of age, grow up, attain majority; mature.

see also 380, 381

134 earliness

n. earliness, primitiveness, anticipation, presentiment, recency, immediacy, punctuality, promptness, promptitude, prematurity; foresight, hunch; early riser, early bird (*inf.*).

adj. early, prior, previous, recent, primitive; new, fresh, budding; premature, in advance, precocious, preceding, anticipatory, preparatory, advanced, prevenient; immediate, precipitant, speedy; imminent; punctual, prompt, timely, on time, sharp.

vb. be early, anticipate, foresee,

forestall, prepare for; precede, take precedence, get a head start, pre-empt, jump the queue.

135 lateness

n. lateness, belatedness, tardiness, retardation, slowness, dilatoriness, backwardness; late hour, high time, last minute; delay, deferment, postponement, adjournment, discontinuation, suspension, procrastination, cooling-off period, moratorium, respite, days of grace, stay, reprieve, remission, wait and see, filibuster; slow starter, late riser.

adj. late, advanced, tardy, dilatory; too late, overdue, belated, delayed, behind, behindhand; last-minute; unready, unpunctual.

vb. be late, stay up, burn the midnight oil; tarry, be slow, linger, saunter, dawdle, dally, shilly-shally; delay, defer, postpone, procrastinate, retard, stay, adjourn, put off, suspend, withhold, hold back, wait and see, play for time, filibuster; put in cold storage, mothball (*inf.*), put in mothballs (*inf.*), put on ice (*inf.*), shelve.

136 timeliness

n. timeliness, opportuneness, opportunism, expediency, fortuity.

opportunity, chance, occasion, right time; crisis, emergency, turning point, dilemma, eleventh hour, nick of time, moment of truth, hour of decision.

adj. opportune, fortuitous, timely, well-timed, punctual, on time, propitious, auspicious, providential, suitable, expedient, advantageous, convenient; critical, crucial, decisive, momentous, significant, key, urgent.

vb. grasp the opportunity, use to the full, take advantage of, cash in on, exploit, capitalize, make capital out of,

opportunize, play on, profit by; hang in the balance.

see also 577, 915

137 untimeliness

n. untimeliness, inopportuness, inexpediency, mistiming; disturbance, interruption, intrusion.

adj. mistimed, ill-timed, untimely, unpunctual, too early, premature, too late; wrong, ill-chosen, improper, untoward, unseemly, intrusive, interrupting, disturbing, inconvenient, disadvantageous, unsuitable, inappropriate, unseasonable, unfavourable, inopportune, inauspicious.

vb. mistime; interrupt, disturb, intrude, break in on (*inf.*); miss an opportunity, let an opportunity slip, miss the boat, fail to exploit.

see also 578, 916

138 frequency

n. frequency, recurrence, reoccurrence, regularity, constancy, oftenness.

adj. frequent, regular, recurrent, successive, reiterated, rhythmic; common, commonplace, customary, not rare, familiar, habitual, general, expected, usual, periodic; incessant, non-stop, perennial, constant, monotonous, continual, steady.

vb. recur, repeat; go on, continue, occur regularly.

adv. often, frequently, usually, generally, as a rule, commonly, regularly, repeatedly; sometimes, now and again, occasionally, at times, from time to time.

see also 140

139 infrequency

n. infrequency, rarity, uncommonness, scarcity, intermittence, unpredictability, irregularity.

adj. infrequent, occasional, rare, sparse, scarce, few, few and far between, scanty, sporadic, meagre, precious; unique, single, individual; uncommon, unusual, bizarre; intermittent; casual, chance, incidental.

adv. infrequently, scarcely, hardly, hardly ever, occasionally, uncommonly, now and then, rarely, seldom.

see also 141

140 regularity

n. regularity, recurrence, periodicity, repetition, frequency; stabilization, evenness, steadiness, constancy; timing, phasing, alternation, oscillation; current, wave, rota, cycle, rotation, swing, circuit, pulsation, beat, rhythm, pulse; routine, daily round; anniversary, birthday, commemoration.

adj. periodical, regular, routine, periodic, systematic, methodical, organized, steady, constant, uniform, serial, cyclic, rotational, pulsating, rhythmic, alternating.

vb. recur, repeat, reiterate, come round again, alternate, undulate, regulate, revolve, throb, beat, pulsate, swing.

adv. periodically, systematically, regularly, at regular intervals, like clockwork; hourly, daily, weekly, monthly, annually.

see also 138

141 irregularity

n. irregularity, fitfulness, jerkiness, unsteadiness, inconstancy, unevenness, variability; jerk, fits and starts, spasm, stop, break, bump.

adj. irregular, sporadic, off and on, fitful, jerky, spasmodic, irregular, uneven; unsteady, shaky; inconstant, random, fluctuating, faltering, wavering, flickering; capricious, changeable, casual.

vb. fluctuate, come and go.

see also 139

F Change

142 change

n. change, variation, alteration, modification, adjustment, qualification, transformation, refinement, evolution, alternation; fluctuation, wavering, modulation; exchange, transference, substitution, mutation, permutation, conversion; transition, diversion, deviation; renewal, innovation, novelty, reconstruction, improvisation, reformation, revision, rearrangement, reorganization, readjustment, metamorphosis, vicissitude, transmutation; deterioration, withdrawal, removal.

modifier. changer, converter, transformer, catalyst, agitator, leaven, adapter.

adj. variable, varying, changeable, modifiable, qualifiable, alternating, inconstant, mutable, plastic, transformable, movable, mobile.

vb. change, alter, vary, modify, qualify, transform, adapt, adjust, improvise; exchange, transfer, substitute; turn, shift, veer; convert, commute; renew, revise, rearrange, reorganize, reform, translate, reconstruct, renovate; refine, moderate, temper; evolve; alternate, fluctuate, waver, modulate.

143 permanence

n. permanence, constancy, invariability, continuity, steadiness, stability; immobility, solidness, consistency; durability, endurance; conservatism, *status quo*, traditionalist, conservative, reactionary, die-hard, stick-in-the-mud.

adj. permanent, immovable, unchangeable, changeless, certain, fixed, uninterrupted, unchanging, continual, constant, lasting; enduring, unwavering, abiding; stable, unremitting; strong, robust, firm, steady, steadfast; conservative, traditional, unprogressive, reactionary, conventional; obstinate, stubborn.

vb. stay, remain, abide, persist; stabilize, maintain, preserve, uphold, sustain, support.

144 cessation

n. cessation, discontinuation, discontinuance, expiration, termination, conclusion.

stop, halt, standstill, closure, interruption, suspense, lapse; industrial action, stoppage, shut-down, strike, go-slow, work-to-rule, sit-in, walkout, unofficial strike, wildcat strike, general strike, lock-out; deadlock, confrontation; ceasefire, armistice, truce; rest, pause, holiday, vacation, respite, lull, breathing space, remission, recess; intermission, interlude, interval, interim, interregnum.

vb. cease, terminate, stop, discontinue, desist, refrain, finish, knock off (*inf.*), break up, quit, shut down, close down, shut up shop, call it a day (*inf.*); pack it in (*inf.*), knock it off (*sl.*); halt, check, restrain, put a stop to, arrest, stall, interrupt; strike, down tools, come out, go out, walk out, lock out, picket, boycott; pause, break, take five (*inf.*), rest, relax, let up (*inf.*); fizzle out (*inf*).

see also **89**

145 continuance

n. continuance, continuation, perpetuation, maintenance, persistence, duration, prolongation.

adj. continual, uninterrupted, unbroken, connected, steady, constant, unceasing, incessant, ceaseless, sustained, inexhaustible.

vb. continue, carry on, keep on, go on, maintain, sustain, uphold, keep at it; stay, remain, last, survive, abide; endure, progress, persist, persevere, stay the course.

see also **535**

146 conversion

n. conversion, convertibility, processing, development, change-over, transformation, alteration; regeneration, new birth, rebirth, evangelization; convert, disciple, follower, believer, proselyte, catechumen.

adj. converted, altered, changed, transformed; regenerate, born again.

vb. convert, turn into, alter, transform, transmute; evangelize, proselytize, save, redeem; camouflage, disguise, mask, hide, conceal, obscure; remodel, improve, mend, reconstruct, reshape, reform, mould, metamorphose.

see also **142**

147 reversion

n. reversion, return, regress, regression, reaction, rebound, flashback, boomerang, recoil, backfire, backlash; restoration, restitution, re-establishment, reconditioning, refreshment, rejuvenation, recovery, reopening; atavism, throwback; resurrection, renewal, revival, comeback; reversal, *volte-face*, about-turn, backsliding, apostasy, lapse, relapse.

adj. reverted; atavistic; apostate, degenerate.

vb. revert, go back, return, turn

back, reverse; recur, reappear, restore, restitute, reinstate, replace; recoil, rebound; regress, retrogress, throw back; backslide, fall away, lapse, relapse, degenerate.

148 revolution

n. revolution, disaster, *débâcle*, explosion, eruption; *coup*, shake-up, overthrow, upheaval, revolt, rebellion, insurrection, anarchy, plot, subversion.

radical, revolutionary, extremist, fanatic, demonstrator, agitator, rebel, anarchist, guerrilla, freedom fighter, insurrectionist, traitor.

adj. revolutionary, radical, progressive, extreme, thorough, deep, complete, rabid; earth-shaking, catastrophic, cataclysmic, shattering; militant, rebellious, revolting, anarchistic, insurgent, underground, subversive, seditious.

vb. revolutionize, subvert, overthrow, upset, shake up; rise up, revolt.

149 substitution

n. substitution, exchange, transference, alternation, commutation, shift, shuffle, switch, rearrangement, transposition, vicariousness.

substitute, transfer, alternative, replacement, understudy, proxy, ghostwriter, locum, reserve, stand-in, standby, relief; deputy, agent, delegate; double, dummy, stopgap, makeshift; scapegoat, whipping boy.

adj. substitutional, alternative, vicarious, reserve, provisional, temporary, makeshift; dummy, mock, imitation.

vb. substitute, exchange, transfer, replace, commute, transpose, shuffle, shift, switch, act for, stand in for, cover for, fill in, relieve, fill in for, put in the place of, ghost, double for, serve in one's stead; take it out on (*inf.*), work off.

adv. instead, in the place of, in lieu.

150 interchange

n. interchange, exchange, transfer, reciprocation, swap, mutuality, interrelation, interchangeability, tit for tat; barter, trade, commerce, correspondence, give and take (*inf.*).

adj. in exchange, mutual, reciprocal, reciprocating, interchangeable, commutable.

vb. interchange, exchange, swap, commute, interact, trade, barter, correspond; give and take (*inf.*).

151 changeableness

n. changeableness, changeability, variability, mutability, irregularity, instability, inconstancy, mobility, fluctuation, vacillation, wavering, fickleness, indecision, unreliability, erraticness, waywardness.

adj. changeable, variable, irregular, inconstant, mobile, vacillating, wavering, fluctuating, volatile, many-sided, versatile, flexible, malleable, adaptable, plastic, unstable, unsteady, protean; fickle, flighty, indecisive, fidgety, capricious, unreliable, erratic, wayward.

vb. vary, range, mutate, chop and change, waver, shift, vacillate, fluctuate, variegate, differ, depart, diverge, dissent.

152 stability

n. stability, immutability, invariability, firmness, permanence, constancy, irreversibility, immobility, immovableness, solidity; regularity; reliability, resoluteness, endurance; stabilization, equilibrium, balance, homeostasis.

fixture, establishment, constant,

invariant; rock, pillar; stabilizer, ballast, counterbalance, counterweight, sandbags.

adj. unchangeable, invariable, changeless, stable, constant, steady, immovable, immobile, stationary; unwavering, inflexible, unadaptable; resolute, reliable, steadfast; stereotyped, uniform; fixed, fast, set, sure, established, entrenched, inveterate.

vb. stabilize, fix, set, steady, secure, sustain, support, fasten; balance; establish, entrench, anchor, transfix.

see also **535**

153 present events

n. eventuality, incidence; event, occurrence, incident, episode, happening, situation, circumstance, development, chance, proceeding, transaction, phenomenon, adventure, experience, triumph, celebration; affair, matter, concern; predicament, accident, misadventure, misfortune, mishap, calamity, emergency, catastrophe.

adj. happening, current, present, afloat, in the air, in the wind, about, prevailing.

vb. happen, take place, occur, come about, follow, ensue, arrive, transpire, fall on, befall, arise, come up, turn up, crop up; be realized, come off, turn out, feel, undergo, experience, meet.

154 future events

n. prospect, outlook, forecast, prediction, approach, promise; fate, destiny; imminence, threat, menace.

adj. impending, approaching, coming, near, close, forthcoming, imminent; threatening, brewing, ominous, certain, inevitable, inescapable, unavoidable, fateful, destined, fated; in prospect, in store, to come, in the offing, on the horizon.

vb. impend, approach, draw on, near, advance, hover, be in store; loom, threaten, hang over, overshadow, menace; forecast, prognosticate; anticipate, expect.

see also **902**

G Causation

155 cause

n. causation, causality, origination, motivation, authorship.

cause, origin, source, root, spring, foundation, seed; beginning, birth, derivation, nativity, genesis; means, basis, grounds, ground, agent, occasion, influence, mainspring, determinant, antecedent; first cause, prime mover, producer, creator, author, originator, inventor, discoverer, founder; motive, inducement, activation; factor, element, rudiment, principle; reason, explanation.

adj. causal, original, determinant; basic, fundamental, primary, radical, initial.

vb. cause, make, create, produce, originate, effect, determine, bring about, provoke, generate, evoke, elicit, induce, call forth, give rise to, arouse, occasion, motivate, suggest, influence, lead to; conduce, contribute to, involve.

156 effect

n. effect, result, consequence, end, outcome, upshot, issue, product; consummation, after-effect, aftermath, repercussion, wake, reaction, backlash, sequel, fruit, harvest, emanation; by-product, spin-off.

adj. caused, consequent, consequential, resultant, resulting, following, ensuing, subsequent, derivative.

vb. result, follow, ensue, spring from,

proceed from, derive from, emanate
from, originate in; become of, come
of.

157 assignment of cause

n. assignment, attribution, imputa-
tion, reference, ascription; association;
explanation, theory, hypothesis,
rationale.

adj. attributable, assignable, refer-
able, imputable, derivable, culpable;
linked, associated; explanatory.

vb. attribute, assign, ascribe, impute,
refer, charge, blame, trace, credit with,
derive from, lay at; connect, associate,
link; explain, account for, solve.

158 chance

n. chance, fortuity, randomness,
unpredictability; odds, risk-taking,
probability; fate, lot, fortune, luck,
good luck, bad luck, pot luck; fluke
(*inf.*), gamble.

adj. casual, chance, accidental, coincidental, fortuitous, random,
haphazard, unthinking, hit-or-miss,
aimless, fluky (*inf.*); unmotivated,
inexplicable, unintentional.

vb. chance, fall to one's lot; chance
upon, stumble on, venture, happen on,
gamble, risk; stand a chance.

adv. by chance, by accident, unexpectedly, unintentionally, fortuitously,
randomly, casually, perchance.

see also 553

159 power

n. power, potency, might, strength,
energy, vigour, life, liveliness,
dynamism; dominance, domination,
omnipotence; sway, control, teeth,
muscle, influence; ability, capability,
skill, potentiality, competence, efficiency, capacity, faculty, efficacy;
force, potential, thrust, pressure, horse-
power, steam, electricity, juice (*sl.*),

gas, nuclear power, solar energy,
hydro-electricity; power station, grid,
pylon.

adj. powerful, mighty, energetic,
vigorous, strong, lively, dynamic,
empowered, forceful, dominant,
potent; omnipotent, almighty; able,
capable, up to (*inf.*), equal to, potential, competent, efficient, effective.

vb. be able, be up to (*inf.*), be
capable of, lie in one's power; be
powerful, perform, operate, accomplish; empower, confer, enable, power,
charge, invest, arm, strengthen, electrify.

see also 161

160 impotence

n. impotence, lifelessness, power-
lessness, ineffectuality, ineffectivity,
helplessness; inability, incapability,
incompetence; unproductiveness,
infertility, barrenness; eunuch, gelding.

adj. powerless, unenergetic, unable,
incapable, incompetent, inefficient,
ineffective, inadequate, disabled,
incapacitated, inept; infirm, helpless,
unprotected, defenceless; spineless,
nerveless, feeble; impotent, sterilized,
sterile, barren, infertile, frigid.

vb. not be able, cannot, not find it in
oneself to; disable, impair, exhaust,
wear down, run down, incapacitate,
disarm, unman, paralyze, put out of
action, throw a spanner in the works;
disqualify, invalidate; castrate, emasculate, spay, geld.

161 strength

n. strength, might, energy, vigour,
force, vitality, toughness, stamina,
hardness, brawn, muscle; invincibility.

adj. strong, mighty, powerful, forceful, energetic, firm; unyielding, unresis-
ting, persistent; brawny, muscular,
stout, hardy, tough, robust, stalwart,

strapping, burly, beefy, big, solid, hefty, virile, athletic; secure, durable.

vb. strengthen, fortify, confirm, reinforce, establish, substantiate, empower, energize, stimulate, bung up, brace, refresh, invigorate.

see also 535, 537

162 weakness

n. weakness, feebleness, frailty, faintness, fragility, flimsiness, delicacy, tenderness; infirmity, debility; effeminacy, femininity.

weakling, coward, cry-baby, sissy (*sl.*), pansy (*sl.*).

adj. weak, powerless, helpless, delicate, puny, frail; fragile, flimsy, brittle, insubstantial, makeshift, unsteady; effeminate, womanly; weakminded, spineless, anaemic (*inf.*), fainthearted, insipid, diluted, wishy-washy (*inf.*); worn, rotten, decrepit.

vb. faint, sicken, languish, crumble, decline; weaken, exhaust, enfeeble, impoverish, debilitate, enervate, disable, handicap; dilute, water down, blunt, sap; fade, give way, fizzle out (*inf.*).

163 production

n. production, productivity, output, performance, through-put; foundation, manufacture, establishment, construction, fabrication, processing; propagation, generation, procreation, fertility, reproduction, breeding, copulation.

product, creation, work, article, piece, goods, merchandise, handiwork, fruit, harvest, produce, yield, result, opus; edifice, building, structure, erection, invention, concoction, brain-child (*inf.*), baby (*sl.*), thing (*sl.*).

adj. productive, generative, creative, manufacturing; fruitful, rich, prolific, fertile; pregnant, expecting, with child,

with young, in the family way (*inf.*), in the club (*sl.*).

vb. produce, create, make, manufacture, put together, make up, fabricate, construct, build; devise, compose; furnish, effect, perform, return, render, provide; invent, concoct, cook up; carve, chisel; yield, blossom, flower; reproduce, generate, procreate, propagate, multiply, conceive, beget, breed.

164 destruction

n. destruction, annihilation, elimination, liquidation, extirpation, disintegration, demolition, eradication, obliteration, nullification, abolition, dissolution, suppression; slaughter; waste, overthrow, subversion, desolation, havoc, wreckage, sabotage, ruin, ravage, downfall, collapse, ruination.

adj. destructive, hurtful, troublesome, harmful, detrimental, ruinous, deadly, fatal, lethal, poisonous, venomous, toxic, internecine, shattering, annihilative.

vb. destroy, terminate, nullify, abolish, suppress, eradicate, wipe out, blot out, obliterate, wipe off the face of the earth, dissolve; annihilate, eliminate, liquidize, extirpate, exterminate, atomize, pulverize, decimate, decapitate; demolish, break, dismantle, knock down, pull down; crush, overthrow, overturn; blitz, bombard, smash, shatter, mutilate, undo; damage, lay waste, devastate, raze, plunder, ruin, pillage, ravage, despoil, sack.

be destroyed, perish, disintegrate, deteriorate, decay, crumble, go to rack and ruin.

165 reproduction

n. reproduction, reconstruction,

remaking, renovation, reforming; regeneration, resurrection; rediscovery, revival, renaissance; duplication, reduplication, reprinting.

adj. reproductive, regenerative, renascent.

vb. reproduce, reconstruct, rebuild, remake, redo, refashion, remould, reform, renovate, renew, revive, rediscover, regenerate, repeat; propagate, multiply; proliferate, duplicate, reprint, copy.

166 producer
n. producer, creator, maker, instigator, mover, manufacturer, constructor, builder, architect, composer, author, writer, originator, inventor, discoverer.

167 destroyer
n. destroyer, breaker; anarchist, terrorist, desperado, gunman, murderer; disrupter, ravager, vandal, defacer, wrecker, iconoclast, nihilist, abolitionist.

plague, pestilence, moth, locust, erosion, rust, cancer, poison, virus, fungus, mildew, blight; demolition expert, demolisher.

see also 370

168 productiveness
n. productiveness, productivity, generative capacity; prolificness, fruitfulness, fertility, proliferation, fecundity; lushness, luxuriance, exuberance, profusion, richness, abundance, wealth, plenty, horn of plenty, cornucopia, bounty, plethora, hotbed, warren; prosperity, boom.

adj. productive, fruitful, prolific, profuse, fertile, rich, fecund; bounteous, spawning, abundant, plenty, copious, lush, luxurious, fulsome,

exuberant, booming; prosperous, wealthy.

vb. be fruitful, blossom, prosper, thrive, flourish, proliferate, grow, swarm.

see also 163

169 unproductiveness
n. unproductiveness, stagnation, unprofitability, incapacity, barrenness, desolateness, infertility; sterilization, contraception; slump, recession, depression, austerity.

adj. unproductive, unprofitable, fruitless, profitless; desolate, barren, poor, unfruitful; ineffectual, ineffective; infertile, unbearing, sterilized, sterile, impotent, frigid, childless, celibate.

vb. stagnate, vegetate, fail; exhaust; castrate, emasculate, spay, geld.

170 parenthood
n. parenthood, ancestry, origin, genealogy, parentage, line, lineage; fatherhood, paternity; parent, progenitor, procreator, begetter; father, dad, daddy, pop (*sl.*); motherhood, maternity; mother, mum, mummy.

adj. generative, procreative, lifegiving; ancestral, genealogical; family, familial; parental, paternal, fatherly, maternal, motherly.

171 offspring
n. offspring, issue, progeny, posterity; lineage, generation, next generation; adoption; descent, sonship, filiation; family, child, son, daughter; heir, descendant; bastard.

adj. descended, familiar, lineal; filial, daughterly; bastard, illegitimate; adopted.

172 operation
n. operation, agency, action, execution, application, performance, run-

ning, management, conduct, function, process, instrumentality, means.

adj. operative, active, functioning, in operation, in action, in force; live, running, working, effective; executive, operational, functional, agential.

vb. operate, function, work, go, move, run; act, behave, perform, handle; produce, bring about.

see also 564, 565

173 vigour

n. vigour, energy, power, dynamism, vehemence, strength, lustiness, élan, dash, verve, vitality, get-up-and-go (*inf.*), go (*inf.*), zest, pep, bounce, zip; drive, push, thrust, enterprise, initiative, aggression.

stimulant, invigorator, activator, incentive, stimulus, fillip, pick-me-up, catalyst, booster, drug, shot.

adj. vigorous, powerful, potent, dynamic, strong, vehement, intense, lively, brisk, energetic; enterprising; aggressive, pushy (*inf.*), self-assertive; stimulating, invigorating, activating.

vb. invigorate, energize, activate, strengthen, fortify, reinforce, stimulate, animate, enliven, vitalize, drive, push, intensify.

see also 159, 161

174 inertness

n. inertness, inertia, inactivity, motionlessness, lifelessness, immobility, dullness, passivity, indolence, idleness, lethargy, listlessness.

adj. inert, lifeless, immobile, motionless, dead, inactive, idle, languid, torpid, lethargic, listless, indolent, passive, slow, still, pacific, dull, sluggish, dormant.

vb. slumber, languish, idle, stagnate, vegetate.

see also 267

175 violence

n. violence, force, boisterousness, turbulence, destructiveness; outburst, outbreak, uproar, explosion, eruption, disruption, clash, clammer, assault, onslaught; disorder, disturbance, turmoil, ferment, fury, frenzy, tumult; storm, blizzard, gale, hurricane, tornado, thunderstorm, hailstorm, cloudburst, tempest.

savage, barbarian, brute, beast, monster, animal, maniac, fiend, terrorist, bully, ruffian.

adj. violent, extreme, severe; vehement, forceful, boisterous, turbulent; rough, raging, wild, stormy, furious, outrageous, rampageous, destructive; aggressive; brutal, brutish, savage, fierce, barbarous.

vb. run wild, rush, mob; erupt, explode, blast, break out; roar, fume, boil, seethe; incite, stir up, whip up, lash; force, coerce; provoke.

176 moderation

n. moderation, assuagement, alleviation, pacification, placating, soothing; reduction; gentleness, calmness, mildness; control.

moderator, balm, consolation, relief, cure, tranquillizer, restraint.

adj. moderate, modest, reasonable; calm, gentle, tranquil; restrained, temperate.

vb. be moderate, be at peace, keep a low profile; keep a happy medium; moderate, restrain, temper, alleviate, reduce, decrease, abate, tone down, cushion, soften the blow, mitigate, mollify, soothe, relieve, console, assuage, pacify, placate, still, quieten; relax, let up.

177 influence

n. influence, weight, dominance,

power, control, force, pressure, sway, authority, pull (*inf.*); significance; prestige, reputation.

adj. influential, weighty, dominant, powerful, forceful, controlling, prevailing, authoritative, important, significant, momentous; prominent, reputable.

vb. influence, determine, affect, convince, persuade, sway, compel, turn, dominate, govern, control, lobby, bring pressure to bear, put pressure on, carry weight with, pull strings (*inf.*), get in with (*inf.*).

see also 420

178 tendency

n. tendency, trend, direction, bent, drift, aim; tenor, thrust, spirit; inclination, bias, leaning, propensity, proneness, predisposition, predilection, penchant, fondness, liking, preference, weakness, proclivity.

adj. tending, conducive, predisposed.

vb. tend, lean, incline, drift, predispose, point to, aim, gravitate towards.

179 liability

n. liability, liableness, susceptibility, amenability; subjection, responsibility.

adj. liable, apt, inclined, disposed, prone, likely to, subject to; answerable, responsible, amenable.

vb. be liable, run the risk of, incur, fall on, be subject to, succumb to, fall prey to, expose oneself to, lay oneself open to.

180 concurrence

n. concurrence, collaboration, cooperation, partnership, working together, joint action; union, concert.

adj. concurrent, combined, allied, united, joint, cooperative; mutual.

vb. concur, cooperate, collaborate, work together, unite, combine; agree, harmonize, accord.

see also 639

181 counteraction

n. counteraction, opposition, polarity, antagonism, contradiction; retroaction, offsetting, neutralization; friction, resistance, drag, counterweight, cross-current, countermeasure; antidote, cure, medicine, relief, preventive, antibiotic, injection.

adj. counter, counteractive, neutralizing, retarding.

vb. counteract, work against, militate against, run counter to; neutralize, cancel out, invalidate, hinder, prevent, frustrate; interfere, oppose, contradict; drag; counterbalance, countervail.

II Space

A Space in general

182 indefinite space

n. space, expanse, extent, expansion, span, area, surface; range, scope, compass, reach, sweep, stretch, gamut, spread; room, open space, clearance, elbow-room, breathing space, latitude, margin, leeway.

adj. spatial; spacious, ample, extensive, roomy, capacious, vast, expansive, deep, broad, wide, long, far-reaching, widespread.

vb. reach, extend, spread, stretch, sweep, flow, range, encompass, span; open, expand, widen.

183 definite space

n. region, area, district, zone; patch, section, sector, quarter, square.

territory, country, state, kingdom,

realm, principality, duchy, province, county, shire, community, city, capital, centre, borough, town, village, hamlet; constituency, ward; diocese, parish; conurbation, metropolitan county, metropolitan district, metropolis, suburb, suburbia; locality, surroundings, environment, neighbourhood, environs, locale, milieu.

adj. territorial, regional; provincial, local, municipal, urban, suburban, rural; parochial, insular.

184 limited space
n. place, spot, position, point, stand, locus, corner; enclosure, field, compound, pen, close, sty, pound, paddock, plot, zone, square, quadrangle, yard, patio, precinct; niche, groove, socket.

185 situation
n. situation, position, location, station, setting, site, place, scene, scenery; whereabouts, bearings.
adj. situated, located, placed, positioned, sited, set, situate.
vb. be situated, be, be found, lie, be there, stand, sit, be located.

186 location
n. location, position, site, place, seat, station, locus, stand, scene, placing, placement, emplacement; encampment, mooring, lodging.
adj. located, positioned, entrenched, installed, settled, encamped.
vb. locate, position, establish, determine, set, place, unearth, discover, search out, come across, find; park, encamp, set up, install, settle, entrench, camp, moor, lodge.

187 displacement
n. displacement, dislocation, derangement, misplacement, shift, unloading, unpacking; loss, mislaying.
adj. displaced, disturbed; dislocated,

uprooted, homeless, rootless; out of place, uncomfortable.
vb. displace, disarrange, disturb, confuse; dislodge, dislocate, disestablish, unseat, uproot, unsettle, derail; shift, move, remove, replace, transpose, transport; discharge, unload, unpack, extract, withdraw, evacuate, vacate; misplace, lose, mislay; feel out of place.

188 presence
n. presence, attendance, participation; occupancy, residence, inhabitance, habitation; ubiquity, omnipresence.
adj. present, in attendance, attendant, resident; available, at one's disposal, at hand, ready, on call, on tap.
vb. be present, be there, be, be around, kick around (*inf.*); attend, visit; haunt, hang around (*inf.*), frequent; live, inhabit, occupy, reside, appear, make an appearance, turn up, show up (*inf.*), present oneself.

189 absence
n. absence, disappearance, non-appearance; absenteeism, non-attendance, truancy, defection, desertion; non-residence, inexistence; emptiness, vacuity, vacuum, bareness, void, loss, vacancy; lack, need, deficiency.
adj. absent, not here, away, missing, lost, out, not in, elsewhere, not at home, moved, removed, vanished, disappeared; wanting, lacking, minus, unavailable, omitted; empty, vacant, bare, vacuous, unoccupied, uninhabited.
vb. be absent, stay away, be missing, lack, want; absent oneself, take no part in, play truant, play hooky (*sl.*), take French leave.

190 inhabitant

n. inhabitant, native, national; citizen, resident, house-dweller, householder; tenant, lodger, paying guest, incumbent, boarder, occupier, squatter; tax-payer, commuter, voter; city-dweller, townsman, town-dweller, suburbanite; denizen; population, populace.

settler, colonist, pioneer; immigrant, foreigner, guest worker; aborigine, autochthon, primitive, ancient.

adj. native, vernacular, common, popular, national, indigenous, domestic, home, local, domesticated, naturalized, aboriginal.

191 habitation

n. habitation, abode, habitat, accommodation, dwelling, residence, residency, domicile, establishment.

house, address; mansion, country house, hall, lodge, grange, manor, castle, villa, chalet, cottage, bungalow; flat, apartment, suite, maisonette, pad (*sl.*), penthouse, bedsitter, block of flats, tenement, mews, skyscraper; high-rise flats; shelter, hut, shanty; home, fireside, hearth, homestead; lodgings, rooms, quarters, billet, berth, barrack, camp, digs (*inf.*), diggings (*inf.*).

inn, hotel, guest house, boarding house, bed and breakfast, hostel, motel, pension; public house, pub (*inf.*), local (*inf.*), tavern, hostelry, club; bar.

restaurant, café, cafeteria, snack bar, buffet, canteen, refreshment room, tearoom, teashop, coffee-bar, ice-cream parlour, take-away; pull-up.

vb. live, dwell, inhabit, people, populate; settle, colonize; reside, abide, stay, visit, sojourn, stop (*inf.*); settle down, take up residence, put down roots; occupy, rent, lodge, keep, squat.

192 contents

n. contents, items, pieces, ingredients, parts, elements, constituents, components; equipment, material, implements, accessories, articles; load, cargo, freight, stuffing.

vb. load, charge, store, freight, ship, weight, pile, mass, take on, pack.

193 container

n. container, receptacle, holder, cover, envelope; depository, reservoir; packet, package, parcel; bag, sack, purse, wallet, pouch, case, suitcase, trunk, briefcase, grip; box, carton, tin, can, chest, coffer, locker, capsule, canister, crate, bin, hopper, bunker, granary, basket, hamper, pannier; pot, jug, glass, beaker, cup, bucket, pail, bowl, plate, vessel, jar, pitcher, urn, basin, boat, crock, vase; bottle, flask, flagon; cauldron, vat; cistern.

B Dimensions

194 size

n. size, proportions, dimension, measurement, distance, area, extent, mass, weight, volume, capacity; largeness, greatness, hugeness, bigness, enormity, vastness, amplitude, immensity, capaciousness, solidness, bulkiness, corpulence, plumpness, obesity, fleshiness, stoutness.

giant, monster, colossus, leviathan, whale.

adj. big, large, great, huge, enormous, vast, jumbo; fat, obese, stout, plump, podgy, corpulent, fleshy, beefy, pot-bellied; overgrown, larger-than-life; bulky, heavy, solid.

see also 32

199

195 littleness

n. littleness, shortness, smallness, minuteness, tininess, slightness, scantiness, exiguity, diminutiveness, brevity.

dwarf, pigmy, midge, midget; atom, particle; reduction, miniature.

adj. little, small, tiny, slight, miniature, limited, puny; dwarfed, stunted, squat, dumpy; minute, microscopic, diminutive, atomic, infinitesimal, wee.

see also 33

196 expansion

n. expansion, increase, growth, spread, enlargement, augmentation, extension, supplementation, reinforcement, development, escalation, elaboration, amplification, intensification; dilation; inflation.

adj. expanded, expansive, dilated, stretched, swollen, tumescent.

vb. expand, grow, spread, increase, develop, boost, enlarge, blow up, extend, augment, supplement, reinforce, escalate, elaborate, amplify, intensify, magnify; dilate, distend, let out, gather, swell, bloat, stretch, protract, inflate.

197 contraction

n. contraction, reduction, lessening, decrease, shortening, abridgment, curtailment, compression, confinement, narrowing; shrinkage, constriction, recession, deflation; compressor, roller, constrictor.

adj. contracted, shrunken, shrivelled, astringent, wizened.

vb. contract, weaken, lessen, reduce, decrease, decline, abate, subside, dwindle; curtail, abridge, shorten; shrink, shrivel, wrinkle; constrict, confine, compress, squeeze, pinch, nip.

198 distance

n. distance, length, reach, extent, range, space, way, mileage; horizon, skyline, background; farness, remoteness, back of beyond, world's end, outpost, foreign parts, outskirts, limit; aloofness, reserve.

adj. distant, far, far-away, far-flung, far-off, furthest, farthest, furthermost, long-distance, long-range, out of range, out of sight, ultimate, hindmost; remote, inaccessible, out-of-the-way, God-forsaken; unapproachable, aloof.

vb. distance, outstrip, outpace, outrun, outspeed; keep one's distance, keep out of the way of.

adv. far, away, at a distance, to the ends of the earth, to the back of beyond; out of reach, out of range, out of bounds.

199 nearness

n. closeness, proximity, vicinity; adjacency, juxtaposition, contiguity.

near place, foreground, neighbourhood, locality; close quarters, close range, short step, stone's throw, earshot, spitting distance, hair's breadth.

adj. near, close, nearest, nearby; local, neighbouring; adjacent, adjoining, next; short-distance, short-range; intimate.

vb. be near, approach, approximate; adjoin, abut, connect, border, neighbour; juxtapose.

adv. nearby, in the neighbourhood, locally; at close quarters, at hand, close at hand; within hearing, within range, within earshot.

nearly, almost, approximately, virtually, practically, nigh; tantamount to, to all intents and purposes, substantially, in effect, all but.

200 interval

n. interval, space, separation, clearance, margin, leeway, gap, hole, ditch, cleft, break, crack, chink, rift, fault, passage, pass, gorge, ravine, gulf, chasm, valley, leap, interstice.

vb. space, keep apart, separate, split, intervene, interspace.

201 contact

n. contact, juxtaposition, contiguity, tangency, junction, connection, meeting, touching.

adj. contiguous, in contact, tangential.

vb. contact, touch, meet, brush, graze, kiss; adjoin, abut, border; juxtapose, bring together; unify.

202 length

n. length, space, measure, span, reach, extent; line, mark, stroke, strip, row, file, string, channel; longness, linearity, longimetry, linear measure; lengthening, extension, prolongation, elongation.

adj. long, lengthy, extensive; high, tall, lofty; lengthened, extended, outstretched, elongated, stretching, drawn out, long drawn out, protracted, enlarged; interminable, limitless, boundless, unending.

vb. be long, stretch out; lengthen, extend, stretch, elongate, draw out, prolong, spin out, protract, enlarge, expand.

203 shortness

n. shortness, briefness, brevity, abridgment, curtailment, reduction, shortening.

adj. short, small, low, slight, tiny, little, stunted, dwarf, compact, square, stunted, dumpy, stubby, chunky, thickset; curt, concise, succinct, terse.

vb. shorten, abbreviate, abridge, condense, abstract, summarize, telescope, epitomize, concentrate, boil down; curtail, cut back, truncate, slash; contract, reduce; cut down, shave, prune, shear, trim, strip, clip, nip, pare, whittle, crop, stunt.

204 breadth; thickness

n. breadth, broadness, width, wideness, expanse, latitude, amplitude; bore, calibre, diameter, girth; thickness, plumpness, density, solidity, crassitude; bulk, mess, body.

adj. broad, wide, extended, large, spacious, extensive, roomy, bulky, massive, full, thick, thickset, stout, compact, squat, dumpy, chunky, stubby.

vb. broaden, widen, thicken, fatten.

205 narrowness; thinness

n. narrowness, confinement, restriction, contraction, thinness, slimness, emaciation, leanness, tenuity, shallowness, delicacy; neck, strait, narrows, bottleneck.

adj. narrow, confined, limited, restrained, close; thin, slender, slim, meagre, lanky, lean, threadlike, fine, delicate, skinny, scraggy, weedy, emaciated, bony, spindly, flimsy; wasted, withered, haggard, shrivelled, wizened.

vb. make narrow, taper, confine, straiten; make thin, attenuate, compress; slim, reduce weight, lose weight, take off weight, diet, go on a diet, bant, watch one's weight, starve; shrink, contract.

206 layer

n. layer, stratum, thickness, bed, course, band, substratum, fold, overlap, overlay; row, tier, level, class, zone, storey, floor; coat, coating, ply, seam, laminate, lamina, sheet, slab, foil, panel, slate, plate, scale, flake, squama; lamination, stratification.

adj. layered, laminated, laminate, flaky, scaly, squamous, laminar, lamellar, lamellate, lamelliform, lamellose, laminose.

vb. laminate, layer, overlay, overlap, cover, stratify, scale, flake; veneer.

207 filament

n. filament, wire, thread, cord, strand, string, rope, cable, twine, twist, wisp, lock, shred, hair, whisker, fibre, tendril, eyelash, gossamer; sinew, tendon; strip, tape, band, ribbon, belt, sash, bandage, scarf, strap.

adj. fibrous, threadlike, wiry, stringy, hairy, capillary, sinewy, tendinous.

208 height

n. height, elevation, altitude; loftiness, highness, tallness, stature; uplands, hill, mountain, rise, slope, escarpment, fell, moor; tower, spire, steeple, mast, skyscraper, pillar, column; summit, top.

adj. high, giant, towering, soaring, elevated, sky-high; multi-storey, high-rise; tall, lanky; eminent, distinguished, sublime, exalted, lofty.

vb. tower, soar, extend above, mount, look over, look out on, overlook, command, dominate, overshadow.

adv. high, up, aloft.

209 lowness

n. lowness, depression, netherness, debasement; lowlands, valley, hollow; depths, floor.

adj. low, low-lying, depressed, sunken, nether; squat, crouched; underlying; lesser, inferior.

vb. be low, lie low, crouch, squat, grovel; lower, depress, debase, sink.

adv. under, underneath, beneath, below, down; underfoot, underground.

210 depth

n. depth, lowness, profundity; drop, depression, bottom, abyss, gorge, pit, space, charm, hollow, trench, mine, chamber, ravine; deeps.

adj. deep, low, profound; deep-seated, deep-rooted; bottomless, fathomless; sunken, buried, immersed; submerged, underwater, deep-sea; subterranean, underground; yawning, gaping.

vb. deepen, hollow, dig, excavate, scrape out, sink, plunge.

adv. deeply, out of one's depth.

211 shallowness

n. shallowness, superficiality; shallow, shoal; covering, veneer, gloss, façade, surface.

adj. shallow, superficial, surface, skin-deep; cosmetic; light, inconsiderable, cursory, slight.

vb. skim, brush, touch on, scratch the surface.

212 summit

n. summit, top, peak, apex, zenith, pinnacle, tip, vertex, acme; consummation, maximum, limit, climax; crown, head, crest, brow, cap, spire.

adj. top, topmost, uppermost, highest, maximal, tip-top; apical, acmic, zenithal; head, capital.

vb. crown, top, tip, head, cap; culminate.

213 base

n. base, root, foundation, support, prop, stand, stay, pier, rest, bottom, basement, floor, basin, substratum, bed, channel, ground, understructure, shaft, substratum, groundwork; foot, toe, pedestal.

adj. bottom, undermost, fundamental, basic, underlying.

214 being vertical

n. verticality, uprightness, perpendicularity, erectness, plumbness, straightness, sheerness; steep, cliff, precipice.

adj. vertical, perpendicular, upright, erect, upstanding, plumb, on end, straight up; steep.

vb. be vertical, stick up, rise; make vertical, erect, raise, elevate.

215 being horizontal

n. horizontality, planeness, flatness, evenness; level, plane.

adj. horizontal, plane, level, even, flush; prostrate, prone, supine, recumbent.

vb. be horizontal, lie down, recline, repose; flatten, level, even out, smooth, plane, squash, prostrate, roll out, straighten.

216 hanging

n. pendency, suspension, hanging; pendant, locket, earring; curtain, hangings; pendulum, stalactite.

adj. hanging, suspended, pendent, dangling, drooping, swaying, pendulous, stalactitic, overhanging.

vb. hang, suspend, fall, hover, float, poise, dangle, drape; droop, sag, swing, sway, oscillate, flap.

217 support

n. support, sustenance, maintenance, reinforcement, back-up; supporter, guide, backing, stiffener, strengthener, sustainer; foundation, base, carriage, bearing, undercarriage, underframe, chassis, bogie, truck; stilt, stay, mainstay, buttress, pole, post, prop, stake, boom, column, pillar, corner-stone, pier, pile, timber, brace, beam, rafter, girder, strut, joist; breakwater, pier,

wall; splint, crutch, truss; back, rest, headrest, backrest, backbone; wedge, chock; pivot, lever, hinge, axis, fulcrum; stand, board, table, seat, saddle, cushion, pillow; shelf, ledge, rack; backer, provider, patron.

adj. supporting, sustaining.

vb. support, hold up, prop, sustain, maintain, carry, bear, keep up; bolster, shore, brace, stay, truss, underpin, undergird, back, buoy up, shoulder; uphold, establish, promote, advance, further, encourage, confirm, strengthen, corroborate, back up, stand by, stick by (*inf.*), stand up for, stand behind, stick up for (*inf.*).

see also 636

218 parallelism

n. parallelism, equidistance, coextension; likeness, correspondence, similarity, affinity; parallelogram; parallelopiped.

adj. parallel, equidistant, not meeting, not converging, coextensive; corresponding, similar, uniform.

vb. parallel, correspond, be equal; match, equate, compare.

219 being oblique

n. obliqueness, obliquity, skewness, curvature, asymmetry; curve, bend, twist, squint, divergence, diagonal; slope, inclination, slide, acclivity, decline, declivity.

adj. oblique, inclined, leaning, angled, skew, askew, skew-whiff (*inf.*), asymmetrical, awry, crooked, askance; sloping, upward, acclivitous, downward, declivitous; divergent, sideways, slanted, bent, curved, twisted, contorted; cross-wise, diagonal, transverse.

vb. incline, lean, slope, tilt, angle, bend, curve, twist, warp; diverge, deviate, slant.

220 inversion

n. inversion, transposition, reversion, reversal; palindrome, about-turn, *volte-face*; upset, capsizal, somersault.

adj. inverted, inverse, opposite, upside-down, back-to-front, topsyturvy.

vb. invert, transpose, rearrange, exchange, reverse, revert, put the cart before the horse (*inf.*); turn over, overturn, overthrow, turn upside down, stand on its head, tip, topple, tilt, capsize, keel over, somersault; turn inside out.

221 crossing

n. crossing, junction, intersection, confluence, crossroads, crossover; cross, crux, crucifix, cruciform, swastika; network, system, intercommunication; wickerwork, lattice, grid, grill, web, net, netting, mesh, textile, fabric, weave, loom, plait.

vb. cross, intersect, interlink, cut, pass across, mesh, weave, loom, knit, sew, plait, twist, interlace, spin, twine, intertwine, interlock, tangle, entangle.

222 being exterior

n. exteriority, extraneousness, externality, outwardness; outside, exterior, surface, top, front, face, appearance, façade, covering.

adj. exterior, outside, external, outward, outer, outermost, outlying; extrinsic, foreign.

vb. be outside; externalize, extrapolate, project, objectify, embody.

see also 825

223 being interior

n. interiority, internality, inwardness; inside, interior; substance, contents, heart, centre, soul.

adj. interior, inside, internal, inward, inner, innermost; intrinsic, inborn, innate; central, integral; inland.

vb. be inside; internalize.

see also 5, 224

224 centrality

n. centrality, centralization; centre, middle, bull's eye; focus, concentration, convergence; nucleus, core, heart, hub, nub, gist, kernel, marrow, pith.

adj. central, centre, middle, inner, focal, pivotal.

vb. centre, centralize, concentrate, focus, converge, draw, attract.

see also 96

225 covering

n. covering, superimposition, cover, lid, flap, box, wrapping; ceiling, roof, shelter, dome, awning, tent, marquee, tarpaulin, canopy, mask, hood, shade, film, blind, umbrella, parasol, sunshade, sheath; sheet, blanket, robe, carpet, rug, mat; coating, varnish, paint, veneer, lacquer, glaze, enamel, wash, polish, stain, distemper, gloss; skin, peel, shell, rind, coat, husk, hull, pod, jacket, integument, tegument.

adj. covered, sheltered, hooded, wrapped, enveloped, veiled, varnished, painted, surfaced.

vb. cover, put on, lay over, protect, shield, shelter, wrap, envelop, enshroud, enclose, veil, superimpose, superpose; roof, carpet, pave, paper; coat, surface, varnish, paint, plate, gloss, glaze, spray, veneer, wax; mask, hide, conceal.

226 lining

n. lining, insulation, interlining; inner surface, inside; filling, stuffing, wadding, padding, quilting, inlay.

vb. line, insulate, interline, inlay,

stuff, wad, pad, fill, quilt, reinforce, overlay, face, encrust.

227 dressing

n. dressing, toilet; dress, clothing, wardrobe, outfit, vesture, garb, gear, guise, raiment, apparel, attire; clothes, garment, vestment, costume, suit, dress; uniform, livery.

adj. dressed, well-dressed, dressed-up, clad.

vb. dress, clothe, turn out, deck out (*inf.*), equip, fit out; wear, have on, be dressed in; put on, get dressed, don, slip on, throw on, assume; dress up, get dressed up, smarten oneself up; change into; wrap up.

228 undressing

n. undressing, divestment; bareness, undress, nakedness, nudism, nudity, naturism, *déshabillé*, stripping, strip-tease; nude, nudist, naturist; baldness, alopecia, shaving, tonsure.

adj. bare, exposed, unveiled, uncovered, unprotected; revealing, *décolleté*; undressed, naked, nude, stark naked, stripped, in one's birthday suit (*inf.*), in the altogether (*inf.*), starkers (*sl.*); bald, hairless, bald-headed, balding, shaven, tonsured, shining, smooth; threadbare, denuded.

vb. uncover, expose, unveil, reveal; remove, take off, cast off; undress, unclothe, strip, disrobe, divest; pluck, peel, pare, shed, bare, skin, flay, scalp, shell, stone, excoriate, decorticate; denude, ravage.

229 being around

n. environment, ambience, circumstances, surroundings; circumjacence; scene, *milieu*, background, setting, habitat, situation, atmosphere, climate; environs, suburbs, vicinity.

adj. environmental, ambient, surrounding, background, situational.

vb. surround, circle, enclose, close in, envelop, girdle, encompass.

adv., prep. around, about.

see also 8

230 being between

n. interposition, intermediacy, inter-currence, intervention, interruption, interjection, interpolation; mediation, intercession; partition, wall, water-shed, fence, hurdle; insert, inset, wedge.

adj. intermediary, intermediate, intervening.

vb. place between, mediate, interpose; insert, intersperse; interrupt, interject, intervene.

prep. between, among.

see also 653

231 circumscription

n. circumscription, encircling, circumnavigation; limitation, demarcation, boundary, restriction.

vb. circumscribe, encircle, ring, encompass, surround, circumambulate, circumnavigate, circumvent; surround; limit, restrict, bound, mark off, confine.

232 outline

n. outline, perimeter, periphery, outside, circumference, circuit, border, boundary, contour; sketch, skeleton, silhouette, profile, framework, tracing, delineation.

vb. outline, sketch, trace, delineate.

233 edge

n. edge, extremity, end, limit, verge; border, frontier, boundary; threshold, brink, brim, rim, side, corner, point, tip, margin, skirt; edging, skirting, fringe, hem.

vb. border, verge, edge, skirt; rim, hem, margin, fringe.

234 enclosure

n. enclosure, confinement; envelope, wrapping; area, ground, pitch, arena; plot, court, yard, garden, park; cell, prison, dungeon, den; pen, cage, pound, aviary, coop, warren.

fence, wire, wall, hedge, fencing, paling, rail, railing, balustrade, barrier, ditch, moat, trench, ha-ha.

vb. enclose, envelop, wrap, enfold, confine, contain, blockade, shut in, shut up, lock up, fence, impound, hedge in, hem in; package, parcel; bottle; jail, imprison.

235 limit

n. limit, end, utmost, extremity, destination, terminus, conclusion; limitation, delimitation, restriction, definition, control; hurdle, barrier, frontier, boundary, border, borderline; threshold, upper limit, ceiling; demarcation line, mark, fringe, edge.

adj. limited, set, defined.

vb. limit, set, settle, define, delimit, demarcate, bound, confine, restrict, draw the line at, curb.

236 front

n. front, frontage, exterior, façade, anterior, foreground, face, head, forehead, vanguard, front line; visage, countenance, physiognomy; semblance.

adj. front, forward, fore, foremost, frontal, frontmost, head, obverse, anterior, leading, advance.

vb. face, front, look out on; border; head, lead; meet, confront, encounter, come face to face with.

adv. in advance, ahead; in the foreground.

237 rear

n. rear, back, tail, end, reverse, posterior, backside, bottom, dorsum; wake, rearguard; background, hinterland, backstage.

adj. rear, back, hind, tail, posterior, after, terminal, final, bottom, dorsal, backmost, hindmost, rearmost, background, backstage.

vb. be behind, follow, back on to; bring up the rear.

adv. at the rear, behind, in the background.

238 sidedness

n. sidedness, laterality; juxtaposition, adjacency; side, hand, flank, shoulder.

adj. side, lateral, sidelong, sidewise, sideways, flanking; adjacent.

vb. be side by side, flank, skirt; juxtapose.

adv. laterally, sideways, abreast, alongside, side by side.

239 being opposite

n. opposition, contraposition, polarity; opposite, converse, reverse, contrary, contrast, contradiction, antipode, antipole.

adj. opposite, contrary, opposing, contradictory.

vb. be opposite, oppose, confront, face.

adv., prep. opposite, over against, facing, *vis à vis.*

240 right side

n. right-handedness, dexterity, dextrality; right, right hand; right-hander, dextral; starboard.

adj. right, right-hand, right-handed, off, offside, dextral, dextrorse.

241 left side

n. left-handedness, sinistrality; left, left hand; left-hander, sinistral; port.

adj. left, left-hand, left-handed, near-side, sinistrorse.

C Form

242 form

n. form, shape, style, look, appearance, fashion, design, outline, profile, contour; structure, construction, formation; morphology.

adj. formed, shaped, developed; formative, impressionable, plastic, mouldable.

vb. form, make, create, fashion, pattern, model, mould; cast, stamp, impress, carve, cut; arrange, construct, build, assemble; take shape, develop, express, grow, materialize.

243 absence of form

n. formlessness, shapelessness, amorphism, fuzziness; chaos, liquid; fluid.

adj. formless, shapeless, amorphous; vague, unclear, indistinct, blurred, fuzzy; indeterminate, indefinite; chaotic, misshapen, unshapely, deformed.

244 symmetry

n. symmetry, regularity, conformity, proportion, equality, evenness, balance, harmony, arrangement, order; shapeliness.

adj. symmetrical, balanced, even, proportioned, harmonious, shapely, regular, well-proportioned.

245 asymmetry

n. asymmetry, disproportion, lopsidedness, irregularity, distortion, contortion, twist, deformity, malformation.

adj. asymmetrical, disproportionate, irregular, misproportioned, uneven, unshapely, grotesque, ugly, hideous, distorted, deformed, malformed, dis-figured, crippled, mangled, hunchbacked, crooked, awry, askew.

vb. distort, contort, twist, pervert, deform, misshape, disfigure, buckle, cripple; writhe, scowl, grimace.
see also 845

246 angular form

n. angularity, pointedness, serration; angle, crotch, elbow, fork, corner, point, zigzag; right angle, acute angle, obtuse angle, reflex angle; triangle; quadrilateral, parallelogram, rhomboid, rectangle, oblong, square, diamond, lozenge, rhombus, rhomb, polygon, pentagon, hexagon, heptagon, octagon, nonagon, enneagon, decagon, endecagon, dodecagon; polyhedron, cube, tetrahedron, pyramid, prism, wedge.

adj. angular, pointed, sharp-cornered, scraggy, jagged, serrated, zigzag, wedge-shaped, cuneiform, cuneate; triangular, rectangular, multilateral.

vb. angle, bend, intersect, serrate, zigzag.
see also 259

247 curved form

n. curvature, bending, flexion, flexure, arcuation; curve, bend, sweep, bow, curl, camber, arc, chord, arcade, rainbow, arch, crook, trajectory; catenary, parabola, hyperbola, circle, ellipse, epicycle; crescent, half-moon, lune, lunula, meniscus, lens, lunate.

adj. curved, bent, rounded, arched, vaulted, crescent, lunate.

vb. curve, turn, arch, bow, curl, crook, buckle, twist, warp, flex; waver, meander, swerve, deviate, veer.

248 straight form

n. straightness, rectilinearity; verticality, perpendicularity; horizontality; bee-line.

adj. straight, even, level, direct; upright, vertical, perpendicular, erect; horizontal; unbroken, uninterrupted.

vb. straighten, order, make straight; untwist, unbend, uncoil, disentangle, unravel, uncurl, unfold.

adv. in a straight line, as the crow flies.

249 round form

n. rotundity, roundness; round, globe, sphere, orb, ball, marble, balloon, bubble, drop, droplet, globule; cylinder, barrel, roll, drum.

adj. round, rotund, rounded, spherical, globular, orbicular, globe-shaped, ;loboid, globose, cylindrical.

vb. round, ball, roll, coil up.

250 simple circularity

n. circularity, roundness; circle, orbit, circuit, ring, loop, halo, crown, corona, aureola, circus, bowl, hoop, quoit, wheel, disc, equator; ellipse, oval, egg; band, belt, wreath, garland; circumference, perimeter, rim, periphery.

adj. round, circular, cyclic, orbicular; oval, elliptical.

vb. encircle, go round; make round. see also 322

251 complex circularity

n. convolution, intricacy, twisting, sinuosity, torsion; coil, turn, twine, twist, plait, kink, loop, spiral, helix, screw, curl, tendril, scroll.

adj. convoluted, intricate, involved; winding, spiral, coiled, helical, flexuous, sinuous, tortuous; serpentine, snake-like; meandering, undulating, wavy.

vb. turn, wind, curl, loop, twist, twirl, fold, twine, plait, intertwine, entwine, sinuate, wrinkle, contort,

wreathe; crimp, ripple; meander, undulate; wriggle, squirm, wiggle.

252 convexity

n. convexity, protuberance, bulginess, outgrowth.

swelling, growth, bump, hump, lump, ridge, protuberance, rising, bulge; tumour, cancer, corn, boil, inflammation, carbuncle, bunion, wart, pimple, bulb; dome, cupola, vault.

adj. convex, arched, raised, curved, bent; bulbous, swollen, bloated; bulging, swelling, excrescent, tumescent, tumid.

vb. swell, bulge, rise, project, protrude, jut.

253 prominence

n. prominence, salience; projection, protuberance, protrusion, extension, spur, spit, promontory, tongue, headland, relief; leader, figure-head, model, example.

adj. prominent, conspicuous, protuberant, extended, jutting, protruding, projecting, salient, obtrusive.

vb. protrude, extend, jut, project, stand out, stick out.

254 concavity

n. concavity, hollowness; hollow, hole, aperture, opening, depression; pit, abyss, mine, shaft, well, trench; corner, niche, recess, alcove, indentation, pocket; valley, dale, bowl, drop, gulf, basin, glen, ravine, crevasse, fissure, crater, gorge, canyon, gully, chasm; dip, dent, dimple, cave, burrow, cavern, grotto, furrow, covert, warren, pothole; excavation, tunnel, passage, retreat, dug-out, dig (*inf.*).

adj. concave, hollow, depressed, excavated, sunken, carved out, indented.

vb. hollow out, excavate, dig, spade,

gouge, delve, mine, tunnel, bore; indent, depress; cave in, fall in, collapse.

255 sharpness

n. sharpness, acuteness; point, tip, prick, thorn, sting, spike, nail, pin, needle, fork, prong; barb, thorn, bramble, prickle, brier, spine; tooth, edge, scissors, shears, knife.

adj. sharp, acute, pointed, fine, keen, cutting, biting, piercing, incisive, trenchant; spiked, spiky, spiny, prickly, thorny, needle-pointed, barbed; pronged, tapered, tapering, acuminate.

vb. be sharp, prick, sting, taper; sharpen, grind, edge, file, hone, whet, strop; barb, point; puncture.

256 bluntness

n. bluntness, obtuseness, flatness.

adj. blunt, unsharpened, unpointed, dull, unsharp, obtuse; toothless.

vb. blunt, dull, take the edge off, round, turn, obtund; be blunt, not cut.

257 smoothness

n. smoothness, flatness, levelness, regularity; stillness, glossiness, silkiness; glass, ice, marble; gloss, varnish, polish, finish.

adj. smooth, flat, plane, level, even, uniform, steady, stable, continuous; quiet, still, sleek, polished, glossy, glassy, lustrous, silky, soft, slippery, oily.

vb. smooth, even, level, plane, scrape, shave, flatten, iron, sand, file, press; polish, shine, burnish, glaze, gloss, varnish; glide, slide, float, skim, drift, stream.

258 roughness

n. roughness, asperity, unevenness, coarseness, harshness, bumpiness, brokenness, irregularity, jaggedness, corrugation.

adj. rough, uneven, coarse, harsh, bumpy, broken, jagged, rugged, choppy, ruffled; bristly, prickly, hairy, hirsute.

vb. roughen, coarsen, break, notch, serrate, crumple, ruffle.

259 notch

n. notch, indentation, cut, zigzag, cleft, trench, trough, gouge, saw, nick, incision, depression, serration.

adj. notched, jagged, saw-toothed, serrated.

vb. notch, serrate, cut, tooth, cog, indent, nick.

260 fold

n. fold, gather, pleat, lapel, overlap, tuck; crease, crimp, wrinkle, corrugation, turn.

adj. folded, gathered, creased, wrinkled, corrugated, pleated, puckered, overlapping.

vb. fold, double, crease, lap, overlap, plicate, pleat, curl, crimp, wrinkle, ruffle, pucker, gather, corrugate.

261 furrow

n. furrow, groove, slit, slot, trench, rut, gouge, moat, channel, canal, ditch, gutter; corrugation.

adj. furrowed, grooved, ribbed, fluted, corrugated, ridged.

vb. furrow, groove, slot, flute, corrugate, channel, plough.

262 opening

n. opening, aperture, orifice, hole, gap, hollow, slit, perforation, slot, break; mouth, throat, gullet; outlet, vent; window, porthole; door, doorway, gate, exit, entrance, hatch, hatchway, channel, passage.

adj. open, unlocked, unfastened, unsealed; clear, accessible; ajar, gaping, wide, yawning; torn, rent.

vb. open, unlock, unbolt, unbar,

unfasten, undo; clear, admit, free, loosen; expose, reveal, unfold; gape, yawn.

see also **264, 462**

263 closure
n. closure, occlusion, stoppage, blockage, obstruction.

adj. closed, unopened, shut, fastened, bolted, blocked, sealed.

vb. close, shut, lock, fasten, bar, bolt.

see also **265**

264 perforator
n. perforator, sponge, sieve, strainer, colander; borer, awl, gimlet, drill, lancet, needle, pin, punch; perforation, porosity.

adj. perforated, porous, pervious, permeable, penetrable, spongy, absorbent, holey.

vb. cut, perforate, pierce, prick, slit, puncture, crack, stick, inject, drill, stab, lance, spear, spike, skewer, impale, bore, mine, tunnel; hole, riddle.

265 stopper
n. stopper, plug, cork, bung, tap, valve, stopcock, wedge, rammer, stuffing, filling, stopping.

adj. stopped up, blocked, obstructed, sealed, impenetrable, impervious, watertight.

vb. block, obstruct, blockade, stop, choke, clog, stuff, ram, fill, dam, seal, cork, plug, bung, occlude, obturate.

D Motion

266 motion
n. motion, mobility, movableness, movement, action, activity, unrest, restlessness, move, passage, progress, advance, ascension, descension; velocity, speed.

adj. moving, in motion, transitional, movable, mobile, restless, nomadic.

vb. move, go, run, progress, proceed; push, impel, stir, set in motion, activate, propel.

267 rest
n. rest, immobility, motionlessness, cessation, stillness, standstill, stop; discontinuance, interval, pause; silence, calm; quiet, calmness, peace, tranquillity.

adj. quiet, peaceful, still, quiescent, asleep; immovable, immobile, motionless, unruffled, peaceful, placid, serene.

vb. rest, stand still, pause, halt, stop, cease; not stir, keep quiet; still, soften, quiesce, relax, lull, becalm, hush.

see also **174**

268 transference
n. transference, transferal, conveyance, movement, removal, shift, relay, conduct, remittance, dispatch, delivery, hand-over; transport, transportation, transit, carriage, shipment, trans-shipment, haulage, freight, consignment.

adj. transferable, transmittable, transmissible, conveyable, movable, portable.

vb. transfer, move, remove, conduct, carry, take, convey, shift; send, direct, remit, relay, dispatch, forward, deliver, hand over, consign; ship, cart, truck, haul, load, post, mail; convoy, escort; import, export; transmit, communicate; relocate, transplant; ply, shuttle.

see also **714**

269 land travel
n. travel, tourism, touring, sightseeing, globe-trotting, roaming; journey, tour, trip, outing, expedition, excursion, day out, picnic; pilgrimage;

venture, adventure; visit, sojourn; exploration, quest, safari.

walk, step, pace, stride, gait, march; stroll, hike, jaunt, saunter, amble, ramble, wayfaring, tramp; promenade, constitutional, perambulation; peregrinations, wanderings.

riding, horse-riding, horsemanship, horse-racing, equestrianism, show-jumping, dressage; cycling, spin, ride; drive; driving, motoring; itinerary, route, course, circuit, direction, map.

adj. journeying, travelling, visiting; peripatetic.

vb. travel, journey, tour, rove, visit, cruise, explore, traverse; walk, step, pace, march, tread, amble, ramble, wander, hike, trek, stroll, ambulate, perambulate, promenade; gad about (*inf.*), gallivant about (*inf.*); ride, cycle, bike (*inf.*); drive, motor.

270 traveller

n. traveller, tourist, sightseer, globe-trotter, holiday-maker, daytripper; visitor, voyager, explorer, adventurer; itinerant, wanderer, roamer, pedlar, vagabond, vagrant, tramp, hobo; migrant, emigrant, immigrant, refugee, gypsy, nomad, bedouin.

pedestrian, walker, foot-passenger, hiker, trekker, rambler, pilgrim, wayfarer, runner, athlete; rider, horse-rider, jockey, show-jumper, hitch-hiker; passenger, commuter, season-ticket holder; motorist, driver.

271 water travel

n. navigation, sailing, cruising, circumnavigation; seamanship, seafaring, exploration; voyage, cruise; water sports, aquatics, sailing, yachting, boating, rowing, canoeing, swimming, diving, surfing.

adj. navigational, sailing, nautical, naval, marine, maritime.

vb. sail, cruise, voyage, ply, run, ferry; set sail; launch, cast off; navigate, steer, pilot, make for, head for, set a course; drop anchor; moor; swim, bathe, dive, dip, paddle, wade, surf, water-ski.

272 mariner

n. mariner, sailor, seaman, seafarer, pilot, boatman, marine, crew, captain, boatswain, navigator, helmsman.

273 air travel

n. air travel, aeronautics, aviation, flying, gliding, flight.
pilot, airman, aviator, flier, aeronaut.
adj. flying; aerial, aeronautical, aerodynamic.
vb. fly, pilot, taxi, take off, climb, rise, soar, zoom; spin, loop, roll; glide, dive, dart, shoot; plunge, plummet, parachute, bail out; touch down, land, come down, crash-land; talk down.

274 space travel

n. space travel, astronautics, cosmonautics; countdown, space flight, space walk; grand tour; re-entry, splashdown.
astronaut, spaceman, cosmonaut, space traveller.
adj. astronautical, cosmonautic, cosmonautical.
vb. take off, orbit, splash down.

275 carrier

n. carrier, bearer, porter, messenger, runner; basket, bag, container; horse, packhorse, llama, beast of burden.
vb. carry, transport, move, convey, transfer, bear.

276 vehicle

n. vehicle, conveyance; cycle, bike, bicycle, pushbike (*sl.*), velocipede, tandem, tricycle; moped, scooter, motor scooter, motorcycle, motorbike; car, automobile, motor, saloon, sports car, G. T., coupé, hard-top, convertible, hatchback, estate car, station wagon, shooting-brake, minibus; taxi, taxicab, minicab, cab, hackney carriage, rickshaw; bus, coach, motor bus, tram, trolley-bus; van, lorry, pickup, dump truck; train, underground, rapid transit; engine, locomotive, diesel locomotive, electric locomotive, steam engine.

cart, trolley, pram, barrow, trailer; carriage, wagon, buggy, trap, gig, hansom.

adj. vehicular, locomotive, wheeled.

277 ship
n. ship, boat, vessel, craft; motorboat, steamer, steamboat, steamship, freighter, barge, lighter, packet, ferry, mail-ship, tanker, supertanker, liner; pilot, tug, launch; destroyer, warship, frigate, battleship, aircraft carrier, submarine; sailing ship, clipper, yacht, rowing boat, paddle boat, canoe, kayak, gondola, junk, galleon.

adj. nautical, marine, maritime, naval, seagoing, seaworthy.

278 aircraft
n. aircraft, aeroplane, plane, airliner, jet, jumbo jet, turbo-prop, shuttle, glider, bomber, seaplane; hovercraft, hydrofoil, helicopter; airship, balloon, Zeppelin.

adj. aviational, aeronautical.

279 spaceship
n. spaceship, spacecraft, capsule, module, space shuttle, space probe; space station, satellite, sputnik; flying saucer, UFO; rocket.

280 velocity
n. velocity, speed, quickness, rapidity, hurry, haste, rush, expedition,

celerity; acceleration, hastening, quickening, speeding up, spurt, burst, charge.

adj. quick, fast, speedy, brisk, swift; nimble, agile, deft, spirited; light-footed, prompt, expeditious.

vb. go fast, speed, hurry, hasten, quicken, race, tear, fly, dash, rush, run, sprint, dart, whiz, zip, pelt, bomb, run like mad, go all out, do a ton (*sl.*), go full pelt (*inf.*); accelerate, go faster, speed up, spurt, put on speed, step on it (*inf.*), put one's foot down (*inf.*), get a move on (*inf.*), get one's skates on (*inf.*), make it snappy (*inf.*); overtake, gain on, catch up, reach, pass, overhaul, go after, outstrip, outpace, outdistance, capture, beat; run for dear life.

adv. fast, quickly, speedily, swiftly, at full speed, flat out, at full pelt.

see also **613**

281 slowness
n. slowness, sluggishness, lethargy, apathy, hesitation, reluctance; deceleration, retardation, slackening, delay, go-slow, brake, curb, restraint.

slowcoach, tortoise, snail, dawdler, lingerer, loiterer, loafer, idler.

adj. slow, slow-moving, dawdling, lingering; sluggish, listless, lethargic, apathetic, inactive, leisurely, hesitant, reluctant.

vb. go slowly, idle, stroll, saunter, dawdle, linger, tarry, take one's time, loiter, loaf, crawl, inch, falter, limp, hobble, shuffle, plod; decelerate, slow down, reduce speed, slacken, relax, let up, ease off, delay, retard, brake, put on the brakes; curb.

282 impulse
n. impulse, thrust, impetus, charge, rush, drive, pressure, momentum, impulsion; bump, shove, shock, jolt,

impact, brunt, clash, crash, collision, pile-up, smash-up; hit, knock, rap, blow, smack.

vb. impel, push, drive, press, propel, move, set in motion, activate, get going, start; collide, crash, run into, bump into, smash, dash, meet, encounter, touch, impinge, clash, butt, bump, jog, shove, jolt, force, scrape, jar.

hit, strike, beat, smite; tap, rap, jab; slap, thump, clout, smack, pummel, thrash, whip, whack, wallop (*sl.*), sock, clap, box, punch, club, cudgel; hammer, pound, bash, slosh (*sl.*), flail; bang, knock, bruise; kick, knee.

283 recoil

n. recoil, reaction, rebound, spring, bounce, repercussion, echo, reverberation, boomerang, backlash, rebuff, answer, reply.

vb. recoil, react, respond, rebound, bounce, spring, kick back, backfire, echo, reverberate; shrink from, draw back, pull back, wince, flinch.

284 direction

n. direction, bearing, orientation, point of the compass, cardinal point, north, south, east, west; destination, aim, object, intention; tendency, thrust, tenor; outlook, standpoint, point of view.

vb. orientate oneself, take one's bearings, locate; direct, signpost, lead, aim for, go for, head for, make for, point to, steer; tend.

adv. towards, in the direction of, via, heading for, on the way to.

285 deviation

n. deviation, misdirection, disorientation, deflection, divergence, turning, departure, diversion, detour; digression, tangent; irregularity, deterioration.

adj. deviating, aberrant, deviant, divergent, misguided, mistaken, lost; tangential, off-beam.

vb. deviate, deflect, swerve, bend, wander, stray, err, depart from, veer, shift, lose one's bearings, get lost, turn aside; disorientate, misdirect; digress, get sidetracked, go off the point, go off at a tangent.

286 precedence

n. precedence, priority, leading, heading, vanguard.

vb. precede, go before, come first, take precedence, herald, go in advance, lead, lead the way, head, take the lead.

adv. in advance, ahead, before.

see also 84, 118

287 following

n. following, succession; follower, disciple, hanger-on, attendant, dependant, adherent, supporter, recruit.

vb. follow, go after, come after, ensue, succeed, attend, wait on; shadow, chase, pursue, track, tail (*sl.*), dog; lag behind, trail.

see also 85, 119

288 progression

n. progression, progress, advance, headway, gain; development, growth, furtherance, advancement, improvement.

adj. forward, progressive, tolerant, broad-minded, forward-looking, enterprising; ongoing.

vb. progress, advance, proceed, move on, forge ahead, press on, strive forward, push ahead, make progress, make headway, gain ground, never look back (*inf.*); further, promote, develop, grow, evolve, become, mature, improve, move with the times.

adv. forward, onward, on, in progress.

289 regression

n. regression, retreat, withdrawal, retirement, return; regress, retrogression, reversal; departure, escape; about-turn, *volte-face*, about-face, U-turn.

adj. backward, backward-looking, reactionary, narrow-minded, reverse, retrograde, retrogressive.

vb. go backwards, regress, recede, retire, back out, withdraw, retreat, draw back, secede, fall back, lose ground; retrogress; go back on one's word, turn around.

290 propulsion

n. propulsion, impulsion, impetus, drive, push, thrust, pressure; missile, projectile, bullet, shell, torpedo, arrow, dart, propellant, shot.

vb. propel, push, move, impel, drive, direct, thrust, press, shove; launch, throw, cast, pitch, toss, chuck (*inf.*); shoot, discharge.

291 pulling

n. pulling, traction, drawing, tow, haul; tug, tractor, traction engine, draught animal; trailer, caravan, train.

vb. pull, draw, haul, drag, heave, tow, tug, take in tow; attract, magnetize; trail.

292 approach

n. approach, advance, arrival, coming; nearness, approximation.

adj. approaching, nearing, forthcoming, coming, looming, drawing near; accessible, get-at-able, approachable, obtainable, available, attainable, convenient, at one's disposal.

vb. approach, draw near, come near, advance, come forward, come into sight, close in on, sidle up to, loom up; approximate, verge on, near.

293 retreat

n. retreat, recession, withdrawal, departure, escape, retirement, removal, evacuation, flight.

vb. retreat, recede, withdraw, back out, depart, run away, fall back, evacuate, escape, retire, remove; fade, die away, sink.

294 attraction

n. attraction, drawing power, gravitation, affinity, pull, draw, influence; magnet, gravity, bait, lure, decoy.

adj. attracting, appealing, magnetic, charismatic.

vb. attract, pull, drag, draw, bring; interest, fascinate.

see also 547

295 repulsion

n. repulsion, rebuff, snub, beating off, dismissal.

adj. repulsive, offensive, repelling.

vb. repel, repulse, drive back, put to flight, beat off, hold off, push back, throw off, turn away, drive away; dismiss, send packing; rebuff, snub; resist.

see also 892

296 convergence

n. convergence, concurrence, confluence, concentration, confrontation, collision course, focalization; union, meeting, encounter.

adj. convergent, concurrent, converging.

vb. converge, come together, focalize, unite, gather, concentrate, meet, tend, narrow the gap, come to a point.

297 divergence

n. divergence, radiation, ramification; fork, bifurcation; fan, spoke, ray.

adj. divergent, deviating, radiating; centrifugal.

vb. diverge, radiate, branch, fork, bifurcate, diffuse, spread, fan out, disperse, scatter, ramify, divaricate.

298 arrival

n. arrival, coming, approach, entrance, entry, appearance, emergence; start, onset; reaching, attainment; return, homecoming; landing, touchdown, disembarkation, alighting, dismounting, docking, mooring.

destination, goal, terminus, journey's end, objective, resting place, harbour, port, dock, berth, landing place, airport.

vb. arrive, come, reach, get to, enter, approach, appear, show up (*inf.*), turn up, return, come home; land, touch down, disembark, alight, dismount, get down, set foot on, dock, moor, drop anchor.

299 departure

n. departure, going, leaving, setting out, exit, withdrawing, abandonment, removal, retreat, flight, take-off, embarkation, sailing; leave-taking, parting, separating, farewell, send-off, dismissal, valediction, parting shot, congé; exodus; emigration.

vb. depart, go, leave, move, quit, retire, withdraw, evacuate, go away, take one's leave, make tracks, set out, start out, be off, push off (*inf.*), push along (*inf.*), shove off (*sl.*); rush off, run away, beat it (*sl.*), scram (*sl.*).

300 entrance

n. entrance, entry, ingress, incoming, induction, initiation, immigration; admittance, admission; introduction, influx, intrusion, infiltration, incursion, penetration, invasion, raid.

vb. enter, come in, step in, go in, set foot in, make one's way into, visit, drop in; intrude, invade, trespass, gatecrash; force into, break in; wriggle in, worm in; insert, put in, admit, introduce, implant, penetrate, infiltrate, percolate.

301 emergence

n. emergence, egress, outflow, emanation, issue, discharge, outflow, effluence, flow; escape, gush, spout, welling, oozing, outpour, leakage, seepage, eruption, secretion.

vb. emerge, go out, come out, come out into the open; emit, eject, discharge, expel, flow out, run out, effuse, give out, exhale, send forth, pour out, gush, spurt, shoot, secrete, seep, erupt, squirt; bleed, leak, empty, weep; exude, ooze.

see also 312

302 reception

n. reception, admission, admittance, acceptance, receptivity; access, welcome, open arms, hospitality, registration, enlistment, enrolment; initiation, baptism, barmitzvah; incorporation, assimilation, absorption, digestion.

adj. admissible, acceptable, receivable; suitable; receptive, sympathetic.

vb. admit, receive, accept, take in; allow in, accommodate, welcome, make welcome; initiate, baptize, introduce, induct, install; assimilate, incorporate, swallow, absorb, digest.

see also 716

303 ejection

n. ejection, expulsion, eviction, removal, elimination; dismissal, discharge, sack (*inf.*), push (*sl.*), deportation, exile, banishment, extradition;

ejector, bouncer (*sl.*), chucker-out;
nausea, sickness, vomiting.

vb. eject, emit, expel, remove,
exclude, eliminate, eradicate, wipe out,
evict; dismiss, get rid of, dispose of,
discharge, sack (*inf.*); depart, exile,
banish, extradite, relegate; urinate,
excrete; be sick, vomit, bring up (*inf.*),
throw up (*inf.*), spew, retch, heave.

304 eating; drinking

n. eating, ingestion, nourishment,
feeding, nutrition, consuming, partak-
ing; feasting, devouring, banqueting;
digestion, chewing, mastication; drinking, imbibation, potation; gastronomy,
epicurism, gourmandise, gluttony.

eater, partaker, consumer, nibbler,
chewer, glutton; drinker, sipper,
drunkard; connoisseur, gourmet, gourmand, epicure.

vb. eat, consume, feed on, partake;
chew, masticate, champ; bite, digest,
swallow; gorge, gobble, bolt, put away
(*inf.*), eat up, tuck into (*inf.*), polish
off (*inf.*), devour, dispose of; breakfast,
lunch, sup; eat out, dine out, wine and
dine, feast, banquet, gourmandize;
stuff, eat one's fill.

nourish, feed, satisfy, provide, maintain, nurture, strengthen, sustain, tend,
gratify; suckle, breast-feed, give suck,
nurse.

drink, gulp, take in, imbibe, wash
down (*inf.*); tipple, guzzle.

305 provisions

n. provisions, food, stores,
sustenance, stock, foodstuffs, groceries,
subsistence, rations, board; fodder,
feed, pasture, pasturage, roughage,
provender; portion, helping, share,
slice, quota, division, ration; larder,
pantry, refrigerator, freezer.

306 food

n. food, meat and drink, foodstuffs,
edibles, comestibles, provisions, nutrition, aliment, nutriment, cooking, grub
(*sl.*), tuck (*sl.*); victuals, pabulum,
viands; delicacy, delicatessen, luxury,
delight.

portion, mouthful, piece, bite, morsel, spoonful.

meal, refreshment, fare; repast,
refection; breakfast, brunch, elevenses,
lunch, luncheon, packed lunch, tea,
afternoon tea, high tea, dinner, supper;
snack, sandwich, bite, nibble, bait,
tiffin; feast, banquet, orgy, blow-out
(*inf.*), beanfeast, beano (*sl.*); picnic,
barbecue; menu, bill of fare, table,
cover, spread; dish, course, hors-
d'oeuvre, appetizer, soup, broth,
pottage, aperitif, entrée, main course,
sweet, dessert, afters (*inf.*), pudding,
savoury.

meat, flesh, game, poultry, fowl;
egg; flour, starch; fish, sea-food; milk
product, butter, cream, cheese; oil, fat,
grease, blubber, margarine, vegetable
fat, vegetable oil; bread, staff of life,
loaf, roll; pastry, patisserie, biscuit,
wafer, cracker, cake; fruit, soft fruit,
berry, jam, conserve, spread, extract,
jelly, gelatin; vegetable, herb, edible
root, greens, tuber, root; cereal, grain;
nut, dried fruit, seed, stone, kernel,
pip; sweet, confectionery, sweetmeat,
confections; cookery, cuisine, catering,
domestic science, home economics.

adj. edible, eatable, comestible,
digestible, nutritious, delicious, succulent, palatable, appetizing, satisfying, tempting, scrumptious (*inf.*);
culinary; prandial, pre-prandial, post-
prandial.

vb. cook, prepare, fix, heat up, warm
up; simmer, steam, boil, coddle; stew,
casserole, braise; bake, roast, spit; grill,

barbecue, broil; fry, sauté, sizzle; poach, scramble; toast, crisp, dry; curry, fricassee; dice, mince; lard, baste.

307 condiment

n. condiment, flavouring, seasoning, additive, sauce, relish, herb, plant, pickle, salt, pepper, mustard.

vb. season, flavour, spice, salt, pepper, bring out the flavour.

308 tobacco

n. tobacco, nicotine, snuff, cigarette, cigar, pipe.

vb. smoke, smoke a pipe, inhale, puff, draw, suck; take snuff.

309 drink

n. drink, beverage, potion, liquid, fluid, juice, sap, whey; infusion, decoction; soft drink, water, milk, tea, coffee, thirst-quencher, nightcap; alcoholic drink, beer, wine, champagne, toast, cocktail; sip, gulp, drop; draught, dram.

310 excretion

n. excretion, urination, evacuation, voiding, discharge, secretion, defecation, expulsion, ejection, excrement, exudation; faeces, excreta; waterworks (*sl.*); urine; bowel movement, diarrhoea, dysentry; offal, dung, droppings, manure; ordure, stool; smegma; perspiration, sweat.

adj. excretive, excretory, secretory; faecal.

vb. excrete, expel, defecate, discharge, evacuate, urinate, secrete, pass, spend a penny, go to the lavatory, be excused.

311 insertion

n. insertion, injection, infusion, introduction, insinuation.

vb. insert, put in, inject, infuse,

introduce, interpolate, include, insinuate, pour in, impregnate, stick in, throw in; force in, drag in (*inf.*), embed, install, fix, implant, bury, sink, immerse.

312 extraction

n. extraction, removal, withdrawal, expulsion, discharge, ejection, extrication, pulling; quarrying, mining; scoop, digger, chisel, extractor, gouge, excavator, dredger.

vb. extract, remove, withdraw, pull out, draw out, pluck, wrench, extricate, cut out, extort, dislodge, uproot, displace, lever out; quarry, mine, excavate, dredge, gouge, chisel; get money out of a stone (*inf.*).

313 passage

n. passage, crossing, journey, trek, voyage; way, thoroughfare, traffic, flow; traffic control, traffic regulation, rule of the road, highway code.

vb. pass, cross, traverse, go through, penetrate, emerge, proceed, drive, weave, thread, ford, span.

314 overstepping

n. overstepping, overrunning, infestation, invasion; transcendence; encroachment, violation, transgression.

vb. go beyond, overstep, encroach, go too far, exceed the limit, overrun, overshoot; invade, infest, plague, swarm, ravage; excel, surpass, outdo, transcend, rise above, eclipse; outdistance, outstrip; trespass, violate, infringe, transgress.

315 shortcoming

n. shortcoming, inadequacy, imperfection, falling short; loss, deficit, shortfall, shortage, dearth, default; need, lack, requirement, deficiency, fault, weakness, lapse, weak point; privation, destitution.

adj. short, deficient, missing, lacking, inadequate, not up to scratch; imperfect, incomplete.

vb. fall short, come short, be deficient, fail, need, miss, lack; lag behind, lose ground; collapse, come to nothing.

316 ascent

n. ascent, ascension, climbing, rise, mount, lift, jump, surge, towering, soaring; ladder, step-ladder, steps, stairs, staircase, escalator, moving staircase, travelator, lift, elevator; hill, mountain, acclivity.

adj. ascending, rising, upward.

vb. ascend, go up, rise, tower, soar, rocket, surge, grow, sprout; take off; climb, mount, scale, surmount, progress, top, scale, conquer, scramble, clamber, creep, work one's way up.

317 descent

n. descent, drop, fall, lapse, swoop, sinking, plunge, downfall, tumble; slump, recession, reduction, declination; subsidence, landslide, hole, cave, chasm.

adj. descending, downward.

vb. descend, go down, fall, drop, subside, decline, swoop, plunge, slump, sink, droop, land, come down, touch down; parachute; crash-land; splash down; topple, push over; tumble, overbalance, lose one's balance, stumble, capsize, turn over, tilt, lurch.

318 elevation

n. elevation, lift, raising, erection; exaltation, ennoblement, sublimation.

adj. raised, lifted, elevated, high, aerial, tall, erect, upstanding, upraised; exalted, noble, sublime, lofty.

vb. lift, elevate, raise, pick up, pull up, help up, uplift, hoist, heave, erect;

support, prop; leaven; boost; glorify, heighten, enhance, exalt.

get up, stand up, get to one's feet, arise; jump up, spring to one's feet.

319 depression

n. depression, lowering, dip; hole, cavity; curtsy, bow, genuflexion; debasement.

adj. depressed; smoothed, even; sitting, sedentary, settled, inactive; prostrate.

vb. depress, lower, press, squash; settle, sink, dip, sag, droop, decline; push down, bring low, ground; fell, cut down, chop down, topple, pull down, demolish, raze to the ground.

drop, let fall, shed, loosen, release, let go, spill; fall, drip, dribble, leak, ooze, seep, drain, permeate, percolate, filter.

sit down, be seated, squat, crouch, kneel, genuflect; perch, roost; bend over, stoop, incline, hunch, bow, curtsy.

320 leap

n. leap, jump, dance, spring, vault, bound, hop, rise, pounce, hurdle, leap-frog, saltation.

adj. lively, frisky, saltatory.

vb. leap, jump, spring, vault, dance, hop, bounce, skip, leapfrog, surge, rise.

321 plunge

n. plunge, jump, rush, dive, drop, fall, plummet, leap, pitch, dip, swoop; ducking, immersion, submergence.

vb. plunge, dive, dip, jump, fall, pounce, cast down; duck, submerge, immerse, drown, souse, dunk; go down, sink, go under; splash down; crash-land; go to the bottom.

322 circulation

n. circulation, circumnavigation; spiral; compass, lap, course, circuit, loop, round trip, orbit, ambit, full circle; by-pass, ring road, detour, diversion.

vb. circle, circulate, go around, revolve around, circumnavigate, circumscribe, circumambulate, lap, tour, ring, gird, wind; by-pass.

see also 250

323 rotation

n. rotation, revolution, turn, circle, spin, cycle, roll, circuit, whirl, twirl, gyration, pirouette; spiral, orbit; whirlpool, eddy, whirlwind, cyclone, tornado, vortex.

adj. rotary, gyratory, rotating, revolving.

vb. rotate, revolve, twist, circle, circulate, spin, cycle, roll, whirl, twirl, loop, swing, spiral; swivel, pivot; swirl, eddy; pirouette.

324 evolution

n. evolution, development, growth, unfolding, unfurling; disentanglement; evolutionism, Darwinism; missing link.

adj. evolving, evolutionary.

vb. evolve, develop, grow, emerge; advance, progress, mature; unfold, open out, unfurl, unroll, unwind, uncurl, uncover, unwrap; unravel, disentangle, free, release, straighten.

325 oscillation

n. oscillation, fluctuation, vacillation, wavering, undulation, quiver, shake, swing, lurch, roll; vibration, tremor, thunder; faltering, hesitancy, uncertainty.

pulse, pulsation, throb, beat, drumming, pound, surge, palpitation, flutter, ripple, wave; earthquake, seismology.

pendulum, oscillator, vibrator, shuttle, see-saw, cradle, rocking-chair, rocking-horse.

adj. oscillating, fluctuating, throbbing, pulsatory; seismic; vacillating, hesitant, undecided, irresolute.

vb. oscillate, alternate, fluctuate, vacillate, vibrate, pulse, throb, beat, pound, surge, flutter, wave, waver, undulate, librate; nod, swing, sway, see-saw, wobble, totter, lurch, roll, rock, quake, quiver, teeter, zigzag; ebb and flow, back and fill; hesitate, falter.

adv. back and forth, to and fro, up and down, from side to side.

326 agitation

n. agitation, disturbance, vibration; jar, jolt, jog, bump, bounce; shudder, quake, tremble, wobble, tremor, jerk; shakes, jitters (*inf.*), shivers, heebie-jeebies (*sl.*), butterflies (*inf.*), apprehension; fit, convulsion, spasm, palsy, seizure, fever, attack, stroke; itch, twitch.

confusion, tumult, turmoil, turbulence; excitation, melodrama, emotion, commotion, fuss, bother, flap (*inf.*), dither (*inf.*), tizzy (*sl.*).

adj. agitated, shaking, unsteady, wavering, shaky, tremulous; jelly-like, itchy, twitching, nervous, apprehensive, jittery (*inf.*).

vb. shake, tremble, vibrate, quiver, quake, shiver, chatter, shudder, palpitate, flap, toss, flutter, totter, wobble, stagger; itch, twitch; twinkle, flicker, glimmer, sparkle.

agitate, sway, rock, swing, beat, disturb, jolt, jar, jerk, bounce; convulse, seize, throw a fit; go out of control.

III Matter

A Matter in general

327 materiality

n. materiality, substantiality, concreteness, corporeality, corporality, tangibility; materialism, Marxism, dialectical materialism.

matter, body, material, stuff, mass, flesh and blood, flesh; thing, object, something, article, commodity, item, being; element, atom, molecule; component, part, ingredient, factor.

adj. material, substantial; corporeal, bodily; physical, concrete, tangible, real, objective, somatic; materialistic, unspiritual, worldly, mundane.

vb. materialize, realize, become real, take form, become flesh, take flesh, objectify, substantialize.

328 immateriality

n. immateriality, insubstantiality, dematerialization, intangibility, disembodiment; spirituality, otherworldliness; shadow, ghost.

adj. immaterial, incorporeal, insubstantial, bodiless, disembodied, intangible, ethereal, shadowy, ghostly, unreal; otherworldly, spiritual.

vb. dematerialize, disintegrate, disembody; spiritualize.

329 universe

n. universe, creation, space, outer space, cosmos, galaxy; world, earth, sphere, globe, orb, nature; heavenly body, celestial body, planet, planetoid, asteroid, moon, satellite, falling star, shooting star, meteor, meteorite, star, sun, constellation, nebula, quasar, pulsar, black hole; heavens, firmament, vault; atmosphere, air, ether, sky, night sky; astronomy, astrophysics, stargazing; observatory, planetarium, telescope; astrology, horoscope, signs of the Zodiac; cosmology, cosmogony, cosmography, geography; map, atlas.

adj. universal, cosmic, galactic; terrestrial, earthly, worldly, mundane; heavenly, celestial, empyrean; extraterrestrial, planetary, solar, astral, lunar; astronomical; geographical.

330 weight

n. gravity, gravitation, attraction; weight, heaviness, pressure, force, mass, bulk; ballast, load, freight, sinker, counterweight, paperweight, stone, rock, sandbags, anchor, plumb; burden.

balance, scales, weighing machine, weighbridge.

adj. heavy, weighty, ponderous, bulky, cumbersome, top-heavy; burdensome, oppressive, troublesome.

vb. weigh, balance, poise, measure, put on the scales, counterpoise, counterbalance; weigh down, weight, load, overload; burden, overwhelm, saddle.

331 lightness

n. lightness, levity, weightlessness, imponderability; buoy, cork; leaven, lightener, ferment, yeast.

adj. light, insubstantial; underweight; weightless; feathery, dainty, airy, fluffy; gentle, delicate, soft; floatable, buoyant, unsinkable; lightweight, summerweight; small, portable.

vb. be light, float, surface, swim; levitate, defy gravity, lighten, raise, ferment; unburden, take off, remove, unload, disencumber, jettison.

B Inorganic matter

332 density

n. density, solidity. thickness, compactness, concreteness, heaviness, concentration, congestion, substantiality; incompressibility, impenetrability, impermeability; consolidation, crystallization, coagulation, solidification, thickening, stiffening; mass, solid, body, substance, lump, conglomerate.

adj. dense, solid, thick, compact, close, heavy, impenetrable, impermeable, condensed, compressed; clotted, curdled; frozen; indivisible, insoluble.

vb. solidify, thicken, coagulate, freeze, clot, fix, crystallize, harden, stiffen, set, congeal, jell (*inf.*), curdle; petrify, ossify; compress, condense, compact.

see also 50

333 rarity

n. rarity, thinness, fineness; low pressure, vacuum, emptiness; rarefaction, attenuation.

adj. rare, thin, light, rarefied, fine, attenuated, airy, ethereal; weak, tenuous, sparse, shrill, flimsy, fragile, insubstantial, subtle; empty, void.

vb. rarefy, lessen, reduce pressure, purify, refine, thin, attenuate.

334 hardness

n. hardness, stiffness, firmness, toughness, rigidity, solidity, impenetrability, inflexibility; hardening, stiffening.

adj. hard, solid, thick, dense, compact; rigid, firm, stiff, taut, tight; tough, unyielding, unbreakable, impenetrable, unbending, inflexible, inelastic, unmalleable, impermeable.

vb. harden, toughen, strengthen, set, stiffen, temper; concentrate, consolidate, solidify, crystallize, freeze,

coagulate, congeal, fossilize, ossify, petrify, starch.

see also 537

335 softness

n. softness, penetrability, flexibility, plasticity, tractability, suppleness, pliancy, litheness; looseness, laxity.

adj. soft, smooth, fluffy, spongy, mellow; gentle, delicate; flimsy, limp; tender, pliant, flexible, plastic, elastic, supple, pliable, lithe, limber, mouldable.

vb. soften, ease, modify, temper, tenderize; subdue, assuage, mollify, appease; knead, mash; give, yield, relax, relent.

336 elasticity

n. elasticity, flexibility, pliability, springiness, spring, bounce, resilience, buoyancy; stretch, extensibility, tensility.

adj. elastic, flexible, pliant, resilient, buoyant; stretching, extensile, tensile.

vb. stretch; spring, bounce.

337 toughness

n. toughness, durability, strength, tenacity, cohesion; bone, gristle, cartilage.

adj. tough, durable, hard, firm, solid, robust, strong, stiff, enduring, unbreakable, tenacious; impervious, unyielding, resistant; fibrous, gristly, sinewy.

vb. toughen, strengthen, stiffen, harden.

338 brittleness

n. brittleness, frailty, fragility, delicacy.

adj. brittle, delicate, frail; breakable, fragile; crispy, crumbly; flimsy, frangible; shaky, unsteady; friable.

vb. break, break easily, split, snap,

shatter, fragment, burst, fall to pieces, splinter, crumble.

see also 48

339 texture

n. texture, pattern, weave, organization, composition, constitution, make-up, form, structure; feel, sense, taste, shape, mould, fibre, fabric, web, weft, tissue.

adj. structural, organizational, constructional. tectonic; textural, granular.

340 powderiness

n. powderiness, pulverulence; crumbling, pulverization; powder, dust, grain, particle, granule, crumb, flake, pollen.

adj. powdery, fine, granulated, pulverized, pulverulent; dusty; impalpable; crumbling, friable.

vb. grind, crush, pulverize, granulate, pound, beat, grate, scrape, crunch, crumble, atomize.

341 friction

n. friction, rubbing, abrasion, erosion, wearing away, grinding, filing, irritation; massage, polishing; stroke.

adj. frictional, abrasive, rubbing.

vb. rub, abrade, scour, grate, graze, rasp, chafe, grind, file, scrape, scrub; wear away, erode; polish, shine, smooth, massage; burnish; brush, clean, wipe.

342 lubrication

n. lubrication, anointment, unction; lubricant, grease, oil, wax, fat, ointment, cream, lotion, balm, salve, unguent; petrol, juice (*sl.*).

vb. lubricate, grease, oil, cream, daub, smear, coat, rub, anoint.

343 fluidity

n. fluidity, liquidity, wateriness, juiciness, solubility, dilution; fluid, liquid, liquor, vapour, solution, solvent, drink, flow.

adj. fluid, liquid, running, flowing, molten, liquefied, watery, juicy, liquescent.

vb. flow, run, pour, stream, swell; liquefy.

344 gaseity

n. gaseity, gaseousness, vaporousness, aeration; gas, vapour, steam, fume, air, smoke, fluid.

adj. gaseous, vaporous, vapory, gassy, gas-like, steaming, aeriform, airy, light, windy, volatile.

vb. gasify, aerate.

345 liquefaction

n. liquefaction, solubility, dissolution, thawing; solvent, dissolvent.

adj. runny, molten, liquefied, melted, thawed, disintegrated; liquefacient, soluble.

vb. liquefy, dissolve, melt, run, thaw, defrost, fuse, flux, condense, fluidify, fluidize, deliquesce, disintegrate.

346 vaporization

n. vaporization, evaporation, condensation, sublimation, gasification, volatization, distillation; vapour, moisture, exhalation, mist, smoke, sublimate.

adj. vaporous, steaming, steamy, gassy, volatile.

vb. vaporize, evaporate, sublimate, distil, diffuse, dissipate, gasify, exhale· smoke, fume, steam.

347 water

n. water, liquid, rain, wet, dampness; ice, steam, water vapour.

adj. watery, aquatic, aqueous,

hydrated, liquid, fluid, wet, moist, hydrous, aqua-, hydro-.

see also 349

348 air

n. air, oxygen, fresh air; airing, exposure, ventilation, air conditioning, aeration; atmosphere, stratosphere, ozone, ether, sky; pneumatics, aerodynamics.

weather, climate, elements; meteorology, forecasting.

adj. airy, aerial; exposed, ventilated, open, aerated; draughty, breezy, windy; pneumatic, aero-; metereological.

vb. air, aerate, ventilate, open, refresh, freshen, cool, aerify, purify, fan.

see also 359

349 moisture

n. moisture, humidity, dampness, wetness, precipitation; drip, damp, dew, rain, wet; moistening, saturation, wettening, humidification.

adj. moist, damp, wet, humid, muggy, dank, misty; saturated, soaked, sodden, waterlogged, awash, drowned, drenched, wet through, like a drowned rat.

vb. moisten, dampen, wet, humidify; sprinkle, dabble, shower, dip, sponge, splash; saturate, drench, soak, bathe, souse, steep, stream, seep, sog; duck, immerse, submerge; waterlog, drown, flood, swamp, inundate, deluge.

350 dryness

n. dryness, aridity, aridness, parchedness, desiccation, dehydration; thirst, drought.

adj. dry, arid, parched, unmoistened, rainless, sapless, evaporated; barren, desert, dusty, baked, scorched,

bleached; dried, dehydrated, thirsty; waterproof, rainproof, watertight.

vb. dry, dehydrate, freeze-dry, dripdry; desiccate, parch, bake, scorch, torrefy; air, evaporate; shrivel, wither; soak up, absorb.

351 ocean

n. ocean, sea, deep, brine, high seas; oceanography.

adj. oceanic, marine, maritime, pelagic; oceanographical.

352 land

n. land, terrain, *terra firma*, mainland, continent; inland, interior; peninsula, neck, isthmus; ground, soil, earth, gravel, sand, rock, pebble; fields, pasture; shore, beach, seaside, strand, bank, coastline, seaboard.

adj. terrestrial, earthy; inland, interior, landlocked, central; coastal, seaside, littoral, riverside, riparian.

353 gulf

n. gulf, inlet, bay, estuary, bight, mouth, harbour, lagoon, sound, fiord, firth, loch, strait, narrows, arm, kyle; cove, cave.

354 lake

n. lake, tarn, loch, lagoon, pool, pond, creek, mere, inland sea, reservoir, basin; puddle.

355 marsh

n. marsh, fen, swamp, mire, bog, quagmire, quicksand, morass, slough, moor, mud.

adj. marshy, soft, fenny, swampy, boggy, wet, waterlogged, squelchy, slushy, muddy, miry, paludal.

356 plain

n. plain, expanse, open country, flat, lowland, champaign, grassland; meadow, field, grass, pasture; steppe, prairie, savannah, pampa, llano; moor,

moorland, common, heath, wold;
upland, plateau, tableland, downs;
tundra, veld.

357 island

n. island, isle, islet, holm, eyot, ait,
archipelago; reef, atoll, ridge, sandbank, cay, key.

358 water in motion

n. river, watercourse, waterway,
tributary, branch, fork, effluent;
stream, brook, rivulet, beck, runnel,
rill, runlet, bourn, creek.

tide, current, flow, course, undercurrent; spring, fountain, spout, gush,
rush, jet, outpouring, uprising;
whirlpool, eddy, vortex, swirl,
maelstrom; wash, backwash.

wave, billow, swell, roller, surge,
crest, ripple, undulation, breaker, tidal
wave, white-caps, white horses; waterfall, cataract, fall, shoot, cascade,
torrent, rapids, weir.

rain, rainfall, precipitation, drizzle,
shower, downpour, thunderstorm,
cloudburst, flood, deluge, inundation,
monsoon; mist.

adj. runny, streaming; rainy, moist,
wet, showery, cloudy, thundery,
stormy; torrential.

vb. flow, run, stream, sweep, rush;
gush, well, spurt, squirt, jet, spout,
issue, flood, inundate; wave, undulate,
billow, swell, ripple, ebb; swirl, eddy,
surge, roll, whirl, tumble; dash, break,
splash; drop, drip, seep, leak, trickle,
dribble, gurgle; spill, overflow, spew,
exude; fall, cascade; drain, empty,
clear, tap, expel, deplete, decant, bleed.

rain, pour, patter, spit, drizzle,
shower.

359 air in motion

n. wind, draught, current, breeze,
whisk, whiff, puff, flutter, waft, zephyr;

gust, blast, flurry, flaw; gale, storm,
squall, blizzard, whirlwind, cyclone,
typhoon, tornado, hurricane, tempest;
trade wind, mistral, föhn.

breathing, respiration, inhalation,
expiration, exhalation, afflatus; breath,
gasp, sigh, pant, cough, sneeze, wheeze.

adj. windy, open, exposed, fresh,
blustery, squally, gusty, stormy, tempestuous; draughty, well-ventilated;
wheezy, asthmatic.

vb. blow, breeze, whiff, waft, flutter,
flap, buffet, sweep, whisk, fling; blast,
rush, roar, howl, wail, stream, whirl;
breathe, respire, inhale, exhale, expire,
puff, pant, gasp; sigh; cough, sneeze,
wheeze; pump, inflate, blow up, swell,
fill.

360 water channel

n. conduit, channel, way, passage,
bed, ditch, trench, trough, moat;
course, canal, aqueduct; tunnel, pipe,
pipeline, tube, main, duct, culvert;
spout, tap, funnel, siphon; drain, drainpipe, gutter, sewer; flume, gully,
cloaca.

361 air-pipe

n. air-pipe, shaft, tube; vent, chimney, flue, ventilator.

362 semiliquidity

n. semiliquidity, viscosity, glutinous-
ness, stickiness, adhesiveness; semiliquid, glue, paste, size, colloid, emulsion, syrup.

adj. semiliquid, semifluid,
gelatinous, viscous, viscid, glutinous,
coagulated, slimy, syrupy, creamy,
sticky, tacky, slushy, gummy, colloid.

363 bubble; cloud

n. bubble, globule, sac, froth, foam,
spray, surf, spume; fizz, head; lather,
suds; effervescence, fermentation,
bubbling.

cloud, haze, haziness, mist, fog, smog, pea-souper (*inf.*), film.

adj. bubbly, foaming, bubbling, soapy, effervescent, sparkling, fizzy, spumous, spumy; cloudy, overcast, dull, grey, unclear, murky, gloomy, dim, misty, hazy, foggy, nebulous.

vb. effervesce, bubble, boil, fizz, foam, ferment.

364 pulpiness

n. pulpiness, sponginess, softness, succulence; pulp, mash, sponge, paste, pap, mulch, mush, jelly, dough, batter, poultice.

adj. pulpy, mushy, doughy, soggy, spongy, pulpous, ripe, fleshy, succulent; thick, smooth.

vb. pulp, mash, crush.

365 unctuousness

n. unctuousness, oiliness, greasiness; oil, fat, grease, blubber; unction, oil, unguent, embrocation, salve, nard, ointment, lubricant, balm, emollient, remedy, cream; resin, gum, pitch, varnish, lacquer, shellac, asphalt, bitumen.

adj. unctuous, oily, greasy, fatty, unguent, creamy.

vb. grease, oil, lubricate; resin, varnish; anoint.

C Organic matter

366 animate matter

n. creation, nature, animals, plants, fauna, flora; creature, organism, cell, protoplasm; biology, natural history, nature study, ecology, genetics, evolution, biochemistry, anatomy, physiology, botany, zoology.

adj. animate, organic, biological.

367 inorganic matter

n. mineral, rock, deposit, ore, metal, coal; geology, mineralogy, metallurgy.

adj. inorganic, inanimate, mineral, metallurgical.

368 life

n. life, existence, being; organism, human, body, creature, man, person, individual, personage, mortal.

soul, spirit, life-blood, breath, heart; élan, verve; vivification, animation, liveliness, vigour, vitality, force, energy.

adj. living, alive, surviving, in the flesh, vital; lively, animated, vigorous, vivacious, forceful, energetic, spirited, alive and kicking, active.

vb. live, exist, be, have life, breathe, respire; move, subsist; be spared, survive.

be born, come to life, come into the world, see the light; bear, beget, conceive, give birth to, bring to life.

vivify, quicken, animate, reanimate, vitalize, enliven, revive, breathe life into.

369 death

n. death, mortality; decease, dying, passing, departure, end, expiration, exit, extinction, parting, separation, release, homecall; loss, bereavement; fatality; demise, dissolution.

last hour, death bed, last breath, swan-song; death list, death toll, casualty list; obituary; the dead, departed, deceased, ancestors, forefathers, those gone before.

adj. mortal, sick, perishing, deathly, moribund, at death's door, on one's last legs; dead, deceased, departed, late, lamented; lifeless, breathless; defunct, extinct, cold; extinguished, terminated, ended, exterminated, lost.

vb. die, depart, go, expire, pass away, give up the ghost, breathe one's last, go the way of all flesh, be taken, kick the bucket (*sl.*); perish, succumb, come to nothing, be no more; be killed, lose one's life; push up daisies (*inf.*).

370 killing

n. killing, slaying, slaughter, destruction, assassination, murder, homicide, manslaughter; bloodshed, carnage, massacre, genocide, butchery, holocaust, liquidation, extermination, annihilation, decimation; shooting, knifing, lynching, poisoning, execution, hanging, strangulation, electrocution, crucifixion, burning, drowning, vivisection; euthanasia, mercy killing; abortion; suicide, self-destruction, hara-kiri, kamikaze.

killer, murderer, assassin, slayer, butcher, cut-throat, poisoner, strangler; gunman, terrorist, gangster; homicidal maniac; hangman, executioner.

adj. killing, lethal, fatal, mortal, deadly, destructive; homicidal, murderous, internecine; suicidal.

vb. kill, murder, slay, destroy, take life, put to death, bump off (*sl.*), knock off (*sl.*), do in (*sl.*), do away with (*inf.*), slaughter, assassinate, massacre, butcher, mow down (*inf.*), gun down (*inf.*), liquidate, annihilate, decimate, exterminate; execute, behead, guillotine, decapitate; shoot, gun, knife, hang, lynch; poison; strangle, suffocate, choke, asphyxiate; put to sleep (*inf.*), put down, put away.

kill oneself, commit suicide, take one's life, do oneself in (*sl.*), blow one's brains out, shoot oneself, cut one's throat.

371 corpse

n. corpse, remains, body, carcass, skeleton, relics, ashes, dust, mummy, cadaver, stiff (*sl.*).

adj. cadaverous, corpse-like, deathlike, deathly, pale.

372 burial

n. burial, funeral, interment, entombment, sepulture; cremation, incineration; embalment, mummification.

burial service, funeral rites, last rites, mourning, obsequies; requiem, elegy, last post, knell, passing bell; epitaph, obituary, in memoriam, RIP; coffin, urn, sarcophagus, pall, mummy case.

mortuary, morgue; undertaker, funeral director; gravestone, headstone, tombstone, monument, memorial; tomb, grave, sepulchre, vault, crypt, mausoleum, barrow; burial ground, graveyard, churchyard, God's acre, cemetery, catacomb, necropolis; pyre, crematorium; war memorial, cenotaph; exhumation, disinterment.

adj. buried, interred; funereal, funeral, mourning, mournful, sad.

vb. bury, inter, inhume, entomb, enshrine, embalm, lay out, lay to rest, sepulture; cremate; exhume, disinter, unearth.

373 animality; animal

n. animality, fauna, zoology; animal, creature, beast, vertebrate, invertebrate; quadruped, biped, man; mammal, marsupial; carnivore, herbivore, omnivore; fish, amphibian, mollusc, crustacean; bird, fowl, bird of prey, waterfowl; insect; reptile; cattle, herd, livestock, poultry, game; pet, domestic animal; rodent, vermin, parasite.

adj. animal, zoological, mammalian; piscine, fishy; amphibian; avian.

374 vegetability; plant

n. vegetability, vegetation, botany;

plant, shrub; plantation, shrubbery, undergrowth, corn, grain, cereal, crop, field; flower, bloom, bud, petal, blossom; flower-bed, garden; foliage, foliation, leafage; grass, pasture, verdure, sod, turf, lawn; herb; weed; tree, sapling, scion; branch, limb, bough, twig, sprig, spray, shoot, stem, stalk, leaf; wood, forest, bush, jungle; copse, spinney, coppice, woodland, thicket, covert, arboretum; forestry, dendrology, conservation; seed, root, bulb.

adj. vegetal, vegetative, botanical, horticultural, floral, verdant, grassy, weedy, arboreal.

375 zoology
n. zoology, life science, anthropology, anatomy, physiology, ichthyology, ornithology, bird-watching, entomology, embryology, taxonomy.

adj. zoological, ornithological.

376 botany
n. botany, plant science, horticulture, ecology, phytology.

adj. botanical, horticultural.

377 management of animals
n. animal husbandry, breeding, stockbreeding, grazing, taming, domestication.

farm, ranch, homestead; fishery, aquarium; zoo, zoological gardens; veterinary science, vet; shepherd, herdsman, herd, cattleherd, cowherd.

vb. keep, husband, breed, rear, raise, herd, drive, ranch, farm, tend, shepherd; feed, fodder, graze, fatten, market; shear, chip, fleece; milk; tame, domesticate, train; groom.

378 agriculture
n. agriculture, farming, cultivation, horticulture, gardening, growing, crop raising, husbandry; strip farming, rotation crops, contour ploughing; landscape gardening.

farm, ranch, homestead, holding, smallholding, grange; kibbutz; farmland, meadow, grassland, farmstead, estate, croft, enclosure, land, field, soil, patch, plot, allotment, plantation; garden, orchard, nursery; greenhouse, vineyard, arboretum.

farmer, husbandman, agriculturalist, cultivator, tiller, planter, grower, rancher, homesteadman, peasant, serf, hiredman, labourer, farmhand; gardener, nurseryman, horticulturalist; landscape gardener.

adj. agrarian, farming, agricultural, rustic, rural, peasant; horticultural, garden.

vb. cultivate, till; fertilize, manure; water, irrigate; dig, plough, harrow; seed, sow, broadcast, disseminate, plant, drill, bed, transplant; weed, hoe; graft; harvest, reap, gather in, glean, winnow, thresh, mow, cut, scythe, bind, stack, pick, pluck.

379 mankind
n. mankind, humanity, human race, human beings, populace, population, the world, flesh; person, man, human being, individual, creature, mortal, body, earthling, *homo sapiens*, Adam, anthropoid; people, public, folk.

society, community, civilization, politics; nation, state, body politic, nationality, statehood; chauvinism, nationalism, imperialism; anthropology, social anthropology, ethnology, sociology.

adj. human, mortal; individual, personal; social, civilized; political, national, state, general, public, civil, federal, social, communal, societal, civic; nationalistic, chauvinist, racialist.

380 male

n. male, man, gentleman, sir; chap, fellow, guy (*sl.*), bloke (*inf.*), boy; virility, masculinity, manliness, manhood.

male animal, cock, drake, gander, dog, tom-cat, hart, stag, stallion, billy-goat, ox, bull; gelding.

adj. male, masculine; manly, virile; gentlemanly.

381 female

n. female, woman, lady, girl; madam, miss; fair sex, weaker sex; femininity, womanliness, girlishness, womanhood; feminism, women's lib; effeminacy; womankind.

female animal, hen, duck, goose, bitch, she-dog, filly, ewe, sow, hind, doe, mare, nanny-goat, cow.

adj. female, feminine, girlish, womanly, lady-like; effeminate.

IV Intellect

1 Formation of ideas

A Intellectual operations in general

382 intellect

n. intellect, mind, brain, consciousness, mentality, intelligence, intellectuality, instinct, faculties; perception, conception, capacity, judgment, understanding, reasoning, genius, wisdom; psychology, behaviourism; psychiatry, psychotherapy.

soul, spirit, psyche, heart, individuality, personality, conscience, self, ego, id, superego, unconscious, subconscious.

adj. mental, intellectual, conceptional, abstract, perceptual, critical, rational, conscious, cognitive, cerebral, intelligent; psychological, psychic, subconscious, subliminal; spiritual.

vb. conceive, cognize, perceive, reason, judge; realize, sense, mark, note.

see also 434

383 absence of intellect

n. unintellectuality, unintelligence, imbecility, stupidity, shallowness, mindlessness, brainlessness.

adj. unintellectual, unintelligent, empty-headed, mindless, brainless.

see also 435

384 thought

n. thought, cogitation, concentration, brain-work; reflection, meditation, rumination, contemplation, thoughtfulness, brooding, pondering, absorption, preoccupation, deliberation; consideration, perception, appreciation, discernment, observation, reasoning, concluding.

adj. thoughtful, pensive, contemplative, reflective, studious; absorbed, engrossed, wrapped up in, dreamy; introspective; discerning, penetrating, intellectual.

vb. think, cogitate, consider, give thought to, concentrate, reflect, meditate, deliberate, ponder, muse, ruminate, contemplate, brood, turn over in one's mind, mull, study, examine, bear in mind, put on one's thinking cap (*inf.*), have on one's mind, take it into one's head (*inf.*); esteem, appraise, weigh up; philosophize, reconsider.

occur to, come to mind, strike, suggest itself, enter one's head.

385 absence of thought
n. thoughtlessness, irrationality, incomprehensibility, folly, senselessness, ignorance, inattention, inconsideration, carelessness, neglect.

adj. thoughtless, irrational, unreasoning, incomprehensible, foolish, blank, vacant, switched off (*inf.*).

vb. not think about, ignore, forget, dismiss, get off one's mind, get out of one's mind, get out of one's head; think no more of, not give another thought to, not give a second thought, not enter one's head.

386 idea
n. idea, notion, concept, conception, thought, mental impression, image, impression; conjecture, fancy, guess, theory, hypothesis, postulate; observation, opinion, assessment, plan.

see also 420

387 topic
n. topic, subject, problem, matter, question; argument, theme, burden, concern, thesis, proposition, thrust, *leitmotif*, issue, point, point in question, moot point.

B Preliminary conditions and operations

388 curiosity
n. curiosity, interest, concern, regard; thirst, quest, desire, eagerness, inclination; inquisitiveness, intrusiveness, nosiness (*sl.*), prying.

questioner; busy-body, snoop, intruder, meddler, Nosy Parker (*sl.*); gossip, backbiter, chatterbox, scandalmonger.

adj. curious, interested, concerned, into (*inf.*), questioning; inquisitive, searching, poking, scrutinizing; intrusive, prying, snooping, meddlesome, nosy (*sl.*).

vb. enquire, question, investigate, seek; show interest, be into (*inf.*), have a thing about (*inf.*); intrude, pry, snoop, meddle, gossip, chatter, backbite.

389 incuriosity
n. incuriosity, apathy, dislike, disinclination.

adj. incurious, unconcerned, inattentive, apathetic, indifferent, uninquisitive, uninterested, bored.

vb. ignore, disregard, be blind to, dismiss, take no interest in, not care less.

390 attention
n. attention, regard, notice, observation, inspection; consideration, study, attentiveness; assiduousness, diligence; mindfulness, heed, heedfulness, vigilance; concentration, preoccupation.

adj. attentive, mindful; heeding, wary, vigilant; considerate, observant; studious, assiduous, diligent.

vb. pay attention, listen, catch, give heed to, observe, notice, take notice, mind, heed, look to, regard, note, take into account; consider, study, inspect, examine, mark, scrutinize, concentrate on; drink in (*inf.*), lap up (*inf.*), hang on someone's every word; lose oneself in; keep one's ear to the ground (*inf.*); attract, draw, pull, focus.

391 inattention
n. inattention, carelessness, inconsideration, unconcern, heedlessness, thoughtlessness; slackness, indolence; neglect, disregard; indifference, cool-

ness, coldness, detachment; absent-mindedness, wandering.

adj. inattentive, careless, inconsiderate, thoughtless, heedless, unobservant; negligent, indifferent, cool, cold, detached; absent-minded, distracted.

vb. be inattentive, dream, daydream, let one's mind wander; not catch, miss, disregard, overlook, neglect; go in one ear and out the other; distract, divert, draw away, turn away, call away, detract, attract from, beguile; upset, disconcert.

392 care

n. care, concern, regard, thought, heed, consideration, solicitude, thoughtfulness, pains; carefulness, scrupulousness, prudence, judiciousness, wisdom; watchfulness, vigilance, alertness; forethought, precaution, caution.

exactness, particularity, thoroughness, meticulousness, neatness, fastidiousness, conscientiousness; economy, conservation, frugality, management, husbandry, stewardship.

oversight, direction, surveillance, supervision, inspection, protection, guarding.

adj. careful, concerned, thoughtful, considerate, courteous, kind, solicitous; prudent, judicious, wise, discreet, unobtrusive, self-possessed, watchful, sober, alert, awake, circumspect, vigilant; diplomatic, politic.

thorough, rigorous, particular, precise, exact, exacting, discriminating, conscientious, meticulous, punctilious, scrupulous; neat, tidy, fussy, finicky; pedantic, fastidious, religious; assiduous, diligent, painstaking, dependable, faithful; economical, sparing, frugal, thrifty, stingy (*inf.*).

vb. be careful, mind, heed, tend, look after, take care of; watch, observe; superintend, supervise, direct, manage, stand over; baby-sit, chaperon; keep vigil; keep tabs on, follow up, protect, support, guard.

393 neglect

n. neglect, carelessness, unconcern, disregard, inconsideration, negligence, neglectfulness, apathy, indifference, omission, dereliction, failure, procrastination; imprudence, rashness, hastiness.

adj. negligent, careless, inconsiderate, unthinking, thoughtless, unmindful, forgetful, oblivious; remiss, lax, inattentive; lackadaisical, imprudent, unguarded, hasty, rash, unwary, reckless, unheeding, injudicious, unwise; apathetic, indifferent, casual, slipshod, lazy; wasteful, extravagant, immoderate.

vb. neglect, omit, miss, forget, dismiss, reject, leave undone, lose sight of, evade, gloss over, skip, skimp; disregard, ignore, overlook, not look at, pass over, make light of, brush aside, laugh off, pooh-pooh, shut one's eyes to, give the go-by, turn a blind eye to.

see also **920**

394 enquiry

n. enquiry, inquiry, examination, investigation, study, analysis, search, probe, quest, perusal; checking, scrutiny, review, inspection; question, query, request, invitation, petition, challenge, feeler; experiment, quiz, test, exam, viva, questionnaire; interrogation, interview, dialogue, cross-examination, grilling, catechism.

questioner, examiner, enquirer, interrogator, interviewer, researcher, investigator, canvasser, pollster.

adj. inquiring, inquisitive, curious, nosy (*sl.*); exploratory, fact-finding.

vb. enquire, ask, put a question, pose, put it to; call upon, request, invite, challenge, charge, bid, petition, canvass; question, interrogate, quiz, cross-examine, interview, grill; seek, look for, search, hunt, turn inside out, peruse; sniff out (*inf.*), smell out; investigate, examine, study, inspect, analyse, probe, scrutinize, check, review, monitor; try; hear; pry, snoop, spy.

395 answer

n. answer, reply, response, acknowledgement; comeback, feedback, rebuttal, rejoinder, retort; repartee, backchat, retaliation.

answerer, replier, correspondent, examinee, candidate.

adj. answering, responsive.

vb. answer, reply, respond, come back to, write back, acknowledge, remark, rejoin, retort, answer back, rebut.

396 experiment

n. experiment, test, research; observation, analysis, inspection, operation, diagnosis, exercise; check, verification, proof, sifting; rehearsal, practice run, trial run, test case, pilot, pilot scheme; feeler, probe; speculation, guess, conjecture, trial and error, hit and miss, shot in the dark, hypothesis; sounding board, guinea pig.

researcher, research worker, scientist, boffin (*sl.*), back-room boy, experimenter, experimentalist, speculator.

adj. experimental, hypothetical; tentative, trial, provisional, temporary, probationary, preliminary, preparatory, unproved, speculative, trial, test.

vb. experiment, investigate, study, examine, scrutinize, explore, research,

search, sound out, prove; analyse, diagnose; check, verify, prove; guess, speculate, hypothesize; put out a feeler, see which way the wind is blowing, spy out the land.

397 comparison

n. comparison, juxtaposition; weighing, estimation, measurement; relation, connection, association, balance, match, parallel, parallelism, correspondence, equation; identification, resemblance, similarity, likening, analogy, illustration, example, picture, metaphor, simile, allegory; contrast, opposition.

vb. compare, juxtapose, parallel, draw a parallel between, put side by side; measure, weigh, confront, collate; liken, relate, associate, link, balance, match, equate; contrast, oppose, separate.

398 discrimination

n. discrimination, discernment, acumen, astuteness, keenness, shrewdness, penetration; distinction, nicety, differentiation; diagnosis, appreciation, critique, judgment, sense, sensitivity, tact, feel, refinement, taste, selection, choice.

adj. discriminating, careful, selective, particular, exacting, choosy (*inf.*), judicious, tactful, discerning, perceptive, sensitive, critical, tasteful, refined.

vb. discriminate, differentiate, discern, tell apart, tell from, distinguish; compare and contrast; choose, pick carefully, select, separate, set apart.

399 indiscrimination

n. indiscrimination, uncriticalness, insensitiveness, tastelessness.

adj. indiscriminate, undiscriminating, unselective, uncritical, undiscerning, careless; mixed, blanket, promiscuous; random, haphazard; aimless, chaotic, confused.

vb. not discriminate, draw no distinction, disregard differences, lump together; confuse, confound, mix, muddle, jumble together.

400 measurement

n. measurement, mensuration; quantification; estimation, determination, computation, calculation, assessment, evaluation, reckoning; graduation, calibration; measure, dimension, distance, degree, pitch, time; size, length, depth, height, width, breadth, thickness; area; mass, weight, density, volume, capacity, pressure, intensity, speed, strength, calibre, viscosity; quantity, magnitude, range, extent; amplitude, frequency, ratio, diameter, radius; temperature.

meter, gauge, scale, rule, ruler, tape-measure, slide-rule, calculator, computer; scales, balance, mark, grade, step, point, limit, standard, criterion; weights and measures, imperial system, avoirdupois, apothecary, troy, metric system, SI unit; metrication.

adj. mensural, dimensional; measurable, assessable, calculable, computable.

vb. measure, quantify, estimate, compute, assess, count, reckon, determine, evaluate, appraise, calculate, survey; gauge, calibrate, graduate; take a reading; level, square; survey, map; average; check; go metric, metricate.

C Materials for reasoning

401 evidence

n. evidence, fact, clue, reason, justification, explanation, grounds, data, case; support, foundation, backing;

sign, indication, trace; document, documentation, information; testimony, witness, statement, plea, assertion, allegation, attestation, exhibit, reference, affidavit; confirmation, corroboration.

adj. suggestive, indicative, symptomatic, corroborative, supporting.

vb. evidence, show, suggest, indicate, evince, illustrate, demonstrate, document, manifest, imply; confirm, verify, support, substantiate, attest, corroborate; testify, bear witness to, witness, affirm; speak for itself (*inf.*), speak volumes (*inf.*).

see also **413**

402 counter-evidence

n. counter-evidence, counterclaim, defence, rebuttal, answer, reply.

adj. rebutting, defending, conflicting; uncorroborative, countervailing; contradictory, contrary, answering, replying.

vb. weigh against, contradict, rebut, refute, squash, deny; be contrary to; cancel out.

see also **414**

403 qualification

n. qualification, modification, limitation, restriction; proviso, exception, reservation; allowance.

adj. qualifying, qualificatory, provisional, contingent, conditional, mitigating, extenuating.

vb. qualify, modify, adjust; limit, restrict, restrain, moderate, mitigate, lessen, temper; condition, colour, make exceptions, exempt, allow for, make allowances for.

see also **700**

404 possibility

n. possibility, potentiality, practicability, feasibility, plausibility, reasonableness, virtuality.

adj. possible, likely, probable; virtual, potential; able, capable, viable, feasible, plausible, practical, practicable, available, attainable, within reach, obtainable, within the bounds of possibility; conceivable, thinkable, imaginable, credible.

vb. be possible, can, may, might, stand a chance; make possible, enable, admit of.

see also **406**

405 impossibility

n. impossibility, impracticability, unavailability, inaccessibility; unreasonableness, no hope, hopelessness, no chance.

adj. impossible, unbelievable, inconceivable, unimaginable, unthinkable; prohibited; insoluble, difficult; unable, implausible, unpracticable, unavailable, insurmountable, insuperable, inaccessible, unobtainable, out of the question, beyond the bounds of possibility.

vb. be impossible, defy possibilities; not dream of (*inf.*); make impossible, exclude.

adv. no way (*inf.*).

see also **407**

406 probability

n. probability, likelihood, likeliness, expectation; prospect, promise, chance, possibility, good chance, hope, opportunity.

adj. probable, likely, expected; reasonable, presumable, on the cards, supposable; promised, well-founded, seeming; feasible, practicable, workable, plausible, credible.

vb. be probable, may well happen, show signs of; make likely, increase the chances of, hope for.

adv. probably, likely, no doubt, in all probability, quite possibly, most likely, to be expected, to be supposed, as likely as not, everything being equal.

407 improbability

n. improbability, unlikelihood, implausibility, inconceivableness, unreasonableness; rarity, infrequency; bare possibility, million to one chance.

adj. improbable, unlikely, unexpected, unreasonable, impracticable, unworkable, implausible, unbelievable, hardly possible, unheard of, doubtful, dubious, questionable; absurd, extraordinary.

vb. be improbable, probably not happen.

408 certainty

n. certainty, certitude; conviction, assurance; reliance, confidence, trust; truth, accuracy, genuineness; dogmatism; unambiguity, conclusiveness; necessity, inevitability, inexorability.

foregone conclusion, safe bet, sure thing (*inf.*), dead cert (*sl.*).

adj. certain, settled, decided, final, definite; absolute, sure, conclusive, solid, irrefutable, indubitable, indisputable, unquestionable, unmistakable, incontrovertible, unassailable, undisputed; reliable, unfailing, unshakable, inerrant, infallible, sound, authoritative, unerring, trustworthy; unambiguous, unequivocal, incontestable; unconditional; ascertained, certified, verified, attested, confirmed, ratified; self-evident, axiomatic.

vb. make certain, guarantee, authenticate, certify, check, confirm, test, prove, verify, corroborate, ratify; ensure, secure, settle, attest, endorse, clinch; commit, engage, take sides; seal, sign, shake hands.

adv. certainly, without doubt, of

course, definitely, at all events, sure thing (*inf.*); in the bag (*inf.*).

409 uncertainty

n. uncertainty, incertitude; unreliability, questionableness, unpredictability, untrustworthiness, ambiguity; vagueness, obscurity; inconclusiveness, indeterminateness, improbability, unlikelihood.

doubt, disbelief, unbelief, suspicion, misgiving, scepticism, agnosticism, faithlessness, doubtfulness, incredulity; indecision, equivocalness, wavering, hesitancy, suspense; perplexity, bewilderment; puzzle, problem, maze, dilemma, quandary, enigma; fog, haziness; anybody's guess.

adj. uncertain, doubtful, undecided; unsure, inconclusive, ambiguous, vague, unclear, indeterminate, unpredictable, unlikely, possible; risky, chancy, insecure; haphazard, random, casual; questionable, unreliable, fallible, erring; shakable, precarious; puzzling, perplexing.

controversial, open, debatable, contentious, problematical, moot; uncertified, unverified, unattested, unconfirmed, unratified.

doubting, unbelieving, suspicious, sceptical, faithless, distrustful, agnostic.

vb. be uncertain, doubt, flounder, grope, fumble; suspect, smell a rat; not know where one stands, not know which way to turn; sit on the fence, waver; fall between two stools; puzzle, bewilder, perplex.

adv. in the air, in question, open to question.

D Reasoning processes

410 reasoning

n. reasoning, rationalizing; judgment, argumentation; reason, rationality, logic, rationalism; thinking, brainwork, cogitation, knowing, realizing; insight, discernment, acumen, penetration, understanding, comprehension, grasp; reflection, deliberation; concluding.

conclusion, inference, deduction, induction, derivation; syllogism; problem, proposition, premise, postulate, thesis, theorem.

discussion, conversation, exchange, dialogue, interview, disputation, argument, dispute, debate, controversy, symposium; apologetics.

adj. rational, reasoning, logical, sound, rationalistic, reasonable; thoughtful, deliberate, collected; arguing, discursive, controversial, polemical; argumentative.

vb. reason, argue, discuss, converse, dispute, talk about, explain; defend, justify, plead, make out a case, support, contend; philosophize; conclude, put two and two together (*inf.*), deduce, infer, derive, syllogize; be reasonable, add up (*inf.*), make sense, hold water.

411 intuition

n. intuition, instinct, sentiment, feeling, sense; insight, inspiration, extra-sensory perception, ESP, sixth sense; automatic reaction, reflex action, hunch, presentiment, premonition, impression.

adj. intuitive, instinctive; involuntary, reflex, automatic, mechanical, unthinking; spontaneous, inspired, impulsive.

vb. feel, sense, feel in one's bones,

guess, just know, have a funny feeling, have the feeling, follow one's nose.

412 false reasoning

n. sophistry, irrationality, unreasonableness, unsoundness, invalidity; delusion, deceit, deception, erroneousness, speciousness, evasion.

fallacy, sophism, ambiguity, solecism, illogicality, paralogism; inconsistency, *non sequitur*, contradiction; circular argument, vicious circle; misinterpretation; miscalculation; preconception; perversion, prejudice, deviation, aberration.

adj. sophistic, fallacious, illogical, specious, inconsistent, loose, contradictory, ambiguous, solecistic; irrational, unreasonable, unsound, untenable, inconsistent, invalid, deceptive, erroneous, heretical.

vb. reason falsely, evade the issue, beat about the bush, miss the point, beg the question; cavil.

413 demonstration

n. demonstration, proof, verification, justification, establishment, affirmation, validation, corroboration; averment; explanation, elucidation, interpretation, illustration; exhibition, presentation, display.

adj. demonstrative; demonstrated, clear, evident, conclusive, certain, decisive; established, concluded, upheld, valid; demonstrable, verifiable, deducible, inferable.

vb. demonstrate, prove, show, verify, make evident, establish, confirm, substantiate, bear out, affirm, authenticate, attest, validate, test, check; declare, testify, witness, document; have a case; settle, determine; justify; explain, illustrate, describe; manifest, exhibit, display.

414 disproof

n. disproof, confutation, refutation, invalidation, rebuttal, contradiction, denial; upset; exposure; clincher.

adj. disproved, confuted, invalidated; shown up, exposed; contradicted.

vb. disprove, prove false, rebut, invalidate, repudiate, contradict, deny; contend, debate, argue, oppose, dispute; show up (*inf.*), discredit, expose; overthrow, overturn, defeat, finish, confound, overwhelm, crush, floor, silence; knock the bottom out of (*inf.*), cut the ground from under one's feet, get the better of.

E Results of reasoning

415 judgment

n. judgment, consideration, contemplation, appraisal, examination, review, weighing, sifting, assessment, estimation, appreciation, evaluation, determination; adjudication, arbitration; report, opinion, view, belief, idea, decree, decision, finding, recommendation, pronouncement, verdict, ruling, resolution.

judge, assessor, examiner, valuer, surveyor, adjudicator, arbitrator, referee, umpire.

adj. judicial, judicious; critical; unprejudiced, unbiased.

vb. judge, consider, contemplate, size up (*inf.*), examine, review, appraise, survey, analyse, weigh, sift, assess, evaluate, estimate, appreciate; decide, conclude, find, recommend, pronounce, rule, decree, settle, adjudicate, arbitrate.

416 misjudgment

n. misjudgment, miscalculation, misconception, misunderstanding, misinterpretation, distortion, overestimation, preconception; underestimation; prejudice, bias; narrow-mindedness, pettiness, narrowness, bigotry.

adj. misjudging, wrong; uncritical, unrealistic; injudicious, unwise, illjudged; partial, unfair, one-sided, biased, prejudiced, intolerant; narrowminded, petty, mean, narrow, shortsighted, bigoted, insular.

vb. misjudge, miscalculate, misconceive, misconstrue, misapprehend, misunderstand, bark up the wrong tree (*inf.*); undervalue, overvalue, overrate; prejudge, presume, suppose, preconceive, jump to conclusions; prejudice, bias, jaundice, twist, sway, warp, influence.

see also 916

417 overestimation

n. overestimation, overvaluation, overrating, exaggeration, overstatement; optimism.

adj. overestimated, exaggerated.

vb. overestimate, exaggerate, overvalue, overrate; maximize, emphasize, make a mountain out of a molehill, make too much of, paint in glowing colours.

see also 481

418 underestimation

n. underestimation, undervaluation, understatement, minimization; pessimism.

adj. underestimated, understated; deprecatory; modest.

vb. underestimate, underplay, play down, underrate, understate, minimize; depreciate, disparage, slight; make light of, not do justice to, think too little of.

419 discovery

n. discovery, finding, disclosure, uncovering; manifestation, revelation; detection, identification, catching; invention; exploration.

adj. on the right track, near, close, warm (*inf.*).

vb. discover, find, hit upon; realize, see, perceive, understand, become aware of, get wise to, get on to, twig (*inf.*); meet, come across, happen upon; expose, disclose, detect, spot, lay bare, reveal, uncover, unearth, bring to light, run to earth (*inf.*), run to ground (*inf.*), track down; catch in the act, catch red-handed.

420 belief

n. belief, credence, trust, acceptance, faith, credit; reliance, dependence, conviction, confidence, persuasion; certainty, surety, assurance, hope; admission, confession, avowal.

creed, doctrine, dogma, credo, revelation; tenet, canon, principle; articles of faith, catechism.

opinion, thought, view, sentiment, idea, notion, conception, impression, assumption; attitude, way of thinking; point of view, position, outlook, angle, stand, stance.

adj. believing, accepting, reliant, dependent, convinced, persuaded, certain, confident; believable, credible, tenable, plausible, trustworthy, reliable, unfailing.

vb. believe, accept, hold, trust, depend, rely, be convicted of, be persuaded of, take at one's word, take on trust, take one's word for; think, consider, regard as, suppose, presume, surmise, fancy, assume, deem, conclude; come round to, change one's views, be converted; have faith in, be a believer, profess, confess.

convince, persuade, bring round, prove, argue, assure, satisfy, make realize, bring home to; teach; captivate, have a way with (*inf.*).

see also 854

421 unbelief

n. unbelief, disbelief, doubt, uncertainty, incredulity, scepticism, misgiving, suspicion, mistrust, distrust, qualm, hesitation, reservation, apprehension, irresolution; faithlessness, rejection; agnosticism, atheism.

adj. unbelieving, disbelieving, doubting, questioning, sceptical, distrusting, incredulous; unbelievable, untenable, unreliable, doubtful, dubious, suspicious, questionable, implausible.

vb. disbelieve, doubt, hesitate, waver, not believe, give no credence to, lack confidence in, set no store by; mistrust, suspect, question, challenge.

422 gullibility

n. gullibility, credulity, simpleness, unsophistication.

adj. gullible, credulous, trusting, unsuspecting, simple, naive, unsophisticated, inexperienced, guileless, simple, green.

vb. be gullible, fall for (*inf.*), be easily persuaded.

423 incredulity

n. incredulity, suspicion, scepticism; sophistication.

adj. incredulous, unbelieving, sceptical, unresponsive, ungullible, sophisticated.

vb. refuse to believe, distrust, doubt; reject, turn a deaf ear to.

see also 421

424 assent

n. assent, affirmative, yes; approval, agreement, acceptance, support, approbation; authorization, permission, consent, empowering, legalization, authority, sanction, guarantee, warrant, authentication, ratification, endorsement, affirmation, go-ahead (*inf.*), green light (*inf.*), nod (*sl.*).

like-mindedness, unanimity, consensus, general agreement; supporter, follower, assenter, signer, subscriber, ratifier, signatory, aye.

adj. assenting, acquiescent; approved, accepted, voted, carried, passed; unanimous, of one mind.

vb. assent, say yes to, agree, concur, affirm, accept, support, subscribe to, approve, vote for, pass, rubber-stamp (*inf.*), put up with (*inf.*), go along with, tolerate, stand for (*inf.*), bear, endure, acquiesce; acknowledge, admit, concede, grant, yield, recognize, defer to.

authorize, grant permission, empower, legalize, ratify, sign, endorse, authenticate, seal.

425 dissent

n. dissent, disapproval, disagreement, dissidence, disapprobation; difference, variance, discord, dissension, protest, controversy, vendetta, animosity, division; non-conformity; non-acceptance, withdrawal, secession; objection, reservation, negative, no.

dissenter, objector, protester, rebel, non-conformist, caviller; interrupter, heckler; separatist; recusant.

adj. dissident, disagreeing, differing; protesting, objecting.

vb. dissent, disagree, disapprove, differ, agree to differ, protest, object, oppose, challenge, heckle, shout down, take exception; reject, refuse, contradict; withdraw, secede.

426 knowledge

n. knowledge, knowing, awareness, consciousness, recognition, realization, understanding, grasp, cognition; intelligence, education, instruction, learning, erudition, scholarship, culture, bookishness; accomplishments, attainments; facts, information, encyclopedia; expertise, know-how, skill, proficiency; wisdom, maturity, experience.

adj. knowing, conscious, mindful, aware, cognizant; discerning, perceptive; acquainted, familiar, well versed in, well grounded in, *au fait;* clever, intelligent, informed, instructed, trained, knowledgeable, educated, well-taught, well-read, learned, erudite, scholarly, cultured, intellectual; mature, wise, experienced.

known, widely known, common, proverbial, commonplace, household name, hackneyed; infamous, notorious.

vb. know, realize, understand, grasp, see, perceive, realize, apprehend, be aware of, discern, appreciate, recognize; experience; be well-informed, be well up on, be into (*inf.*), know backwards, know inside out, know like the back of one's hand.

see also **434, 460**

427 ignorance
n. ignorance, unawareness, unconsciousness, unknowingness, nescience; unenlightenment, incomprehension, darkness, fog, haziness, vagueness; inexperience, immaturity, greenness, naivety, simplicity, empty-headedness, stupidity; unlearnedness, unintellectuality, illiteracy; unskilfulness, awkwardness.

smattering, shallowness; unknown, unknown quantity, unexplored ground,

virgin territory, mystery, closed book, sealed book.

adj. ignorant, unaware, unknowing; unmindful, unconscious, disregarding; inexperienced, immature, green, inept, simple, stupid, thick, dense; unenlightened, in the dark, unfamiliar with, not conversant, a stranger to, none the wiser; untaught, illiterate, uneducated, untrained, backward, unscholarly, unlearned, uncultivated, unread, uncultured, Philistine, unintellectual; unknown, untold, unseen, mysterious, secret, undiscovered, virgin, uncharted.

vb. not know, be ignorant, be in the dark, not have any idea, not have the foggiest idea (*inf.*); pass (*inf.*).

see also **435**

428 student
n. student, scholar, schoolchild, learner, disciple; philosopher, scientist, researcher, expert, man of letters, wise man, savant, sage; professor, don, teacher, doctor; bookworm, intellectual, egghead (*inf.*); genius, brain, know-all, mine of information, walking encyclopedia.

see also **473, 474**

429 ignoramus
n. ignoramus, know-nothing, dunce, fool, blockhead; greenhorn, raw recruit, babe, simpleton.

see also **437**

430 truth
n. truth, fact, reality, the case, gospel truth, plain truth, real thing, real McCoy (*inf.*).

trueness, verity, correctness, exactitude, accuracy, precision, perfection, rectitude, faithfulness, sincerity, honesty; authenticity, infallibility, genuineness, validity.

adj. true, truthful, veracious, real,

right, factual, correct, objective, actual; historical; genuine, authentic, original, official, veritable; unadulterated, unmixed; attested, valid, guaranteed; undisputed, conclusive, final; accurate, exact, precise, faithful, infallible; sincere, honest, upright.

vb. be true, be the case; ring true; hit the nail on the head (*inf.*); come true, come about, happen, occur.

see also 476

431 error

n. error, mistake, fault, blunder, failure, fall, flaw, lapse, omission, lie, untruth, wrong, deviation, sin; *faux pas*, slip, slip-up (*inf.*); misjudgment, misunderstanding, misconception, inaccuracy, mismanagement; misprint, literal; bloomer (*sl.*), clanger (*sl.*), howler (*sl.*).

erroneousness, falsity, inaccurateness, inexactness.

adj. wrong, incorrect, unreal, untrue; unauthentic, unoriginal, spurious; inaccurate, inexact, imprecise; erroneous, mistaken, lying, untruthful, in error; unfaithful, disloyal, deceitful, corrupt, unsound; deceptive, fallacious, misleading, pretended, sham, counterfeit, faked, mocked; misunderstood; fallible.

vb. go wrong, make a mistake, err, blunder, slip up (*inf.*), bungle; be wrong, be mistaken; misconceive, misunderstand; not hold water, fall down, fall to the ground; mislead, lead astray, lead up the garden path (*inf.*), pervert, deceive, trick, hoax.

see also 477, 478

432 maxim

n. maxim, proverb, saying, truth, text, dictum, motto, slogan, watchword, moral, aphorism, adage, axiom; banality, truism, platitude, commonplace, cliché; epigram, witticism.

adj. aphoristic, proverbial, epigrammatic; brief, concise, pithy, terse; trite, commonplace.

433 absurdity

n. absurdity, ridiculousness, ludicrousness, outrageousness, folly, silliness, stupidity, nonsense; spoonerism, malapropism; jest, trick, practical joke, prank, farce, buffoonery, clowning, wildness; extravaganza.

adj. absurd, ridiculous, crazy, farcical, nonsensical, senseless, inane, wild, foolish, silly, stupid, bizarre, extravagant, fantastic.

vb. be absurd, talk nonsense, fool around; play tricks.

see also 451

434 intelligence; wisdom

n. intelligence, understanding, brightness, cleverness, brilliance; genius, talent, brains, grey matter, intellect, sense, common sense, wit.

wisdom, experience, erudition, sagacity, sapience; shrewdness, discernment, judgment, acumen, insight, perspicacity, sharpness, acuteness, penetration, prudence, foresight.

adj. intelligent, clever, bright, brilliant, able, knowledgeable; wise, sagacious, shrewd, prudent, knowing, contemplative, reasoning, thoughtful, sober, sensible, judicious, circumspect, discreet, considerate, astute, perceptive, perspicacious, far-sighted, discerning, quick, acute, sharp, penetrating, keen, discriminating, having one's wits about one, not born yesterday (*inf.*).

vb. be wise, understand, discern; have one's head screwed on the right way (*inf.*).

see also 426

435 unintelligence; folly

n. unintelligence, stupidity, dullness, slowness, heaviness; foolishness, folly, weakness, shallowness, silliness, simplicity, childishness, puerility, imbecility; imprudence, short-sightedness, indiscretion.

adj. unintelligent, unthinking, unreasoning; stupid, dull, slow, weak, shallow, superficial, vacant, simple, dumb, thick, dense, empty-headed, slow-witted, feeble-minded, simple-minded, weak-minded, half-witted, blockish, oafish, feather-brained, doltish; foolish, crazy, silly, insane, inane, idiotic, imbecile, puerile, childish; backward, retarded, handicapped, subnormal, deprived; unwise, imprudent, short-sighted, undiscerning.

vb. be foolish, act the fool, fool around, lark about (*inf.*).

see also 427

436 sage

n. sage, wise man, man of learning, savant, pundit, expert, doctor, scholar, master, great thinker, authority, oracle, elder statesman, connoisseur, luminary; wiseacre, know-all, sciolist.

see also 428, 473

437 fool

n. fool, simpleton, dunce, idiot, ignoramus, scatterbrain, half-wit, fathead, thickhead, blockhead, nitwit, nincompoop, moron, cretin, imbecile, numskull, bore, dolt, ass, buffoon, chump (*sl.*), lout, oaf, ninny, jerk (*sl.*), twit (*sl.*).

see also 429, 630

438 sanity

n. sanity, saneness, balance, normality, clearmindedness, lucidity, wholesomeness, *mens sana*, rationality, reason.

adj. sane, normal, sound-minded, healthy-minded, sound, right-minded, sober, lucid, in one's right mind, self-possessed, all there (*inf.*).

439 insanity

n. insanity, insaneness, madness, lunacy; imbecility, cretinism, idiocy; phobia, mania, craze, passion, obsession, infatuation, fixation, compulsion; mental illness, nervous breakdown, nervous disorder; nervousness, nerves; hysteria, frenzy, fever, attack, fit, rage; peculiarity, eccentricity, abnormality, oddity.

adj. insane, mad, unsound, unbalanced, crazy, deranged, confused, demented, rabid, berserk, out of one's mind, off one's head, off one's rocker (*sl.*); obsessed, infatuated; frenzied, wild, raging, furious; eccentric, odd, cranky, peculiar.

vb. be mad, wander, ramble; go mad, lose one's sanity, take leave of one's senses, go out of one's mind, crack up (*inf.*), go off one's rocker (*sl.*); madden, drive mad, unbalance.

440 madman

n. madman, lunatic, mental case, loony (*sl.*), bedlamite; maniac, psychopath, psychotic, paranoid, hysteric, neurotic, manic-depressive, melancholic, hypochondriac, kleptomaniac; imbecile, idiot, moron, cretin, mongol; fool, crank, nut (*sl.*), eccentric, freak, weirdo (*inf.*), crackpot (*inf.*).

F Extension of thought

441 memory

n. memory, recollection, reminiscence, retrospection, recall, review, flashback, afterthought, hindsight, reconsideration, reflection, thought; retention, good memory, photographic memory, *déjà vu.*

memorandum, memo, reminder, record, note, jotting, scribble, mark; notes, summary, agenda, minutes; mnemonic, aid to memory; souvenir, memento, token, keepsake, relic, trinket; testimonial, memorial, monument, trophy, commemoration; warning, advice, suggestion, hint; prompt, prompter; memoirs, reminiscences, recollections, memories, memorabilia; diary, journal, album, scrapbook, notebook.

adj. remembered, recalled, retained, unforgotten, fresh, vivid; half-remembered, at the back of one's mind; reminiscent, reminding, evocative; memorable, unforgettable, indelibly fixed on one's mind; commemorative, memorial.

vb. remember, recollect, recall, bring to mind, be reminded of, think of, not forget; review, retrace, go back, flash back, look back, turn one's thoughts back, reminisce, call up, revive, rake up the past, drag up (*inf.*), dredge up (*inf.*); recognize, identify, know again, make out.

come to mind, ring a bell, stay in the memory, never be forgotten, haunt, recur, penetrate, stay in one's mind, not leave one's thoughts, not get out of one's mind.

memorize, learn, commit to memory, know by heart, learn by rote, master, impress, retain, fix in the mind; keep always, hold dear, treasure, cherish, commemorate, enshrine in the memory, keep the memory alive.

remind, prompt, suggest, hint, bring back, make one think of, jog one's

memory, refresh one's memory; warn, throw the book at (*inf.*).

442 oblivion

n. oblivion, forgetfulness, unmindfulness, absent-mindedness, amnesia, memory like a sieve, loss of memory, blankness, complete blank, mental block; insensibleness, indifference, carelessness.

adj. forgotten, unremembered, lost, out of one's mind, clean forgotten, unrecalled, unretained, in one ear and out the other; out of sight, out of mind; almost remembered, on the tip of one's tongue.

oblivious, forgetful, unmindful, heedless, inattentive, preoccupied, distracted, absent-minded.

vb. forget, fail to remember, have no recollection, put out of one's mind, have a short memory, think no more of, not give another thought, one's memory be a blank, escape one; be forgotten, sink into oblivion, fade from one's memory.

443 expectation

n. expectation, expectancy, looking forward, contemplation, anticipation, prospect, outlook; confidence, trust, hope, high hopes; preparedness; suspense, apprehension, pessimism.

adj. expectant, waiting, in anticipation, looking forward to, in suspense, on tenterhooks, itching, on edge, with bated breath; hoping, hopeful, confident; eager, watchful, vigilant, prepared; apprehensive, pessimistic.

expected, awaited, anticipated, foreseen, predicted, prophesied, longed for, looked for; on the cards, prospective.

vb. expect, look forward to, promise oneself, hope for, anticipate, contemplate, foresee, long for, bargain for (*inf.*), predict, prophesy, forecast, see coming, take for granted; wait for, await, bide one's time, mark time, hold one's breath, be in suspense; rely on, bank on, count on; be expected, lead one to expect, not put it past (*inf.*), be just like one.

444 non-expectation

n. inexpectation, unpreparedness, unexpectedness; surprise, shock, start, jolt, blow, bombshell, bolt from the blue, thunderbolt; turn-up for the book (*sl.*).

adj. unexpected, unforeseen, sudden, surprising, astonishing, staggering; unheralded, unpredicted, uncontemplated; unheard of, not thought of; more than one bargained for, not on the cards, without warning, out of the blue.

surprised, startled, thunderstruck, off one's guard, unready, unprepared, caught napping.

vb. not expect, not bargain for; surprise, take by surprise, catch unawares, catch in the act, catch red-handed, make one jump, startle, astonish, bowl over (*inf.*), knock down with a feather; come unexpectedly, turn up.

445 disappointment

n. disappointment, foiling, bafflement; discouragement, despondency, dissatisfaction, unfulfilment, discontent, frustration, disillusionment, regret, distress, displeasure.

bad news, setback, adversity, defeat, failure, anti-climax, miscarriage, let-down (*inf.*).

adj. disappointed, discouraged, dissatisfied, thwarted, baffled, unsuccessful, defeated, foiled, let-down (*inf.*), disconcerted, depressed, frustrated, disillusioned, full of regrets, despon-

dent; disappointing, unsatisfactory, inadequate, insufficient, not up to expectations.

vb. disappoint, fail, let down (*inf.*), thwart, foil, baffle; come short of, dash one's hopes, not come up to expectations, leave much to be desired; frustrate, disconcert, disillusion, dissatisfy, let the side down (*inf.*).

446 foresight

n. foresight, second sight, foresightedness, anticipation; forethought, premeditation, preconsideration, preconception.

adj. foreseeing, foresighted, looking ahead, anticipatory.

vb. foresee, prophesy, forecast, anticipate; see ahead, look into the future, have a premonition, feel in one's bones.

447 prediction

n. prediction, forecast, foretelling, prophecy, prognostication, prognosis, foresight, forethought, foreknowledge, precognition, prescience, prevision; augury, divination, vaticination, astrology, clairvoyancy, soothsaying, fortune-telling, crystal-gazing, palmistry, casting lots; parapsychology, extrasensory perception; telepathy, telesthesia.

omen, sign, indication, symptom, portent, clue, hint, auspice, writing on the wall; warning, forewarning, foreboding, presentiment; guess, estimate, conjecture, budget; foretoken; presage; horoscope, fortune; herald, harbinger.

oracle, forecaster, prognosticator, prophet, prophetess, seer; fortune-teller, soothsayer, clairvoyant, augur, diviner, palmist, astrologer, crystal-gazer, gipsy; witch, wizard, medium; sibyl, haruspex; thought-reader, mind-reader, telepath, parapsychologist; weatherman, meteorologist.

adj. predicting, predictive, prognostic, divinatory, clairvoyant, portentous, significant; auspicious, favourable; ominous, foreboding; psychic, second-sighted; supernatural, paranormal, parapsychological; predictable, foreseen, expected, likely; divinable.

vb. predict, forecast, prognosticate, foresee, foretell, prophesy, vaticinate; forewarn; promise; bode, forebode, betoken, portend, foreshadow, presage; divine, augur, tell the future, tell fortunes, cast lots, read one's hand, read one's palm, read tea leaves.

see also **984**

G Creative thought

448 supposition

n. supposition, guesswork, speculation, theorizing, postulation.

guess, surmise, notion, fancy, conjecture, inkling, hint, intimation, shrewd idea, vague idea, sneaking suspicion, rough guess, wild guess, shot in the dark.

premise, presupposition, postulate, proposition; inference, deduction, conclusion; thesis, hypothesis, working hypothesis, theory.

theorist, scientist, theorizer, academic, thinker, speculator, backroom boy, boffin (*sl.*).

adj. suppositional, unproved, tentative, speculative, conjectural, hypothetical, theoretical; supposed, assumed, presupposed, presumed, reputed, alleged, postulated, putative.

vb. suppose, believe, imagine, think, fancy, deem, guess, venture a guess, conjecture, speculate, estimate, divine,

surmise, suspect, gather, assume, presume, presuppose; postulate, posit; infer, imply, deduce, theorize.

449 imagination

n. imagination, inventiveness, creativity, originality, visualization; fantasy, diversion, whimsy, daydreaming, castle-building, pipedreaming, wishful thinking, escapism; utopia, paradise, world of fantasy, cloud-cuckoo land, dream world.

idea, figment of the imagination, invention, notion, fancy, whim, caprice, vagary, chimera, will-o'-the-wisp, vision, appearance, day-dream, castles in the air, romance, flight of fancy, dream, nightmare.

visionary, prophet, seer, idealist, escapist, Quixote, dreamer, daydreamer.

adj. imaginative, inventive, creative, resourceful, inspired, visionary, idealistic, with one's head in the clouds, quixotic, impractical, unrealistic; imaginary, fanciful, fantastic, capricious, whimsical, chimerical, dreamlike, ideal, utopian, fictitious, pretended, make-believe, illusory, fabulous.

vb. imagine, picture, conjure up, envisage, conceive, suppose, visualize; invent, create, make up, think of, devise, fabricate, coin, hatch; dream, muse, fancy, fantasize, idealize, romanticize, build castles in the air, daydream, pretend, make believe.

2 Communication of ideas

A Nature of ideas communicated

450 meaning

n. meaning, sense, significance, interpretation, implication, explanation; intent, aim, import, drift, tenor, thrust, purport; substance, essence, content.

meaningfulness, expressiveness; signification, connotation, denotation; reference, referendum, definition; unambiguity, equivalence, synonymity; synonym, related word.

adj. meaningful, significant, indicative, expressive, suggestive, evocative; substantial, pithy, full of meaning, pregnant; unambiguous; literal, verbal, word for word, verbatim, exact, faithful, true; semantic, linguistic.

vb. mean, signify, designate, refer to, drive at (*inf.*), denote, connote, indicate, symbolize, suggest, express, convey, declare, state, assert, spell; intimate, hint, betoken, bode, purport, import; imply, involve, speak of, touch on, point to.

451 meaninglessness

n. meaninglessness, senselessness, inexpressiveness, expressionlessness, nonsensicalness; misinterpretation, illogicality, ambiguity.

nonsense, balderdash, rubbish, twaddle, blather, rot (*sl.*), poppycock (*sl.*), trash, inanity, drivel, bunkum, prattle, baloney (*sl.*), bunk (*sl.*), ballyhoo, piffle (*sl.*); hot air (*sl.*), empty talk, humbug; cliché, truism, platitude.

adj. meaningless, insignificant, unindicative, inexpressive, unevocative; insubstantial, empty, void, vacant, blank; irrelevant, unimportant; senseless, aimless, purposeless; vague, ambiguous, tautological; trite, trivial, absurd, nonsensical, foolish; unintended, misinterpreted.

vb. be meaningless, mean nothing;

talk nonsense, babble, prattle, blather, twaddle; talk through one's hat (*sl.*).

452 intelligibility

n. intelligibility, comprehensibility; recognizability, cognizability; lucidity, clarity, transparency; precision, plainness, explicitness, unambiguousness; readability, legibility, decipherability; audibility; plain speech; plain English.

adj. intelligible, comprehensible, understandable; clear, obvious, lucid, precise, plain, explicit, clear-cut, distinct, unambiguous, unequivocal; simple, straightforward, popular, made simple, for the beginner, made easy, without tears, for the million; recognizable, readable, legible, decipherable; audible.

vb. understand, apprehend, comprehend, grasp, follow, take in, figure out (*inf.*), catch on (*inf.*), get the meaning of, get the hang of (*inf.*), twig (*inf.*); fathom, penetrate, get to the bottom of, read between the lines, get the idea, get the gist of; know, have knowledge of, realize, perceive, appreciate; discern, distinguish, make out (*inf.*), work out (*inf.*); conceive, be aware of, recognize, sense, be conscious of.

be intelligible, make sense, be clear, click (*sl.*); make clear, put in plain English, put in words of one syllable.

see also 502

453 unintelligibility

n. unintelligibility, incomprehensibility, meaninglessness, unrecognizability, unsearchableness, impenetrability; unclearness, obscurity, illegibility, ambiguity, indecipherability, unreadability; inaudibility; gibberish, incoherence, double Dutch, Greek; puzzle, mystery, enigma, sealed book, closed book.

adj. unintelligible, incomprehensible, meaningless, beyond one's comprehension; indistinct, vague, indefinite, hazy, inexact, ill-defined, loose, unclear, ambiguous, equivocal; incoherent, mixed up; obscure, puzzling, hard, complicated, intricate, profound, academic, over one's head, abstruse, recondite; concealed, mysterious, hidden, enigmatic, esoteric; illegible, indecipherable, unreadable; inaudible; unrecognizable, impenetrable, unsearchable, inexplicable; inscrutable, unfathomable, unutterable, ineffable.

vb. not understand, not have the first idea, not get the hang of (*inf.*), not make head or tail of, be baffled, be beyond one, get hold of the wrong end of the stick (*inf.*); be unintelligible, talk above someone's head; not make sense, escape one, be all Greek to one.

see also 503

454 ambiguity

n. ambiguity, equivocalness; vagueness, uncertainty; ambivalence, equivocation, incongruity, inconsistency, prevarication; play on words, pun, *double entendre.*

adj. ambiguous, ambivalent, equivocal, uncertain, vague, vacillating, prevaricating; two-edged, backhanded; incongruous.

vb. cut both ways; play on words, pun; quibble, equivocate, prevaricate.

455 figure of speech

n. figure of speech, metaphor, transference, figurativeness; symbolism, imagery; rhetoric; comparison, simile, likeness, allegory, trope, fable, parable, allusion, personification; euphemism, irony, satire; understatement; onomatopoeia.

adj. figurative, metaphorical, extended, transferred, allusive; rhetorical;

symbolic; comparative, allegorical, parabolic; euphemistic, euphuistic, ironical, satirical.

456 interpretation

n. interpretation, explanation, exposition, commentary, elucidation, clarification, illumination, explication; background, reason; analysis, diagnosis, review, criticism, critique, survey, investigation, appraisal, evaluation; significance, importance; annotation, note, comment; example, illustration, instance.

translation, equivalent, dynamic equivalent, paraphrase, rendering, rendition, adaptation, rewording, restatement, gloss, transcription, transliteration, version, reading.

interpreter, commentator, reviewer, critic, analyst, exponent, writer, editor, annotator, expositor, preacher, exegete; translator, linguist, polyglot; hermeneutics, exegetics, homiletics.

adj. interpretive, explanatory, expository, explicatory; analytical, diagnostic, critical, evaluatory; defining, descriptive, illuminating, discursive, exegetical; exemplary, illustrative; editorial, glossarial; literal, faithful, word-for-word; free, rough.

vb. interpret, explain, account for, give reasons for, give reasons why, make sense of; expound, lay bare the meaning, give an account of, state the significance of, read between the lines; make clear, elucidate, make plain, clarify, illuminate, throw light on, cast light on; simplify, expand on, emphasize; demonstrate, illustrate, exemplify, show by example; set forth, reveal, expose, lay bare, unfold, spell out.

translate, render, put in other words, put into, reword, restate, rephrase, paraphrase; transliterate, transcribe; decipher, decode, crack, solve; annotate, comment on, remark on, edit, gloss.

457 misinterpretation

n. misinterpretation, misreckoning, misconception, misunderstanding, misconstruction, falsification, distortion, perversion, delusion, error, mistake; mistranslation.

vb. misinterpret, misunderstand, get hold of the wrong end of the stick (*inf.*), misquote, falsify, distort, pervert, read into, misconstrue, not give a true account of, give a false impression of.

see also 453

B Modes of communication

458 manifestation

n. manifestation, revelation, showing, demonstration, disclosure, expression, presentation, exhibition; publishing, telling, announcement; divulgence, betrayal.

appearance, vision, apparition; exhibit, show, layout, example, specimen, showpiece; parade, procession, pageant; evidence, sign, miracle, theophany.

adj. manifest, apparent, clear, visible, perceptible, observable, obvious, patent, open, evident, self-evident, unmistakable, crystal-clear, staring one in the face, written all over one, express, explicit, conspicuous, noticeable, prominent, bold, striking, pronounced, flagrant, glaring, salient.

vb. manifest, appear, reveal, show, disclose, express; present, produce, publish, tell, announce, proclaim, betray, divulge, demonstrate, exemplify, indicate, show signs of, evince; make manifest, make plain, lay bare, expose, show forth; display, exhibit, set out, uncover, unfold, unmask, parade; promote, publicize.

see also 462, 823

459 latency

n. latency, secrecy, subtlety, dormancy; insidiousness; undercurrent, implication, suggestion, hint, allusion, connotation, inference, more than meets the eye, snake in the grass.

adj. latent, hidden, veiled, dormant, quiescent, lurking, subtle, insidious, beneath the surface, between the lines, underlying, undercover; underdeveloped, potential, possible; implied, inherent, inferred, suggested, intimated, hinted, supposed, tacit, understood, unmentioned, unspoken, unexpressed; suggestive, indicative, provocative.

vb. be latent, be beneath the surface, lurk, lie low; imply, indicate, infer, suggest, mean, intimate, hint, insinuate, involve, provoke, entail.

see also 461

460 information

n. information, knowledge, facts, info (*inf.*), gen (*sl.*), low-down (*sl.*); briefing, run-down (*inf.*); proof, evidence, notes, details, results, figures, tables, statistics, data; intelligence; news, message, report, notice, communication, notification, declaration, presentation, proclamation, broadcast, transmission; narration, account, description, story, tale, paper; tidings, discovery, revelation, enlightenment; dispatch, release, hand-out, announcement; telephone call, telex, telegram, cable, wire, teletext.

hint, mention, advice, aside, wink, whisper, word in one's ear, tip-off (*inf.*), warning, intimation, suspicion, glimmer, indication, suggestion.

informant, spokesman, narrator, story-teller, messenger, newsman, reporter, authority, announcer, broadcaster, correspondent, journalist; dispatcher, courier, herald, emissary, envoy, ambassador, carrier; guidebook, manual, chart, itinerary, map, timetable.

informer, spy, secret agent, observer, wire tapper, snoop, grass (*sl.*), squealer (*sl.*); gossip, tell-tale, eavesdropper, newsmonger, tattler, scandalmonger.

adj. informative, instructive, enlightening, educational, enriching, newsy (*inf.*), chatty (*inf.*), communicative.

vb. inform, speak, say, tell, notify, let know, communicate, give the facts, put over, put across, get across, get over, present, give to understand, convey, declare, announce, express, proclaim; relate, narrate, recite, report, describe, set forth, make known, let in on, tip off (*inf.*), have a word in someone's ear; enlighten, put in the picture; broadcast, spread the news, circulate, disseminate, promulgate; telephone, ring, call, telex, cable, wire; report back, debrief (*inf.*).

bring up to date, fill in on (*inf.*); keep up with, keep tabs on (*inf.*), keep track of, keep one's finger on the pulse, keep up to date, keep posted; hint, suggest, get at, insinuate, intimate, advise, warn; tell on, inform on, betray, grass on (*sl.*), squeal (*sl.*).

see also 464, 597

461 concealment

n. concealment, covering, hiding, confinement, burying, secretion; suppression, evasion; seclusion, privacy, isolation, solitude; camouflage, disguise, shroud, veil, curtain, screen, mask, cloak, purdah; cabal.

adj. concealed, hidden, out of sight, behind the scenes, covered, eclipsed, buried, obscured, unseen, unexposed; disguised, camouflaged, incognito; furtive, stealthy, secret, hush-hush, clandestine, underhand, sly.

vb. conceal, hide, cover, bury, suppress, screen, cloak, shroud, veil, curtain, evade, withhold, pull the wool over someone's eyes (*inf.*), keep secret, lie low, keep in the dark, keep under one's hat (*inf.*), sweep under the carpet (*inf.*), secrete; cloud, obscure, envelop, ensconce, camouflage, disguise, dissemble; confine, store, harbour, cache, shelter, stash (*inf.*); close, seal, lock.

sneak, prowl, creep, lurk, steal, slink.

see also 463, 466, 826

462 disclosure

n. disclosure, exposure, opening, uncovering, revelation, apocalypse; show-down; betrayal, manifestation, give-away; acknowledgement, admission.

adj. disclosed, uncovered, exposed, conspicuous, open; indicative, betraying, tell-tale.

vb. disclose, reveal, give away, expose, divulge, lay open, lay bare, make plain, uncover, unfold, unveil, unfurl, unmask, take the wraps off; not contain oneself for, bring into the open; declare, make known, spit it out (*inf.*); put one's cards on the table, nail one's colours to the mast, show one's colours; open up (*inf.*), unburden oneself, unbosom, confide, get out of one's system (*inf.*), get off one's chest (*inf.*); come out of one's shell.

confess, admit, acknowledge, concede, grant, own up (*inf.*), come clean, avow, plead guilty, make a clean breast of; one's sins will find one out.

betray, not keep a secret, blurt out, let on, let out, blabber, leak, let the cat out of the bag (*inf.*), spill the beans, come out with, talk out of turn, give the game away.

see also **458, 460**

463 hiding

n. hiding, deceit, faking, deception; hiding place, hide-out, hidey-hole, refuge, retreat, covert, den, shelter.

disguise, camouflage, mask, blind, masquerade, cloak, cover, veil, guise, façade, envelope, shade, blackout, masking; ambush, snare, trap, pitfall, net, noose.

vb. ambush, trap, ensnare, waylay, lay in wait, set a trap for, decoy.

see also **459, 801**

464 publication

n. publication, announcement, communication, revelation, disclosure, notification, proclamation, declaration, promulgation, broadcasting, dissemination.

broadcast; book, booklet; newspaper, periodical, magazine, journal; publicity, promotion, canvassing, advertisement, poster, sign, bill, placard, notice, broadsheet, leaflet, folder, brochure, pamphlet, circular, hand-out, handbill, flysheet, blurb, plug (*inf.*).

adj. published, in print, available, obtainable, in circulation; current, public.

vb. publish, issue, bring out, put into circulation, print, distribute; reissue, reprint; be published, come out, circulate, get around.

make known, announce, notify, proclaim, declare, pronounce, impart, send forth, communicate, reveal,

disclose, spread, broadcast, diffuse, pass the word round, put about, blazon, promulgate, disseminate; publicize, promote, advertise, canvass, circularize, sell, plug (*inf.*), tell the world.

465 news

n. news, tidings, information, facts, events, current affairs; headlines, front-page news, stop press, newsflash, scoop, sensation; description, account, report, story, bulletin, message, release, communiqué, press release, announcement, hand-out, dispatch.

rumour, gossip, hearsay, scandal, whisper, popular report, fabrication, tale, chit-chat; grapevine, bush telegraph.

vb. report, tell, broadcast, publish, circulate, spread; make news, hit the headlines.

466 secret

n. secret, mystery, puzzle, riddle, brain-teaser, enigma, arcanum; code, cipher, cryptogram, hieroglyph; confidence; skeleton in the cupboard; suppression, blackout, censure.

adj. secret, strange, mysterious, hidden, unknown, puzzling, mystical, cryptic, enigmatic; private, confidential, classified, top secret, hush-hush; secretive, reticent, taciturn; secluded.

vb. keep secret, keep to oneself, not tell, hide, conceal, keep mum (*inf.*), suppress, stifle, sit on (*inf.*), hush up, censor.

adv. in secret, in private, confidentially, under one's breath, between ourselves; between you, me, and the bedpost.

see also **461**

467 messenger

n. messenger, dispatcher, dispatch bearer, carrier, courier, runner, crier, bearer, office-boy, message-boy, errand-boy, page-boy, buttons; spokesman, intermediary, go-between, ambassador, envoy, emissary, internuncio; herald, forerunner, precursor, harbinger, trumpet; minister, angel, prophet.

post, mail, correspondence; post office; telecommunications, telephony, telegraphy; broadcasting, radio, transistor, wireless, television, the box; telephone, phone, receiver; radio set, two-way radio, intercom (*inf.*), pocket radio, walkie-talkie, field radio; telegram, wire, cable, cablegram, telegraph; teleprinter, telex, teletext, semaphore, flag, beacon, smoke-signal.

468 affirmation

n. affirmation, assertion, statement, declaration, proposition, profession, pronouncement, explanation, answer, report, observation, expression, formulation; admission, acknowledgement, attestation, avowal; agreement, ratification, endorsement.

swearing, asseveration; oath, vow, testimony, sworn statement, affidavit, promise, contract, pledge.

adj. affirmative, assertive, affirmatory, declarative; emphatic, strong, forceful, dogmatic, positive, assured, solemn, sworn, on oath.

vb. affirm, assert, state, declare, profess, pronounce, express, explain, maintain, contend, submit, asseverate, aver; confirm, endorse, ratify; admit, acknowledge; emphasize, stress, underline, highlight, impress, urge, reinforce, rub in (*inf.*), make much of, plug; speak out, have one's say, put one's foot down (*inf.*); swear, vow, promise, pledge, testify, attest, assure, guarantee,

vouch; swear in, put on oath, charge, adjure.

see also **514, 698**

469 negation

n. negation, denial, contradiction, repudiation, refusal, renunciation, disclaimer, disavowel; abnegation, recusance.

adj. negative, denying, contrary, contradictory, disavowing, recusant, repugnant.

vb. negate, deny, belie, give the lie to, contradict, contravene, gainsay, renounce, repudiate, disown, disavow, disclaim, abjure, abnegate; refuse, reject; cancel, nullify, invalidate.

see also **694**

470 teaching

n. teaching, education, pedagogy, pedagogics, didactics; instruction, training, study, schooling, direction, guidance, tuition, tutoring, coaching, tutelage; preparation, discipline, cultivation, enlightenment, edification; indoctrination, brainwashing, inculcation, conditioning, propagandism, proselytism; spoon-feeding.

course, curriculum, class, lesson, lecture, talk; catechism, sermon; homework, prep (*inf.*), assignment, exercise, task, work.

adj. educational, informative, instructive, enlightening, edifying; academic, pedagogical, didactic, scholastic.

vb. teach, educate, instruct, impart, inform, acquaint, familiarize, direct, guide, discipline, advise, counsel; convince, explain; prepare, initiate; school, coach, cram, prime, put through the mill (*inf.*); enlighten, edify; cultivate, nurture, train, exercise, practise, groom, drill, ground, bring up, foster, rear, breed, lick into

476

shape (*inf.*); indoctrinate, inculcate, din into, force down someone's throat, ram down someone's throat (*inf.*), instill, imbue, condition; proselytize; catechize; hold classes, lecture, hold forth, expound, preach, sermonize, moralize.

471 misdirection

n. misdirection, misguidance, misinstruction, misteaching, misrepresentation, falsification, perversion, mistake, error, blind leading the blind.

vb. misdirect, misinform, mislead, misrepresent, pervert, distort, deceive.

472 learning

n. learning, knowledge, scholarship, training, erudition, lore; self-improvement, self-education, 'self-instruction; attainments, study, reading, application, studiousness, industry; lesson, class, course, class-work, homework, prep (*inf.*), assignment; revision, refresher course.

adj. knowledgeable, academic, studious, well-read, learned, industrious, scholarly, erudite; self-taught, self-instructed, self-made.

vb. learn, acquire, pick up, attain; experience, understand, grasp, discover, appreciate; master, become familiar with, get off pat (*inf.*), get the hang of (*inf.*); memorize, learn by heart; study, read, go into, go in for, specialize; absorb, assimilate, digest, drink in, imbibe; read up on, revise, review, refresh oneself, cram, prepare, get up, brush up, improve; pore over, bury oneself in; contemplate; burn the midnight oil; browse, scan, thumb through, flick through (*inf.*), dip into; improve one's mind, teach oneself; study under, sit at the feet of.

see also 426

473 teacher

n. teacher, educator, advisor, guide, counsellor; school-teacher, head-master, principal, head; professor, lecturer, don, reader, fellow, doctor, dean; tutor, instructor, pedagogue, coach, trainer, guru, governess.

see also 436

474 learner

n. learner, pupil, scholar, student, schoolchild; undergraduate, fresher, freshman, graduate, postgraduate; swot, bookworm; follower, disciple, adherent; apprentice, trainee, probationer, novice, beginner, recruit, newcomer, tyro; class, set, form, grade, stream.

see also 428

475 place of learning

n. school; nursery, kindergarten, crèche; college, polytechnic, university, academy, institute, institution, seminary, varsity (*inf.*), *conservatoire, lycée, gymnasium;* classroom, schoolroom, study, lecture theatre, auditorium; library, carrel.

476 truthfulness

n. truthfulness, veracity, integrity, frankness, openness, candour, straightforwardness, forthrightness; accuracy, honesty, reliability, sincerity, uprightness, guilelessness, impartiality.

adj. truthful, veracious, sincere, guileless, impartial; frank, open, candid, unreserved, plain, direct, straight, straightforward, forthright, blunt, ingenuous.

vb. be truthful, not lie; speak plainly, tell someone straight, not hesitate, make no bones about, speak one's mind, paint in its true colours, call a

87

spade a spade, tell all; not to put too fine a point on it (*inf.*).

see also **430, 508**

477 falsehood

n. falsehood, fraudulence, falsification, fabrication, inaccuracy, deception, dishonesty, lying, mendacity, perjury; misrepresentation, distortion, perversion; double dealing, two-facedness, duplicity, hypocrisy, insincerity, guile; mockery, pretence, make-believe, façade.

adj. false, lying, untruthful, mendacious; fabricated, inaccurate, misrepresented, distorted, put on (*inf.*), make-believe, counterfeit, bogus, pretended, fake, invented, spurious; fraudulent, dishonest, insincere, hypocritical; double-dealing, two-faced; roguish, corrupt, oily, smooth, disingenuous, perfidious.

vb. falsify, lie, fib, exaggerate, understate, tell a white lie, bear false witness, perjure oneself, forswear; prevaricate, equivocate; deceive, mislead, misrepresent, distort, manipulate, doctor, adulterate, make up, invent, concoct, construct, contrive, fabricate, hatch, get up (*inf.*), trump up, spin a yarn; fake, counterfeit, forge; feign, put on (*inf.*), put on a brave face, go through the motions, play, pretend, make believe, sham, simulate, dissemble; laugh off (*inf.*).

see also **431**

478 deception

n. deception, misleading, deceit, misrepresentation, cheating, trickery, craftiness, treachery, fraudulence, dishonesty; lying, guile, furtiveness, beguilement, betrayal, treason; hoax, crying wolf, delusion, self-deception, wishful thinking, hallucination, illusion.

trick, dodge, ruse, trap, artifice, stratagem, subterfuge; fraud, swindle, fiddle, rip-off (*sl.*), bamboozle (*inf.*), skulduggery (*inf.*), underhand dealing, sharp practice, sleight of hand, legerdemain.

adj. deceiving, deceptive, illusory, false, sham, fake, fraudulent, dishonest, underhand, behind someone's back, furtive, treacherous, crafty, wily, cunning, shifty.

vb. deceive, mislead, delude, fool, trick, trap, trip up, catch, entrap, ensnare, hoodwink, beguile, dupe, pull the wool over someone's eyes (*inf.*); outwit, outmanoeuvre; go behind someone's back.

cheat, trick, defraud, swindle, fleece, rip off (*sl.*), bamboozle (*inf.*), chisel (*sl.*), cozen; go down (*inf.*), diddle (*sl.*), cross (*sl.*), double-cross, pull a fast one (*sl.*), stack the cards against, put one over on (*inf.*), victimize; take advantage of, get the better of, take for a ride (*inf.*); hoax, cry wolf; play a joke on, kid (*sl.*), pull someone's leg, have on (*inf.*); trifle with, cajole; betray, commit treason.

479 dupe

n. dupe, fool, victim, sucker (*sl.*), sitting duck, simpleton, greenhorn, gull.

480 deceiver

n. deceiver, beguiler, dodger, trickster, swindler, crook, cheat, rogue, impostor, con man (*sl.*), phoney (*sl.*), wolf in sheep's clothing, charlatan, chisel (*sl.*), knave, cozener, sharper; hypocrite, actor, dissembler, Tartuffe; liar, fibber, story-teller; betrayer, traitor, quisling, rat (*sl.*), informer, double-crosser, victimizer; underground, fifth columnist, saboteur, terrorist.

481 exaggeration

n. exaggeration, overstatement, extravagance, hyperbole, misrepresentation, misjudgment, stretching; storm in a teacup, much ado about nothing, stretch of the imagination, fantasy, tall story.

adj. exaggerated, extravagant, preposterous, fabulous, hyperbolic, excessive, superlative, overdone, out of all proportion, coloured, high-falutin, boastful, bombastic.

vb. exaggerate, overstate, overestimate, overplay, hyperbolize, make too much of, overdo, strain, misrepresent; amplify, enlarge, magnify, emphasize, highlight, maximize, heighten, intensify, aggravate; colour, embroider; make a mountain out of a molehill, stretch a point, lay it on thick, pile it on (*inf.*), out-herod Herod.

see also 417

C Means of communicating ideas

482 indication

n. indication, calling, identification, designation, symbolization, signification; sign, badge, emblem, figure, design, symbol, representation, type, token, logo; colophon, flag, banner, pennant, standard, ensign, colours, pendant, bunting, streamer, Union Jack, Stars and Stripes; coat of arms, crest, insignia, medal, regalia.

label, ticket, name, card, notice, bill, stub, counterfoil, docket, form, voucher, counter, chip, tab, tag; indicator, marker, pointer, needle, arrow, index, gauge; stamp, seal, imprint, impression, fingerprint, footprint; signature, autograph, initials, monogram.

signal, gesticulation, gesture; wink, nod, wave, call, shout, whistle, nudge; alarm, siren, hooter, bell; light, beacon.

evidence, hint, suggestion, note, explanation, proof, clue, intimation, symptom, hallmark.

adj. indicative, suggestive, symptomatic, symbolic, typical, representative.

vb. indicate, call, mean, signify; identify, designate, show, name, specify, appoint, assign, symbolize, point to; manifest, express, imply, bear the marks of, evince, intimate, denote, betoken; mark, point, gauge, brand, score, scratch, spot.

label, tag, docket, tab, earmark; stamp, seal, print, punch, impress, emboss, emblazon; sign, initial, autograph; annotate, number, letter, paginate.

gesticulate, gesture, signal, motion, wave, beckon, wink, nod, hoot, ring, shout, whistle, nudge.

483 record

n. record, register, catalogue, account, document, report, statement; brief, memo, memorandum, note; newspaper, bulletin, gazette, almanac; diary, journal, log; certificate, ticket; archives, public records, proceedings, minutes, annals, chronicle, scroll, inscription, manuscript; tape-recording, photograph, film, videotape.

souvenir, memento; relic, mark, trace, remains, evidence; trail, footprint, impression, scent; wash, wake; monument, testimony, witness, memorial, statue, column, cenotaph, remembrance, testimonial, mausoleum, shrine.

adj. recorded, documented, noted, reported.

vb. record, note, mark, report,

account, write down, take down, jot down; register, write in, enter, fill in, insert, inscribe, enrol, matriculate; document, list, catalogue, minute, chronicle; tape, tape-record, photograph, film.

adv. on record, in black and white, in writing, on the books.

484 recorder

n. recorder, registrar, secretary, clerk, accountant; diarist, chronicler, annalist, historian, biographer, journalist, archivist, scribe, amanuensis.

tape-recorder, stereo-recorder, cassette-recorder, video-recorder; record, disc.

485 obliteration

n. obliteration, deletion, erasure, effacement, blotting out, eradication, cancellation, expunction; eraser, rubber, sponge, duster.

vb. obliterate, wipe out, rub off, delete, efface, erase, blot out, black out, strike out, write out, leave no traces, remove, iron out, raze, cancel, expunge.

486 representation

n. representation, description, depiction, illustration, portrayal, exemplification, enactment, personification; reproduction, copy, imitation, image, likeness; picture, sketch, diagram, chart, map, model; art, painting, sculpture; photography, photograph, photo, snapshot, slide, transparency.

adj. representative, characteristic, typical, illustrative.

vb. represent, stand for, stand in the place of, serve as; render, realize, draw, depict, describe, portray, illustrate, picture, reproduce, delineate; reflect, mirror; exemplify, typify, embody, symbolize; designate, express.

487 misrepresentation

n. misrepresentation, distortion, perversion, twisting, falsification, exaggeration, understatement; caricature, parody, travesty, burlesque, counterfeit; misinterpretation.

vb. misrepresent, distort, twist, garble, warp, pervert, falsify, caricature, parody, give the wrong impression; misinterpret, misstate.

488 painting

n. painting, art, graphics, fine art; picture, illustration, mural, depiction, canvas, fresco, wall-painting, collage; work, study, sketch, drawing, outline, silhouette, cartoon, representation, copy, composition, likeness; abstract painting, landscape, portrait, self-portrait, still-life; watercolour, oil painting, miniature, masterpiece, old master.

technique, treatment, design, pattern, atmosphere, tone, shadow, values, perspective.

adj. graphic, visual, pictorial, picturesque, scenic.

vb. paint, portray, depict, compose, illustrate, draw, sketch, design, represent, copy, crayon, pencil, silhouette, ink, shade, tint, limn.

489 sculpture

n. sculpture, carving, stone-carving, cutting, casting, moulding; ceramics, pottery; statue, bust, cast, embossment, relief, marble, plaque, cameo; figure, representation, image.

adj. carved, sculptured, glyptic, glyphic.

vb. sculpture, sculpt, carve, chisel, cut, hew, shape, fashion, model, mould, emboss, cast.

490 engraving

n. engraving, etching, carving, chiselling, incising, printing, photogravure, lithography; inscription, print, lithograph, block, woodcut, linocut, plate.

vb. engrave, etch, inscribe, cut, carve, chisel, incise, chase, print, impress, stamp.

491 artist

n. artist, creator, composer, painter, designer, draughtsman, architect, drawer, sketcher, cartoonist, photographer, cameraman; sculptor, carver, modeller, statuary, lapidary; potter, ceramist; engraver, etcher, lithographer; printer, typographer.

492 language

n. language, communication, speech, tongue, talk, style, diction, parlance; utterance, expression, voice, articulation; idiom, dialect, provincialism, *patois*, jargon, pidgin, *koine*, *lingua franca*; mother tongue, vernacular, common speech, British English, American English, Standard English, Queen's English, Received Pronunciation; artificial language, world language, Esperanto; Babel, confusion of tongues.

linguistics, grammar, syntax, semantics, phonetics, phonology, historical linguistics, comparative linguistics, etymology, philology, dialectology, lexicography; linguist, polyglot, philologist, grammarian, lexicographer.

adj. linguistic, lingual, grammatical, standard, current, vernacular, idiomatic.

see also 514

493 letter

n. letter, symbol, consonant, vowel; capital, upper case, large letter, majuscule; small letter, lower case, minuscule; rune, cuneiform, hieroglyph; syllable, character, ideogram, pictogram; alphabet, ABC; orthography, spelling, spelling-pronunciation.

adj. literal, alphabetical, orthographic, syllabic.

vb. spell, letter, form letters; syllabify.

494 word

n. word, expression, term, name, designation, vocable, sound, syllable, utterance, phrase, construction, locution; neologism, slang, colloquialism, jargon, provincialism, cliché, vogue word, catch phrase, slogan; archaism; root, derivative, derivation; synonym, antonym, homonym.

vocabulary, lexicon, wordlist, dictionary, glossary, thesaurus, concordance, index; lexicology, lexicography, etymology, terminology.

adj. verbal, literal, lexical, lexicographical.

495 neologism

n. neologism, new word, new usage, coinage, neology; formation, translation, loan-word, borrowing, calque, portmanteau, blend, hybrid; corruption, barbarism, nonce word; cliché, vogue word, slang, vulgarism, argot, cant, colloquialism, informal usage, journalese, Americanism, Anglicism, Briticism.

adj. newly-coined, newfangled, colloquial, informal, slang, foreign, borrowed, translated, nonce, vogue.

496 nomenclature

n. nomenclature, naming, calling, appellation, designation, identification, terminology, classification.

name, title; Christian name, first name, given name, forename; surname, last name, family name, signature; sign, style, label, tag; nomen, denomination; nickname, description, epithet.

adj. nominal, titular; named, known as.

vb. name, call, designate, identify, specify, term, title, dub, label, tag, style; classify, characterize, describe, define, nominate, denominate; christen, baptize; be known as, be called, go by the name of, go under the name of.

497 misnomer

n. misnomer, misnaming, malapropism; nickname, pet name, pen name, pseudonym, fictitious name, assumed name, alias, *nom de plume*, stage name, sobriquet, *nom de guerre.*

anonymity, namelessness; what's-its-name, thinggamy (*inf.*), thingumabob (*inf.*), what-d'you-call-it, so-and-so, A. N. Other, Mr. X.

adj misnamed, in name only, professed, pretended, pseudo-, quasi-, self-styled, so-called, *soi-disant;* anonymous, unknown, unidentified, nameless, unknown.

vb. misname, nickname, dub, mislabel, mistake.

498 phrase

n. phrase, clause, sentence, group of words; idiom, figure of speech; expression, utterance, locution; slogan, maxim, saying, formula, cliché.

vb. phrase, word, reword, express, state, put into words, formulate, verbalize.

499 grammar

n. grammar, usage, syntax, word order, sentence structure, analysis, parsing; inflection, case-ending, morphology, accidence.

part of speech, noun, substantive,

proper noun, collective noun, mass noun, count noun, case, gender, number, declension; pronoun; verb, participle, gerund, copula, infinitive, split infinitive, person, tense, active, passive, conjugation; adjective, qualifier, modifier, comparative, superlative, comparison; adverb, particle; preposition; interjection; conjunction; article, definite article, indefinite article, determiner; subject, predicate; affix, prefix, suffix, infix.

adj. grammatical, syntactic, correct, proper, well-formed, acceptable, appropriate.

vb. parse, analyse, inflect, conjugate, decline.

500 solecism

n. solecism, ungrammaticalness, bad grammar, misusage, mistake, error, barbarism, blunder; mispronunciation, slip of the tongue; malapropism, spoonerism, cacology, catachresis.

adj. ungrammatical, incorrect, solecistic; slovenly, slipshod, loose; inappropriate, unacceptable, badly-formed.

vb. use bad grammar, make a mistake, murder the language.

see also 511

501 style

n. style, manner, characteristics, presentation; command, fluency, mastery, skill; manner of speaking, diction, phrasing, phraseology, wording, composition, writing; usage, mode of expression, expression, vocabulary, word-power, parlance, choice of words, way of putting it, feeling for words, *sprachgefühl;* mannerism, idiosyncrasy, intonation.

see also 510, 514

502 lucidity

n. lucidity, clearness, clarity, perspicuity, transparency, unambiguousness, intelligibility, directness, plain speech, simplicity, exactness, precision.

adj. lucid, clear, perspicuous, unambiguous, distinct, obvious, direct, plain, intelligible, explicit, easily understood, limpid, pellucid.

see also 452, 802

503 obscurity

n. obscurity, imperspicuity, vagueness, opaqueness, ambiguity, imprecision, unintelligibility, complexity, abstruseness.

adj. obscure, cloudy, blurred, fuzzy, vague, unclear, imperspicuous, imprecise, indistinct, ambiguous, unintelligible, incomprehensible, complicated, involved, intricate, abstruse.

see also 453, 803

504 conciseness

n. conciseness, succinctness, brevity, terseness, curtness, pithiness, laconism; contraction, ellipsis.

adj. concise, brief, succinct, condensed, compressed, shortened, short, precise, pithy, terse, compact, summary, laconic, sententious; elliptic, telegraphic.

vb. be concise, condense, compress, shorten, abridge, abbreviate, summarize, come to the point, put in a nutshell.

adv. in short, in brief, in a nutshell, to the point, to cut a long story short.

505 diffuseness

n. diffuseness, profuseness, abundance; wordiness, verbosity, discursiveness; digression, departure, deviation, excursus; tautology, redundancy, verbiage, repetition, padding, circumlocution, periphrasis, pleonasm.

adj. diffuse, discursive, wordy, lengthy, long-winded, verbose, tedious, rambling, digressive, redundant, repetitious, protracted, prolix, pleonastic, roundabout, periphrastic, circumlocutory.

vb. amplify, enlarge on, develop, expatiate; digress, ramble, wander, deviate, go off at a tangent, go off the subject, get off the point, get sidetracked, beat about the bush (*inf.*); go on and on, talk at length, repeat oneself.

see also 516

506 vigour

n. vigour, power, strength, intensity, force, effectiveness, forcefulness, urgency, piquancy; sparkle, spirit, punch (*sl.*), fervour, vehemence, verve, animation, vitality, fire, glow, warmth.

adj. vigorous, powerful, strong, forceful, trenchant, incisive, bold, tough, lively, inspired, sparkling, racy, fervent, vehement, insistent, impassioned, fiery, ardent, passionate, persuasive; vivid, graphic; pointed.

see also 173, 755

507 feebleness

n. feebleness, weakness, faintness, frailty, flaccidity, enfeeblement, pauperism, barrenness, lifelessness.

adj. feeble, weak, faint, frail, thin, poor, limp, lifeless, flaccid, insipid, meagre, scant, slight, shallow, diluted, wishy-washy, uninspired, stale, flat, tame, forced.

see also 162

508 plainness

n. plainness, simplicity, plain speech, naturalness, straightforwardness, modesty, unpretentiousness, severity.

adj. plain, simple, natural, unaffected, artless, naive, straightforward, modest, ordinary, undramatic, severe, restrained, unadorned, unpretentious, unsophisticated, common, homely, homespun, unimaginative, matter-of-fact; direct, frank, open, blunt.

vb. speak plainly, call a spade a spade, come straight to the point.

see also 476

509 ornament

n. ornamentation, adornment, embellishment, elaboration, enrichment, enhancement, decoration, embroidery, floweriness.

ornament, colour, frills, rhetoric, metaphor, euphemism, verbosity, grandiloquence, bombast, fustian.

adj. ornate, adorned, embellished, grand, rich, lofty, elaborate, lavish, grandiose; vivid, dazzling, scintillating; fancy, extravagant, pretentious, showy, flashy, loud, flaunting, boastful, big, high-falutin, high-flown, big-sounding, magniloquent; rhetorical, voluble, pompous, flowery, euphemistic, euphuistic, grandiloquent.

vb. embellish, adorn, enrich, colour; talk big, lay it on (*inf.*).

see also 846

510 elegance

n. elegance, tastefulness, style, grace, graciousness, dignity, beauty, correctness, refinement, propriety, polish, finish; harmony, balance, proportion, rhythm; artificiality, affectation.

adj. elegant, tasteful, gracious, graceful, dignified, artistic, delicate, refined, pure, stylized, polished; proper, appropriate, happy, well-expressed, right, correct, felicitous, seemly; harmonious, balanced, well-proportioned, well-turned, mellifluous; affected, artificial.

see also 848

511 inelegance

n. inelegance, tastelessness, bad taste, gracelessness, impropriety; barbarism, coarseness, vulgarity; incorrectness, stiltedness, formality, awkwardness, clumsiness.

adj. inelegant, tasteless, graceless, unseemly, improper, incorrect, laboured, stilted, forced, heavy, stiff, formal, ponderous, clumsy, awkward, inappropriate; coarse, crude, vulgar, rude, uncouth.

see also 849

512 voice

n. voice, sound, speech, language, utterance; vocal organs, vocal chords, tongue, lips, larynx, lungs, breath; articulation, pronunciation, vocalization, enunciation, delivery, inflection, intonation, pitch, rhythm, tone, accent, timbre, stress, emphasis; vowel, consonant, phoneme; phonetics.

adj. vocal, expressed, uttered, spoken, oral, lingual, vocalic, phonetic, voiced, sonant, sounded; clear, distinct, articulate.

vb. voice, speak, express, sound, pronounce, utter, articulate, get one's tongue round, vocalize, enunciate; nasalize, palatalize, aspirate; roll, trill, burr; stress, emphasize.

513 muteness

n. muteness, aphonia, voicelessness, inarticulation, dumbness, silence.

adj. mute, voiceless, speechless, tongueless, unsounded, unvoiced, unvocal, surd, inarticulate, tongue-tied, dumb, silent, mum, inaudible.

vb. mute, silence, dumbfound, strike dumb, still, soften, deaden, muffle, suppress, smother.

see also 517, 779

514 speech

n. speech, language, talk, discourse, utterance, articulation, expression, pronunciation, communication; eloquence, fluency, expressiveness, facility, vivacity, style, poise, delivery, rhetoric, vigour, force, gift of the gab (*inf.*).

speaker, talker, conversationalist; public speaker, orator, lecturer, after-dinner speaker, expositor, rhetorician, declaimer, preacher; spokesman, mouthpiece.

adj. speaking, talking, verbal, oral; articulating; eloquent, fluent, voluble, expressive, forceful, meaningful.

vb. speak, say, talk; vocalize, pronounce, voice, enunciate; express, utter, tell, affirm, converse, communicate, chat; repeat, rattle off, trot out (*inf.*).

address, discuss, lecture, teach, instruct, plead, argue, make a speech, give a talk, deliver a lecture, have the floor, hold forth, preach, speechify (*inf.*), rant, spout.

see also **468, 516**

515 imperfect speech

n. imperfect speech, speech defect, aphasia, impediment, stammer, stutter, faltering, hesitation, mispronunciation, lisp, twang, nasalization, drawl.

adj. inarticulate, indistinct, throaty, shaking, stuttering, stammering, hesitant.

vb. stammer, stutter, hesitate, pause, falter, stumble, lisp, drawl, slur, speak through one's nose, mispronounce, mumble, mutter, garble, swallow one's words.

516 talkativeness

n. talkativeness, gift of the gab (*inf.*), loquacity, garrulity, verbosity, long-windedness.

chatter, chat, jabber, babble, prattle, blather, prittle-prattle (*inf.*), chit-chat, idle talk, chinwag (*sl.*), palaver, small talk; nonsense, drive, twaddle, hot air (*sl.*), yap (*inf.*), yackety-yack (*sl.*); gossip, scandal.

chatterbox, prattler, jabberer, tattler, windbag (*inf.*), gasbag (*sl.*); gossip, muckraker (*inf.*).

adj. talkative, chatty, voluble, loquacious, garrulous; chattering, babbling; glib, eloquent, fluent; long-winded, verbose; gossipy.

vb. chat, keep on, go on about (*inf.*), chatter, talk idly, waffle, ramble on; babble, jabber, prattle, gabble, yackety-yack (*sl.*), yack (*sl.*), yap (*inf.*); gossip, tell tales.

see also **505**

517 taciturnity

n. taciturnity, reserve, reticence, silence, uncommunicativeness, no comment, curtness, brusqueness; modesty, hesitance.

adj. taciturn, reserved, reticent, silent, dumb, mute, quiet, uncommunicative, secretive, tight-lipped, close-lipped, mum, restrained, hesitant, modest, retiring; curt, brusque, laconic; aloof, distant.

vb. say nothing, refuse to comment, keep quiet, keep one's mouth shut, hold one's tongue, save one's breath; stand aloof.

see also **779**

518 address

n. address, speech, talk, lecture, oration, discourse, reading, recitation, recital, exhortation, paper, pep talk (*sl.*), spiel (*sl.*), appeal, invocation, homily, sermon, allocution; harangue, tirade, declamation.

inaugural address, opening; greeting, salutation; farewell address, goodbye, valediction.

oratory, rhetoric, speech-making.

public speaking, elocution, preaching, homiletics.

519 conversation

n. conversation, chat, talk, discussion, interview, exchange of views, interchange, expression, repartee, colloquy, interlocution; chatter, chit-chat, prattle; *tête-à-tête*, heart-to-heart.

conference, debate, dialogue, consultation, conflab (*inf.*), powwow, summit conference, summit, congress, symposium, convention, seminar, parley, council, audience, hearing.

vb. converse, chat, discuss, hold a conversation, communicate, counsel, confer, exchange views, debate, negotiate, put one's heads together, confabulate.

520 monologue

n. monologue, soliloquy, monody; apostrophe, aside.

vb. soliloquize, talk to oneself.

521 writing

n. writing, script, lettering, calligraphy, stroke, flourish; handwriting, hand, fist, longhand; graphology, chirography; mark, scribble, scrawl; transcription, inscription, printing, copying, shorthand, stenography, typing; correspondence, letter-writing; journalism, reporting.

written matter, copy, work, composition, document, paper, manuscript, transcript, typescript, parchment, scroll.

writer, calligrapher, scribe, copyist, transcriber, secretary, stenographer, typist; author, novelist, journalist.

adj. written, graphic, in writing, handwritten, in black and white, roman, italic.

vb. write, pen, compose, prepare, draft, write out, report, document,

write down, record, put pen to paper; scribble, scrawl; transcribe, inscribe, copy, engrave, print, type.

522 printing

n. printing, typography; composition, typesetting; publishing; print, impression, stamp, page, sheet, copy, printed matter; type, lead, leading, rule, letter, fount, space; galley, proof, slip, bromide.

printer, typographer, typesetter, compositor; proofreader, reader; copy editor.

adj. printed, in print, typographical.

vb. print, impress, imprint, stamp, engrave; compose, set type, set up; run off, go to press, put to bed; publish, issue, bring out.

523 correspondence

n. correspondence, communication, exchange of letters, post, mail; letter, postcard, note, message, report, missive, dispatch, epistle, chit, acknowledgement, reply, answer; business letter, love letter, valentine, fan letter, poison pen letter, chain letter, round robin, circular; address, destination.

correspondent, letter-writer, pen-friend, pen-pal (*inf.*), addressee, recipient.

adj. epistolary, postal.

vb. correspond, write to, communicate, exchange letters, drop a line, send, post, mail, dispatch.

524 book

n. book, publication, work, volume, tome, copy, text, manuscript, bestseller, paperback, hardback, booklet, edition, reprint, offprint; study book, course book, textbook, set book, primer, workbook; reader, companion volume, selected readings; complete works, omnibus edition.

magazine, periodical, journal, review, gazette; back number, back issue.

reference book, encyclopedia, cyclopedia, handbook, manual, dictionary, bible, guidebook; index, concordance; bibliography, reading list.

library, collection of books, lending library, public library, mobile library, inter-library loan.

writer, author, novelist, biographer, essayist, reporter, ghost-writer, hack; editor, publisher, reviewer, critic; man of letters, man of learning, bookworm, scholar, book-collector, bibliophile.

525 description

n. description, account, report, statement, record, summary, information, explanation, characterization, specification; portrayal, sketch, portrait, representation, illustration, picture, image, profile; narrative, story, tale, yarn, anecdote, saga, epic; fiction, myth, legend, fairy-tale, fairy story, fantasy, fable, parable, allegory; plot, story-line, subject, argument.

narrator, reciter, story-teller, novelist, raconteur, anecdotist, fabricator.

adj. descriptive, narrative, expressive; graphic, vivid, true-to-life, lifelike, telling, detailed, pictorial; fictional, made-up, legendary, mythical, fabulous, parabolic, allegorical.

vb. describe, portray, sketch, set forth, represent, outline, trace, illustrate, picture, draw, paint, imagine, delineate, characterize, define, specify, mark out, express; account, report, state, record, explain, summarize; narrate, tell, recount, relate, recite, rehearse.

526 dissertation

n. dissertation, essay, paper, composition, commentary, exposition, thesis, treatise, monograph, discourse, disquisition; survey, review, analysis, examination, enquiry, investigation, study, discussion, story, comment, write-up, critique.

essayist, expositor, commentator; critic, reviewer.

vb. discuss, treat, handle, concern, deal with, consider, comment; analyse, survey, examine, explain, interpret; review, criticize, write up.

527 compendium

n. compendium, summary, resumé, precis, abridgment, abstract, summing up, syllabus, survey, outline, synopsis, skeleton, reduction, analysis, conspectus, epitome; core, essence; digest, miscellany, anthology, selections, readings.

adj. compendious, concise, brief, succinct, abbreviated.

vb. summarize, sum up, abstract, abridge, condense, reduce, shorten, digest, outline, survey; boil down to.

528 poetry; prose

n. poetry, song, rhyme, poem, verse, stanza, sonnet, ode, lyric, idyll, epic, ballad, jingle, limerick; chorus, refrain; prosody, versification, scansion, rhythm, metre, stress, beat, foot; prose, writing, literature, composition, story.

poet, writer, composer, versifier, poet laureate, bard, minstrel, troubadour.

adj. poetic, rhythmic, lyrical, idyllic, tuneful.

vb. poetize, sing, versify; rhyme, scan; write, conceive, imagine, compose.

529 drama

n. theatre, the stage; hall, opera

house, cinema, playhouse; play, drama, show, opera, melodrama, tragicomedy, tragedy, comedy, farce, slapstick, pantomime, mime, variety, cabaret, pageant, revue, spectacle, carnival; presentation, appearance, exhibition, production; dramatics, stagecraft, showmanship, acting, performance, histrionics.

actor, actress, performer, player, role, part, character, Thespian, lead, star, understudy, extra; cast, characters, *dramatis personae*.

adj. dramatic, theatrical; impressive, spectacular.

vb. dramatize, direct, produce, present, stage, produce, put on, perform, enact, play.

V Volition

1 Individual volition

A Volition in general

530 will

n. will, volition, intention, resolution, power, mind, conviction, determination, willpower, choice, free will, discretion, conation; desire, wish, inclination.

adj. volitional, willing, minded, voluntary, free, intentional, wilful, deliberate, wished, premeditated, conative.

vb. will, wish, want, desire, incline, choose, resolve, make a decision, decide, make up one's mind, determine, purpose, see fit, take it into one's head to (*inf.*), have one's own way; conclude, come to the conclusion.

adv. at will, at pleasure, as one thinks, of one's own accord.

531 necessity

n. necessity, compulsion, obligation; inevitability, unavoidability, certainty, inexorableness, inescapableness; determinism, predestination, foreordination, fatalism; involuntariness, spontaneity, reflex action, instinct, intuition.

no choice, no alternative, Hobson's choice, six of one and half a dozen of the other; must (*inf.*), essential, prerequisite; fate, the inevitable, whatever will be shall be, *che sara, sara*.

adj. necessary, inevitable, unavoidable, inescapable, inexorable, certain, sure, foreordained, predetermined, destined, predestined, irresistible; essential, indispensable, imperative; compulsory, obligatory; deterministic, fatalistic; involuntary, unintentional, instinctive, unconscious, automatic, reflex, mechanical.

vb. necessitate, compel, oblige, constrain, force, dictate; destine, foreordain; need, require, cry out for.

adv. of necessity, necessarily, inevitably, certainly, willy-nilly.

532 willingness

n. willingness, readiness, disposition, inclination, compliance; eagerness, enthusiasm, zeal, earnestness.

adj. willing, prepared, ready, disposed, inclined, game, desirous, compliant, eager, enthusiastic, zealous; voluntary, uninvited, unasked, unprompted.

vb. be willing, like to, want, desire, choose, feel like, show willing (*inf.*), be inclined towards; volunteer, take on the responsibility, offer oneself; be eager, enthuse, jump at, leap at, lean over backwards (*inf.*), fall over oneself to (*inf.*); gush over, go overboard about (*inf.*), go to town on (*inf.*).

adv. willingly, gladly, eagerly, readily; voluntarily, of one's own accord; off one's own bat.

see also **611**

533 unwillingness

n. unwillingness, disinclination, unreadiness, hesitation, reluctance, scruple, qualm, aversion, demur; non-cooperation, protest, abstention.

adj. unwilling, unready, disinclined, reluctant, hesitant, averse, opposed, loath, not in the mood, unenthusiastic, indifferent, half-hearted.

vb. be unwilling, not feel like, not want to, would rather not, refuse, hesitate, hold back, balk at, shirk, demur, fight shy of, shy away, shrink, dodge, evade; force oneself.

adv. unwillingly, without enthusiasm, against one's will, against one's better judgment, under protest, grudgingly.

see also **612**

534 resolution

n. resolution, determination, resolve, certainty, persistence, constancy, doggedness, conviction, perseverance, boldness, tenacity, fortitude, steadfastness; firmness, willpower, strength of will, mettle; self-control, self-reliance, self-possession.

adj. resolute, determined, steadfast, firm, steady, strong, certain, serious, strong-willed, iron-willed, inflexible, bold, persistent, tenacious, constant, dogged; single-minded, wholehearted, committed, decided; unyielding, unhesitating, unflinching, unwavering, unswerving, unbending.

vb. be resolute, determine, resolve, decide, be bent on; have one's heart set upon, stand fast, take one's stand, hold one's ground, not give in, stick to one's guns, stand no nonsense, put one's foot down; take the bull by the horns; commit oneself, dedicate, put one's heart and soul into.

535 perseverance

n. perseverance, tenacity, steadfastness, firmness, persistence, continuance, constancy, endurance, indefatigability, undauntedness, doggedness; stamina, guts (*inf.*), staying power, backbone, stickability (*sl.*), moral fibre, stiff upper lip.

stayer, bulldog.

adj. persevering, persistent, determined, tenacious, steadfast, constant, steady, firm, unmoved, undaunted, indefatigable, untiring, obstinate, enduring, continuing; diligent, industrious, assiduous.

vb. persevere, remain, persist, endure, continue to the end, go on, carry on, have what it takes, keep at it, keep going (*inf.*), stick at it (*inf.*), soldier on, plod (*inf.*), plug away (*inf.*), slog away, see it through (*inf.*), stick it out (*inf.*); stick out for, hold out for; hold a job down (*inf.*).

536 irresolution

n. irresolution, indecision, vacillation, wavering, fluctuation; inconstancy, hesitation, fickleness, instability.

adj. irresolute, indecisive, undecided, fluctuating, wavering, vacillating, fickle, hesitant, in two minds, unstable, infirm, inconstant, changeable.

vb. be irresolute, vacillate, waver, fluctuate, hesitate, falter, shilly-shally.

537 obstinacy

n. obstinacy, stubbornness, inflexibility, rigidity, tenacity, hardness, relentlessness, obduracy, intransigence, intractableness; bigotry, dogmatism, narrow-mindedness, intolerance, fanaticism.

dogmatist, bigot, fanatic, die-hard, mule, intransigent; pedant, stickler.

adj. obstinate, stubborn, inflexible, tenacious, uncompromising, intransigent, unyielding, unrelenting, hardened, hard, intractable, headstrong, self-willed, set in one's ways; stiff-necked, pig-headed, recalcitrant, refractory, obdurate, pertinacious; dogmatic.

vb. be obstinate, not give in, stick to one's guns; resist, oppose, dig one's heels in.

see also 534, 535

538 change of mind

n. change of mind, second thoughts, afterthought, change of heart, *volte-face*, repentance; retraction, withdrawal, backing out, reversal, abandonment, desertion, defection, renunciation, recantation; tergiversation, backsliding, apostasy.

turncoat, time-server, rat, renegade, traitor, deserter, apostate.

adj. fickle, irresolute, unfaithful, inconstant.

vb. change one's mind, have second thoughts, think beter of, change one's tune; take back, withdraw, back out, back down, climb down (*inf.*), disown, deny, retract, revoke, recant, disclaim; nullify; trim; apologize, eat humble pie, eat one's words; fall away, apostasize.

539 caprice

n. caprice, whim, fancy, vagary, notion, quirk, prank, crotchet, freak, craze, whimsy, whim-wham, flash; jest,

witticism; capriciousness, whimsicality; fickleness, inconstancy.

adj. capricious, whimsical, fanciful, inconstant, fickle, changeable, flighty, frivolous, freakish, crotchety, unpredictable, erratic, fitful.

540 choice

n. choice, option, decision, determination, selection, adoption; alternative, preference, substitute.

vote, ballot, poll, election, representation, referendum, plebiscite; suffrage, franchise; voter, elector, electorate, constituency, ward.

adj. optional, elective, selective, discretional, discriminating, choosy (*inf.*), fastidious; electoral, voting.

vb. choose, pick, decide on, opt, adopt, sort, prefer, take up, go for, plump for (*inf.*), like, fancy, favour, appoint, co-opt, elect, nominate, commit oneself; separate, select, isolate, segregate, cull, glean, sift, winnow, divide the sheep from the goats, separate the wheat from the chaff; weigh, judge, discriminate, make up one's mind; vote, cast votes, poll, ballot, draw lots, vote in, return.

541 absence of choice

n. no choice, Hobson's choice, first come first served; impartiality, neutrality, no preference, indifference; abstention, don't know.

adj. choiceless, neutral, impartial, disinterested, unbiased, indifferent.

vb. be neutral, abstain, not commit oneself, sit on the fence, not take sides.

542 rejection

n. rejection, dismissal, repudiation, denial, refusal, renunciation, rebuff, disownment, disapproval, exclusion, expulsion.

adj. rejected, repudiated, excluded, renounced, spurned.

vb. reject, not accept, dismiss, exclude, repudiate, renounce, deny, refuse, disapprove, rebuff, spurn, decline, disown, disclaim, despise, turn up one's nose at (*inf.*), expel, jettison, discard, brush aside, have nothing to do with, turn one's back on, laugh in someone's face (*inf.*).

see also **556, 694**

543 predetermination

n. predetermination, predestination, preordination, inevitability, necessity, finality; prediction, forecast; doom, fate; premeditation, predeliberation, foregone conclusion.

adj. predetermined, planned, proposed, designed, fixed, deliberate.

vb. predetermine, foreordain, predestine, appoint, destine, predestinate; predict, forecast, foretell, determine beforehand; premeditate, preconceive.

544 spontaneity

n. spontaneity, spur of the moment; improvisation, extemporization; involuntariness, reflex action; impetuosity, impulsiveness, hastiness, suddenness, rashness; impulse buying.

adj. spontaneous, impulsive, unpremeditated, unthinking, unconsidered; involuntary, automatic, instinctive, reflex; extempore, impromptu, improvised, ad lib (*inf.*); hasty, sudden, rash, precipitate; casual, offhand, throwaway.

vb. act impulsively; blurt out, say the first thing that comes into one's mind; improvise, extemporize, ad lib (*inf.*), play by ear.

adv. on impulse, on the spur of the

moment, impulsively, rashly, instinctively, automatically.

see also **613, 859**

545 habit

n. habit, custom, mode, practice, wont, usage, fashion, style, rule, procedure; tendency, propensity, bent, disposition, predisposition, weakness, bias, penchant, second nature, instinct; routine, ritual, rut, groove, treadmill, regularity; convention, precedent, tradition, etiquette, protocol, the done thing; conditioning, accustoming, adaptation, familiarization, training, acclimatization.

addict, habitué, fiend, creature of habit, devotee, client, patron, regular (*inf.*).

adj. usual, customary, normal, common, general, accepted, expected, prevalent, current, conventional, orthodox, established; habitual, frequent, regular, routine, stereotyped; mechanical, seasoned, inveterate; confirmed, ingrained, deep-seated; besetting, clinging, persistent; accustomed, used to, adapted.

vb. accustom, get used to, take to, adapt, adjust, accommodate, condition, train, familiarize, orientate, acclimatize, harden, season, inure, habituate; catch on.

be wont to, be in the habit of, make a practice of.

adv. usually, as is usual, generally.

546 absence of habit

n. disuse, unaccustomedness, desuetude; cessation, relinquishment; decay, neglect, deterioration.

adj. unused, unaccustomed, not used to, not in the habit of; unskilled, inexperienced.

vb. break a habit, abandon, neglect, relinquish, discard, discontinue, rid oneself of, throw off, wean from; not get used to, not take to; not catch on.

see also 607

547 motive

n. motive, cause, reason, purpose, ground, basis, spring, spur, impetus, urge, prod, goad, carrot, lure, bait; influence, stimulus, incentive, inspiration, prompting, instigation; persuasion, inducement, coaxing, cajolery, wheedling; charm, attraction, glamour; enticement, temptation, bribery.

motivator, instigator, prompter, animator, coaxer, wheedler; pressure group, lobby, lobbyist.

adj. motivating, persuasive, convincing, impelling, forceful; provocative, stimulating, rousing; fascinating, alluring, charming, captivating, enthralling; enticing, tantalizing.

vb. motivate, cause, inspire, stimulate, prompt, instigate, insist, induce, drive, push, egg on, spur, urge, prod, goad; provoke, elicit, call forth, evoke; influence, encourage, support; persuade, sway, prevail on, talk into, win over, wear down resistance, brainwash (*inf.*), twist round one's little finger (*inf.*), pull strings; coax, cajole, wheedle; captivate, fascinate, charm, attract, interest, entice, tempt, tantalize, beguile, enrapture; lobby, put pressure on; bribe, buy, get at (*inf.*), oil, corrupt.

548 dissuasion

n. dissuasion, discouragement, hindrance, deterrent, disincentive, damper, restraint, cold water, wet blanket; spoilsport, killjoy.

adj. dissuasive, discouraging.

vb. dissuade, deter, hinder, prevent, advise against, discourage, talk out of, wean from, dampen, stifle, disparage, pour cold water on.

549 pretext

n. pretext, excuse, plea, apology, justification, pretence, gesture, show, guise, veil, cloak, mask, appearance, alibi.

adj. ostensible, alleged, specious.

vb. allege, pretend, claim, profess, excuse; apologize, make excuses, bluff.

550 good

n. good, benefit, gain, profit, success, advantage, service, boon, windfall, godsend, pennies from heaven, providence, blessing, good turn; well-being, welfare, prosperity, fortune, happiness, weal; improvement, betterment, edification, progress.

adj. good, beneficial, advantageous, helpful, useful, edifying.

see also 899, 935

551 evil

n. evil, misfortune, ill, harm, ruin, nuisance, disadvantage, bane, accident, tragedy, disaster, catastrophe, calamity, affliction, trial, crying shame, raw deal; foul play, wrong, injury, pain, anguish, hurt; wickedness, corruption.

adj. evil, bad, wicked; unfortunate, ill, tragic, catastrophic, disastrous, painful, distressing, hurtful.

see also 900, 936

B Prospective volition

552 intention

n. intention, purpose, aim, intent, meaning; goal, object, end, objective, mark, destination, target; plan, design, idea, proposal; dream, desire, aspiration, expectation, ambition.

adj. intended, designed, planned, proposed, deliberate; intending, purposeful, teleological.

vb. intend, aim, go for, attempt, try for, pursue; plan, propose, project, design, purpose, mean; dream, expect, hope, aspire, have designs on (*inf.*); consider, think about, contemplate, study, have in mind, have in view, calculate, work out, decide, determine, resolve.

553 chance

n. chance, randomness, uncertainty, fortuity; fate, fortune, luck, coincidence, fluke, toss-up (*inf.*); speculation, venture, risk, hazard; bet, gamble, wager, stake, flutter, draw, lottery.

speculator, gambler, better, backer, punter; bookmaker, turf accountant, bookie (*inf.*).

adj. chance, lucky, fortuitous, unintentional, haphazard, aimless, random, risky, hazardous, touch-and-go.

vb. chance, risk, venture, hazard, speculate, gamble, bet, wager, back
see also 158

554 pursuit

n. pursuit, hunt, chase, race, pursuance, quest, search, tracking; hunter, chaser, pursuer, seeker, quester, follower.

adj. pursuing, following.

vb. pursue, look for, search, follow up, seek, quest, prosecute; hunt, go after, chase, give chase, hound, tail, trail, stalk, shadow, track, sniff out (*inf.*), smell out, dog.

prep. after, in pursuit of, on the track of.

555 avoidance

n. avoidance, evasion, escape, flight, withdrawal, retreat, shunning, abstinence, circumvention; shirker, fugitive, runaway, absconder, eloper, deserter, refugee, truant.

adj. avoiding, evasive, elusive.

vb. avoid, escape, evade, elude, keep away, keep off, boycott; flee, shrink, flinch; get out of, shun, shirk, dodge, flunk, turn away, duck, hedge; steer clear of, keep one's distance, take no part in, leave alone, not get involved in, disregard, give the go-by; abstain, refrain; retreat, withdraw.

556 relinquishment

n. relinquishment, abandonment, giving up, surrender, renunciation, discontinuance, withdrawal, desertion, quitting.

vb. relinquish, abandon, give up, renounce, forgo, abdicate, waive, surrender, throw in the towel; turn over to, turn in; leave, quit, withdraw, back out, go back on, retreat, secede, forsake; discontinue, break with, break off with, drop, let go, throw away, cast off, discard, part with, shed, desert, chuck (*inf.*), ditch, jilt; leave in the lurch, have done with (*inf.*), walk out on (*inf.*).

see also 542, 713

557 business

n. business, affairs, dealings, trade; job, employment, post, appointment, position, situation, engagement, incumbency; vocation, calling, pursuit, occupation, profession; line of business, speciality, *métier*, craft; career, life-work, life, mission; work, task, undertaking, activity, assignment, affair, concern; function, office, role, capacity, responsibility, duty, charge, commission, terms of reference, scope, area, field, realm, province, portfolio.

adj. businesslike, efficient, professional, official, prompt; busy, tied up with (*inf.*).

vb. employ, occupy, appoint, select, recruit, engage, contract, take on, give a job to, commission, enlist, hire, rope in (*inf.*), take on the payroll; work, undertake, be busy, be occupied with, be engaged on, be about.

558 plan

n. plan, scheme, project, design, programme, proposal, schedule; scope, outline, sketch; method, procedure, guidelines, principles; policy, course of action, strategy; representation, chart; master-plan, long-range plan; blueprint, draft, rough draft, pilot scheme, dummy run; plot, conspiracy, intrigue, cabal, little game (*inf.*).

planner, director, designer, organizer, architect, engineer, administrator; conspirer, plotter, schemer.

adj. planned, projected, prospective, on the drawing board, procedural.

vb. plan, design, work out, draw up, organize, arrange, propose, devise, create, dream up (*inf.*), frame, undertake, proceed, outline, sketch, draft; forecast, project, think ahead, phase; scheme, plot, conspire, concoct, hatch.

559 way

n. way, manner, fashion; method, means, procedure, process; tactics, measures, steps; direction, passage, entrance, access, approach, route, itinerary, course.

path, track, footpath, walk; road, street, avenue, lane, drive, crescent, close, alley, terrace, park, garden, green, hill, grove, boulevard, square, place, court, circus, arcade, piazza, market, mall, embankment; ring-road, by-pass, arterial road, motorway, dual carriageway, clearway, primary route, trunk road, highway.

railway, underground, tube; main line, branch line, feeder.

560 mid-course

n. centre, mean, middle course, middle of the road, half-way house.

adj. middle, central, medial, neutral, middle-of-the-road, unextreme, moderate, intermediate, midway, half-way.

561 circuit

n. circuit, detour, by-pass, roundabout way; digression, deviation.

adj. circuitous, roundabout, indirect, out-of-the-way.

see also 250

562 requirement

n. requirement, requisite, stipulation, need, want, demand; condition; essential, imperative, necessity, must (*inf.*), desideratum; needfulness, obligation, compulsion, indispensability, emergency, urgency, matter of life and death, essentiality.

adj. necessary, essential, imperative, indispensable, vital, needful, urgent; wanted, in demand.

vb. require, need, want, wish; lack, be in need of, miss; demand, call for, ask, invite, cry out for; necessitate, force, compel.

563 instrumentality

n. instrumentality, mediation, subservience, intervention; help, aid, assistance, agency, medium, vehicle, intermediary, organ.

adj. instrumental, intermediate, conducive, assisting, subsidiary, auxiliary, subservient, contributory, helpful; effective.

vb. be instrumental, help, aid, mediate.

see also 172

564 means

n. means, wherewithal, resources, ways and means, equipment, supplies, assets, reserves, provisions; power, potential; factor, agent, medium, channel, organization.

vb. find the means, provide, equip, supply.

565 instrument

n. instrument, implement, apparatus, equipment, appliance, gadget, device, invention, contrivance, contraption; machine, mechanism, machinery, engine; tool, utensil; computer, robot, automaton.

adj. instrumental, mechanical, automatic.

566 materials

n. materials, resources, supplies, assets, means, wherewithal, stuff, raw materials.

567 store

n. store, collection, accumulation, heap, pile, stack, load, mass, stock, hoard, bulk, deposit, bundle; crop, harvest; hoard, treasure, reserves, savings, nest-egg; backlog; fountain, well, spring, gold-mine, reservoir; abundance, profusion, fullness.

storage, safekeeping; warehouse, stockroom, storeroom, depot, depository; library, museum, archives.

adj. stored, accumulated, saved, kept.

vb. store, keep, put away, put aside, put by, stow away, stash away (*inf.*); accumulate, pile up, heap, stack, amass, bulk, bundle, stockpile, lay in; collect, save, deposit, invest, hoard, salt away (*inf.*); harvest, gather; put by for a rainy day.

adv. aside, in store, in reserve, in stock.

568 provision

n. provision, equipment, supply, furnishings, fittings, fixtures, reserve, store, facilities, belongings, accessories,

accompaniments, outfit, paraphernalia, apparatus, appliance; catering, purveying.

adj. provided, furnished, equipped, well-equipped.

vb. provide, equip, supply, furnish, fit, prepare, rig, dress, assemble, deck; give, afford, lend, invest, endow; maintain, stock, cater; supplement, complement; replenish, fill up.

569 waste

n. waste, ruin, decay, devastation, desolation, dilapidation, deterioration, erosion, wear and tear, loss, exhaustion, depletion, decline; consumption, disuse, misuse, squandering, uselessness, dissipation; extravagance, wastefulness, prodigality; excess.

adj. wasteful, extravagant, prodigal, squandering, spendthrift; wasted, squandered, depleted, worthless.

vb. waste, consume, expend, eat up, eat away, exhaust, reduce, deplete, empty, drain, devour, dissipate; squander, lavish, abuse; destroy, erode, decay, dry up, dwindle, wither, run dry, wear out; be of no avail, come to nothing.

570 sufficiency

n. sufficiency, adequacy, enough to go on with; right amount.

adj. sufficient, adequate, enough, satisfactory, acceptable; plenty, abundant, generous, liberal, full, complete, replete.

vb. be sufficient, suffice, be enough, avail, do, comply with, qualify; fill the bill, come up to, live up to, satisfy requirements, make the grade, prove acceptable; lick into shape (*inf.*).

571 insufficiency

n. insufficiency, inadequacy, deficiency, scarcity, meagreness, scantiness, slightness, poverty, paucity, dearth, lack.

adj. insufficient, inadequate, not enough, unacceptable, meagre, thin, slight, scanty, poor, bankrupt, sparing, unsatisfactory, wanting, lacking, missing, failing, disappointing; miserly, parsimonious.

vb. be insufficient, not come up to, fall short, come short, fail, want, need, lack, require.

prep. without, in want of, short of.
see also 35

572 excess

n. excess, redundance; exorbitance, inordinacy, superfluity, oversufficiency, abundance, plenty, lavishness, plethora, profusion, glut, surfeit, surplus, over-supply, saturation, exuberance, superabundance, inundation, flood, deluge, torrent, avalanche, bounty, bonanza, cornucopia, congestion; enough and to spare, more than enough; luxury, extravagance, too much of a good thing.

adj. excessive, inordinate, exorbitant, extravagant, immoderate, unreasonable, saturated, plentiful, superfluous, overfull, congested, surplus, redundant, to spare, extra; plenty, abundant.

vb. abound, teem, swarm; overdo; saturate, glut, inundate, flood, overwhelm, choke, drench.

573 importance

n. importance, significance, consequence; seriousness, gravity; substance, matter, weight, moment, import; prominence, eminence; be-all and end-all, priority, urgency.

adj. important, significant, momentous, decisive, critical, relevant, consequential, crucial, considerable, valuable; great, extensive; serious,

grave, weighty, ponderous, heavy, solemn; famous, well-known, eminent, notable, distinguished, prominent, impressive, imposing, influential, illustrious, extraordinary, outstanding, exceptional, top-notch (*inf.*), heavyweight (*inf.*), mainline (*inf.*); basic, essential, fundamental; chief, main, primary, principal, foremost, leading, paramount, salient.

vb. be important, carry weight, influence, matter, deserve attention; make important, emphasize, underline, stress; value, prize, set great store by, think much of.

574 unimportance

n. unimportance, insignificance, triviality, worthlessness, immateriality, paltriness, irrelevance; red herring, trifle, nothing to speak of, nothing to write home about, nonentity, drop in the ocean.

adj. unimportant, insignificant, immaterial, worthless, inconsequential, irrelevant, trivial, worthless, paltry, petty, trifling, inconsiderable, slight, common, ordinary, superficial.

vb. be unimportant, not matter; play second fiddle, make light of, play down, make nothing of.

575 utility

n. utility, usefulness; utilization, employment, helpfulness, efficacy; suitability, applicability, practicability, serviceableness.

advantage, benefit, profit, worth, value, merit; service, application, convenience.

adj. useful, valuable, beneficial, profitable, advantageous, suitable, practicable, convenient, helpful, handy, available, ·applicable; utilitarian, functional, sensible, pragmatic.

vb. be useful, help, serve a purpose, perform a function, come in handy; profit, benefit, stand one in good stead, avail.

use, employ, have the use of, exploit, exercise, utilize, take advantage of, turn to, take up, adopt, practise, apply, avail oneself of; handle, operate; spend, consume.

see also **606**

576 inutility

n. inutility, uselessness, worthlessness, fruitlessness, ineffectiveness, unsuitability, impracticability; futility, hopelessness, vanity.

lost labour, waste of time, wild-goose chase; dead wood; waste, refuse, rubbish, waste-product, litter, dregs, dust, muck.

adj. useless, of no use, worthless, purposeless, futile, vain, pointless, empty, ineffective, incompetent, counter-productive; thankless, unrewarding; unusable, unsuitable, impracticable, inconvenient, unhelpful, disadvantageous, unavailable; out of order, broken down, inoperative; unnecessary, uncalled for.

vb. be useless, be of no help, come to nothing; flog a dead horse, labour in vain, have no future, beat the air.

577 expedience

n. expedience, suitability, appropriateness, fitness, rightness, advisability, propriety, desirability, advantageousness, usefulness.

adj. expedient, advantageous, suitable, fitting, appropriate, apposite, desirable, advisable, seemly; practical, useful, convenient; wise, politic.

vb. suit, fit; help, do, benefit.

see also **136, 915**

578 inexpedience

n. inexpedience, unsuitability, inappropriateness, inadvisability, undesirability, unfitness, impropriety, inconvenience, disadvantage, prejudice.

adj. inexpedient, unsuitable, inappropriate, undesirable, inadvisable, unfitting, unseemly, unwise, inopportune, imprudent, unfavourable, detrimental, disadvantageous, inconvenient.

vb. not do, not help; inconvenience, put out, embarrass, bother, trouble, hinder.

see also **137, 916**

579 goodness

n. goodness, excellence, fineness, greatness, magnificence, superiority; quality, value, price, worth, merit.

top people, elite, cream, pick of the bunch, salt of the earth, treasure, gem, one in a million, champion, corker (*sl.*).

adj. good, excellent, fine, great, superb, splendid, magnificent, marvellous, wonderful, attractive, lovely; masterly, skilled, competent; praiseworthy, commendable; admirable, desirable, enticing, surprising, astonishing; super, terrific, out of this world (*inf.*), cool (*sl.*), neat (*sl.*), magic (*sl.*).

best, first-class, first-rate, optimum, premium, prime, highest, supreme, superlative, A-1, top-notch (*inf.*), tops; exceptional, incomparable, surpassing, incredible, unbelievable, excelling, exemplary; choice, select, exquisite, superior, capital (*inf.*); valuable, priceless, inestimable.

fair, pretty good, not bad, all right, O K., passable, tolerable, adequate, middling, fair to middling.

vb. be good, have value, have quality; do good, benefit, help, edify.

see also 550, 844

580 badness

n. badness, nastiness, wickedness, vileness, foulness; inferiority, unsatisfactoriness, mediocrity; bane, ill wind, woe, spanner in the works, fly in the ointment.

adj. bad, wrong, awful, nasty, terrible, horrid, horrible; inferior, imperfect, defective, worthless, poor, second-rate, below average, deficient, unsatisfactory, mediocre, ordinary, unwholesome, shoddy, trashy, crummy (*sl.*), shabby; lousy (*sl.*), rotten; pitiful, contemptible, paltry.

harmful, damaging, detrimental, hurtful, destructive, fatal, deadly, corrupting, poisonous, corroding, toxic, venomous, subversive.

vb. be bad, have no value; do bad, harm, injure, hurt, wound, ruin, destroy, corrupt, subvert; vex, trouble, wrong.

see also 551

581 perfection

n. perfection, excellence, impeccability, faultlessness, stainlessness; maturity, completion, culmination, consummation.

ideal, standard, model, paragon, summit, ultimate, height, acme; showpiece, masterpiece, *pièce de résistance.*

adj. perfect, faultless, pure, flawless, impeccable, immaculate, untainted, unblemished, untarnished, stainless, spotless, unstained, uncontaminated, unadulterated, irreproachable, beyond compare, brilliant; supreme, ideal.

whole, sound, complete, entire, finished, developed, fulfilled, completed, accomplished, consummate.

vb. perfect, develop, complete, finish, bring to fruition, get down to a fine art, consummate.

582 imperfection

n. imperfection, impurity, defectiveness, inadequacy, immaturity; disfigurement, defacement, deformity, discoloration.

blemish, flaw, stain; fault, mistake, defect, lack, drawback, snag, loophole, weak spot, weak link in the chain.

adj. imperfect, flawed, defective, deficient, malformed, distorted, tainted, adulterated, blemished, damaged, injured, impaired.

incomplete, unfinished, unsound, uneven, unsatisfactory, faulty, inadequate, fallible.

vb. be imperfect, show faults, fall short, not come up to, be found wanting.

see also 847

583 cleanness

n. cleanness, cleanliness, pureness, spotlessness, whiteness; neatness, tidiness, orderliness, trimness; cleaning, washing, scrubbing, scouring, sprinkling; sterilization, disinfection; cleansing, purification, purgation, ablution.

adj. clean, tidy, neat; immaculate, white, spotless, stainless, untarnished, unblemished, unstained, unsullied, unpolluted, unsoiled, dirtless, spick and span, starched, laundered, polished; germ-free.

vb. clean, tidy, clear; wash, lather, shampoo; bathe, scrub, scour, sponge, mop, swab; brush, sweep; freshen, ventilate; disinfect, fumigate; sterilize, pasteurize; launder, starch, iron; cleanse, purify, sprinkle, purge, expurgate.

584 uncleanness

n. uncleanness, impurity, untidiness, disorderliness, muckiness, filthiness, pollution, defilement.

dirt, filth, spot, stain, smear, smudge, blot, muck, grime, grease, slime; squalor.

adj. unclean, dirty, soiled, polluted, tarnished, sullied, spotted, smeared, daubed, smudged, besmirched; filthy, grimy, greasy, muddy, sooty; squalid, foul, mucky; contaminated, decayed, rotten, rancid, putrid; sloppy, untidy, messy, slovenly, dishevelled, bedraggled, unkempt, like something the cat brought in (*inf.*), unwashed; defiled, unrefined, unpurified.

vb. be dirty, rust, decay, rot, collect dust; dirty, soil, sully, tarnish, daub, bedaub, smudge, blot, pollute, foul; mess up, untidy; corrupt, defile, debase, taint, contaminate, infect.

585 health

n. health, wholeness, soundness, healthfulness, healthiness, salubrity, wholesomeness, balance, vitality; sanity; fitness, strength, well-being, good health, rosy cheeks.

hygiene, sanitation, public health, cleanliness.

adj. healthy, well, sound, whole, wholesome, fit, strong, robust, vigorous, energetic, hale, hearty; all right, rosy-cheeked, flourishing, never feeling better, in fine fettle, in good shape, fighting fit.

healthful, invigorating, stimulating, bracing, beneficial, salubrious; nutritious, nourishing, body-building, restorative, therapeutic, corrective; good for one, what the doctor ordered; hygienic, sanitary.

vb. be healthy, flourish, feel fine; be good for.

586 ill health

n. ill health, poor health, bad health, frailty, weakness, infirmity, invalidity, unhealthiness, indisposition.

illness, disease, ailment, malady, sickness, complaint, disability, affliction, condition, disorder, breakdown, collapse, relapse; fever, infection, virus (*inf.*), bug (*sl.*), pain; bout, spell; stroke, fit, attack, seizure, spasm, convulsions.

lack of hygiene, insalubrity, uncleanliness, contagiousness, infectiousness.

adj. ill, unwell, ailing, weak, unhealthy, poorly, frail, infirm, sick; suffering, down with, indisposed, disabled; drooping, languishing, declining, bedridden, laid up, confined; run down, exhausted; under the weather (*inf.*), out of sorts, seedy (*inf.*), groggy (*inf.*).

unhygienic, insanitary, polluted, bad for, insalubrious; infectious, contagious, endemic; poisonous, toxic, deadly.

vb. be ill, be down with, suffer; fall ill, catch, become ill with, contract, go down with, get, be stricken with; show symptoms of, sicken for; waste away, droop, languish; be bad for, disagree with.

587 improvement

n. improvement, betterment, change, advance, development, refinement, progress, reformation, face-lift, amelioration; enrichment, promotion, furtherance, reform, modernization; revision, correction, amendment.

adj. improved, corrected, amended, revised, reformed, touched up; progressive, reformatory.

vb. improve, develop, further, better, reorganize, promote, reform, straighten out, mend, ameliorate; revise, update, upgrade, correct, rectify; polish, refine, enrich; decorate, beautify, touch up, refurbish; progress, make progress, get better, advance, profit; pick up, come on, rally; pull one's socks up (*inf.*); mellow, mature.

see also **288**

588 deterioration

n. deterioration, impairment, degeneration, decay, rotting, decomposition, erosion, rust; dilapidation, ruin, collapse, decadence, disintegration; impoverishment, adulteration, defilement, corruption, spoiling, detriment, pollution; retrogression; damage, injury, wound, lesion, cut, gash, sore, bruise.

adj. deteriorated, impaired, spoiled, decadent, ruined; damaged, harmed, desolate, ravaged, plundered, robbed, marred, mutilated; decayed, decomposed, rotten, putrified, foul, putrid; worn away, wasting away, emaciated, depleted; ramshackle, tumbledown.

vb. deteriorate, worsen, degenerate, decay, decline, slide, fall, slump, sink, go downhill, fall away, depreciate; go bad, rot, wither, crumble, the rot set in (*inf.*); wither, shrivel; spoil; go to pieces, break up, decompose, fade away, waste away, die; collapse, break down, founder, go to wrack and ruin, go to the dogs (*inf.*), go to pot (*inf.*); go off the rails (*inf.*).

impair, pervert, ruin, corrupt, distort; lower, pull down, reduce, degrade, dehumanize; adulterate, defile, deprave, infect, contaminate; eat away, erode, corrode.

harm, damage, injure, wound, savage, cripple, lame; maltreat, misuse; disgrace, dishonour, discredit; exacerbate, aggravate; hold against (*inf.*), count against; confuse, mess up (*inf.*)

589 restoration

n. restoration, healing, cure, recovery, convalescence, recuperation; renovation, repair, reconditioning, refurbishing, reconstruction, remaking; rehabilitation, re-establishment, resumption, reinstatement, return, getting back to normal; reparation, restitution, amends; reclamation, salvage, rescue.

revival, renewal, reawakening, reinvigoration, resuscitation, rebirth, regeneration, resurrection, renaissance, resurgence, rejuvenation; Indian summer, face-lift, new look, comeback.

adj. restored, repaired, re-established, back to normal; restorative, corrective, remedial, recuperative, therapeutic, soothing, curative.

vb. restore, rebuild, reconstruct, remodel, refashion, reorganize, recondition, reform, remake, revamp, renovate, modernize; repair, mend, fix; refurbish, touch up; darn, patch, sew.

put right, correct, rectify, amend, redress; return, recompense, refund, make amends, make restitution, reinstate, put back, reinstall, re-establish, resume, return to normal; reclaim, salvage, rescue, retrieve, redeem.

revive, refresh, renew, recreate, reanimate, regenerate, resurrect, resuscitate, rejuvenate, reawaken, revitalize, rekindle.

cure, heal, treat, minister to, nurse, rehabilitate, put on one's feet again.

be restored, recover, convalesce, recuperate, get well, get better, fall on one's feet (*inf*), pick up, rally, pull through, gain strength, get back into circulation (*inf.*); come up smiling (*inf.*).

see also **618**

590 relapse

n. relapse, return, reversion, retrogression, regression; deterioration, declension; apostasy.

vb. relapse, regress, retrogress, deteriorate, degenerate, sink back, slip back, revert, suffer, relapse; backslide, fall from grace, apostasize.

see also 289

591 remedy

n. remedy, cure, relief, assistance, treatment, medication; medicine, medicament, preparation, prescription, pharmaceutical, drug; mixture, dose, potion, linctus; pill, tablet, capsule, lozenge; vaccine, injection, inoculation, jab (*inf.*), shot (*inf.*); lotion, ointment, balm salve; tonic, pick-me-up, stimulant, restorative, refresher, tranquillizer. sedative; panacea, cure-all, elixir; operation, surgery.

adj. remedial, therapeutic, healing, medicinal, corrective, curative, restorative.

vb. remedy, cure, heal, restore; treat, attend, practise; relieve, support, help, mitigate, soothe, palliate; send for the doctor, send to hospital, dial 999, hospitalize, operate; undergo treatment, take pills, take one's medicine.

592 bane

n. bane, curse, plague, evil, scourge, affliction, trial, cross, thorn in the flesh; pain in the neck (*inf.*); weakness, besetting sin; poison, venom, virus; blight, mildew, rust, mould, rot, fungus, gangrene, cancer.

adj. baneful, evil, pestilent; deadly, poisonous, venomous; harmful, destructive.

593 safety

n. safety, security, surety, impregnability, invulnerability, immunity; protection, defence, safekeeping, custody, guardianship, supervision, care; law and order.

protector, guard, defender; custodian, warden, curator, keeper, trustee; life-guard, bodyguard, guardian; patrol, lookout, scout, night watchman, watchdog, vigilante, sentry, policeman.

adj. safe, secure, impregnable, invulnerable, unassailable; protected, guarded, safeguarded, defended, shielded, sheltered; unharmed, unhurt, safe and sound, unscathed; waterproof, bulletproof.

vb. make safe, safeguard, protect, keep, guard, defend, shelter, screen, shield, harbour; supervise, care for, mind, look after, take charge of, keep an eye on, attend to, take under one's wing; keep order, patrol, police, be on the lookout, keep vigil, keep cave (*sl.*); hide, lie low, go to earth.

adv. out of danger, in the clear, out of harm's way, in safe hands, under one's wing, under lock and key.

see also 595

594 danger

n. danger, peril, risk, hazard, jeopardy; menace, threat; dangerousness, perilousness, riskiness, insecurity, precariousness, vulnerability, exposure, openness, helplessness; weak spot.

adj. dangerous, perilous, hazardous, risky, insecure, precarious, alarming, unsafe, treacherous, slippery, shaky, unstable; unsheltered, unshielded, vulnerable, exposed, open, naked, unfortified; menacing, threatening, ominous; critical, serious, delicate, explosive.

vb. endanger, jeopardize, put in jeopardy, expose, lay open to, risk, run the risk of, render liable to, court disaster, tempt providence.

595 refuge

n. refuge, shelter, sanctuary, asylum, retreat; home, ivory tower, port, harbour, haven; den, lair, nest, covert; castle, fortress, stronghold; safeguard, protection, defence; cover, screen, shade, shield, umbrella, wind-break; escape, way out, recourse, last resort.

see also 593, 646

596 pitfall

n. pitfall, trap, snare, ambush, booby-trap; reef, rock, sandbank, quicksand, undercurrent; danger spot, black spot, trouble spot; trouble-maker, wrecker, snake in the grass.

597 warning

n. warning, caution, lesson, example, advice, counsel, caveat; alert, hint, intimation, admonition, tip-off (*inf.*), early warning, writing on the wall, symptom, sign, omen, augury; foreboding, premonition; notice, indication, notification; call, cry, shout.

adj. warning, cautionary, advisory, instructive.

vb. warn, caution, advise, alert, admonish, counsel, encourage, exhort, hint, prompt, suggest; forewarn, tip off (*inf.*); notify, inform, give notice, apprise.

see also 460

598 indication of danger

n. alarm, alert, bell, alarm bell, fire alarm; siren, horn, fog-horn, klaxon, tocsin; light, red light, warning light; red alert; SOS, distress signal; beacon; war-cry, drum-beat; false alarm, hoax, scare.

vb. give the alarm, raise the alarm, dial 999, alert, put on the alert; cry wolf.

599 preservation

n. preservation, protection, maintenance, saving, keeping, conservation; storage, canning, freezing, refrigeration, dehydration.

adj. preservative, protective; preserved, kept, intact, protected; fresh, well-preserved.

vb. preserve, maintain, keep, protect, look after; conserve, keep fresh, bottle, can, tin, season, cure, salt, dry, smoke, freeze, refrigerate, freeze-dry, dehydrate, pickle, spice, marinade; embalm, mummify.

600 escape

n. escape, flight, departure, getaway; evasion, avoidance, abdication, desertion, disappearance; freedom, release, deliverance, rescue; retreat, withdrawal; narrow escape, close shave, near miss, near thing.

exit, way out, overflow, vent, waste-pipe, exhaust, leak, leakage, life-line, loophole.

escaper, runaway, truant, dodger, fugitive, refugee.

adj. escaped, free, out, at large, at liberty, missing, wanted.

vb. escape, flee, take flight, abscond, leave, depart, break loose, break out, decamp, free, get clear of, get away with, make one's getaway, make oneself scarce, give the slip, slip through one's fingers, elude, avoid, evade, elope, play truant; emerge, issue, burst out.

see also 921

601 deliverance

n. deliverance, saving, rescue, release, freeing, liberation, relief; extrication, unbinding, loosening, disentanglement; ransom, forgiveness, pardon; remission, discharge, acquittal, reprieve, exoneration; emancipation, affranchisement, manumission.

vb. deliver, rescue, release, free, discharge, relieve; remit, acquit, let off (*inf.*), exonerate; extricate, loosen, untie; emancipate, liberate; salvage, retrieve; save, redeem, ransom, pardon, forgive.

see also 680, 911

602 preparation

n. preparation, plan, step, arrangement; outline, draft, scheme, foundation, groundwork, spadework; rehearsal, practice, training, dummy run; approach, run-up (*inf.*); preparedness, readiness, fitness, experience, all systems go (*inf.*); red alert.

adj. preparatory, introductory, initial; prepared, ready, alert, waiting, on call, standing by, all set; experienced, skilled, qualified, versed, seasoned, broken in.

ready-made, prefabricated, ready-mixed, treated; frozen, pre-cooked, processed, dehydrated, ready-to-eat, oven-ready, instant; off-the-peg.

vb. prepare, get ready, arrange, plan, make preparations; settle, decide; adapt, adjust, fit, equip, supply, deck out, fit out, provide; take steps, take measures; practise, rehearse, train, study, hold in readiness; clear the decks, lay the foundations, prepare the ground, pave the way, smooth the way, blaze a trail, do the groundwork, do one's homework, break the ice.

see also 558

603 non-preparation

n. non-preparation, unpreparedness, lack of training, inexperience; immaturity, rawness, naivety.

adj. unprepared, unready, napping, surprised, taken aback, unguarded, off one's guard, with one's pants down (*sl.*); unorganized, makeshift, hasty, rush (*inf.*); thoughtless; inexperienced,

unskilled, uninstructed, untrained, unqualified, unequipped; new, naive, raw, immature; undeveloped, half-baked; backward, developing; fallow, virgin.

vb. be unprepared, be taken unawares, be caught napping; not plan, make no provision for; improvise.

604 attempt

n. attempt, try, effort, trial, experiment, endeavour, essay, undertaking, enterprise, venture.

adj. experimental, probationary, tentative, trial.

vb. attempt, try, have a try, make an effort, endeavour, venture, seek, aim for, strive, contend, risk, aspire, contest, have a go, lift a finger, put oneself out, have a crack at (*inf.*), have a shot at (*inf.*), have a stab at (*inf.*).

605 undertaking

n. undertaking, enterprise, project, plan, programme, cause, pursuit, campaign, operation, exercise, venture, exploit, feat; occupation, business, job, task, work, concern, matter in hand, proposition, engagement, commitment, obligation.

adj. enterprising, adventurous, venturesome, daring, go-ahead, pioneering, progressive, up-and-coming; ambitious, aspiring.

vb. undertake, engage in, go in for, do, take part in, participate in, devote oneself to; manage, engage, promise, contract; take upon oneself, put one's hand to, commit oneself to, take on, assume, shoulder, bear the burden of, tackle, embark on, enter upon, get down to (*inf.*), launch into, plunge into, commence, begin, start, set to, broach, set about; get down to business, get one's teeth into (*inf.*), take the bit between the teeth (*inf.*), get down to brass tacks (*inf.*), get to grips with.

adv. in hand, under control, in order.

see also **88**

606 use

n. use, usage, application, practice, exercise, employment, management, conduct, realization, adoption, conversion, treatment, handling, performance, control; method, technique; utility, usefulness.

adj. used, applied, utilized, adopted, accepted, practised; in use, in service, in force; old, second-hand.

vb. use, employ, apply, utilize, put to use, put into service; realize, adopt, draw on, take advantage of; adapt, convert, relate, bring to bear, resort to, have recourse to, fall back on; manage, conduct, deal with, treat, handle; exploit, use to the full, get the most out of, cash in on (*inf.*), capitalize, get the benefit of.

see also **575**

607 disuse

n. disuse, non-use, discontinuance, suspension, abolition, rejection, relinquishment, abandonment, unemployment, abeyance; obsolescence.

adj. disused, neglected, abandoned, idle, abolished, deserted, derelict; unused, unemployed, unspent; out of order, out of service, inactive; extra, spare.

vb. disuse, suspend, abolish, put aside, have done with, reject, get rid of, throw out, jettison, discard, scrap, throw on the scrap-heap, neglect, abandon, desert, relinquish.

608 misuse

n. misuse, abuse, misapplication, misemployment, mishandling, mismanagement, misappropriation; perversion, debasement, degradation, prostitution, desecration, defilement, profanation, pollution; outrage, violation; error, mistake.

vb. misuse, abuse, mistreat, ill-treat, maltreat, mishandle, misemploy, misappropriate; pervert, prostitute, debase, desecrate, defile, violate, deprave, profane; wrong, insult, injure, hurt, harm, malign; squander, waste.

C Voluntary action

609 action

n. action, doing, execution, commission, operation, management, handling.

act, deed, thing, work, job, activity, feat, exploit; performance, achievement, undertaking, accomplishment; move, step, measure; blow, stroke.

doer, performer, worker, workman; instrument.

adj. doing, in operation, in process, operative.

vb. act, do, conduct, operate, work, function.

achieve, accomplish, complete, fulfil, carry out, bring about, execute, realize, effect, perform, dispose of, commit, transact, put into effect, put into action, put into operation.

take action, take steps, do something about, specialize in, concern oneself with, make it one's business, go in for; persist, persevere, keep going.

see also **611, 615**

610 inaction

n. inaction, rest, waiting, inertia, suspension, abeyance; laissez-faire, dormancy, neglect, stagnation.

adj. inoperative, idle, unemployed; suspended, in abeyance.

vb. not act, wait, pause, hang fire, bide one's time, twiddle one's thumbs, hold your horses (*inf.*); wait and see, do nothing, abstain, refrain; leave alone, have nothing to do with, let sleeping dogs lie.

see also **612**

611 activity

n. activity, liveliness, agility, nimbleness, alertness, alacrity, readiness, keenness, eagerness; energy, life, vigour, spirit, verve, zest, dynamism, enthusiasm, get-up-and-go (*inf.*); hurry, bustle, flurry, rush, commotion, rat-race.

industry, diligence, assiduousness, perseverance, resolution, determination, application, concentration; enterprise, initiative; activism, militancy, aggressiveness.

busy person, enthusiast, zealot, activist, fanatic, militant, live wire.

adj. active, lively, energetic, dynamic; busy, hard at it, eventful, bustling, dashing, raring to go; alert, agile, nimble, sharp, spry, wire, alive, restless, fidgety.

enthusiastic, keen, zealous; pushy (*inf.*), ambitious, aggressive, forceful, activist, militant, go-ahead, enterprising; industrious, diligent, hardworking, studious.

vb. be active, be busy, rush around, bustle about, have one's hands full, have a finger in every pie; have many irons in the fire; busy oneself in, stir oneself, rouse onself; persevere, keep going, keep at it; work hard, not have a moment to spare, never stop, overwork, overdo it, have no time to call one's own.

see also **532, 609**

612 inactivity

n. inactivity, stillness, inertia; lethargy, slackness, sluggishness, torpor, lifelessness, listlessness; apathy, indifference, carelessness; idleness, laziness, indolence, sloth.

fatigue, tiredness, weariness, sleepiness; sleep, slumber, rest, doze, nod, snooze, shut-eye, catnap, forty winks, siesta, repose, dormancy; breather, pause, holiday, vacation.

lazy person, idler, loafer (*inf.*), good-for-nothing, lazy-bones, bum (*sl.*), tramp, sluggard, wastrel, parasite, sponger.

adj. inactive, still, stable; unemployed, unoccupied, fallow, barren; idle, lazy, slothful, indolent, lethargic, slack, sluggish, listless, torpid, languid; unadventurous, unenterprising, stay-at-home; apathetic, indifferent, uninterested.

tired, weary, drowsy, sleepy, fatigued, somnolent, dormant; exhausted, run down, overworked, worn out, washed out, drooping, faint, weak, stale.

vb. be inactive, rest, relax, pause, bide one's time; drift, vegetate, stagnate.

idle, loaf about (*inf.*), mooch about (*sl.*), loiter about, hang about (*inf.*), bum around (*sl.*); dilly-dally, shilly-shally, languish; kill time, waste time, while away the time.

sleep, slumber, doze, drowse, snooze, take a nap, nod off, have forty winks, yawn, dream; go to bed, turn in, kip down (*sl.*), hit the sack (*sl.*).

see also **533, 617, 841**

613 haste

n. haste, rush, hurry, scramble, scurry, flurry, hurly-burly; dash, spirit, spurt, run, burst, sprint, bolt, race;

hurriedness, hastiness, urgency, promptness, precipitation, rashness, impulsiveness, impetuosity.

adj. hasty, quick, fast, swift, speedy, hurried, dashing; impetuous, impulsive, rash, inconsiderate, reckless, foolhardy, precipitate, headlong, impatient.

vb. hasten, quicken, speed up, accelerate, expedite, dispatch, stimulate, fillip, urge, goad, whip, incite, push through, rush through, railroad through (inf.).

rush, sprint, spurt, scurry, scuttle, dash, bustle, zoom, tear, bomb (inf.), go all out (inf.), step on it (inf.).

see also 280, 544, 859

614 leisure

n. leisure, free time, spare time, time off, recreation, relaxation, rest, respite, breather, break, pause, lull, recess; holiday, leave, leave of absence, vacation, sabbatical, furlough, home leave.

adj. leisurely, resting, unoccupied.

vb. have time to spare, be off, take one's ease, relax, rest.

adv. off, off duty, on holiday; at leisure, at one's convenience, at an early opportunity.

see also 281, 840

615 exertion

n. exertion, effort, panic, trouble, toil, labour, work, travail, strife, strain, tension, elbow grease, drudgery; hard work, handful (inf.), uphill task, sweat (sl.), drudge.

adj. laborious, arduous, hard, difficult, strenuous, onerous, painstaking, gruelling, punishing, uphill, back-breaking.

vb. exert oneself, try, attempt; take pains, work, labour, fight, toil, contend, struggle, strive, sweat blood; knuckle

down (inf.), get down to it (inf.), buckle down (inf.); drudge, grind, plod (inf.), plug away (inf.), slog away, sweat one's guts out (sl.); make heavy weather of, make a meal of; put oneself out, do one's best, do one's utmost, go to all lengths, go all out, leave no stone unturned, move heaven and earth, pull out all the stops (inf.); overdo it, have one's work cut out.

see also 535, 611

616 repose

n. repose, rest, relaxation, inaction, breather, break, pause, coffee-break, tea-break, lunch-break, lunch-hour, rest period; day of rest, Sabbath, Lord's Day; ease, quiet, quietness, tranquillity.

adj. restful, tranquil, quiet, calm, peaceful; sabbatical.

vb. rest, be quiet, stop, halt; take a rest, take it easy, let up, ease off, slow down, stretch one's legs, have a break; get away from it all (inf.).

see also 610, 618

617 fatigue

n. fatigue, tiredness, weariness; sleepiness, heaviness, drowsiness, doziness, somnolence; faintness, weakness. exhaustion, collapse, staleness, jadedness; lassitude, languor.

adj. tired, weary, exhausted, run down, fagged out (inf.), worn out, ready to drop (inf.), dog-tired, dead beat, all in, whacked (inf.); heavy, dozy (inf.), drowsy, sleepy; weak, faint, dropping, haggard; washed out, drained, stale, jaded.

vb. be tired, drop, collapse, flag, jade, peg out (inf.), flake out (sl.); faint, pass out (inf.), lose consciousness; work too hard, overdo it.

weary, tire, fatigue, wear out,

exhaust, take it out of (*inf.*), fag out (*inf.*), strain; bore.

see also **612, 841**

618 refreshment

n. refreshment, enlivenment, invigoration, recovery, restoration, convalescence, recuperation, relief.

adj. refreshing, restoring, invigorating, exhilarating, bracing, stimulating, arousing; refreshed, invigorated, like a new man.

vb. refresh, restore, arouse, revive, enliven, animate, strengthen, stimulate, invigorate, renew, reawaken, bring round, give new life to, energize, improve, relieve, resuscitate, vivify; encourage, cheer.

recover, recuperate, pick up, perk up, recharge one's batteries, get one's breath back.

see also **589, 616**

619 agent

n. agent, doer, actor, performer, participant, instrument, medium, practitioner, executor; worker, workman, operator, mechanic, labourer, operative, craftsman, skilled worker; apprentice; hack, drudge, slave, fag.

workforce, employees, staff, personnel, labour, payroll, manpower, resources.

620 workshop

n. workshop, workplace, establishment, installation, institution, plant, factory, works, foundry, yard; shop, house, office, bureau, branch, station, laboratory; firm, company, concern, industry.

621 conduct

n. conduct, behaviour, manner, deportment, demeanour, air, carriage, bearing, posture, attitude, comportment, mien, delivery, appearance,

guise; guidance, control, oversight, supervision, superintendence, execution, government, management, organization; strategy, tactics, policy, campaign, programme.

adj. behavioural; tactical, strategical.

vb. behave, act, conduct; acquit oneself, bear oneself, comport onself, pose, appear, seem; behave oneself, mind one's manners, mind one's P's and Q's, be on one's best behaviour; manage, guide, supervise, direct, regulate, administer.

622 management

n. management, conduct, guidance, direction, control, order, charge, power, execution, government, organization, administration, decision making, handling, regulation, legislation, jurisdiction; oversight, supervision, superintendence, surveillance, command, authority, leadership; stewardship, husbandry, housekeeping, economics.

adj. directive, managerial, controlling, supervisory; executive, administrative, governmental, gubernatorial, legislative; official, bureaucratic.

vb. manage, conduct, run, guide, direct, lead, control, regulate, order, govern, command, steer, point the way, decide; handle, execute, administer, organize, legislate; supervise, superintend; steward.

623 director

n. manager, director, controller, leader, executive, governor, politician, minister, legislator, commander; dictator; superintendent, supervisor, inspector, overseer, foreman; steward; administrator, official, bureaucrat, functionary, secretary; guide, organizer.

see also **34, 675**

624 advice

n. advice, suggestion, opinion, view, counsel, guidance, encouragement, information, instruction, recommendation; warning, admonition, criticism, dissuasion; caution, notice; notification.

advisor, counsellor, right-hand man, friend, confidant, teacher, informant, helper, consultant; think-tank.

adj. advisory, consultative.

vb. advise, guide, direct, tell, have a word with, suggest; exhort, urge, prompt, encourage, persuade, recommend, counsel; warn, admonish, dissuade; inform, notify, acquaint.

consult, ask, discuss, talk over, seek the opinion of, seek advice, turn to, confide in.

625 council

n. council, cabinet, committee, government, parliament, board, directorate, board of governors; congress, conference, assembly, convention, synod, convocation, diet; panel, forum, brains trust.

councillor, minister, member of parliament, back-bencher, parliamentarian, statesman, senator, congressman; delegate, representative, officer.

626 precept

n. precept, maxim, command, direction, instruction, prescription, principle, law, statute, commandment, rule; canon, doctrine, law, charge, mandate, injunction, edict; formula, recipe.

see also **103, 954**

627 skill

n. skill, capability, proficiency, competence, skilfulness, expertness, ability, aptitude, talent, gift, genius, endowment, flaw, strong point, forte, what it takes, knack; experience, practice, training, qualifications, expertise, know-how, judgment; adeptness, deftness, adroitness, facility.

adj. skilful, capable, able, proficient, competent, effective, clever; experienced, trained, qualified, fit, suited, cut out for (*inf.*), accomplished, well-versed, expert, veteran; gifted, endowed; handy, adept, deft, adroit, agile, dexterous; all-round, versatile; enterprising, inventive.

vb. be good at, shine at, have what it takes; be expert, know backwards, know the ropes (*inf.*), know the ins and outs (*inf.*).

628 unskilfulness

n. unskilfulness, inability, ineptitude, inexperience, greenness, weak point, incompetence, inefficiency, mismanagement; awkwardness, clumsiness; botch-up, hash, mess, cock-up (*inf.*).

adj. unskilful, inexperienced, uneducated, unqualified, incompetent, amateur, unsuited, unused to, lay, amateurish, unprofessional, do-it-yourself, scratch; butterfingers; awkward, clumsy, heavy-handed, bungling, maladroit; impracticable, home-made, Heath Robinson; unwieldy, cumbersome, bulky.

vb. be no good at (*inf.*), spoil, bungle, ruin, botch, mismanage, mishandle, make a mess of, make a hash of, mess up (*inf.*), louse up (*sl.*), screw up (*sl.*), cock up (*sl.*), put one's foot in it; misfire.

629 expert

n. expert, master, adept, proficient,

handyman, Jack-of-all-trades, man of many parts, man of many talents; professional, authority, specialist, scholar, genius, whizz-kid (*inf.*), veteran, old hand; man of the world.

see also **436**

630 bungler

n. bungler, fumbler, botcher, muddler, dunce, idiot, blockhead, scatterbrain, ignoramus; butterfingers; beginner, novice, greenhorn; amateur, layman; lout, lubber.

see also **437**

631 cunning

n. cunning, craftiness, intrigue, deceit, guile, artfulness, craft, subtlety, slyness, wiliness, cleverness, shrewdness, chicanery, finesse.

stratagem, artifice, trick, deception, plot, scheme, ruse, wile, dodge, trap, little game (*inf.*), con (*sl.*), hoax, fabrication, double-dealing, casuistry.

artful dodger, hypocrite, fraud, cheat, plotter, con-man (*sl.*), trickster, slippery customer (*inf.*), smooth talker (*inf.*).

adj. cunning, shrewd, crafty, artful, sly, wily, deceptive, subtle, dishonest, fraudulent, unscrupulous, underhand, shifty, smart, shady, smooth, slippery, sharp, clever (*inf.*), too clever by half (*inf.*).

vb. be cunning, trick, deceive, fraud, cheat, trap, hoax, con (*sl.*), plot, scheme, contrive, pull a fast one (*sl.*), put one over on (*inf.*), put one across (*inf.*), outwit, get the better of.

632 artlessness

n. artlessness, simplicity, innocence, naivety, simple-mindedness, guilelessness, ingenuousness; child, babe.

adj. artless, innocent, simple, naive, simple-minded, guileless, unaffected, natural, uncomplicated, straightforward, ingenuous, childlike, unsophisticated, genuine, frank, open, candid, forthright.

vb. be natural, wear one's heart on one's sleeve; speak one's mind, not mince words.

D Antagonism

633 difficulty

n. difficulty, problem, headache, trouble, tall order, handful, heavy going; dilemma, predicament, quandary, strait, plight, embarrassment, fix, pickle (*inf.*), scrape, tight spot (*inf.*), hole (*sl.*); hardship, arduousness, laboriousness, troublesomeness; perplexity.

adj. difficult, hard, tough, laborious, arduous, uphill, strenuous; awkward, burdensome, trying, troublesome, bothersome, wearisome; unclear, obscure, knotty, thorny, baffling, perplexing, complicated, intricate.

vb. be in difficulties, flounder, have a hard time, strike a bad patch, make heavy weather of, make a meal of, not keep one's head above water; get into difficulty, get into hot water; put one's foot in it (*inf.*); beset, trouble, harm, disconcert, discourage, inconvenience, embarrass; baffle, perplex, put on the spot (*inf.*).

adv. in deep water, in difficulty, on the horns of a dilemma, in a quandary, in a spot, in hot water, in trouble.

see also **615, 635**

634 ease

n. ease, facility, straightforwardness; child's play, plain sailing, piece of cake (*inf.*), nothing to it (*inf.*), walk-over (*inf.*), push-over (*inf.*), cinch (*sl.*).

adj. easy, simple, cushy (*inf.*), manageable, facile; obvious, apparent; pleasant, comfortable; clear, uncomplicated; effortless.

vb. be easy, require no effort, present no difficulties, give no trouble, run smoothly, go like clockwork; take in one's stride.

ease, facilitate, smooth the way, free, relieve, rid, get rid of, lighten, release, disentangle; take a weight off someone's mind (*inf.*).

635 hindrance

n. hindrance, impedance, intervention, interruption; restriction, prohibition, restraint, check, blockage; retardation, curb, arrest, drag; inconvenience, hitch, setback, hold-up, bottleneck, catch, snag, spanner in the works (*inf.*), encumbrance, chain, menace.

obstacle, obstruction, barrier, impediment, interference, stumbling-block, barricade, hurdle, bar, impasse, cul de sac.

adj. hindering, restraining, preventive.

vb. hinder, prevent, thwart, frustrate, hamper, trammel; stop, check, restrain, foil, confine, retard, arrest; deter, prohibit, restrict, bar, forbid, encumber, burden, chain, fetter, shackle; interfere, meddle; obstruct, block, impede, barricade; spoil, gum up the works (*sl.*).

see also **633, 665**

636 aid

n. aid, help, assistance; helping hand, leg up; encouragement, comfort, relief, succour, alleviation, mitigation; favour, benevolence, service; advice, backing, guidance.

financial aid, giving, support, maintenance, charity; compensation, allowance, grant, subsidy, benefit, stipend, honorarium, expenses; patronage, sponsorship, promotion, advancement.

adj. helpful, beneficial, assisting; auxiliary.

vb. help, aid, assist, cooperate; encourage, stand by, back up, sustain, bolster, relieve, comfort, succour, save, rescue, abet; lend a hand, play one's part; befriend, advise, serve, minister to, take under one's wing.

patronize, finance, support, keep, maintain, promote, subsidize, foster, shoulder, sponsor, sanction.

see also **217, 639**

637 opposition

n. opposition, antagonism, confrontation, repugnance, defiance, hostility, abhorrence, aversion, incompatibility, polarity; dislike, dissension, contradiction.

adj. opposing, antagonistic, defiant; hostile.

vb. oppose, counter, conflict with, fly in the face of, run counter to; confront, fight, combat, hinder, obstruct, thwart, object, dispute, contradict; resist, defy; deny, not have any part in, part company with, disapprove, disagree.

see also **648, 883**

638 opponent

n. opponent, antagonist, adversary, enemy, foe, the opposition, competitor, challenger, candidate, entrant, rival, contestant.

see also **883**

639 cooperation

n. cooperation, collaboration, participation, partnership, fellowship, brotherhood, harmony; give and take, teamwork, solidarity; amalgamation, merger, fusion, affiliation, membership; help, assistance.

adj. cooperative, collaborative, participatory; associated.

vb. cooperate, collaborate, give and take, help each other out, play ball with; contribute, help.

join, combine, unite, merge, club together, affiliate, join forces, pool together, pool resources, stand together, stick together (*inf.*), pull together; share, take part in, participate, throw in one's lot, go along with, team up with, take sides; gang up against (*inf.*); put one's heads together (*inf.*).

see also 180, 709

640 auxiliary

n. auxiliary, helper, assistant, aid, ancillary, collaborator, helping hand, partner, associate, colleague, fellow-worker, co-worker, team-mate, sidekick (*inf.*); accomplice, confederate; friend, companion, ally, comrade; follower, adherent, disciple; hanger-on; patron, backer, supporter; right-hand man, stalwart, tower of strength.

see also 636

641 party

n. party, group, movement, organization, society, band, body; council, congress, alliance, association, confederation, federation, league, coalition, union; community, fellowship, brotherhood; company, firm, establishment, concern, cooperative, cartel, syndicate.

faction, sect, denomination, tradition, splinter-group, clique, coterie, inner circle.

adj. federal, allied, confederate,

cooperative; exclusive, cliquish, partisan, sectarian.

vb. join, enrol, become a member of, affiliate, subscribe; associate with, side with.

642 discord

n. discord, dissension, trouble, difference, disagreement, misunderstanding, cross purposes, variance, ill feeling, tension, friction; divisiveness, troublesomeness, quarrelsomeness, rivalry.

dispute, quarrel, row, fight, argument, squabble, bickering, tiff, vendetta, feud; schism, split, rift, parting of the ways.

adj. discordant, disagreeing, divisive; contradictory; quarrelsome, troublesome, violent, factious, pugnacious, harsh, uncooperative, bolshie (*sl.*).

vb. differ, clash, conflict, dissent; fall out with, part company with; break up.

dispute, contend, fight, struggle, strive, come to blows, complain, object, argue, disagree; quarrel, wrangle, squabble, bicker; have a bone to pick with, have words with, take issue with; look for trouble (*inf.*), ask for it (*inf.*), rub up the wrong way (*inf.*), tread on someone's toes.

adv. at loggerheads, at odds, at variance, at sixes and sevens, not on speaking terms.

see also 25, 893

643 concord

n. concord, agreement, harmony, conformity, understanding, consonance, rapport, goodwill, friendship, amity, concert, accord, consensus, unanimity, unity, détente, *rapprochement*, entente, entente cordiale.

adj. agreeing, harmonious, friendly.

peaceful, amicable, reconciled, unanimous, united.

vb. agree, get on with, get along with, hit it off (*inf.*), see eye to eye, be at one with; come to an understanding.

see also **24, 699**

644 defiance

n. defiance, disobedience, rebellion, insubordination, insolence, obstinacy; mutiny, revolt, revolution; challenge, dare.

adj. defiant, bold, daring, proud, unruly, rebellious, disobedient, insubordinate; independent, lawless, anarchistic, militant.

vb. defy, confront, brave, challenge, dare, fling down the gauntlet, call one's bluff; resist, disobey, oppose, disregard, flout, spurn, laugh at, scorn, taunt; rebel, revolt, insult, protest, kick against, kick against the pricks.

see also **648**

645 attack

n. attack, assault, onslaught, aggression, advance, charge, push, thrust, drive, outbreak, outburst, raid, offensive, storm, skirmish, foray, sally, sortie; invasion, intrusion, inroad, incursion, encroachment; siege, barrage, bombardment, blitz; mugging, rape.

attacker, aggressor, assailant, fighter, raider, stormer, invader, enemy, intruder, sniper, ravager; mugger, rapist.

adj. attacking, assaulting, aggressive.

vb. attack, assault, advance, charge, rush, push, thrust, assail, fight; raid, invade, storm, sally, sortie, foray; intrude, encroach; besiege, lay siege to, blockade; ravage, lay waste; fire, shoot, snipe; bomb, bombard; beat up, do over (*sl.*), smash somone's face in (*inf.*), mug, rob, rape.

646 defence

n. defence, protection, guarding, security; fortification, castle, fort, fortress, stronghold, keep, bastion, citadel, garrison; trenches, ditch, moat; embankment, rampart, battlement, earthworks; armour.

defender, guard, watch, sentry; protector, champion.

adj. defended, guarded, safe; defensive, armed, watchful.

vb. defend, protect, guard, keep, keep safe, safeguard, secure, shield, shelter, screen; withstand, beat off, ward off, fend off, drive back, take evasive action; spring to someone's defence; strengthen, reinforce, fortify; arm, cover, camouflage.

see also **593**

647 retaliation

n. retaliation, reprisal, revenge, reaction, backlash, counterattack, counterinsurgence, second-strike capability; measure for measure, an eye for an eye, tit for tat, just deserts; requital, repayment, vengeance, punishment, retribution; recrimination; retort, riposte.

adj. retaliatory, retributive, reciprocal.

vb. retaliate, hit back, strike back, fight back, get back (*inf.*), defend oneself; requite, avenge, revenge, punish, return, repay, vindicate, pay back, settle up, get square, get one's own back, give tit for tat, get even with; reciprocate, return the compliment, give someone a dose of his own medicine; retort, counter, recriminate.

see also **912**

648 resistance

n. resistance, withstanding, defence, stand, check; steadfastness, renitence.

adj. resisting, recalcitrant, hard-hearted.

vb. resist, withstand, not give in, not submit, repel, stand up to, not take lying down, stand fast; stay, defend, hold off, oppose, prevent, thwart, foil, frustrate, obstruct, attack; counteract, neutralize; endure, suffer, tolerate; persevere, hold out, stick it out (*inf.*); maintain, take one's stand, stand one's ground, stick one's heels in (*inf.*), stick to one's guns, hold one's own.

see also 535, 644

649 contest

n. contest, engagement, fight, battle, war, encounter, confrontation, action, skirmish, feud, *mêlée*, set-to, tussle, scrap (*sl.*), brush, affray, altercation; duel, joust, warfare, hostilities; conflict, strife, struggle, bloodshed, onslaught, carnage.

game, match, event, rally, race, challenge; competition, round, tournament; sport, recreation.

adj. contending, contestant; competitive.

vb. contend, fight, oppose, combat, confront, challenge, encounter, engage in battle, campaign, battle, brush with, dispute, strive, struggle, scrap (*sl.*), set to, take on, tussle, joust, assert oneself; compete, contest, race, vie with.

see also 651, 655

650 peace

n. peace, absence of hostilities, armistice, truce, treaty; pacification, conciliation, reconciliation, love, friendship, agreement, harmony, accord; cold war, peaceful coexistence.

adj. peaceful, quiet, tranquil; bloodless, nonaggressive; pacifist; appeasing, conciliatory, peace-making.

see also 24, 652

651 war

n. war, hostilities, combat, fighting, warfare, attack, battle, campaign, operation, mission, action, contention.

aggressiveness, warlikeness, belligerence, militancy, warmongering, pugnacity.

adj. warlike, aggressive, militant, pugnacious, belligerent, martial, threatening, contentious, warmongering, unfriendly, bellicose, up in arms, on the warpath; fighting, warring.

vb. wage war, engage in hostilities, attack, invade, contend, strive; declare war, go to war; mobilize, call up, recruit, enlist, conscript, muster.

see also 645, 649

652 pacification

n. pacification, peace-making, appeasement, conciliation, reconciliation, reparation, satisfaction, assuagement, alleviation, mollification, soothing, calming; propitiation, atonement.

peace-offering, sacrifice, placation, gift; white flag, olive branch.

adj. pacificatory, placatory, propitiatory; irenic.

vb. pacify, conciliate; appease, satisfy, sacrifice, atone, propitiate; quiet, calm, still, moderate, quell, soften, alleviate, assuage, mollify, placate, tranquillize; reconcile, harmonize, bring together, bring to terms, settle one's differences, accommodate; make peace, bury the hatchet; make it up, shake hands.

see also 650

653 mediation

n. mediation, arbitration, interposition, intervention, shuttle diplomacy.

mediator, arbitrator, go-between, intermediary, arbiter, negotiator, peace-maker, trouble-shooter, intercessor, third party; judge, referee, umpire; adjudicator, assessor; neutral, independent.

adj. mediatory, intercessory.

vb. mediate, arbitrate, negotiate, reconcile, hear both sides, intercede, interpose, intervene; judge, umpire, rule; interfere, meddle.

see also 230

654 submission

n. submission, yielding, obedience; acquiescence, resignation, deference; submissiveness, docility, meekness, humility, passivity.

adj. submissive, obedient; compliant, amenable, tractable, mouldable; resigned, subdued; acquiescent, reconciled, patient; docile, humble, lowly, tame.

vb. submit, give in, yield, surrender, capitulate, resign, relinquish, give up, throw in the towel, admit defeat.

obey, defer, bow to, comply, acquiesce; take the line of least resistance.

see also 673, 679

655 combatant

n. combatant, fighter, contender, opponent, serviceman, soldier, conscript, recruit, pressed man; casual, irregular; mercenary, hireling; warrior, veteran.

armed forces, services, troops, forces, military force, army, infantry, cavalry, artillery; navy, air force; unit, group, division, section, squad, troop, patrol; party; task force; formation, column, line, array.

656 non-combatant

n. non-combatant, pacifist, conscientious objector, neutral, dove, flower people, conchie (*sl.*); peace-maker.

657 arms

n. arms, weapons, armament, munitions; armour, mail, panoply; small arms, firearm, gun; revolver, rifle, shotgun, machine gun, automatic; cannon, mortar; bazooka; hand-grenade bomb, explsoive, dynamite, gunpowder; atomic bomb, hydrogen bomb, H-bomb, neutron bomb; armoury, arsenal; ballistics.

658 arena

n. arena, battlefield, battleground, scene of action, field of action, theatre of war, trenches, front; field, ground, centre, scene, sphere, track, court, course; stadium, gymnasium, playground, campus, coliseum, amphitheatre, circus, forum, pit.

E   Results of action

659 completion

n. completion, finish, end, conclusion, achievement, performance, accomplishment, fulfilment, perfection, realization, execution.

finishing touch, crown, *coup de grâce;* last straw, limit (*sl.*).

adj. complete, finished, accomplished, fulfilled, perfect, entire, whole; conclusive, final, last.

vb. complete, finish, end, conclude, terminate; achieve, perform, carry out, implement; bring off (*inf.*), pull off (*inf.*), succeed; knock off (*inf.*), polish off (*inf.*), wrap up (*inf.*); get over with (*inf.*), get over and done with (*inf.*); accomplish, work out, hammer out, see through, go through with, realize, effect, fulfil, discharge, settle; be resolved, things work out, perfect, consummate, ripen, mature; culminate, come to a head.

see also 56, 609

660 non-completion

n. non-completion, failure, non-performance, neglect, defeat; fault, blemish, deficiency, defect.

adj. uncompleted, failed, neglected, incomplete, half-done, partial, imperfect, deficient.

vb. not complete, leave undone, neglect; miss, fail, drop out, leave, not stay the course.

see also 57, 582

661 success

n. success, completion, achievement, attainment, accomplishment; successfulness, happy ending, favourable outcome, prosperous issue; triumph, victory, conquest, push-over (*inf.*), walk-over (*inf.*); breakthrough, advance, progress; prosperity, luck, happiness, bed of roses; success story, hit, smash hit (*sl.*).

winner, victor, champion, hero, title-holder, conqueror.

adj. successful, winning, victorious, triumphant, champion, in the lead, unbeaten, invincible; beneficial, advantageous; fruitful, prosperous, fortunate, thriving, flourishing.

vb. succeed, make a success of, achieve, attain, accomplish, reach, complete, fulfil, obtain, get, capture, gain, pull off (*inf.*), bring off (*inf.*); be successful, come off (*inf.*), do the trick (*inf.*); advance, get on, make it (*inf.*), make a go of (*inf.*), make a breakthrough, proceed, progress, benefit, reap, profit, prosper, flourish, thrive, prevail, score a hit, hit the jackpot.

win, beat, conquer, defeat, get the better of, gain the upper hand, clobber (*sl.*), overcome, ride out the storm, crush, overwhelm, win hands down, walk away with (*inf.*), come out on top (*inf.*), come off with flying colours; survive, get by, hang on.

662 failure

n. failure, misadventure, breakdown, collapse, fiasco, disaster, débâcle, disappointment, flop (*inf.*), wash-out (*inf.*); defeat, overthrow, downfall, ruin, landslide; unsuccessfulness, ineffectiveness, defectiveness; neglect, omission, shortcoming; no-go (*inf.*), wild goose chase, utter defeat, clobbering (*sl.*), rout.

loser, underdog, has-been (*inf.*), also-ran (*inf.*), non-starter, dud.

adj. unsuccessful, futile, vain, useless, fruitless, profitless; unfortunate, disastrous; inadequate, ineffective, abortive; overthrown, defeated, fallen, outmatched, thwarted, frustrated, foiled, pipped at the post, outvoted.

vb. fail, go amiss, fall down, let one down; abandon, neglect, miss; thwart, frustrate; fall short, break down, fall through (*inf.*), miscarry, come to nothing, flounder, falter, go on the rocks, flop (*inf.*), fizzle out (*inf.*); lose, be defeated, suffer defeat, go down, go under; bark up the wrong tree (*inf.*), not get to first base (*inf.*); get no change out of (*inf.*).

663 trophy

n. trophy, prize, reward, award, honour, medal, badge, cup, memorial, decoration, ribbon, order, crown, palm, laurel, accolade, mention, citation; consolation prize, booby prize, wooden spoon.

booty, loot, spoil, plunder, premium, capture.

see also 724

664 prosperity

n. prosperity, good fortune, happiness, welfare, well-being, successfulness, luckiness, affluence, wealth, riches, luxury, benefits, blessings; golden age, good old days, heyday, boom, bed of roses, halcyon days, summer.

adj. prosperous, flourishing, thriving, successful, well-to-do, well-off, comfortable, rich, auspicious; up-and-coming, born with a silver spoon in one's mouth; golden, glorious, cloudless, sunny, halcyon.

vb. prosper, thrive, flourish, increase, blossom, be successful, fare well, turn out well; get on in the world, make one's mark, be rich, make a fortune; Fortune smile upon.

see also 661

665 adversity

n. adversity, misfortune, trouble, hardship, unluckiness, bad luck, hard times, bad patch, ill wind, deep water, difficulty, misadventure, unhappiness; disaster, distress, catastrophe, crisis, calamity, burden, pressure, affliction, blight, curse, plague, scourge.

adj. adverse, unfavourable, hostile, unfriendly, sinister; disastrous, catastrophic; afflicted, troubled, wretched, stricken; unfortunate, unlucky, unhappy, ill-starred, ill-fated, down on one's luck, in a bad way, in the wars.

vb. be in trouble, hit a bad patch, be in for it (*inf.*), have a hard time of it, feel the pinch, fall on hard times, decline, sink, stew in one's own juice, go under, get out of one's depth, fall flat on one's face (*inf.*), fall by the wayside.

see also 633

666 mediocrity

n. mediocrity, commonness, ordinariness, averageness, passableness, tolerableness.

adj. mediocre, average, ordinary, indifferent, middling, fair, poor, feeble, common, commonplace, dull, monotonous, stale, insipid, wishy-washy, tolerable, fair-to-middling, passable, humdrum, run of the mill, so-so, nothing to write home about, much of a muchness.

vb. make do, just exist, struggle along, muddle through, scrape through, manage somehow, get by, just keep one's head above water, stagnate, vegetate.

2 Intersocial volition

A General

667 authority

n. authority, power, control, right, prerogative, command, rule, sway; dominion, sovereignty, ascendancy, upper hand, supreme authority, last word; influence, prestige, power behind the throne, arm of the law.

government, democracy, *vox populi*, officialdom, bureaucracy, administration, establishment, them, powers that be; open government, devolution.

adj. authoritative, commanding, dominant, lawful, powerful, sovereign; in office, in power; official, executive, administrative, bureaucratic, governmental, democratic, gubernatorial, political.

vb. rule, govern, control, direct, dominate, lord it over, domineer, command, sway, reign; assume control, take over, take the reins, have power, rule the roost; authorize, empower, back, devolve, decentralize.

see also 671

668 laxity

n. laxity, slackness, looseness, flexibility; anarchy, lawlessness, mob rule, disorder, chaos, turmoil.

adj. lax, slack, loose, remiss, soft, flabby, relaxed, flexible; anarchic, uncontrolled, lawless, chaotic, rebellious.

vb. be lax, tolerate, not enforce, stretch a point; misrule, misgovern; give a free hand to, give free rein to; take the law into one's own hands, do what is right in one's own eyes.

see also **670**

669 severity

n. severity, strictness, austerity, firmness, rigidity, inflexibility, rigour; hardness, cruelty; firm hand, strong hand, heavy hand, rod of iron, tight rein, pound of flesh, letter of the law.

tyranny, oppression, despotism, fascism; tyrant, dictator, despot, autocrat, taskmaster, authoritarian, disciplinarian.

adj. severe, stern, strict, harsh, hard, austere, extreme, puritanical; firm, rigid, unbending, inflexible, immovable, unchanging; rigorous, exacting, uncompromising, stringent; grim, cruel, forbidding; unfeeling, hard-hearted; tyrannical, overbearing, domineering, despotic, totalitarian, authoritarian, oppressive, heavy-handed.

vb. be severe, be hard on, discipline, come down on (*inf.*), deal harshly with, insist, crack down on (*inf.*), clamp down on (*inf.*), put one's foot down (*inf.*), keep a tight rein on, rule with an iron hand, domineer, lord it over, dominate, oppress, tyrannize.

see also **963**

670 lenience

n. lenience, softness, tolerance, mildness, forbearance; mercy, clemency, forgiveness, pardon; kindness, compassion, favour.

adj. lenient, soft, gentle, mild, kind, compassionate, loving, soft-hearted, tender, sympathetic, easy-going; tolerant, forbearing, long-suffering; merciful, forgiving, clement.

vb. be lenient, go easy on, spare the rod; pass over, forbear, refrain; forgive, pardon; tolerate, bear.

671 command

n. command, direction, rule, charge, ordinance, mandate, directive, dictate, injunction, behest; bidding, call, summons; decree, ruling, law, act, fiat, canon, edict, bull, proclamation; writ, warrant, subpoena; demand, claim, request, requirement; final demand, ultimatum.

adj. commanding, powerful, authoritative.

vb. command, rule, direct, dictate, order, charge, decree, proclaim, ordain; lay down, prescribe; demand, claim, request, ask, require, exact; bid, call, summon, invite, send for.

see also **667, 954**

672 disobedience

n. disobedience, violation, disregard, neglect, non-observance, infringement, transgression, sin; misbehaviour, naughtiness; waywardness, stubbornness, insubordination, defiance, intractableness, unruliness; mutiny, revolt, rebellion, revolution, desertion, riot, insurgence.

rebel, revolutionary, radical, anarchist, reactionary, extremist, insurrectionist, insurgent, rioter, terrorist, mutineer, deserter; trouble-maker, brawler.

adj. disobedient, insubordinate; naughty, misbehaving; defiant, refractory, unsubmissive, disloyal, rebellious, intractable, unruly, lawless, uncontrollable, obstreperous; stubborn, wayward, insolent; revolutionary, mutinous, riotous, anarchistic, dissident, factious, insurgent.

vb. disobey, defy, fly in the face of, disregard, neglect, ignore, pay no attention to, not heed, violate, infringe, transgress, sin, break rules; misbehave; revolt, rebel, mutiny.

673 obedience
n. obedience, submission, compliance, loyalty, devotion, faithfulness, fidelity, constancy; meekness, docility.

adj. obedient, submissive, complaisant; law-abiding, well-behaved, good; devoted, loyal, faithful, respectful, dutiful, subservient, docile, acquiescent; round one's little finger (*inf.*), at one's beck and call, on a string, henpecked.

vb. obey, submit, do, keep, observe, follow, pay attention to, bow to, heed, comply, fulfil, agree, behave, do what one is told, do one's duty, do what is expected of one.

see also **654, 679**

674 compulsion
n. compulsion, force, drive, necessity, need, obligation, pressure, constraint, coercion, violence, strong arm, duress; urgency; conscription.

adj. compelling, compulsive, necessary, driving, pressing, coercive, unavoidable, irresistible, compulsory, urgent.

vb. compel, force, drive, coerce, constrain, impel, dictate, necessitate, oblige, require, urge, bring pressure to bear on, inflict.

675 master
n. master, mistress, chief, leader, head, superior, principal, lord; direc-tor, manager, supervisor, boss, management, overseer, authority, officer, official, mayor, mayoress; governor, governess, ruler, president, executive, sovereign, king, queen, prince, princess, emperor, empress, regent; captain, commander, lieutenant; big Chief (*sl.*), bigwig.

see also **34, 623**

676 servant
n. servant, dependant, assistant, right-hand man, subordinate, employee, worker, staff, personnel; slave, serf, vassal, captive, bondman, fag; orderly, menial; drudge, hack; chauffeur, butler, domestic, housekeeper, maid, nurse; porter, janitor, doorman; steward, stewardess, waiter, waitress, barman, barmaid; charwoman, cleaner.

adj. serving, ministering, attending, helping.

vb. serve, work for, be in the employment of, minister, aid, help, wait upon, care for, look after, nurse, mother; attend, do for (*inf.*).

677 sign of authority
n. badge of office, insignia, symbol, emblem, livery, uniform, regalia, rod, sceptre, mace, crown, staff, wand, rod, sword, stripe, decoration, flag.

678 freedom
n. freedom, liberty, independence, autonomy, democracy, self-determination; freedom of choice, free will; immunity, exemption, privilege, *carte blanche*, blank cheque, unrestraint; range, scope, play, field, room, leeway, latitude, opportunity, full play, free rein, elbow room.

adj. free, released, liberated, freed, at liberty, at large, let out, scot free; clear, extricated, unshackled, unfettered, unattached, unengaged, unconfined, unimpeded, unhindered, unrestrained; independent, autonomous, self-governing, democratic, enfranchised.

vb. free, have a free hand, have the run of; be independent, please oneself, do as one wishes, fend for oneself, stand on one's own two feet, go it alone.

see also **680**

679 subjection

n. subjection, subservience, servitude, dependence, subordination, inferiority; allegiance, service; bondage, slavery, serfdom, servility, thrall.

adj. subject, dependent, subordinate, submissive, inferior, junior, accessory, subsidiary, satellite, auxiliary; accountable, answerable, liable, contingent.

vb. subject, enslave, dominate, subordinate, master, rule, hold captive, conquer, tame, subdue, subjugate, hold under one's thumb; repress, suppress, sit on.

be subject to, depend on, lean on; be at the mercy of, serve.

see also **35**

680 liberation

n. liberation, release, discharge, deliverance, rescue; extrication, disengagement, unravelling, loosing, unfettering, loosening, untying; emancipation, enfranchisement, manumission.

adj. freed, liberated, released, loose.

vb. liberate, free, release, discharge, deliver, save, rescue, set at liberty, restore, let out; extricate, loose, remove fetters, unfetter, untie, remove, unbind, undo, cut loose, disengage, unravel, let slip; ransom, pardon, dismiss, acquit; emancipate, enfran-

chise; shake off, free oneself of, get rid of, lose.

see also **601, 961**

681 restraint

n. restraint, control, constraint, discipline, self-control, self-discipline, self-restraint, reticence, reserve, caution; repression.

restriction, limitation, barrier, check, hindrance, impediment, obstacle, block, bar, curb, blockade, embargo, ban, veto; curfew; closed shop; censorship, news blackout; monopoly, cartel, protectionism.

custody, detention, imprisonment, confinement, impounding; chain, bond, irons, fetter, shackle.

adj. restraining, restrictive, controlling, limiting, strict, narrow, repressive; restrained, under control, in check, controlled, disciplined, reserved, cautious, calm, reticent, withdrawn, repressed, pent-up, bottled-up.

in custody, under arrest, imprisoned, detained, confined, in prison, in detention, behind bars, inside (*sl.*), in jug (*sl.*), in clink (*sl.*).

vb. restrain, control, limit, govern, check, arrest, curb, keep in check, hold back, narrow; discipline, bridle; repress, suppress, keep back, bottle up, muzzle, gag, subdue, quell, quash; hinder, impede, restrict, hamper; control oneself, pull oneself together, take a grip on oneself (*inf.*), sort oneself out (*inf.*), get organized.

take into custody, apprehend, help police with their inquiries, run in, turn in (*inf.*), turn over to, pick up, arrest, convict, take prisoner; imprison, detain, confine, put into prison, put away (*inf.*), shut up, lock up, put behind bars, intern, impound; tie, bind, chain, fetter, manacle.

682 prison

n. prison, gaol, jail, lock-up, nick (*sl.*), clink (*sl.*), jug (*sl.*), maximum-security prison, police station; cell, cage, guardroom; dungeon; detention camp, internment camp, concentration camp; Borstal, detention centre, approved home, remand centre.

683 keeper

n. keeper, custodian, warden, curator, attendant, official, guard; caretaker, porter, janitor, concierge, housekeeper, gatekeeper; watchman, lookout, patrol, scout; baby-sitter, governess, nurse, nanny, guardian; escort, bodyguard; gamekeeper, ranger; jailer, warder, prison governor, screw (*sl.*).

see also 593

684 prisoner

n. prisoner, convict, culprit, con (*sl.*), inmate, star, gaolbird, young offender, captive, prisoner of war, internee; defendant, the accused, detainee; criminal, rogue.

see also 906, 940

685 vicarious authority

n. commission, delegation, deputation, representation, authorization, committal, trusteeship; appointment, nomination, assignment; mission, embassy, envoy, legation, agency; devolution, decentralization; inauguration, installation, investiture, induction, ordination, coronation; accession.

trust, charge, mandate, authority, warrant; task, duty, errand, employment.

adj. commissioned, delegated, vicarious, deputed.

vb. commission, delegate, appoint, empower, grant authority to, authorize, charge, commit, assign, entrust; devolve, decentralize; name, nominate; inaugurate, invest, induct, ordain, install, place, establish; crown, enthrone; employ, engage, hire, contract.

represent, deputize, act on behalf of, stand in for.

686 annulment

n. annulment, cancellation, abrogation, dissolution, revocation, retraction, invalidation, nullification, reversal, repeal, abolition, countermand.

dismissal, removal, displacement, the sack (*inf.*), the boot (*sl.*), the push (*sl.*); retirement, lay-off, redundancy, natural wastage; deposal, dethronement, impeachment.

demotion, downgrading, degradation.

adj. annulled, cancelled, null and void; rained off, abandoned, postponed.

vb. annul, cancel, abolish, repeal, revoke, dissolve, rescind, quash, render void, nullify, invalidate; refute, counteract, reverse, repudiate, countermand.

dismiss, oust, overthrow, unseat, remove from office, discharge, depose, dethrone, displace, suspend, sack, fire, give the push to (*sl.*), give the boot to (*sl.*), give papers to, show the door to, strike off the register, write out, pension off; relieve, replace, recall; impeach, unfrock; demote, degrade, downgrade.

687 resignation

n. resignation, abdication, retirement, relinquishment, renunciation, withdrawal, departure, leaving, surrender, desertion; pension, golden handshake, leaving gift, leaving present, gratuity, superannuation.

adj. resignatory; retired, former,

previous, outgoing, one-time, sometime, emeritus.

vb. resign, quit, leave, depart, vacate office, relinquish, abandon, step down, stand down, stand aside, retire, abdicate, give up office, walk out of, hand in one's notice, tender one's resignation, hand in one's papers.

688 consignee

n. consignee, delegate, representative, substitute, deputy; trustee, executor, nominee, proxy; intermediary, middleman, negotiator, broker; committee, board, panel, group, organization, deputation, cabinet, decision maker.

ambassador, envoy, commissioner, delegation, emissary, diplomat, consul, attaché, plenipotentiary, nuncio; embassy, consulate, mission.

see also **619, 689**

689 deputy

n. deputy, assistant, second-in-command, right-hand man; delegate, substitute, representative, proxy, surrogate, stand-in, agent, proxy, vicar; ambassador, commissioner; spokesman, mouthpiece.

adj. deputy, deputizing, vice, pro, acting.

vb. deputize, substitute, represent, stand in for, act on behalf of.

B Special

690 permission

n. permission, liberty, leave, freedom, consent; authorization, legalization, confirmation, endorsement, affirmation, sanction; authority, permit, grant, charter, licence, certificate, concession, allowance; pass, passport, visa, pass-

word; letter of commendation; go-ahead, green light (*inf.*), all-clear, clearance, nod; free hand, free rein, *carte blanche*, blank cheque.

adj. permitting, allowing; tolerant, lenient, permissive; permitted, granted, allowed, authorized, approved.

vb. permit, let, allow, grant, give permission; consent, approve, favour, have no objections; authorize, warrant, legalize, sanction, certify, charter, franchise, license; give the go-ahead, give the green light (*inf.*), give clearance, rubber-stamp (*inf.*); tolerate, concede, bear, suffer.

691 prohibition

n. prohibition, forbiddance, obstruction, suppression, repression, refusal, interdiction, injunction, disallowance, countermand, ban, veto, embargo, boycott, taboo.

adj. prohibiting, forbidding; prohibitive, excessive, restrictive; prohibited, forbidden, illegal, illicit, unlawful, taboo, impermissible.

vb. prohibit, forbid, refuse, withhold, deny, disallow, prevent, hinder, hamper, preclude, restrain, interdict; ban, veto, boycott, say no to, debar, exclude, shut out; obstruct, oppose, suppress, repress, restrict, stop, halt.

692 consent

n. consent, acceptance, agreement, allowance, permission, approval, assent, concurrence, acquiescence, compliance.

adj. consenting, agreeable, willing, acquiescent.

vb. consent, accept, allow, agree, approve, assent, say yes to, be in favour of, concur, acquiesce, accede; concede, grant, yield, acknowledge, vouchsafe.

see also **690**

693 offer

n. offer, tender, bid, submission; approach, advance, overture; proposal, proposition, presentation, suggestion.

adj. on offer, available, for sale, advertised.

vb. offer, hold out, present, suggest, propose, submit, extend, move, put forward, put forth, tender, bid, approach; make overtures, make advances; lay at one's feet, sacrifice, proffer.

volunteer, offer oneself, come forward, stand for.

694 refusal

n. refusal, rejection, denial, declension; rebuff, snub, slap in the face, insult; veto, ban, exclusion.

adj. refusing, unwilling, uncompliant, resisting, hard-hearted, reluctant.

vb. refuse, reject, not want, decline, resist, ignore, turn down, say no to, not hear of, exclude, disallow, shun, repudiate, repel, spurn, rebuff, scorn, snub, repulse, turn one's back on, turn a deaf ear to, set one's face against, wash one's hands of, harden one's heart against; slam the door in someone's face (*inf.*); withhold, deny, hold back.

see also **469, 542**

695 request

n. request, call, petition, invitation, bid, application, demand, appeal, plea, address; inquiry, question; offer, proposal, proposition; prayer, entreaty, intercession, invocation, supplication; importunity, urgency.

adj. requesting, petitioning, supplicatory, imprecatory, invocatory, prayerful, begging, on bended knees; urgent, importunate, persistent, clamorous.

vb. request, call, ask, express a wish, apply for, summon, demand, implore, beseech, beg, appeal, entreat, pray, call on, petition, crave, plead, adjure; inquire, invite.

urge, ply, press, persist, pester, bother, coax, clamour.

canvass, solicit, importune, tout, hawk; appeal for money, pass the hat round (*inf.*), have a whip-round (*inf.*), make a collection.

696 protest

n. protest, deprecation, disapproval, objection, complaint, dissent, expostulation, remonstrance.

demonstration, demo (*inf.*), rally, sit-in, mass meeting, march, protest march, strike, hunger strike.

adj. protesting, deprecatory, expostulatory, remonstrative.

vb. protest, depreciate, speak against, lodge a protest, ask not to, disapprove, object, disagree, oppose, criticize, demur, remonstrate, expostulate; groan, jeer, murmur, heckle, sneer; demonstrate, march, strike, go on strike, picket.

see also **144**

697 petitioner

n. petitioner, supplicant, suppliant, applicant, claimant, candidate, bidder; inquirer, advertiser; lobby, lobbyist, pressure group, canvasser, hawker, tout, pedlar, vendor; beggar, scrounger, cadger, sponger, loafer, idler, vagabond, tramp, down-and-out.

C Conditional

698 promise

n. promise, covenant, pledge, contract, pact, undertaking, commitment, consent, word, vow, word of honour; gentleman's agreement.

engagement, betrothal; fiancée, fiancé, intended (*inf.*).

adj. promised, committed, pledged, bound; engaged, betrothed.

vb. promise, agree, undertake, commit, declare, covenant, pledge, contract, consent, vow, swear; warrant, guarantee; bind onself, give one's word, pledge one's honour; become engaged, betrothe.

699 contract

n. contract, agreement, covenant, undertaking, pact, concordat, promise, pledge, understanding, arrangement, settlement, transaction, bargain, deal (*inf.*); negotiation, compromise, give and take; treaty, convention, alliance, league, charter, entente; gentleman's agreement.

adj. contractual, conventional, promissory.

vb. contract, agree, covenant, undertake, pledge, promise, arrange, bargain, deal, negotiate, hammer out, stipulate; sign, sign on the dotted line, agree on terms, settle, come to an agreement, accept an offer, shake on it (*inf.*); ratify, confirm.

see also 24, 643

700 conditions

n. conditions, terms, provisions, specifications, frame of reference, strings, proviso, contingencies, arrangements, limitations, restrictions, reservations, exceptions, escape clause, *sine qua non*.

adj. conditional, provisional, contingent, with strings attached, granted on certain terms, dependent on, subject to.

vb. negotiate, discuss; propose conditions, postulate, stipulate, attach strings, insist on, impose.

see also 403

701 security

n. security, surety, warranty, covenant, bond, promise, pledge, earnest, token, certainty; deposit, caution money, money in advance, forfeit, stake, insurance, bail, pawn, mortgage, collateral; liability, responsibility; hostage, captive, prisoner.

adj. guaranteed, pledged, pawned, on deposit.

vb. give security, guarantee, pledge, sign for, insure, assure, underwrite, mortgage, stake, pawn; give bail, go bail; stand surety, bail out; stand for, back.

702 observance

n. observance, attention, performance, doing, carrying out, keeping, heeding, practice; obedience, compliance, devotion.

adj. observant, practising, professing; diligent, conscientious; exact, scrupulous, pedantic; dependable, responsible; loyal, faithful, devoted, obedient.

vb. observe, heed, keep, do, carry out, follow, adhere to, perform, discharge, practise, adopt, conform to, fulfil, comply; keep on the right side of the law; hold fast, stand by, embrace, profess, give allegiance to, be loyal to.

703 non-observance

n. non-observance, neglect, disregard, omission; breaking, infringement, violation, transgression, trespass, breach, sin; disobedience, disloyalty, infidelity; inattention, carelessness, indifference, irresponsibility.

adj. non-observant, negligent,

careless, indifferent; unfaithful, disobedient.

vb. not observe, not practise, not keep; break, disobey, violate, infringe, transgress, breach, contravene; neglect, disregard, omit; break faith, be faithless.

704 compromise

n. compromise, bargaining, agreement, understanding, settlement; give and take, concessions, mutual concessions; middle course, middle ground, half-way house; composition; *modus vivendi.*

vb. compromise, make concessions, give and take, meet half-way, go fifty-fifty, steer a middle course, split the differences; negotiate, come to an agreement, come to an understanding, reconcile, settle, adjust, agree to differ.

D Possessive relations

705 acquisition

n. acquisition, getting, obtainment, procuration; recovery, retrieval, redemption.

gain, benefit, advantage, reward, income, earnings, wages, salary, grant, profit, receipts, proceeds, emolument; collection, gathering, produce, output, yield, fruit, harvest, crop; addition, accrual, accumulation.

adj. obtainable, available; acquisitive, hoarding, grasping.

profitable, fruitful, productive, advantageous, worthwhile, lucrative, paying its way, remunerative.

vb. acquire, get, obtain, take possession of, make one's own, appropriate, lay hold of, procure; force from, grab, seize, capture, pocket, secure, draw, tap; gain, accept, receive, make,

collect, earn, benefit, win, accumulate; gather, harvest, glean, reap.

get back, recover, retrieve, regain, redeem.

buy, purchase; profit, capitalize on, cash in on (*inf.*); inherit, come into, be left.

see also **716**

706 loss

n. loss, mislaying, misplacement; dispossession, deprivation, forfeiture, want, bereavement; insolvency, bankruptcy.

adj. lost, missing, misplaced, mislaid, nowhere to be found, hidden, obscured, vanished, strayed, gone; lacking, wanting, deprived of, bereft; overdrawn, insolvent, bankrupt; unprofitable, disadvantageous, wasted, irretrievable, desperate, hopeless, futile.

vb. lose, mislay, misplace, not find; let slip, drop, miss, fail, forfeit; deprive; displace; waste, squander; incur losses, go bankrupt.

707 possession

n. possession, ownership, occupancy, residence, tenancy, tenure; possessorship, proprietorship; hold, mastery, grasp, control, custody; purchase.

adj. possessing, having, owning, possessive, exclusive, monopolistic, selfish; possessed, owned, purchased, enjoyed, in possession of.

vb. possess, own, have, hold, keep, retain, grasp, occupy, control, maintain, use, boast of, enjoy; have title to, have rights to, have claim upon; monopolize, hog (*inf.*), have all to oneself, corner; include, comprise, contain; belong, appertain.

708 non-possession

n. non-possession, loss, deprivation, surrender of rights; lease; no man's land.

adj. not owning, lacking; destitute, poor, impoverished, penniless; unowned, unoccupied, unpossessed, unattached, free, ownerless, virgin, unclaimed, lost, independent, unbound.

see also 706

709 joint possession

n. joint possession, co-ownership, cooperation, participation, partnership, sharing; socialism, communism, public ownership, nationalization, worker participation, profit-sharing; community, cooperative, collective, kibbutz; joint fund, kitty, pool; share, portion.

participator, partner, member, partaker, shareholder, worker-director.

adj. cooperative, joint, participatory, common, communal, profit-sharing; involved, committed, dedicated, connected with.

vb. participate, share, cooperate, join, take part in, partake, go halves.

see also 639

710 possessor

n. possessor, owner, holder, master, partner; buyer, purchaser; occupant, occupier, tenant, resident, lodger, lessee, landlord, landlady, landowner, landholder, proprietor, proprietress; heir, heiress, inheritor.

711 property

n. property, land, assets, resources, means, goods, riches, wealth, valuables, inheritance, capital, investment, equity, land, holding, estate.

belongings, equipment, paraphernalia, things, trappings, fixtures, furniture, furnishings, goods and chattels; appurtenances, accoutrements; personal effects, luggage, baggage; burden, encumbrance, impedimenta.

712 retention

n. retention, holding, keeping; hold, grasp, clench, clinch, grip, hug, embrace, clasp; confinement, stranglehold, tight grip, straitjacket.

adj. retentive, holding; retained, held, kept.

vb. retain, hold, keep, keep hold of, grasp, clench, grip, clinch, clasp, clutch, embrace, hug, squeeze, press; cling to, stick to, fasten on, secure, hold fast; contain, restrain, enclose, confine; maintain, preserve; cherish, nurture, harbour; detain, reserve, withhold.

713 non-retention

n. relinquishment, abandonment, renunciation, disposal; exemption, dispensation, release; divorce, dissolution.

adj. abandoned, thrown away, rejected, marooned.

vb. not retain, relinquish, abandon, renounce, let go, part with, dispose of, discard, throw away, jettison, release; waive, lift restrictions, derestrict, exempt.

see also 556, 921

714 transfer

n. transference, conveyancing, assignation; changeover, change of hands; devolution, delegation; exchange, conversion, interchange; sale, lease; bequest, endowment, legacy.

adj. transferable, negotiable, interchangeable, exchangeable; transferred, made over.

vb. convey, transfer, sell, sign,

consign, assign, change over, deliver, make over; entrust, commit; exchange, convert; devolve, delegate, decentralize; bequeath, will, make a will, pass on, hand down.

see also 268

715 giving

n. giving, bestowal, conferral, granting, imparting, delivery.

gift, present, donation, grant, award, presentation, prize; allowance, subsidy, aid, assistance; tip, gratuity; bounty, largesse, windfall; leaving present, golden handshake; charity, hand-out, alms; bequest, legacy; blessing, favour, grace, mercy.

sacrifice, offering, worship, dedication, consecration; offering, collection, offertory.

giver, donor, contributor.

adj. giving, charitable, generous, liberal, sacrificial; given, free.

vb. give, donate, grant, award, present, contribute, render, remit, convey, supply, furnish, provide, afford, dispense, hand out, dole out, distribute, administer, deal out, mete out, subsidize, give towards; bestow, confer, endow, invest with, impart, communicate; expend, spend, lavish; offer, sacrifice.

716 receiving

n. receiving, reception, acquisition, acceptance, admission, collection; receipts, proceeds, dues, monies, toll.

recipient, receiver, beneficiary; object, target, victim, guinea pig; customer, client; trustee, payee, addressee, earner; heir, heiress.

adj. receiving, receptive, welcoming, hospitable, sensitive.

vb. receive, accept, admit, be given, get, gain, acquire, collect, obtain, draw, take in, derive, come by, attract, come

in for, be on the receiving end; take up, levy, charge; be received, accrue, come in, fall to one.

see also 302, 705

717 apportionment

n. apportionment, allotment, sharing, division, distribution, dealing, rationing.

portion, share, allocation, section, piece, part, fraction, fragment; helping, serving, slice, ration; proportion, quota, allowance; cut (*sl.*), split, parcel, lot.

vb. apportion, allot, distribute, divide, share out, hand out, dole out, dish out (*inf.*), farm out, parcel out, deal, assign, dispose, administer, give away, dispense, ration.

see also 55

718 lending

n. lending; loan, advance, mortgage, allowance, credit, investment, credit card, credit account, hire purchase, never-never (*inf.*).

bank, building society, pawnbroker, pop-shop (*sl.*); banker, bank manager, lender, financier, money-lender, creditor; usurer, shark, angel (*sl.*), Shylock.

vb. lend, let out, allow to borrow, trust with, entrust, hire out, let, lease, charter; loan, finance, support, back, advance, grant, lend on security, put out at interest, give credit, risk.

719 borrowing

n. borrowing, rental, hire, loan; assumption; appropriation, adoption, importation; imitation, copy.

vb. borrow, rent, hire, lease, charter; take on tick (*inf.*), raise money, pawn, cadge; touch for (*sl.*); obtain, use, adopt.

720 taking

n. taking, possession, acceptance, appropriation, requisition; seizure, grab, capture; kidnapping, abduction; dispossession, deprivation, extortion, confiscation; recovery, retrieval.

taker, possessor; seizer, grabber, raider; kidnapper, abductor.

adj. taking, grasping, greedy, rapacious, extortionate, ravenous.

vb. take, possess, accept, receive, get, obtain, win, gain; seize, lay hold of, appropriate, take for oneself, acquire, avail oneself of, adopt, assume; grip, clasp; catch, apprehend, grasp; grab, trap, snatch, capture, raid; take away, steal, kidnap, abduct; confiscate, commandeer; recover, retrieve; take from, remove, deprive of, divest of, dispossess, extort, strip, disinherit.

see also 722

721 restitution

n. restitution, restoration, return, giving back, reinstatement; retrieval, recovery, repossession, repatriation; recompense, repayment, refund, amends, compensation, reimbursement, remuneration, reparation, indemnification, redemption, satisfaction.

adj. restitutive, restoring, compensatory, redemptive.

vb. restore, return, give back, reinstate, reinstall; rehabilitate, repair; recover, get back, retrieve, recoup, regain, retake, reclaim.

make restitution, refund, make amends, reimburse, repay, compensate, indemnify, redeem, ransom.

see also 589

722 stealing

n. stealing, theft, larceny, robbery, burglary, house-breaking, shop-lifting; vandalism, looting, pilfering, ransack-ing, pillage, plunder, sacking; hijacking, skyjacking (*inf.*); kidnapping, abduction; hold-up, stick-up (*inf.*), mugging (*inf.*), hit-and-run-raid, smash-and-grab-raid, job (*sl.*); embezzlement, misappropriation, extortion, fraud.

adj. thieving, light-fingered.

vb. steal, take, burgle, thieve, rob, remove, go off with, get away with, make off with, run off with, seize, pilfer, pick-pocket, pinch (*sl.*), nick (*sl.*), filch, fleece, nobble (*sl.*), knock off (*sl.*), rip off (*sl.*), screw (*sl.*), shop-lift, purloin; abduct, kidnap, mug (*inf.*), hijack, skyjack; embezzle, misappropriate, defraud, swindle, cheat, fiddle, peculate, smuggle; loot, rifle, sack, raid, ransack, plunder, pillage.

be stolen, fall off the back of a lorry (*inf.*).

723 thief

n. thief, robber, stealer; burglar, house-breaker, shop-lifter, mugger, attacker; pilferer, pick-pocket; hijacker, skyjacker (*inf.*), highwayman; safe-blower, safe-cracker; kidnapper, abductor; plunderer, looter; embezzler, swindler, cheater, fiddler; crook, rogue, thug, smuggler, pirate.

see also 684

724 booty

n. booty, prize, haul, loot, swag (*sl.*), takings, plunder, spoil, winnings, stolen goods, goods fallen off the back of a lorry (*inf.*), capture, premium, contraband, prey.

725 business

n. business, trade, commerce, business affairs, traffic; negotiations, bargaining, transactions, marketing, buying and selling; barter, exchange, swap (*inf.*).

adj. business, trading, commercial, mercantile.

vb. transact business, trade, traffic, deal in, handle, market, buy and sell; negotiate, bargain; exchange, barter, swap (*inf.*).

726 purchase

n. purchase, buying, obtaining, acquisition; shopping, payment, investment, marketing.

buyer, purchaser, consumer, shopper, customer, patron, client, clientele, custom, market, patronage.

vb. purchase, buy, get, obtain, gain, acquire; go shopping, pay for, invest, exchange, bargain, sign; patronize; go window-shopping, buy back, redeem.

727 sale

n. sale, disposal, selling, marketing, trading; clearance, sell-out; bazaar, jumble sale, rummage sale; auction, public sale; sales talk, salesmanship, high-pressure salesmanship, sales patter, promotion, advertising.

seller, vendor, retailer, shopkeeper, shop assistant, salesman, commercial traveller, sales rep.

adj. saleable, marketable, in demand; available, on the market.

vb. sell, dispose, market, flog (*sl.*), retail, trade, dump, vend; ask, demand; transfer, transact, exchange; peddle, hawk; reduce prices, sell off; auction, come under the hammer.

728 trader

n. trader, dealer, retailer, shopkeeper, tradesman, middleman, wholesaler, exporter, importer, shipper, trafficker, merchant; businessman, industrialist, capitalist, manager, financier, entrepreneur, tycoon, stockbroker, speculator.

pedlar, hawker, tinker, huckster; tout; rag-and-bone man.

729 merchandise

n. merchandise, commodities, stock, wares, articles, goods, property, product, possessions; things, stuff; line, supplies; consumer goods, consumer durables.

730 market

n. market, mart, square, mall, arcade, shopping centre, shopping precinct, exchange, emporium; shop, store, supermarket, department store, multiple, chain store, boutique, hypermarket; kiosk, stand, stall, booth, barrow, bazaar; place of business, premises, concern, establishment.

731 money

n. money, currency, legal tender, cash, bank notes, bread (*sl.*), dough (*sl.*), lolly (*sl.*); change, small change; cheque, credit card, hire purchase; pay, salary, wages, pocket money; pin money; sum, amount, balance; funds, credit, finance, reserves, capital, wealth, wherewithal.

adj. monetary, pecuniary, financial.

vb. mint, coin, issue, monetize, put in circulation; withdraw, remove from circulation, call in, demonetize.

732 treasury

n. treasury, bank, exchequer, repository, coffer, vault, strongroom, depository, safe, cash box; cash register, till; money-box, piggy bank; wallet, purse, bag.

733 treasurer

n. treasurer, receiver, cashier, banker, purser, bursar, paymaster, accountant, teller, steward, trustee.

734 wealth

n. wealth, riches, money, affluence, luxury, opulence, prosperity, fortune, money to burn; profits, assets, means, resources.

rich man, millionaire, moneybags, man of means, capitalist.

adj. rich, wealthy, affluent, prosperous, luxurious, well-off, in the money, well-to-do, well provided for, made of money (inf.), rolling in it (inf.).

vb. get rich, make a fortune, come into money, line one's pocket; live comfortably, afford, bear the expense of, make both ends meet.

735 poverty

n. poverty, impoverishment, poorness; destitution, scarcity, privation, penury, pennilessness, pauperism, indigence, insolvency; beggary, mendicancy; poor man, pauper, beggar.

adj. poor, needy, destitute, under-privileged, distressed; impecunious, poverty-stricken, penniless, hard up, broke (inf.), bankrupt, insolvent; begging, mendicant; starving, hungry, empty-handed, down-and-out.

vb. be poor, find it hard going, live from hand to mouth, starve; impoverish, ruin, eat out of house and home.

736 credit

n. credit, trust, reliability; loan, account, credit account, credit card; creditor, mortgagee.

vb. credit, charge, charge to an account, credit one's account; give credit, defer payment, lend.

737 debt

n. debt, liability, obligation, claim, commitment, indebtedness, due, duty; debts, bills, amount due, amount owing, accounts outstanding, score, deficit, arrears.

debtor, borrower, purchaser, buyer, mortgagor.

adj. indebted, liable, answerable, responsible, committed, under obligation; owing, in debt, overdrawn, in the red; unpaid, due, outstanding, payable, unsettled, in arrears, overdue.

vb. be in debt, owe, be under obligation, overdraw, run up a bill, fall into debt, be in Queer Street (sl.).

738 payment

n. payment, remittance; settlement, clearance, reckoning; recompense, restitution, compensation, reimbursement, refund, subsidy; deposit, instalment, down payment, first payment.

pay, wages, salary, earnings, remuneration, emolument; fee, stipend, allowance, expenses, honorarium; pay packet, pay slip; payroll.

adj. paying, remunerative, not owing; paid, discharged, out of debt.

vb. pay, make payment for; repay, reward, remunerate; settle, discharge, defray, meet, bear the cost of, foot the bill; recompense, reimburse, compensate, recoup, refund; subsidize; pay on the nail; contribute, chip in (inf.), fork out (inf.), cough up (sl.); spend, expend; stand, treat.

739 non-payment

n. non-payment, failure to pay, default, bankruptcy, insolvency, liquidation, crash, ruin; overdraft, overdrawn account; debts.

non-payer, defaulter, bankrupt, lame duck; embezzler.

adj. non-paying, defaulting, insolvent, bankrupt, failed, ruined, on the rocks (inf.), bust (inf.), liquidated.

vb. not pay, default, fall into arrears, go bankrupt, go into liquidation, go to the wall, fold up (*inf.*), fail, be wound up, go bust (*inf.*), crash, go under; write off; bankrupt, ruin, wind up, put in the hands of a receiver, liquidate.

740 expenditure

n. expenditure, outlay, payment, disbursement, spending, costs, expenses, outgoings, investment.

vb. spend, expend, pay, pay out, lay out, invest, foot the bill; exhaust, discharge, consume; squander, waste, lavish.

741 income

n. income, receipts, revenue, returns, earnings, salary, wages, profit, assets, proceeds, dividends, gains, takings, turn-over, box-office receipts, gate-money.

receipt, acknowledgement, slip, voucher, record.

742 accounts

n. accounts, bookkeeping; account, bill, invoice, reckoning, statement, balance sheet; ledger, log, cash-book; budget.

accountant, chartered accountant, auditor, bookkeeper, actuary, cashier.

adj. accounting, budgetary.

vb. account, keep the books, enter, debit, credit, balance; budget; cook the books (*inf.*), falsify, fiddle (*sl.*).

743 price

n. price, cost, expense, amount, charge, toll, fee, fare; rent, rental, hire charge; value, face value, worth; evaluation, valuation, estimate, quotation.

taxation, tax, duty, levy, tariff, inland revenue; excise, custom, impost, tribute, dues; rates, rateable value, assessment.

price control, price freeze, austerity,

squeeze; cost of living, price index; price tag, label, ticket.

adj. priced, marked, charged, valued, worth.

vb. price, value, charge, assess, estimate, put a price on, reckon, rate; demand, ask; reduce, mark down; increase, mark up.

cost, be worth, go for, sell for, fetch, come to, amount to.

tax, exact, levy, put a tax on, raise taxes; pay taxes.

744 discount

n. discount, reduction, rebate, allowance, deduction, cut, subtraction, remission, concession; depreciation; subsidy.

vb. reduce, lower, rebate, deduct, cut, take off, knock off, subtract, allow; depreciate.

745 dearness

n. dearness, expensiveness, expense, costliness; exorbitance, excessiveness, extravagance.

adj. dear, expensive, costly, high-priced, pricey (*inf.*); exorbitant, too high, overpriced, excessive, prohibitive, extortionate, immoderate, unreasonable, extravagant, lavish, steep (*inf.*), stiff (*inf.*).

vb. be dear, cost a lot, cost a pretty penny (*inf.*); go up, increase, revalue; overcharge, exploit, bleed, fleece, extort.

746 cheapness

n. cheapness, inexpensiveness, competitiveness, reasonableness; bargain, good value, good buy.

adj. cheap, inexpensive, low-priced, moderate, reasonable, fair, peanuts (*sl.*).

family-sized, economy-sized, economy, bargain, standard; reduced, cut-price, half-price, marked down, dirt cheap.

free, gratuitous, for nothing, without charge, complimentary, gratis, on the house, for love.

vb. be cheap, get one's money's worth; fall in price, decrease, cheapen, depreciate, mark down, devalue.

747 liberality

n. liberality, generosity, benevolence, bounteousness, bounty, largesse; kindness, giving, charity, hospitality, cordiality.

adj. liberal, generous, big-hearted, open-handed, bountiful, lavish, unsparing, unstinting, munificent; kind, benevolent, unselfish, charitable, beneficient.

vb. be liberal, give generously, lavish, heap upon, spare no expense, go beyond what one can afford.

748 economy

n. economy, thrift, care, prudence, housekeeping, stewardship, management, frugality, husbandry, providence, parsimony, stinginess; saving; retrenchment.

adj. economical, economizing, careful, prudent, good, saving, thrifty, frugal, sparing, stingy, mean; convenient, time-saving, labour-saving.

vb. economize, cut back, keep costs down, cut costs, cut corners, tighten one's belt (*inf.*), make ends meet, live within one's means; manage, steward, husband, save, conserve.

749 extravagance

n. extravagance, wastefulness, squandering, prodigality, lavishness, immoderateness; money to burn, shopping spree, spending spree, no thought of tommorow; prodigal, wastrel, spendthrift, squanderer.

adj. extravagant, wasteful, squandering, prodigal, lavish, over-generous, immoderate, exorbitant, reckless, careless, profligate.

vb. waste, squander, throw away, have money to burn, spend money like water, hang the expense, blow (*sl.*), blue (*sl.*); fritter away, dissipate; go too far, overdo it.

750 parsimony

n. parsimony, parsimoniousness, stinginess, scrimping, niggardliness, penny-pinching, cheese-paring, meanness, miserliness, penuriousness; niggard, miser, screw; greed, avarice, covetousness, avidity, voracity, gluttony.

adj. parsimonious, stingy, niggardly, miserly, mean, tight-fisted, close-fisted, penny-pinching, scrimping; sparing, chary,

greedy, avaricious, voracious, possessive, acquisitive, grasping, grabby (*inf.*), itchy (*inf.*), rapacious, covetous, avid.

vb. be parsimonious, scrimp, stint, skimp; over-economize; be greedy, always want more.

VI Affections

A Affections in general

751 affections

n. affections, qualities, character, nature, make-up; personality, psyche, heart, soul, breast, inner self; temperament, disposition, spirit, temper, mood, state of mind, frame of mind, humour; tendency, inclination, bent, bias.

adj. affected, characterized, formed,

moulded, disposed, inclined, predisposed.

see also 5, 58

752 feeling

n. feeling, emotion, affection, sentiment, passion; experience, sense, impression, consciousness, sensation, perception, sympathy, warmth, tenderness, sensitivity, empathy; fervour, ardour, enthusiasm.

adj. feeling, emotional, sentimental, romantic, passionate, fervent, intense, impassioned, dramatic, burning, earnest, moving, tender; felt, experienced, heart-felt, thrilled, moved, affected, touched.

vb. feel, sense, experience, go through, enjoy, suffer, undergo, bear, endure.

move, affect, touch, stir, impress, excite, influence, quicken, touch one's heart, touch to the quick; appreciate, respond; thrill, tingle.

753 sensitivity

n. sensitivity, sensibility, susceptibility, awareness, consciousness, responsiveness, excitability.

five senses, sight, hearing, smell, taste, touch; sixth sense, intuition, feminine intuition; extra-sensory perception.

adj. sensitive, aware, conscious of, alive to, awake to, susceptible, impressionable, receptive, sensible; sensory, sentient.

raw, tender, bare, sore, bruised, delicate, painful, oversensitive, hypersensitive; exposed, open, vulnerable.

754 insensitivity

n. insensitivity, insensibility, unawareness, unresponsiveness, inexcitability, impassivness; apathy, indifference, lethargy, aloofness, coldness; hypnosis, numbness, paralysis; dream, trance, coma, stupor; hardness of heart, callousness; stoic, ascetic; iceberg.

adj. insensitive, insusceptible, unimpressionable, unresponsive, inexcitable, unmoved, unaffected, unaware, unconscious, dead to, blind to, oblivious to, lost to, insensible; lethargic, dull, unenthusiastic, apathetic, indifferent, cool, aloof; unfeeling, unemotional, passionless, unresponsive, frigid, cold, numb, paralyzed; blank, poker-faced, dead pan, expressionless; thick-skinned, hard-hearted, callous, cold-blooded.

vb. deaden, numb, paralyze, stupefy, stun, harden, sear, blunt, dull, drug; turn off (*inf.*), switch off (*inf*); be unaffected, leave cold.

755 excitation

n. excitation, stimulation, activation, animation, inspiration, quickening; incitement, provocation, agitation, excitement; captivation, fascination, interest.

adj. exciting, stimulating, inspiring, moving, sparkling, exhilarating, thrilling, delightful; captivating, fascinating, interesting, absorbing, gripping, stirring, tantalizing, compelling, impressive, dramatic, sensational.

vb. excite, stimulate, arouse, activate, move, stir, work up, whip up, incite, influence, affect, provoke, awaken, touch, interest, animate, quicken, inspire; inflame, intensify, kindle, fire, light up; electrify, galvanize, energize.

absorb, fascinate, attract attention, impress, intrigue; tantalize, tease, anger, cause a stir; catch one's attention, come home, arrest, compel, engage; make one's mouth water, whet the appetite; knock for six (*inf.*), take one's breath away; delight, thrill, exhilarate, turn on (*inf.*), switch on (*inf.*).

see also 756, **829**

756 excitability

n. excitability, impetuousness, boisterousness, instability, emotionalism, restlessness, agitation, irritability, intolerance.

excitement, exhilaration, thrill, ecstasy, transport; rage, fury, outburst, agony; hysterics, delirium; fuss, big song and dance (*inf.*), hullabaloo, tizzy (*sl.*), tiz-woz (*sl.*), dither (*inf.*), fluster, stew (*inf.*), to-do.

adj. excited, moved, stirred, inspired, thrilled, quickened, enthusiastic, eager, impressed, delighted, pleased, happy, joyful, touched.

excitable, sensitive, highly-strung, nervous, easily excited, emotional; impulsive, quick-tempered, impetuous; moody, temperamental; impatient, irritable, touchy, edgy, jumpy, jittery, restless, fidgety; tense, uptight, all worked up (*inf.*), keyed up, a bundle of nerves (*inf.*); distraught, beside onself; mad, fuming, raging.

vb. be excited, thrill; let oneself go, get carried away, abandon oneself, freak out (*sl.*); tingle, glow, palpitate, pant; tremble, quiver, shake.

get excited, work oneself up; feet, flap (*inf.*), shuffle, fuss; rage, fume, explode, flare up, boil over (*inf.*).

see also 755

757 inexcitability

n. inexcitability, imperturbability, stability, composure, calmness, coolness, level-headedness, even temper, steadiness; peace of mind, serenity, tranquillity; self-possession, self-control, self-restraint, self-assurance; detachment, aloofness; stoicism.

patience, endurance, forbearance, long-suffering, submission, humility, meekness, resignation.

adj. inexcitable, calm, cool, composed, collected, self-possessed, dispassionate, imperturbable, unflappable (*inf.*), unruffled, immovable, stable, level-headed, even-tempered, easygoing, moderate, sedate, serene, tranquil, placid, inoffensive, mild, phlegmatic; patient, forbearing, uncomplaining, meek, submissive, philosophic, stoical; detached, aloof, disinterested, spiritless, nonchalant, blasé, casual.

vb. keep calm, keep one's temper, keep one's cool (*sl.*), keep one's shirt on (*sl.*), not bat an eyelid; calm down, compose oneself, control oneself, relax, take hold of oneself, pull oneself together, cool it (*sl.*), simmer down (*inf.*), cool off.

bear, tolerate, endure, put up with, stomach (*inf.*), stick it out (*inf.*), swallow, brook, resign oneself to, grin and bear it, submit to, make the best of.

B Sensation

758 touch

n. touch, feeling, contact, tactility; feel, touching, stroking, massage, manipulation; tickle, titillation, itching; scratching, pricking, stinging, shivers.

adj. tactile, tactual, tangible, touchable, palpable.

vb. touch, feel, press, squeeze, stroke, rub, finger, paw, smooth, caress, fondle, massage, manipulate, lick, kiss; tap, pat, hit, strike; explore, feel for, grope, fumble; grasp, grip, grab, grapple, clasp, clutch; tickle, titillate, itch; graze, scratch, prick, sting.

759 heat

n. heat, hotness, warmth, tepidity; temperature, thermometer; thermostat, hot weather, summer, heatwave, scorcher (*inf.*), dog days; fire, blaze, glow, light, sparkle, flicker, conflagration; ardour, fervour, zeal, passion, intensity.

adj. thermal; hot, very warm, torrid, parched; burning, fiery, blazing, ignited, lit, alight, on fire, in flames, glowing, incandescent, smoking; heated, molten; sweltering, baking, scorching, sizzling, scalding, grilling, roasting; tropical, humid, sticky, close, sultry, muggy, stifling, oppressive; warm, tepid, lukewarm; temperate, mild, fair, sunny, summery; bright, clear; intense, fervent, vehement, passionate, ardent, excited.

vb. be hot, burn, flame, burst into flames, catch fire, flare up, flicker, glow; smoke, fume, reek, smoulder, smother, suffocate; cook, boil, scald, seethe, fry, sizzle, roast, parch, scorch, bake, swelter.

760 cold

n. cold, coldness, chilliness, frigidity, frozenness, iciness, frostiness, congelation; chill, nip, shivers, shivering; cold snap, arctic conditions; ice, icicle, glacier, iceberg, black ice; frost, rime, hoar-frost; hail, hailstorm; snow, snowflake, snowdrift, snowstorm, blizzard, avalanche, sleet, slush.

adj. cryoscopic, cold, cool, chilly, fresh, crisp, brisk, nippy, frigid; piercing, biting, cutting, numbing, stinging; raw, sharp, keen; wintry, brumal, bleak, Siberian, arctic, polar; freezing, icy, gelid, frosty, hoary.

vb. be cold, freeze, shiver, shudder, quiver; chatter.

761 heating

n. heating, warming; combustion, burning, incineration, flaming, kindling, ignition, scorching, incandescence.

adj. heating, warming, calefactory; combustible, flammable; glowing, incandescent.

vb. heat, warm, heat up, reheat, put on the fire; ignite, kindle, set fire to, strike a light, put a match to, touch off; burn, scorch, consume, scald, incinerate, reduce to ashes, cremate; fire, smelt; thaw, defrost, de-ice, unfreeze, melt, liquefy; insulate.

762 refrigeration; incombustibility

n. refrigeration, cooling, chilling, freezing, glaciation, glacification.

incombustibility, non-flammability; asbestos, safety curtain.

adj. cooled, chilled; frozen, icy.

incombustible, non-flammable, fireproof.

vb. refrigerate, cool, chill, make cold, freeze, deep-freeze, ice, frost, congeal, glaciate.

extinguish, put out, blow out, quench, stifle, smother, damp, choke, snuff, douse, drown.

763 furnace

n. furnace, boiler, kiln, stove, cooker, oven; incinerator; crematorium; fire, heater, radiator; hearth, fireplace, fireside, grate, hob.

764 refrigerator

n. refrigerator, fridge, freezer, deepfreeze, icebox, icepack, cool-bag, coolbox, cooling apparatus, cold storage; air-conditioner, fan, ventilator.

765 fuel

n. fuel, combustible; coal, coke, charcoal, briquette, wood, log, gas, oil, petrol, electricity, juice (*sl.*), hydro-electricity, nuclear power, solar energy.

match, lighter, firelighter, fuse, touch-paper, vesta, detonator, torch, firebrand, tinder, flint.

adj. combustible, flammable, explosive.

vb. fuel, fire, power; feed, stoke.

766 thermometer

n. thermometer, calorimeter, thermostat, mercury, clinical thermometer, pyrometer, thermocouple, thermopile, thermograph; Fahrenheit, centigrade, Celsius, Réamur, kelvin; degree.

767 taste

n. taste, flavour, relish, savour, smack, sapor; tang, after-taste; tongue, palate, taste buds; gustation.

adj. tasty, palatable, delicious, appetizing, gustatory.

vb. taste, relish, enjoy, eat, smack one's lips; try, sample, sip; taste of, savour of.

768 tastelessness

n. tastelessness, insipidity, flavourlessness, dullness, flatness, staleness.

adj. tasteless, unsavoury, insipid, flavourless, dull, flat, bland, stale, wishy-washy, unseasoned, unspiced, plastic (*inf.*), uninteresting.

see also 507, 843

769 pungency

n. pungency, piquancy, sharpness, keenness, spiciness, tanginess; zest, bite, edge, tang, kick (*inf.*), zing (*sl.*), punch (*sl.*).

adj. pungent, sharp, piquant, penetrating, poignant, strong, tangy,

racy; spiced, curried, hot; tart, sour, bitter.

see also 307

770 savouriness

n. savouriness, palatability, deliciousness, tastiness, richness, lusciousness.

delicacy, luxury, treat, rarity, delight, titbit, dainty, *bonne bouche*, chef's special, dish fit for a king; caviar; ambrosia, nectar.

adj. palatable, delicious, savoury, tasty, nice, dainty, delightful, choice, rich, luscious, delectable, exquisite, heavenly (*inf.*), scrumptious (*inf.*), yummy (*inf.*); fit for a king, fit for the gods; well done, done to a turn.

appetizing, mouth-watering, tempting, inviting, enticing, tantalizing, moreish (*inf.*).

vb. taste good; enjoy, like, relish, savour, appreciate.

771 unsavouriness

n. unsavouriness, unpalatability, unpleasantness, flavourlessness; bread and water, bitter pill, yuk (*sl.*).

adj. tasteless, flavourless, bland, dull, inedible; undrinkable; underdone; gone off; yukky (*sl.*); uninteresting, unappealing, unappetizing, uninviting, disagreeable, horrible, revolting.

vb. nauseate, disgust, turn one's stomach; disagree with, turn off (*inf.*); dislike, loathe.

772 sweetness

n. sweetness, sweetening, sugariness; sweet, sweetener, sugar, honey, molasses, syrup, treacle, saccharin.

adj. sweet, sweetened, sugared; sugary, saccharine, sirupy, rich, luscious, delicious; sticky; bitter-sweet, sweet-and-sour.

vb. sweeten, make sweet, sugar; dulcify.

773 sourness

n. sourness, acidity, bitterness, sharpness; acid, vinegar, gall, wormwood.

adj. sour, acid, tart, bitter, caustic, cutting, pungent, sharp, biting, dry; acidulous, vinegary, acetous; unsweetened, unsugared, unripe.

vb. sour, turn sour, set one's teeth on edge; ferment, curdle, tartarize.

774 odour

n. odour, smell, scent, trace, trail, exhalation, emanation, effluvium; fragrance; stench.

sense of smell, smelling, olfaction, detection.

adj. smelling, scented, odorous; strong, pungent, redolent; olfactory.

vb. smell, smell of, give out, give off, emit, scent, exhale; sniff, whiff, detect, perceive, smell out.

see also 776, 777

775 inodorousness

n. inodorousness, no smell; deodorization, ventilation, fumigation; deodorant, deodorizer; fumigant, fumigator, cleanser.

adj. inodorous, odourless, unscented, scentless.

vb. deodorize, fumigate, aerate, clean, purify.

776 fragrance

n. fragrance, aroma, bouquet, scent, perfume, spice, balm.

adj. fragrant, aromatic, scented, perfumed, spicy, sweet-scented, sweet-smelling, redolent, odoriferous, odorous, ambrosial.

vb. smell, scent, be fragrant; scent, perfume, embalm.

777 stench

n. stench, smell, stink, fetor, reek, fume, mephitis, miasma; foulness, uncleanness, smelliness, mustiness, rancidity; B.O. (*inf.*), body odour; skunk, polecat; stink-bomb.

adj. smelly, stinking, foul, unclean, fetid, strong-smelling, foul-smelling, nasty, vile, repulsive, offensive, rank, noxious, noisome; stale, musty, rancid, putrid, decaying, high, putrescent.

vb. smell, stink, reek, smell to high heaven (*inf.*).

778 sound

n. sound, noise, vibration, resonance, report, reverberation, echo, ringing; loudness, softness; note, level, accent, cadence, tenor, intonation, tone, timbre; acoustics, phonetics.

adj. sounding, heard, audible, distinct, within earshot; loud, resonant, sonorous; auditory, acoustic, phonetic.

vb. sound, make a noise, give out, emit, produce; hear, listen.

see also 795

779 silence

n. silence, inaudibility, quietness, stillness, noiselessness; peace, quiet, still, hush; loss of signal, blackout, news blackout, security blackout, censorship.

adj. silent, inaudible, noiseless, hushed, quiet, still, soundless, unuttered, unspoken, unvoiced; soundproof.

vb. silence, hush, quiet, still, calm, muffle, reduce to silence, mute, stifle; subdue, deaden, repress, tone down, put the lid on.

see also 513, 517

780 loudness

n. loudness, noisiness, audibility, rowdiness; noise, racket, roar, boom, blast, swell, din, clamour, tumult, outcry, uproar, hubbub, hullabaloo, pandemonium.

adj. loud, noisy, clamorous, vociferous, loud-mouthed; boisterous, rumbustious, rowdy, obstreperous; thundering, deafening, ringing, booming, ear-splitting, resounding, piercing, blaring, crashing, stentorian, enough to wake the dead.

vb. be loud, boom, roar, thunder, fulminate, resound, bellow, blare, peal, crash, rattle, deafen, be unable to hear oneself think.

781 faintness

n. faintness, softness, inaudibility; whisper, breath, undertone, murmur, mutter, sigh, rustle, ripple, hum.

adj. faint, soft, quiet, hushed, inaudible; indistinct, stifled, muted, muffled, deadened, subdued; feeble, weak, low, distant, muttering.

vb. whisper, speak softly, murmur, mutter, sigh, hum, rustle, purr, creak, squeak.

782 sudden and violent sound

n. bang, blast, shot, report, boom, detonation, eruption, explosion; thud, whack, knock, slap, tap, rap, snap; crash, crackle; shout, cry, yelp.

vb. crash, crack, knock, slap, smack, whack, tap, rap, snap; click; plop, plonk, thud; thunder, boom, detonate, bang, pop, slam, burst, explode, blow up, set off.

783 repeated and prolonged sound

n. roll, clang, clatter; rattle, rustle; chuckle, cackle; whistle, hum, whirr, purr, buzz, strum; throb.

vb. roll, clang, clatter; rattle, rustle; ripple, swish, hum, drone, whirr, purr, buzz, strum, whistle, trill; thump, throb, palpitate, tick, beat, pound,

patter; chime, peal, toll; chuckle, cackle; rumble, grumble, growl.

784 resonance

n. resonance, vibration, tintinnabulation; ringing, clanging, echo, resounding, thunder, boom; chime, bell, gong, jingle, tinkle.

adj. resonant, vibrant, reverberating, loud, echoing, ringing, clanging, chiming, deep-sounding.

vb. resound, reverberate, boom, vibrate, echo, re-echo, ring, gong, chime, tinkle, jingle, clang, whirr, buzz, drone, whine, purr, hum.

785 non-resonance

n. non-resonance, thud, bump, plop, plump, thump, plonk, clonk, clunk.

adj. non-resonant, deadened, muffled, dead, heavy, dull.

vb. thud, bump, plonk, plump, plop, thump, clonk, clunk; muffle, stifle, dull, damp, deaden.

786 hissing sound

n. hiss, hissing, sibilance, buzz, swish, rustle, whirr, whistle, splash, squelch, whoosh, zip.

adj. hissing, sibilant.

vb. buzz, hiss, swish, rustle, whistle, splash, whoosh, zip, fizz, whiz, whirr, squelch, sizzle, sneeze, wheeze, effervesce, sibilate.

787 harsh sound

n. harshness, hoarseness, gruffness, discord, dissonance, cacophony; shrillness, whistle, croak, squawk, squeal, screech, shriek.

adj. strident, shrill, high-pitched, piercing, sharp, penetrating; squealing, creaking, grating, scratchy, tinny, metallic; clanging, clashing, screeching, jarring, discordant, dissonant; hoarse, gruff, harsh, raucous, loud, husky, throaty, guttural, dry.

vb. clang, clatter, clunk, crash, bang, clash, jangle; croak, quack, squawk, caw, cluck; saw, grind; shrill, whistle, shriek, screech, scream, squeal, yelp, squeak, creak; grate, rasp, irritate, jar, set one's teeth on edge, get on one's nerves.

788 human sound

n. cry, exclamation, utterance, shout, call, noise, shouting, clamour, outcry; scream, shriek, yell, moan, groan, wail, bellow, howl, whimper.

adj. clamorous, noisy, loud, yelling, vociferous.

vb. cry, exclaim, call, speak, utter, shout, scream, yell, shriek, screech, squeal, squeak, caterwaul, bawl, bellow, hoot, vociferate, whoop, hoop, hollo; groan, moan, complain, howl, wail, whine, whimper, sob.

cheer, chant, clamour, support; shout down, hiss, boo, ridicule, disapprove, censure.

789 animal sound

n. call, cry, ululation, barking.

vb. cry, yelp, yap, squeal, squawk; cackle, cluck, quack; caw, crow; screech, croak; coo, cuckoo; gobble, gaggle; chuckle, chirp, chirrup, cheep; tweet, twitter, whistle, pipe, trill, sing; warble; purr, miaow, mew, caterwaul; hum, drone, buzz; bark, bay, howl, woof, roar, bellow, bell; grunt, snort, snap, growl, snarl, whine, oink; neigh, bray, whinny; bleat, baa; moo, low.

790 melody

n. melody, melodiousness, tunefulness, concord, consonance, euphony, harmony, unison, accord, concert, music, blending.

adj. melodious, musical, euphonic, tuneful, rhythmical, melodic, lyrical, harmonious, in tune, accordant; sweet-sounding, dulcet, soothing, pleasing, mellow, soft, rich; catchy, memorable, singable, popular.

791 discord

n. discord, discordance, unmelodiousness, inharmoniousness, dissonance, atonality; noise, din, racket, cacophony.

adj. discordant, dissonant, atonal, unmelodious, inharmonious, unmusical, untuneful, out of tune, off key, flat, sharp; cacophonous, clashing, jarring, grating.

792 music

n. music, composition, work, opus, piece; arrangement, adaptation, setting, transcription, orchestration, instrumentation; incidental music, background music, accompaniment; record, recording; concert, recital.

classical music, chamber music, light music, country and western, folk music, pop music, electronic music, jazz, blues, reggae, punk, rock, soul, ragtime.

symphony, concerto, suite; overture, prelude; sonata; ballet, dance; opera, operetta; song, air, solo, hymn, strain; tune, chorus, refrain, round; duo, trio, quartet; passage, movement, phrase.

adj. musical, tuneful, pleasing; vocal, choral; scored, arranged, adapted.

vb. compose, write, set to music, arrange, score; perform, render, play, make music, interpret; sing, chant, croon; listen.

793 musician

n. musician, artist, player, performer, virtuoso, soloist, instrumentalist, concert artist; singer, vocalist, chorister, bard, minstrel, artiste, choir, chorus, singing group; orchestra, band, ensemble, symphony orchestra, chamber orchestra; group; dancer, ballerina; composer.

794 musical instrument

n. musical instrument, brass, woodwind, stringed instruments, percussion; record player, gramophone, stereo, hifi, music centre, stereogram, juke-box; record, disc, single, LP; tape-recorder, cassette-recorder; recording tape.

795 hearing

n. hearing, sense of hearing; good hearing, an ear for; earshot, range, carrying distance, sound; listening, auscultation; eavesdropping, wiretapping.

listener, hearer, auditor, witness; eavesdropper, wire-tapper, peeping Tom; audience, auditorium; audition, interview, reception.

adj. auditory, hearing, auricular.

vb. hear, listen to, catch, take in, pick up, lend an ear, be all ears, give a hearing to, hark; attend to, pay attention to; perceive, detect, get wind of; overhear, listen in, eavesdrop, tap, bug.

796 deafness

n. deafness, inaudibility, deaf-and-dumbness, deaf-mutism; lip reading, deaf-and-dumb alphabet, deaf-and-dumb language, dactylology.

adj. deaf, hard of hearing, stonedeaf, deaf-and-dumb, deaf-mute; deafening, stunning, ear-splitting; deaf to, unaware of.

vb. deafen, stun.

797 light

n. light, illumination, lighting, radiance, brilliance, splendour, brightness, clearness, lightness; luminosity, phosphorescence.

beam, ray, gleam, shaft, streak, laser, pencil, stream, glint, chink; flash,

streak, blaze, flame, flare, glow, spark, sparkle, twinkle, flicker, glimmer, glitter, dazzle, shimmer; glare, gloss, shine, lustre; polish, reflection; daylight, sunshine; sunrise, daybreak, dawn.

adj. luminous, light, bright, clear, shining, brilliant, beaming, glowing, glittering, sparkling, gleaming, dazzling; shiny, glossy, sheeny; illuminated, lighted, lit; cloudless.

vb. shine, burn, glow, blaze, glitter, glimmer, glisten, gleam, sparkle, dazzle, blind; flash, shimmer, flicker, twinkle, scintillate, blink, flare, beam; dance, play, reflect, glare.

illuminate, switch on, lighten, brighten, enlighten, dawn, shed light on, light up, irradiate; polish, burnish.

798 darkness

n. darkness, dark, night, nightfall, Cimmerian gloom, blackness, blackout, eclipse, shade, shadow, umbra, penumbra, adumbration, obscuration; gloom, sombreness.

adj. dark, unlit, unlighted, unilluminated; black, starless, dull, overcast, cloudy; indistinct, obscure, shady, nebulous, shaded, shadowy; tenebrous, obfuscous; dismal, gloomy, sombre, dreary, bleak, desolate, murky, dim.

vb. darken, blacken, black out, switch off, cover, eclipse, obscure, overshadow, becloud, place in shadow, cast a shadow over, obfuscate, adumbrate.

799 dimness

n. dimness, murkiness, shadiness, obscurity; dusk, twilight, half-light, gloaming, gloom.

adj. dim, dull, faint, vague, indistinct, obscure, blurred, opaque, fading, evanescent; grey, cloudy, foggy, hazy, misty, shadowy, gloomy.

vb. dim, dull, fade out, blur, obscure, shade, becloud, cloud over, dull, vanish, wane, evanesce.

800 source of light

n. light, luminary, sun, moon, planet, star, halo, aurora, corona, nimbus; meteor, shooting star; lightning, flash; fireworks.

lamp, torch, bulb, spotlight, searchlight, flashlight, floodlight, headlamp, side-light, indicator; neon light, fluorescent tube, strobe light, lantern; beacon, lighthouse.

candle, wick, spill, taper, wax; match, flame, flare; coal, ember, brand.

801 shade

n. shade, covering, veil, shield, screen, blind, curtain, shutter, drape; sunglasses, blinkers, goggles; visor, hood; shelter, awning, canopy; umbrella, parasol.

adj. shady; screened.

vb. shade, cover, veil, screen, shield, shelter, protect, curtain, blinker.

see also 463, 593

802 transparency

n. transparency, clearness, glassiness, vitreosity, translucence, lucidity.

adj. transparent, translucent, clear, see-through, revealing, unobstructed, glassy, vitreous, crystal, lucid, diaphanous, pellucid, limpid.

vb. be transparent, see through, show, show through.

see also 502

803 opacity

n. opacity, opaqueness, cloudiness, murkiness, obscurity, darkness; smoke, mist, cloud, film.

adj. opaque, non-transparent, absorbing light, impervious, dark, unclear, smoky, misty, cloudy, muddy, blurred,

filmy, dull, murky, dim, darkened, turbid.

vb. make opaque, devitrify, obscure, darken, cloud, smoke, obstruct one's vision.

see also 503

804 semitransparency

n. semitransparency, translucence, pearliness, milkiness; smoked glass, frosted glass, opal glass; dark glasses, sunglasses.

adj. semitransparent, semitranslucid, semiopaque, frosted, pearly, smoked, milky.

805 colour

n. colour, hue, shade, tinge, tone, dash, touch, tint, tincture, cast; paint, pigment, dye, wash, stain, lake; prism, spectrum; glow, brilliance, warmth, intensity; coloration, colouring, pigmentation, complexion, chromatism.

adj. coloured, chromatic, tinted, tinged, touched, dyed, painted, stained; constant, fast.

colourful, bright, warm, glowing, intense, strong, deep, rich, brilliant; garish, glaring, gaudy, loud, showy, flashy, lurid, harsh, clashing, painful.

soft, pastel, subdued, refined, tender, delicate, matt; faded, dingy, dull, drab, cold, uninviting.

vb. colour, shade, tinge, paint, touch up, stain, wash, coat, put on, lay on; contrast, set off, throw into relief; clash, not go with, conflict, grate.

806 absence of colour

n. colourlessness, achromatism, discoloration, fading, paleness, dullness, dimness, faintness, flatness; anaemia, sallowness, whitening, bleaching.

adj. colourless, hueless, toneless, lacklustre, dull, lifeless, cold, dim, faint, weak; faded, washed out, pale, pallid, sallow, ashen, white, anaemic, pasty; transparent.

vb. fade, lose colour, lose brightness, bleach, blanch, wash out, whiten, drain, turn pale, discolour, grow dim, etiolate.

807 white
n. white, whiteness, whitishness, lightness, fairness, paleness; milkiness, chalkiness, silveriness, snowiness.

adj. white, fair, light, blonde, hoary; snowy, snow-white, frosted, milky, lactescent, chalky, silvery, pearly, ivory, albescent; whitish, cream, off-white; pale, ashen, anaemic, sallow, wan; clean, spotless, pure.

vb. whiten, whitewash, bleach, blanch, snow; clean, purify.

808 black
n. black, blackness, darkness, inkiness, sootiness.

adj. black, blackish; jet-black, pitch-black, coal-black; inky, sooty, stained; dark, murky; sable, swarthy.

vb. blacken, ink, ink in, darken, shade.

809 grey
n. grey, greyness, dinginess, drabness, dusk, shade.

adj. grey, greyish, shaded, dull, drab, dingy, sombre, neutral; dusty, smoky; silver-haired, hoary; speckled, pepper-and-salt.

810 brown
n. brown, tan, beige, mahogany.

adj. brown, brownish, beige, khaki, maroon, auburn, buff, bronze, copper, chocolate, coffee, rust-coloured, reddish-brown, bay, chestnut, russet, sepia, ochre, hazel.

811 red
n. red, redness, blush, glow, colour, cochineal, carmine.

adj. red, reddish, ruddy, scarlet, crimson, vermilion, ruby, cherry-red, blood-red, coral, brick-red, maroon, rust, magenta, russet, auburn, pink, salmon-pink, rosy; glowing, warm; blushing, embarrassed, burning.

vb. redden, blush; glow, flush.

812 green
n. green, verdure; lawn, turf.

adj. green, greenish, grassy, verdant, leafy, lime, emerald, sage, olive, beryl, blue-green, aquamarine, sea-green, pea-green; bilious, sickly, pale; fresh, unripe.

813 yellow
n. yellow, cream, tan, lemon; buttercup, daffodil, crocus, jasmine.

adj. yellow, yellowish, cream, saffron, sand, gold, golden, buff, tan, khaki, light-brown; sallow, bilious, jaundiced.

814 purple
n. purple; violet, pansy, lavender.

adj. purple, purplish, reddish-blue, bluish-red, violet, indigo, mauve, lilac, lavender, plum-coloured.

815 blue
n. blue, sky, azure, indigo.

adj. blue, bluish, turquoise, azure, royal blue, navy blue; sapphire, sky-blue, indigo.

816 orange
n. orange, tangerine, apricot, peach, mandarin, carrot, salmon, coral.

adj. orange, orangey, reddish-yellow, gold, old gold, copper, bronze, brass, ginger.

817 variegation
n. variegation, diversification, diversity, motley, spectrum, rainbow,

kaleidoscope; chequerwork, tartan, mosaic, parquetry, marquetry.

adj. variegated, kaleidoscopic, many-coloured, multi-coloured; spotted, mottled, motley, patched, piebald, pied, dappled, speckled, freckled; striped, streaked, checked.

vb. diversify, variegate, chequer, checker; stud, mottle, spatter, dapple, speckle, stipple, streak, strip.

818 vision

n. vision, sight, eyesight, perception, recognition; observation, inspection, scrutiny, investigation, notice, once-over (*inf.*); bird's eye view, survey, panorama, overview.

look, view, regard, glance, glimpse, eye; squint, peep, peek; leer; wink, twinkle.

viewpoint, standpoint, position, outlook, perspective, attitude; lookout, observation point, watch-tower, gallery, grandstand.

adj. visual, ocular, opthalmic, optical; observant; watchful, vigilant.

vb. see, look at, view, watch, look on, observe, perceive, discern, recognize, notice, catch sight of, set eyes on, eye; glance, glimpse, catch a glimpse of, peep; blink, wink, twinkle; gaze, gape, stare, fix one's eyes on; leer, ogle, glare, glower.

scrutinize, investigate, survey, inspect; scan, look through, look over, flick through (*inf.*), thumb through (*inf.*).

819 blindness

n. blindness, sightlessness, colour-blindness, night-blindness, snow-blindness; blind spot, blind side, failing, mote in one's eye.

adj. blind, sightless, unseeing, eyeless, colour-blind; blinded, blind-fold, blinkered, hoodwinked, in the dark.

vb. be blind, lose one's sight, strike blind, put someone's eyes out; obscure, hide, mask, screen, blindfold, blinker, hoodwink.

820 imperfect vision

n. imperfect vision, partial vision, shortsightedness, myopia; longsightedness, presbyopia; double vision; colour-blindness; squint, strabism, cross-eye, astigmatism, conjunctivitis, cataract.

adj. dim-sighted, purblind, half-blind; shortsighted, myopic; long-sighted, presbyopic; colour-blind, astigmatic, cross-eyed, squinting, strabismic.

vb. see double, squint, screw up one's eyes, see blurred.

821 spectator

n. spectator, viewer, onlooker, observer, watcher, eye-witness, bystander, passer-by, looker-on, beholder, sight-seer; peeper, peeping Tom; spy, snoop, meddler.

spectators, crowd, public, supporters, fans, followers, turn-out, audience.

822 optical instrument

n. glasses, spectacles, bifocals, goggles, specs (*inf.*), contact lenses, monocle, eye-glasses, lorgnette, pince-nez; binoculars, opera glasses, field glasses, telescope; microscope, magnifying glass, lens; camera; mirror, looking glass, reflector, glass, speculum.

823 visibility

n. visibility, perceptibility, clarity, distinctness, plainness, prominence, conspicuousness.

adj. visible, apparent, in view, in sight, observable, perceptible, noticeable, before one's very eyes; evident, clear, plain, obvious, patent; prominent, conspicuous, pronounced, standing out; unmistakable, glaring; open, exposed; distinct, well-defined, definite, clear-cut.

vb. show, show through, show itself, manifest itself, be revealed, come into sight, come into view; stand out, stand out a mile (*inf.*), stick out like a sore thumb (*sl.*), hit in the face, leap to the eye.

see also **458**, **825**

824 invisibility

n. invisibility, concealment, seclusion, latency, obscurity, indistinctness, imperceptibility, indefiniteness, vagueness, indiscernibility, cloudiness, darkness, haziness, fuzziness.

adj. invisible, imperceptible, indiscernible; hidden, out of sight, concealed, obscure; inconspicuous; indistinct, unclear, ill-defined, vague; intangible, unseen, spiritual; cloudy, nebulous, shadowy, mysterious, hazy, blurred, fuzzy.

see also **461**, **826**

825 appearance

n. appearance, look, aspect, feature, shape, form, outline, profile, face; condition, presentation, expression; posture, pose, bearing; mien, countenance, manner, behaviour; externals, appearances, outward show, first impression, face value.

phenomenon, spectacle, display, exhibition, show, demonstration, scene, parade, pageant.

adj. apparent, visible, manifest; seeming, ostensible, supposed, specious, plausible, alleged, outward, superficial, external, to look at (*inf.*).

vb. appear, look, seem, show, take

the form of; emerge, arise, come into view, be revealed, turn up, show up, put in an appearance, crop up (*inf.*), pop up (*inf.*), occur, happen, present itself, express itself, manifest itself, materialize, come to light, come into the picture, come onto the horizon, see the light of day.

adv. apparently, to all appearances, superficially, at first sight, on the face of it, for show, to all intents and purposes.

see also **222**, **458**, **823**

826 disappearance

n. disappearance, vanishing, fading, fade-out, evanescence, evaporation, dematerialization; departure, retirement, flight, escape, removal, withdrawal, loss.

adj. disappearing, fading, evanescent; disappeared, vanished, missing.

vb. disappear, vanish, fade, evaporate, dematerialize, dissolve; pass out of sight, leave no trace, disappear into thin air, go up in smoke, vanish from sight, be eclipsed, be swallowed up, be lost to view.

go away, depart, remove, withdraw, retire, escape, flee; cease, be no more, die, perish, sink.

see also **824**

C Personal

827 pleasure

n. pleasure, joy, happiness, gladness, delight, enjoyment, satisfaction, fulfilment; serenity.

enchantment, bewitchment, exultation, relish, gusto, zest, glee, cheer, thrill, kick (*inf.*), ecstasy, elation, bliss, rapture, euphoria, transport; luxury, ease, convenience, comfort, paradise, bed of roses, golden age, halcyon days, lap of luxury.

gratification, indulgence, self-indulgence, revelry, hedonism, sensuousness, sensuality, sexuality.

adj. pleasant, satisfying, enjoyable, delightful, exciting, adorable, welcome; comfortable, snug, cosy, homely, comfy (*inf.*), congenial, convenient, palatial, luxurious; gratifying, pleasurable, sensuous, bodily, physical, hedonistic, voluptuous, self-indulgent, carnal.

happy, pleased, joyful, glad, delighted, joyous, satisfied; thrilled, excited, tickled pink (*inf.*), exhilarated, starry-eyed, bubbling over, in the seventh heaven; smiling, laughing, genial, convivial, delirious; merry, in good spirits, cheery, jolly, blithe, gladsome, blissful; overjoyed, ecstatic, in ecstasies, enraptured, in raptures enthusiastic, carried away; peaceful, contented, at peace.

vb. enjoy, like, take delight in, derive pleasure from, rejoice in, love, fancy, be keen on, appreciate, relish, revel in, get a kick out of (*inf.*), rave about (*inf.*), enjoy oneself, have a good time, tread on air.

see also **829, 836, 840**

828 pain

n. pain, hurt, distress, discomfort, affliction, anguish, misery, agony, shock, blow, injury, suffering, unhappiness, sorrow, grief, sadness, regret, melancholy, despair, broken heart, weeping, wretchedness, tribulation, trial, ordeal, torment, torture, martyrdom, crucifixion, hell; bereavement, sense of loss, mourning, grieving; ache, twinge, pang, spasm, stitch, wound, sting, burn, illness, sickness.

worry, anxiety, heartache, vexation, fretting, uneasiness, discontent, disquiet, dissatisfaction; problem, care, burden.

sufferer, victim, prey, scapegoat, wretch, guinea pig.

adj. painful, hurtful, tormenting, excruciating, suffering, writhing, agonizing, harrowing; unpleasant, extreme, sharp, severe, grievous, sore, sensitive.

unfortunate, unhappy, sad, miserable, troubled, afflicted, heavy-laden, burdened, anxious, worried, vexed, uneasy; sorrowful, weeping, mournful, wretched, cut up (*inf.*), heart-broken.

vb. undergo, suffer, go through, bear, endure, put up with (*inf.*), persevere; ache, smart, throb, sting, burn; be tender, be sore, be bruised; regret, despair, mourn, weep.

see also **830**

829 pleasurableness

n. pleasurableness, pleasantness, niceness, enjoyableness, loveliness; charm, fascination, glamour, prestige, attractiveness, winsomeness, allurement.

delight, treat, surprise, amusement, fun, gift, joy, honeymoon, benefit, refreshment, titbit, feast, banquet, manna.

adj. pleasant, nice, enjoyable, agreeable, pleasing, lovely, charming, fascinating, attractive, beautiful, picturesque; glamorous, prestigious, appealing, enchanting, winsome, luring, seductive; delightful, exquisite, delicious, luscious, tasty.

vb. please, satisfy, delight, gladden, rejoice, thrill, gratify; turn on (*inf.*), turn on to (*inf.*), switch on (*inf.*), stimulate, excite; interest; attract, charm, enchant, enthrall, captivate, bewitch, enrapture; amuse, tickle, titillate.

see also **755, 827**

830 painfulness

n. painfulness, hurtfulness, unpleasantness, bitterness, disagreeableness; sorrow, pain, disappointment, irritation, annoyance, nuisance, difficulty, problem, care, burden, trouble, load, cross, concern, nightmare, bitter cup, bitter pill; embarrassment.

adj. unpleasant, disagreeable, bothersome, upsetting, disturbing, troublesome, annoying, irritating, trying, tiresome; distressing, awful, grim, shocking, appalling, tragic, extreme, dreadful.

vb. hurt, grieve, injure, wound, afflict, pain; distress, worry, trouble, outrage, bother, upset, disturb, annoy, irritate, vex, needle; torment, harass, pester, tease, pick on (*inf.*), have it in for (*inf.*); harrow, agonize, excruciate, crucify, martyr, torture, obsess, haunt, plague; lose sleep over (*inf.*); discomfort, put out, inconvenience.

see also **828, 893**

831 content

n. content, contentment, peace, peace of mind, happiness, satisfaction; self-satisfaction, complacency; ease, rest, comfort, serenity, solace.

adj. contented, content, pleased, peaceful, satisfied, happy, carefree, without cares, uncomplaining.

vb. be content, be satisfied, sit pretty, have one's wishes granted, have all that one could wish for, have nothing to worry about, have nothing to complain of, can't complain.

satisfy, gratify, indulge, suffice; go down well, put at ease; appease, reconcile.

832 discontent

n. discontent, dissatisfaction, unhappiness, sadness, depression, resentment, regret, unrest, uneasiness, tension, strain; grudge, chip on one's shoulder.

complainer, grumbler, fault-finder, grouch; reactionary, radical, protester, angry young man.

adj. discontented, unhappy, uneasy, restless, disgruntled, dissatisfied, cheesed off (*sl.*), browned off; grumbling, complaining, critical, hyper-critical, hard to please, never satisfied.

vb. be discontented, grumble, criticize, find fault, go on about, pick holes in (*inf.*), speak out against, moan; dissatisfy, disappoint, disconcert, disgruntle, discourage, dishearten.

833 regret

n. regret, sorrow, misgiving, compunction, scruple, qualm, pang of conscience, apology, repentance, change of heart, contrition, penitence, self-reproach, remorse, soul-searching.

adj. regretful, apologetic, penitent, humble, sorry, remorseful, contrite, repentant, broken, conscience-stricken.

vb. regret, apologize, be sorry for, cry over, repent, humble oneself, admit, own up, grieve, weep over, mourn, bewail, bemoan; rue.

834 relief

n. relief, alleviation, mitigation, assuagement; help, aid, comfort, consolation, relaxation, ease, load off one's mind; remedy, cure.

adj. relieving, easing, comforting, consoling, consolatory, soothing, comfortable, breathing easily.

vb. relieve, alleviate, mitigate, ease, soften, comfort, cushion, assuage, soothe, lighten, ease the strain, console, cheer up.

be relieved, feel better, recover; heave a sigh of relief, breathe again.

see also **176**

835 aggravation

n. aggravation, exacerbation, worsening, heightening, intensification, sharpening, deepening, strengthening, inflammation; annoyance, irritation, exasperation.

adj. aggravated, worsened, made worse, not improved.

vb. aggravate, worsen, exacerbate, make things worse, complicate, increase, magnify, multiply, heighten, intensify, deepen, go from bad to worse, get worse and worse; annoy, irritate.

836 cheerfulness

n. cheerfulness, good humour, happiness, gladness, joy; high spirits, vitality, animation, sparkle, liveliness, jollity, merriment, mirth, gaiety, glee; laughter, fun and games; light-heartedness, levity, breeziness; stoicism, stiff upper lip.

adj. cheerful, glad, happy, joyful; genial, animated, lively, in good humour, sparkling, vivacious, exuberant, full of beans (*inf.*), in high spirits, high-spirited, on top of the world, jolly, merry, gay, jovial, jocular, playful, sporty; light-hearted, perky, chirpy, breezy, carefree, debonair.

cheering, heartening, encouraging, inspiring, heartwarming.

vb. cheer, gladden, cheer up, perk up (*inf.*); brighten, encourage, comfort; enliven, animate, inspire, uplift, raise the spirits, warm the heart.

be cheerful, take heart, snap out of it (*inf.*); persevere, keep smiling (*inf.*), grin and bear it, keep one's chin up (*inf.*), keep a stiff upper lip, keep one's end up (*inf.*).

see also **827, 838**

837 dejection; seriousness

n. dejection, despondency, melancholy, sorrow, sadness, grief, depression, despair, gloom, misery, heaviness of spirit, low spirits, blues, dumps, doldrums, mopes, *weltschmerz*.

seriousness, earnestness, solemnity, gravity, sedateness, sobriety, coolness; dead pan (*inf.*), straight face.

adj. dejected, unhappy, despondent, downcast, sad, sorrowful, down-hearted, depressed, low, troubled, desolate, dispirited, broken-hearted, crushed, heart-broken, upset, cut up (*inf.*), discouraged, crestfallen, blue, down, moping, down in the mouth, down in the dumps, in the doldrums (*inf.*), out of sorts; melancholy, world-weary, careworn; gloomy, miserable, dismal, forlorn, doleful, wretched, cheerless, dull; suicidal, despairing.

serious, earnest, grave, sober, solemn; thoughtful, pensive; stern, strict; straight-faced, dead pan (*inf.*), expressionless.

vb. be dejected, lose heart; regret, grieve, mourn, sorrow; fret, brood, mope; languish, droop, wilt, pull a long face, beat one's breast.

sadden, oppress, break a person's heart, cut up (*inf.*), discourage, deject, depress, unnerve, dismay, demoralize, get down (*inf.*); cast down; drive to drink (*inf.*); dampen, pour cold water on.

be serious, keep a straight face, take life seriously, not see the joke.

see also **828, 839**

838 rejoicing

n. rejoicing, happiness, celebration, congratulation, jubilation, exultation, revelry, festivity, merrymaking, mirth, thanksgiving; cheers, shouts, hurrahs, applause; laughter, laugh, chuckle, chortle, giggle, snigger, cackle, titter, roar, guffaw; smile, grin, smirk, beam.

adj. rejoicing, jubilant, elated, exultant, rollicking.

vb. rejoice, be happy, sing for joy, leap for joy, dance, exult, celebrate, revel, have a party; clap one's hands, applaud, say thankyou to, congratulate.

laugh, chuckle, chortle, guffaw, giggle, titter, snigger; burst out laughing, roar, fall about laughing, double up with laughter, be convulsed with laughter, split one's sides, roll in the aisles (*inf.*), be in stitches (*inf.*); smile, beam, smirk, grin, twinkle; laugh at, ridicule, poke fun at, deride.

see also **840**, **842**

839 lamentation

n. lamentation, mourning, grief, sorrow, weeping, sobbing, tears, waterworks (*sl.*); cry, weep, good cry, sob, bawl, wail, whimper; lament, elegy, requiem, dirge, funeral oration.

adj. lamenting, sad, mournful; weeping, sobbing, in tears, tearful.

vb. lament, grieve, sorrow; cry, weep, burst into tears, break down, dissolve into tears, shed tears, turn on the waterworks (*sl.*), sob, cry one's eyes out (*inf.*), sob one's heart out (*inf.*), blubber, snivel, whimper, whine, howl, bawl, wail.

see also **837**

840 amusement

n. amusement, pleasure, fun, good time; leisure; hobby, pastime, diversion, relaxation, entertainment, recreation, sport, play, game; television, radio, cinema, concert, theatre; meal, picnic, party, barbecue, banquet,

feast; fete, fair, carnival, gala, fiesta, festivity; holiday, excursion, outing, pleasure trip, jaunt.

adj. entertaining, amusing, engaging, diverting, pleasant, witty; amused, entertained.

vb. amuse, entertain, delight, cheer, enliven, brighten up.

amuse oneself, enjoy oneself, relax, play games, go out, have fun, have a good time, let off steam (*inf.*), have a ball (*sl.*), let one's hair down (*inf.*), live it up (*inf.*), whoop it up (*inf.*), paint the town red (*sl.*), carouse, revel.

see also **614, 827, 842**

841 weariness

n. weariness, tiredness, exhaustion, fatigue, lassitude; tedium, boredom, apathy, listlessness, world-weariness, ennui, monotony, sameness, humdrum, the same old thing (*inf.*).

misery, wet blanket, drip; pain in the neck.

adj. wearisome, tiresome; tedious, boring, uninteresting, uninspiring, heavy, monotonous, dreary, flat, stale, repetitious, repetitive, soporific; tired, weary, exhausted, drowsy, jaded, worn out.

vb. weary, fatigue, tire, tire out, send to sleep, bore, exhaust, depress, leave cold; flag, droop.

see also **612, 617, 843**

842 wit

n. wit, wittiness, humour, joking, fun; jocularity, whimsicality, facetiousness, flippancy, drollery.

joke, witticism, repartee, pun, play on words, quip, jest, Spoonerism, *double entendre*, whimsy, sally, wisecrack, gag, funny story, shaggy-dog story, chestnut, aphorism, epigram; satire, sarcasm, irony; banter, burlesque, badinage.

humorist, comedian, joker, wag, life and soul of the party, jester, clown, buffoon, satirist.

adj. witty, humorous, funny, amusing, jocular, quick-witted, whimsical, quick, keen, lively, nimble; waggish; clownish; teasing, bantering.

vb. be witty, crack a joke, joke, jest, pun, bring the house down (*inf.*), sparkle, scintillate; tease, pull a person's leg, banter, rib (*inf.*), rag (*sl.*), make fun of, ridicule, kid (*sl.*).

843 dullness

n. dullness, heaviness, tediousness, mediocrity, insipidity, colourlessness, drabness, dreariness, tameness, flatness, dryness, stuffiness, slowness; familiarity, triteness, banality.

adj. dull, heavy, ponderous, tedious, boring, uninteresting, dry, stuffy, stodgy, sluggish, mediocre, flat, uninspired, lifeless, dead, drab, dreary, gloomy; long-winded, prosaic; conventional, stereotyped, common, commonplace, trite, banal, pointless.

844 beauty

n. beauty, elegance, attractiveness, good looks, loveliness, prettiness, fairness, handsomeness, shapeliness, pulchritude; glamour, grace, charm, appeal; magnificence, gloriousness, splendour, brilliance; beautification, face-lift, hair-dressing, adornment; cosmetics, make-up; plastic surgery.

good looker, smasher (*inf.*), stunner (*inf.*), belle, raving beauty, peach (*sl.*), pin-up (*inf.*), dream, Venus; ornament, masterpiece, showpiece.

adj. beautiful, attractive, good-looking, lovely, pretty, swell (*inf.*), smashing (*inf.*), glamorous, fair, handsome, appealing, pleasing, sightly, graceful, elegant, refined, comely, char-

ming; shapely, well-formed, well-proportioned.

splendid, magnificent, brilliant, wonderful, glorious, marvellous, gorgeous, grand, fine, resplendent, excellent, impressive, exquisite.

vb. beautify, improve the appearance of, pretty up (*inf.*), doll up (*inf.*), tart up (*sl.*), dress up (*inf.*), adorn, decorate, ornament, trim, embellish.

see also **579, 846**

845 ugliness

n. ugliness, hideousness, unloveliness, uncomeliness, inelegance, disfigurement, offensiveness; mutilation, deformity, distortion.

eyesore, defacement, horror, mess, blemish, blot, graffiti, slum.

adj. ugly, hideous, inelegant, unbecoming, unprepossessing; frightful, horrid, shocking, offensive; unlovely, unseemly, uncomely; disfigured, deformed, misshapen, monstrous, grotesque.

vb. make ugly, disfigure, deface, distort, mutilate.

see also **245**

846 ornamentation

n. ornamentation, decoration, adornment, embellishment, enhancement, trimming, frill, foil; embroidery, needlework; illumination, lettering, illustration; jewellery, jewel, gem, stone, precious stone; tinsel, ribbon, lace, gilt, tassel, bunting.

adj. ornamental, decorative, adorning, embellishing, garnishing, cosmetic; florid, dressy, ornate, fancy, gaudy, garish.

vb. decorate, adorn, beautify, enhance, brighten up, embellish, garnish, embroider, deck, bedeck, gild, festoon, array, set off.

see also **509, 844**

847 blemish

n. blemish, defect, flaw, stain, smudge, blot, blur, taint, daub, spot, speck, smirch, blotch, tarnish, rust, stigma, dent, impurity, disfigurement, deformity.

adj. blemished, spoilt, disfigured, defective, imperfect.

vb. blemish, stain, smudge, blot, daub, smear, smirch, tarnish, sully, soil, spoil, mar, damage, deface, disfigure.

see also **582, 845**

848 good taste

n. good taste, refinement, tastefulness, elegance, grace, polish; discrimination, good judgment, culture, sophistication; decorum, decency, soberness, seemliness, properness, restraint, simplicity, delicacy, daintiness.

good judge, connoisseur, expert, critic, gourmand, *bon vivant*.

adj. tasteful, in good taste, refined, polished, elegant, dignified, graceful, delicate; decent, sober, becoming, seemly, proper, simple, aesthetic; cultured, discriminating, sophisticated, cultivated.

see also **510**

849 bad taste

n. bad taste, tastelessness; vulgarity, coarseness, rudeness, barbarism; pretension, artificiality; showiness, gaudiness; ugliness, unloveliness, hideousness; dowdiness, unfashionableness; cad, bounder (*sl.*).

adj. tasteless, in bad taste, unrefined, unpolished; vulgar, coarse, rude, gross, crass, uncouth; pretentious, artificial,

florid, ostentatious, flashy, showy; inelegant, ugly, unsightly, unlovely; dull, tawdry, shoddy, low, common, plebeian.

see also **511**

850 fashion

n. fashion, style, mode, trend; new look, latest style, the latest; fad, craze, rage, all the rage, the last word; society, high society, set, right people; upper cut, upper crust.

adj. fashionable, stylish, trendy, latest, in fashion, in vogue, in (*inf.*), all the rage (*inf.*), modern, up-to-the-minute.

vb. catch on (*inf.*), become popular, grow in popularity, find favour; jump on the bandwagon (*inf.*), follow the crowd.

851 ridiculousness

n. ridiculousness, ludicrousness, funniness, outrageousness, absurdity.

adj. ridiculous, funny, comic, droll, amusing, hilarious, farcical, whimsical, side-splitting, too funny for words, rich, priceless (*sl.*), killing (*sl.*), absurd, ludicrous, preposterous, outrageous, fantastic.

vb. be ridiculous; laugh; bring the house down (*inf.*); play the fool, look silly.

see also **853**

852 affectation

n. affectation, pretentiousness, pretense; artificiality, unnaturalness; show, sham, foppery, put-on (*sl.*), play-acting, front, façade, act, airs, airs and graces.

pretender, actor; play-actor; charlatan, impostor, humbug, dandy, fop.

adj. affected, pretentious, put-on, tongue in cheek, pretended, assumed, artificial, unnatural, theatrical; showy, for effect; awkward; superficial, shallow, hollow; insincere.

vb. be affected, pretend, assume, put on, feign, simulate, act out the part of, pose, fake, sham, go through the motions of; talk big; put up a front.

853 ridicule

n. ridicule, mockery, contempt, scorn, disdain, derision, sneering, jeering, scoffing; satire, parody, caricature, burlesque; irony, sarcasm.

laughing-stock, target, victim, butt, dupe, fool.

adj. derisory, contemptuous; scoffing; ironical.

vb. ridicule, mock, laugh at, deride, sneer, jeer, scoff, revile, gibe; boo, hiss, hoot; pour scorn on, run down, make fun of, pull a person's leg; banter, taunt; laugh on the other side of one's face (*inf.*); parody, caricature, satirize.

see also 924

854 hope

n. hope, faith, trust, reliance, confidence, assurance; promise; expectation, anticipation; aspiration, dream, vision, pipe-dream, desire, wish, longing, yearning, ambition; optimism, cheerfulness, high hopes; false optimism, wishful thinking, pious hopes, fool's paradise.

hoper, aspirant, competitor, candidate, optimist, idealist.

adj. hoping, trusting, expecting, hopeful, assured, expectant, optimistic, relying on, confident, sanguine, bold, fearless, ambitious; promising, auspicious, favourable.

vb. hope, trust, believe, have faith in, rely, rest on, depend, lean on, bank on, rest assured, expect, anticipate; aspire, dream, wish, desire, long for, yearn for, contemplate; look on the bright side, see things through rose-coloured spectacles.

raise one's hopes, inspire, promise, lead one to expect, have the makings of, show signs of promise, bid fair, bode well.

see also 420, 836

855 hopelessness

n. hopelessness, despair, desperation, despondency; irrevocability, irredeemability; defeatism, pessimism; pessimist, Job's comforter.

adj. hopeless, irrevocable, irredeemable, incurable, irreversible, beyond hope, vain, to no avail, futile; unfortunate, bad, disastrous, impossible, helpless, lost, gone; pessimistic, defeatist.

vb. despair, lose heart, give up hope, abandon all hope, give up; dash one's hopes.

see also 837

856 fear

n. fear, fright, terror, horror, dread, scare, tremor, panic, despair, alarm, blue funk (*sl.*), consternation, awe, trepidation; timidity, fearfulness, timorousness.

anxiety, hesitation, worry, concern, uneasiness; nervousness, apprehension, cold feet, butterflies (*inf.*), nerves, jitters (*inf.*), willies (*sl.*), heebie jeebies (*sl.*), cold sweat.

adj. afraid, frightened, terrified, dreading, scared, scared stiff, shocked, in awe, trembling, panicking, panic-stricken, startled, petrified, shrinking.

uneasy, worrying, anxious, troubled, bothered, disturbed, hesitant, timid, shy, timorous, cautious; nervous, apprehensive, fidgety, jittery (*inf.*), jumpy, edgy, on edge, tense.

terrible, frightful, awful, dreadful, horrifying, ghastly, atrocious, frightening, terrifying, appalling, harrowing, traumatic, inconceivable; disturbing, disquieting.

vb. fear, be afraid, panic; dread, shake, quiver, quake, cringe, tremble, shudder, one's knees be knocking, be scared out of one's wits, break out in a cold sweat; funk, shrink, flinch; go to pieces, crack up (*inf.*), break down.

frighten, scare, terrify, shock, startle, make one jump; intimidate; give cause for alarm, appal, petrify, frighten out of one's wits, make one's hair stand on end, make one's blood run cold; put the fear of God into (*inf.*); disturb, trouble, bother, concern, dismay, daunt, disquiet, unnerve, worry, torment.

see also **858**

857 courage

n. courage, valour, bravery, fearlessness, boldness, intrepidity, audacity, daring, fortitude; pluck, mettle, heart, backbone, guts (*inf.*), what it takes, stamina, staying power, spunk (*inf.*), grit (*inf.*); Dutch courage; gallantry, chivalry, heroism, prowess, manliness, self-reliance, resolution, determination, firmness, strength; enterprise, initiative.

brave person, hero, heroine, stalwart.

adj. courageous, brave, valiant, bold, confident, fearless, intrepid, audacious, daring, dauntless, undaunted, unflinching; determined, resolute, strong, tough; plucky, heroic, chivalrous, gallant; game; enterprising, adventuresome.

vb. be courageous, have what it takes; keep one's chin up (*inf.*); face, brave, encounter, confront, handle, look in the face, face up to, meet face

to face, take the bull by the horns; have the nerve to; make a stand, risk.

pluck up courage, take heart, summon, muster, nerve oneself.

hearten, encourage, strengthen, fortify, inspire, assure, boost.

see also **534, 535**

858 cowardice

n. cowardice, cowardliness, faint-heartedness, weakness, shrinking, funk, cold feet, weak knees, yellow streak; fear, apprehension; shyness, timidity.

coward, scaredy-cat (*inf.*), cry-baby; deserter, shirker, slacker; poltroon, dastard, sneak.

adj. cowardly, craven, faint-hearted, timid, shy, weak, weak-kneed, scared, lily-livered, yellow (*inf.*), chicken (*sl.*); dastardly, pusillanimous.

vb. lose one's courage, get cold feet, back out, chicken out (*inf.*), funk, shrink, quail, show the white feather.

859 rashness

n. rashness, temerity, imprudence, impulsiveness; hurriedness, overhastiness, carelessness, recklessness, foolhardiness; indiscretion; daring, presumption; flippancy, levity; daredevil, harum-scarum (*inf.*).

adj. rash, impulsive, impetuous, hurried, sudden, precipitous, overhasty, premature, breakneck, headlong, frenzied, furious; reckless, foolhardy, careless, thoughtless, imprudent, inconsiderate; headstrong, unthinking, heedless; wild, brash, illconsidered.

vb. be rash, stick one's neck out (*inf.*), jump to conclusions, rush to conclusions, play with fire, burn one's fingers, court danger, court disaster, ask for trouble (*inf.*), ask for it (*inf.*), fools rush in where angels fear to tread, throw caution to the winds, tempt providence.

see also **544, 613**

860 caution

n. caution, prudence, cautiousness, care, heed, alertness, vigilance, wariness, suspicion; discretion, circumspection, deliberation, forethought, precaution, presence of mind, foresight.

adj. cautious, watchful, wary, circumspect, careful, prudent, vigilant.

vb. be cautious, play safe, take precautions, take care, look out, provide for, look before one leaps, watch one's step.

861 desire

n. desire, wish, need, want; liking, fondness, fancy, weakness, predilection, inclination, urge, aspiration, ambition; ardour, longing, yearning, pining; nostalgia, homesickness; craze, frenzy, lust, covetousness.

hunger, thirst, ravenousness, craving, voracity, relish, appetite, famine, drought.

adj. desiring, wanting, wishing, liking, desirous, fond, inclined, partial, longing, yearning, pining, itching (*inf.*), dying; eager, keen, crazy, mad, keen, craving; covetous.

hungry, greedy, ravenous, starving, famished, voracious, dry, parched; unsatisfied; peckish (*inf.*).

vb. desire, want, wish, need; like, be fond of, enjoy, choose, fancy, take a fancy to, incline towards, love, take to, be sweet on, have a soft spot for, go for in a big way, set one's heart on (*inf.*), set one's sights on, prize, esteem; aspire, dream; long for, crave, yearn, pine, hanker, make one's mouth water, lust, covet; relish.

be hungry, hunger, starve, famish; be thirsty, be dry, thirst.

see also **889**

862 dislike

n. dislike, distaste, disinclination, dissatisfaction; hate, hatred, loathing, aversion, repugnance.

adj. disliking, disinclined, averse to, loath to, fed up with, allergic, squeamish.

disliked, objectionable, repugnant, loathsome, abhorrent, abominable, disagreeable, unpopular.

vb. dislike, not feel like, not care for, hate, loathe, detest, not take kindly to, have nothing to do with, avoid, turn up one's nose at (*inf.*), not go for, not stomach.

see also **892**

863 indifference

n. indifference, unconcern, apathy, coldness, insensitivity, neutrality; half-heartedness, lukewarmness; unambitiousness.

adj. indifferent, cold, neutral; lukewarm, half-hearted; unconcerned, impassive, dispassionate, unresponsive, unmoved, uninvolved, lackadaisical, listless, inattentive; isolated, uncommunicative.

vb. be indifferent, not mind, not care, not care less, not give a damn (*inf.*), take no interest in, not matter, be all the same to, leave one cold; take it or leave it.

see also **754**

864 fastidiousness

n. fastidiousness, fussiness, meticulousness, scrupulousness, punctiliousness, pedantry, conscientiousness; perfectionism, idealism.

perfectionist, idealist, stickler, purist, pedant; fuss-pot (*inf.*).

adj. fastidious, particular, exact, precise, meticulous, exacting, scrupulous, rigorous, choosy (*inf.*), discriminating, selective, squeamish, finicky, pernickety (*inf.*), over-scrupulous, overparticular, overprecise, hypercritical; hard to please; pedantic; delicate, nice.

vb. be fastidious, fuss, be hard to please, split hairs, pick and choose; make a fuss about, make a song and dance about (*inf.*).

865 satiety

n. satiety, repletion, saturation, fill, surfeit, glut, plethora, jadedness, too much of a good thing.

adj. sated, satiated, replete, gorged, glutted, cloyed, overfull, overflowing; full, satisfied.

vb. satiate, fill, surfeit, glut, gorge, stuff, cloy, overfill, overfeed, satisfy, gratify; have one's fill, have enough.

866 wonder

n. wonder, surprise, amazement, awe, astonishment, bewilderment, fascination, stupefaction, incredulity.

sensation, miracle, sign, phenomenon, portent, spectacle, freak, marvel, drama, the unbelievable, prodigy, curiosity, oddity, rarity, something to write home about.

adj. surprising, amazing, astonishing, marvellous, fantastic, unbelievable, incredible, dramatic, remarkable, sensational, phenomenal, miraculous, stupendous, unprecedented, unparalleled, extraordinary, unusual, freakish, unique.

surprised, amazed, astonished, lost in wonder, bewildered, flabbergasted, spellbound, speechless, dumbfounded, thunderstruck, aghast.

vb. wonder, marvel, be surprised, be amazed, be taken aback, stare, gape, not believe, not get over.

amaze, astonish, surprise, bewilder, stupefy, dumbfound, flabbergast, overwhelm, take one's breath away.

867 absence of wonder

n. non-wonder, blankness; expectation; ordinariness, just as one thought, nothing much to write home about.

adj. unastonishing, expected, common, ordinary, usual; unamazed, unsurprised, unimpressed.

vb. not wonder, not be surprised, not bat an eyelid, not turn a hair; expect, take for granted, presume.

868 repute

n. repute, good standing, reputation, name, good name, renown, character, credit, respectability, reliability, trustworthiness, dependability; respect, favour, prestige, honour, glory, regard, kudos (*inf.*); fame, distinction, eminence, prominence, popularity; greatness, dignity, superiority, exaltation, majesty; rank, position, station, status.

big name, somebody, celebrity, star, dignitary, VIP, bigwig, big shot (*sl.*), grand old man.

adj. reputable, respectable, reliable, trustworthy, dependable, respected, well thought of, esteemed, acclaimed; renowned, of renown, famous, popular, celebrated, notable, leading, well-known; prestigious, honourable, distinguished, illustrious, eminent, prominent.

dignified, noble, great, grand, superior, high, exalted, elevated, sublime, majestic.

vb. be somebody, have a name, leave one's mark, make a name for oneself, go down in history.

honour, regard, respect, esteem, hold in high regard, admire, revere, praise, worship; exalt, glorify, crown, enthrone, ennoble, knight, immortalize.

869 disrepute

n. disrepute, disfavour, dishonour, ill-repute, bad name, bad character, unreliability, poor reputation; notoriety, infamy; disgrace, disrespect, reproach, shame, humiliation, degradation, abasement, ignominy, contempt.

scandal, gossip, backbiting, slander, calumny, defamation; slur, slight, insult, stain, stigma, brand, blot.

adj. disreputable, dishonourable, discreditable, ignominious; humiliating, lowering, degrading; notorious, infamous, shady, questionable; disgraceful, scandalous, shameful, outrageous, shocking, contemptible, despicable, corrupt, offensive, flagrant, base, mean, low, shabby, shoddy.

disgraced, humiliated, unable to show one's face.

undistinguished, obscure, unknown, unheard of, unrenowned.

vb. disgrace oneself, lose one's reputation, lose face, lapse from grace, fall from grace, fade; condescend, stoop, descend, lower oneself.

put to shame, disgrace, discredit, dishonour, expose, mock, show up; ridicule, embarrass, humiliate, humble; debase, degrade, snub, confound, unfrock; stain, tarnish, smear, sully, blot; take down a peg or two (*inf.*), cut down to size (*inf.*), drag through the mire (*inf.*).

870 nobility

n. nobility, dignity, grandeur, greatness, distinction, eminence; rank,

descent, birth, blood, high birth, blue blood; royalty, majesty, court; aristocracy, gentry, landed gentry, peerage, ruling class, privileged class, elite, gentility; society, high society, upper classes, upper ten thousand, upper crust (*inf.*), higher-ups (*inf.*).

nobleman; peer, peeress; archbishop; duke, duchess; marquis, marchioness; earl; count, countess; viscount, viscountess; bishop; baron, baroness; lord, lady; baronet; knight, dame; life peer; dowager.

adj. noble, dignified, grand, great, magnificent, lofty, imposing, distinguished; royal, majestic, monarchic, regal, reigning, princely; aristocratic, courtly, titled, lordly; highborn, of gentle birth, born in the purple.

871 common people

n. commonalty, common people, commons; people, the masses, general public, rank and file, grass roots; bourgeoisie, middle class; working class, lower class, have-nots, underdogs, proletariat; rabble, crowd, herd, riffraff, *hoi polloi*, ragtag and bobtail, the great unwashed, scum, dregs.

commoner, plebeian, citizen, civilian, man in the street, Mr. Average; countryman, rustic, yokel, country bumpkin, peasant, serf.

adj. common, plebeian, bourgeois, ordinary, average, lowly, humble, of low estate, mean, ignoble; rustic.

872 title

n. title, name, designation; courtesy title, handle (*inf.*), honorific; order, privilege, honour; decoration, ribbon, medal, crest, emblem.

873 pride

n. pride, self-respect, self-regard, self-esteem, dignity, self-love; conceit, vanity, haughtiness, vainglory; self-exaltation, self-glorification; ego-trip; arrogance, insolence.

proud person, bighead (*inf.*), swank (*inf.*), boaster, bragger.

adj. self-respecting, pleased with oneself, self-assured, self-satisfied; dignified, lofty, stately, elevated, high-falutin; egotistic, conceited, bigheaded (*inf.*), patronizing.

vb. be proud, hold one's head high; take pride in, pride oneself on, glory in, boast.

see also 875

874 humility

n. humility, humbleness, self-abasement, self-effacement; submission, obedience, meekness, lowliness, modesty, subservience, subjection; unobtrusiveness.

humiliation; abasement; mortification; come-down (*inf.*), let-down (*inf.*), deflation, crushing, shame.

adj. humble, lowly, meek, submissive, modest, self-effacing, subservient, servile; unassuming, unpretentious; humiliated, humbled, let down (*inf.*), deflated, squashed, crushed, crestfallen, chastened; embarrassed, ashamed.

vb. humble oneself, submit, obey; condescend, stoop, deign; eat humble pie, come down from one's high horse; be humiliated, not dare show one's face, feel small, feel squashed.

humiliate, humble, shame, embarrass, deflate, crush, squash, let down (*inf.*), bring low, put to shame, disconcert, make one feel small, take down a peg or two (*inf.*), teach one his place, reduce to tears.

see also 881

875 vanity

n. vanity, conceit, self-importance, self-glorification, egotism, vainglory,

self-applause, boastfulness; self-worship, narcissism; show, ostentation, exhibitionism; futility, emptiness, uselessness.

egotist, show-off, exhibitionist, know-all, smart aleck (*inf.*), toffee-nose (*sl.*), Narcissus.

adj. vain, conceited, haughty, self-centred, self-important, self-glorifying, self-applauding, full of oneself, boastful, cocky, swollen-headed, stuck up (*inf.*), puffed up, too big for one's boots (*sl.*), swanky (*inf.*), snooty (*inf.*), high and mighty (*inf.*), pompous, arrogant, insolent, supercilious, pretentious, snobbish, toffee-nose (*sl.*), stand-offish; showy, exhibitionist.

vb. be vain, be puffed up, get too big for one's boots (*sl.*), have a high opinion of oneself, think too much of oneself, come the high and mighty with (*inf.*), know it all, boast, show off; turn up one's nose at (*inf.*); go to one's head, puff up.

see also 879

876 modesty; shyness

n. modesty, unassumingness, unpretentiousness, unobtrusiveness, restraint, meekness, retiring nature; chastity, purity, virtue.

shyness, timidity, bashfulness, reserve, reticence, coyness; inhibition, nervousness.

adj. modest, retiring, restrained, meek, unassuming, unobtrusive, diffident, shrinking; restrained, tasteful, undecorated; chaste, pure, innocent.

shy, timid, bashful, quiet, reserved, coy, reticent, reluctant, backward, inhibited, secretive, demure, proper; blushing, embarrassed, red.

vb. hold back, hide one's face, keep in the background, take a back seat, hide one's light under a bushel, retire into one's shell; blush, go red.

877 ostentation

n. ostentation, exhibitionism, showiness, pretension; pomp, pompousness, magnificence, splendour, grandeur, majesty, pageantry; blatancy, flagrancy, flashiness, gaudiness, loudness; flourish, parade, fuss, splurge, showing off; bravado, histrionics, theatricality, sensationalism, effect, showmanship; exhibitionist, show-off, showman.

adj. ostentatious, showing off, proud, pompous, grandiose, extravagant, bombastic, high-flown, fancy, jazzy, showy, garish, gaudy, flashy, flamboyant, flaunting, blatant, flagrant, obtrusive, conspicuous, loud, screaming; spectacular, sensational, theatrical, histrionic, for effect, for show.

vb. show off, flaunt, parade, flourish, splurge, play to the gallery, do for show, make an exhibition of oneself, give oneself airs; sensationalize.

878 celebration

n. celebration, commemoration, honouring, keeping, observance; anniversary, jubilee, birthday, red-letter day, centenary, bicentenary, tercentenary, ceremonial; solemnization; ceremony, function, occasion, festive occasion, do (*inf.*); clapping, applause, praise, acclaim, cheers, hurrahs, cries, ovation, standing ovation, salute.

adj. celebrative, commemorative, anniversary, congratulatory, ceremonial, festive.

vb. celebrate, commemorate, observe, keep, remember,˙ honour, congratulate, crown; throw a party, make merry, kill the fatted calf.

879 boasting

n. boasting, self-glory, self-glorification; boast, brag, empty talk, big talk, hot air, bombast, bluster, braggadocio, gasconade.

boaster, big mouth, swank (*inf.*), gas-bag (*sl.*), braggart, Gascon.

adj. boastful, bragging, big-mouthed, pretentious, inflated, self-glorifying, vaunting.

vb. boast, vaunt, brag, show off, talk big, bounce, exaggerate; blow one's own trumpet, have a high opinion of oneself, pat oneself on the back, congratulate oneself, flatter oneself.

880 insolence

n. insolence, rudeness, boldness, audacity, effrontery, impudence, impertinence, arrogance, presumption, forwardness, shamelessness, officiousness, sauciness, defiance, lip (*sl.*), cheek, nerve (*inf.*), sauce, brass.

upstart, wise guy (*sl.*), pup.

adj. insolent, impudent, impertinent, arrogant, high-handed, disrespectful, insulting, rude, offensive, officious, outrageous, defiant, cheeky, saucy, uppity (*inf.*); presumptious, forward.

vb. be insolent, have the cheek, have a nerve (*inf.*), get fresh, come the high and mighty with (*inf.*), get on one's high horse (*inf.*), throw one's weight about (*inf.*); give lip (*sl.*), brazen it out, answer back, presume, take for granted.

881 servility

n. servility, obsequiousness, meniality, sycophancy, toadyism; sycophant, toady, back-scratcher, yes-man, sponger, parasite, hanger-on, boot-licker.

adj. servile, menial, beggarly, slavish, subservient, obsequious, cringing, toadyish, boot-licking, ingratiating, fawning, grovelling, snivelling.

vb. be servile, suck up to (*sl.*), crawl (*inf.*), grovel, go down on one's knees, lick the boots of, ingratiate oneself with, toady, fawn, curry favour; flatter.

D Sympathetic

882 friendship

n. friendship, companionship, amity, comradeship, fraternity, intimacy, familiarity; friendliness, affection, amicability, sociability, good terms, neighbourliness, understanding, compatibility, matiness, warmth, cordiality.

friend, companion, mate, pal, chum, buddy, comrade; boy-friend, girl-friend; acquaintance, neighbour; close friend, best friend, bosom friend, confidant, intimate.

adj. friendly, close, familiar, intimate, inseparable, confiding; faithful, loyal, devoted, true, trusted, staunch, firm; amicable, sympathetic, compatible, sociable, affectionate, warm-hearted, brotherly, matey, pally; kind, benevolent.

vb. be friendly, know, be acquainted with, be on good terms with; befriend, get to know, make friends with, get in with (*inf.*), get pally with, chum up with, break the ice; go out with (*inf.*), go with, knock about with (*inf.*), go around with, keep company with, go together, see (*inf.*), run after (*inf.*), go after (*inf.*), chase, try to get, take out, accompany, court, woo, make advances; be just good friends.

see also **889**

883 enmity

n. enmity, hostility, inimicality; antipathy, unfriendliness; hatred, antagonism, dislike, repugnance, animosity; ill-feeling, hard feelings; separation, estrangement, alienation; bitterness, acrimony, coolness.

enemy, foe, antagonist, opponent, adversary, arch-enemy, invader; public enemy; rival, informer.

adj. inimical, hostile, antagonistic, unfriendly, ill-disposed, opposed; irreconcilable, alienated, estranged; at odds, at daggers drawn, at loggerheads, not on speaking terms, on bad terms; cool, cold, chilly, uncordial; opposite, contrary, conflicting; quarrelsome, unsympathetic, grudging, resentful.

vb. be opposed to, differ, be at odds with, conflict, clash; antagonize, provoke, alienate, estrange.

see also **637, 638**

884 sociability

n. sociability, geniality, friendliness, cordiality, gregariousness, conviviality, affability, hospitality, open house, social intercourse.

party, social, get-together, ball, meeting, reunion, rendezvous, reception, at home, soirée; visit, call, appointment, engagement, date, interview, stay; arrangement.

visitor, dropper-in, guest, caller; mixer, good mixer, life and soul of the party; gate-crasher, uninvited guest.

adj. sociable, friendly, genial, cordial, affable, gregarious, neighbourly, hospitable.

vb. be sociable, invite, welcome, receive, entertain, throw a party; keep open house; visit, drop in on, look in, call by.

885 unsociability

n. unsociability, unfriendliness, uncommunicativeness, shyness; distance, unapproachability, aloofness; seclusion, privacy, separateness, isolation, retirement, withdrawal, solitariness, loneliness; backwater, back of beyond, backwoods, refuge, retreat, cloister, ivory tower, shell, desert island.

recluse, hermit, monk, anchorite, backwoodsman; loner, stay-at-home; outcast, castaway; refugee, evacuee; outlaw, bandit; orphan, leper.

adj. unsociable, unfriendly, distant, shy, uncommunicative, unapproachable, aloof, stand-offish, antisocial, inhospitable; lonesome, solitary, lonely, friendless, desolate, retiring, withdrawn; secluded, forsaken, isolated, rustic, out-of-the-way, remote, God-forsaken, unexplored, uninhabited, deserted.

vb. be unsociable, stand aloof, keep oneself to oneself, keep one's distance, go into seclusion, shut oneself up, retire into one's shell; seclude, exclude, expel, excommunicate, repel, cold-shoulder, keep at arm's length, keep at bay, beat off.

886 courtesy

n. courtesy, thoughtfulness, consideration, politeness, manners, good manners, civility, culture, refinement, breeding, gentility, respect, kindness, friendliness, generosity, gallantry, chivalry; condescension, flattery, oiliness.

good turn, favour, compliment; greeting, handshake, smile, embrace, hug, kiss.

adj. courteous, polite, well-mannered, civil, amiable, affable, thoughtful, considerate, kind, friendly, generous, obliging; cultivated, cultured, refined, polished, well-bred; politic, diplomatic; gentlemanly, lady-like; gallant, chivalrous; condescending, obsequious, ingratiating, patronizing.

vb. be courteous, behave oneself, mind one's P's and Q's, be on one's best behaviour; give one's regards, give one's compliments, send best wishes, pay one's respects, compliment; greet, welcome, hail, exchange greetings, hold out one's hand, shake hands, smile, wave, hug, embrace, kiss.

887 discourtesy

n. discourtesy, impoliteness, bad manners, misbehaviour, incivility, ill breeding; disrespect, impudence, unfriendliness, brusqueness; meanness, nastiness, unpleasantness, rudeness, vulgarity, boorishness, coarseness, grossness, shamelessness.

adj. discourteous, impolite, bad-mannered, uncivil, uncultured, unrefined, unbecoming, misbehaved, ungentlemanly, rude, unfriendly, unkind, ungracious, unpleasant, nasty, obstreperous, disrespectful, offensive, crude, coarse, vulgar, shameless; loutish, rowdy, disorderly, boorish; thoughtless, careless, inconsiderate, tactless, gauche, outspoken; brusque, abrupt, curt, offhand, rough, gruff, surly, difficult; audacious, brash; cheeky, high-handed.

vb. be rude, insult, affront, outrage; give the cold shoulder; irritate, annoy, shout down, interrupt; snub, disregard, ignore.

888 congratulation

n. congratulation, felicitation, best wishes, compliments, happy returns; applause, appreciation, bouquet, praise, acknowledgement, toast.

adj. congratulatory, complimentary.

vb. congratulate, compliment, felicitate, pay one's respects, offer one's congratulations, salute, praise, honour, acclaim, sound the praises of, appreciate, admire, adulate; toast, celebrate; mob.

889 love

n. love, fondness, affection, attachment, devotion, adoration; passion, Eros, ardour, amorousness, lust, infatuation, crush (*sl.*), pash (*sl.*); first love, calf-love, puppy love; emotion, sentiment; attractiveness, charm, winsomeness, appeal, sex-appeal, fascination; love affair, affair, romance, liaison, relationship, flirtation, amour, eternal triangle.

lover, admirer, suitor, wooer, boy-friend, girl-friend, date (*inf.*), steady (*inf.*), blind date; Romeo, Juliet, fiancé, fiancée; mistress; cohabitant.

adj. loving, fond, affectionate, devoted, adoring, attached; emotional, sentimental, tender, soft; yearning, longing, passionate, ardent, amorous, glowing.

enamoured, attracted, enchanted, fascinated, caught, charmed, captivated, enraptured, taken with, sweet on, keen on, infatuated, gone on, crazy, wild, mad, smitten, in love, head over heels in love.

lovable, winsome, attractive, charming, appealing, captivating, irresistible, dear; loved, beloved, cherished.

vb. love, like, be fond of, care for, delight in, adore, fancy; treasure, hold dear, take to one's heart (*inf*), admire, regard, cherish, appreciate, esteem, value, prize; be in love, dote on, be enraptured by; fall in love, fall for, be crazy about, have it bad (*inf.*); lose one's heart to, have a crush on, be swept off one's feet (*inf.*), be infatuated with; long, yearn, copulate, have intercourse, make love to, have sex with (*inf.*), sleep with (*inf.*), sleep together (*inf.*), go to bed with, have it off with (*sl.*); live with, live together, cohabit, live in sin (*inf.*).

attract, appeal, fascinate, captivate, charm, enchant, allure, draw, rouse, enrapture, infatuate, sweep off one's feet (*inf.*).

see also **861, 882**

890 endearment

n. endearment, affection, attachment, fondness, love, soft nothings, embrace, kiss, cuddle, stroke, fondling, petting, necking (*sl.*); courtship, courting, wooing, pass, advance, dating, flirtation, amorous intentions; love-letter, Valentine; proposal, offer of marriage, engagement.

vb. woo, court, go out with (*inf.*), run after (*inf.*), pursue, chase, date, pay attentions to, make overtures, make advances, make passes, make eyes at (*inf*), ogle, flirt; propose, pop the question (*inf.*).

be fond of, cherish; embrace, hug, clasp, draw close, snuggle, kiss, cuddle; stroke, fondle, caress, pat, pet, neck, smooch (*inf.*).

see also **882**

891 darling; favourite

n. darling, dear, love, beloved, dearest, sweetheart, angel, pet, sweet, sweetie (*inf.*), sweetie-pie (*inf.*), sugar (*inf.*), honey (*inf.*), precious (*inf.*), treasure (*inf.*), jewel (*inf.*); favourite, mother's darling, teacher's pet, blue-eyed boy, apple of one's eye.

892 hate

n. hate, hatred, dislike, antipathy, aversion, loathing, abhorrence, repugnance, repulsion, disgust, scorn, detestation, nasty look.

anathema, abomination, menace, pest, *bête noire*, bitter pill.

adj. detestable, hateful, odious, abominable, abhorrent, loathsome, accursed, offensive, repugnant, disgusting, revolting, repulsive, vile; averse to, hostile, antagonistic.

vb. hate, dislike, loathe, abhor, detest, abominate, denounce, condemn, object to, spurn, spit upon, curse, reject, have it in for (*inf.*).

offend, rub up the wrong way, repel, disgust, shock, alienate, estrange, antagonize, make one's blood run cold.

see also 295, 862

893 resentment; anger

n. resentment, bitterness, hurt, soreness, malice, grudge, bone to pick; sore point.

anger, indignation, displeasure, antagonism; rage, fury, wrath, vehemence, passion, vexation, exasperation, annoyance, impatience, ire; bad temper, outburst, fit, tantrum, huff, tiff, quarrel, argument, fight.

adj. resentful, indignant, sore, hurt, grudging, bitter, embittered, with a chip on one's shoulder, acrimonious.

angry, cross, irate, furious, raging, fiery, mad (*inf.*), hopping mad (*inf.*), fuming, displeased; antagonized, enraged, exasperated, infuriated, annoyed, irritated, peeved (*sl.*), impatient, irritable, ratty (*sl.*), shirty (*sl.*), provoked, affronted, riled, vexed, worked up, het up (*inf.*), up in arms, in a huff, hot under the collar, foaming at the mouth (*inf.*).

vb. resent, feel bitter towards, take umbrage, take exception, be insulted, bear a grudge, bear malice, have a bone to pick.

get angry, get cross, lose one's temper, blow one's top (*inf.*), hit the

roof (*inf.*), fly off the handle (*inf.*), blow up (*inf.*), explode; get worked up, get het up (*inf.*), get hot under the collar, go up the wall (*inf.*), go off the deep end (*inf.*).

be angry, burn, roar, rage, rant and rave, fume, storm, boil, seethe, foam at the mouth (*inf.*); snap, bite someone's head off (*inf.*), jump down someone's throat (*inf.*); criticize, nag, get at.

anger, enrage, incense, infuriate, madden, antagonize, exasperate, provoke, bother, harass, vex, annoy, incite, irritate, needle, nettle, rankle, rile, stir, get someone's back up (*inf.*), get someone's blood up, make one's blood boil, send up the wall, rub up the wrong way (*inf.*), tread on someone's toes (*inf.*), get on someone's nerves, get under someone's skin, get someone's goat (*sl.*), upset, ruffle, discompose, put out.

see also 642

894 irritability

n. irritability, sensitivity, nervousness, uneasiness, exasperation, impatience, touchiness, bad temper.

adj. irritable, sensitive, susceptible, touchy, oversensitive, prickly, edgy, short-tempered, ratty (*sl.*), shirty (*sl.*), uptight, gruff, grumpy; nervous, anxious, jumpy, jittery (*inf.*); temperamental, moody; irritated, annoyed, needled, riled, rankled, nettled, rubbed up the wrong way, with a chip on one's shoulder; irascible, choleric, querulous, cantankerous.

895 sullenness

n. sullenness, moroseness, glumness, moodiness, unsociability, sourness, bad temper, gruffness, spleen; frown, scowl, grimace, sneer, dirty look (*inf.*), wry face.

adj. sullen, morose, glum, silent,

unsociable; moody, surly, grouchy, churlish, sulky, cross, mopish, ill-humoured, ill-natured, disagreeable, sour, mournful, saturnine; scowling, frowning; gloomy, dismal, sad, dim, dark, cheerless, sombre.

vb. scowl, frown, grimace, make a face, pull a face, glower, growl, sulk, grouch, mope, sneer.

896 marriage

n. marriage, matrimony, wedlock, conjugality, union, match, alliance, marriage tie, marriage bed; wedding, pledging, ceremony, nuptials, espousals; church wedding, civil marriage, registry-office wedding; elopement, abduction; shotgun wedding; reception, wedding breakfast, party, dance; honeymoon, consummation.

man and wife, bride and groom, bridal pair, newlyweds, honeymooners; partner, spouse, mate; husband; man; wife, helpmeet, better half (*inf.*), the missus (*sl.*).

adj. matrimonial, marital, nuptial, conjugal, married, wed, united, matched; newly-wed; honeymooning, going-away, marriageable, eligible, suitable, of marriageable age.

vb. marry, get married, wed, espouse, take to oneself, lead to the altar, plight one's troth, become one, get hitched (*sl.*), get spliced (*sl.*), make an honest woman of (*inf.*); honeymoon, go away, consummate; run away, leave home, elope; join, unite, pronounce man and wife, marry, give in marriage, give away; marry into, marry out of; marry off, match, matchmake, find a match for, find a mate for; catch, find, hook (*sl.*).

see also **889**

897 celibacy

n. celibacy, singleness, bachelorhood, virginity, spinsterhood; celibate, bachelor, confirmed bachelor; spinster, bachelor girl, old maid, virgin.

adj. celibate, single, unmarried, unwed, not the marrying kind; eligible, unattached, free; virgin.

898 divorce; widowhood

n. divorce, separation, annulment, dissolution, decree nisi, desertion; breakdown of marriage.

widowhood; survivor, widow, dowager, relict; widower; grass widow, golf widow.

adj. divorced, parted, separated, living apart.

vb. divorce, get a divorce, annul, cancel, put asunder, sue for a divorce, desert, split up (*inf.*), separate, live apart; widow, bereave; leave, survive.

899 benevolence

n. benevolence, kindness, helpfulness, thoughtfulness, kindheartedness, graciousness, courtesy, charity, altruism, philanthropy, fellow-feeling, the golden rule; service, good deed, good turn, aid, relief, favour, benefit, alms.

kind person, good Samaritan, good neighbour, altruist, humanitarian, do-gooder, philanthropist, heart of gold.

adj. kind, benevolent, charitable, helpful, careful, thoughtful, well-meaning, well-intentioned, well-meant, gracious, good, pleasant, generous, obliging, neighbourly, kindhearted, warm-hearted, compassionate, sympathetic, unselfish, altruistic, humanitarian, philanthropic; merciful, pitying.

vb. be kind, help, do a good turn, do a favour, benefit, support, encourage, comfort, relieve, bless, mean well, wish well, do as one would be done by, bend over backwards to help.

see also 550, 905, 935

900 malevolence

n. malevolence, unkindness, hate, animosity, malice, malignity, spite, bitterness, acrimony; cruelty, inhumanity, wickedness, ruthlessness, relentlessness, harshness, severity, callousness; tyranny, oppression, despotism, intolerance; brutality, beastliness, savagery, barbarousness, brutishness, monstrousness.

ill, harm, misfortune, mischief, blow, outrage, foul play, catastrophe, disaster, atrocity, torture.

adj. unkind, unfriendly, unloving, uncharitable, stepmotherly, inconsiderate, thoughtless; spiteful, malicious, catty, hateful, resentful, bitter, acrimonious, caustic.

cruel, malevolent, malicious, inhuman, wicked, harsh, severe, relentless, fierce, savage, barbarous, brutal, beastly; pitiless, unmerciful, intolerant, ruthless, cold, callous, hardhearted, oppressive, despotic, devilish, diabolical.

vb. be malevolent, hurt, harm, abuse, maltreat, damage, injure, oppress, tyrannize, not tolerate, persecute, torture, torment, victimize, have it in for (*inf.*), take it out on (*inf.*).

see also 551, 906, 936

901 curse

n. curse, malediction, denunciation, execration, abuse, vilification, vituperation, scurrility; profanity, swearing, oath, imprecation, expletive, swearword, naughty word, bad language, blasphemy, sacrilege, profanation.

adj. maledictory, imprecatory, damnatory; abusive, scurrilous, profane,

sacrilegious, blasphemous, blue, naughty, indecent, obscene.

vb. curse, wish on (*inf.*), invoke, summon, call down on; abuse, defame, denounce, pour abuse, call names, revile, vituperate, vilify, damn; swear, swear like a trooper, blaspheme.

902 threat

n. threat, menace, warning, intimidation, blackmail; writing on the wall, danger signal, distress signal; threatening, commination.

adj. threatening, menacing, intimidating, frightening; ominous, imminent.

vb. threaten, menace, intimidate, blackmail, frighten, scare, torment, bully, push around (*inf.*), order about (*inf.*); be brewing, loom, be imminent.

see also 154

903 philanthropy

n. philanthropy, humanitarianism, utilitarianism, altruism, social conscience; welfare state, social services; patriotism, love of one's country, loyalty, public spirit; nationalism, chauvinism; internationalism.

philanthropist, humanitarian, dogooder; idealist, altruist, visionary, man with a vision, missionary; patriot, lover of one's country, loyalist, nationalist, chauvinist; internationalist, citizen of the world, cosmopolitan.

adj. philanthropic, humanitarian, humane, kind, altruistic, patriotic; chauvinistic; public-spirited, reforming.

vb. have a social conscience, be public-spirited, show public spirit; love one's country.

904 misanthropy

n. misanthropy, selfishness, egotism, cynicism, unsociability, incivism;

misanthrope, man-hater, misogynist, woman-hater, cynic, egoist.

adj. misanthropic, antisocial, unsocial, unsociable, inhuman, cynical; unpatriotic.

see also **885**

905 benefactor

n. benefactor, benefactress, helper, good neighbour, do-gooder, giver, donor, contributor; protector, guard, watch, champion, guardian; patron, supporter, backer, rescuer, deliverer, liberator, redeemer; angel, guardian angel.

see also **640**

906 evildoer

n. evildoer, wrongdoer, troublemaker, mischief-maker; criminal, lawbreaker, offender, transgressor, sinner, public enemy; crook, villain, rogue; thief, gangster, con man (*inf.*); murderer, assassin; ruffian, thug, hooligan, layabout (*inf.*); nasty piece of work (*inf.*); beast, brute, monster, vampire, viper.

see also **684, 723, 940**

907 pity

n. pity, compassion, goodness, kindliness, benevolence, understanding, charity; tenderness, soft-heartedness, warm-heartedness; condolence, sympathy, commiseration, fellow feeling, comfort, solace, consolation; mercy, favour, grace, clemency, forbearance, forgiveness, second chance.

adj. pitying, compassionate, kind, tender, gentle, lenient; merciful, gracious, clement, forbearing, forgiving, generous; sympathetic, consoling, commiserating, comforting, sorry; pitiful, pitiable.

vb. pity, show mercy, take pity on, pardon, spare, forgive, reprieve, give a second chance; relent, relax, repent; put out of one's misery.

sympathize, feel for, feel with, put oneself in someone's shoes, be understanding, express sympathy, commiserate, share another's sorrow, grieve with, weep for, love, console, comfort, support, uphold, encourage, sit by, put one's arm round.

908 pitilessness

n. pitilessness, ruthlessness, mercilessness, relentlessness, cruelty, heartlessness, callousness, hardness of heart; letter of the law, pound of flesh.

adj. pitiless, unpitying, unmerciful, merciless, relentless, unrelenting, unforgiving, barbarous, tyrannical, vindictive, revengeful; rough, harsh, severe; cruel, brutal, savage; cold, unsympathetic, unfeeling, unmoved, inflexible; hard-hearted, stony-hearted, cold-blooded.

vb. show no pity, stop at nothing (*inf.*), harden one's heart, turn a deaf ear to, give no quarter, exact one's pound of flesh; one's heart bleed for (*inf.*).

909 gratitude

n. gratitude, thankfulness, appreciation, gratefulness, sense of obligation; thanks, thank-you, acknowledgment, response, recognition, praise, tribute, vote of thanks, honour, credit; blessing, grace, prayer, benediction; bread-and-butter letter; reward, trip; leaving-present.

adj. grateful, thankful, appreciative, responsive; indebted, obliged, much obliged; pleased, gratified, overwhelmed.

vb. thank, say thank you, show one's gratitude, respond, appreciate, show one's appreciation, acknowledge, recognize, praise, pay a tribute to, never forget, applaud; reward, tip; give thanks, say grace, return thanks.

910 ingratitude

n. ingratitude, ungratefulness, lack of appreciation, thanklessness, no sense of obligation; thoughtlessness, rudeness.

adj. ungrateful, unappreciative, unmindful, forgetful, rude; thankless, unrewarding, unprofitable, worthless; unthanked, unacknowledged, unrewarded.

vb. be ungrateful, not thank, take for granted, presume upon.

911 forgiveness

n. forgiveness, pardon, free pardon, absolution; remission, acquittal, release, discharge; exoneration, exculpation; justification, reconciliation, redemption, atonement; reprieve, amnesty, indemnity; grace, mercy, patience, forbearance.

adj. forgiven, pardoned, excused, absolved, let off, acquitted, free, not guilty, released, reinstated, reconciled, restored, taken back, welcomed home; redeemed, justified, adopted.

vb. forgive, pardon, excuse, remit, reprieve, clear, absolve, discharge, acquit, free, declare not guilty, let off (*inf.*), let go; let pass, disregard, ignore, shut one's eyes to, grant amnesty to; show mercy, tolerate, forbear; redeem, reconcile, justify; purge, blot one's sins out, wipe the slate clean; bury the hatchet, make it up, kiss and make up; forgive and forget, let bygones be bygones.

see also **921, 961**

912 revenge

n. revenge, vengeance, requital, reprisal, retaliation; vindictiveness,

spitefulness, rancour; avenger, vindicator.

adj. revengeful, vengeant, spiteful, retaliatory, unrelenting, rancorous, unappeasable, implacable.

vb. avenge, take revenge, take vengeance, requite, vindicate, retaliate, get even with, get one's own back.

see also **647**

913 jealousy

n. jealousy, resentment, intolerance, distrust, suspicion, green eye, green-eyed monster; rivalry, unfaithfulness, hostility; vigilance, watchfulness, possessiveness.

adj. jealous, green-eyed, resentful, distrustful, suspicious, vigilant, watchful, possessive.

914 envy

n. envy, covetousness, resentment.

adj. envious, covetous, jealous.

vb. envy, covet, lust after, desire, crave, hanker; grudge, begrudge.

E Moral

915 right

n. right, justice, rightfulness, lawfulness, legality, legitimacy, fairness, equity, impartiality, poetic justice; suitability, reasonableness, fittingness; the right thing, what is right, the proper thing, square deal, fair play.

adj. right, correct, precise, true, valid, accurate; appropriate, proper, suitable, apt, fit, on the right track; fair, honest, upright, righteous, just, rightful, lawful, legitimate, equitable, impartial, objective, unprejudiced, unbiased, disinterested, dispassionate, straightforward, plain; fair and square, straight, fair-minded, sporting.

vb. be just, play the game, try to be

fair, do justice to, do the right thing, give the Devil his due.

see also 577

916 wrong

n. wrong, wrongness, injustice, wrongfulness, inequity, unfairness, partiality, partisanship, prejudice, bias, favouritism; foul play, raw deal, irregularity; grievance, injury; preferential treatment, discrimination, reverse discrimination, nepotism.

adj. wrong, unjust, wrongful, unreasonable, unfair, inequitable, partial, biased, prejudiced, partisan, uneven, unbalanced; below the belt, not cricket (*inf.*), unsportsmanlike; erroneous, imprecise, inaccurate, on the wrong track, at fault; injurious, harmful; wicked, sinful; unsuitable, unfitting, inappropriate, improper; unjustifiable, inexcusable, unforgivable; inadmissible, illegal, illicit, illegitimate.

vb. do wrong, break the law, wrong, hurt, injure, harm, treat unfairly, maltreat, cheat; discriminate, favour, prefer, show preference, be biased, show partiality; not play the game properly, not play fair, hit below the belt.

see also 416, 578

917 dueness

n. dueness, due; deserts, comeuppance, just deserts, merits; right, human rights, rights of man, women's rights; dues, fees, levy, contribution; reward, compensation; punishment; privilege, responsibility, prerogative.

adj. due, owing, payable, overdue, outstanding, unpaid, unsettled, in arrears, chargeable; deserved, well-deserved, merited, worthy, just, warranted, entitled, deserving, worthy, needy, rightful, meritorious.

vb. be due, become due, mature, deserve, merit, have the right to, be entitled to; be worthy of, warrant, expect, earn, claim, lay claim to; demand one's rights; have it coming to one (*inf.*), have only oneself to thank, serve someone right.

918 undueness

n. undueness, unfittingness; presumption, assumption, overstepping, arrogation, violation, encroachment; dispossession, disentitlement, forfeiture, disfranchisement.

adj. undue, undeserved, unmerited, unwarranted, uncalled for, improper, unnecessary, immoderate; unworthy, unjust, unfair, undeserving; unentitled, unprivileged.

vb. have no right to, presume, venture, overstep, assume, usurp, violate, not be entitled to, take liberties; not expect; disqualify; invalidate, disentitle, disfranchise.

919 duty

n. duty, obligation, liability, responsibility, burden, onus; accountability; engagement, commitment, pledge, contract, debt; call of duty, sense of duty, moral obligation, conscience, still small voice; loyalty, faithfulness, allegiance.

adj. incumbent, up to one, behoving; obliged, duty-bound, under obligation; liable, responsible, answerable, subject to, accountable; obligatory, binding, compulsory, necessary; dutiful, obedient, submissive, tractable, compliant.

vb. be one's duty, be the duty of, should, ought, had better, behove; be responsible for, rest with, devolve on, rest on the shoulders of, fall to, fall to one's lot; accept responsiblity, commit oneself; do one's duty, do what is expected of one, perform, fulfil, acquit oneself well, meet one's obligations; impose a duty, call upon, enjoin, look to; oblige, bind, saddle with, put under obligation.

920 neglect of duty

n. neglect, disregard, omission, evasion, non-observance, dereliction, negligence; carelessness, slackness, remissness, slovenliness; absence, absenteeism, truancy; defection, desertion, mutiny; disloyalty, unfaithfulness.

adj. negligent, inattentive, careless, slack, undutiful; disloyal, unfaithful; rebellious, mutinous.

vb. neglect, fail, break, violate; pass over, let slip, let go, omit, ignore, evade, shirk; defer, postpone, procrastinate; suspend, discard, dismiss; rebel, mutiny; absent oneself, play truant; let someone down, not trouble oneself.

see also 393

921 exemption

n. exemption, immunity, privilege; freedom, liberation, release, dispensation, exception, absolution; permission, leave; lifting of restrictions; escape-clause.

adj. exempt, free, clear, non-liable, not subject to, not chargeable; immune, privileged; unaffected, unrestrained, uncontrolled, unbound, unrestricted; outside.

vb. exempt, free, clear, release, acquit, discharge; lift restrictions; shrug off, pass the buck (*inf.*); be exempt, be free, enjoy immunity, get away with murder (*inf.*).

see also **680, 961**

922 respect

n. respect, regard, honour, esteem, appreciation, favour, admiration, recognition, high opinion, high regard, deference, liking, love; praise, reverence, veneration, awe, worship; respects, bow, curtsy, salute, greeting, salutation.

adj. respectful, deferential, courteous, polite, admiring, showing respect for; attentive, reverential; on one's knees, prostrate.

respected, highly regarded, valued, appreciated, esteemed, honoured, time-honoured, important, well thought of.

vb. respect, regard highly, think well of, think a great deal of, have a high opinion of, admire, take off one's hat to (*inf.*), value, appreciate, honour, hold dear; praise, extol, revere, worship; pay one's respects, bow, kneel, curtsy, welcome, greet; scrape, grovel; keep in with (*inf.*), keep on the right side of; stand in awe of.

command respect, impress, overawe, awe, stun, overwhelm, humble.

923 disrespect

n. disrespect, discourtesy, impoliteness, irreverence, dishonour, low opinion, low regard; insult, affront, offence, humiliation, slight, snub, rebuff, slap in the face, backhanded compliment.

adj. disrespectful, discourteous, impolite, irreverent, dishonourable, insulting, offensive, slighting, cutting, humiliating, rude, scornful, impertinent, depreciating, pejorative.

vb. have no respect for, show disrespect for, have a low opinion of, have no time for, underrate, dishonour, offend, insult, affront, slight, snub, rebuff, scorn, despise, look down on (*inf.*), humiliate, interrupt.

924 contempt

n. contempt, scorn, disdain, ridicule, mocking, derision, disrespect, disdainfulness, contemptuousness, scornfulness, snobbishness, haughtiness; sneer, slight, scoff, cold shoulder.

adj. contemptuous, disdainful, scornful, disrespectful, haughty, supercilious, insolent, snooty, snobbish; contemptible, mean, poor, base, worthless, shameful, despicable, beneath contempt.

vb. despise, disdain, spurn, scorn, pour scorn on, turn one's nose up at (*inf.*), sneer at, mock, laugh at, ridicule, deride; pity, look down on (*inf.*), look down one's nose at (*inf.*); disregard, cut dead; avoid, shun, steer clear of; cheapen, belittle, pooh-pooh, not care a fig for.

see also 853

925 approval

n. approval, recognition, acknowledgement; satisfaction; agreement, permission, sanction, adoption, acceptance; admiration, esteem, credit, honour; compliment, bouquet, commendation, citation, write-up; praise, glorification; applause, clapping, ovation, acclaim.

adj. approving, favourable, complimentary, commendatory, laudatory; approvable, commendable, laudable, praiseworthy, creditable, acceptable; approved, popular, praised, uncensored.

vb. approve, recognize, acknowledge; agree, give permission, allow, sanction; accept, adopt, favour; not reject, not sniff at; praise, admire, esteem, compliment, commend, speak well of, write up, crack up (*inf.*), take off one's hat to (*inf.*), give full marks to, must hand it to (*inf.*); find no fault with, have nothing but praises for; sing the praises of, rave about (*inf.*); clap, applaud, cheer, acclaim, hail, give a big hand to.

926 disapproval

n. disapproval, disagreement, non-acceptance, objection, criticism, complaint, opposition, rejection, contradiction, denunciation, censure, fault-finding, reprehension, judgment, blame, reproach, sneer, taunt.

rebuke, reprimand, reproof, admonition, talking to, telling off, lecture, piece of one's mind; brickbat; dissatisfaction, discontent, displeasure.

adj. disapproving, critical, hostile, reproachful, sneering, taunting, reproving, chiding, censorious, condemnatory, defamatory; niggling, fault-finding; unfavourable, uncomplimentary, disparaging; shocked, not amused.

objectionable, blameworthy, reprehensible, not good enough, in person's bad books, not all it is cracked up to be (*inf.*).

vb. disapprove, disagree, not accept, not think much of, not hold with, hold no brief for, frown on; run down, disparage, belittle; object to, oppose, contradict; boo, hiss; blame, reproach, incriminate; snub, taunt, sneer.

criticize, complain, denounce, find fault with, pick holes; reprehend, reprove, rebuke, reprimand, admonish, upbraid, judge, knock (*sl.*), slam (*sl.*), condemn, censure, punish, put someone in his place; tell off, talk to, tick off (*inf.*), speak to, lecture, have words with (*inf.*), dress down (*inf.*), dust down (*inf.*), tear off a strip (*sl.*), chide, scold, take to task, rap over the knuckles (*inf.*), haul over the coals (*inf.*); give a piece of one's mind to, give a person what for (*sl.*).

927 flattery

n. flattery, adulation, compliment,

soft soap (*inf.*), eyewash (*sl.*), false praise, insincerity, obsequiousness, fawning, cajolery, wheedling.

flatterer, cajoler, wheedler, hypocrite, toady.

adj. flattering, adulatory, blandishing, complimentary, over-complimentary, unctuous, ingratiating, insincere, smooth, smarmy (*inf.*).

vb. flatter, butter up (*inf.*), suck up to (*sl.*), soft-soap (*inf.*), cajole, wheedle, inveigle; lay it on thick (*inf.*), lay it on with a trowel (*inf.*).

see also **881**

928 disparagement

n. disparagement, depreciation, detraction, degradation, debasement, vilification, discrediting, belittling, defilement, denigration, smear campaign, whispering campaign, muckraking, mud-slinging, backbiting; slander, libel, calumny, defamation; aspersion, slur, smear, insinuation, innuendo, scandal, gossip.

disparager, critic, slanderer, libeller, backbiter, scandal-monger, muckraker, mud-slinger; mocker, scoffer, cynic, satirist.

adj. disparaging, deprecatory, derogatory, pejorative, denigratory, slanderous, libellous, defamatory, slighting; cynical.

vb. disparage, depreciate, belittle, play down, run down (*inf.*), decry, discredit, cut down to size (*inf.*); denounce, denigrate, blacken; attack, cast aspersions on; criticize, revile, defame, vilify, malign, slight, slur, tarnish, defile, sully, knock (*sl.*), smear; slander, libel; hound; deride, scoff, mock, ridicule.

929 vindication

n. vindication, justification,

establishment, support, plea, defence, excuse, extenuation; ground, right, basis; exoneration, exculpation.

adj. vindicating, justifying, excusing; extenuating; justifiable, arguable, defensible, plausible.

vb. vindicate, justify, establish, support, bear out, uphold, confirm, show, prove, demonstrate, maintain, defend, give grounds for; absolve, acquit, clear, exonerate, excuse, make excuses for, make allowances for.

930 accusation

n. accusation, indictment, prosecution, arraignment, impeachment, charge, censure, incrimination, insinuation, slur, exposé, complaint, denunciation, smear, blame, allegation, action, case; frame-up (*inf.*), put-up job.

accuser, plaintiff, prosecutor.

adj. accusing, denunciatory, incriminating, defamatory.

vb. accuse, censure, charge, bring charges, prefer charges, arrest, arraign, impeach, indict, impute, complain, bring a complaint, find fault with, blame, pin blame on, denounce, incriminate, implicate, involve, reprove, slur, attack, recriminate, slander, libel; point the finger at; frame (*sl.*), trump up, concoct, invent, fabricate, construct, bear false witness.

931 probity

n. probity, uprightness, rectitude, honesty, integrity, fidelity, faithfulness, loyalty, morality, goodness, virtue, reliability, conscientiousness, truthfulness, character, principles, high principles.

adj. honourable, upright, moral, right, fair, good, straight, square, virtuous, honest, law-abiding, reputable, reliable, trustworthy, dependable, conscientious, faithful, loyal, straightforward, sincere, frank, candid, principled, scrupulous.

see also 935, 951

932 improbity

n. improbity, dishonesty, immorality, badness, evil, wickedness, criminality, corruption; cunning, guile; disloyalty, faithlessness, double-dealing, double-crossing, sell-out, duplicity, betrayal, defection, treason, treachery, perfidy, foul play, trick, prank.

adj. dishonest, immoral, bad, wicked, corrupt, evil, criminal, fraudulent; unscrupulous, unprincipled, disreputable; unreliable, undependable, faithless; betraying, treacherous, perfidious, insidious, two-faced, insincere, deceitful, double-dealing; underhand, sly, crafty, devious, shady, dubious, suspicious, questionable, fishy (*sl.*).

vb. be dishonest, lie, cheat, swindle, deceive, betray, double-cross, sell out (*inf.*), two-time (*sl.*).

see also 936, 952

933 disinterestedness

n. disinterestedness, impartiality, indifference, non-involvement, unconcern, detachment, objectivity, neutrality; selflessness, self-sacrifice, self-denial.

adj. disinterested, impartial, indifferent, unconcerned, unbiased, unprejudiced, dispassionate, objective, fair, unselfish, selfless, self-denying, self-sacrificing, self-effacing, self-forgetful; generous, liberal, magnanimous.

934 selfishness

n. selfishness, self-indulgence, greed, meanness, narrowness; self-worship, narcissism, egoism, vanity, self-interest, self-seeking.

self-seeker, egoist, individualist, time-server, narcissist, number one.

adj. selfish, self-centred, self-indulgent, greedy, miserly, mean, narrow; wrapped up in oneself, self-absorbed, self-seeking, egoistic.

vb. be selfish, look after number one.

935 virtue

n. virtue, morality, goodness, uprightness, righteousness, narrow way, sanctity, rectitude; honesty, temperance, kindness, excellence; quality, character, integrity; purity, chastity, innocence; ethics, morals.

adj. virtuous, moral, good, upright, righteous, holy, saintly, angelic; honest, kind, excellent, worthy, proper; perfect, irreproachable, unblemished, immaculate, impeccable; chaste, pure, innocent.

vb. be good, behave oneself, acquit oneself well, keep to the straight and narrow; set a good example.

see also 931, 951

936 vice

n. vice, wickedness, corruption, iniquity, evil, immorality, perversity, baseness, meanness, malignity, malevolence, grossness, wantonness; degeneration, deterioration; unrighteousness, transgression, ungodliness; bad habit, besetting sin, failing, weakness, fault.

adj. wicked, evil, bad, corrupt, immoral, wayward, dissolute, perverse, gross, wanton, base, mean, malevolent, perverted, depraved, degenerate, irreligious, sinful, unrighteous, ungodly, unregenerate.

offensive, shocking, outrageous, scandalous, atrocious, abominable, heinous, repugnant, monstrous, unforgivable.

vb. err, stray, fall, lapse, degenerate, transgress, go off the rails (*inf.*); make wicked, corrupt, demoralize, defile, lead astray.

see also 932, 952

937 innocence

n. innocence, guiltlessness, blamelessness, inculpability, irreproachability, faultlessness, integrity, probity, uprightness, perfection, purity, impeccability; clear conscience, clean hands, clean slate.

adj. innocent, not guilty, above suspicion, in the clear, pure, clean, spotless, unsoiled, untainted, undefiled, blameless, irreproachable, faultless, upright, perfect, impeccable; unoffending, simple, unsophisticated, inexperienced, guileless.

vb. be innocent, have a clear conscience, have nothing to confess.

938 guilt

n. guilt, blame, culpability; responsibility, liability, answerability; criminality, sinfulness; bad conscience, guilty conscience.

crime, offence, transgression, trespass, misdeed, sin, misdemeanour, misconduct, misbehaviour, error, fault, lapse, slip.

adj. guilty, wrong, at fault, offending, to blame, culpable, reproachable; blamed, condemned, judged, incriminated; red-handed, caught in the act.

939 good person

n. good person, good example, model, standard, pattern, ideal, paragon; one in a million, salt of the earth, last word, ultimate; saint, angel, hero, pillar; perfect gentleman; good fellow, good sort, good egg, sport (*sl.*).

see also 905

940 bad person

n. bad person, wrongdoer, evildoer, sinner, transgressor; reprobate; scoundrel, wretch, villain, miscreant, rogue, rascal, blackguard, knave; bully, scallywag, scamp, scapegrace; wastrel, bum (*sl.*), idler, loafer, prodigal, beggar, tramp; ugly customer, nasty piece of work (*inf.*), bad lot, bad egg; good-fornothing, ne'er-do-well, black sheep; criminal, crook, liar, cheat, traitor, impostor; rat, louse (*sl.*), worm.

941 penitence

n. penitence, repentance, change of heart, confession, contrition; sorrow, regret, remorse; sackcloth and ashes, hair shirt; penitent, convert, prodigal son.

adj. penitent, repentant, confessing, humble, contrite, conscience-stricken, convicted; regretful, sorry, compunctious, apologetic, full of regrets.

vb. repent, confess, acknowledge, plead guilty, humble oneself, own up, admit; feel shame, deplore; be penitent, be sorry, regret, apologize; turn from sin, see the light, be converted.

942 impenitence

n. impenitence, hardness of heart, heart of stone, seared conscience, obduracy; no regrets; hardened sinner.

adj. impenitent, unrepentant, uncontrite; hard, insensitive, callous, stubborn, obdurate, unashamed; incorrigible, irredeemable; dead, lost.

vb. be impenitent, have no regrets, show no remorse; harden one's heart.

943 atonement

n. atonement, satisfaction, amends,

apology, redress, compensation, indemnity, retribution, requital, repayment, restitution, reparation.

propitiation, reconciliation, sacrifice, offering; substitute, representative; scapegoat; expiation; penance; purgatory.

adj. atoning, satisfying, indemnificatory, compensatory; propitiatory, reconciliatory, sacrificial, redemptive; substitutionary, representative, vicarious.

vb. atone, make amends, redress, compensate, indemnify, requite, repay; apologize; propitiate, reconcile, appease, satisfy, redeem.

944 temperance

n. temperance, moderation, abstemiousness, restraint, self-restraint, self-control, self-discipline; self-denial, abstinence, teetotalism; abstainer, total abstainer, teetotaller.

adj. temperate, moderate, restrained, disciplined, careful; self-denying, self-controlled, abstinent; continent; sparing, frugal, plain; abstemious, sober.

vb. be temperate, exercise self-control, control oneself, deny oneself, abstain, refrain; know when to stop, know when one has had enough.

945 intemperance

n. intemperance, excess, extravagance, inordinateness, self-indulgence; sensuality, voluptousness, carnality, flesh; luxury, high living; dissipation, debauchery; hedonism, epicureanism.

adj. intemperate, immoderate, unrestrained, inordinate, excessive, self-indulgent; sensual, sensuous, voluptuous, carnal, bodily, fleshly, gluttonous, debauched; high-living, pleasure-loving, epicurean, hedonistic.

vb. be intemperate, indulge oneself, have one's fling, sow one's wild oats, paint the town red (*sl.*), not know when to stop, overeat, drink too much.

946 ascetism

n. ascetism, austerity, abstinence, abstemiousness, mortification, plain living.

ascetic, self-denier, recluse, hermit, anchorite, stylite; fakir, dervish, flagellant.

adj. ascetic, austere, plain, severe, rigid, stern, abstemious, puritanical, rigorous.

947 fasting

n. fasting, abstinence, hunger, starvation; fast, bread and water, short commons, diet, slimming; fast-day, Lent, Ramadan.

adj. fasting, abstinent, abstaining, starving, hungry, unfed, famished, Lenten.

vb. fast, eat nothing, go hungry, starve, famish; go on hunger strike; diet, reduce weight, slim, take off weight.

948 gluttony

n. gluttony, greed, voracity, rapacity, unsatiability, intemperance, excess, indulgence.

glutton, pig (*inf.*), guzzler, hog, greedy-guts (*sl.*); gourmand, epicure.

adj. greedy, gluttonous, ravenous, devouring, guzzling.

vb. overeat, stuff oneself, make a pig of oneself (*inf.*), eat like a horse, devour, guzzle, gobble, gulp down, bolt down; eat out of house and home.

949 soberness

n. soberness, sobriety, temperance, abstinence, teetotalism, prohibition.

sober person, abstainer, teetotaller, total abstainer, prohibitionist, Band of Hope, Temperance League.

adj. sober, temperate, abstinent, teetotal, on the wagon (*sl.*), off drink, clear-headed, in one's right mind, in possession of one's senses, unintoxicated, stone-cold sober, dry.

vb. be sober, not drink, sign the pledge; hold one's drink, have a good head for drink; sober up, sleep it off (*inf.*).

950 drunkenness

n. drunkenness, intoxication, inebriety, insobriety, intemperance; alcoholism, dipsomania; a drop too much, tipsiness; drinking-bout, pub-crawl, party, celebration, orgy; pink elephants; hangover, head, headache.

drunkard, drinker, heavy drinker, hard drinker, tippler, boozer, alcoholic, drunk (*sl.*).

adj. drunk, intoxicated, inebriated, under the influence, tipsy, befuddled; on the bottle; happy, high, lit up (*inf.*); seeing double, glassy-eyed; groggy; the worse for drink, sloshed (*sl.*), tight (*inf.*), stoned (*sl.*), blotto (*sl.*), canned (*sl.*), sozzled (*sl.*), plastered (*sl.*), under the table.

vb. drink, booze, guzzle, tipple, wet one's whistle (*inf.*), hit the bottle, drink like a fish, drown one's sorrows; be merry, be tipsy, have a drop too much, have one over the eight; be drunk, have more than one can hold, see double, get stoned out of one's mind (*sl.*); intoxicate, inebriate, go to one's head.

951 purity

n. purity, cleanness, cleanliness, whiteness; sinlessness, perfection; untaintedness, unsulliedness, spotlessness, immaculateness.

morality, chastity, virtue, decency, abstemiousness, virginity; prudery, primness, prudishness, overmodesty, false modesty, squeamishness; prude, prig, old maid.

adj. pure, clean, perfect, sinless; unsullied, untainted, spotless, undefiled, unadulterated, unc .taminated; decent, demure, abstemious; edifying; chaste, virtuous; continent, celibate, virgin, platonic; prudish, prim, squeamish, shockable, narrow, strict, Victorian, puritanical, strait-laced, old-maidish; simple, innocent, guileless, artless; inexperienced.

see also 931, 935

952 impurity

n. impurity, uncleanness, sinfulness, imperfection, taintedness, sulliedness, contamination, pollution, adulteration.

immorality, unchastity, indecency, looseness of morals, permissive society; lewdness, prurience, profligacy, incontinence, lechery, wantonness, licentiousness, dissoluteness, salaciousness, lasciviousness; lust, sensuality, eroticism; obscenity, filth, dirt, smut, pornography; free love, promiscuity, adultery, wife-swapping (*inf.*), sleeping around (*inf.*), fornication, unfaithfulness, infidelity, affair, relationship, liaison, eternal triangle; seduction, rape, assault, violation, defilement; prostitution, street-walking, harlotry, whoredom; homosexuality, lesbianism, sodomy, incest.

adj. impure, unclean, imperfect, tainted, sullied, contaminated, polluted, adulterated; immoral, unchaste, indecent, loose, slack, of loose morals, easy, fast, wild, promiscuous, of easy virtue, permissive; lewd, profligate, lecherous, licentious, lascivious, wanton, dissolute, salacious, debauched; sensual, erotic; vulgar, coarse, risqué, spicy; obscene, filthy, dirty, smutty, lurid, sexy, pornographic, blue, unprintable, unexpurgated; homosexual, gay (*sl.*), queer (*sl.*), lesbian; extramarital, unlawful, illicit, adulterous, incestuous.

vb. be impure, commit adultery, fornicate, sleep around (*inf.*); seduce, take advantage of (*inf.*), rape, assault, violate; go on the streets, walk the streets, prostitute, adulterate, contaminate; sully, taint, pollute.

see also 932, 936

953 libertine

n. libertine, profligate, Don Juan, rake, womanizer, lecher, adulterer, seducer, rapist, fornicator; homosexual, homo (*inf.*), queer (*sl.*), gay (*sl.*), fairy (*sl.*), pansy (*inf.*), nancy (*sl.*), butch (*sl.*), transvestite, pervert; lesbian.

adultress, woman of easy virtue, loose woman, flirt, tart (*sl.*), slut, pick-up (*inf.*); mistress; prostitute, pro, call-girl, fallen woman, whore, harlot, street-walker, hustler (*sl.*).

954 legality

n. legality, legitimacy, lawfulness, permissibility, validity, constitutionality; legislation, law-giving, law-making, authorization, codification, sanction, enactment; right, authority, justice; jurisprudence.

law, statute, decree, ordinance, act, edict, order, code, regulation, rule, by-law, constitution.

adj. legal, legitimate, lawful, right, just; constitutional; permissible, permitted, valid, sanctioned, codified, authorized, prescribed, within the law, statutory; jurisprudential, nomothetic.

vb. legalize, permit, authorize,

sanction, approve, validate, establish, enforce, pass, license, charter, empower; legislate.

see also 103, 626

955 illegality

n. illegality, unlawfulness, unconstitutionality, miscarriage of justice, injustice; law-breaking, violation, transgression, trespass, contravention, encroachment, infringement, offence, wrong, crime.

lawlessness, antinomianism, irresponsibility, terrorism, anarchism, mob rule, chaos, disorder, breakdown of law and order.

illegitimacy, bastardy; bastard, illegitimate child, natural child, love child.

adj. illegal, unlawful, illicit, forbidden, prohibited, banned, unauthorized, wrong, against the law, outside the law; stolen, black-market, smuggled, contraband; lawless, wild, chaotic, anarchic, irresponsible; illegitimate, bastard, natural, born out of wedlock, born on the wrong side of the blanket, born without benefit of clergy (*inf.*).

vb. break the law, disobey, commit, violate, transgress, contravene, infringe; take the law into one's own hands, be a law unto oneself; nullify, abrogate, void, annul, cancel.

956 jurisdiction

n. jurisdiction, authority, control, direction, supervision; right, power, responsibility, capacity, competence; executive, corporation, administration; domain, extent, scope, range, territory.

police, police force, constabulary; police officer, policeman, constable, officer, copper (*sl.*), cop (*sl*) rozzer (*sl.*), fuzz (*sl.*); traffic warden, meter maid.

adj. jurisdictional, judiciary, competent, responsible, judicial, executive.

vb. administer, preside, direct, supervise; judge; police, keep order, control.

957 tribunal

n. tribunal, court, assizes, session, bench, bar; judgment seat, mercy seat, throne; dock, witness-box; courthouse.

958 judge

n. judge, justice, J.P., recorder, magistrate, stipendiary, beak (*sl.*); judiciary; marshal; jury, panel, tribunal; juror, juryman, jurywoman, foreman.

see also 653, 960

959 lawyer

n. lawyer, legal practitioner; the bar, legal profession; defender, counsel, barrister, advocate, bencher; legal adviser, attorney, procurator, solicitor; prosecution; notary, commissioner for oaths; legist, jurist, jurisconsult; pettifogger.

vb. practise law, plead; be called to the bar, take silk; argue, defend, advocate; allege, prosecute.

960 lawsuit

n. lawsuit, case, suit, action, legal proceedings, hearing, indictment; litigation, judicature; summons, writ, subpoena; affidavit, bill; pleadings, argument, prosecution, cross-examination, defence, plea, summing-up; verdict, finding, decision, ruling, pronouncement, sentence, decree, award, precedent; appeal; litigant, party, suitor, plaintiff, defendant.

vb. go to law, prosecute, sue, litigate, bring an action against, bring to trial, file a claim; try, hear, give a hearing to, judge, arbitrate, adjudicate; rest one's case; sum up; rule, find, pron-

ounce, declare, return a verdict, bring in a verdict, pass sentence, sentence, convict, acquit.

961 acquittal

n. acquittal, discharge, reprieve, release, remission, pardon, clearance, dismissal, exoneration, exculpation; innocence; suspended sentence.

adj. acquitted, not guilty, clear, discharged, released, set free, liberated, justified; forgiven.

vb. acquit, declare not guilty, discharge, pardon, absolve, forgive, clear, dismiss, grant remission, reprieve, release, set free, let off (*inf.*); exempt; exonerate, exculpate; justify, vindicate; save, rescue, redeem.

see also 601, 921

962 condemnation

n. condemnation, denunciation, conviction.

adj. condemnatory, damnatory.

vb. condemn, find guilty, sentence, pass sentence on, judge, convict, punish, doom, damn, curse; proscribe, denounce, criticize, find fault with, blame, rebuke.

963 punishment

n. punishment, reproof, discipline, chastisement, correction, reprimand, retribution; penalty, imposition, fine, damages, costs, compensation; exile, banishment; hard labour; bread and water.

corporal punishment, slap, rap, cuff, blow, clout; capital punishment, death sentence, execution, decapitation, beheading, hanging, electrocution, strangling, strangulation, poisoning, crucifixion, impalement, drowning; torture; slaughter, genocide, mass murder, massacre, annihilation.

punisher; executioner, hangman, firing squad; inquisition.

adj. punitive, penal, castigatory, disciplinary, corrective.

vb. punish, reprove, discipline, chastise, correct, sentence, take to task, admonish, rebuke, reprimand, dress down (*inf.*), come down on like a ton of bricks (*inf.*), crack down on (*inf.*); make an example of; retaliate, get one's revenge, get even with.

expel, exile, banish, deport, transport, outlaw, isolate, send to Coventry; imprison, jail; penalize, fine, endorse one's licence.

strike, hit, slap, rap over the knuckles, box on the ears; flog, whip, beat, thrash, scourge, flay; spank, give a good hiding (*inf.*), thrash the living daylights out of (*sl.*), lick (*sl.*), tan (*sl.*), belt, strap, clout, wallop (*sl.*), cane, whack (*inf.*).

kill, put to death, shoot, execute, behead, guillotine, decapitate; hang, lynch; hang, draw, and quarter; crucify, impale; electrocute, gas; strangle; burn at the stake; drown; poison; slaughter, annihilate, massacre; torture, martyr, put on the rack, break on the wheel, tar and feather.

be punished, suffer, pay the penalty, get one's just deserts, have it coming, deserve; face the music, take the rap.

see also **926**

964 means of punishment

n. scourge, birch, whip, lash, belt, cane, rod, stick, switch, cat-o'-nine-tails; pillory, stocks, ducking stool, whipping post; torture chamber, rack, wheel, screw, water torture; axe, guillotine; block, scaffold; cross, stake; gallows, gibbet, noose, rope; electric chair, gas chamber, death chamber; condemned cell.

965 reward

n. reward, pay, payment, compensation, recompense, remuneration, reimbursement, reparation, redress; allowance, expenses, honorarium; tip, gratuity; prize, award, trophy, bonus, premium, bounty, accolade, guerdon.

adj. rewarding, remunerative, compensatory; profitable, advantageous, worthwhile; charitable, liberal, generous, open-handed, unsparing.

vb. reward, pay, recompense, reimburse, redress, compensate; award, recognize, pay tribute, present, give, bestow, confer, grant, thank.

see also **663, 715**

F Religious

966 divinity

n. divinity, divineness, deity, godhead; God, Spirit, Supreme Being, Creator, prime mover, Providence.

adj. divine, spiritual; godlike, godly; heavenly, celestial, sublime; transcendent, immanent, self-existent; eternal, everlasting, immortal; almighty, omnipotent, all-powerful, infinite, supreme; omniscient, all-knowing; just, merciful, gracious, loving, personal.

967 God

n. God; Trinity; Father, Lord, Yahweh, Jehovah, Almighty, King of Kings; Son of God, Jesus Christ, Son of Man, Immanuel, Word, Messiah, Saviour, Redeemer; Holy Spirit, Holy Ghost, Comforter, Paraclete.

god, goddess, object of worship; idol, false god; golden calf; pantheon; numen; totem, fetish; mumbo-jumbo.

supreme deity, Zeus, Jupiter; goddess of women and marriage, Hera, Juno; goddess of crops, Demeter,

Ceres; god of the sun, Phoebus, god of music, medicine, and poetry, Apollo; god of war, Ares, Mars; god of commerce, eloquence, and cunning, Hermes, Mercury; god of the sea, Poseidon, Neptune; god of metal-working, Hephaestus, Vulcan; god of wine and revelry, Dionysus, Bacchus; god of the underworld, Hades, Pluto, Dis; god of agriculture, Kronos, Saturn; god of love, Eros, Cupid; goddess of love and beauty, Aphrodite, Venus; goddess of the moon and hunting, Artemis, Diana; goddess of wisdom, Athena, Minerva; god of the countryside, Pan, Faunus.

Allah; Brahma, Atman, Vishnu, Shiva; Buddha.

968 good spirit

n. good spirit, angel, ministering spirit, seraph, cherub, host, principalities, authorities, powers, thrones, dominions; archangel.

adj. angelic, ministering, heavenly, celestial.

969 evil spirit

n. devil, Satan, fallen angel, father of lies, Beelzebub, prince of this world, prince of darkness; demon, evil spirit, unclean spirit, powers of darkness; imp, fiend, vampire; adversary.

adj. satanic, devilish, diabolic, diabolical, wicked.

see also **984**

970 mythical being

n. fairy, spirit, elf, brownie, goblin, hob, bogle, body, kobold, hobgoblin, dryad, pixie, gnome, peri; sprite, genie, jinnee; nymph; wood-nymph, hamadryad; mountain-nymph, oread; water-nymph, naiad; sea-nymph, nereid; siren, mermaid, water-spirit, water-elf, nix, nixie, kelpie; imp, puck,

leprechaun, gremlin, urchin; changeling; sylph; dwarf, troll.

adj. fairy, mythical, imaginary, fabulous; elfin, elfish, impish.

971 ghost

n. ghost, spectre, spook (*inf.*), apparition, vision, phantom, phantasm, appearance, shade, presence, poltergeist, wraith, *doppelgänger*, double, fetch, visitant, spirit, departed spirit, zombie.

adj. ghostly, spooky (*inf.*), supernatural, evil, haunted, eerie, weird, uncanny, phantom.

vb. haunt, visit, walk, return from the dead.

972 heaven

n. heaven, paradise, bliss, glory, kingdom of heaven, Abraham's bosom, heavenly city, next world, world to come, eternal rest, kingdom-come (*sl.*), happy hunting ground, Elysium; rapture, resurrection, translation, ascension, glorification.

adj. heavenly, celestial, blessed, glorious, glorified, empyrean.

973 hell

n. hell, perdition, underworld, lower world, nether regions, bottomless pit, abyss, inferno, everlasting fire, lake of fire and brimstone, place of the lost, place of torment, pandemonium, Sheol, Gehenna.

adj. hellish, infernal.

974 religion

n. religion, belief, faith, dogma, teaching, doctrine, creed, tenet, revelation, articles of faith, confession; theology.

deism, theism, monotheism, polytheism, pantheism; animism; gnosticism.

Christianity, Judaism; Islam,

Buddhism, Hinduism, Brahmanism, Taoism, Confucianism.

teacher; prophet, apostle; preacher, lay-preacher, exponent, interpreter, commentator, evangelist, missionary.

adj. religious, spiritual, divine, holy, sacred; theological, doctrinal; devout, godly, believing, practising, faithful, regenerate, converted.

see also **980**

975 irreligion

n. irreligion, ungodliness, godlessness, unholiness, unspirituality, wickedness, sinfulness; idolatry, heathenism, paganism; atheism, unbelief; disbelief, scepticism, doubt, agnosticism; heresy, antichristianity; rationalism, free thinking, materialism.

unbeliever, atheist; agnostic, doubter, sceptic, doubting Thomas; idolater; heathen, pagan; infidel, heretic, dissenter.

adj. irreligious, ungodly, godless, wicked, sinful, idolatrous, heathen, pagan; unbelieving, atheistic; heretical, unorthodox; disbelieving, sceptical, agnostic; materialistic, secular, worldly, profane; unregenerate, unconverted, lost, damned.

see also **981**

976 revelation

n. revelation, disclosure; inspiration, afflatus, prophecy, vision; signs, foreshadowing; Scripture, Bible, Word of God, canon; Talmud, Torah, Ten Commandments; Law, Gospel.

Koran, Vedas.

adj. revelational, inspirational, inspired, revealed, prophetic, biblical, scriptural, canonical; evangelical; authoritative.

977 orthodoxy

n. orthodoxy, soundness, faithfulness, strictness, truth, adherence, observance.

the Church, body of Christ, Church invisible, Church militant, Church triumphant, Christendom; believer, true believer, Christian, practising Christian, church member, the saints, the faithful.

adj. orthodox, sound, correct, right, pure, true, faithful; evangelical, conservative, strict, literal, fundamentalist; practising, believing.

978 heresy

n. heresy, heterodoxy; divergence, aberration, distortion, perversion, unorthodoxy, unauthenticity, apostasy, infidelity.

adj. heretical, heterodox, divergent, different, unorthodox, unsound, unscriptural, unbiblical.

979 sectarianism

n. sectarianism, partisanship, schismatism, separatism; denominationalism; party-spirit.

sect, schism, split, section, faction, division, branch; denomination, communion, tradition; off-shoot, secession; sectarian, party-man, seceder, dissident, non-conformist, rebel.

adj. sectarian, partisan, schismatic, party-minded; denominational; dissident, non-conformist; separatist, secessionist, break-away; exclusive.

980 piety

n. piety, devoutness; devotion, single-mindedness; trust, faith; loyalty, submission, dedication, commitment, faithfulness, adherence, perseverance, allegiance, zeal, ardour, earnestness; adoration, worship, reverence, fear, awe, prayerfulness; holiness, sanctity, consecration, godliness, saintliness, humility, spirituality.

saint, believer, convert, man of prayer, man of God; follower, disciple, pilgrim; pietist.

adj. pious, devout, devoted, faithful, loyal, dedicated, committed, single-minded, zealous, earnest; believing, practising, holy, godly, saintly, spiritual, sanctified, consecrated, other-worldly, humble, meek.

vb. be pious, repent and believe, have faith, trust, fear God; keep the faith, persevere; worship, pray; sanctify, consecrate, make holy, dedicate, hallow.

981 impiety

n. impiety, godlessness, irreverence, unrighteousness, unholiness, sinfulness, disobedience; worldliness; blasphemy, sacrilege, desecration, defilement, violation.

hypocrisy, sanctimoniousness, false piety, self-righteousness, religiosity, formalism, hallowness, churchianity (*inf.*), religious show, façade, lip service, cant.

sinner, blasphemer; scoffer, mocker; materialist, worldling; hypocrite, Pharisee, scribe.

adj. impious, irreligious, ungodly, godless, irreverent, unholy, unrighteous, sinful, wicked, disobedient; unbelieving, atheistic, agnostic, non-practising; unhallowed, unsanctified, unregenerate, hardened; blasphemous, sacrilegious, profane; sanctimonious, hypocritical, pharasaical, false, deceitful, insincere, dishonest.

vb. be impious, sin, blaspheme; desecrate, profane, pay lip service.

982 worship

n. worship, honour, reverence, praise, adoration, exaltation, homage, veneration; service, devotions; prayer, private devotion, quiet time, meditation; confession; thanksgiving, grace; supplication, request, entreaty, appeal, petition, intercession, rogation; hymn, song, psalm, chant, anthem, canticle, chorus.

worshipper, church-goer, Christian, communicant; suppliant, petitioner, intercessor, man of prayer; congregation, church, flock, assembly.

adj. worshipping, devoted, reverent, religious, devout, prayerful, on one's knees, supplicant; worshipful, reverential, solemn, holy, serious, dignified, sublime, majestic, glorious.

vb. worship, adore, praise, glorify, bless, exalt, honour, magnify, revere, venerate, pay homage to, laud, revere, bow down, humble oneself; idolize; pray to, seek; confess; thank, give thanks, ask, invoke, entreat, petition, implore, intercede, say one's prayers, beseech; sing; meditate, contemplate, consider, reflect.

see also 977

983 idolatry

n. idolatry, idolism, idol worship, irreligion, heathenism, paganism, fetishism, demonism, devil-worship, hero-worship, iconolatry, image-worship, mumbo-jumbo; idolization, deification, apotheosis.

idol, false god, image, graven image, icon, statue, golden calf, totem, fetish.

idolater, idolizer, pagan, heathen, image-maker.

adj. idolatrous, heathen, pagan, idol-worshipping.

vb. idolatrize, idolize, worship, enshrine, deify; sing the praises of, put on a pedestal, admire, dote on, treasure.

984 sorcery

n. sorcery, magic, superstition, witchcraft, diabolism, black magic, occultism, cabbala, exorcism, divination; miracle-working, thaumaturgy; spell, incantation, bewitchment, enchantment, influence, possession, trance, hocus-pocus, mumbo-jumbo, open sesame, abracadabra; charm, amulet, talisman, mascot, fetish, good-luck charm.

spiritism, spiritualism, spirit communication; séance, sitting; ouija board, planchette, automatic writing; levitation.

sorcerer, wizard, witch, enchanter, spell-binder, magician, conjurer; soothsayer, clairvoyant; astrologer; shaman, witch-doctor, medicine-man; voodoo; thaumaturgist, miracle-worker; diviner; exorcist; occultist, necromancer, spiritualist.

adj. sorcerous, devilish, diabolical, occult, necromantic; spell-binding; magical, supernatural, weird, uncanny, eerie; charmed, bewitched, enchanted; mystic, esoteric, transcendental.

vb. divine, conjure; wave a wand; exorcise, lay ghosts; call up spirits; bewitch, enchant, charm, fascinate, mesmerize, obsess, possess, put under a curse; hold a séance; go into a trance; materialize, dematerialize.

see also 447

985 churchdom

n. churchdom, Christendom, the church, ministry; call, vocation; office, holy orders; pastorship, pastorate, priesthood, clerical order, cure of souls, spiritual guidance, pastoral case, service, preaching, administration of the sacraments, prayer; fellowship communion.

adj. ecclesiastical, ministerial, pastoral, cleric, priestly, sacerdotal.

vb. call, ordain, consecrate, present, nominate; take holy orders.

986 clergyman

n. clergyman, servant of God, shepherd; pastor, preacher, minister, incumbent, priest, vicar, parson, rector; curate, chaplain, cleric, padre, father, reverend; abbot, prelate, bishop, archbishop, prior, dean, archdeacon, canon, primate, Pope; metropolitan, patriarch, cardinal; monk, friar; nun, sister; rabbi, teacher.

adj. clerical, ordained.

vb. be ordained, enter the ministry.

987 laity

n. laity, layman, lay people, parish, congregation, church, fold, flock, assembly, church member, parishioner, brethren; elder, deacon; lay-preacher, lay-reader.

adj. lay, unordained, non-clerical, secular, temporal, of the world, civil, profane, unholy, unconsecrated, unsacred.

vb. laicize, secularize, deconsecrate.

988 religious service

n. ceremony, ordinance, rite, ritual, custom, institution, observance; order, form, litany; administration, celebration, officiation.

service, divine worship, service of worship, morning service, matins, evening service, evensong, vespers, compline, fellowship, prayer meeting, Bible Study, Sunday School; Holy Communion, Lord's Supper, mass, Eucharist; baptism.

adj. ritual, ceremonial, customary, formal, liturgical.

vb. observe, keep, celebrate, minister, administer, officate, perform, dedicate, bless, pray, baptize, worship; encourage, share, fellowship.

989 vestment

n. vestment, cloth, clerical dress, canonicals, robes, surplice, gown, mantle, cassock, rochet, chasuble, cape, hood; mitre, staff, crook, crosier.

990 church building

n. church, chapel, sanctuary, house of prayer, house of God, Lord's house, bethel, kirk, tabernacle; mission, house-church, meeting-house; cathedral, minster, abbey; monastery, priory, friary, convent, nunnery; synagogue; mosque, shrine, temple.

Index

The index does not list every word or phrase in the main part of the book. In particular, many words derived from other related words, e.g. adverbs ending in *-ly* derived from adjectives, have been excluded. If you want to look up a word that is not in the index, you should therefore look up the word closest to it, and refer to the categories in the main part of the book, looking at the part of speech of the word you originally wanted. Further, a reference to a particular entry does not necessarily mean that the word looked up will appear at that entry – but since you are interested in other words related to this one, the fact that it does not occur at the entry is of no consequence.

Numbers printed in darker, bold type show the main categories for the particular words. The titles of the categories are also printed in the bolder typeface. For further help on finding the word you want, see the section 'How to use this thesaurus' at the front of the book.

Index

A

accolade *n.* 663, 965

accommodate *vb.* 105, 302, 545, 652

accommodation *n.* 191

accompaniment *n.* 60, 792

accompany *vb.* 60, 122, 882

accomplice *n.* 640

accomplish *vb.* 159, 609, 659, 661

accomplished *adj.* 581, 627, 659

accomplishment *n.* 609, 659, 661

accord *n.* 24, 643; *vb.* 16, 24, 105, 180

account *n.* (description) 460, 465, 483, 525; (money) 736, 742; *vb.* (describe) 157, 456, 483, 525; (pay) 742

accountable *adj.* 679, 919

accountant *n.* 733, 742

accounts *n.* 742

accretion *n.* 40, 41

accrue *vb.* 36, 40, 705, 716

accumulate *vb.* 36, 40, 94, 567, 705

accurate *adj.* 430, 476, 915

accursed *adj.* 892

accusation *n.* 930

accuse *vb.* 930

accustom *vb.* 105, 545

ache *n.* 828; *vb.* 828

achieve *vb.* 609, 659, 661

achievement *n.* 89, 609, 659, 661

achromatism *n.* 806

acid *n.* 773; *adj.* 773

acknowledge *vb.* 395, 424, 468, 692, 909, 925, 941

acme *n.* 212, 581

acoustics *n.* 778

acquaintance *n.* 882

acquiesce *vb.* 424, 654, 673, 692

acquire *vb.* 472, 705, 716, 720, 726

acquisition *n.* 705, 716, 726

acquisitive *adj.* 705, 750

acquit *vb.* 601, 680, 911, 921, 961

acquit oneself well *vb.* 919, 935

acquittal *n.* 601, 911, 961

acrimonious *adj.* 893, 900

act *n.* 609, 852, 954; *vb.* 172, 529, 609, 692

acting *n.* 529; *adj.* 689

action *n.* 172, 266, 609, 651, 960

activate *vb.* 88, 266, 282

active *adj.* 172, 368, 611

activism *n.* 611

activist *n.* 611; *adj.* 611

activity *n.* 266, 557, 609, 611

actor *n.* 529, 619

actress *n.* 529

actual *adj.* 1, 3, 120, 430

actuary *n.* 742

acumen *n.* 434

acute *adj.* 255, 434

acute angle *n.* 246

adage *n.* 432

Adam *n.* 379

adapt *vb.* 24, 105, 125, 142, 602, 606

adaptable *adj.* 105, 151

adaptation *n.* 456, 545, 792

add *vb.* 36, 40

addendum *n.* 41

addict *n.* 545

addition *n.* 38, 40, 41, 705

additional *adj.* 6, 40

additive *n.* 307

address *n.* 191, 518, 523, 695; *vb.* 514

addressee *n.* 523, 716

adept *n.* 629; *adj.* 627

adequate *adj.* 570, 579

adhere *vb.* 50

adherent *n.* 474, 640

adhesive *n.* 49; *adj.* 50

ad infinitum *adv.* 78

adjacent *adj.* 199, 238

adjective *n.* 499

adjoin *vb.* 199, 201

adjournment *n.* 89, 135

adjudicate *vb.* 415, 960

adjudicator *n.* 415, 653

adjunct *n.* 41, 60

adjure *vb.* 468, 695

adjust *vb.* 24, 105, 142, 403, 704

ad lib *adj.* 544; *vb.* 544

administer *vb.* 621, 622, 956, 988

administration *n.* 622, 667, 956

administrator *n.* 558, 623

admirable *adj.* 579

admire *vb.* 868, 888, 922, 925

admissible *adj.* 302

admission *n.* 98, 300, 302, 420, 462, 468, 716

admit *vb.* 98, 262, 300, 302, 424, 462, 468, 716, 833

admit defeat *vb.* 654

admonish *vb.* 597, 624, 926, 963

adolescent *n.* 131; *adj.* 129, 131

adopt *vb.* 540, 575, 606, 702, 720

adopted *adj.* 40, 100, 171, 606

adoption *n.* 171, 540, 606

adorable *adj.* 827

adore *vb.* 889, 982

adorn *vb.* 509, 844, 846

adroit *adj.* 627

adulation *n.* 927

adult *n.* 133; *adj* 133

adulterate *vb.* 45, 477, 582, 952

adulterer *n.* 953

adultery *n.* 952

adulthood *n.* 133

adumbrate *vb.* 798

advance *n.* **288**, 292, 587, 645, 693, 718, 890; *adj.* 236; *vb.* **288**, 292, 587, 645, 661, 718

advanced *adj.* 125

advantage *n.* 34, 550, 575

advantageous *adj.* 550, 575, 577, 661, 965

adventure *n.* 153, 269

adventurer *n.* 270

adventurous *adj.* 605

adverb *n.* 499

adversary *n.* 638, 883, 969

adverse *adj.* 14, 665

adversity *n.* 445, **665**

advertisement *n.* 464

advertising *n.* 727

advice *n.* 460, 597, **624**, 636

advisable *adj.* 577

advise *vb.* 460, 597, 624, 636

advisor *n.* 473, 624

advisory *adj.* 597, 624

advocate *n.* 959; *vb.* 959

aerate *vb.* 344, 348, 775

aerial *adj.* 273, 318, 348

aerodynamics *n.* 348

aeronautical *adj.* 273, 278

aeronautics *n.* 273

aeroplane *n* 278

aesthetic *adj* 848

affable *adj.* 884

affair *n.* 153, 557, 889, 952

affect *vb.* 177, 752, 755

affectation *n.* 510, **852**

affected *adj.* 510, 751, 752, 852

affection *n.* 752, 882, 889, 890

affections *n.* 751

affidavit *n.* 401, 468, 960

affiliate *vb.* 11, 52, 639, 641

affinity *n.* 18, 105, 218, 294

affirm *vb.* 401, 413, 424, 468, 514

affirmation *n* 413, 424, **468**, 690

affirmative *n.* 424; *adj.* 468

affix *n.* 499; *vb.* 40, 47

afflict *vb.* 830

affliction *n.* 551, 586, **592**, **665**, 828

affluence *n.* 664, 734

afford *vb.* 568, 715, 734

affront *n.* 923; *vb.* 887, 923

affronted *adj.* 893

afloat *adj.* 153

aforementioned *adj.* 84

afraid *adj.* 856

after *adj.* 119; *adv.* 85

after-effect *n.* 87, 156

afterlife *n.* 123

aftermath *n.* 87, 156

afternoon *n.* 128

afterthought *n.* 87, 441, 538

afterwards *adv.* 85

again *adv.* 62, 77

age *n.* 109, 130; *vb.* 130

aged *adj.* 130

ageless *adj.* 114, 129

agency *n.* 172, 563, 685

agenda *n* 83, 441

agent *n.* 149, 155, 564, **619**, 689

aggravation *n* 835

aggregate *n.* 54; *adj.* 54

aggressive *adj.* 173, 175, 645, 651

aggressor *n.* 645

aghast *vb* *adj.* 866

agile *adj.* 280, 611, 627

agitation *n.* 80, 326, 755, 756

agitator *n.* 142, 148

agnostic *n.* 975; *adj.* 409, 975, 981

agnosticism *n.* 409, 421, 975

ago *adv.* 124

agonize *vb.* 830

agonizing *adj.* 828

agony *n.* 756, 828

agrarian *adj.* 378

agree *vb.* 24, 105, 180, 424, 692, 925

agreeable *adj.* 692, 829

agreed *adj.* 24

agreement *n.* 24, 105, 424, 643, 650, 692, 699, 704, 925

agriculture *n.* 378

ahead *adv.* 236, 286

ahead of *adj.* 118

aid *n.* 563, **636**, 640, 834, 899; *vb.* 563, 636

ailment *n.* 586

aim *n.* 178, 284, 450, 552; *vb.* 178, 284, 552

aimless *adj.* 158, 399, 451, 553

air *n.* 329, 344, **348**, 621, 792; *vb.* 348, 350

air conditioning *n.* 348

aircraft *n.* **278**

airing *n.* 348

air in motion *n.* 359

airman *n.* 273

air-pipe *n.* **361**

airport n. 298
airs n. 852
air travel n. 273
airy adj. 4, 331, 333,
  344, 348
ajar adj. 262
akin adj. 11
alacrity n. 611
alarm n. 482, 598, 856
alarming adj. 594
album n. 441
alcoholism n. 950
alcove n. 254
alert n. 597, 598; adj.
  392, 602, 611; vb. 597,
  598
algebra n. 38
alias n. 497
alibi n. 549
alien n. 100; adj. 100
alienate vb. 883, 892
alight adj. 759; vb. 298
alike adj. 13, 18
alive adj. 368, 611, 753
all n. 54; adj. 54, 56
Allah n. 967
allegation n. 401, 930
allege vb 549, 959
alleged adj. 448, 549,
  825
allegiance n. 679, 919,
  980
allegory n. 397, 455,
  525
all-embracing adj. 54,
  98
allergic adj. 862
alleviate vb. 176, 652,
  834
alley n. 559
alliance n. 641, 699, 896
allied adj. 11, 47, 180,
  641
all-inclusive adj. 54, 98
allocation n. 717
allot vb 55, 717
allotment n. 378, 717

allow vb. 690, 692, 744,
  925
allowance n. 31, 690,
  715, 717, 718, 738, 744,
  965
allow for vb. 31, 403
alloy n. 45; vb. 45
all right adj. 579, 585;
  adv. 79
all-round adj. 627
allure vb. 547, 829, 889
allusion n. 455, 459
ally n. 640
ally with vb. 47
almanac n. 116, 483
Almighty n. 967
almighty adj. 159, 966
almost adv. 199
alms n. 715, 899
aloft adv. 208
alone adj. 48, 59
alongside adv. 238
aloof adj. 198, 517, 754,
  757, 885
alphabet n. 493
also adv. 40
alter vb. 142, 146
alternate vb. 12, 140,
  142, 325
alternative n. 149, 540;
  adj. 149
altitude n. 208
altogether adv. 54, 56
altruistic adj. 899, 903
always adv. 114
amalgamate vb. 45, 52
amass vb. 94, 567
amateur n. 630; adj.
  628
amaze vb. 866
ambassador n. 460, 467,
  688, 689
ambience n. 8, 229
ambiguity n. 409, 412,
  451, 453, 454, 503
ambition n. 552, 854,
  861

ambitious adj. 605, 611,
  854
ambivalent adj. 454
amble n. 269; vb. 269
ambrosia n. 770
ambulate vb. 269
ambush n. 463, 596; vb.
  463
amelioration n. 587
amenable adj. 179, 654
amend vb. 589
amendment n. 587
amends n. 31, 589, 721,
  943
amiable adj. 886
amicable adj. 643, 882
amity n. 643, 882
amnesia n. 442
amnesty n. 911
among prep. 230
amorous adj. 889
amorphous adj. 243
amount n. 26, 731, 743;
  vb. 743
amphibian n. 373; adj.
  373
amphitheatre n. 658
ample adj. 32, 75, 182
amplify vb. 36, 196,
  481, 505
amplitude n. 32, 194,
  204, 400
amputate vb. 42
amulet n. 984
amuse vb. 829, 840
amusement n. 829, 840
amusing adj. 840, 842,
  851
anachronism n. 117
anachronistic adj. 117,
  126
anaemic adj. 162, 806,
  807
analogy n. 9, 18, 397
analysis n. 38, 48, 53,
  394, 396
analyst n. 456
analytical adj. 38, 456

anarchist *n.* 148, 167, 672

anarchistic *adj.* 148, 644, 672

anarchy *n.* 80, 148, 668

anathema *n.* 892

anatomy *n.* 366, 375

ancestor *n.* 11, 86

anchor *n.* 330; *vb.* 152

ancient *adj.* 124, 126

ancillary *n.* 640; *adj.* 35, 60

and *adv.* 40

anecdote *n.* 525

anew *adv.* 77, 125

angel *n.* 467, 891, 905, 939, **968**

angelic *adj.* 935, 968

anger *n.* **893**; *vb.* 755, 893

angle *n.* 246, 420; *vb.* 219, 246

angry *adj.* 893

anguish *n.* 551, 828

angular form *n.* **246**

animal *n.* 175, 373, *adj.* 373

animality *n.* 373

animal sound *n.* **789**

animate *adj.* 366; *vb.* 173, 368, 618, 755, 836

animate matter *n* **366**

animism *n.* 974

animosity *n.* 425, 883, 900

annals *n* 116, 483

annex *vb.* 40

annexe *n.* 41

annihilate *vb.* 164, 370, 963

anniversary *n.* 140, 878; *adj.* 878

annotate *vb.* 456, 482

announce *vb.* 458, 460, 464

announcement *n.* 458, 460, 464, 465

announcer *n.* 460

annoy *vb.* 830, 835, 887, 893

annoyed *adj.* 893, 894

annually *adv.* 140

annulment *n.* **686**, 898

anoint *vb.* 342, 365

anonymous *adj.* 497

answer *n.* 283, 395, 402, 468, 523; *vb.* 395

answerable *adj* 179, 679, 737, 919

answer back *vb.* 395, 880

antagonism *n.* 181, 637, 883, **892**, 893

antagonist *n.* 638, 883

antagonistic *adj.* 637, 883, 892

antecede *vb.* 118

antecedent *n.* 86, 118, 155; *adj.* 84, 118

antedate *vb.* 117

antediluvian *adj.* 126

anterior *n.* 236; *adj.* 84, 118, 236

anthem *n.* 982

anthology *n.* 527

anthropoid *n.* 379

anthropology *n* 375, 379

anticipate *vb.* 134, 154, 443, 446, 854

anti-climax *n* 445

antidote *n.* 181

antinomianism *n.* 955

antiquated *adj.* 126

antique *adj.* 126

antiquity *n.* 124, 126

antisocial *adj.* 885, 904

anxious *adj.* 828, 856, 894

any *adj.* 26

anyhow *adv.* 80

apart *adj.* 48

apartheid *n.* 99

apartment *n.* 191

apathy *n.* 281, 389, 393, 612, 754, 841, 863

ape *n.* 20

aperitif *n.* 306

aperture *n.* 254, 262

aphasia *n.* 515

apocalypse *n.* 462

apolegetics *n* 410

apologetic *adj.* 833, 941

apologize *vb.* 538, 549, 833, 941, 943

apology *n.* 549, 833, 943

apostasy *n.* 147, 538, 590, 978

apostle *n* 974

appal *vb* 856

appalling *adj.* 830, 856

apparatus *n.* 565, 568

apparent *adj.* 458, 634, 823, 825

apparently *adv.* 825

apparition *n.* 4, 458, 971

appeal *n.* 518, 695, 960; *vb.* 695, 829

appear *vb.* 188, 298, 458, 621, **825**

appearance *n.* 222, 242, 298, 458, 621, **825**

appease *vb.* 335, 652, 831, 943

append *vb.* 40, 85

appendage *n* 41, 60, 87, 89

appendix *n.* 41

appertain *vb.* 707

appertaining *adj.* 9

appetite *n.* 861

appetizer *n.* 306

appetizing *adj.* 306, 767, 770

applause *n.* 838, 878, 888, 909, 925

appliance *n.* 565, 568

applicable *adj.* 9, 105, 575

applicant *n.* 697

application *n.* 172, 472, 575, 606, 611, 695

assemblage n. 47, **94**

assemble vb 47, 58, 94, 242, 568

assembly n. 59, 94, 625, 982, 987

assent n. **424**, 692; vb. 24, 424, 692

assert vb. 450, 468

assert oneself vb. 649

assess vb. 400, 415, 743

assessor n. 415, 653

assets n. 564, 566, 711, 734, 741

asseverate vb. 468

assiduous adj. 390, 392, 535

assign vb. 685, 714, 717

assignable adj. 157

assignment n. 470, 557

assignment of cause n. 157

assimilate vb. 302, 472

assist vb. 636

assistance n. 563, 636, 639

assistant n. 640, 676, 689

assizes n. 957

associate n. 640; vb. 9, 47, 94, 157, 397

associated adj. 60, 157, 639

association n. 52, 60, 397, 641

assorted adj. 45

assuage vb. 176, 652, 834

assume vb. 448, 720, 852

assumption n. 420, 918

assurance n. 408, 420, 854

assure vb. 420, 468, 701, 857

asthmatic adj. 359

astigmatism n. 820

astonish vb. 444, 866

astonishing adj. 444, 579, 866

astrologer n. 447, 984

astrology n. 329, 447

astronaut n. 274

astronomy n. 329

astute adj. 434

asylum n. 595

asymmetry n. 17, 219, **245**

atavism n. 147

at hand adj. 123, 188; adv. 199

atheism n. 421, 975

atheist n. 975

athlete n. 270

athletic adj. 161

at home n. 884

atlas n. 329

at last adv. 89

atmosphere n. 8, 229, 329, 348, 488

atoll n. 357

atom n. 33, 195, 327

atomic adj. 195

atomic bomb n. 657

atomize vb. 53, 164, 340

atonal adj. 791

at once adv. 115

atonement n. 31, 652, 911, **943**

atrocious adj. 856, 936

atrocity n. 900

attach vb. 40, 47

attaché n. 688

attached adj. 47, 889

attachment n. 41, 50, 60, 889, 890

attack n. 326, 439, 586, 645, 651; vb. 645, 648, 651, 928, 930

attacker n. 645, 723

attain vb. 472, 661

attainable adj. 292, 404

attainments n. 426, 472

attempt n. **604**; vb. 552, 604, 615

attend vb. 188, 287, 591, 676

attendant n. 60, 287, 683; adj. 60, 188

attending adj. 60, 676

attend to vb. 593, 795

attention n. **390**, 702

attentive adj. 390, 922

attenuate vb. 205, 333

attest vb. 401, 408, 413, 468

attested adj. 408, 430

at the same time adv. 122

attire n. 227

attitude n. 7, 420, 621, 818

attorney n. 959

attract vb. 224, 291, 294, 390, 547, 889

attract attention vb. 755

attraction n. 294, 330, 547

attractive adj. 579, 829, 844, 889

attributable adj. 157

attribute n. 5; vb. 157

atypical adj. 19

auburn adj. 810, 811

auction n. 727; vb. 727

audacious adj. 857, 887

audacity n. 857, 880

audible adj. 452, 778

audience n. 519, 795, 821

audition n. 795

auditorium n. 475, 795

augment vb. 36, 196

augur n. 447; vb. 447

augury n. 447, 597

aunt n. 11

aurora n. 127, 800

auspicious adj. 136, 447, 664, 854

austere adj. 669, 946

austerity n. 169, 669, 743, 946

balance *n.* 28, 31, 44, 152, 244, 330, 400, 731; *vb.* 28, 31, 152, 330, 397, 742
balance sheet *n.* 742
bald *adj.* 228
balderdash *n.* 451
balk at *vb.* 533
ball *n.* 249, 884
ballad *n.* 528
ballast *n.* 31, 152, 330
ballerina *n.* 793
ballet *n.* 792
ballistics *n.* 657
balloon *n.* 249, 278
ballot *n.* 540
ballyhoo *n.* 451
balm *n.* 176, 342, 365, 591, 776
balustrade *n.* 234
bamboozle *vb.* 478
ban *n.* 99, 681, 691, 694; *vb.* 99, 691
banality *n.* 432, 843
band *n.* 49, 94, 207, 250, 641, 793; *vb.* 47
bandage *n.* 49, 207
bandit *n.* 885
bane *n.* 551, 580, **592**
bang *n.* 782; *vb.* 282, 782, 787
banish *vb.* 99, 303, 963
bank *n.* 352, 718, 732
banker *n.* 718, 733
bank on *vb.* 443, 854
bankrupt *adj.* 571, 706, 735, 739; *vb.* 739
banner *n.* 482
banquet *n.* 306, 829, 840; *vb.* 304
banter *vb.* 842, 853
baptism *n.* 302, 988
baptize *n.* 302, 496, 988
bar *n.* (inn) 191; (restraint) 681; (tribunal) 957; *vb.* 99, 263, 635; *prep.* 42, 99

barb *n.* 255; *vb.* 255
barbarian *n.* 175
barbarism *n.* 495, 500, 511, 849
barbarous *adj.* 175, 900, 908
barbecue *n.* 306, 840
bard *n.* 528, 793
bare *adj.* 189, 228, 753; *vb.* 228
barely *adv.* 33
bargain *n.* 699, 746; *vb.* 699, 725, 726
bargain for *vb.* 443
bargaining *n.* 704, 725
barge *n.* 277
bark *vb.* 789
barman *n.* 676
baron *n.* 870
barrack *n.* 191
barrage *n.* 645
barrel *n.* 249
barren *adj.* 160, 169, 350, 612
barricade *n.* 635; *vb.* 635
barrier *n.* 234, 235, 635, 681
barrister *n.* 959
barrow *n.* 276, 372, 730
barter *n.* 150, 725; *vb.* 150, 725
base *n.* 89, **213**, 217; *adj.* 869, 924, 936
basement *n.* 213
bash *vb.* 282
bashful *adj.* 876
basic *adj.* 88, 155, 213, 573
basin *n.* 193, 213, 254, 354
basis *n.* 23, 155, 547
basket *n.* 193, 275
bastard *n.* 171, 955
baste *vb.* 306
bastion *n.* 646
batch *n.* 26, 94
bathe *vb.* 271, 349, 583

battle *n.* 649, 651
battleground *n.* 658
battlement *n.* 646
battleship *n.* 277
bawl *vb.* 788, 839
bay *n.* 353; *adj.* 810; *vb.* 789
bazaar *n.* 727, 730
be *vb.* 1, 185, 188, 368
beach *n.* 352
beacon *n.* 467, 482, 598, 800
beaker *n.* 193
be-all and end-all *n.* 573
beam *n.* 217, 797, 838; *vb.* 797, 838
beanfeast *n.* 306
bear *vb.* 217, 275, 368, 828
bearer *n.* 275, 467
bearing *n.* 9, 217, 284, 621, 825
bearings *n.* 185
bear in mind *vb.* 384
bear malice *vb.* 893
bear out *vb.* 413, 929
bear upon *vb.* 9
bear witness to *vb.* 401
beast *n.* 175, 373, 906
beastly *adj.* 900
beast of burden *n.* 275
beat *n.* 140, 325, 528; *vb.* 140, 282, 325, 340, 661, 783, 963
beat about the bush *vb.* 412, 505
beat off *vb.* 295, 646, 885
beat one's breast *vb.* 837
beat up *vb.* 645
beautiful *adj.* 844
beautify *vb.* 587, 844, 846
beauty *n.* 510, **844**
becalm *vb.* 267
beck *n.* 358

beckon *vb.* 482

becloud *vb.* 798, 799

become *vb.* 1, 142, 288

become of *vb.* 156

becoming *n.* 1; *adj.* 848

bed *n.* 206, 213, 360; *vb.* 378

bed and breakfast *n.* 191

bedaub *vb.* 584

bedeck *vb.* 846

Bedlam *n.* 80

bedlamite *n.* 440

bed of roses *n.* 661, 664, 827

bedouin *n.* 270

bedraggled *adj.* 584

bed-ridden *adj.* 586

be drunk *vb.* 950

be dry *vb.* 861

bedsitter *n.* 191

beefy *adj.* 161, 194

bee-line *n.* 248

Beelzebub *n.* 969

beer *n.* 309

be excited *vb.* 756

be excused *vb.* 310

befall *vb* 153

before *adj.* 118; *adv.* 84, 286

beforehand *adj.* 117

be found *vb.* 1, 185

befriend *vb.* 636, 882

befuddled *adj.* 950

beg *vb.* 695

beget *vb.* 163, 368

begetter *n.* 170

beggar *n.* 697, 735, 940

beggarly *adj.* 881

begin *vb.* 88, 605

begin again *vb.* 88

beginner *n.* 474, 630

beginning *n.* 88, 155

begrudge *vb.* 914

beg the question *vb* 412

beguile *vb.* 391, 478, 547

beguiler *n.* 480

behave oneself *vb.* 621, 886, 935

behead *vb.* 48, 370, 963

behest *n.* 671

behind *adj.* 135; *adv.* 85, 237

behind bars *adj.* 681

behindhand *adj.* 135

behind someone's back *adj.* 478

behind the scenes *adj.* 461

behind the times *adj.* 126

beholder *n.* 821

behove *vb.* 919

beige *n.* 810; *adj.* 810

being *n.* 1, 5, 327, 368; *adj.* 1

being according to external form *n.* 6

being according to internal form *n.* 5

being around *n.* 229

being between *n.* 230

being exterior *n.* 222

being horizontal *n.* 215

being interior *n.* 223

being oblique *n.* 219

being opposite *n.* 239

being vertical *n.* 214

belated *adj.* 135

belie *vb.* 469

belief *n.* 415, 420, 974

believable *adj.* 420

believe *vb.* 420, 448, 854

believer *n.* 146, 977, 980

believing *adj.* 420, 974, 977, 980

belittle *vb.* 924, 926, 928

bell *n.* 482, 598, 784; *vb.* 789

belle *n.* 844

belligerent *adj.* 651

bellow *vb.* 780, 788, 789

belong *vb.* 9, 58, 60, 202, 707

belonging *adj.* 9, 60

belongings *n.* 60, 568, 711

beloved *n.* 891; *adj.* 889

below *adv.* 209

below average *adj.* 580

below par *adj.* 35

below the belt *adj.* 916

belt *n.* 49, 207, 250, 964; *vb.* 963

bemoan *vb.* 833

bench *n.* 957

bencher *n.* 959

bend *n.* 219, 247; *vb.* 105, 219, 246, 285

bend over *vb.* 319

bend over backwards to help *vb.* 899

beneath *adv.* 209

beneath contempt *adj.* 924

beneath the surface *adj.* 459

benediction *n.* 909

benefactor *n.* 905

beneficial *adj.* 550, 575, 585, 636, 661

beneficiary *n.* 716

beneficient *adj.* 747

benefit *n.* 550, 575, 636, 705, 829, 899; *vb.* 575, 577, 579, 661, 705, 899

benevolence *n.* 636, 747, 899, 907

bent *n.* 178, 545, 751; *adj.* 219, 247, 252

bequeath *vb.* 714

bequest *n.* 714, 715

bereave *vb.* 898

bereavement *n.* 369, 706, 828

bereft *adj.* 706

berry *n.* 306

berserk *adj.* 439

berth *n* 191, 298

beryl *adj.* 812
beseech *vb.* 695, 982
beset *vb.* 633
besetting sin *adj.* 545
besetting sin *n.* 592, 936
beside oneself *adj.* 756
besides *adv.* 40
besiege *vb.* 645
be situated *vb.* 1, 185
besmirched *adj.* 584
best *adj.* 34, 579
best friend *n.* 882
bestow *vb.* 715, 965
bestseller *n.* 524
best wishes *n.* 888
be subject to *vb.* 179, 679
bet *n.* 553; *vb.* 553
bête noire *n.* 892
be the duty of *vb.* 919
bethel *n.* 990
betoken *vb.* 447, 450, 482
betray *vb.* 458, 462, 478, 932
betrayer *n.* 480
betrothal *n.* 698
betrothed *adj.* 698
better *n.* 34, 553; *adj.* 34; *vb.* 587
better half *n.* 896
betterment *n.* 550, 587
between *prep.* 230
between ourselves *adv.* 466
between the lines *adj.* 459
be up to *vb.* 159
beverage *n.* 309
bewail *vb.* 833
bewilder *vb.* 409, 866
bewitch *vb.* 829, 984
bewitched *adj.* 984
be worth *vb.* 743
beyond compare *adj.* 34, 581
beyond hope *adj.* 855
bi- *adj.* 61

bias *n.* 178, 416, 545, 751, 916; *vb.* 416
biased *adj.* 416, 916
Bible *n.* 524, 976
biblical *adj.* 976
bibliography *n.* 83, 524
bicker *vb.* 642
bicycle *n.* 276
bid *n.* 693, 695; *vb.* 394, 671, 693
bidder *n.* 697
bide one's time *vb.* 443, 610, 612
bifurcate *vb.* 63, 297
big *adj.* 32, 161, 194, 509
bigheaded *adj.* 873
big-hearted *adj.* 747
big-mouthed *adj.* 879
big name *n.* 868
bigot *n.* 537
bigoted *adj.* 416
big-sounding *adj.* 509
big talk *n.* 879
bigwig *n.* 675, 868
bike *n.* 276; *vb.* 269
bilateral *adj.* 61
bilious *adj.* 812, 813
bill *n.* 464, 482, 742, 960
billet *n.* 191
billion *n.* 70
bill of fare *n.* 306
billow *vb.* 358
billy-goat *n.* 380
bin *n.* 193
binary *adj.* 39, 61
bind *vb.* 47, 378, 681, 698, 919
binding *adj.* 919
binoculars *n.* 822
biographer *n.* 484, 524
biology *n.* 366
bipartite *adj.* 61
birch *n.* 964
bird *n.* 373
bird's eye view *n.* 818
bird-watching *n.* 375
birth *n.* 88, 155, 870

birthday *n.* 140, 878
biscuit *n.* 306
bisection *n.* 63
bishop *n.* 870, 986
bit *n.* 33, 55, 59
bit by bit *adv.* 55
bitch *n.* 381
bite *n.* 306, 306, 769; *vb.* 304
bite someone's head off *vb.* 893
biting *adj.* 255, 760, 773
bitter *adj.* 769, 773, 893, 900
bitter-sweet *adj.* 772
bitumen *n.* 365
bizarre *adj.* 139, 433
blabber *vb.* 462
black *n.* 808; *adj.* 798, 808; *vb.* 99
blacken *vb.* 798, 808, 928
blackguard *n.* 940
black hole *n.* 329
blackish *adj.* 808
blacklist *vb.* 99
black magic *n.* 984
blackmail *n.* 902; *vb.* 902
black-market *adj.* 955
black out *vb.* 485, 798
blackout *n.* 463, 466, 779, 798
black sheep *n.* 940
black spot *n.* 596
blame *n.* 926, 930, 938; *vb.* 157, 926, 930, 962
blameless *adj.* 937
blameworthy *adj.* 926
blanch *vb.* 806, 807
bland *adj.* 768, 771
blank *n.* 2; *adj.* 2, 385, 451, 754
blank cheque *n.* 678, 690
blanket *n.* 225; *adj.* 54, 101, 399
blankness *n.* 442, 867

blare *vb.* 780
blasé *adj.* 757
blaspheme *vb.* 901, 981
blast *n.* 359, 780, 782;
  vb. 175, 359
blatant *adj.* 877
blather *n.* 451, 516; *vb.*
  451
blaze *n.* 759, 797; *vb.*
  797
blazon *vb.* 464
bleach *vb.* 806, 807
bleached *adj.* 350
bleak *adj.* 760, 798
bleat *vb.* 789
bleed *vb.* 301, 358, 745
blemish *n.* 582, 660,
  845, 847; *vb.* 847
blend *n.* 45, 495; *vb.* 52
bless *vb.* 899, 982, 988
blessed *adj.* 972
blessing *n.* 550, 715,
  909
blessings *n.* 664
blight *n.* 53, 167, 592,
  665
blind *n.* 225, 463, 801;
  adj. 754, 819; *vb.* 797
blinded *adj.* 819
blindfold *adj.* 819; *vb.*
  819
blindness *n.* 819
blind spot *n.* 819
blink *vb.* 797, 818
blinker *vb.* 801, 819
blinkers *n.* 801
bliss *n.* 827, 972
blithe *adj.* 827
blitz *n.* 645; *vb.* 164
blizzard *n.* 175, 359,
  760
bloat *vb.* 196
bloated *adj.* 252
block *n.* 490, 681, 964;
  vb. 263, 265, 635
blockade *n.* 99, 681; *vb.*
  234, 265, 645
blockage *n.* 263, 635

blockhead *n.* 429, 437,
  630
blonde *adj.* 807
blood *n.* 11, 870
blood relationship *n.*
  11
bloodshed *n.* 370, 649
bloom *n.* 374
bloomer *n.* 431
blossom *n.* 374; *vb.*
  163, 168, 664
blot *n.* 584, 845, 847,
  869; *vb.* 584, 847, 869
blotch *n.* 847
blot out *vb.* 164, 485,
  911
blow *n.* 282, 444, 609,
  828, 900, 963; *vb.* 359,
  749
blowout *n.* 48, 306
blow up *vb.* 196, 359,
  782, 893
blubber *n.* 306, 365; *vb.*
  839
blue *n.* 815; *adj.* 815,
  837, 901, 952
blue blood *n.* 870
blue-eyed boy *n.* 891
blueprint *n.* 23, 558
blues *n.* 792, 837
bluff *vb.* 549
blunder *n.* 431, 500; *vb.*
  431
blunt *adj.* 256, 476, 508;
  vb. 162, 256, 754
bluntness *n.* 256
blur *n.* 847; *vb.* 799
blurb *n.* 464
blurred *adj.* 243, 503,
  799, 803, 824
blurt out *vb.* 462, 544
blush *n.* 811; *vb.* 811,
  876
bluster *n.* 879
blustery *adj.* 359
board *n.* 217, 305, 625,
  688
boarder *n.* 190

boast *n.* 879; *vb.* 873,
  875, 879
boaster *n.* 873, 879
boastful *adj.* 481, 509,
  875, 879
boasting *n.* 879
boat *n.* 193, 277
bode *vb.* 447, 450
bode well *vb.* 854
bodiless *adj.* 4, 328
bodily *adj.* 327, 827,
  945
body *n.* 3, 327, 368, 371
body-building *adj.* 585
bodyguard *n.* 593, 683
body odour *n.* 777
boffin *n.* 396, 448
bog *n.* 355
bogie *n.* 217
bogus *adj.* 477
boil *n.* 252; *vb.* 175,
  306, 363, 759, 893
boil down *vb.* 203, 527
boiler *n.* 763
boil over *vb.* 756
boisterous *adj.* 175,
  756, 780
bold *adj.* 458, 506, 534,
  644, 854, 857
boldness *n.* 534, 857,
  880
bolshie *adj.* 642
bolster *vb.* 217, 636
bolt *n.* 49, 613; *vb.* 47,
  263, 304
bolt down *vb.* 948
bomb *n.* 657; *vb.* 280,
  613, 645
bombard *vb.* 164, 645
bombast *n.* 509, 879
bombastic *adj.* 481, 877
bomber *n.* 278
bombshell *n.* 444
bonanza *n.* 75, 572
bond *n.* 49, 681, 701
bondage *n.* 679
bone *n.* 337
bone to pick *n.* 893

bonus *n.* 41. 965
boo *vb.* 788. 853. 926
booby prize *n.* 663
booby-trap *n.* 596
book *n.* 464. 524; *vb.* 83
bookishness *n.* 426
bookkeeping *n.* 742
booklet *n.* 464. 524
bookmaker *n.* 553
bookworm *n.* 428. 474. 524
boom *n.* 168. 217. 664. 780. 782. 784; *vb.* 780. 782. 784
boomerang *n.* 147. 283
boon *n.* 550
boorish *adj.* 887
boost *vb.* 36. 196. 318. 857
booster *n.* 173
booth *n.* 730
booty *n.* 663. 724
booze *vb.* 950
boozer *n.* 950
border *n.* 232. 233. 235; *vb.* 199. 201. 233. 236
bore *n.* 204. 437; *vb.* 254. 264. 617. 841
boredom *n.* 841
borer *n.* 264
boring *adj.* 77. 841. 843
borough *n.* 183
borrow *vb.* 719
borrowed *adj.* 100. 495
borrower *n.* 737
borrowing *n.* 495. **719**
boss *n.* 34. 675
botany *n.* 366. 374. 376
botch *vb.* 628
both *adj.* 61
bother *n.* 326; *vb.* 578. 695. 830. 856. 893
bothered *adj.* 856
bothersome *adj.* 633. 830
bottle *n.* 193; *vb.* 234. 599

bottleneck *n.* 205. 635
bottle up *vb.* 681
bottom *n.* 89. 210. 213. 237; *adj.* 213. 237
bottomless *adj.* 210
bough *n.* 374
bounce *n.* 173. 283. 326. 336; *vb.* 283. 320. 326. 336. 879
bouncer *n.* 303
bound *n.* 320; *vb.* 231. 235
boundary *n.* 89. 231. 232. 233. 235
boundless *adj.* 78. 202
bounteous *adj.* 168. 747
bounty *n.* 168. 572. 715. 747. 965
bouquet *n.* 776. 888. 925
bourgeois *adj.* 871
bout *n.* 586
boutique *n.* 730
bow *n.* 247. 319. 922; *vb.* 247. 319. 654. 673. 922
bow down *vb.* 982
bowl *n.* 193. 250. 254
bowl over *vb.* 444
box *n.* 193. 225; *vb.* 282. 963
boy *n.* 131. 380
boycott *n.* 99. 691; *vb.* 99. 144. 555. 691
boy-friend *n.* 882. 889
brace *n.* 217; *vb.* 161. 217
bracing *adj.* 585. 618
brag *vb.* 879
braid *n.* 49
brain *n.* 382. 428
brain-child *n.* 163
brainwash *vb.* 470. 547
braise *vb.* 306
brake *n.* 281; *vb.* 281
bramble *n.* 255
branch *n.* 55. 97. 358. 374. 620. 979; *vb.* 297

brand *n.* 97. 800. 869; *vb.* 482
brand-new *adj.* 125
brash *adj.* 859. 887
brass *n.* 794. 880; *adj.* 816
brat *n.* 131
brave *adj.* 857; *vb.* 644. 857
brawler *n.* 672
brawn *n.* 161
brawny *adj.* 161
bray *vb.* 789
brazen it out *vb.* 880
breach *n.* 703; *vb.* 703
bread *n.* 306
breadth *n.* 26. 204. 400
break *n.* 92. 200. 262. 614. 616; *vb.* 48. 92. 144. 164. 338. 703. 920
breakable *adj.* 338
break-away *adj.* 979
break down *vb.* 53. 588. 662. 839. 856
breakdown *n.* 48. 53. 586. 662
breaker *n.* 167. 358
breakfast *n.* 306
break in *vb.* 300
break in on *vb.* 137
breakneck *adj.* 859
break off *vb.* 89
break out *vb.* 88. 175. 600
break the law *vb.* 916. 955
breakthrough *n.* 661
break up *vb.* 53. 144. 588. 642
breakwater *n.* 217
break with *vb.* 556
breath *n.* 4. 359. 368. 512. 781
breathe *vb.* 359. 368
breather *n.* 92. 612. 614. 616
breathing space *n.* 144. 182

breathless *adj.* 369
breed *n.* 11, 97; *vb.* 163, 377, 470
breeding *n.* 377, 886
breeze *n.* 359
breezy *adj.* 348, 836
brevity *n.* 195, 203, 504
brewing *adj.* 154
bribe *vb.* 547
brickbat *n.* 926
bride *n.* 896
bridge *n.* 49; *vb.* 47
bridle *vb.* 681
brief *n.* 483; *adj.* 113, 203, 432, 504, 527
briefcase *n.* 193
briefing *n.* 460
brier *n.* 255
bright *adj.* 434, 759, 797, 805
brighten *vb.* 797, 836
brighten up *vb.* 840, 846
brilliant *adj.* 434, 581, 797, 805, 844
brim *n.* 233
brine *n.* 351
bring *vb.* 294
bring about *vb.* 155, 172, 609
bring back *vb.* 441
bring out *vb.* 464, 522
bring round *vb.* 420, 618
bring together *vb.* 94, 201, 652
bring to mind *vb.* 441
bring up *vb.* 303, 470
brink *n.* 233
brisk *adj.* 173, 280, 760
bristly *adj.* 258
brittleness *n.* 162, 338
broach *vb.* 605
broad *adj.* 101, 182, 204
broadcast *n.* 460, 464; *vb.* 95, 378, 460, 464, 465
broadcaster *n.* 460

broaden *vb.* 36, 101, 204
broad-minded *adj.* 288
brochure *n.* 464
broil *vb.* 306
broke *adj.* 735
broken *adj.* 833
broken down *adj.* 576
broken-hearted *adj.* 837
broken in *adj.* 602
broker *n.* 688
bronze *adj.* 810, 816
brood *n.* 94; *vb.* 384, 837
brook *n.* 358; *vb.* 757
broth *n.* 306
brother *n.* 11, 987
brotherhood *n.* 11, 639, 641
brow *n.* 212
brown *n.* 810; *adj.* 810
browned off *adj.* 832
browse *vb.* 472
bruise *n.* 588; *vb.* 282
bruised *adj.* 753
brunt *n.* 282
brush *n.* 649; *vb.* 201, 211, 341, 583, 649
brush aside *vb.* 393, 542
brush up *vb.* 472
brusque *adj.* 517, 887
brutal *adj.* 175, 900, 908
brute *n.* 175, 906
brutishness *n.* 900
bubble *n.* 249, 363; *vb.* 363
bubbling over *adj.* 827
bucket *n.* 193
buckle *vb.* 245, 247
buckle down *vb.* 615
bud *n.* 374
Buddha *n.* 967
Buddhism *n.* 974
budding *adj.* 125, 129, 134
buddy *n.* 882

budget *n.* 447, 742; *vb.* 742
buff *adj.* 810, 813
buffet *n.* 191, 306; *vb.* 359
buffoon *n.* 437, 842
buffoonery *n.* 433
bug *n.* 586; *vb.* 795
buggy *n.* 276
build *vb.* 36, 163, 242
builder *n.* 166
building *n.* 163
building society *n.* 718
build up *vb.* 36, 161
built-in *adj.* 55
bulb *n.* 252, 374, 800
bulbous *adj.* 252
bulge *n.* 252; *vb.* 56, 252
bulk *n.* 32, 75, 204, 330, 567
bulkiness *n.* 194
bull *n.* 380, 671
bulldog *n.* 535
bullet *n.* 290
bulletin *n.* 465, 483
bulletproof *adj.* 593
bull's eye *n.* 224
bully *n.* 175, 940; *vb.* 902
bump *n.* 141, 252, 282, 326, 785; *vb.* 282, 785
bunch *n.* 94
bundle *n.* 94, 567; *vb.* 567
bung *n.* 265; *vb.* 265
bungalow *n.* 191
bungle *vb.* 431, 628
bungler *n.* 630
bunion *n.* 252
bunk *n.* 451
bunker *n.* 193
bunting *n.* 482, 846
buoy *n.* 331
buoyant *adj.* 331, 336
burden *n.* 387, 665, 828, 919; *vb.* 330, 635

burdensome *adj.* 330,
633
bureau *n.* 620
bureaucracy *n.* 667
bureaucrat *n.* 623
bureaucratic *adj.* 622,
667
burglar *n.* 723
burglary *n.* 722
burial *n.* 372
buried *adj.* 210, 372,
461
burlesque *n.* 487, 842,
853
burly *adj.* 161
burn *n.* 828; *vb.* 759,
761, 797, 828, 893
burning *n.* 370, 761;
adj 752, 759, 811
burnish *vb.* 257, 341,
797
burr *vb.* 512
burrow *n.* 254
bursar *n.* 733
burst *n.* 48, 280, 613;
vb. 48, 338, 782
burst forth *vb.* 88
burst into flames *vb.*
759
burst into tears *vb.* 839
burst out *vb.* 600
bury *vb.* 311, 372, 461,
472
bus *n.* 276
bush *n.* 374
business *p.* 557, 605,
725
businesslike *adj.* 79,
557
businessman *n.* 728
bust *n.* 489; *adj.* 739
bustle *n.* 611; *vb.* 611,
613
busy *adj.* 557, 611
busy-body *n.* 388
butcher *n.* 370; *vb.* 370
butler *n.* 676
butt *n.* 853; *vb.* 282

butter *n.* 306
buttercup *n.* 813
butterfingers *n.* 630;
adj. 628
butterflies *n.* 326, 856
butter up *vb.* 927
buttress *n.* 217
buy *vb.* 547, 705, 726
buyer *n.* 710, 726, 737
buzz *n.* 783, 786; *vb.*
783, 784, 786, 789
by accident *adv* 158
by chance *adv.* 158
bygone *adj.* 124
by-law *n.* 954
by-pass *n.* 322, 559,
561; *vb.* 322
by-product *n.* 87, 156
bystander *n.* 821
by the way *adv.* 10

C

cab *n.* 276
cabal *n.* 461, 558
cabaret *n.* 529
cabinet *n.* 625, 688
cable *n.* 49, 207, 460,
467; *vb.* 460
cackle *n.* 783, 838; *vb.*
783, 789
cacophony *n.* 787, 791
cad *n.* 849
cadge *vb.* 719
cadger *n.* 697
café *n.* 191
cage *n.* 234, 682
cajole *vb.* 478, 547, 927
cajoler *n.* 927
cake *n.* 306
calamity *n.* 153, 551,
665
calculate *vb.* 38, 400,
552
calculation *n.* 38, 400
calculator *n.* 38, 400

calculus *n.* 38
calendar *n.* 116
calibrate *vb* 27, 400
calibre *n.* 204, 400
call *n.* 788, 789, 884;
vb. 482, 496, 788
call away *vb.* 391
call by *vb.* 884
caller *n.* 884
call for *vb.* 562
call forth *vb.* 155, 547
call-girl *n.* 953
calligraphy *n.* 521
call in *vb.* 731
calling *n.* 557
call of duty *n.* 919
call on *vb* 695
callous *adj.* 754, 900,
942
callow *adj.* 129
call up *vb.* 94, 441, 651
call upon *vb.* 394, 919
calm *n.* 267; *adj.* 176,
616, 681, 757; *vb.* 652,
779
calm down *vb.* 757
calque *n.* 495
calumny *n.* 869, 928
camber *n.* 247
cameo *n.* 489
camera *n.* 822
cameraman *n.* 491
camouflage *n.* 18, 461,
463; *vb.* 146, 461, 646
camp *n.* 191; *vb.* 186
campaign *n.* 605, 621,
651; *vb.* 649
campus *n.* 658
can *n.* 193; *vb.* 404, 599
canal *n.* 261, 360
cancel *vb.* 485, 686, 955
cancel out *vb.* 181, 402
cancer *n.* 167, 252, 592
candid *adj.* 476, 632,
931
candidate *n.* 395, 638,
697, 854
candle *n.* 800

candour *n.* 476

cane *n.* 964; *vb.* 963

canister *n.* 193

cannon *n.* 657

canoe *n.* 277

canoeing *n.* 271

canon *n.* 420, 626, 671, 976, 986

canonical *adj.* 976

canonicals *n.* 989

canopy *n.* 225, 801

cant *n.* 495, 981

cantankerous *adj.* 894

canteen *n.* 191

canticle *n.* 982

canvas *n.* 488

canvass *vb.* 394, 464, 695

canvasser *n.* 394, 697

canyon *n.* 254

cap *n.* 212; *vb.* 34, 212

capable *adj.* 159, 404, 627

capacious *adj.* 182, 194

capacity *n.* 26, 159, 194

cape *n.* 989

capillary *adj.* 207

capital *n.* 493, 711, 731; *adj.* 34, 212, 579

capitalist *n.* 728, 734

capitalize *vb.* 136, 606, 705

capital punishment *n.* 963

capitulate *vb.* 654

caprice *n.* 449, 539

capricious *adj.* 141, 151, 449, 539

capsize *vb.* 220, 317

capsule *n.* 193, 279, 591

captain *n.* 272, 675

captivate *vb.* 420, 547, 829, 889

captivation *n.* 755

captive *n.* 676, 684, 701

capture *n.* 663, 720, 724; *vb.* 705, 720

car *n.* 276

caravan *n.* 291

carcass *n.* 371

card *n.* 482

cardinal *n* 986; *adj.* 34

cardinal point *n.* 284

care *n.* (carefulness) 392, 860; (worry) 828, 830; *vb.* 593, 676, 889

career *n.* 557

carefree *adj.* 831, 836

careful *adj.* 392, 398, 748, 860

careless *adj.* 391, 393, 703, 749, 859, 920

caress *vb.* 758, 890

caretaker *n.* 683

cargo *n.* 192

caricature *n.* 20, 22, 487, 853; *vb.* 20, 487, 853

carnage *n.* 370, 649

carnal *adj.* 827, 945

carnival *n.* 529, 840

carnivore *n.* 373

carouse *vb.* 840

carpet *n.* 225

carrel *n.* 475

carriage *n.* 217, 268, 276, 621

carried away *adj.* 827

carrier *n.* 275, 460, 467

carrot *n.* 547, 816

carry *vb.* 217, 268, 275

carry on *vb.* 91, 145, 535

carry out *vb.* 609, 659, 702

cart *n.* 276; *vb.* 268

carte blanche *n.* 678, 690

cartel *n.* 641, 681

cartilage *n.* 337

carton *n.* 193

cartoon *n.* 488

cartoonist *n.* 491

carve *vb.* 48, 163, 242, 489, 490

carver *n.* 491

cascade *n.* 358; *vb.* 358

case *n.* 7, 193, 401, 499, 930, 960

cash *n.* 731

cash-book *n.* 742

cash box *n.* 732

cashier *n.* 733, 742

cash in on *vb.* 136, 606, 705

cash register *n.* 732

casserole *vb.* 306

cassette-recorder *n.* 484, 794

cassock *n.* 989

cast *n.* 22, 94, 489, 529; *vb.* 242, 489

castaway *n.* 885

cast down *vb.* 321, 837

caste *n.* 97

castle *n.* 191, 595, 646

castles in the air *n.* 449

cast lots *vb.* 447

cast off *vb.* 228, 271, 556

castoffs *n.* 44

castrate *vb.* 160, 169

casual *n.* 655; *adj.* 139, 158, 393, 409

casuistry *n.* 631

catacomb *n.* 372

catalogue *n.* 83, 483; *vb.* 83, 483

catalyst *n.* 142, 173

cataract *n.* 358, 820

catastrophe *n.* 153, 551, 665, 900

catastrophic *adj.* 148, 551, 665

catch *n.* 635; *vb.* 478, 720, 795

catch-all *n.* 54; *adj.* 54

catch in the act *vb.* 419, 444, 938

catch on *vb.* 452, 545, 850

catch sight of *vb.* 818

catch up *vb.* 280

catchy *adj.* 790

chase n. 554; vb. 287,
490, 554, 882, 890
chaser n. 554
chasm n. 200, 254, 317
chassis n. 217
chaste adj. 876, 935,
951
chastened adj. 874
chastise vb. 963
chat n. 516, 519; vb.
514, 516, 519
chatter n. 516, 519; vb.
326, 388, 516, 760
chatterbox n. 388, 516
chatty adj. 460, 516
chauffeur n. 676
chauvinist n. 903; adj.
379
cheap adj. 746
cheapen vb. 746, 924
cheapness n. 746
cheat n. 480, 631, 940;
vb. 478, 631, 722, 916,
932
cheater n. 723
check n. 396, 635, 648,
681; vb. 37, 144, 394,
396, 408, 413, 635, 681
checker vb. 817
checklist n. 83
cheeky adj. 880, 887
cheer n. 827; vb. 618,
788, 834, 836, 840, 925
cheerfulness n. 836, 854
cheerless adj. 837, 895
cheers vb. 838, 878
cheese n. 306
cheesed off adj. 832
cheese-paring n. 750
cheque n. 731
chequer vb. 817
cherish vb. 441, 712,
889, 890
cherub n. 968
chest n. 193
chestnut n. 842; adj.
810
chew vb. 304

chicanery n. 631
chicken adj 858
chicken out vb. 858
chide vb. 926
chief n. 34, 675; adj. 34,
573
child n. 11, 131, 171
childhood n. 129
childish adj. 129, 131,
435
childless adj. 169
childlike adj. 129, 131,
632
chill n. 760; vb. 762
chilly adj. 760, 883
chime n. 784; vb. 783,
784
chimney n. 361
chink n. 200, 797
chip n. 33, 55, 482; vb.
48, 377
chip in vb. 738
chip on one's shoulder
n. 832
chirp vb. 789
chirpy adj. 836
chirrup vb. 789
chisel n. 312, 480; vb.
163, 312, 478, 489, 490
chit n. 523
chit-chat n. 465, 516,
519
chivalry n. 857, 886
chocolate adj. 810
choice n. 398, 530, 540;
adj. 579, 770
choiceless adj. 541
choir n. 793
choke vb. 265, 370, 572,
762
choleric adj. 894
choose vb. 398, 530,
532, 540, 861
choosy adj. 398, 540,
864
chop vb. 48, 319
chop and change vb.
151

choppy adj. 258
choral adj. 792
chord n. 247
chorister n. 793
chortle vb. 838
chorus n. 528, 792, 793,
982
christen vb. 496
Christendom n. 977,
985
Christian n. 977, 982
Christianity n. 974
chromatic adj. 805
chronicle n. 116, 483;
vb. 483
chronicler n. 484
chronological adj. 116
chronometer n. 116
chronometry n. 116
chuck vb. 290, 556
chuckle n. 783, 838; vb.
783, 789, 838
chum n. 882
chunky adj. 203, 204
church n. 977, 982, 985,
987, 990
church building n. 990
churchdom n. 985
church-goer n. 982
church member n. 977,
987
churchyard n. 372
churlish adj. 895
cigar n. 308
cigarette n. 308
cinema n. 529, 840
cipher n. 39, 466
circle n. 94, 247, 250,
323; vb. 229, 322, 323
circuit n. 140, 232, 250,
269, 322, 323, 561
circular n. 464, 523;
adj. 250
circulate vb. 322, 323,
460
circulation n. 322
circumambulate vb.
231, 322

circumference *n.* 232, 250

circumlocution *n.* 505

circumscription *n.* 231

circumspect *adj.* 392, 434, 860

circumstance *n.* 8, 153

circumstances *n.* 8, 229

circumstantial *adj.* 8

circumvent *vb.* 231, 555

circus *n.* 250, 559, 658

cistern *n.* 193

citadel *n.* 646

citation *n.* 663, 925

citizen *n.* 190, 871

city *n.* 183

city-dweller *n.* 190

civic *adj.* 379

civil *adj.* 379, 886, 987

civilian *n.* 871

civility *n.* 886

civilization *n.* 379

civilized *adj.* 379

clad *adj.* 227

claim *n.* 671, 737; *vb.* 549, 671, 917

claimant *n.* 697

clairvoyant *n.* 447, 984

clamber *vb.* 316

clammer *n.* 175

clamorous *adj.* 695, 780, 788

clamour *n.* 780, 788; *vb.* 695, 788

clamp *vb.* 47

clamp down on *vb.* 669

clan *n.* 11

clandestine *adj.* 461

clang *n.* 783; *vb.* 783, 784, 787

clanger *n.* 431

clanging *n.* 784; *adj.* 784, 787

clap *vb.* 282, 838, 878, 925

clarify *vb.* 456

clarity *n.* 452, 502, 823

clash *n.* 175, 282; *vb.*

14, 282, 642, 787, 791, 805, 883

clasp *n.* 49, 712; *vb.* 50, 712, 720, 758, 890

class *n.* 7, 55, 97, 122, 206, 470, 472, 474; *vb.* 97

classified *adj.* 81, 466

classify *vb.* 81, 83, 97, 496

classroom *n.* 475

clatter *vb.* 783, 787

clause *n.* 498

clean *adj.* 46, 583, 937, 951; *vb.* 341, 583, 775, 807

cleaner *n.* 676

cleanliness *n.* 583, 585, 951

cleanness *n.* 583, 951

cleanse *vb.* 583

cleanser *n.* 775

clear *adj.* 46, 413, 452, 458, 502, 512, 678, 797, 802, 823, 921; *vb.* 320, 583, 921, 961

clearance *n.* 182, 200, 690, 727

clear-cut *adj.* 452, 823

clear-headed *adj.* 949

clearmindedness *n.* 438

cleavage *n.* 48

cleave *vb.* 48, 50

cleft *n.* 200, 259

clemency *n.* 670, 907

clergyman *n.* 986

cleric *n.* 986; *adj.* 985

clerical *adj.* 986

clerical dress *n.* 989

clerk *n.* 484

clever *adj.* 426, 434, 627, 631

cliché *n.* 495, 498

click *vb.* 24, 452, 782

client *n.* 545, 716, 726

cliff *n.* 214

climate *n.* 8, 229, 348

climax *n.* 89, 212

climb *vb.* 273, 316

climb down *vb.* 538

clinch *n.* 712; *vb.* 47, 50, 408, 712

clincher *n.* 414

cling *vb.* 50, 712

clip *vb.* 203

clipper *n.* 277

clippings *n.* 44

clique *n.* 94, 641

cloak *n.* 461, 463, 549; *vb.* 461

clock *n.* 116

clog *vb.* 265

cloister *n.* 885

clonk *n.* 785; *vb.* 785

close *n.* 89, 184, 559; *adj.* 47, 50, 154, 199, 419, 759, 882; *vb.* 144, 263, 461

closed book *n.* 427, 453

closed shop *n.* 99, 681

close-fisted *adj.* 750

close friend *n.* 882

close in on *vb.* 292

close-lipped *adj.* 517

close shave *n.* 600

closure *n.* 89, 144, 263

clot *vb.* 332

cloth *n.* 989

clothe *vb.* 227

clothes *n.* 227

cloud *n.* 363, 803; *vb.* 461, 799, 803

cloudburst *n.* 175, 358

cloudless *adj.* 664, 797

cloudy *adj.* 358, 363, 503, 799, 803, 824

clout *n.* 963; *vb.* 282, 963

clown *n.* 842

clowning *n.* 433

cloy *vb.* 56, 865

club *n.* 96, 191; *vb.* 282, 639

cluck *vb.* 787, 789

clue *n.* 401, 447, 482

clumsy *adj.* 511, 628

cluster *n.* 94
clutch *vb.* 712, 758
clutter *n.* 80
coach *n.* 276, 473; *vb.* 470
coagulate *vb.* 332, 334
coagulated *adj.* 362
coal *n.* 367, 765, 800
coalesce *vb.* 13, 52
coalition *n.* 641
coarse *adj.* 258, 511, 849, 887, 952
coastline *n.* 352
coat *n.* 206, 225; *vb.* 225, 342, 805
coating *n.* 206, 225
coat of arms *n.* 482
coax *vb.* 547, 695
cock *n.* 380
cocktail *n.* 309
cock-up *n.* 628
cocky *adj.* 875
coddle *vb.* 306
code *n.* 103, 466, 954
codification *n.* 954
coerce *vb.* 175, 674
coexist *vb.* 60, 122
coextensive *adj.* 28, 218
coffee *n.* 309; *adj.* 810
coffee-bar *n.* 191
coffee-break *n.* 616
coffer *n.* 193, 732
coffin *n.* 372
cog *vb.* 259
cogitation *n.* 384, 410
cognition *n.* 426
cognitive *adj.* 382
cognizability *n.* 452
cognizant *adj.* 426
cohabit *vb.* 889
cohabitant *n.* 889
cohere *vb.* 50
coherence *n.* 50, 337
cohesive *adj.* 50
coil *n.* 251; *vb.* 249
coin *vb.* 449, 731
coinage *n.* 495

coincide *vb.* 13, 24, 28, 60, 122
coincidence *n.* 24, 60, 105, 122, 553
coincidental *adj.* 60, 158
coke *n.* 765
cold *n.* 760; *adj.* 754, 760, 806, 863
cold-blooded *adj.* 754, 908
cold feet *n.* 856, 858
cold shoulder *n.* 924; *vb.* 885
cold war *n.* 650
coliseum *n.* 658
collaborate *vb.* 180, 639
collaborator *n.* 640
collage *n.* 488
collapse *n.* 164, 588, 617, 662; *vb.* 254, 588, 617
collate *vb.* 397
collateral *n.* 701; *adj.* 11
colleague *n.* 640
collect *vb.* 94, 567, 705, 716
collective *n.* 709; *adj.* 24
collectively *adv.* 60
college *n.* 475
collide *vb.* 282
collision course *n.* 296
colloid *n.* 362; *adj.* 362
colloquial *adj.* 495
colloquialism *n.* 494, 495
colonist *n.* 190
colonize *vb.* 191
colony *n.* 94
coloration *n.* 805
colossal *adj.* 32
colour *n.* 509, 805, 811; *vb.* 403, 509, 805
colour-blind *adj.* 819, 820
colourful *adj.* 805

colourlessness *n.* 806, 843
colours *n.* 482
column *n.* 91, 208, 217
coma *n.* 754
combat *n.* 651; *vb.* 637, 649
combatant *n.* 655
combination *n.* 45, 52
combine *vb.* 45, 47, 52, 639
combustible *n.* 765; *adj.* 761, 765
combustion *n.* 761
come *vb.* 298
come about *vb.* 153, 430
come across *vb.* 186, 419
come after *vb.* 85, 119, 287
comeback *n.* 147, 395, 589
come back to *vb.* 395
come before *vb.* 84, 118
come by *vb.* 716
come clean *vb.* 462
comedian *n.* 842
come down *vb.* 273, 317
come-down *n.* 874
come down on *vb.* 669, 963
comedy *n.* 529
come first *vb.* 286
come forward *vb.* 292, 693
come home *vb.* 298, 755
come in *vb.* 300, 716
come into *vb.* 705
come into conflict with *vb.* 25
come into sight *vb.* 292, 823
come into view *vb.* 823, 825
comely *adj.* 844

come near *vb.* 292
come next *vb.* 85
come of *vb.* 156
come of age *vb.* 133
come off *vb.* 153, 661
come on *vb.* 587
come out *vb.* 88, 144, 301, 464
come out with *vb.* 462
come round again *vb.* 140
come round to *vb.* 420
come short *vb.* 315, 445, 571
comestible *adj.* 306
comet *n.* 329
come to *vb.* 743
come to a head *vb.* 659
come to an agreement *vb.* 699, 704
come to an end *vb.* 89
come to blows *vb.* 642
come together *vb.* 94, 296
come to life *vb.* 368
come to light *vb.* 825
come to mind *vb.* 384, 441
come to nothing *vb.* 2, 315, 369, 576, 662
come to the point *vb.* 504
come up *vb.* 153
come up against *vb.* 25
come up to *vb.* 28, 570
comfort *n.* 636, 834; *vb.* 636, 834, 836, 899, 907
comfortable *adj.* 634, 664, 827, 834
comforting *adj.* 834, 907
comic *adj.* 851
coming *n.* 292, 298; *adj.* 123, 154
coming out *n.* 88
command *n.* 501, 622, 626, 667, 671; *vb.* 208, 622, 667, 671

commandeer *vb.* 720
commander *n.* 623, 675
commanding *adj.* 667, 671
commandment *n.* 626
commemorate *vb.* 441, 878
commemorative *adj.* 441, 878
commence *vb.* 88, 605
commend *vb.* 925
commendable *adj.* 579, 925
commensurate *adj.* 28
comment *n.* 456, 526; *vb.* 456, 526
commentary *n.* 456, 526
commentator *n.* 456, 526, 974
commerce *n.* 150, 725
commercial *adj.* 725
commercial traveller *n.* 727
commiserate *vb.* 907
commission *n.* 94, 557, 609, 685; *vb.* 557, 685
commissioner *n.* 688, 689
commissioner for oaths *n.* 959
commit *vb.* 609, 685, 698, 714
commit adultery *vb.* 952
commitment *n.* 605, 698, 737, 919, 980
commit oneself *vb.* 534, 540, 605, 919
commit suicide *vb.* 370
committed *adj.* 534, 698, 737, 980
committee *n.* 94, 625, 688
commodities *n.* 729
commodity *n.* 327
common *n.* 356; *adj.*

35, 138, 508, 666, 709, 843, 867
commoner *n.* 871
commonly *adv.* 138
common people *n.* 871
commonplace *n.* 432; *adj.* 138, 666, 843
common sense *n.* 434
commotion *n.* 326, 611
communal *adj.* 379, 709
communicant *n.* 982
communicate *vb.* 460, 464, 514, 519, 523
communication *n.* 460, 464, 492, 514, 523
communicative *adj.* 460
communion *n.* 979
communiqué *n.* 465
communism *n.* 709
community *n.* 183, 379, 641, 709
commutable *adj.* 150
commutation *n.* 149
commute *vb.* 142, 149, 150
commuter *n.* 190, 270
compact *adj.* 50, 203, 204, 332, 334, 504; *vb.* 332
companion *n.* 640, 882
company *n.* 94, 620, 641
comparable *adj.* 28
comparative *adj.* 27, 455
compare *vb.* 27, 218, 397
comparison *n.* 18, 27, 397, 455, 499
compartment *n.* 55
compass *n.* 182, 322
compassion *n.* 670, 907
compassionate *adj.* 670, 899, 907
compatible *adj.* 24, 105, 882
compatriot *n.* 11

compel *vb.* 177, 531, 562, 674, 755

compelling *adj.* 674, 755

compendious *adj.* 54, 527

compendium *n* 527

compensation *n.* 31, 721, 738, 917, 965

compensatory *adj.* 31, 721, 943, 965

compete *vb.* 649

competence *n.* 159, 627, 956

competent *adj.* 159, 579, 627, 956

competition *n.* 649

competitive *adj.* 649

competitor *n.* 638, 854

compile *vb.* 58

complacency *n.* 831

complain *vb.* 642, 788, 832, 926, 930

complainer *n.* 832

complaint *n.* 586, 696, 926, 930

complement *n.* 28, 60

complete *adj.* 54, 56, 581, 659; *vb.* 581, 609, 659, 661

completely *adv.* 54, 56

completeness *n.* 54, 56

completion *n.* 89, 581, 659, 661

complex circularity *n.* 251

complexion *n.* 805

complexity *n.* 503

compliance *n.* 532, 673, 692, 702

compliant *adj.* 532, 654, 919

complicate *vb.* 835

complicated *adj.* 453, 503, 633

compliment *n.* 886, 888, 925, 927; *vb.* 886, 888, 925

comply *vb* 105, 570, 654, 673, 70£

component *n.* 55, 192, 327

compose *vb.* 58, 81, 163, 521, 528, 792

composed *adj.* 757

composer *n.* 166, 491, 528, 793

composite *adj.* 45

composition *n.* 45, 58, 81, 339, 488, 521, 522, 526, 528, 792

compositor *n.* 522

composure *n.* 757

compound *n.* 45, 184; *vb.* 36, 52

comprehend *vb.* 58, 98, 452

comprehensible *adj.* 452

comprehension *n.* 410, 452

comprehensive *adj.* 54, 56, 98, 101

compress *vb.* 37, 197, 205, 332, 504

compressed *adj.* 332, 504

compressor *n.* 197

comprise *vb.* 58, 98

compromise *n.* 30, 699, 704; *vb.* 704

compulsion *n.* 439, 531, 562, 674

compulsive *adj.* 674

compulsory *adj.* 531, 674, 919

compunction *n.* 833

compunctious *adj.* 94!

compute *vb.* 38, 400

computer *n.* 38, 400, 565

comrade *n.* 640, 882

con *n.* 631, 684; *vb.* 631

concatenation *n.* 47, 85

concavity *n.* 254

conceal *vb.* 225, 461, 466

concealment *n.* 461, 824

concede *vb.* 424, 462, 690, 692

conceited *adj.* 873, 875

conceivable *adj.* 404

conceive *vb.* 88, 163, 368, 382, 449

concentrate *vb.* 96, 296, 334, 384, 390

concentration *n.* 296, 332, 384, 390, 611

concept *n.* 386

conception *n.* 382, 386, 420

concern *n.* 387, 392, 557, 605, 620; *vb.* 9, 526, 609, 856

concerned *adj.* 388, 392

concerning *adv., prep.* 9

concert *n.* 180, 643, 790, 792, 840

concerto *n.* 792

concession *n.* 690, 704, 744

conciliation *n.* 650, 652

concise *adj.* 203, 432, 504, 527

conciseness *n.* 504

conclude *vb.* 56, 89, 410, 530

conclusion *n.* 89, 144, 235, 410, 659

conclusive *adj.* 408, 413, 430, 659

concoct *vb.* 163, 477, 558, 930

concomitant *n.* 60; *adj.* 60

concord *n.* 24, 643, 790

concordance *n.* 494, 524

concordat *n.* 699

concrete *adj.* 3, 327, 332

concur *vb.* 24, **180**, 424, 692

concurrence *n.* 24, **180**, 296, 692

concurrent *adj.* 24, 60, 122, 180, 296

condemn *vb.* 892, 926, **962**

condemnation *n.* **962**

condemned *adj.* 938

condemned cell *n.* 964

condensation *n.* 346

condense *vb.* 203, 332, 345, 504, 527

condescend *vb.* 869, 874, 886

condiment *n.* 307

condition *n.* 7, 562, 825; *vb.* 470, 545

conditional *adj.* 403, 700

conditioning *n.* 470, 545

conditions *n.* 8, **700**

condolence *n.* 907

conduce *vb.* 155

conducive *adj.* 178, 563

conduct *n.* 172, 606, **621**, 622; *vb.* 268, 606, 609, 621, 622

conduit *n.* 360

confectionery *n.* 306

confederate *n.* 640: *adj.* 641; *vb.* 47

confederation *n.* 641

confer *vb.* 159, 519, 715, 965

conference *n.* 94, 519, 625

confess *vb.* 420, 462, 941, 982

confession *n.* 420, 941, 974, 982

confidant *n.* 624, 882

confide *vb.* 462, 624

confidence *n.* 408, 420, 443, 466, 854

confident *adj.* 420, 443, 854, 857

confidential *adj.* 466

confine *vb.* 205, 234, 681, 712

confirm *vb.* 401, 408, 413, **468**, 699, 929

confiscate *vb.* 720

conflict *n.* 649; *vb.* 637, 642, 805, 883

confluence *n.* 221, 296

conform *vb.* 16, 24, **105**, 702

conformist *n.* 20, 105

conformity *n.* 16, **105**, 244, 643

confound *vb.* 82, 399, 414, 869

confront *vb.* 239, 637, 644, 649

confrontation *n.* 637, 649

confuse *vb.* 82, 187, 399

confused *adj.* 80, 399, 439

confusedly *adv.* 80

confusion *n.* 80, 326

confuted *adj.* 414

congeal *vb.* 332, 334, 762

congelation *n.* 760

congenial *adj.* 827

congenital *adj.* 5

congestion *n.* 332, 572

conglomerate *n.* 332

conglomeration *n.* 45

congratulate *vb.* 838, 878, **888**

congratulate oneself *vb.* 879

congratulation *n.* 838, **888**

congregate *vb.* 50, 94

congregation *n.* 94, 982, 987

congress *n.* 94, 519, 625, 641

congressman *n.* 625

congruity *n.* 16, 24, 105

conjecture *n.* 386, 396, 447, **448**; *vb.* 448

conjugal *adj.* 896

conjugate *vb.* 499

conjunction *n.* 499

conjunctivitis *n.* 820

conjure *vb.* 449, 984

conjurer *n.* 984

con man *n.* 480, 631, 906

connect *vb.* 47, 81

connected *adj.* 9, 47, 52, 60, 81

connection *n.* 9, 47, 49, 201

connoisseur *n.* 304, 436, 848

connotation *n.* 450, 459

conquer *vb.* 316, 661, 679

conqueror *n.* 661

conscience *n.* 382, 919

conscience- stricken *adj.* 833, 941

conscientiousness *n.* 392, 864, 931

conscious *adj.* 382, 426, 753

conscript *n.* 655; *vb.* 651

conscription *n.* 674

consecrate *vb.* 980, 985

consecration *n.* 715, 980

consecutive *adj.* 85, 91

consensus *n.* 24, 424, 643

consent *n.* 424, 690, 692, 698; *vb.* 690, 692, 698

consequence *n.* 60, 85, 87, 156, 573

consequent *adj.* 85, 156

consequential *adj.* 119, 156, 573

conservation *n.* 374, 392, 599

conservatism *n*. 143

conservative *n*. 105, 143; *adj*. 143, 977

conserve *n*. 306; *vb*. 599, 748

consider *vb*. 384, 390, 415, 420, 526, 982

considerable *adj*. 32, 75, 573

considerate *adj*. 390, 392, 434, 886

consideration *n*. 384, 390, 392, 415, 886

consign *vb*. 268, 714

consignee *n*. 688

consignment *n*. 268

consist *vb*. 1, 58, 98

consistency *n*. 50, 105, 143

consistent *adj*. 16, 24, 105

consolation *n*. 176, 834, 907

consolation prize *n*. 663

console *vb*. 176, 834, 907

consolidate *vb*. 52, 334

consolidation *n*. 332

consonance *n*. 24, 643, 790

consonant *n*. 493, 512; *adj*. 24, 105

conspicuous *adj*. 253, 458, 462, 823, 877

conspiracy *n*. 558

conspire *vb*. 558

conspirer *n*. 558

constable *n*. 956

constancy *n*. 16, 91, 114, 140, 143, 152, 535

constant *n*. 152; *adj*. 91, 140, 143, 145, 152, 535

constellation *n*. 329

consternation *n*. 856

constituency *n*. 183, 540

constituent *n*. 55, 192; *adj*. 55, 73

constitute *vb*. 58, 98

constitution *n*. 5, 58, 339, 954

constitutional *n*. 269; *adj*. 954

constrain *vb*. 531, 674

constraint *n*. 674, 681

constrict *vb*. 197

construct *vb*. 58, 163, 242, 477, 930

construction *n*. 163, 242, 494

constructor *n*. 166

consul *n*. 688

consult *vb*. 624

consultant *n*. 624

consultation *n*. 519

consultative *adj*. 624

consume *vb*. 304, 569, 575, 740, 761

consumer *n*. 304, 726

consummate *adj*. 89, 581; *vb*. 56, 581, 659, 896

consummation *n*. 89, 156, 212, 581, 896

consumption *n*. 569

contact *n*. 47, 201, 758; *vb*. 201

contagious *adj*. 586

contain *vb*. 98, 234, 707, 712

container *n*. 193, 275

contaminate *vb*. 584, 588, 952

contemplate *vb*. 384, 415, 552

contemplative *adj*. 384, 434

contemporaneous *adj*. 120, 122

contemporary *n*. 122; *adj*. 60, 120, 122, 125

contempt *n*. 853, 869, 924

contemptible *adj*. 580, 869, 924

contemptuous *adj*. 853, 924

contend *vb*. 414, 615, 649, 651

contender *n*. 655

content *n*. 450, 831; *adj*. 831

contented *adj*. 827, 831

contentious *adj*. 409, 651

contents *n*. 192, 223

contest *n*. 649; *vb*. 604, 649

contestant *n*. 638; *adj*. 649

context *n*. 8

contiguity *n*. 199, 201

continent *n*. 352; *adj*. 944, 951

contingencies *n*. 700

contingent *adj*. 8, 403, 679, 700

contingent duration *n*. 111

continual *adj*. 114, 138, 143, 145

continuance *n*. 91, 107, 145, 535

continue *vb*. 91, 107, 112, 138, 145, 535

continuity *n*. 50, 91, 143

continuous *adj*. 91, 257

contort *vb*. 245, 251

contour *n*. 232, 242

contraband *n*. 724; *adj*. 955

contraception *n*. 169

contract *n*. 24, 468, 698, 699, 919; *vb*. 197, 203, 205 557, 698, 699

contraction *n*. 197, 205, 504

contractual *adj*. 699

contradict *vb*. 14, 25,

12, 18, 24, 105, 397, 521, 523

correspondent *n.* 395, 460, 523

corroborate *vb.* 217, 401, 408

corroborative *adj.* 401

corrode *vb.* 588

corrosion *n.* 53

corrugate *vb.* 260, 261

corrupt *adj.* 431, 477, 869, 932, 936; *vb.* 547, 580, 584, 588, 936

corruption *n.* 495, 551, 588, 932, 936

cosmetic *adj.* 211, 846

cosmetics *n.* 844

cosmic *adj.* 329

cosmology *n.* 329

cosmonaut *n.* 274

cosmopolitan *n.* 903; *adj.* 101

cosmos *n.* 329

cost *n.* 743; *vb.* 743

costly *adj.* 745

costs *n.* 31, 740, 963

costume *n.* 227

cosy *adj.* 827

cottage *n.* 191

cough *n.* 359; *vb.* 359

cough up *vb.* 738

council *n.* 94, 519, 625, 641

councillor *n.* 625

counsel *n.* 597, 624, 959; *vb.* 470, 519, 597, 624

counsellor *n.* 473, 624

count *n.* 38, 870; *vb.* 38, 400

countable *adj.* 38

count against *vb.* 588

countdown *n.* 274

countenance *n.* 236, 825

counter *n.* 482; *adj.* 181; *vb.* 637, 647

counteract *vb.* 31, 181, 648, 686

counteraction *n.* 181

counterattack *n.* 647

counterbalance *n.* 31, 152; *vb.* 31, 181, 330

counter-evidence *n.* 402

counterfeit *n.* 20, 487; *adj.* 20, 431, 477; *vb.* 20, 477

counterfoil *n.* 482

countermand *n.* 686, 691; *vb.* 686

countermeasure *n.* 181

counterpart *n.* 18, 20, 22, 28

counterpoise *vb.* 330

counter-productive *adj.* 576

counterweight *n.* 152, 181, 330

countless *adj.* 75, 78

count on *vb.* 443

country *n.* 183

countryman *n.* 871

county *n.* 183

coup n. 148

coup de grâce n. 659

coupé *n.* 276

couple *n.* 61; *vb.* 47, 61

couplet *n.* 61

coupling *n.* 47, 49

courage *n.* 857

courier *n.* 460, 467

course *n.* 269, 306, 358, 360, 470, 559

course of action *n.* 558

course of time *n.* 110

court *n.* 234, 559, 658, 870, 957; *vb.* 882, 890

court danger *vb.* 859

courteous *adj.* 392, 886, 922

courtesy *n.* 886, 899

courtship *n.* 890

cousin *n.* 11

cove *n.* 353

covenant *n.* 698, 699, 701; *vb.* 698, 699

cover *n.* 193, 225, 306, 463, 595; *vb.* 206, 225, 461, 646, 798, 801

cover for *vb.* 149

covering *n.* 211, 222, 225, 461, 801

covert *n.* 254, 374, 463, 595

covet *vb.* 861, 914

covetous *adj.* 750, 861, 914

covetousness *n.* 750, 861, 914

cow *n.* 381

coward *n.* 162, 858

cowardice *n.* 858

cowardly *adj.* 858

co-worker *n.* 640

coy *adj.* 876

crack *n.* 200; *vb.* 264, 456, 782

crack down on *vb.* 669, 963

cracker *n.* 306

crackle *n.* 782

crack up *vb.* 439, 856, 925

cradle *n.* 325

craft *n.* 277, 557, 631

craftsman *n.* 619

crafty *adj.* 478, 631, 932

cram *vb.* 56, 470, 472

crank *n.* 106, 440

cranky *adj.* 439

crash *n.* 282, 739, 782; *vb.* 282, 739, 780, 782, 787

crash-land *vb.* 273, 317, 321

crass *adj.* 849

crate *n.* 193

crater *n.* 254

crave *vb.* 695, 861, 914

craven *adj.* 858

craving *n.* 861

crawl *vb.* 281, 881

crawl with *vb.* 75

crayon *vb.* 488

craze *n.* 125, 439, 539, 850, 861

crazy *adj.* 433, 435, 439, 861, 889

creak *vb.* 781, 787

cream *n.* 306, 342, 365, 579, 813; *adj.* 807, 813; *vb.* 342

creamy *adj.* 362, 365

crease *n.* 260; *vb.* 260

create *vb.* 155, 163, 242, 449, 558

creation *n.* 21, 163, 329, 366

creative *adj.* 21, 163, 449

creator *n.* 155, 166, 491, 966

creature *n.* 366, 368, 373, 379

crèche *n.* 475

credence *n.* 420

credible *adj.* 404, 406, 420

credit *n.* 420, 718, 731, 736, 868, 909, 925; *vb.* 736, 742

creditable *adj.* 925

credit card *n.* 718, 731, 736

creditor *n.* 718, 736

credulous *adj.* 422

creed *n.* 420, 974

creek *n.* 354, 358

creep *vb.* 316, 461

cremate *vb.* 372, 761

cremation *n.* 372

crematorium *n.* 372, 763

crescent *n.* 247, 559; *adj.* 36, 247

crest *n.* 212, 358, 482, 872

crestfallen *adj.* 837, 874

cretin *n.* 437, 440

crevasse *n.* 254

crew *n.* 94, 272

crib *n.* 22; *vb.* 20

crier *n.* 467

crime *n.* 938, 955

criminal *n.* 684, 906, 940; *adj.* 932

criminality *n.* 932, 938

crimp *n.* 260; *vb.* 251, 260

crimson *adj.* 811

cringe *vb.* 856

cringing *adj.* 881

cripple *vb.* 245, 588

crisis *n.* 80, 136, 665

crisp *adj.* 760; *vb.* 306

crispy *adj.* 338

criterion *n.* 23, 27, 103, 400

critic *n.* 456, 524, 526, 848, 928

critical *adj.* 136, 382, 398, 415, 573, 594, 926

criticism *n.* 456, 624, 926

criticize *vb.* 696, 832, 893, 926, 962

critique *n.* 398, 456, 526

croak *vb.* 787, 789

crocodile *n.* 91

crocus *n.* 813

croft *n.* 378

crook *n.* 247, 480, 723, 906, 940, 989; *vb.* 247

crooked *adj.* 29, 219, 245

crop *n.* 374, 567, 705; *vb.* 203

crop up *vb.* 153, 825

cross *n.* 221, 592, 830, 964; *adj.* 893, 895; *vb.* 45, 221, 313, 478

cross-examination *n.* 394, 960

cross-eyed *adj.* 820

crossing *n.* 221, 313

cross purposes *n.* 642

crotchety *adj.* 539

crouch *vb.* 209, 319

crow *vb.* 789

crowd *n.* 75, 94, 821, 871; *vb.* 75, 94

crown *n.* 212, 250, 659, 663, 677; *vb.* 212, 685, 868, 878

crucial *adj.* 136, 573

crucifix *n.* 221

crucifixion *n.* 370, 828, 963

crucify *vb.* 830, 963

crude *adj.* 511, 887

cruel *adj.* 669, 900, 908

cruise *n.* 271; *vb.* 269, 271

crumb *n.* 33, 340

crumble *vb.* 162, 164, 338, 340, 588

crumple *vb.* 258

crunch *vb.* 340

crush *n.* 94, 889; *vb.* 164, 340, 364, 414, 661, 874

crushed *adj.* 837, 874

crushing *n.* 874

crustacean *n.* 373

crutch *n.* 217

crux *n.* 221

cry *n.* 597, 782, 788, 789, 839; *vb.* 788, 789, 833, 839

cry-baby *n.* 162, 858

cry out for *vb.* 531, 562

cry over *vb.* 833

cryptic *adj.* 466

crystal *adj.* 802

crystal-clear *adj.* 458

crystallize *vb.* 332, 334

cry wolf *vb.* 478, 598

cube *n.* 246

cuckoo *vb.* 789

cuddle *vb.* 890

cudgel *vb.* 282

cuff *n.* 963

cuisine *n.* 306

cul de sac *n.* 635

culinary *adj.* 306

cull *vb.* 540

culminate *vb.* 56, 212, 659

culmination *n.* 89, 581

culpable *adj.* 157, 938

culprit *n.* 684

cultivate *vb.* 378, 470

cultivated *adj.* 848, 886

cultivator *n.* 378

culture *n.* 426, 848, 886

cultured *adj.* 426, 848, 886

culvert *n.* 360

cumbersome *adj.* 330, 628

cumulative *adj.* 36

cuneiform *n.* 493; *adj.* 246

cunning *n.* 631, 932; *adj.* 478, 631

cup *n.* 193, 663

curate *n.* 986

curative *adj.* 589, 591

curator *n.* 593, 683

curb *n.* 281, 635, 681; *vb.* 37, 235, 281, 681

curdle *vb.* 332, 773

cure *n.* 176, 181, 589, 591, 834; *vb.* 589, 591, 599

curfew *n.* 128, 681

curiosity *n.* 388, 866

curious *adj.* 388, 394

curl *n.* 247, 251; *vb.* 247, 251, 260

currency *n.* 731

current *n.* 140, 358, 359; *adj.* 120, 125, 153, 464, 492, 545

current affairs *n.* 465

curriculum *n.* 470

curried *adj.* 769

curry *vb.* 306

curry favour *vb.* 881

curse *n.* 592, 665, 901; *vb.* 892, 901, 962

cursory *adj.* 113, 211

curt *adj.* 203, 504, 517, 887

curtail *vb.* 37, 197, 203

curtain *n.* 216, 461, 801

curtsy *n.* 319, 922; *vb.* 319, 922

curve *n.* 219, 247; *vb.* 219, 247

curved form *n.* 247

cushion *n.* 217; *vb.* 176, 834

custodian *n.* 593, 683

custody *n.* 593, 681, 707

custom *n.* 545, 726, 743, 988

customary *adj.* 126, 138, 545, 988

customer *n.* 716, 726

cut *n.* 43, 55, 259, 717, 744; *vb.* 48, 259, 264, 490, 744

cut back *vb.* 37, 42, 203, 748

cut down *vb.* 203, 319

cut out *vb.* 312

cut out for *adj.* 627

cut-price *adj.* 746

cut-throat *n.* 370

cutting *adj.* 255, 760, 773, 923

cut up *adj.* 828, 837; *vb.* 837

cycle *n.* 109, 140, 276, 323; *vb.* 269, 323

cyclic *adj.* 109, 140, 250

cycling *n.* 269

cyclone *n.* 323, 359

cyclopedia *n.* 524

cylinder *n.* 249

cylindrical *adj.* 249

cynic *n.* 904, 928

cynical *adj.* 904, 928

cynicism *n.* 904

D

dabble *vb.* 349

dad *n.* 170

daffodil *n.* 813

daily *adv.* 140

dainty *n.* 770, 848; *adj.* 331, 770

dally *vb.* 135

dam *vb.* 265

damage *n.* 588; *vb.* 164, 582, 588, 847

damages *n.* 31, 963

damaging *adj.* 580

damn *vb.* 901, 962

damned *adj.* 975

damp *n.* 349; *adj.* 349; *vb.* 762

dampen *vb.* 349, 548, 837

dampness *n.* 347, 349

dance *n.* 792, *vb.* 320, 838

dancer *n.* 793

dandy *n.* 852

danger *n.* 594

dangerous *adj.* 594

dangle *vb.* 216

dank *adj.* 349

dapple *vb.* 817

dare *n.* 644; *vb.* 644

daredevil *n.* 859

daring *n.* 857, 859; *adj.* 644, 857

dark *n.* 798; *adj.* 798, 803, 808

darken *vb.* 798, 803, 808

darkness *n.* 427, 798, 803, 808

darling *n.* 891

darn *vb.* 589

dart *n.* 290; *vb.* 273, 280

dash *n.* 33, 173, 613; *vb.* 280, 282, 613

dashing *adj.* 611, 613

dastardly *adj.* 858

data *n.* 38, 401, 460

date *n.* 107, 116, 884; *vb.* 116

dated *adj.* 107, 126

daub *n.* 847; *vb.* 342, 584, 847

daughter *n.* 171

daunt *vb.* 856

dauntless *adj.* 857

dawdle *vb.* 135, 281

dawn *n.* 127, 797; *vb.* 797

day *n.* 109, 116

daybreak *n.* 127, 797

day-dream *n.* 449; *vb.* 391, 449

daylight *n.* 797

dazzle *n.* 797; *vb.* 797

dazzling *adj.* 509, 797

deacon *n.* 987

dead *adj.* 2, 174, **369**, 754, 785, 843

deaden *vb.* 513, 754, 779, 785

deadlock *n.* 144

deadly *adj.* 164, 370, 580, 586, 592

deaf *adj.* 796

deafen *vb.* 780, 796

deafening *adj.* 780, 796

deafness *n.* **796**

deal *n.* 26, 699; *vb.* 9, 526, 606, 699, 717, 725

dealer *n.* 728

dealings *n.* 557

deal out *vb.* 715

dean *n.* 986

dear *n.* 891; *adj.* 745, 889

dearness *n.* 745

dearth *n.* 315, 571

death *n.* 89, **369**

death chamber *n.* 964

deathly *adj.* 369, 371

death sentence *n.* 963

débâcle *n.* 148, 662

debar *vb.* 691

debase *vb.* 209, 584, 608, 869

debasement *n.* 209, 319, 608, 928

debatable *adj.* 409

debate *n.* 410, 519; *vb.* 414, 519

debauched *adj.* 945, 952

debilitate *vb.* 162

debility *n.* 162

debit *vb.* 742

debonair *adj.* 836

debrief *vb.* 460

debris *n.* 44

debt *n.* 737, 919

debts *n.* 737, 739

début *n.* 88

decade *n.* 70, 109

decadent *adj.* 588

decamp *vb.* 600

decant *vb.* 358

decapitate *vb.* 164, 370, 963

decay *n.* 53, 126, 588; *vb.* 53, 164, 588

decaying *adj.* 777

deceased *n.* 369; *adj.* 369

deceit *n.* 412, 463, 478, 631

deceitful *adj.* 431, 932, 981

deceive *vb.* 431, 471, 477, 478, 631, 932

deceiver *n.* **480**

deceleration *n.* 281

decent *adj.* 848, 951

decentralize *vb.* 53, 95, 667, 714

deception *n.* 463, 477, 478, 631

deceptive *adj.* 431, 478, 631

decide *vb.* 415, 530, 534, 552, 622

decided *adj.* 408, 534

decimal *n.* 39; *adj.* 39, 70

decimate *vb.* 164, 370

decipher *vb.* 456

decipherable *adj.* 452

decision *n.* 415, 540, 960

decisive *adj.* 136, 413, 573

deck *vb.* 227, 568, 602, 846

declaim *vb.* 468

declaimer *n.* 514

declaration *n.* 460, 464, 468

declare *vb.* 413, 450, 460, 462, 468, 651, 698, 960, 961

declension *n.* 37, 499, 694

decline *n.* 37, 126, 219, 317, *vb.* 37, 130, 162, 197, 317, 319, 499, 542, 588

declining *adj.* 37, 586

decode *vb.* 456

decollate *vb.* 48

decompose *vb.* 48, 53, 588

decomposition *n.* 53, 588

deconsecrate *vb.* 987

decorate *vb.* 587, 844, 846

decoration *n.* 509, 663, 677, 846, 872

decorum *n.* 848

decoy *n.* 294; *vb.* 463

decrease *n.* 37, 42, 43, 57, 197; *vb.* 37, 176, 197, 746

decree *n.* 415, 671, 898, 954, 960; *vb.* 415, 671

decrepit *adj.* 126, 130, 162

decry *vb.* 928

dedicate *vb.* 534, 980, 988

dedicated *adj.* 709, 980

dedication *n.* 715, 980

deduce *vb.* 410, 448

deduction *n.* 42, 43, 87, 410, 744

deed *n.* 609

deem *vb.* 420, 448

deep n. 351; adj. 148, 182, 210, 805

deepen vb. 36, 210, 835

deep-freeze n. 764; vb. 762

deep-seated adj. 210, 545

deface vb. 845, 847

defamation n. 869, 928

defamatory adj. 926, 928, 930

default n. 315, 739; vb. 739

defeat n. 445, 660, 662; vb. 414, 661

defeatist adj. 855

defecate vb. 310

defect n. 43, 57, 582, 660, 662, 847

defection n. 189, 538, 920, 932

defective adj. 55, 57, 580, 582, 847

defence n. 402, 593, 595, 646, 648, 929, 960

defenceless adj. 160

defend vb. 410, 593, 646, 647, 648, 929, 959

defendant n. 684, 960

defer vb. 135, 424, 654, 920

deference n. 654, 922

defiance n. 637, 644, 672, 880

deficiency n. 29, 35, 57, 189, 315, 571, 660

deficient adj. 29, 35, 57, 315, 582, 660

deficit n. 57, 315, 737

defile vb. 584, 588, 608, 928, 936

defilement n. 584, 588, 608, 928

define vb. 102, 235, 496, 525

defining adj. 456

definite adj. 408, 823

definite article n. 499

definite space n. 183

definition n. 235, 450

deflate vb. 874

deflated adj. 874

deflation n. 197, 874

deflect vb. 285

deformed adj. 243, 245, 845

deformity n. 245, 582, 845, 847

defraud vb. 478, 722

defrost vb. 345, 761

deft adj. 280, 627

defunct adj. 369

defy vb. 25, 331, 637, 644, 672

degenerate n. 940; adj. 147, 936; vb. 53, 147, 588, 590, 936

degradation n. 608, 686, 869, 928

degrade vb. 588, 686, 869

degree n. 7, 27, 93, 400, 766

dehydrate vb. 350, 599

de-ice vb. 761

deification n. 983

deign vb. 874

deism n. 974

deity n. 966

déjà vu n. 441

dejection n. 837

delay n. 135, 281; vb. 135, 281

delegate n. 149, 625, 688, 689; vb. 685, 714

delete vb. 42, 485

deliberate adj. 410, 530, 543, 552; vb. 384

deliberation n. 384, 410, 860

delicacy n. 162, 205, 306, 338, 770, 848

delicate n. 753; adj. 162, 205, 331, 338, 510, 594, 735, 848, 864

delicatessen n. 306

delicious adj. 306, 767, 770, 772, 829

delight n. 306, 770, 827, 829; vb. 755, 829, 840, 889

delighted adj. 756, 827

delightful adj. 755, 770, 827, 829

delineate vb. 232, 486, 525

delirious adj. 827

delirium n. 756

deliver vb. 268, 601, 680, 714

deliverance n. 600, 601, 680

delivery n. 268, 512, 514, 621, 715

delude vb. 478

deluge n. 358, 572; vb. 349

delusion n. 412, 457, 478

demand n. 562, 671, 695; vb. 562, 671, 695, 727, 743

demarcation n. 48, 231, 235

dematerialize vb. 2, 328, 826, 984

demeanour n. 621

demented adj. 439

demise n. 89, 369

democracy n. 667, 678

demolish vb. 164, 319

demolition n. 164

demon n. 969

demonism n. 983

demonstrate vb. 401, 413, 456, 458, 696

demonstration n. 413, 458, 696, 825

demonstrator n. 106, 148

demoralize vb. 837, 936

demote vb. 686

demur n. 533; vb. 533, 696

demure *adj.* 876, 951

den *n.* 234, 463, 595

dendrochronology *n.* 116

denial *n.* 414, 469, 542, 694

denigrate *vb.* 928

denomination *n.* 496, 641, 979

denominational *adj.* 979

denominator *n.* 39

denote *vb.* 450, 482

dénouement n. 89

denounce *vb.* 892, 928, 930, 962

dense *adj.* 75, 332, 334, 435

density *n.* 204, 332, 400

dent *n.* 254, 847

denude *vb.* 228

denunciation *n.* 901, 926, 930, 962

deny *vb.* 402, 414, 469, 542, 637, 691, 694, 944

deodorant *n.* 775

depart *vb.* 151, 285, 293, 299, 600, 687, 826

department *n.* 55, 97

departure *n.* 285, 293, 299, 369, 600, 687, 826

depend *vb.* 420, 679, 854

dependable *adj.* 392, 702, 868, 931.

dependant *n.* 132, 287, 676

dependence *n.* 9, 420, 679

dependent *adj.* 420, 679, 700

depict *vb.* 20, 486, 488

deplete *vb.* 358, 569

depleted *adj.* 57, 569, 588

deplore *vb.* 941

deport *vb.* 99, 963

deposit *n.* 55, 367, 567, 701, 738; *vb.* 567

depository *n.* 193, 567, 732

depot *n.* 567

deprave *vb.* 588, 608

depreciate *vb.* 696, 744, 746, 928

depreciation *n.* 37, 43, 744, 928

depress *vb.* 209, 254, 319, 837, 841

depression *n.* 37, 169, 209, 210, 254, 259, 319, 837

deprive *vb.* 706, 720

deprived *adj.* 435, 706

depth *n.* 26, 209, 210, 400

deputation *n.* 685, 688

deputize *vb.* 685, 689

deputy *n.* 149, 688, 689; *adj.* 689

derail *vb.* 187

deranged *adj.* 439

derelict *adj.* 607

dereliction *n.* 393, 920

deride *vb.* 838, 853, 924, 928

derivation *n.* 155, 410, 494

derivative *n.* 494; *adj.* 156

derive *vb.* 156, 157, 410, 716

derogatory *adj.* 928

descend *vb.* 317, 869

descendant *n.* 11, 171

descent *n.* 11, 171, 317, 870

describe *vb.* 413, 460, 496, 525

description *n.* 460, 465, 486, 496, 525

descriptive *adj.* 456, 525

desecrate *vb.* 608, 981

desert *adj.* 350; *vb.* 556, 607, 898

deserter *n.* 538, 555, 672, 858

desertion *n.* 189, 556, 600, 672, 898, 920

deserts *n.* 917

deserve *vb.* 573, 917, 963

desiccate *vb.* 350

design *n.* 23, 58, 242, 482, 488, 552, 558; *vb.* 58, 488, 543, 552, 558

designate *adj.* 119, 123; *vb.* 102, 450, 482, 486, 496

designer *n.* 491, 558

desirable *adj.* 577, 579

desire *n.* 388, 530, 552, 854, 861; *vb.* 530, 532, 854, 861, 914

desist *vb.* 89, 144

desolate *adj.* 169, 588, 837

desolation *n.* 164, 569

despair *n.* 828, 837, 855, 856; *vb.* 828, 855

desperate *adj.* 706

desperation *n.* 855

despise *vb.* 542, 923, 924

despondency *n.* 445, 837, 855

despotism *n.* 669, 900

dessert *n.* 306

destination *n.* 235, 284, 298, 552

destined *adj.* 154, 531, 543

destiny *n.* 154

destitute *adj.* 708, 735

destroy *vb.* 82, 164, 370, 569

destroyer *n.* 167, 277

destruction *n.* 2, 53, 164, 370

destructive *adj.* 164, 175, 370, 580

detach *vb.* 48, 51

detached *adj.* 48, 391, 757

detachment *n.* 48, 391, 757, 933

detail *n.* 8, 55, 460

detailed *adj.* 8, 525

detain *vb.* 681, 712

detect *vb.* 419, 774, 795

détente *n.* 643

detention *n.* 681

deter *vb.* 548, 635

deteriorate *vb.* 37, 164, 588, 590

deterioration *n.* 126, 142, 569, 588, 590

determination *n.* 400, 415, 530, 534, 540, 857

determine *vb.* 89, 155, 177, 400, 413, 530, 534, 543, 552

determined *adj.* 534, 535, 857

determinism *n.* 531

deterrent *n.* 548

detest *vb.* 862, 892

detonate *vb.* 782

detonator *n.* 765

detour *n.* 285, 322, 561

detract *vb.* 42, 391

detriment *n.* 580, 588

detrimental *adj.* 164, 578, 580

devastate *vb.* 164

devastation *n.* 569

develop *vb.* 36, 196, 242, 288, 324, 587

developing *adj.* 36, 129, 603

development *n.* 36, 153, 196, 288, 324, 587

deviate *vb.* 15, 219, 247, 285, 505

deviation *n.* 15, 29, 142, 285, 431

device *n.* 565

devil *n.* 969, 984

devilish *adj.* 900, 969, 984

devious *adj.* 932

devise *vb.* 58, 163, 449, 558

devolution *n.* 667, 685, 714

devolve *vb.* 667, 685, 714, 919

devoted *adj.* 673, 702, 882, 889, 982

devotee *n.* 545

devote oneself to *vb.* 605

devotion *n.* 673, 702, 889, 980

devour *vb.* 304, 569, 948

devout *adj.* 974, 980, 982

dew *n.* 349

dexterity *n.* 240

dexterous *adj.* 627

diabolical *adj.* 900, 969, 984

diabolism *n.* 984

diagnosis *n.* 396, 398, 456

diagonal *n.* 219; *adj.* 219

diagram *n.* 486

dial 999 *vb.* 591, 598

diameter *n.* 204, 400

diametrical *adj.* 14

diamond *n.* 246

diarrhoea *n.* 310

diary *n.* 116, 441, 483

dice *vb.* 48, 306

dichotomy *n.* 63

dictate *n.* 671; *vb.* 531, 671, 674

dictator *n.* 623, 669

dictionary *n.* 83, 494, 524

didactic *adj.* 470

die *n.* 23; *vb.* 2, 89, 293, 369, 588, 826

die-hard *n.* 143, 537

diet *n.* 625, 947; *vb.* 205, 947

differ *vb.* 14, 15, 19, 151, 425, 642

difference *n.* 10, 15, 19, 104, 106, 425, 642

different *adj.* 14, 15, 19, 104, 106

differentiate *vb.* 15, 398

different time *n.* 121

differing *adj.* 25, 425

difficult *adj.* 405, 615, 633, 887

difficulty *n.* 633, 665, 830

diffuse *adj.* 505; *vb.* 95, 297, 346, 464

diffuseness *n.* 505

dig *n.* 254; *vb.* 210, 254, 378

digest *n.* 527; *vb.* 304, 472, 527

digestible *adj.* 306

digger *n.* 312

digit *n.* 39

dignified *adj.* 510, 848, 868, 870, 873, 982

dignity *n.* 510, 868, 870, 873

dig one's heels in *vb.* 537

digression *n.* 285, 505, 561

digs *n.* 191

dilapidated *adj.* 126

dilapidation *n.* 569, 588

dilated *adj.* 196

dilatory *adj.* 135

dilemma *n.* 136, 409, 633

diligent *adj.* 390, 392, 535, 611, 702

discriminating *adj.* 392, 398, 434, 540, 848, 864

discrimination *n.* 15, 398, 848, 916

discuss *vb.* 410, 514, 519, 526, 624, 700

disdain *n.* 853, 924; *vb.* 924

disease *n.* 586

disembark *vb.* 298

disembodied *adj.* 4, 328

disentangle *vb.* 46, 48, 81, 248

disfigure *vb.* 245, 845, 847

disfigurement *n.* 582, 845, 847

disfranchise *vb.* 918

disgrace *n.* 869; *vb.* 588, 869

disgraceful *adj.* 869

disgruntle *vb.* 832

disgruntled *adj.* 832

disguise *n.* 18, 461, 463; *vb.* 20, 146, 461

disgust *n.* 892; *vb.* 771, 892

dish *n.* 306

dishearten *vb.* 832

dishevel *vb.* 82

dishevelled *adj.* 584

dishonest *adj.* 477, 478, 631, 932

dishonour *n.* 869, 923; *vb.* 588, 869, 923

dish out *vb.* 717

disillusion *vb.* 445

disinclination *n.* 389, 533, 862

disinfect *vb.* 583

disingenuous *adj.* 477

disinherit *vb.* 720

disintegrate *vb.* 48, 53, 164, 328

disintegration *n.* 48, 53, 164, 588

disinter *vb.* 372

disinterested *adj.* 541, 757, 915, 933

disinterestedness *n.* 933

dislike *n.* 637, 862, 883, 892; *vb.* 771, 862, 892

dislocate *vb.* 48, 82, 187

dislodge *vb.* 187, 312

disloyal *adj.* 431, 672, 920

disloyalty *n.* 703, 920, 932

dismal *adj.* 798, 837, 895

dismantle *vb.* 164

dismay *vb.* 837, 856

dismembered *adj.* 48

dismiss *vb.* 99, 295, 303, 389, 542, 686, 920, 961

dismount *vb.* 298

disobedience *n.* 644, 672, 703, 981

disobey *vb.* 644, 672, 703, 955

disorder *n.* 80, 175, 584, 586, 668, 955; *vb.* 82

disorderly *adj.* 82, 887

disorganized *adj.* 80, 82

disorientate *vb.* 285

disown *vb.* 469, 538, 542

disparage *vb.* 418, 548, 926, 928

disparagement *n.* 928

disparate *adj.* 15, 19, 29, 104

dispassionate *adj.* 757, 863, 915, 933

dispatch *n.* 268, 460, 465, 523; *vb.* 268, 523, 613

dispatch bearer *n.* 467

dispel *vb.* 95

dispensation *n.* 713, 921

dispense *vb.* 95, 715, 717

disperse *vb.* 48, 82, 95, 297

dispersion *n.* 95

dispirited *adj.* 837

displace *vb.* 85, 187, 312, 706

displacement *n.* 187, 686

display *n.* 413, 825; *vb.* 413, 458

displeasure *n.* 445, 893, 926

disposal *n.* 81, 713, 727

dispose *vb.* 81, 717

disposed *adj.* 81, 179, 532, 751

dispose of *vb.* 89, 303, 609, 713, 717

disposition *n.* 5, 532, 545, 751

dispossession *n.* 706, 720, 918

disproof *n.* 414

disproportion *n.* 10, 29, 245

disproportionate *adj.* 25, 29, 245

disprove *vb.* 414

dispute *n.* 25, 410, 642; *vb.* 25, 410, 414, 637, 642, 649

disqualify *vb.* 99, 160, 918

disquiet *n.* 828; *vb.* 856

disregard *n.* 391, 393, 672, 703, 920; *vb.* 99, 389, 391, 393, 555, 644, 672, 703, 887, 924

disreputable *adj.* 869, 932

disrepute *n.* 869

disrespect *n.* 869, 887, 923, 924

disrespectful *adj.* 880, 887, 923, 924

disrupt *vb.* 82

disruption *n.* 175

dissatisfaction *n.* 445, 828, 832, 862, 926

dissect *vb.* 48, 53

dissemble *vb* 461, 477

disseminate *vb*. 95, 378, 460, 464

dissension *n*. 25, 425, 637, 642

dissent *n*. 425, 696; *vb*. 151, 425, 642

dissenter *n*. 106, 425, 975

dissertation *n* 526

dissident *n*. 979; *adj*. 106, 425, 672, 979

dissimilarity *n*. 19, 25, 29, 106

dissimulation *n*. 19

dissipate *vb*. 95, 346, 569, 749

dissipation *n*. 95, 569, 945

dissociation *n*. 10, 48

dissolute *adj*. 936, 952

dissolution *n*. 48, 53, 164, 345, 369, 686, 898

dissolve *vb*. 2, 53, 164, 345, 686, 826

dissonance *n*. 25, 787, 791

dissuade *vb*. 548, 624

dissuasion *n*. 548, 624

distance *n*. 194, **198**, 400, 885; *vb* 198

distant *adj*. 198, 517, 781, 885

distaste *n*. 862

distemper *n* 225

distend *vb* 196

distil *vb*. 346

distinct *adj* 48, 102, 452, 512, 778, 823

distinction *n*. 398, 868, 870

distinctive *adj*. 5

distinguish *vb*. 15, 398, 452

distinguished *adj*. 208, 573, 868, 870

distort *vb*. 245, 457, 471, 477, 487, 588, 845

distorted *adj*. 245, 477, 582

distortion *n*. 245, 416, 457, 477, 487, 845

distracted *adj*. 391, 442

distraught *adj*. 756

distress *n*. 445, 665, 828; *vb*. 830

distressed *adj*. 735

distressing *adj*. 551, 830

distress signal *n*. 598, 902

distribute *vb*. 95, 464, 715, 717

distribution *n*. 81, 717

district *n*. 183

distrust *n*. 421, 913; *vb*. 423

disturb *vb*. 82, 137, 187, 326, 856

disturbance *n*. 80, 137, 175, 326

disunite *vb*. 48, 51

disunity *n*. 17

disuse *n*. 546, 569, 607; *vb*. 607

ditch *n* 261, 360, 646; *vb*. 556

dither *n*. 326, 756

ditto *adv* 77

dive *n*. 321; *vb*. 271, 273, 321

diverge *vb*. 15, 48, 95, 151, 219, **297**

divergence *n*. 285, **297**

divergent *adj*. 15, 219, 285, 297, 978

diverse *adj*. 15, 104

diversified *adj*. 17, 104

diversify *vb* 817

diversion *n*. 142, 285, 449, 840

diversity *n*. 15, 17, 19, **104**, 817

divert *vb*. 391

diverting *adj*. 840

divest *vb*. 228, 720

divide *vb*. 38, 48, 55, 63, 95, 97, 717

dividends *n*. 741

divination *n*. 447, 984

divine *adj*. 966, 974; *vb*. 447, 448, 984

divinity *n*. **966**

divisibility *n*. 51

division *n*. 25, 38, 48, 55, 97, 425, 655, 717

divisive *adj*. 642

divorce *n*. 48, 713, **898**; *vb*. 48, 898

divulge *vb*. 458, 462

do *n*. 878; *vb*. 570, 577, 605, **609**, 673, 702

do away with *vb*. 370

docile *adj*. 654, 673

dock *n*. 298, 957; *vb*. 298

docket *n*. 482; *vb*. 482

doctor *n*. 428, 436, 473; *vb*. 477

doctrine *n*. 420, 626, 974

document *n*. 401, 483, 521; *vb*. 401, 483, 521

dodge *n*. 478, 631; *vb*. 533, 555

dodger *n* 480, 600

doe *n*. 381

doer *n*. 609, 619

dog *n*. 380; *vb*. 287, 554

doggedness *n*. 534, 535

dogma *n*. 420, 974

dogmatic *adj* 468, 537

do-gooder *n*. 899, 903, 905

do in *vb*. 370

doing *n*. 609, 702; *adj*. 609

do-it-yourself *adj*. 628

doldrums *n*. 837

doleful *adj*. 837

dole out *vb*. 95, 715, 717

doll up *vb*. 844

doltish *adj*. 435

domain *n.* 956

dome *n.* 225, 252

domestic *n.* 676; *adj* 190

domestic animal *n.* 373

domesticate *vb.* 377

domesticated *adj.* 190

domestic science *n.* 306

domicile *n.* 191

dominance *n.* 34, 159, 177

dominant *adj.* 159, 177, 667

dominate *vb.* 177, 208, 667, 669, 679

domineer *vb.* 667, 669

dominion *n.* 667

don *n.* 428, 473; *vb.* 227

donate *vb.* 715

donor *n.* 715, 905

doom *n.* 543; *vb.* 962

door *n.* 262

doorman *n.* 676

do over *vb.* 645

dormancy *n.* 459, 610, 612

dorsal *adj.* 237

dose *n.* 26, 591

dot *n.* 33

dotage *n.* 130

dote on *vb.* 889, 983

double *n.* 28, 149, 971; *adj.* 62; *vb.* 62, 149, 260

double-cross *vb.* 478, 932

double dealing *n.* 477, 631, 932; *adj.* 477, 932

double entendre n. 454, 842

double-sidedness *n.* 61

doubt *n.* 409, 421, 975; *vb.* 409, 421, 423

doubtful *adj.* 407, 409, 421

dough *n.* 364, 731

douse *vb.* 762

dove *n.* 656

dovetail *vb.* 24, 47

dowager *n.* 870, 898

dowdiness *n.* 849

down *adj.* 837; *adv.* 209

down-and-out *n.* 697; *adj.* 735

downcast *adj.* 837

downfall *n.* 164, 317, 662

downgrade *vb.* 686

down-hearted *adj.* 837

down-payment *n.* 55, 738

downpour *n.* 358

downward *adj.* 219, 317

doze *n.* 612, 617; *vb.* 612

dozen *n.* 70

drab *adj.* 805, 809, 843

draft *n.* 558, 602; *vb.* 521, 558

drag *n.* 181, 635; *vb.* 181, 291, 294

drag up *vb.* 441

drain *n.* 360; *vb.* 319, 358, 569, 806

drained *adj.* 617

drake *n.* 380

dram *n.* 309

drama *n.* 529, 866

dramatic *adj.* 529, 752, 755, 866

dramatis personae n. 529

drape *n.* 801; *vb.* 216

draught *n.* 309, 359

draught animal *n.* 291

draughtsman *n.* 491

draughty *adj.* 348, 359

draw *n.* 28, 294, 553; *vb.* 28, 291, 294, 308, 312, 390, 486, 488, 525, 705, 889

drawback *n.* 582

drawer *n.* 491

drawing *n.* 291, 488

drawl *n.* 515; *vb.* 515

draw up *vb.* 558

dread *n.* 856; *vb* 856

dreadful *adj.* 830, 856

dream *n.* 4, 449, 552, 854; *vb* 391, 449, 552, 612, 854, 861

dream up *vb.* 558

dreamy *adj.* 384

dreary *adj.* 798, 841, 843

dredge *vb.* 312

dredge up *vb.* 441

dregs *n.* 44, 576, 871

drench *vb.* 349, 572

dress *n.* 227; *vb.* 227, 568, 844

dressage *n.* 269

dress down *vb.* 926, 963

dressing *n.* 227

dribble *vb.* 319, 358

dried *adj.* 350

drift *n.* 178, 450; *vb.* 178, 257, 612

drill *n.* 264; *vb.* 264, 378, 470

drink *n.* 309, 343; *vb.* 304, 950

drinker *n.* 304, 950

drink in *vb.* 390, 472

drinking *n.* 304

drip *n.* 349, 841; *vb.* 319, 358

drip-dry *vb.* 350

drive *n.* 173, 269, 282, 290, 559, 645, 674; *vb.* 173, 269, 282, 290, 295, 377, 547, 674

drive at *vb.* 450

drivel *n.* 451

driver *n.* 270

driving *n.* 269; *adj.* 674

drizzle *n.* 358; *vb.* 358

droll *adj.* 851

drone *n.* 783, 784, 789

droop *vb.* 216, 317, 319, 837, 841

drop *n.* 37, 210, 249, 254, 309, 317, 321; *vb.*

37, 317, 319, 358, 556, 617, 706

drop anchor *vb.* 271, 298

drop in *vb.* 300

drop out *vb.* 660

droppings *n.* 310

drought *n.* 350, 861

drown *vb.* 321, 349, 370, 963

drowsy *adj.* 612, 617, 841

drudge *n.* 615, 619, 676; *vb.* 615

drug *n.* 173, 591; *vb.* 754

drum *n.* 249

drumming *n.* 325

drunk *n.* 950; *adj.* 950

drunkard *n.* 304, 950

dry *adj.* 350, 773, 787, 843, 949; *vb.* 306, 350

dryness *n.* 350, 843

dualism *n.* 61

duality *n.* 61

dub *vb.* 496, 497

dubious *adj.* 407, 421, 932

duchess *n.* 870

duchy *n.* 183

duck *n.* 74, 381; *vb.* 321, 349, 555

duct *n.* 360

dud *n.* 662

due *n.* 737, 917; *adj.* 737, 917

duel *n.* 649

dueness *n.* 917

dues *n.* 716, 743, 917

dug-out *n.* 254

duke *n.* 870

dull *adj.* 174, 256, 435, 666, 754, 768, 771, 785, 798, 799, 806, 843; *vb.* 256, 754, 785, 799

dullness *n.* 174, 435, 768, 806, **843**

dumb *adj.* 435, 513, 517

dumbfound *vb.* 513, 866

dummy *n.* 22, 23, 149; *adj.* 149

dump *vb.* 727

dumpy *adj.* 195, 203, 204

dunce *n.* 429, 437, 630

dung *n.* 310

dungeon *n.* 234, 682

duo *n.* 792

dupe *n.* 479, 853; *vb.* 478

duple *adj.* 61

duplicate *n.* 22; *adj.* 13, 62; *vb.* 62, 165

duplication *n.* **62**, 77, 165

duplicity *n.* 477, 932

durability *n.* 143, 337

durable *adj.* 112, 161, 337

duration *n.* 107, 145

duress *n.* 674

during *adv., prep.* 107

dusk *n.* 128, 799, 809

dust *n.* 340, 371, 576

duster *n.* 485

dusty *adj.* 340, 350, 584, 809

dutiful *adj.* 673, 919

duty *n.* 557, 685, 737, 743, **919**

dwarf *n.* 195, 970; *adj.* 203

dwell *vb.* 191

dwindle *vb.* 37, 197, 569

dye *n.* 805

dying *n.* 369; *adj.* 130, 861

dynamic *adj.* 159, 173, 611

dynamite *n.* 657

dysentry *n.* 310

E

eager *adj.* 443, 532, 756, 861

earl *n.* 870

earlier *adj.* 84, 118; *adv.* 121

earliness *n.* 134

early *adj.* 117, 134

early warning *n.* 597

earmark *vb.* 482

earn *vb.* 705, 917

earner *n.* 716

earnest *n.* 701; *adj.* 532, 752, 837

earnings *n.* 705, 738, 741

earring *n.* 216

earshot *n.* 199, 795

earth *n.* 329, 352

earthquake *n.* 325

earthworks *n.* 646

earthy *adj.* 352

ease *n.* 616, 634, 827, 831, 834; *vb.* 335, 634, 834

ease off *vb.* 281, 616

east *n.* 284

easy *adj.* 634, 952

easy-going *adj.* 670, 757

eat *vb.* 304, 569, 767

eat away *vb.* 569, 588

eating *n.* 304

eavesdropping *n.* 460, 795

ebb *vb.* 37, 358

eccentric *n.* 106, 440; *adj.* 106, 439

ecclesiastical *adj.* 985

echo *n.* 22, 283, 778, 784; *vb.* 77, 283, 784

eclipse *n.* 798; *vb.* 34, 314, 461, 798

ecology *n.* 366, 376

economical *adj.* 392, 748

economics *n.* 622

economize *vb.* 37, 748

economy *n.* 392, **748**; *adj.* 746

ecstasy *n.* 756, 827

eddy *n.* 323, 358; *vb.* 323, 358

edge *n.* 233, 235, 255, 769; *vb.* 233, 255

edgy *adj.* 756, 856, 894

edible *adj* 306

edict *n.* 626, 671, 954

edifice *n.* 163

edify *vb.* 470, 550, 579

edit *vb.* 456

edition *n.* 524

editor *n.* 456, 524

educate *vb.* 470

educated *adj.* 426

education *n.* 426, 470

educational *adj.* 460, 470

eerie *adj.* 971, 984

efface *vb.* 485

effect *n.* 87, 156, 877; *vb.* 155, 163, 609, 659

effective *adj.* 159, 172, 563, 627

effeminate *adj.* 162, 381

effervesce *vb.* 363, 786

efficacy *n.* 159, 575

efficient *adj.* 159, 557

effluent *n.* 301, 358

effort *n.* 604, 615

effortless *adj.* 634

effrontery *n.* 880

egg *n.* 250, 306

egg-timer *n.* 116

ego *n.* 382

egoist *n.* 904, 934

egotism *n.* 875, 904

ego-trip *n.* 873

eight *n.* 70; *adj.* 70

eject *vb.* 301, 303

ejection *n.* 99, 303, 310, 312

elaborate *adj.* 509; *vb.* 196

elapse *vb.* 107, 110

elasticity *n.* **336**

elated *adj.* 756, 827, 838

elbow *n.* 246

elder *n.* 34, 132, 987; *adj.* 130

eldest *adj.* 130

elect *adj.* 119; *vb.* 540

election *n.* 540

electorate *n.* 540

electric chair *n.* 964

electricity *n.* 159, 765

electrify *vb.* 159, 755

electrocute *vb.* 370, 963

electronic *adj.* 125

elegance *n.* **510**, 844, 848

elegy *n.* 372, 839

element *n.* 5, 55, 155, 327

elementary *adj.* 88

elements *n.* 192, 348

elevated *adj.* 208, 318, 868, 873

elevation *n.* 208, **318**

elevator *n.* 316

eleven *n.* 70

elevenses *n.* 306

eleventh hour *n.* 136

elf *n.* 970

elicit *vb.* 155, 547

eligible *adj.* 896, 897

eliminate *vb.* 46, 99, 164, 303

elite *n.* 579, 870

elixir *n.* 591

ellipse *n.* 247, 250

ellipsis *n.* 504

elliptic *adj.* 504

elocution *n.* 518

elongated *adj.* 202

elope *vb.* 600, 896

eloquent *adj.* 514, 516

elsewhere *adj.* 189

elucidate *vb.* 413, 456

elude *vb.* 555, 600

emaciated *adj.* 205, 588

emanation *n.* 156, 301, 774

emancipation *n.* 601, 680

emasculate *vb.* 160, 169

embalm *vb.* 372, 599, 776

embankment *n.* 559, 646

embargo *n.* 99, 681, 691

embarkation *n.* 299

embark on *vb.* 605

embarrass *vb.* 578, 633, 869, 874

embarrassed *adj.* 811, 830, 874, 876

embassy *n.* 685, 688

embed *vb.* 311

embellish *vb.* 509, 844, 846

ember *n.* 800

embezzle *vb.* 722

embezzler *n.* 723, 739

embittered *adj.* 893

emblazon *vb.* 482

emblem *n.* 482, 677, 872

embody *vb.* 52, 98, 222, 486

emboss *vb.* 482, 489

embrace *n.* 886, 890; *vb.* 50, 98, 702, 886, 890

embrocation *n.* 365

embroider *vb.* 481, 509, 846

embryology *n.* 375, 376

embryonic *adj.* 88

emerald *adj.* 812

emerge *vb.* 301, 313, 324, 600, 825

emergence *n.* 298, **301**

emergency *n.* 136, 153, 562

emigrant *n.* 100, 270

emigration *n.* 299

eminent *adj.* 34, 208, 573, 868, 870

emissary *n.* 460, 467, 688

emit *vb.* 301, 303, 774, 778

emollient *n* 365

emolument *n.* 705, 738

emotion *n.* 326, 752, 756, 889

empathy *n.* 752

emperor *n.* 675

emphasize *vb.* 417, 456, 468, 481, 512, 573

employ *vb.* 107, 557, 575, 606, 685

employee *n.* 619, 676

emporium *n.* 730

empower *vb.* 159, 161, 667, 685, 954

emptiness *n.* 2, 189, 333, 875

empty *adj.* 189, 333, 451; *vb* 301, 358, 569

empty-handed *adj.* 735

empty-headed *adj.* 383, 427, 435

emulate *vb.* 20

emulsion *n.* 362

enable *vb.* 159, 404

enact *vb.* 529

enactment *n.* 486, 954

enamel *n.* 225

enamoured *adj.* 889

encampment *n.* 186

enchant *vb.* 827, 829, 889, 984

encircle *vb.* 231, 250

enclose *vb.* 98, 225, 229, 234

enclosure *n.* 184, 234, 378

encompass *vb* 182, 229, 231

encore *n* 62, 77; *adv.* 77

encounter *n* 296, 649; *vb* 649, 857

encourage *vb.* 217, 547, 618, 624, 636, 836, 857, 907

encroachment *n.* 314, 645, 918, 955

encrust *vb.* 226

encumbrance *n.* 635, 711

encyclopedia *n.* 426, 524

end *n.* 89, 156, 235, 237, 369, 552, 659; *vb.* 89, 659

endanger *vb.* 594

endearment *n.* 890

endeavour *n.* 604; *vb.* 604

endemic *adj.* 586

endless *adj.* 78, 91, 114

endless duration *n.* 114

endorsement *n.* 408, 424, 468, 690, 963

endow *vb.* 568, 715

endowment *n.* 5, 627, 714

endurance *n.* 112, 114, 143, 152, 337, 535, 757

endure *vb.* 91, 112, 145, 535, 648, 752, 757, 828

enemy *n.* 638, 645, 883

energetic *adj.* 32, 159, 161, 173, 368, 585, 611

energize *vb.* 161, 173, 618, 755

energy *n.* 159, 161, 173, 368, 611

enfeeble *vb.* 130, 162, 507

enforce *vb.* 954

enfranchise *vb.* 678, 680

engage *vb.* 557, 605

engaged *adj.* 698

engage in battle *vb.* 649, 651

engagement *n.* 557, 605, 649, 698, 890

engine *n.* 276, 565

engineer *n.* 558

engrave *vb.* 490, 521, 522

engraver *n.* 491

engraving *n.* 490

engrossed *adj.* 384

enhance *vb.* 36, 318, 509, 846

enigma *n.* 409, 453, 466

enjoy *vb.* 752, 770, 827, 861

enjoyable *adj.* 827, 829

enjoy immunity *vb.* 921

enjoy oneself *vb.* 827, 840

enlarge *vb.* 36, 40, 196, 202, 505

enlighten *vb.* 460, 470, 797

enlist *vb.* 83, 302, 557, 651

enliven *vb.* 173, 368, 618, 836, 840

enmity *n.* 883

ennoble *vb.* 318, 868, 870

ennui *n.* 841

enormous *adj.* 32, 194

enough *adj.* 75, 570

enquire *vb.* 388, 394

enquiry *n.* 394, 526

enrage *vb.* 893

enrapture *vb.* 547, 827, 829, 889

enrich *vb.* 509, 587

enrol *vb.* 83, 483, 641

ensconce *vb.* 461

ensemble *n.* 54, 793

enshrine *vb.* 372, 983

enshroud *vb.* 225

ensign *n.* 482

enslave *vb.* 679

ensnare *vb.* 463, 478

ensue *vb.* 85, 119, 153, 156, 287

ensure *vb.* 408

entail *vb.* 98, 459

entangle *vb.* 82, 221

entente *n.* 643, 699

enter *vb.* 298, 300, 483, 742

enterprise *n.* 173, 288, 604, **605**, 611, 627, 857
entertain *vb.* 840, 884
enter upon *vb.* 88, 605
enthralling *adj.* 547, 829, 866
enthrone *vb.* 685, 868
enthusiasm *n.* 532, 611, 752
enthusiastic *adj.* 532, 611, 756, 827
entice *vb.* **547**, 770
entire *adj.* 54, 56, 581, 659
entirety *n.* 54, 56, 59
entitled *adj.* 917
entity *n.* 1, 3, 59
entomb *vb.* 372
entomology *n.* 375
entrance *n.* 262, 298, **300**, 559
entrant *n.* 638
entrap *vb.* 478
entreat *vb.* 695, 982
entrée *n.* 306
entrench *vb.* 152, 186
entrepreneur *n.* 728
entrust *vb.* 685, 714, 718
entry *n.* 298, 300
entwine *vb.* 251
enumerate *vb.* 38, 83, 102
enunciate *vb.* 512, 514
envelop *vb.* 225, 229, 234, 461
envelope *n.* 193, 234
envious *adj.* 914
environment *n.* 8, 183, 229
envisage *vb.* 449
envoy *n.* 460, **467**, 685, 688
envy *n.* **914**; *vb.* 914
ephemeral *adj.* 113
epic *n.* 525, 528
epicure *n.* 304, 945, 948
epigram *n.* 432, 842

epilogue *n.* 87, 89
episode *n.* 153
epistle *n.* 523
epitaph *n.* 372
epithet *n.* 496
epitome *n.* 527
epitomize *vb.* 203
epoch *n.* 109
equal *n.* 28; *adj.* 13, **28**, 159
equality *n.* 13, **28**, 244
equalize *vb.* 28, 31
equate *vb.* 13, 218, 397
equation *n.* 28, 397
equator *n.* 63, 250
equestrianism *n.* 269
equidistant *adj.* 90, 218
equilibrium *n.* 28, 152
equip *vb.* 227, 564, 568, **602**
equipment *n.* 568, 711
equity *n.* 711, 915
equivalence *n.* 12, 28, 450
equivalent *n.* 18, 28, 456; *adj.* 12, 13, 18, 28
equivocal *adj.* 409, 453, 454
equivocate *vb.* 454, 477
era *n.* 109
eradicate *vb.* 164, 303, 485
erase *vb.* 485
erect *adj.* 214, 248, 318; *vb.* 214, 318
erection *n.* 163, 318
erode *vb.* 37, 53, 164, 341, 569, **588**
Eros *n.* 889, 967
erotic *adj.* 952
err *vb.* 285, 431, 936
errand *n.* 685
errand-boy *n.* 467
erratic *adj.* 151, 539
erring *adj.* 409
erroneous *adj.* 412, 431, 916
error *n.* 431, 457, 471

erudite *adj.* 426, 472
eruption *n.* 148, 175, 301, 782
escalate *vb.* 36, 196
escalator *n.* 316
escape *n.* 293, 301, 555, 595, **600**, 826; *vb.* 293, 555, **600**, 826
escapism *n.* 449
escarpment *n.* 208
escort *n.* 683; *vb.* 268
esoteric *adj.* 453, 984
especial *adj.* 34, 102
Esperanto *n.* 492
espouse *vb.* 896
essay *n.* 526, 604
essence *n.* 1, 5, 450
essential *n.* 5, 531, 562; *adj.* 1, 5, 531, 562, 573
establish *vb.* 81, 88, 152, 161, 413, 685, 929, 954
established *adj.* 126, 152, 413, 545
establishment *n.* 88, 152, 191, 413, 620, 641, 667, 730
estate *n.* 7, 378, 711
esteem *n.* 922, 925; *vb.* 384, 861, 868, 889, 925
estimate *n.* 447, 743; *vb.* 38, 400, 415, 448, 743
estrange *vb.* 883, 892
estuary *n.* 353
etcher *n.* 491
etching *n.* 490
eternal *adj.* 78, 114, 966
eternity *n.* 78, 108, 112, **114**
ethereal *adj.* 4, 328, 333
ethics *n.* 935
ethnic *adj.* 11, 379
etiquette *n.* 545
etymology *n.* 492, 494
Eucharist *n.* 988
eunuch *n.* 160
euphemism *n.* 455, 509

exhibitionist *n.* 875, 877; *adj.* 875

exhilarate *vb.* 618, 755, 827

exhilaration *n.* 756

exhort *vb.* 518, 597, 624

exhume *vb.* 372

exile *n* 303, 963; *vb.* 303, 963

existence *n.* 1, 368

existent *adj.* 120

existentialism *n.* 1

exit *n.* 262, 299, 369, 600

exodus *n.* 299

exonerate *vb.* 601, 911, 929, 961

exorbitant *adj.* 572, 745, 749

exorcise *vb.* 984

exotic *adj.* 100

expand *vb.* 36, **196**

expand on *vb.* 456

expanse *n.* 26, 182, 204, 356

expansion *n.* 36, 182, **196**

expatriot *n.* 100

expect *vb.* 154, 443, 552, 854

expectation *n.* 406, 443, 552, 854, 867

expected *adj.* 123, 138, 406, 443, 447, 545, 867

expecting *adj.* 163, 854

expedience *n* 136, 577

expedite *vb.* 613

expedition *n.* 269, 280

expel *vb* 99, 301, 303, 310, 542, 885, 963

expend *vb.* 569, 715, 738, 740

expenditure *n* **740**

expense *n.* 743, 745

expenses *n* 636, 738, 740, 965

experience *n.* 130, 153, 426, 434, 602, 627, 752; *vb.* 153, 426, 472, 752

experiment *n.* 394, **396**, 604; *vb.* 396

expert *n.* 428, 436, **629**, 848; *adj.* 130, 627

expertise *n.* 426, 627

expiation *n.* 943

expiration *n.* 89, 144, 359, 369

explain *vb.* 157, 410, 413, 456, 470, 525, 526

explanation *n.* 155, 157, 413, 450, 456, 525

expletive *n.* 901

explicit *adj.* 452, 458, 502

explode *vb.* 175, 756, 782, 893

exploit *n.* 605, 609; *vb.* 136, 575, 606, 745

exploration *n.* 269, 271, 419

exploratory *adj.* 86, 394

explore *vb.* 269, 396, 758

explorer *n.* 270

explosive *n* 657; *adj.* 594, 765

exponent *n.* 456, 974

exponential *adj.* 39

export *vb.* 268

exporter *n.* 728

expose *vb.* 228, 262, 414, 419, 458, 462

exposed *adj.* 228, 348, 414, 462, 753, 823

expose oneself to *vb.* 179

expositor *n.* 456, 514, 526

expostulate *vb.* 696

expound *vb.* 456, 470

express *adj.* 458; *vb.* 242, 450, 458, 460, 514, 525

expression *n* 242, 458, 468, 492, 494, 498, 825

expressionless *adj.* 451, 754, 843

expulsion *n.* 99, 303, 310, 312, 542

expunge *vb.* 485

expurgate *vb.* 583

exquisite *adj.* 579, 770, 829, 844

extant *adj.* 1

extemporize *vb.* 544

extend *vb.* 6, 182, 196, 202, 208, 253, 693

extended *adj.* 202, 204, 253, 455

extension *n.* 36, 41, 196, 202, 253

extensive *adj.* 32, 54, **182**, 202

extent *n.* 26, 27, 107, 182, 194, 198, 202, 400, 956

extenuating *adj.* 403, 929

exterior *n.* 222, 236; *adj.* 6, 222

exterminate *vb.* 164, 369, 370

external *n.* 6; *adj.* 6, 100, 222, 825

extinct *adj.* 2, 126, 369

extinguish *vb.* 164, 369, 762

extol *vb.* 922

extort *vb.* 312, 720, 722, 745

extra *n.* 529; *adj.* 40, 572, 607; *adv.* 40

extract *n.* 55, 306; *vb.* 187, 312

extraction *n.* 312

extradite *vb.* 303

extramarital *adj.* 952

extraneousness *n.* 6, 40, **100**, 222

extraordinary *adj* 407, 573, 866

extrapolate *vb.* 6, 222

extra-sensory perception *n.* 411, 447, 753

extraterrestrial *adj.* 329

extravagance *n.* 481, 569, 572, 745, **749**, 945

extravagant *adj.* 481, 509, 569, 572, 745, 749, 877

extreme *n.* 89; *adj.* 89, 148, 175, 669, 828, 830

extremely *adv.* 32

extremist *n.* 148, 672

extremity *n.* 89, 233, 235

extricate *vb.* 312, 601, 678, 680

extrinsic *adj.* 6, 100, 222

exuberant *adj.* 168, 572, 836

exudation *n.* 310

exude *vb.* 301, 358

exultation *n* 827, 838

eye *n.* 818; *vb* 818

eye for an eye *n.* 647

eyelash *n.* 207

eyesight *n.* 818

eyesore *n* 845

eye-witness *n.* 821

F

fable *n.* 455, 525

fabric *n* 221, 339

fabrication *n.* 163, 465, 477, 631

fabulous *adj.* 449, 481, 525, 970

façade *n.* 211, 222, 236, 477, 852

face *n.* 222, 236, 825; *vb.* 226, 239, 857

face-lift *n* 587, 589, 844

facet *n.* 7, 55

facetiousness *n.* 842

face value *n* 743, 825

facility *n.* 514, 568, 627, **634**

facsimile *n.* 20, 22

fact *n.* 1, 401, 426, 430, 460

fact-finding *adj.* 394

faction *n* 641, 979

factious *adj.* 25, 642, 672

factor *n* 8, 55, 155, 327

factory *n* 620

factual *adj.* 1, 430

faculties *n.* 382

faculty *n.* 159

fad *n.* 125, 850

fade *vb.* 162, 588, 806, 826

fade out *vb.* 799

faeces *n.* 310

failing *n.* 819, 936

failure *n* 315, 393, 431, 445, 571, 660, **662**

faint *vb.* 162, 617

faint-hearted *adj.* 162, 858

faintness *n.* 162, 507, 617, **781**, 799, 806

fair *n.* 840; *adj.* (average) 30, 666; (of weather) 759; (whitish) 807; (good-looking) 844; (just) 915, 931, 933

fairy *n.* 953, 970

fairy story *n.* 525

faith *n.* 420, 854, 974, 980

faithful *adj.* 430, 456, 673, 702, 882, 977

faithless *adj.* 409, 421

fake *n.* 20; *adj.* 20, 477, 478; *vb.* 20, 477, 852

fall *n.* 37, 317, 321, 358; *vb.* 37, 317, 321, 588, 936

fallacy *n* 412, 431

fall apart *vb.* 51

fall away *vb.* 538, 588

fall back *vb.* 289, 293

fall back on *vb.* 606

fall down *vb* 431, 662

fallen *adj* 662

fallen angel *n* 969

fallen woman *n.* 953

fall for *vb* 422, 889

fallible *adj* 431, 582

fall ill *vb.* 586

fall in *vb.* 254

falling star *n* 329

fall in love *vb.* 889

fall on *vb.* 153, 179

fallow *adj.* 603, 612

fall short *vb* 29, 35, 315, 571, 582, 662

fall through *vb.* 662

fall to *vb* 716, 919

false *adj.* 2, 477, 478

falsehood *n.* 431, 477

false reasoning *n.* 412

falsification *n.* 457, 471, 477, **487**

falter *vb.* 325, 515, 536, 662

fame *n.* 868

familiar *adj* 138, 426, 545, 882

familiarize *vb.* 470, 545

family *n.* 11, 55, 97, 171

famished *adj.* 861, 947

famous *adj.* 573, 868

fan *n.* 764; *vb.* 348

fanatic *n.* 148, 537, 611

fanciful *adj.* 449, 539

fancy *n.* 448, 449, 539, 861; *adj.* 509, 846; *vb.* 448, 449, 540, 861, 889

fan out *vb.* 297

fantastic *adj.* 433, 449, 851, 866

fantasy *n.* 449, 481

far *adj.* 198

farce *n* 433, 529, 851

fare *n.* 306, 743

farewell *n.* 299

far-flung *adj.* 198

farm *n.* 377, 378; *vb* 377

farm out *vb.* 717

far-reaching *adj.* 32, 182

far-sighted *adj.* 434

farthest *adj.* 198

fascinate *vb.* 294, 547, 755, 889

fascinating *adj.* 547, 755, 829

fascism *n* 669

fashion *n.* 125, 242, 545, 559, **850**

fast *n.* 947; *adj.* 280, 613, 805; *vb.* 947; *adv.* 280

fasten *vb.* 47, 50, 152, 263

fastidiousness *n.* 392, 540, **864**

fasting *n.* **947**; *adj.* 947

fat *n.* 306; *adj.* 194

fatal *adj.* 164, 369, 370

fatalism *n.* 531

fate *n.* 123, 154, **158**, 531, 543, 553

fat-head *n.* 437

father *n.* 11, 170

fathom *vb.* 452

fathomless *adj.* 210

fatigue *n* **617**, 841

fatten *vb.* 204, 377

fatty *adj.* 365

fault *n* 200, 315, 431, 582

faultless *adj.* 581, 937

faulty *adj.* 582

fauna *n* 366, 373

faux pas *n.* 431

favour *n.* 636, 670, 715, 886, 899, 907, 922; *vb* 540, 925

favourable *adj.* 854, 925

favourite *n.* **891**

favouritism *n.* 916

fawning *n.* 927; *adj.* 881

fear *n.* **856**, 858, 980; *vb.* 856

fearless *adj.* 857

feasible *adj.* 404, 406

feast *n.* 306; *vb* 304

feat *n.* 605, 609

feathery *adj.* 331

feature *n.* 5, 8, 55, 825

fecundity *n.* 168

federal *adj.* 379, 641

federation *n.* 641

fed up with *adj.* 862

fee *n.* 738, 743, 917

feeble-minded *adj.* 435

feebleness *n.* 160, 162, 507, 666, 781

feed *vb.* 304, 377

feedback *n.* 395

feeder *n.* 559

feel *n.* 339, 398, 758; *vb.* 411, 752, 758

feel better *vb.* 834

feeler *n.* 394, 396

feel for *vb.* 758, 907

feeling *n.* 411, 752, 758; *adj.* 752

feel like *vb.* 532

feel small *vb.* 874

fees *n.* 917

feign *vb.* 477, 852

felicitate *vb.* 888

felicitous *adj.* 510

fell *n.* 208; *vb.* 48

fellow *n.* 11, 122, 131, 380, 473

fellow-feeling *n.* 899, 907

fellowship *n* 60, 639, 641, 988; *vb* 988

fellow-worker *n.* 640

female *n.* **381**; *adj.* 381

femininity *n.* 162, 381

feminism *n.* 381

fen *n.* 355

fence *n.* 230, 234

fend for oneself *vb.* 678

fend off *vb* 646

ferment *n.* 80, 175; *vb.* 331, 363, 773

ferry *n.* 277; *vb.* 271

fertile *adj.* 163, 168

fertilize *vb.* 378

fervour *n.* 506, 752, 759

festive *adj.* 878

festivity *n.* 838, 840

festoon *vb.* 846

fetch *vb.* 705, 718, 743

fete *n.* 840

fetid *adj.* 777

fetish *n.* 967, 983, 984

fetter *n.* 681; *vb.* 635, 681

feud *n.* 642, 649

fever *n.* 326, 439, 586

few *adj.* 33, 76, 139

fewness *n.* 33, **76**

fiancée *n.* 698, 889

fiasco *n.* 662

fib *vb.* 477

fibber *n.* 480

fibre *n.* 207, 339

fibrous *adj.* 337

fickle *adj* 151, 536, 538, 539

fiction *n.* 525

fictitious *adj.* 2, 449

fiddle *n.* 478; *vb.* 722, 742

fidelity *n.* 673, 931

fidgety *adj.* 151, 611, 756, 856

field *n.* 184, 352, 356, 378, 557, 658

fiend *n* 175, 969

fierce *adj.* 175, 900

fiery *adj.* 506, 759, 893

fiesta *n* 840

fifth columnist *n* 480

fight *n.* 642, 649, 651; *vb.* 25, 615, 637, 642, 645, 649

fight back *vb.* 647

fighter *n.* 645, 655

figurative *adj.* 455

figure *n.* 39, 489; *vb.* 38

figure-head n. 253

figure of speech n. 455, 498

figure out vb. 452

filament n. 207

filch vb. 722

file n. 83, 202; vb. 83, 91, 255, 257, 341

filial adj. 171

filibuster n. 135; vb. 135

fill n. 865; vb. 56, 107, 265, 865

fill in vb. 149, 460, 483

fillip n. 173; vb. 613

fill up vb. 568

filly n. 381

film n. 225, 363, 483, 803; vb. 483

filter vb. 319

filth n. 584, 952

final adj. 89, 237, 408, 659

finality n. 543

finance n. 731; vb. 636, 718

financier n. 718, 728

find vb. 415, 419, 960

find fault with vb. 832, 926, 930, 962

fine n. 963; adj. 205, 255, 333, 340, 579, 844; vb. 963

finesse n. 631

finger vb. 758

fingerprint n. 482

finicky adj. 392, 864

finish n. 56, 89, 257, 510, 659; vb. 89, 144, 414, 581, 659

fiord n. 353

fire n. 506, 759, 763; vb. 645, 686, 755, 761, 765

firearm n. 657

fireproof adj. 762

fireside n. 191, 763

fireworks n. 800

firing squad n. 963

firm n. 620, 641; adj. 143, 152, 161, 334, 337, 534, 535, 669

first adj. 34, 88

first-class adj. 34, 579

first hand adj. 21

firth n. 353

fish n. 306, 373

fishy adj. 373, 932

fissure n. 254

fit n. 326, 439, 586, 893; adj. 585, 915; vb. 47, 105, 568, 602

fitful adj. 141, 539

fit in vb. 24

fit out vb. 227, 602

fitting adj. 577, 915

fittings n. 568

five and over n. 70

fix n. 633; vb. 47, 152, 311, 589

fixation n. 439

fixative n. 49

fixed adj. 47, 143, 152, 543

fixtures n. 152, 568, 711

fizz n. 363; vb. 363, 786

fizzle out vb. 144, 162, 662

flabbergasted adj. 866

flabby adj. 668

flaccid adj. 507

flag n. 467, 482, 677; vb. 617, 841

flagellant n. 946

flagon n. 193

flagrant adj. 458, 877

flail vb. 282

flake n. 33, 206, 340; vb. 206

flake out vb. 617

flamboyant adj. 877

flame n. 797, 800; vb. 759

flammable adj. 761, 765

flank n. 238; vb. 238

flap n. 225, 326; vb. 216, 326, 359, 756

flare n. 797, 800; vb. 756, 797

flash n. 115, 539, 797, 800; vb. 797

flashback n. 147, 441

flashlight n. 800

flashy adj. 509, 805, 849, 877

flask n. 193

flat n. 191, 356; adj. 215, 257, 768, 791, 843

flat out adv. 280

flattery n. 881, 886, 927

flaunt vb. 877

flavour n. 767; vb. 307

flavourless adj. 768, 771

flaw n. 431, 582, 847

flawless adj. 54, 581

flay vb. 228, 963

fleck n. 33

fledgling n. 125

flee vb. 555, 600, 826

fleece n. 377, 478, 722

fleeting adj. 113

flesh n. 306, 327, 379

flesh and blood n. 3, 327

fleshly adj. 945

fleshy adj. 194, 364

flex vb 247

flexible adj. 151, 335, 336, 668

flexuous adj. 251

flicker vb. 326, 759, 797

flickering adj. 141

flick through vb. 472, 818

flight n. 273, 293, 299, 555, 600, 826

flighty adj. 151, 539

flimsy adj. 162, 205, 335, 338

flinch vb. 283, 555, 856

fling vb. 359

flint n. 765

flippancy n. 842

flirt n. 953; vb 890

flirtation *n* 889. 890

flit *vb* 113

float *vb* 216. 257. 331

flock *n* 75. 94. 982. 987; *vb* 75. 94

flog *vb* 963

flood *n.* 358. 572; *vb.* 349. 358. 572

floodlight *n.* 800

floor *n* 206. 209. 213

flop *n.* 662

flora *n.* 366

floral *adj* 374

florid *adj* 846. 849

flounder *vb.* 409. 633. 662

flourish *n.* 877; *vb.* 36. 168. 585. 661. 664. 877

flout *vb.* 644

flow *n* 85. 91. 301. 313. 343. 358

flower *n.* 374; *vb.* 163

flowering *n.* 127; *adj.* 129

flowery *adj.* 509

fluctuate *vb* 141. 142. 151. 325. 536

flue *n.* 361

fluency *n.* 501. 514. 516

fluffy *adj.* 331. 335

fluid *n* 243. 309. 343; *adj* 343. 347

fluidity *n.* 343. 345

fluke *n.* 158. 553

flurry *n.* 359. 611. 613

flush *adj.* 28. 215; *vb.* 811

fluster *n.* 756

fluted *adj.* 261

flutter *vb.* 325. 326. 359

flux *vb.* 345

fly *vb* 110. 113. 273. 280

foam *n* 363; *vb.* 363. 893

focal *adj* 90. 96. 224

focalize *vb.* 296

focus *n* 90. **96.** 224; *vb* 96. 224. 390

fodder *n.* 305; *vb.* 377

foe *n* 638. 883

fog *n* 363. 409. 427. 799

foil *vb* 445. 635. 648. 662

fold *n.* 206. **260;** *vb* 251. 260. 739

foliage *n.* 374

folk *n.* 379

follow *vb.* 85. 105. 119. 237. **287.** 452. 673. 702

follower *n* 119. 287. 424. 474. 554. 640. 821

following *n.* 85. **287;** *adj.* 85. 119. 156. 554

follow up *vb* 392. 554

follow-up *n.* 87

folly *n.* 385. 433. **435**

fond *adj* 861. 889

fondle *vb.* 758. 890

fondness *n.* 861. 889. 890

food *n.* 305. **306**

fool *n.* 429. 437. 440. 479; *vb* 478

fool around *vb.* 433. 435

foolhardy *adj.* 613. 859

foolish *adj.* 385. 433. 435. 451

foot *n.* 213. 528

footing *n.* 93

footpath *n.* 559

footprint *n.* 482. 483

fop *n.* 852

foray *n.* 645

forbearance *n.* 670. 757. 907. 911

forbears *n.* 11. 86

forbid *vb.* 99. 635. 691. 955

forbidding *adj.* 669. 691

force *n* **159.** 161. 175. 177. 506. 674; *vb.* 175. 282. 531. 562. **674**

forced *adj.* 507. 511

force in *vb* 300. 311

force oneself *vb* 533

forces *n.* 655

ford *vb* 313

fore *adj.* 236

foreboding *n* 447. 597; *adj.* 447

forecast *n* 154. 348. 447; *vb* 154. 443. 446. 447. 558

foregoing *adj.* 84. 118

foreground *n* 199. 236

foreign *adj.* 100. 222

foreknowledge *n.* 447

foreman *n.* 623. 958

foremost *adj.* 236. 573

foreordain *vb.* 531. 543

forerun *vb.* 84. 118

forerunner *n.* 86. 467

foresee *vb.* 443. 446. 447

foreshadow *vb.* 447. 976

foresight *n.* 134. 434. 446. 447. 860

forest *n.* 374

forestall *vb.* 134

foretaste *n.* 55. 118

foretell *vb.* 447. 543

forethought *n.* 392. 446. 447. 860

forever *adv.* 114

forewarn *vb.* 447. 597

foreword *n.* 86. 88

forfeit *n.* 43. 701; *vb.* 706

forge *vb.* 477

forge ahead *vb.* 288

forgery *n.* 20. 22

forget *vb.* 385. 393. 442

forgiveness *n.* 601. 670. 907. **911**

forgo *vb* 556

forgotten *adj* 124. 126. 442

fork *n.* 246. 255. 297. 358; *vb* 63. 297

fork out *vb* 738

forlorn *adj.* 837

form *n.* 242, 339, 474, 482, 825; *vb* 58, 242

formal *adj* 511, 988

formalism *n.* 981

formalize *vb.* 81

formation *n.* 242, 655

formative *adj.* 129, 242

former *adj.* 84, 118, 124, 126

formless *adj.* 243

formula *n.* 39, 103, 498, 626

formulate *vb.* 81, 468, 498

fornicate *vb.* 952

fornicator *n.* 953

forsake *vb.* 556

forswear *vb.* 477

forte *n.* 627

forthcoming *adj.* 154, 292

forthright *adj.* 476, 632

forthwith *adv.* 115

fortification *n.* 646

fortify *vb.* 161, 173, 646, 857

fortitude *n.* 534, 857

fortress *n.* 595, 646

fortuitous *adj.* 136, 158, 553

fortunate *adj.* 661

fortune *n.* 158, 447, 550, 553, 734

forum *n.* 96, 625, 658

forward *adj.* 236, 288, 880; *vb.* 268; *adv.* 288

forward-looking *adj.* 125, 288

fossilize *vb.* 334

foster *vb.* 470, 636

foul *adj.* 584, 777; *vb.* 584

foul play *n.* 551, 900, 916, 932

found *vb.* 88

foundation *n.* 88, 155, 213, 217, 401, 602

founder *n.* 155; *vb* 588

foundry *n* 620

fountain *n.* 358, 567

four *n.* 67; *adj.* 67

fourfold *adj.* 68

fowl *n* 306, 373

fracas *n* 80

fraction *n.* 39, 73, 717

fracture *n.* 48; *vb.* 48

fragile *adj.* 162, 338

fragment *n.* 33, 55, 73, 717; *vb.* 48, 338

fragrance *n.* 774, 776

frail *adj.* 162, 338, 507, 586

frame *n.* 5; *vb.* 558, 930

frame of mind *n.* 751

frame of reference *n.* 700

framework *n.* 5, 232

franchise *n.* 540; *vb.* 690

frangible *adj.* 338

frank *adj.* 476, 508, 632, 931

fraternity *n.* 11, 882

fraud *n.* 478, 631, 722

fraudulent *adj.* 477, 478, 631, 932

freak *n.* 440, 539, 866

freckled *adj.* 817

free *adj.* 10, 530, 600, **678**, 708, 715, 897, 911; *vb.* 48, 600, 601, 678, 680, 921

freedom *n.* 600, **678**, 690, 921

freedom from mixture *n.* **46**

free thinking *n.* 975

free time *n.* 614

free will *n.* 530, 678

freeze *vb.* 332, 334, 599, 760, 762

freight *n.* 192, 268

frenzied *adj.* 439, 859

frenzy *n.* 80, 175, 439, 861

frequency *n* 27, **138**, 140, 400

frequent *adj* 138, 545; *vb.* 188

fresh *adj.* 125, 359, 599, 760

freshen *vb.* 348, 583

fret *vb.* 837

fretting *n.* 828

friable *adj.* 338, 340

friar *n.* 986

friary *n* 990

friction *n* 181, 341, 642

fridge *n.* 764

friend *n* 640, 882

friendless *adj.* 885

friendly *adj.* 643, 882, 884, 886

friendship *n.* 643, 650, **882**

frighten *vb.* 856, 902

frightful *adj.* 845

frigid *adj.* 160, 169, 754, 760

frill *n.* 509, 846

fringe *n.* 233, 235

frisky *adj.* 320

fritter away *vb.* 749

frivolous *adj.* 539

front *n.* 222, **236**, 658, 852; *adj.* 236

frontier *n.* 233, 235

frost *n.* 760; *vb.* 762

frosted *adj.* 804, 807

froth *n.* 363

frown *n.* 895; *vb.* 895

frown on *vb.* 926

frozen *adj.* 332, 760, 762

frugal *adj.* 392, 748, 944

fruit *n.* 156, 163, 306

fruitful *adj.* 163, 168, 661

fruitless *adj.* 169, 576, 662

frustrate *vb.* 181, 445, 635, 648, 662

fry *vb.* 306, 759

gentleman's agreement
n. 698, 699

gentry n. 870

genuine adj. 1, 21, 430,
632

geography n. 329

geology n. 367

geometry n. 38

gesticulate vb. 482

gesture n. 482, 549; vb.
482

get vb. 705, 716, 720,
726

get across vb. 460

get along with vb. 24,
643

get around vb. 464

get at vb. 460, 547, 893

get-at-able adj. 292

getaway n. 600

get away with vb. 600,
722, 921

get back vb. 647, 705,
721

get by vb. 661, 666

get down vb. 298, 837

get down to vb. 605

get dressed vb. 227

get even with vb. 647,
912, 963

get in with vb. 177, 882

get on vb. 661, 664

get one's own back vb.
647, 912

get on one's nerves vb.
787, 893

get on with vb. 24, 643

get over vb. 460, 659

get ready vb. 602

get rid of vb. 303, 607,
634, 680

get the hang of vb. 452,
472

get to vb. 298

get-together n. 884

get up vb. 318, 472, 477

get-up-and-go n. 173,
611

get used to vb. 545

get well vb. 589

ghastly adj. 856

ghost n. 328, 971

ghostly adj. 4, 328, 971

ghost-writer n. 149, 524

giant n. 194; adj. 208

gibberish n. 453

gibe vb. 853

gift n. 627, 652, 715, 829

gifted adj. 627

gift of the gab n. 514,
516

giggle vb. 838

gild vb. 846

ginger adj. 816

gipsy n. 447

gird vb. 322

girder n. 217

girdle n. 49; vb. 229

girl n. 131, 381

girl-friend n. 882, 889

girth n. 204

gist n. 224

give vb. 335, 568, 715,
965

give and take n. 150,
639, **704**

give away vb. 462, 717,
896

give in vb. 654

given adj. 1, 715

give off vb. 301, 774

give out vb. 301, 774,
778

giver n. 715, 905

give up vb. 556, 654,
855

give up office vb. 687

give way vb. 162

giving n. 636, **715**, 747

glaciate vb. 762

glacier n. 760

glad adj. 827, 836

gladden vb. 829, 836

gladly adv. 532

glamorous adj. 829, 844

glamour n. 547, 829,
844

glance n. 818; vb. 818

glare n. 797; vb. 797,
818

glaring adj. 458, 805,
823

glass n. 193, 257, 822

glasses n. 822

glassy adj. 257, 802

glaze n. 225; vb. 225,
369, 257

gleam n. 797; vb. 797

glean vb. 378, 540, 705

glee n. 827, 836

glib adj. 516

glide vb. 257, 273

glider n. 278

glimmer n. 460, 797;
vb. 326, 797

glimpse n. 818; vb. 818

glint n. 797

glisten vb. 797

glitter n. 797; vb. 797

global adj. 101

globe n. 249, 329

globe-trotter n. 270

globule n. 249, 363

gloom n. 798, 799, 837

gloomy adj. 798, 799,
837, 843, 895

glorification n. 925, 972

glorify vb. 318, 868, 982

glorious adj. 664, 972,
982

glory n. 868, 972; vb.
873

gloss n. 211, 225, 257,
456, 797; vb. 225, 257,
456

glossary n. 83, 494

gloss over vb. 393

glossy adj. 257, 797

glow n. 759, 797, 805;
vb. 759, 797, 811

glue n. 49, 362; vb. 50

glum adj. 895

glut n. 572, 865

glutton n. 304, 948

gluttony n. 304, 750, 945, **948**

gnome n. 970

go vb. 172, **266**, **299**

goad vb. 547, 613

go after vb. 85, 119, 287, 554, 882

go-ahead n. 424, 690; adj. 605, 611

goal n. 89, 298, 552

go along with vb. 424, 639

go around vb. 322

go around with vb. 882

go away vb. 299, 826, 896

go back vb. 147, 289, 441

go back on vb. 556

go bad vb. 588

gobble vb. 304, 789, 948

go before vb. 84, 118, 286

go behind vb. 85

go-between n. 467, 653

go beyond vb. 314

goblin n. 970

God n. 966, **967**

goddess n. 967

God-forsaken adj. 198, 885

godhead n. 966

godless adj. 975, 981

godly adj. 966, 974, 980

go down vb. 317, 321, 586, 662

godsend n. 550

go for vb. 284, 540, 552, 743, 861

goggles n. 801, 822

go in vb. 300

go in for vb. 472, 605

go into vb. 394, 472

go it alone vb. 678

gold adj. 813, 816

golden adj. 664, 813

golden age n. 664, 827

golden calf n. 967, 983

golden handshake n. 687, 715

golden rule n. 899

gold-mine n. 567

go mad vb. 439

gondola n. 277

gone adj. 124, 706, 855

gone off adj. 771

gone on adj. 889

gong n. 784

good n. **550**; adj. 550, 579, 585, 673, 899, 931

goodbye n. 518

good deed n. 899

good example n. 939

good-for-nothing n. 612, 940

good health n. 585

good humour n. 836

good-looking adj. 844

good luck n. 158

good manners n. 886

good memory n. 441

good name n. 868

good neighbour n. 899, 905

goodness n. 579, 907, 931, 935

good person n. 939

goods n. 163, 711, 729

good spirit n. **968**

good taste n. **848**

good time n. 840

good turn n. 550, 886, 899

goodwill n. 643

go off at a tangent vb. 285, 505

go off with vb. 722

go on vb. 1, 138, 145, 535

go on about vb. 516, 832

go on strike vb. 696

goose n. 381

go out vb. 144, 301

go out of control vb. 326

go out with vb 882, 890

go over vb. 77

gorge n. 200, 210, 254; vb. 56, 304, 865

gorgeous adj. 844

go round vb. 250

go shopping vb. 726

go-slow n. 144, 281

gospel n. 430, 976

gossamer n. 207

gossip n. 388, 516, 516, 869, 928; vb. 388, 516

go through vb. 313, 752, 828

go through the motions vb. 477, 852

go through with vb. 659

go together vb. 60, 882

go to law vb. 960

go to pieces vb. 588, 856

go to press vb. 522

go to the bottom vb. 321

gouge n. 259, 261, 312; vb 254, 312

go under vb. 321, 662, 665, 739

go up vb. 316, 745

gourmand n. 304, 848, 948

gourmandise n. 304

gourmet n. 304

govern vb. 177, 622, 667, 681

governess n. 473, 675, 683

government n. 621, 622, 625, 667

governmental adj. 622, 667

governor n. 623, 675

go with vb. 24, 60, 882

go wrong vb. 431

grab vb. 705, 720, 758

grace n. 844, 848, 907, 911

graceful adj. 510, 844, 848

gracious adj. 510, 899, 907, 966

gradation n. 27

grade n. 27, 93, 400, 474; vb. 27, 97

gradual adj. 27

graduate n. 474; vb. 27, 400

graft vb. 378

grain n. 33, 306, 340, 374

grammar n. 492, **499**

grammarian n. 492

grammatical adj. 492, 499

granary n. 193

grand adj. 509, 844, 868, 870

grandeur n. 870, 877

grandiloquent adj. 509

grandiose adj. 509, 877

grandstand n. 818

grange n. 191, 378

grant n. 636, 715; vb. 424, 690, 692, 715

grant permission vb. 424

granular adj. 339

granulate vb. 340

granule n. 340

grapevine n. 465

graphic adj. 488, 506, 521, 525

graphics n. 488

grapple vb. 758

grasp n. 410, 707, 712; vb. 50, 426, 452, 472, 707, 712, 720, 758

grasping adj. 705, 720, 750

grass n. 356, 374, 460

grassland n. 356, 378

grassy adj. 374, 812

grate n. 763; vb. 341, 787, 805

grateful adj. 909

gratify vb. 829, 831, 865

grating adj. 787, 791

gratitude n. **909**

gratuity n. 715, 965

grave n. 372; adj. 573, 837

graven image n. 983

gravestone n. 372

gravitate towards vb. 178

gravity n. 294, 330, 573, 837

graze vb. 201, 341, 377, 758

grease n. 306, 342, 365, 584; vb. 342, 365

greasy adj. 365, 584

great adj. 32, 573, 579, 868, 870

greater adj. 34

greatness n. 26, 32, 194, 579, 868, 870

greedy adj. 720, 750, 861, 934, **948**

greedy-guts n. 948

green n. 559, **812**; adj. 129, 422, 427, 812, 913

greenhorn n. 429, 479, 630

greenhouse n. 378

greet vb. 886, 922

greeting n. 518, 886, 922

gregarious adj. 884

gremlin n. 970

grey n. **809**; adj. 30, 130, 363, 799, 809

grey matter n. 434

grid n. 159, 221

grief n. 828, 837, 839

grievance n. 916

grieve vb. 830, 833, 837, 839

grill n. 221; vb. 306, 394, 759

grim adj. 669, 830

grimace n. 895; vb. 245, 895

grimy adj. 584

grin n. 838; vb. 838

grin and bear it vb. 757, 836

grind vb. 341, 615, 787

grip n. 193, 712; vb. 50, 712, 720, 758

gripping adj. 755

gristle n. 337

groan n. 788; vb. 696, 788

groceries n. 305

groggy adj. 586, 950

groom vb. 377, 470

groove n. 184, 261, 545; vb. 261

grope vb. 409, 758

gross n. 70; adj. 54, 56, 849, 936

grotesque adj. 245, 845

grotto n. 254

grouch n. 832; vb. 895

ground n. (reason) 155, 401, 547, 929; (land) 213, 352, 658; vb. 319, 470

groundwork n. 213, 602

group n. 55, **94**, 97, 641, 793; vb. 52, 94, 97

grovel vb. 209, 881, 922

grow vb. 36, 168, 196, 242, 288, 316, 324

growl vb. 783, 789, 895

grown-up n. 133; adj. 133

growth n. 36, 196, 252, 288, 324

grow up vb. 133

grudge n. 832, 893; vb. 914

grudgingly adv. 533

gruelling adj. 615

gruff adj. 787, 887, 894

grumble vb. 783, 832

grumbler n. 832

grumpy *adj.* 894

grunt *vb.* 789

guarantee *n.* 424; *vb.* 408, 468, 698, 701

guard *n.* 593, 646, 683; *vb.* 392, 593, 646

guardian *n.* 593, 683, 905

guardroom *n.* 682

guerdon *n.* 965

guerrilla *n.* 148

guess *n.* 386, 396, 447, 448; *vb.* 396, 411, **448**

guest *n.* 100, 884

guffaw *vb.* 838

guidance *n.* 470, 624

guide *n.* 103, 217, 473, 623; *vb.* 470, 621, 622, **624**

guidebook *n.* 460, 524

guile *n.* 477, 478, 631, 932

guileless *adj.* 422, 476, **632**, 937, 951

guillotine *n.* 964; *vb.* 370, 963

guilt *n.* **938**

guilty *adj.* 938

guinea pig *n.* 396, 716, 828

guise *n.* 227, 463, 549

gulf *n.* 200, 254, 353

gullibility *n.* **422**

gully *n.* 254, 360

gulp *n.* 309; *vb.* 304, 948

gum *n.* 365; *vb.* 50

gun *n.* 657; *vb.* 370

gunman *n.* 167, 370

gunpowder *n.* 657

gurgle *vb* 358

guru *n.* 473

gush *vb.* 301, 358, 532

gust *n* 359

gusto *n.* 827

gusty *adj.* 359

guts *n.* 535, 857

gutter *n.* 261, 360

guzzle *vb.* 304, 948, 950

gypsy *n.* 270

gyration *n.* 323

H

habit *n.* 79, 138, **545**

habitat *n.* **191**, 229

habitation *n.* 188, **191**

hack *n.* 524, 619, 676

hackneyed *adj.* 426

haggard *adj.* 205, 617

hail *n.* 760; *vb.* 886, 925

hair *n.* 207

hair-dressing *n.* 844

hairless *adj.* 228

hairy *adj.* 207, 258

halcyon days *n.* 664, 827

hale *adj.* 585

half *n.* 63; *adj.* 63

half a dozen *n.* 70

half-and-half *adj.* 45

half-done *adj.* 55, 57, 660

half-hearted *adj.* 533, 863

half-price *adj.* 746

half-remembered *adj.* 441

halfway *n.* 30, 704; *adj.* 30, 90, 560; *adv.* 90

half-wit *n.* 437

half-witted *adj.* 435

hall *n.* 191, 529

hallmark *n.* 482

hallow *vb.* 980

hallucination *n.* 478

halo *n.* 250, 800

halt *n.* 144; *vb.* 144, 267, 691

halve *vb.* 63

hamlet *n.* 183

hammer *vb.* 282

hammer out *vb.* 659, 699

hamper *n.* 193; *vb.* 635, 681, 691

hand *n.* 238, 521

handbook *n.* 524

hand down *vb.* 714

handful *n.* 26, 76, 633

handicap *vb.* 162

hand in one's notice *vb.* 687

handiwork *n.* 163

handle *n.* 872; *vb.* 172, 606, 609, 622, 725

hand out *vb.* 715, 717

hand-out *n.* 464, 465, 715

hand over *vb.* 268

handshake *n.* 886

handsome *adj.* 844

handwriting *n.* 521

handy *adj.* 575, 627

handyman *n.* 629

hang *vb.* 216, 370, 963

hang around *vb.* 188, 612

hanger-on *n.* 287, 640, 881

hanging *n.* 216, 370, 963

hangman *n.* 370, 963

hangover *n.* 44, 950

hanker *vb.* 861, 914

haphazard *adj.* 158, 399, 409, 553

happen *vb.* 1, 107, 153, 825

happening *n.* 153

happiness *n.* 550, 661, 664, 831, **836**

happy *adj.* 827, 831, **836**, 950

happy medium *n.* 30

happy returns *n.* 888

harangue *n* 518

harass *vb.* 830, 893

harbour *n.* 298, 353, 595; *vb.* 461, 593, 712

hard *adj.* 334, 337, 537, 633, 669, 942

harden *vb.* 332, 334, 337, 754

hardened *adj.* 537, 942

hard-hearted *adj.* 648, 754, 908

hard labour *n.* 963

hardly *adv.* 33, 139

hardness *n.* 334, 537, 633, 669, 754

hardship *n.* 633, 665, 735

hard-working *adj.* 611, 615

hardy *adj.* 161

harlot *n.* 953

harm *n.* 551, 900; *vb.* 580, 608, 900, 916

harmful *adj.* 164, 580, 592, 916

harmonious *adj.* 24, 79, 105, 244, 643, **790**

harmony *n.* 24, 244, 510, 643, 650, **790**

harness *n.* 49; *vb.* 47

harrow *vb.* 378, 830

harrowing *adj.* 828, 856

harsh *adj.* 258, 642, 669, 787, 900, 908

harsh sound *n.* 787

harvest *n.* 128, 163, 567; *vb.* 378, 567

haste *n.* 280, **613**

hasty *adj.* 393, 544, 603, 613

hatch *n.* 262; *vb.* 449, 477, 558

hatchway *n.* 262

hate *n.* 862, **892,** 900; *vb.* 862, **892**

hatred *n.* 862, 883, 892

haughty *adj.* 873, 875, 924

haul *n.* 291, 724; *vb.* 268, 291

haunt *vb.* 188, 441, 830, 971

have *vb.* 707

have a go *vb.* 604

have fun *vb.* 840

have in mind *vb.* 552

have it in for *vb.* 892, 900

haven *n.* 595

have nothing to do with *vb.* 10, 542, 862

have no time for *vb.* 923

have-nots *n.* 871

have on *vb* 227, 478

have one's own way *vb.* 530

have one's say *vb.* 468

have on one's mind *vb.* 384

havoc *n.* 164

hawk *vb.* 695, 727

hawker *n.* 697, 728

hazard *n.* 553, 594; *vb.* 553

hazel *adj.* 810

hazy *adj.* 363, 799, 824

H-bomb *n.* 657

head *n.* 89, 236, 675; *vb.* 212, 236, 284, 286

headache *n.* 633, 950

headlines *n.* 465

headlong *adj.* 613, 859

headmaster *n.* 473

headquarters *n.* 96

head start *n.* 34

headstone *n.* 372

headstrong *adj.* 537, 859

headway *n.* 288

heal *vb.* 589, 591

health *n.* **585**

heap *n.* 567; *vb.* 567, 747

hear *vb.* 778, **795**, 960

hearing *n.* **795**, 960

hearsay *n.* 465

heart *n.* 223, 224, 368, 751, 857

heart-broken *adj.* 828, 837

heartening *adj.* 836, 857

hearth *n.* 191, 763

heartlessness *n.* 908

heart-to-heart *n.* 519

heartwarming *adj.* 836

hearty *adj.* 585

heat *n.* **759**, 763; *vb.* 306, 761

heath *n.* 356

heathen *n.* 975, 983

heating *n.* **761**

heatwave *n.* 759

heave *vb.* 291, 303, 318, 834

heaven *n.* 329, **972**

heavenly *adj.* 770, 966, **972**

heavy *adj.* 330, 332, 511, 573, 617, 841

heavy drinker *n.* 950

heavy-handed *adj.* 628, 669

heavy-laden *adj.* 828

heavyweight *adj.* 573

heckle *vb.* 425, 696

hedge *n.* 234; *vb.* 555

hedonistic *adj.* 827, 945

heed *n.* 390, 392, 860; *vb.* 390, 392, 673, 702

heedless *adj.* 391, 442, 859

hefty *adj.* 161

height *n.* 26, **208**, 400, 581

heighten *vb.* 36, 318, 481, 835

heinous *adj* 936

heir *n.* 171, 710, 716

helicopter *n.* 278

helix *n.* 251

hell *n.* 828, **973**

helmsman *n.* 272

help *n.* 563, **636**, 639, 834; *vb.* 563, 575, 577, **636**, 639, 676

helper *n.* 624, 640, 905

helpful *adj.* 550, 575, 636

helping *n.* 305, 717

helpless *adj.* 160, 162, 855

hem *n.* 233; *vb.* 233

hem in *vb.* 234

hemisphere *n.* 63

hen *n.* 381

henpecked *adj.* 673

herald *n.* 86, 467; *vb.* 118, 286

herb *n.* 306, 307, 374

herbivore *n.* 373

herd *n.* 94, 373, 377, 871; *vb.* 377

hereafter *n.* 123; *adv.* 123

hereditary *adj.* 5

heresy *n.* 106, 975, **978**

heretical *adj.* 106, 412, 975, **978**

heritage *n.* 11

hermit *n.* 885, 946

hero *n.* 661, 857, 939

heroic *adj.* 857

hesitant *adj.* 515, 533, **536**, 856

hesitate *vb.* 325, 409, 421, 515, 533, 536

heterodox *adj.* 978

heterogeneous *adj.* 15, 17, 45, 104

hew *vb.* 48, 489

hexagon *n.* 70, 246

heyday *n.* 664

hidden *adj.* 453, 459, 461, 466, 824

hide *vb.* 225, 461, 466, 593

hideous *adj.* 245, 845

hide-out *n.* 463

hiding *n.* 461, 463

hierarchy *n.* 97

hi-fi *n.* 794

high *adj.* 32, **208**, 318, 777, 868

high birth *n.* 870

highest *adj.* 212, 579

high-flown *adj.* 509, 877

high-handed *adj.* 880, 887

high hopes *n.* 443, 854

highlight *vb.* 468, 481

high living *n.* 945

highly-strung *adj.* 756

high opinion *n.* 922

high-pitched *adj.* 787

high principles *n.* 931

high-rise *adj.* 208

high spirits *n.* 836

high tea *n.* 306

high time *n.* 135

highway *n.* 559

highway code *n.* 313

highwayman *n.* 723

hijack *vb.* 722

hijacker *n.* 723

hike *n.* 269; *vb.* 269

hiker *n.* 270

hilarious *adj.* 851

hill *n.* 208, 316, 559

hind *n.* 381; *adj.* 237

hinder *vb.* 181, 548, 635, 637, 681

hindmost *adj.* 198, 237

hindrance *n.* 548, **635**, 681

hindsight *n.* 441

hinge *n.* 49, 217

hint *n.* 459, **460**, 482; *vb.* 459, 460

hire *vb.* 557, 685, 719

hire out *vb.* 718

hire purchase *n.* 718, 731

hiss *vb.* **786**, 788, 853, 926

hissing sound *n.* 786

historian *n.* 484

historical *adj.* 124, 430

history *n.* 124

histrionics *n.* 529, 877

hit *n.* 282, 661; *vb.* 282, 758, 963

hit and miss *n.* 396

hit back *vb.* 647

hitch *n.* 635

hitch-hiker *n.* 270

hit it off *vb.* 24, 643

hit-or-miss *adj.* 158

hit upon *vb.* 419

hive off *vb.* 48

hoard *n.* 567; *vb.* 567

hoarse *adj.* 787

hoary *adj.* 126, 807, 809

hoax *n.* 478, 598, 631; *vb.* 478, 631

hob *n.* 763, 970

hobble *vb.* 281

hobby *n.* 840

hoe *vb.* 378

hog *n.* 948; *vb.* 707

hoist *vb.* 318

hold *n.* 707, 712; *vb.* 50, 420, 707, 712

hold against *vb.* 588

hold back *vb.* 533, 681, 694, 876

hold dear *vb.* 441, 889, 922

holder *n.* 193, 710

hold forth *vb.* 470, 514

holding *n.* 378, 711, 712

hold off *vb.* 295, 648

hold one's breath *vb.* 443

hold out *vb.* 648, 693

hold out for *vb.* 535

hold up *vb.* 135, 217, 635

hold-up *n.* 635, 722

hold water *vb.* 410

hole *n.* 254, 262, 319; *vb.* 264

holiday *n.* 144, 612, 614, 840

holiday-maker *n.* 270

hollow *n.* 210, 254, 262; *adj.* 254, 852; *vb.* 210, 254

holocaust *n.* 370

holy *adj.* 935, 974, 980, 982

Holy Communion *n.* 988

holy orders n. 985
Holy Spirit n. 967
homage n. 982
home n. 11, 191, 595;
    adj. 190
homecoming n. 298
homeless adj. 59, 187
homely adj. 508, 827
home-made adj. 628
homesickness n. 861
homestead n. 191, 377,
    378
homework n. 470, 472
homicide n. 370
homogeneity n. 13, 16,
    46, 59
homo sapiens n. 379
homosexual n. 106,
    953; adj. 952
honest adj. 430, 476,
    915, 931
honey n. 772, 891
honeymoon n. 829,
    896; vb. 896
honour n. 663, 868,
    872, 909, 922, 982; vb.
    868, 878, 922, 982
honourable adj. 868,
    931
hood n. 225, 801, 989
hooded adj. 225
hoodwink vb. 478, 819
hook n. 49; vb. 47, 896
hooligan n. 906
hoop n. 250; vb. 788
hoot vb. 482, 788, 853
hooter n. 116, 482
hop n. 320; vb. 320
hope n. 406, 420, 443,
    854; vb. 406, 443, 552,
    854
hopeful adj. 443, 854
hopelessness n. 405,
    576, 855
horizon n. 198
horizontal adj. 215, 248
horn n. 598
horn of plenty n. 168

horology n. 116
horoscope n. 329, 447
horrible adj. 580, 771
horrid adj. 580, 845
horrifying adj. 856
horror n. 845, 856
horse n. 275
horsemanship n. 269
horse-power n. 159
horse-racing n. 269
horse-rider n. 270
horticultural adj. 374,
    376, 378
hospitable adj. 716, 884
hospitality n. 302, 747,
    884
host n. 75, 968
hostage n. 701
hostel n. 191
hostile adj. 637, 665,
    883, 892
hostilities n. 649, 651
hot adj. 759, 769
hotel n. 191
hour n. 109
hour-glass n. 116
hourly adv. 140
house n. 191, 620
household n. 11; adj.
    426
householder n. 190
housekeeper n. 676,
    683
housekeeping n. 622,
    748
hover vb. 154, 216
hovercraft n. 278
howl vb. 359, 788, 789,
    839
hub n. 96, 224
huddle n. 94; vb. 94
hue n. 805
hug n. 712, 886; vb. 50,
    712, 886, 890
huge adj. 32, 194
hull n. 225
hum n. vb. 781, 783,
    784, 789

human n. 368; adj. 379
human being n. 379
humane adj 903
humanitarian adj. 899,
    903
humanity n. 379
human rights n. 917
human sound n. 788
humble adj. 35, 654,
    833, 871, 874, 941, 980;
    vb. 869, 874, 922
humble oneself vb. 833,
    874, 941, 982
humid adj. 349, 759
humiliate vb. 869, 874,
    923
humility n. 654, 874,
    980
humorous adj. 842
humour n. 5, 751, 842
hump n. 252
hunch n. 134, 411; vb.
    319
hunchbacked adj. 245
hundred n. 70
hunger n. 861, 947; vb.
    861
hunger strike n. 696
hungry adj. 735, 861,
    947
hunt n. 554; vb. 394,
    554
hurdle n. 230, 235, 320,
    635
hurricane n. 175, 359
hurried adj. 613, 859
hurry n. 280, 611, 613;
    vb. 280, 613
hurt n. 828; adj. 893;
    vb. 580, 608, 830, 900,
    916
hurtful adj. 164, 551,
    580, 828, 830
husband n. 896; vb.
    377, 748
husbandry n. 378, 622,
    748

247

hush n. 779, 781; vb. 267, 779

hush-hush adj. 461, 466

hush up vb. 466

husk n. 225

husky adj. 787

hut n. 191

hybrid n. 45, 495

hydrated adj. 347

hydro- adj. 347

hydro-electricity n. 159, 765

hydrogen bomb n. 657

hygienic adj. 585

hymn n. 792, 982

hyperbole n. 481

hyper-critical adj. 832, 864

hyper-sensitive adj. 753

hypnosis n. 754

hypochondriac n. 440

hypocrisy n. 477, 981

hypocrite n. 480, 631

hypothesis n. 157, 386, 396, 448

hypothetical adj. 2, 396, 448

hysteria n. 439, 756

hysteric n. 440

I

ice n. 347, 760; vb. 762

iceberg n. 754, 760

icon n. 983

icy adj. 760, 762

idea n 386, 415, 420, 449, 552

ideal n. 581, 939; adj. 449, 581

idealist n. 449, 864, 903

identical adj. 13

identification n. 397, 419, 482, 496

identify vb. 482, 496

identity n. 13

idiom n. 492, 498

idiosyncractic adj. 102

idiosyncrasy n. 5, 102, 501

idiot n. 437, 440, 630

idiotic adj. 435

idle adj. 174, 610, 612; vb. 107, 174, 281, 612

idler n. 281, 612, 940

idol n. 967, 983

idolatry n. 975, 983

idolize vb. 982, 983

idyllic adj 528

ignite vb. 761

ignited adj. 759

ignoble adj. 871

ignominious adj. 869

ignoramus n. 429, 437, 630

ignorance n. 385, 427

ignorant adj. 427

ignore vb. 385, 389, 393, 672, 694, 887, 911

ill n. 551, 900; adj. 586

illegal adj. 691, 916, 955

illegality n. 955

illegible adj. 453

illegitimate adj. 171, 916, 955

ill feeling n. 642, 883

ill health n. 586

ill-humoured adj 895

illicit adj. 691, 916, 952, 955

illiterate adj. 427

illness n. 586, 828

illogical adj. 412, 451

illuminate vb. 456, 797

illusion n. 4, 449, 478

illustrate vb. 413, 456, 486, 488, 525

illustration n. 23, 397, 413, 456, 486, 488, 525

illustrative adj. 456, 486

illustrious adj. 573, 868

image n. 386, 486, 489, 525, 983

imagery n. 455

imaginable adj. 404

imaginary adj. 2, 449, 970

imagination n. 449

imagine vb. 448, 449

imbecile n. 437, 440; adj. 435

imbecility n. 383, 435, 439

imitate vb. 18, 20

imitation n. 20, 486, 719; adj. 149

immaculate adj. 581, 583, 935

immanent adj. 5, 966

immateriality n. 4, 328, 574

immaturity n. 129, 427, 582, 603

immeasurable adj. 78

immediate adj. 115, 134

immensity n. 194

immerse vb. 311, 321, 349

immersed adj. 210

immigrant n. 100, 190, 270; adj. 100

immigration n. 300

imminent adj. 123, 134, 154, 902

immobile adj. 152, 174, 267

immoderate adj. 32, 393, 572, 749, 918, 945

immoral adj. 932, 936, 952

immortal adj. 114, 966

immortalize vb. 114, 868

immovable adj. 143, 152, 267, 669, 757

immunity n. 593, 678, 921

immutability n. 152

imp n. 969, 970

impact n. 282

impair vb. 160, 588

impale *vb.* 264, 963

impart *vb.* 464, 470, 715

impartial *adj.* 476, 541, 915, **933**

impassioned *adj.* 506, 752

impassive *adj.* 863

impatient *adj.* 613, 756, 893

impeach *vb.* 686, 930

impeccable *adj.* 581, 935, 937

impede *vb.* 635, 681

impediment *n.* 515, 635, 681

impel *vb.* 266, 282, 290, 674

impend *vb.* 123, 154

impenetrable *adj.* 265, 332, 334, 453

impenitence *n.* 942

imperative *n.* 562; *adj.* 531, 562

imperceptible *adj.* 33, 824

imperfect *adj.* 35, 57, 315, 582, 847, 952

imperfection *n.* 35, 315, 582, 952

imperfect speech *n.* 515

imperfect vision *n.* 820

imperialism *n.* 379

imperishable *adj.* 114

impermeable *adj.* 332, 334

impersonation *n.* 20

impertinent *adj.* 880, 923

imperturbable *adj.* 757

impervious *adj.* 265, 337, 803

impetuous *adj.* 613, 756, 859

impetus *n.* 282, 290, 547

impiety *n.* 981

impinge *vb.* 282

implacable *adj.* 912

implant *vb.* 300, 311

implausible *adj.* 405, 407, 421

implement *n.* 192, 565; *vb.* 659

implicate *vb.* 930

implication *n.* 450, 459

implicit *adj.* 5

implore *vb.* 695, 982

imply *vb.* 401, 448, 450, 459, 482

impolite *adj.* 887, 923

imponderability *n.* 4, 331

import *n.* 450, 573; *vb.* 268, 450

importance *n.* 456, 573

important *adj.* 177, 573, 922

importer *n.* 728

importunity *n.* 695

impose *vb.* 700, 919

imposing *adj.* 573, 870

imposition *n.* 963

impossibility *n.* 405

impossible *adj.* 405

impostor *n.* 480, 852, 940

impotence *n.* 160, 169

impoverish *vb.* 162, 735

impracticable *adj.* 407, 576, 628

impractical *adj.* 449

imprecatory *adj.* 695, 901

imprecise *adj.* 431, 503, 916

impregnable *adj.* 593

impregnate *vb.* 311

impress *vb.* 242, 441, **468**, 482, 490, **522**, 752, 755, 922

impression *n.* 22, 386, 411, 420, 482, 483, 522, 752

impressionable *adj.* 242, 753

impressive *adj.* 529, 573, 755, 844

imprint *n.* 482; *vb.* 522

imprison *vb.* 234, 681, 963

improbability *n.* **407**, 409

improbity *n.* 932

improper *adj.* 137, 511, 916, 918

improve *vb.* 288, 472, **587**, 618

improvement *n.* 288, 550, **587**

improvise *vb.* 142, 544, 603

imprudent *adj.* 393, 435, 859

impudent *adj.* 880, 887

impulse *n.* 282

impulsive *adj.* 411, 544, 613, 756, 859

impurity *n.* 582, 584, 847, **952**

impute *vb.* 157, 930

inability *n.* 160, 628

inaccessible *adj.* 198, 405

inaccurate *adj.* 431, 477, 916

inaction *n.* 610, 616

inactive *adj.* 174, 281, 607, **612**

inactivity *n.* 174, **612**

inadequate *adj.* 315, **571**, 582, 662

in advance *adj.* 134; *adv.* 84, 236, 286

inadvisable *adj.* 578

inane *adj.* 433, 435

inanimate *adj.* 367

inanity *n.* 451

inapplicable *adj.* 10, 106

inappropriate *adj.* 10, 106, 137, 500, 511, 578

in arrears *adj.* 737, 917

inarticulate *adj.* 513, 515

indiscretion *n.* 435 859

indiscriminate *adj.* 15, 54, 399

indiscrimination *n.* 399

indispensable *adj.* 531, 562

indisputable *adj.* 408

indissoluble *adj.* 54

indistinct *adj.* 243, 503, 515, 781, 799, 824

indistinguishable *adj.* 13

individual *n.* 368, 379; *adj.* 59, 102, 139, 379

individualist *n.* 934

indivisibility *n.* 50, 59

indivisible *adj.* 50, 54, 59, 332

indoctrinate *vb.* 470

indolent *adj.* 174, 612

indubitable *adj.* 408

induction *n.* 300, 410, 685

indulge *vb.* 831, 945

indulgence *n.* 827, 948

industrialist *n.* 728

industrious *adj.* 472, 535, 611

industry *n.* 472, 611, 620

inebriated *adj.* 950

inedible *adj.* 771

ineffable *adj.* 453

ineffably *adv.* 32

ineffective *adj.* 160, 169, 576, 662

inefficient *adj.* 160, 628

inelegance *n.* 511, 845, 849

inept *adj.* 160, 427, 628

inequality *n.* 14, 29

inequity *n.* 14, 916

inerrant *adj.* 408

inertia *n.* 174, 610, 612

inertness *n.* 174

inescapable *adj.* 154, 531

inevitable *adj.* 123, 154, 408, 531, 543

inexact *adj.* 19, 431, 453

inexcitability *n.* 754, 757

inexcusable *adj.* 916

inexhaustible *adj.* 145

inexpedience *n.* 137, 578

inexpensive *adj.* 746

inexperience *n.* 129, 427, 603, 628

inexperienced *adj.* 125, 129, 422, 546, 628, 937

inexplicable *adj.* 158, 453

infallible *adj.* 408, 430

infamous *adj.* 426, 869

infancy *n.* 88, 129

infant *n.* 131; *adj.* 129

infantry *n.* 655

infatuated *adj.* 439, 889

infatuation *n.* 439, 889

infect *vb.* 45, 584, 588

infection *n.* 586

infectious *adj.* 586

infer *vb.* 101, 410, 448, 459

inferable *adj.* 413

inference *n.* 410, 448, 459

inferiority *n.* 29, 35, 580, 679

infernal *adj.* 973

inferno *n.* 973

infertile *adj.* 160, 169

infest *vb.* 314

infidel *n.* 975

infidelity *n.* 703, 952, 978

infiltrate *vb* 45, 300

infinite *adj.* 78, 114

infinitely *adv.* 78

infinitesimal *adj.* 33, 195

infinity *n.* 78, 114

infirm *adj.* 130, 160, 586

infirmity *n.* 126, 130, 162, 586

inflammation *n.* 252, 835

inflate *vb.* 196, 359

inflated *adj.* 879

inflation *n* 196

inflect *vb.* 499

inflection *n.* 499, 512

inflexible *adj.* 152, 334, 537, 908

inflict *vb.* 674

influence *n.* 155, 159, 177, 294, 547; *vb.* 155, 177, 547, 573, 755

influential *adj.* 177, 573

influx *n.* 300

in force *adj.* 172, 606

inform *vb.* 460, 470, 597, 624

informal *adj.* 495

informant *n.* 460, 624

information *n.* 401, 426, 460, 465, 525, 624

informative *adj.* 460, 470

informed *adj.* 426

informer *n.* 460, 480, 883

infrequency *n.* 139, 407

infringement *n.* 672, 703, 955

infuriate *vb.* 893

infusion *n* 309, 311

ingenuity *n.* 21

ingenuous *adj.* 476, 632

ingratiating *adj.* 881, 886, 927

ingratitude *n.* 910

ingredient *n.* 55, 192, 327

inhabit *vb.* 188, 191

inhabitant *n.* 190

inhale *vb.* 308, 359

inharmonious *adj.* 791

inhere *vb.* 5

inherent *adj.* 5, 55, 459

inherit *vb.* 705

inheritance *n.* 711
inheritor *n.* 710
inhibition *n.* 876
inhuman *adj.* 900, 904
inimical *adj.* 25, 883
iniquity *n.* 936
initial *adj.* 88, 155, 602; *vb.* 482
initiation *n.* 88, 300, 302, 470
initiative *n.* 173, 611, 857
inject *vb.* 264, 311
injection *n.* 181, 311, 591
injudicious *adj.* 393, 416
injunction *n.* 626, 671, 691
injure *vb.* 580, 588, 608, 830, 900, 916
injured *adj.* 582
injury *n.* 551, 588, 828, 916
injustice *n.* 916, 955
ink *vb.* 488, 808
inkling *n.* 448
inland *n.* 352; *adj.* 223, 352
inland revenue *n.* 743
inlay *n.* 226; *vb.* 226
inlet *n.* 353
in lieu *adv.* 149
in love *adj.* 889
inmate *n.* 684
in memoriam *n.* 372
inn *n.* 191
innate *adj.* 5, 223
inner *adj.* 223, 224
innermost *adj.* 223
inner self *n.* 751
innocence *n.* 632, 935, 937, 961
innocent *adj.* 632, 935, 937, 951
innovation *n.* 125, 142
innuendo *n.* 928
inoculation *n.* 591

inodorousness *n.* 775
inoffensive *adj.* 757
in operation *adj.* 172, 609
inoperative *adj.* 576, 610
inopportune *adj.* 137, 578
in order *adv.* 79, 605
inordinate *adj.* 572, 945
inordinately *adv.* 32
inorganic matter *n.* 367
in part *adv.* 55
in progress *adj.* 57; *adv.* 288
inquire *vb.* 695
inquirer *n.* 697
inquiry *n.* 394, 695
inquisition *n.* 963
inquisitive *adj.* 388, 394
inroad *n.* 645
insalubrious *adj.* 586
insane *adj.* 435, 439
insanitary *adj.* 586
insanity *n.* 439
inscription *n.* 483, 490, 521
inscrutable *adj.* 453
insect *n.* 373
insecure *adj.* 409, 594
insensible *adj.* 754
insensitive *adj.* 754, 942
insensitivity *n.* 754, 863
inseparable *adj.* 47, 50, 54, 882
insert *n.* 230; *vb.* 40, 230, 311, 483
insertion *n.* 311
inside *n.* 223, 226; *adj.* 223, 681
insidious *adj.* 459, 932
insight *n.* 410, 411, 434
insignia *n.* 482, 677
insignificant *adj.* 451, 574
insincere *adj.* 477, 852, 927, 932, 981

insinuate *vb.* 311, 459, 460
insinuation *n.* 311, 928, 930
insipid *adj.* 162, 507, 666, 768, 843
insist *vb.* 547, 669, 700
insistent *adj.* 506
insobriety *n.* 950
insolence *n.* 644, 672, 873, 880, 924
insolent *adj.* 332, 405
insoluble *adj.* 332, 405
insolvent *adj.* 706, 735, 739
inspect *vb.* 390, 394, 818
inspection *n.* 390, 392, 394, 396, 818
inspector *n.* 623
inspiration *n.* 411, 755, 976
inspire *vb.* 547, 755, 836, 854, 857
inspired *adj.* 411, 449, 506, 756, 976
instability *n.* 17, 151, 536, 756
install *vb.* 186, 302, 311, 685
installation *n.* 620, 685
instalment *n.* 55, 738
instance *n.* 23, 456
instant *n.* 115; *adj.* 602
instantaneous *adj.* 115
instantly *adv.* 115
instead *adv.* 149
instigate *vb.* 547
instigator *n.* 166, 547
instill *vb.* 470
instinct *n.* 382, 411, 531, 545
instinctive *adj.* 411, 531, 544
institute *n.* 475; *vb.* 88
institution *n.* 475, 620, 988
in store *adj.* 154; *adv.* 567

instruct *vb.* 470, 514
instructed *adj.* 426
instruction *n.* 103, 426, 470, 624, 626
instructive *adj.* 460, 470, 597
instructor *n.* 473
instrument *n.* 565, 609, 619
instrumental *adj.* 563, 565
instrumentalist *n.* 793
instrumentality *n.* 172, 563
insubordinate *adj.* 644, 672
insubstantial *adj.* 4, 328, 331, 333, 451
insufficiency *n.* 315, 571
insular *adj.* 183, 416
insulate *vb.* 226, 761
insult *n.* 869, 923; *vb.* 644, 887, 923
insulting *adj.* 880, 923
insuperable *adj.* 405
insurance *n.* 701
insurgence *n.* 672
insurgent *n.* 672; *adj.* 148, 672
insurmountable *adj.* 405
insurrection *n.* 148
insurrectionist *n.* 148, 672
insusceptible *adj.* 754
intact *adj.* 54, 599
intangible *adj.* 4, 328, 824
integer *n.* 39
integral *adj.* 5, 39, 54, 55, 56, 223
integrate *vb.* 52, 105
integration *n.* 24, 45, 52, 56, 59
integrity *n.* 56, 476, 931, 935, 937
intellect *n.* 382, 434

intellectual *n.* 428; *adj.* 382, 384, 426
intelligence *n.* 382, 426, 434, 460
intelligent *adj.* 382, 426, **434**
intelligibility *n.* **452**, 502
intemperance *n.* **945**, 948, 950
intend *vb.* 552
intended *n.* 698; *adj.* 552
intense *adj.* 173, 752, 759, 805
intensification *n.* 196, 835
intensify *vb.* 36, 173, 196, 481, 835
intensity *n.* 27, 32, 506, 759, 805
intention *n.* 284, 530, **552**
intentional *adj.* 530
interact *vb.* 12, 150
intercession *n.* 230, 653, 695, 982
intercessor *n.* 653, 982
interchange *n.* 12, **150**, 519, 714; *vb.* 150
interdiction *n.* 691
interest *n.* 41, 388, 755; *vb.* 294, 547, 755, 829
interested *adj.* 388
interesting *adj.* 755
interfere *vb.* 181, 635, 653
interior *n.* 223, 352; *adj.* 223, 352
interjection *n.* 230, 499
interlude *n.* 144
intermediary *n.* 653; *adj.* 230
intermediate *adj.* 30, 90, 230, 560, 563
interminable *adj.* 78, 114, 202
intermingle *vb.* 45

intermission *n.* 92, 144
intermittent *adj.* 92, 139
internal *adj.* 5, 223
international *adj.* 101
internationalism *n.* 903
internecine *adj.* 164, 370
internee *n.* 684
internment camp *n.* 682
interplay *n.* 12; *vb.* 12
interpose *vb.* 230, 653
interpret *vb.* 456
interpretation *n.* 450, 456
interpreter *n.* 456, 974
interrogate *vb.* 394
interrupt *vb.* 92, 137, 144, 230, 887, 923
interruption *n.* 92, 230
intersect *vb.* 221, 246
intersperse *vb.* 230
interval *n.* 92, 109, 144, **200**, 267
intervention *n.* 92, 230, 563, 635, 653
interview *n.* 394, 410, 519, 884; *vb.* 394
interviewer *n.* 394
intimacy *n.* 882
intimate *n.* 882; *adj.* 199, 882; *vb.* 450, 459, 460, 482
intimation *n.* 448, 460, 482, 597
intimidate *vb.* 856, 902
intolerance *n.* 537, 900
intonation *n.* 501, 512, 778
intoxicate *vb.* 950
intractable *adj.* 537, 672
intransigent *adj.* 537
intrepid *adj.* 857
intricate *adj.* 251, 453, 503, 633
intrigue *n.* 558, 631; *vb.* 755

intrinsic *adj.* 1, 5, 223
introduce *vb.* 84, 88, 300, 302, 311
introductory *adj.* 86, 88, 602
introspective *adj.* 384
intrude *vb.* 137, 300, 388, 645
intruder *n.* 388, 645
intrusive *adj.* 137, 388
intuition *n.* **411**, 531, 753
inundate *vb.* 349, 358, 572
in use *adj.* 606
inutility *n.* 576
invade *vb.* 314, 645, 651
invader *n.* 100, 645, 883
invalid *adj.* 412, 586
invalidate *vb.* 414, 469, **686**
invariability *n.* 13, 16, 143, 152
invasion *n.* 300, 314, 645
inveigle *vb.* 927
invent *vb.* 163, 449, 477, 930
invention *n.* 88, 163, 419, 449
inventive *adj.* 21, 449, 627
inventor *n.* 155, 166
inventory *n.* 83
inversion *n.* **220**
invertebrate *n.* 373
invest *vb.* 159, 568, 715, 726, 740
investigate *vb.* 388, 394, 396, 818
investigation *n.* 394, 526, 818
investigator *n.* 394
investiture *n.* 685
investment *n.* 718, 726, 740
inveterate *adj.* 152, 545
in view *adj.* 823

invigorate *vb.* 161, 173, 618
invigorating *adj.* 173, 585, 618
invincible *adj.* 161, 661
invisibility *n.* **824**
invitation *n.* 394, 695
invite *vb.* 562, 695, 884
invocation *n.* 518, 695
invoice *n.* 742
invoke *vb.* 901, 982
involuntary *adj.* 411, 531, 544
involve *vb.* 9, 98, 155, 450
involved *adj.* 9, 251, 503, 709
inward *adj.* 5, 223
iota *n.* 33
irate *adj.* 893
iron *vb.* 257, 583
ironical *adj.* 455, 853
iron out *vb.* 485
irony *n.* 455, 842, 853
irrational *adj.* 39, 385, 412
irreconcilability *n.* 10, 14
irreconcilable *adj.* 883
irredeemable *adj.* 855, 942
irrefutable *adj.* 408
irregular *adj.* 17, 80, 92, 104, 106, 141, 151, 245
irregularity *n.* 17, 106, **141**, 151, 245, 258, 285, 916
irrelevant *adj.* 10, 451, 574
irreligion *n.* **975**, 983
irreligious *adj.* 936, 975, 981
irreproachable *adj.* 581, 935, 937
irresistible *adj.* 531, 674, 889
irresolution *n.* 421, **536**, 538

irresponsible *adj.* 955
irretrievable *adj.* 706
irreverent *adj.* 923, 981
irreversibility *n.* 152, 855
irrevocable *adj.* 855
irrigate *vb.* 378
irritability *n.* 756, 893, **894**
irritate *vb.* 830, 835, 893
irritation *n.* 341, 830, 835
Islam *n.* 974
island *n.* 357
isolate *vb.* 48, 102
isolated *adj.* 885
isolation *n.* 59, 461, 885
issue *n.* 11, 87, 156, 171, 301, 387; *vb.* 358, 464, 522, 600, 731
italic *adj.* 521
itch *vb.* 326, 758
itching *adj.* 443, 861
item *n.* 59, 192, 327
itinerant *n.* 270
itinerary *n.* 269, 460, 559
ivory *adj.* 807
ivory tower *n.* 595, 885

J

jab *n.* 591; *vb.* 282
jacket *n.* 225
jaded *adj.* 617, 841, 865
jagged *adj.* 246, 258, 259
jail *n.* 682; *vb.* 234, 963
jailer *n.* 683
jam *n.* 306
jangle *vb.* 787
janitor *n.* 676, 683
jar *n.* 193, 326; *vb.* 282, 326, 787, 791
jargon *n.* 492, 494

jaundice *vb.* 416, 813

jaunt *n* 269, 840

jazz *n.* 792

jealousy *n.* **913**, 914

jeer *vb.* 696, 853

jell *vb.* 332

jelly *n.* 306, 364

jeopardize *vb.* 594

jerk *n.* 92, 141, 326, 437; *vb.* 326

jest *n.* 433, 539, 842; *vb.* 842

jet *n.* 278, 358; *vb.* 358

jettison *vb.* 331, 542, 607, 713

jewel *n.* 846, 891

jilt *vb.* 556

jittery *adj.* 326, 756, 856, 894

job *vb.* 557, 605, 609, 722

jockey *n.* 270

jocular *adj* 836, 842

jog *n.* 326; *vb.* 282, 441

join *vb.* 40, 45, 47, 52, 639, 709

joint *n.* 49; *adj.* 180, 709

joint possession *n.* **709**

joke *n.* 842; *vb.* 842

jolly *adj.* 827, 836

jolt *n.* 282, 326, 444; *vb.* 282, 326

jot *n.* 33

jot down *vb.* 441, 483

journal *n.* 116, 441, 464, 483, 524

journalist *n.* 460, 484, 521

journey *n.* 269, 313; *vb.* 269

jovial *adj.* 836

joy *n.* 827, 829, 836

J.P. *n.* 958

jubilant *adj.* 838

jubilee *n.* 109, 878

Judaism *n.* 974

judge *n.* 415, 653, **958**; *vb.* 382, 415, 540, 653, 956, 960

judgment *n.* 382, 398, 410, **415**, 434, 627, 926

judicious *adj.* 392, 398, 415, 434

jug *n.* 193, 682

juice *n.* 309, 343

jumble *n.* 45; *vb.* 45, 82, 399

jump *n.* 316, 320, 321; *vb.* 320, 321

jump at *vb.* 532

jump the queue *vb.* 134

jumpy *adj.* 756, 856, 894

junction *n.* 47, 49, 201, 221

jungle *n.* 374

junior *n.* 35, 131; *adj.* 35, 129, 679

junk *n.* 277

jurisdiction *n.* 622, **956**

jurisprudence *n.* 954

jurist *n.* 959

juror *n.* 958

jury *n.* 958

just *adj.* 915, 917, 954, 966

just deserts *n.* 647, 917

justice *n.* 915, 954, 958

justification *n.* 401, 413, 549, 911, 929

justify *vb.* 410, 413, 911, 929, 961

jut *vb.* 252, 253

juvenile *n.* 131; *adj.* 129, 131

juxtaposition *n.* 94, 199, 201, 238, 397

K

kaleidoscope *n.* 817

keel over *vb.* 220

keen *adj.* 255, 434, 611, 760, 842, 861

keenness *n.* 611

keen on *adj.* 889

keep *n.* 646; *vb.* 377, 567, 593, 599, 673, 702, 707, 712

keep apart *vb.* 48, 200

keep away *vb.* 198, 555, 885

keep back *vb.* 681

keeper *n.* 593, **683**

keep in with *vb.* 24, 922

keep off *vb.* 555

keep on *vb.* 145, 516

keep one's temper *vb.* 757

keep order *vb.* 593, 956

keepsake *n.* 441

keep up *vb.* 217, 460

kernel *n.* 90, 224, 306

key *n.* 357; *adj.* 136

keyed up *adj.* 756

kick *n.* 769, 827; *vb.* 282

kick against *vb.* 644

kid *n.* 131; *vb.* 478, 842

kidnap *vb.* 720, 722

kidnapper *n.* 720, 723

kill *vb.* 370, 963

killing *n.* 370; *adj.* 370, 851

killjoy *n.* 548

kill time *vb.* 612

kiln *n.* 763

kind *n.* 97; *adj.* 882, 886, 899, 903, 935

kindergarten *n.* 475

kindhearted *adj.* 899

kindle *vb.* 755, 761

kindness *n.* 670, 747, 886, 899, 935

kindred relations *n.* **11**

king *n.* 675

kingdom *n.* 183

kingdom of heaven *n.* 972

kink *n.* 251

kinship *n.* 11

kiosk *n.* 730

kip down *vb.* 612

747, **749**; *vb.* 569, 740, 747

law *n.* 103, 626, 671, 954, 976

lawful *adj.* 667, 915, 954

lawless *adj.* 80, 644, 668, 672, 955

lawn *n.* 374, 812

lawsuit *n.* **960**

lawyer *n.* **959**

laxity *n.* 51, 335, 393, **668**

lay *adj.* 628, **987**

layabout *n.* **906**

lay at *vb.* 157, 693

lay bare *vb.* 419, 456, 458, 462

lay claim to *vb.* 917

lay down *vb.* 671

layer *n.* **206**; *vb.* 206

lay hold of *vb.* 705, 720

lay in wait *vb.* 463

lay it on *vb.* 481, 509, 927

layman *n.* 630, 987

lay-off *n.* 686

lay on *vb.* 805

lay out *vb.* 372, 740

lay-preacher *n.* 974, 987

lay siege to *vb.* 645

lay waste *vb.* 164, 645

lazy *adj.* 393, 612

lead *n.* 286, 529; *vb.* 34, 84, 236, 284, **286**, 573, 622

lead astray *vb.* 431, 936

leader *n.* 125, 253, 623, 675

leading *n.* (printing) 522

lead to *vb.* 155

leaf *n.* 374, 812

leaflet *n.* 464

league *n.* 641, 699

leak *n.* 600; *vb.* (es-

cape) 301, 358; (disclosure) 462

lean *adj.* 205; *vb.* (tend) 178; (incline) 219

lean on *vb.* 679, 854

leap *n.* 200, **320**, 321; *vb.* 320

leapfrog *n.* 320; *vb.* 320

leap year *n.* 109

learn *vb.* 441, 472

learner *n.* 428, 474

learning *n.* 426, 472

lease *n.* 708, 714; *vb.* 718, 719

leave *n.* 614, 690, 921; *vb.* 299, 556, 600, 660, 687

leave alone *vb.* 555, 610

leaven *n.* 142, 331; *vb.* 318

leave of absence *n.* 614

leave out *vb.* 99

leave-taking *n.* 299

leave undone *vb.* 393, 660

leavings *n.* 44

lechery *n.* 952, 953

lecture *n.* 470, 518, 926; *vb.* 470, 514, 926

lecturer *n.* 473, 514

lecture theatre *n.* 475

ledge *n.* 217

ledger *n.* 742

leer *n.* 818; *vb.* 818

leeway *n.* 182, 200, 678

left *n.* 241; *adj.* 44, 241

legacy *n.* 714, 715

legal adviser *n.* 959

legality *n.* 915, **954**

legalize *vb.* 424, 690, 954

legal proceedings *n.* 960

legal tender *n.* 731

legation *n.* 685

legend *n.* 525

legerdemain *n.* 478

legible *adj.* 452

legion *n.* 75; *adj.* 75

legislation *n.* 622, 954

legislative *adj.* 103, 622

legislator *n.* 623

legist *n.* 959

legitimacy *n.* 915, 954

leisure *n.* 614, 840

leisurely *adj.* 281, 614

leitmotif *n.* 387

lemon *n.* 813

lend *vb.* 568, 718, 736

lending *n.* 718

length *n.* 26, 198, **202**, 400

lengthen *vb.* 36, 202

lengthy *adj.* 202, 505

lenience *n.* 670

lenient *adj.* 670, 690, 907

lens *n.* 247, 822

Lent *n.* 947

leper *n.* 885

leprechaun *n.* 970

lesbian *n.* 106, 953; *adj.* 952

lesion *n.* 588

lessee *n.* 710

lessen *vb.* 37, 76, 197, 333, 403

lesser *adj.* 35, 209

lesson *n.* 470, 472, 597

let *vb.* 690, 718

let down *vb.* 445, 874

let fall *vb.* 319

let go *vb.* 556, 713

lethal *adj.* 164, 370

lethargy *n.* 174, 281, **612**, 754

let off *vb.* 601, 911, 961

let on *vb.* 462

let out *vb.* 196, 462, 680, 718

let pass *vb.* 911

let slip *vb.* 680, 706, 920

letter *n.* 493, 522, 523; *vb.* 482, 493

lettering *n.* 521, 846

letter of the law   n. 669,
908
let up   vb. 144, 176, 281,
616
level   n. 27, 93, 206, 215;
adj 28, 215, 248, 257;
vb. 16, 257, 400
level-headed   adj. 757
lever   n. 217
leviathan   n. 194
levitation   n. 331, 984
levity   n. 331, 836, 859
levy   n. 743, 917; vb.
716, 743
lewdness   n. 952
lexical   adj. 494
lexicography   n.   492,
494
lexicology   n 494
lexicon   n. 83, 494
liability   n. 179, 701,
737, 919, 938
liaison   n. 889, 952
liar   n. 480, 940
libel   n. 928; vb. 928,
930
liberal   adj. 570, 715,
747, 965
liberated   adj. 678, 680,
961
liberation   n. 601, 680,
921
liberator   n. 905
libertine   n. 953
liberty   n. 678, 690
library   n. 475, 524, 567
librate   vb. 325
licence   n 690
license   vb. 690, 954
licentiousness   n. 952
lick   vb. 758, 963
lick into shape   vb. 470,
570
lid   n. 225
lie   n. 431; vb. 185, 477,
932
lie down   vb. 215

lie low   vb. 209, 459,
461, 593
lieutenant   n. 675
life   n. 107, 159, 368,
557, 611
life-blood   n. 368
life-giving   adj. 170
life-guard   n. 593
lifeless   adj. 174, 369,
507, 612, 843
lifelike   adj. 18, 525
life-line   n. 600
life peer   n 870
life science   n. 375
lifetime   n. 112
life-work   n. 557
lift   n. 316, 318; vb 318
lift restrictions   vb. 713,
921
ligature   n. 49
light   n. 797, 800; adj.
(not heavy) 331, 333,
344; (of colour) 797,
807
lighted   adj. 797
lighten   vb. 634, 797,
834
lighter   n. 277, 765
light-hearted   adj. 836
lighthouse   n. 800
lighting   n. 797
light music   n. 792
lightness   n. 331, 797,
807
lightning   n. 800
light up   vb. 755, 797
like   adj. 13, 18; vb. 540,
770, 827, 861, 889
like clockwork   adv. 140
likely   adj. 123, 404, 406,
447; adv. 406
likely to   adj. 179
like-minded   adj.   24,
424
liken   vb. 18, 397
likeness   n. 18, 20, 22,
486, 488
like to   vb. 532

liking   n. 178, 861, 922
lilac   adj. 814
lily-livered   adj. 858
limb   n. 374
limber   adj. 335
lime   adj. 812
limerick   n. 528
limit   n. 89, 233, 235,
400, 659; vb. 231, 235,
403, 681
limitation   n. 231, 235,
403, 681
limitations   n. 700
limited   adj. 195, 205,
235
limited space   n. 184
limitless   adj. 78, 202
limp   adj. 335, 507; vb.
281
limpid   adj. 502, 802
line   n. 11, 170, 202, 655,
729; vb. 81, 226
lineage   n. 11, 170, 171
lineal   adj. 171
linearity   n. 202
liner   n. 277
linger   vb. 112, 135, 281
lingua franca   n. 492
linguist   n. 456, 492
linguistic   adj. 450, 492
lining   n. 226
link   n. 9, 49; vb. 9, 47,
52, 157, 397
lip reading   n. 796
lip service   n. 981
liquefaction   n. 345
liquefied   adj. 343, 345
liquefy   vb. 343, 345,
761,
liquescent   adj. 343
liquid   n. 309, 343, 347;
adj. 343, 347
liquidate   vb. 164, 370,
739
liquidize   vb. 164
liquor   n. 343
lisp   n. 515; vb. 515

list *n.* **83**, 97; *vb.* 38, 83, 483

listen *vb.* 390, 778, 792, 795

listless *adj.* 174, 281, **612**, 863

lit *adj.* 759, 797

litany *n.* 988

literal *n.* 431; *adj.* 456, 493, 494, 977

literature *n.* 528

lithe *adj.* 335

lithographer *n.* 491

lithography *n.* 490

litigation *n.* 960

litter *n.* 576

little *adj.* 33, 195, 203; *adv.* 33

little by little *adv.* 27

liturgical *adj.* 988

live *adj.* 172; *vb.* 1, 188, 191, 368

live apart *vb.* 898

live comfortably *vb.* 734

lively *adj.* 173, 368, **506**, 611, 836

livery *n.* 227, 677

livestock *n.* 373

live together *vb.* 889

live up to *vb.* 28, 570

live wire *n.* 611

live with *vb.* 889

llama *n.* 275

llano *n.* 356

load *n.* 26, 192, 330, 830; *vb.* 192, 268, 330

loaf about *vb.* 612

loafer *n.* 281, 612, 697, 940

loan *n.* 718, 719, 736; *vb.* 718

loan-word *n.* 495

loath *adj.* 533

loathe *vb.* 771, 862, 892

loathsome *adj.* 862, 892

lobby *n.* 547, 697; *vb.* 177, 547

local *n.* 191; *adj.* 183, 190, 199

locality *n.* 183, 199

locate *vb.* 186, 284

location *n.* 185, **186**

loch *n.* 353, 354

lock *n.* 207; *vb.* 263, 461

locker *n.* 193

locket *n.* 216

lock out *vb.* 144

lock-out *n.* 99, 144

lock up *vb.* 234, 681

lock-up *n.* 682

locomotive *n.* 276; *adj.* 276

locust *n.* 167

lodge *n.* 191; *vb.* 186, 191

lodger *n.* 190, 710

lodging *n.* 186

lodgings *n.* 191

loftiness *n.* 208

lofty *adj.* 208, 318, 870

log *n.* 116, 483, 742, 765; *vb.* 83

logic *n.* 410

logo *n.* 482

loiter *vb.* 281, 612

lone *adj.* 59

loneliness *n.* 59, 885

long *adj.* 182, 202; *vb.* 443, 854, 861, 889

long-distance *adj.* 198

long duration *n.* 112

longhand *n.* 521

longing *n.* 854, 861; *adj.* 861, 889

long-lasting *adj.* 112

longness *n.* 202

long-range *adj.* 198

longsighted *adj.* 820

long-standing *adj.* 112

long-suffering *n.* 757; *adj.* 670

long-term *adj.* 112

long-winded *adj.* 505, 516, 843

look *n.* 242, 818, 825; *vb.* 818, 825

look after *vb.* 392, 593, 599, 676

look back *vb.* 441

look down on *vb.* 923, 924

looker-on *n.* 821

look for *vb.* 394, 554

look forward to *vb.* 443

look in *vb.* 884

looking glass *n.* 822

look like *vb.* 18

look out *vb.* 860

lookout *n.* 593, 683, 818

look out on *vb.* 208, 236

look over *vb.* 208, 818

look through *vb.* 818

look to *vb.* 390, 919

loom *n.* 221; *vb.* 154, 221, 292, 902

loop *n.* 250, 251, 322; *vb.* 251, 273, 323

loophole *n.* 582, 600

loose *adj.* 335, 453, 500, 668, 680, 952; *vb.* 48, 680

loosen *vb.* 262, 319, 601

loot *n.* 663, 724; *vb.* 722

lopsidedness *n.* 29, 245

loquacious *adj.* 516

lord *n.* 675, 870, 967

lord it over *vb.* 34, 667, 669

Lord's Day *n.* 616

Lord's Supper *n.* 988

lore *n.* 472

lorgnette *n.* 822

lorry *n.* 276

lose *vb.* 116, 187, 662, **706**

lose consciousness *vb.* 617

lose face *vb.* 869

lose ground *vb.* 289, 315

lose heart *vb.* 837, 855

loser *n.* 662
lose weight *vb.* 205
loss *n.* 43, 189, 369, 569, 706
lot *n.* (many) 26, 32, 75, 94; (fate) 158; (apportionment) 717
lotion *n.* 342, 591
lottery *n.* 553
loud *adj.* 778, **780**, 787, 788, 805, 877
loudness *n.* 778, **780**, 877
louse *n.* 940
louse up *vb.* 628
lousy *adj.* 580
lout *n.* 437, 630
love *n.* 650, **889**, 890, 891, 922; *vb.* 827, 861, **889**
love affair *n.* 889
love child *n.* 955
love letter *n.* 523, 890
lovely *adj.* 579, 829, 844
lover *n.* 889
loving *adj.* 670, 889, 966
low *adj.* 35, 209, 210, 781, 837, 849, 869; *vb.* 789
lower *adj.* 35; *vb.* 209, 319, 588, 744
lower class *n.* 871
lowland *n.* 356
lowlands *n.* 209
lowly *adj.* 35, 654, 871, 874
low-lying *adj.* 209
lowness *n.* 209, 210
low opinion *n.* 923
low-priced *adj.* 746
low regard *n.* 923
low spirits *n.* 837
loyalist *n.* 105, 903
loyalty *n.* 673, 702, 919, 931
lozenge *n.* 246, 591
LP *n.* 794

lubber *n.* 630
lubricate *vb.* 342, 365
lubrication *n.* 342
lucidity *n.* 438, 452, 502, 802
luck *n.* 158, 553, 661, 664
lucrative *adj.* 705
ludicrous *adj.* 433, 851
luggage *n.* 711
lukewarm *adj.* 30, 759, 863
lull *n.* 144, 614; *vb.* 267
luminary *n.* 436, 800
luminous *adj.* 797
lump *n.* 55, 252, 332
lump together *vb.* 399
lunacy *n.* 439
lunar *adj.* 329
lunate *n.* 247; *adj.* 247
lunatic *n.* 440
lunch *n.* 306; *vb.* 304
lunch-break *n.* 616
lunch-hour *n.* 616
lune *n.* 247
lungs *n.* 512
lurch *n.* 325; *vb.* 317, 325
lure *n.* 294, 547
lurid *adj.* 805, 952
luring *adj.* 829
lurk *vb.* 459, 461
luscious *adj.* 770, 772, 829
lushness *n.* 168
lust *n.* 861, 889, 952; *vb.* 861, 914
lustiness *n.* 173
lustre *n.* 257, 797
luxurious *adj.* 168, 734, 827
luxury *n.* 572, 664, 734, 747, 827, 945
lynch *vb.* 370, 963
lyric *n.* 528
lyrical *adj.* 528, 790

M

mace *n.* 677
machinery *n.* 565
mad *adj.* **439**, 756, 861, 889, 893
madam *n.* 381
madden *vb.* 439, 893
made-up *adj.* 525
madman *n.* **440**
madness *n.* 439
magazine *n.* 464, 524
magic *n.* 984; *adj.* 579
magistrate *n.* 958
magnanimous *adj.* 933
magnetic *adj.* 294
magnetize *vb.* 291
magnification *n.* 36
magnificent *adj.* 579, 844, 870
magnify *vb.* 36, 196, 481, 835, 982
magnifying glass *n.* 822
magnitude *n.* 26, 32, 400
maid *n.* 676
maiden *n.* 897; *adj.* 88
mail *n.* 467, 523, 657; *vb.* 268, 523
main *n.* 360; *adj.* 34, 573
mainland *n.* 352
maintain *vb.* 91, 143, 145, 217, 304, 468, 568, 599, 636, 712, 929
majesty *n.* 868, 870, 877
major *adj.* 34, 130
majority *n.* 72, 75, 133
make *n.* 97; *vb.* 155, 163, 242, 705
make advances *vb.* 882, 890
make a face *vb.* 895
make a fortune *vb.* 664, 734
make a go of *vb.* 661

make amends *vb.* 31.
589, 721, 943

make a mess of *vb.* 628

make a mistake *vb.* 431.
500

make an example of *vb.*
963

make a noise *vb.* 778

make a speech *vb.* 514

make-believe *n.* 477;
adj. 449, 477

make certain *vb.* 408

make clear *vb.* 452, 456

make do *vb.* 149, 606,
666

make exceptions *vb.*
403

make excuses *vb.* 549

make eyes at *vb.* 890

make for *vb.* 271, 284

make friends with *vb.*
882

make fun of *vb.* 842,
853

make headway *vb.* 288

make it *vb.* 661

make it up *vb.* 652, 911

make known *vb.* 460,
462, 464

make light of *vb.* 393,
418, 574

make love to *vb.* 889

make nothing of *vb.*
574

make off with *vb.* 722

make one jump *vb.* 444,
856

make one think of *vb.*
441

make out *vb.* 288, 441,
452

make over *vb.* 714

make passes *vb.* 890

make peace *vb.* 652

make plain *vb.* 456,
458, 462

make possible *vb.* 404

make preparations *vb.*
602

make progress *vb.* 288,
587

maker *n.* 166, 967

make sense *vb* 410,
452, 456

makeshift *adj.* 149, 162,
603

make the best of *vb.*
757

make too much of *vb.*
417, 481

make up *vb.* 58, 163,
449, 477

make-up *n.* 5, 58, 339,
751, 844

make up for *vb.* 31

make up one's mind
vb. 530, 540

malady *n.* 586

malapropism *n.* 433,
497, 500

male *n.* 380; *adj.* 380

malevolence *n.* 900,
936

malformed *adj.* 245,
582

malice *n.* 893, 900

malign *vb.* 608, 900,
928, 936

malleable *adj.* 151

maltreat *vb.* 588, 608,
900, 916

mammal *n.* 373

man *n.* 133, 368, 373,
379, 380

manage *vb.* 392, 605,
606, 621, 622, 661, 666,
748

manageable *adj.* 634

management *n.* 392,
606, 609, 621, 622, 675

management of animals
n. 377

manager *n.* 623, 675,
728

manage to *vb.* 661

mandate *n.* 626, 671,
685

mangled *adj.* 245

manhood *n* 133, 380

mania *n.* 439

maniac *n.* 175, 440

manifest *adj.* 458, 825;
vb. 401, 413, 458, 482,
823, 825

manifestation *n.* 419,
458, 462

manipulate *vb.* 477, 758

mankind *n.* 379

manliness *n.* 380, 857

manner *n.* 501, 559,
621, 825

mannerism *n.* 501

manners *n.* 886

man of learning *n.* 428,
436, 524

man of many talents *n.*
629

man of means *n.* 734

man of the world *n.* 629

manor *n.* 191

manpower *n.* 619

mansion *n.* 191

manslaughter *n.* 370

manual *n.* 460, 524

manufacture *n.* 163; *vb.*
163

manufacturer *n.* 166

manure *n.* 310; *vb.* 378

manuscript *n.* 483, 521,
524

many *adj.* 72, 75

many-coloured *adj.* 817

many-sided *adj.* 151

map *n.* 269, 460, 486;
vb. 400

mar *vb.* 847

march *vb.* 91, 269, 696

mare *n.* 381

margarine *n.* 306

margin *n.* 44, 182, 200,
233; *vb.* 233

marine *n.* 272; *adj.* 271,
277, 351

mariner *n* 272

marital *adj.* 896

maritime *adj.* 271, 277, 351

mark *n.* 97, 202, 235, 400, 441, **483**, 521, 522; *vb.* 382, 390, 482, 483

mark down *vb.* 743, 746

marker *n.* 482

market *n.* 96, 559, 726, **730**; *vb.* 377, 725, 727

mark up *vb.* 743

maroon *adj.* 810, 811

marooned *adj.* 713

marquee *n.* 225

marquis *n.* 870

marred *adj.* 588

marriage *n.* 47, **896**

marrow *n.* 224

marry *vb.* 47, 896

marsh *n.* 355

marshal *n.* 958; *vb.* 81

marsupial *n.* 373

martial *adj.* 651

martyr *n.* 980; *vb.* 830, 963

martyrdom *n.* 828

marvel *n.* 866; *vb.* 866

marvellous *adj.* 32, 579, 844, 866

Marxism *n.* 327

mascot *n.* 984

masculine *adj.* 380

mash *vb.* 335, 364

mask *n.* 225, 461, 463, 549; *vb.* 146, 225, 819

mass *n.* 26, 75, 94, 194, 327, 330, 332, 567, 988; *vb.* 75, 192

massacre *n.* 370, 963

massage *vb.* 341, 758

masses *n.* 26, 32, 871

massive *adj.* 32, 204

mast *n.* 208

master *n.* 34, 131, 436, 629, **675**; *vb.* 441, 472, 679

masterly *adj.* 579

masterpiece *n.* 488, 581, 844

master-plan *n.* 558

mastery *n* 501, 707

masticate *vb.* 304

mat *n.* 225

match *n.* 397, 649, 765, 800, 896; *vb.* 24, 28, 61, 218, 397, 896

matchless *adj.* 34

mate *n.* 882, 896; *vb.* 61, 889

material *n.* 192, 327; *adj.* 3, 327

material existence *n.* 3

materialist *n.* 981

materialistic *adj.* 327, 975

materiality *n.* 3, 327

materialize *vb.* 242, 327, 825, 984

materials *n.* 566

maternal *adj.* 11, 170

mathematics *n.* 38

matriculate *vb.* 83, 483

matt *adj.* 805

matter *n.* 3, 153, 327, 387, 573; *vb.* 573

matter in hand *n.* 605

matter-of-fact *adj.* 508

matter of life and death *n.* 562

mature *adj.* 133, 426; *vb.* 130, 133, 288, 324, 587, 659

maturity *n.* 126, 130, 133, 581

mauve *adj.* 814

maxim *n.* 103, 432, 498, 626

maximize *vb* 417, 481

maximum *n.* 212

mayor *n.* 675

maze *n.* 409

meadow *n.* 356, 378

meagre *adj.* 33, 57, 205, 507, 571

meal *n.* 306, 840

mean *n.* 30, 90, 560; *adj.* (average) 30, 90; (stingy) 748, 750; (disreputable) 869, 871, 924, 936; (selfish) 934; *vb.* **450**, 459, 482, 552

meander *vb.* 247, 251

meaning *n.* 450, 552

meaningful *adj.* 450, 514

meaninglessness *n.* 451, 453

meanness *n.* 750, 887, 934, 936

means *n.* 155, 172, 559, 564, 566, 711, 734

means of punishment *n.* 964

meanwhile *adv., prep.* 107

measure *n.* 26, 27, 400, 559, 609; *vb.* 26, 27, 330, 397, 400

measure for measure *n.* 647

measurement *n.* 27, 194, 397, 400

meat *n.* 306

Mecca *n.* 96

mechanic *n.* 619

mechanical *adj.* 411, 531, 545, 565

mechanism *n.* 565

medal *n.* 482, 663, 872

meddle *vb.* 388, 635, 653

meddler *n.* 388, 821

medial *adj.* 90, 560

median *n.* 30, 90

mediation *n.* 230, 563, 653

mediator *n.* 653

medicine *n.* 181, 591

mediocre *adj.* 30, 35, 580, **666**, 843

mediocrity *n.* 35, 580, **666**, 843

meditate *vb.* 384, 982

medium *n.* 30, 447, 563, 564, 619; *adj.* 30
medley *n.* 45, 104
meekness *n.* 654, 673, 757, 874, 876
meet *vb.* 94, 153, 201, 296, 419
meet half-way *vb.* 704
meeting *n.* 94, 201, 296, 884
meeting place *n.* 96
melancholy *n.* 828, 837; *adj.* 837
mellow *adj.* 335, 790; *vb.* 130, 587
melodious *adj.* 790
melodrama *n.* 326, 529
melody *n.* 790
melt *vb.* 345, 761
member *n.* 55, 709
member of parliament *n.* 625
membership *n.* 639
memo *n.* 441, 483
memoirs *n.* 116, 441
memorable *adj.* 441, 790
memorial *n.* 372, 441, 483, 663; *adj.* 441
memorize *vb.* 441, 472
memory *n.* 124, 441
menace *n.* 154, 594, 892, 902; *vb.* 154, 902
mend *vb.* 146, 587, 589
menial *n.* 676; *adj.* 35, 881
meniscus *n.* 247
mensuration *n.* 400
mental *adj.* 382
mental block *n.* 442
mental illness *n.* 439
mention *n.* 460, 663; *vb.* 460, 514
menu *n.* 306
mercantile *adj.* 725
mercenary *n.* 655
merchandise *n.* 163, 729

merchant *n.* 728
merciful *adj.* 670, 899, 907, 966
merciless *adj.* 908
mercury *n.* 766, 967
mercy *n.* 670, 715, 907, 911
mere *n.* 354; *adj.* 1, 46
merge *vb.* 45, 47, 52, 639
merger *n.* 36, 45, 52, 639
meridian *n.* 127
merit *n.* 575, 579, 917; *vb.* 917
mermaid *n.* 970
merry *adj.* 827, 836
merrymaking *n.* 838
mesh *n.* 221; *vb.* 221
mesmerize *vb.* 984
mess *n.* 80, 204, 628, 845
message *n.* 460, 465, 523
messenger *n.* 275, 460, 467
Messiah *n.* 967
mess up *vb.* 584, 588, 628
messy *adj.* 584
metal *n.* 367
metallic *adj.* 787
metallurgy *n.* 367
metamorphosis *n.* 142
metaphor *n.* 397, 455, 509
metaphysics *n.* 1
meteor *n.* 329, 800
meteorologist *n.* 447
meteorology *n.* 348
mete out *vb.* 715
meter *n.* 400
method *n.* 79, 81, 558, 559, 606
methodical *adj.* 79, 81, 140
meticulous *adj.* 392, 864

metre *n.* 528
metric system *n.* 400
metropolis *n.* 183
metropolitan *n.* 986
mettle *n.* 534, 857
mew *vb.* 789
miaow *vb.* 789
microscope *n.* 822
microscopic *adj.* 195
mid *adj.* 90
mid-course *n.* 560
midday *n.* 127
middle *n.* 30, 90, 224; *adj.* 30, 90, 224, 560
middle age *n.* 130
middle class *n.* 871
middleman *n.* 688, 728
middle of the road *adj.* 560
middling *adj.* 30, 579, 666
midget *n.* 195
midnight *n.* 128
midpoint *n.* 30, 90
midsummer *n.* 127
midway *adj.* 560; *adv.* 90
midwinter *n.* 128
mien *n.* 621, 825
might *n.* 32, 159, 161
mighty *adj.* 32, 159, 161
migrant *n.* 100, 270
mild *adj.* 176, 670, 757, 759
mildew *n.* 53, 167, 592
mileage *n.* 198
milieu *n.* 8, 183, 229
militant *n.* 611; *adj.* 148, 611, 644, 651
militate against *vb.* 181
milk *n.* 309; *vb.* 377
milk product *n.* 306
milky *adj.* 804, 807
millenium *n.* 70, 109
million *n.* 70
millionaire *n.* 734
mime *n.* 529
mimic *n.* 20; *vb.* 20

mince *vb* 306

mind *n.* 382, 530; *vb.* 390, 392, 593

mindful *adj.* 390, 426

mindless *adj.* 383

mind-reader *n.* 447

mine *n.* 210, 254; *vb.* 254, 264, 312

mineral *n.* 367

mingle *vb.* 45

miniature *n.* 195, 488; *adj.* 33, 195

minibus *n.* 276

minimal *adj.* 33

minimize *vb.* 418

mining *n.* 312

minister *n.* 467, 623, 625, 986; *vb.* 589, 636, 676, 988

ministerial *adj.* 985

ministry *n.* 985

minor *n.* 131; *adj.* 33, 35, 129

minority *n.* 76, 129; *adj.* 11

minstrel *n.* 528, 793

mint *n.* 23; *vb.* 731

minus *adj.* 189; *adv.., prep.* 42

minute *n.* 109; *adj.* 33, 195; *vb.* 483

minutes *n.* 441, 483

minutiae *n.* 102

miracle *n.* 458, 866

miracle-working *n.* 984

miraculous *adj.* 866

mirage *n.* 4

mire *n.* 355

mirror *n.* 822; *vb.* 20, 486

mirth *n.* 836, 838

misadventure *n.* 153, 662, 665

misanthropy *n.* **904**

misapprehend *vb.* 416

misappropriation *n.* 608, 722

misbehaviour *n.* 672, 887, 938

miscalculation *n.* 412, 416

miscarriage *n.* 445

miscarriage of justice *n.* 955

miscarry *vb.* 662

miscellany *n.* 45, 104, 527

mischief *n.* 900

mischief-maker *n.* 906

misconception *n.* 416, 431, 457

misconduct *n.* 938

misconstrue *vb.* 416, 457

misdate *vb.* 117

misdemeanour *n.* 938

misdirection *n.* 285, **471**

misemployment *n.* 608

miser *n.* 750

miserable *adj.* 828, 837

miserly *adj.* 571, 750, 934

misery *n.* 828, 837, 841

misfire *vb.* 628

misfit *n.* 10

misfortune *n.* 153, 551, 665, 900

misgiving *n.* 409, 421, 833

misgovern *vb.* 668

misguidance *n.* 471

misguided *adj.* 285

mishandle *vb.* 608, 628

mishap *n.* 153

mishmash *n.* 45

misinform *vb.* 471

misinstruction *n.* 471

misinterpretation *n.* 412, 416, 451, 457, 487

misjudgment *n.* 416, 431, 481

mislay *vb.* 187, 706

mislead *vb.* 431, 471, 477, 478

mismanagement *n.* 431, 608, 628

misnomer *n.* **497**

misogynist *n.* 904

misplace *vb.* 187, 706

misprint *n.* 431

mispronunciation *n.* 500, 515

misquote *vb.* 457

misrepresentation *n.* 471, 477, 478, 481, **487**

miss *n.* 131, 381; *vb.* 137, 315, 391, 393, 660, 662, 706

misshapen *adj.* 243, 245, 845

missile *n.* 290

missing *adj.* 189, 315, 571, 600, 706, 826

missing link *n.* 92, 324

mission *n.* 557, 651, 685, 688, 990

missionary *n.* 903, 974

mist *n.* 4, 346, 358, 363, 803

mistake *n.* 431, 457, 471, 500, 582, 608; *vb.* **497**

mistaken *adj.* 285, 431

mistiming *n.* 117, 137

mistranslation *n.* 457

mistreat *vb.* 608

mistress *n.* 675, 889, 953

mistrust *n.* 421; *vb.* 421

misty *adj.* 349, 363, 799, 803

misunderstanding *n.* 25, 416, 431, 457, 642

misusage *n.* 500

misuse *n.* 569, **608**; *vb.* 588, 608

mite *n.* 131

mitigate *vb.* 176, 403, 591, 834

mitigation *n.* 636, 834

mitre *n.* 989

mix *vb.* **45**, 52, 58, 82, 399

mixed up *adj.* 80, 453

mixer *n.* 884

mixture *n.* **45**, 52, 104, 591

mix-up *n.* 80

mnemonic *n.* 441

moan *vb.* 788, 832

moat *n.* 234, 261, 360, 646

mob *n.* 75, 94; *vb.* 175, 888

mobile *adj.* 142, 151, 266

mobilization *n.* 94, 651

mob rule *n.* 668, 955

mock *adj.* 18, 20, 149; *vb.* 853, 869, 924, 928

mocker *n.* 928, 981

mockery *n.* 477, 853

mock-up *n.* 23

modal *adj.* 8

mode *n.* 7, 545, 850

model *n.* 22, 486, 581, 939; *vb.* 23, 242, 489

modeller *n.* 491

moderate *adj.* 176, 560, 746, 757, 944; *vb.* 142, 176, 403, 652

moderation *n.* 176, 944

modern *adj.* 120, 125, 850

modernization *n.* 125, 587, 589

modest *adj.* 33, 176, 418, 508, 517, 874, **876**

modesty *n.* 508, 517, 874; **876**

modify *vb.* 15, 142, 335, 403

modulation *n.* 142

module *n.* 279

moist *adj.* 347, 349, 358

moisten *vb.* 349

moisture *n.* 346, **349**

molecule *n.* 327

mollify *vb.* 176, 335, 652

molten *adj.* 343, 345, 759

moment *n.* 115, 573

momentary *adj.* 113

momentous *adj.* 136, 177, 573

momentum *n.* 282

monarchic *adj.* 870

monastery *n.* 990

money *n.* 731, 734

money-lender *n.* 718

mongol *n.* 440

mongrel *n.* **45**; *adj.* 45

monitor *vb.* 394

monk *n.* 885, 986

monocle *n.* 822

monograph *n.* 526

monologue *n.* **520**

monopolize *vb.* 707

monopoly *n.* 681

monotony *n.* 16, 91, 841

monsoon *n.* 358

monster *n.* 175, 194, 906

monstrous *adj.* 845, 936

month *n.* 109

monthly *adv.* 140

monument *n.* 372, 441, 483

moo *vb.* 789

mooch about *vb.* 612

mood *n.* 5, 751

moody *adj.* 756, 894, 895

moon *n.* 329, 800

moor *n.* 208, 355, 356; *vb.* 186, 271, 298

moot *adj.* 409

moot point *n.* 387

mop *vb.* 583

mope *vb.* 837, 895

moral *n.* 432; *adj.* 931, 935

moralize *vb.* 470

moral obligation *n.* 919

moratorium *n.* 135

more *adj.* 72

moreish *adj.* 770

moreover *adv.* 40

more than enough *n.* 572

morgue *n.* 372

moribund *adj.* 130, 369

morning *n.* **127**; *adj.* 127

moron *n.* 437, 440

moroseness *n.* 895

morphology *n.* 242, 499

morsel *n.* 33, 306

mortal *adj.* 368, 379; *adj.* 369, 370, 379

mortgage *n.* 701, 718

mortgagee *n.* 736

mortgagor *n.* 737

mortification *n.* 874, 946

mortuary *n.* 372

mosaic *n.* 817

mosque *n.* 990

motel *n.* 191

moth *n.* 167

mothball *vb.* 135

moth-eaten *adj.* 126

mother *n.* 11, 170; *vb.* 676

motion *n.* 266; *vb.* 482

motionless *adj.* 174, 267

motivate *vb.* 155, 547

motivator *n.* 547

motive *n.* 8, 155, **547**

motley *adj.* 17, 45, 104, 817

motor *n.* 276; *vb.* 269

motorcycle *n.* 276

motoring *n.* 269

motorist *n.* 270

motorway *n.* 559

mottled *adj.* 817

motto *n.* 432

mould *n.* 23, 53, 339, 592; *vb.* 146, 242, 489

mouldable *adj.* 242, 335, 654

mount *n.* 316; *vb.* 32, 208, 316

mountain *n* 208, 316

mourn *vb.* 828, 833, 837

mournful *adj.* 372, 828, 839, 895

mouth *n.* 262, 353

mouthful *n.* 26, 306

mouthpiece *n.* 514, 689

mouth-watering *adj.* 770

movable *adj.* 142, 266, 268

move *n* 266, 609; *vb.* 172, 187, 266, 268, 282, 290, 299, 693, 752, 755

moved *adj.* 189, 752, 756

movement *n.* 266, 268, 641, 792

move on *vb.* 288

mover *n.* 166

moving *adj* 752, 755

mow *vb.* 378

mow down *vb.* 370

Mr. X *n.* 497

much *adj.* 75; *adv.* 32

muck *n.* 576, 584

muckraker *n.* 516, 928

mucky *adj.* 584

mud *n.* 355

muddle *n.* 80; *vb.* 82, 399

muddler *n.* 630

muddle through *vb.* 666

muddy *adj.* 355, 584, 803

mud-slinging *n.* 928

muffle *vb.* 513, 779, 785

muffled *adj.* 781, 785

mugging *n.* 645, 722

muggy *adj.* 349, 759

mulch *n.* 364

mule *n.* 537

mull *vb.* 384

multi-coloured *adj* 817

multifarious *adj.* 104

multilateral *adj* 246

multiple *n* 730; *adj.* 39, 72

multiplication *n.* 38

multiplicity *n.* 72, 75

multiply *vb* 36, 38, 163, 165, 835

multisection *n.* 71

multi-storey *adj.* 208

multitude *n.* 75

mum *n.* 170; *adj.* 513, 517

mumble *vb.* 515

mumbo-jumbo *n.* 967, 983, 984

mummify *vb.* 372, 599

mundane *adj.* 327, 329

municipal *adj.* 183

munificent *adj.* 747

munitions *n.* 657

mural *n.* 488

murder *n.* 370; *vb.* 370

murderer *n.* 167, 370, 906

murky *adj.* 363, 798, 803, 808

murmur *n.* 781; *vb.* 696, 781

muscle *n.* 159, 161

muse *vb.* 384, 449

museum *n.* 567

mush *n.* 364

music *n.* 790, **792**

musical instrument *n.* **794**

musician *n.* **793**

must *n.* 531, 562

mustard *n.* 307

muster *vb.* 94, 651, 857

musty *adj.* 777

mutability *n.* 151

mutation *n.* 142

mute *adj.* 513, 517, 781; *vb.* 513, 779

muteness *n.* 513

mutilate *vb.* 164, 845

mutineer *n.* 672

mutiny *n.* 644, 672, 920; *vb* 672, 920

mutter *n.* 781; *vb.* 515, 781

mutual *adj* 9, 12, 150, 180

muzzle *vb* 681

myriads *n.* 75

mystery *n.* 427, 453, 466

mystic *adj.* 984

myth *n* 525

mythical being *n* **970**

N

nag *vb.* 893

nail *n.* 255; *vb* 47

naive *adj.* 131, 422, 632

naked *adj.* 228, 594

name *n.* 482, 494, 496, 868, 872; *vb* 482, 496

nanny *n.* 683

nanny-goat *n.* 381

nap *n.* 612

narcissism *n.* 875, 934

narrate *vb.* 460, 525

narrative *n.* 525; *adj.* 525

narrow *adj.* 205, 416, 681, 934; *vb.* 27, 681

narrow-mindedness *n.* 416, 537

narrowness *n.* **205**, 416, 934

narrows *n.* 205, 353

nasalization *n.* 515

nasty *adj.* 580, 777, 887

nation *n.* 379

national *n.* 190; *adj.* 190, 379

nationality *n.* 379

nationalization *n.* 709

native *n.* 190; *adj.* 5, 190

nativity n. 155

natural adj. 3, 508, 632, 955

natural history n. 366

naturalized adj. 100, 190

nature n. 5, 58, 329, 366, 751

naturism n. 228

naughty adj. 672, 901

nausea n. 303

nautical adj. 271, 277

naval adj. 271, 277

navigate vb. 271

navy n. 655

near adj. 154, 199, 419; vb. 154, 292

nearby adj. 199; adv. 199

nearly adv. 199

nearness n. 199, 292

nearside adj. 241

neat adj. 79, 392, 579, 583

nebula n. 329

nebulous adj. 363, 798, 824

necessary adj 531, 562, 674, 919

necessities n. 8

necessity n. 408, 531, 543, 562, 674

neck n. 205, 352; vb. 890

nectar n. 770

need n. 57, 189, 315, 562, 674, 861; vb. 76, 315, 531, 562, 571, 861

needle n. 255, 264, 482; vb. 830, 893

needlework n. 846

needy adj. 735, 917

negation n. 469

negative n. 23, 425; adj. 39, 469

neglect n. 385, 391, 393, 546, 610, 660, 662, 672, 703, 920; vb. 391, 393,

546, 607, 660, 662, 672, 703, 920

negligent adj. 391, 393, 703, 920

negligible adj. 76

negotiable adj. 714

negotiate vb. 519, 653, 700, 704, 725

neigh vb. 789

neighbour n. 882

neighbourhood n. 183, 199

neighbouring adj. 199

neighbourly adj. 884, 899

neologism n. 494, **495**

nephew n. 11

nerve n. 880

nerveless adj. 160

nerves n. 439, 856

nervous adj. 326, 756, 856, 894

nervousness n. 439, 856, 876, 894

nest n. 595

net n. 221, 463

nether adj. 209

netting n. 221

network n. 221

neurotic n. 440

neutral n. 653, 656; adj. 90, 541, 560, 863

neutrality n. 541, 863, 933

neutralize vb. 31, 181, 648

never adv. 108

new adj. 40, 125, 134, 603

newborn adj. 131

newcomer n. 100, 474

newest adj. 120

newly adv. 125

newly-wed adj 896

newness n. 21, **125**

news n. 460, 465

newspaper n. 464, 483

next adj. 85, 119, 199

nibble n. 304, 306

nice adj. 770, 829, 864

niche n. 184, 254

nick n. 259, 682; vb. 259, 722

nickname n. 496, 497; vb. 497

nicotine n. 308

niece n. 11

niggardly adj. 750

nigh adv. 199

night n. 128, 798; adj 128

nightfall n. 128, 798

nightmare n. 449, 830

nihilist n. 167

nil n. 74

nimble adj. 280, 611, 842

nimbus n. 800

nine n. 70

nip n. 760; vb. 197, 203

no n. 425

nobility n. 34, **870**

noble adj. 32, 318, 868, 870

nobody n. 74

nocturnal adj. 128

nod n. 424, 482, 612, 690; vb. 325, 482

node n. 49

nod off vb. 612

noise n. 778, 780, 788, 791

noiseless adj. 779

noisome adj. 777

nomad n. 270

nomadic adj. 266

nom de plume n. 497

nomenclature n. **496**

nominal adj. 496

nominate vb. 496, 540, 685, 985

nominee n. 688

non-acceptance n 425, 926

non-adhesive adj. 51

non aggressive adj. 650

nonce *adj.* 495
nonchalant *adj.* 757
non-combatant *n.* 656
non-completion *n.* 660
nonconformist *n.* 106, 425, 979; *adj.* 25, 106, 979
none *n.* 74
nonentity *n.* 2, 574
non-existence *n.* 2
non-expectation *n.* 444
non-flammable *adj* 762
non-imitation *n.* 21
non-material existence *n.* 4
non-observance *n.* 672, 703, 920
non-payment *n.* 739
non-possession *n.* 708
non-preparation *n.* 603
non-resonance *n.* 785
non-retention *n.* 713
nonsense *n.* 433, 451, 516
non sequitur n. 412
non-starter *n.* 662
non-stop *adj.* 138
non-uniformity *n.* 17, 29
noon *n.* 127
no one *n.* 74
noose *n.* 463, 964
norm *n.* 30, 103
normal *adj.* 438, 545
normalize *vb.* 16
normative *adj.* 103
north *n.* 284
nostalgia *n.* 861
nosy *adj.* 388, 394
notable *adj.* 32, 573, 868
notary *n.* 959
notation *n.* 39
notch *n.* 259; *vb.* 258, 259
note *n.* 41, 441, 456, 460, 482, 483, 523, 778; *vb.* 382, 390, 483

nothing *n.* 74
notice *n.* 390, 460, 464, 482, 597, 624, 818; *vb.* 390, 818
noticeable *adj.* 458, 823
notify *vb.* 460, 464, 597, 624
notion *n.* 386, 420, 448, 449
notorious *adj.* 426, 869
nought *n.* 74
noun *n.* 499
nourish *vb.* 304
nourishing *adj.* 585
novel *n.* 525; *adj.* 125
novelist *n.* 521, 524, 525
novelty *n.* 21, 125, 142
novice *n.* 474, 630
now *adv.* 120
nowadays *adv.* 120
no way *adv.* 405
noxious *adj.* 777
nuance *n.* 27
nucleus *n.* 224
nude *n.* 228; *adj.* 228
nudge *n.* 482; *vb.* 482
nuisance *n.* 551, 830
null *adj.* 74
nullify *vb.* 2, 164, 469, 686
numb *adj.* 754; *vb.* 754
number *n.* 26, 39, 72, 499; *vb.* 38, 482
numbering *n.* 38
numbing *adj.* 760
numeral *n.* 39
numeration *n.* 38
numerous *adj.* 32, 72, 75
nun *n.* 986
nunnery *n.* 990
nuptial *adj.* 896
nurse *n.* 676, 683; *vb.* 304, 589, 676
nursery *n.* 378, 475
nurture *vb.* 304, 470, 712
nut *n.* 49, 306, 440

nutrition *n.* 304, 306
nutritious *adj.* 306, 585
nymph *n.* 970

O

oaf *n.* 437
oafish *adj.* 435
oath *n.* 468, 901
obdurate *adj.* 537, 942
obedience *n.* 654, 673, 702, 874
obedient *adj.* 654, 673, 702, 919
obesity *n.* 194
obey *vb.* 105, 654, 673, 874
obituary *n.* 369, 372
object *n.* 327, 552, 716; *vb.* 25, 425, 637, 642, 696, 892, 926
objection *n.* 425, 696, 926
objectionable *adj.* 862, 926
objective *n.* 298, 552; *adj.* 3, 6, 327, 430, 933
obligation *n.* 531, 562, 605, 674, 737, 919
oblige *vb.* 674, 919
obliged *adj.* 909, 919
obliging *adj.* 886, 899
oblique *adj.* 219; *vb.* 531
obliteration *n.* 164, 485
oblivion *n.* 442
oblivious *adj.* 393, 442, 754
oblong *n.* 246
obscene *adj.* 901, 952
obscure *adj.* 453, 503, 798, 799, 824; *vb.* 461, 798, 799
obscurity *n.* 453, 503, 799, 803, 824

obsequious *adj.* 881, 886

observable *adj.* 458, 823

observance *n.* **702**, 878, 977, 988

observant *adj.* 390, 702, 818

observation *n.* 101, 384, 386, 390, 396, 818

observatory *n.* 329

observe *vb.* 105, 390, 392, 673, 702, 818, 878, 988

observer *n.* 460, 821

obsess *vb.* 830, 984

obsessed *adj.* 439

obsolete *adj.* 2, 126

obstacle *n.* 635, 681

obstinacy *n.* 537, 644

obstinate *adj.* 143, 535, 537

obstruct *vb.* 265, 635, 637, 648, 691

obtain *vb.* 1, 661, 705, 716, 720, 726

obtainable *adj.* 292, 404, 464, 705

obtrusive *adj.* 253, 877

obtuse *adj.* 256

obtuse angle *n.* 246

obvious *adj.* 452, 458, 502, 634, 823

occasion *n.* 136, 155, 878; *vb.* 155

occasionally *adv.* 138, **139**

occult *adj.* 984

occupancy *n.* 188, 707

occupation *n.* 557, 605

occupier *n.* 190, 710

occupy *vb.* 107, 188, 191, 557, 707

occur *vb.* 1, 107, 153, 384, 430, 825

ocean *n.* 351

octagon *n.* 70, 246

octave *n.* 70

octet *n.* 70

odd *adj.* 29, 39, 439

oddity *n.* 439, 866

odds *n.* 158

ode *n.* 528

odious *adj.* 892

odorous *adj.* 774, 776

odour *n.* 774

of course *adv.* 408

off *adj.* 53, 240; *adv.* 614

offal *n.* 310

offence *n.* 923, 938, 955

offend *vb.* 892, 923

offender *n.* 906

offensive *n.* 645; *adj.* 295, 777, 845, 869, 880, 887, 892, 923, 936

offer *n.* **693**, 695; *vb.* 532, 693, 715

offering *n.* 715, 943

offertory *n.* 715

offhand *adj.* 544, 887

office *n.* 557, 620, 985

office-boy *n.* 467

officer *n.* 625, 675, 956

official *n.* 623, 675, 683; *adj.* 430, 557, 622, 667

officious *adj.* 880

offset *n.* 31; *vb.* 31

off-shoot *n.* 979

offside *adj.* 240

offspring *n.* 11, **171**

often *adv.* 138

ogle *vb.* 818, 890

oil *n.* 306, 342, 365, 765; *vb.* 342, 365, 547

oiliness *n.* 365, 886

oily *adj* 257, 365, 477

ointment *n.* 342, 365, 591

O.K. *adj.* 579; *adv.* 79

old *adj.* 124, 126, 130, 606

old-fashioned *adj.* 126

old maid *n.* 897, 951

old master *n.* 488

oldness *n.* **126**, 130

olive *adj.* 812

olive branch *n.* 652

omen *n.* 447, 597

ominous *adj.* 154, 447, 594, 902

omission *n.* 57, 99, 393, 431, 662, 703, 920

omitted *adj.* 189

omnibus *n.* 524; *adj.* 54

omnipotent *adj.* 159, 966

on *adv.* 288; *adv.*, *prep.* 9

on and on *adv.* 114

once *adj.* 124

one *n.* 59; *adj.* 13, 59

on edge *adj.* 443, 856

on end *adj.* 214

oneness *n.* 13, 59

onerous *adj.* 615

one-sided *adj.* 416

one-time *adj.* 118, 124, 687

ongoing *adj.* 288

onlooker *n.* 821

only *adj.* 46, 59

onomatopoeia *n.* 455

onset *n.* 88, 298

onslaught *n.* 175, 645, 649

on time *adj.* 134, 136

ontological *adj.* 1

onus *n.* 919

onward *adv.* 288

ooze *vb.* 301, 319

opacity *n.* 803

opal glass *n.* 804

opaque *adj.* 799, 803

open *adj.* 262, 348, 409, 458, 462, 476, 508, 632, 753, 823; *vb.* 88, 182, 262, 348

open-handed *adj.* 747, 965

opening *n.* 88, 254, **262**, 462, 518; *adj.* 88

openness *n.* 476, 594

open up *vb.* 462

opera n. 529, 792
opera glasses n. 822
operate vb. 159, 172,
575, 591, 609
operation n. 172, 396,
591, 605, 609, 651
operative n. 619; adj.
172, 609
ophthalmic adj. 818
opinion n. 386, 415,
420, 624
opponent n. 638, 655,
883
opportune adj. 136
opportunity n. 136,
406, 678
oppose vb. 14, 25, 181,
239, 414, 425, 637, 644,
648, 649, 696, 926
opposed adj. 533, 883
opposite n. 239; adj. 14,
220, 239, 883; adv.,
prep. 239
opposition n. 181, 239,
397, 637, 926
oppress vb. 669, 837,
900
oppressive adj. 330,
669, 759, 900
opt vb. 540
optical adj. 818
optical illusion n. 4
optical instrument n.
822
optimism n. 417, 854
optimum adj. 579
option n. 540
opulence n. 734
opus n. 163, 792
oracle n. 436, 447
oral adj. 512, 514
orange n. 816; adj. 816
oration n. 518
orator n. 514
orb n. 249, 329
orbit n. 250, 322, 323;
vb. 274
orchard n. 378

orchestra n. 793
ordain vb. 671, 685, 985
ordeal n. 828
order n. 79, 81, 85, 93,
103, 622, 663, 872; vb.
79, 248, 622, 671, 902
orderliness n. 79, 583
orderly n. 676; adj. 79;
adv. 79
ordinance n. 103, 671,
954, 988
ordinary adj. 508, 574,
580, 666, 867, 871
ordure n. 310
ore n. 367
organ n. 563
organic adj. 366
organism n. 366, 368
organization n. 58, 79,
81, 564, 622, 641
organize vb. 58, 79, 81,
558, 622
organizer n. 558, 623
orgy n. 306, 950
orientate vb. 284, 545
orifice n. 262
origin n. 88, 155, 170
original n. 23; adj. 21,
88, 102, 125, 155, 430
originality n. 21, 102,
449
ornament n. 509, 844;
vb. 844
ornamentation n. 509,
846
ornate adj. 509, 846
ornithology n. 375
orphan n. 885
orthodox adj. 545, 977
orthodoxy n. 977
orthography n. 493
oscillation n. 140, 325
ostentation n. 875, 877
ostracize vb. 99
other adj. 40
otherworldly adj. 328,
980
ought vb. 919

oust vb. 686
out adj. 189, 600
outbreak n. 88, 175, 645
outburst n 175, 645,
756, 893
outcast n. 885; adj. 44
outclass vb 29
outcome n 87, 156
outcry n. 780, 788
outdated adj. 126
outdistance vb. 280,
314
outdo vb. 314
outer adj. 222
outer space n. 329
outfit n. 227, 568
outflow n. 301, 301
outgoing adj. 687
outgoings n. 740
outgrowth n. 252
outing, n. 269, 840
outlast vb. 112
outlaw n. 885; vb. 963
outlay n. 740
outlet n. 262
outline n. 232, 242, 488,
558, 602, 825; vh. 232,
525, 558
outlive vb. 112
outlook n. 154, 284,
420, 443
outlying adj. 222
outmanoeuvre vb. 478
outmatch vb. 34
outmoded adj. 126
outnumber vb. 75
out of date adj. 126
outpace vb. 198, 280
outpost n. 198
outpour n. 301
output n. 163, 705
outrage n. 608, 900; vb.
830, 887
outrageous adj. 175,
433, 851, 869, 880, 936
outright adj. 54
outrun vb. 198
outset n. 88

outside n. 222, 232; adj
  6, 100, 222, 921
outskirts n 198
outspeed vb 198
outspoken adj. 887
outstanding adj. 44,
  573, 737, 917
outstay vb. 112
outstretched adj. 202
outstrip vb. 29, 198,
  280, 314
outward adj. 6, 100,
  222, 825
outwit vb. 478, 631
oval n. 250; adj. 250
ovation n. 878, 925
oven n 763
over adj. 44
over again adv. 77
over against adv., prep.
  239
overall ¯ adj. 98, 101
over and above adv. 40
overawe vb. 922
overbalance vb. 317
overbearing adj. 669
overcast adj. 363, 798
overcharge vb. 745
overcome vb 661
overcompensate vb. 31
overdo vb. 481, 572,
  611, 615, 617
overdraft n. 739
overdrawn adj. 706,
  737
overdue adj. 117, 135,
  737, 917
overeat vb. 945, 948
overestimation n. 416,
  417
overfeed vb. 865
overfill vb 865
overflow n. 600; vb. 56,
  358
overflowing adj. 75,
  865
over-generous adj. 749
overgrown adj 194

overhanging adj. 216
overhaul vb. 280
overhear vb. 795
overjoyed adj. 827
overlap n. 206, 260; vb.
  206, 260
overlay n. 206; vb. 206,
  226
overload vb. 330
overlook vb. 208, 391,
  393
overlord n. 34
overplay vb. 481
overrate vb. 416, 417
overrun vb. 314
overseer n. 623, 675
oversensitive adj. 753,
  894
overshadow vb. 34,
  154, 208, 798
overshoot vb. 314
oversight n. 392, 621,
  622
overstatement n. 417,
  481
overstepping n. 314,
  918
overtake vb. 280
overthrow n. 148, 164,
  662; vb. 148, 164, 220,
  414, 686
overture n. 693, 792
overturn vb. 82, 164,
  220, 414
overvalue vb. 416, 417
overwhelm vb. 414,
  572, 661, 866, 922
overwhelming adj. 32
overwork vb. 611
owe vb. 737
owing adj. 737, 917
own vb. 707
owner n. 710
ownership n. 707
own up vb. 462, 833,
  941
ox n. 380

oxygen n. 348
ozone n. 348

P

pace n. 269; vb. 269
pacesetter n. 125
pacification n. 176, 650,
  652
pacifist n. 656; adj. 650
pack n. 94; vb. 56, 75,
  192
package n. 193; vb. 234
packet n. 193, 277
pact n. 698, 699
pad vb. 226
padding n. 226, 505
paddle vb. 271
paddock n. 184
padre n. 986
pagan n. 975, 983
page n. 467, 522
pageant n. 458, 529, 825
pageantry n. 877
pail n. 193
pain n. 551, 586, **828**,
  830; vb. 830
painful adj. 551, 753,
  805, 828
painfulness n. **830**
pain in the neck n. 592,
  841
pains n. 392
painstaking adj. 392,
  615
paint n. 225, 805; vb.
  225, 488, 525, 805
painter n. 491
painting n. 486, **488**
pair n. 61; vb. 61
pal n. 882
palatable adj. 306, 767,
  770
palatalize vb. 512
palate n. 767
palatial adj. 827

palaver n. 516
pale adj. 371, 806, 807, 812
palindrome n. 220
paling n. 234
pall n. 372
palliate vb. 591
pallid adj. 806
pally adj. 882
palm n. 663
palmist n. 447
palpable adj. 758
palpitate vb. 326, 756, 783
palpitation n. 325
palsy n. 326
paltry adj. 574, 580
pampa n. 356
pamphlet n. 464
panacea n. 591
pandemonium n. 780, 973
panel n. 206, 625, 688, 958
pang n. 828, 833
panic n. 615, 856; vb. 856
pannier n. 193
panoply n. 657
panorama n. 54, 818
pansy n. 162, 814, 953
pant n. 359; vb. 359, 756
pantheism n. 974
pantheon n. 967
pantomime n. 529
pantry n. 305
pap n. 364
paper n. 460, 518, 521, 526; vb. 225
paperback n. 524
par n. 30
parable n. 455, 525
parabola n. 247
parabolic adj. 455, 525
parachute vb. 273, 317
parade n. 458, 825, 877; vb. 91, 458, 877

paradise n. 449, 827, 972
paragon n. 581, 939
parallel n. 397; adj. 28, 218; vb. 218, 397
parallelism n. 218, 397
parallelogram n. 218, 246
paralysis n. 754
paralyze vb. 160, 754
paramount adj. 34, 573
paranoid n. 440
paranormal adj. 447
paraphernalia n. 568, 711
paraphrase vb. 20, 456
parapsychology n. 447
parasite n. 373, 612, 881
parasol n. 225, 801
parcel n. 193, 717; vb. 234, 717
parch vb. 350, 759
parchment n. 521
pardon vb. 601, 670, 680, 907, 911, 961
pare vb. 203, 228
parent n. 11, 86, 170
parenthood n. 170
parish n. 183, 987
parishioner n. 987
parity n. 28
park n. 234, 559; vb. 186
parliament n. 625
parochial adj. 183
parody n. 20, 487, 853
parrot n. 20; vb. 20
parse vb. 499
parsimony n. 748, 750
parson n. 986
part n. 55, 73, 327, 529, 717; vb 48, 55, 637, 642, 898
partake vb. 304, 709
partial adj. 55, 73, 660, 861, 916
participant n. 619, 709

participate vb. 605, 639, 709
participation n. 188, 639, 709
participle n. 499
particle n. 33, 195, 340, 499
particular adj. 5, 8, 102, 392, 398, 864
particularize vb. 102
particularly adv. 34
parting n. 48, 299, 369, 642
partisan adj. 641, 916, 979
partition n. 230; vb. 48
partly adv. 55
partner n. 640, 709, 710, 896
partnership n. 60, 180, 639, 709
part of speech n. 499
part with vb. 556, 713
party n. 94, 641, 655, 840, 884, 896, 950, 960
party-minded adj. 979
pass n. 200, 690, 890; vb. 107, 110, 310, 313, 424, 427, 954
passable adj. 579, 666
passage n. 200, 262, 266, 313, 360, 559, 792
pass away vb. 369
passé adj. 126
passenger n. 270
passer-by n. 821
pass for vb. 18
passing n 369
passion n. 752, 889, 893
passionate adj. 506, 752, 759, 889
passive n 499; adj. 174
pass on vb. 714
pass out vb. 617
pass over vb. 393, 670, 920
passport n. 690
pass sentence vb. 960

perfection n. **581**, 659, 937, 951

perfectionist n. 864

perforation n. 262, 264

perforator n. **264**

perform vb. 163, 172, 529, 609, 659, 702, 792, 919, 988

performance n. 163, 172, 529, 609, 659, 702

performer n. 529, 609, 619, 793

perfume n. 776; vb. 776

peril n. 594

perimeter n. 232, 250

period n. **109**

periodic adj. 109, 138, 140

periodical n. 464, 524; adj. 140

peripatetic adj. 269

periphery n. 232, 250

periphrastic adj. 505

perish vb. 164, 369, 826

perishable adj. 113

perjury n. 477

perk up vb. 618, 836

permanence n. 112, **143**, 152

permeable adj. 264

permeate vb. 45, 319

permissible adj. 954

permission n. 424, **690**, 692, 921, 925

permissive society n. 952

permit n. 690; vb. 690, 954

permutation n. 142

pernickety adj. 864

perpendicular adj. 214, 248

perpetual adj. 78, 91, 114

perpetuate vb. 114

perpetuation n. 91, 145

perpetuity n. 78, 91, 114

perplex vb. 409, 633

perplexing adj. 409, 633

persecute vb. 900

perseverance n. 534, 535, 611, 980

persevere vb. 145, 535, 611, 648, 980

persist vb. 112, 143, 145, 535, 695

persistence n. 145, 534, 535

person n. 368, 379, 499

personal adj. 379, 966

personal effects n. 711

personality n. 5, 58, 382, 751

personification n. 455, 486

personnel n. 619, 676

perspective n. 488, 818

perspicacity n. 434

perspicuity n. 502

perspiration n. 310

persuade vb. 177, 420, 547, 624

persuasion n. 420, 547

perturb vb. 82

peruse vb. 394

perverse adj. 936

perversion n. 412, 457, 471, 477, 487, 608, 978

perversity n. 936

pervert n. 953; vb. 431, 457, 487, 588, 608

perverted adj. 936

pessimism n. 418, 443, 855

pest n. 892

pester vb. 695, 830

pestilence n. 167

pestilent adj. 592

pet n. 373, 891; vb. 890

petal n. 374

peter out vb. 37

petition n. 394, 695, 982; vb. 394, 695, 982

petitioner n. 697, 982

petrify vb. 332, 334, 856

petrol n. 342, 765

petty adj. 416, 574

phantom n. 971; adj. 971

Pharisee n. 981

pharmaceutical n. 591

phase n. 109; vb. 558

phasing n. 140

phenomenal adj. 866

phenomenon n. 153, 825, 866

philanthropy n. 899, **903**

philosopher n. 428

philosophic adj. 757

philosophize vb. 384, 410

phlegmatic adj. 757

phobia n. 439

phoneme n. 512

phonetics n. 492, 512, 778

phoney n. 480; adj. 20

phosphorescence n. 797

photograph n. 483, 486; vb. 483

photographer n. 491

photography n. 486

phrase n. 494, 498, 792; vb. 498

phraseology n. 501

physical adj. 3, 327, 827

physiognomy n. 236

physiology n. 366, 375

piazza n. 559

pick vb. 378, 398, 540

picket vb. 144, 696

pickle n. 307, 633; vb. 599

pick-me-up n. 173, 591

pick on vb. 830

pick-pocket n. 723; vb. 722

pick up vb. 318, 472, 587, 589, 618

picnic n. 269, 306, 840

pictogram n. 493

pictorial *adj.* 488, 525

picture *n.* 397, 486, 488, 525; *vb.* 449, 486, 525

picturesque *adj.* 488, 829

piece *n.* 55, 59, 306, 717, 792

pièce de résistance n. 581

piecemeal *adv.* 55

pier *n.* 213, 217

pierce *vb.* 264

piercing *adj.* 255, 760, 780, 787

piety *n.* **980**

pig *n.* 948

pigment *n.* 805

pigmy *n.* 195

pile *n.* 217, 567; *vb.* 192

pile-up *n.* 282

pile up *vb.* 94, 567

pilfer *vb.* 722

pilferer *n.* 723

pilgrim *n.* 270, 980

pilgrimage *n.* 269

pill *n.* 591

pillage *n.* 722; *vb.* 164, 722

pillar *n.* 152, 208, 217, 939

pillow *n.* 217

pilot *n.* 272, 273, 277, 396; *vb.* 271, 273

pilot scheme *n.* 396, 558

pimple *n.* 252

pin *n.* 255, 264

pinch *vb.* 197, 722

pine *vb.* 861

pink *adj.* 811

pinnacle *n.* 212

pin-up *n.* 844

pioneer *n.* 86, 125, 190; *vb.* 84

pious *adj.* 980

pip *n.* 306

pipe *n.* 308, 360; *vb.* 789

pipe-dreaming *n.* 449, 854

pipeline *n.* 360

piquancy *n.* 506, 769

pirate *n.* 723

pirouette *n.* 323; *vb.* 323

pit *n.* 210, 254, 658

pitch *n.* 234, 321, 365, 400, 512; *vb.* 290

pitfall *n.* 463, **596**

pith *n.* 224

pithy *adj.* 432, 450, 504

pitiable *adj.* 907

pitiful *adj.* 33, 580, 907

pitilessness *n.* **908**

pity *n.* 907; *vb.* 907, 924

pivot *n.* 90, 217; *vb.* 323

pivotal *adj.* 224

pixie *n.* 970

placard *n.* 464

placate *vb.* 176, 652

place *n.* 184, 185, 186, 559; *vb.* 186

placement *n.* 85, 186

place of business *n.* 730

place of learning *n.* 475

placid *adj.* 267, 757

plagiarize *vb.* 20

plague *n.* 167, 592, 665; *vb.* 314, 830

plain *n.* 356; *adj.* 46, 452, 476, 502, **508**, 823

plain living *n.* 946

plainness *n.* 46, 452, **508**, 823

plain speech *n.* 452, 502, 508

plaintiff *n.* 930, 960

plait *n.* 49, 221, 251; *vb.* 221, 251

plan *n.* 23, 81, 386, 552, **558**, 602, 605; *vb.* 58, 81, 552, **558**, 602

plane *n.* 215, 278; *vb.* 215, 257

planet *n.* 329, 800

planetarium *n.* 329

planned *adj.* 543, 552, 558

plant *n.* 307, 374, 620; *vb.* 378

plantation *n.* 374, 378

planter *n.* 378

plants *n.* 366

plaque *n.* 489

plastic *adj.* 142, 151, 242, 335, 768

plastic surgery *n.* 844

plate *n.* 23, 193, 206, 490; *vb.* 225

plateau *n.* 356

platitude *n.* 432, 451

platonic *adj.* 951

plausible *adj.* 404, 406, 420, 825, 929

play *n.* 529, 678, 840; *vb.* 477, 529, 792, 797

play-acting *n.* 852

play down *vb.* 418, 574, 928

player *n.* 529, 793

playful *adj.* 836

play games *vb.* 840

playground *n.* 658

playhouse *n.* 529

play on words *n.* 454, 842

plea *n.* 401, 549, 695, 929, 960

plead *vb.* 410, 514, 695, 959

plead guilty *vb.* 462, 941

pleadings *n.* 960

pleasant *adj.* 827, 829, 840

please *vb.* 829

pleased *adj.* 756, 827, 831, 909

pleased with oneself *adj.* 873

please onself *vb.* 678

pleasing *adj.* 790, 792, 829, 844

pleasurableness *n.* **829**

portrait *n.* 20, 22, 488, 525

portray *vb.* 20, 486, 488, 525

portrayal *n.* 20, 486, 525

pose *n.* 825; *vb.* 23, 394, 621, 852

position *n.* 7, 93, 184, 185, 186, 420, 557; *vb.* 186

position in a series *n.* 93

positive *adj.* 39, 468

possess *vb.* 707, 720, 984

possession *n.* 707, 720, 729, 984

possessive *adj.* 707, 750, 913

possessor *n.* 710, 720

possibility *n.* 404, 406

possible *adj.* 404, 409, 459

post *n.* 217, 467, 523, 557; *vb.* 268, 523

postdate *vb.* 117

poster *n.* 464

posterior *n.* 237; *adj.* 85, 119, 237

posteriority *n.* 119

posterity *n.* 171

postgraduate *n.* 474

post office *n.* 467

postpone *vb.* 89, 135, 920

postscript *n.* 41, 87, 89

postulate *n.* 386, 410, 448; *vb.* 448, 700

posture *n.* 7, 621, 825

pot *n.* 193

pot-bellied *adj.* 194

potent *adj.* 159, 173

potential *n.* 159, 564; *adj.* 159, 404, 459

pothole *n.* 254

potion *n.* 309, 591

pot luck *n.* 158

potter *n.* 491

pottery *n.* 489

pouch *n.* 193

poultry *n.* 306, 373

pounce *n.* 320; *vb.* 321

pound *n.* 184, 234, 325; *vb.* 282, 325, 340, 783

pound of flesh *n.* 669, 908

pour *vb.* 343, 358

pour out *vb.* 301

poverty *n.* 571, 735

powder *n.* 340

powderiness *n.* 340

power *n.* 159, 173, 177, 506, 530, 564, 622, 667; *vb.* 159, 765

powerful *adj.* 159, 161, 173, 177, 506, 667, 671

powerless *adj.* 160, 162

power station *n.* 159

practicable *adj.* 404, 406, 575

practical *adj.* 404, 577

practical joke *n.* 433

practically *adv.* 199

practice *n.* 396, 545, 602, 627, 702

practise *vb.* 470, 591, 602, 702

practised *adj.* 606

practising *adj.* 702, 974, 977, 980

practitioner *n.* 619

pragmatic *adj.* 575

prairie *n.* 356

praise *n.* 909, 922, 925, 982; *vb.* 868, 909, 922, 925, 982

praiseworthy *adj.* 579, 925

pram *n.* 276

prank *n.* 433, 539, 932

prattle *vb.* 451, 516

pray *vb.* 695, 980, 982, 988

prayer *n.* 695, 909, 982, 985, 988

prayerful *adj.* 695, 980, 982

preach *vb.* 470, 514

preacher *n.* 456, 514, 974, 986

preaching *n.* 518, 985

preamble *n.* 86; *vb.* 84

precarious *adj.* 409, 594

precaution *n.* 392, 860

precede *vb.* 84, 118, 134, 286

precedence *n.* 84, 286

precedent *n.* 23, 84, 86, 118, 545, 960; *adj.* 84

preceding *adj.* 84, 118, 134

precept *n.* 103, 626

precinct *n.* 184

precious *adj.* 139

precious stone *n* 846

precipice *n.* 214

precipitate *adj.* 544, 613

precipitation *n.* 349, 358, 613

precipitous *adj.* 859

precis *n.* 527

precise *adj* 392, 504, 864

preclude *vb.* 99, 691

precocious *adj.* 134

preconception *n.* 412, 416, 446

precursor *n.* 86, 467

predate *vb.* 117

predecessor *n.* 86

predestination *n.* 531, 543

predetermination *n.* 543

predicament *n.* 153, 633

predict *vb.* 443, 447, 543

predictable *adj.* 447

prediction *n.* 154, 447, 543

predilection *n.* 178, 861

predisposed

predisposed *adj.* 178, 751

predisposition *n.* 178, 545

predominate *vb.* — 34, 101

pre-eminent *adj.* 34

pre-empt *vb.* 134

pre-existence *n.* 118

prefabricated *adj.* 602

preface *n.* 86, 88; *vb.* 84

prefer *vb.* 540, 916

preference *n* 84, 178, 540

prefix *n.* 41, 86, 499; *vb.* 40

pregnant *adj.* 163, 450

prehistoric *adj.* 124, 126

prejudge *vb* 416

prejudice *n* 412, 416, 578, 916

preliminary *n.* 86, 88; *adj.* 86, 396

prelude *n.* 86, 88, 792; *vb.* 84

premature *adj.* 134, 137, 859

premeditated *adj.* 530, 543

première *n.* 88

premise *n.* 410, 448

premises *n* 730

premium *n.* 663, 724, 965; *adj.* 579

premonition *n.* 411, 597

preoccupation *n.* 384, 390

preoccupied *adj.* 442

prep *n.* 470, 472

preparation *n.* 81, 86, 470, 591, 602

preparatory *adj.* 86, 396, 602

prepare *vb* 81, 306, 470, 521, 568, 602

prepared *adj.* 443, 532, 602

preposition *n.* 499

preposterous *adj* 481, 851

prerequisite *n.* 531

prerogative *n.* 34, 667, 917

prescribe *vb.* 671

prescribed *adj.* 954

prescription *n.* 591, 626

prescriptive *adj.* 103

presence *n.* 188, 971

presence of mind *n.* 860

present *n.* 120, 715; *adj.* 1, 120, 153, 188; *vb.* 460, 529, 693, 715, 825, 965

presentation *n.* 413, 458, 460, 501, 529, 693, 715, 825

present-day *adj.* 120, 125

present events *n.* 153

present time *n.* 120

preservation *n.* 599

preserve *vb.* 599, 712

preside *vb.* 956

president *n.* 675

press *vb.* 257, 282, 290, 319, 695, 712, 758

pressed man *n.* 655

pressing *adj.* 674

pressure *n.* 159, 177, 282, 290, 330, 665, 674

pressure group *n.* 547, 697

prestige *n.* 177, 667, 829, 868

prestigious *adj.* 829, 868

presumable *adj.* 406

presume *vb.* 416, 420, 448, 867, 880, 910, 918

presuppose *vb.* 448

pretend *vb.* 20, 449, 477, 549, 852

pretender *n* 852

pretentious *adj.* 509, 849, 852, 875, 877, 879

pretext *n.* 549

pretty *adj.* 844

prevail *vb.* 1, 34, 101, 112, 661

prevail on *vb.* 547

prevalent *adj* 32, 75, 545

prevaricate *vb.* 454, 477

prevent *vb.* 99, 181, 548, 635, 648, 691

preview *n.* 118

previous *adj.* 84, 118, 134, 687

prey *n.* 724, 828

price *n.* 579, 743; *vb.* 743

priceless *adj.* 579, 851

prick *vb.* 255, 264, 758

prickly *adj.* 255, 258, 894

pride *n.* 873

pride oneself on *vb.* 873

priest *n.* 986

prig *n.* 951

prim *adj* 951

primary *adj.* 21, 155, 573

primate *n* 986

prime *n.* 129; *adj.* 39, 579; *vb.* 470

prime mover *n.* 155, 966

primer *n.* 88, 524

primitive *n* 190; *adj.* 88, 124, 126, 134

prince *n.* 675

princely *adj* 870

princess *n.* 675

principal *n.* 473, 675; *adj.* 34, 573

principality *n.* 183

principle *n.* 5, 23, 103, 155, 420, 626

principles *n.* 558, 931

print *n.* 490, 522; *vb.* 464, 482, 490, 521, 522

printer *n.* 491, 522
printing *n.* 490, 521, 522
prior *n.* 986; *adj.* 84, 118, 134
priority *n.* 84, 118, 286, 573
priory *n.* 990
prism *n.* 246, 805
prison *n.* 234, **682**
prisoner *n.* **684**, 701
privacy *n.* 461, 885
private *adj.* 466
privilege *n.* 34, 678, 872, 917, 921
prize *n.* 663, 715, 724, 965; *vb.* 573, 861, 889
pro *n.* 953; *adj.* 689
probability *n.* 158, **406**
probable *adj.* 404, 406
probationary *adj.* 396, 604
probationer *n.* 474
probe *n.* 394, 396; *vb.* 394
probity *n.* 931, 937
problem *n.* 387, 409, 410, 633, 828, 830
problematical *adj.* 409
procedure *n.* 103, 545, 558, 559
proceed *vb.* 110, 266, 288, 313, 558, 661
proceedings *n.* 483
proceeds *n.* 705, 716, 741
process *n.* 172, 559
processed *adj.* 602
processing *n.* 146, 163
procession *n.* 91, 458
proclaim *vb.* 458, 460, 464, 671
procrastinate *vb.* 135, 920
procreation *n.* 163
procuration *n.* 705
procure *vb.* 705
prod *n.* 547; *vb.* 547

prodigal *n.* 749, 940; *adj.* 569, 749
prodigality *n.* 569, 749
prodigal son *n.* 941
prodigy *n.* 866
produce *n.* 163, 705; *vb.* 155, 163, 172, 458, 529
producer *n.* 155, **166**
product *n.* 38, 156, 163, 729
production *n.* 163, 529
productive *adj.* 163, 168, 705
productiveness *n.* 168
profanation *n.* 608, 901
profane *adj.* 901, 975, **981**, 987; *vb.* 608, 981
profess *vb.* 420, 468, 549, 702
profession *n.* 468, 557
professional *n.* 629; *adj.* 557
professor *n.* 428, 473
proffer *vb.* 693
proficiency *n.* 426, 627
proficient *n.* 629; *adj.* 627
profile *n.* 232, 242, 525, 825
profit *n.* 550, 575, 705, 734, 741; *vb.* 136, 575, 587, 661, 705
profitable *adj.* 575, 705, 965
profitless *adj.* 169, 662
profit-sharing *n.* 709; *adj.* 709
profligate *n.* 953; *adj.* 749, 952
profound *adj.* 210, 453
profuse *adj.* 32, 56, 75, 168, 505
profusion *n.* 26, 32, 75, 168, 567, 572
prognosis *n.* 447
prognosticate *vb.* 154, 447

programme *n.* 83, 558, 605, 621
progress *n.* 266, **288**, 550, 587, 661; *vb.* 130, 145, 266, 288, 324, 587, 661
progression *n.* 36, 85, 91, **288**
progressive *adj.* 91, 125, 148, 288, 587, 605
prohibit *vb.* 99, 635, **691**
prohibition *n.* 99, 635, **691**, 949
prohibitive *adj.* 99, 691, 745
project *n.* 558, 605; *vb.* 6, 222, 252, 253, 552, **558**
projectile *n.* 290
projection *n.* 6, 253
prolegomena *n.* 86
proletariat *n.* 871
proliferate *vb.* 36, 165, 168
prolific *adj.* 163, 168
prolix *adj.* 505
prologue *n.* 86
prolongation *n.* 36, 112, 145, 202
promenade *n.* 269
prominence *n.* **253**, 573, 823, 868
prominent *adj.* 177, 253, 458, 573, 823, 868
promiscuous *adj.* 399, 952
promise *n.* **698**, 699, 701, 854; *vb.* 698, 699, 854
promised *adj.* 406, 698
promised land *n.* 96
promontory *n.* 253
promote *vb.* 217, 288, 458, 464, 587, 636
promotion *n.* 464, 587, 636, 727
prompt *adj.* 115, 134,

279

publish *vb.* 458, **464**, 465, 522
publisher *n.* 524
publishing *n.* 458, 522
puck *n.* 970
pucker *vb.* 260
pudding *n.* 306
puddle *n.* 354
puerile *adj.* 129, 131, 435
puff *n.* 359; *vb.* 308, 359
puff up *vb.* 875
pugnacious *adj.* 642, 651
pull *n.* 177, 294; *vb.* 291, 294, 390
pull a person's leg *vb.* 478, 842, 853
pull down *vb.* 164, 319, 588
pulling *n.* 291, 312
pull off *vb.* 659, 661
pull oneself together *vb.* 681, 757
pull one's socks up *vb.* 587
pull out *vb.* 312
pull through *vb.* 589
pull together *vb.* 639
pull up *vb.* 318
pull-up *n.* 191
pulp *n.* 364; *vb.* 364
pulpiness *n.* 364
pulsar *n.* 329
pulsate *vb.* 140
pulsation *n.* 140, 325
pulse *n.* 140, 325; *vb.* 325
pulverize *vb.* 164, 340
pummel *vb.* 282
pump *n.* 359
pun *n.* 454, 842
punch *n.* 264, 506, 769; *vb.* 282, 482
punctiliousness *n.* 392, 864
punctual *adj.* 115, 134, 136

puncture *n.* 48; *vb.* 48, 255, 264
pungency *n.* 769
pungent *adj.* 769, 773, 774
punish *vb.* 647, 926, 962, **963**
punishment *n.* 647, 917, 963
punk *n.* 792
puny *adj.* 162, 195
pup *n.* 880
pupil *n.* 131, 474
purchase *n.* 707, 726; *vb.* 705, 726
purchaser *n.* 710, 726, 737
purdah *n.* 461
pure *adj.* 46, 581, 583, 935, 937, 951, 977
purgatory *n.* 943
purge *vb.* 583, 911
purify *vb.* 46, 333, 348, 583, 775, 807
purist *n.* 864
puritanical *adj.* 669, 946, 951
purity *n.* 46, 876, 935, 937, 951
purloin *vb.* 722
purple *n.* 814; *adj.* 814
purport *n.* 450; *vb.* 450
purpose *n.* 547, 552; *vb.* 530, 552
purposeful *adj.* 552
purposeless *adj.* 451, 576
purr *vb.* 781, 783, 784, 789
purse *n.* 193, 732
purser *n.* 733
pursue *vb.* 287, 552, 554, 890
pursuer *n.* 554
pursuit *n.* **554**, 557, 605
push *n.* 303, 645; *vb.* 282, **290**, 547, 645
push ahead *vb.* 288

push along *vb.* 299
push around *vb.* 902
push back *vb.* 295
push down *vb.* 319
push off *vb.* 299
push-over *n.* 634, 661
pushy *adj.* 173, 611
put *vb.* 186
put about *vb.* 464
put across *vb.* 460
put aside *vb.* 567, 607
put a stop to *vb.* 144
put asunder *vb.* 898
putative *adj.* 448
put away *vb.* 304, 370, 567, 681
put back *vb.* 589
put by *vb.* 567
put down *vb.* 370
put forward *vb.* 693
put in *vb.* 300, 311
put into *vb.* 456
put into action *vb.* 609
put it to *vb.* 394
put off *vb.* 135
put on *vb.* 225, 227, 477, 529 805, 852
put-on *n.* 852; *adj.* 477, 852
put on a brave face *vb.* 477
put oneself out *vb.* 604, 615
put out *vb.* 578, 762, 830, 893
put over *vb.* 460
putrefaction *n.* 53, 777
putrid *adj.* 584, 588, 777
put right *vb.* 589
put together *vb.* 47, 52, 163
put up *vb.* 191
put-up job *n.* 930
put up with *vb.* 424, 757, 828
puzzle *n.* 409, 453, 466; *vb.* 409

pylon *n.* 159
pyramid *n.* 246
pyre *n.* 372

Q

quack *vb.* 787, 789
quadrangle *n.* 67, 184
quadratic *adj.* 67
quadrilateral *n.* 67, 246
quadrisection *n.* **69**
quadruped *n.* 373
quadruple *adj.* 68; *vb.*
68
quadruplet *n.* 67
quadruplication *n.* **68**
quagmire *n.* 355
quail *vb.* 858
quake *n.* 326; *vb.* 325,
326, 856
qualification *n.* 41, 142,
403
qualifications *n.* 627
qualified *adj.* 130, 602,
627
qualify *vb.* 142, 403,
570
quality *n.* 5, 58, 579,
935
qualm *n.* 421, 533, 833
quandary *n.* 409, 633
quantify *vb* 26, 400
quantitative *adj.* 26
quantity *n.* **26**, 32, 75,
400
quarrel *n* 25, 642, 893;
vb. 25, 642
quarrelsome *adj.* 642,
883
quarry *vb.* 312
quart *n* 69
quarter *n* 69, 183; *vb*
69
quartet *n* 67, 792
quasar *n.* 329
quash *vb.* 681, 686

quasi- *adj.* 497
quaternity *n.* 67
queen *n* 675
Queen's English *n.* 492
queer *n.* 106, 953; *adj*
952
quell *vb.* 37, 89, 652,
681
quench *vb.* 762
query *n.* 394
quest *n.* 269, 388, 394,
554; *vb.* 554
question *n.* 387, **394**,
695; *vb* 388, **394**, 421
questionable *adj.* 407,
409, 421, 869, 932
questioner *n.* 388, 394
questionnaire *n.* 394
queue *n.* 91; *vb.* 91
quibble *vb.* 454
quick *adj.* **280**, 434,
613, 842
quicken *vb.* **280**, 368,
613, 752, 755
quicksand *n.* 355, 596
quick-tempered *adj.*
756
quick-witted *adj.* 842
quiescent *adj.* 267, 459
quiet *n.* 267, 616, 779;
adj. 517, 616, 650, 779,
781, 876; *vb.* 652, 779
quieten *vb.* 176
quiet time *n.* 982
quilt *vb.* 226
quintessence *n.* 5
quintet *n.* 70
quintuple *adj.* 70
quintuplet *n* 70
quip *n* 842
quirk *n.* 539
quisling *n.* 480
quit *vb* 299, **556**, 687
quite *adv* 56
quiver *n* 325; *vb* 325,
326, 756, 760, 856
Quixote *n* 449
quiz *n* 394; *vb.* 394

quoit *n.* 250
quota *n* 305, 717
quotation *n* 743
quote *vb.* 20
quotient *n.* 38

R

rabbi *n.* 986
rabble *n.* 871
rabid *adj.* 148, 439
race *n.* 11, 554, 613,
649; *vb.* 280, 649
racialist *adj.* 379
rack *n.* 217, 964
racket *n.* 780, 791
raconteur *n.* 525
racy *adj.* 506, 769
radiate *vb.* 297
radiation *n.* 297
radiator *n.* 763
radical *n.* 148, 672, 832;
adj. 56, 148, 155
radio *n.* 467, 840
radius *n.* 400
rafter *n.* 217
rag *n.* 33; *vb.* 842
rage *n.* 439, 756, 850,
893; *vb.* 756, 893
ragtime *n.* 792
raid *n.* 300, 645; *vb*
645, 720, 722
rail *n.* 234
railing *n.* 234
railway *n.* 559
rain *n.* 347, 349, 358;
vb. 358
rainbow *n.* 247, 817
rainfall *n.* 358
rainproof *adj* 350
raise *vb.* 214, 318, 331,
377
rake *n* 953
rally *n* 649, 696; *vb*
94, 587, 589
ram *vb.* 265

Ramadan *n.* 947
ramble *n.* 269; *vb.* 269, 439, 505
rambler *n.* 270
rambling *adj.* 505
ramification *n.* 297
rampart *n.* 646
ramshackle *adj.* 588
ranch *n.* 377, 378
rancid *adj.* 53, 584, 777
rancorous *adj.* 912
random *adj.* 141, 158, 399, 409, 553
range *n.* 27, 182, 198, 400, 678, 795, 956; *vb.* 81, 182
ranger *n.* 683
rank *n.* 7, 93, 97, 870; *adj.* 777; *vb.* 27, 97
rankle *vb.* 893
ransack *vb.* 722
ransom *n.* 601; *vb.* 601, 680, 721
rant *vb.* 514
rap *n.* 282, 782, 963; *vb.* 282, 782
rape *vb.* 645, 952
rapidity *n.* 280
rapids *n.* 358
rapist *n.* 645, 953
rapport *n.* 643
rapprochement *n.* 643
rapture *n.* 827, 972
rare *adj.* 21, 33, 139, 333
rarefied *adj.* 333
rarely *adv.* 139
rarity *n.* 76, 139, 333, 770
rascal *n.* 940
rashness *n.* 393, 544, 613, 859
rasp *vb.* 341, 787
rat *n.* 480, 538, 940
rate *n.* 27; *vb.* 743
rates *n.* 743
ratify *vb.* 408, 424, 468, 699

ratio *n.* 27, 400
ration *n.* 305, 717; *vb.* 717
rational *adj.* 39, 382, 410
rationale *n.* 157
rationalism *n.* 410, 975
rationality *n.* 410, 438
rat-race *n.* 611
rattle *n.* 783; *vb.* 780, 783
raucous *adj.* 787
ravage *n.* 164; *vb.* 164, 228, 314, 645
ravaged *adj.* 588
rave *vb.* 439, 827, 925
ravenous *adj.* 720, 861, 948
ravine *n.* 200, 210, 254
raw *adj.* 129, 603, 753, 760
raw deal *n.* 551, 916
raw materials *n.* 566
ray *n.* 297, 797
raze *vb.* 164, 319, 485
re *adv.*, *prep.* 9
reach *n.* 182, 198, 202; *vb.* 182, 280, 298, 661
reaction *n.* 147, 156, 283, 647
reactionary *n.* 143, 672, 832; *adj.* 143, 289
read *vb.* 456, 472, 482
readable *adj.* 452
reader *n.* 473, 522, 524
reading *n.* 456, 472, 518
read into *vb.* 457
readjustment *n.* 142
ready *adj.* 188, 532, 602
ready reckoner *n.* 38
real *adj.* 1, 3, 327, 430
realistic *adj.* 18
realize *vb.* 327, 382, 419, 426, 452, 486, 659
really *adv.* 1
realm *n.* 183, 557
reanimate *vb.* 368, 589

reap *vb.* 48, 378, 661, 705
reappear *vb.* 77, 147
rear *n.* 237; *adj.* 237; *vb.* 377, 470
rearguard *n.* 237
rearrange *vb.* 142, 220
reason *n.* 8, 155, 401, 410, 438, 456, 547; *vb.* 382, 410
reasonable *adj.* 176, 406, 410, 746
reasoning *n.* 382, 384, 410; *adj.* 410, 434
reawaken *vb.* 589, 618
rebate *n.* 43, 744; *vb.* 744
rebel *n.* 106, 148, 425, 672; *vb.* 644, 672
rebellion *n.* 148, 644, 672
rebellious *adj.* 148, 644, 668, 672
rebirth *n.* 146, 589
rebound *n.* 147, 283; *vb.* 147, 283
rebuff *n.* 283, 295, 542, 694, 923; *vb.* 295, 542, 694, 923
rebuild *vb.* 165, 589
rebuke *n.* 926; *vb.* 926, 962, 963
rebuttal *n.* 395, 402, 414
recalcitrant *adj.* 537, 648
recall *n.* 441; *vb.* 441, 686
recantation *n.* 538
recapitulate *vb.* 77
recede *vb.* 37, 289, 293
receipts *n.* 705, 716, 741
receive *vb.* 302, 705, 716, 720, 884
receiver *n.* 467, 716, 733
receiving *n.* 716; *adj.* 716
recency *n.* 134

283

recent *adj.* 125, 134

receptacle *n.* 193

reception *n.* 94, 98, 302, 716, 795, 884, 896

receptive *adj.* 302, 716, 753

recess *n.* 144, 254, 614

recession *n.* 169, 197, 293, 317

recipe *n.* 626

recipient *n.* 523, 716

reciprocal *adj.* 9, 12, 28, 39, 150, 647

recital *n.* 518, 792

recite *vb.* 77, 460, 525

reckless *adj.* 393, 613, 749, 859

reckon *vb.* 38, 400, 743

reckoning *n.* 38, 400, 738, 742

reclaim *vb.* 589, 721

recline *vb.* 215

recluse *n.* 885, 946

recognition *n.* 426, 818, 909, 925

recognize *vb.* 426, 441, 452, 818, 909, 925

recoil *n.* 147, 283; *vb.* 147, 283

recollect *vb.* 441

recommend *vb.* 415, 624

recompense *n.* 31, 721, 738, 965; *vb.* 31, 589, 738, 965

reconcile *vb.* 24, 105, 652, 653, 704, 831, 911, 943

reconciled *adj.* 643, 654, 911

reconciliation *n.* 24, 650, 652, 911, 943

recondite *adj.* 453

reconditioning *n.* 147, 589

reconsider *vb.* 384

reconsideration *n.* 441

reconstruct *vb.* 142, 146, 165, 589

record *n.* 83, 441, **483**, 484, 525, 792, 794; *vb.* 83, 483, 525

recorder *n.* **484**, 958

recount *vb.* 525

recoup *vb.* 31, 721, 738

recourse *n.* 595

recover *vb.* 589, 618, 720, 721, 834

recovery *n.* 147, 589, 618, 705, 720, 721

recreation *n.* 614, 649, 840

recriminate *vb.* 647, 930

recruit *n.* 287, 474, 655; *vb.* 557, 651

rectangle *n.* 246

rectify *vb.* 587, 589

rector *vb.* 986

recuperate *vb.* 589, 618

recur *vb.* 77, 138, 140, 441

recurrent *adj.* 109, 138

red *n.* **811**; *adj.* 811, 876

redeem *vb.* 31, 146, 601, 721, 726, 911, 943

redeemer *n.* 905, 967

rediscover *vb.* 165

red-letter day *n.* 878

redress *n.* 943, 965; *vb.* 589, 943, 965

reduce *vb.* 37, 76, 197, 203, 588, 743, 744

reduction *n.* 37, 42, 195, 197, 527, 744

redundancy *n.* 505, 686

redundant *adj.* 505, 572

reduplication *n.* 62, 165

re-echo *vb.* 784

reef *n.* 357, 596

reek *n.* 777; *vb.* 759, 777

re-entry *n.* 274

re-establish *vb.* 589

refer *vb.* 9, 157, 450

referee *n.* 415, 653

reference *n.* 157, 401, 450

reference book *n.* 524

referendum *n.* 450, 540

refill *n.* 56

refine *vb.* 142, 333, 587

refined *adj.* 398, 510, **805**, 844, 848, 886

reflect *vb.* 384, 486, 797, 982

reflection *n.* 22, 384, 441, 797

reflector *n.* 822

reflex *adj.* 411, 531, 544

reform *n.* 587; *vb.* 142, 146, 587, 589

reforming *n.* 165; *adj.* 903

refractory *adj.* 537, 672

refrain *n.* 528, 792; *vb.* 89, 144, 555, 610, 944

refresh *vb.* 161, 348, 472, 589, 618

refresher *n.* 591

refreshment *n.* 147, 306, **618**, 829

refresh one's memory *vb.* 441

refrigeration *n.* 599, 762

refrigerator *n.* 305, 764

refuge *n.* 463, 595, 885

refugee *n.* 270, 600, 885

refund *n.* 31, 721, 738; *vb.* 31, 589, 721, 738

refurbish *vb.* 125, 587, 589

refusal *n.* 469, 542, 691, **694**

refuse *n.* 576; *vb.* 425, 469, 533, 542, 691, **694**

refutation *n.* 414

refute *vb.* 402, 686

regain *vb.* 705, 721

regal *adj.* 870

regalia *n.* 482, 677

regard *n.* 388, 390, 392,

rendezvous *n.* 96, 884; *vb.* 94

renegade *n.* 538

renew *vb.* 77, 125, 142, 165, 589

renounce *vb.* 469, 542, 556, 713

renovate *vb.* 125, 142, 165, 589

renown *n.* 868

rent *n.* 743; *adj.* 48, 262; *vb.* 191, 719

renunciation *n.* 469, 538, 542, 556, 713

reoccurrence *n.* 77, 138

reorganization *n.* 81, 142

reorganize *vb.* 142, 587, 589

repair *n.* 589; *vb.* 589, 721

reparation *n.* 31, 589, 721, 943, 965

repartee *n.* 395, 519, 842

repatriation *n.* 721

repay *vb.* 647, 721, 738, 943

repeal *n.* 686; *vb.* 686

repeat *n.* 77; *vb.* 20, 62, 77, 138, 140, 165

repeated and prolonged sound *n.* 783

repel *vb.* 295, 648, 885, 892

repent *vb.* 833, 907, 941

repercussion *n.* 156, 283

repetition *n.* 62, 77, 140, 505

repetitive *adj.* 77, 841

replace *vb.* 147, 149, 187, 686

replay *n.* 77

replenish *vb.* 56, 568

replete *adj.* 56, 570, 865

replica *n.* 20, 22

reply *n.* 283, 395, 402, 523; *vb.* 395

report *n.* 415, 460, 465, 468, 483, 523, 525, 778, 782; *vb.* 460, 465, 483, 521, 525

reporter *n.* 460, 524

repose *n.* 612, **616**; *vb.* 215

repository *n.* 732

reprehensible *adj.* 926

represent *vb.* 20, **486**, 488, 525, 685, 689

representation *n.* 20, 22, **486**, 488, 489, 525, 558, 685

representative *n.* 625, 688, 689; *adj.* 18, 101, 482, 486

repress *vb.* 679, 681, 691, 779

reprieve *n.* 135, 601, 911, 961; *vb.* 907, 911, 961

reprimand *n.* 926, 963; *vb.* 926, 963

reprint *n.* 20, 22, 77, 524; *vb.* 165, 464

reprisal *n.* 647, 912

reproach *n.* 869, 926; *vb.* 926

reproduce *vb.* 20, 163, 165, 486

reproduction *n.* 22, 77, 163, **165**, 486

reprove *vb.* 926, 930, 963

reptile *n.* 373

repudiate *vb.* 414, 469, 542, 686, 694

repugnance *n.* 637, 862, 883, 892

repugnant *adj.* 862, 892, 936

repulse *vb.* 295, 694

repulsion *n.* **295**, 892

repulsive *adj.* 295, 777, 892

reputable *adj.* 177, 868, 931

reputation *n.* 177, 868

repute *n.* **868**

request *n.* 394, 671, **695**, 982; *vb.* 394, 671, 695

requiem *n.* 372, 839

require *vb.* 531, 562, 571, 671, 674

requirement *n.* 8, 315, **562**, 671

requital *n.* 31, 647, 912, 943

rescue *n.* 589, 600, 601, 680; *vb.* 589, 601, 636, 680

research *n.* 396; *vb.* 396

researcher *n.* 394, 396, 428

resemblance *n.* 18, 105, 397

resentful *adj.* 883, 893, 900, 913

resentment *n.* 832, **893**, 913, 914

reservation *n.* 403, 421, 425, 700

reserve *n.* 149, 198, 517, 568, 681, 876; *adj.* 149; *vb.* 712

reserves *n.* 564, 567, 731

reservoir *n.* 193, 354, 567

reside *vb.* 188, 191

residence *n.* 188, 191, 707

resident *n.* 190, 710; *adj.* 188

residual *adj.* 44

residue *n.* 44

resign *vb.* 654, 687

resignation *n.* 654, **687**, 757

resilience *n.* 336

resin *n.* 365; *vb.* 365

resist *vb.* 295, 537, 637, 644, **648**, 694

resistance *n.* 181, **648**

resistant *adj.* 337

resolute *adj.* 152, 534, 857

resolution *n.* 415, 530, **534**, 611, 857

resolve *n.* 534; *vb.* 53, 530, 534, 552

resonance *n.* 778, **784**

resort to *vb.* 606

resounding *n.* 784; *adj.* 780

resourceful *adj.* 449

resources *n.* 564, 566, 711, 734

respect *n.* 868, 886, **922**; *vb.* 868, 922

respectful *adj.* 673, 922

respiration *n.* 359

respite *n.* 135, 144, 614

respond *vb.* 283, 395, 752, 909

responsibility *n.* 179, 557, 701, 917, 919, 956

responsible *adj.* 133, 179, 702, 919, 956

responsive *adj.* 395, 909

rest *n.* 44, 92, 144, 213, 217, **267**, 610, 612, 614, 616; *vb.* 144, 267, 612, 614, 616

restate *vb.* 77, 456

restaurant *n.* 191

restitution *n.* 31, 147, 589, **721**, 738, 943

restless *adj.* 266, 611, 756, 832

restoration *n.* 147, **589**, 618, 721

restorative, *n.* 591; *adj.* 585, 589, 591

restore *vb.* 147, 589, 591, 618, 680, 721, 911

restrain *vb.* 37, 144, 176, 403, 635, **681**, 691

restrained *adj.* 176, 508, 517, 681, 876, 944

restraint *n.* 37, 176, 281, 548, 635, **681**, 876, 944

restrict *vb.* 99, 231, 235, 403, 635, 681, 691

restrictions *n.* 700

result *n.* 44, 87, 156, 163, 460; *vb.* 85, 119, 156

resumé *n.* 527; *vb.* 589

resumption *n.* 77, 589

resurgence *n.* 589

resurrection *n.* 147, 165, 589, 972

resuscitate *vb.* 589, 618

retail *vb.* 727

retailer *n.* 727, 728

retain *vb.* 441, 707, 712

retaliate *vb.* 647, 912, 963

retaliation *n.* 395, **647**, 912

retard *vb.* 135, 281, 635

retarded *adj.* 435

retch *vb.* 303

retention *n.* 441, **712**

reticent *adj.* 466, 517, 681, 876

retinue *n.* 91

retire *vb.* 289, 293, 299, 687

retired *adj.* 118, 124, 687

retirement *n.* 89, 293, 687, 826

retiring *adj.* 517, 876, 885

retort *n.* 395, 647; *vb.* 395, 647

retrace *vb.* 441

retraction *n.* 538, 686

retreat *n.* 289, **293**, 299, 463, 595, 600, 885; *vb.* 289, 293, 556

retribution *n.* 647, 943, 963

retrieve *vb.* 589, 601, 705, 720, 721

retrograde *adj.* 289

return *n.* 147, 289, 298, 721; *vb.* 147, 163, 298, 589, 647, 721

reunion *n.* 47, 884

revalue *vb.* 745

reveal *vb.* 228, 262, 419, 456, 458, 462

revealed *adj.* 976

revealing *adj.* 228, 802

revel *vb.* 827, 838, 840

revelation *n.* 419, 420, 458, 462, 464, 974, **976**

revenge *n.* 647, **912**; *vb.* 647

revengeful *adj.* 908, 912

revenue *n.* 741

reverberate .*vb.* 283, 784

reverberation *n.* 283, 778

revere *vb.* 868, 922, 982

reverence *n.* 922, 980, 982

reverend *n.* 986

reversal *n.* 147, 220, 289, 538, 686

reverse *n.* 237, 239; *adj.* 14, 289; *vb.* 147, 220, 686

reversion *n.* 147, 220, 590

review *n.* 394, 415, 456, 524, 526; *vb.* 394, 415, 441, 472, 526

reviewer *n.* 456, 524, 526

revile *vb.* 853, 901, 928

revise *vb.* 142, 472, 587

revitalize *vb.* 589

revival *n.* 147, 165, 589

revive *vb.* 77, 165, 368, 441, 589, 618

revoke *vb.* 538, 686

revolt *n.* 148, 644, 672; *vb.* 148, 644, 672

revolting *adj.* 148, 771, 892

287

revolution n. 148, 323, 644, 672

revolve vb. 140, 323

revolver n. 657

revue n. 529

reward n. 663, 705, 909, 917, 965; vb. 738, 909, 965

reword vb. 77, 456, 498

rhetorical adj. 455, 509

rhetorician n. 514

rhombus n. 246

rhyme n. 528; vb. 528

rhythm n. 140, 510, 512, 528

rhythmical adj. 790

rib n. 842

ribbon n. 49, 207, 663, 846, 872

rich adj. 163, 168, 509, 664, 734, 770, 772, 790, 805

riches n. 664, 711, 734

rickshaw n. 276

rid vb. 634

riddle n. 466; vb. 264

ride n. 269; vb. 269

rider n. 41, 270

ridge n. 252, 357

ridicule n. 853, 924; vb. 788, 842, 853, 869, 924, 928

ridiculousness n. 433, 851

riding n. 269

rifle n. 657; vb. 722

rift n. 200, 642

rig vb. 568

right n. 240, 667, 915, 917, 929, 954, 956; adj. 240, 430, 915, 931, 954, 977

right angle n. 246

righteous adj. 915, 935

right-hand man n. 624, 640, 676, 689

right side n. 240

rigid adj. 334, 669, 946

rigorous adj. 392, 669, 864, 946

rigour n. 669

riled adj. 893, 894

rim n. 233, 250; vb. 233

rind n. 225

ring n. 250; vb. 231, 322, 460, 482, 784

ringing n. 778, 784; adj. 780, 784

riot n. 80, 672

ripe adj. 364

ripen vb. 659

ripple n. 325, 358, 781; vb. 251, 358, 783

rise n. 36, 41, 208, 316, 320; vb. 32, 34, 36, 88, 214, 252, 273, 316, 320

risk n. 553, 594; vb. 158, 553, 594, 604, 718, 857

risqué adj. 952

rite n. 988

ritual n. 16, 545, 988; adj. 988

rival n. 638, 883; vb. 28

rivalry n. 642, 913

river n. 358

riverside adj. 352

road n. 559

roamer n. 270

roaming n. 269

roar n. 780, 838; vb. 175, 359, 780, 789, 838, 893

roast vb. 306, 759

rob vb. 645, 722

robber n. 723

robbery n. 722

robe n. 225

robes n. 989

robot n. 565

robust adj. 143, 161, 337, 585

rock n. 152, 330, 352, 367, 792; vb. 325, 326

rocket n. 279; vb. 316

rod n. 677, 677, 964

rodent n. 373

rogue n. 480, 723, 906, 940

roguish adj. 477

role n. 529, 557

roll n. 83, 249, 306, 323, 325, 783; vb. 249, 323, 325, 358, 783

roller n. 197, 358

roman adj. 521

romance n. 449, 889

romantic adj. 752

roof n. 225; vb. 225

room n. 182, 678

roomy adj. 182, 204

roost vb. 319

root n. 39, 88, 155, 213, 306, 374, 494

rooted adj. 47

rope n. 49, 207, 964

roster n. 83

rosy adj. 585, 811

rot n. 53, 451, 592; vb. 53, 584, 588

rota n. 83, 140

rotary adj. 323

rotate vb. 323

rotation n. 140, 323

rotten adj. 53, 162, 580, 584, 588

rotund adj. 249

rough adj. 57, 175, 258, 887, 908

roughage n. 305

roughness n. 258

round n. 249, 649, 792; adj. 249, 250; vb. 249, 256

roundabout adj. 505, 561

rounded adj. 247, 249

round form n. 249

rouse vb. 611, 889

rousing adj. 547

rout n. 662

route n. 269, 559

routine n. 16, 79, 91,

140, 545; *adj.* 16, 140, 545
rove *vb.* 269
row *n.* 85, 202, 206, 642
rowdy *adj.* 780, 887
rowing *n.* 271
royal *adj.* 870
rub *vb.* 341, 342, 758
rubber *n.* 485
rubbish *n.* 451, 576
rub in *vb.* 468
ruby *adj.* 811
rude *adj.* 511, 849, 880, 887, 910, 923
rudiment *n.* 155
rudimentary *adj.* 88
rue *vb.* 833
ruffian *n.* 175, 906
ruffle *vb.* 82, 258, 260, 893
rug *n.* 225
rugged *adj.* 258
ruin *n.* 164, 551, 569, 588, 662, 739; *vb.* 164, 588, 628, 735
rule *n.* 103, 400, 522, 626, 667, 671, 954; *vb.* 415, 653, 667, 671
ruler *n.* 400, 675
rumble *vb.* 783
ruminate *vb.* 384
rumour *n.* 465
run *n.* 613; *vb.* 110, 172, 266, 280, 343, 345, 358, 622
run away *vb.* 293, 299, 896
runaway *n.* 555, 600
run down *vb.* 160, 853, 926, 928
run-down *n.* 460; *adj.* 586, 612, 617
rung *n.* 93
run in *vb.* 681
run into *vb.* 282
runner *n.* 270, 275, 467
running *n.* 172; *adj.* 91, 172, 343

runny *adj.* 51, 345, 358
run off with *vb.* 722, 896
run out *vb.* 89, 301
rupture *n.* 48; *vb.* 48
rural *adj.* 183, 378
ruse *n.* 478, 631
rush *n.* 280, 282, 358, 611, 613; *adj.* 603; *vb.* 280, 358, 359, 613, 645
russet *adj.* 810, 811
rust *n.* 167, 588, 592, 847; *adj.* 810, 811; *vb.* 53, 584
rustic *n.* 871; *adj.* 378, 871, 885
rustle *vb.* 781, 783, 786; *vb.* 781, 783, 786
rusty *adj.* 126, 810, 811
rut *n.* 261, 545
ruthless *adj.* 900

S

Sabbath *n.* 616
sabbatical *n.* 614; *adj.* 616
sable *adj.* 808
sabotage *n.* 164
saboteur *n.* 480
saccharin *n.* 772
sack *n.* 193, 303, 686; *vb.* 164, 303, 686, 722
sackcloth and ashes *n.* 941
sacred *adj.* 974
sacrifice *n.* 652, 715, 943; *vb.* 652, 693, 715
sacrilege *n.* 901, 981
sad *adj.* 828, 837, 839, 895
sadden *vb.* 837
saddle *n.* 217; *vb.* 330, 919
safari *n.* 269

safe *n.* 732; *adj.* 54, 593, 646
safe-blower *n.* 723
safeguard *n.* 595; *vb.* 593, 646
safekeeping *n.* 567, 593
safety *n.* 593
safety curtain *n.* 762
sag *vb.* 216, 319
saga *n.* 525
sage *n.* 428, 436
sail *vb.* 271
sailing *n.* 271, 299
sailing ship *n.* 277
sailor *n.* 272
saint *n.* 939, 977, 980
saintly *adj.* 935, 980
salacious *adj.* 952
salad days *n.* 129
salary *n.* 705, 731, 738, 741
sale *n.* 714, 727
salesman *n.* 727
sales talk *n.* 727
salient *adj.* 253, 458, 573
sallow *adj.* 806, 807, 813
sally *n.* 645, 842; *vb.* 645
salmon *n.* 811, 816
saloon *n.* 276
salt *n.* 307; *vb.* 307, 599
salt away *vb.* 567
salt of the earth *n.* 579, 939
salubrious *adj.* 585
salutation *n.* 518, 922
salute *n.* 878, 922; *vb.* 888
salvage *n.* 44, 589; *vb.* 589, 601
salve *n.* 342, 365, 591
same *adj.* 13, 16, 28
sample *vb.* 767
sanctify *vb.* 980
sanctimonious *adj.* 981

sanction *vb* 690, 925, 954

sanctity *n* 935, 980

sanctuary *n.* 595, 990

sand *n.* 352; *adj.* 813; *vb.* 257

sandbags *n.* 152, 330

sandbank *n.* 357, 596

sandwich *n.* 306

sane *adj.* 438

sanguine *adj.* 854

sanitation *n* 585

sanity *n.* 438, 585

sap *n.* 309; *vb* 162

sapling *n.* 374

sapphire *adj* 815

sarcasm *n.* 842, 853

sarcophagus *n.* 372

sash *n* 207

Satan *n.* 969

sated *adj.* 56, 865

satellite *n.* 60, 279, 329; *adj.* 679

satiety *n* 865

satire *n.* 455, 842, 853

satirist *n.* 842, 928

satisfaction *n.* (pacification) 652, 721, 943; (enjoyment) 827, 831

satisfactory *adj.* 570

satisfied *adj* 827, 831, 865

satisfy *vb* (of food) 304, 865; (enjoy) 829, 831

satisfying *adj* 306, 827, 943

saturation *n* 56, 349, 572, 865

sauce *n.* 307, 880

saunter *n* 269; *vb.* 135, 281

savage *n* 175; *adj* 175, 900, 908; *vb.* 588

save *vb.* 567, 601, 680, 748, 961

saving *n* 567, 599, 601, 748

Saviour *n* 967

savour *n.* 767; *vb.* 767, 770

savouriness *n.* 770

savoury *n* 306; *adj.* 770

saw *n.* 259; *vb.* 48, 787

say *vb* 460, 514

saying *n* 432, 498

scaffold *n.* 964

scald *vb.* 759, 761

scale *n.* 27, 206, 400; *vb.* 206, 316

scales *n.* 330, 400

scallywag *n.* 940

scalp *vb.* 228

scamp *n.* 940

scan *vb.* 472, 528, 818

scandal *n* 465, 516, 869, 928

scandalmonger *n.* 388, 460, 928

scandalous *adj.* 869, 936

scant *adj.* 76, 507

scanty *adj.* 33, 139, 571

scapegoat *n.* 149, 828, 943

scarce *adj* 139

scarcity *n.* 33, 76, 139, 571, 735

scare *n.* 598, 856; *vb.* 856, 902

scared *adj.* 856, 858

scarf *n.* 207

scarlet *adj* 811

scatter *vb* 82, 95, 297

scene *n.* 185, 186, 658

scenery *n* 185

scenic *adj.* 488

scent *n.* 483, 774, 776; *vb.* 774, 776

scented *adj.* 774, 776

sceptic *n.* 975

sceptical *adj.* 409, 421, 423, 975

sceptre *n.* 677

schedule *n* 83, 116, 558; *vb.* 83

scheme *n* 558, 602, 631; *vb.* 558, 631

schemer *n.* 558

schism *n.* 106, 642, 979

scholar *n* 428, 436, 474, 524, 629

scholarly *adj* 426, 472

scholarship *n.* 426, 472

school *n.* 94, 475; *vb.* 470

schoolchild *n.* 131, 428, 474

schooling *n.* 470

school-teacher *n* 473

scientist *n.* 396, 428, 448

scintillate *vb.* 797, 842

scintillating *adj.* 509

scissors *n.* 255

scoff *n.* 924; *vb* 853, 928

scoffer *n.* 928, 981

scold *vb* 926

scoop *n.* 312, 465

scooter *n.* 276

scope *n.* 182, 557, 558, 678, 956

scorch *vb.* 350, 759, 761

scorcher *n.* 759

score *n.* 70, 737; *vb.* 38, 482, 792

scorn *n.* 853, 892, 924; *vb.* 644, 694, 923, 924

scornful *adj.* 923, 924

scoundrel *n.* 940

scour *vb.* 341, 583

scourge *n.* 592, 665, 964; *vb.* 963

scout *n.* 86, 593, 683

scowl *n.* 895; *vb* 245, 895

scraggy *adj.* 205, 246

scram *vb.* 299

scramble *n.* 613; *vb.* 45, 306, 316

scrap *n.* 55, 649; *vb* 607, 649

scrapbook *n* 441

scrape *n.* 633; *vb.* 257, 341

scrape out *vb.* 210

scrape through *vb.* 666

scrappy *adj.* 57

scratch *adj.* 628; *vb.* 482, 758

scratch the surface *vb.* 211

scratchy *adj.* 787

scrawl *n.* 521; *vb.* 521

scream *n.* 788; *vb.* 787, 788

screech *vb.* 787, 788, 789

screen *n.* 461, 595, 801; *vb.* 461, 593, 646, 801

screw *n.* 49, 251

scribble *n.* 441, 521; *vb.* 521

scribe *n.* 484, 521, 981

script *n.* 521

Scripture *n.* 976

scroll *n.* 251, 483, 521

scrounger *n.* 697

scrub *vb.* 341, 583

scrumptious *adj.* 306, 770

scruple *n.* 533, 833

scrupulous *adj.* 392, 702, 864, 931

scrutinize *vb.* 390, 394, 396, 818

scrutiny *n.* 394, 818

sculptor *n.* 491

sculpture *n.* 486, 489; *vb.* 489

scum *n.* 44, 871

scurrilous *adj.* 901

scurry *n.* 613; *vb* 613

scythe *vb* 378

sea *n.* 351

seaboard *n.* 352

seafaring *n.* 271

sea-food *n.* 306

seagoing *adj.* 277

seal *n.* 482; *vb.* 265, 408, 424, 461, 482

sealed book *n.* 427, 453

seam *n.* 49, 206

seaman *n.* 272

séance *n.* 984

sear *vb.* 754

search *vb.* 394, 396, 554

searching *adj.* 388

searchlight *n.* 800

seared conscience *n.* 942

seaside *n.* 352; *adj.* 352

season *n.* 107, 109; *vb.* 307, 545, 599

seasoned *adj.* 130, 545, 602

seat *n.* 186, 217

secede *vb.* 289, 425, 556

secession *n.* 425, 979

secluded *adj.* 466, 885

seclusion *n.* 461, 824, 885

second *n.* 109, 115; *adj.* 62

secondary *adj.* 35

secondhand *adj.* 126, 606

second nature *n.* 545

second-rate *adj.* 580

second thoughts *n.* 87, 538

secrecy *n.* 459

secret *n.* 466; *adj.* 427, 461, 466

secret agent *n.* 460

secretary *n.* 484, 521, 623

secrete *vb.* 301, 310, 461

secretive *adj.* 466, 517, 876

sect *n.* 641, 979

sectarian *n.* 979; *adj.* 641, 979

sectarianism *n.* 979

section *n.* 55, 73, 97, 183, 717

sectional *adj.* 73

sector *n.* 55, 183

secular *adj.* 975, 987

secure *adj.* 47, 161, 593; *vb.* 47, 152, 408, 646, 705, 712

security *n.* 593, 646, 701

sedateness *n.* 757, 837

sedative *n.* 591

sedentary *adj.* 319

sediment *n.* 44

seditious *adj.* 148

seducer *n.* 953

seduction *n.* 952

seductive *adj.* 829

see *vb.* 419, 426, 818, 882

see ahead *vb.* 446

seed *n.* 155, 306, 374; *vb.* 95, 378

see double *vb.* 820, 950

seedy *adj.* 586

see fit *vb.* 530

see it through *vb.* 535

seek *vb.* 388, 394, 554, 604, 982

seem *vb.* 18, 621, 825

seeming *adj.* 406, 825

seemly *adj.* 510, 577, 848

seep *vb.* 301, 319, 349, 358

seer *n.* 447, 449

see-saw *n.* 325; *vb.* 325

seethe *vb.* 175, 759, 893

see through *vb.* 659, 802

segment *n.* 55, 73

segregate *vb.* 99, 540

segregation *n.* 48, 99

seismic *adj.* 325

seize *vb.* 326, 705, 720, 722

seizure *n.* 326, 586, 720

seldom *adv.* 139

select *adj* 579; *vb.* 398, 540, 557

selection *n.* 398, 527, 540

selective *adj.* 398, 540, 864

self *n.* 382

self-abasement *n.* 874

self-assurance *n.* 757, 873

self-centred *adj.* 875, 934

self-control *n.* 534, 681, 757, 944

self-deception *n.* 478

self-denial *n.* 933, 944

self-destruction *n.* 370

self-determination *n.* 678

self-discipline *n.* 681, 944

self-effacing *adj.* 874, 933

self-esteem *n.* 873

self-evident *adj.* 408, 458

self-forgetful *adj.* 933

self-glory *n.* 879

self-important *adj.* 875

self-improvement *n.* 472

self-indulgent *adj.* 827, 934, 945

self-instruction *n.* 472

self-interest *n.* 934

selfishness *n.* 904, 934

selfless *adj.* 933

self-love *n.* 873

self-made *adj.* 472

self-portrait *n.* 488

self-possessed *adj.* 392, 438, 757

self-regard *n.* 873

self-reliance *n.* 534, 857

self-respect *n.* 873

self-sacrifice *n.* 933

selfsameness *n.* 13

self-satisfied *adj.* 831, 873

self-seeking *n.* 934; *adj.* 934

self-styled *adj.* 497

self-taught *adj.* 472

sell *vb.* 464, 714, 727

sell-out *n.* 727, 932

semantic *adj.* 450

semantics *n.* 492

semaphore *n.* 467

semblance *n.* 22, 236

semi- *adj.* 63

semiliquidity *n.* **362**

seminar *n.* 519

seminary *n.* 475

semitransparency *n.* **804**

senator *n.* 625

send *vb.* 268, 523

send for *vb.* 671

send forth *vb.* 301, 464

send-off *n.* 299

send up *vb.* 20

senility *n.* 126, 130

senior *n.* 34, 132; *adj.* 130

sensation *n.* 465, 752, 866

sensational *adj.* 755, 866, 877

sense *n.* 398, 411, 434, 450, 752; *vb.* 382, 411, 452, 752

senseless *adj.* 433, 451

sense of duty *n.* 919

sense of hearing *n.* 795

sense of smell *n.* 774

sensibility *n.* 753

sensible *adj.* 434, 575, 753

sensitive *adj.* 398, 716, 753, 756, 828, 894

sensitivity *n.* 398, 752, 753, 894

sensory *adj.* 753

sensual *adj.* 945, 952

sensuality *n.* 827, 945, 952

sentence *n.* 498, 960; *vb* 960, 962, 963

sententious *adj.* 504

sentient *adj.* 753

sentiment *n.* 411, 420, 752, 889

sentimental *adj.* 752, 889

sentry *n.* 593, 646

separability *n.* 48, 51

separate *vb.* 48, 55, 95, 398, 540, 898

separation *n.* 48, 898

separatism *n.* 979

separatist *n.* 106, 425; *adj.* 979

sepia *adj.* 810

septet *n.* 70

sepulchre *n.* 372

sequel *n.* 87, 119, 156

sequence *n.* 85, 91

seraph *n.* 968

serenity *n.* 267, 757, 827, 831

serf *n.* 378, 676, 871

serfdom *n.* 679

serial *adj.* 85, 91, 140

serial position *n.* 93

series *n.* 85

serious *adj.* 534, 573, 594, **837**, 982

seriousness *n.* 573, **837**

sermon *n.* 470, 518

serrate *vb.* 246, 258, 259

servant *n.* 35, **676**

serve *vb.* 636, 676, 679

serve as *vb.* 486

service *n.* 550, 575, 679, 982, 988

service of worship *n.* 988

services *n.* 655

servility *n.* 679, **881**

serving *n.* 717

session *n.* 957

set *n.* 94, 474, 850; *adj.* 152, 185, 235; *vb.* 47, 81, 152, 186, 235, 332, 334

set about *vb.* 88, 605

set apart *vb.* 48, 398

setback n. 445, 635
set fire to vb. 761
set forth vb. 456, 460, 525
set free adj. 961; vb. 48, 961
set great store by vb. 573
set in motion vb. 88, 266, 282
set in order vb. 81
set no store by vb. 421
set off vb. 782, 805, 846
set one's heart on vb. 861
set one's teeth on edge vb. 773, 787
set out vb. 299, 458
set sail vb. 271
setting n. 8, 185, 229, 792
settle vb. 186, 191, 319, 408, 413, 652, 659, 699, 738
settle down vb. 191
settlement n. 699, 704, 738
settler n. 190
settle up vb. 647
set to vb. 605, 649
set up vb. 186, 522
seven n. 70; adj. 70
sever vb. 42, 48
several adj. 75
severe adj. 175, 508, 669, 828, 908, 946
severity n. 508, 669, 900
sew vb. 221, 589
sewer n. 360
sex-appeal n. 889
sextet n. 70
sexuality n. 827
sexy adj. 952
shabby adj. 580, 869
shackle n. 681; vb. 635
shade n. 225, 463, 595, 798, 801; vb. 799, 801

shadow n. 4, 328, 798; vb. 287, 554
shadowy adj. 4, 328, 798, 799, 824
shady adj. 631, 798, 801, 869, 932
shaft n. 213, 254, 361, 797
shake vb. 45, 51, 326, 756, 856
shake hands vb. 408, 652, 699, 886
shake off vb. 680
shake-up n. 148
shaky adj. 141, 326, 338, 594
shallow adj. 211, 435, 507, 852
shallowness n. 211, 383, 427, 435
sham n. 20, 852; adj. 20, 431, 478; vb. 477, 852
shambles n. 80
shame n. 869, 874; vb. 874
shameful adj. 869, 924
shameless adj. 887
shampoo n. 583
shanty n. 191
shape n. 242, 339, 825; vb. 489
shapeless adj. 243
shapely adj. 244, 844
share n. 55, 305, 709, 717; vb. 55, 639, 709, 988
shareholder n. 709
share out vb. 717
sharing n. 709, 717
shark n. 718
sharp adj. 255, 434, 769, 773, 787, 791, 828
sharpen vb. 255
sharpness n. 255, 434, 769, 773
sharp practice n. 478
shatter vb. 164, 338

shattering adj. 148, 164
shave vb. 203, 257
shaving n. 228
shear vb. 203, 377
shears n. 255
sheath n. 225
shed vb. 95, 228, 319, 556
shed light on vb. 797
sheep n. 20
sheer adj. 46, 214
sheet n. 206, 225, 522
shelf n. 217
shell n. 23, 225, 290, 885; vb. 228
shellac n. 365
shelter n. 191, 225, 463, 595, 801; vb. 225, 461, 593, 646, 801
shelve vb. 135
Sheol n. 973
shepherd n. 377, 986
shield n. 595, 801; vb. 225, 593, 646, 801
shift n. 149, 187, 268; vb. 142, 149, 151, 187, 268, 285
shifty adj. 478, 631
shilly-shally vb. 135, 536, 612
shimmer n. 797; vb. 797
shine n. 797; vb. 257, 341, 797
shine at vb. 627
ship n. 277; vb. 192, 268
shipment n. 268
shipper n. 728
shirk vb. 533, 555, 920
shirker n. 555, 858
shirty adj. 893, 894
shiver vb. 326, 760
shoal n. 94, 211
shock n. 282, 444, 828; vb. 856, 892
shockable adj. 951
shocked adj. 856, 926

shocking *adj.* 830, 845, 869, 936

shoddy *adj.* 580, 849, 869

shoot *n.* 374; *vb.* 290, 370, 645, 963

shooting star *n.* 329, 800

shop *n.* 620, 730

shop assistant *n.* 727

shop-lifter *n.* 723

shop-lifting *n.* 722

shopper *n.* 726

shopping *n.* 726

shopping centre *n.* 730

shopping spree *n.* 749

shore *n.* 352; *vb.* 217

short *adj.* 57, 113, 203, 315, 504

shortage *n.* 57, 315

shortcoming *n.* 29, 35, 43, 57, 315, 662

short duration *n.* 113

shorten *vb.* 37, 42, 197, 203, 504, 527

shortfall *n.* 57, 315

shorthand *n.* 521

short-lived *adj.* 113

shortness *n.* 33, 195, 203

short-sighted *adj.* 416, 435, 820

short-sightedness *n.* 435, 820

short-tempered *adj.* 894

short-term *adj.* 113

shot *n.* 173, 290, 782

shoulder *n.* 238; *vb.* 217, 605, 636

shout *n.* 482, 597, 782, 788; *vb.* 482, 788

shout down *vb* 425, 788, 887

shove *n.* 282; *vb.* 282, 290

show *n.*
(manifestation) 458;
(drama) 529; (vanity)

852, 875; *vb.* (be visible) 458, 802, 823, 825; (demonstrate) 413; (indicate) 482

show-down *n.* 462

shower *n.* 358; *vb.* 349, 358

show-jumper *n.* 270

show-jumping *n.* 269

showman *n.* 877

showmanship *n.* 529, 877

show off *vb.* 419, 875, 877, 879

show-off *n.* 875, 877

show one's colours *vb.* 462

showpiece *n.* 458, 581, 844

show through *vb.* 802, 823

show up *vb.* 188, 298, 414, 825, 869

show willing *vb.* 532

showy *adj.* 509, 852, 875, 877

shred *n.* 33, 207

shrewd *adj.* 434, 631

shrewd idea *n.* 448

shrewdness *n.* 398, 434, 631

shriek *n.* 787, 788

shrill *adj.* 333, 787; *vb.* 787

shrine *n.* 483, 990

shrink *vb.* 37, 197, 205, 283, 533, 555, 856, 858

shrivel *vb.* 197, 350, 588

shroud *vb.* 461

shrub *n.* 374

shrug off *vb.* 921

shudder *vb.* 326, 760, 856

shuffle *vb.* 82, 149, 281, 756

shun *vb.* 555, 694, 924

shut *vb.* 263

shut down *vb.* 144

shut-eye *n.* 612

shut in *vb.* 234

shut oneself up *vb* 885

shut out *vb.* 691

shutter *n.* 801

shuttle *n.* 278, 325; *vb* 268

shut up *vb.* 144, 234, 681

shy *adj.* 856, 858, 876, 885

shy away *vb.* 533

shyness *n.* 858, 876, 885

sibilant *adj.* 786

sick *adj.* 369, 586

sicken *vb.* 162, 586

sickly *adj.* 812

sickness *n.* 303, 586, 828

side *n.* 11, 233, 238

side by side *adv.* 238

sidedness *n.* 238

side-splitting *adj.* 851

sideways *adj* 219, 238; *adv.* 238

side with *vb.* 641

sidle up to *vb.* 292

siege *n.* 645

siesta *n.* 612

sieve *n.* 264

sift *vb.* 46, 415, 540

sigh *n.* 359, 781

sight *n.* 753, 818

sightly *adj.* 844

sightseeing *n.* 269

sightseer *n.* 270, 821

sign *n.* 401, 447, 458, 482, 597; *vb.* 424, 482, 699, 701, 714, 726

signal *n.* 482; *vb.* 482

signatory *n* 424

signature *n.* 482, 496

significance *n.* 450, 456, 573

significant *adj.* 136, 450, 573

signify *vb.* 450, 482

sign of authority *n.* 677

signpost *vb* 284

silence *n.* 267, 513, 517, 779; *vb.* 414, 513, 779

silent *adj.* 513, 517, 779, 895

silhouette *n.* 232, 488; *vb.* 488

silky *adj.* 257

silly *adj.* 433, 435

silver-haired *adj.* 809

silvery *adj.* 807

similarity *n.* **18**, 105, 218, 397

simile *n.* 397, 455

simmer *vb.* 306

simmer down *vb.* 757

simple *adj.* (not mixed) 46; (gullible) 422, 632, 937, 951; (foolish) 427, 435; (easy to understand) 452, 502, 508; (easy) 634

simple circularity *n.* 250

simple-minded *adj.* 435, 632

simpleton *n.* 429, 437, 479

simplify *vb.* 46, 53, 456

simulate *vb.* 20, 477, 852

simultaneous *adj.* 60, 122

sin *n.* 431, 672, 703, 938; *vb.* 672, 981

sincere *adj.* 430, 476, 931

sine qua non *n.* 60, 700

sinew *n.* 207

sinful *adj.* 916, 936, 938, 952, 975, 981

sing *vb.* 528, 789, 792, 982

singer *n.* 793

single *adj.* 54, 59, 139, 897

single-minded *adj.* 534, 980

single out *vb.* 102

singular *adj.* 59

sinister *adj.* 665

sinistral *n.* 241

sink *vb* 209, 210, 317, 319, 321, 588

sink back *vb.* 590

sinker *n.* 330

sinless *adj.* 951

sinner *n.* 906, 940, 981

sinuate *vb.* 251

sip *n.* 309; *vb.* 767

siphon *n.* 360

sir *n.* 380

siren *n.* 116, 482, 598, 970

sirupy *adj.* 772

sister *n.* 11, 986

sit *vb.* 23, 185

sit down *vb.* 319

site *n.* 185, 186

sit-in *n.* 144, 696

sit on *vb.* 466, 679

sit on the fence *vb.* 409, 541

sit pretty *vb.* 831

sitting *n.* 984

sitting duck *n.* 479

situation *n.* 8, 93, 153, 185, 229, 557

six *n.* 70; *adj.* 70

sixth sense *n.* 411, 753

size *n.* 26, 27, 32, **194**, 362, 400

size up *vb.* 415

sizzle *vb.* 306, 759, 786

skeleton *n.* 232, 371, 527

sketch *n.* 232, 486, 488, 525, 558; *vb.* 232, 488, 525, 558

sketchy *adj.* 57

skew *adj.* 219

skewer *vb.* 264

skilful *adj.* 627

skill *n.* 159, 426, 501, 627

skilled *adj.* 579, 602

skilled worker *n.* 619, 629

skim *vb.* 211, 257

skimp *vb.* 393, 750

skimpy *adj.* 57

skin *n.* 225; *vb.* 228

skinny *adj.* 205

skip *vb.* 320, 393

skirmish *n.* 645, 649

skirt *n.* 233; *vb.* 233, 238

skunk *n.* 777

sky *n.* 329, 348, 815

skyjacking *n.* 722

skyline *n.* 198

skyscraper *n.* 191, 208

slab *n.* 206

slack *adj.* 391, 612, 668, 920, 952

slacken *vb.* 281

slacker *n.* 858

slag *n.* 44

slam *vb.* 782, 926

slander *n.* 869, 928; *vb.* 928, 930

slanderer *n.* 928

slang *n.* 494, 495; *adj.* 495

slant *vb.* 219

slap *n.* 782, 963; *vb.* 282, 782, 963

slap in the face *n.* 694, 923

slapstick *n.* 529

slash *vb.* 203

slate *n.* 206

slaughter *n.* 164, 370, 963; *vb.* 370, 963

slave *n.* 35, 619, 676

slavery *n.* 679

slavish *adj.* 881

slay *vb.* 370

sleek *adj.* 257

sleep *n.* 612; *vb.* 612

sleep around *vb.* 952

sleep together *vb.* 889

sleep with *vb.* 889

sleepy *adj.* 612, 617

sleet *n.* 760
sleight of hand *n.* 478
slender *adj.* 33, 205
slice *n.* 55, 305, 717
slide *n.* 219, 486; *vb.* 257, 588
slide-rule *n.* 400
slight *n.* 869, 923, 924; *adj.* 33, 195, 203, 571; *vb.* 418, 923, 928
slim *adj.* 33, 205; *vb.* 205, 947
slime *n.* 584
slimy *adj.* 362
slink *vb.* 461
slip *n.* 431, 500, 522, 741, 938
slip back *vb.* 590
slippery *adj.* 51, 257, 594, 631
slipshod *adj.* 393, 500
slip-up *n.* 431
slit *n.* 261, 262; *vb.* 48, 264
sliver *n.* 55
slogan *n.* 432, 494, 498
slog away *vb.* 535, 615
slope *n.* 208, 219; *vb.* 219
sloppy *adj.* 584
slot *n.* 261, 262; *vb.* 261
slothful *adj.* 612
slough *n.* 355
slovenly *adj.* 500, 584, 920
slow *adj.* 174, **281**, 435; *vb.* 281, 616
slowcoach *n.* 281
slowness *n.* 135, **281**, 435, 843
sluggard *n.* 612
sluggish *adj.* 174, 281, 612, 843
slum *n.* 845
slumber *vb.* 174, 612
slump *n.* 169, 317; *vb.* 317, 588

slur *n.* 869, 928, 930; *vb.* 515, 928, 930
slush *n.* 760
slushy *adj.* 355, 362
slut *n.* 953
sly *adj.* 461, 631, 932
smack *vb.* 282, 782
smack one's lips *vb.* 767
small *adj.* 33, 195, 203, 331
small arms *n.* 657
small change *n.* 731
smallholding *n.* 378
smallness *n.* 33, 195
small talk *n.* 516
smarmy *adj.* 927
smart *adj.* 125, 631; *vb.* 828
smart aleck *n.* 875
smash *vb.* 164, 282, 645
smash-and-grab-raid *n.* 722
smash hit *n.* 661
smash-up *n.* 282
smattering *n.* 76, 427
smear *n.* 584, 928, 930; *vb.* 342, 847, 869, 928
smell *n.* 753, 774, 777; *vb.* 774, 776, 777
smell out *vb.* 394, 554, 774
smelly *adj.* 777
smelt *vb.* 761
smile *n.* 838, 886; *vb.* 838, 886
smirch *n.* 847; *vb.* 847
smirk *n.* 838; *vb.* 838
smite *vb.* 282
smitten *adj.* 889
smog *n.* 363
smoke *n.* 344, 346, 803; *vb.* 308, 346, 599, 759, 803
smoke-signal *n.* 467
smoking *adj.* 759
smoky *adj.* 803, 809
smooth *adj.* 228, **257**,

335, 364, 477, 631, 927; *vb.* 16, 215, **257**, 341, 758
smoothness *n.* 257
smother *vb.* 513, 759, 762
smoulder *vb.* 759
smudge *vb.* 584, 847
smuggle *vb.* 722
smuggled *adj.* 955
smuggler *n.* 723
smut *n.* 952
snack *n.* 306
snack bar *n.* 191
snag *n.* 582, 635
snail *n.* 281
snake in the grass *n.* 459, 596
snake-like *adj.* 251
snap *vb.* 338, 782, 789, 893
snap out of it *vb.* 836
snapshot *n.* 486
snare *n.* 463, 596
snarl *vb.* 789
snatch *vb.* 720
sneak *n.* 858; *vb.* 461
sneer *n.* 895, 924, 926; *vb.* 696, 853, 895, 924, 926
sneeze *vb.* 359, 786
sniff *vb.* 774
sniff out *vb.* 394, 554
snigger *n.* 838; *vb.* 838
snip *vb.* 48
sniper *n.* 645
snivel *vb.* 839
snobbish *adj.* 875, 924
snoop *n.* 388, 460, 821; *vb.* 388, 394
snooty *adj.* 875, 924
snooze *n.* 612; *vb.* 612
snort *vb.* 789
snow *n.* 760; *vb.* 807
snowball *n.* 36; *vb.* 36
snowdrift *n.* 760
snowflake *n.* 760
snowstorm *n.* 760

snub *n.* 295, 694, 923; *vb.* 887, 923, 926

snuff *n.* 308; *vb.* 762

snug *adj.* 827

snuggle *vb.* 890

soak *vb.* 56, 349

soak up *vb.* 350

so-and-so *n.* 497

soapy *adj.* 363

soar *vb.* 32, 208, 273, 316

sob *n.* 839; *vb.* 788, 839

sober *adj.* 837, 848, 944, 949

soberness *n.* 848, 949

so-called *adj.* 497

sociability *n.* 882, 884

social *n.* 884; *adj.* 379

social conscience *n.* 903

socialism *n.* 709

social services *n.* 903

society *n.* 379, 641, 850, 870

sociology *n.* 379

socket *n.* 184

sod *n.* 374

sodden *adj.* 349

sodomy *n.* 952

soft *adj.* 257, 331, 335, 670, 781, 805, 889

soft drink *n.* 309

soften *vb.* 267, 335, 513, 652, 834

soft-hearted *adj.* 670, 907

softness *n.* 335, 364, 670, 778, 781

soft nothings *n.* 890

soft soap *n.* 927

sog *vb.* 349

soggy *adj.* 364

soi-disant adj. 497

soil *n.* 352, 378; *vb.* 584, 847

soirée *n.* 884

sojourn *n.* 269; *vb.* 191

solace *n.* 831, 907

solar *adj.* 329

solar energy *n.* 159, 765

solder *vb.* 50

soldier *n.* 655

soldier on *vb.* 535

sole *n.* 59

solecism *n.* 412, 500

solemn *adj.* 468, 573, 837, 982

solicit *vb.* 695

solicitor *n.* 959

solicitous *adj.* 392

solid *n.* 3, 332; *adj.* 3, 50, 161, 332, 334, 337

solidarity *n.* 50, 639

solidify *vb.* 332, 334

solidity *n.* 3, 152, 204, 332, 334

soliloquize *vb.* 520

soliloquy *n.* 520

solitary *adj.* 885

solitude *n.* 59, 461

solo *n.* 792

soloist *n.* 793

soluble *adj.* 345

solution *n.* 343

solve *vb.* 157, 456

solvent *n.* 343, 345

sombre *adj.* 798, 809, 895

some *adj.* 26, 72

somebody *n.* 868

somersault *n.* 220; *vb.* 220

something *n.* 327

sometime *adj.* 124, 687; *adv.* 121

sometimes *adv.* 138

somnolence *n.* 612, 617

son *n.* 171

sonata *n.* 792

song *n.* 528, 792, 982

sonnet *n.* 528

sonorous *adj.* 778

soothe *vb.* 176, 591, 834

soothing *adj.* 589, 790, 834

soothsayer *n.* 447, 984

sooty *adj.* 584, 808

sophism *n.* 412

sophisticated *n.* 848; *adj.* 423, 848

sophistry *n.* 412

soporofic *adj.* 841

sorcery *n.* 984

sore *n.* 588; *adj.* 753, 828, 893

sore point *n.* 893

sorrow *n.* 828, 830, 833, 837, 839, 941; *vb.* 837, 839

sorry *adj.* 833, 907, 941

sort *n.* 97; *vb.* 97, 540

sortie *n.* 645; *vb.* 645

SOS *n.* 598

soul *n.* 223, 368, 382, 751

sound *n.* 353, 512, 778, 795; *adj.* 410, 438, 581, 585, 977; *vb.* 512, 778

sounding board *n.* 396

sound out *vb.* 396

soundproof *adj.* 779

soup *n.* 306

soupçon *n.* 33

sour *adj.* 769, 773, 895

source *n.* 88, 155

source of light *n.* 800

sourness *n.* 773, 895

souvenir *n.* 441, 483

sovereign *n.* 675; *adj.* 667

sow *n.* 381; *vb.* 95, 378

space *n.* 182, 198, 200, 202, 329

space-age *adj.* 125

spaceman *n.* 274

spaceship *n.* 279

space travel *n.* 274

space traveller *n.* 274

spacious *adj.* 32, 182, 204

spade *vb.* 254

spadework *n.* 602

span *n.* 109, 182, 202; *vb.* 47, 182, 313

spank *vb.* 963

spanner in the works *n.* 580, 635

spare *adj.* 44, 607; *vb.* 670, 907

spare time *n.* 614

sparing *adj.* 748, 750, 944

spark *n.* 797

sparkle *n.* 506, 759, 797, 836; *vb.* 326, 797, 842

sparse *adj.* 33, 76, 139, 333

spasm *n.* 141, 326, 586, 828

spasmodic *adj.* 92, 141

spatial *adj.* 182

spatter *vb.* 817

spay *vb.* 160, 169

speak *vb.* 460, 512, 514, 788

speak against *vb.* 25, 696

speaker *n.* 514

speak for itself *vb.* 401

speak one's mind *vb.* 476, 632

speak out *vb.* 468

speak out against *vb.* 832

speak volumes *vb.* 401

spear *n.* 264

special *adj.* 59, 102

specialist *n.* 629

speciality *n.* 102, 557

specialize *vb.* 472, 609

species *n.* 97

specific *adj.* 5, 59, 102

specification *n.* 97, 525

specifications *n.* 102, 700

specify *vb.* 102, 482, 496, 525

specimen *n.* 458

specious *adj.* 412, 549, 825

speck *n.* 33, 847

speckle *vb.* 817

spectacle *n.* 529, 825, 866

spectacles *n.* 822

spectacular *adj.* 529, 877

spectator *n.* **821**

spectre *n.* 971

spectrum *n.* 805, 817

speculation *n.* 396, 448, 553

speculator *n.* 396, 448, 553, 728

speech *n.* 492, 512, 514, 518

speech defect *n.* 515

speechless *adj.* 513, 866

speech-making *n.* 518

speed *n.* 27, 266, 280, 400; *vb.* 280

speed up *vb.* 280, 613

speedy *adj.* 134, 280, 613

spell *n.* 109, 586, 984; *vb.* 450, 493

spell-binder *n.* 984

spellbound *adj.* 866

spelling *n.* 493

spell out *vb.* 456

spend *vb.* 575, 715, 738, 740

spendthrift *n.* 749; *adj.* 569

spend time *vb.* 107

spew *vb.* 303, 358

sphere *n.* 249, 329, 658

spice *n.* 776; *vb.* 307, 599

spick and span *adj.* 583

spicy *adj.* 769, 776, 952

spike *n.* 255; *vb.* 264

spill *n.* 800; *vb.* 319, 358

spin *n.* 269, 323; *vb.* 221, 273, 323

spine *n.* 255

spineless *adj.* 160, 162

spinney *n.* 374

spin-off *n.* 87, 156

spin out *vb.* 202

spinster *n.* 897

spiral *n.* 251, 322, 323; *adj.* 251; *vb.* 323

spire *n.* 208, 212

spirit *n.* 4, 368, 382, 506, 611, 751, 966, 968, 969

spirited *adj.* 280, 368

spiritism *n.* 984

spiritless *adj.* 757

spiritual *adj.* 4, 328, 382, 966, 974, 980

spiritualist *n.* 984

spirituality *n.* 328, 980

spit *n.* 253; *vb.* 306, 358

spiteful *adj.* 900, 912

splash *n.* 786; *vb.* 349, 358, 786

splash down *vb.* 274, 317, 321

spleen *n.* 895

splendid *adj.* 579, 844

splendour *n.* 797, 844, 877

splice *n.* 49; *vb.* 47, 896

splint *n.* 217

splinter *n.* 55; *vb.* 338

splinter-group *n.* 641

split *n.* 642, 717, 979; *adj.* 48; *vb.* 48, 63, 200, 338

split hairs *vb.* 864

spoil *n.* 663, 724; *vb.* 588, 628, 635, 847

spoilsport *n.* 548

spoke *n.* 297

spokesman *n.* 460, 467, 514, 689

sponge *n.* 264, 364, 485; *vb.* 349, 583

sponger *n.* 612, 697, 881

spongy *adj.* 264, 335, 364

sponsor *vb.* 636

spontaneity *n.* 531, 544

spontaneous *adj.* 115, 131, 411, 544

standpoint *n.* 284, 818
standstill *n.* 144, 267
stand together *vb.* 639
stand up *vb.* 318
stand up for *vb.* 217
stand up to *vb.* 648
stanza *n.* 528
star *n.* 329, 529, 684, 800, 868
starboard *n.* 240
starch *n.* 306; *vb.* 334, 583
stare *vb.* 818, 866
starless *adj.* 798
start *n.* 34, **88**, 298, 444; *vb.* **88**, 282, 605
startle *vb.* 444, 856
start out *vb.* 299
starve *vb.* 205, 735, 861, 947
stash away *vb.* 567
state *n.* 7, 183, 379; *adj.* 379; *vb.* **468**, 498, 525
statehood *n.* 379
stately *adj.* 32, 873
statement *n.* 83, 401 **468**, 483, 525, 742
statesman *n.* 625
station *n.* 7, 93, 185, 186, 620, 868
stationary *adj.* 152
statistics *n.* 38, 460
statue *n.* 483, 489, 983
stature *n.* 208
status *n.* 7, 93, 868
status quo *n.* 143
statute *n.* 626, 954
statutory *adj.* 954
staunch *adj.* 882
stay *n.* 135, 213, 217, 884; *vb.* (of time) 112, 135, 143, 145; (dwell) 191; (support) 217; (resist) 648
stay-at-home *n.* 885; *adj.* 612
stay away *vb.* 189

staying power *n.* 535, 857
stay up *vb.* 135
steadfast *adj.* 112, 143, 152, 534, 535
steady *n.* 889; *adj.* 16, 140, 143, 145, 152, 534, 535; *vb.* 152
steal *vb.* 461, 720, 722
stealing *n.* **722**
stealthy *adj.* 461
steam *n.* 159, 344, 347; *vb.* 306, 346
steam engine *n.* 276
steamer *n.* 277
steep *adj.* 214, 745; *vb.* 349
steeple *n.* 208
steer *vb.* 271, 284, 622
steer clear of *vb.* 555, 924
stem *n* 374
stench *n.* 774, 777
stenography *n.* 521
step *n.* 269, 400, 602, 609; *vb.* 269
step by step *adv.* 27
step down *vb.* 687
step in *vb.* 300
stepmotherly *adj.* 900
step on it *vb.* 280, 613
steppe *n.* 356
steps *n.* 316, 559
stereogram *n.* 794
stereo-recorder *n.* 484
stereotyped *adj.* 16, 152, 545, 843
sterile *adj.* 160, 169
sterilization *n.* 169, 583
stern *adj.* 669, 837, 946
stew *n.* 756; *vb.* 306
steward *n.* 623, 676, 733; *vb.* 622, 748
stewardship *n.* 392, 622, 748
stick *n.* 964; *vb.* 47, 50, 264
stick by *vb.* 217

stick-in-the-mud *n.* 143
stick it out *vb.* 535, 648, 757
stickler *n.* 537, 864
stick one's heels in *vb.* 648
stick one's neck out *vb.* 859
stick out *vb.* 253, 823
stick out for *vb.* 535
stick to *vb.* 712
stick together *vb.* 639
stick to one's guns *vb.* 534, 537, 648
stick-up *n.* 722
stick up for *vb.* 217
sticky *adj.* 50, 362, 759, 772
stiff *n.* 371; *adj.* 334, 337, 511, 745
stiffen *vb.* 332, 334, 337
stiff-necked *adj.* 537
stiff upper lip *n.* 535, 836
stifle *vb.* 466, 548, 762, 779, 785
stifled *adj.* 781
stifling *adj.* 759
stigma *n.* 847, 869
still *adj.* 174, 257, 267, 612, 779; *vb.* 176, 267, 513, 652, 779
still-life *n.* 488
stilt *n.* 217
stilted *adj.* 511
stimulant *n.* 173, 591
stimulate *vb.* 173, 547, 618, 755, 829
stimulus *n.* 173, 547
sting *n.* 255, 828; *vb.* 255, 758, 828
stinginess *n.* 748, 750
stink *n.* 777; *vb.* 777
stint *n.* 109; *vb.* 750
stipend *n.* 636, 738
stipendiary *n.* 958
stipple *vb.* 817
stipulate *vb.* 699, 700

strong *adj.* 32, 159, **161**, 173, 337, 506, 534, 585, 769, 774

stronghold *n.* 595, 646

strong point *n.* 627

strongroom *n.* 732

strong-smelling *adj* 777

strong-willed *adj.* 534

structure *n* 5, 47, 163, 242, 339

struggle *n.* 649; *vb.* 615, 642, 649

strum *n.* 783; *vb.* 783

strut *n.* 217

stub *n.* 482

stubborn *adj.* 143, 537, 672, 942

stubby *adj.* 203, 204

stuck up *adj.* 875

stud *vb* 817

student *n.* 131, **428**, 474

studious *adj.* 384, 390, 472, 611

study *n.* 390, 394, 472, 475, 488, 526; *vb.* 384, 390, 394, 472, 602

stuff *n.* 3, 327, 566, 729; *vb.* 56, 75, 226, 265, 304, 865, 948

stuffing *n.* 192, 226, 265

stuffy *adj.* 843

stumble *vb.* 317, 515

stumble on *vb.* 158

stumbling-block *n.* 635

stun *vb.* 754, 796, 922

stunner *n.* 844

stunted *adj.* 195, 203

stupefy *vb.* 754, 866

stupendous *adj.* 32, 866

stupid *adj.* 427, 433, 435

stupidity *n.* 383, 427, 433, 435

stupor *n.* 754

stutter *n.* 515; *vb.* 515

sty *n.* 184

style *n.* 242, 492, **501**, 510, 850; *vb.* 496

stylish *adj* 125, 850

subconscious *adj.* 382

subdivide *vb.* 48

subdue *vb.* 335, 679, 681, 779

subdued *adj.* 654, 781, 805

subject *n.* 387, 499, 525; *vb.* 679

subjection *n.* 35, 179, 679, 874

subject to *adj.* 35, 179, 679, 700, 919

subjugate *vb.* 679

sublimation *n.* 318, 346

sublime *adj.* 32, 208, 318, 868, 966, 982

subliminal *adj.* 382

sublimity *n.* 34

submarine *n.* 277

submerge *vb.* 321, 349

submerged *adj.* 210

submission *n.* 654, 673, 757, 874

submissive *adj.* **654**, 673, 679, 757, 874

submit *vb.* 468, 654, 673, 693, 757, 874

subnormal *adj.* 435

subordinate *n.* 35, 676; *adj.* 35, 679; *vb.* 679

subpoena *n.* 671, 960

subscribe *vb.* 424, 641

subscriber *n.* 424

subsequent *adj.* 85, 119, 156

subservient *adj.* 563, 673, 679, 874, 881

subside *vb.* 37, 197, 317

subsidiary *adj.* 563, 679

subsidize *vb.* 636, 715, 738

subsidy *n.* 636, 715, 738, 744

subsist *vb.* 1, 368

subsistence *n.* 1, 305

substance *n.* 3, 5, 223, 332, 450, 573

substandard *adj.* 35

substantial *adj.* 1, 3, 327, 450

substantiate *vb.* 161, 401, 413

substitute *n* 149, 540, 688, 99, 943; *vb.* 142, **149**, 689

substitution *n.* 142, **149**

substratum *n.* 206, 213

subsume *vb.* 98

subterfuge *n.* 478

subterranean *adj* 210

subtle *adj.* 333, 459, 631

subtraction *n.* 38, **42**, 744

suburb *n.* 183

suburban *adj.* 183

subversion *n.* 148, 164

subversive *adj.* 148, 580

subvert *vb.* 148, 580

succeed *vb.* 85, 119, 287, 659, **661**

success *n.* 550, **661**

successful *adj.* 661, 664

succession *n.* 85, 91, 119, 287

successor *n.* 119

succinct *adj.* 203, 504, 527

succour *n.* 636

succulence *n.* 364

succulent *adj.* 306, 364

succumb *vb.* 179, 369

suck *vb.* 308

sucker *n.* 479

suckle *vb.* 304

suckling *n.* 131

suck up to *vb.* 881, 927

sudden *adj.* 115, 444, 544, 859

sudden and violent sound *n.* 782

suds *n.* 363

sue *vb.* 960

suffer *vb.* 586, 590, 648, 752, **828**, 963

suffer defeat *vb.* 662

sufferer *n.* 828

suffice *vb.* 28, 570, 831

sufficiency *n.* 570

sufficient *adj.* 75, 570

suffix *n.* 41, 87, 499; *vb.* 40

suffocate *vb.* 370, 759

suffrage *n.* 540

sugar *n.* 772, 891; *vb.* 772

sugary *adj.* 772

suggest *vb.* 155, 401, 441, 450, 459, 460, 597, 624, 693

suggestion *n.* 441, 459, 460, 482, 624, 693

suggestive *adj.* 401, 450, 459, 482

suicide *n.* 370

sui generis adj. 59, 102

suit *n.* 227, 960; *vb.* 105, 577

suitable *adj.* 136, 302, 575, 577, 896, 915

suitcase *n.* 193

suite *n.* 91, 191, 792

suitor *n.* 889, 960

sulk *vb.* 895

sullenness *n.* 895

sullied *adj.* 584, 952

sully *vb.* 584, 847, 869, 928, 952

sultry *adj.* 759

sum *n.* 26, 54, 731; *vb.* 40

summarize *vb.* 203, 504, 525, 527

summary *n.* 441, 525, 527; *adj.* 504

summer *n.* 127, 664, 759; *adj.* 127

summer time *n.* 116, 127

summery *adj.* 127, 759

summing up *n.* 527, 960

summit *n.* 89, 208, 212, 519, 581

summon *vb.* 94, 671, 695, 857, 901

summons *n.* 671, 960

sum up *vb.* 527, 960

sun *n.* 329, 800

Sunday School *n.* 988

sunder *vb.* 63

sundown *n.* 128

sunglasses *n.* 801, 804

sunken *adj.* 209, 210, 254

sunny *adj.* 664, 759

sunrise *n.* 127, 797

sunset *n.* 128

sunshine *n.* 797

sup *vb.* 304

super *adj.* 579

superabundance *n.* 32, 572

superannuated *adj.* 130

superannuation *n.* 687

superb *adj.* 579

supercilious *adj.* 875, 924

superficial *adj.* 211, 435, 574, 825, 852

superfluity *n.* 32, 572

superimpose *vb.* 225

superintend *vb.* 392, 622

superintendent *n.* 623

superior *n.* 34, 675; *adj.* 34, 579, 868

superiority *n.* 34, 84, 579, 868

superlative *n.* 499; *adj.* 34, 481, 579

supermarket *n.* 730

supernatural *adj.* 447, 971, 984

superpose *vb.* 225

supersede *vb* 85

superstition *n.* 984

supervision *n.* 392, 593, 621, 622, 956

supervisor *n.* 623, 675

supper *n.* 306

supplant *vb.* 85

supple *adj.* 335

supplement *n.* 40, 41, 87; *vb.* 40, 196, 568

supplementary *adj.* 40

supplicant *n.* 697, 982; *adj.* 982

supplication *n.* 695, 982

supplies *n.* 564, 566, 729

supply *n.* 568; *vb.* 564, 568, 602, 715

support *n.* 213, **217**, 401, 424, 636, 929; *vb.* 152, 217, 392, 401, 410, 424, 636, 907

supporter *n.* 217, 287, 424, 640, 821, 905

suppose *vb.* 416, 420, 448, 449

supposed *adj.* 448, 459, 825

supposition *n.* **448**

suppress *vb.* 164, 461, 466, 513, 679, 681, 691

supreme *adj.* 34, 579, 581, 667, 966

sure *adj* 152, 408, 531

surety *n.* 420, 593, 701

surf *n.* 363; *vb.* 271

surface *n.* 182, 211, 222; *adj.* 211; *vb.* 225, 331

surfeit *n.* 572, 865; *vb.* 865

surge *vb.* 316, 320, 325, 358

surgery *n.* 591

surly *adj.* 887, 895

surmise *n.* 448; *vb.* 420, 448

surmount *vb.* 316

surname *n.* 496

surpass *vb.* 6, 34, 314

surpassing *adj.* 32, 34, 579

surplice *n.* 989

surplus *n* 44, 572

T

tab *n.* 482; *vb.* 482
table *n.* 83, 217, 306
tablet *n.* 591
taboo *n.* 691; *adj.* 691
tacit *adj.* 459
taciturnity *n.* 517
tackle *vb.* 88, 605
tack on *vb.* 40
tacky *adj.* 362
tactful *adj.* 398
tactical *adj.* 621
tactics *n.* 559, 621
tactless *adj.* 887
tag *n.* 482, 496; *vb.* 482, 496
tail *n.* 87, 89, 91, 237; *adj.* 237; *vb.* 37, 287, 554
taint *n.* 847; *vb.* 584, 952
take *vb.* 268, 720, 722
take action *vb.* 609
take advantage of *vb.* 136, 478, 575, 606, 952
take after *vb.* 18, 20
take away *vb.* 42, 720
take back *vb.* 31, 538
take care *vb.* 860
take care of *vb.* 392
take charge of *vb.* 593
take exception *vb.* 425, 893
take for granted *vb.* 443, 867, 880, 910
take from *vb.* 720
take heart *vb.* 836, 857
take in *vb.* 98, 302, 304, 452, 716, 795
take into account *vb.* 390
take it out of *vb.* 617
take it out on *vb.* 149, 900
take liberties *vb.* 918
take life *vb.* 370

take measures *vb.* 602
take notice *vb.* 390
take off *vb.* 20, 228, 273, 744
take on *vb.* 557, 605, 649
take out *vb.* 882
take over *vb.* 667
take pains *vb.* 615
take part in *vb.* 605, 639, 709
take place *vb.* 1, 153
take precautions *vb.* 860
take sides *vb.* 408, 639
take steps *vb.* 602, 609
take to *vb.* 545, 861
take umbrage *vb.* 893
take up *vb.* 540, 575, 716
take upon oneself *vb.* 605
taking *n.* 720
takings *n.* 724, 741
tale *n.* 460, 465, 525
talent *n.* 434, 627
talisman *n.* 984
talk *n.* 470, 492, 514, 518, 519; *vb.* 514
talkativeness *n.* 516
talk down *vb.* 273
talker *n.* 514
talk into *vb.* 547
talk out of *vb.* 548
talk over *vb.* 624
tall *adj.* 32, 202, 208, 318
tally *vb.* 24, 38
tame *adj.* 507, 654; *vb.* 377, 679
tan *n.* 810, 813; *adj.* 813; *vb.* 963
tandem *n.* 61, 276
tang *n.* 767, 769
tangency *n.* 201
tangent *n.* 285
tangerine *n.* 816
tangible *adj.* 3, 327, 758

tangle *n.* 45, 82; *vb.* 221
tangy *adj.* 769
tanker *n.* 277
tantalize *vb.* 547, 755
tantamount *adj.* 28; *adv.* 199
tantrum *n.* 893
tap *n.* 265, 360, 782; *vb.* 282, 358, 758, 782
tape *n.* 207; *vb.* 483
tape-measure *n.* 400
taper *n.* 800; *vb.* 37, 205, 255
tape-recorder *n.* 484, 794
tape-recording *n.* 483
tardy *adj.* 135
target *n.* 552, 716, 853
tariff *n.* 743
tarnish *n.* 847; *vb.* 584, 847, 869, 928
tarpaulin *n.* 225
tarry *vb.* 135, 281
tart *adj.* 769, 773
tartan *n.* 817
tart up *vb.* 844
task *n.* 557, 605
tassel *n.* 846
taste *n.* 339, 398, 753, 767; *vb.* 767
tasteful *adj.* 398, 510, 848, 876
taste good *vb.* 770
tasteless *adj.* 511, 768, 771, 849
tastelessness *n.* 399, 511, 768, 771, 849
tasty *adj.* 767, 770, 829
taunt *n.* 926; *vb.* 644, 853, 926
taut *adj.* 334
tautological *adj.* 451
tautology *n.* 505
tavern *n.* 191
tawdry *adj.* 849
tax *n.* 743
taxi *n.* 276; *vb.* 273
taxonomy *n.* 97, 375

tea n. 306, 309

tea-break n. 616

teach vb. 420, 470

teacher n. 428, 473, 624, 974, 986

teaching n. 470

team n. 94

team-mate n. 640

team up with vb. 639

teamwork n. 639

tear vb. 48, 280, 613

tea-room n. 191

tears n. 839

tease vb. 755, 830, 842

technique n. 488, 606

tedious adj. 841, 843

teem vb. 75, 572

teenager n. 131

teens n. 70, 129

teeter vb. 325

teeth n. 159

teetotalism n. 944, 949

telecommunications n. 467

telegram n. 460, 467

telegraphic adj. 504

telepathy n. 447

telephone n. 467; vb. 460

telescope n. 329, 822; vb. 203

television n. 467, 840

tell vb. 38, 460, 465, 514, 525, 624

tell apart vb. 398

teller n. 733

tell fortunes vb. 447

telling adj. 525

tell off vb. 926

tell on vb. 460

tell-tale n. 460; adj. 462

tell tales vb. 516

tell the future vb. 447

temerity n. 859

temper n. 5, 751; vb. 142, 176, 334, 335, 403

temperament n. 5, 751

temperamental adj. 756, 894

temperance n. 935, 944, 949

temperate adj. 176, 759, 944, 949

temperature n. 400, 759

tempest n. 175, 359

tempestuous adj. 359

temple n. 990

temporal adj. 107, 116, 987

temporary adj. 113, 149, 396

tempt vb. 547

temptation n. 547

tempting adj. 306, 770

tempt providence vb. 594, 859

ten n. 70; adj. 70

tenable adj. 420

tenacious adj. 50, 337, 534, 535, 537

tenancy n. 707

tenant n. 190, 710

tend vb. 178, 284, 377, 392

tendency n. 178, 284, 545, 751

tender n. 693; adj. 129, 335, 670, 752, 753, 889; vb. 693

tenderize vb. 335

tendril n. 207, 251

tenement n. 191

tenet n. 420, 974

tenor n. 178, 284, 450, 778

tense n. 499; adj. 756, 856

tension n. 25, 615, 642, 832

tent n. 225

tentative adj. 396, 448, 604

tenuous adj. 333

tenure n. 707

tepid adj. 759

tergiversation n. 538

term n. 93, 109, 494; vb. 496

terminal n. 89; adj. 89, 237

terminate vb. 89, 144, 164, 659

terminology n. 494, 496

terminus n. 89, 235, 298

terms n. 700

terms of reference n. 557

terrace n. 559

terra firma n. 352

terrain n. 352

terrestrial adj. 329, 352

terrible adj. 580, 856

terrific adj. 579

terrify vb. 856

territory n. 183, 956

terror n. 856

terrorism n. 955

terrorist n. 167, 175, 370

terse adj. 203, 432, 504

test n. 394, 396; vb. 408, 413

testify vb. 401, 413, 468

testimonial n. 441, 483

testimony n. 401, 468, 483

tether vb. 47

text n. 432, 524

textbook n. 524

textile n. 221

textural adj. 339

texture n. 339

thank vb. 909, 965

thankful adj. 909

thankless adj. 576, 910

thanks n. 909

thanksgiving n. 838, 982

thaw vb. 345, 761

theatre n. 529, 840

theatrical adj. 529, 852, 877

theft n. 722

theism *n.* 974

theme *n.* 387

theology *n.* 974

theorem *n.* 410

theoretical *adj.* 448

theorist *n.* 448

theorize *vb.* 448

theory *n.* 157, 386, 448

therapeutic *adj.* 585, 589, 591

thermal *adj.* 759

thermometer *n.* 759, 766

thermostat *n.* 766

thesaurus *n.* 83, 494

thesis *n.* 387, 410, 448, 526

thick *adj.* 204, 332, 364, 435

thicken *vb.* 204, 332

thicket *n.* 374

thickness *n.* 204, 206, 332

thickset *adj.* 203, 204

thick-skinned *adj.* 754

thief *n.* 723, 906

thin *adj.* 33, 76, 205, 333, 507, 571; *vb.* 27, 333

thing *n.* 3, 163, 327, 609

thing added *n.* 41

thing subtracted *n.* 43

think *vb.* 384, 420, 448

thinkable *adj.* 404

think about *vb.* 552

think ahead *vb.* 558

thinker *n.* 448

think-tank *n.* 624

thinness *n.* 76, 205, 333

third *n.* 66; *adj.* 65

third party *n.* 653

thirst *n.* 350, 388, 861; *vb.* 861

thirst-quencher *n.* 309

thirsty *adj.* 350

thorn *n.* 255, 255

thorn in the flesh *n.* 592

thorny *adj.* 255, 633

thorough *adj.* 56, 148, 392

thoroughfare *n.* 313

thought *n.* **384**, 386, 392, 420, 441

thoughtful *adj.* 384, 392, 410, 434, 837, 886

thoughtless *adj.* 385, 391, 393, 603, 859, 887, 900, 910

thousand *n.* 70

thrall *n.* 679

thrash *vb.* 282, 963

thread *n.* 49, 207; *vb.* 313

threadbare *adj.* 228

threadlike *adj.* 205, 207

threat *n.* 154, 594, **902**

threatening *adj.* 154, 594, 651, 902

three *n.* 64; *adj.* 64

thresh *vb.* 378

threshold *n.* 233, 235

thrifty *adj.* 392, 748

thrill *n.* 756, 827; *vb.* 752, 755, 756, 829

thrive *vb.* 36, 168, 661, 664

throat *n.* 262

throaty *adj.* 515, 787

throb *n.* 325, 783; *vb.* 140, 325, 783, 828

throne *n.* 957

throng *n.* 75, 94; *vb.* 75, 94

throughout *adv., prep.* 107

throw *vb.* 290

throw away *vb.* 556, 713, 749

throwaway *adj.* 544

throw in *vb.* 311

throw in the towel *vb.* 556, 654

throw light on *vb.* 456

throw off *vb.* 295, 546

throw out *vb.* 607

throw up *vb.* 303

thrust *n.* 173, 178, 282, 290, 645; *vb.* 290, 645

thud *vb.* 782, 785

thug *n.* 723, 906

thumb through *vb.* 472, 818

thump *vb.* 282, 783, 785

thunder *n.* 325, 784; *vb.* 780, 782

thunderbolt *n.* 444

thunderstorm *n.* 175, 358

thunderstruck *adj.* 444, 866

thundery *adj.* 358

thwart *vb.* 445, 635, 637, 648, 662

tick *vb.* 783

ticket *n.* 482, 483, 743

tickle *vb.* 758, 829

tick off *vb.* 926

tide *n.* 358

tidy *adj.* 79, 392, 583; *vb.* 583

tie *n.* 28, 49; *vb.* 28, 47, 681

tier *n.* 93, 206

tie-up *n.* 47

tight *adj.* 47, 334, 950

tight-fisted *adj.* 750

tight-lipped *adj.* 517

till *n.* 732; *vb.* 378

tilt *vb.* 219, 220, 317

timber *n.* 217

timbre *n.* 512, 778

time *n.* **107**, 109, 116, 400; *vb.* 116

time-honoured *adj.* 126, 922

timekeeping *n.* 116

timelessness *n.* 108, 114

timeliness *n.* **136**

timepiece *n.* 116

time-saving *adj.* 748

time-server *n.* 538, 934

timetable *n.* 116, 460

timid *adj.* 856, 858, 876

timing *n.* 116, 140

307

timorous *adj.* 856

tin *n.* 193; *vb.* 599

tincture *n.* 45, 805

tinder *n.* 765

tinge *n.* 805; *vb.* 805

tingle *vb.* 752, 756

tininess *n.* 33, 195

tinker *n.* 728

tinkle *n.* 784

tinny *adj.* 787

tinsel *n.* 846

tint *n.* 27, 805; *vb.* 488

tinted *adj.* 805

tiny *adj.* 33, 195, 203

tip *n.* 212, 233, 255, 715, 965; *vb.* 212, 220, 909

tip-off *n.* 460, 597

tipple *vb.* 304, 950

tipsy *adj.* 950

tirade *n.* 518

tire *vb.* 617, 841

tired *adj.* 612, 617, 841

tiresome *adj.* 830, 841

tissue *n.* 339

titbit *n.* 770, 829

tit for tat *n.* 150, 647

titillate *vb.* 758, 829

title *n.* 496, 872

titled *adj.* 870

title-holder *n.* 661

titter *n.* 838

titular *adj.* 496

tizzy *n.* 326, 756

toady *n.* 881, 927; *vb.* 881

to and fro *adv.* 325

toast *n.* 309, 888; *vb.* 306, 888

tobacco *n.* 308

today *n.* 120

toddler *n.* 131

to-do *n.* 80, 756

toe *n.* 213

together *adj.* 47; *adv.* 60

togetherness *n.* 60

toil *n.* 615; *vb.* 615

toilet *n.* 227

token *n.* 4, 441, 482, 701

tolerable *adj.* 579, 666

tolerant *adj.* 288, 670, 690

tolerate *vb.* 670, 690, 911

toll *n.* 716, 743; *vb.* 783

tomb *n.* 372

tomorrow *n.* 123; *adv.* 121, 123

tone *n.* 488, 512, 778, 805

tone down *vb.* 176, 779

toneless *adj.* 806

tongue *n.* 253, 492, 512, 767

tongue in cheek *adj.* 852

tongue-tied *adj.* 513

tonic *n.* 591

tonsure *n.* 228

too *adv.* 40

tool *n.* 565

tooth *n.* 255; *vb.* 259

toothless *adj.* 130, 256

top *n.* 89, 208, 212, 222; *adj.* 212; *vb.* 34, 212, 316

top-heavy *adj.* 29, 330

topic *n.* 387

topical *adj.* 125

top-notch *adj.* 573, 579

topple *vb.* 220, 317, 319

topsy-turvy *adj.* 220

top up *vb.* 56

Torah *n.* 976

torch *n.* 765, 800

torment *n.* 828; *vb.* 830, 856, 900, 902

torn *adj.* 48, 262

tornado *n.* 175, 323, 359

torpedo *n.* 290

torpid *adj.* 174, 612

torrent *n.* 358, 572

torrential *adj.* 358

tortoise *n.* 281

tortuous *adj.* 251

torture *n.* 828, 900, 963; *vb.* 830, 900, 963

toss *vb.* 290, 326

toss-up *n.* 553

tot *n.* 131

total *n.* 40, 54; *adj.* 54; *vb.* 38, 40

totalitarian *adj.* 669

totality *n.* 54

totem *n.* 967, 983

totter *vb.* 325, 326

touch *n.* 753, 758, 805; *vb.* 201, 752, 755, 758

touch-and-go *adj.* 553

touch down *vb.* 273, 298, 317

touched *adj.* 752, 756

touch on *vb.* 211, 450

touch up *vb.* 587, 589, 805

touchy *adj.* 756, 894

tough *adj.* 161, 334, 337, 506, 633, 857

toughen *vb.* 334, 337

toughness *n.* 161, 334, 337

tour *vb.* 269, 322

tourism *n.* 269

tourist *n.* 270

tournament *n.* 649

tout *n.* 697, 728; *vb.* 695

tow *vb.* 291

towards *adv.* 284

tower *n.* 208; *vb.* 32, 34, 208, 316

towering *adj.* 32, 208

tower of strength *n.* 640

town *n.* 183

townsman *n.* 190

toxic *adj.* 164, 580, 586

trace *n.* 33, 401, 483, 774; *vb.* 157, 232, 525

tracing *n.* 22, 232

track *n.* 559, 658; *vb.* 287, 554

track down *vb.* 419

tractable *adj.* 654, 919

tractor *n.* 291

unconverted *adj.* 975
uncooperative *adj.* 642
uncouple *vb.* 48
uncouth *adj.* 511, 849
uncover *vb.* 419, 462
uncritical *adj.* 399, 416
unctuousness *n.* 365,
927
uncultured *adj.* 427,
887
uncurl *vb.* 248, 324
undamaged *adj.* 54
undated *adj.* 117
undaunted *adj.* 535, 857
undecided *adj.* 325,
409, 536
undefiled *adj.* 937, 951
undependable *adj.* 932
under *adv.* 209
undercarriage *n.* 217
undercover *adj.* 459
undercurrent *n.* 358,
459, 596
underdeveloped *adj.*
459
underdog *n.* 35, 662,
871
underdone *adj.* 771
underestimation *n.* 416,
418
underfoot *adv.* 209
underframe *n.* 217
undergo *vb.* 153, 752,
828
undergraduate *n.* 474
underground *n.* 276,
480, 559; *adj.* 148, 210;
adv. 209
undergrowth *n.* 374
underhand *adj.* 461,
478, 631, 932
underline *vb.* 468, 573
underlying *adj.* 209,
213, 459
underneath *adv.* 209
underplay *vb.* 418
under-privileged *adj.*
735

underrate *vb.* 418, 923
understanding *n.*
(knowledge) 382, 410,
426, 434; (agreement)
24, 643, 699, 704;
(pity) 907
understate *vb.* 418, 477,
487
understood *adj.* 459
understudy *n.* 149, 529
undertaker *n.* 372
undertaking *n.* 557,
604, 605, 609, 698, 699
undertone *n.* 781
undervalue *vb.* 416, 418
underwater *adj.* 210
underworld *n.* 973
underwrite *vb.* 701
undeserved *adj.* 918
undesirable *adj.* 578
undeveloped *adj.* 603
undiscerning *adj.* 399,
435
undiscovered *adj.* 427
undiscriminating *adj.*
399
undisputed *adj.* 24, 408,
430
undistinguished *adj.*
869
undivided *adj.* 54, 56
undo *vb.* 48, 164, 262,
680
undress *n.* 228; *vb.* 228
undressing *n.* 228
undueness *n.* 918
undulate *vb.* 140, 251,
325, 358
unearth *vb.* 186, 372,
419
uneasy *adj.* 828, 832,
856
uneducated *adj.* 427,
628
unemotional *adj.* 754
unemployed *adj.* 607,
610, 612
unending *adj.* 202

unenterprising *adj.* 612
unenthusiastic *adj.* 533,
754
unequal *adj.* 29, 59
unequipped *adj.* 603
unequivocal *adj.* 408,
452
unerring *adj.* 408
uneven *adj.* 17, 29, 92,
141, 245, 258
unexpected *adj.* 158,
407, 444
unexplored *adj.* 885
unexpurgated *adj.* 952
unfailing *adj.* 408, 420
unfair *adj.* 416, 916, 918
unfaithful *adj.* 431, 538,
703, 920
unfamiliar *adj.* 106
unfashionableness *n.*
849
unfasten *vb.* 262
unfavourable *adj.* 137,
578, 665, 926
unfeeling *adj.* 669, 754,
908
unfinished *adj.* 57, 582
unfitting *adj.* 578, 916
unflinching *adj.* 534,
857
unfold *vb.* 262, 324,
458, 462
unforeseen *adj.* 444
unforgettable *adj.* 441
unforgivable *adj.* 916,
936
unforgiving *adj.* 908
unfortunate *adj.* 662,
665, 828
unfounded *adj.* 2
unfreeze *vb.* 761
unfriendly *adj.* 883,
885, 887, 900
unfrock *vb.* 686, 869
unfruitful *adj.* 169
unfurl *vb.* 324, 462
ungodly *adj.* 936, 975,
981

unwise adj. 393, 416, 435, 578

unworthy adj. 918

unwrap vb. 324

unyielding adj. 112, 161, 334, 337, 534, 537

up adv. 208

update vb. 125, 587

upgrade vb. 587

upheaval n. 80, 148

uphill adj. 615, 633

uphold vb. 143, 145, 217, 929

upland n. 356

uplands n. 208

uplift vb. 318, 836

upper adj. 34

upper classes n. 870

uppermost adj. 212

upraised adj. 318

upright adj. 214, 248, 430, 915, 931, 935

uprising n. 358

uproar n. 80, 175, 780

uproot vb. 187, 312

upset n. 220, 414; adj. 837; vb. 82, 148, 830, 893

upshot n. 87, 156

upside-down adj. 220; adv. 80

upstanding adj. 214, 318

upstart n. 125, 880

upsurge vb. 36

uptight adj. 756, 894

up-to-date adj. 125

upward adj. 219, 316

urban adj. 183

urchin n. 970

urge n. 547, 861; vb. 468, 547, 613, 624, 674, 695

urgency n. 506, 562, 573, 613, 674, 695

urinate vb. 303, 310

urn n. 193, 372

usage n. 499, 501, 545, 606

use n. 606; vb. 575, 606, 707, 719

used adj. 126, 606

used to adj. 545

useful adj. 550, 575, 577

useless adj. 576, 662

usher in vb. 84

usual adj. 138, 545, 867

usurer n. 718

usurp vb. 918

utensil n. 565

utilitarian adj. 575

utilitarianism n. 903

utility n. 575, 606

utilize vb. 575, 606

utmost n. 235

utopia n. 449

utter adj. 56; vb. 512, 514, 788

utterance n. 492, 494, 498, 512, 514, 788

V

vacant adj. 189, 385, 435, 451

vacate vb. 187

vacation n. 144, 612, 614

vaccine n. 591

vacillate vb. 151, 325, 536

vacuity n. 2, 189

vacuum n. 2, 189, 333

vagabond n. 270, 697

vagrant n. 270

vague adj. 4, 243, 409, 454, 503, 799, 824

vain adj. 576, 662, 855, 875

valentine n. 523, 890

valiant adj. 857

valid adj. 413, 430, 915, 954

validate vb. 413, 954

validity n. 430, 954

valley n. 200, 209, 254

valour n. 857

valuable adj. 573, 575, 579

valuables n. 711

value n. 575, 579, 743; vb. 573, 743, 889, 922

valuer n. 415

valve n. 265

vampire n. 906, 969

van n. 276

vandal n. 167

vandalism n. 722

vanished adj. 2, 189, 706, **826**

vanity n. 576, 873, **875**, 934

vaporization n. 346

vaporous adj. 4, 344, 346

vapour n. 4, 343, 344, 346

variable n. 39; adj. 15, 17, 104, 142, **151**

variance n. 15, 425, 642

variant n. 15; adj. 15

variation n. 15, 19, 104, 142

variegation n. 817

variety n. 19, 72, 104, 529

various adj. 104

varnish vb. 225, 257, 365

vary vb. 15, 142, 151

vase n. 193

vast adj. 32, 78, 182, 194

vastly adv. 32

vat n. 193

vault n. 252, 320, 329, 372, 732; vb. 320

vaulted adj. 247

vaunt vb. 879

veer vb. 142, 247, 285

vegetability n. 374

vitalize *vb.* 173, 368
vitreous *adj.* 802
vivacious *adj.* 368, 836
vivacity *n.* 514
vivid *adj.* 441, 506, 509, 525
vivisection *n.* 370
vocabulary *n.* 494, 501
vocal *adj.* 512, 792
vocalist *n.* 793
vocalize *vb.* 512, 514
vocation *n.* 557, 985
vociferous *adj.* 780, 788
vogue *n.* 125; *adj.* 495
voice *n.* 492, 512; *vb.* 512, 514
void *n.* 2, 74, 189; *adj.* 2, 333, 451; *vb.* 955
volatile *adj.* 151, 344, 346
volition *n.* 530
volte-face *n.* 147, 220, 289, 538
voluble *adj.* 509, 514, 516
volume *n.* 26, 194, 400, 524
voluntary *adj.* 530, 532
volunteer *vb.* 532, 693
voluptuous *adj.* 827, 945
vomit *vb.* 303
voodoo *n.* 984
voracity *n.* 750, 861, 948
vortex *n.* 323, 358
vote *n.* 540, 909; *vb.* 424, 540
voted *adj.* 424
voter *n.* 190, 540
vouch *vb.* 468
voucher *n.* 482, 741
vow *n.* 468, 698; *vb.* 468, 698
vowel *n.* 493, 512
voyage *n.* 271, 313; *vb.* 271
voyager *n.* 270

vulgar *adj.* 511, 849, 887, 952
vulnerable *adj.* 594, 753

W

wadding *n.* 226
wade *vb.* 271
wafer *n.* 306
waffle *vb.* 516
waft *vb.* 359
wag *n.* 842; *vb.* 325
wager *n.* 553
wages *n.* 731, 738, 741
wagon *n.* 276
wail *n.* 788, 839; *vb.* 788, 839
wait *vb.* 443, 610
wait and see *vb.* 135, 610
waiter *n.* 676
wait on *vb.* 287, 676
waive *vb.* 556, 713
wake *n.* 237
walk *n.* 269, 559; *vb.* 269
walk away with *vb.* 661
walker *n.* 270
walkie-talkie *n.* 467
walk out *vb.* 144, 556, 687
walkout *n.* 144
walk-over *n.* 634, 661
wall *n.* 217, 230, 234
wallet *n.* 193, 732
wallop *vb.* 282, 963
wan *adj.* 807
wand *n.* 677
wander *vb.* 269, 285, 505
wanderer *n.* 270
wandering *n.* 391
wane *n.* 37; *vb.* 37, 799
want *n.* 57, 562, 706, 861; *vb.* 57, 189, 530, 532, 562, 571, **861**

wanted *adj.* 562, 600
wanton *adj.* 936, 952
war *n.* 649, **651**
warble *vb.* 789
ward *n.* 183, 540
warden *n.* 593, 683
warder *n.* 683
ward off *vb.* 646
wardrobe *n.* 227
wardship *n.* 129
warehouse *n.* 567
wares *n.* 729
warfare *n.* 649, 651
warlike *adj.* 651
warm *adj.* 419, 759, 805; *vb.* 306, 761, 836
warm-hearted *adj.* 882, 899
warmth *n.* 506, 752, 759, 805, 882
warm up *vb.* 306
warning *n.* 447, 460, 597, 902; *adj.* 597
warp *vb.* 219, 247, 416, 487
warrant *n.* 424, 671, 685; *vb.* 690, 698, 917
warranty *n.* 701
warren *n.* 234, 254
warrior *n.* 655
wart *n.* 252
wary *adj.* 390, 860
wash *n.* 358, 805; *vb* 583, 805
washed out *adj.* 612, 617, 806
wash-out *n.* 662
waste *n.* 44, 164, **569** 576; *vb.* 569, 608, 749
waste away *vb.* 53, 586, 588
wasted *adj.* 205, 569
wasteful *adj.* 393, 569, 749
waste-pipe *n.* 600
waste time *vb.* 612
wastrel *n.* 612, 749, 940

watch *n.* 116, 646; *vb.* 392, 818

watchdog *n.* 593

watcher *n.* 821

watchful *adj.* 392, 443, 818, 860

watchman *n.* 683

watchword *n.* 432

water *n.* 309, 347; *vb.* 378

water channel *n.* 360

water down *vb.* 45, 162

waterfall *n.* 358

water in motion *n.* 358

waterlogged *adj.* 349, 355

waterproof *adj.* 350, 593

watershed *n.* 230

water sports *n.* 271

watertight *adj.* 265, 350

water travel *n.* 271

waterway *n.* 358

watery *adj.* 343, 347

wave *n.* 325, 358, 482; *vb.* 325, 482, 886

wavering *n.* 142, 151, 325, 409, 536; *adj.* 141, 151, 326, 536

wavy *adj.* 251

wax *n.* 342, 800; *vb.* 36, 225

way *n.* 198, 313, **559**

wayfarer *n.* 270

way out *n.* 301, 600

wayward *adj.* 151, 672

weak *adj.* 162, 507, 586, 617, 628, 781, 858

weak-minded *adj.* 162, 435

weakness *n.* 162, 178, 315, 507, 586, 617, 858, 936

weak spot *n.* 582, 594

wealth *n.* 168, 664, 711, 731, 734

wean from *vb.* 546, 548

weapons *n.* 657

wear *vb.* 227

wear and tear *n.* 569

wear away *vb.* 341

wear down *vb.* 160, 547

weariness *n.* 612, 617, 841

wearisome *adj.* 633, 841

wear out *vb.* 569, 617

weather *n.* 348

weave *n.* 339; *vb.* 221, 313

web *n.* 221, 339

wed *adj.* 47; *vb.* 896

wedding *n.* 896

wedge *n.* 230, 246, 265

weed *n.* 374; *vb.* 378

weedy *adj.* 205

week *n.* 109

weep *vb.* 301, 833, 839, 907

weigh *vb.* 330, 397, 415

weight *n.* 26, 177, 194, 330, 400, 573; *vb.* 330

weighting *n.* 31

weightless *adj.* 331

weigh up *vb.* 384

weird *adj.* 971, 984

welcome *n.* 302; *adj.* 827; *vb.* 302, 884, 886

welcoming *adj.* 716

weld *n.* 49; *vb.* 50

welfare *n.* 550, 664

well *n.* 254, 567; *adj.* 585; *vb.* 301, 358

well-behaved *adj.* 673

well-being *n.* 550, 585, 664

well-dressed *adj.* 227

well-formed *adj.* 499, 844

well grounded *adj.* 426

well-meaning *adj.* 899

well-off *adj.* 664, 734

well-proportioned *adj.* 244, 510, 844

well-read *adj.* 426, 472

well thought of *adj.* 868, 922

well-turned *adj.* 510

well-versed *adj.* 426, 627

weltschmerz n. 837

west *n.* 284

wet *n.* 347, 349; *adj.* 347, 349; *vb.* 349

wet blanket *n.* 548, 841

whack *n.* 782; *vb.* 282, 782, 963

whacked *adj.* 617

whale *n.* 194

what's-its-name *n.* 497

wheedle *vb.* 547, 927

wheel *n.* 250

wheeled *adj.* 276

wheeze *vb.* 359, 786

when *adv., prep.* 107

whereabouts *n.* 185

wherewithal *n.* 564, 566

whet *vb.* 255, 755

while *adv., prep.* 107

while away *vb.* 107, 612

whim *n.* 449, 539

whimper *vb.* 788, 839

whimsical *adj.* 449, 539, 842, 851

whine *vb.* 784, 788, 789, 839

whip *n.* 964; *vb.* 282, 963

whip up *vb.* 175, 755

whirl *n.* 323; *vb.* 323, 358, 359

whirlpool *n.* 323, 358

whirlwind *n.* 323, 359

whirr *n.* 783, 786; *vb.* 783, 784, 786

whisk *n.* 359; *vb.* 359

whisper *n.* 460, 781; *vb.* 781

whistle *n.* 482, 786, 787; *vb.* 482, 786, 787, 789

white *n.* 807, 951; *adj.* 583, 806, 807

white flag n. 652

whittle vb. 203

whiz vb. 280, 786

whizz-kid n. 629

whole n. 26, 54, 59; adj. 39, 54, 56, 581, 585

wholehearted adj. 534

wholesale adj. 54, 56, 98

wholesome adj. 438, 585

whoop vb. 788, 840

whore n. 953

wicked adj. 551, 580, 900, 916, 932, 936, 981

wickerwork n. 221

wide adj. 101, 182, 204

widen vb. 36, 182, 204

widespread adj. 32, 54, 101, 182

widow n. 898; vb. 898

widowhood n. 898

width n. 26, 204, 400

wife n. 896

wiggle vb. 251

wild adj. 175, 433, 439, 859, 889

wilful adj. 530

will n. 530; vb. 530, 714

willies n. 856

willingness n. 532, 692

willpower n. 530, 534

wilt vb. 837

wily adj. 478, 631

win vb. 661, 705, 720

wince vb. 283

wind n. 359; vb. 251, 322

windfall n. 550, 715

window n. 262

wind up vb. 89, 116, 739

windy adj. 344, 348, 359

wine n. 309

wink n. 482, 818; vb. 482, 818

winner n. 661

winnings n. 724

winnow vb. 46, 48, 378

win over vb. 547

winsome adj. 829, 889

winter n. 128; adj. 128

wintry adj. 128, 760

wipe vb. 341

wipe out vb. 164, 485, 911

wire n. 207, 460, 467; adj. 611; vb. 460

wireless n. 467

wiry adj. 207

wisdom n. 382, 392, 426, 434

wisecrack n. 842

wish n. 530, 854, 861; vb. 530, 854, 861

wishful thinking n. 449, 478, 854

wishy-washy adj. 162, 507, 666, 768

wisp n. 4, 207

wit n. 434, 842

witchcraft n. 984

withdraw vb. 42, 289, 293, 299, 312, 538, 556, 600, 687, 731, 826

withdrawn adj. 681, 885

wither vb. 350, 588

withhold vb. 461, 694, 712

within hearing adv. 199

within reach adj. 404

without adv., prep. 42; prep. 571

with reference to adv., prep. 9

withstand vb. 646, 648

with strings attached adj. 700

with the exception of adv., prep. 42

with young adj. 163

witness n. 401, 483; vb. 401, 413

witty adj. 840, 842

wizard n. 447, 984

wizened adj. 197, 205

wobble n. 326; vb. 325, 326

woe n. 580

wold n. 356

woman n. 133, 381

woman-hater n. 904

womanizer n. 953

women's rights n. 917

wonder n. 866; vb. 866

wonderful adj. 32, 579, 844

wont n. 545

woo vb. 882, 889, 890

wood n. 374, 765

woodwind n. 794

word n. 494, 698; vb. 498

word for word adj. 450, 456

wording n. 501

Word of God n. 976

word order n. 499

wordy adj. 505

work n. 163, 488, 521, 524, 557, 605, 615, 792; vb. 172, 557, 615, 676

workable adj. 406

work against vb. 181

worked up adj. 893

worker n. 609, 619, 676

work off vb. 149

work oneself up vb. 756

work one's way up vb. 316

work out vb. 38, 452, 552, 558, 659

workshop n. 620

work together vb. 52, 180

work up vb. 755

world n. 329, 379

worldliness n. 327, 329, 981

world-weariness n. 837, 841

worldwide adj. 32, 101

319

X, Y, Z